AUSTRALIA NEW ZEALAND AND THE SOUTH PACIFIC

FODOR'S TRAVEL GUIDES

are compiled, researched, and edited by an international team of travel writers, field correspondents, and editors. The series, which now almost covers the globe, was founded by Eugene Fodor in 1936.

OFFICES
New York & London

Fodor's Australia, New Zealand, and the South Pacific

Editor: Debra Bernardi
Area Editors: Lois Brett, John P. Campbell, Chris Farrant, Heidi Gordon, Sonny Gordon, Jeff Greenwald, Kathleen Hancock, Graeme Kennedy, Pauline Murphy, Jan Prince, Jennifer Pringle-Jones, David Swindell, James Tully, John Young
Contributing Editor: Emery Barcs
Drawings: Michael Kaplan, Sandra Lang, Don Mulligan
Photographs: Australian Tourist Commission, Lois Brett, New Zealand Tourist Office, Victoria Arts Centre, Western Samoa Visitors Bureau
Maps and Plans: Arlene Goldberg & Jaye Zimet, Pictograph

SPECIAL SALES

Fodor's Travel Guides are available at special quantity discounts for bulk purchases (50 copies or more) for sales promotions or premiums. Special travel guides or excerpts from existing guides can also be created to fit specific needs. For more information write Special Marketing, Fodor's Travel Guides, 2 Park Avenue, New York, NY 10016.

AUSTRALIA
NEW ZEALAND
AND THE
SOUTH PACIFIC
1987

HODDER AND STOUGHTON
LONDON SYDNEY AUCKLAND

Copyright © 1987 by FODOR'S TRAVEL GUIDES
ISBN 0-679-01314-8
ISBN 0-340-40022-6 (Hodder & Stoughton edition)

No part of this book may be reproduced in any form without permission in writing from the publisher.

The following Fodor's Guides are current; most are also available in a British edition published by Hodder & Stoughton.

Country and Area Guides

Australia, New Zealand & the South Pacific
Austria
Bahamas
Belgium & Luxembourg
Bermuda
Brazil
Canada
Canada's Maritime Provinces
Caribbean
Central America
Eastern Europe
Egypt
Europe
France
Germany
Great Britain
Greece
Holland
India, Nepal & Sri Lanka
Ireland
Israel
Italy
Japan
Jordan & the Holy Land
Kenya
Korea
Mexico
New Zealand
North Africa
People's Republic of China
Portugal
Province of Quebec
Scandinavia
Scotland
South America
South Pacific
Southeast Asia
Soviet Union
Spain
Sweden
Switzerland
Turkey
Yugoslavia

City Guides

Amsterdam
Beijing, Guangzhou, Shanghai
Boston
Chicago
Dallas & Fort Worth
Greater Miami & the Gold Coast
Hong Kong
Houston & Galveston
Lisbon
London
Los Angeles
Madrid
Mexico City & Acapulco
Munich
New Orleans
New York City
Paris
Philadelphia
Rome
San Diego
San Francisco
Singapore
Stockholm, Copenhagen, Oslo, Helsinki & Reykjavik
Sydney
Tokyo
Toronto
Vienna
Washington, D.C.

U.S.A. Guides

Alaska
Arizona
California
Cape Cod
Chesapeake
Colorado
Far West
Florida
Hawaii
I–95: Maine to Miami
New England
New Mexico
New York State
Pacific North Coast
South
Texas
U.S.A.
Virginia

Budget Travel

American Cities (30)
Britain
Canada
Caribbean
Europe
France
Germany
Hawaii
Italy
Japan
London
Mexico
Spain

Fun Guides

Acapulco
Bahamas
Las Vegas
London
Maui
Montreal
New Orleans
New York City
The Orlando Area
Paris
Puerto Rico
Rio
St. Martin/Sint Maarten
San Francisco
Waikiki

Special-Interest Guides

Selected Hotels of Europe
Ski Resorts of North America
Views to Dine by around the World

MANUFACTURED IN THE UNITED STATES OF AMERICA
10 9 8 7 6 5 4 3 2 1

CONTENTS

Foreword — viii

Planning Your Trip
Tourist Information, 2; Entry Requirements, 4; Health Certificates, 4; What to Pack, 4; How to Go, 6; What Will It Cost? 7; Money Matters, 7; How to Get There by Air, 8; Stopovers, 9; How to Get There by Sea, 9; Tours, 10; Tour Operators, 11; Special-Interest Travel, 12; Inter-Island Ships, 13; Motoring, 15; Bus Service, 17; Trains, 18; Taxis; 18; Motorscooters and Bicycles, 19; Hotels, 19; Meet the People, 20; Roughing It, 21; Dining Out, 23; Liquor Laws, 25; Drinking Water, 25; Electrical Current, 25; Telephones, 25; Mail, 26; Medical Treatment, 26; Languages, 27; Sports, 27; Metric Conversion, 28; Shopping, 29; Hints to Handicapped, 30; U.S. Customs, 30

AUSTRALIA

Map of Australia, 32–33

Facts at Your Fingertips for Australia
Planning Your Trip, 35; Passports and Visas, 35; Tourist Offices, 36; Currency and Credit Cards, 36; What Will It Cost? 36; When to Go, 37; Average Temperature and Rainfall, 37; Time Zones, 38; What to Take, 38; How to Get There, 39; Cruises, 39; How to Get Around, 39; Tours, 40; Driving in Australia, 41; Electricity, 41; Tipping, 42; Drinking Laws, 42; Departure Tax, 42

Australia: Continent or Island? — 43
  Emery Barcs

New South Wales: The Oldest of the Six States — 68
  Emery Barcs and Pauline Murphy
  Sydney, 69
    Map of Sydney, 71
    Map of Sydney Harbour and Beaches, 82
  Practical Information for Sydney, 83
  New South Wales beyond Sydney, 99
    Map of New South Wales, 100–101
  Practical Information for New South Wales beyond Sydney, 115

Australian Capital Territory: Canberra and Environs — 142
  Map of Canberra, 145
  Practical Information for Canberra, 147

Victoria: The Garden State — 154
  Sonny and Heidi Gordon
  Melbourne, 154
    Map of Melbourne, 158
  Practical Information for Melbourne, 160
  Victoria beyond Melbourne, 173
    Map of Victoria, 175
  Practical Information for Victoria beyond Melbourne, 184

Queensland — 197
  David Swindell
  Map of Coastal Queensland, 199
  Far North Queensland: Cairns and the Far Northern Great Barrier Reef, 200

CONTENTS

Practical Information for Far North Queensland, 203
Northern Queensland: Townsville and the Northern
  Great Barrier Reef, 206
Practical Information for Northern Queensland, 207
The Whitsunday Islands and Coast, 209
Practical Information for the Whitsunday Region, 212
Southern Queensland, 214
Practical Information for Southern Queensland, 220

South Australia 226
  Chris Farrant
Adelaide: The Capital, 227
Practical Information for Adelaide, 227
South Australia beyond Adelaide, 231
Practical Information for South Australia beyond Adelaide, 235

Western Australia: Home of "the Most Fortunate People" 239
The Perth Area, 241
  Map of Perth, 242
Practical Information for the Perth Area, 245
Western Australia beyond Perth, 250
Practical Information for Western Australia beyond Perth, 256

The Northern Territory 266
Practical Information for the Northern Territory, 271

Tasmania: An Island State 282
  Jennifer Pringle-Jones
Practical Information for Tasmania, 288

NEW ZEALAND

Map of New Zealand, 306
Facts at Your Fingertips for New Zealand
  Tourist Information, 307; Passports, Visas, Customs, 307; Climate, 308; Packing, 308; What Will It Cost? 308; Currency, 309; How to Get There, 309; Stopovers, 309; How to Get About, 309; Hints to the Motorist, 310; Taxis, 311; Accommodations, 311; Farm Holidays, 311; Food, 312; Dining Out, 312; Drinking Laws, 312; Time Zone and Business Hours, 313; Festivals and Special Events, 313; Sightseeing, 314; Sports, 314; Fishing and Hunting, 316; Beaches, 316; Shopping, 316; Gambling, 316; Hints to Handicapped Travelers, 316; Electricity, 317; Telephones, 317

New Zealand: Land of the Long White Cloud 318
  John P. Campbell
National Parks: A Legacy of Grandeur 329
Fishing and Hunting: Trout Marlin, Shark, Chamois, and Thar 334
The North Island: "The Fish of Maui" 338
  John P. Campbell
  Map of Auckland, 343
  Map of Wellington, 363
  Practical Information for the North Island 367
The South Island: "The Mainland" 380
  Practical Information for the South Island 404

CONTENTS

THE SOUTH PACIFIC

The Pacific Way: An Introduction to the South Pacific — 415
Jan Prince
Map of the South Pacific, 416–417

French Polynesia: The Bustling Paradise — 428
Jan Prince
Map of Tahiti and Moorea, 429

The Cook Islands: The Goose Gets Fatter — 472
Graeme Kennedy

American Samoa: Polynesia Imperfect — 479
Graeme Kennedy
Map of the Samoas, 480

Western Samoa: Where It's Really At — 485
Graeme Kennedy

Tonga: Ancient Polynesia Still — 494
Graeme Kennedy

Niue Island: Hidden Coral Wonderland — 502
Graeme Kennedy

Wallis and Futuna: French Fantastic — 507
Graeme Kennedy

Fiji Islands: Crossroads of the South Pacific — 511
James Tully
Map of Fiji, 513

Kiribati and Tuvalu: Recently Independent Nations — 528
Lois K. Brett

Vanuatu — 536
Kathleen Hancock

New Caledonia: The Island of Light — 550
Kathleen Hancock

Solomon Islands: Battlefields in the South Pacific — 569
Jeff Greenwald and Don Hook

Papua New Guinea: Adventurous, Exciting, and Exotic — 580
Lois K. Brett
Map of Papua New Guinea, 583

Index — 607

FOREWORD

From the sophistication of Sydney to the rugged wilderness of the Outback, Australia is a paradise for sports lovers, sightseers, sun worshippers—everyone who wants to see the world down under. New Zealand is a smaller country of glacial mountains, rich green forests and pastures, long deserted beaches—natural wonders that attract hikers, skiers, fishing enthusiasts, and the more sedentary who just want to drink in the scenery. The islands of the South Pacific have been the stuff of dreams for hundreds of years: white-sand beaches, blue waters, glorious flowers, warm people. *Fodor's Australia, New Zealand, and the South Pacific* is designed to help you plan your own trip here—based on your time, your interests, your budget, your idea of what this trip should be. Perhaps having read this guide you'll have some new ideas. We have, therefore, tried to offer you the widest range of activities and within that range selections that will be safe, worthwhile, and of good value. The descriptions we provide are designed to help you make your own intelligent choices from among our selections.

The first section of this book, Planning Your Trip, consists of material designed to help you to decide where and how to travel around these Pacific destinations, providing you with general information on what sorts of activities, amenities, methods of transportation, and the like are available.

Next the book breaks into the three specific areas covered. The Australia and New Zealand sections open with Facts at Your Fingertips, consisting of information about each country as a whole: climate, time zones, tipping practices, and such. Then there are introductions to each country, to help you with the background of the area: some history, the people and their way of life, and so on. Following comes the detailed descriptions of the countries by area. Each area is at first broadly described; following is Practical Information to help you explore each place: how to get there, how to get around, hotels, restaurants, sports, tours, and more. The South Pacific section opens with an introduction to the islands, and then each island is described in depth: again, broadly at first, with all the Practical Information following.

All selections and comments in *Fodor's Australia, New Zealand, and the South Pacific* are based on personal experiences. Errors are bound to creep into any travel guide, however. Much change can and will occur even while we are on press, and also during the succeeding twelve months or so that this edition is on sale. We sincerely welcome letters from our readers on these changes, or from those whose opinions differ from ours, and we are ready to revise our entries for next year's edition when the facts warrant it.

Send your letters to the editors at Fodor's Travel Guides, 2 Park Avenue, New York, NY 10016. Continental or British Commonwealth readers may prefer to write to Fodor's Travel Guides, 9–10 Market Place, London W1N 7AG, England.

PLANNING YOUR TRIP

by
LOIS K. BRETT

Speaking in today's terms, perhaps one of the most notable comments one can make about the South Pacific is that it is a safe destination. Almost without exception, tourists can roam at will and feel comfortable wherever they travel. It is still possible to stroll the streets almost anywhere without fear, especially on the small islands. Except for the major cities in Australia and New Zealand, most towns are small, many like the village towns in England. Some towns in Australia and New Zealand, are very much like the towns and cities as they were in the 1940s in the United States—both as to their Victorian structures and in the leisurely style of that time. Some of the small villages in the island communities are very much as they were 50 or 100 years ago.

The 1980s, however, brought dramatic changes to the South Pacific—all to the better for the tourist. Before that time, it was not only expensive to get there, but it was confusing, owing to the multiplicity of standards in accommodations and services. There were no international hotels in the real sense, and air fares were almost prohibitive.

Much of that has been changed, and today travelers will find the South Pacific recovering from an almost total face lift. The entry of world-class hotels throughout the area triggered many renovations, with hotels everywhere sprucing up their properties and management becoming very conscious of the expectations of the international traveler.

Fortunately for the visitor to the South Pacific, hotel rates did not go sky high with all the building of new hotels, upgrading, and renovations. Instead, tourists came out ahead and will find many accommodations well below U.S. rates for equivalent hotels in North America—including the Hyatt, Hilton, Regent, and Sheraton. These hotels played a major role bringing the South Pacific up to world standards, and today the international traveler will find some of the best hotels and resorts in the world. Today almost all of the major hotels in regions covered in this book have been brought up to the standards expected by world travelers.

The strength of the dollar in past years has made the South Pacific a tremendous bargain. Though some air fares may be considered high compared to fares to Europe, once you are in the South Pacific, hotels, meals, and sights become inexpensive because of the break the tourists get with the U.S. dollar.

The variety of hotels and price ranges are as wide as the number of hotels—from plush to downright inexpensive. As an extra, and one that most American hotels do not offer, most of the hotels in the South Pacific offer tea-and coffee-making facilities, along with complimentary coffee, tea, sugar, and cream. (This is particularly so where there was once British-colonial influence.) And for the benefit of those on a budget, most of the smaller motel and hotel units have kitchenettes—some even have washers and dryers. Almost all hotels have irons, ironing boards, and hair dryers—along with converters, so you can plug into their 220-watt system.

Another bit of good news is that air fares are competitive, bringing the price of an airline ticket to the South Pacific within the reach of anyone who may have thought that only Europe was affordable. Each of the airlines flying to the South Pacific offers packages or special air fares for special seasons. Some tour operators offer packages that include hotel and airfare at prices almost equivalent to the regular economy air fare to the same area. Other savings are available with fly-drive or fly-drive-hotel packages (see Tour Operators).

Because of the distances covered across the Pacific, many tour operators offer multiple-destination packages. Such a package might include Australia, New Zealand, Cook Islands, Tahiti, and Fiji, complete with hotel and airfare. Another may include Australia with Fiji, Papua New Guinea, or another country in the South Pacific, with hotels and air fare included. There are many possibilities worth looking into, especially those that include more than one destination in a South Pacific holiday.

PLANNING YOUR TRIP

When planning your trip, it is worth looking into traveling during low season. Most of the countries have seasons that are the reverse of those in North America. Air fares during that period can mean big savings on tickets. And with many of the countries on or near the equator, the "best season" is almost year round.

Be aware, however, that air carriers to the South Pacific (Air New Zealand, Continental, Qantas, United Airlines, and UTA French Airlines) do not all travel the same route. Depending on your time, and what you want to see, there are many advantages to flying one air carrier over another (see Stopovers).

Air New Zealand allows the most free country stopover privileges to the South Pacific. From Los Angeles, you can visit Honolulu and Fiji on your way to New Zealand (Auckland). This fare also includes stopovers in Wellington and Christchurch (New Zealand), and you can spend time in the Cook Islands and/or Tahiti, on your way home—all for $US1,050. For $US50 more, you can add either Sydney or Brisbane (Australia) and still stop over in the Cook Islands and Tahiti enroute to Los Angeles (1986 air fares).

Qantas has a similar $US1,100 fare from San Francisco or Los Angeles, but the routing is different. Stopovers include Honolulu, Sydney, Brisbane, Cairns (Australia), Tahiti, and the choice of either Fiji or New Zealand on your return route.

UTA French Airlines has special packages to Tahiti, and *Continental Airlines* has packages to Australia and Fiji. (See Tour Operators for air carrier–air tour packages.)

Flying is not the only way to get to the South Pacific. In 1986, there were more cruise ships in the Pacific than ever before. Some offered long cruises; others offered short or segmented (port-to-port) travel packages. This latter plan makes it easy to fly to one destination and leisurely cruise to another. (See Cruises).

If you want a change from your usual holiday and in complete contrast to your normal routine, try variety. It brings an extra dimension to travel which should be just the thing to give your vacation added zip. For specific information, write to the national government tourist office. Your special interest may be one which has clubs or other activities in which you may wish to become involved.

TOURIST INFORMATION. All the major tourist countries maintain official information bureaus in important cities: New York, San Francisco, London, Toronto, and many others. They have a wealth of free printed matter to help you in planning your trip and they are at your service to give you any additional special information you may require. There is no charge for any of this. They do not, however, issue tickets or make hotel reservations.

There are many special holidays and events in the Pacific that are well worth seeing. Take advantage of these cultural experiences by planning ahead. Write to the tourist bureaus listed below for specifics.

Remember that in the case of Australia and New Zealand the amount of information available is so great that you should try to specify which areas within these two countries you wish to visit or indicate your special interests.

Addresses of the official tourist information bureaus in the South Pacific Islands, Australia, New Zealand, the United States, Canada, and the United Kingdom are:

American Samoa. Head Office: *Economic Development–Tourism Office,* American Samoa Government, Box 1147, Pago Pago, American Samoa 96799. Tel. 684/633–5187. Tlx 782501. Australia: 327 Pacific Holiday, North Sydney, NSW, 2060. Tel. 929-7027. Tlx AA70183.

Australia. *Australian Tourist Commission.* Head Office: 324 St. Kilda Road, Melbourne, Victoria, 3004. Tel. (03) 690–3900. Tlx 31911. Cable AUSTOUR. Sydney: 5 Elizabeth St., Sydney, NSW, 2000 Tel. (02) 233–7233. Tlx 22322. **North America:** 3550 Wilshire Blvd., Suite 1740, Los Angeles, CA 90010. Tel. (213) 380–6060. Tlx USA 674940. Cable AUSTOUR. 1270 Avenue of the Americas, New York, NY 10020. Tel. (212) 489–7750. Tlx USA 640747. Cable AUSTOUR. 636 Fifth Ave., Suite 467, New York, NY 10111–0043; **United Kingdom:** 4th floor, 20 Savile Row, London W1X 1AE. Tel. (01) 434–4371 & 2. Tlx. 266039. Cable ATCLON. **New Zealand:** 15th floor, Quay Tower, 29

PLANNING YOUR TRIP

Customs St., West, Auckland 1. Tel. (09) 79–9594. Tlx 21007. Cable AUSTOUR.

Cook Islands. *Cook Islands Tourist Authority:* Head Office: Box 14, Rarotonga, Cook Islands. Tel. 29–435. Tlx 2006. Cable COOKTOUR. **North America:** Any *Air New Zealand* office. **United Kingdom:** Any *Air New Zealand* office. **Australia:** Any *Air New Zealand* office; Walshes World, Box R177, Sydney, NSW, 2000. Tel. 232–7226. Tlx 70655. **New Zealand:** Box 3647, Auckland. Tel. 794–314. Tlx 21419.

Fiji. *Fiji Visitors Bureau:* Head Office: GPO Box 92, Thomson Street, Suva. Tel. 22867. Tlx FJ2180. Cable TOURIST FIJI. Or Box 9217, Nadi Airport, Nadi, Fiji. **Australia:** 38–40 Martin Place, Sydney, NSW, 2000. Tel. 231–4251. Cable FIJITOUR. **New Zealand:** Room 605, Tower Block, Canterbury Arcade, 47 High St., Box 1179, Auckland 1. Tel. 732–132. Cable FIJI HOLIDAY. **North America:** 3701 Wilshire Blvd., Suite 316, Los Angeles, CA 90010. Tel. (213) 389–0292; (800) 621–9604. Tlx (0230) 759972. **United Kingdom:** Marketing Services (Travel and Tourism) Ltd., Suite 433, High Holborn House, 52–54 High Holborn, London WC1V 6RL. Tel. (01) 242–3131. Cable SUPER EPS.

Kiribati. *Government of the Republic of Kiribati,* Box 261, Bikenibeu, Tarawa, Kiribati. Central Pacific. Tlx K177039 RESOURCES. Cable: RESOURCES.

New Caledonia. *Office Territorial du Tourisme.* Head Office: B.P. 688, 25 avenue du Marechal Foch, Noumea. Tel. 27–2632; Tlx 063 NM. Cable TOURISME. **Australia:** 13th floor, 39 York Street, Erskine House, Sydney, NSW, 2000. Tel. 292–573. Tlx 10101 INTSY. **New Zealand:** *UTA French Airlines,* 11 Commerce St., Auckland. Tlx TRAVSERV NZ21419.

New Zealand. *New Zealand Government Tourist Office.* Head Office: New Zealand Government Tourist & Publicity Dept., Private Bag, Wellington. Tel 728–860 Tlx NZ 3491. Cable TOURISTO. **United States.** Alcoa Bldg., Suite, One Maritime Plaza, San Francsico, CA 94111. Tel. (415) 788–7404. Tlx 34271. Cable HINAU. 10960 Wilshire Blvd., Suite 1530, Tishman Bldg., Los Angeles, CA 90024. Tel. (415)–7404. Tlx 34271. 630 5th Ave., Suite 530, New York, NY 10111. Tel. (212) 477–8241. Tlx 23012088. Cable WHANAKE. **Canada:** 701 W. Georgia Street, Suite 1120, Vancouver, BC V7Y 1B6. Tel. (604) 684–2117. Tlx 04–55186. Cable POHUTUKAWA. **United Kingdom:** New Zealand House, Haymarket, London SW1Y 4TQ. Tel (01) 930–8422. Tlx: 24368. Cable DEPUTY LONDON SW1. **Australia:** 115 Pitt St., GPO Box 614, Sydney, NSW, 2000. Tel. 233–6633. Tlx AA20781. Cable ENZEDTOURS. 330 Collins Street, Box 2136T, Melbourne, Victoria, 3000. Tel. 676–621. Tlx AA 30482. 288 Edward St., Box 62, Brisbane, Queensland, 4000 Tel. 221–3722. TLX 41803. 16 Georges Terrace, Box X2227, Perth 6000. Tel. 325–7347. Tlx 93700.

Papua New Guinea. *Tourist Association of Papua New Guinea.* Head Office: Box 773, Port Moresby. Tel. 27–2287. Tlx 22375. Cable PANGTOUR. **North America:** *Air Niugini National Airline Papua New Guinea,* Box 1801, Laguna Beach, CA 92652. Tel. (714) 752–5440. Tlx 910–596–1501 NW PT BCH NPB.

Solomon Islands. *Solomon Islands Tourist Authority.* Box 321, Honiara., Tel. 442. Cable TOURIST.

Tahiti. *Tahiti Tourist Promotion Board.* Head Office: Fare Mankhini, Blvd. Papeete, BP 65, Papeete. Tel. 29–626. Tlx OFFTOUR 254 FP. Cable OFFTOUR. **United States:** 4405 Riverside Dr., Suite 204–205, Burbank, CA 91505. Tel. (800) 272–3282. Tlx 66–2743. 20 Park Pl., Suite 611, Boston, MA 02116. Tel. (617) 426–6108. 35 E. Wacker Dr., Chicago, IL 60601. Tel. (312) 372–5628. 3300 W. Mockingbird La., Suite 534, Executive Tower, Dallas, TX 75235. Tel. (214) 350–1592. One Penn Plaza, Suite 2206, New York, NY 10119. Tel. (212) 563–3830. TLX 968928. 212 Sutter St., Suite 600, San Francisco, CA 94109. Tel. (415) 956–8501. 1411 Fourth Ave., Suite 630, Seattle, WA 98101. Tel. (206) 624–7537. 550 Palea St., Honolulu, HI 96319. **Canada:** 2 Carlton Street, Suite, 1519, Toronto, Ontario M5B 1K2. Tel 416/977–5321. **Australia:** B.N.P. Bldg. 12 Casterleigh Street, Sydney, NSW 2000. TLX INTSY AA10101. Tel. 231–5244.

Vanuatu. *Vanuatu Visitors Bureau.* Head Office: Box 209, Port Vila, Vanuatu. Tel. 2813. Cable: TOURIST.

Western Samoa. *Department of Economic Development,* Box 862, Government of Western Samoa, Apia. **North America:** *Samoa Mission of the United Nations,* 820 2nd Ave., New York, NY 10017. *Polynesian Airlines,* 9841 Airport Blvd., Suite 808, Los Angeles, CA 90045.; **Australia:** c/o WS Representative in Australia (Tourist), 12th Floor, 95–99 York Street, Sydney, NSW, 2000;

PLANNING YOUR TRIP

W. Samoa Visitors Bureau, 1st Floor, Clarence Street, Sydney, NSW, 2000.
New Zealand: Western Samoa Consul Agent, 3rd Floor, Maota Samoa, 283–293 Karangahape Road, Auckland;

ENTRY REQUIREMENTS. A valid passport is required for all destinations in this book. For other requirements see Facts at Your Fingertips for Australia and New Zealand and Practical Information for the specific islands.

Health Certificates. In 1986, the *International Association for Medical Assistance to Travelers (IAMAT)* issued a release warning tourists of the malaria increase throughout the world, including many destinations in the South Pacific. Chloroquine has been the usual treatment; however, in Papua New Guinea and the Solomon Islands, there is a tolerance problem and visitors should consult their doctors. Malaria medication *must be continued for six weeks after leaving infected areas.* For IAMAT's free folder *How to Protect against Malaria,* which gives complete details about the disease, its control, and high-risk areas, write: IAMAT, 736 Center Street, Lewiston, NY 14092. In Australia: St. Vincent's Hospital, Victoria Parade, Melbourne, 3065; Canada: 188 Nicklin Road, Guelph, Ontario N1H 7L5.

Other Medical Assistance Associations: Intermedic, 777 Third Ave., New York, NY 10017, (212) 303–1777, consists of an international network of English-speaking physicians in over 90 countries throughout the world. The cost for a one-year membership is $6.00. Membership includes a directory of participating physicians along with their addresses and both home and office telephone numbers. These doctors will respond promptly to calls from members.

Worldcare Travel Assistance Association, Inc. is staffed worldwide 24 hours a day by American physicians, nurses, and paramedics as well as a team of multilingual assistance coordinators. Worldcare provides medical assistance, evacuation, and hospitalization coverage, as well as immediate advances of funds for medical costs incurred abroad. If a member is hospitalized for more than 10 days, round-trip airfare and up to $1,000 living expenses is provided for minors if left unattended as a result of member's hospitalization. Individual and family memberships are available for any length of trip. For information: Write 2000 Pennsylvania Ave., NW, Suite 7600, Washington, DC 20006, or call (202) 293–0335 or (800) 521–4822.

I.T.C. Travellers Assistance Ltd. This international group offers assistance service with coordination centers in 174 countries. Trained, local, multilingual personnel provide free medical aid 24 hours a day. Worldwide membership includes: free telephone access to any of eight ITC emergency control centers, all required medical assistance (ambulatory, hospitalization, prescribed medication, transportation), repatriation, free return tickets for children left unattended because of the member's hospitalization. Individual or family membership is available for any length of trip up to 180 days. Write the above: Box G-759, Station G, Calgary, Alberta, Canada T3A 2G6. Or call (403) 228–4685. Telex 03–825754.

The U. S. Department of Health and Human Services, Public Health Service Centers for Disease Control, Atlanta, GA 30333, makes the following suggestions for visitors to South Pacific destinations: gamma globulin, typhoid-tetanus: two shots 30 days apart, if you've had no immunization before, or typhoid-tetanus booster and polio booster if it has been ten years since your last. *These are not requirements to enter these countries, but they are strongly recommended.* Please consult your physician. You may also wish to check with your doctor about the gamma globulin shot; because of the AIDS scare, some people have preferred not to take this shot. This is totally your decision, but it would be wise to have professional advice.

The health requirements for each island are in their Practical Information sections.

WHAT TO PACK. The smart, sophisticated traveler usually packs light. And don't forget to save space in your suitcase for purchases. A plus for travelers to the Pacific, according to Air New Zealand, is that your baggage allowance has been changed for the old 44- and 66-pound weight. Now you are allowed two pieces of luggage, plus one carry-on. The total for economy is two pieces with an overall length-width-height no more than 104 inches. No

PLANNING YOUR TRIP 5

single piece may be over 62 inches. For first-class passengers, the rules are the same, except they have a 124-inch limit. Total weight for both classes is 70 pounds per piece of luggage. Carry-on luggage may not exceed 44 inches.

What to wear. Australians, New Zealanders, and South Pacific islanders dress casually for most occasions. Generally, the best approach is to dress as you would in your home city, and this goes for both men and women. However, a coat and tie are worn when dining in international hotels or for any formal occasion. Men everywhere tend to be more casual in their dress than women. Resort wear in the South Pacific is the same as it is in any part of the world. Bright colors and prints are worn on most of the islands.

City wear for women: Casual dress or skirts and blouses with jacket or sweater. In the evening, however, women enjoy dressing up a lot more than the men—from casual to cocktail attire, depending on the occasion. It's a good idea to have a sweater for cool evenings anywhere.

For men: Lightweight suits and ties are worn by most businessmen or when going to dinner, but slacks and sport shirt are proper most everywhere, except for formal occasions.

Island and resort wear for women: Loose-fitting casual summer clothing—drip-dry cotton or wash-and-wear are ideal. Lightweight skirts and blouses are practical. Shorts and bathing suits are worn on beaches, around pools, and at private clubs or homes, but *never* in public. In the villages, South Pacific islanders are very modest.

In Tahiti and some of the other islands, the *pareau* (a single cloth worn as a wrap-around) can take the place of a dress and is worn from breakfast to dinner. At most, all you'll need are one or two dinner dresses, two pairs of shorts, blouses, a skirt, and a couple of bathing suits, sandals (for the beach), one pair of dress shoes, and a good pair of walking shoes. At international hotels, such as the Hyatt or Regent, women dress up for dinner. You might consider saving some of your travel-wardrobe money for a shopping spree in Tahiti or New Caledonia, where you can buy items from France, Italy, and London at the local boutiques. There are also many good boutiques in Australia.

For Men: Casual clothing will be the most comfortable—lightweight slacks and open-neck, short-sleeve sport shirts. Neckties and a very lightweight jacket are usually worn in the evening to international-type restaurants or formal events. Otherwise, open-neck shirt with or without jacket is acceptable. Two pairs of street shorts, shirts, a couple of bathing suits, and a sweater are about all you'll need, plus walking shoes, sandals for the beach, and one pair of street shoes. Many men wear Bermuda shorts with *long* socks in the day. For the posh resorts and hotels, enjoy yourself and dress in whatever is fashionable. Tropical clothes and shirts are seen everywhere.

Island Dress Customs: While island dress is casual, there are two exceptions—what is worn on Sunday and what is worn in villages. Just about everywhere, including Australia and New Zealand, everything shuts down on Sundays. Mornings are devoted to church services—and evenings, too, in most of the island communities. Everyone dresses in their best and the entire day is devoted to religion and family outings. Women and children usually wear white to church and many women wear broad-brimmed Panama-type hats. Men wear white shirts and ties, and some wear a lightweight jacket. If possible, you should plan on bringing along something to wear to at least one Sunday service. The choirs on any of the islands are worth going to hear. Church visitors are expected to honor the same custom they have at home and not wear shorts, slacks, or inappropriate clothing to services.

In town, women do not wear shorts or revealing attire. Revealing clothing on streets draws unfavorable attention and is offensive to island people. They expect you to kindly conform to their request for modesty when you are a guest in their country and not to take their request lightly. Shorts, bikinis, and other resort wear is acceptable at resorts, beaches, and your hotel.

Extras: Bring a tape recorder to bring back the sounds of the country and to enjoy while you are there. Don't forget medication for diarrhea, insect repellent, and your camera. Converter and adapter plugs for electric razor or hair dryer (see Electricity in the appropriate chapters). Bring extra tapes, batteries for your tape recorder and camera, and lots of film—they're very expensive everywhere except in Australia. Remember, you'll be in the tropics, so bring film that will function well in the glare.

If you wear glasses, take along an extra pair or a prescription. Be aware that there are few optical shops, if any, on the small islands. Sunglasses are extremely important in the tropical area—it is wise to have a pair even if you don't usually wear them. The reflection of sky, water, or white sandy beaches can create big problems. If you plan on relaxing under that palm tree reading, it may be worth the investment of purchasing a pair of sunglass reading spectacles.

It is important to take care of your skin in this tropical land. For protection, you'll need a powerful sunscreen. Make sure you apply this your first few days. After that, you can reduce the number of the screen. If your skin is fair, take the sun a little at a time and keep your skin lubricated. A sun hat will help keep your face from turning to leather (it will also keep your hair healthy). Keep in mind reflection problems. If you are unprotected, it can cause serious sunburns. If your skin is oily, it is best to keep it clean. The more you perspire, the more you may wish to rinse your face to keep your oil glands and perspiration from completely clogging your pores. Small disposable towelettes are ideal for purse or pocket—but remember, fresh, cool water will also do the same job.

HOW TO GO. Between the all-expenses-paid-in-advance type of travel and the pay-as-you-go there are enormous variations, and unless you are a widely experienced traveler you will be wise to consult a travel agent on the various possibilities. We list below the four principal ways of traveling:

The group tour, in which you travel with others, following a prearranged itinerary hitting all the high spots and paying a single all-inclusive price that covers everything—transportation, meals, lodging, sightseeing tours, guides. These can range from two weeks to several months and can be taken on luxury or budget levels. Usually accompanied by experienced multilingual guides.

Furthermore, there are possibilities for special-interest tours in which you are assured of companions with similar interests or hobbies to your own. Whether you want to visit World War II sites or enjoy the South Pacific horticulture, your travel agent will be able to find you a specialized tour.

The freelance tour is now defined as following a set itinerary planned for you by the travel agent or by tour operators, with all costs in advance. You are strictly on your own, not with any group. This type of tour allows for a great deal of flexibility. Hotel reservations and transportation facilities are all taken care of by the travel agent, but no sightseeing is included—you do this on your own. If your arrangements are through one of the larger operators, their representative may meet you on arrival and help you with your luggage. This same rep can book you on sightseeing tours, if you want them, but you will pay extra for this.

The FIT (foreign independent travel) tour is the custom-made type of program, all arranged for you by your travel agent prior to your departure. The agent tailors the tour to your preferences. There's a charge for this type of service, so it's an expensive way to travel. Your air or sea travel is paid in advance; you can pay for tours as you go.

The majority of the islands in the Pacific and Australia and New Zealand require you have a visa and a paid-for onward ticket to your next destination. You must also be able to prove you have enough money, traveler's checks, or a bank draft to be able to stay within their country for the period of your visit.

Travel Agents. Travel agents are experts in the increasingly complicated business of tourism. A good travel agent (and they are everywhere) can save you time and money through knowledge of details which you could not be expected to know about. Your agent can help you take advantage of special reductions in air fares and the like, save you time by making it unnecessary for you to waste precious days abroad trying to get tickets and reservations. In the all-important phase of planning your trip, even if you wish to travel independently, it is wise to take advantage of the services of these specialists. Whether you select a large or small organization is only a matter of your preference. But be sure the agent is reliable.

If you wish your agent merely to arrange a steamship or airline ticket or to book you on a package tour, the services should cost you nothing as the agent almost certainly has a commission from the tour operator.

If, on the other hand, you wish your agent to plan an individual itinerary for you, there will be a service charge on the total cost of the work done. This may amount to 10 or 15 percent, but it will save you money on balance. If your travel budget is limited, you should frankly explain this to your agent and have an interesting itinerary worked out accordingly.

PLANNING YOUR TRIP

If your travel agent does not have brochures on the countries in this book or if you wish to know more about a specific destination, you can write to the tourist-information offices listed in this book (See Tourist Information), or you can write to the *Pacific Asia Travel Association (PATA)*. PATA is a nonprofit corporation to promote and facilitate travel and tourism to and among Pacific destinations. Write to them for information on any country in the Pacific basin: 228 Grant Ave., San Francisco, CA 94108.

If you cannot locate a travel agent near your home, we recommend writing to the following: *American Society of Travel Agents,* 3 East 54th Street, New York, NY 10022. In Britain, write: *Association of British Travel Agents,* 55 Newman Street, London W1P 4AH. Any agency affiliated with these organizations is almost sure to be thoroughly reliable.

WHAT WILL IT COST? In general, it will cost two people about $US155 per day, excluding liquor, car rental, and gasoline. However, this is a deceptive figure that will vary from island group to island group, from the main island to the outer islands, and from cities to small towns. The figure may seem high, but it includes the cost of a half-day tour as well as local transportation.

TYPICAL DAILY BUDGET ($US) FOR TWO PERSONS

Accommodation at moderate hotel	$US60
Breakfast (American style)	14
Lunch (at moderately priced restaurant)	16
Dinner (moderate to expensive restaurant)	30
*Half-day tours and local excursions/transportation	35
	US$155

Note: This fee may be a one time charge, reducing the daily rate to approximately $120 per day for two. Also, because of the climate, most travelers to the South Pacific tend to eat only one big meal and a Continental-type breakfast, so this figure can change dramatically.

One money-saving feature about the South Pacific islands is the no-tipping custom of hospitality. It will also be to your advantage to check the currency exchange rate. The cost of meals, as mentioned in the budget above, may be on the high side, since it is in U.S. dollars. Many South Pacific island countries are tremendous bargains, especially where the currency has been fluctuating. New Zealand, Cook Islands, New Caledonia, Tahiti, and Western Samoa are cases in point.

Local transportation in Australia and New Zealand and wherever else it's available is easy to use and fairly inexpensive. However, be aware that in the small island communities, there are no street signs—except in Papeete (Tahiti) —so it's usually a matter of playing it by ear and depending on the kindness of the local people to help you find where you are going. (See Motoring, Bus Service, etc., below.)

MONEY MATTERS. The press-time exchange rates for Australia and New Zealand are in their Facts at Your Fingertips sections; currency and exchange rate information is given in the Practical Information section for each island. Be advised that this information varies, so you should get the most current information before you go.

Exchange facilities are available at international airports. Most foreign currencies can be exchanged at the airport where you arrive. City banks will exchange currencies Monday to Friday (check each country for banking hours). It is recommended that you change money at the airport or city banks. Banks and larger hotels will cash traveler's checks but it will be difficult elsewhere.

In Australia and New Zealand, you can use your **credit cards** freely in most of the large towns—same with traveler's checks. However, in the small towns in Australia, New Zealand, and on all the small islands in the South Pacific, you may have problems. Most small hotels, stores, gas stations, and restaurants not only do not accept credit cards but will not cash traveler's checks. This is not

PLANNING YOUR TRIP

to be discourteous, but because they are usually mom-and-pop-type operations without the facilities or the business to warrant accepting anything other than local currency. One way to get around this is to go to a local bank on arrival and draw enough local funds for your entire stay or draw enough local currency with you before starting out each day. Another way is to draw traveler's checks in local currency, if you do not wish to carry large sums of cash. The disadvantage to the latter two is that banks have strange hours in the South Pacific, except in major cities, and except in the large centers, many banks close for several hours at noon. Worse—you may have problems even finding a bank. Consequently, it is wise to have enough local currency with you before starting out each day.

Not all credit cards are accepted everywhere. International resorts, international restaurants, and some of the large department stores will accept *American Express* and *Diners Club. Visa* and *MasterCard* are just now making an impact, but don't count on their being acceptable anywhere but in the largest of cities of Australia and New Zealand and then perhaps only at a bank or at some of the larger international hotels and international restaurants.

HOW TO GET THERE BY AIR. There are three possibilities: by air, sea, or a combination of these. *From North America:* Look into the possibility of (1) using the maximum stopover privileges and side trips at little or no extra cost on your airline ticket (note that not all carriers offer the same routing to or through the South Pacific); (2) going around the Pacific in a circle-type tour, picking up local airlines but not retracing the same route when you head back; (3) taking advantage of various combinations of plane and ship tours that will give you an exciting itinerary; and (4) making side trips by local airlines and/or shipping companies within your destination, if you have time and can go with an open schedule. (See section How to Get There: by Sea, below.)

Except for the many international air carriers traveling to and from Australia and New Zealand, there are only five *direct* international carriers that fly to the South Pacific from the United States. *Air New Zealand, Continental Airlines, Qantas, UTA French Airlines,* and *United Airlines. CP Air* flies from Vancouver, Victoria, Montreal, or Toronto.

From Europe: You can travel by air over the North Pole through Moscow and Siberia to Tokyo, then south to your Pacific destination. You can also go through New York or from San Francisco, Seattle, or Los Angeles, to the Pacific. Another routing could be London, Bahrain, Singapore, Sydney, then to the island destinations. There are other routings, but these are the most widely used, so consult your travel agents and ask that they be imaginative.

MAJOR INTERNATIONAL AIRPORTS:

American Samoa. *Pago Pago International Airport* (7 miles from town).
Australia. International airports: *Adelaide* (about 4 miles from city), *Brisbane* (6 miles from city), *Cairns* (3 miles from city center), *Darwin* (5 miles from city), *Melbourne* (14 miles from city), Perth (8 miles from city), *Sydney Kingsford Smith International Airport* (about 6 miles from town).
Cook Islands. *Rarotonga International Airport* (3 miles from town).
Fiji. *Nadi International Airport* (5 miles from Nadi town or 15 miles from Nausori Airport in Suva).
Kiribati. *Bonriki, Tarawa International Airport* (3 miles from town).
New Zealand. International airports: *Auckland* (14 miles from town), *Christchurch* (7 miles from town), and *Wellington* (5 miles from town).
Niue. *Niue International Airport* (2 miles from town).
Papua New Guinea. *Jackson International Airport* (5 miles from Port Moresby).
Solomon Islands. *Henderson International Airport* (8 miles from Honiara).
Tonga. *Tongatapu International Airport* (14 miles from Nuku'lofa).
Vanuatu. *Bauerfield International Airport* (4 miles from Port Vila).
Western Samoa. *Faleola International Airport* (23 miles form Apia).
Wallis & Futuna. *Wallis Island Airport.* (3 miles from town). Direct flights from Nadi and Noumea.

PLANNING YOUR TRIP

STOPOVERS. There are a number of exciting ways to see the Pacific at no extra cost to you—or for very little extra cost. If you plan on going as far as New Zealand or Australia, it is possible to take advantage of airline stopover privileges. The airlines flying *directly* to the South Pacific that offer stopovers are: *Air New Zealand, Continental Airlines, Qantas, United Airlines,* and *UTA French Airlines.* Each has a unique route pattern, and it is the wise tourist who takes advantage of creative ways to get to other destinations. Note, however, that not all carriers offer the same stopover privileges.

Generally, if you have an economy or first-class ticket, you can have a number of stopovers included at no extra cost. However, if you are traveling by *excursion* or *package tour,* your stopovers will be limited. Here are the major on-line stopover possibilities to the South Pacific from North America: Hawaii, Fiji, Tahiti, Cook Islands, and numerous cities in New Zealand and Australia. If you plan on purchasing a *Circle Pacific* type ticket through Australia, it is possible —depending on the price of your ticket—to route yourself through some or all of the following destinations: Singapore, Hong Kong, Philippines, Taiwan, or Japan, with return to the West Coast. Ask your travel agent.

HOW TO GET THERE BY SEA. Cruising combines the best of everything and provides a very special kind of holiday. Because it is the largest body of water in the world, the Pacific is cruised at a leisurely pace, with plenty of time for you to enjoy the meals, entertainment, activities, elegance, and beauty of the royal-blue water. You have the opportunity to meet new people and share in their cultures. Having your floating home carry you in the dark of night from one port to the next, is travel with maximum convenience and comfort. It offers a new and exciting challenge—all without having to pack and unpack each day.

Many of the small South Pacific islands are difficult to get to, and most of the big air carriers simply fly over them, so cruising the Pacific is a great opportunity and a relaxing way for the passenger to visit these islands, many untouched by much outside influence. Sailing into one of these small ports can be one of the most rewarding experiences of the cruise, and to the islanders, it may be the greatest event of the month, so they greet cruise ships with great fanfare. At some ports of call, islanders perform on arrival with colorful and enthusiastic entertainment, and many entertainment groups go aboard and perform. The poignant farewell is quite memorable.

Today's deluxe cruise ships, which cater to every whim of the passenger, are a far cry from the whalers and trading ships that called on these South Pacific ports long ago. While ships have improved, life has changed little on many of these islands. As in years past, the arrival of a big cruise ship is somewhat important to the local people and gives them an opportunity to show their handicrafts and to earn, while it gives the passenger an opportunity to buy some exotic gifts. (*Note:* While some bargaining may be warranted, the prices of the handicrafts are usually small compared to the craft hours involved in the making, so please consider this when buying handcrafted items.)

Cruising the South Pacific really took off in a big way during the early 1980s. Cruise lines discovered that the Pacific was not only popular but profitable. Since then, more and more cruise lines have entered the Pacific, and this competition has brought better service, more and exciting ports of call, and competitive prices—all to the advantage of the traveler.

As the number and variety of cruises grow each year, each cruise line tries to come up with new ideas to lure you aboard their ships. If you are single, are dieting, want to stop smoking, are interested in theater, or would like to meet people, on board or living in ports of call, there's a special-interest cruise to fill your need. Some cruise lines have even added personal-computer courses for those who want to catch up with the electronic world.

If you have a lot of friends or want to plan a family reunion but don't want the fuss or muss at home, many families or groups of friends have found cruising the way to go. If you can put together a group of about 15 passengers, many lines will offer you a free trip. And any group, large or small, may travel as a party on almost any scheduled cruise, complete with facilities for seminars, screening special films, or whatever they need.

After you've done some of your own your research (in the Sunday newspapers, the library, your friends, and the cruise lines listed below), see your travel agent for specific advice and booking. Remember, however, your agent cannot predict what your fellow passengers will be like but can advise you about the types of people who travel on certain lines or cruises.

Ship accommodations, all meals, the voyage itself, entertainment, cruise staff services, and landing and embarkation facilities are included in the price. And you'll never go hungry. Ships today offer as many as a dozen possibilities around the clock to satisfy your appetite—and if you're still hungry, there's always room service. Cruise lines also cater to people who want to watch their calories.

The cost of the average cruise comes to about $150 per day per person. Not included in your fare are transportation to and from port of embarkation (unless it is a fly-cruise package), wines and liquors consumed on board, personal laundry, shore excursions (unless otherwise stated), port taxes, personal services such as beauty or barbershop, and tips. Some tipping suggestions follow:

Cabin steward—$5–$5.50 per person per day (he shares with cabin boy, etc.).

Dining room steward—same (he shares with busboy).

Deck steward—$6 per person per trip.

Head dining room steward (maitre d'hotel)—$40, half on departure. Some may refuse a tip.

Table captain (if any)—$20 per couple for the trip, maybe more if he prepares many special dishes at your table.

Wine steward—15% of the wine bill.

Night steward—75 cents to $2 per service, or proportionately for the whole trip if you use his services frequently.

Bartender—15% to 20% of the bar bill each time.

Most tips should be given on the last evening of your trip, with two exceptions: the bartender and the maitre d'. If you are concerned about a "good" table, the maitre d' can be of service to you only at the beginning of the trip.

Tipping on a ship is a little different from other places; you will be seeing your stewards each day and often develop a personal kind of relationship with them. As a matter of fact, you ought to, because you find out a lot that way.

If the cruise is longer than about 14 days, the daily tip average may be a little less, and half might be given after one week; the crew can use the money in port.

All South Pacific cruises are not alike, nor are all cruise ships. Each line tries to offer something unique. Some cruise lines offer bonus plans or hotel packages which allow you to stay at certain destinations at either end of your cruise at cut-rate prices. With careful selection, you can save a great deal of money or add days to your holiday. Some packages will help cut your airfare from certain "gateway" cities. Always ask your travel agent if your home city is one of the gateways; there could be a great savings here.

Like airlines, all cruise lines do not go to the same destinations. But some do, and this is where you must do your homework—selecting the cruise that fits your pocketbook and your desires. Contact your travel agent or the cruise lines listed here for more information: *Princess Cruises.* 2029 Century Park East, Los Angeles, CA 90067; or, *P & O Cruises Australasia,* 6P0546, Sydney 2001, Australia.

Sitmar Cruises, 10100 Santa Monica Blvd., Los Angeles, CA 90067; or 39 Martin Place, Sydney, 2000, Australia.

Holland America Line, Westours Inc., 300 Elliott Ave. West, Seattle, WA; (206) 281–3535. The company has a 114-year history of cruising and a policy of no tipping.

Royal Viking Line, 750 Battery St., San Francisco, CA 94111; (800) 422–8000.

Society Expeditions Cruises, 723 Broadway East, Seattle, WA 98102; (800) 426–7794; (206) 285–9400.

Exploration Holidays and Cruises, 1500 Metropolitan Park Bldg., Olive Way at Boren Ave., Seattle, WA 98101.

American Hawaii Cruises. 550 Kearny St., San Francisco, CA 94108; (415) 392–9400.

Cunard Line, 555 5th Ave., New York, NY 10017; (800) 327–9501.

TOURS. Traveling by a package or group tour, you are free of all the petty, everyday financial problems. All expenses, including hotels, transportation, meals, sightseeing, taxis and guides are paid in advance. (Meals are not included in all tours, so make certain you check with your agent as to exactly what is included in the tour you purchase.)

PLANNING YOUR TRIP

It assures you of companionship and saves you the trouble of coping with strange language and moneys. Your tour or package takes in all the important points of interest and has the advantage of leaving you free to enjoy them with never a care about the irksome details of travel. Someone else worries about train and bus connections, someone else looks after your luggage, and someone else pays the bills for you as you go along. Finally, you are able to anticipate every expense.

For first-time travelers to the South Pacific, Australia, or New Zealand, it is probably advisable you handle all your arrangements with your travel agent. (Except for small details more easily arranged after arrival.) This is where you can save considerable money on accommodations and other pleasures of the islands.

On tours or packages, you will usually find you can fairly well relax and do as you please if you do not want to take a coach tour the day one is arranged. The coach will just go off without you and you will be able to do as you please. (Just be sure you advise your tour guide ahead of time.)

In instances where the tour will move on without you to another island for overnight stays, you will have to pay your own accommodation for staying behind plus any meals involved. (This is the decision you must make before you buy your package or group tour—when you occasionally want to individualize, you will want to be prepared and make certain you'll have enough funds to cover the extra expenses.) When your group returns from their overnight elsewhere, your costs go back to the original arrangement.

Listed in each chapter are some tours offered by responsible and reliable operators. Their packages are arranged so you can sample what you want. Some of the tours are adventurous, others for sun worshipers who just want to sit and relax, some are special interest. The listings are only samplings of the vast number of the exciting South Pacific, Australia, and New Zealand trips available.

Tour Operators: There are a number of tour operators who specialize in the South Pacific and prepare excellent trips. These South Pacific specialists have many years of experience behind them and know the area well. All work closely with air carriers to provide single- or multiple-country destinations. The four types of packaged tours available are: *escorted; independent; independent and escorted;* and *special interest.* Your travel agent knows these operators and can supply you with brochures or can get one for you if you mention the tour operator listed below.

Australian Travel Service/Tour Pacific, 1101 E. Broadway, Glendale, CA 91205. All sightseeing—motorcoach, air and camping tours, apartment rentals, fly-rail and self-drive tours. Escorted and independent tours. (818) 247–4564, local; (800) 232–2121, Calif.; (800) 423–2880, U.S.

Bird Bonanzas, Box 611563, North Miami, FL 33181. Moderately priced birdwatching tours. (305) 895–0607.

Brendan Tours, 510 W. Sixth St., Los Angeles, CA 90014; (213) 488–9191, local; (800) 252–0351, Calif.; (800) 423–2880, U.S. All sightseeing and self-drive tours. Escorted and independent tours.

Club Universe, 1671 Wilshire Blvd., Los Angeles, CA 90057. (213) 484–8910. First-class deluxe escorted tours.

Globus Gateway Cosmos, 69–15 Austin St., Forest Hills, NY 11375; (718) 268–7000 (collect from N.Y. State). Deluxe first-class escorted tours.

Gold Discovery Tours, Box 4660, Sylmar, CA 91342. (818) 362–7078. Moderately priced gold-and gem-prospecting tours. Escorted group tours.

Hemphill Harris Travel Corp, 16000 Ventura Blvd., Suite 200, Encino, CA 91436; (818) 906–8086, local; (800) 252–2103, Calif.; (800) 421–0454 U.S.; (818) 906–8086 Canada, Alaska, Hawaii (collect). Luxury fully escorted all-inclusive tours. Also individual and custom tours.

Hunts of the Pacific, 760 Market Street, Suite 445, San Francisco, CA 94102. Tours to Fiji; cruise on schooner; scuba diving. 415/989–1153; 800/624–6163.

Jetabout Holidays, Los Angeles International Airport, 9800 Sepulveda Blvd., Los Angeles, CA 90045. All price ranges, sightseeing tours. Also hotel bookings, transportation passes, cruises, motorcoach, air and camping tours, and self-drive tours. Independent tours. (213) 641–8770, local; (800) 641–8773, Calif.; 213/641–8770 Alaska, Hawaii, and Canada (collect).

Jetset Tours (North America), 8383 Wilshire Blvd., Suite 432, Beverly Hills, CA 90211. (213) 651–4050, local; (800) 252–2035, Calif.; (800) 421–4603, U.S.; (213) 651–4050 Canada (collect). Complete range of South Pacific tours featuring Australia; budget, moderate, and deluxe fully escorted tours. Over 50 independent programs. Super car-rental and fly-drive vacation plans.

Maupintour, 1515 St. Andres Dr., Lawrence, KA 66046. (913) 843–1211. Luxury escorted group tours.

Omni International Tours, Box 1198, Oak Harbor, WA 98277; (206) 679–3141, local; (206) 679–3141, Wash. (collect); (800) 426–1716, U.S. Moderate, locally escorted independent sightseeing tours.

Percival Tours, 1 Tandy Center Plaza, Ft. Worth, TX 76102. (817) 870–0300, local; (800) 433–5656, U.S. and Canada. Luxury escorted tours.

Poseidon Venture Tours, 359 San Miguel Dr., Suite 303, Newport Beach, CA 92660. (714) 644–5344; (800) 854–9334, U.S.; (714) 644–5344, Calif., Alaska, Hawaii, and Canada (collect). Moderate, locally escorted group and individual scuba-diving tours.

Questers Tours and Travel, 257 Park Ave. South, New York, NY 10010–7369; (212) 673–3120. Moderate, escorted natural-history and special-interest tours for groups.

Royal Road Mutual Holiday, 1600 Kapolani Blvd., Honolulu, HI 96814; (808) 946–6909, local; (800) 367–5277, U.S. and Alaska; (800) 663–5335 (HI). Moderate, budget, and independent fly-drive tours to South Pacific.

Sobek Expeditions, One Sobek Tower, Suite DA, Angels Camp, CA 95222; (209) 736–4524, (local); (800) 441–1455, Calif.; (800) 344–3284, U.S. First-class escorted adventure expeditions for groups and individuals including whitewater rafting, trekking, ballooning, camel treks, and scuba diving.

TransNiugini Tours, c/o Greg Stathakis, 408 East Islay St., Santa Barbara, CA 90131. Or, Australia Travel Service/Tour Pacific: in California (800) 232–2121, Calilf.; (800) 423–2880, U.S.; (805) 569–2448, Canada (collect). Arranges tours to Papua New Guinea. Offers tours throughout the country. Special southern highlands extension by four-wheel drive into remote areas. Also excursion to Baiyer River Bird of Paradise Wildlife Sanctuary and village cultural tours.

Valor Tours, Schoonmaker Point Blvd., Foot of Spring St., Sausalito, CA 94965; (415) 332–7850. Specialists in veteran tours with organized programs throughout the South Pacific.

SPECIAL-INTEREST TRAVEL. More and more people are looking for unusual methods of travel and offbeat but purposeful pastimes. The standard tours are still popular with those on limited time or those who expect to be in the Pacific only once in their lifetime. However, special-interest tours are extremely popular. There are literally hundreds of different tours in categories ranging from hunting for artifacts and birdwatching to finding World War II battle sites. The problem is to select the right one from so many. No matter what your interest, there is most probably a package holiday or a club to share on arrival. If you don't like package tours, you can still go it alone, putting purpose into travel by arranging for special visits before you leave home. If you don't want to plan ahead, you can wait until you arrive and check with the tourist offices.

If you want a change from your usual holiday or a complete contrast to your normal routine, try variety—such as those listed below. It brings an extra dimension to travel and can be just the thing to give your vacation added zip. For specific information, write to the national government tourist office (see Tourist Information).

Here are examples of the diverse interests to be enjoyed or explored.

American Samoa. Anthropology. This is the country Margaret Mead wrote about in *Coming of Age in Samoa.* Reading this book before you arrive will give you an insight to the culture at the time of Mead's visit. If your interest is literature, there's more for you here. Somerset Maugham wrote of Samoa; the hotel where Maugham placed his character Sadie Thompson is now Max Halleck's store No. 3. Robert Louis Stevenson wrote lovingly of Samoa, and almost any book written by him will give you some insight to the country. If you don't read them before you arrive, take these books along and enjoy them while you sit under a palm tree at the Rainmaker Hotel in Pago Pago. Other special interests you can pursue here: tapa cloth, dressmaking, LBJ Tropical Medical Center, photography, tuna canneries.

Australia. Australia has, perhaps, more special interests than any other country in the world. Whatever your hobby or lifetime pursuit, Australia has

PLANNING YOUR TRIP

one to match yours. From the arts to animal life (kangaroos, wallabies, koala bears, water buffalo, crocodiles, and a great variety of bird life), astronomy, camping, casino gambling, cattle, crafts, farming, fauna, flora (eucalyptus trees, wildflowers—especially in Western Australia and varied parts of the desert), gems and minerals, historical sights, horse breeding, horticulture, national parks, ornithology, railroading, sheep, sports (tennis, yachting, fishing, lawn bowling, and cricket are only a few), trekking, train travel, wine making, and World War II veteran tours. These are only a few of the hundred.

Cook Islands. Fruit processing, horse racing (but not the serious type—Cook Islanders never guarantee their horses will cross the finish line; a lot depends on how the horses feel that day), numismatics, philately. Stamps and coins from the Cooks are sought by collectors throughout the world.

Fiji. Flora, Fijian dancing and firewalking, philately, photography, pottery making, rail touring through sugar-cane fields, tapa-cloth making, and weaving.

Kiribati. Bird sanctuaries (largest in the Pacific is on Christmas Island), World War II (Tarawa is the site of one of the most vicious battles in the war), Robert Louis Stevenson (site and hotel on Abemama Island).

New Caledonia. Aquariums, botanical gardens and zoos, nickel mining, shopping for French items: lingerie, shoes, fabrics, and clothing for women, as well as ties and shoes for men.

New Zealand. Like Australia, New Zealand offers a wide variety of special interests: anthropology, archaeology, cultural artifacts, dairying, farming, fiords, glaciers, meat industry (65% of world exports of lamb and mutton come from New Zealand), greenstone (a type of jade), railway museum and train travel, research museum of New Zealand Geological Survey, wool industry, trekking, tramping, and national parks.

Papua New Guinea. Anthropology, archaeology, bush walking and trekking, historical walks (covering trails from World War II, including the Kokoda Trail), ornithology, plantation visits (coffee, tea, rubber, and coconut), philately, shells, singsings (village festivals).

Solomons. Birdwatching, garden touring, philately, veteran tours and World War II artifacts.

Tahiti. Aerial sightseeing, anthropology, archaeology, botany, exploring different islands of French Polynesia, Gauguin Museum.

Tonga. Birdwatching, Captain Cook's discovery tour, Christianity affinity tours, coconut processing, dancing-feasting, farming, handicrafts (Tonga weaving, basketware, and tapa cloth are among the best in the Pacific), philately, whale watching.

Vanuatu. Artifacts, art centers, bird watching, Pentecost land divers, shell collecting, Stone Age people (the Big Nambas).

Western Samoa. Aerial tours, feasts and dancing, island exploring, plantation visiting (copra), shell collecting, tapa-cloth making, basketware and weaving (among some of the finest in the Pacific). See also American Samoa, above.

INTER-ISLAND SHIPS. You may be able to schedule a number of unusual and adventurous trips by checking out the ships that travel from port to port in the list below. Many ships that travel between small islands carry everything from chickens to light freight, mail, and hearty, adventurous passengers. Write: *Bank Line Pty Ltd.,* 18th floor, One York St., Sydney, NSW, 2000, Australia; *Chandris Lines,* Chandris House, 135 King St., Sydney, NSW, 2000, Australia; *Lloyd Triestino,* 8 Spring St., Sydney, NSW; *Nauru Pacific Line,* 80 Collins St., Melbourne, Victoria 3000, Australia. Comparing shipping companies on a regional basis, it is possible to travel for months on end by arranging your trip between local shipping lines and regional air carriers. This type of travel is not for those in a hurry, as much of the shipping schedule of these boats depends on the loading and unloading of goods and cargo. Contact the addresses below for additional information.

American Samoa: An inter-island boat runs from Pago Pago to Apia in Western Samoa and to Manu'a Islands in American Samoa. *Government of American Samoa, Office of Tourism,* Pago Pago, American Samoa 96799.

Australia: The *Elizabeth E* has 4-day cruises in and around the Whitsunday Islands and the outer Barrier Reef. *Elizabeth E Cruises,* 102 Goldsmith St., Mackay, Qld., 4740. Roylen Cruises offers a 5-day cruise to the Great Barrier Reef through the Whitsunday Islands. *McLean's Roylen Cruises,* River St., East Mackay, Qld., 4740, Australia. *M. V. Coonawarra P/L,* 289 Flinders St., Adelaide, South Australia, 5033. Offers 42-passenger diesel-engine paddlewheeler *Coonawarra* making 5-day trip on Murray River. *Murray River Queen,* c/o South Australian Government Tourist Bureau, 151 Franklin St., Adelaide, South Australia, 5000. Paddle wheeler makes a 5-day cruise from Goolwa to Swan Reach and back. *M. V. Kurrukajarra,* Box 1901, Townsville, Qld., Australia 4810. Offers 5-day cruises from Townsville through the Hinchinbrook Channel visiting the Palm Islands Group, Family Islands Group, Dunk Island, Bedarra Island and the Great Barrier Reef.

Cook Islands: *Silk and Boyd Ltd.,* Box 131, Rarotonga, operates cargo vessels between the islands of the Cook Group on the 400-ton *Manuvai,* 17-passenger ship.

Fiji: *Blue Lagoon Cruises, Ltd.,* Box 54, Lautoka, Fiji; tel: 61–612. *Seafarer Cruises,* c/o Hunts of the Pacific, 760 Market St., San Francisco, CA 94102. In Fiji: tel. 61–500. A three-masted schooner for the very adventurous.

Kiribati: There is no scheduled passenger service. Local transport would be questionable for the average tourist. However, the *Gilbert Islands Shipping Corp.* offers occasional service according to cargo requirements. For details, write to *Kiribati Tourist Bureau,* Box 77, Bairiki, Tarawa, Kiribati, Central Pacific.

Tuvalu: *Ministry of Communications and Transport Vaiaku,* Funafuti, Tuvalu, Central Pacific. Service between Tuvalu Islands, Kiribati, and Fiji.

New Caledonia: Cruises to the coral reef and nearby islands. Write *Office of Tourism of New Caledonia,* 27 rue de Sebastopol, Noumea, New Caledonia.

New Zealand: Wellington to Picton service (52 miles across the Cook Strait) is operated by *New Zealand Railways* aboard four ferries for passengers, automobiles, and railway freight cars. Daily sailings from Wellington.

Papua New Guinea: Cargo/passenger service between Madang and Lae is offered by *Lutheran Shipping M.V. Totol,* Box 789, Madang, PNG.

Melanesian Tourist Services Pty. Ltd., P.O. Box 707, Madang, Papua New Guinea, or UNIREP through your travel agent. Offers cruises on the *Melanesian Explorer.*

Solomon Islands: Local companies operate scheduled services to a number of islands and several other companies provide nonscheduled service. The government Marine Department runs scheduled and non-scheduled services and, like the commercial operators mentioned, can carry a limited number of passengers. The most regular services run from Honiara to the Western Solomons and Malaita. *Solomon Islands Government,* Ministry of Transport & Communications, Marine Division, Box G22, Honiara, Solomon Islands. *Ysabel Development Company,* Commonwealth St., Box 92, Honiara. *Melan-Chine Shipping Co.,* Box 71, Honiara. *Coral Seas Limited,* Commonwealth St., Box 9, Honiara. *Saratoga Shipping Company,* off Commonwealth St., Box 611, Honiara, Solomon Islands.

Tahiti: Daily boat service departs Papeete Mon.-Sun. at 9:15 A.M. Departs Moorea at 4 P.M. Takes about 50 min. on the *Keke III.* Other Moorea boats are car ferries. The *Raromatai Ferry* connects Tahiti with Huahine, Raiatea, Tahaa, Bora Bora. The *Temehani II,* operated by Société de Navigation Temehani, B.P. 9015, Papeete (Mota Uta), Tahitia, travels between Tahiti and Huahina, Rauatea, Bora Bora, Tahaa, Raiatea, Huahine, and Papeete.

Tahiti Yachting. Arue Nautical Center, Box 363, Papeete. Offers 28- to 65-foot sailboats for rental on daily or weekly basis. Write for information and rates.

Compagnie Française Maritime De Tahiti, B.P. 368, Papeete, Tahiti, Society Islands operates the *Taporo III* from Papeete (Tahiti) to Huahine Island, Raiatea, and Bora Bora islands. Fare (excluding meals) is $US15.

The *Taporo V* sails from Papeete to the atolls in the Tuamotus and the Marquesas Islands.

Ocean Voyages, 1709 Bridgeway, Sausalito, CA 94965, offers cruises aboard: 72-foot ketch *Galaxie,* 46-foot ketch *Roscop,* and 38-foot sloop *Vanessa.* Also contact *Exploration Holidays and Cruises;* See "cruises," above.

Tonga: *The Pacific Navigation Company* operates a local shipping service which connects Nuku'alofa with 'Eua, Ha'apai, Vava'u, and the Niuas. The Nuku'alofa, Ha'apai, Vava'u run is generally one round trip per week and is operated by the inter-islands ferry *Olovaha.* There are no advance bookings on the inter-island ferry due to frequent changes in service due to local commitments and weather. Write to *Tonga Visitors Bureau,* 37, Nuku'alofa, Tonga.

PLANNING YOUR TRIP

Western Samoa. Passenger/vehicle ferry service between *Upolu* and *Savaii* islands daily. The *Apia/Pago ferry* (passenger/car) leaves Apia Sun., Tues., Thurs. at 10 P.M. and returns from Pago Pago on Mon., Wed., and Fri. at 4 P.M. Bookings through *Western Samoa Shipping*, Matafele, Apia. There are several Savaii, Apia, Pago sailings each day. Make arrangements only after arrival in Samoa and confirm well in advance.

MOTORING. There is a great deal of difference in the road systems in the South Pacific—both as to upkeep and type and existence of pavement. The information below should give you an idea and help you to determine how many days you may need or want a rental car.

Australia and New Zealand have sophisticated road systems, similar to those in North America. However, you should be aware that many of the roads on the smaller islands are not asphalt but crushed coral or rock. In some areas because of the rain, roads may have a number of potholes; therefore, caution should be considered when driving these roads, especially at night.

Lightweight motor scooters are the mode of transportation for many of the local people on the small islands.

American Samoa. Roads are good in Apia and a 50-mile asphalt road runs the length of Tutuila Island from east to west, but it does not circle the island. While most roads are fairly good, there are some unpaved roads that cross the mountains to the north shore villages. It is possible to drive to the Chiefs Burial Grounds and the Ancient Site, two of American Samoa's favorite tourist sites. Worth renting a car for at least one day. *Requirements:* Local or international driver's license required. Drivers keep to the right.

Australia. Australia has over half a million miles of good roads and over 60,000 milies of express routes. It is a sophisticated and well-maintained system around all the major areas. Because Australia is about the size of the United States, most people fly from point to point (major city to major city) and then pick up a rental car within each state. There is an excellent automobile association in the country with a reciprocal plan for members of some automobile associations. The association in Australia supplies a great many maps, helps with your travel plans, and generally does the same as AAA in the United States. It's worth renting a car any or all days—but you may want to think about the long stretches between states and rent a car after arrival in each capital city and fan out from there. *Requirements:* International driving licenses are preferred and recognized for a maximum of one year. Compulsory third-party insurance is sold with each rental. Comprehensive insurance is extra and strongly recommended. *Caution:* In the outback, or regions where the roads are not paved, watch for potholes, especially during the rainy season. Drivers keep to the left.

Cook Islands. There is a road that encircles this tiny island (the island is only 20 miles around), and it is fairly good. There are a few other roads that lead off from the main highway, but most are unpaved. This is lovely island to drive around and to enjoy—stopping by beaches to picnic or swim or to just sit on the beach or under a coconut tree and read a good book. Worth having a car for one or more days. *Requirements:* You should take out a Cook Islands driver's license, which you get at the police department. Show your driver's license for identification. *Caution:* Watch for potholes and motor scooters. Drivers keep to the left.

Fiji. There are approximately 1,500 miles of roads, about 1,000 of which are all weather, and you can circle the main island of Viti Levu. There is a good road between Nadi and Suva, and most of the hotels on this island are along this road. If you want to take a leisurely drive between these two cities, there are a number of good hotels where you can enjoy lunch. The Polynesian Cultural Center—well worth visiting—is about two-thirds of the way from Nadi, en route to Suva. Without rushing, you can get to the center in about two hours from Nadi area; from there, it is only about a half hour into Suva. Worth renting a car for one or more days. *Requirements:* Home-state driver's license. *Caution:* Watch for potholes and be cautious on rainy days. Drivers keep to the left.

Kiribati and Tuvalu. It is possible to rent cars, but there are few roads. It is pleasant, however, to drive through the villages on what roads they do have. The people are pleasant and enjoy waving as you drive by. The roads are paved, but they are limited to the urban areas. There is little reason for car rental beyond one day. *Requirements:* Home-state driver's license. *Caution:* Because automobile traffic is very light, local people tend to walk in the road; be especially aware of small children both day and night. You may wish to toot your horn *lightly* when approaching people on the road so they move to the side. Drivers keep to the left.

New Caledonia. There are approximately 3,000 miles of roads in the country. Most are paved two-lane roads. Although the country dirt roads are normally well tended, there can be a problem in rainy weather. New Caledonia is like one long cigar, and it is possible to drive from Poum at the northern tip to Quen on the southern tip. There are a number of very pleasant drives. Worth renting a car one or more days. *Requirements:* A temporary driving permit is given to visitors holding a valid driver's license and passport. Drivers keep to the right. *Caution:* Drive carefully when roads are slick and watch for potholes on the unpaved roads.

New Zealand. The country has a sophisticated road system. It is an easy country to get around and drive in. It is only 1,200 miles long (about 500 on North Island and approximately 700 miles on South Island). You can drive from Bay of Islands on the northern tip to Wellington on the southern tip of North Island, on a leisure four- to six-day trip, stopping anywhere you want along the way. The road between Auckland and Wellington is only 430 miles. If you have a week, it would be pleasant to take advantage of these traffic-free roads to explore this wonderful country. There are delightful villages all along the way, with many places for you to stop to eat or stay at one of the small hotels en route. North Island is more tropical.

If you want to go to South Island from Wellington, you can cross by ferry or drop off you car and fly, then pick up another car at the airport on South Island. The south is lush and green with a number of national parks down its mountain spine. Wherever you drive north or south, you are never more than 17 miles from water (either lakes or ocean). If you have the time, New Zealand's South Island is worth exploring by car, especially if you can take four to seven leisurely days. There are many small hotels and lots of small resorts. The roads are good, and the automobile association in this country, as in Australia, is extremely helpful. Well worth the time to drive anywhere and everywhere. It is also possible to fly from point to point, and most rental-car companies will arrange to have a car for you at each stop. Suggest you rent from the company that allows you free pickup and drop-off privileges. *Requirements:* International driving licenses or hometown driver's licenses. Third-party and comprehensive insurance required. *Caution:* In some areas there are a number of one-way bridges. Watch for these and be aware of the traffic; you may have to back up all the way to allow the other driver her or his right of way. It is especially important to be aware of this, especially at dusk or at night. Drivers keep to the left.

Papua New Guinea. There are approximately 7,000 miles of paved and graded roads that connect villages, plantations, jungle and mountain areas, but there are no cross-country routes. Because of the terrain, most people travel by air. However, in each of the large towns, car rental is available and it is possible to drive around these areas. There are many delightful roads to travel on—to parks or picnic areas and beaches. Especially around Port Moresby, Lae, or Madang. It is not recommended that tourists drive anywhere in the mountain country during the rainy season or after heavy rains, except where the roads are paved. On many of the small islands, where the Germans once had a number of plantations, the road systems are quite good. While they may not be paved, they are fairly wide and usually take you through beautiful areas of white sandy beaches and past lush plantations. Worth exploring areas around the big cities, or on the small islands, for at least one day in every destination. *Requirements:* International driver's license required. *Caution:* Do not drive in the rain; watch for potholes. Drivers keep to the left.

Solomon Islands. While it is possible to rent a car in the Solomons, most of the roads are rough and lead only to main towns. The local people travel mostly by boat. You can drive around Honiara, but it is, perhaps, better to rent a car and driver or take the tours available. *Requirements:* Drivers must be 21, and you must have a current driver's license. Drivers keep to the left.

Tahiti. There are about 135 miles of asphalt roads and about 230 miles of stone-surfaced roads in the country. It is possible to drive around all the islands. You may have to follow maps fairly closely, since there are few or no road signs on most islands. It is almost impossible to get lost on any of the islands, since the roads generally circle the island or go only in one direction and then

PLANNING YOUR TRIP

stop—meaning you just have to turn around and go back. The roads on the island of Tahiti are fairly good, and it is possible to leisurely drive all around the island in a day, with plenty of time to stop along the way for picnics or to have lunch in one of the small villages. It is suggested you check with the tourist department, when you pick up your maps, and have them mark the villages where it is possible to get a restaurant meal. Worth renting a car for all or a part of your stay. *Requirements:* Drivers must be 21 years of age. Unlimited public liability insurance and maintenance are included when you rent a car. Renter's liability for collision is extra and recommended. Home-state driver's license required. Drivers keep to the right. *Caution:* The town of Papeete, on Tahiti—the capital and major city in the country—can be rather hectic during the commuting hours, so be wary during the morning hours between 6:30 and 8 A.M. and between 4:30 and 6 P.M. While not hazardous, except for the motor-scooter crowd, it is extremely busy on main roads to and around Papeete. On the outer islands, there is no problem, except for a few potholes. On the outer islands, people tend to walk in the road; be wary at all times, day or night.

Tonga. There are about 150 miles of paved and gravel roads on Tongatapu, 44 miles on Vava'u, 11 on Haapai, and 9 on Eau. It is possible to rent a car in Tonga, but you may have to make arrangements for a car and driver elsewhere on arrival. On Tonga, the road in Nuku'alofa town is fairly good; however, the roads tend to be a little rough once you leave the main center. Most tourists rent the small minimokes (small, colorful open-air vehicles similar to jeeps). Cars are available, however. There are many places to take leisurely drives on Tongatapu, and there are many delightful beaches where you can enjoy a picnic or swim. The tourist bureau will give you a map and mark out the beach areas for you. Worth renting a minimoke for the whole time or a car part of the time. Tonga is fun to explore. *Requirements:* You can get a driver's license at the police department in Nuku'alofa, by showing your local driver's license. *Caution:* Look out for potholes once you're out of town and be cautious when it rains. Drivers keep to the left.

Vanuatu. Roads are not permanently surfaced, except for short stretches on Efate and Santo. In some areas four-wheel-drive vehicles are the usual form of motor transport. It is up to you whether you wish to drive and how comfortable you are with four-wheel drive. *Requirements:* Public liability and property damage; passenger insurance and collision insurance required. Current driver's license or international license required. *Caution:* Watch for potholes. Drivers keep to the right.

Western Samoa. There are some 500 miles of roads; about half are main roads, but not all are surfaced. There are a number of rough secondary and plantation roads. It is possible to drive all around Savai'i and Upolu, but the roads can get a bit rough. There are a lot of beautiful areas to see and villages to visit. Worth renting a car for a day or more. Because of certain village protocols, it may be easier to hire a car and driver the first time you want to explore, then do it on your own the second time. But, be sure to settle on the price beforehand. *Requirements:* Insurance required. International driver's license honored. *Caution:* Watch for potholes. Do not drive through villages at night or on Sunday or at vesper hours—dusk. These are vesper or private hours and are spent in prayer, meetings, or with their families. Drivers keep to the right.

BUS SERVICE. On some of the small islands a local bus trip can turn out to be one of the truly delightful experiences of your travels. Some buses are the open-air type with usually enough room to squeeze in everyone on the island. Most people will want to talk to you and know where you are from and "Why you come Samoa?"

While some buses have unscheduled routes—and the routes rather irregular—you'll reach your destination eventually and make many friends along the way. Buses such as the ones on American Samoa start early in the morning and stop about 5 P.M. They do not run on Sundays or holidays.

In Tahiti a small bus is called "le truck." As with the buses in Samoa, you can't help but have fun. They are decoratively painted, fares are cheap, and you meet loads of locals with the same spirit mentioned above.

Some territories have scheduled services; many do not. Just be prepared to wait—take photos, make notes, write those post cards you keep promising to

PLANNING YOUR TRIP

send home. Most probably, you'll have just as much fun watching the passing parade.

The major cities or main tourist cities have guided tour buses (some buses holding up to 40–45 passengers) that travel between capital cities or make tours of special interest. Local agents can arrange these tours from one to as many days required for your particular project. (See individual cities for tour details.)

Smaller eight to twelve passenger buses are also available, usually for one to three-hour sightseeing tours of the major highlights.

Buses arranged by travel agents have guides to point out the sites of interest. A *Kiwi Coach Pass* allows reduced fares for bus travel in New Zealand.

TRAINS. Australia. There are 45,000 km of national and state-owned and operated railroads connecting all state capitals (except Hobart and Darwin) and many other urban and centers. The principal services follow the coast from the main terminals; an east to west line provides unbroken rail link from Sydney to Perth (via Broken Hill and the Nullabor Plain). All trains on the main trunk lines are air conditioned and have first- and second-class seats and sleeping cars. Dining cars are available on most trains. Some of the cabins and roomettes on the express trains have private toilet facilities and showers with hot and cold water. Overseas passengers are entitled to carry 80 kg. of luggage.

Accommodations. There is little difference between first and second class (economy), except that economy seating may not have reclining seats. First-class sleeping compartments have their own facilities, while those for economy class are at the end of the particular car. Some trains have motorail facilities for transporting cars.

Bookings. Reservations must be made in advance, even months ahead of time for such popular expresses as the Indian-Pacific and other long-distance trains. Peak travel periods for Australians are the summer months from Dec. through Feb.; the school holidays in May and from Aug. through Sept.; and Easter week.

Rail and Motorcoach Passes: These are great bargains but must be purchased before arrival. Allow unlimited first-class travel. See Facts at Your Fingertips for Australia.

Fiji. The South Pacific Sugar Mills offers a free service during crushing season (May-Dec.) through 400 miles of cane fields. Tourists usually take a one-hour ride out of Lautoka and then take a taxi back to town.

New Zealand. *New Zealand Government Railways,* Railways Private Bag, Wellington. Offers rail service throughout both North and South islands. The Northerner overnight express between Auckland and Wellington runs both ways nightly and is made up mainly of seat cars with a limited number of sleeping cars; has licensed dining car. There is rail/ferry service between Wellington and Picton with a number of round trips daily. In the South Island, the "Southerner" train service runs Mon. through Sat. between Christchurch, Dunedin, and Invercargill.

The New Zealand Railways Travelpass is available for rail service and for ferry service between Picton and Wellington. See Facts at Your Fingertips for New Zealand.

TAXIS. Taxi services are available throughout the South Pacific territory. However, rates and services vary to such a degree, it is best to refer to the guide listed below to judge whether or not you should use taxi services or hire a car with driver. All prices are approximate.

American Samoa. Rates are approximate. $1.00 for short ride; $16 for circle island tour, or $6 per hour. Confirm rates before journey.

Australia. Readily available throughout the country. Rates vary from place to place.

Cook Islands. Taxis operate 7:00 A.M. to midnight. Rate NZ$.30 flag fall, NZ $.40 first mile, and NZ$.35 additional mile.

Fiji. Rates are by car, not per person. Plentiful and reasonable. Local trips about $.30 first mile. Journey out of town: agree on fare in advance.

New Caledonia. Rates Fr 20 per km or Fr 12 per mile.

New Zealand. Available in all major centers. Rates vary according to distance. Meters in all cabs.

PLANNING YOUR TRIP

Papua New Guinea. In district centers at $.20 per mile. Considered best means of public transportation.

Solomon Islands. In Honiara and Auki. Negotiate before riding as taxis have no meters.

Tahiti. Flag fall Fr 60 plus 45 per km, with minimum of Fr 100, in Papeete limits; Fr 90 outside city. Fares double after 11:00 P.M. Circle trip around Tahiti Island, with stops at restaurants and points of interest, approximately Fr 4,000 (1–4 passengers).

Tonga. Open air 3-wheel taxis called "Ve'etolu." Fix price beforehand.

Vanuatu (formerly New Hebrides). Rates fixed by law. No bargaining.

Western Samoa. 20–30 Sene for trips in Apia. Agree on fare out of town in advance.

MOTORSCOOTERS AND BICYCLES. Available in Australia, Cook Islands, New Zealand, American Samoa, and Tahiti. Some of the other small islands may have invested in motorscooter rentals by the time this book goes to press. Check with the local tourist bureau on arrival. Bicycles are available on some of the islands and can usually be rented through your hotel.

Special Note: While motorscooters are very popular with local people and tourists, please be warned about driving in the island communities. The accident rate is high with scooters—mostly because of potholes, soft road shoulders, and the slick conditions of the roads during and after the rains. Since traffic is usually light on the small islands, many drivers of cars and scooters tend to drive in the middle of the road and do not necessarily abide by any speed limits. So, be aware of this situation and do not drive motorscooters at night unless you know the road conditions well. Also, be aware that because traffic is light, local people tend to use the road as their sidewalk—both day and night. Insurance is strongly recommended.

HOTELS. Variety is the spice of life in the South Pacific. There's a place for every pocketbook, but you may discover a fine distinction between the sophisticated hotels of the major cities and resorts and the small motel-hotel types in the small towns or villages.

Australia and New Zealand have excellent international hotels in their major cities, and in Sydney, Melbourne, Brisbane, and Auckland, you'll find some of the finest hotels in the world—Hyatt, Hilton, Inter-Continental, Regent, and Sheraton—all with high standards, up-to-date interiors, and international know-how.

When these international giants entered the picture a few years ago, the older hotels throughout the South Pacific set about upgrading their properties and began offering the amenities expected by the international traveler—all to the advantage of the traveler, because hotel rates remained much the same. Most of the local hotels in the major cities are unique from the international chain hotels and have a different atmosphere—usually low key and usually not high-rise. They offer English charm and English facilities—pubs and ladies' cocktail lounges, which are now used by everyone.

Fiji and Tahiti have world-class hotels and resorts. The large resorts on these islands are plush and have swimming pools, tennis courts, lawn bowling, fishing boats, snorkeling, scuba diving, glass-bottom boats, water-skiing equipment, or a number of other facilities. Some have golf, and many are putting in fitness centers. The larger the hotel, the more is offered.

One money-saving way to stay at these large resorts without having to pay the high cost, $150 per day and up, is to look into packages offered by large tour operators.

Many of the small hotels in Australia and New Zealand are very much like the small hotels in the island communities. Most of the small hotels and motels are owned and run by couples, many retired, who take special pride in their operation. While the hotels are not fancy, they are comfortable, most with a small kitchenette and utensils, a bed-sitting room, and private bath. Some have swimming pools; others are close to or on the beach. What they all have is amazingly low prices. One of the reasons for the proliferation of small hotels in the South Pacific is that Australians and New Zealanders love to travel, and they do it frequently. Most prefer spending their money getting there—the hotel is secondary. Many do their own cooking and laundry.

While these small island hotels are not resorts, they usually offer some sport activities or access to nearby clubs that welcome overseas visitors. The proprietors are quite willing to assist in helping you discover the community. Large hotels have travel tour desks.

On some islands you can rent self-contained cottages by the week or month—allowing you to do as you please and to find out what getting away from it all *really* means. So you are not completely out of touch, restaurants and small grocery stores are usually nearby. If the hotel doesn't have a swimming pool, there are always the everpresent white-sand beach, palm trees, and magnificent scenery.

The small islands, like the Samoas, Tonga, or the Cooks, are unsophisticated and delightful, offering many opportunities to discover what Polynesia is all about. You'll meet many outgoing and friendly Australians and New Zealanders who enjoy sharing experiences.

Whether large or small hotel, one important point to remember is that service will vary with the climate. Learn to relax and don't expect the same rapid service you might receive in the United States. Enjoy the slow pace, whether at the dining table or awaiting room service. The climate and humidity will slowly catch up with you, and it will become easy to understand why service, regardless of how plush the hotel, takes just a little longer than in cooler destinations.

MEET THE PEOPLE. Visits to homes, farms, or ranches have become very popular in Australia and New Zealand. Accommodations range from simple to plush. All offer the hospitality of the host family, from bed and breakfast to farms and ranches, some complete with swimming pools and all the comforts of a resort. On the farms and ranches you are not obligated to do anything other than enjoy. However, many guests have wanted to find out what life on a farm or a horse or sheep ranch is really like and have enjoyed pitching in and performing some of the ranch or farm chores.

What has made the home-ranch-farm stays so popular is the sharing of common interests, news, and lifestyles and getting to know one another—country to country, family to family.

The Australian and New Zealand programs have grown tremendously over the past few years. More due to word of mouth—and by guests who have returned and brought their friends and families—than by direct advertising, other than information to travel agents.

On the small islands, it is possible to stay with local families, but such programs are not promoted by the tourist bureaus. Perhaps the easiest way to get to know the people in the islands is to stay in one of the local boarding or guesthouses. Names of these can be obtained from the tourist office and are generally quite inexpensive. If you enjoy that experience, then seek out local people for the possibility of a home stay.

If you are determined to stay awhile (more than two or three days), and with a family, write to the government tourist office and state your case. In most instances, they will respond, but it is possible that some bureaus will not; if they do not respond, it is because they might not be sanctioning stays with local families at the time. The reason for this, most probably, is that some people have taken advantage of their island hospitality, without understanding the customs.

In **Australia,** you can contact the following organizations: *Victorian Tourism Commission,* North American Office, 3550 Wilshire Blvd., Suite 1736, Los Angeles, CA 90010. Offers unique and inexpensive vacation to sheep farms in the scenic state of Victoria. All farms are within easy reach of Melbourne. For a free brochure write to the above.

Home Accommodation, 9 Westbourne Rd., Kensington, Victoria, 3031, Australia; (03) 376–1525. *Australian Home Hosting,* 35 Jacka Cres, Campbell, ACT, 2601, Australia; (062) 47–9642; tlx AA 62614 Public Telex. *Goway Travel,* 40 Wellington St. East, Toronto, ONT M5E 1C7; (416) 863–0799 (collect); and 402 West Pender St., Suite 716, Vancouver, BC V6B 1T9; (604) 687–4004 (collect). Tlx 0451170. *Bed & Breakfast Australia,* 18 Oxford St., Box 442, Woollahra, NSW, 2025; (02) 33–4235; tlx AA 27229 VACSAM or, in the United States, *Islands in the Sun,* 760 W. 16th St., Costa Mesa, CA 92627; (711) 645–8300. *Blue Haze Ranch,* Box 51, Crows Nest, Qld., 4355, Australia; (6176) 98–4949. *Farm Holidays,* 9 Fletcher St., Woollahra, NSW 2025, Australia. Tel (02) 387–681. *Host Farms Association,* 7 Abbott St., North Balwyn, Victoria,

PLANNING YOUR TRIP

3104, Australia. (03) 857–6767. *Quirindi Host Farms,* Box 293, Quirindi, NSW, 2343, Australia.

In **New Zealand,** *Bed & Breakfast, New Zealand Style,* Box 309, Nelson; (54) 82–424; tlx 39114. Between October 1 and May 31 only. Prepurchased vouchers entitle each user to a list of names of hosts whom they can contact at 24 hours' notice for bed & breakfast (dinner by arrangement at many homes). Only holders of vouchers accepted at host homes. This is a very popular program with inexpensive to medium prices. *N.Z. Farm Holidays,* Private Bag, Parnell, Auckland, New Zealand; 394–780. Developers of the original farm holidays offer more than 250 farms: working farms, sheep, dairy, horticulture, cattle, mixed pasture, as well as high-country sheep farms. Prices range from: NZ$50–NZ$55 per day including accommodation and farm-cooked meals. *N.Z. Life Vacations,* R.D. 2, Ngaruawahi, Te Akau, New Zealand; tel. 4864 Te Akau. 2 hours from Auckland or Waitomo. Provides farm life at NZ$65 a day, including all meals and accommodation. *Country Life Timaru,* C/-Kirk, R.D. 14, Cave, New Zealand; tel. 734 Cave. Cattle, sheep, pigs, turkeys, and cropping farms. Activities available: swimming, tennis, barbecues, horse riding, golf, Maori rock drawings, walking; only one hour from skiing. *Inexpensive.*

Farmhouse Holidays, 83 Kitchener Rd., Milford, Auckland 9, New Zealand; 492–171. Farm vacations for those who do not wish to be confined to a set itinerary. *Inexpensive.*

Rural Tours: The Country Experience New Zealand, Box 228, Cambridge; tel. (07127) 5091 Cambridge; (071232) 872 Maugatatari. Homes, farms, and ranches in beautiful Cambridge district, known for English heritage, antique shops, horse studs, and wealthy farms, plus 60 host homes. *Farm Stays Limited,* Box 630, Rotorua; tel. 24 895. Farms in North Island. Most farms offer leisure activities, tennis, swimming, horse riding, etc. *The Friendly Kiwi Home Hosting Service,* Box 5049, Port Nelson; tel. 85–575. Farms in Waitomo, Wairarapa, Nelson, and Murchison areas. Special emphasis on outdoor activities with professional guides for trout fishing, game shooting, wilderness trekking. *New Zealand Home Hospitality Ltd.,* Box 309, Nelson, New Zealand; Tlx NZ3697 HOMEHOSP. 350 host families throughout NZ on a paying-guest basis. *Rural Holidays,* Box 2155, Christchurch, N.Z.; tel. 61919. Farms located throughout the South Island. Cottage accommodations from top quality to old, basic cottages. Own food, linen, or sleeping bags needed. Blankets usually provided. 2-night min.; $60–$75; up to 7 nights at $135–180. Maximum occupancy 6 persons. *Fisherman Live-In Home Holidays,* offered by Club Pacific's Angler-to-Angler program. A dozen itineraries for 17–30 days, ranging in price from NZ$2,420 to NZ$3,192, including air fare from Los Angeles via Air New Zealand or Pan American. Write Mel Krieger, Club Pacific, 790–27th Ave. San Francisco, CA 94121.

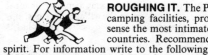

ROUGHING IT. The Pacific has some youth hostels and camping facilities, providing an inexpensive and in a sense the most intimate way of getting to know various countries. Recommended for the young in body and spirit. For information write to the following:

U.S.A.: *American Youth Hostels, Inc.,* 1332 Eye St. N.W., Washington, DC 20005; *Campgrounds Unlimited,* Blue Rapids, KS 66411; *National Campers & Hikers Association,* 7172 Transit Road, Buffalo, NY 14221.

Canada: *Canadian Youth Hostels Association,* National Office, 333 River Rd., Vanier City, Ottawa, Ontario K1L 8B9.

Great Britain: *Camping Club of Great Britain and Ireland,* 11 Lower Grosvenor Place, London S.W.1.; *The Youth Hostels Association,* 14 Southhampton Street, Strand, London W.C.2; *Worldwide Student Travel,* 37 Store St., London, W.C.1.

Australia and New Zealand have wonderful camping facilities. You can rent your equipment there, and it is fairly easy to get space in the parks year round, but it is wise to plan well ahead during the busy summer months and school holidays. Christmas—approximately mid-Dec. to early Feb.; Easter holidays; two middle weeks in May; late Aug. to second week in Sept.; and public holidays are busy times when you should make reservations.

New Zealand: *Youth Hostel Association,* 36 Customs St. East, Auckland. For camping in New Zealand, come during the summer months (December through Easter). There are two kinds of camps: "motor" or "camping" sites.

Motor camp: Provides additional and/or superior equipment and amenities.

Camping site: Provides lesser standard of equipment and is usually in remote area.

A directory, issued by the Camp and Cabin Association, is obtainable from the National Tourist Office. Reservations advisable during the December-to-Easter season.

For further information, write to the nearest *National Tourist Bureau* (see Tourist Information), or *Automobile Association* offices: 33 Wyndham St. Post to Box 5, Auckland; 166 Willis St. also Box 1053, Wellington; 210 Hereford St., and Box 994, Christchurch.

Australia: There are over 90 Youth Hostels, each state with its own association. Members of other hostels which are affiliated with the International Y.H.A. are welcome to join the Australian Association.

Inquiries concerning Youth Hostels in Australia should be directed to: *Australian Youth Hostels Association*, 26 King St., Sydney, NSW, 2000.

Campmobiles are for hire and accommodate up to five persons. They are self-contained. Rates range about $A300 per week plus mileage.

Caravan (Trailer) Hire & Camping Equipment: Equipment that can be towed behind cars and camping equipment are for hire or purchase. Camping sites have independent water supply, sewerage, hot showers, laundry facilities, and electricity supply.

Australia offers a wide variety of camping tours and safaris from 3 to 44 days. The most popular camping tours run from 8 to 21 days. Everything is well-planned, but campers pitch in and help with some of the camp chores. You can help the cook prepare the meals or set up the campfire, and you must do your own laundry. You do no heavy work, and you sleep in weatherproof two-person tents.

The tours are usually taken by the under-30 crowd, but if you have the right attitude, anyone from 16 to 70 is welcome. On these tours, you travel by 40 passenger air-conditioned coaches, complete with toilet facilities. Night stops are at camping grounds with showers and laundry facilities.

If you are on your own: standards vary from one caravan park to another, but basic amenities include electricity hookup, hot and cold water, showers, toilets, and laundry facilities. Site fees are between $A6 and $A12 per day. At some caravan parks you can rent on-site vans or cabins from A$16 to $A35 for two or more. In most cases linen and blankets can be rented. Areas are set aside for people who wish to use tents.

Australian motoring organizations and state government tourist offices will provide you with a guide to camping and caravan parks. For details, write the *Australian Tourist Commission*. (See Tourist Information.)

Small Islands: Most of the small islands discourage camping, but it is possible. However, there are specific unwritten rules. Never, under any circumstances, take it on your own to camp unless you ask permission of the owner or the chief of the local village. Most of the areas you may consider as ideal campsites are actually private property or belong to the village. The best approach is to write ahead and ask tourist bureaus what is expected and what is available.

Hospitality on the small islands is fragile. Most villagers are extremely generous and expect nothing for their hospitality, but you should realize that in many instances, local people feel that what is theirs is yours, and in return—*what is yours is theirs*. So be wary of what you wish to share, or if it is worth a campsite for what you might have that they may wish to share.

As the children and most the adults in the villages are very curious about visitors, because most tourists do not take the approach you seek, be prepared to know a little about the culture of the people before you move in on them. This is especially important so that you do not break the rules of protocol. In the Samoas, for instance, children are cherished, older people are respected, vesper hours (quiet hours at dusk) are for prayers—no one moves about in the village at that time, and no one passes a chief's house during a meeting of the village elders. There are many other customs, and other islands have similar unspoken rules.

Another reason camping is not encouraged in the islands, is that campers in the past have taken advantage of the local people—by accepting the hospitality of their hosts and not remembering that accepting hospitality requires you give something in return. Usually a few dollars given to your host or the village chief for each day you stay, or canned or bottled goods (find out what the locals buy and give what you feel is fair for the hospitality you've received). If you give money, you must do it unobtrusively—stating that you would like to buy something for the village or that you would like to buy some staples or canned goods and ask if they handle this for you. You might want to bring along some small gifts to share with children—Frisbees, balloons, ballpoint pens, pencils, small note pads, or similar gifts. And most important, remember, you may be the only contact these people have with westerners. The impression you leave behind is critical for the person who follows you and wishes to share village hospitality.

Papua New Guinea: It is possible to camp in the national parks of this country and on some of the beaches. There are a number of expatriates living in the country who enjoy roughing it and camping out, especially when bird-watching, bush walking, or trekking—which are very popular. Write to the tourist bureau for the names of local clubs where you might share club facilties or hospitality.

DINING OUT. At all the resorts and international hotels in the South Pacific, you will find good-to-excellent restaurants offering everything from a simple meal to continental cuisine. Where there is a French influence, you will find outstanding restaurants—but expensive. The better the resort or the hotel, the better chance you'll find an excellent internationally trained chef. In the smaller hotels, you will usually have to settle for less—but quite frequently you will be pleasantly surprised at the high quality. There is such a variety of food, it would be impossible to describe specialties for all the countries in this book in a paragraph or two. Listed below, however, are some of the kinds of food that can be expected and the types of restaurant facilities available. Liquor is very expensive everywhere in the South Pacific. You may want to bring your own hard liquor. Australian and New Zealand wines are fairly priced, but some others can be out of sight. Check each country's Practical Information section for particular ideas of where to dine.

American Samoa. Don't expect gourmet food here, although there are a number of different dining establishments: from pizza parlors to American food mixed with Samoan style to Chinese restaurants. Try a *fia-fia* (Samoan feast) that consists of suckling pig, chicken, fish, *pulusami* (young taro leaves cooked in coconut sauce), breadfruit, coconut, bananas, lime and mango, and other exotic fruits and vegetables. Guests at these feasts usually sit cross-legged on straw mats and are entertained by Samoan singers and dancers. Worth trying at least once.

Australia. The past few years have changed the eating patterns of the Australians and have made a lot of tourists happy. Many nationalities have immigrated to the country over the past few years, and many of these new immigrants have opened small but excellent restaurants. Most of these small places are family run and the owners take a great deal of pride in their work. Meals at many are equal to gourmet restaurants in the international class establishments. All this has brought the restaurant food picture in Australia way up on the scale of good cuisine. The introduction of many new international hotels brought many chefs with international reputations. Unlike the case in North America, some of the best restaurants in the town are in the international hotels. Hotels and restaurants in the smaller towns and villages tend to be less exciting, but the food is usually quite good.

Specialties to look for: seafood, meat (beef and lamb in particular), and tropical fruit. Oysters are outstanding, as is most shellfish. Most cities have sophisticated dining rooms, and some offer dinner dancing. Many private clubs offer meals and entertainment at reasonable prices, and overseas visitors are welcome.

Besides Australian cuisine, you'll find French, Chinese, Middle Eastern, Japanese hibachi, along with hamburgers, pizza, fish and chips, and other fast foods—including McDonalds and Kentucky Fried Chicken.

Cook Islands. Restaurants and dining facilities on Rarotonga are limited. Most tourists eat at the hotels where they are staying. There are a few small restaurants and cafes around town. Small motel-hotels usually have kitchen facilities, and many tourists cook their own meals. Moderately priced meals.

Fiji. It used to be that good food was available only at a few of the hotels. Today, however, Fiji has a number of quality resorts where you can dine alfresco on international cuisine, complete with entertainment and a live band for dancing. Meals are reasonably priced. In Suva there are a number of excellent restaurants serving everything from French to Chinese to Indian delicacies at reasonable prices. A few Fijian and Indian foods worth trying: *kokoda*—a marinated local fish steeped in coconut cream and lime; *rourou*—a special taro-leaf dish; *kassava* (tapioca) is used in a variety of dishes and is boiled, baked, or grated and cooked in coconut cream with sugar and mashed bananas. An unusual vegetable is the *daruka*—an asparaguslike vegetable (in season only during April and May). Meals: inexpensive to expensive.

Kiribati and Tuvalu. You will have to depend on your hotel. You can get excellent seafood at your hotels on both Tarawa and Christmas Island. Food on Tarawa is geared for the Australian or New Zealander. There are no tourist restaurants. On Christmas Island, you can have a huge juicy lobster or the fish you've just caught that day. Moderately priced meals.

New Caledonia. You might suspect you are in France when you taste some of the outstanding French food available here. And, there is a great variety of other foods: Indonesian, Chinese, Indian, Spanish, Vietnamese. Take your pick. The *bougna*, a native feast, consists of roast pig, fish, or chicken wrapped in banana leaves and cooked on white-hot stones covered with sand. Moderate to expensive meals.

New Zealand. In the past few years, more and more international hotels have entered the scene bringing with them chefs with international reputations. As in Australia, some of the best restaurants are in the international hotels. Many of the small restaurants offer international cuisine but most are mom-and-pop establishments, and the owners take great pride in preparation and in service.

New Zealand lamb is probably the best known, but you will find excellent beef and pork dishes on most menus, and portions are usually very generous. There is also a wide range of fish—John Dory, snapper, grouper, as well as oysters, crayfish, scallops, and game birds. If you catch your own trout, you can ask your hotel to prepare it for your dinner. The kiwi fruit is probably the best-known fruit. Other fruits and vegetables are always deliciously fresh. Recommend is *favlova*, the country's traditional dessert, a special type of large meringue. New Zealand wines are inexpensive to moderately priced. Meals from inexpensive to expensive.

Niue. There are no fancy restaurants—you will have to settle for food at your hotel. Moderately priced.

Papua New Guinea. Beef and poultry from the highlands, plus fresh vegetables and fruit are the choices you have in hotels and restaurants around the country. Seafood is delicious, and you can dine on crabs, prawns, crayfish, and barranumdi. Papua New Guineans claim their local fruit—strawberries, pineapples, papaws, mangoes, passionfruit, bananas—are the best buys in the South Pacific. There are excellent restaurants in all the international hotels and resorts. Moderate to expensive meals.

Solomons. Except for those in the Hotel Mendana and the Hotel Honiara, there are few restaurants worth writing home about. However, 28 miles west of Honiara is the Tambea Village Resort, which serves both Western and Chinese food. While you are exploring the country, it will be worth a stop for lunch or dinner. Try the fresh fruits, vegetables, and seafood anywhere. Meals will be moderately priced.

Tahiti. You can dine on goumet French food in the most elegant or simple atmosphere—but it will be expensive. You can settle for Chinese food or pizza in one of the many small inexpensive restaurants, or on the foods of Normandy and Brittany, such as frog legs or smoked salmon, for not too much money. For a few francs, you can buy the long, slender, delicious crusty French bread—as fresh as the loaves you buy in Paris. With it, and a little cheese and something to drink, you can sit along the waterfront and watch the life of French Polynesia pass by—or take off for a picnic along the beach roads. One reminder—if you want French food every day, your food expenses can go out of sight if you don't plan carefully.

Tonga. In addition to the dining rooms at the various hotels, the main street of Nuku'alofa has several small restaurants featuring Tongan food such as *'ufi* (a large white yam), taro, or *lu pulu* (meat and onions, marinated in coconut milk and baked in taro leaves in an underground oven). If you want to enjoy an evening out with music, dancing, and special entertainment, try a Tongan feast with roast suckling pig, crayfish, and chicken, with local fruits and vegetables—cooked in an underground oven. You can do this at the International Dateline Hotel, or you can try one of the feasts offered tourists at a beach setting.

PLANNING YOUR TRIP

For a special picnic try some of Tonga's huge and delicious avocados with some cheese and bread. A few good restaurants in or near town offer French, Chinese, and German food. All meals are fairly moderate to inexpensive.

Vanuatu. The best restaurants are French and situated in the hotels (mostly in Vila) or on the island resorts. All hotels in Santos have restaurants. Many cafes in Vila have French, Chinese, Vietnamese, and European menus that are not too expensive. There are also a few inexpensive pizza and spaghetti restaurants. Meals will be moderate to expensive.

Wallis and Futuna. Don't count on anything fancy here, not even in your hotel—which is just about the only place to eat. Moderate.

Western Samoa. Aggie Grey's Hotel, the Samoan Hideaway Beach Resort and the Hotel Tusitala serve the best of Samoan and Western meals. The *fia fia* in Western Samoa is the same feast as in American Samoa and worth a try. There are a few small restaurants patronized by the local people. It would be best to ask at your hotel for recommendations. Moderately priced meals.

LIQUOR LAWS in the South Pacific vary from city to city, state to state, and country to country. These different laws have frequently made a problem to the uninitiated. Some restaurants, in Australia or New Zealand for instance, do not have liquor licenses; however, you can BYOB (bring your own bottle), and the restaurant will provide the setups—glasses and mix. Bar hours can vary a great deal in these two countries, so check with your local tourist office—particularly for information on Sunday hours.

The sabbath throughout the South Pacific is greatly respected, and many restaurants and bars are closed on Sunday. This revelation frequently comes as a shock to many tourists, so be forewarned. International or world-class hotels are the exception; they can legally serve alcohol seven days a week. But, you should be aware that many of the small hotels in the South Pacific do not have restaurants or bars.

DRINKING WATER. Generally speaking, the water in most of the South Pacific Islands, Australia, and New Zealand is safe to drink in the major areas and capital cities. If there is a question about the local water, you will usually find bottled water in your hotel room and in the dining rooms. In the outlying areas of American Samoa, Western Samoa, and Tonga, drink bottled water. Drink only bottled water in the Cook Islands and Papua New Guinea.

In Tahiti the water is not all safe to drink; tourists will be safer buying bottled water.

Special note: If you are heading for remote areas, you might take a supply of Halazone, a small pill available in most drugstores. It may make the water taste peculiar, but it renders it potable.

If you plan on driving long distances, it is wise to take bottled water, no matter what country you visit.

ELECTRICAL CURRENT. The electric current varies to such a degree in the South Pacific that it is wise to carry a mini-converter. This device converts 220V foreign current into 110V domestic. The Franzus Co. (see below for address) Number 18/21 converter handles all portable appliances up to 1000 watts. Their F-11 model works with equipment up to 50 watts.

Most foreign wall outlets usually require *round* pins. In some areas you may have to use a 3-pronged plug. A plug adapter is required to fit American appliances to foreign wall outlets, but remember that adapters *do not convert voltage*. For complete information and a list of the type of equipment you may need, write to the *Franzus Co.*, 352 Park Ave. South, New York, NY 10010.

TELEPHONES. All hotels catering to the international tourist have telephone service. In many instances, costly surcharges can be added on international calls placed from a guest's room. These fees can vary from country to country and from hotel to hotel within a country. In most instances, rates are not published, so be sure to ask before you place your call. Many of the

PLANNING YOUR TRIP

smaller hotels may have have only the owner's personal telephone. In that case, go to the overseas telephone office, usually in the local post office.

There are some coin-operated phone booths in some of the larger cities and countries. Telephone service in the outlying areas, once you are away from the major tourist spots, is almost nonexistent, so don't count on phone booths along the roadway.

Phone service to North America can take a while in some of the small island communities, so be prepared.

American Samoa. Country code: 684. Coin-operated booths in Pago Pago. Telephone service available at major hotels. Limited service elsewhere.

Australia. Country code: 61. Then dial city area code and number. Coin operated phones, and phone booths, throughout the country with excellent telephone service. All tourist hotels have direct international dial service.

Cook Islands. Country code: 682. Major hotels have room telephone service. Limited service elsewhere.

Fiji. Country code: 679. Coin-operated booths in Suva. All major tourist hotels have room telephone service. Limited service elsewhere.

Kiribati. Country code: 686. Limited service throughout the country.

New Caledonia. Country code: 687. Coin-operated phones in major areas. Telephone room service at major hotels.

New Zealand. Country code: 64. Then dial city area code and number. Coin-operated phones and phone booths throughout the country with excellent telephone service. All tourist hotels have direct international dial service.

Niue. No direct phone service.

Papua New Guinea. Country code: 675. Public telephones in Port Moresby. Telephone service in major hotels. Limited in outlying areas.

Solomon Islands. Country code: 677. Available at international hotels but very limited elsewhere.

Tonga. Country code: 676. Some public phones available. Major hotels have room telephone service.

Wallis and Futuna. No direct phone service.

Western Samoa. Country code: 685. Tourist hotels have telephone service, but there is limited service elsewhere in the country.

To dial direct to the Pacific area from the United States, dial 011 (international access code) plus the country code (see above), plus the city code, if any, plus the local number. After dialing the entire number, allow at least a minute for the ring to start. Some areas, such as Kiribati, Niue, Wallis and Futuna, do not have direct dialing and you may have to place your call through an operator in Sydney, Australia—in which case your call can take anywhere from ten minutes to three hours, or longer. Contact in remote areas may be by radiophone.

MAIL. Mail to and from the island communities varies a great deal, so prepare well in advance if you are planning to use the mail for any reason. The main post office may also serve as the cable office and the telephone exchange. In many instances you may have to make your overseas calls from there. Usual post-office hours are from 8 A.M. to 4:30 P.M. but vary from island to island. A few are open on Saturday from 8 to 11 A.M. Mail boxes are few, except in the main cities. Aerograms and post cards from the South Pacific average about 50 cents mailed to North America.

You will usually have to write to post-office boxes when writing to hotels or tour operators. Few islands have direct mail services to homes or business establishments. Just make sure you write no less than six weeks in advance of any request, and expect two to six weeks for a response. Telex or telephone seems to be the fastest way to contact hotels or other businesses.

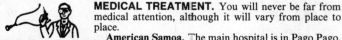

MEDICAL TREATMENT. You will never be far from medical attention, although it will vary from place to place.

American Samoa. The main hospital is in Pago Pago. Dispensaries are situated in the outer islands.

Australia. Modern hospital facilities throughout the country.

Cook Islands. The main hospital is in Rarotonga. Cottage hospitals are situated in the smaller islands.

Fiji. Medical attention available throughout the islands.

PLANNING YOUR TRIP

Kiribati. Small hospitals on Tarawa and Christmas islands. Simple medical facilities elsewhere.
New Caledonia. Hospital facilities available in Noumea. Services limited elsewhere.
New Zealand. Modern hospital facilities throughout the country.
Papua New Guinea. Hospitals in major centers. Medical attention close at hand in all other instances.
Solomon Islands. The main hospital is on Guadalcanal. Church missions have medical facilities on other islands.
Tahiti. Government hospitals and private clinics available on Tahiti. Infirmaries and dispensaries available on Moorea, Raiatea, and Huahine.
Tonga. Medical facilities available throughout the main centers of the kingdom.
Vanuatu (formerly New Hebrides). Hospitals in main centers. Small clinics in outlying areas.
Western Samoa. Main hospital is in Apia. Medical attention available in all other areas of the country.

LANGUAGES. English is widely understood throughout the South Pacific and especially in the larger cities. English-speaking visitors will have little language difficulty in the leading hotels, restaurants, travel agencies, airports, and shops.

SPORTS. It is obvious that with all that water and beach in the South Pacific, any sport remotely connected with the two is extremely popular—and there are many experts to help you swim, water ski, surf, snorkel, skin and scuba dive, sail, and fish.

However, sports activities are by no means limited to water contact. The climate is most conducive to play, and in Australia, New Zealand, and the South Pacific islands you will find much action—whether participant or spectator—all the way from skin diving in Fiji to snow skiing in Australia and New Zealand (during the northern hemisphere's summer months).

Golf, yachting, tennis, fishing, horseback riding, lawn bowling, polo clubs—members of overseas organizations devoted to any of these are usually given honorary membership rights at social and club facilities.

We recommend a letter from your home secretary written a month or so in advance to the club secretary, which will perhaps bring you a calendar of coming events and should guide you ahead of time regarding club rules. Write to local government tourist office for club addresses.

Here is a thumbnail sketch of activities. For more details, see country chapters.

American Samoa. Fishing, snorkeling, surfing, swimming, tennis, golf, skin diving, scuba diving, yachting, cricket.
Australia. Cricket, football, fishing, hunting, golf, greyhound racing, horse racing, lawn bowling, motor racing, polo, skiing, skin diving, target shooting, tennis, trail riding, trotting, yachting.
Cook Islands. Fishing, golf, horse racing and riding, lawn bowling, sailing, skin diving.
Fiji. Fishing, golf, lawn bowling, scuba and skin diving.
Kiribati. Lobster and big-game fishing, swimming.
New Caledonia. Cricket, horseback riding, snorkeling, spear fishing, swimming, tennis.
New Zealand. Fishing, golf, hiking and bush walking, horse racing, hunting, lawn bowling, skiing, tennis, rugby football, cricket, yachting and rowing.
Papua New Guinea. Bush walking, game fishing, golf, horseback riding, polo-crosse, sailing, scuba diving, squash, water skiing.
Solomon Islands. Fishing, golf, skin diving, swimming, tennis, yachting, water skiing.
Tahiti. Fishing, golf, horseback riding and racing, scuba diving, swimming, tennis, yachting.
Tonga. Boating, fishing, horseback riding, skin diving, surfing, swimming.
Vanuatu (formerly New Hebrides). Sailing, fishing, skin diving, and tennis.
Western Samoa. Boating, cricket, fishing, golf, horseracing, lawn bowling, longboat races, skin diving, swimming, tennis, track and field.

METRIC CONVERSION

CONVERTING METRIC TO U.S. MEASUREMENTS

Multiply:	by:	to find:
Length		
millimeters (mm)	.039	inches (in.)
meters (m)	3.28	feet (ft.)
meters	1.09	yards (yd.)
kilometers (km)	.62	miles (mi.)
Area		
hectare (ha)	2.47	acres
Capacity		
liters (L)	1.06	quarts (qt.)
liters	.26	gallons (gal.)
liters	2.11	pints (pt.)
Weight		
gram (g)	.04	ounce (oz.)
kilogram (kg)	2.20	pounds (lb.)
metric ton (MT)	.98	tons (t.)
Power		
kilowatt (kw)	1.34	horsepower (hp)
Temperature		
degrees Celsius	9/5 (then add 32)	degrees Fahrenheit

CONVERTING U.S. TO METRIC MEASUREMENTS

Multiply:	by:	to find:
Length		
inches (in.)	25.40	millimeters (mm)
feet (ft.)	.30	meters (m)
	Length	
yards (yd.)	.91	meters
miles (mi.)	1.61	kilometers (km)
Area		
acres	.40	hectares (ha)
Capacity		
pints (pt.)	.47	liters (L)
quarts (qt.)	.95	liters
gallons (gal.)	3.79	liters
Weight		
ounces (oz.)	28.35	grams (g)
pounds (lb.)	.45	kilograms (kg)
tons (t.)	1.11	metric tons (MT)
Power		
horsepower (hp)	.75	kilowatts
Temperature		
degrees Fahrenheit	5/9 (after subtracting 32)	degrees Celsius

PLANNING YOUR TRIP

SHOPPING. American Samoa. Tapa cloth, shell beads, purses, wood carvings, woven laufala table and floor mats. U.S. citizens can bring home $800 duty free, including one gallon of liquor from duty-free shop.

Australia. Opals, aboriginal art, handbeaten copper and silver, leather goods, toy koalas and kangaroos. Store hours: M–F 9–5:30, Sat. 9–12.

Cook Islands. Wood carvings, traditional patterns, pearl shells, woven products, embroidery, Panama hats, baskets, hand-made ukeleles. Coins and stamps are good collector's items. Duty-free shops: M–F 7:30–3:30, Sat. 7:30–11:30.

Fiji. Tortoiseshell work, filigree jewelry, wooden carvings, kava bowls. Clothing from local cloth can be made in a few days at moderate prices. (No bargaining.) M–F 8–5; closed 1–2 P.M. Sat. 8–1. Duty-free shops.

Gilbert Islands. Baskets, table mats, fans in all sizes and shapes plus a variety of other handicrafts made from pandanus leaves, coconut leaves. Shells are a big items from turtle shells to sea shells. Seashell necklaces are popular local items. Tourists usually snatch up the models of Gilbertese canoes, houses, and swords. (The swords are made from sharks' teeth.) Items are available at the handicraft store in Beito. Hours: M–F 8–5. Closed from noon to 1 P.M. Sat. 8–noon.

New Caledonia. Items of shell, coral, wood carvings and handpainted materials, aloha shirts, tapa cloth, Polynesian music records. French best buys: lingerie, shoes, fabrics and clothing for women. Ties and continental shoes for men. Boutiques with Italian shoes, sportswear from London. Store hours: M–F 7:30–5:30, closed 11–2; Sat. 7:30–11.

New Zealand. Greenstone items (jade) such as brooches, earrings, tie pins, and tikis; shell items, wood items: bowls, cribbage boards, Maori gods, walking sticks, war clubs, woolen car robes, lambswool rugs and sweaters.

Papua New Guinea. Carvings, statuettes, ceremonial masks from Angoram and Sepik, crocodile carvings from Trobriands, Buka basketware, arrows, bows and decorated axes from the highlands. Carvings and artifacts can be bought in most towns and settlements at reasonable prices. Some stores ship purchases. In Port Moresby, *Trobriand Crafts* on Douglas St. and *Paua Agencies* offer packing, shipping, and air-freight services. (Note: The health authority at the port of embarkation probably will require certificates of fumigation for most artifacts.) *Girl Guides Handicraft Shop* is a museum for the crafts of Papua New Guinea and has excellent small gifts such as buka trays or carvings. It has one of the largest selections in Port Moresby; Lakatoi artifacts near Koki has simple to valuable crafts, including Chambri Lakes pots and wood carvings from the Trobriands. Other shops include: *South Pacific Artifacts Higoadi's* for collection of handwoven ponchos, blankets, rugs and embroidered table linens. Hours: 9–5 daily except Sunday.

Solomon Islands. Walking sticks, mother-of-pearl work, war clubs and other curios in carved and inlaid wood. Conch shells and rare varieties of cowrie. *New Georgia* (western district) has carved fish, turtles and birds. Carvings in ebony, inlaid shell are unique. Tailors in Chinatown have bargain rates. Note: Replicas of artifacts may be freely exported. The genuine ones, including shell money, dress ornaments and weapons may not be taken from the Solomons without special permission. Hours: M–F 8–5, closed 12:30–2; Sat. 8–12:30. Chinese stores have extended hours.

Tahiti. Wooden tikis, war clubs, carved shells, costume jewelry of mother-of-pearl, baskets and woven hats. Tahitian fashions (from bikinis to ball gowns) in hand-blocked materials. French perfume is lower than in Paris, as are crystalware and French liquors. Duty-free shop at Tahiti-Faaa International Airport.

Tonga. Tapa cloth and woven goods, considered among the finest in the South Pacific. Baskets and mats, grass skirts, fans, model wood carvings, tortoise shell ornaments, brooches, earrings, rings and silver-inlaid knives. *Langa Fonua,* the women's organization of Tonga, sells fine, inexpensive handicrafts at Langa Fonua House. Arrangements can also be made to have lunch or tea in the society's attractive old house. Hours: M–F 8:30–5; Sat. 9–12.

Vanuatu (formerly New Hebrides). Grass shirts and baskets from Futuna and Tanna. *Pentecost:* Carved ferns and masks from Ambrym and Malekula; woodwork from Tongoa and Santo; pig's tusks (rare and expensive), necklaces made of shells or colorful seeds from villages near Vila. Hours: M–F 7:30–5, closed 11:30–2; Sat. 7:30–11:30.

Western Samoa. Woven baskets, trays, tortoise shells and carved wooden items, tapa cloth. *Western Samoa Handicrafts Corp.* in Apia has authentic handicrafts and is sponsored by the government to preserve Samoan culture. Hours: M–F 8–4, closed noon–1:30; Sat. 8–12:30.

HINTS TO HANDICAPPED. Australia and New Zealand are very aware of the need for facilities for the disabled, but they are not equipped to handle the severely handicapped or those in wheelchairs in any way like the services now available to people in the United States. It is suggested that you give advance notice, with relevant details of your disability, to the airline, hotel, or railway office, which will attempt to ensure the best possible assistance. Theaters and restaurants are happy to assist the disabled, but most have no wheelchair access, ramps, or wheelchair toilet facilities.

There are no special facilities for handicapped people in the small South Pacific islands. The main problem would be wheelchair access. And although many hotels are ground level and you'd have easy access to the beaches, there would be problems in the dining areas or with hotel-room toilet facilities.

In other words, any handicapped person planning a trip to the South Pacific will have to be adventurous and plan to do it almost on his or her own. But don't consider it impossible—the South Pacific is worth the challenge.

In Australia, booklets listing facilities in each capital city are available from *Australian Council for Rehabilitation of the Disabled* (ACROD), Box 60, Curtin, ACT, 2605; (062) 82-4333.

U.S. CUSTOMS. Beginning July 7, 1986, the U.S. Customs Service began charging $5 per person for inspecting the luggage of travelers entering the United States by plane or by ship.

Fees will not be levied on passengers arriving from Canada, Mexico, Caribbean nations, or U.S. territories unless they come aboard their own planes or boats. Fees will not be charged for commercial transactions.

AUSTRALIA

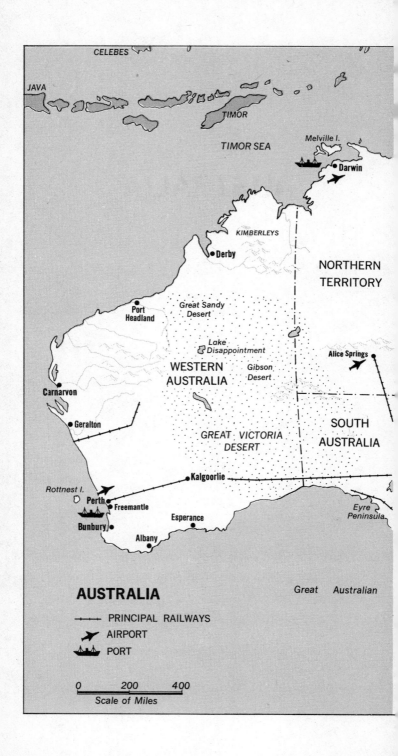

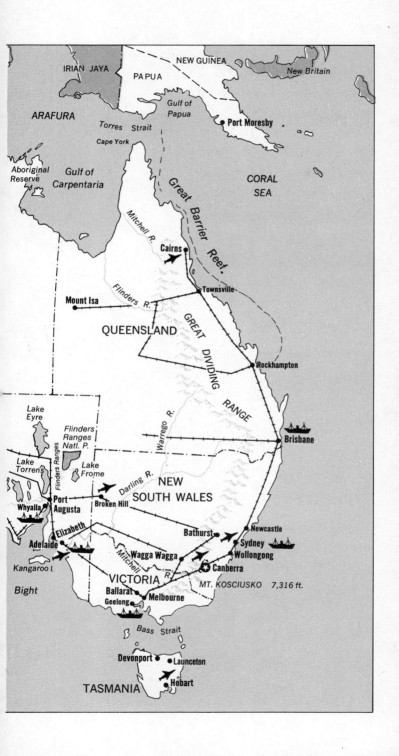

FACTS AT YOUR FINGERTIPS FOR AUSTRALIA

PLANNING YOUR TRIP. Australia has become the "in" destination for the eighties. Once considered the absolute end of the earth, the Land Down Under is now in the mainstream of travel. The sliding of the Australian dollar has played a big part in luring visitors over the last few years, but equally important has been the image of Australia, portrayed in movies, rock videos, and television commercials, as a wide-open, free-and-easy place to vacation. Australia is also considered a "safe" destination, far from the cares of the world—in other words, just the type of setting one hopes to find in a vacation spot. Add to all this the fact that Australia is an island in the South Pacific with good weather, thousands of miles of beaches, and plenty of sunshine and it's no wonder that tourism is now one of the nation's largest industries and one of its most important sources of foreign currency.

Thousands find excitement visiting the huge, sophisticated cities that line the Australian coasts and seem to mirror the metropolises of America and England. Others would just as soon see nothing more than the vast and amazing Outback, where the earth looks and feels the way it must have felt hundreds of millions of years ago. The wildlife of Australia is magnet enough for even more travelers, those who want to see the koala, the kangaroo, the platypus, the wombat, or the emu in their native habitat.

A few questions about Australia should be answered before you plan your trip Down Under. The answers may amaze you. First, Australia is a long way from just about everywhere. It's a 15- to 17-hour journey to Sydney from Los Angeles, San Francisco, or Vancouver and even a few hours longer than that from London and other cities in Europe. But the airlines do try to limit the boredom with movies (two are usually shown between the United States and Australia) and a couple of inflight meals, and heaven knows, there's lots of time left over to sleep.

Second, Australia is a very big country, about the size of the continental United States, and it's the only country on earth to occupy an entire continent all by itself. When planning a trip to Australia, keep distances in mind. For example, if you plan to fly from Sydney in the east to Perth in the west, you'll be on the plane for five hours, or about as long as it takes to fly from New York to Los Angeles. If you decide you'd like to take the trip across Australia by rail, plan to spend four days and three nights crossing the continent. And if you want to drive around the country, factor in plenty of road time and plan to stay overnight at motels if you're driving far. If you're going to an island on the Great Barrier Reef, it could take you the better part of a day to fly to the nearest landside city and transfer by helicopter, light plane, or boat to the island.

To give you an idea of distances in Australia, the Australian Tourist Commission has prepared this chart:

Journey from Sydney to	Road Miles	kms	Jet time	Rail time hours	Coach time
Adelaide	885	1,416	1.50	25.15	23.40
Alice Springs	1,844	2,950	5.20	64.30	56.25
Brisbane	630	1,014	1.10	15.30	17.45
Cairns	1,712	2,853	3.0	53.0	44.0
Canberra	192	307	0.30	5.00	4.45
Darwin	2,533	4,053	6.30	–	92.50
Hobart	717	1,147	2.30	18.00	14.30
Perth	2,717	4,347	5.20	65.45	72.15

PASSPORTS AND VISAS. A valid passport and an ongoing ticket out of the country are required of all visitors to Australia. Visitors might also be asked by customs-and-immigration officials to verify that they have enough funds with them to sustain their stay in Australia. All visitors to Australia, except holders of New Zealand and Australian passports, must also

AUSTRALIA

have visas. Visas are free and available from all Australian consulates and government offices.

TOURIST OFFICES. *USA.* New York: 489 Fifth Ave., 31st floor, New York, NY 10017. Tel: (212) 687–6300. Los Angeles: 3550 Wilshire Blvd., Los Angeles, CA 90010. Tel: (213) 380–6060.

United Kingdom. London: Qantas House, 49 Old Bond Street, London W1X 4PL Tel: (01) 499–2247.

Canada: 120 Eglinton East, Suite 220, Toronto, Ont. M4P 1E2. Tel: (416) 487–2126.

Europe. Federal Republic of Germany: Neue Mainzerstrasse 22 D6000/Frankfurt am Main 1. Tel: (0 611) 235071.

New Zealand. 29 Customs Street West, Auckland 1. Tel: (09) 79–9594.

Japan. Sankaido Building, 7th floor, 9–13 Akasaka, 1-Chome, Minato-ku, Tokyo 107. Tel: (03) 585–0705.

Singapore: 400 Orchard Road, Singapore 0923. Tel: 235–2295.

Travelers can write directly to the Australian Tourist Commission Head Office, 324 St. Kilda Road, Melbourne 3004, Victoria, Australia.

CURRENCY AND CREDIT CARDS. The Australian dollar is the unit of currency, and it is divided into 100 cents. It is symbolized "$A". Major credit cards honored at hotels, restaurants, and stores throughout the nation are *American Express, Diners Club, Visa, MasterCard,* and *Access.* (For exchange rates, see below.)

WHAT WILL IT COST? Australia is neither the most nor the least expensive country to visit. Australians enjoy one of the highest standards of living on earth, and this is reflected in the price of many consumer items. The once-formidable Australian dollar has lost ground on international money markets since 1980, and persistent inflation has helped keep many prices high. At presstime, mid-1986, $A1 = $US0.72, and although the U.S. dollar has slipped a bit against the Aussie dollar, no one is predicting a return to the early days of the decade when the exchange rate was almost the reverse of what it is now. **Prices in this section are in Australian dollars unless otherwise noted.**

That said, visitors to Australia can nonetheless find plenty of bargains and money-saving plans that help keep the lid on vacation costs. There are deluxe and first-class hotels in every city in Australia that, like their counterparts in North America and Europe, can cost more than $US100 per night for a room, but there are even more budget accommodations, such as motels and tourist hotels, that cost half that or less. For families traveling together, reasonably priced self-catering apartments are found in most cities. There are restaurants throughout Australia that cater to every taste and pocketbook; thus, there's no problem should you want to splurge on a gourmet meal one night and eat hamburgers the next. Likewise, there are numerous transportation bargains that bring down the cost of domestic travel in Australia (see How to Get Around).

The information below gives some idea of what a moderately priced day might cost a visitor in Australia:

Motorcoach sightseeing tour: $A16 half day; $A25 full day. Cruise on Sydney Harbour: $A11.50. Theater ticket: $A12–$A25, depending on seats. Concert, opera, or ballet ticket: $A15 and up, depending on seats. Rock concert ticket: $A18–$A20, depending on seats. Ticket to a movie: $A6.50. Entrance to museum or art gallery: free to $A3. Ticket to a sports event: $A7–$A9. Hotel room per day, single: $A85 premier; $A50 moderate; $A30 budget. Breakfast in a coffee shop: $A4 per person. Lunch at a café or bistro: $A6 per person. Dinner at a fine restaurant: $A50 per person. Bottle of Australian wine: $A3 and up. Glass of beer at a pub: $A.70. Cocktail: $A3. Commuter rail ticket: .60–$A4. City bus fare: .60–$A2. City tram fare: .60–$A4. Ferry ride: .65 one way.

FACTS AT YOUR FINGERTIPS

WHEN TO GO. There is no "wrong" time of the year to visit Australia, but depending on what you want to do, here are a few pointers. If you want to visit the Great Barrier Reef, rainiest months are January and February. If you want to ski in Tasmania or Victoria, June and July are the only months with sufficient snow. If you like hot weather, visit November to March. If you like it cooler but not cold, any other month is fine. If you like it cold, don't go to Australia. If you plan a trip to the Outback, the hottest and driest months are November to March. April and May seem about the best time to explore the Outback.

AVERAGE TEMPERATURE AND RAINFALL. (A quick and fairly accurate conversion from Centigrade to Fahrenheit is to double the Centigrade figure and add 30.)

TEMPERATURES

Average rainfall in inches; average temperature max/min Fahrenheit.

Adelaide

	Jan	Feb	Mar	Apr	May	Jun	July	Aug	Sep	Oct	Nov	Dec
Max.°F	85	85	80	73	66	60	59	61	66	72	77	82
Min.°F	61	62	59	55	51	47	45	46	48	52	55	59
Rainfall	.8	.8	.9	1.7	2.7	2.8	2.6	2.4	2.0	1.7	1.2	1.0

Alice Springs

	Jan	Feb	Mar	Apr	May	Jun	July	Aug	Sep	Oct	Nov	Dec
Max.°F	98	96	91	83	73	68	67	71	79	88	93	95
Min.°F	72	70	65	56	48	43	40	44	51	60	65	68
Rainfall	1.3	1.5	.9	.5	.7	.6	.5	.5	.2	.8	.9	1.2

Brisbane

	Jan	Feb	Mar	Apr	May	Jun	July	Aug	Sep	Oct	Nov	Dec
Max.°F	85	84	82	79	74	69	69	71	75	79	82	84
Min.°F	69	69	67	62	56	51	49	50	55	60	64	67
Rainfall	6.6	6.3	5.7	3.5	2.7	2.7	2.1	1.9	1.9	2.9	3.7	5.0

Cairns Great Barrier Reef

	Jan	Feb	Mar	Apr	May	Jun	July	Aug	Sep	Oct	Nov	Dec
Max.°F	89	88	87	84	81	78	77	80	82	85	87	88
Min.°F	74	75	72	71	68	65	62	64	66	69	72	74
Rainfall	15.7	17.4	18.3	7.0	3.6	2.0	1.2	1.0	1.4	1.4	3.3	6.7

Canberra

	Jan	Feb	Mar	Apr	May	Jun	July	Aug	Sep	Oct	Nov	Dec
Max.°F	82	80	76	67	59	54	52	55	60	66	72	79
Min.°F	56	55	51	44	37	34	33	33	37	42	47	52
Rainfall	2.4	2.4	2.1	1.9	1.9	1.5	1.5	1.8	2.0	2.9	2.5	2.2

Darwin

	Jan	Feb	Mar	Apr	May	Jun	July	Aug	Sep	Oct	Nov	Dec
Max.°F	90	89	90	92	90	88	87	89	91	92	93	92
Min.°F	77	77	77	76	72	69	67	69	74	77	78	78
Rainfall	15.4	12.9	10.2	4.0	.6	.1	.04	.1	.5	2.0	4.9	9.6

Hobart

	Jan	Feb	Mar	Apr	May	Jun	July	Aug	Sep	Oct	Nov	Dec
Max.°F	71	71	68	63	58	53	53	55	59	62	65	68
Min.°F	53	53	51	48	44	41	40	41	43	45	48	51
Rainfall	1.9	1.7	1.8	2.2	1.9	2.3	2.1	1.9	2.0	2.5	2.2	2.2

Melbourne

	Jan	Feb	Mar	Apr	May	Jun	July	Aug	Sep	Oct	Nov	Dec
Max.°F	78	78	75	68	62	57	56	59	63	67	71	75
Min.°F	57	58	55	51	47	44	42	44	46	49	51	55
Rainfall	1.9	2.0	2.1	2.8	2.2	2.0	1.9	2.0	2.7	2.7	2.3	2.3

	Jan	Feb	Mar	Apr	May	Jun	July	Aug	Sep	Oct	Nov	Dec
Perth												
Max.°F	85	86	82	76	69	65	63	64	67	70	76	81
Min.°F	64	64	62	57	53	50	48	48	50	53	57	61
Rainfall	.31	.43	.8	1.8	4.9	7.3	6.9	5.4	3.2	2.2	.8	.5
Sydney												
Max.°F	78	78	76	72	67	62	60	63	67	71	74	77
Min.°F	65	65	63	58	52	48	46	48	51	56	60	63
Rainfall	3.9	4.5	5.2	5.0	4.8	5.2	4.1	3.2	2.7	3.0	3.1	3.1

Fahrenheit to Celsius

F	32	41	50	59	68	77	86	95	104	113	122	131	140
C	0	5	10	15	20	25	30	35	40	45	50	55	60

TIME ZONES. Australia has three time zones: Eastern Standard Time is ten hours ahead of Greenwich Mean Time; Central Australian Time, 9½ hours ahead; and Western Time, 8 hours ahead. Therefore, when it is noon in Perth, it is 1:30 in Adelaide and 2 P.M. in Sydney, Melbourne, Canberra, Brisbane, and Hobart. During the summer months most States introduce daylight saving of an hour.

WHAT TO TAKE. The first rule of packing for a trip to Australia is that it is an informal country. Unless you're planning black-tie nights on the town, leave the dress-up clothes at home. Even if you decide to go to the opera or a symphony one evening, you needn't dress up. Many people will indeed be dressed up, but many others will not, so essentially, dress to please yourself. Much of Australia lies in the tropics, so dress light if you're heading into the Outback or to the resorts along the Great Barrier Reef. Even in the big cities, you'll find plenty of people walking downtown in shorts and T-shirts when the temps top out. You'll need a hat to protect against the strong Aussie sun and tennis shoes for walking on top of the Great Barrier Reef. Sturdy, comfortable walking shoes are a must for Australia. It is doubtful you'll ever feel cold in Australia no matter the time of year you visit, but if you go in winter, early spring, or late fall (remember, Australian seasons are the opposite of North America's and Europe's), take a light jacket or sweater for cooler evenings. Since it is apt to rain any time along the Australian coast, pack an umbrella or a raincoat. You needn't bother with either if you're heading for the arid heart of the nation.

It's easy to find dry cleaners, laundries, and self-service laundries anywhere in any Australian city. Hotels provide cleaning services, but they are nowhere near as cheap as if you clean your clothes yourself.

Take prescribed medicines with you. Australian pharmacists (called chemists) will not fill a prescription written in North America by American or Canadian doctors. If you run out, take your old prescription to a local doctor and ask if he or she will write a new prescription. Over-the-counter drugs and cosmetics are readily available at all drugstores.

If you shop for clothes in Australia, you'll find sizes marked in centimeters rather than inches. See the chart for conversion.

Women's dresses and suits

Australian	10	12	14	16	18	20	22
American	10	12	14	16	18	20	22

Men's suits, overcoats and sweaters

Australian	92	97	102	107	112	117	122
American	36	38	40	42	44	46	48

FACTS AT YOUR FINGERTIPS

Shirts and collars

Australian	36	37	38	39	40	41	42	43
American	14	14½	15	15½	16	16½	17	17½

HOW TO GET THERE. The only way these days to get to Australia is by air. A few cruise lines include Australian ports in their itineraries, but there has been nothing approaching regular ship service since the jet age dawned more than a quarter century ago. Today, there is a near glut of air services to Australia from North America, Europe, and Asia, so choosing a flight that fits into your travel plans is easy. From North America, *Qantas*, Australia's national airline; *United Airlines, Air New Zealand, Continental Air Lines, UTA French Airlines,* and *CP Air* fly from Los Angeles, San Francisco, Honolulu, and Vancouver to Sydney, Melbourne, Brisbane, and Cairns, depending on the airline. From the United Kingdom, *Qantas* and *British Airways* fly to Sydney, Melbourne, and Perth, and *Singapore Airlines* flies to those cities via Singapore. From Europe, *Lufthansa, KLM, Alitalia,* and *JAT/Yugoslavian Airlines* fly to Australia. From Asia, *Thai Airways, Singapore Airlines,* and *Japan Air Lines* are the major carriers to Australia.

The air fare to Australia is not as high as it once was and has even dipped below $1,000 for a round-trip coach ticket between the U.S. West Coast and Sydney, and similar bargains are always being offered between London and Sydney. Ticket prices are normally higher during the Australian summer (December through February) than in winter (June through August). In spring and fall in Australia, fares are higher than in winter but lower than in summer. The airlines are forever offering promotional fares to Australia; any savvy travel agent will know about them. Or call the airline direct and ask for the lowest fare, but be prepared for the barrage of restrictions cheap fares always seem to entail. Travel agents can also tell you about fares that accompany tours and fly-drive plans, if you want to travel in a group or do your own driving. Some airlines offer group fares but do not require travel on an organized group tour, so ask about these fares as well.

CRUISES. No cruise line calls regularly at Australian ports. Occasionally, a ship from one of the following lines pulls into an Australian port on part of a larger itinerary: *Cunard/NAC,* 555 Fifth Ave., New York, NY 10017 (800) 221–4770 or (212) 661–7777 U.S.; (800) 268–3705 Canada; *P&O/Princess Cruises,* 2029 Century Park East, Los Angeles, CA 90067 (213) 553–7000; *Royal Viking Line,* 750 Battery St., San Francisco, CA 94111 (800) 422–8000 U.S.; (800) 233–8000 Canada.

HOW TO GET AROUND. Domestic air travel in Australia is convenient, modern, and efficient. It is the only way to see a lot of Australia in a short amount of time. But it is not cheap. Australians who have been to the United States and had a taste of deregulated air fares, for example, return home complaining bitterly about the high cost of air travel in their own country. *Ansett Airlines of Australia* and *Australian Airlines* are the two major domestic airlines. A brash newcomer is *East-West Airlines,* once a regional carrier that expanded its services nationwide at costs approaching reality. Ansett and Australian Airlines are often referred to as the Siamese twins because their schedules are virtually identical and their fares are equally high.

In their defense, both Ansett and Australian Airlines have devised discount tickets that help bring down the cost of air travel within Australia, but only for foreign nationals holding round-trip tickets in and out of Australia and non-Australian passports. Go Australia Airpass and See Australia Airfares are two of the plans that chop as much as 40 percent off normal coach fares. East-West's Passfare is similar. Your travel agent sells these tickets; or contact the tourist-information office.

If you have lots of vacation time and can travel on the ground, Australia has a comprehensive rail system and bus routes that cover the nation. *Railways of Australia* (ROA) operates passenger trains between all major cities in the country. Three of its most popular trains are the Indian Pacific from Sydney to Perth, the Ghan from Sydney to Alice Springs, and the Sunlander from Brisbane to Cairns. Austrailpass and the less expensive Budget Austrailpass allow unlimited travel on ROA for specified periods of time, ranging from $A400 for 14 days for first-class travel to $A990 for three months' travel in first class. Budget Austrailpass uses second-class coaches and ranges from $A290 for 14 days to $A730 for three months. Travel agents in the United States sell these tickets and can book a seat and sleeper compartment on Australian trains; or contact the tourist-information office.

There are two major interstate bus companies, *Ansett Pioneer* and *Greyhound Australia*. Although there are main express routes between the major cities, both bus lines operate to smaller towns across Australia. Ansett Pioneer's Aussiepass and Greyhound's Aussie Explorer fare allow unlimited travel for specified periods, beginning at about $A225 for a two-week ticket. Again, travel agents in North America sell the tickets.

An important reminder: Many of the discount travel tickets must be purchased outside Australia, so check with your travel agent when purchasing your air ticket to Australia about any one of them; or contact the tourist-information office.

TOURS. Dozens of tour wholesalers and virtually all the airlines that fly to Australia market a variety of tours Down Under through your hometown travel agent. Generally speaking, tour wholesalers do not sell their products directly to the public. You'll have to consult an airline or travel agent if you wish to visit Australia as part of an organized or prepackaged tour. *Qantas*, for example, works with a number of tour wholesalers in North America, Europe, and Asia in marketing all sorts of tours—fly-drive, fly-rail, fly-camper, Outback safaris, luxury 'round Australia motorcoach programs, and vacations at the resorts along the Great Barrier Reef, to name a few.

Although most tour wholesalers won't sell you a tour directly, they will gladly send you brochures about group and independent tours they are operating this year. These contain such information as price, departure dates, airlines, and even the number of meals included in the tour package. Ask for brochures about tours to Australia from *Adventure Center*, 5540 College Ave., Oakland, CA 94618 (camping safaris, Great Barrier Reef resorts, sailing and yacht charters); *Tour-Pacific*, 1101 E. Broadway, Glendale, CA 91205 (motorcoach tours, camping tours, fly-drive, fly-rail); *Bali Hai Holidays*, 433 Brookes Ave., San Diego, CA 92103 (city tours, motorcoach tours); *Australian Explorers*, Professional Building, Parlin, NJ 08859 (Outback sightseeing tours).

Several tour operators concentrate on what are known in the travel industry as special-interest tours. These tours explore a particular aspect of Australian life. For example, there are wildlife tours that visit game reserves, mining tours that visit opal and gold fields, ornithology tours that birdwatch their way through Australia, and tours that visit the aboriginal areas of the great Australian Outback. Some of the major wholesalers with special-interest tours are *Voyages of Discovery*, 1298 Prospect, La Jolla, CA 92037 (astronomy tours); *World of Oz*, 3 E. 54th St., New York, NY 10022 (complete range of special-interest tours); *Wilderness Travel*, 1760 Solano Ave., Berkeley, CA 94707 (bush-camping expeditions); *Sobek Expeditions*, Angels Camp, CA 95222 (scuba-diving tours); *Evergreen Travel Service*, 19505 L 44th Ave., Lynnwood, WA 98036 (tours for the disabled); *Nature Expeditions International*, Box 11496, Eugene, OR 97440 (natural-history tours); *Veterans Tours International*, Box 633, Brunswick, ME 04011 (tours of interest to World War II veterans); *Gold Discovery Tours*, Box 4660, Sylmar, CA 91342 (gold- and gem-prospecting tours).

Still other tour operators offer luxurious escorted tours with tour managers to handle all the details of travel and guides to point out all the places of interest. They include *Maupintour*, 1515 St. Andrews Dr., Lawrence, KS 66044; *Olson Travelworld*, 5855 Green Valley Circle, Culver City, CA 90230; *Percival Tours*, 1 Tandy Center Plaza, Ft. Worth, TX 76102; *Travcoa*, 4000 MacArthur Blvd., Newport Beach, CA 92660; *Four Winds*, 175 Fifth Ave., New York, NY 10010; *Globus-Gateway*, Box 482, Forest Hills, NY 11375.

Station Tours: There are a number of tours to sheep and cattle properties. Some are within easy reach of major centers; others are deep in the outback. In many cases overnight accommodations are offered to the visitor. In addition

FACTS AT YOUR FINGERTIPS

to observation of station life, there are swimming, fishing, wildlife observation, tennis and horseback riding.

Visitors can embark on an adventurous Outback camping tour with *Bill King's Australian Adventure Tours,* c/o Australian Travel Service, 1101 E. Broadway, Glendale, CA 91205. *Koala Tours,* 18521 Des Moines Way South, Seattle, WA 98148, also markets farmstay vacations in Australia.

For tours from Brisbane: *Dagworth Sheep and Cattle Station,* via Winton, Queensland 4735. Offers wildlife, tours to historic sites, daily routine, tennis, swimming and horseback riding. Road transportation from Winton by arrangement.

For tours from Sydney: *Ansett Airlines,* 9841 Airport Blvd., Los Angeles, CA 90045. Pelican sheep station, 136 miles from Sydney, offers demonstrations of sheep mustering and shearing, opportunity to attend sheep and cattle sales. Sapphire-hunting safaris can also be arranged. "Jolly Swagman" tour includes travel by air to Dubbo, a country town in New South Wales, where visitors are shown and participate in a wide variety of rural activities including sheep mustering and shearing, boomerang-throwing demonstrations, and visiting a wildlife sanctuary.

DRIVING IN AUSTRALIA. Valid foreign driver's licenses are honored in Australia. If your license is printed in a language other than English, it may be a good idea to obtain an International Driver's License. On a population basis, Australia ranks among the most highly motorized nations in the world, with about one vehicle for every three persons. Hence, facilities for motorists—such as petrol (gasoline) stations, repair shops, and motor inns (motels)—along the main roads and in the towns and cities are plentiful and range from good to excellent. The roads, even some of the major and most traveled highways, are of mixed quality, but few meet the high standards of American or European expressways. On the whole, Australian roads are not made for driving at high speeds. While signs along some highways indicate safe maximum speeds for normal weather conditions, motorists should always obtain information about the conditions of roads (especially secondary roads and tracks) before setting out on a lengthy trip. This is especially important after heavy rains, when even main highways can be flooded and impassable for days.

Opinions about the ability and manners of Australian drivers differ a great deal but a few suggestions are in order: If you are involved in an accident, even a minor one, insist on calling a police officer, note the other car's registration number, and do not argue about who has been at fault. Also be aware that in Australia it is a serious offense, punishable by law, not to stop after an accident or to refuse assistance to a person injured in an accident regardless of whether one was involved in the accident. In other words, assistance is obligatory.

Traffic in Australia keeps to the left side of the road; in most instances, those approaching from the right have the right of way at an intersection. Stop signs mean just what they say; it is not enough to slow down—you must stop completely. And "give way" signs mean you must give way to all other traffic whether you are on another driver's right or not. On zebra-crossings, pedestrians have absolute right of way as soon as they have stepped on them. Therefore, motorists must halt in front of the crossing and wait until the pedestrian has passed them before proceeding. It's the law in Australia that all occupants in a car wear seat belts. Penalties for contravening regulations are severe and include minimum fines of $A20, loss of license and, if the offense is very serious, jail.

ELECTRICITY. The electrical current in Australia is 240–250 volts, 50 Hz AC, and wall outlets are three-pronged, with the 2 prongs at top set at an angle. North American visitors, therefore, need both a voltage converter and a three-pin adapter to operate such small travel appliances as hair dryers and electric shavers. (The set of adapter plugs you have may not work here.) These are for sale at hardware and variety stores in North America and Australia (though they are somewhat hard to find) and many full-service hotels in Australia provide them free for guests.

TIPPING. There was a time when tipping was unheard of in Australia, and even today, many Aussies are hard-pressed to pay gratuities. Visitors, however, are usually expected to tip, but only if the service was worth a little something extra. Service charges are not included in hotel and restaurant bills, so if you tip, 10 percent of the total bill is sufficient. Round off a taxi fare in favor of the driver and tip porters at railway and ship terminals small change over the set charge for their services. Bartenders at pubs do not expect tips, but those at hotel and restaurant bars won't turn them down if offered.

DRINKING LAWS. These laws vary by state, but commonly, pubs close around 11:00 P.M. Other bars, such as those in hotels and clubs, stay open later. Each state, city, and community has quirks in its drinking laws, so check locally about age requirements and where and when drinks are served. Australian laws are quite severe on the topic of driving while intoxicated, and no concessions are granted to foreign visitors who break them. You'll find police giving "breathalyzer" tests, as they're known in Australia, on city streets and national highways. Be careful—or go to jail.

DEPARTURE TAX. Everyone departing Australia must pay a $A20 departure tax, one of the highest such taxes in the world. There is some current discussion in Australian Parliament about reducing or eliminating the tax, but at press time, it is still being collected.

AUSTRALIA

Continent or Island?

by
EMERY BARCS

Emery Barcs, a Sydney resident for over 40 years, writes for Australia's top newsweekly the Bulletin. *His most recent book, the critically acclaimed* Backyard of Mars, *deals with his first five years in Australia.*

Whether one calls Australia the world's smallest continent or the largest island, it is a land of fascinating contrasts. Almost the size of the United States (excluding Alaska and Hawaii) and one and a half times the land area of Europe (excluding the Soviet Union) Australia had 15,750,000 people in June 1985. Australia is also the only continent inhabited by a single nation, although one in five Australians was born overseas. Australia's tropical north is a short jet hop from the equator; yet, from its southernmost point, one-day trips by plane can be organized for tourists to the frozen reaches of Antarctica. While the major resort areas of the big cities provide maximum creature comforts for the most demanding visitor, trips off the beaten track or to the sparsely populated hinterland, called the Outback, need careful preparation by competent experts. For there the traveler will be left very much alone.

In Australia, untamed nature is never far from the amenities of technological civilization. While this proximity is a major attraction to the visitor, it also poses risks that may not be obvious. Let's suppose you are driving along one of the thousands of golden beaches studding the Australian coast. The day may be hot and the water inviting. But sharks may occasionally lurk in those blue waters, especially if the sea happens to be flat that day. The calm waters around Australia may also turn into rip currents that can drag the swimmer far out to sea or churn up giant waves that sweep cliff-climbers or rock fishermen into the seething water from seemingly safe ledges.

On land, that innocent looking Australian bush stretching from the roadside is likely to be a treacherous thicket. Hardly a weekend goes by without search parties seeking bush walkers—often allegedly experienced—who have become lost in the maze. Mostly they are found; sometimes they are not. But these are sensible warnings only. They are not intended to dampen the traveler's interest in surfing, fishing, or exploring the bush. On the contrary, by using common sense, prudence, and readily available advice, the visitor will enjoy a safe Australian vacation, mixing adventure with a pleasant holiday schedule.

The overseas visitor should also be prepared to look at the Australian scenery with fresh eyes. There is great beauty in the Australian landscape: Sydney's harbor, with its flamboyant opera house, has been favorably compared with Rio de Janeiro; the huge canyons of the Blue Mountains in New South Wales rank among the world's finest sights; and the riot of color in suburban gardens is lasting inspiration to horticulturists.

But the Australian countryside rarely radiates mellow serenity. More often it appears harsh and alien at first sight. Indeed, one's first encounter with nature in Australia is perhaps akin to the experience of looking at abstract paintings or listening to atonal music for the first time—there may be a feeling of puzzlement, even dismay. The first Europeans who landed in Australia were shocked when they surveyed their surroundings. One may, therefore, need time to discover for oneself the often austere and melancholy beauty of much of the continent.

The Land

There are a number of reasons that make Australia vastly different from the other continents. The first is its age: Australia is one of the oldest of the earth's land masses—older than Europe or America. Second, it has been physically isolated from the rest of the world for some 50 million years, perhaps even longer. This isolation assured the survival of unique strains of flora and fauna. And the remoteness, coupled with the continent's uninviting shoreline, discouraged western explorers from colonizing the continent until about two centuries ago.

Bounded by the Arafura Sea on the north, the Coral and Tasman seas of the South Pacific Ocean on the east, and the Indian Ocean on the west and south, Australia's coastline runs 12,446 miles (19,914 kilometers)—about equal to the distance between Sydney and London via Suez. It is surrounded by a rather shallow continental shelf averaging 100 fathoms (600 ft) deep and ranging between 20 and upwards of 150 miles (32–240 kilometers) wide. One of the coast's unsurpassed glories is the Great Barrier Reef, a wonderland of coral reefs and coral islands extending more than 1,250 miles (2,000 kilometers) north of Brisbane, capital of Queensland, to the island of New Guinea.

Varying greatly in size, the six states and two territories that make up the Commonwealth of Australia occupy the continent's 2,967,909 square miles (7,716,563 square kilometers) of land. Largest is Western Australia, 975,920 square miles—four times larger than Texas and eleven times the size of Great Britain, followed by Queensland, 667,000 square miles, South Australia, 380,070 square miles, New South Wales, 309,433 square miles, Victoria, 87,884 square miles, and the island state of Tasmania, 26,383 square miles. The sparsely populated Northern Territory sprawls over 520,280 square miles, while the Australian

Capital Territory, which includes the federal capital of Canberra, is hemmed into 939 square miles and is fast becoming too small for its rapidly growing population.

Although Australia has often been described as an empty bowl, since parts of its edges are higher than its center, it is in fact, the flattest of the continents mainly because of its age. The elements have had time to plane land. The continent has an average height of only 1,000 feet above sea level, compared with a world mean of 2,300 feet. The enormous plateau that rises in the west spreads over approximately three-quarters of the total area and occupies almost the whole of Western Australia, the greater part of the Northern Territory, a sizable chunk of South Australia, and parts of Western Queensland. East of the Great Western Plateau are the Central Eastern Lowlands, mostly a dry belt crossing Australia from north to south, which at one point—Lake Eyre in South Australia—drop to some 36 feet below sea level. In prehistoric times, roughly 60 million years ago, the Lowlands were part of the sea floor. East of them rise the Eastern Highlands, otherwise known as the Great Dividing Range, which follows the contours of the coast from the top of Australia to the bottom of Tasmania. Although the average altitude of the Highlands is a mere 2,700 feet, its highest peak, Mount Kosciusko, in the picturesque Australian Alps in New South Wales, rises to 7,316 feet. The great majority of Australians live in the 30–250-mile-wide coastal strip east of the Great Divide.

Climate and Weather

While the relatively small Australian nation owns a huge amount of land, much of it remains uninhabited. This has inspired wild fantasies about "limitless possibilities" of settling large numbers of the world's land-hungry landless masses in Australia. However, sober surveys have found that the empty continent simply could not maintain more than—at most—between 25 and 28 million people. The reason is that almost all of the unsettled land—about 70 percent of the federation's total territory—is so arid as to be unfit for civilized habitation in its undeveloped state. In recent years, the discovery of impressive mineral wealth in the deserts has led to the establishment of mining towns provided with all modern conveniences, including air-conditioned homes and offices. But water for these settlements has had to be piped long distances, and everything people need for survival must be brought from far away. Even in the somewhat more habitable areas on the fringe of the arid "dead heart" of Australia, water is so scarce and vegetation so sparse that several square miles of land are needed to keep one sheep alive.

The total annual run-off of all Australian rivers is only a fraction of that carried by some of the world's mighty waterways—only about two-thirds that of the St. Lawrence in North America, for instance, and half that of the Amazon. Australia's largest river, the 1,600-mile-long Murray, is one of the continent's most important streams. With the Darling, it forms Australia's most wide-ranging river system, draining an area of more than 400,000 square miles. But most of Australia's rivers are small and coastal, flowing into the sea. Maps may show various internal river systems but these are usually little more than dry sandy beds or a series of rapidly evaporating water holes, some flowing into great salt "lakes" as dry as the river beds, such as Lake Eyre in South Australia.

But while Australia is the world's driest continent, the majority of travelers will want to visit only the more closely settled regions where the action takes place. Only a few will journey into the desert lands in the remote Outback.

As for water—it continues to be a problem in all parts of Australia but scientists have utilized the most advanced technology in the world to harness available resources. For instance, Sydney's water storage dams contain enough water to see the city through seven or eight rainless years—longer than the worst drought on record. So, except for occasional, severe, prolonged dryness which may entail some restrictions on water use, visitors will suffer no privations. In fact they may never become aware of the situation, for Australians themselves are among the world's most spendthrift water-users. Although in Australia water is by no means a cheap commodity, in normal times suburban garden-sprinklers may be on for hours and the average Aussie would feel deprived to miss a daily shower or two.

Sometimes the problem is of course too much rather than too little water—and in the wrong place. When the rains come, dry river beds become raging torrents, flooding the countryside and isolating townships by making roads impassable. Motorists would therefore be wise to read weather reports, including information on the state of roads, whenever there is heavy rainfall.

Australians are great sun-worshippers—hardly surprising in a sun-drenched land. The average daily sunshine in the capital cities ranges from 5.9 hours in Hobart to 8.4 hours in Darwin. Inland the average is even higher. Years ago, one of Australia's most popular humorists, the late Lennie Lower, reported from Marble Bar (Western Australia): "I am now in that part of the British Empire on which the sun never sets." Still, only about 39 percent of Australia (half of Queensland, a bit more than one-third of Western Australia, and four-fifths of the Northern Territory) lies within the hot, tropical zone. The remaining areas, including the whole of New South Wales, Victoria, South Australia, and Tasmania, are in the temperate zone. Still, even there it is wise to apply generously some genuinely medicated suntan lotion or creme before exposing the body to an over-supply of the sun's ultraviolet rays.

The Seasons

"I could never get used to that," said the legendary English schoolboy when his geography teacher explained that in Australia everything is upside down. Winter in Australia arrives when the northern hemisphere swelters in summer heat, and Sydneysiders and Melbournites prepare for bed when it is midday in London. But while visitors have little difficulty in adjusting to a reversal of seasons, Australia's close observance of northern hemisphere traditions at Christmas time is somewhat incongruous when one sees posters of Santa Claus in Arctic garb against a background of reindeer and snow, while the mercury is climbing to 100°F.

Except in the high mountains, where plenty of snow falls in winter (it has been calculated that Australia's snowfields occupy a larger area than those of Switzerland) and the heath is fragrant with alpine flowers in summer, the seasons in Australia are not as marked as they are in the northern hemisphere. Most plants keep their foliage all year round. In general the summer months are December, January, and February; autumn includes March, April, and May; winter comes in June, July, and August; spring runs through September, October, and November. The rainy season in the tropical north is during the summer months.

Only in a few regions, such as the Alps and other high mountain ranges in southern Tasmania and at night in some of the deserts, does the thermometer dip below freezing, though cold snaps may occur elsewhere. Summer can be very warm: temperatures of around 100°F are not exceptional even in the temperate zone, but they rarely continue for more than a day or two. Maximum summer averages in capital cities vary between 90°F in Darwin and 70°F in Hobart. Minimum summer averages range from Darwin, 77°F to Hobart, 52°F. The maximum average winter temperatures range from 87°F in Darwin and 53°F in Canberra, while minimums range from 69°F in Darwin to 33°F in Canberra.

Throughout the year, one can always find some region in Australia where the climate is excellent for touring. But some months are better than others for visiting certain parts of the continent. Three of the State capitals—Sydney, Melbourne, and Perth—are really all-season cities. Brisbane and Darwin are rather hot in summer. Adelaide, Hobart, and Canberra, on the other hand, are on the cold side in winter. The best months for exploring the Great Barrier Reef are between April and November; for the Northern Territory and Central Australia (Alice Springs, Ayers Rock) between April and October; and for the Gold Coast of Queensland, between April and November. The skiing season usually begins at the end of May or early June and lasts until the end of September.

Plants and Animals

Fossil evidence indicates that in the Cretacious period (from Latin *creta*, meaning chalk) some 65 million years ago, when dinosaur reached the peak of their development and birds and possum-like mammals proliferated, Australia was still connected by land with Asia. But dating from perhaps 50 million years ago, when the sea cut off Australia and turned it into a separate landmass, plant and animal life there developed almost independent of the rest of the world until the arrival of the white man a couple of centuries ago. We say "almost" because some migratory birds kept coming and going to and from other continents.

Hence all plants and animals stranded in Australia had to adapt themselves to the continent's special conditions. The most impressive plants are the 450 species of eucaliptus or gum trees which thrive practically in every soil and in every climate—the tropical north, the freezing Alps, the deserts, and the rain-soaked forests. One of its species, the mountain ash (to be found in Victoria and Tasmania) is the tallest hardwood in the world, growing to 300 feet and more. There are 600 species of acacias; the most common of them is the wattle—so called because early settlers found its saplings useful for constructing hut walls and roofs of interlaced (wattled) branches and mud, a technique known as "wattle and daub." Thousands of species of wildflowers thrive all over Australia. Western Australia has the largest number of species, about 2,000.

While Australia has neither indigenous hoofed beasts nor primates, some unique animals live here. The oldest of them is probably the platypus, which, although a mammal, lays eggs, suckles its young from enlarged pores, has webbed feet and a ducklike bill, lives on river banks, but is not really an aquatic creature and cannot stay under water for more than about a minute. Some zoologists assert that it is a "living fossil," a surviving example of the transition from reptiles to mammals.

Another strange fellow is the echidna or spiny anteater, which looks like a kind of hedgehog. While it is difficult to find platypus and echidnas in their natural habitat (both are protected animals and cannot be hunted or captured without authorization) every major Australian zoo has a few of them.

About half of Australia's 230 species of native mammals consists of a wide variety of marsupials—from giant 8-foot-tall kangaroos to mouselike creatures. Their one common characteristic is that they carry and feed their young in pouches. The best known Australian marsupials belong to the family of kangaroos which abound on the continent. The name "kangaroo" is aboriginal, but its meaning is uncertain. (The story that it means "don't know"—because when the first white settlers asked aboriginals what they called the strange animal they muttered "kanguru," meaning they didn't understand the question—is a fiction.) Kangaroos, using their powerful hind legs and their strong tails, can clear 27 feet or more in a single leap and can hop along at speeds of 25 miles an hour for short distances. They breed fast, and because they live mainly on grass, sheep and cattle breeders consider them a nuisance.

No one knows the size of the kangaroo population but there are millions in Australia. A recent survey has estimated their number in New South Wales alone at some 3.5 million. For a while conservationists fearing their extinction, fought for a total prohibition on hunting them, and, in 1973, the federal government forbade the export of kangaroo skins. The prohibition, however, led to such an increase in the number of kangaroos that it has been withdrawn and replaced with regulations limiting the number of animals allowed to be shot in the whole of Australia. A small fee is charged for a hunting license. But whether a pest or not, the kangaroo has become a symbol of Australia. It figures in the national coat of arms together with that other exclusively Australian creature, the flightless but fast-running bird, the emu.

The most endearing Australian indigenous animal is undoubtedly that sleepy, bearlike, harmless tree-dweller, the cuddly koala. The aboriginal name means "one who doesn't drink," which is more or less true, for the koala seems to obtain most of the liquid it needs from the leaves of certain eucalyptus trees—which seem to make him permanently drowsy. The koala is also a protected animal and the Australian prohibition on hunting koalas since the early 1930s may have come just in time to prevent the extinction of the inoffensive, defenseless, and charming animal which had been killed by the millions for their skins.

Australia's only large predatory mammal, the doglike dingo, is not indigenous to the continent. Some zoologists now believe that its ancestor was the Indian plains wolf. It is generally accepted, however, that the dingo was brought to Australia by the aborigines 7,000 to 10,000 years ago as a semiwild hunting dog.

Another predatory mammal, the Tasmanian tiger, was thought to have become extinct but some naturalists now believe it may have survived in the impenetrable and unexplored forests of western and southwestern Tasmania.

Australia is a veritable paradise for ornithologists and bird watchers. There are some 720 kinds of birds, 530 of them exclusively Australian. They include 60 species of parrots and 70 species of honey eaters. Other distinguished Australian birds are the aristocratic black swan, the Cape Barren goose, the dancing and singing lyrebird, and the slightly sinister looking kookaburra, whose sepulchral laughter has earned it the name of "laughing jackass." The widespread belief that Australian birds don't sing is nonsense; some of them perform veritable arias.

Someone once wrote, "Name anything that jumps, slithers, or crawls and Australia has it." An exaggeration of course, but it is true that the continent is the home of considerable variety of insects, spiders, and 6.6 percent of the world's reptiles, including giant crocodiles. Yet one can live years, even a lifetime, in Australia without ever confronting any of the nastier species. Indeed it takes considerable expense and effort to see the large estuarian crocodile which lives in northern salt waters. None of the 240 species of lizards is dangerous though some of them—such as the dramatic frilled lizard—may look threatening. Some 20 of the 140 species of land and freshwater snakes are dangerous to man,

AUSTRALIA

but there is only minimal chance of encountering them on the usual tourist itinirary. (The story may be different if one ventures into the bush.)

An Australian Chronology

First Aboriginal settlers reach Australia	c. 28,000 B.C.
Ptolemy's theory of a southern Terra Incognita	A.D. c. 150
Luis de Torres sails through the strait between Australia and New Guinea	1606
Willem Jansz sails into the Gulf of Carpentaria	1606
Dirk Hartog examines the west coast of Australia	1612
Abel Tasman discovers Van Diemen's land (Tasmania)	1642
William Dampier lands on the northwest coast	1688
James Cook lands at Botany Bay	1770
The first British convict fleet arrives	1788
Captain Arthur Phillip formally takes possession of eastern Australia, including Tasmania and establishes colony of New South Wales	1788
Sheep breeding begins	1796
Crossing of the Blue Mountains opens up new regions for settlement	1813
Establishment of five additional colonies:	
Tasmania	1825
Western Australia	1829
South Australia	1834
Victoria	1851
Queensland	1859
Transportation of convicts ends:	
Eastern colonies	1840
Tasmania	1853
Western Australia	1868
Australian Colonies Government Act paves way for responsible government	1850
Discovery of gold	1851
Commonwealth of Australia, a federation of six former colonies (now States) comes into being	January 1, 1901
Australia enters World War I on the side of the Allies	1914
Australia enters World War II on the side of the Democracies	1939

Australia's Past

There are many theories about when and how the first humans, the ancestors of the present aboriginals, reached Australia. Estimates have varied between 10,000 and 30,000 years ago—now the latter seems to be the accepted figure. Some scientists argue that those ancient dark-skinned hunters and food-gatherers wandered into Australia when it still formed a continuous land mass with Asia. Others assert that the aboriginals came by rafts and canoes. Whatever the fact, once they reached Australia they developed in the same kind of isolation as the animals and plants. During the thousands of years between their arrival and the landing of white explorers no record has survived of any contact with outsiders.

A remarkable feature of the aboriginals' isolated evolution is that while they created a complex social order, fascinating expressions of art, and a mythology, their technology—except for the aerodynamically complicated boomerang—stagnated in the Stone Age. They had no agriculture and no domesticated animals except the dingo and they did not know how to work metals. They lived in small tribal groups, established no permanent settlements and developed no writing. Their numbers at the time of the first European arrivals two centuries ago is also a mystery. At present 300,000 seems to be the most widely accepted figure but no one really knows.

One may assume that at some time Asian seafarers ventured as far south as Australia. But if they landed, they left no mark. As for the Europeans, Ptolemy, the Greek mathematician, astronomer, and geographer (A.D. 126–161) suspected the existence of a Terra Incognita (Unknown Land) in what is now the Southern Indian Ocean, but it took another 15 centuries before the first European sailed within sight of that mysterious land. A ship under the command of the Spaniard Luis de Torres sailed through the strait (named after him) between Australia and New Guinea in 1606, but whether he actually sighted Australia is not known. Willem Jansz, a captain of the Dutch East India Company, arrived in the same year. His pinnace *Duyfken* sailed into the Gulf of Carpentaria, and he charted 200 miles of the coastline, although Jansz mistook it for part of New Guinea.

Thirst for knowledge and adventure played only a minor part in these and subsequent voyages to the antipodes. The main purpose, like those of the great explorations in previous centuries, was the furthering of trade and the acquisition of new resources. On both counts, Australia disappointed the early sailors, many of them Dutch. Dutch navigators had learned from experience that after rounding the Cape of Good Hope they could reach the Dutch East Indies faster if they took a strait eastern course as far as Australia before turning north. These navigators included Dirk Hartog, probably the first European to land on Australian soil—on an island (now carrying his name) off the Western Australian coast, which his ship, *Eendracht,* reached October 25, 1616. A pewter plate that Hartog left on the island is now in the National Museum of Amsterdam. In 1642 another Dutchman, Abel Tasman, discovered what is now Tasmania. Rather modestly, he gave it the name of Van Diemen's Land in honor of the governor-general of the Dutch East Indies. Although Tasman raised the Dutch flag and declared that the island was henceforth a possession of Holland, his fellow countrymen were not interested when they heard of the event. Neither did they show much enthusiasm for Willem de Flaming's report in 1697 that he had reached the Swan River. Today Perth—the Western Australian capital—stands on its banks.

William Dampier, an English buccaneer, was the first Briton to land in New Holland (as Australia was then called.). The date was 1688 and the place King Sound in the northwest. He thought it a desolate spot and gave us the first description of the aborigines: "the miserablest people in the world." Eleven years later, he returned in a Royal Navy ship and explored a bit more of the inhospitable northwest coast. During the next decades Britons, Dutch, and essentially everyone else forgot New Holland, which became a sort of fantasy land. Here, Jonathan Swift located "the country of the Yahoos," the degraded, brutish creatures, visited by Gulliver.

The misconception that Captain James Cook discovered Australia still lingers on. He did not, nor did he claim to have done so. It is true, however, that discovery and exploration of the east coast of Australia during the voyage of Cook's ship, the *Endeavour,* became one of the most important of all the early voyages of discovery. Cook's instructions from the British Admiralty were, first, to make certain astronomical observations from Tahiti; then to sail southward, and then, if necessary, westward, to look for a "continent or land of great extent." On April 20, 1770, Cook sighted the southeastern corner of Australia at Point Hicks. On the 29th, he landed in a large bay in what is today south Sydney and called it Botany Bay because of the variety of hitherto unknown plants that the English botanist Joseph Banks and his Swedish colleague, the naturalist Daniel Carl Solander, found there. A week later, Cook continued his voyage north, charted the coast, and, eventually, on the small Possession Island off Cape York in the north took eastern Australia for Britain. Upon reaching home, Cook gave an enthusiastic report about the economic possibilities of eastern Australia, which he named New South Wales. Although his book *The Voyages of Captain Cook* became a best seller and was translated into several languages, Britons were only mildly interested in the newest extension of their possessions.

Early Colonists

It took the American Revolutionary War to provide the British Government with the necessary impetus to pay attention to Australia. Loss of the American colonies meant that there was no longer a viable place to ship law breakers sentenced to exile. Australia looked like a suitable alternative. It was sufficiently remote, and, as Prime Minister William Pitt declared in Parliament, it offered the cheapest way to reduce the prison population which was overcrowding Britain's jails. So Australia became the new repository for convicts and on May 13, 1787, the First Fleet of eleven ships sailed from England with approximately 1,030 people, including roughly 760 convicts under the command of Captain Arthur Phillip, who was to be the first governor of the new colony. After a voyage lasting eight months the fleet reached Botany Bay on January 18, 1788.

Captain Phillip, however, regarded the bay as unsuitable for a settlement. But a few miles north he found "the finest harbour in the world, in which a thousand sail of the line may ride in the most perfect security" and transferred the operation to that site. He named the place Sydney (after Lord Sydney, secretary of state for the colonies)—where Australia's premier city with a population in excess of three million now stands. The date of the landing in Sydney Harbour at Sydney Cove was January 26, 1788, now celebrated as Australia Day.

At the time it was a miserable settlement, in physical and human terms. Some of the convicts were political offenders and petty rascals, but the majority were hardened criminals. Only a few had learned any trade or knew anything about agriculture. In addition, most of the European plants and the cattle transported by the fleet soon died in the new surroundings. During the early years the colonists had to rely upon food supplies imported from overseas and there were many times when the venture appeared doomed. However, in due course land with better soil for farming was found farther inland and new settlements were established. By 1792 when Governor Phillip retired for health reasons and returned to England the colony was almost self-sufficient in staple foods.

For the next twenty years or so, the newcomers still occupied only a small coastal strip. A few exploratory voyages were made, the most important being the expedition of Captain Matthew Flinders who circumnavigated the continent for the first time in 1802–1803. Flinders is credited with having first used the name Australia; previously the continent had been called New Holland, New South Wales, or Botany Bay. For some time the early settlers could not move much farther inland because of the barrier of the Blue Mountains. But in 1813 Gregory Blaxland, a farmer, Lieutenant William Lawson, a former member of the New South Wales Corps, and acting Provost Marshal William Charles Wentworth found a way across the mountains, following the ridges instead of gullies and ravines. The successful crossing eventually led to the opening of the country for settlement farther afield from Sydney. Exploration continued throughout the nineteenth century, and, although almost the whole of Australia has now been surveyed and mapped, some little-known areas still remain. Later explorers had the advantage of setting out on expeditions from newly established settlements, five of which became capitals of new colonies: Hobart, Tasmania, established in 1804; Brisbane, Queensland, 1824; Perth, Western Australia, 1829; Melbourne, Victoria, 1835; and Adelaide, South Australia, 1836. In 1839, the harbor of Darwin was discovered by H.M.S. *Beagle* and named in honour of Charles Darwin, who had been a naturalist with an earlier expedition of the *Beagle*. It is now the site of the capital of the Northern Territory, which was a Commonwealth territory governed by Canberra until 1978 when it became self-governing.

Gold and Fleece

Two factors have been of the utmost importance in the relatively fast development of Australia. One was the successful breeding of sheep; the other, the discovery of gold.

Although the saying that "Australia rides on the sheep's back" is no longer quite valid, without the establishment of a large wool growing industry at an early date, the continent's development would have been a great deal slower and probably quite different. At the start, Australia produced nothing that could be sold to the rest of the world to create sufficient income and encourage outside investment and development. It was Captain Henry Waterhous, an officer of the First Fleet, who brought the quality sheep, Spanish merinos, to Australia. He bought them during an official mission to the Cape Colony (South Africa) in 1797, paying £4 for each of the dozen or so animals. Soon after, other merinos were purchased from the Royal Merino stud at Kew, England. Experiments with the new imports were almost immediately successful and by the beginning of the nineteenth century New South Wales already produced the world's finest wool. In 1807 the first wool consignment (245 pounds) produced on a few NSW farms was sent to London. It was a great success. In the mid-1980s some 80,000 Australian properties grazed more than 150 million sheep producing 1,700 million pounds of wool, worth about A$2,000 million. Although in the late 1970s Australia had lost to the Soviet Union the number one rank of sheep ownership, Australian wool production remained about 50 percent higher than that of the USSR. Australia still produces about 30 percent of the world's wool.

The early settlers—immigrants, freed convicts, marines, and discharged military personnel who chose to stay in Australia—received land free of charge. There was so much of it, especially after the crossing of the Blue Mountains. Some people took possession of the land on the western plains simply by squatting. The only condition for obtaining official approval of ownership was the obligation to employ convicts, which really meant cheap labor for minimal costs of food and clothing. Still, for the growing number of free settlers, the system of transportation of criminals and attendant problems became intolerable and the demand for abolition grew. Regular convict transportation to the eastern colonies ceased in 1840 and to Tasmania in 1853. Western Australia on the other hand continued to receive transported convicts to overcome an acute shortage of labor, but the system finally was terminated in 1868. During eighty years of transportation approximately 168,000 convicts were sent from Britain to Australia. During the first six of these eight decades Australia's population increased very slowly—to only 405,000 by 1850. It was the discovery of gold which gave the first big boost to populating the continent.

Gold had been found in Australia more than a quarter of a century earlier than the usual date—1851—given to its discovery. A government surveyor, J. McBrien, reported in 1823 his find of alluvial gold on the Fish River, about 15 miles east of what is today the town of Bathurst. Similar reports followed. However, the governing strata, fearing a rush of already-scarce labor from the farms to the goldfields, kept the secret as long as possible. In 1844 when the geologist W. B. Clarke showed some gold nuggets to the then governor of New South Wales, Sir Goerge Gipps, and to several members of the NSW legislative council, telling them that there was plenty more of the stuff where he had found them, Gipps said: "Put them away Mr. Clarke, or we shall all have our throats cut."

Gold was found in California in 1848 and was followed by a rush to the promised land from many parts of the world, including Australia, where life became difficult for most people. A severe drought for several seasons had reduced the woolclip to almost nil, ruining the entire economy.

Thousands made up their mind that California was the place to emigrate. To stop the exodus Governor Fitz Roy asked London to send out a competent geologist who, it was hoped, would find metals and minerals in economic quantities. The job fell to Samuel Stutchbury, a competent professional who did what was expected of him: he found the metals and minerals including gold. The rush overseas stopped and was replaced by a mass immigration: the gold boom was on. It was rather short lived, lasting about twenty years—from the early 1850s to the early 1870s. But it had at least one lasting effect. It more than quadrupled Australia's population: from 405,000 to almost 1,650,000. When the boom petered out many "diggers" decided to stay in the country as tradesmen, merchants, and farmers. But in 1854, gold caused Australia's only bloody uprising against government authority, the Eureka Stockade, resulting in the death of about thirty men. The miners' chief grievance was a decision of the government of Victoria to license gold mining and the refusal of some miners to pay the license fee. The trouble, which originally started over a broken window in the Eureka Hotel in the town of Ballarat, has been transformed into a legend of social rebellion of the underdog against authority.

Evolution of a Commonwealth

Until federation in 1901 the Australian continent was divided between six self-governing British colonies established at different times: New South Wales in 1823; Tasmania in 1825; Western Australia, 1829; South Australia, 1834; Victoria, 1851; and Queensland, 1859. Despite close ties—such as the majority's British/Irish descent and their common English language—the six colonies developed separately, paying scant regard to common interests. Not only did they introduce different laws, but instead of developing a uniform railway system to conquer the immense distances of their sprawling new land, they even laid railroads with different gauges.

Gradually, however, economic and political necessities prevailed over parish-pump attitudes as it became obvious that Australia would develop as a whole only if it were treated as one political and economic identity. The process of unification began at irregularly held "intercolonial conferences" upgraded in 1891 to a National Australasian Convention, which opened in Sydney in March of that year. The convention drew up a draft of a federal constitution. A further convention in 1897–98 used the draft to fashion the Australian Constitution and it took another two years before the "indissoluble Federal Commonwealth of Australia" came into being on January 1, 1901. The Earl of

Hopetown became its first governor general and Sir Edmund Barton, a former speaker of the New South Wales Legislative Assembly, its first Prime Minister.

The Constitution provided for Federal Parliament to sit in Melbourne until a federal capital territory was selected and established. The present Australian Capital Territory was ceded from New South Wales to become federal territory in 1911, and the name of the national capital, Canberra, was chosen in 1913. The first Federal Parliament to meet in Canberra was opened by the Duke of York, later King George VI, on May 9, 1927.

Australia today is an independent and sovereign parliamentary democracy—a member of the (no longer entirely British) Commonwealth of Nations. Despite her independence Australia maintains a close official relationship with Britain. The British monarch, Queen Elizabeth II, is also formally Queen of Australia and as such is the head of state. Her representatives in the country are the governor general and the six state governors. All are designated by the elected (federal or state) governments and appointed by the monarch on their recommendation. Except in extraordinary circumstances the governors act on the advice of the elected ministers. But the governors do have so-called "reserve powers" which enable them to act independently in cases of extreme crisis. Such a situation arose in 1975 when the governor general, Sir John Kerr, summarily dismissed the then Prime Minister Gough Whitlam and appointed the leader of the Liberal Country Party opposition, Malcolm Fraser, to form a new government.

Also called a commonwealth herself, Australia's political structure resembles in parts that of Britain and in parts that of the United States. She has an elected two-chamber federal parliament consisting of the 76-member Senate and the 148-seat House of Representatives. The six states that form the Commonwealth of Australia also each have their own parliament. In 1978 the Northern Territory—until then administered by Canberra—became a self governing entity. For all practical purposes its government is similar to all other state governments, although the titles are different.

Rights and duties of federal and state governments are clearly delineated—in theory. Canberra looks after over-all economic subjects (finance, foreign affairs, defense) and collects most taxes; the states deal with education, police matters, social welfare, and local government issues in their own respective territories. In practice, lines of responsibility frequently overlap each other, causing problems. At present five parties are represented in the Australian (federal) parliament: the Liberal Party, a moderately conservative group; the National Country Party, with mainly rural backing (these too form a coalition); the Australian Labor Party, which is akin to the British Labour Party; the Australian Democrats, a small middle-of-the-road group; and the recently formed Anti Nuclear Party, which has one representative in the Senate. The last federal elections in December 1984 returned a 16-seat majority for Labor in the 148-seat House of Representatives.

The present governor general is Sir Ninian Stephen, a former High Court judge. The prime minister is Bob Hawke (Labor).

The Judiciary

One of Australia's most cherished and respected institutions is its independent judiciary. Each state has its own structure of civil, criminal, and children's courts, and industrial tribunals. The highest judicial authority is the High Court of Australia, established by the Constitution and consisting of a chief justice and six justices appointed for life. The High Court deals with all matters arising from the Constitution as well as with appeals against the decisions of any of the six state supreme courts. Until March, 1986, it was possible to appeal High Court decision to Britain's Privy Council; but during a visit to Australia that month the Queen signed a proclamation ending Australian appeals to the Privy Council and the power of the United Kingdom to legislate in effect Australian law. While the Australia Act 1986 severed links between the UK parliamentary and legal systems it did not affect the Queen's position. But it did end possible implied limitations on state powers originating in their former colonial status.

Social Security and Health

Australia was one of the first "social welfare states" in the world. Some of its initiatives in this field have been considered almost revolutionary. For instance, old age pensions were introduced in 1909; invalid pensions a year later; and maternity allowances in 1912. At present, social security payments represent the largest single item in the federal government's budget. In addition, the states are still responsible for a number of social welfare services including housing, public health, and maternal and child welfare.

Australia's medical services hold to a very high standard. Most Australian universities have medical schools offering five- or six-year training courses, after which graduate doctors must serve at least a year in an approved hospital before they are registered. Only registered doctors may practice. Five Australian universities have dental schools. In mid-1986 there were about 19,000 medical practitioners (14 percent of them women) and 5,500 dentists. About three quarters of the 1,115 hospitals are government owned. There is a government-run medical insurance plan, Medicare, financed by a 1 percent levy on taxable income; everyone must be part of it. But in addition to Medicare one may also insure oneself privately for supplementary benefits. There is no free medicine in Australia except for pensioners and for people on the lowest income category who are not taxed.

Visitors needing medical attention may be sure of excellent care once they have contacted a doctor. The problem could be to find a doctor, especially on weekends and holidays or at night when even Australians may encounter difficulties in summoning one. However, the better hotels and larger motels in the urban centers have one or more doctor and dentist on whom they can call in a medical emergency. One can also go to the casualty department of a public hospital. In normal circumstances, ambulance services in urban areas are good and, if necessary, they will transport a sick person to the casualty department of the nearest public hospital.

A unique Australian institution is the Royal Flying Doctor Service which provides medical attention and care for people in the vast and isolated regions of the Australian inland. The doctors operate from a number of centralized bases and keep in touch with their patients by two-way radios. There is a separate government-operated aerial medical service in the Northern Territory and aerial ambulance services function in New South Wales and South Australia.

The Economy

A wealthy country by any standards, Australia is self-sufficient in most raw materials except for crude oil, sulphur, and phosphate. It is among the world's major producers of wool, grain, beef, and a long list of metals and minerals, especially iron ore. Huge quantities of it have been discovered mainly in the "wastelands" of Western Australia together with large amounts of industrial diamonds. Australia's high standard of living and her prosperity depend on the export of her farm and mineral products which make up about 80 percent of all goods sold overseas. Manufactured products account for only 20 percent of the total.

Before World War II, Britain was Australia's best customer, buying about half of all exports. Now she takes only 7 percent of the total. Since the late 1960s Japan has emerged as Australia's number one customer.

In mid-1986 Australia's main socioeconomic problems stemmed from low international commodity prices; a result of a (by and large successful) struggle against inflation and unemployment. The high cost of labor is an important factor in the constant effort to keep overseas markets and, if possible, to extend them. Despite these efforts Australia's share of the world's export markets has slipped from 2.6 percent to 1.2 percent in the past 30 years. Her rank as a world exporter has fallen in the same period from eighth to twenty-third position.

Foreign Affairs and Defense

Australia's foreign policy is committed to its own territorial security amd to peaceful coexistence in the family of nations. Despite the international economic problems which have hit Australia hard, aid to less fortunate countries totals roughly A$500,000,000 a year or about A$33.3 for every Australian man, woman, and child. Although in lifestyle, culture, and civilization Australia is a western nation, conscious efforts have been and are being made to establish closer ties with eastern civilizations in Australia's near north. However, like most other nations Australians have closer and friendlier relations with some countries than with others. Britain, Canada, New Zealand, and, to a lesser extent, the United States are considered members of the same family. Despite the recent tensions between New Zealand and the US (caused by New Zealand's strong antinuclear policy, which has meant the barring of US warships), ANZUS, the alliance between Australia, New Zealand, and the US in 1951, remains the cornerstone of the country's defense planning. There are also close contacts with the Association of South East Asian Nations (ASEAN), a group which comprises Indonesia, Singapore, Malaysia, Thailand, and the Philippines. Australia was also a founding member of the United Nations and has been involved in many of its activities.

The task of designing an efficient defense system for a country as huge as Australia with a coastline of 22,983 miles—almost equal to the distance between Sydney and London—has focused on the creation of a highly trained, combat-ready nucleus for each of the country's three services: Army, Navy, and Air Force. Their organization and training are based on experiences gained in past wars in which Australia fought with distinction with the western Allies. In World War I (1914–1918) when the population was fewer than five million, 417,000 Australians served in the armed forces—322,000 of them overseas in Gallipoli, Europe, and Palestine. In World War II (1939–1945) about one million persons—eight out of ten males between 18 and 35 years of age—enlisted in the forces. About 550,000 served overseas; 34,300 died on active service. Australian contingents also fought in the Korean and Vietnam wars. While no enemy force ever landed in Australia, Japanese planes bombed Darwin heavily in World War II; two Japanese submarines fired a few shells at Sydney and Newcastle and three of their midget two-men submarines penetrated Sydney Harbour.

But while Australians are justly proud of their war records, they refuse to impose stringent military regulations in peacetime. As a result, there is no peacetime compulsory military service. All fighting forces are volunteers who sign contracts for various periods of time. Many make soldiering their lifelong careers. At present some 72,000 Australians are on active defense service. In addition there are about 32,000 reservists. Total annual defense expenditure hovers around A$6 billion.

Peoples of Australia

Out of a total population of 15.75 million, the overwhelming majority of Australians belong to the Caucasian race. Some thirty or forty years ago, one could have added that, except for a small minority, the major part of the population came from Anglo-Saxon and Irish stock. To a lesser extent this is still true. However, since the end of World War II in 1945, there has been an influx of about 4,000,000 immigrants from more than 60 countries—the majority from the British Isles. The large-scale immigration has been an important factor in changing a people with an insular mentality into an outward looking and cosmopolitan nation. As one would expect, the change is most marked among the nation's youth.

Old, ingrained attitudes have not, of course, completely disappeared in the last two generations, but only traces of the once prevalent xenophobia have survived. For example, until the late 1940s many Australians resented when people talked in a foreign language in a public place. Today, one may speak Swahili or Tagalog, Russian or Chinese without causing the slightest stir.

Officially, the so-called "White Australia" policy, which made it virtually impossible for non-whites to settle in this country, never existed. But when it was quietly abandoned (in the 1950s) Australia became one of the world's major ethnic melting pots. As the last published census (1981) shows by that time 21.9 percent of the population—3,308,000 persons—was born outside Australia. In the 1947 census the proportion was 10 percent. Major immigrant groups included the Ireland, U.K., New Zealand, Germany, Greece, Italy, Lebanon, Yugoslavia, Poland, and Holland. The newcomers included 322,000 Asians and more than 90,000 Africans.

To these figures should be added the unknown number of second and even third generation immigrants who, although born and raised in Australia still retain close cultural ties with their parent's homeland. Australian government encourages foreign-born residents to become naturalized citizens, retaining the cultural heritage of their native countries and sharing their inheritance with "old Australians." Despite islands of discontent among certain ethnic groups, the process of adaptation has been astonishingly fast and successful in Australia. A large number of foreign-born residents occupy distinguished positions in the economic, artistic, scientific, and cultural life of the country. Some have been knighted, others have been elected to parliaments and appointed to courts.

The Aborigines

The aborigines' ancestors came to Australia from Asia perhaps 60,000 years ago. But they do not look much like any other Asians, though their limbs are somewhat similar to those of Indians. The shape of their heads and their features is quite unique: they tend to have a wide faces with large, flat noses, deep-set eyes (to give protection from the sun), bushy eyebrows, and strong protruding jaws. The color of a full-blooded aboriginal is dark brown; that of mixed bloods—now the great majority—varies from a deep sun tan to almost white. Very few aborigines still roam the vast expanses of the continent's arid center as nomadic hunters and food gatherers. Of the statistically ascertained aboriginals—160,000, or 1¼ percent of the total Australian population—about 60,000 now live in rural areas including mission stations and aboriginal reserves, and 100,000 live in urban areas. Yet as recently as 1962, an expedition that entered the Woomero Rocket Range area in Central Australia discovered seventy-one aborigines who had apparently never been in contact with white people.

The aborigines' experience under white rule in the past is not an attractive story. When the First Fleet arrived, an estimated 300,000 of them roamed the wide expanses of Australia. They lived in some 450 tribes of various sizes but even the largest contained only a few scores of families. Each tribe had its own territory for hunting and food gathering and clashes between tribes over border transgressions and other infringements are supposed to have been rare. They had few weapons and tools—spears, boomerangs, stone axes, sticks for making fire, and grass bags. They wore no clothes; the dog was their only domesticated animal.

Whether they lived the lives of miserable Stone Age savages or were a happy breed in a paradise, saved for so long from destructive civilization, may be open for argument. But it is hardly surprising that the newly arrived whites stood uncomprehendingly before the aboriginal enigma. They did not understand the deeper meaning of what appeared to them a near animal existence that filled them with revulsion and horror. After all, most of the early newcomers found themselves in Australia very much against their wishes. Even the free settlers had come only with the aim of getting rich and getting out as fast as possible. Because aborigines were useless as exploitable slave laborers and a nuisance as occupiers of the land they were brushed aside—peacefully, if possible, brutally, if necessary. As a result, whatever their original number might have been, within a century only a small fraction survived. By 1921 only about 60,000 were left.

Until recently it has been asserted that on the mainland the aborigines gave up the struggle for their ancient land without resistance. However, new research has found that, especially at the beginning, the new settlers had to fight for the possession of land with the old owners. Finally, the fire-arm won against the spear and the boomerang. The aborigines resisted most fiercely on the island of Tasmania where hunting parties were organized to exterminate them. By 1835 only 203 of the estimated 5,000 Tasmanian aborigines survived and they were deported to the small and barren Flinders Island between Tasmania and the mainland. The Tasmanian race became extinct in 1888.

Towards the end of the last century it was believed that the aboriginal was doomed to die out in a few decades. Yet the contrary has happened. With more enlightened government policies, the aborigines have not only survived but their numbers are fast increasing. Past wrongs inflicted on them cannot be undone but they are being compensated, to some extent, with specific efforts to assist their economic, social, and cultural development. Since the referendum of 1967 that endorsed the abolition of all discriminatory laws, aborigines have become full-fledged Australian citizens. Large areas of crown land have been transferred to their ownerships, their educational and industrial training has been stepped up. One of them, Sir Douglas Nicholls, became governor of South Australia and another, Neville Bonner, was a member of the federal parliament's Senate. Well-known singer, pastoralist, and businessman, Ernie Bridge, an aborigine, is now minister of aboriginal affairs in the West Australian cabinet.

In the past, official policy has been to attempt assimilation of the aborigines with the white body politic. Now the emphasis is on what most aboriginal leaders seem to strive for: full citizenship and equal rights, with the right to maintain a separate cultural and social identity. Without question, the lot of the aboriginal in Australian society has made great strides in recent years. But there is plenty of room for further improvement. Even the most inveterate optimists must admit that it will be a long time before the legally equal aboriginal becomes a fully accepted member of Australian society.

But how long aboriginal culture will survive as a separate, living force when full acceptance is achieved is anybody's guess. At any rate, great effort is being taken to save what has survived in aboriginal culture and art. As the people had no written language, their laws, myths, and lore were passed from generation to generation by word of mouth. Their often enchanting stories explaining life's phenomena from the world's creation (Dreamtime) as well as their bark paintings, tribal customs, and taboos are carefully collected. Wall paintings, when discovered, become protected by law in order to save them from the ravages of man and nature. There are wall paintings in the Northern Territory which may be 5,000 years old (coach tours from Darwin are organized to inspect them). A number of works, including landscapes, bark paintings, and boomerangs, are on sale in Darwin, Alice Springs, and in souvenir shops in the capital cities. Aboriginal reserves located all over Australia are now governed by their own elected councils; one must request their permission to visit. As a rule, aborigines do not mind visitors but they dislike being gaped at as if they were exhibits in some human zoo.

The Australian Way of Life

Multicultural Australia's future is nowadays one of the most keenly discussed topics among intelligent Australians who realize that the annual influx of some 100,000 "people" from dozens of countries and cultures will steadily alter the lifestyle of this developing nation. But so far the Anglo-Saxon way of life has maintained its dominant position.

Australians are easy to live with. This may be too sweeping a generalization and many Australians who criticize their own nationals for bourgeois attitudes may energically refute this statement. Yet compared with the people of many other nations, Australians are more tolerant and more resistant to injustice than most.

These traits are not unmitigated blessings in every situation. For instance, the tendency of so many Australians to side with the real or imagined underdog in all circumstances has led them to believe that "authority is always wrong." Some analysts of the Australian scene have explained this phenomenon as an inheritance from the country's early colonial period when forebears of the present Australians had often misused authority in their effort to survive.

The distrust of authority, a basic feature of Australian life, is expressed on many levels. The Commonwealth Constitution, for example, provides that the people must be asked by referendum whether they will agree to change certain laws. During the past 86 years, only a few of these referenda have ended with an affirmative vote. But latent suspicion of power is manifested in more pedestrian ways. Police in a chase can count on very little help from passersby, not so much because Australians are afraid of becoming involved, but because so many of them instinctively bestow the benefit of the doubt on the chased.

The popular Australian practice of "cutting down tall poppies to size" has nothing to do with gardening, but is another form of the anti-authority phenomenon: an attempt to cut down people who have climbed "too high" in their respective fields.

Australians as a whole seem to be immune to hero worship in politics or government. In its nearly two centuries of history, Australia has never had anyone approaching the status of a charismatic leader even for a brief period. Internationally successful sportsmen and women become temporary heroes as long as they don't appear to think that they are "better" than others. The same may be true for those who have achieved international recognition as artists, scientists, musicians, and writers. It is the talented rather than the humble or the average who must "know their place" to live happily ever after.

This attutude has given rise to the legend that Australian society is classless and egalitarian. It is neither. It is true, however, that class is far less important in Australia than in most Western countries; also on a personal level, the feeling of equality is more genuine than it is elsewhere. Australia has no home-bred aristocracy, and titled immigrants (including British) play an unimportant part in social life. Nor is money the necessary rope for climbing to the top of the social pyramid. Upward social mobility is fairly widespread, and, except for a few ultra-conservative strongholds, it matters more what persons are than what social stratum they come from.

Public opinion polls have consistently shown that most Australians consider themselves middle class. The population includes a large proportion of trade union members who represent about 55 percent of the total work force. This is not surprising. While pockets (even large ones) of poverty exist, mainly among the uneducated and untrained, the old and the aborigines, Australia is hardly a country of paupers. Some 60 percent of all dwellings, for example, are occupied by people who own them or are paying them off. Thousands more are saving for a deposit on a home. There are few families without a motor car, a refrigerator, radio, and TV. In a population of 15.75 million there are close to 4 million telephone subscribers. Middle class *is* a rather flexible concept and it consists of a number of economic strata; most Australians will fit into one of them between the thin layer of have-nots at the bottom and thinner ceiling of the very rich on top.

The ambition of most Australians to own a home surrounded by a plot of land has largely created the environment in which they live—the sprawling dormitory garden suburb with all its merits and disadvantages. Few Australians will live in a rented flat if they can help it, even an apartment of one's own (or "home unit" as they are called here) is considered second-rate except when it is in the luxury class. Despite its vast expanses, Australia is one of the world's most urbanized countries. About 85 percent of the population live in city and town conglomerates while only 15 percent live in rural areas. Still, the small garden plot is important because Australians are genuinely fond of being outdoors.

What do Australians look like? No answer is satisfactory. The variety of types in Australia defies any general description. But, alas, certainly the image of the average Australian as a tall, muscular, bronzed outdoor type is a fiction.

If it is difficult to generalize about the outward appearance of Australians, it is even harder to find common denominators in their character. And there are plenty of exceptions to the following rules.

As mentioned before, they are easy to live with. They are also a gregarious people—a likable lot, friendly to strangers. Australians are supposed to be among the world's most inveterate gamblers and drinkers. While there are surely millions of Australians who never gamble and hardly ever touch alcohol, this generalization may be rather near the mark. The latest available figure (1983–84) indicates an annual alcohol consumption of 140.1 liters for every man, woman, and child. Drug addiction is as much a curse in Australia as in most Western countries and in 1986 the federal and state governments have embarked on a A$100 million campaign to combat it.

There are a number of legal gambling casinos in New South Wales, Queensland, Tasmania, South Australia, and the Northern Territory. But their appearance has hardly reduced the number of illegal gambling places, mostly in capital cities. Most of them are said to be fairly well run; the main risk in visiting them is a police raid which will inevitably land the tourist in a court and result in a fine. Other legally approved gambling outlets include horse and dog racing, lotteries, and in New South Wales and Canberra, poker machines. According to informed calculations people in the state of Victoria "invested" (an Australian euphemism for legal betting) $900,000 in gambling every hour of the day and night in the calendar year 1984. Of course, some of this amount was returned to the "investors" in winnings, and the government also reaped large sums in taxes.

The Australian Language

One of the obstacles to an acquaintance between foreign visitors and Australians may be language. Australians do, of course, speak English. But Australian English is spoken even by some of the educated with an accent which is quite noticeable and, in its extreme form is sometimes unintelligible to the untrained ear. Lengthy and rather inconclusive arguments have been going on for many years about the origins, or nature, and aesthetics of this accent. Some like it, asserting it is an expression of Australian patriotism to use it; others are outraged by it. Long ago, a poem appeared in the *Bulletin,* Sydney, January 13, 1894, which ended "T'were better if you never sang/Than voiced it in Australian twang." Australians can be quite touchy on this subject and it may be wiser to accept their perfectly valid argument that it is their sweet right to pronounce their language as they want. However, there is one consolation. When the ears become accustomed to equating something like "oi" with "i" and "aye" with "a" ("aye noice daye today"), one need not worry about regional variations. Surprisingly enough, considering the enormous size of the country, there are no regional dialects though some people assert that there are slight differences between Sydney and Melbourne pronunciations.

Besides a distinct accent of debatable felicity, Australians have also developed a large number of superb slang words. Take the word "wowser," which the late Sidney J. Baker defined in his *Dictionary of Australian Slang* as "a puritanical enthusiast, a blue-stocking, a drab-souled philistine haunted by the mockery of others' happiness." And Baker rightly quotes the *Daily Telegraph* (of Sydney) which commented on July 31, 1937: "If Australia had given nothing more to civilisation than that magnificent label for one of its melancholy products—the word wowser—it would not have been discovered in vain." Now, almost half a century later, the average Australian would still agree with this judgment.

Here are a few examples of Australian contributions to colorful English. An "abo" means, of course, an aboriginal. Originally an "Anzac" meant a member of the Australian and New Zealand Army Corps who fought on Gallipoli in World War I; now the term includes all who served in any subsequent wars. "Aussie" can mean Australia or an Australian. "Back of beyond" is the remote inland. To "barrack for" is to shout encouragement to one's side. "Battlers" are persons who struggle for an existence; they are usually spoken of with compassion. A "black tracker" is an aboriginal employed mainly by police to find a lost or wanted person. An "idler" or a "loafer" who imposes on another is a "budger." A red-haired person is nicknamed "Bluey." A "bloke" is a chap or a fellow, and "bonzer" means good or excellent, hence a "bonzer bloke" is a very nice chap. "Bulsh" is a contemptuous term for nonsense or a baseless statement but, because of its derivation, it is not used in polite society.

To be on "compo" is to receive worker's compensation for an accident on the job. "Cooee" is a penetrating cry used especially in wild country to make contact with a person some distance away; not to be in cooeeing distance means to be fairly far away from someone. To "feel crook" is to be ill or off-color. A "digger" is an Australian soldier. "Dinkum" or "fair dinkum" means genuine, true, or honest. A "dinkum Aussie" is an Australian in every sense of the word. "I'm easy" expresses indifference; one doesn't really care one way or another. To plead for a "fair go" is to plead for reasonableness or for giving or receiving a fair chance. To "get stuck into" something is to do a job with zest.

"Goodoh" is a loose statement which, depending on the way it is said can mean different degrees of approval from excellent to a sceptical perhaps. On the other hand, "my oath" is a very strong affirmation. To be "on the outer" means to be broke. "Plonk" is poor quality wine. A "squatter" is not necessarily someone who settles on property he doesn't own; the term can also mean a large landowner. Hence, squattocracy is the nearest thing to an Australian landed aristocracy. The poetic sounding "sundowner" really means a work-shy tramp who arrives at a property to ask for food and shelter at sundown in order to dodge work in return. "Tucker" is food and "yabber" is chatter.

The same words can have several meanings. An invitation to dinner is usually for an evening meal, except on Sunday when it means lunch. "Tea" can be afternoon tea or (evening) dinner except on Sundays and holidays, when it is always the evening meal.

Women

One of the most widely held beliefs about Australia is that it is a man's world—meaning that in Australia women are permitted to play an important role only in the home and, to be tolerably happy, must know their greatly restricted place everywhere else. If notions of this kind have ever been valid, which is rather doubtful, they are certainly antiquated now. The Commonwealth and most of the states have adopted sex discrimination acts which make it unlawful to discriminate against another person on the grounds of sex, marital status, and pregnancy in practically every field of employment except as combatants in the armed forces. This law is being strictly applied especially since the celebrated verdict in the case of thirty-four women against Australia's mammoth Broken Hill Pty Ltd. (BHP) brought down at the end of 1985. BHP refused to employ the thirty-four in its steelworks mainly on the grounds that a New South Wales law prohibits employing women in jobs where they may have to lift objects weighing more than sixteen kilograms—equivalent to an average four-year-old child or two buckets of water. (No limit is set for adult men.) The court decided in favor of the women, who got their jobs.

Australian women were among the first to obtain the right to vote at parliamentary elections. The first Australian state to introduce female suffrage was South Australia in 1894 (a year after New Zealand, which pioneered that reform in the British Commonwealth). Women obtained the vote in Australian Commonwealth elections at the time of federation. By 1908, all states had passed similar legislation and by 1923 women had the right not only to vote but also to sit in any of the nation's seven parliaments (federal and state). In the federal parliament at present 13 of the 76 members of the Senate and 7 of the 148-seat

House of Representatives are women. Joan Child is speaker of the house.

Many women occupy distinguished positions in the professions, the arts, the judiciary, education, science, and journalism. Of course, many more are members of the "work force" in which the rule is equal pay for equal work for both sexes. The proportion of women in the work force has steeply increased in recent years. In the late 1960s they represented 35 percent of the total, now they represent more than 45 percent. In the 1950s only 15 percent of married women worked. Now 50 percent of all married women are working. The proportion of working women among immigrants is especially high—about 36 percent of the total female work force was born outside Australia. The main reason is that a single wage rarely enables a person with a family to save money for a house, a car, and other amenities of the Australian standard of living. It is very often the woman's salary that makes the quick attainment of this standard possible.

Another exploded myth about male social dominance in Australia is that at social gatherings men and women group separately because men dislike discussing serious matters with women. The truth is that men and women mix—or separate—in Australia much as they do in any other Western society.

Arts and Learning in Australia

Within a short two centuries Australians have not only succeeded in establishing a flourishing economy and one of the world's most advanced social organizations; they have also created a culture, based on British-Western traditions, which has taken on an increasingly national character. The achievement becomes all the more impressive if one considers its brief past: the first Australian public library was opened in 1826, the first permanent theater in 1830, the first university (Melbourne) in 1850, and the first art gallery (consisting almost entirely of casts and copies) in 1861.

One of the important features of Australian culture is its geographic dispersal. Each of the six state capitals, as well as the federal capital of Canberra, is a cultural center well provided with universities, libraries, art galleries, museums, symphony orchestras, theaters, and cultural and scientific associations. To live in Perth in the "Far West" or in Hobart in the "Deep South" imposes no cultural deprivation on Australians.

Literature

The first poets of note dealing specifically with Australian themes and emotions were Adam Lindsay Gordon (1833–70), A. B. (Banjo) Patterson (1864–1941), whose "Waltzing Matilda" has become the country's best-known song, and Henry Lawson (1867–1922), followed by C. J. Brennan, R. D. Fitzgerald, Kenneth Slessor, Douglas Stewart, A. D. Hope, James McAuley, Judith Wright, and Nancy Kessing.

The convict James R. Tucker (1808–86) was the first Australian author who received international attention with his autobiographical novel, *Ralph Rashleigh,* in which he describes the arrest of a bank robber in London, his deportation, and his life in the penal colony of New South Wales. Other noteworthy authors of this epoch were Marcus Clarke (1846–81), who also wrote about the life of a convict in *For the Term of His Natural Life* and Thomas Alexander Browne (1826–1915) who, under the name of Rolf Boldrewood wrote *Robbery under Arms,* the saga of cattle thieves. Between the two World Wars, Norman Lindsay, Katharine Susannah Pritchard, Kylie Tennant, Brion Penton, and Henry Handel Richardson (Mrs. J. G. Robertson) became internationally known. A number of distinguished contemporary writers include Patrick White, Nobel Prize winner (1973), the best-selling author Morris West, as well as Xavier Herbert, Hal Porter, Christina Stead, Alan Moorehead, Thomas Keneally, Russel Braddon, Donald Horne, Ronald McKie, and John O'Grady.

Colleen McCullough's *The Thorn Birds,* a compelling saga of three generations of Australians, remained on all best seller lists in the United States throughout much of 1977. Ross Campbell was an outstanding humorist; Ray Lawler and David Williamson are among the more popular Australian playwrights.

Painting and Sculpture

There has been an explosion in the output and appreciation of art in Australia during the past three or four decades. Only since World War II can one speak of a truly Australian school of painters. Their predecessors, distinguished and talented as they were, imitated European models and trends. While the earliest Australian painters were mainly convicts whose portraits and landscapes had historical significance but little artistic value, the first Australian painters of artistic importance were German-born Conrad Martens and Swiss-born Abram Buvelot (second half of the last century).

At the turn of the century the Heidelberg School (Heidelberg is a suburb of Melbourne) tried to add some Australian content to French impressionist spirit. Practitioners Eliot Gruner and Hans Heysen have a secure place in the history of Australian art. But the Australian school begins only with the rise to prominence of such painters as William Dobell, Russell Drysdale, Sydney Nolan, Arthur Boyd, and Lloyd Rees whose works can be found in the art galleries of many countries. A number of foreign-born artists, mainly from totalitarian countries, have also enriched Australia's art world. They include Hungarian-born Desiderius Orban and Judy Cassab and Sali Hermann of Swiss origin.

In this connection, one should again mention aboriginal art. Rock and cave paintings, some of them centuries old, and the bark paintings, mainly in Arnhem Land in the north and other parts of the Northern Territory, are expressions of considerable artistic talent. Among aboriginal artists who adopted the western idiom, Albert Namatjira, painter of Australia's "dead heart" was a highly gifted craftsman.

Music

It is a rare day in the Australian capital cities—except perhaps in midsummer—when music loving tourists cannot find a concert, or even an opera performance, worth attending. Every state capital has at least one symphony orchestra, maintained by the Australian Broadcasting Corporation (ABC). Some have a second or third supported by private associations. While the ABC is the largest musical entrepreneur in the country, organizing some 800 concerts a year, there are a large number of musical societies which provide the means for local and overseas artists to present themselves to Australian audiences. The most important is Musica Viva of Australia, a chamber music association with headquarters in Sydney and branches in all capitals, including Canberra. Symphony concerts have been so much in demand that the ABC had had to organize three subscription series of twenty concerts each in Sydney alone. Each is attended by about 2,800 people. Musica Viva's concerts have some 10,000 subscribers.

Rock and roll from Australia is also making its mark on the rest of the world. The band Men at Work, for example, has had huge success in the US with their first two albums.

Among the many Australian singers and instrumentalists who have achieved international fame are or were Dame Nellie Melba, Peter Dawson, Florence Austral, Eileen Joyce, John Sutherland, John Brownlee, Dame John Hammond, Geofrey Parsons, June Bronhill, and Marie Collier. Well-known composers include Richard Meale, Peter Schulthorpe, Malcolm Williams, George Dreyfus, Felix Werder, Colin Brumby and Nigel Butterley. The country's major opera company is the Australian Opera which performs in most capital cities. The more recent additions to buildings for music, opera and ballet performances are the world famous Sydney Opera House on the harbor, the Festival Theatre in Adelaide, the concert hall in Perth, the Seymour Centre in Sydney, and the opera theatre in Melbourne.

The Media

Australians rank among the world's most avid newspaper readers, radio listeners, and television viewers. Altogether there are some 600 newspapers, ranging from small four- or six-page local sheets published once or twice weekly to mass circulation metropolitan dailies. Neither the government nor any political party owns a daily newspaper. The 17 dailies published in the capital cities are controlled by three publishing groups which also hold shares or controlling interests in the radio and TV stations. The 17 capital city newspapers have an average daily circulation of one copy for every two people. Large, high quality newspapers (all morning) include *The Age* of Melbourne; *The Sydney Morning Herald; The Advertiser* of Adelaide; and *The West Australian* of Perth. *The Sun-News-Pictorial,* a morning daily paper in Melbourne, has the largest circulation of all—about 600,000 net paid copies per day. Except for *The Australian,* a quality national morning newspaper with a modest circulation (about 200,000 daily) which is printed in Sydney, Melbourne, and Brisbane, all other papers are sold almost entirely in the cities and states in which they are published.

Australia has a lively and extensive periodical press. *The Australian Women's Weekly* (despite its name it is a monthly now) sells almost 1,000,000 copies a month while the weekly *Woman's Day* circulation hovers around the half million mark. Among the weeklies, the 104-year-old *Bulletin* of Sydney (circulation about 130,000 per week) maintains a high standard of reporting and comment on politics, social issues, economics, and the arts. There are also innumerable specialized magazines including some published in foreign languages for the immigrant community.

While neither federal nor state governments have any special rights enabling them to interfere with print media, the story is rather different with broadcasting. Ownership of Australian broadcasting is part public and part private. The Australian Broadcasting Corporation, a statutory body similar to the BBC, runs the national radio and television stations. Private companies operate commercial radio and TV stations under license from the Minister for Posts and Telecommunications. The transmitters are operated by the Australian Telecommunications Commission. A 3-person radio and television tribunal monitors standards. To date, no government, Conservative or Labor, has attempted to interfere with programming. At present there are 93 national and 118 commercial radio stations and 84 national and 48 commercial TV stations. The ABC maintains a special "rock radio" station (2jj Sydney) targeted at youth between the ages of about 18 and 25. There are also radio transmissions in the languages of immigrants ("ethnic radio").

Probably the most popular foreign broadcasts in the whole of Southeast Asia are the transmissions of Radio Australia in Melbourne which include 51 news bulletins a day in nine languages: English, Indonesian, Mandarin, Cantonese, Japanese, Vietnamese, Thai, French, and Pidgin English.

Some 8,000 journalists are employed by the Australian media. With the exception of a few top men and women in executive jobs, practically all journalists belong to the Australian Journalists' Association (AJA) which is registered as a trade union. In general, journalistic standards are high. But Humbert Wolfe's oft-quoted lines about the British journalists can also be applied to the Australian species:
"You cannot hope to bribe or twist/(Thank God) the British journalist/But seeing what the man will do/Unbribed, there's no occasion to."

Science

Australian science has been one of the greatest beneficiaries of the enormous advance in international communications. Australian scientists no longer work in isolation; scores of them visit overseas countries to keep abreast of the latest developments in their fields and many of their foreign colleagues come to Australia to lecture and to learn. More than 200 Australian societies are engaged in scientific pursuits, the best known being the Australian Academy of Science and the Australian and New Zealand Association for the Advancement of Science. Two Australian scientists working in Australia have received Nobel Prizes: the virologist Sir Frank Macfarlane Burnet (1960) and the neurologist Sir John Carew Eccles (1963). Australians have also been prominent in many branches of science including radio-astronomy in which they have done considerable pioneering work.

Education

In Australia, education is compulsory up to the age of fifteen (except for Tasmania where it is sixteen), and, at all three levels (primary, secondary, and tertiary) it is free except for nongovernmental schools. While the Constitution mandates education to be a responsibility of each state, the federal government, which has complete responsibility for education in the territories, grants huge subsidies to the states to enable them to meet the soaring costs of maintaining and expanding their educational institutions. A dispute has been going on for years between those who want to nationalize all education and others who wish to maintain the present two-tier system with the corollary that private schools (called "public schools" as in England) would continue to receive government financial support. There are about 7,400 government schools; "public schools" total 2,200, mostly run by churches. Some 2.5 million children attend government schools; 638,000 go to private schools. For children who live in the Outback, or who are handicapped by illness or physical disability, the states maintain correspondence schools supplemented by Schools of the Air. These use two-way radios enabling teachers to give the same lessons to children hundreds of miles apart. Teachers are also able to talk to their pupils, who, in turn, can talk to each other.

Australia has 19 universities with a total student body of 167,400. There are also 78 colleges of advanced education which place greater emphasis on practical than theoretical training and research, and 167 technical colleges. Total expenditure on education in the 1985–86 financial year was almost A$9 billion or 6 percent of the gross domestic product. Whether Australia gets its money's worth from the spiralling amounts spent on education is hotly debated. Still, at present it appears that educational opportunities will continue to expand. Every year thousands of foreign students, partly through Australian scholarships and partly with private support, study at Australian schools and universities. Most are from Asian countries.

In Sum

No matter what one thinks of Australia, one can hardly fail to admire what has gone on here in less than two centuries. Australia was founded in the epoch of the international sailing ship, when it took the better part of six months to receive an answer to a letter sent to London. It took even longer to get goods ordered from "home"—that is, England.

The first steamer reached Sydney in 1831; the first cable service between Europe and Australia was established in 1872; regular plane service between Sydney and London opened shortly before World War II.

On remembers all this, looks around, and thinks: "What an achievement!"

NEW SOUTH WALES

The Oldest of the Six States

by
EMERY BARCS and PAULINE MURPHY

Pauline Murphy is a free-lance writer who has worked for some years in the Australian travel industry.

If you have comparatively little time to spend in Australia yet want to get the feel of the immense country, you would be wise to concentrate on the oldest of the six states: New South Wales. There is no substitute in the rest of Australia for such unique places as Queensland's Great Barrier Reef or the ochre-colored lonely charm of the central desert; yet New South Wales can offer most of what the rest of the country has. New South Wales people assert that their state has more, and what it has is better. There is at least some truth in this assertion. Though New South Wales, with around 5½ million inhabitants, is Australia's most populous state, it ranks fourth in area. Yet it is still so large that it could accommodate the combined territories of the United Kingdom, Germany, Austria, Holland, Denmark, and Switzerland. Within its boundaries, New South Wales offers a great variety of tourist attractions, from the near-tropical north to the snowy mountains of the Australian Alps in the south. Its 1,300 km of coastline is studded with golden beaches, and it has picturesque waterways including inland and scenic coastal rivers with good fishing opportunities. Climatically the whole state is in the temperate zone.

Getting around New South Wales is no problem, for the state is well equipped with all means of transport and has an extensive road network ranging from expressways to dirt tracks. There are plenty of opportunities to participate in organized tours, or to set out on your own by hiring almost anything that moves, from bicycles, motor boats, automobiles (with or without campers, called caravans here) to airplanes. New South Wales is Australia's richest and economically most developed state where you can not only pay a quick visit to some of the world's most advanced farms, but also spend a holiday in the country as a paying guest on some of them. Connoisseurs may spend pleasurable hours tasting some of Australia's best wines in the Hunter Valley vineyards. Should the visitor be confronted with any special problem he or she may get expert advice from the staff of the travel centers the Government of New South Wales maintains in Sydney (Corne Pitt and Spring streets), in Melbourne (353 Little Collins Street), in Brisbane (Corne Queen and Edward streets), as well as in tourist-information centers in the New South Wales country towns of Albury and Tweed Heads. Like all Australian states, New South Wales has its own parliament and government. The parliament consists of two chambers: the Legislative Assembly and the Legislative Council. The state premier (in Australia the head of the federal government is called prime minister, and the leaders of state governments have the title premier) and his or her ministers are all members of parliament. They look after such issues as education, transport, health, social welfare, justice, and police (although the federal government is also involved with some of them). At present three parties are represented in the New South Wales parliament: Labor is in power (1981) led by Premier Neville Wran. The crown's representative in the state is Air Marshal Sir James Rowland.

SYDNEY

Sydney, capital of New South Wales, is not only Australia's oldest, largest, and liveliest city, where about 22 percent of all Australians live, but also one of the few cities in the world that tourists find easily manageable. This may sound paradoxical, because what is generally known as "Sydney"—a conglomerate of seven separately administered cities (Sydney, Parramatta, Liverpool, Penrith, Campbelltown, Blacktown, and Bankstown), four shires (Sutherland, Baulkham Hills, Hornsby, and Warringah), and 33 municipalities—occupies a larger area (12,061 square kilometers) than Greater London or New York. Still, the tourist can effortlessly cope with Sydney because the main attractions are so close together, many of them within easy walking distance of the city center, Martin Plaza. It takes only ten minutes to saunter from there to Circular Quay, the birthplace of Australia as we know it today, and the terminal of the ferry boats that ply one of the world's largest and most enchanting harbors. From the quay, or from the many stops in the city en route, one can reach any of several ocean and harbor beaches for surfing or swimming in less than 30 minutes by bus. A few minutes' bus or train ride will take the visitor to King's Cross, Sydney's nightclub and entertainment center so fondly remembered by thousands of visitors, including mariners from dozens of nations and American soldiers, sailors, and airmen who spent quite some time (and money) there while on leave during World War II and the Korean and Vietnam wars.

To be in Sydney and not take a boat trip on the harbor would be as strange and unthinkable as to be in Venice and not hire a gondola. Unless you have seen the city from the water, you have not seen it at all. There are several choices; you may simply board a commuter ferry like thousands of Sydneysiders do or take part in one of several daily harbor cruises lasting two or three hours or hire a motor launch and explore many of the arms and bays that border the harbor's 240km of foreshores. The most rewarding way, however, is to get an invitation on a sailing boat. It is from the water that one can fully appreciate the lofty elegance of the Harbor Bridge, the largest single-span bridge in the world—affectionately called the Coathanger. It connects the city proper with the north shore and has been as much a symbol of Sydney as the Eiffel Tower is of Paris.

It is also from the water that one experiences the most thrilling views of another world-famous landmark: the masterpiece of the Danish architect Joern Utzon, the Sydney Opera House. Situated at Bennelong point, between Sydney Cove and Farm Cove, the mighty building gives the impression of being about to break its moorings and glide over the water with the help of the billowing glazed concrete "sails" of its roof. The Opera House has now challenged the Harbor Bridge as the tourist symbol of Sydney. Behind the Opera House and also on the opposite shore, "mini-Manhattan" office towers look down on the busiest port of the South Pacific, and on the cradle of the Australian nation.

Growth of a Metropolis

In two centuries that "cradle"—once a lonely campsite at the bottom of the world—has grown into the fourth most populous city of the commonwealth—after London, Bombay, and Calcutta. This rapid growth has not been an unmitigated blessing, for much that could have turned Sydney into an incomparably more beautiful place has been lost in the hasty process. For instance, there is no drive around the harbor; except for a few short stretches of public parks and beaches, the foreshores are occupied by private gardens, or are used for commercial purposes. Or another example: After World War II, when building activities were resumed on a large scale, the authorities could have made the widening of the narrow streets—originally footpaths or ox cart tracks—a condition for issuing building permits. Instead they acquiesced in the creation of concrete canyons of skyscrapers, which have dramatized the city skyline but made traffic congestion worse. Traditionally, Sydney's trouble has been its builders' assertion that what was good for them was also good for the public. Another reason for the slapdash development of the inner city was a lack of civic pride. In any contest between the aesthetic and the profitable the latter was sure to win. Lately this attitude has changed. The few surviving mementos of Sydney's past, such as the Rocks area with its century-old houses, are being carefully restored, and once dreary business thoroughfares such as Martin Place—now rebaptized Martin Plaza—are being transformed into places for public enjoyment, including free concerts for lunch-hour crowds.

Sydney undoubtedly shares the woes of many other cities. Traffic congestion and overcrowding of public transport at peak hours are as bad as anywhere. But smog has not become a serious problem yet. The sun still shines 342 days out of every 365. And although Sydney suffers from housing problems, and substandard dwellings are not unknown, it has no wretched slums of the kind one finds in Europe or North America. On the other hand, it has no super-luxury district either. A few grand homes situated in large grounds—survivors of an age when domestic help was not such a problem as it is today—still exist, but most of them are marked for demolition and will soon be replaced by homes of more modest proportions and much better design. Rich Sydneysiders live lavishly but not ostentatiously. The reputedly posh dis-

NEW SOUTH WALES

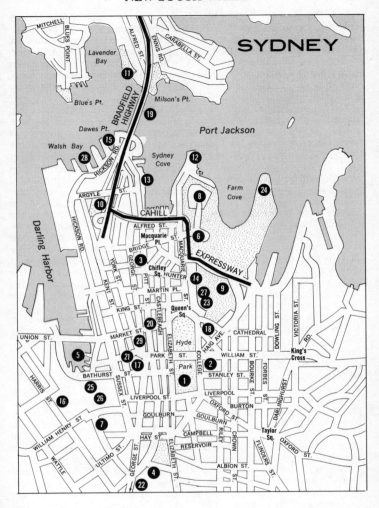

Points of Interest

1) Anzac War Memorial
2) Australian Museum
3) Australia Square
4) Central Railway Station
5) Darling Harbour Development (Conference and Exhibition Center)
6) Conservatorium of Music
7) Sydney Technical College
8) Government House
9) National Art Gallery
10) Observatory
11) Olympic Swimming Pool
12) Opera House
13) Overseas Passenger Terminal
14) Parliament
15) Pier One
16) Power House Museum
17) St. Andrew's Cathedral
18) St. Mary's Cathedral
19) Sydney Harbor Bridge
20) Sydney Tower
21) Sydney Town Hall
22) University of Sydney
23) The Barracks Museum
24) Mrs. Macquarie's Point
25) Entertainment Centre
26) Chinatown
27) The Mint Museum
28) The Wharf Theatre
29) Queen Victoria Building

tricts of Sydney—Bellevue Hill, Darling Point, Vaucluse in the eastern suburbs, the upper North Shore between Roseville and Wahroonga, and Palm Beach and its surroundings farther out at the seaside—are no more than upper-middle-class precincts, even if a Rolls or a Mercedes stands next to a more modestly priced second or third car in the garage, and a barbecue and a swimming pool (which has become so commonplace that no one would think of it as a status symbol) have been built in the backyard.

Sydney has shared with other Australian cities the misfortune that its adolescence and early adulthood coincided with what some consider to be a rather poor period of Western architecture. This has left its mark not only on its many Victorian public buildings but also on many of the older suburbs with their acres of red or liver-colored cottages with tiled roofs of the same hue. Thousands of them were built by speculators, frequently to the plans of some London architectural firm and designed for English climatic conditions. The Anglo-Irish immigrants obviously liked these reminders of their origins. A change in architectural styles and tastes came only after World War II, when local and immigrant architects began to build homes in harmony with Sydney needs and environment. To carry out their ideas they often had to fight the ultraconservative tastes of building authorities, but now there is little opposition to their work and, whatever other drawbacks they may have, Sydney's newer suburbs look all the better for the change. Compared with the rest of the world's, housing standards have remained high and the aim of most Sydneysiders is still to own a home in which each member of the family has its own room.

Changes in Sydney during the past 30 years or so have not been restricted to physical appearance. The mentality of its people has also changed. The old jibe that Sydney is "the world's smallest big city"—originally directed at the narrow-minded insularity of its citizens and not at the size of the place—is no longer valid. Sydneysiders may not be as suave and sophisticated as Parisians, Londoners, or New Yorkers, but neither are they clumsy colonial oafs, suspicious of all outsiders. This is hardly surprising, since Sydney has become one of the most polyglot and cosmopolitan cities in the world. On the whole they are friendly, approachable, and hospitable. They seem to genuinely like visitors (especially Americans—a nice change for U.S. travelers who are not always greeted warmly in more "elegant" cities). There's a high value placed on sports, the outdoors, and leisure time in general.

Sydney is the oldest civilized settlement not only in Australia and New Zealand, but in the whole southwestern Pacific. A few physical mementos—some churches and public buildings—that date back to the first decades of its founding in January 1788 have survived as witnesses to the city's early history. However, considering the sordid beginnings of the place as a penal colony, what is surprising is not that so little has remained, but that there has been anything worth preserving. The founder of the city was Captain Arthur Phillip, commander of the First Fleet, who realized that the place to establish a settlement was not Botany Bay, discovered by Captain Cook, but "the finest harbor in the world," which Phillip found a few miles farther north, and where Sydney stands today. The early history of Sydney is, in fact, the early history of the whole of Australia, and we have dealt with it there. Here is a short chronological list of some of the events in the city's development from the establishment of a miserable camp at the edge of the continent to a mighty metropolis.

1788   Settlement at Farm Cove

1789   James Ruse granted land at Rose Hill (now Par-

NEW SOUTH WALES

ramatta) and became the first settler there

1792	First foreign trading vessel, *Philadelphia*, arrived
1793	First church built (on Hunter Street)
1802	First book (*General Standing Orders*) printed in Sydney
1803	First newspaper, *Sydney Gazette and N.S.W. Advertiser*, published
1809	First post office opened
1810	First race track opened (Hyde Park)
1823	Legislative council appointed to assist the governor in colonial affairs
1831	First immigrant ship arrives and the first steamer, *Sophia Jane*, reaches Sydney
1838	David Jones (now Australia-wide chain department store) opened first shop
1841	Gas used for street lighting
1842	First omnibus licensed
1844	Exports exceed imports for the first time
1849	Last convict ship arrives
1850	University of Sydney founded
1856	Registration of births, deaths, and marriages inaugurated
1858	First electric telegraph line opened
1871	National Art Gallery founded
1883	Railroad from Sydney to Melbourne established
1898	Sydney and Newcastle connected by phone
1910	Saturday half-holiday established
1915	Conservatorium of Music opened and first policewoman appointed
1932	Harbour Bridge opened

Exploring Sydney

If you are in a hurry or don't like treading the sidewalk for hours, the best way to see Sydney is to join a conducted coach or coach-and-ferry-boat tour. You could combine coach and foot by catching the red Sydney Explorer bus operated by the Urban Transit Authority. The bus travels throughout the city and will deposit you or pick you up again at any of 20 tourist stops. (See Tours under Practical Information.) Or you may view the city from the Sydney Tower, in the heart of the city. Sydney Tower opened in 1981 and is the tallest building south of the equator, rising 324.8m above sea level. Double-decker lifts transport visitors (ticket: $3.50) up to the nine-story turret at the peak of the tower in around 40 seconds. The turret has two restaurants with rotating floors and an observation level, from which you can see horizons some 70km away.

More energetic visitors will probably enjoy exploring the city on foot; the mildly undulating terrain will hardly strain people in reasonable physical shape, and the rewards of seeing the town and the people at a leisurely pace make the effort worthwhile. One can of course decide on innumerable variations for this sort of exploration, but here are a few easy half-day itineraries.

Before you begin, a word of warning: be prepared for a very quiet day if you are visiting Sydney on Christmas Day or Good Friday, when most attractions are closed.

Circular Quay, The Rocks, Opera House

At Circular Quay, at one of the ferry wharves, you may get timetables for ordinary ferry runs and harbor cruises. Turning left (toward the Bridge), a few minutes' walk brings you to Sydney's oldest quarter, the Rocks. It was here, after landing on January 26, 1788, that Captain Arthur Phillip established the first settlement, and the nation was born. The Rocks was the site of Australia's first prison, barracks, store, and hospital. However, a few decades later the district became the roughest, toughest, and most miserable slum of the new city. These conditions were mainly responsible for the outbreak of bubonic plague there at the end of the last century. After the disease was eradicated, the Rocks remained a slum, though situated in what was potentially one of the city's most valuable sites. Fears that the Rocks would completely disappear if it were allowed to become another concrete jungle led to the establishment in 1968 of the Sydney Cove Redevelopment Authority, with a charter to restore, renovate, and redevelop the area. Much of this has already been done with loving care, and today the Rocks appears more or less as it looked at the beginning of the nineteenth century. It has no buildings of outstanding architectural value but it has atmosphere. Erected in 1815, Cadman's Cottage, near the Overseas Passenger Shipping Terminal, is Sydney's oldest building. John Cadman, Governor Lachlan Macquarie's superintendent of boats, lived there. It is now a museum and visitor center. The Argyle Centre (open 10 A.M. to 5:30 P.M. seven days a week), where artists and craftspeople exhibit and sell their wares, is a large convict-built brick building dating from the 1820s. Originally a bond store in which convicts were housed in the cellars, it is now a major tourist attraction. Proceeding through the Argyle Cut, hewn from the rocky hillside by convicts in 1843, one reaches Argyle Place, with its early terrace houses, and the Garrison

Church designed by architect Henry Ginn, begun in 1840. The insignia of the regiments that worshiped there are displayed in the church. Nearby is Sydney Observatory (1858) on Observatory Hill with fine views of the harbor. Lower Fort Street has a number of fine colonial houses, and at Dawes Point, cannons, which were once supposed to defend Sydney, are exhibited. Walking back around Circular Quay you reach the Sydney Opera House, where conducted tours of the complex lasting about one hour are held daily between 9 A.M. and 4 P.M. The dramatic design of the building by Danish architect Joern Utzon was selected in 1957 from entries in an international competition. It took about 14 years (1959–1973) to build it. The cost of $A102 million was mainly provided by state lotteries. The Concert Hall seats 2,700 people, the Opera Theatre 1,550, the Drama Theatre 550, and the Cinema and Chamber Music Hall 420. After visiting the Opera House you can lunch in one of the two restaurants in the complex: the formal and rather expensive Bennelong or the self-service Harbor Restaurant, which has an open-air terrace. Provided the weather is suitable, it is pleasant to sit and watch the ships and ferries glide by.

Royal Botanic Gardens, Art Gallery, N.S.W. State Library

From the Opera House, stroll through the Royal Botanic Gardens on the shores of Farm Cove. The Gardens are open from 8 A.M. to sunset every day. Guided walks are conducted on Wednesdays and Fridays at 10 A.M., except on public holidays. Here Australia's first farm was established. There are wide expanses of lawns, with Australian and overseas plants, and its special attractions include azaleas (September), roses (early spring and autumn), and lots of fountains and statues. Adjoining the Botanic Gardens are Government House, the residence of the governor of New South Wales (not open for visits), and the Conservatorium of Music, originally built in 1817 as the Government House stables. Leaving the gardens at Shakespeare Place, a short walk across the Domain—a grassy expanse where speakers on all kinds of topics harangue the crowd on Sunday afternoons—takes you to the Art Gallery of New South Wales. The gallery has a fine collection of Australian Art. From the gallery retrace your steps to Shakespeare Place. There stands the State Library of New South Wales, a fine yellow sandstone building in the classical museum style, which also houses the Mitchell and Dixson Libraries and Galleries. Exhibitions are held in the Galleries. The Library contains the world's greatest collection of Australiana, developed from the nucleus of some 61,000 books, manuscripts, maps, views, and portraits left to the nation by David Scott Mitchell, a wealthy nonpracticing lawyer, and collector, on his death in 1907. Sir William Dixson (1870–1952) gave the library a further fine collection of Australiana and Pacific artifacts. Among the library's treasures are a 1623 first-folio Shakespeare and a first edition of *Julius Caesar.*

Macquarie Street and Hyde Park

The library is on Macquarie Street, probably the only street in Sydney that one could justifiably call elegant. Many professionals, especially doctors, have their offices there. No. 133, now headquarters of the Royal Australian Historical Society, is one of the few surviving witnesses of the early nineteenth century, when the street was one of Sydney's choicest residential areas.

Farther up the left side of Macquarie Street away from Circular Quay is the early nineteenth-century area now occupied by the New South Wales State Parliament House, Sydney Hospital, the Old Mint building, and the Law Courts. This was the site of the Rum Hospital, so called because in 1810 Governor Lachlan Macquarie gave a license to import 45,000 gallons of rum to two businessmen, Garnham Blaxcell and Alexander Riley, and to the colony's chief surgeon, D'Arcy Wentworth, in return for their financing a badly needed hospital. The hospital section was demolished to make way for the Victorian bulk of Sydney Hospital (opened 1894), but the surgeons' barracks have survived. One part of the surgeons' quarters now forms a section of the State Parliament House, and the other, known as the Old Mint Building, is now a museum housing Australian decorative arts, stamps, coins, and flags. These surviving sections of the old Rum Hospital suggest that with its colonnaded facade it must have looked quite attractive. At the end of Macquarie Street stands Hyde Park Barracks, the work of Francis Howard Greenway, the most important architect of Sydney's convict period. Himself a convict, transported to Australia for 14 years for concealing his assets at a bankruptcy trial in 1814, Greenway designed several of early Sydney's best buildings. Hyde Park Barracks was originally built for convicts doing public works, such as roadmaking. It was also a place of punishment. However, by the middle of the nineteenth century, after transportation of convicts to New South Wales had ceased, the barracks were transformed into a reception center for English, Scottish, and Irish immigrants; here they received food and shelter until they found jobs. In 1878 the building was reconstructed to house the District Law Court of New South Wales. It is now New South Wales' only museum of social history from colonial days to the 1950s. The clock that decorates the facade was made in Sydney and carries the inscription "L. Macquarie Es., Governor, 1817." There is a pleasant indoor-outdoor cafe on the grounds of the museum. Opposite the barracks, on the other side of Queen's Square (now a plaza), stands a rather commonplace statue of Queen Victoria (unveiled in 1888).

Hyde Park extends from Queen's Square to Liverpool Street, between Elizabeth and College streets. It is one of the inner city's open spaces, with well-kept paths, trees, and flower beds. However, complaints are mounting about the encroachment of statues, fountains, and restrooms on the green space. Originally established by that great town planner and builder Governor Macquarie as a town common, and named by him after London's Hyde Park, the expanse was first used for military drill, cricket, and horse racing. Park Street, which (with its continuation William Street) connects the city with the eastern suburbs via Kings Cross, bisects Hyde Park. In the middle of the northern half of the park stands one of Sydney's best-known landmarks, the Archibald Fountain, the work of the French sculptor Francois Sicard. The fountain, completed in 1933, was a gift to the city by the late J. F. Archibald, one of the founders in 1880 of Australia's top-ranking weekly quality magazine, the *Bulletin,* to commemorate the French-Australian alliance in World War I. Apollo stands in the middle of the fountain, surrounded by other mythological figures. The Anzac War Memorial dominates the southern section of Hyde Park. The 33m concrete construction faced with red granite on the outside and white marble inside, and decorated with statues of World War I soldiers by Rayner Hoff, was opened in 1934. Opposite the eastern side of the park rises the brown stone neo-Gothic St. Mary's (Roman Catholic) Cathedral built by William Wardell from 1866 to 1886, with further additions in 1900 and 1928. At the corner of College and William streets is the Australian Museum. A visit, even if only a short one, is highly recommended, for the museum, founded in 1827, has the world's best collection of Aboriginal art and a permanent exhibition of the art of the South Seas.

NEW SOUTH WALES

Park Street and Martin Plaza

Park Street has become a dividing line between the city's smarter part (down to Circular Quay) and more modest section (up to Central Station), where the cinema complexes and the many Chinese restaurants (on Dixon and Campbell streets) are the main tourist attractions. Nearby is the Sydney Entertainment Centre, where indoor sports events, rock concerts, and exhibitions of all kinds are held. It seats up to 12,500 people. Due for completion for the bicentennial year in 1988 is the massive Darling Harbour Complex, where recreational and convention facilities and accommodations are being built on the water's edge. At the junction of Park and George streets stands the Town Hall, a massive building erected between 1868 and 1889 and designed by eight or more architects who seemed unable to agree on the Italian or French Renaissance styles. The modern office tower that the City Council has erected behind it has not helped to improve the appearance of the older edifice. The Town Hall Auditorium, which seats 2,500 people, is equipped with a large organ of 6 keyboards, 127 stops, and 8,672 pipes. A small plaza separates the Town Hall from St. Andrew's (Anglican) Church, the oldest cathedral in Australia. It is a pleasant neo-Gothic church opened in 1868 after many delays. It seats some 850 people. Opposite the Town Hall toward Circular Quay, the Queen Victoria Building, an architectural curiosity, occupies a whole city block.

Designed in 1893 for the City Council by architect George McRae to accommodate shops and a fruit and vegetable market (but never used as such), the Queen Victoria Building used to house the municipal library. It is due to reopen mid-1986, as an impressive shopping and tourist complex after extensive renovation. Continuing along George Street toward the Quay one reaches Martin Plaza with its well-proportioned General Post Office (built 1866 to 1886) and impressive bank and office buildings on both sides. In front of the GPO is the Cenotaph, a memorial to Australian soldiers killed in wars, where a changing of the guard takes place every Thursday (except during the Christmas break and on wet days) between 12:30 and 12:50 P.M. Until 1973 Martin Place (as it was known until recently) was a busy traffic thoroughfare. Since then it has been gradually transformed into a pedestrian plaza and public entertainment area with sunken amphitheater, where musicians of varying quality entertain the lunchtime crowd between noon and about 2 P.M. The atmosphere is cheerful and the sight is serene despite an excess of concrete (some of it colored). Between Martin Plaza and Circular Quay is the territory of Sydney's (and indeed much of Australia's) big business. Here are most of the international airlines and multinational enterprises, the two most exclusive clubs (Union and Australian), the Commonwealth and New South Wales government buildings, the stock exchange, and the head offices of Australian and overseas (mainly British) insurance companies. A short distance from Martin Plaza (on George Street) is Wynyard, Sydney's busiest suburban railroad station, which also has an entrance in York Street.

Kings Cross and the Harborside Suburbs

A bus from Park Street or from Hyde Park corner of Elizabeth and Park streets follows William Street—Sydney's new car-sales center—to Kings Cross. The Cross, as Sydneysiders call it, is strictly speaking the junction of William Street, Victoria Street, Darlinghurst Road, and Bayswater Road. But in Sydney parlance, living "at the Cross" can mean anything from the junction proper to Potts Point, Elizabeth Bay, or Woolloomooloo. Although this is where most of Sydney's nightspots are concentrated, it is nothing like London's Soho, Hamburg's Reeperbahn, or the Pigalle area of Paris. For it is not really a red-light district but a rather odd mixture of sleazy and smart, rough and bohemian. It has strip joints and elegant restaurants, which come to life in the evening, while during the late morning and early afternoon its main streets, Darlinghurst Road and Macleay Street, teem with all kinds of show people who do their shopping in the supermarkets and food stores or meet in the cafes. Elizabeth Bay House on Onslow Avenue, designed in 1832 by John Verge and built for Colonial Secretary Alexander Macleay, has been declared a historic building and is now administered by the Historic Houses Trust of New South Wales. Originally it stood in large grounds full of Australian and South Sea plants but it is now surrounded by high-rise buildings. At the end of Macleay Street, the short winding Wylde Street (nicknamed the Burma Road) leads down to Woolloomooloo Bay. The name is Aboriginal, and the area is supposed to have been an Aboriginal burial ground. In recent years the district has been a bone of contention between conservationists who want to improve the slum but retain its present character and developers who wish to turn it into a modern business and residential quarter. As a result of a compromise, redevelopment is in progress. A large part of the shore of Woolloomooloo Bay is occupied by wharves, and on the bay's eastern side the Royal Australian Navy has a large establishment that dates back to 1788. The tip of the navy complex, called Garden Island, was indeed an island until World War II, when the Captain Cook Graving Dock was built and the narrow channel dividing it from the mainland was filled in. But the old name has stuck. From Woolloomooloo you may take a bus to the city or walk there in 15 or 20 minutes. Or you can return to the Cross, which is a good starting point for inspecting Sydney's harborside eastern suburbs, the city's most expensive residential districts. The Main Harbour Cruises, which depart seven times daily from #6 Wharf Circular Quay, touch most eastern suburb harborside bays. But of course, they must be seen from the land to appreciate them thoroughly. Distances between the bays are too long for comfortable walks. Use a bus or taxi.

Take a Darling Point bus at the Cross (on Bayswater Rd.) and alight at St. Mark's church (Anglican). It was designed by Edmund Blacket, Australia's most prolific church-builder—50 of them in New South Wales—and consecrated in 1852. It is Sydney society's favorite church for weddings. Walking down Greenoaks Avenue next to the church you reach Ocean Avenue, which leads to a small park on Double Bay. The Double Bay shopping center, a short way from the Harbor, is one of the smartest in Sydney. (Note: in Australia "shopping center" means one or more streets where most of the shops of a suburb are situated.) Although the charge that wealthy European immigrants have appropriated Double Bay for themselves is exaggerated, the suburb is certainly one of the city's most cosmopolitan and polyglot areas. It is no coincidence that Cosmopolitan is the name of the hotel on Knox Street, Double Bay's geographical heart. You may feel like having a rest and a snack before boarding another bus on New South Head Road for Rose Bay. En route you pass by Point Piper (named after a customs collector of the early days) with its elegant villas. Getting off the bus at Rose Bay police station, stroll along the few hundred yards of one of the rare harborside walks left in Sydney and enjoy the view across Rose Bay itself, the largest bay in the harbor. Another possibility is to take bus 324 (from the Quay) or 327 (from Central Railway) and travel via Rose Bay to a stop near Vaucluse House on Wentworth Road. Vaucluse House was owned by William Charles Wentworth, one of the most important and wealthy Australian politicians of the first half of

NEW SOUTH WALES

the nineteenth century. He was the son of D'Arcy Wentworth (one of the partners in the Rum Hospital deal) and a convict girl. Vaucluse House, surrounded by a beautiful garden, is interesting for its historic memories (the Constitution of New South Wales was drawn up there) and for its furniture and paintings, which reflect the lifestyle of a prominent Sydney family some 150 years ago. Nearby Nielsen Park includes one of the pleasant harbor beaches, Shark Bay—but don't be nervous, it has shark netting. From there one may take a bus to Watson's Bay, near the entrance to Sydney Harbour. It is an enchanting place with beautiful views of the harbor that can be enjoyed while lunching at Doyles seafood restaurant on the water's edge. A little farther on is small sheltered Camp Cove, where Captain (later Governor) Phillip and his party came ashore and rested on January 22, 1788, when they discovered the magnificent harbor on the shore of which Sydney now stands. Between Camp Cove and the Heads is out-of-the-way Lady Jane Beach, one of Sydney's two "official" nudist beaches. On the high cliffs above Watson's Bay looking out over the Pacific stands a copy of Australia's first lighthouse, named after Governor Macquarie, designed by Francis Greenway, and completed in 1818. It was replaced in 1883 with the present building, which resembles Greenway's design.

Seeing the Harbor

During his voyage in 1770, Captain James Cook sailed past the heads of Sydney Harbour. He marked them on his chart as the entrance of a "safe anchorage," which he called Port Jackson after George Jackson, a secretary of the British Admiralty. But Cook did not have time to find out what lay beyond those heads; the discovery was left to Captain Phillip, who unfurled the British flag at Sydney Cove on Monday, January 26, 1788. January 26 or the following Monday is now celebrated as Australia Day. Sydney Harbour—or Port Jackson, as it is still officially called—is about 26km long, and its average width is 1.5km. But its foreshores meander along many arms and sheltered bays and total about 240km. The harbor was created over thousands of years by the confluence of two freshwater rivers, the Parramatta and Lane Cove, which meet between the suburbs of Greenwich and Drummoyne. Ferries leave Circular Quay regularly (see *Practical Information*).

Before their confluence the two rivers form the peninsula of Hunters Hill, one of Sydney's most charming suburbs, where a number of well-to-do French immigrants settled in the mid-nineteenth century. They built the attractive stone houses with cast-iron railings and decorations, which stand in leafy gardens. Many of them have pleasant views of the river and of Sydney's skyline.

By the end of World War II, many of these old buildings had fallen into disrepair and could be bought for a song. However, their new owners have restored most of them, modernizing the interiors while keeping the old architectural appearance. Today Hunters Hill is one of Sydney's most coveted residential areas. Other noteworthy sights on a cruise include St. Ignatius College; a Jesuit school known as Riverview, which overlooks the Lane Cove River and has a famous observatory founded in 1909; the 330m-long single-span concrete arch Gladesville Bridge, the longest of its kind in the world; and four small islands in the mouth of the Parramatta River. The largest of them, Cockatoo, which now houses a dockyard, was until the last quarter of the nineteenth century Sydney's most horrible prison for reconvicted criminals. Goat Island, which served a similar purpose, now houses a modern shipbuilding yard that constructs wooden hulled boats; there is also a small maritime museum. Spectacle and Schnapper islands are used by the navy. Goat Island is the only one of the four islands open to visitors. (Goat Island Cruises operate Wednesday–Friday at 11 A.M. and 1 P.M. and on Saturday and Sunday at 11 A.M. and 2 P.M. Contact the Maritime Services Board, 240–2111.)

Opposite Cockatoo Island is Balmain, named after William Balmain, who served as a surgeon with the First Fleet. In recent years Balmain has become an artists' and intellectuals' colony despite its industrial character.

Several regular daily harbor cruises by ferries and hydrofoil leave Circular Quay (for details see *Practical Information*). Most of them offer refreshments and running commentaries about the most notable sights.

Fort Denison, off Mrs. Macquarie's Point, was nicknamed Pinchgut, probably because in the early days recalcitrant convicts were sent to the barren little island with bread and water. But stories of terrible sufferings inflicted on prisoners in the Fort's dungeons are false. There have never been dungeons there. Fortification of the little island was first planned to guard Sydney from an invasion after two United States cruisers had managed to slip into Port Jackson undetected on a dark night in 1839, without any hostile intentions. The project was later dropped, then revived to protect the colony from a feared Russian attack after the Crimean War. A Martello tower with thick walls was completed in 1875. The fort was named after the state governor of the time, Sir William Denison. Pinchgut with its old cannons, 3½ m-thick walls, and beautiful views of the city, is worth a visit.

Off Point Piper are two other small islands—Clark and Shark—which are open for visits or picnics from dawn to dusk. For details contact the National Parks and Wildlife Service, 189 Kent St., Sydney. Tel. 237–6500.

On the north side of the harbor in the pleasant inner suburb of Kirribilli are Admiralty House and Kirribilli House, both owned by the commonwealth government. The former is used by the governor-general and the latter by the prime minister when they are in Sydney. But the main attraction of this area is Taronga Park Zoo, open every day 9 A.M.–5 P.M. The most pleasant way to get there is by ferry from #5 Jetty, Circular Quay. Housing a unique collection of Australian and 5,000 other animals, Taronga is beautifully situated, with enchanting views of the harbor. (The Aboriginal name Taronga, in fact, means "lovely sea-views.") Farther around the northern side of the harbor is Balmoral Beach, a pleasant place for a swim, protected by shark-netting. Much of the land in this area is occupied by military reserves. Past Balmoral is Middle Harbour with the Spit Bridge, and farther on Roseville Bridge which leads to the northern ocean beaches through French's Forest. Middle Harbour, which reminds one of the dreamy charm of some northern Italian lakes, is one of the most picturesque areas of Sydney, despite the densely settled shores of its many bays and arms. It is worthwhile paddling in a canoe to the upper reaches that abound in water birds. However, don't swim in the quiet waters of Middle Harbour; that's the sort of environment sharks favor.

Manly is the last (or if one enters the heads by ship, the first) of the northern harborside suburbs. It was Governor Phillip who gave it the name when, during a visit to the area in May 1788, he found that the Aborigines there had qualities "that gave me a much higher opinion of them than I had formed from the behavior of those seen in Captain Cook's voyage, and their confidence and manly behavior made me give the name Manly Cove to this place." Manly was separated from the other Sydney settlements for many years; the first ferry service between it and the city began in 1847, and a road link was established only in 1924. Now there are regular ferry, hydrofoil, and bus services. Manly has one of Sydney's finest ocean beaches and a swimming pool in the harbor near the ferry wharf. Australia's great sport, surfing, began at Manly back in 1902 as an act of rebellion. The more or less authenticated story has it that a Manly journalist, William Gocher, entered the water in defiance of the law that forbade daylight surf bathing. There is an international standard hotel at Manly right on the surfing beach, along with a range of good restaurants and, of course, some excellent take-out fish-and-chip shops to provide you with lunch or dinner in a spot where you've chosen your own view.

Darlinghurst Jail and Court House, Victoria Barracks, and Paddington

All buses that connect the city with the suburbs of Bondi, Watsons Bay, Bronte, Clovelly, Coogee, Maroubra, and the districts around Botany Bay stop at Taylor Square in front of the iron fence that separates the street from the interesting buildings of Darlinghurst Jail and Court House. When they were built in the 1840s this was the limit of closely settled Sydney. The great stone Court House, designed in neo-Greek style by Mortimer Lewis, still serves its original purpose. But the jail has been converted from a place for punishing criminals into one for educating youth; since 1921 it has housed the East Sydney Technical College and its art school. One building, the women's prison, has been reconstructed as an auditorium called the Cell Block Theatre, with mementos of its grim past still visible. The Court House and Jail was built from the beautiful yellow sandstone found near Sydney Harbour, which gives a special character to many surviving buildings of the city's early period.

About 15 minutes' walk along Oxford Street from the Darlinghurst Court House is Sydney's most impressive military-building complex: Victoria Barracks. They are open to the public on Tuesday at 10:30 A.M. (February to November), when there is a changing of the guard. Conducted tours are also arranged. The Barracks, designed by Colonel George Barney, an architect who also worked on the construction of Circular Quay and Fort Denison, were commenced in 1841 and finished seven years later. "Finished" is perhaps not the right word, because new buildings have frequently been added to the old ones. Paddington is now considered a part of the city. The British-colonial-style buildings, with their airy verandas, are of considerable architectural value. The buildings are arranged around a spacious, grassy parade ground with the 225m main block, originally designed to house the soldiers and their families, parallel to Oxford Street. Until 1870 Victoria Barracks housed British troops. Now only a few soldiers actually live there; the buildings are used as army offices.

Until the 1950s Paddington, the district that developed around Victoria Barracks, was one of Sydney's worst slums. Then journalists, writers, theater people, and the like settled there because they found that here they could buy an old house near the city. These new settlers were followed by a second generation of developers who carried the rejuvenation of the area further. Today Paddington is no longer cheap or neglected. It has chic restaurants, bars, art galleries, boutiques, and shops that sell objets d'art, including costume jewelry—some of it made on the premises. The district has been likened to London's Chelsea. The atmosphere is genuinely Victorian, and if its inhabitants have their way it will remain so, whatever changes progress brings in future.

AUSTRALIA

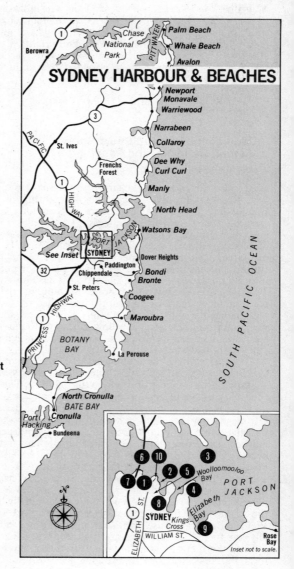

Points of Interest

1) Circular Quay
2) Farm Cove
3) Fort Denison
4) Garden Island
5) Government House
6) Harbour Bridge
7) The Rocks
8) Royal Botanic Gardens
8) Rushcutter's Bay
10) Sydney Opera House

Botany Bay

No visit to Sydney would be complete without a trip to Botany Bay, where Captain Cook's *Endeavour* dropped anchor on April 29, 1770. It can be reached by taking a bus from the city to the suburb of La Perouse. The Comte de La Pérouse, commander of two ships, *L'Astrolabe* and *La Boussole,* arrived off Botany Bay in January 1788, three days after the First Fleet under Governor Phillip. Whether Phillip and La Pérouse ever met is doubtful, but it is certain that the French officers dined and wined their British fellow officers on board their ships. The French made no attempt to dispute British ownership of the place, although they stayed in Botany Bay for some six weeks. Some time after that both French ships disappeared, probably perishing in a storm near Vanuatu. Today there are two reminders of the short French visit to Botany Bay: a column erected in 1829 by the French explorer H. Y. P. de Bougainville and next to it the grave of Father Louis Receveur, a Franciscan priest who traveled with La Pérouse and who died in Botany Bay on February 17, 1788.

The ships of the First Fleet were at first anchored at the entrance of Botany Bay near Bare Island, named after an entry in Captain Cook's journal that spoke of "a small bare island which lies close to the north shore" within Botany Bay. Bare Island—just off La Perouse—is now linked to the mainland by a causeway. In 1885 the government of New South Wales built a fort there following the Russian invasion scare. Today it is a protected historic site open to visitors every day from 9 A.M.–5 P.M. Opposite La Perouse, on the southern shore of Botany Bay, is the suburb of Kurnell and the spot where Captain Cook landed. The Captain Cook's Landing Place Museum, containing displays featuring the famous seafarer's voyages, was opened in 1967.

PRACTICAL INFORMATION FOR SYDNEY

For information about New South Wales in general, including how to get there, see *Practical Information for New South Wales beyond Sydney.*

TOURIST INFORMATION. For tourist information and tour arrangements, contact the *Travel Centre of New South Wales,* Cnr Pitt and Spring streets, Sydney, tel. 231-4444; or *Tourist Newsfront,* Suite 3, Penrhyn House, 22 Playfair Street, the Rocks, Tel. 27-7197.

USEFUL ADDRESSES. *American Consulate General,* Cnr Park and Elizabeth streets Sydney; 02-264-7044. *British Consulate General,* Goldfields House, 1 Alfred Street, Circular Quay, Sydney; 02-27-7521.

TELEPHONES. The area code for Sydney and environs is 02.

ACCOMMODATIONS. Sydney has a wide variety of hotels, motels, serviced apartments, and private hotels in its city and suburbs. For information and bookings contact the Travel Centre of NSW at 231-4444. Categories are: *Deluxe,* $A100; *Expensive,* $A80–$A100; *Moderate,* $A60–$A79; *Inexpensive,* $A35–$A60; *Budget,* below A$35 Rates are for double rooms per day.

# AUSTRALIA

DELUXE

Boulevard. 90 William Street; 02-357-2277. 274 rooms, 13 suites. A very good hotel in an up-and-coming environment. Midway between city and the Kings Cross nightclub district. Air conditioned.

Hilton International. 259 Pitt Street; 02-266-0610. 582 rooms, 34 suites. Mid-city, center of main theater and shopping areas. All first-rate international hotel services including swimming pool, restaurants, bars, cafeterias, parking. Air conditioned.

Holiday Inn Menzies. 14 Carrington Street, City Center; 02-2-0232. 426 rooms, 15 suites. Frequented mainly by businesspeople. First-class international standard. Wide choice of restaurants including Japanese. Air conditioned. Pool.

Hyatt Kingsgate. Kings Cross Road; Kings Cross; 02-357-2233. Off Sydney's nightclub area. Good international standard. 389 rooms, 5 suites. Spectacular views of city and harbor from upper-floor rooms. Air conditioned. Pool.

Inter-Continental. 117 Macquarie Street; 02-230-0200. Completed late 1985. Luxury hotel in the colonial treasury building. Harbor views; gourmet dining. Air conditioned.

Regent of Sydney. 199 George Street; 02-238-0000. 578 rooms, 42 suites. International class. Close to Circular Quay for rail, bus, or ferry travel. Swimming pool, sun lounges, boutiques, health club; all business facilities available. Restaurants, bars, cafeterias. Air conditioning; parking.

Sebel Town House. 23 Elizabeth Bay Rd, Elizabeth Bay; 02-358-3244. 165 rooms, 25 suites. Smaller hotel with attentive service; popular with celebrities. Harbor views. Pool.

Sheraton-Wentworth. 61-101 Phillip Street; 02-230-0700. 485 rooms, 33 suites. Main banking, insurance, and big-business district. Government offices nearby. All first-rate international hotel services. A very good restaurant on 5th floor. Shopping arcade, beauty and barbershops, and car rental. Air conditioned.

EXPENSIVE-DELUXE

The Southern Cross. Cnr Elizabeth and Goulburn streets; 02-2-0987. 176 rooms. Near Central Station, cinema area, and Chinatown. Air conditioned. Pool.

The York Apartments. 5 York Street; 02-264-7747. 35 units, 88 suites. Modern serviced apartments near transport and business district. Air conditioned. Pool.

EXPENSIVE

Manly Pacific International. 55 North Steyne, Manly; 02-977-7666. 156 units, 24 suites. Luxury hotel on the beach at Manly. Short trip to the city by hydrofoil or leisurely trip by bus or ferry. Restaurants, swimming pool, parking facilities, boutiques, cafeterias.

Old Sydney Parkroyal. 55 George St., the Rocks; 02-27-8220. 176 units. A modern hotel inside the facade of an old warehouse in the historic Rocks area. Close to Circular Quay. Air conditioned. Pool.

The Park Apartments. 16 Oxford St.; 02-331-7728. 135 units. Comfortably furnished self-contained apartments, near Hyde Park. Pool and restaurants.

MODERATE

The Russell. George Street, the Rocks; 02-241-3543. A charming Old World private hotel in the historic heart of Sydney. Some shared bathrooms.

INEXPENSIVE

Clairmont Village Inn. 5 Ward Ave., Kings Cross; 02-358-2044. 72 units. Free parking. Air conditioned. Pool. In the center of the Kings Cross area.

Imperial. 221 Darlinghurst Road, Kings Cross; 02-331-4051. 150 units, most with bath. Essential services. A private hotel.

NEW SOUTH WALES

RESTAURANTS. No visit to Sydney would be complete without an adequate sampling of its more than 2,000 restaurants. Sydneysiders dine out quite regularly, and the climate makes gardens, terraces, courtyards, and pavements, sometimes with the added bonus of a harbor or beach view, popular selections.

There are restaurants in Sydney serving fine food to suit every mood and every wallet. A diverse ethnic background among the city's population, the excellent quality and availability of fresh ingredients, the layout of the city around a magnificent harbor, and the talent of its chefs combine to produce a wide enough range of restaurants to make your choice difficult. What will it be for lunch today? A small vegetarian cafe serving the freshest salads and long, cool fruit juices? Or grilled John Dory fillets and a crisp white wine at a seafood restaurant by the harbor? And for dinner? Do you feel like silver service, elegant decor, fine Australian and imported wines, and the best French cuisine? Or will you take your own wine to a no-frills cafe serving spicy Malay sate or Thai curry expertly prepared and simply presented?

If your time in Sydney is limited, so is the number of culinary experiences you can manage. Musts on your sampling lists should include seafood fresh from local or nearby waters: fat Sydney rock oysters, the prehistoric-looking, crustaceous Balmain bugs, sweet king prawns, or fish such as snapper or John Dory, popular among discerning locals.

You should also taste a selection of Australian wines; the Hunter and Barossa valleys are only two of the Australian areas producing world-class wines. You will notice that wine in restaurants is priced much higher than in hotels or liquor stores. This is the result of the very high price restaurants must pay for wine licenses. Before selecting a restaurant, check the type of liquor license it has. Licensed restaurants usually serve a range of beers, spirits, and wines. Unlicensed restaurants are not permitted to sell alcohol, and you will have to buy your own from a hotel or liquor store—some restaurants then charge you a corkage fee to open and serve these wines. Unlicensed restaurants are usually referred to as BYO (bring your own).

For dessert, either fresh fruits such as mango, papaw, pineapple, or strawberries or a selection of fine Australian cheeses should delight.

Price Classifications and Abbreviations: The price classifications (in Australian dollars) for the restaurants listed are based on the average price of a three-course dinner for one. This does not include drinks or tip. Tipping in Australian restaurants is at your discretion for good service. It is generally around 10 percent of the bill. There may be a surcharge on weekends or public holidays, when penalty rates must be paid to staff. *Deluxe* means over $A35; *Expensive,* $A25–$A35; *Moderate,* $A15–$A24; *Inexpensive,* less than $A15. Abbreviations for credit cards are: AE, American Express; BC, Bank Card; DC, Diners Club; MC, MasterCard; V, Visa.

Many of Sydney's best restaurants are away from the city center; the approximate distance in kilometers and miles from the center of Sydney is indicated where relevant. Cabs can easily take you to the outlying restaurants.

Sydney's international hotels offer excellent dining. The fifth-floor restaurant at the Sheraton Wentworth is very pleasant, and equally good food and service are offered at **Kables** at the Regent, the **San Francisco Grill** at the Hilton, and the **Treasury** at the Inter-Continental.

AUSTRALIAN

Perry's. *Expensive.* 495 Oxford Street, Paddington (4km/2½ mi. east); 33-3377. A stylish restaurant within an old manse. Perry's chef describes his cooking as modern Australian, with a French base and Asian influence. Ingredients are the freshest, with some interesting local dishes such as buffalo from the Northern Territory, when available. Licensed. D, Tue.–Sat. Reservations recommended. AE, BC.

CHINESE

Choy's 1000 A.D. *Inexpensive-Moderate.* Cnr Harbour and Hay streets; 211-4213. A busy restaurant with blackboard menu offering a pleasing selection of dishes. Very close to entertainment center. Licensed. Reservations recommended. L, D, daily, AE, BC, DC.

AUSTRALIA

Dixon. *Moderate.* 51 Dixon Street; 211–1619. In the heart of Chinatown and an old favorite of Sydneysiders. Open until 2 A.M. Licensed. L, D, daily. AE, BC, DC, MC, V.

Imperial Peking Harbourside. *Expensive.* 15 Circular Quay West, the Rocks; 27–7073 or 27–6100. Innovative Chinese cuisine, specializing in Pekingese food. More up-market than most of Sydney's Chinese restaurants. Licensed. L, D, daily. Reservations recommended. AE, BC, DC, MC, V.

FRENCH

Berowra Waters Inn. *Deluxe.* Berowra Waters (40km/25 mi. north); 456–1027. Gay Bilson has a battalion of keen patrons who return again and again to sample some of the finest cuisine in Australia. Hers is also a popular restaurant for special occasions. For an unusual day's outing (and a really expensive experience!) take a small Aquatic Airways seaplane (919–5966) from Rose Bay to this restaurant perched right on the water's edge of Berowra Creek. Licensed. L, D, Friday–Sunday. Reservations essential. AE, BC, DC.

Brussels. *Moderate.* 8 Heeley Street, Paddington (5km/3 mi. east); 33–4958. Traditional and classic Belgian and French food is served here. There are only nine tables in an intimate restaurant. A delicious Belgian specialty is *sambre et meuse:* roast-chicken pieces in a sauce of dried juniper berries, white wine, and veal stock. BYO, L, Monday–Friday; D, Monday–Saturday. Reservations advisable on weekends. BC, MC.

Claude's. *Expensive.* 10 Oxford Street, Woollahra (4km/2½ mi. east); 331–2325. Chefs Josephine and Damien Pignolet run one of the best French restaurants in Sydney. It is small and charming, and service is excellent. Popular nights are the first Friday of each month—bouillabaisse night—and the first Saturday, when a *Fine Bouche* menu is offered—this is a gourmet night, with a set menu of up to six courses. BYO, D, Tuesday–Saturday. Reservations are essential—sometimes up to three weeks ahead for weekends. No cards.

Pegrum's. *Expensive.* 36 Gurner Street, Paddington (5km/3 mi. east); 357–4776. Another successful husband-and-wife team on Sydney's French-restaurant scene, with Mark Armstrong as chef and Lorinda at the front of the house. Imaginative cuisine and interesting specials that vary according to what is available at the markets, such as buffalo from the Northern Territory or crayfish from Tasmania. Licensed. L, Friday; D, Tuesday–Saturday. Reservations a must. AE, BC, DC, MC, V.

GREEK

Diethnes. *Inexpensive–Moderate.* 336 Pitt Street; 267–8956. Cheerful, friendly, and always busy. Offers all the Greek favorites. Licensed. L, D, Monday–Saturday. Reservations advisable. AE, BC.

INTERNATIONAL

Butlers. *Expensive–Deluxe.* 123 Victoria Street, Potts Point (2km/1 mi. east); 357–1988. A fashionable eating place, pretty and elegant. The food shows a nouvelle-cuisine influence and alters daily according to the fresh ingredients available. Dining on the terrace gives you magnificent views across the rooftops to the landmarks of the city. Licensed. L, Monday–Friday; D, Monday–Saturday. Reservations recommended. AE, BC, DC, MC, V.

Eliza's Garden Restaurant. *Expensive–Deluxe.* 29 Bay Street, Double Bay (4.5km/3 mi. east); 32–3656. This pleasant restaurant attracts the eastern suburbs social set, and no wonder: It's in the heart of their shopping area, and the smorgasbord or a la carte meals are imaginatively prepared. A shaded garden area is perfect for summer dining, and there are open fires in winter. Licensed. L, D, daily. Reservations recommended. AE, BC, DC, MC, V.

ITALIAN

Beppi's. *Expensive.* Cnr Stanley and Yurong streets, East Sydney (2km/1 mi. east); 357–4558 or 357–4391. Beppi has delighted Sydney palates for over 30 years. Friendly and efficient waiters in black tie tempt you with a wide menu and delicious specials. Ask for a table in the cellar area and you'll be surrounded

NEW SOUTH WALES

by floor-to-ceiling wine. Licensed. L, Monday–Friday; D, Monday–Saturday. Reservations advised. AE, BC, DC, MC, V.

No Name. *Inexpensive.* 81 Stanley Street, East Sydney (2km/1 mi. east); 357–4711. There's often a line waiting on the stairs, tables are shared, and service is speedy. Included in your two-course meal is bread, milk or cordial, and a basic salad. The *Arch Coffee Lounge* downstairs serves great coffee. BYO. L, D, daily. No cards.

Taylor's. *Expensive.* 203 Albion Street, Surry Hills (2km/1 mi. southeast); 33–5100. Set in a row of beautifully restored colonial cottages, Taylor's with its Georgian decor does not look very Italian. The food, however, is: northern-Italian cuisine imaginatively prepared and attractively presented. Book a garden table when the weather obliges with its best. Licensed. L, Friday; D, Tuesday–Saturday. Reservations advisable. AE, BC, DC, MC, V.

JAPANESE

Suntory. *Expensive–Deluxe.* 529 Kent Street; 267–2900. A favorite with Japanese business people and the expense-account set, Suntory is Sydney's most exclusive Japanese restaurant. Only the best ingredients are used, and the service is excellent. The restaurant and bar overlook a pretty Japanese garden and pool. Licensed. L, D, Monday–Saturday. Reservations are essential. AE, BC, DC, V.

SEAFOOD

Doyle's on the Beach. *Expensive.* 11 Marine Parade, Watson's Bay (11km/7 mi. east); 337–2007. For a really comprehensive view of Sydney Harbour you might well do a seafood-restaurant crawl, and enjoy it from all sides. Here is a perfect place to start, where dining indoors (ask for a table near the front) or outdoors allows you a view up the harbor to the city skyscape across sparkling water, or of brilliant sunsets and the night lights of Sydney. The Doyle family has been catching and serving fish for many years and is an institution on the Sydney restaurant scene. Casual dress. BYO. L, D, daily. BC, DC, MC.

Mischa's Seafood Restaurant. *Moderate–Expensive.* The Esplanade, Balmoral Beach (8km/5 mi. north); 969–9827 or 969–3720. Mischa's is on the northern side of the harbor where you can enjoy a stroll along Balmoral Esplanade after your meal. Mischa, who looks as though he enjoys his fare, serves delicious seafoods, exotic cocktails, and breakfasts like the Balmoral Schooner: hot cakes, eggs and bacon, fried potatoes, toast, and coffee. Licensed. B, L, D, daily. Reservations recommended; the earlier you book, the closer you get to the window and the view. AE, BC, DC, MC.

Waterfront. *Expensive.* 27 Circular Quay West, the Rocks; 27–3666. You will probably meet lots of other tourists here because of the Waterfront's magnificient views of the harbor and the Opera House and its location in the historic Rocks area. Dine inside or on the stone-flagged pavement outside beneath masts and sails of an old schooner. Delicious fresh food, including memorable hot or cold mixed seafood platters. Licensed. L, D, daily. Reservations recommended. AE, BC, DC, MC, V.

STEAK

Clock Cellar. *Moderate.* 470 Crown Street, Surry Hills (2km/1 mi. southeast); 331–1832. Excellent fresh, juicy steaks of all sorts are available here with great sauces. It's a popular venue for the discriminating carnivores of Sydney and can be packed with the business set at lunchtime. Licensed. L, Monday–Friday; D, Mon.–Sat. Reservations recommended. AE, BC, DC.

VEGETARIAN

Metro. *Inexpensive.* 26 Burton Street, Darlinghurst (2km/1 mi. east); 33–5356. Well known and constantly busy; you may have to stand in line. The food is innovative and rich, with the emphasis on homemade and fresh ingredients—pastas, pastries, salads, etc. It's worth the wait to experience Metro's delights. BYO. D, Thursday–Sunday. No reservations.

AUSTRALIA

FOR THE TOURIST

Bennelong. *Expensive.* Sydney Opera House, Bennelong Point; 241–1371. Bennelong has extensive harbor views and an interesting a la carte menu. There is often a chamber group playing to add to the elegant atmosphere. A table d'hote menu is available for pretheater diners, 5:30–7:30 P.M. Licensed. L, D, Monday–Saturday. Reservations recommended. AE, BC, DC, MC, V.

Summit. *Expensive.* Level 47, Australia Square Tower; 27–9777. A la carte and smorgasbord menus available. Diners have marvelous views of Sydney. There is a dance floor, and supper is served Mon.–Sat. Licensed. L, D, daily. Reservations recommended. AE, BC, DC, MC, V.

Sydney Tower. Centrepoint, Market Street; 233–3722. There are two revolving levels of restaurants atop this enormous tower. Expansive views of Sydney distract diners from their meals in the the a la carte restaurant on Level 1 *(expensive)* and in the self-service restaurant on Level 2. The self-service restaurant offers a fixed-price three-course meal for a *moderate* sum. Licensed. Level 1: L, Monday–Friday; D, Monday–Saturday. Level 2: L, D, Tuesday–Sunday. AE, BC, DC, MC, V.

COFFEE SHOPS, TEA SHOPS, BRASSERIES

Bayswater Brasserie. 32 Bayswater Road, Kings Cross; 357–2749. There's something for everyone here: a light or a more substantial meal, brunch, or just excellent coffee with a pastry. Fashionable spot, offers courtyard or indoor tables. Licensed. Mon.–Saturday, midday–midnight; Sunday, 11 A.M.–5 P.M. No reservations. BC, MC, V.

Cafe Roma. 189 Hay Street; 211–3909. Great coffee is dispensed in this authentic Italian cafe, and there's a display window bursting with delicious cakes and pastries. A wide variety of veal, poultry, pasta, and other dishes also available. Decor is no frills: laminex tables and orange vinyl chairs. BYO. Monday–Friday 7:30 A.M.–5:30 P.M.; Saturday 7:30 A.M.–3 P.M.

Cosmopolitan. Knox Street, Double Bay (4.5km/3 mi. east); 327–1866 or 327–5520. The Cosmopolitan is both restaurant and coffee shop and has a piano-bar area besides. From the sidewalk-cafe area watch all manner of flashy and expensive cars come and go and the fashionable people around town stroll by. Licensed. Daily, 8:00 A.M.–2 A.M. AE, BC, DC, MC, V.

Gelato Bar. 140 Campbell Parade, Bondi Beach (9km/5½ mi. east)); 30–4033 or 30–3211. The Gelato Bar serves meals throughout the day and is always busy. Gelato, ice cream, and amazing cakes bring customers from far and near. The cake display in their front window usually draws a pavement crowd! BYO. Tuesday–Sunday, 10 A.M.–11:45 P.M.

Hyde Park Barracks Cafe. Hyde Park Barracks, Macquarie Street; 223–1155. Delicious light meals and morning and afternoon teas on the doorstep of a major Sydney tourist attraction. Licensed. Daily 10 A.M.–5 P.M.

HOW TO GET AROUND. From airport to the city or suburb: The cheapest transport to and from the airport is via the *Urban Transport Authority* buses, tel. 29–2622, which run every 20 to 30 minutes between Circular Quay (Jetty 2) and the International and Domestic Air Terminals stopping at 5 points en route. $A2 for adults. *Kingsford Airport Bus Service* runs smaller coaches on request between 6 A.M. and 8 P.M. $A3 for adults, $A1.50 for children. Bookings must be made at least an hour before pickup time; tel. 667–3221. Taxis are available at the airport. The fare from the airport to city center is between $A10 and $A12. Chauffeur-driven cars are also available (*Legion Limousines,* 38 Mountain Street, Broadway, tel. 211–2844; *Hughes Chauffeured Limousines,* 34–36 Young St., Redfern, tel. 699–2233). Rent-a-car companies also service the airport.

Sydney's transport system of government buses, electric trains, and ferries suffers from an ailment common to most fast-growing cities: it is overtaxed in peak hours and insufficiently used in between. In addition, it is organized in such a way that most traffic lines radiate from the city to groups of suburbs in more or less straight lines, without adequate connections between suburbs on either side of those lines. Only electric trains run from one end of Sydney to the other; bus trips start and terminate in the city. Ferries run from Circular Quay.

NEW SOUTH WALES

Trains: Sydney's electric trains are part of the state railway system and they are fairly fast and reliable. The city proper is serviced by an underground loop—the City Circle, from Central Railway Station to Town Hall, Wynyard, Circular Quay, St. James, and Museum and back to Central. It is an economical way to travel in the city. A second recent and very convenient rail extension goes from Central Railway Station to Town Hall, Martin Place, Kings Cross, Edgecliff, Bondi Junction, and back. Inquiries: 2–0942 or 29–2622.

Buses: The government bus service is being modernized and is adequate except at peak hours. Most bus lines connect the city with the suburbs, though there are a few shuttle services to suburban railroad stations and a few intersuburb private buses. Inquiries: 29–2622.

The minimum bus and train fare is 50¢. Train tickets must be bought at the station where the trip begins. (Mounting a train without a ticket may result in a fine of $A200.) Bus fares are usually paid on the bus, and having the exact fare ready is appreciated but not mandatory. Maps of the transportation system are not readily available, but an excellent street directory—*Gregory's*—is on sale in bookshops and at many newsagents. (In Australia, a newsagent is a seller of newspapers, magazines, and cheaper books, as well as stationery.)

Ferries. In good weather the most pleasant, though not the fastest, means of transport is the ferry. Even if the temperature is fairly high you get the benefit of an ocean breeze on the harbor. There are ways to combine a ferry from Circular Quay and bus to reach one's destination. There are both government-run and private ferry companies. Inquiries: 29–2622.

Some special fares available on the Sydney transport system include: Day Rover ($A5.00). One day's unlimited travel by train, government bus, and ferry (except hydrofoils and special buses) within the Sydney and Newcastle areas. Ticket is valid after 9 A.M. Monday–Friday or any time weekends and public holidays. Travelpass (weekly) Rover ($A24.00 adult): one week's unlimited travel on trains, Government bus, and ferry services (except hydrofoil and special buses) around the city and suburbs.

Taxis: may be hailed, hired from official ranks, or booked by phone for a small added charge. Main city taxi ranks are at St. James Station, Circular Quay, Carrington St., and Foveaux Street (near Central Station). Radio-cab services include: *De Luxe Red and Yellow*, tel. 332–8888; *Legion*, tel. 2–0918; *RSL*, tel. 699–0144. You can also order air-conditioned chauffeur-driven **limousines** for short city trips or for long tours. These cars are usually excellent and their drivers are careful and competent. Companies offering tours are *Astra*, tel. 699–2223, and *Hughes*, tel. 332–3344.

Motoring: Parking is very difficult in the city. Street parking is controlled by coin-operated meters. Space is usually difficult to find, especially between 8 A.M. and 7 P.M. After 6 P.M. no street parking fees are charged. Motorists who disregard advisory signs, overstay meters, or park in loading zones and other restricted areas are liable to fines. The motorist has the right to explain why he or she contravened regulations, but dispensation from paying the fine is rarely given. It is cheaper and safer to park in one of the 40 privately owned parking stations in the city (see Parking Stations in the yellow pages of the telephone directory), although they are by no means cheap. Fees are lower at the three parking stations operated by the Sydney City Council, but is difficult to find a space in them between 8:30 A.M. and 1:30 P.M. Traffic drives on left; seat belts are mandatory.

SEASONAL EVENTS. January. *The Festival of Sydney* begins with a dramatic boat procession and fireworks over Sydney Harbour on New Year's Eve and continues to the end of January. It is Sydney's biggest celebration of the year and includes drama, music, sporting events, fairs, and processions. Among its highlights are outdoor musical events such as Opera in the Park, starring Dame Joan Sutherland. **March–April.** *The Royal Easter Show* is the state's major agricultural show, when the country comes to town. **September.** *Carnivale:* celebrates the many cultures that make up Australian society. **December 26.** Start of the *Sydney-to-Hobart Yacht Race;* from Rush Cutter's Bay. Watch from ferries, Watson's Bay, North Head, Dobroyd Point, Nielson Park.

AUSTRALIA

TOURS. Coach: A wide range of half-day and one-day tours around Sydney and its environs in comfortable, air-conditioned coaches are organized by 6 main operators—*ATT Kings,* 46 Kent Rd., Mascot, tel. 66–9544; *Ansett Pioneer,* Cnr Oxford and Riley streets, Darlinghurst, tel. 268–1331; *Australian Pacific,* 109–123 O'Riordan Street, Mascot, tel. 693–2222; *Clipper,* 5–7 Alma Road, Ryde, tel. 888–3022; *Murrays,* Box 123, Waterloo, 2017, tel. 319–1266. Competition between them is keen, and consequently the services are good. Most tours depart from Circular Quay West, opposite the Maritime Services Board Building (while at Circular Quay's overseas passenger shipping terminal is being rebuilt, departures are from the George St. North side of this building). Coaches will also pick up passengers—if arrangements are made when booking—from city and Kings Cross hotels and motels.

Half-day tours offered include city sights and trips to the northern and southern beaches and Taronga Zoo. Full-day tours visit the Blue Mountains, Jenolan Caves, the Hawkesbury River, Old Sydney Town, Canberra, and the Hunter Valley wine region. Also available are full day tours of Sydney and a trip to a winery and farm on the outskirts of the city called Gledswood for an Australian barbecue and a sheep-shearing demonstration. Especially good value is the Sydney Explorer, a 17km bus trip around Sydney's top tourist spots. One can set off at any of 20 stops, walk as much as one likes, then climb aboard again at the same or any other stop. Sydney Explorer buses run every 25 minutes from 9:30 A.M. to 5 P.M. seven days a week. A pamphlet explaining the tour and what can be seen near each stop is available from the Travel Centre of New South Wales (Cnr Pitt and Spring streets, tel. 231–4444). All-day ticket $A7 for adults, $A3.50 for children. Family rates are available.

Trains: Day tours from Sydney include trips to the Blue Mountains, Jenolan Caves, Hawkesbury River, Old Sydney Town, Canberra, the Hunter Valley, Port Stephens, and the South Coast. For bookings contact the *State Rail Authority* at 217–8819.

Harbour Cruises: *Captain Cook Cruises* (all cruises depart No. 6 Jetty, Circular Quay, tel. 27–9408). Coffee Cruise daily all year at 10 A.M. and 2 P.M.; 2 1/2 hours, Harbour and Middle Harbour. Adults $A14.50, children $A9; coffee included. Luncheon River Cruise, Harbour, Parramatta, and Lane Cove rivers. Daily all year at 12:30 P.M. Adults $A10; children $A7; buffet luncheon $A10 extra. Sydney Harbour Budget Cruise, 9:30 A.M., 11 A.M., 2:30 P.M. Main harbor points. Adults $A8.00, children $A5.00. Harbourside Sydney in a Day. Full-day tour; reservations essential. Monday–Friday. Departs 9 A.M. and includes harbor highlights, guided Rocks-quarter walk, and visit to Opera House, where luncheon is served. Adults $A31. Candlelight Dinner Cruise, August 1–May 31, Tuesday–Saturday; June and July, Friday and Sat. only. Departs 7 P.M., returns 9:30 P.M. and 11 P.M. Dinner and dancing. $A36.

Tours to Fort Denison (Pinchgut) leave Jetty 2, Circular Quay, at 10:15 A.M., 12:45 P.M., and 2:15 P.M., Tuesday–Saturday. Book at the *Maritime Services Board* Public Relations Section, tel. 240–2111. For information on other harbor cruises and cruises on Sydney's other beautiful waterways (the Hawkesbury, Pittwater, Botany Bay, and the George's River) phone the *Travel Centre of New South Wales,* 231–4444.

Walking Tours: For those who enjoy exploring by foot, choose from the following: *Maureen Fry's* tours of historic Macquarie Street, Glebe, or Observatory Hill, tel. 660–7157. *The Rocks Walking Tours,* tel. 27–6678 or 27–4416. *Sydney Opera House:* regular daily guided walks begin at 9 A.M. and last about 45 minutes; the last walk is at 4 P.M. On Sunday there are backstage tours 9 A.M.–5 P.M., tel. 2–0525. *Royal Botanic Gardens:* free guided tours leave from the visitor center (gate nearest the art gallery) at 10 A.M. Wednesday and Friday except public holidays, tel 231–8111. Catered bush walks in *Ku-ring-gai Chase National Park,* tel 810–4518. *Harbour Walks,* tel. 95–1755. Guided tours of art galleries, tel. 498–6776 or day walks in the Blue Mountains (*Balmain Hiking and Bushwalking Expeditions,* tel. 810–8187).

Air Tours: To see Sydney by air a number of companies offer tours. Some require minimum numbers of 2 to 4 people for departures: *Aquatic Air,* tel. 919–5966 has sea planes that do scenic flights, as well as commuter trips, between Rose Bay and Palm Beach. They will also deliver you to the door of several excellent restaurants on the banks of the Hawkesbury River. *Heli-Aust,* tel 660–2288, for scenic harbor flights and day trips to the Blue Mountains and

NEW SOUTH WALES 91

Hunter Valley. *Air New South Wales,* tel. 268–1889, gives you a taste of the Outback experience on its Jolly Swagman day tour to Dubbo.

NATIONAL PARKS. The Sydney region has three large national parks: Royal National Park to the south; Ku-ring-gai National Park to the north, and Sydney Harbour National Park, which includes part of the foreshores and a number of small harbor islands.

Sydney Harbour National Park. Tel. 337–5355. Massive headlands rising out of the sea and gentler slopes and sandy beaches. There are numerous picturesque spots to picnic, walk, or swim. The park includes South Head, Nielsen Park, Middle Head, Dobroyd, North Head, and the former quarantine station. You must book in advance to visit the quarantine station (tel. 977–6229) as well as Rodd, Shark, and Clark islands.

The Royal National Park. Tel. 521–2230. Established in 1878. Covers an area of 14,000 hectares (around 35,000 acres). It can be reached by car by turning off Princes Highway at Loftus or Waterfall (32km—19 mi.—from the city). The electric train stops at Royal National Park station, from which a road leads to the entrance to the park at Audley (1km). Here a causeway separates the fresh and tidal waters of the Hacking River. It is a pleasant spot for picnicking, boating, or even staying overnight in the local motel. The park has sealed (paved) roads for motoring and many well-kept paths for exploring on foot. The place is loveliest in spring and early summer, when most of the 700 species of wildflowers are in bloom.

Set around a flooded river valley, **Ku-ring-gai Chase National Park** is 24km (14 mi.) from Sydney. It also has a number of excellent surfing beaches. Tel. 457–9853. Access is by car, bus, and ferry. Drive along Pacific Highway through some of Sydney's choicest northern suburbs and turn off at Pymble or Mt. Colah for Bobbin Head or go past Gordon onto Mona Vale Road and follow it as far as Terrey Hills, then turn to Coal and Candle Creek and Commodore Heights until reaching the end of the road at West Head. The views from here over wide sweeps of river and ocean are among the most spectacular in Australia. Ku-ring-gai Chase National Park may also be reached by the ferry, which runs from Palm Beach (connected by bus with Sydney); inquiries, tel. 918–2747. The Palm Beach–Patonga–Bobbin Head ferry leaves 11:30 A.M. and takes about 4 hours 20 minutes. Or take a train to Turramurra Station and then travel by bus to Bobbin Head; inquiries, tel. 450–2277.

Lane Cove River Park is 12 km (7 mi.) from the city. Access is by car, turning off Pacific Highway at Chatswood onto Fullers Bridge Road, or by bus from Chatswood Station. It is a popular picnic place, crowded on weekends and holidays. The river is rather polluted, and swimming is discouraged. A paddle-wheeler plies the Lane Cove River on scenic cruises. Tel. 46–5907).

CITY PARKS AND GARDENS. Sydney is blessed with three of the world's largest and most beautiful human-made parks, Hyde Park, the Royal Botanic Gardens, and Centennial Park. All are very popular with picnickers, joggers, and leisurely walkers. There are also numerous smaller parks set on the harbor's edge and throughout the suburbs.

Hyde Park is a semiformal park of lawns, flowerbeds, and shade trees in the center of the city. It features the magnificent Archibald Fountain in its northern part and the pink granite war memorial at the southern end. It is the site of a festival village each January during the Sydney Festival. The *Royal Botanic Gardens* are magnificently sited on the edge of the harbor at Farm Cove, next to the Opera House. Open 8 A.M.–sunset daily. *Centennial Park* was opened in 1888 to commemorate Australia's first hundred years. It is about 10 minutes from the city center and beckons with over 220 hectares (528 acres) of lakes, grasslands, magnificent trees, and sports fields. It attracts cyclists and horseback riders as well as picnickers and has a road for motorists as well. Closes at sunset.

THE BEACHES. It is no exaggeration to say that Sydney's beaches range from excellent to magnificent. From about the middle or the end of October until the end of April the water is usually pleasantly warm—although there are hardy "icebergs" who swim the whole year round. In addition to their excellence Sydney's main beaches can be all reached by public transport, and all are patrolled (from October till Easter) by volunteer members of the Surf Life Saving Association of Australia. They are expert in saving people from drowning. The association was founded in 1907 and since then has been credited with rescuing more than 100,000 people. But you get into trouble only if you don't follow the rules. Surf only between the flags placed on the beach by lifeguards, who know where currents can be dangerous. They are also on the lookout for sharks and ring a warning siren when they spot one, before going out in a surf boat to chase it away. Lifesavers also treat people stung by bluebottles (Portuguese men-o'-war), nasty creatures with stinging tentacles. For information on getting to the beaches by public transport, phone the Urban Transit Authority 2–0543 or the State Rail Authority, 219–4517.

Sydney has two groups of ocean beaches, all of which are sandy—one north, the other south of the harbor. Beaches are free unless you want to use the dressing sheds and a locker, when a small fee is sometimes charged. Distance from the city is shown in parentheses, and symbols represent the following: Pt: patrolled in season; DS: dressing sheds; P: parking; P(F): parking with a fee; S: shops; SB: surfboard riding permitted—generally in specially marked areas or outside swimmers' areas.

NORTHERN OCEAN BEACHES

The beaches north of the harbor are beautiful. One follows another as you move north along Barrenjoey Road to Palm Beach.

Manly (9 1/2 mi., 16km). Consists of three beaches: Manly, North Steyne, and Queenscliff. A popular commercial beach, 1 mi. long. Pt, DS, S, P, SB. Swimming pool and rock pool. Surf-o-Planes are available from kiosk. Easily accessible from Sydney by ferry.

Harbord (111/2 mi., 19km). 1/2 mi. long. Pt, DS, S, P(F), SB. Rock pool. Waves are rather gentle, making this a favorite beach for body surfing.

Curl Curl (13 mi., 21km) 1 mi. long. Pt, DS, P(F), SB.

Dee Why (131/3 mi., 22km) 2 mi. long. Pt, DS, P(F), SB. Body surfing is good here.

Long Reef (14 mi., 22km). 2 mi. long. Pt, DS, P(F). Surfing is considered consistently good here.

Collaroy (141/2 mi., 23km). 4 mi. long. Pt, DS, P(F), SB. Rock pool and snack bar.

Narrabeen (16 mi., 26km). 4 mi. long. Pt, DS, P(F). Rock pool and snacks. North Narrabeen is a favorite surfing beach.

Warriewood Beach (171/2 mi., 28km). 1 mi. long. Pt, P(F), SB. Snack bar.

Mona Vale Beach (181/2 mi., 30km). 1 mi. long. Pt, DS, P(F), SB. Swimming pool.

Newport Beach (21mi., 34km). 1/2 mi. long. Pt, DS, S, P(F), SB.

Bilgola Beach (221/2 mi., 36km). 1/2 mi. long. Pt, DS, P(F), SB. Swimming pool and snack bar.

Avalon Beach (228/10 mi., 37km). 1 mi. long. Pt, DS, S, P(F), SB. Rock pool.

Whale Beach (231/2 mi., 38km). 1/2 mi. long. Pt, DS, P(F), SB. Rock pool and snack bar.

Palm Beach (27 mi., 43km). This fashionable beach is beautiful and sandy, and 1 1/2 mi. long. High-priced houses look out over the Pacific. Pt, DS, S, P(F), SB. Rock pool and snack bar.

SOUTHERN OCEAN BEACHES

Bronte Beach (5 mi., 8km east). Beach is wider and more open than Tamarama. 1/4 mi. long. Swimming pool, rock pool, snack bar, first-aid room.

Coogee (5 mi., 8km south). Family beach, 1/4 mi. long. Pt, DS, P, SB. Rock pool.

Bondi Beach (51/2 mi., 9km east of Sydney). Sydney's most famous beach, with the archetypal bronzed surfers everywhere. Very busy and commercial. 1 mi. long. Pt, DS, P(F), SB. Swimming pool, rock pool, snack bar, first-aid room, and children's playground. Beach equipment for hire.

Tamarama (51/2 mi., 9km east). Beach is quieter than Bondi, surrounded by cliffs, and 1/2 mi. long. Pt, DS. Snack bar and first-aid room. Surfboard riding is not permitted.

NEW SOUTH WALES

Maroubra (7 mi., 11km south). Family beach. 1/2 mi. long. Pt, DS, P(F), SB.
Malabar (8 mi., 13km south). 1/8 mi. long. Pt, P, DS, SB.
Cronulla Beaches (Cronulla, North Cronulla, Wanda, and Elouera Beach). (18 mi., 30km south). 2 mi. long. Rock pools and snack bar. Pt, DS, P, SB.

HARBOR BEACHES

There are also beaches on both northern and southern harbor foreshores: some have protected swimming enclosures. Harbor beaches include:
Balmoral. A very pretty beach on the north side (with shark net), a good place to watch yachts on weekends. Shops, restaurant nearby. Popular with families.
Camp Cove. A small beach at Watsons Bay, in front of houses, with a grassy headland. Snack bar. Topless bathing popular. Usually crowded with families on weekends.
Lady Jane. Popular nude beach at Watsons Bay. You must descend ladders down a cliff face here.
Nielsen Park. at Vaucluse. A narrow sandy beach with grassy headlands and a large park behind it. Snack bar and dressing sheds. A favorite spot for watching the start of the Sydney–Hobart yacht race.

When at the beach remember these two warnings: Don't dive into the calm water of the harbor—that's where sharks like to lurk; and protect your skin from the powerful Sydney sun.

ZOOS AND ANIMAL PARKS. *Featherdale Wildlife Park,* 217–229 Kildare Road, Doonside (14km/25 mi. west); 622–1705. Open daily (except Christmas Day) 9 A.M.–5 P.M. Koalas, possums, wallabies, wombats, kangaroos. Have your photo taken holding a koala.

Koala Park, Castle Hill Road, West Pennant Hills (25km/15 mi. north); 84–3141. Open daily (except Christmas Day) 9 A.M.–5 P.M. Enjoy Australian native animals in a natural bushland setting. You may pose with koalas and handfeed kangaroos at intervals during the day.

Taronga Zoo & Aquarium, Bradley's Head Road, Mosman; 969–2777. Open daily 9 A.M.–5 P.M. Can be reached by ferry from Circular Quay, Jetty 5. The zoo exhibits more than 4,000 native and exotic mammals, birds, reptiles, and fish and has the world's finest collection of Australian fauna.

Waratah Park, Namba Road, Duffy's Forest (30-min. drive from Harbour Bridge); 450–2377. Open daily (except Christmas Day) 10 A.M.–5 P.M. Pet and photograph tame koalas and kangaroos. Walk-in koala enclosure.

THEME PARKS. *Australia's Wonderland.* Walgrove Road, Eastern Creek, west of Sydney; 675–0111. Largest theme park in the southern hemisphere. Attractions include a giant wooden roller-coaster and a shoot-the-rapids raft ride. Open 10 A.M.–8 P.M. daily during school holidays and on weekends and public holidays between August and May.

Luna Park. Milsons Point, northern side of Sydney Harbour Bridge; 922–6977. Its famous laughing face can be seen from all over the harbor. A variety of games and rides are offered Friday night, Saturday, and Saturday night, Sunday, and public holidays.

SPORTS. Sydneysiders are outdoor people and enjoy participating in and watching a wide variety of sports.
Boating: Sydney's waterways are alive with boats. See Harbour Cruises under Tours, above, for rental contacts. and How to Get Around in *Practical Information for NSW beyond Sydney.*

Fishing: Fishing from the many ocean beaches and coastal cliffs you may catch mullet, sole, snapper, and whiting. Bream, flathead, snapper, whiting, blackfish, and crabs are caught in the waters of Sydney Harbour, Botany Bay, and the Georges and Hawkesbury rivers. The Travel Centre of NSW, tel. 231–4444, can tell you about fishing charters and where to get a fishing license.

Golf: There are 40 public golf courses in and around Sydney ready to welcome overseas visitors. Book a day in advance. *Bondi Golf Links,* tel. 30–1981; *Castle Cove Country Club,* Deepwater Road, Castle Cove, tel. 406–5444; *Kuring-gai Golf Course,* 361 Bobbin Head Road, Turramurra, tel. 44–5110; *Moore Park Golf Course,* Anzac Parade, Moore Park, tel. 663–3960; *Northbridge Golf Club,* Sailor's Bay Road, Northbridge, tel. 95–2169.

Hang Gliding: For lessons (equipment included) contact *Stanwell Soaring Centre,* 5 Sheridan Cr, Stanwell Park, tel. (042) 944–2648. Book in advance.

Surfing: Excellent surfing facilities are available at Sydney's beaches (see Beaches, above).

Tennis: The yellow pages telephone directory lists courts for hire all over Sydney. Book in advance. Near the city is *Rushcutter's Bay,* tel. 357–1675, and *Ridge Street Tennis Centre,* North Sydney, tel. 929–7172.

SPECTATOR SPORTS

Cricket: *Sydney Cricket Ground,* Moore Park, tel. 357–6601, for international and interstate matches in season (October–March). Tickets available through Bass, tel. 264–2800. Sydney's first-grade cricket competition is played on various city and suburban grounds.

Football: Four codes are played fast and furiously throughout winter: Rugby Union (amateur), Rugby League (professional), Australian Rules (a fast and open game featuring spectacular high kicks and leaps), and soccer (European football). Daily newspapers tell who is playing where, and tickets can be bought at the grounds.

Greyhound Racing: *Wentworth Park.* Wentworth Park Road, Glebe, tel. 660–6964; *Harold Park,* Ross Street, Glebe, tel. 660–5313.

Harness Racing: Trotting meetings regularly at *N.S.W. Trotting Club,* Ross Street, Glebe, tel. 660–3688.

Horse Racing: This is one of Sydney's most popular year-round spectator sports, and regular meetings are held at the *Australian Jockey Club,* Alison Road, Randwick, tel. 663–8400; *Sydney Turf Club,* King Street, Canterbury, tel. 799–8000; *Rosehill,* Grand Avenue, Rosehill, tel. 682–1000; and *Warwick Farm,* Hume Highway, Warwick Farm, tel. 602–6199. The most important events are the autumn Doncaster Handicap and Sydney Cup and spring Epsom and Metropolitan handicaps. Races are held each Saturday throughout the year.

Motor Racing: This has a strong year-round following with stock-car, racing-car, drag, and motorcycle events held in various city and out-of-town locations such as the *Amaroo Park,* Annangrove Road, Annangrove, tel. 679–1122, and the *Oran Park Raceway,* Oran Park Road, Narellan, tel. (046) 46–1004.

Sailing: Sydney Harbour is almost congested with sailing races on weekends. Among the most exciting craft to watch racing are the 18-footers, with huge sails and hardworking crews. Their speed is often over 20 knots, and they can be airborne in a good blow. A spectator's ferry follows the races on Saturday from the *Sydney Flying Squadron,* 76 McDougall Street, Milson's Point at 2:15 P.M. on race days between September and March, and on Sundays from the *NSW 18-ft. Sailing League Clubhouse,* Bay Street, Double Bay at 2:15 P.M.

Surfing Carnivals: Held from November to March. Contact *Australian Surf Life Saving Association* at 663–4298 for details.

Tennis: During the summer season major matches are played at *White City Courts,* 30 Alma Street, Paddington, 331–4144, and at the *Sydney Entertainment Centre,* Harbour Street, 211–2222. Tickets available through Bass, 264–2800.

 MUSEUMS AND HISTORIC SITES. More complete descriptions of most of the following museums and historic sites are given in the section "Exploring Sydney," above.

Art Gallery of New South Wales. Art Gallery Road, the Domain; 221–2100. Entry to the gallery is free, but there is a charge to see the larger visiting exhibitions. Open Monday to Saturday 10 A.M.–5 P.M., Sunday, noon–5 P.M., and public holidays 10 A.M.–5 P.M. Closed Christmas Day and Good Friday. Colonial paintings, Australian Impressionists, late 19th- and early 20th-century and contemporary Australian art.

NEW SOUTH WALES

Australian Museum. College Street; 339–8111. Open Tuesday to Sunday and public holidays, 10 A.M.–5 P.M.; Monday noon–5 P.M. Closed Christmas Day and Good Friday. Good exhibits of Australia's natural and cultural history.

Captain Cook's Landing Place. Kurnell; 668–9923. Open weekdays and public holidays 10:30 A.M.–5 P.M. Closed Christmas Day and Good Friday. Museum, highlighting Captain Cook's discovery of Botany Bay. Park, barbecue facilities, and beach.

Elizabeth Bay House. 7 Onslow Avenue, Elizabeth Bay; 358–2344. It is open Tuesday–Friday 10 A.M.–4:30 P.M., Saturday 10 A.M.–5 P.M., and Sunday noon–5 P.M. Closed Monday except public holidays, when it is open 10 A.M.–5 P.M. Restored 1835 home, authentically furnished.

Geological and Mining Museum. 36 George Street North, the Rocks; 251–2422. Open Monday–Friday 9:30 A.M.–4 P.M., Saturday 1–4 P.M., Sunday and public holidays 11 A.M.–4 P.M. Houses displays of gold, gemstones, minerals, rocks, and fossils.

The Hyde Park Barracks. Queens Square, Macquarie Street; 217–0111. The museum is open daily, except Tuesday 10 A.M.–5 P.M.; Tuesday noon–5 P.M. Closed Christmas Day and Good Friday. NSW history from colonial days to the 1950s.

The Mint. Queens Square, Macquarie Street; 217–0111. The museum is open daily, except Wednesday, 10 A.M.–5 P.M.; Wednesday noon–5 P.M. Closed Christmas Day and Good Friday. Australian decorative arts, stamps, coins, flags.

The Observatory, Observatory Hill, The Rocks; 241–2478. Open Monday, Tuesday, Thursday, Friday 10 A.M.–noon; Wednesday 10 A.M.–5 P.M.; weekends 1–5 P.M. Closed Christmas Day and Good Friday. A charming colonial building constructed in local sandstone. The Observatory is now a museum with exhibitions on time-keeping and astronomy. Evening observation of the stars sessions may be booked.

Power House Museum, Mary Ann Street, Ultimo; 217–0111. Open daily 10 A.M.–5 P.M. Closed Christmas Day and Good Friday. Stage One of this technological museum includes historic exhibits such as New South Wales' first locomotive, a monoplane, and one of Australia's first manufactured cars. Stage Two is due for completion in 1988.

The State Archives. 2 Globe Street; 237–0100. Open Monday, Tuesday, Thursday, Friday 9 A.M.–5 P.M.; Wednesday 9 A.M.–9 P.M.; Saturday and public holidays 10 A.M.–4 P.M. The archives house the official records of the governments of New South Wales from the First Fleet convicts to plans of the Opera House.

Vaucluse House. Wentworth Avenue, Vaucluse; 337–1957. The house is open Tuesday to Sunday 10 A.M.–4:30 P.M. The grounds are open 7 A.M.–5 P.M. on the same days. Closed Christmas Day and Good Friday. A tearoom serves Devonshire teas and light meals. Historic colonial house, 1829–1847.

Victoria Barracks. Oxford Street, Paddington; 339–3543. Telephone for information on the changing-of-the-guards ceremony and guided tours. Military barracks built 1841.

LIBRARIES. *State Library of New South Wales.* Macquarie Street; 230–1414. Galleries are open Monday–Saturday 10 A.M.–5 P.M.; Sunday 2–6 P.M. The general reference library's hours are Monday–Saturday 9 A.M.–9 P.M.; Sunday 2–6 P.M. Frequent exhibits of paintings, drawings, documents, and rare books that are part of NSW history.

GALLERIES. Art in Australia is booming, and a large number of Australians buy Australian paintings and sculptures. As a result, the number of art galleries has increased and many are of high quality. In a stroll around the suburbs of Paddington and Woollahra you will discover many interesting galleries. Some galleries to visit: *Aboriginal Art Centre,* 7 Walker Lane, Paddington, 357–6839; open Tuesday–Saturday, 11 A.M.–6 P.M. *Collectors Gallery of Aboriginal Art,* 40 Harrington Street, City, 27–8492; open Monday–Friday, 9 A.M.–5 P.M., Saturday 10 A.M.–5 P.M. For contemporary Australian art visit *Holdsworth Galleries,* Cnr Holdsworth Street and Jersey Road, Woollahra, 33–1364; open Monday–Saturday 10 A.M.–5 P.M., Sunday noon–5 P.M. *Barry Stern Galleries,* 19 Glenmore Road, Paddington, 357–5492, and 12 Mary

Place, Paddington, 357–5492. *Rudy Komon Gallery*, 124 Jersey Road, Woollahra, 32–2533; open Monday–Saturday 10 A.M.–5 P.M.

SHOPPING. In Sydney you can buy practically anything that the wide world can offer—provided you are ready to pay the price. Candidly, Sydney is not a bargain hunter's paradise. Except for a few products like kangaroo-skin or opals, nothing can be bought here more cheaply than elsewhere. One should be careful about where one buys opals. The wisest thing is to go to one of the city's several well-established jewelers. They will charge the fair price. Some **opal** specialists are: *Flame Opals*, 119 George Street, the Rocks, 27–3446, and *Allison's Opal Rooms*, 15 Park Street, 267–7133. If you show your passport you can purchase opals duty free. For **Australiana**, an interesting shop is *Coo-ee Australian Emporium* at 98 Oxford Street, Paddington, 356–1544. Some of its fabric designs are done by the Tiwi Aboriginal tribe.

Sydney has a profusion of high-class department stores, trendy boutiques, intimate arcades, and high-tech towers. In the city center, George, Pitt, and Castlereagh streets run parallel, north-south, and contain the bulk of the really good stores. International credit cards are accepted in virtually every shop. Long ago it used to be said that Australian stores stocked last season's fashions from Europe and North America. Not any more. Australian fashion designers can and do hold their own against the world's best, and you will find their creative designs and fine-quality clothes in many of the big stores as well as the ritzier boutiques of Double Bay.

Department Stores. *David Jones* has long been Sydney's premier department store. It is to Sydney what Saks is to New York or I. Magnin is to San Francisco. There are two DJs stores in the city center. The Elizabeth Street store (which occupies almost an entire block between Market and Castlereagh) is known as the women's store because it specializes in everything a woman could want, as well as many items of general merchandise. On the sixth floor, *Georges of Melbourne* (perhaps the most exclusive clothing and accessories retailer in Melbourne) has set up its own little store within a store. DJs' men's store is right across the street on the corner of Castlereagh and Market and takes a particular pride in stocking a man's every need. The men's store also stocks a wide range of home furnishings. In the basement of the men's store is a newly renovated Harrods-style gourmet food hall, known as *Food, Glorious Food*. It carries the best of imported as well as Australian-made food products. They bake their own bread, and there are half a dozen cozy little sit-down bars selling everything from cake and coffee to fish, oysters, and chilled Australian wines.

Not far down Market Street is *Grace Bros.*, another very big department store, which is very much a part of the inner-city retail landscape. It sells general merchandise, although not quite the range or quality of DJs. A second store is at Broadway past Central Railway Station.

Gowings, Lowes, and *Waltons* are smaller department stores that stock budget items.

Arcades. Sydney is blessed with some marvelous old-fashioned arcades. Far and away the best of them is the *Strand Arcade*, between Pitt and Castlereagh. Built in the late 1880s, it was once described as "undoubtedly the finest public throughfare in the Australasian Colonies." The Strand has been beautifully restored and today offers a basement and five galleried floors crammed with a delightful array of tiny shops and boutiques selling everything from jewelry to antiques and men's and women's fashion. There's also a profusion of eateries and health-food shops. The *St. James Arcade* (between Elizabeth and Castlereagh, just north of DJs), much more modern, also features some very elegant boutiques and jewelery shops.

Centrepoint. In the heart of the city and beneath Sydney Tower is a shopping complex that features scores of outlets for everything from bikinis to bread rolls. A pedestrian walkway links Centrepoint with two David Jones stores and Grace Bros. and offers a convenient way to move around without having to suffer the fits and starts of traffic.

Double Bay. Although Sydney is full of trendy designer boutiques, people seem to attach a special aura to the same merchandise when it is sold in Double Bay. Double Bay (also known as Double Pay) is just a few minutes' ride out of the city center along New South Head Road. The shopping here is really excellent. The affluent middle class who inhabit the swank eastern suburbs don't hesitate to pay top dollar for the finest products, and that goes for everything

NEW SOUTH WALES

from meat, poultry, and fish to the latest Italian and French clothing. There are also some very good restaurants and small eateries in Double Bay. Well worth the visit.

Mid-City Centre. On four levels between George and Pitt, King and Market. Dozens of trendy boutiques plus four good coffee shops on the gallery level. On the Pitt Street level restaurants offer Asian, Lebanese, Mexican, and Italian delights

MLC Centre. *Gucci* is here, and so are a lot of other top-quality shops. At the base of the giant white granite cylinder known as the MLC Centre between Martin Place and Castlereagh and King streets. Good eateries, including takeout.

THEATER AND ENTERTAINMENT. For information on entertainment in Sydney, consult the *Sydney Morning Herald's* Friday and Saturday editions. Tickets for many shows can be booked through Bass agencies, tel. 264–2800. Live theater in Sydney has not as large a following as one would expect in a city of more than 3 million people. Yet there is nothing "provincial" about Sydney's theatrical life, and performances range from professional to excellent.

The *Opera House* is the center for the performing arts in Sydney. It offers opera, theater, music, ballet, and film. There is a good package available called "An Evening at the Opera House." It includes dinner at the Bennelong Restaurant, a guided tour, and a show. Cost varies according to whether you select drama, ballet, or opera. For information on the Opera House phone 250–7111 and for tickets, 2–0525.

Opera. The *Australian Opera Company* has a summer and winter season (January–February and June to October).

Dance. The *Australian Ballet,* 357–1200, the national classical company, performs here March to May and November–December. The *Sydney Dance Company,* 358–4600, presents fascinating contemporary dance and modern ballet, with the focus on Australian works. Its season is generally July–August and November. If you're a dance fan, make it a point to see them if they're in town.

Theater. The Opera House is also one of the homes of the *Sydney Theatre Company,* 250–1700, which presents a mixture of classics and modern Australian plays. Its other venue is a new complex called the Wharf at Pier 4, Hickson Road, Walsh Bay. This is a renovated wharf building and has a restaurant. The other main live theaters are *Seymour Centre for the Performing Arts,* Cnr City Road and Cleveland Street, Chippendale (information tel. 692–0555, box office 692–3351); the *Theatre Royal,* MLC Centre, King Street, Sydney, 231–6111; *Her Majesty's Theatre,* Railway Square, 107 Quay Street, Sydney (information tel. 212–3411, box office tel. 212–1120). Smaller theaters presenting quality theater are: *Ensemble,* 78 McDougall Street, Milsons Point (information tel. 929–8877, box office tel. 929–0644); *Northside Theatre Company,* 2 Marian Street, Killara, tel. 498–3166.

Kinsela's, 383–387 Bourke Street, Darlinghurst, 331–6200, a fashionable Sydney nightspot, is a combination of restaurant, bars, and cabaret. *Les Girls,* 2C Roslyn Street, Kings Cross, 358–2333, features female impersonators. *Jolly Swagman Show,* Argyle Tavern, 18 Argyle Street, the Rocks, 27–7728, is an Australiana Show complete with sheep shearing and bush music.

Music. Orchestral concerts, chamber music, and other music recitals are also presented at the Opera House. For information phone 250–7111 and for bookings, 2–0525. There are also some great free Sunday afternoon outdoor concerts there, usually jazz, starting at 2:30 P.M., and the view is fantastic. Other popular jazz spots are *The Basement,* 29 Reiby Place, Circular Quay, 27–9927, which offers one of the most interesting and varied jazz programs in Sydney. Dinner is also available. *Don Burrows Supper Club,* the Regent of Sydney, 199 George Street, 238–0000, is a sophisticated nightspot where some of the best Australian and international jazz musicians and vocalists perform. Major international and local rock-pop artists generally perform at the *Entertainment Centre,* Harbour Street, Haymarket, 211–2222. See also Nightlife.

AUSTRALIA

NIGHTLIFE. Sydney is *the* city in Australia for nightlife. Although some of its bars, clubs, and discotheque-nightclubs can be quiet early in the week, as the week goes on the crowds get bigger and noisier and the hours later. Sydneysiders enjoy a variety of entertainments. Some like to dress up and go dancing until they drop at one of Sydney's fashionable discotheques. Others enjoy a quiet drink at a piano bar; some would rather jostle crowds for a beer in a friendly pub. There are cabaret evenings at the local licensed club, or bawdy entertainment and boisterous singing at a theater restaurant. Jazz buffs might choose a sophisticated supper club or a casual jazz restaurant for entertainment, while a young punk rocker finds a pub dispensing her or his style of music on the edge of town. Singles will find that although in Sydney there are no bars especially for them, most of the bars mentioned, as well as discotheques and supper clubs, are even better. See also Theater and Entertainment, above.

BARS

Often called hotels, due to an old licensing law that required overnight accommodations to be available, many bars close around 11:00 P.M.

Arthur's. 155 Victoria Street, Kings Cross; 358-5097. You can get anything from a drink to a full meal here or dance the night away on the small mirrored dance floor. This fashionable spot attracts patrons colorful and bizarre from far and near, and its cocktails are well worth a try. Monday–Saturday 6:00 P.M.–3:00 A.M.; Sunday midday–6:30 P.M.

Hero of Waterloo. 81 Lower Fort Street, the Rocks; 27-8471. Situated in Sydney's historic Rocks area, the Hero is a charming and authentic "pub" and a great spot to enjoy an Aussie beer. Monday–Saturday 10 A.M.–10:45 P.M., Sunday midday–6:30 P.M.

Lord Nelson. 19 Kent Street; 27-6198. The oldest licensed hotel in Australia. Monday–Friday 11 A.M.–11 P.M., Saturday noon–11 P.M.

Kinsela's. 387 Bourke Street, Darlinghurst; 331-6200. One of *the* Sydney nightspots; offers restaurant, cabaret, and bar facilities in a refurbished funeral parlor. Monday–Thursday 6:30 P.M.–1 A.M., Friday–Saturday 6:30 P.M.–2 A.M.

Marble Bar. Sydney Hilton, 259 Pitt Street; 266-0610. Elegant and ornate bar has been re-created from the old Adams Hotel originally on the site. Monday–Saturday 4:30 P.M.–midnight.

Orient Hotel. Cnr George and Argyle streets, the Rocks; 27-2464. Entertainment nightly, a popular "watering hole." Open seven days to 11 P.M.

CLASS ACTS

Sydney Hilton Hotel. 259 Pitt Street; 266-0610. Three cabaret seasons a year are performed here, with top international and Australian stars.

DISCOTHEQUES, NIGHTCLUBS, DANCING

Arthur's. 155 Victoria Street, King's Cross; 358-5097. Join Sydney's young glitterati—if you can get in among the Friday- and Saturday-night crush—for drinks, a snack, supper, or dancing till late. Monday–Saturday 6 P.M.–3 A.M., Sunday 11 A.M.–midnight.

Cauldron. 207 Darlinghurst Road, Darlinghurst; 331-1523 or 331-5730. A restaurant and discotheque, the Cauldron is extremely popular and gets very crowded. Its clients include the glamorous model set. May be difficult to get in unless you're dining at the restaurant or you pass the doorman's scrutiny. Open Monday–Sunday.

Juliana's. Sydney Hilton, Reception floor, 295 Pitt Street; 266-0610. Dress up for this elegant disco. It is a piano bar Thursday and Friday, 5–9 P.M. and a discotheque Tuesday–Saturday until 3 A.M. Cover charge; no minimum.

Rogue's. 10 Oxford Street, Darlinghurst; 33-6924. Preference is given to members at this glamorous restaurant-cum-bar-disco—unless you have a reservation at the restaurant. There's also a piano bar with live music. Daily 7:30 P.M.–3 A.M., with disco from about 11:30 P.M.

William's. 100 William Street, Sydney; 356-2222. William's has two very comfortable lounge bars, an elegant restaurant, and a dance floor. Monday–

Saturday. Entry is by membership, dinner reservation, or payment of cover charge.

NEW SOUTH WALES BEYOND SYDNEY

Blue Mountains

The City of the Blue Mountains, a favorite holiday resort near Sydney, is not a city at all, but a collection of 24 separate townships dispersed over an area of 1,350 square km of mountainous bushland traversed by the Great Western Highway. The largest of the townships, Katoomba, center of the "city," is 106km by road or rail from Sydney. You can easily see the Blue Mountains in a day, but if possible, spend a few days there. Besides lovely bush walks and excursions on horseback, the area offers scenically attractive golf courses. They are interesting to low-handicap golfers but not too challenging for the weekend player. The courses at Blackheath and at Leura are exceptionally attractive, with spectacular views of the mountains. There are rather arduous walks, but don't forget the first rule of the inexperienced bushwalker—never wander away from the beaten track.

Popular walks include the 6km Federal Pass Walk, which takes about 2½ hours and skirts the foot of the cliffs between Leura and Katoomba Falls. One descends near Leura Falls by way of 1,330 graded steps between lush vegetation—mountain ash, cedar, bloodwoods, and all kinds of gums abound—and follows the trail that passes Linda Falls, Leura Falls, Weeping Rock, and one of Katoomba's great sights, the Three Sisters rocks, before arriving at the foot of the 245m Katoomba Falls. The scenic railway can take the wayfarer back to the top. The scenic railway, only 415m long, is reputedly the steepest in the world, and it's quite a thrill to travel on it down into Jamieson Valley, a drop of 230m. The scenic skyway, which takes passengers from one clifftop to another over a void of 275m, is another tourist attraction in Katoomba.

Upper Hawkesbury

This attractive river area on the northwestern outskirts of Sydney was discovered by a rowing expedition under the command of Governor Arthur Phillip in 1789. Twenty-one years later, in 1810, Governor Macquarie established five towns—Windsor, Richmond, Castlereagh, Pitt Town, and Wilberforce (the Five Macquarie Towns)—in the area. Castlereagh has almost disappeared, but the other four are still expanding; it won't be very long before the Sydney suburban sprawl swallows them.

There are several early-nineteenth-century buildings in the area well worth seeing. These include St. Matthew's Church of England in Windsor, designed by Francis Greenway; the restored courthouse at Windsor; and the Anglican Church of St. Peter at Richmond. At Richmond the Royal Australian Air Force maintains an air base.

The Hawkesbury itself offers scenic beauty and excellent water skiing from Windsor Bridge to Wiseman's Ferry. A one-day excursion from Sydney by car to Windsor—with a 10km drive from Windsor to the Hawkesbury at Wiseman's Ferry—may also take in, on the return trip, the city of Parramatta. Although Sydneysiders consider Parramatta an outer suburb, not a separate city, this view is not shared by the residents, who think that its founder, Governor Phillip, should have stuck

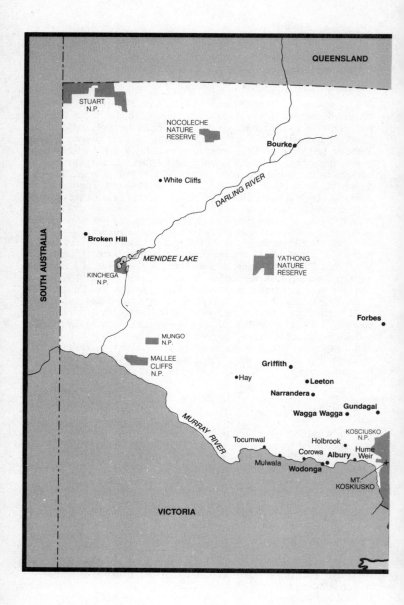

NEW SOUTH WALES

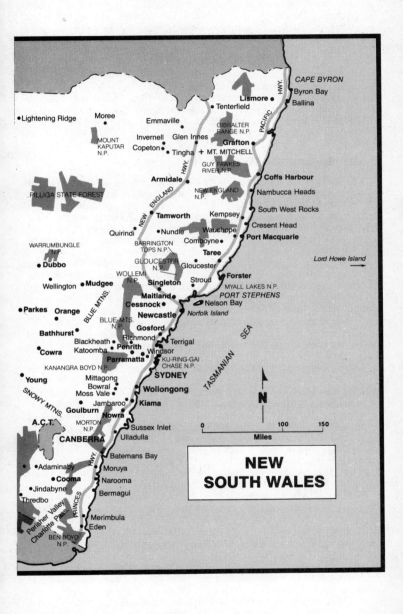

to his original idea and made Parramatta the capital of the young colony. Today the city is mainly industrial and has little charm, although it has retained a number of good buildings from the early days. They include the carefully restored Old Government House, the oldest surviving public building in Australia, completed in 1816 and now surrounded by Parramatta Park; Experiment Farm Cottage (1820) on Ruse Street, which stands on the site of James Ruse's farm, memorable as the first land grant given in New South Wales (1792); Elizabeth Farm House, built by John Macarthur in 1793, the oldest existing building in Australia; and Hambledon (1824), built by John Macarthur for Penelope Lucas, the governess of his children. Two other buildings worth a visit are the Lancer Barracks on Smith Street (1820), which contains a military museum, and St. John's Church, founded in 1799 but rebuilt twice since.

The Illawarra and Southern Highlands

The 242km of coastline, skirted by the Princes Highway, is the dream come true of people who love water sports and don't want to be crowded but wish to enjoy the comforts of our technological age. But if you leave the Princes Highway, say at Oak Flats, and drive for less than an hour along the Illawarra Highway, you will be in the heart of the southern highlands, where the atmosphere recalls the countryside of England. The southern highlands have none of the majesty of the Australian Alps or the wild beauty of certain parts of the Blue Mountains. But they are mellow, lovely, and charming. Although winter days can be cold and summer days hot, the climate is pleasant in spring, and in autumn simply wonderful. Small wonder that many people settle there after retirement.

Illawarra is an Aboriginal term meaning "high place near the sea," and indeed, for lengthy stretches the Princes Highway runs through hills that advance to the seashores, offering spectacular vistas of the coastline.

Setting out from Sydney, the first and last big city on the Princes Highway is Wollongong, with a population of about 208,650. Wollongong is now the third largest city in New South Wales. It is a bustling industrial city with a large percentage of "New Australians," who give the place a distinctly cosmopolitan character. Port Kembla—part of Wollongong—is the site of one of the world's largest steelworks, established in 1928. Between Port Kembla and Shellharbour is Lake Illawarra, a 42-square-km "pool" with popular camping sites and a reputation for excellent prawns. Shellharbour itself is an attractive secluded spot that got its name from the many shells once found on its shores. There are plans for a major marina to be built here.

Kiama, 120km from Sydney, is the next important resort. Cattle breeders know it as the place where the famous Australian Illawarra Shorthorn (AIS) cattle were developed. One of Kiama's main tourist attractions is the blowhole, a few minutes' walk from the main shopping center. When strong southeasterly seas are running, as they often do, a large volume of water surges high into the air and falls back into the sea. At night the blowhole is illuminated with multicolored floodlights. Visitors to Kiama should not miss the Minnamurra Falls Reserve, a natural rainforest area only 15km from the sea.

Another 45km on is Nowra-Bomaderry, where the South Coast railway terminates and buses take passengers heading farther south. Nowra is a busy tourist center with all kinds of sporting facilities on water and land—including a beautifully laid out 18-hole golf course on the Shoalhaven River. It is also the focal point of nine smaller resorts nearby and a starting point for a large number of excursions to scenic attractions within a radius of 40km, including the beautiful Kangaroo Valley, which links the coast with the southern highlands behind.

Staying at one of the hotels or motels in the favorite tourist resorts of the southern highlands—Mittagong, Bowral, Moss Vale, and Bundanoon—you will find a large proportion of New Australians of central-European origin among the guests, especially in spring and in autumn when the trees in bloom or rust-colored foliage awake memories of their native lands. The four townships are relatively near to Sydney, and communications between them and the city by road and rail are good. The main railway line from Sydney to the southwest and to Melbourne traverses the area, as does the Hume Highway, although only Mittagong—now connected with Sydney by a new 80km expressway—is situated directly on the highway. There are many easy bushwalks, and short drives lead to scenic lookouts over hundreds of square kilometers of wildlife reserves and parks.

Early in Australia's history, in 1798, John Wilson, an ex-convict turned explorer who lived for some time with Aborigines, penetrated the southern highlands. In 1803, John Macarthur received the grant of land at Camden, where he carried out the wool-growing experiments that played such an important part in Australia's economic development. The well-kept farms and properties and the beautifully tended gardens surrounded by hawthorn hedges give the area an especially neat and friendly appearance.

There are several popular festivals in the area: in February Mittagong stages the dahlia festival; in March Moss Vale holds a Bush Week in conjunction with the annual agricultural show; and in October Bowral's tulip festival takes place. Every second year at Easter the Australian Musica Viva Society turns Mittagong into a music center for four days with lectures and chamber-music performances, usually by at least one ensemble of international renown. The Morton National Park, with headquarters at Fitzroy Falls near Moss Vale on the Nowra Road, has spectacular lookouts and pleasant picnic grounds.

The Wombeyan limestone caves are also popular attractions in the Mittagong area. Four km from Mittagong along the Hume Highway a road turns off and runs for 65km through breathtaking mountain scenery to Wombeyan. Five of the caves are fully developed for inspection, and tours accompanied by expert guides start from the Kui Kiosk at Wombeyan five times a day. The road between Mittagong and the Wombeyan Caves is only partly sealed but quite good, though careful driving is necessary. A longer road (162km) to the Caves from Mittagong via Moss Vale, Goulburn, and Taralga is easier going, especially for cars towing campers. Accommodation is available at Goulburn, about 80km from Wombeyan.

The Central Coast

The central coast, 50km to 120km north of Sydney—midway between Sydney and Newcastle—is aptly known as the playground of two cities. The township of Gosford at its heart can be reached by electric train. The road includes a 40km stretch of express turnpike, one of the few in Australia. (Instead of the turnpike you can drive along the less comfortable but scenically more rewarding old Pacific Highway, which has been maintained in good repair.) The central coast's greatest attractions are connected with water sports, fishing and surfing, but the area also has large tracts of unspoiled bushland for quiet walks along lakes and rivers. In vacation periods the main resorts are rather noisy and overcrowded, for the area has been developed into one of Sydney's main school-holiday areas. It has an equable climate and is sheltered from the winds. The area's proximity to Sydney (about an hour by electric train from Gosford) has also persuaded an increasing number of people to retire here or to buy or build weekend houses. The main townships are Gosford, which serves as a gateway for the area, Woy Woy and Ettalong off Brisbane Water, and Terrigal. An interesting tourist attraction is Old Sydney Town, near Gosford—a re-creation of Sydney Cove and its surroundings as they were in the early nineteenth century.

The Hunter Region

If you believe that coal-mining regions must look drab and bleak, you should see the verdant Hunter area of New South Wales. Here the god of coal must share his power and influence with a more cheerful deity—Bacchus. For after coal, wine is a most important product of this rich and beautiful part of the state. It begins about 100km north of Sydney at Catherine Hill Bay and extends 145km north, to just past Taree and 275km west to the Great Dividing Range, covering an area of 30,000 square km. Comparing places is rarely a rewarding exercise, but in the Hunter region one is often tempted because the scenery changes so rapidly, reviving memories of past travels. You may be looking down on the blue waters of some Mediterranean shoreline or faced with an Italian lake or a vineyard that could be in France. And all this without leaving the region named after its main river, the 470km Hunter, which rises in the Mount Royal Range and flows into the Pacific at Newcastle, Australia's sixth largest city.

The Hunter region's modern history begins with that permanently present character of early Australian history—the convict. In 1797, when Lieutenant John Shortland, commander of a Royal Navy whaleboat stationed at Sydney, received orders to sail north, he wasn't entrusted with the task of discovering anything but of finding some runaway convicts. Instead he found the mouth of a large river about 105km north of Sydney, which he named Hunter after John Hunter, who had succeeded Phillip as governor. A settlement for twice-convicted criminals was established there in 1801, and three years later—it was a very English epoch in Australian history—the place was named Newcastle and the surrounding district Northumberland. Gradually, however, the newly founded settlement followed the usual Australian pattern. With the influx of immigrants, the jail became transformed into a thriving colony. By the 1820s the settling and opening of the Hunter region was well under way. The discovery of huge reserves of high quality coal, which in turn encouraged the establishment of industry, greatly helped the region's development.

Although Newcastle (pop. 270,000) is looked upon as being an industrial center and is proud of its reputation as Australia's "City of Enterprise," it can also be a pleasant holiday resort, since there are beaches nearby. The city's pride is the War Memorial Cultural Centre, established from the donations of business firms and private citizens, which houses a good library and serves as a venue for cultural activities including concerts, art exhibitions, lectures, and the like.

About 18km south of Newcastle is Australia's largest seaside lake, Lake Macquarie, with an area of 110 square km and 150km of foreshores. The lake is one of Australia's most delightful water-sport centers: excellent for fishing, sailing, yachting, and water skiing. Because of its sheltered situation it is very pleasant in winter, and it receives enough sea breezes to be agreeably ventilated in summer. The little lakeside townships and villages have a large population of retired people. One of Australia's most distinguished artists, the painter Sir William Dobell, lived in Wangi Wangi, one of the attractive resorts. His home is now a museum dedicated to his memory.

NEW SOUTH WALES

About 50km north of Newcastle is Port Stephens, which takes in a number of resorts such as Nelson Bay, Shoal Bay, Fingal Bay, Tea Gardens, Lemon Tree Passage, Karuah and Soldiers Point. The area has been aptly described as a blue-water wonderland and offers the visitor a wide range of sports and entertainments. You may fish in the morning and play golf and tennis, bowls, or squash in the afternoon.

In the Port Stephens area are the twin towns of Tea Gardens and Hawks Nest, situated on the picturesque Myall River, which joins the Myall Lakes. A large national park surrounds them. Suggestions that the sands of the lake should be mined have caused a stormy controversy, and mining has now ceased. Still farther north, 325km from Sydney and 147km from Newcastle, is yet another excellent holiday center in the town of Forster. There are some 20 ocean beaches in its immediate vicinity, and the township has a long frontage on Wallis Lake, the water of which is rarely less than 20°C (68°F), even in winter.

The next large town north is Taree (pop. 16,697) on the banks of the Manning River. There are several pleasant fishing villages in the district as well as the Ellenborough Falls with a spectacular drop of 160m. This makes them one of the highest falls in the southern hemisphere.

The centers of the Hunter region's coal-mining industry are the towns of Maitland (pop. 44,125) and Cessnock (pop. 12,152). But neither resembles the sooty coal towns of Britain, Belgium, France, or Germany. They have managed to look like any other Australian working-class suburb, with neat houses and well-tended gardens. Although both Maitland and Cessnock are built on coal they are also the centers of prosperous farming districts, for they have some of the most fertile soil in New South Wales. Several farm homesteads near the two towns built in the first half of the last century are still in use. They are not open for inspection, but the Maitland City Council has issued a booklet titled *Historical Buildings of Maitland and District,* which describes them. Near Cessnock are the famous vineyards of Pokolbin, which produce some of the country's best wine. Many are open to visitors for tasting and sales, and have either restaurants or picnic facilities.

Stroud is not one of the larger settlements of the Hunter region (its population is only about 570), but besides having a few early-nineteenth-century buildings such as the Anglican Church of St. John (1833) and a well-designed courthouse, its international fame rests on the brick-throwing ability of its citizens. Every year there is a brick-throwing and rolling-pin-throwing contest among four towns called Stroud in different parts of the world—the U.S., Canada, England, and Australia. In this competition six men from each Stroud compete at throwing housebricks, and the results from each center are collated to decide the international winner. The women of the four Strouds compete in the rolling-pin-throwing competition.

The North Coast Region

Overseas visitors to Australia, or even Australians, who set out from Sydney to drive north—perhaps to Surfers' Paradise in Queensland—may never arrive there. Not because they face any serious dangers en route, but because they may succumb to the attractions of places on the way. The Pacific coast north and south of Sydney is among the world's most beautiful and pleasant seashores. In addition, though most holiday resorts along it are provided with the amenities of modern civilization, few are overcrowded even during the peak holiday season.

Nowhere is this more true than on the north coast of New South Wales, which is studded with holiday spots whose existence is not primarily based on the tourist business. Most of them are centers of thriving agricultural areas, attractive places where people go about their business in a leisurely way and where courtesy and service are still not merely memories of the past. The north-coast region (adjacent to the Hunter Valley region) is about 560km long, with the Wang Wauk River at its southern and Queensland at its northern border. Its average width between the Pacific Ocean and the Great Dividing Range is 80km. There are few secondary industries in this narrow strip of land (some people wish there were more) and not many factory chimneys to spoil the idyllic landscape of undulating farmland with herds of grazing cows, green fields of sugar cane and maize, extensive tropical-fruit gardens with their fine pineapples, bananas, melons, mangos, papaws, avocados, peanuts, and macadamia nuts. There are picturesque fishing villages in sheltered bays and mountains rising to more than 1,000m broken by deep ravines with cascading creeks. North-coast local patriots even assert, with some justification, that the sun rises in Australia in their territory because Cape Byron is the most easterly point of the mainland.

The first larger resort on the way is Port Macquarie, which is a great spot for a vacation. Established in 1821 as a convict settlement on the banks of the Hastings River, the Port, as it is affectionately known, is a favorite long-weekend target of Sydneysiders. It has 40 motels including some very good ones, a couple of licensed hotels, and two restaurants of respectable quality—one German, the other French. Port Macquarie's St. Thomas Church of England is the third oldest church in Australia (built between 1824 and 1828), and there is an interesting collection of convict relics in the local museum. There are the usual water-sport facilities and an interesting and fairly flat golf course, which will tax your skill but not your stamina. Two cruisers operate along the placid Hastings River. Situated up the river 19km away is Wauchope, an important timber center and railhead for Port Macquarie. Timbertown, 3km west of Wauchope, is the re-creation of a typical Australian timber town of the 1880s and is well worth a visit; activities include traveling on an old steam train, taking a wagon ride, seeing a bullock team working, and watching craftspeople in period dress demonstrating their skills. The Wauchope district also claims a record: It has the biggest blackbutt forest in the world.

Another worthwhile excursion from Port Macquarie is by car or coach to the Comboyne Plateau, a largely inaccessible wilderness of dense forest, waterfalls, and cascades, including the spectacular 150m Ellenborough Falls near the little township of Comboyne. The view—from Forster to Port Macquarie—is breathtaking. There is a difficult motor road to the world's largest blackbutt tree, a 300-year-old, 70m giant with a girth of 11m. It is advisable to join an organized tour to the Plateau.

North of Port Macquarie is Kempsey, a pretty town and headquarters for the Macleay River, with nine motels, six hotels, and five camper parks with on site vans and cabins. In the vicinity are a number of popular resorts: South West Rocks, Stuarts Point, Crescent Head, and Grassy Heads. They have excellent beaches for surfing and are patrolled by lifeguards during the season. There are two tourist attractions near South West Rocks—the old Trial Bay Jail with a museum and the Smoky Cape Lighthouse (open for inspection on Tuesday and Thursday) with beautiful views of long stretches of beaches and surf. A drive from Kempsey upstream along the Macleay River is well worthwhile. Nambucca Heads, 526km from Sydney, is another popular resort, and Shelley Beach, one of its beauty spots, has been favored by Australian and overseas painters. The next important town is Coffs Harbour, center of the largest banana-producing district in Australia (587km from Sydney). Among popular attractions there is the pet porpoise pool situated at Park Beach, where porpoises and Australian seals perform twice daily. Coffs Harbour has a championship 18-hole golf course and several very well-appointed camper parks. About 80km from Coffs Harbour is Grafton, situated on both sides of the Clarence River and famous for its Jacaranda Festival in the first week of November, when thousands of jacaranda trees are in full bloom.

The largest center on the New South Wales North Coast north of Newcastle is Lismore on the Richmond River—the longest navigable coastal river in the state. Thirty-one km from there is Ballina, one of the main fishing ports of the North Coast and a good place for fishing, surfing and sun-bathing. Cape Byron, 47km from Lismore, is the spot where the sun first greets Australia. Australia's most powerful lighthouse (claimed to be the second most powerful in the world, with a light of 3,000,000 candlepower) stands there. Cape Byron was named by Captain Cook in May 1770 after the grandfather of the poet Lord Byron, John Byron, who commanded a round-the-world voyage in 1764–1766. Near the Queensland border is one of the region's most attractive areas, the Tweed Valley, where the Tweed River meanders through its rich farmlands. The valley itself is dominated by the 1,157m Mt. Warning, which is accessible from the town of Murwillumbah. There is a marvelous vista from its peak—a rather arduous ascent for untrained climbers.

New England Region

Tourists who have had their fill of surf and beaches may find a pleasant change by driving from the ocean westward over one of the three highways to the New England region, the hinterland of the north coast.

The name New England has a nostalgic air—and not by chance. The region discovered by the explorer John Oxley in 1818, has an English atmosphere, especially in autumn (April, May) on the tablelands, which are situated at an average altitude of 900m above sea level with peaks up to 1,610m (Round Mountain). Here the thousands of trees imported from England and planted by English settlers shed their golden leaves in autumn. Winter is *really* winter, with snow and frost. However, only the mountains and the higher slopes of New England remind one of the northern hemisphere. Farther to the west, where the region's rich black soil plains spread out endlessly, you are in the "real Australia" again.

Although New England can offer much to the traveler, its tourist attractions are rather for the leisurely wayfarer than for the tourist with limited time. One of the unusual pastimes in the region is "fossicking" for gemstones. Looking for them has become so popular that a special reserve has been set aside in the Glen Innes district for amateur fossickers. It is unlikely that a find will make you rich, but it is good fun and needs neither great effort nor expensive equipment. What is necessary can be bought or hired from hardware stores in the township nearest to the localities where gemstones are found. The stones include beryl, aquamarine, emerald, topaz, sapphire, zircon, spinel, and diamonds. (New England is not opal country.) The best localities for fossicking are Emmaville, Torrington, Glen Innes, Inverell, Copeton, Tingha, Kingsgate, Oban, Uralla, Bendemeer, Hall Creek (in the Moonbi Range), Nundle and Bingara. A fossicker must obtain a license ($A2.50 single, $A5.00 for families) to fossick on Crown land. No license is necessary on private land available for fossicking. The Crown land license can be obtained either from the Department of Mineral Resources, 8 Bent Street, Sydney, tel. 231–0922, from the Mining Registrar in Armidale, or the Inverell Tourist Information Centre. Nullamunna Fossicking Reserve (tel. 067–22–1693) might be a good place to start your hunt. It is about 20km north east of Inverell and a $A3,000, 70-carat blue sapphire was found here in 1970. If you are not so lucky there are picnic and barbecue facilities to use instead of the pick.

Traveling north on the New England Highway the first important town is Tamworth, 449km from Sydney. It is a pleasant and prosperous agricultural center (pop. 29,656), and it claims to have been the first Australian city to use electricity for street lighting. Tamworth is also the country-music capital of Australia. The town comes alive during the last week of January, when the Australasian Country Music Awards attract artists and their audiences from throughout Australia. Some 94km farther is Uralla, which offers good angling in the downstream waters of the Macdonald River. "Thunderbolt," one of Australia's most notorious bushrangers (an euphemism for bandit), is buried in Uralla cemetery. He was shot dead by a policeman in May 1870.

A short drive (23km) from here is Armidale (pop. 21,500), the largest center of the New England Tablelands. It is 1,000m above sea level. The numerous educational institutions, including the University of New England and the Armidale College of Advanced Education, have stamped their mark on the city. With a large population of academics and students, Armidale has a lively cultural life. Its Hinton Benefaction Art Gallery contains what is probably the best collection of Australian paintings outside Sydney.

As Armidale is about halfway between Sydney and Brisbane on the New England Highway, it is a favorite resting place. However, it is well worth staying there not only overnight but for a full day to fully enjoy the surrounding beauty. Glen Innes, 99km from Armidale, is at the intersection of the New England and Gwydir highways, 1073m above sea level. It is another good stopover, with comfortable hotel and motel accommodation and several camper parks. Winter snowfalls can be rather severe there, as all along the tablelands section of the New England Highway.

The last large town on the highway before reaching Queensland is Tenterfield at the junction of the New England, Bruxner, and Mt. Lindesay highways. Tenterfield considers itself the birthplace of Australian Federation because it was in its School of Arts on October 24, 1889, that Sir Henry Parkes, then premier of New South Wales, delivered a speech that started the movement that, some 11 years later, brought about the Australian Commonwealth (the union of the six Australian states into one nation). Incidentally, in Australian usage, a school of arts may be but is usually not a place where the arts (painting, sculpture, etc.) are taught. It is a cultural center with a public library, lecture room, or hall and similar amenities. The Tenterfield School of Arts is now a national monument. The Boonoo Boonoo Falls (pronounced *bunnabernoo*), where a stream cascades 210m to the valley below, is some 30km along a rough road from the town.

The New England region has magnificent National Parks. For details see Practical Information, below.

The Northwest Country Region

The northwest region is not conventional tourist country, but those who like wide horizons and a sort of prairie atmosphere will be attracted to the seemingly unending expanses of the rich sheep and cattle raising and wheat growing part of Australia. The region is especially pleasant in spring and autumn when the days are mild and the nights are cool. It has a number of picturesque rivers—the Macquarie, Bogan, Castlereagh, Namoi, Gwydir and Macintyre—where fishing is good.

They flow northward and northwestward into the Darling, which empties into the Murray, which, in turn, ends in the Southern Ocean some 3,000km away. Most of the time they are friendly, useful waterways, but when rains swell them they become broad seas inundating hundreds of square kilometers of the countryside, drowning beasts and devastating property.

If you want to obtain the real feel of the region, travel all the way to Bourke, called the gateway to the Outback. Situated on the Darling, 789km by road from Sydney, the town is the hub of the world's richest wool producing area. There are some 300 sheep and cattle properties in the Bourke area, which produces an average of 50,000 bales of wool a year. A rodeo held at Bourke late in winter (July, August) is good fun if you like a spectacular show.

Besides sheep, cattle, and wheat, the most famous products of the region are opals, and the best place to find them is around Lightning Ridge, 766km by road from Sydney. The nearest town and railhead to the ridge is Walgett. One can stay either at Walgett or in the hotel or motels in the middle of the opal fields, which also have a number of all-amenities camper parks. Drop in and chat with the locals at the hotel for hints on how to find the opals and for some colorful stories.

The Lightning Ridge fields are the only source of the famous black opals. There, as well as in the nearby Glengarry and Grawin fields, you may find, in addition to opals, other semiprecious stones including agate, jasper, and topaz.

Australia's best-known spa for rheumatic complaints, Moree, is east of Lightning Ridge. The water is obtained from a well more than 900m deep. On the town's outskirts you will find vast cotton farms, harvested in April and May, and leafy green pecan farms.

The Outback Region

There could hardly be a better introduction to the Outback region than the warning of the NRMA to motorists intending to travel in the outback:

"1. The vehicle should be in first-class mechanical order and the driver, or some member of the party, should have a reasonable knowledge of running repairs. In addition to the normal spare, an extra wheel with tyre and tube should be carried. 2. In addition to the normal tool kit, which should include a good jack, tyre pump, shovel, axe and tow rope a dozen other items should be carried. [For full list ask for an NRMA pamphlet.] 3. A well equipped first aid kit, 4½ liters of drinking water per person, food and a reserve drum of petrol are essentials. 4. Advice should be sought from police or other responsible persons regarding road and weather conditions ahead. The advice should be rechecked at each opportunity en route. Your proposed itinerary should be known so that, if necessary, a search could be made more easily. If in need of assistance stay with your vehicle. Do not over-exert yourself and conserve your water supply."

That is the sort of advice you need in the region "back o' Bourke" if you venture off the highways and sealed roads. It's a big place—more than 12,000,000 hectares (29,600,000 acres), and it is inhabited only by some 2,000,000 sheep, who produce an average of 60,000 bales of wool annually. It is an arid place, and for hundreds of kilometers its borders with Queensland in the north and South Australia in the west are fenced against dingos (a sort of wild dog). Yet forbidding as most of the region is, it also has a strange wild beauty that attracts many tourists who like to face a challenge. This goes only for visitors who decide to organize their own expedition off the beaten track. Users of the regular transport systems are not exposed to any greater risks than commuters traveling between their suburbs and the city.

The main destination of the regular transport systems is the Outback region's only important urban center: Broken Hill, or the Silver City as it is nicknamed. Broken Hill, a city of 26,913 inhabitants, owes its existence to the world's richest known silver-lead and zinc deposits, on top of which it stands. Discovered by chance in 1883 by Charles Rasp, a German-born boundary rider (horsemen who check that fences of sheep and cattle paddocks are intact), the deposits are now mined by several big companies.

Although almost everything that humans and industry need must be brought to Broken Hill from considerable distances—the main water supply is pumped from the Darling River some 110km away—the city today is a very pretty place with well-kept gardens surrounding substantial dwellings and public buildings, including a modern civic center that would be the pride of much larger cities.

One of the most interesting peculiarities of Broken Hill is that for all practical purposes it is run by the Barrier Trades and Labour Council, the central body of the local trade unions. Together with the employers, it has worked out an effective mechanism for negotiating issues between the two sides.

Another unusual feature of Broken Hill is its very low crime rate and its thriving cultural activities. There are, for instance, several art galleries; one of Australia's most prominent painters who turned to art from mining, Pro Hart, lives there. It is the center of the Royal Flying Doctor Service and of the School of the Air. Its tourist attractions include organized inspections of some of the mines.

Outside Broken Hill, visitors to the Outback region may also enjoy a swim in the 16,200-hectare (40,000-acre) human-made Menindee Lake, 110km southeast of the city, where there are other water sports including water skiing. There is a camper park at the lake, connected to Broken Hill by a good road. The Kinchega National Park, 113km southeast of Broken Hill, is the home of the emu and the red kangaroo. Mootwingee, meaning "green grass," 132km north of Broken Hill, is a sacred Aboriginal tribal ground rich in rock engravings, cave paintings, and stencils of kangaroos, lizards, emu, and dingo tracks, some dating back 2,000 or 3,000 years. White Cliffs, northeast of Broken Hill, is worth a visit for opals.

A relaxing way to see the southern end of the vast Outback is by houseboat or paddlesteamer. Houseboats can be chartered at Wentworth and the Coonawarra.

The Murray Riverina Region

If you wish to spend a holiday in relaxing rather than scenically spectacular surroundings, somewhat off the main tourist track, one of a number of serene little towns along the New South Wales section of the mighty Murray River may be the place to go. The river, which rises in the Australian Alps and after a course of 2,600km empties its waters into the sea at Lake Alexandrina in South Australia, is a fisher's paradise. It also teems with bird life. A special attraction of the Murray region is the properties that take in paying guests for farm holidays.

The Murray was discovered by the explorers Hume and Hovell during their overland trip from Sydney to Port Phillip (Melbourne) in 1824. They called it the Hume. But six years later, in 1830, Captain Charles Sturt "discovered" it again and named it Murray after the British Colonial Secretary of that time. For about a quarter of a century between the early 1850s and the late 1870s the Murray and its tributaries were important trading and transportation channels, with some 100

NEW SOUTH WALES

paddlesteamers and 200 barges plying them. But with the development of the faster rail and road transport, shipping on the Murray began to decline; it finally ceased after World War II. However, in recent years several of the rusting old paddle-wheel river boats have been reconditioned and new ones built, and they are now being used as pleasure boats taking tourists on half-day excursions or week-long trips on several stretches of Australia's "Ol' Man River."

Albury (pop. 39,800) with its twin town of Wodonga across the Murray River in Victoria, was chosen as one of Australia's main "growth centers" in the Australian government's master plan, now suspended, to divert people from the state capitals on the coast. The choice was a good one. For Albury has many of the requirements of a potentially large urban center. It is situated along the main railway line and on one of the two main highways that connect Sydney (581km to the north) with Melbourne (308km to the south). The national capital of Canberra is 357km by road. About 3km from Albury is the airport with connections to all state capitals and many other places within and outside New South Wales. The Murray provides almost inexhaustible water supplies. The mainly agricultural hinterland is prosperous, and for pleasure and relaxation Albury is well provided with cultural and sporting amenities. In addition it is close to the playgrounds of the Australian Alps.

Those pleasant little townships along the Murray River include Corowa, with a first-class airfield and a fine 18-hole golf course; Mulwala (on a lake near Corowa) with a "boatel," where guests can moor their boats underneath their units (tel. 057–3928); Tocumwal, with good river beaches nearby; and Moama and Barham.

The Riverina part of this region will fascinate those interested in agricultural activities and irrigation schemes. Except for its mountainous southeastern part, the Riverina consists of a succession of sprawling plains with sheep and cattle pastures, wheat fields, and, on the irrigated land, orchards and vineyards. The 1690km Murrumbidgee (an Aboriginal word for "big river"), one of Australia's largest waterways, rolls through it, supplying the irrigation channels of the Murrumbidgee Irrigation Area (MIA)—1,300 square km of verdant oasis in an otherwise dry countryside.

Tourists driving from Sydney to Melbourne who wish to visit the MIA may stop at Wagga Wagga, "capital" of the Riverina (4485km southwest of Sydney), a thriving and developing town on the Murrumbidgee River with a population of about 36,832. A tour of Wagga Wagga and of the three main centers off the MIA, Narrandera, Leeton, and the wine town of Griffith, can fit into a day's outing.

The Snowy and South Coast Regions

The snowy and south-coast regions of New South Wales have some of the most varied concentrations of tourist attractions in Australia. The enchantingly beautiful south coast is world famous among big-game fishers. It has 250km of dreamy bays, inlets, and friendly little towns where visitors can stay at modern and well-run hotels, motels, or caravan parks. And a couple of hundred kilometers away the towering peaks of the Snowy Mountains and of the Kosciusko National Park gaze down on slopes that are snow covered in winter and bedecked with fragrant wildflowers in spring and summer. Here in the mountains is one of the world's greatest hydroelectric schemes with its picturesque artificial lakes and fast-flowing streams, which abound in trout and fish.

Until after World War II it was not easy to reach either the south coast or the Snowy Mountains from Sydney or Melbourne. Today travel is very good. The Princes Highway is a scenically charming road that meanders through lengthy stretches of timbered country near quiet inlets and bays. Motorists are advised not to drive very fast and to pass with great care on the winding, narrow road.

The seaside between Nowra and Durras Lake is studded with bays and lakes with well-developed holiday amenities. Jervis Bay (172km south of Sydney), which is partly Commonwealth of Australia territory and is the site of the Royal Australian Naval College and other naval establishments, is one of them. Others include Sussex Inlet at the mouth of the St. Georges Basin, Lake Conjola, Burrill Lake, Tabourie Lake, and Durras Lake. Just off Princes Highway, north of Ulladulla, is a lovely little spot called Mollymook with some of the south coast's finest beaches and a pleasant little golf course near the surf.

The Marlin Hotel, in neighboring Ulladulla, is well known among Australian and international big-game fishers for its service, accommodation, and cuisine. Fishing is the most important local industry, most of the fishers being of Italian descent. Their blessing-of-the-fleet festival, stretching over four days at Easter, includes the colorful ceremony of blessing the fishing boats by Catholic priests.

Some 50km south of Ulladulla one reaches the resort of Batemans Bay on the estuary of the Clyde River. Batemans Bay is just one of many south-coast towns excellent for fishing and for water sports. Fishing villages include Narooma (Aboriginal for "clear blue water") and Bermagui ("canoe-like"), which became internationally famous after the American novelist Zane Grey wrote about their exceptional big-game-fishing qualities. Two other popular resorts are beautifully situated Merimbula (473km from Sydney) and, about 50km farther to the south, Eden, a tuna-fishing center.

There are two good roads from the southeast coast to Cooma, the gateway to the Snowy Mountains. One leads from Batemans Bay through Braidwood and Canberra and another, the Snowy Mountains Highway (branching off Bermagui and Merimbula) through Nimmitabel. Cooma is the most cosmopolitan town in Australia; its 8,000 inhabitants were born in 50 different countries. People of 27 nationalities helped build the Snowy Mountains Hydro-Electric Scheme and their national colors are displayed on high poles in the Avenue of Flags in the town's Centennial Park. Every year thousands of visitors descend on Cooma—mainly skiers in winter and a good many trout fishers in summer—and many spend a night in the town before dispersing to their destinations in the mountains the following morning.

Mountains and Skiing

The Snowy Mountains cover an area of hundreds of square kilometers and have Australia's highest peaks, including the tallest of them all, the 2230m Mount Kosciusko. Why Kosciusko? Because the Polish explorer Paul Edmund de Strzelecki, who found it in 1840, named it after his country's national hero. The national park of the same name, with an area of 6,143 square km, is the largest national park in the New South Wales and contains all the state's snowfields. In Australia skiing has become a popular sport only since World War II. Before the war there were only a state-owned hotel and two chalets in the whole vast snow country. Now there are dozens of hotels, motels, and lodges for the general public and many clubs have built "huts," some quite substantial, for their members. One of the main ski centers is Thredbo Village on the Alpine Way at the foot of Mt. Crackenback (1936m), a wilderness some 25 years ago and now a lively playground with ski lifts and tows on the slopes and shops and nightclubs for after-ski in the village. It was Charles Anton, an Austrian refugee from Hitler and a ski enthusiast, who saw the potential of the area in the late 1940s and started the movement for a ski village at Thredbo. The Ramshead Range divides Thredbo from the other two main ski centers of the Kosciusko National Park: Smiggin Holes and Perisher Valley. The old chalet at Charlotte's Pass, near the top of Mt. Kosciusko, is open in the ski season and in the summer holidays. It has been recently refurbished, has excellent ski slopes nearby, and is the best starting point for day-long excursions into the silent white world of the Main Range. If you want to spend a few days in the snow country but have no gear, you need not worry. Practically everything can be hired in Sydney, in Melbourne, or on the spot.

Electricity and Trout Fishing

How to use water instead of letting it run to waste in the sea is an old preoccupation of Australians. It was in 1884 that the New South Wales surveyor-general of that time, P. F. Adams, made a revolutionary proposal. He suggested that the waters of the Snowy River, which rises on the eastern slopes of the Snowy Mountains near Mt. Kosciusko and enters the Tasman Sea after winding southward for about 435km, should be turned inland and used for irrigation. It took another 65 years before work on the scheme was started, in August 1949, by the newly created Snowy Mountains Hydro-Electric Authority. But then the work was executed on a truly grand scale. Since then the waters of the Snowy Mountains have been diverted into the Murray-Murrumbidgee river system and used not only for irrigation but also for the generation of electric power. Sixteen large dams and many smaller ones, seven power stations, about 130km of roads, and 80km of aqueducts have been built. The last generator began production in 1974. Total generating capacity of electric power is 4 million kilowatts, and 2,500 million cubic meters of water are available annually for irrigation.

The human-made lakes and dams and the opening of the rugged Snowy Mountains by roads have enabled the Snowy Mountains Hydro-Electric Authority to create a large trout-fishing region, which is surely the best in Australia and a very good one by world standards. The anglers who flock there have added to the development of the mountains as a winter-summer resort paradise that is growing year by year. But the controlled growth is not allowed to threaten the environment or the scenery. Many establishments are now open all the year except for a few weeks around May, a midseason period when the weather in the area is least favorable for vacationing.

The Golden West Region

The golden-west region is a vast, prosperous, mainly pastoral area of New South Wales with one main tourist attraction: the Jenolan Caves. Yet if you want to spend a few days or even weeks relaxing in a rural atmosphere, living the life of the people on the land, this is an excellent area in which to do it. Several homesteads take in paying guests, giving the visitor a sheep-station holiday where he or she can watch or participate in work on the property. Most of these places are near the towns of Bathurst, Orange, Cowra and Parkes.

The region is full of places closely connected with Australia's early history. Bathurst, for instance, is Australia's oldest inland city, founded by Governor Lachlan Macquarie in 1815, two years after the crossing of the Blue Mountains by Blaxland, Wentworth, and Lawson. It was near this town that gold was discovered, starting Australia's colorful gold-rush days. This was also one of the most notorious bushranger areas, where outlaws made life insecure until well into the second half of the last century.

Cowra, a town of the golden-west region, saw one of the most dramatic, behind-the-front-line episodes of the Pacific zone in World War II. On August 4, 1944, Japanese prisoners of war in the Cowra camp attempted a mass break for freedom. It was a suicidal venture in which some 250 Japanese and four Australian soldiers died. They are buried in separate well-tended cemeteries adjacent to each other.

Dubbo, with a population of 32,285, is the largest town in the region and has 25 motels for travelers. It is a popular stopping-off place for motorists traveling between Melbourne and Brisbane on the Newell Highway.

There are several ways to visit the region's most interesting tourist attraction, the Jenolan Caves. They are 183km by road from Sydney and can be seen in one day's return trip. But it is advisable to spend at least one night at Jenolan Caves House, a pleasant old-fashioned hotel built in 1898 (and several times extended and renovated since) where accommodation is comfortable and the tariff reasonable. (Book through Travel Centre of N.S.W., tel: 02–231–4444.) Another, and perhaps even more pleasant way is to combine a visit to the caves with a holiday in the Blue Mountains near Sydney, for the caves are only 77km from Katoomba.

The discovery of the Jenolan Caves is connected with an episode in the "romantic" history—as it is now regarded—of the bushranger era. In the 1830s an escaped convict called James McKeown was the terror of travelers along the Western Road in the Blue Mountains. In 1838, one of his victims, James Whalan, decided to take revenge by hunting down the bushranger in his hideout. He found McKeown's tracks and followed them on horseback through unexplored country until—after riding through a huge natural archway that he called the Devil's Coachhouse—he looked down on a peaceful valley with a small farm at the bottom. He concluded that it must be the bushranger's refuge, and next day he returned with his brother Charles and a couple of troopers. They captured McKeown in a big cave in the mountainside—now known as McKeown's Hole—and found that the place was full of similar "holes." After delivering McKeown to the authorities, the brothers returned and explored more of the caves.

In 1866 the New South Wales government declared the caves and their environment a reserve. A lot of work has been done on both over the years, and now the caves can be comfortably inspected.

Jenolan has two types of caves, great natural archways, which can be inspected independently, and underground "dark" caves, which can be visited only in the company of a guide. Cave tours depart throughout the day, and there is one at night. They last about an hour and a half. No special clothing is necessary, but well-soled shoes are advisable.

Another group of caves at Abercrombie, some 76km from Bathurst, are not as spectacular as the Jenolan Caves but have a grand arch claimed to be the greatest natural tunnel in the world. It is 221m long, 60m wide, and in places more than 30m high.

Wellington also has caves, with regular tours daily and excellent picnic facilities nearby, as well as a camper park and cabins. Accommodations here may be booked by phoning (068) 45–2970.

Lord Howe Island

The tiny—11km long, 2km wide—Lord Howe Island is a heavily forested green speck 702km east of Sydney in the Pacific Ocean. What it can offer to tourists is pleasant climate the year round, relaxing holidays with such unsophisticated pastimes as fishing, bushwalking,

NEW SOUTH WALES

or bicycling, and accommodation in simple guest houses. The island has a permanent population of some 250. Many of its visitors are "regulars" who return for a holiday year after year. There is a golf course.

Transport from the mainland to Lord Howe (which is a dependency of New South Wales) is by air.

Norfolk Island

Norfolk Island, 1449km off the east coast of Australia, is a beautiful little (8km long, 4km wide) spot of volcanic origin in the Pacific Ocean. Since 1914 it has been a territory of the Australian Commonwealth. (Before that it belonged to New South Wales.)

Every year some 10,000 people spend their holidays on the island; fishing, swimming, walking, playing golf (on a nine-hole course) and bowls—or simply lazing in the mellow sunshine.

Norfolk Island has an interesting history. Sighted by Captain Cook in 1774, it became a penal colony in 1788. Until 1855, when it was closed, the most intractable prisoners were sent there. Some of the buildings they erected are still in use; they form the nucleus of Kingston, the administrative headquarters of the island.

In 1856, the year after the last convict had been taken from the island, the place was voluntarily settled by the 194 residents of Pitcairn Island. They were the descendants of the mutineers of the *Bounty* who, in 1789, had cast adrift in an open boat their captain, William Bligh, with 18 of the men who wished to go with him. The mutineers, commanded by Fletcher Christian, then settled on Pitcairn Island with some Polynesian (Tahitian) women. Today half of Norfolk Island's permanent population of about 1,000 have a *Bounty* ancestry.

PRACTICAL INFORMATION FOR
NEW SOUTH WALES BEYOND SYDNEY

PHONE NUMBERS: When ringing Sydney and its suburbs from other areas the prefix code is 02. For all areas other than Sydney the prefix codes are shown in parentheses before the telephone number.

HOW TO GET THERE. Sydney, the capital of New South Wales, is the main gateway of eastern Australia. Passenger ships from overseas call at Sydney Harbour, and scheduled international passenger aircraft land at the city's *Kingsford Smith* airport. From North America, *Qantas, United, Continental, Air New Zealand,* and *UTA French Airlines* all fly to Sydney. Sydney is also well provided with transport to and from other capital cities by rail, air, and road. You can sometimes book a berth on a ship that happens to be sailing between Sydney and another Australian port.

By rail: Two overnight trains run between Sydney and Melbourne seven days a week (about a 13-hour trip). They are the *Southern Aurora* (sleeper only) and the *Spirit of Progress*. The daytime *Intercapital Daylight* runs from Monday to Saturday. The best trains between Sydney and other capital cities are: Brisbane, *the Brisbane Limited* (15 ¾ hours); Canberra, the *Canberra XPT* (4 hours)— both daily; Perth, *the Indian Pacific* (2 ½ days)—Sunday, Thursday, and Saturday.

By air: Both *Australian Airlines* (16 Elizabeth Street, Sydney, 02–693–3333) and *Ansett* (Cnr Oxford and Riley streets, Darlinghurst, 02–268–1111) operate frequent flights daily between Sydney and all other state capitals. *East West Airlines* (02–2–0940) also services a number of interstate routes.

By bus: *Ansett Pioneer, Greyhound, Deluxe, Olympic East West Express,* and *VIP* run express coach services from Adelaide, Brisbane, Melbourne, and Perth to Sydney. Ansett Pioneer also services the Canberra-to-Sydney route. Further information from: Ansett Pioneer, Cnr Oxford and Riley streets, Darlinghurst, 02–258–1881; Greyhound, same address, 02–268–1414; Deluxe Coachlines, Cnr Hay and Castlereagh streets, Sydney, 02–212–4888; Olympic East West Express, 405 Pitt Street, Sydney, 02–212–3100; Australian VIP Leisure Tours, 700 George Street, Sydney, 02–211–3166.

TOURIST INFORMATION. For information on traveling in NSW and to make bookings for transport tours or accommodation contact the *Travel Centre of New South Wales,* Cnr Pitt and Spring streets, Sydney; 02–23 –1444; Cnr Queen and Edward streets, Brisbane; 07–31–1838; 353 Little Collins Street, Melbourne, 03–67–7461.

The Blue Mountains. Blue Mountains Tourist Information Centre, Echo Point, Katoomba; (047) 82–1833. Open daily.

Upper Hawkesbury. Hawkesbury Tourist and Information Centre, Cnr Windsor Road and Groves Avenue, McGrath's Hill; (045) 77–5915. Parramatta Tourist Information Centre, Market Street, Parramatta; (02)–630–3703

The Illawarra. Bomaderry-Nowra: Princes Highway, Bomaderry; (044) 21–0778 Open daily. Gerringong: 100 Fern Street; (042) 34–1175. Kiama: Council Chambers, Princes Highway; (042) 32–1122. Open Monday–Friday. Mittagong: Southern Highlands Visitors Centre, Hume Highway; (048) 71–2888. Open daily. Wollongong: Leisure Coast Visitors Centre, Crown Street; (042) 28–0300. Open daily.

Central coast. The Visitors Information Centre, 200 Mann Street, Gosford; (043) 25–2835. Open daily.

The Hunter. Cessnock, Cnr. Wollombi and Mount View Roads; (049) 9–0477. Open daily. Forster, Tourist Information Centre, Little Street; (065) 54–8541. Open Monday–Friday mornings and weekends. Hexham, Tourist Information Centre, Cnr. Pacific and New England highways; (049) 64–8006. Open 9 A.M.–4 P.M., Monday–Friday, 10 A.M.–2 P.M. Saturday and Sunday. Hunter Valley Wine Society, 4 Wollombi Road, Cessnock; (049) 90–6699. Maitland, King Edward Park, New England Highway, East Maitland; (049) 33–6200. Open weekends and public holidays. Maitland City Council, High Street; (049) 33–6200. Open Monday-Friday. Nelson Bay, Victoria Parade; (049) 81–1579. Open daily. Newcastle, City Hall, King Street; (049) 26–2323. Open Monday–Friday. Singleton, Townhead Park, Maitland Road; (065) 72–3973. Open Friday–Sunday and public holidays. Taree, Pacific Highway; (065) 52–1801. Open daily.

The NRMA maintains more than a dozen depots in the Hunter region where motorists in trouble can obtain help on the road. If not in possession of an NRMA list of depots call the Association's Newcastle branch 8 Auckland Street, (049) 2–4821, for information.

The North Coast. There are several regional tourist associations with headquarters at important centers and knowledgeable staffs. Coffs Harbour, Park Ave.; (066) 52–1522. Grafton, Duke and Victoria streets; (066) 42–4677. Lismore, Tourist Information Centre, Ballina Street; (066) 21–1519. Murwillumbah: Pacific Highway; (066) 72–1340. Port Macquarie, Horton Street; (065) 83–1293. Kempsey, off Pacific Highway; (065) 62–5444. Tweed Heads, Pacific Highway; (075) 36–2634.

New England. Armidale: 135 Rusden Street; (067) 72–3771. Glen Innes: 94 Church Street; (067) 32–2397; Inverell: Cnr Captain Cook Drive and Campbell Street; (067) 22–3830; Tenterfield: Shire Council Chambers, Rouse Street; (067) 36–1744. Open Monday–Friday.

North West. North West Tourist Association, Anzac Park, Oxley Highway, Gunnedah; (067) 42–1564. Moree: Jellicoe Park, Alice Street; (067) 52–9559. Tamworth: CWA Park, Cnr New England Highway and Kable Avenue; (067) 66–36. Bourke: Tourist Information Centre, 14 Richmond St.

The Outback. Broken Hill, Information Center, Cnr Bromide and Blend streets, Broken Hill; (080) 60–77.

The Murray Riverina. Albury: Travel Centre of NSW, Wodonga Place, Hume Highway; (060) 21–2655. Open daily. Albury Travel Bureau, 550 Dean

Street; (060) 21–1477. Open Monday–Saturday. Deniliquin: End Street, Tel. (058) 81–2878. Open Monday–Saturday. Griffith: Cnr Banna and Jondaryn Avenue; (069) 62–4145. Open daily. Gundagai: Sheridan Street; (069) 44–1341. Open daily. Hay: Moppet Street; (069) 93–1003. Open Monday–Friday. Leeton: Chelmsford Place; (069) 53–2611. Open daily. Narrandera: Narrandera Park, Newell Highway; (069) 59–1766. Open Monday–Friday and school-holiday weekends. Wagga Wagga: Tarcuttas Street; (069) 21–3361. Open Monday–Friday.

The Snowy. Cooma: Sharp Street; (0648) 2–1177 or 2–1108. Open daily. Goulburn: 2 Montague Street; (048) 21–5343. Jindabyne: Snowy River Information Centre, Petamin Plaza; (0648) 6–2444. Open daily. Queanbeyan: Farrer Place; (062) 98–0241. Open Monday–Friday, and Saturday morning. Thredbo: Thredbo Resort Centre; (0648) 7–6360. Open daily in winter; variable hours in summer. Tumut: Fitzroy Street; (069) 47–1849. Open daily. Yass: Shire Council Building; (062) 26–2557. Open daily. Kosciusko National Park: Visitors' Centre, Sawpit Creek (on Mt. Kosciusko Road); (0648) 6–2102. Open daily.

South Coast. Bateman's Bay, Princes Highway; (044) 72–4225. Open daily. Bega, Gipps Street; (0649) 2–2045. Open Monday to Friday, and Saturday and Sunday mornings during school holidays. Bermagui, 24 Bridge Street; (0649) 3–4565. Open daily. Eden, Princes Highway, South Eden; (0649) 6–1953. Open daily. Merimbula, Town Centre; (0649) 5–1129. Open Monday–Friday and mornings on weekends and public holidays. Moruya, Council Chambers, Moruya; (044) 74–1000. Open Monday–Friday. Narooma, Princes Highway; (044) 76–2881. Open Monday–Friday and mornings on weekends. Nowra/Bomaderry, Princes Highway, Bomaderry; (044) 21–0778. Open daily. Tathra, Andy Poole Drive; (0649) 4–1487. Open daily. Ulladulla, Civic Centre; (044) 55–1269. Open Monday–Saturday and Sunday morning.

Golden West. Bathurst, Court House, Russell Street; (063) 33–6288. Open daily. Cowra, Civic Centre, Kendall and Darling streets; (063) 42–4333. Open daily. Dubbo, 232 Macquarie Street; (068) 82–5359. Open daily. Forbes, 69 Lachlan Street; (068) 52–2330. Open Monday–Friday and Saturday morning. Mudgee, 64 Market Street; (063) 72–1944. Open daily. Orange, Civic Gardens, Byng Street; (063) 62–4215. Open daily. Parkes, Dubbo Road; (068) 62–1011. Open daily. Wellington, Cameron Park, Nanima Crescent; (068) 45–2001. Open daily. Young, Cnr Lynch and Boorowa streets; (063) 82–3394. Open Monday–Friday, and Saturday morning.

Lord Howe Island. Lord Howe Island Tourist Centre, 20 Loftus Street, Sydney 2000; 02–27–2867. The Travel Centre of NSW.

Norfolk Island. Norfolk Island Government Tourist Bureau offices: Taylors Road, Burnt Pine, Norfolk Island, tel: Norfolk Island 2147; 64 Castlereagh St., Sydney, 02–235–3937; Jolimont Centre, Northbourne Avenue, Canberra City; (062) 45–6435; 247 Collins St., Melbourne; (03) 654–1393.

HOW TO GET AROUND. The state has very extensive air, rail, and road transport services. **By air:** Air services sometimes extend their reach into country New South Wales by car services from the airport to other towns. These extensions are indicated in parentheses. *East West Airlines* (323 Castlereagh Street, Sydney 02–2–0940) carries passengers to Albury-Wodonga (Falls Creek in Victoria), Canberra, Glen Innes, Gold Coast in Queensland, Grafton, Inverell, Kempsey (Macksville, Nambucca Heads), Port Macquarie (Wauchope), Tamworth (Gunnedah), Taree (Forster). *Air New South Wales* (Building 49, Keith Smith Avenue, Kingsford Smith Airport, Mascot, 02–268–1242): Broken Hill, Canberra, Casino (Ballina, Byron Bay, Lismore), Coffs Harbour, Cooma (Jindabyne, Perisher, Thredbo), Coonabarabran, Coonamble, Dubbo (Narromine, Warren), Gold Coast, Griffith, Merimbula (Bega, Eden), Moree, Mudgee, Narrabri, Narrandera (Leeton), Wagga Wagga, Walgett (Lightning Ridge). Smaller airlines offer commuter services between Sydney and a number of New South Wales towns, or between towns. Special Fares and discounts on normal fares are offered by both major intrastate airlines. East West Airlines offers a 35% discount fare to major destinations, but you must stay a minimum of one night and a maximum of one month at your destination. Air New South Wales offers a Network 30 fare to overseas visitors (this must be ticketed outside Australia, but you can book your flights on arrival): 30% discount on any of its services, except Norfolk Island, with a minimum of one night's stopover required between sectors.

AUSTRALIA

By rail: The *State Rail Authority* (Rail Travel Center, Ground Floor, Transport House, 11–31 York Street, Sydney, 02–217–8819) operates trains from Sydney to destinations throughout the state as well as a coach link from some railheads to other country towns. The government has been upgrading the rail services in the past five years and there are now fast and comfortable XPT trains operating on many routes. On commuter services discount fares are available. The Nurail Pass offers 14-day unlimited first-class travel within NSW for $A120. The SRA also offers a variety of day or extended tours, incorporating rail, coach and launch travel, in NSW. A range of holidays from 2 to 8 days includes four days in Snowy River country and Canberra, 6 to 8 days on a sheep station where one can become acquainted with life on an Australian property (including horse riding, sheep mustering and shearing, etc.) but with all the comforts provided, or up to a week of surf and sun at coastal towns such as Port Macquarie, Byron Bay or Coffs Harbour.

By bus: Some towns in NSW are connected to Sydney by bus services; however, government regulations generally do not allow buses to service areas that are accessible by rail. There are express buses from Sydney to: Ballina (*Kirklands Australia,* 4 Magellan Street, Lismore, 02–267–5030 or 06–21–2755), Cessnock (*Batterhams Bus Lines,* 181 Vincent Street, Cessnock, 049–90–5000), Port Macquarie (*Skennars Coachlines,* 52 Clarence Street, Port Macquarie, 065–83–1488 or 200 George Street Sydney, 02–27–7951), Cooma and the snowfields (*Ansett Pioneer,* 02–268–1363). To reach South Coast towns, the train operates to Nowra and is then met by the bus (Pioneer Motor Services, Stewart Place, Nowra, 044–21–7722). In addition to day tours from Sydney (see *Practical Information for Sydney*), a variety of tours are offered in comfortable air-conditioned coaches through country New South Wales. Departures are not always frequent, but include 3- to 5-day trips to Canberra and the Snowy Mountains, 11 days to Brisbane via opal country at Lightning Ridge and the North Coast, and a 7-day "Red Carpet" tour to Melbourne. Companies offering bus tours are *AAT Kings Tours,* 46 Kent Road, Mascot, 02–669–5444; *Australian Pacific Tours,* 109–123 O'Riordan Street, Mascot, 02–693–2222 or 008–42–5353; *Clipper Tours,* 9–11 Alma Road, North Ryde, 02–888–3144; *Newmans Coach Holidays,* 1st Floor, Network House, 84 Pitt Street, Sydney, 02–231–6511; *Sunbeam Tours,* 3rd Floor, Dymocks Building, 428 George Street, Sydney, 02–231–2355.

RENTING CARS, CAMPERS, AND BOATS. The independently minded who wish to move around by themselves and camp may rent all they need for that purpose.

Cars. *Avis Rent-a-Car,* 140 Pacific Highway, North Sydney, 02–922–8181; *Budget Rent-a-Car,* 93 William Street, Sydney, 02–339–8888; *Hertz Rent-a-Car,* 65 William Street, Sydney, 02–357–6621.

Campervans. *John Terry Motors,* Cnr Hill Crest Street and Parramatta Road, Homebush, 02–764–3444; *Meridian Holidays,* Box 90, Mosman 2088, 02–29–3880; *Holiday Motorhome Rentals,* 314 Princes Highway, Banksia, 02–597–2533; *Newmans Sunseeker Campervan Rentals,* 16–20 Parramatta Road, Summer Hill, 02–797–6133; *Campervans Australia* (national licensee of Budget Rent-a-Car), 745 Princes Highway, Tempe, 02–559–1511.

Campers. *Parravans,* Cnr Windsor and Grove roads, McGraths Hill, 045–77–577. If you do not wish to tow your own van many caravan parks in NSW have on-site vans to hire.

Houseboats. *Aquapark Holidays,* River Road, Wisemans Ferry, 045–66–4308; *Fenwicks Hawkesbury River Houseboats,* Box 55, Brooklyn NSW 2253, 02–455–1333; *Holidays-a-Float,* 65 Brooklyn Road, Brooklyn, 02–455–1368; *Newcastle Holiday Houseboats,* Box 29, Buladelah 2423, 049–97–4221; *Manning River Houseboats,* 36 Crescent Avenue, Taree, 065–52–6271; *Gold Coast Houseboat Hire,* 161 Pacific Highway, Murwillumbah, 066–72–3525; *Aquavilla Houseboats,* Box 173, Wentworth 2648, 050–27–3396.

Boats. Cruisers: *Clippers Anchorage,* Akuna Bay, Hawkesbury River, Coal and Candle Creek in Ku-ring-gai Chase National Park, 02–450–1888; *Halvorsen Boats,* Ku-ring-gai Chase National Park, Bobbin Head, 02–457–9011. Sailing Boats, Aweekaway Yacht Charters. Box 520, Newport NSW 2106, 02–997–2566; *Broken Bay Yacht Charter,* Box 317, Mona Vale NSW 2103, 02–99–2043; *Meridian Boating Services,* Box 90, Mosman 2088. 02–29–3880; *Sail Australia,* Sydney Harbour: 23A King George Street, North Sydney, 02–957–2577; Pittwater: Church Point Ferry Wharf, Church Point, 02–977–3171.

NEW SOUTH WALES

ACCOMMODATIONS. The same price classifications have been used for country New South Wales as for Sydney. Throughout the state you will find most of the motel rates fall within the $A30–$A40 range for a double room with its own bathroom; you will not find any plush, deluxe accommodations in the country.

THE BLUE MOUNTAINS

Besides hotels and motels, there are many charming guest houses to choose from. The Blue Mountains are a popular weekend retreat for Sydneysiders looking for fresh air, Old World but comfortable accommodations, and excellent restaurants. In guest houses rooms do not usually have private bathrooms.

BLACKHEATH. Cleopatra. *Expensive.* Cleopatra Street; (047) 87–8456. 5 rooms, most without private bathroom. Australian colonial country house, excellent meals. Unlicensed. Open Friday–Sunday night. All meals included.
 Kubba Roonga. *Moderate.* 9 Brentwood Avenue; (047) 87–8330. 7 rooms without private bathrooms. French-Vietnamese cuisine. Large garden. Dinner and breakfast included.
 Redleaf Motel. *Inexpensive.* Brightlands Avenue; (047) 87–8108. 42 units, 4 suites, all with showers. Pool, sauna.

LEURA. Everglades Village Inn. *Moderate.* 70 Gladstone Road; (047) 84–1317. 54 units, private showers, heated pool, tennis, squash, sauna. Near golf course.
 Little Company Guesthouse. *Moderate.* 2 Eastview Avenue; (047) 82–4023. 10 rooms. Once a convent. Tennis, croquet. Dinner and breakfast included.

KATOOMBA. Balmoral House. *Moderate.* 196 Great Western Highway; (047) 82–2264. 8 rooms (1 with private bathroom). Restored Victorian-era guesthouse. Breakfast included, restaurant open for dinner.
 Alpine Motor Inn. *Inexpensive.* Cnr Great Western Highway and Orient Street; (047) 82–2141. 19 units, 6 suites, all with showers; pool, sauna.

UPPER HAWKESBURY

PARRAMATTA. Parramatta City Motel. *Inexpensive.* Cnr Great Western Highway and Marsden Street; 02–635–7266. 44 units with showers. Pool.

WINDSOR. Alexander the Great Motel. *Inexpensive.* Windsor Road; (045) 77–5555. 24 units with showers. Pool.

THE ILLAWARRA

BERRIMA. Berrima Bakehouse. *Inexpensive.* Cnr. Wingecarribee Street and Hume Highway; (048) 77–1381. 18 units with showers, central heating, pool.

BOWRAL. Berida Manor Country Retreat. *Expensive.* David Street; (048) 61–1177. 40 units with showers. Excellent restaurant.
 Craigieburn. *Moderate.* 66 Centennial Road; (048) 61–1277. 66 rooms (62 with showers/baths). TV lounge, pool, golf course.
 Golf View. *Inexpensive.* Boronia Street; (048) 61–2777. 23 units with showers. Restaurant (closed Sunday). Pool, tennis.
 Tudor Motor Inn. *Inexpensive.* Cnr Moss Vale & Links roads; (048) 612–1911. 28 units with showers, central heating, air cooling.

BUNDANOON. Bundanoon Hotel. *Inexpensive.* Erith Street; (048) 83–6005. 46 rooms, some private bathrooms.
 Tree Tops Guesthouse. *Inexpensive.* 101 Railway Parade; (048) 83–6372. 6 rooms without private bathrooms. Dinner and breakfast included.

AUSTRALIA

JAMBEROO. Gundarimba Guest House and Restaurant. *Expensive.* 45 Allowrie Street; (042) 36–0228. 6 rooms without private bathrooms.

KIAMA. Briggdale Seaside. *Inexpensive.* Princes Highway; (042) 32–1767. 7 units with showers, heaters and fans, barbecue.
Gibsons Beachfront. *Inexpensive.* 9 Bong Bong Street; (042) 32–1372. 17 units with showers and baths. Overlooks beach.
The Pines. *Inexpensive.* Bong Bong Street; (042) 32–1000. 28 units with showers. Pool, sauna; on surf beach.

MITTAGONG. Melrose. *Inexpensive.* Hume Highway; (048) 71–1511. 6 units with showers. Central heating.
Poplars. *Inexpensive.* Hume Highway; (048) 89–4239. 15 units, 1 suite with shower.

MOSS VALE. Bong Bong Motel. *Inexpensive.* 238 Argyle Street; (048) 91–1033. 10 units.
Dormie House Private Hotel. *Inexpensive.* Arthur Street; (048) 91–1033. 31 rooms, 3 suites with showers. Adjoins golf course. Dinner and breakfast included.

WOLLONGONG. Northbeach International. *Expensive.* Cliff Road, North Wollongong; (042) 27–1188. 72 units, 1 suite, all with showers. Pool, restaurant; overlooks water.
Boat Harbour Motel. *Inexpensive.* 7 Wilson Street; (042) 28–9166. 44 units with showers. Air conditioned, restaurant (closed Sundays and public holidays).

CENTRAL COAST

GOSFORD. Willows Motel. *Moderate.* 512 Pacific Highway; (043) 28–4666. 50 units, 4 suites with showers. Pool. Air conditioning.
Gosford Motor Inn. *Inexpensive.* 23 Pacific Highway; (043) 23–1333. 36 units with showers. Pool, barbecue, air conditioning.

TERRIGAL. Cobb & Co Motor Inn. *Moderate.* 154 Terrigal Drive; (043) 84–1166. 48 units with showers and baths. Pool, spa, sauna. Near beach.

THE ENTRANCE. Ocean Front Motel. *Moderate.* 102 Ocean Parade; (043) 32–5911. 12 units with showers. On the beach.

TOOWOON BAY. Kim's Camp. *Expensive.* Charlton Avenue; (043) 32–1566. 34 units with showers. Cabin-style accommodations right on the beach. Delicious meals; a favorite retreat for families.

WOY WOY. Glades Country Club Colonial Motor Inn. *Inexpensive.* Cnr Durban Road and Everglades Crescent; (043) 41–7374. 22 units with showers. Air conditioned, pool.

THE HUNTER

Besides hotels and motels in the Hunter, holiday flats and cottages are also available, as are farm holidays. Inquire at the tourist information center or National Roads and Motorists Association, 151 Clarence St., Sydney; 02–260–9222.

CESSNOCK. Cumberland Motor Inn. *Inexpensive.* 57 Cumberland Street; (049) 90–6633. 29 units with showers. Air conditioned. Pool. Restaurant (closed Sunday).

FORSTER. Forster Motor Inn. *Inexpensive.* 11 Wallis Street; (065) 54–6877. 28 units, 2 suites with showers. Air conditioned. Barbecue, pool, restaurant (closed Sunday).

NEW SOUTH WALES

GLOUCESTER. Altamira (Farm Property). *Inexpensive.* Bakers Creek Road; (065) 50–6558. Motel-style units. All meals. Horse riding, bushwalking, pool, tennis.

MAITLAND. Toll Bar Motor Inn. *Inexpensive.* 279 New England Highway, Rutherford; (049) 32–5255. 40 units with showers. Air conditioning, heating, pool, restaurant.

NELSON BAY. Peninsula Motor Inn. *Inexpensive.* 52 Shoal Bay Road; (049) 81–3666. 26 units with showers. Air conditioned; barbecue, pool.

NEWCASTLE. Telford. *Moderate.* Cnr Shortland Esplanade and Zaara Street; (049) 2–5181. 90 units, 1 suite with shower. Air conditioning, pool, restaurant. On beachfront.
   Travelodge. *Moderate.* Shortland Esplanade; (049) 25–5576. 72 units with showers. Air conditioned; pool, restaurant. Overlooks beach.

SINGLETON. Charbonnier of the Hunter Motel. *Inexpensive.* 44 Maitland Road; (065) 72–2333. 68 units, 4 suites with showers. Air conditioned. Barbecue, pool, spa and sauna, restaurant. A very good motel with a wide range of services offered.

TAREE. El Greco Motor Inn. *Inexpensive.* Oxley Street (Pacific Highway); (065) 52–1455. 16 units with showers. Air conditioned; pool, playground.

THE NORTH COAST

There are a very large number caravan parks and camp grounds in the region. However, it is advisable to book well ahead, especially during the holiday season. Bookings by telephone can be made either directly to the caravan parks or through the regional tourist centers. (See Camping, below.)

Since the north coast is such a popular holiday area for Australians, there is no shortage of good-quality accommodations. These include holiday apartments and cottages, hotels and motels, and farm-holiday properties. Many are within walking distance of fine beaches.

BALLINA. All Seasons Motor Inn. *Budget–Inexpensive.* 301 Pacific Highway, (066) 86–2922. 40 units with showers. Restaurant, air conditioning, pool.
   El Rancho Motor Inn. *Budget–Inexpensive.* Cnr Chevy and Fox streets, (066) 86–3333. 19 units with showers. Air conditioning, restaurant, barbecue, pool, playground; good for family groups.

BYRON BAY. Cape Byron Resort Motel. *Budget–Inexpensive.* 16 Lawson Street; (066) 85–7663. 15 units with showers. Air conditioning, cooking facilities, restaurant, pool, spa, barbecue, children's playground. Two minutes' walk to beach.

COFFS HARBOUR. Coffs Harbour Holiday Village Motor Inn. *Inexpensive.* 97 Park Beach Road; (066) 52–2055. 28 units with showers. Restaurant, barbecue, pool, spa, sauna.
   Nautilus Beach Resort. *Inexpensive to moderate* (some apartments *expensive*). Pacific Highway, Kororo (7km north of Coffs Harbour); (066) 53–6699. 44 units with showers; restaurant, barbecue, pool, spa, sauna, tennis and golf. Beach frontage.

GRAFTON. Abbey Motor Inn. *Budget–Inexpensive.* 59 Fitzroy St; (066) 42–6122. 24 units, 1 suite with shower. Air conditioned.

LISMORE. Centre Point Motel. *Inexpensive.* 202 Molesworth Street; (066) 21–8877. 33 units, 8 suites with showers. Air conditioning, restaurant, barbecue.

AUSTRALIA

MUWILLUMBAH. Attunga Park Motel. *Expensive.* Nobbys Creek Road (11km north of Murwillumbah); (066) 79-1455. 4 units with showers; restaurant, pool. All meals included.

PORT MACQUARIE. Pelican Shores Resort. *Inexpensive–Deluxe.* Park Street; (065) 833-9999. 86 units, 4 suites with showers; air conditioning, restaurant, pool, barbecue, sauna, tennis court. The resort has well-landscaped gardens, and each unit has a private balcony overlooking the water. A marina is right alongside.
    Sand Castle Motor Inn. *Budget–Inexpensive.* 20 William Street; (065) 83-3522. 45 units, 10 suites with showers. Restaurant, barbecue, pool. Opposite Town Beach.
    Town Beach Motel. *Budget–Inexpensive.* 5 Stewart Street; (065) 83-1733. 26 units with showers. Restaurant, pool. Overlooks the entrance to the Hastings River and Town Beach.

TWEED HEADS. Cooks Endeavour Motor Inn. *Inexpensive.* 26 Frances Street; (075) 36-5399. 21 units with showers. Pool, spa. Within walking distance of shops, licensed clubs, and Coolangatta and Greenmount beaches.

WAUCHOPE. Mt. Seaview Resort. *Budget–Inexpensive.* Yarras via Wauchope (55km west); (065)87-7133. Motel, lodge and bunkhouse accommodations and tent sites on a beef-cattle property. All meals available. Four-wheel drive safaris to wilderness areas and horse riding are enjoyable activities for guests.

NEW ENGLAND

ARMIDALE. Cattlemans Motor Inn. *Inexpensive.* 31 March Street; (067) 72-7788. 44 units with shower. Air conditioned. Pool, spa and sauna, barbecue, restaurant.
    Moore Park Inn. *Inexpensive.* New England Highway; (067) 72-2358. 21 units with showers. Air conditioned. Pool and spa, restaurant.

GLEN INNES. Alpha. *Budget.* New England Highway; (067) 32-2688. 16 units with showers. Central heating. Dinner brought to room. Barbecue.

INVERELL. Cousins Motor Inn. *Inexpensive.* Glen Innes Road; (067) 22-3566. 18 units with showers. Air conditioned. Dinner brought to units. Pool.

TENTERFIELD. Tenterfield Motor Inn. *Budget.* 114 Rouse Street; (067) 36-1177. 22 units with showers. Pool, spa and sauna, restaurant.

NORTH WEST

BOURKE. Major Mitchell Motel. *Inexpensive.* 44 Merlin Street; (068) 72-2556. 12 units with showers. Air conditioned.

COONABARABRAN. Coachman's Rest Motor Lodge. *Inexpensive.* Oxley Highway; (068) 42-2111. 20 units with showers. Air conditioned. Pool, restaurant. Closest accommodation to Warrumbungle National Park.

LIGHTNING RIDGE. Lightning Ridge Motor Village. *Inexpensive.* Onyx Street; (068) 29-0304. 24 units with showers. This is a licensed hotel-motel. Air conditioned. Barbecue, restaurant.

MOREE. Alexander Motor Inn. *Budget.* Cnr Gwydir and Newell highways; (067) 52-4222. 22 units with showers. Air conditioned. Pool, unlicensed restaurant.

NEW SOUTH WALES

QUIRINDI. Surrounding this town, a group of farmers has combined to offer guest accommodations on their properties. At each your rooms are in the homestead and meals are with the family. For inquiries: (067) 46-1545.

TAMWORTH. Country Comfort Motel. *Inexpensive.* 293 Marius Street (New England Highway); (067) 66-2903. 51 units, 2 suites with showers. Air conditioned. Barbecue, pool, restaurant.

THE OUTBACK

BROKEN HILL. Broken Hill Overlander Motor Inn. *Inexpensive.* 142 Iodide Street; (080) 88-2566. 15 units with showers. Air conditioned. Barbecue, pool, spa and sauna. Dinner brought to units.
  Old Willyama Motor Inn. *Inexpensive.* 466 Argent Street (cnr Iodide Street); (080) 83-3355. 25 units, 4 suites with showers. Air conditioned. Barbecue, pool, spa, restaurant.

WENTWORTH. Avoca Station. *Inexpensive.* Pomona Road via Wentworth; (050) 27-3020. Self-contained log cabins on a 28,500-hectare sheep and cattle grazing property 27km north of Wentworth. Cook your own meals.
  Nindethana Station. *Inexpensive.* Pooncarie Road, via Wentworth; (050) 26-0210. A 12,950-hectare Merino sheep station with fully self-contained homestead accommodations where you may prepare your own meals.
  Two Rivers Motel. *Inexpensive.* Silver City Highway; (050) 27-3268. 24 units, 12 suites with showers. Air conditioned. Price includes a light breakfast. Barbecue.

WHITE CLIFFS. Post Office Family Inn. *Budget.* Post Office Residence; (080) 9161-60. 3 rooms. Price includes breakfast. Unlicensed restaurant.

THE MURRAY RIVERINA

For information on farm stays in the region, contact the tourist bureau, (060) 21-1477.

ALBURY. There is a wide choice of good-quality motel accommodation in Albury.
  Travelodge. *Moderate.* Cnr Dean and Elizabeth streets; (060) 21-5366. 139 units, 3 suites with showers. Air conditioned. Pool and restaurant. Popular with conference groups.
  Ellis Townhouse. *Inexpensive.* Cnr Wilson and David streets; (060) 21-3000. 21 units with showers. Air conditioned. Barbecue, spa, sauna. Light breakfast included.

COROWA. Wingrove Motel. *Budget-Inexpensive.* Federation Avenue; (060) 33-2055. 10 units with showers. Air conditioning. Pool.

GRIFFITH. Acacia Motel. *Inexpensive.* Jondaryan Avenue; (069) 62-4422. 30 units with showers. Air conditioned. Pool.

GUNDAGAI. Moonlite Motel. *Budget.* Cnr Mount and Cross streets, Gundagai South; (069) 44-1433. 20 units with showers. Air conditioned. Restaurant.

HAY. Inlander Motor Inn. *Inexpensive.* 83 Lachlan Street; (069) 93-1901. 42 units. Air conditioned. Pool, playground. Restaurant.

HOLBROOK. Glenfalloch. *Budget.* Holbrook; (060) 36-7203. Accommodation is on a sheep farm and is in self-contained renovated shearers' quarters, or you may pitch a tent. It is not luxurious, but the property and accommodations are well maintained and clean, and hosts, Mr. and Mrs. Murdoch, make guests very welcome.

AUSTRALIA

HUME WEIR. Lake Hume Resort. *Inexpensive-moderate.* Riverina Highway; (060) 26–2444. On-site vans and cabin accommodations on the edge of Lake Hume. Licensed club on grounds.

LEETON. Leeton Gardens Motel. *Inexpensive.* Wade Avenue; (069) 53–3044. 23 units with showers. Air conditioned. Pool. Restaurant (closed Sunday and public holidays).

NARRANDERA. Camellia Motel. *Budget–Inexpensive.* 80 Whitten Street; (069) 59–2633. 16 units with showers. Air conditioned. Pool, unlicensed restaurant.

TOCUMWAL. Kingswood Motel. *Inexpensive.* Cnr Kelly and Jerilderie streets; (058) 74–2444. 13 units with showers. Air conditioned. Barbecue and pool.

WAGGA WAGGA. Carriage House Motel. *Inexpensive.* Sturt Highway; (069) 22–7374. 37 units with showers. Air conditioned. Barbecue and pool.
Old Wagga Inn. *Moderate.* Cnr Morgan and Tarcutta streets; (069) 21–6444. 38 units with showers. Air conditioned. Pool and sauna, restaurant.

THE SNOWY

In the Snowy Mountains visitors can choose from farm properties, self-contained apartments, cabins, hotels and motels, and ski lodges. Staying on the snowfields at Perisher-Smiggins, Thredbo, Charlotte Pass, or Guthega is usually more expensive than staying in the town below the snowline such as Jindabyne, Cooma, and Berridale.

ADAMINABY. Reynella Holidays. *Inexpensive.* Bolaro Road; (0648) 4–2386. Full board in bunkhouse accommodations on a sheep-and-cattle property. Trail rides and overnight camping can be arranged in summer and skiing in winter.
San Michele. *Inexpensive.* Snowy Mountains Highway; (0648) 4–2229. Full board in motel style units on a sheep property. Visitors can share in farm activities, horse ride and fish, swim, and play tennis.

CHARLOTTE PASS. Kosciusko Chalet. *Moderate.* Kosciusko Road; (0648) 7–5245. 40 rooms, 2 suites, with showers. Central heating and restaurant. One of the original accommodation houses in the mountains and in winter accessible only by over-snow transport. Not luxurious but set in a pretty little village.

COOMA. The Marlborough Motel. *Inexpensive–Moderate.* Monaro Highway; (0648) 2–1133. 60 units with showers. Central heating.

GOULBURN. Posthouse Motor Lodge. *Inexpensive.* 1 Lagoon Street (Hume Highway); (048) 21–5666. 38 units with showers. Air conditioned; central heating. Pool, restaurant.

JINDABYNE. Aspen Chalet. *Inexpensive* (summer)–*Expensive* (winter). Kosciusko Road; (0648) 6–2372. (Hotel/motel.) 43 rooms with showers. Central heating. Pool, spa and sauna, restaurant (closed Sunday).
Alpine Gables. *Inexpensive.* Cnr Kosciusko and Kalkite streets; (0648) 62–5555. 42 units with showers. Serviced apartments with cooking facilities. Central heating. Pool, spa and sauna, restaurant.

PERISHER VALLEY. Perisher Valley Hotel. *Deluxe.* Mt. Kosciusko Road; (0648) 7–5030. 10 units, 11 suites with showers. Central heating. Dinner brought to room. Spa and sauna. Situated at ski lifts and open during ski season only. Price includes dinner and breakfast.
Marritz Chalet. *Expensive.* (0648) 7–5220. 21 units with showers. A very hospitable ski lodge with Austrian cuisine in the restaurant. Price includes all

NEW SOUTH WALES

meals; rooms are very comfortable, many with enclosed balconies overlooking the ski fields. Open during ski season only.

QUEANBEYAN. Airport International Motor Inn. *Inexpensive-Moderate.* 57 Yass Road; (062) 97-7877. 61 units, 3 suites with showers. Air conditioned. Pool and sauna, tennis court and gym, barbecue, restaurant.

SMIGGIN HOLES. Smiggins Hotel. *Inexpensive-Expensive.* Kosciusko Road; (0648) 7-5375. 45 rooms with showers. Open in winter only. A short walk to ski lifts. Central heating. Restaurant.

THREDBO VILLAGE. Thredbo Alpine Hotel. *Inexpensive-Moderate.* (0648) 7-6333. 64 rooms, 2 suites with showers. Central heating. Pool, spa and sauna, barbecue, restaurant.
  Bernti's Mountain Inn. *Inexpensive.* (0648) 7-6216. 28 units with showers. Central heating. Spa and sauna, restaurant.

TUMUT. Ashton Motel. *Inexpensive.* 124 Wynyard Street; (069) 47-1999. 18 units with showers. Air conditioning and central heating. Pool and barbecue.

SOUTH COAST

BATEMANS BAY. Clyderiver Lodge Motel. *Expensive.* 3 Clyde Street; (044) 72-4308. 30 units with showers. Air conditioned. Pool, restaurant (closed Sunday).
  Mariners Lodge. *Inexpensive.* Orient Street; (044) 72-4707. Hotel/motel. Air conditioned. Waterfront site. Pool, restaurant.

BERMAGUI. Beachview Motel. *Inexpensive.* 12 Lamont Street; (0649) 3-4155. 8 units with showers. A good base for game fishing.

BOYDTOWN. Sea Horse Inn Hotel. *Inexpensive.* Off Princes Highway, 8km south of Eden; (0649) 6-1361. Restaurant. This charming old inn from past whaling days is classified by the National Trust. It is set right on the beachfront of Twofold Bay. Rooms are basic but the setting superb.

EDEN. Coachman's Rest Motor Inn. *Inexpensive.* Princes Highway; (0649) 6-1900. 26 units with showers. Air conditioned. Pool and spa, restaurant.

MERIMBULA. Black Dolphin Motel. *Budget-Inexpensive.* Princes Highway; (0649) 5-1500. 45 units with showers. Air conditioned. Pool, spa and sauna, small tennis court, restaurant.

MOLLYMOOK. Beachpoint Motor Inn. *Inexpensive.* Shepherd Street; (044) 55-3022. 10 units with showers. Garden setting; pool. Adjacent to golf course.

MORUYA. Moruya Motel. *Budget-Inexpensive.* Princes Highway; (044) 74-2511. 8 rooms with showers. Air conditioned. Dinner brought to units. Price includes a light breakfast.

NAROOMA: Highway Motel. *Inexpensive.* 153 Princes Highway; (044) 76-2311. 55 units with showers. Pool. Restaurant.
  Whale Motor Inn. *Inexpensive.* Wagonga Street; (044) 76-2411. 4 units, 8 suites with showers. Pool, restaurant (closed Sunday).

NOWRA. Coolangatta Historic Village Resort. *Inexpensive.* Shoalhaven Heads Road, Coolangatta (12km northeast of Nowra); (044) 48-7131. 23 units, 4 suites with showers. Barbecue, pool, tennis court, restaurant. Rooms are in cottages and other buildings of the old village.
  Leprechaun Hotel-Motel. *Inexpensive.* Princes Highway, cnr Kalandar Street; (044) 21-5222. 62 units, 7 suites with showers. Air conditioned. Pool, sauna, tennis and squash courts, restaurant.

ULLADULLA. Pigeon House Motor Inn. *Budget–Inexpensive.* Princes Highway; (044) 55–1811. 16 units with showers. Room service. Barbecue, pool, boat-parking facilities.

GOLDEN WEST

BATHURST. Atlas Motel. *Inexpensive.* 272 Stewart Street (Great Western Highway); (063) 31–5055. 26 units with showers. Air conditioned. Unlicensed restaurant (closed Sunday).
  Newhaven Park. *Inexpensive.* Georgian Plains; (063) 372–376. A cattle shed, with accommodation and full board available in the homestead or a large dormitory. Activities include horse riding, tennis, swimming (pool); gold panning nearby.

COWRA. Alabaster Motel. *Budget–Inexpensive.* Lynch St.; (63) 412–3133. 10 units with showers. Air conditioned. Barbecue, pool and spa.

DUBBO. Atlas Motel. *Inexpensive.* 140 Bourke St.; (068) 827–244. 31 units with showers. Air conditioning; pool. Dinner can be brought to units.
  Blue Diamond Motor Inn. *Inexpensive.* 113 Wingewarra St.; (068) 820–666 or toll free on (008) 02–7236. 20 units with showers. Air conditioned. Barbecues, pool, and half court tennis available.
  Country Comfort Motel. *Inexpensive.* Peek Hill Rd. (Newell Hwy.); (068) 82–4777. 39 units with showers. Air conditioned. Barbecue, pool, sauna, tennis court, restaurant.

FORBES. Town & Country Motor Inn. *Inexpensive.* Newell Hwy.; (068) 523–444. 20 units, 2 suites with showers. Air conditioned. Barbecue, pool and spa, restaurant.

MUDGEE. Cudgegong Valley Motel. *Inexpensive.* 212 Market St.; (063) 722–308. 16 units with showers. Air conditioned. Barbecue and pool. Inquire at the tourist information center (063–72–1944) for touring suggestions around the local wineries.

ORANGE. Apple City Flag Inn Motel. *Inexpensive.* 146 Bathurst Rd.; (063) 62–6033. 50 units, 1 suite with shower. Air conditioned. Restaurant.

PARKES. Bushman's Motor Inn. *Inexpensive.* Currajong Road (Newell Highway); (068) 62–2199. 20 units with showers. Air conditioned. Pool, restaurant (closed Sunday).

WELLINGTON. Bridge Motel. *Inexpensive.* 40 Gobolian Street; (068) 45–2555. 11 units with showers.

YOUNG. Tadlock Motor Inn. *Inexpensive.* Olympic Way; (068) 82–3300. 12 units with showers. Air conditioned. Restaurant.

LORD HOWE ISLAND

Accommodations on the island are either in a choice of 17 guest houses or in self-contained apartments, generally cottage or cabin style, set in attractive gardens.
  Pinetrees Lodge. *Expensive.* Book through the Travel Centre of NSW, Sydney; 02–231–4444. Pinetrees is the largest guesthouse on the island. Many of the single-story motel-style units have private facilities and covered verandas. Tennis court, access to the lagoon beach, all meals provided.
  Leanda Lei Apartments. *Moderate–Expensive.* Middle Beach Road; tel. Lord Howe Island 2015 or 2195. 14 self-contained apartments. Hire cars and push bikes available and guests have access to a 37-ft. Hire Cruiser. Mountain and ocean views.

NEW SOUTH WALES

NORFOLK ISLAND

As on Lord Howe Island, the accommodations are unsophisticated but comfortable and generally set in attractive gardens. They include hotels, guesthouses, and self-contained apartments and cottages.

Ross-Haven Luxury House. *Expensive–Deluxe.* Point Ross; Tel: Norfolk Island 2539. A luxurious house with one double and two twin bedrooms, only 10 minutes' drive from the center of the island. It is surrounded by 16 acres of wooded clifftops and has a swimming pool.

Hotel Norfolk. *Moderate.* Queen Elizabeth Avenue; tel. Norfolk Island 2177 or 2677, 51 units with showers; barbecue, swimming pool and restaurant.

CAMPING. Sydney region prepared campsites include: *La Mancha Cara-Park,* 9 Pacific Highway, Berowra; 02–456–1766. *Dural Carapark,* 269 New Line Road, Dural; 02–651–2555. *Sundowner,* cnr Lane Cove and Fontenoy roads, North Ryde; 02–88–1933. *Van Village Caravan Park,* Plassey Road, North Ryde; 02–88–3649. *OK Caravan Corral,* 134 Terry Road, Rouse Hill; 02–629–2652.

Seaside Camping: Terrigal, Avoca, Port Macquarie, Coffs Harbour, Forster, Ballina, Tweed Heads, Nambucca Heads, Port Stephens, South West Rocks, Narooma, Bateman's Bay, Merimbula, Kiama, Ulladulla, Jervis Bay. *Lake Sites:* Burrinjuck Dam, Burrendong Dam, Menindee Lakes, Lake Macquarie, Wyangala Dam. *Country Towns:* Many country towns have caravan parks that provide tent sites, including: Katoomba, Cooma, Dorrigo, Gundagai, Bathurst, Dubbo, Albury, Wagga, Armidale, Wellington, Cowra, Broken Hill. For information on the sites and facilities of campsites and caravan parks for tourists throughout NSW, contact the *National Roads and Motorists Association* (NRMA), 151 Clarence Street, Sydney; 02–260–9222.

Roadside rest areas: The NSW Department of Main Roads has provided frequent rest areas for motorists on the major highways. The sites are usually in attractive spots and most have shelters, tables, seats, fireplaces, drinking water, and litter bins. Using these special areas helps to prevent the bush fires that sometimes result from building fires beside the road and helps to keep the highway environment unlittered.

FARM HOLIDAYS. The demand for experience of the Outback has been big enough to persuade some farmers and graziers to open their homesteads (and add new facilities) for tourists. There are quite a few country properties where people can spend their holidays. The quality of accommodation varies a great deal. In some of them people must bring their own sleeping bags and tents or perhaps sleep in a converted shearing shed; in others all modern conveniences (including hot showers and toilets) are attached to your room in the homestead, or you may stay in a spare cottage on the property. It can be great fun if you like a civilized introduction to bucolic life for a week or two. The better of these farms include San Michele, a sheep station, tel. (0648) 4–2229 and *Reynella* (R & J Rudd), tel. (0648) 4–2386 in the foothills of the Snowy Mountains. The owners of Reynella organize horseback safaris into the Kosciusko National Park from December to February. It's a good way to lose weight (if you can stand the exercise) and to enjoy the season when the Alpine heaths are at their fragrant best. *Berrebangalo Country Resort* at Gunning, tel. (048) 45–1135, is an Apaloosa stud farm where the visitors' room is in the homestead and home-cooked meals and horse riding are offered. For information and bookings on an extensive range of farm holidays contact the Travel Centre of New South Wales, cnr Pitt and Spring streets, Sydney, 02–231–4444.

RESTAURANTS. Many of the accommodations listed above also offer meals. Dollar ranges for price categories are as in Practical Information for Sydney.

THE BLUE MOUNTAINS. Cleopatra. *Deluxe.* Cleopatra Street, Blackheath; (047) 87–8456. This small French restaurant is within a charming guesthouse, but there is room for some casual meal guests to sample the marvelous cuisine. Unlicensed. L, D Friday–Sunday. No cards.

Glenella. *Expensive–Deluxe.* 56 Govetts Leap Road, Blackheath; (047) 87-8352. A well-established and excellent French restaurant that is also a guesthouse. Many Sydneysiders make regular visits to the Blue Mountains just for a meal at Glenella. Licensed. L, Friday–Sunday; D, Thursday–Sunday. AE, MC.

Kubba Roonga. *Expensive.* 9 Brentwood Avenue, Blackheath; (047) 87-8330. Another excellent restaurant in a Blackheath guesthouse: it appears the perfect formula to produce memorable eating. This time French food mixes with an interesting Vietnamese influence. Unlicensed. D, Thursday–Sunday. BC.

The Paragon. Katoomba Street, Katoomba; (047) 82-2928. Art-deco restaurant and confectionary shop—a favorite spot to stop for Devonshire teas, waffles, and sweets.

THE ILLAWARRA. Baker & Bunyip. *Moderate.* 23 Prince Alfred Street, Berry; (044) 64-1454. The restaurant features a walk-in wine cellar with some excellent Australian and French wines, piano music on weekends, and a gallery of art. The cuisine is French and very good. Licensed. L, Sunday (winter); D, Tuesday–Sunday. BC, MC.

Berida Manor. *Expensive.* David Street, Bowral; (048) 61-1177. The restaurant has "healthy meals" for in-house patrons staying there to get in shape, or a delicious a-la-carte international menu for those who choose it. Licensed. L, D, daily. AE, BC, MC.

Gundarimba. *Expensive.* 45 Allowrie Street, Jamberoo; (042) 36-0228. Set in a 1930s-style guesthouse, the restaurant offers French cuisine, tasty and beautifully presented. Licensed. L, Sunday; D, Tuesday–Sunday. BC.

THE HUNTER. Clos de Corne. *Expensive.* Hermitage Road, Pokolbin; (049) 98-7635. The French restaurant is set in the Hermitage Estate vineyards and offers a-la-carte lunches and a fixed-price dinner from the same menu. The appetizers are so good that you may like to make a meal of them. Licensed. L, Monday–Wednesday, Saturday–Sunday; D, Monday–Wednesday, Friday–Saturday. Closed in February. AE, BC, DC, MC, V.

Old George and Dragon. *Expensive.* 48 Melbourne Street, East Maitland; (049) 33-7272. Despite the English-sounding name, the style here is French provincial. This very good restaurant is in a former country pub. Licensed. L, Wednesday–Friday, Sunday; D, Tuesday–Saturday. AE, BC, DC, V.

Pokolbin Cellar. *Expensive.* Hungerford Hill Wine Village, Broke Road, Pokolbin, (049) 98-7584. The French-provincial cuisine is innovative and the surrounds inviting. Licensed. L, daily; D, Wednesday–Saturday. BC, V.

Loxton House. *Moderate.* 142 Bridge Street, Muswellbrook; (065) 43-3468. Tasty cooking and a comprehensive selection of Hunter Valley wines are offered. Licensed. L, Tuesday–Friday; D, Tuesday–Saturday. AE, BC, MC, V.

THE NORTH COAST. Cafe Cezanne. *Deluxe.* 18 Elizabeth Street, Coffs Harbour; (066) 52-4144. A stylish and elegant restaurant with excellent French food made from fresh local ingredients. Licensed. D, Tuesday–Saturday. AE, BC, DC.

Le Petit Escargot. *Moderate–Expensive.* RSL Club, Short Street, Port Macquarie; (065) 83-1343. A small French restaurant within the RSL Club priding itself on good food and service. Not far to the club's poker machines if you want to try to win back the price of dinner. Licensed. D, Wednesday–Saturday.

Seashells. *Moderate-Expensive.* 123 Park Beach Road, Coffs Harbour; (066) 52-5050. Seafood is a specialty and there is a pleasant outdoor section. On most nights there is entertainment offered and in winter an open fire. Licensed. L, D daily. AE, BC, V.

Bellowing Bull. *Moderate.* Bruxner Highway, Alstonville, (15km east of Ballina); (066) 28-0715. A friendly restaurant serving excellent steak; plenty of good Australian beer on tap. Licensed. D, Tuesday–Sunday.

NEW SOUTH WALES

SEASONAL EVENTS. January. *Australasian Music Festival*, Tamworth. **February.** *Dahlia Festival*, Mittagong. **March.** *Motorcycle races* (Easter), Bathurst. *The Great Goat Race* (Easter), Lightning Ridge. *Musica Viva* (Easter), Mittagong. *Blessing of the fleet* (Easter Sunday), Ulladulla. *Hunter Valley Wine Festival* (March-April of alternate years). *Apple Country Fair,* Orange. St. Patrick's Day horseraces, Broken Hill. **April.** *Australian Jazz Festival,* Grafton. *Festival of the Falling Leaf* (April–May), Tumut. **June.** *Great Lakes Country Music Festival,* Forster–Tuncurry. **July.** *Yulefest,* traditional Christmas fare in Blue Mountains hotels and guesthouses. **August.** *Lightning Ridge Opal Festival. Polo Carnival,* Quirindi. **September–November.** *Springtime Festival in the Blue Mountains.* **October.** *Forster–Tuncurry Oyster Festival.* **James Hardie 1000-Car Race,** Bathurst. **Apple-blossom festival,** Batlow. **Annual spring flower show,** Leura. **Leura Gardens Festival and Village Fair. Tulip Time,** Bowral. **Festival of the Waters,** Gosford. **October–November. Jacaranda Festival** Grafton. **November.** *Snowy Mountains Festival,* Adaminaby. **Rhododendron Festival,** Blackheath.

TOURS. See also How to Get Around, above, for rail and coach tour operators. See also Tours in Sydney for day trips out of the city. Tourist Information, above, has the phone numbers for the information offices mentioned here. **The Blue Mountains.** *AAT, Ansett Pioneer, Australian Pacific,* and *Clipper* run day tours to the Blue Mountains (See Practical Information for Sydney.) The State Rail Authority (SRA), 02–217–8819, also runs day tours to the Blue Mountains and Jenolan Caves as well as overnight trips including accommodation. In the Mountains *Golden West Tours,* 283 Main Street, Katoomba (047) 82–1866, operates full- and half-day tours. The *Blue Mountains Explorer,* (047) 82–1833, does an hour's circuit of the major Blue Mountains attractions each weekend. Passengers may leave or join the bus at any of its 14 stops, and may also do some interesting bushwalks between some spots.

Upper Hawkesbury. *Hawkesbury River Cruise Boats* operates 2 boats from the Windsor Wharf, (045) 77–2310, and offers 1-hour cruises on weekends and public holidays. *Del Rio Cruises,* (045) 66–4300, cruise the Wisemans Ferry area on weekends and public and school holidays. *Sydney Footnotes,* (02) 646–3119 or 679–1513, will lead you on a leisurely stroll of historic Windsor.

The Illawarra. From Sydney the SRA runs day tours to both the Illawarra coast and southern highlands and offers one- and two-night trips to the coast; 02–217–8819. For tours to Kiama and Wollongong contact *Leisure Coast Tours,* (042) 71–3320; to *Nowra Area: Sampsons Tours,* (044) 21–3922. Regular tours do not operate within the southern highlands, but Thrifty Rent-a-Cars are available through the Tourist Information Centre, (048) 71–2888.

Central Coast. From Sydney, *AAT, Ansett Pioneer, Australian Pacific,* and *Clipper* run coach day tours from Sydney to Old Sydney Town, as does the SRA. (See Sydney Tours.) On the Coast, *Dragon Cruise Lines,* Gosford Public Wharf, (043) 82–1291; offer scenic cruises on Brisbane Waters in a Chinese junk. *MV Lady Kendall,* (043) 42–4438, has daily cruises on Brisbane Waters. *Hawkesbury River Ferries,* Brooklyn, (02) 455–1566, have historic riverboat mail-run and half-day tours on the Hawkesbury River.

The Hunter. Day trips from Sydney are available. By rail visit the Hunter Valley wine area and Port Stephens Rose Farm, (02) 217–8819. By bus: *AAT, Ansett Pioneer,* and *Australian Pacific* offer a Hunter Valley wine tour (see Sydney Tours.). A 6-day rail-coach trip to the Hunter Valley includes Newcastle and Port Stephens; a five-day rail-coach tour to Forster includes a cruise on Wallis Lake and free time for relaxing on the beach; and two- to eight-day tours to a farm-holiday property, Altamira, at Gloucester, (call 02–217–8819).

In the Hunter tours from Newcastle to the Upper Hunter vineyards, Port Stephens and Barrington Tops, are available from Sid Fogg & Sons, (049) 28–1088. *Wangi Queen Showboat* cruises on Lake Macquarie (except July), (049) 58–3211. From Forster there are tours of the beaches and Port Macquarie district from *Forster Bus Service,* (065) 54–6431. Daily cruises on Lake Wallis: *Amaroo II,* (065) 54–7478. From Port Stephens there are local tours and trips to the Hunter Vineyards, through Port Stephens Buses, (049) 81–1207. Cruising Port Stephens and the Myall Lakes on board *Tamboi Queen,* (049) 81–1959. In Maitland *Royal Newcastle Aero Club* has scenic flights over the coast and wineries; (049) 32–8888.

AUSTRALIA

North Coast. Enjoy a barbecue or dinner cruise on the Richmond River aboard the *Richmond Princess* at Ballina (066) 86–3669. There are also cruises on the Nambucca River at Nambucca Heads, (065) 68–6922. *Byron Bus & Coach Service,* (066) 85–6554, has a variety of tours that visit the Gold Coast, some magnificent rain forests and national parks, and a macadamia plantation. Tours also visit the "alternative society" area of Nimbin, which attracted a new wave of hippie settlers in the 60s and 70s, and Terania Creek, the center of a current issue for "greenies" who are trying to stop logging there. From Coffs Harbour, *North Coast Tours,* (066) 52–7193, venture as far afield as Grafton and Yamba, the Bellinger Valley and Dorrigo Plateau as well as to the Coffs Harbour attractions such as the Big Banana (for a tourist's view of the local banana industry) and a wildlife park. The lush rain forests of the far North Coast are difficult to appreciate from main roads and lend themselves to exploration by four-wheel drive; contact *Off the Beaten Track Experiences* at Mullumbimby for day safaris, (066) 84–2277. In Port Macquarie, cruises, coach tours, and four-wheel-drive tours are all available: the *Waterbus,* (065) 83–5911, has an Everglades tour on the Mariah River, while *Port Macquarie River Cruises,* (065) 83–3058, offers barbecue cruises on the Hastings River. *Skennar's Coaches* include in their itineraries day trips to Timbertown as well as historic highlights of the Macleay Valley and Trial Bay. Four-wheel-drive safaris of Port Macquarie's forest area are led by *Ben's Tours,* (065) 82–0433. In Tweed Heads, the *Palm Island and Tweed River Cruise Company,* (075) 35–6888, offers a novel package: a cruise to the Murwillumbah Services Club, where you can dine and try your hand at the poker machines before returning by coach. The company also offers a free bus service to the Coolangatta–Tweed Heads Gold Club.

The SRA, has a choice of extended sunny north-coast holidays that give you time to laze on the beach and include some local touring. Destinations offered are Nambucca Heads, Coffs Harbour, Grafton, Byron Bay and a farm stay at Mount Seaview, via Wauchope.

New England. Day Tours: *Armidale Tableland Tours,* (067) 72–1105, will show you the highlights of Armidale City including the university as well as local beauty spots such as Dangar Falls and Wollomombi Falls. In Tenterfield, tours of the district can be organized by *Tally Ho Tours* for a minimum of 14 people, (067) 36–1577. The SRA has a four-day rail-coach tour from Sydney to Armidale that highlights the beautiful parks, gardens, churches, and cathedrals of Armidale and includes a visit to the Wollombi Falls, the highest in Australia. Also available is a seven-day tour to Sherwood Park Manor, a gracious homestead with open fireplaces, spacious rooms and sweeping verandas. Activities on the property include horse riding, tennis, archery, mini golf, and swimming in the pool. Call 02–217–8819.

North West. In Bourke, *Ron Davidson,* (068) 72–2277, runs mini bus tours of the district that include the cotton farms and "Back o' Bourke" artists. Also, the tourist-information center at 14 Richard Street can supply you with "Mud Map" tours on paper. Mud maps are the traditional bushman's way of showing directions on a map he has drawn in a smooth patch of earth.

Black Opal Tours in Lightning Ridge, (068) 29–0666, has tours of the Ridge and the surrounding opal fields or can help you with self-drive tours in a rent-a-moke. If you wish to see the pecan farms, cotton gins, and the overseas-telecommunication station at Moree, contact *Jones Tours* at Pallamallawa, (067) 54–9357. *Jim's Joy Tours* can take you touring around Tamworth by mini coach, (067) 66–4269.

From Sydney the SRA's tour programs, 02–217–8819, has a six-day farm-stay holiday in the Quirindi area. You can stay at one farm or a number of farms and experience Australian country life. There are also a four-day tour to Tamworth and a tour to the Dubbo area that includes the Warrumbungles, and a four-day rail-coach trip to opal country at Lightning Ridge. *Air New South Wales,* 02–268–1242, also has tours to Lightning Ridge with an opportunity for you to fossick for opals during the trip.

The Outback. *Wanderer Tours,* (080) 7750, escorts day and half-day tours to the sights of Broken Hill such as an underground mine, the Flying Doctor Service, School of the Air and visits to some of the art galleries. There are also day trips to the ghost town of Silverton, the Opal Fields at White Cliffs, and to the vast Menindee Lakes and Kinchega National Park. For an unusual and authentic view of life in the Outback, *Barrier Air Taxi Service,* (080) 88–4307, takes passengers on its bush mail deliveries to 25 stations, and passengers have

NEW SOUTH WALES 131

lunch and morning tea at a station homestead. You can also join their mail run to White Cliffs and have a look at its opal fields and underground houses. From Wentworth, the *M. V. Loyalty,* (080) 27-3330, offers a two-hour cruise to the junction of the Murray and Darling rivers and then up the Darling.

Air New South Wales, 268-1242, and the *SRA,* 217-8819, both offer tours to the Outback from Sydney. *Destrek International* in Broken Hill, (080) 2356, has a four-day tour that includes White Cliffs and Mootwingee. Five-day paddlesteamer holidays depart from Mildura on the *Coonawarra,* (050) 23-3366.

Murray Riverina. In Albury: *Mylon Motorways,* (060) 24-1877, has half-day tours around the parks and gardens of Albury-Wodonga and through the Murray Valley to the Wineries of Rutherglen in Victoria. A range of half-day tours includes trips to the pretty towns of Myrtleford, Bright, and Beechworth in Northern Victoria and through pioneering and bushranger country around Albury. There are also daily cruises on the paddlesteamer *Cumberoona* from Nourial Park, (060) 21-1477. In Leeton: the visitors' information center, (069) 53-2832, can arrange tours based on local industries, to the cannery, rice mill, juice factory, and rice farm and orchards and inspection of the irrigation system. In Griffith the visitors' center has information on tours to the districts' wineries and farm inspections. In Mulwala cruises operate on Lake Mulwala on weekends and school holidays. Inquire at Albury's tourist bureau, (060) 21-1477. The SRA offers extended rail/coach tours to Albury and district from Sydney, one of which includes a Murray River cruise on the *P.S. Pride of the Murray.*

The Snowy. *Ansett Pioneer* runs day bus tours to the Snowy Mountains from Canberra, (062) 45-6624, and to the snowfields and Snowy Mountains Hydro-Electric Scheme from Cooma, (0648) 2-1422. Tours of the dams, power stations, and pretty Tumut countryside are available from *Tumut Valley Tours,* (069) 47-1043. Scenic air tours over Cooma, Lake Jindabyne, Lake Eucumbene, and Mount Kosciusko depart from Cooma airport. Details from Cooma Visitors' Centre. *Kosciusko Expeditions,* (0648) 6-2458, leads day walks in the Kosciusko National Park.

Ansett Pioneer has a range of two- to five-day tours from Sydney and Canberra to the Snowy Mountains, 02-268-1363 in Sydney or (062) 45-6624 in Canberra. The SRA has a four-day rail-coach tour combining Canberra and the Snowy Mountains, 02-217-8819. Adventure tours are also available; see "Sports."

South Coast. Enjoy a discovery cruise on the Clyde River in Batemans Bay, with *Merinda Cruises,* (044) 72-6103. In Eden there are coach tours of the district with *Edwards,* (0649) 6-1780, and a cruise on Twofold Bay aboard the *Snug Cove Ferry Service's* boat *Cat Balou,* (0649) 6-2027. In Merimbula there are cruises on Merimbula Lake, on glass-bottom boats (0649) 5-2134 or (0649) 5-1129. Cruise Wagonga Inlet from Narooma aboard the *Wagonga Princess,* (044) 76-2825. *Sampsons Tours* in Nowra has day trips available, (044) 21-3922, four-wheel-drive half-day and day tours in the area are offered by *Shoalhaven Adventure Camps* (044) 21-6424. In Pambula (near Merimbula), the *Sinbad* cruises on Pambula Lake and River, (0649) 5-6478. The SRA's Jewel of the South is a five-day rail-coach tour that visits Lake Tabourie, Ulladulla, and Batemans Bay as well as Pebbly Beach where kangaroos can be hand fed.

Golden West. From Sydney, the SRA has one-day trips to the Jenolan Caves, as do the coach companies *AAT, Ansett Pioneer,* and *Australian Pacific.* In Bathurst half-day local sightseeing and full-day tours to the historic gold-mining towns of Sofala and Hill End leave from the tourist-information center, (063) 33-6288. In Dubbo, *Countrywide Tours,* (068) 82-2249, offers trips to the Western Plains Zoo and the Wellington district. *Dubbo Bus and Coachlines,* (068) 82-2572, has tours to the Wellington Caves and Burrendong Dam, a gold-mining tour, a shearing-shed and property tour, and a tour to the historic town of Gulgong. The tourist-information center has self-drive itineraries for motorists to Wellington, Parkes, Warrumbungles, and Mudgee and Gulgong. From Mudgee, take tours of the local wineries and historic Gulgong and trips to a horse farm and to a sheep and sheep-dog farm: *Mudgee Personalised Tours,* (063) 72-3237. From Orange there are tours with *Big Apple Country Tours,* (063) 62-4215; visit the old gold-mining town of Ophir and local sights. *Lyons Country Safari,* (063) 69-6251, shows visitors round the Yarrawonga sheep and cattle property. The SRA, and *Country Wide Tours Dubbo,* (068) 82-2249, combine to offer two- to five-day tours of Dubbo and district that may include the zoo, Wellington Caves, and the Warrumbungles. These may be picked up in Sydney or Dubbo. There are also two-night combined rail-coach tours to the Jenolan Caves staying at Caves House.

Lord Howe Island. *Seaview Aviation Scenic Flights,* tel. Lord Howe Island 2058, has a window seat for everyone taking an aerial look at Lord Howe or the Maritime Graveyards of the Pacific—120 mi. north. 1½-hour glass bottom boat cruises on *M.V. Coral Princess* give close-up views of varied corals and fish life. Snorkeling equipment is provided free and the company also rents underwater cameras, sailboards, canoes and surf skis. Inquire on the island for details. Two-hour scenic cruises aboard the *TSMV Lulawei* can be booked by phoning Lord Howe Island 2195. Bus tours are also available; check with your host for times of regular island tours.

From Sydney, transport to the island and accommodation can be arranged by: The Travel Centre of NSW, *The Lord Howe Island Tourist Centre,* 20 Loftus Street, Sydney, 02–27–2867, *Pacific Unlimited Holidays/Norfolk Airlines,* 50 York Street, Sydney, 02–290–2266.

Norfolk Island. *Pinetree Tours,* tel. Norfolk Island 2424, and *Marie's Tours,* tel. Norfolk Island 2174 or 2420, show visitors the remains of Norfolk's convict and Pitcairn Island past and its many scenic spots by minicoach; they have barbecue breakfast walks as well. Inquire at the tourist-information center at Burnt Pine, Norfolk Island, for glass-bottomed-boat tours.

From Sydney you can book packages that include transport, accommodation, and rental car through *Pacific Unlimited Holidays,* 3rd floor, 50 York Street, Sydney, 02–290–2266, or *Pacific Island Travel Centre,* 20 Loftus Street, Sydney, 02–27–2867, or *East West World Travel Centre,* 70 Pitt Street, Sydney, 02–233–3700

PARKS, GARDENS, AND FORESTS. The Blue Mountains. *Blue Mountains National Park.* (047) 87–8877. Magnificent sandstone canyons, tall bluegum forests, and a variety of habitats such as heath, swamp, mallee, and grassland. A mecca for bushwalkers. Visitors' centers at Glenbrook and Blackheath: *The Everglades,* Denison Street, Leura. 6 acres of landscaped terraced gardens with fabulous mountain views. Open daily.

The Illawarra. *Morton National Park.* (044) 21–9969. Within walking distance of Bundanoon. Colorful sandstone cliffs form impressive gorges with cascading waterfalls and patches of subtropical rainforest.

Minnamurra Falls and Reserve. (042) 36–0147. Situated in dense subtropical rainforest. Picnic facilities.

Wollongong Botanic Gardens. Northfields Avenue, North Wollongong. 19 hectares (47 acres) of gardens divided into areas representing different parts of the world.

Central Coast. *Bouddi National Park.* (043) 24–4911. Coastal sandstone scenery with a variety of coastal heaths and forests. Access is south of McMasters Beach. The first marine national park in New South Wales.

Brisbane Water National Park. (043) 24–4911. Panoramic vistas spread from steep cliffs that rise vertically from the flooded valley of the Hawkesbury River.

Dharug National Park. (043) 24–4911. On the northern side of the Hawkesbury River, near Wisemans Ferry. Its prime importance is for its wealth of Aboriginal rock engravings.

The Fragrant Gardens, Portsmouth Road, Erina. (043) 67–7546. Specializes in herbs, herb teas, and fragrant plants. Open daily, 9:30 A.M.–5 P.M., except Christmas.

The Hunter. *Barrington Tops National Park.* (049) 87–3108. Features rainforest and grasslands and subalpine woodlands on the plateau top. Very popular with bushwalkers and campers. 38km from Gloucester.

Myall Lakes National Park. (049) 87–3108. This 31,000-hectare (76,600-acre) park boasts expanses of beautiful lakes and beaches, eucalypt forests and a diversity of animal life. Fishing, swimming, sailing, and canoeing are typical water sports enjoyed here. 16km east of Bulladelah. Seal Rocks is a pleasant place to camp.

Tomaree National Park. (049) 87–3108. This narrow coastal park has a number of beaches overlooked by spectacular headlands and rocky points, immediately south of Port Stephens. Swimming, surfing, bushwalking, and nature study are the main attractions.

The North Coast. The north-coast area has a number of spectacular national parks. Some favorites with the locals are: *Bundjalung National Park.* (066)

NEW SOUTH WALES

28–1177. The park extends along 38km of coastline from Evans River estuary in the north to Iluka on the Clarence River in the south. There are a camping area at Woody Head and beachside picnic facilities on the Iluka peninsula. Bushwalking is particularly worthwhile in the central wilderness area.

Guy Fawkes River National Park. (066) 57–2309. This is a rugged wilderness river with spectacular rapids and waterfalls. The park's vegetation ranges from woodlands to rain forest and you may sight large mobs of kangaroos. Overnight camping facilities are available. 60km from Dorrigo.

Hat Head National Park. (065) 83–5518. Coastal dunes, dune lakes, and coastline stretches from Smoky Cape to Crescent Head. Enjoy coastal walks at Hat Head and Smoky Cape and camping at South West Rocks. 20km east of Kempsey.

Mount Warning National Park. (066) 28–1177. The park is dominated by the sharp, jagged neck of Mt. Warning, a volcanic plug surrounded by rain forest, woodlands, and heath. The Park is 16km southwest of Muwillumbah, and there is camping on the Muwillumbah-Kyogle access road.

Nymboida National Park. (066) 42–0613. All canoeists know this park: it straddles the junction of two spectacular rivers, the Nymboida and the Mann. Access is by foot or canoe, and you can take a car along the Grafton-Glen Innes Road to the Ramomie State Forest camping area at the southern end of the park.

Arakoon State Recreation Area. (065) 66–6168. Its features are small cores with intimate beaches, rocky headlands, and coastal vistas over Gap Beach. It is also the site of the historic ruins of Trial Bay Gaol. There are picnic and barbecue facilities as well as campsites. 37km north of Kempsey.

New England. *Bald Rock National Park.* (067) 32–1177. Bold Rock is the focal point of the park: it is 213m high and believed to be the largest granite dome in the southern hemisphere. If you climb the northeastern side and follow the white trail markings there are panoramic views of the Queensland and NSW border areas. The park is north of Tenterfield along the Mt. Lindesay Road.

Gibralter Range National Park. (067) 32–1177. This is a plateau with deep gorges and spectacular waterfalls. The variety of vegetation attracts abundant wildlife, and platypus are known to inhabit the mountain streams. However, they are elusive little creatures and you will do well to spot one. Camping, picnicking, swimming, and fishing are activities available at Gibralter Range. The park is 70km west of Glen Innes on the Gwydir Highway.

New England National Park. (066) 57–2309. Beautiful rain forests with heath and snowgums covering the cliff tops. There are panoramic views of the Macleay River from Point Lookout. Cabin accommodations are available, as is camping. The park is 80km east of Armidale on the Ebor Road.

North West. *Keepit Dam and State Recreation Area.* (067) 69–7605. A center for aquatic sports about 41km west of Gunnedah. Barbecue and picnic facilities are available, and there are camper and camping areas.

Mount Kaputar National Park. (067) 92–7222. Set among many deep and narrow gorges, precipitous cliffs, and fascinating rock formations of volcanic origins. There are cabin accommodations and a camping area. The park is 53km east of Narrabri along a steep and narrow road.

Warrabah National Park. (067) 72–1733. The park is on the western slopes of the Namoi River and gives visitors one of the few opportunities to enjoy the flora and fauna of the inland rivers. It is 80km by road from Tamworth.

Warrumbungle National Park. (068) 25–4364 for cabin and camping bookings. Spectacular scenery of spires and domes is all that remains of ancient volcanic activity in the area. Siding Spring Observatory, with its giant 3.9m optical telescope, is within the park. Its Exploring the Universe exhibition is open Monday-Wednesday and daily during school holidays; the observation deck of the telescope is open daily. The park is 37km west of Coonabarabran.

The Outback. *Kinchega National Park.* (080) 88–0286. Red-sand dunes and black-soil flats with a complex system of saucer-shaped overflow lakes. There are old aboriginal campsites to see, and overnight camping facilities are available. The park is 2km west of Menindee and 111km southeast of Broken Hill.

Mootwingee National Park. (080) 88–0253. Set in a semiarid environment and on a sandstone range with permanent waterholes in narrow gorges lined with red river gums. There are basic camping facilities within the park and a number of self-guided walks to try. The park is 132km northeast of Broken Hill.

Mungo National Park. (050) 28–1278. Mungo is part of an ancient lake system that dried up after the last ice age, 15,000 years ago. It is the site of some of the earliest known Aboriginal occupation, dating back 40,000 years. A feature is the "Walls of China," white sand dunes marking the edge of the former lake. Camping and picnic areas are available. The park is 110km north east of Mildura, although the dirt roads are impassable after heavy rains.

Murray Riverina. *Albury Botanic Gardens.* Off Wodonga Place. A peaceful and pretty garden for a picnic stop.

Cocoparra National Park. (069) 62–0255. Its stands of cypress pine and narrow-leafed ironbark trees contrast well with a large variety of acacias and wildflowers. Bush camping is permitted. The park is 25km northeast of Griffith.

Wagga Wagga Botanic Gardens & Zoo. Williams Hill, Macleay Street. As well as a rain-forest area, the gardens include a children's play area and miniature railway.

The Snowy. *Kosciusko National Park.* (0648) 6–2102. The major attraction of the Snowy region. It is Australia's largest alpine area, snow covered in winter and a mass of wildflowers in summer. In winter cross-country and downhill skiing are the major activities, and in summer alpine walks (with plenty of snowgums to see), horseriding, canoeing, and fishing are favorite pastimes. There are cabins and camping area at Sawpit Creek. Access is via Jindabyne or Tumut.

Tumut. Nestled in the foothills of the Snowy Mountains, its contrasting scenery makes it a paradise for photographers and painters. Each Autumn in April–May the town celebrates the Festival of the Falling Leaf, when the trees look particularly beautiful.

South Coast. *Ben Boyd National Park.* (0649) 6–1434. Named after one of the Eden district's earliest whalers, the park features rugged cliffs, caves, and beaches. Basic camping is available. The park is 8km north of Eden.

Jervis Bay Nature Reserve. 2km along Cave Beach Road, Jervis Bay. This is an annex to the National Botanic Gardens and contains a large variety of native plants from all parts of Australia. Open weekdays and the first Sunday of the month.

Kangaroo Valley. Not strictly a park or garden, this picturesque valley lies between Nowra and the Southern Highlands.

Mimosa Rocks National Park. (044) 76–2798. Rocky headlands, caves, and beaches form a picturesque coastline. Popular for fishing, swimming, and snorkeling. 22km north of Bega.

Morton National Park. (044) 21–9969. Here colorful sandstone cliffs form impressive gorges with cascading waterfalls and patches of subtropical rainforest. Access from Nowra and Ulladulla. Camping and picnic areas are available.

Golden West. *Burrendong Arboretum and Lake Burrendong Park.* (068) 46–7345. Situated 27km southeast of Wellington, the lake area is popular for picnicking, fishing, and water skiing, and the arboretum contains the largest collection of native trees and shrubs in Australia.

Japanese Garden and Cultural Centre. Cowra; (006) 42–1488. Open daily. This is the largest traditional garden outside Japan and includes a teahouse and an exhibition of Japanese art and craft.

Kanungra Boyd National Park. (047) 87–8877. Adjoins the Blue Mountains National Park; a large wilderness area accessible from Jenolan Caves or from Oberon.

Machattie Park. Russell Street, Bathurst. Magnificent gardens and trees in the center of Bathurst featuring duck ponds and an excellent begonia display. Begonias normally flower mid-February until Easter.

BEACHES. The Illawarra. Surfing beaches include *Kiama; Werri Beach* near Gerringong; *Seven Mile Beach*, east of Berry. Still-water beaches include *Green Patch* on Jervis Bay, which has a pleasant camping area in a nature reserve. For information, call (044) 43–0977 from 10 A.M.–4 P.M.

Central Coast. The best beaches on the central coast are (from north to south) *Kilcare, McMasters Beach, Avoca Beach, Terrigal, the Entrance.* Avoca, Terrigal, and the Entrance are all close to shops and other amenities. They are patrolled in summer.

The Hunter. *Newcastle Beach* is only 180m from Hunter Street, the main street of the city. Eight Newcastle beaches are patrolled daily by lifesavers between August and May. *Bar Beach* is floodlit at night. (Pt means patrolled; DS—dressing sheds; SB—surfboard riding; P—parking; P(f)—pay parking. *Fingal Bay:* ½ m. long. Pt, DS, SB, P. Toilets and caravan park adjacent. *Shoal Bay:* ½ m. long. P, SB. *Hawks Nest:* 25 m. long. A popular holiday area for families. Pt, DS, P, SB. Camping ground nearby. *Seal Rocks:* 2 m. long. SB. A popular beach with surfers but lacking in amenities, although there is access to adjacent camping area for bathrooms. *Forster:* 2 mi. long. DS, P, SB. Rock pool and picnic areas. *Tuncurry:* 1 m. long. DS, P, SB. Swimming pool.

The North Coast. *Town Beach:* Port Macquarie. 2 mi. long. Pt. DS. P. SB. *Park Beach:* Coffs Harbour. 1 m. in length. Pt, DS, P, SB. *South West Rocks:* 2 beaches of ⅛ m. and 2 mi. Pt. weekends and public holidays only. DS, P(f), SB on main beach only. *Red Rock:* Not patrolled. DS, P(f), SB. *Angourie Point:* 4 mi. long. Pt, DS, P, SB. *Seven Mile Beach:* Lennox Head. 7 mi. long. Pt. Christmas–New Year. DS, Pt, SB. Camping nearby. *Byron Bay:* 5 mi. long. Pt, DS, P, SB. *Duranbah Beach:* Tweed Heads. 300 yards long. Pt, DS, P, SB.

South Coast. *Seven Mile Beach:* 7 mi. long and not patrolled. DS, P, SB. *Pebbly Beach:* 2 mi. long and unpatrolled. SB. At dusk kangaroos graze on the edge of the beach. Access is via a forest road. *Moruya:* 1½ mi. long. Pt in season. DS, SB. *Narooma:* ½ mi. long. Pt in season. DS, P, SB. *Tathra:* 3 m. long. Pt in season. DS, P, SB. *Merimbula:* 4 mi. long. Pt in season. DS, P, SB.

Lord Howe Island: *Neds Beach:* Over 21 different species of fish come to be hand fed here. *Old Settlement Beach* and *North Beach* on the lagoon are the most popular beaches for swimming, and there are barbecue areas and dressing sheds. Snorkeling here is rewarding. *Blinky Beach:* the island's surfing beach.

ZOOS AND ANIMAL PARKS. See also Parks, Gardens, and Forests, above, for more good spots for wildlife watching. **Central Coast.** *Eric Worrell's Australian Reptile Park.* Pacific Highway, 1km north of Gosford; (043) 28–4311. Open daily 8 A.M.–6 P.M.

North Coast. *Pet Porpose Pool,* Orlando Street, Coffs Harbour; (066) 52–2164. Open daily. There are two daily shows by porpoises and seals. *Kumbaingerie Animal Park,* Pacific Highway, 14km north of Coffs Harbour. This is an 80-hectare sanctuary of mainly Australian fauna.

New England. *Goonoowigall Wildlife Refuge* 5km south of Inverell, just off the Tingha road. It is regarded as one of the most valuable wildlife refuges in northern NSW, and over 120 species of native birds have been recorded there. Vehicular access is limited.

North West. *Macquarie Marshes.* The marshes occupy a natural depression filled by water from the Macquarie River and are surrounded and protected on all sides by tall reeds and unusual plant life. There are large numbers of swans, brolgas, pelicans, ducks, ibis, and spoonbills. The marshes are about 100km north of Warren.

Murray Riverina. *Murray Cod Hatcheries Fauna Park.* 8km east of Wagga on the Sturt Highway. It features the largest and oldest Murray cod in captivity and is Australia's largest fish hatchery.

Golden West. *Western Plains Zoo.* (068) 82–5888, Dubbo. Australia's only official open-range zoo. Visitors can drive on the 6km of sealed roads, hire a bicycle or mini moke, or walk along the road and bush trails. Coach tours to the zoo are operated by Country Wide. For tours call (068) 82–2249. Open daily.

Lord Howe Island. Lord Howe Island is listed by the United Nations World Heritage Committee as of "Outstanding Universal Value"; it is the natural home of a wide variety of sea-birds and plant life and attracts many naturalists.

SPORTS. Blue Mountains. *Bushwalking.* Since the Blue Mountains National Park is so accessible to Sydney it is a very popular for bushwalking. The following companies will escort you on bushwalking tours in the area: *Australian Himalayan Expeditions,* (02) 264–3366, overnight excursions from Sydney; *Blue Mountains Guide Service,* (047) 82–3782 or (047) 82–1833, 1½-hour walks on weekends and 4- to 6-hour walks daily.

Upper Hawkesbury. *Grass Skiing.* Facilities at the *Kurrajong Heights Grass Ski Park,* (045) 67–7260, include beginner and advanced slopes, equipment hire, tows, and lessons. Open weekends and school and public holidays from 9 A.M.

Golf. Windsor Country Golf Club, McQuade Avenue, (045) 77–4390; *Richmond Golf Club,* Bourke Street, (045) 78–1739.

Horseracing. Hawkesbury Race Club, (045) 77–2263. The historic *Clarendon Racecourse* is the oldest racing institution in Australia, outside the Australian Jockey Club. Its first meeting was held in 1829. It is still a leading club in Australia and has an excellent trotting track. There are 20 race days (gallops) and 20 trotting nights each year, usually on Thursdays. Check with the tourist-information center for details, (045) 77–2310.

Horseriding. The Hawkesbury is a very "horsey" area. Casual riding and lessons are available from many local groups. These include: *Valley View* at Grose Vale, (045) 72–1260; *Lyndrian Trails* at St. Albans, (045) 68–2106; *Farm Equestrian Centre* (lessons only) at Kurrajong Hills, (045) 73–1276.

Water Skiing: Del Rio Aquatic Club, (045) 66–4330 offers lessons as well as camper accommodations and tent sites, a restaurant and club, and all facilities for skiers bringing their own boats.

The Illawarra. *Horseriding. Tugalong Station,* Tugalong Road, Canyon Leigh, (048) 78–9171. Enjoy a bush holiday here, with up to 5 hours' daily trail riding. *Bundanoon Horseriding,* Erith Street, Bundanoon, (048) 83–6434, half-hour, hour, and day rides.

Sailboarding. Wollongong Sailboard School, (042) 28–7878. Sailboarding at Brighton Beach, Wollongong, 9 A.M.–4 P.M. Thursday–Sunday, weather permitting.

The Hunter. The Hunter region is a mecca for water-sport enthusiasts. Surfing, swimming and fishing, boating are the major activities. *Sailing.* At Myall Lakes yachts are available for charter from *Myall Lakes Water Safaries,* (049) 97–4664, who also offer sailing tours, and *Appollo Yacht Charters,* (049) 43–6239. In Port Stephens, yachts are available from *Sail-Cruise,* (049) 81–2405.

Cruising. In Port Stephens, cruisers for charter are from *Leisure Time Charter Cruise,* (049) 81–4144

Houseboats. Newcastle Holiday Houseboats, (049) 63–5700; *Myall Lake Houseboats,* (049) 97–4221; *Taree-Manning River Houseboats,* (065) 52–6271.

Hot-Air Ballooning. From April to November early-morning balloon flights are made over the winelands and farms of the Hunter. They finish with a champagne breakfast. Book with *Balloon Aloft,* (02) 607–2255.

North Coast. *Sailing.* Contact *Ballina Quays Marina,* (066) 86–4643. Sailboards and catamarans are available at Grafton, (066) 72–3525.

Cruising. Skipper-a-Clipper, Port Macquarie (small craft), (065) 83–1940.

Houseboats. Manning River Houseboats, Taree, (065) 52–6271. *Gold Coast Houseboat Hire,* Murwillumbah, (066) 72–3525.

Canoeing. Within an hour's drive of Grafton there is good canoeing for the inexperienced-to-the-expert canoeist. Hire canoes and kayaks at Grafton, (066) 42–6284.

Diving. For access to diving in almost all weather conditions, Byron Bay with clear warm water is the place. Dive charters from *Byron Bay Dive Centre.* By diving here in the Julian Rocks Marine Park you will see the coming together of the tropical and temperate sealife species; (066) 85–6857.

Fishing. At *Iluka Boatshed and Marina* you can hire boats for fishing as well as buy tackle and other supplies; (066) 46–6106.

Golf. Coolangatta–Tweed Heads Golf Club, Soorley Street, Tweed Heads South, (075) 36–2799. *Terranora Lakes Country Club,* Maranana Street, Belambil Heights, (075) 54–9223

Horse Racing. Grafton has been called the horse-racing capital of New South Wales. There is a year-long racing calendar, the highlight being the July Racing Carnival, where some of Australia's top thoroughbreds and riders compete. Contact *Clarence River Jockey Club,* (066) 42–2566, and *South Grafton Jockey Club,* (066) 42–5353.

The Outback. *Houseboating.* Houseboat holidays on the Murray or Darling rivers commence at Wentworth. The boats are spacious, with plenty of deck room for relaxing. You can swim, fish, picnic on a secluded sandy beach and visit attractions on the shore. All for hire from: *Aqua Sun,* (050) 27–3322; *Aquavilla,* (050) 27–3396; and *Liba Liba,* (050) 27–3355.

Murray Riverina. *Boating.* Canoes, kayaks, sailing, and fishing boats can be hired in Albury-Wodonga, at Walwa, Lake William Hovell, Lake Guy, Rocky Valley Dam, Lake Hume, and Lake Mulwala. For full details contact the travel bureau, (060) 21–1477. In Corowa, for both boat and bike hire, contact *Bindeere Holiday Park,* (060) 33–2500. In Griffith, paddleboats can be hired on Lake Wyangan on weekend afternoons.

Ballooning. Early morning hot-air-balloon flights can be experienced over the rice fields and orchards of the Murrumbidgee Irrigation Area between July and October. Book with the visitor-information center at Leeton, (069) 53–2611.

NEW SOUTH WALES

Canoeing. Hire a canoe and explore the region's waterways yourself (see Boating) or let *Adventure Tours* at Albury, (060) 25–6755, arrange the trip. They'll accommodate beginners for a 3- to 4-hour leisurely paddle, set the adrenaline pumping on a day's white-water canoeing, or organize combined canoeing and camping trips.

Fishing. The lakes and rivers of the southern part of the region are a fisher's paradise. You should be well armed with information on fishing licenses and fishing seasons. Contact the *Inland District Fisheries Office,* 512 Dean Street, Albury, (060) 23–0941, or have a chat with Mr. Russell Mason, 320b Urana Road, Lavington, (060) 25–1346, a local expert.

Golf. There are a number of excellent golf courses along the Murray; some have on-course accommodations or are planning them. *Albury Golf Club,* North Street, Albury, (060) 21–3411—a championship 18-hole golf course. *Hume Country Golf Club,* Logan Road, North Albury, (060) 25–2766—18-hole course; it is being expanded to 36 holes and will have on-course accommodations.

Gliding. The *Leeton Gliding Club* offers joy flights and instructions on weekends. Bookings through the visitor-information center, (069) 53–2611. In *Tocumwal,* the *Sportavia Soaring Centre* offers complete gliding instruction for beginners to the advanced, daily, (058) 74–2063.

Water Skiing. Boats and equipment are for hire at Lake Hume and Lake Mulwala. Phone the Albury Travel Bureau, (060) 21–1477, for details.

The Snowy. For details on the many sporting holidays available in the Snowy, inquire at the Travel Centre of NSW, (02) 231–4444. A sample, only, is given here: *Canoeing and Rafting.* There is a wide choice of canoeing and rafting trips in the Snowy region departing from either Sydney or Cooma. For some examples, contact *Australian Himalayan Expeditions,* Sydney, (02) 264–3366, or *Wilderness Expeditions* in Cooma, (0648) 2–1581.

Cycling. 2-day cycling tours through the Snowy River Valley are available from *Kosciusko Expeditions,* (0648) 6–2458.

Fishing. There is a wide variety of trout-fishing sites, from fast, cascading streams in the high mountains, to the more placid waters of lakes and dams. The best way to approach the trout waters, like the snowfields, is via Cooma. The 188km stretch of the Snowy Mountains Highway between Cooma and Tumut—which runs partly through Kosciusko National Park—is studded with excellent trout-fishing places. The main lakes and dams, well stocked with rainbow trout, brown trout, and some Atlantic salmon, are: Jindabyne, Lake Eucumbene (the largest of them all, containing nine times as much water as Sydney Harbour), the Tantangara, Talbingo, and Jounama dams, and Lake Blowering. The best trout streams can be approached from the centers of Cooma, Dalgety, Jindabyne, Thredbo Alpine Village, Khankoban, Adaminaby, Kiandra, Bombala, and Nimmitabel. *Trout Tours,* (0648) 42–2276, operates from Anglers Reach Lakeside Village, Lake Eucumbene (via Adaminaby), and organizes half, one- and two-day fishing trips on Lake Eucumbene. Their boats are comfortable, and top-quality tackle is supplied. You can also hire your own boat and gear. Inquire from the Cooma Visitors' Centre, (0648) 21–177, regarding fishing licenses.

Gliding. Alpine Soaring, Barry Way, 3km south of Jindabyne, (0648) 6–2348: instruction and joy flights in a powered glider over the Snowy Mountains.

Horse Riding. You will find many opportunities for day rides or horseback safaris in the Snowy Mountains, the home of poet Banjo Patterson's legendary horseman the Man from Snowy River. Operators include: *Reynella Safaris,* via Adaminaby, (0648) 44–2386, accommodation and day rides, or horseback camping trips; *Thredbo Riding School,* Thredbo Alpine Village, (0648) 7–6275, hour-long rides along the Thredbo River, half-day rides, or a five-day riding holiday; *Talbingo Trails,* Tumut, (069) 47–2173; weekend or five- to six-day trail rides.

Sailboarding. Lake Jindabyne Sailboards, next to Snow-hire Caravan Park, Thredbo turnoff, Jindabyne, (0648) 6–7091. Hire boards available.

Sailing. Sundance Sailing School, next to Snow-Line Caravan Park, Thredbo turnoff, Jindabyne, (0648) 6–7091. Rental of Hobie Cats with all equipment and jackets supplied. Instruction available.

Skiing. Equipment can be hired on the snowfields, in Jindabyne, Cooma, and Sydney. Daily or weekly passes must be bought at each skifield to use the skilifts. The price is around $A25–$A28 per day for adults. There are many ski tours from Sydney during the season (June to early October) for downhill skiers. They usually include coach transport, accommodation, and meals. Operators include *Ansett Pioneer*, (02) 268–1363, and *Deanes Clipper Tours*, (02) 888–3022. Cross-country skiing trips for beginners are organized by *Australian Himalayan Expeditions*, (02) 264–3366, and *Wildtrek*, (02) 29–2307.

South Coast. *Boating.* Small pleasure craft are available for hire right along the coast. Inquire at local tourist-information centers.

Diving. In Huskisson (on Jervis Bay), dive charter vessels are available from *Sea Life III*, (044) 41–5012, and on the *Bay Explorer*, (044) 41–5255. In Moruya, boats and equipment available from *Dive-About*, (044) 74–2454, or after hours (044) 71–1247.

Fishing. From Clyde River (Bateman's Bay); a boat leaves the public wharf twice daily. Book at *Harry's Bait and Tackle Shop*. In Merimbula, enjoy fishing cruises aboard the *Matilda* on Merimbula Lake. Rods and bait supplied, (0649) 5–1129. For big-game fishing, the *Warrigul* departs from Ulladulla Harbour; (044) 55–8589. Bermagui is one of the state's best starting sports for game fishing. *Shiralee Lodge and Charter Service* can provide you with accommodation and also runs fishing trips on the vessels *Parpin* and *Binjarra*. Phone (047) 73–8071 for details.

Sailboarding. Jervis Bay Windsurfing School, 55 Owen Street, Huskisson (at Sailor's Beach), (044) 41–5055.

Golden West. *Ballooning.* The *Adventure Travel Centre*, (02) 264–6033, and *Australian Himalayan Expeditions*, (02) 264–3366, can arrange hot-air-ballooning trips to Canowindra for you between April and November.

Car Racing. Bathurst is the home of the internationally known James Hardie 1,000 race. It is held annually on the Mount Panorama Motor Racing Circuit on the first weekend in October. Visitors can drive on the track when its not in use.

Motor Cycle Racing. Huge crowds of fans flock to Bathurst for the Easter Motor Cycle Races held annually on the Mount Panorama Motor Racing Circuit.

Lord Howe Island. *Boating.* Charter boat representatives will call at your lodge. *Sailboards and Surfskis.* For hire from Michael Thompson, of the MVCoral Princess. Diving. Diving tours from Sydney allow divers to experience the diverse sea life of the "Crossroads of the Pacific," fed by currents from the Great Barrier Reef, New Caledonia, New Zealand, and Australia. Contact: *Sealife International*, 27 Alfred Street, Coogee; (02) 665–6335.

Fishing. Enjoy a half- or full-day fishing trip aboard the TSMV *Lulawei* in the Pacific waters around Lord Howe Island. All bait and tackle supplied, tel: Lord Howe Island 2195.

Golf. The *Lord Howe Island Golf Club* has a nine-hole golf course overlooking the lagoon. Clubs and balls are available for hire.

Norfolk Island. Inquire at the visitor-information center for details about tennis-court hire, boat and bicycle hire, and the best fishing spots and fishing tours. They will also tell you about how to arrange a game of golf on the islands picturesque course and of its unusual hazards, suprisingly relaxed-looking cattle.

During winter (June–August) the island hosts the Dewar's Winter Sport Carnival, and there is plenty of activity for both spectators and participants. Sports include bowls, scuba diving, snorkeling, photography, golf, tennis, billiards, and snooker. There are also bridge tournaments, backgammon, chess, and mahjong. All events are designed for the not so serious as well as the experienced.

MUSEUMS AND HISTORIC SITES. The Blue Mountains. There are numerous small museums, galleries, and antique shops in the Blue Mountains. *Norman Lindsay Gallery and Museum*, 128 Chapman Parade, Faulconbridge, via Springwood (047) 51–1067, was home of the artist Norman Lindsay from 1912 until his death in 1969. It now houses a large collection of his works. Surrounded by gardens. Open 11 A.M.–5 P.M., Friday–Sunday. *Tranter Museum of Australiana*, 7 Rupert Street, Katoomba (047) 82–2552. Open weekends and school and public holidays. Specializes in Australian bushranger history.

Upper Hawkesbury. Parramatta: *Experiment Farm Cottage*. Harris Street, (02) 635–5655. Open Tuesday-Sunday and public holidays from 10 A.M.–4 P.M.. Georgian-style cottage built c. 1835. Site of James Rude's experiment farm. First

NEW SOUTH WALES

land grant made by Governor Phillip; here Ruse sowed Australia's first wheat crop. *Lancer Barracks,* Smith Street. *Elizabeth Farm House,* Alice Street, (02) 635-9488. Open Tuesday–Sunday and public holidays from 10 A.M.–4:30 P.M. Oldest existing building in Australia; prototype of the early colonial farmhouse. *Hambledon Cottage,* Hassall Street, (02) 635-6924. Open Wednesday–Sunday and public holidays 11 A.M.–4 P.M.

Court House. Court Street, Windsor, (045) 77-3023. A beautifully restored sandstock brick building stands as it was when erected (1821–1822), by William Cox with convict labor. Designed by Francis Greenway, it is still used as a courthouse. Open Monday–Wednesday 10 A.M.–12:20 P.M.; weekends 11 A.M.–noon, 1–4 P.M.

Pitt Town. One of the 5 Macquarie towns, it is very peaceful and set in beautiful rural countryside. Although most of the buildings are privately owned and not open to visitors, a stroll through the town will evoke the historic atmosphere.

The Illawarra. *Wollongong City Art Gallery.* Cnr Keira and Burrelli streets, (042) 28-7802 As well as a permanent Australian collection, the gallery has monthly traveling exhibitions.

The Hunter. *Dobell House,* 47 Dobell Drive, Wangi Wangi. Formerly the artist William Dobell's residence, the house has been retained much as it was in his lifetime. Open Sundays and public holidays (except Christmas Day and Good Friday) 2–4 P.M.

Newcastle Region Maritime Museum. At Fort Scratchley, (049) 2-2588. Exhibits include maritime-technology and marine-art works. Open Tuesday–Sunday noon–4 P.M.

The North Coast. *Ballina Maritime Museum.* Norton Street, (066) 86-3484. Features the La Balsa Raft, which landed in November 1973 having drifted 13,760km across the Pacific in 178 days from Ecuador. It thus proved that South Americans could have crossed the Pacific in a similar fashion centuries before. Open daily.

Coffs Harbour and District Historical Museum. 191 High Street, (066) 52-5794. Includes some aboriginal artifacts in its display.

Lismore Regional Art Gallery. Molesworth Street, (066) 21-1536. Open Tuesday–Saturday. This is the only permanent public collection in the region.

"The Pub With No Beer." (The Cosmopolitan) at Taylors Arms, about a half hour's drive west from Macksford. This hotel, built in 1903, was made famous by a song of the bush balladeer Gordon Parsons. It has good picnic and barbecue facilities.

St. Thomas' Church. Cnr. Hay and William streets, Port Macquarie. Built by convict labor between 1824 and 1828. Inspections daily except Friday afternoon and Sunday.

Trial Bay Gaol. Trial Bay. 35km northeast of Kempsey. The restored front section of the old gaol, dating back to 1886, houses a museum and kiosk. Swim at the sheltered beach alongside, enjoy your picnic lunch, and camp here too.

Tweed Heads Historic Site. Kirkwood Rd., South Tweed Heads, (066) 28-117. This is the location of the Minju Bal Resource Museum and Study Centre as well as a fine aboriginal bora ring. The museum is operated by the Tweed Aboriginal Co-operative. Open Tuesday–Friday 10 A.M.–3 P.M.

Newcastle Regional Art Gallery. (049) 26-3644. Contains a Dobell collection and other national art treasures, as well as Australia's largest collection of contemporary Japanese ceramics. Open Monday–Saturday 10 A.M.–5 P.M. and Sunday and public holidays 2–5 P.M.

New England. *Centenary Cottage.* Logan Street, Tenterfield, was built in 1871 and contains items of historical interest. Open weekends.

Convict-Carved Road Tunnel. Midway between Glen Innes and Grafton. A vivid reminder of the harsh early days of NSW, the tunnel is set among beautiful mountain and riverside scenery.

Folk Museum. Cnr Rusden and Faulkner streets, Armidale, (067) 72-8666. The building that houses displays on early transport, handicrafts, and lifestyles has been classified by the National Trust.

Hillview Doll Museum. Palham Street, Tenterfield, (067) 36-1491. There are more than 1,000 dolls from all over the world; locally made "applehead" dolls are a feature.

Land of the Beardies History House and Museum. Glen Innes. A working model of Glen Innes life more than a century ago. Local crafts are for sale. Open daily.

New England Regional Art Museum. Kentucky Street, Armidale, (067) 72-3771. The museum houses the famous Hinton Art Collection, the Armidale City Art Collection, and the Coventry Collection. Open daily.

Pioneer Village. 2km south of Inverell Post Office, (067) 22-3348. A collection of authentic 1840-1930 buildings moved here from their original sites. Picnic and barbecue facilities are provided.

Smith's Mining and Natural History Museum, on the banks of Smiths Creek, Tingha, (067) 23-3479. The display includes a good mineral and gemstone collection. Telephone for hours of opening.

The Outback. *The Broken Hill City Art Gallery.* Civic Center, Chloride Street; open Monday-Saturday. Established in 1904, this is the oldest regional art gallery in New South Wales. As well as an interesting general collection of Australian art, there are many works by the acclaimed local artists called "The Brushmen of the Bush," such as Pro Hart and Jack Absalom.

Daydream Mine. Broken Hill, (080)-2241. Discovered in 1881. For those wearing comfortable walking shoes a walk down to the workings is most interesting.

Silverton Ghost Town. 25km from Broken Hill. Once a mining town, now a popular set for movie producers—parts of *Road Warrior* were filmed here. A camel farm operates at Silverton, and rides are available.

Murray Riverina. *Albury Regional Art centre.* (060) 21-6384. There is a permanent collection of paintings, prints, photographs, and ceramics as well as monthly visiting exhibitions.

Albury Regional Museum. Housed in the Turks Head Hotel, (060) 21-4550. Built in 1854, near the historic Union Bridge between New South Wales and Victoria. Open daily.

Jindera Pioneer Museum. Jindera, (060) 26-3221. Named NSW Museum of the Year in 1982, this museum features a store stocked with authentic goods of the 19th century, while the living area at the rear is furnished in its original style. Open daily.

Pioneer Park Museum. Airport Road, 2km north of Griffith, (069) 62-4196. A complex of buildings from last century including a homestead, gadhouse, schoolhouse, and church. Open daily.

Woolpack Inn Museum. Albury Street, Holbrook, (060) 36-2131. Open daily. The museum was a two-story hotel; rooms and yard are in the style of yesteryear.

The Snowy. *Bedervale,* Via Braidwood, (048) 42-2421. A colonial homestead. Built in 1840, Bedervale is on a working grazing property. Its original furniture, silverware, and books are on display. Open the first Sunday of each month, with tours of the homestead at 2, 3, and 4 P.M.

Riversdale. North of Goulburn, just past Goulburn Gaol, (048) 21-4741. A National Trust building, Riversdale is a colonial Georgian residence built from locally hand-made sandstock bricks in 1838. Open daily. Inquire at information centre, (048) 21-5343, for hours.

South Coast. *Kameruka Estate.* Off the Princes Highway between Bega and Merimbula; one of the oldest dairy farms in Australia. Open daily.

Central Tilba. 15km south of Narooma; has been declared a historic village by the National Trust and is set amid the rolling green hills of dairy country.

Eden Whaling Museum. A small museum, it gives the background to the industry upon which Eden was founded. Open daily.

Golden West. *Carcoar.* a small village classified by the National Trust, 48km from Bathurst on the Mid Western Highway.

Gulgong. Famous as the town on Australia's $10 note, Gulgong grew from a gold discovery in 1867. The main street is much as it was when the town first developed and the Pioneers Museum, (063) 74-1513, is worth a visit (open daily).

Hill End and Sofala. The gold rush of the 1870s brought 60,000 people to these towns. Some of the original buildings remain, but the population is now very small.

Old Dubbo Gaol. Macquarie Street, Dubbo, (068) 82-8122. Closed as a jail since 1966, it has been faithfully restored as a tourist attraction and a reminder of its colonial past. Open daily.

Yerranderie Ghost Town. Situated on the edge of the Blue Mountains National Park Yerranderie was once a thriving silver-mining town and now consists of only a few residences. Bush camping is available, and there are lodge

NEW SOUTH WALES

rooms at the historic post office. Chester coaches runs weekend tours to Yerranderie from Sydney, (02) 644–7980.

WINERIES. The Hunter Valley Wine Society will provide a lengthy list of vineyards you can visit and a map. There are more than 35 wineries in the region, and at least one bottle each of red and white wine should be on your shopping list. *Hungerford Hill Wine Village,* Broke Road, Pokolbin, (049) 98–7666. Open daily. A recreational complex in a bushland setting. A good food and wine pavilion. *Hunter Estate,* Hermitage Road, Pokolbin, (049) 98–7577. Open daily. Licensed French restaurant (closed Thursday). *Rothbury Estate,* Broke Road, Pokolbin, (049) 98–7555. Open daily.

GALLERIES. The North Coast. *Bentinck Galleries, Antiques and Fine Arts.* Bentinck St., Ballina, (066) 86–4065. Paintings by leading Australian artists are for sale.

The Outback. For details of the dozen or so artists' galleries open to visitors in Broken Hill, inquire at the tourist-information center, see above.

SHOPPING. The Illawarra. *Berkelouws Book Barn,* Hume Highway, Berrima, (048) 77–1370. Contains more than 75,000 volumes embracing a wide range of interests. Also sells rare and antique books, as well as books, maps, and prints. Open daily.

Victoria House, Hume Highway, Mittagong, (048) 71–1682. The largest selection of tapestry and embroidery kits in Australia and a comprehensive range of craft accessories. Open daily. There are also many fine *antique shops* in the Southern Highlands region: contact the information center at Mittagong for details, see above.

Norfolk Island. Norfolk Island is a duty-free port and for such a small township, Burnt Pine shops sell a wide variety of electronic equipment, cameras, imported ornaments, clothing, tableware and jewelry. All stores are within an easy walk of each other.

ENTERTAINMENT AND NIGHTLIFE. Most towns in New South Wales have one licensed club, if not half a dozen, that offers sporting and social facilities for members. Most welcome visitors. On the far North Coast are some of the biggest clubs in New South Wales. They attract visitors from Queensland (to play the poker machines) and from Victoria (to soak up north-coast sunshine, as well as play "the pokies"), locals, and other tourists on holidays. They offer bars, restaurants, and top entertainers. Two favorites: *Seagulls Rugby League Football Club,* Gollan Drive, West Tweed Heads, (075) 36–3433; *Twin Towns Services Club,* Pacific Highway, Tweed Heads, (075) 36–2277.

The licensed clubs along the Murray are among the best in the state. They have developed as such because of the large numbers of Victorians vacationing along the river to enjoy the sports and to play the poker machines at the clubs because they are not available within their own state. Visitors are welcome at the clubs, to play sport or "pokies" or to eat and drink at their very good restaurants and bars. A good example is the *Commercial Club,* 618 Dean Street, Albury, (060) 21–1133. It has four squash courts, two bowling greens, snooker and billiards, a coffee and snack bar, a bistro, and a dining room. Saturday nights there is a cabaret and dinner dance and there are film nights and regular live entertainment.

AUSTRALIAN CAPITAL TERRITORY

Canberra and Environs

In 1901 when the federation of Australia became established the new country had a proper government—without a proper home. Australia had no capital; it was governed mainly from Melbourne, where parliament also sat. Certainly, the constitution provided that a capital should be built. It had to be somewhere within the area of New South Wales at least 160km from Sydney. On selection of the site it would be transferred from state to commonwealth jurisdiction. Many communities, wanting to become the future center of Australian political and administrative life, had offered themselves for the role. None was accepted. It was eight years before, in 1908, a suitable site was chosen on the western slopes of the Great Dividing Range, about 310km from Sydney and 660km from Melbourne. The area of 2,359 square km was transferred from New South Wales to the Commonwealth. It consisted mainly of cleared grazing land with two tiny villages (Hall and Tharwa), five mountain peaks above 1,500m and the narrow Mologolo River, a tributary of the Murrumbidgee, running through it. But what should the new capital be called? Suggestions poured in but it was not until 1913—when the first buildings were begun—that the choice was made. Australia's capital was to be called Canberra, an Aboriginal word meaning "meeting place."

An international competition to select the design of the new capital was won by the distinguished American architect Walter Burley Griffin in 1909. But more than 40 years passed before Canberra's development really got under way. Earlier, because of the two world wars and the depression in between, there was no money available for the ambitious project. Besides, few people wanted to live in a place that was nominally a city but in reality a huge building site with empty spaces between the few houses standing in forlorn isolation. A temporary parliament building was finished in 1927—with extensions it is still in use; a small shopping center was erected—it is still there; comparatively modest homes for the governor-general and the prime minister were constructed—they still live in them; and a few government departments, including the prime minister's, managed to function from crowded quarters in Canberra. But as soon as parliament was adjourned on Fridays for the weekend the great scramble home began, and for a while after World War II a roster system had to be introduced so that at least one minister, in addition to the prime minister, stayed in the capital on Saturdays and Sundays. In the 1950s, when the federal government began to insist that diplomatic representatives should move from Sydney to Canberra, a veil of gloom descended on the illustrious ambassadors and their staffs.

Seeing Canberra today one would hardly believe that this was the situation only about three decades ago. For whatever its shortcomings may be, the national capital is one of the world's most beautiful modern planned cities. Some 12 million trees and shrubs planted in its open spaces have transformed the former grazing paddocks into continuous parklands. Damming of the Molonglo has created Lake Burley Griffin, a peaceful expanse of water with 36km of park shores including the Commonwealth Nursery Gardens. The architectural style of the public building ranges from good to excellent and many of the new embassies, built by some of the 61 foreign diplomatic representations in the national capital, are showpieces. Occasionally some of them open their doors for public inspection—at a small charge, which goes to charity.

Canberra's rate of growth has outstripped that of any other place in Australia. In 1957 only some 36,000 people lived here, 20 years later more than 200,000, and by today the population is in excess of 240,000 people. A large proportion of the population consists of New Australians and many of them work in the service industries, including tourism. More than two and a half million tourists a year now flock to Canberra merely to see the country's capital. They can stay in numerous hotels or motels—some of the best in the country. The best season to visit Canberra is spring, when the thousands of Australian and exotic trees and bushes are in bloom, or in autumn, when the mellow sun shines on rusty foliage. Summer, on the other hand, can be hot and winter rather cold.

Although politics and government provide most of the jobs in Canberra—about 60 percent of the population is in the public service—the capital is fast developing into an artistic and intellectual center. The National University is here, and so are the headquarters of several scientific institutions, including the Commonwealth Scientific and Industrial Research Organisation (CSIRO) and the Academy of Science. The attractive civic center provides theater and concerts. For those who wish to spend their holidays in Canberra, the city offers a wide choice of sporting activities including rowing, swimming, horse riding, golf, and even a nude-bathing beach on the banks of the Murrumbidgee River. Certainly, Canberra has many critics who bewail the social stratification that automatically puts one into a niche according to his or her political pecking order or public service rank; the loneliness, especially of young wives and mothers who had to move to Canberra leaving behind their close relations and friends; the boredom, such as felt by some foreign diplomats used to pulsating urban life and unable to become reconciled to the slow-motion provincialism of Australia's national capital. Still, the advantages of living in a beautiful city away from the hectic bustle, pollution, and traffic problems of the major cities obviously outstrip the drawbacks.

Canberra proper occupies only the northern part of the Australian Capital Territory (ACT)—the area acquired by the commonwealth—and three new townships, Woden, Belconnen, and Tuggeranong, have been developed to cope with the swelling population, for Canberra is tearing at its seams. The ACT has a fully elected 18-member house of assembly but is primarily administered by a federal minister for the capital territory. The people of Canberra elect two members to the House of Representatives and two to the Senate of the Federal Parliament.

Exploring Canberra

Parliament House is the obvious place to begin an inspection of Canberra's important buildings. It was erected as a transitional solution—"something more than provisional and less than permanent"—between 1923 and 1927. The founding fathers of federation dreamed of something more grandiose. But by 1923 the parliamentarians who had assembled in Melbourne since Federation in 1901 realized that if they insisted on carrying out the founder's plans they would have to wait longer before they could move to the national capital. Hence they decided to make do with something more modest for the next 50 years or so. At that time (1923) the federal parliament had only 36 senators and 74 members of the House of Representatives, so the building to which they moved in 1927 was at least adequate for their needs. Today the Senate has 76 members and the House of Representatives has 148. With additions during the past half century the number of rooms stands now at 638 and even this is insufficient, so construction of a new Parliament House, planned for completion in 1989, has begun on Capitol Hill.

But the old building will probably be maintained, and rightly so. Admittedly, its architecture is not memorable, but it is quite a pleasant building. And, after all, it is a historical relic that will be better appreciated with the passing of time. The interior of Parliament House, though not spectacular, is in muted good taste. The main entrance leads to the colonnaded King's Hall, decorated with portraits of the queen, by Australian artists, and of past governors-general, prime ministers, presidents of the Senate, and speakers of the House of Representatives. The most interesting exhibit in King's Hall is one of the three surviving copies of Magna Carta in its 1297 version. On the right of King's Hall (looking into it from the entrance) is the chamber of the Senate and to the left is that of the House of Representatives.

Visitors may sit in the galleries and listen to the proceedings of either the Senate or the House of Representatives. Tickets of admission may be obtained on application to the principal attendant in writing, or by telephone: (062) 72–1211. There are no tours of inspection when both houses are sitting. However, when only one house is in session, public tours of the other chamber are provided. When sittings commence in the afternoon, tours operate in the morning. The house is open daily.

The National Library, designed by the Sydney architects Bunning, Madden, and O'Mahoney, stands on the southern shore of Lake Burley Griffin. It was built between 1964 and 1968 at a cost of about $A8 million. It is a building of classical simplicity, and its perfect proportions make it look smaller than it really is (110m long and 52m wide). Many fine Australian materials, including timber, have been used in its interior decoration. There are several exhibition areas, a theater seating 300 people, and a main reading room seating 150. There are other reading rooms for special studies and for newspapers and periodicals.

AUSTRALIAN CAPITAL TERRITORY

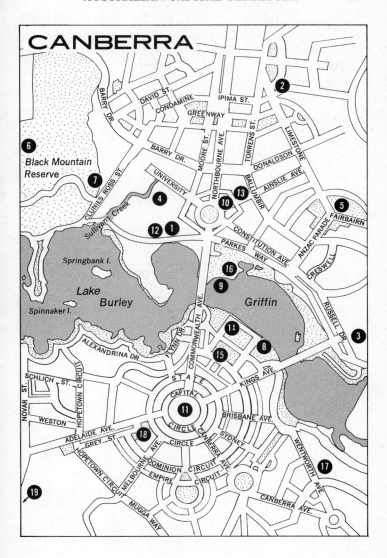

Points of Interest

1) Academy of Science
2) All Saints Church
3) Australian American Memorial
4) Australian National University
5) Australian War Memorial
6) Black Mountain Lookout and Telecom Tower
7) Botanic Garden
8) National Gallery and High Court
9) Capt. Cook Memorial Water Jet
10) Civic Square and Theatre Center
11) Capital Hill, construction site of new Parliament House
12) National Sound and Film Archive
13) Monaro Mall
14) National Library
15) Parliament House
16) Regatta Point Planning Exhibition
17) Railway Station
18) Prime Minister's lodge
19) Royal Australian Mint

Altogether the library has more than three million volumes, but it can be extended to store many more. Artistic features of the National Library include a copper relief above the entrance door by Australian sculptor Tom Bass; on the lake side of the building a bronze casting by Henry Moore; in the foyer three tapestries designed by Mathieu Mategot and woven of Australian wool at Aubusson, France. The library also exhibits relics of Captain Cook's voyages. Guided tours of the library start at 11:15 A.M. and 2:15 P.M. Monday to Friday. It is open seven days a week. The High Court building, opposite the library, was completed in 1980 and is another of the attractions in the Parliamentary Triangle. Next to it stands the new National Gallery, opened in October 1982. Visiting hours are 10 A.M.–5 P.M. daily.

Some Memorials

Erected to commemorate the men and women of Australia who gave their lives in their country's wars, the War Memorial is one of the world's most important military museums. It was originally started to commemorate Australian servicemen and women of World War I but when it was opened on November 11, 1941, World War II was well on its way. The exhibition galleries contain an enormous wealth of war equipment and pictures. The library and records section has a collection of more than 12,000 paintings, sketches, and sculptures, more than 250,000 photographic negatives and prints, and in excess of 1,200,000m of historic film. The library also holds 75,000 books, 5,000 volumes of bound periodicals, and 150,000 diaries and memoirs. The Australian War Memorial is open to visitors every day except Christmas Day.

Canberra has paid tribute to the memory of Captain Cook by installing a powerful water jet in the central basin of Lake Burley Griffin in the cove below Regatta Point, some 180m from the shoreline. The jet can spout a column of water weighing some six tons about 150m into the air. The sight is as beautiful as it is impressive. A mechanism automatically turns off the jet when the wind reaches a velocity of 19.2km per hour and turns it on again when the wind speed drops below that figure. A globe on the shore, 3m in diameter, shows the routes taken by Captain Cook, and they are described on the handrail surrounding it. The Captain Cook Memorial operates daily from 10 A.M. to noon, from 2 to 4 P.M.; from 8:30 to 9:30 P.M. (with floodlights) during daylight-saving time (end of October to the beginning of March), and other special occasions as directed by the Department of Capital Territory.

The Canberra Carillon, which stands on Aspen Island near Kings Avenue Bridge in Lake Burley Griffin, is a gift from the United Kingdom government to mark Canberra's 50th birthday. It is one of the largest of its kind in the world and has 53 bells. The biggest of them weighs six tons and the smallest 7kg. The three-column tower was built by the British Ministry of Buildings and Public Works; the bells were cast and the "clavier" (playing keyboard and frame) was constructed by John Taylor and Sons, Loughborough, England. Recitals are given regularly, and the Westminster chimes, which sound every quarter of an hour between 8 A.M. and 9 P.M., are relayed by landline to the city center.

The Australian-American Memorial, a 79m aluminium shaft surmounted by an eagle, commemorates America's help in the defense of Australia in World War II. It stands in the center of a building complex housing the Defence departments at Russell. The Australian National University's grounds are open to the public. Tours may be arranged for interested groups through the University Information Office in Balmain Crescent. The headquarters of the Australian Academy of

AUSTRALIAN CAPITAL TERRITORY

Science is one of Canberra's landmarks: a copper-covered shell concrete dome, 46m in diameter. Opposite, in the Institute of Anatomy buildings, there is an interesting exhibition of Aboriginal history and culture. The Civic Square and Theatre Centre are on a rather small scale. The center consists of two buildings: the larger Canberra Theatre, really an auditorium, seating 1,200 people, and the smaller Playhouse seating 312. Outside the city proper on the Murrumbidgee River, within the limits of the Tuggeranong new town development, stands Lanyon homestead, owned by the Australian government. Nearby is a gallery, which houses an exhibition of Sidney Nolan paintings, a gift of the famous artist to the nation. The Royal Military College, Duntroon, can be seen by joining a conducted tour held every day at 2:30 P.M. from Monday to Friday between April and October. People interested in Australian flora should visit the National Botanic Gardens (entry from Clunies Ross Street), which are devoted entirely to Australian native plants. The gardens are laid out on the slopes of Black Mountain, on the summit of which rises the Telecom Tower.

PRACTICAL INFORMATION FOR CANBERRA

HOW TO GET THERE. By car: from Sydney via the Hume and Federal highways; from Melbourne via the Hume and Barton highways or the Princes Highway and Monaro Highway via Cooma. **By rail:** from Sydney, daily XPT services run to Canberra (4 hours), the Canberra-Monaro Express runs Monday–Saturday, and the Canberra Express on Sunday (4½ hours). From Melbourne, disembark at Yass Junction and complete the journey by coach. **By air:** from Sydney: *Ansett,* (02) 268–1111, *Air Australian Airlines,* (02) 693–3333, *East West,* 2–0940 and *Air New South Wales,* (02) 268–1678 have daily flights to Canberra. There are also flights from Adelaide, Brisbane, Melbourne (TAA or Ansett), Coffs Harbour (Air NSW), Newcastle (East West), Wagga (*Western NSW Airlines*), Griffith, Orange, and Dubbo. **By bus:** *Ansett Pioneer,* (02) 268–1881, has express services between Sydney and Canberra, and from Cooma. *Murrays,* (062) 95–3677, links Canberra with Batemans Bay, Narooma, Moss Vale, and Wollongong. Express coach services from Melbourne to Sydney will drop passengers in Canberra and there are express coaches from Adelaide.

TOURIST INFORMATION. *Canberra Tourist Bureau,* Jolimont Centre, Northbourne Avenue, Canberra City, (062) 45–6464, open Monday–Friday and Saturday morning. The visitor-information center, Northbourne Avenue (just south of junction of Federal and Barton highways), open daily. **Useful Addresses:** *American Embassy:* State Circle, Yarralumla, (062) 73–3711. *UK Embassy:* Commonwealth Avenue, Yarralumla, (062) 73–0422

ACCOMMODATIONS. Canberra accommodations range from the deluxe to budget level, and despite the city's modest size there is a wide choice of good-quality rooms available. This situation has emerged in response to the demands for the best in service and hospitality from visiting politicians, diplomats, businesspeople, and tourists. Rates for double rooms without meals, are classified as follows: *Deluxe* $A90 and up; *Expensive* $A70–$A89; *Moderate* $A50–$A69; *Inexpensive* $A35–$A50; *Budget* below $A35.

Deluxe

Canberra International Motor Inn. 242 Northbourne Avenue; (062) 47–6966. 117 units with showers, set around a garden atrium with tropical rainforest plants. Air conditioned. Pool, restaurant, bar, coffee shop. Some rooms are apartment style with kitchen and lounge.

Noahs Lakeside International Hotel, London Circuit, Canberra City; (062) 47-6244. 216 units, 7 suites, with showers. Air conditioned. Pool and restaurant. Some rooms have views of the lake.

Parkroyal Motor Inn. 102 Northbourne Avenue, Braddon (2km northeast); (062) 49-1411. 77 units with showers. Pool. The Silver Grill Restaurant is an award winner.

TraveLodge Canberra City. 74 Northbourne Avenue, Canberra City; (062) 49-6911. 72 units with showers. Air conditioned. Restaurant and pool. The closest hotel to the city center.

EXPENSIVE

Canberra Rex Hotel. Northbourne Avenue, Braddon (2km northeast); (062) 48-5311. 156 rooms, 2 suites with showers. Air conditioned. Restaurant. Pool, leisure and sporting facilities.

Capital Motor Inn. 108 Northbourne Avenue, Braddon (2km northeast); (062) 48-6566. 48 units with showers. Air conditioned. Restaurant. The newest motel in the Canberra business district and within an easy walk to the city.

Diplomat International Motor Inn. Cnr Canberra Avenue and Hely Street, Griffith (5km south); (062) 95-2277. 68 units, 10 suites, with showers. Pool, sauna, tennis and squash facilities. The motel is not far from Canberra's parliamentary triangle and is set among safe, leafy walks

Kingston Court. 4 Tench Street, Kingston (4km south); (062) 95-2244. 36 self-contained, two-bedroom spacious apartments with quality fittings. Air conditioned. Swimming pool, half-court tennis, barbecue area.

The Manna Guest House. Turallo Terrace, Bungendore NSW (35km northeast); (062) 38-1582. Pool. The Manna is a beautifully restored Edwardian Josephite Convent. Tariff includes breakfast, and dinner is available.

MODERATE

Embassy Motel. Cnr Hopetoun Circuit and Adelaide Avenue, Deakin (5km southwest); (062) 81-1322. 86 units, 4 suites, with showers. Air conditioned cooling and central heating. Pool and sauna, restaurant.

Town House Motor Inn. 65 Ainslie Street, Canberra City; (062) 48-8011. 61 units, 2 suites, with showers. Air conditioned. Restaurant. Close to theater, cinema, and shops.

INEXPENSIVE

Kythera Motel. 98-100 Northbourne Avenue, Braddon (2km northeast); (062) 48-7611. 72 units with showers. Air conditioned. Pool. Restaurant.

New Deakin Inn. 70 Kent Street, Deakin; (062) 81-1011. Hotel-motel of 24 units with showers. 2 restaurants: a Malay-Chinese and an Italian. Nearby are the prime minister's lodge and new Parliament House site.

Nineteenth Hole Motel. 311 Goyden Street, Narrabundah (7km southeast); (062) 95-3477. 23 units with showers. Air conditioned. Pool and spa. Restaurant. Overlooks the Capital Golf Course.

Regency Motor Inn. 47 McMillan Cnr Griffith (5km south); (062) 95-0074. 62 units, 9 suites, with showers. Air conditioned. Pool, 2 restaurants.

BUDGET

Motel 7. Cooma Road, Narrabundah (7km southeast); (062) 95-1111. 63 units with showers, pool, restaurant (closed Monday).

RESTAURANTS. Canberra can offer diners a variety of ethnic cuisines and an assortment of atmospheres in which to enjoy them: aboard a cruise, atop a lookout, in a farmhouse or old pub, and international standard restaurants. Price categories for meals for one person are as follows: *Expensive,* $A25-$A35, *Moderate,* $A15-$A24, *Inexpensive,* less than $A15. For credit card abbreviations see Restaurants in Practical Information for Sydney.

AUSTRALIAN CAPITAL TERRITORY

AUSTRALIAN

Gundaroo Pub Restaurant. *Inexpensive.* Gundaroo; (062) 95–3677. The pub was opened in 1865 and is now famous for its colonial meal of Gundaroo soup, sizzling T-bone steaks, freshly baked bush damper with jam and cream, and real billy tea. Entertainment is provided by bush musicians and in the evening there's a dance band. A set price includes meal, unlimited beer, wine, soft drinks, and entertainment. Licensed. L, Sunday; D, Thursday–Saturday. Inquire about free bus transport when booking.

FRENCH-AUSTRALIAN

Chats. *Moderate.* Cnr Burke Crescent and Canberra Avenue, Kingston; 95–0650. Daily menu changes and beautifully presented meals put together with fresh and tasty ingredients make this small restaurant an attractive one. Licensed L, Monday–Friday; D, Monday–Saturday, AE, BC, DC, MC, V.

Hill Station Homestead. *Expensive.* Shepperd Street, Hume; 60–1393. At this country-style restaurant visitors may dine in a large and airy pavilion or in smaller private dining rooms. There is an open fire in winter and furnishings are colonial in style. Licensed. L, Wednesday–Sunday; D, Tuesday–Sunday. AE, BC, DC, MC, V.

Le Carousel Jean Pierre. *Expensive.* Red Hill Lookout, Red Hill; 73–1808. Classic French cuisine, which has won the restaurant's host the coveted Golden Plate Award, can be enjoyed with magnificent views of Canberra. Licensed. L, Monday–Friday; D, Monday–Saturday. AE, BC, DC, MC, V.

Le Rustique. *Expensive.* 24 Garema Place; 48–6514. A blackboard menu sets out the regularly changing and high-quality French-provincial selection. Licensed. L, Monday–Friday; D, Monday–Saturday. AE, BC, DC, MC, V.

Nobbs. *Expensive.* The Lawns, Boungainville Street; Manuka; 95–9744. One of Canberra's best restaurants, where the atmosphere is elegant and the food is a rich assortment of French dishes with Australian influences. Licensed. L, Monday–Friday; D, Monday–Saturday. AE, BC, DC, MC, V.

Peaches. *Expensive.* Cnr Franklin and Furneaux streets, Manuka; 95–9795. One of Canberra's several excellent French-Australian restaurants with interesting and exotic dishes beautifully presented. Licensed. L, Monday–Friday; D, daily. AE, BC, DC, MC, V.

Warrens of Manuka. *Moderate–Expensive.* Cnr Franklin and Furneaux streets, Manuka; 95–9795. A small but stylish tavern serving French-Australian food, and a handy place for supper up to 11:15 P.M. Licensed. L, Sunday–Friday; D, daily; Supper daily. AE, BC, DC, MC, V.

Chats. *Moderate.* Cnr Burke Crescent and Canberra Avenue, Kingston, 95–0650. Daily menu changes and beautifully presented meals put together with fresh and tasty ingredients make this small restaurant an attractive one. Licensed. L, Monday–Friday; D, Monday–Saturday. AE, BC, DC, MC, V.

ITALIAN

La Cucina. *Moderate.* Plaza Level, Boulevard Centre, Canberra; 47–4849. Pasta with tasty sauces and good veal are the restaurant's backbone. It is a friendly and popular eating place. Unlicensed. L, Wednesday–Friday; D, Tuesday–Saturday. AE, BC, MC.

TOURIST

High Court Cafe. *Inexpensive.* High Court Building, overlooking Lake Burley Griffin; 70–6828. A pleasant venue for morning or afternoon tea or lunch. The food is fresh, well prepared, and inexpensive. L, daily. Morning and afternoon tea from 9:45 A.M.–4:15 P.M.

HOW TO GET AROUND. By bus. Canberra and its suburbs are serviced by the *ACTION* public bus network. Route maps and timetables are available from the Bus Interchange, City Walk, or at the Canberra Tourist

Bureau, (062) 45–6405. They list all the tourist attractions and the bus number to catch to get to them.

By car. rental cars are available from *Avis,* (062) 49–6088; *Budget,* (062) 48–9788; *Hertz,* (008) 42–5332; and *Thrifty,* (062) 47–7422. Driving around Canberra is simplified by following the routes of five tours marked with arrowed sign posts in the city and surroundings. There is also a travel-tape commentary for sale to go with the main arrow tour. Inquire at the tourist bureau.

TOURS. Day Tours. By bus: *The Canberra Explorer,* (062) 95–3677, links major tourist attractions every hour, and sightseers may leave and rejoin the bus at any of the 24 stops. A day ticket is $A7 for adults, and an hour ticket is $A2.50. *Ansett Pioneer,* (062) 45–6624, and *Murrays Australia,* (062) 95–3677, have day and half-day tours of Canberra and its rural environs. Ansett's day tour includes the snowfields and the Snowy Mountains Hydro Electric Scheme. Murrays has some tours offering dinki-di Aussie experiences at the Gundaroo Pub and Burbong Sheep Station. **Cruises:** Book with Murrays (see above) for cruises on Lake Burley Griffin and the Molongolo River and for lunch or dinner cruises aboard the *City of Canberra.* **By taxi:** *Canberra Taxi Tours,* (062) 48–6310, can suggest tours for you or design them to suit your requirements. **From Sydney.** The major day-tour operators in Sydney all have trips to Canberra in their programs. See Practical Information for Sydney.

Extended Tours. By coach: *Ansett Pioneer* (see above) has 2- to 10-day tours to Canberra and the Snowy Mountains region from Sydney, Melbourne, Adelaide, and Brisbane. **By rail-coach:** the *SRA,* (02) 27–8819, has a three-day tour to Canberra from Sydney that includes local sightseeing and a scenic cruise on the lake, and a four-day tour combining Canberra and the Snowy Mountains.

PARKS, GARDENS, FORESTS. Canberra is a garden city, and by driving through its streets and suburbs visitors will reap the rewards of many hours of hard work by resident domestic gardeners.

Australian National Botanic Gardens, entry from Clunies Ross Street, Black Mountain. Almost entirely devoted to Australian flora, the gardens are open daily 9 A.M.–5 P.M. Guided tours on Sundays at 10 A.M. and 2 P.M.

Commonwealth Plant Nursery, off Weston Park Road. Open daily.

Lake Burley Griffin Foreshores. There are numerous picnic and fishing spots along its 35km of shoreline. Cruises and boat and cycle hire operate from the terminal at Acton.

Tidbinbilla Nature Reserve, 40km southwest of Canberra, is being developed as a reserve to enable visitors to see Australian flora and fauna in natural surroundings. Picnic facilities and walking trails. Open daily.

BEACHES. *Lake Burley Griffin:* Beaches for swimming have been established at Black Mountain Peninsula, Yarralumla Bay, and Springback Island.

ZOOS AND ANIMAL PARKS. *Canberra Wildlife Gardens,* Mugga Lane, Red Hill. Here there are more than 100 varieties of native and exotic animals and birds, some wandering free of enclosure. They include kangaroos and wombats. Open daily.

Rehwinkels Animal Park, Macks Reef Road, 24km north. A natural bush setting for koalas, wombats, free-roaming kangaroos, and other animals and birds. Open daily.

SPORTS. *Australian Institute of Sport.* Leverrier Street, Bruce. This impressive modern complex provides access to top coaching and training facilities for young Australian athletes. Currently the Institute has more than 280 resident athletes in ten sports in Canberra, while the squash and diving units are based in Brisbane and hockey in Perth. Public tours of the National Sports Centre are on Saturday at 2 P.M. Facilities may also be used by the public, outside training and competition times. Inquire on (062) 52–1111.

AUSTRALIAN CAPITAL TERRITORY

Boating. Boats may be hired at Acton terminal on the shores of Lake Burley Griffin.

Cycling. Canberra has extensive cycleways for commuter and recreational use. Inquire at the tourist-information center for route maps or follow the signs. Cycles can be hired from *Mr. Spokes Bike Hire,* Acton Park, Acton, near the ferry terminal, (062) 31-0428. All size bikes, tandems, baby seats, and backpacks are available.

Fishing. No licenses are needed to fish in the ACT. Open-water fishing is permitted in the Murrumbidgee and Molongolo rivers, below Coppins Crossing. Trout fishing is good in all the other waters in the territory and Lakes Burley Griffin and Ginninderra. (Inquire at the Canberra Tourist Bureau regarding prohibited waters.) Trout season is between October and May, and the bag limit is 10 fish per person per day.

Golf. Golf courses in Canberra and nearby are:
Belconnen Public Golf Course, Drake Brockman Drive, Holt.
Federal Golf Club, Red Hill.
Gloucester Public Golf Course, Jerrabomberra Avenue, Narrabundah.
Queanbeyan Golf Club, Brown Street, Queanbeyan.
Royal Canberra Golf Club, Westbourne Woods, Yarralumia.
Yowani Country Club, Federal Highway, Lyneham.

MUSEUMS AND HISTORIC OR NATIONAL SITES.
All Saints Church, Cowper Street, Ainslie. This was previously the mortuary station at Rookwood in Sydney and was reerected on this site in 1958.

GALLERIES. Australian National Gallery, Parkes Place, Parkes; (062) 71-2501. It stands within the parliamentary triangle on the shores of Lake Burley Griffin. The building is an interesting monument to modern architecture, and its galleries contain Australia's finest collection of visual arts. As well as many international masterpieces, the gallery contains an extensive collection of Australian and Aboriginal art. Free guided tours are available daily, and the educational program includes lunchtime lectures, exhibitions, and audiovisual presentations. There is a gallery shop and restaurant overlooking the sculpture garden. Open daily 10 A.M.-5 P.M. $A2 admission.

Australian War Memorial, at the top of Anzac Parade, is a museum commemorating the more than 102,000 Australian war dead. The impressive building houses a vast collection of historic aircraft, relics, models, dioramas, photographs, and artworks representing all theaters of war. Open daily.

Blundell's Farmhouse, near Royal Military College, Duntroon. The cottage was built in 1858 by the pioneer Robert Campbell, of Duntroon, for his plowman. It has now been furnished according to that period and is open to visitors daily from 2-4 P.M. and from 10 A.M.-noon on Wednesday, but in winter closed Wednesday morning and Monday.

Church of St. John the Baptist. Constitution Avenue, Reid. The church and adjacent schoolhouse preserve much of Canberra's history. Open Wednesday 10 A.M.-noon and weekends 2-4 P.M.

General Post Office. Alinga Street. In a display gallery above the GPO is Australia's largest and most valuable collection of stamps, assembled from Australia Post's archives. Open 9:30 A.M.-5P.M. Monday-Thursday.

Government House. Dunrossil Drive, Yarralumla, is the official residence of Australia's governor-general. The house and grounds are not open to visitors, but there is a good view of it from a lookout on Lady Denman Drive between the Cotter Road and Scrivener Dam.

Lanyon Homestead, on the banks of the Murrumbidgee, 30km south of Canberra. The homestead, gardens, and cluster of outbuildings in their rural setting are classified by the National Trust. Open 10 A.M.-4 P.M. Tuesday-Sunday and public holidays.

National Film and Sound Archive, McCoy Circuit, is housed in an art-deco-styled building. Visitors aware of the prominent place Australian films are now taking on the international scene may be interested in visiting the archives. Public screenings and exhibitions of historic films and television and radio programs are frequently held. Open daily, 10 A.M.-4 P.M.

New Parliament House Construction Site, Capital Hill. An exhibition of the new House and an observation platform overlooking the site are reached from the turnoff from State Circle almost opposite St. Andrew's Church. Open daily 9 A.M.–6 P.M.

Nolan Gallery, near Lanyon Homestead, 30km south of Canberra; (062) 37-5192. It has both permanent and changing exhibitions of works by the famous Australian artist Sydney Nolan. Open Tuesday–Sunday and public holidays 10 A.M.–4 P.M.

Parliament House, Parkes Place. The House is open daily (except Christmas Day) 9 A.M.–5 P.M. Visitors may observe Parliament when it is sitting or join the guided tours of the Senate and House of Representatives when it is not. Tickets for admission to the Senate galleries are not usually required, but it is advisable to write or telephone (062) 72-1211 in advance to the principal attendant for tickets to the House of Representatives. The tours run approximately every half hour between 9 A.M. and 4:30 P.M. Monday–Thursday and 9:30 A.M.–8:30 P.M. Friday.

Regatta Point Planning Exhibition, on Lake Burley Griffin's shore near the northern end of Commonwealth Avenue Bridge. Presents in model form audio-visual screenings, diagrams and photos the development of Canberra. Open daily 9 A.M.–5 P.M.

Royal Australian Mint, via Kent and Denison streets, Deakin. There is a visitors' gallery from which production-floor processes can be viewed, and an extensive coin exhibition in the foyer. Open 9 A.M.–4 P.M. Monday–Friday (with a break between noon and 12:40 P.M.); there is no production on public holidays or from Christmas to New Year's.

Royal Military College, Duntroon. Duntroon House is the oldest home in the ACT. The grounds of Australia's military academy are open to the public, and there are conducted tours from April to October on Monday–Friday at 2:30 P.M. There are no tours on public holidays and the college grounds are closed on Good Friday.

Southlands Gallery, off Athlon Drive, Woden, (062) 86-5330. Features paintings for sale by leading Australian artists as well as Australian handicrafts. Open Tuesday–Saturday 10 A.M.–5 P.M. and Sunday 2–5 P.M.

LIBRARIES *National Library of Australia,* off King Edward Terrace on the shores of Lake Burley Griffin. The five-story library features white Carrara marble columns, marble walls, foyer and staircase. It houses more than three million volumes as well as maps, plans, pictures, prints, photographs, and films. The three-level foyer has extensive exhibition areas with constantly changing displays. The exhibitions are open Monday–Thursday 9 A.M.–4:45 P.M. Friday–Sunday and public holidays 9 A.M.–4:45 P.M. Guided tours are 11:15 A.M. and 2:15 P.M. Monday–Friday.

SHOPPING. If you are looking to buy something uniquely Australian, the following may appeal. **Fashion:** *Carla Zampatti Designer Boutique,* 30 Giles Street, Kingston, (062) 95-6955; *Wendy Heather Design Boutique,* Manuka Village, (062) 95-0666. These shops feature clothing designed by two women very prominent in the Australian fashion industry.

Opals: You can buy this beautiful Australian stone at *The Opal Studio,* Cinema Centre Arcade, Bunda Street, Canberra, (062) 47-5474, or at *Hansen's Opal Centre,* 16 Garema Place, Canberra, (062) 47-8623.

Wool Products: *Scope Arts Sheepskins and Cottons,* top level, Monaro Mall, Canberra, (062) 49-7410. Specializes in lambskin and woollen products such as mittens, boots, and jackets.

ENTERTAINMENT. Full details of entertainment are available in the daily paper, the *Canberra Times.* The Canberra Tourist Bureau publishes a seasonal listing of events that includes art exhibitions, concerts and exhibitions, ballet, and drama.

The focus of Canberra's cultural life is the *Canberra Theatre Centre,* Civic Square, London Circuit, (062) 57-1077. It opened in 1965 as the first performing-arts center in Australia and became a model for the development of venues in other states. Its theater seats 1,200 people, and the playhouse has 310 seats. Between them they stage a wide variety of drama, music, dance, opera, and

Sydney is where Australia began, and, as the country's largest city, much that affects the entire nation still begins here. *(Photo: Australian Tourist Commission)*

Ayers Rock in Australia's Northern Territory continually changes color throughout a day—a particularly vivid show at sunset. *(Photo: Australian Tourist Commission)*

Australia's second largest city, Melbourne combines sophistication and small-town charm. *(Photo: Victorian Arts Center, courtesy Australian Tourist Commission)*

Visitors will glory in the natural beauty of New Zealand. Here the steamer *Earnslaw* is arriving at Queenstown Bay, Otago. *(Photo: New Zealand Tourist Office)*

The stereotype of Fiji—as an ideal spot for the traveler looking to escape civilization—is remarkably accurate. Pictured is the Fiji Cultural Center. *(Photo: Brett)*

The Samoas are the heartland of Polynesia. Here is Rainmaker Mountain on Pago Pago, the capital of American Samoa. *(Photo: Brett)*

Many of the people of Western Samoa can be seen living their lives in traditional native fashion. *(Photo: Western Samoa Visitors Bureau)*

comedy. The major Australian companies such as the Australian Opera, the Australian Ballet, the Sydney Theatre Company, and the Melbourne Theatre Company perform there. Canberra also has its own opera company, philharmonic society, symphony orchestra, and Theatre A.C.T., who use the center. From time to time international artists also play the center. Lunchtime theater is regularly presented in the rehearsal room or the playhouse during the week. Exhibitions and displays are featured in the Gallery and the Link, and the center has a cafe for light meals and drinks.

For music lovers, the *Canberra School of Music* presents a program of music throughout the year. It is at William Herbert Place, Canberra, (062) 46–7811. The music is varied: You might catch a Mozart piano sonata, some contemporary Australian music, a jazz performance, or a brass choir.

NIGHTLIFE. If you feel like mixing with the Canberra night owls, having a drink, and listening to some music, explore some of these: *Dorette's Bistro,* Garema Place, Cicic; 47–6244. Listen to live jazz while you eat on Tuesday, Thursday, Friday, and Saturday. *Juliana's Discotheque,* Noah's Lakeside International Hotel, London Circuit, Canberra; 47–6244. *Top of the Cross,* Hindmarsh Drive, Phillip; 82–5222.

VICTORIA

The Garden State

by
SONNY and HEIDI GORDON

Sonny and Heidi Gordon are travel writers who divide their time between Melbourne and Los Angeles.

When the peaches, pears, and apricots of the Goulburn Valley are in spring bloom and the acacias explode across the land, Victoria seems to become an enormous garden, which only goes to underline the reason for its nickname: the Garden State.

Every season is a kaleidoscope of colors: the poplars, beech, and oaks of a Melbourne autumn; the soft blanket of summer wildflowers in the high country; the winter reds and pinks of the flowering gums along the coast. Victoria *is* a garden state—a state for all seasons.

Victoria's Rich Heritage

There is a deep, abiding pride among Victorians. To express and maintain that pride, the state has become a veritable marketplace of museums. Even the smallest township now seems to have a collection of implements, bric-a-brac, and household items that form a visual narrative of its past.

An itinerary that includes Moe (early explorers), Korumburra (coal), Beechworth (bushrangers), Echuca (the river trade), Swan Hill (rural pioneers), Bendigo (the Chinese immigrants), Ballarat (gold-rush days), and Warrnambool (the tall ships) will provide a keen

VICTORIA

insight into a history that, although relatively brief, is unique in the world owing to the lifestyles forced upon its participants by a terrain and climate the like of which few of them had previously experienced.

A New Breed

Those coming to Victoria were the new breed of Australians, wishing to be known and recognized as separate from the convict-based origins of New South Wales. Landing was refused to convict ships arriving from England, and the separatist movement grew in strength until, in 1851, what until then had been the Port Phillip District of New South Wales was constituted as the colony of Victoria. (Victoria still comprises the same 87,884 square miles, making it the smallest state on the Australian mainland and taking up just 3 percent of the country's total land mass. Yet its population accounts for nearly a third of the country's inhabitants and it contributes similarly to the national wealth.)

Within a year of being declared a separate colony, Victoria became the scene of a gold rush that contributed much to opening up its inland regions. The precious metal was discovered in many parts of the state and led to the establishment of several substantial country towns, many of which still survive and prosper while others indicate their one-time existence only by deserted churches, rusting machinery, garbage-filled mine shafts, and piles of rubble that once formed houses, shops or hotels.

It was on the gold fields that Australia experienced the one and only revolution in its history. Miners seeking gold at Ballarat revolted against conditions imposed upon them by the authorities and demanded the abolition of the licensing system and of the ownership of property as a qualification for voting rights. They burned their licenses, built a stockade at Eureka, and rallied around a new Australian flag. The "revolution" occurred on December 3, 1854, and resulted in the deaths of five policemen and 22 rebels. The leaders were eventually found not guilty, and more important, most of their urgent demands were met.

Today, a park and diorama commemorate the Eureka Stockade incident and the timber head of the mineshaft is a landmark for an historical park where visitors can participate in the life of miners in the 1850s. In the park you can hire a gold pan and "fossick" (pick over old claims) for gold; but travel a few miles farther and you can stand alone amid the scattered remnants of once-thriving settlements and more vividly recapture those rumbustious days of not so long ago.

Older residents claim there is still plenty of gold to be extracted from the ground in this part of Victoria, though it seems unlikely there will be a repeat of the days when 319,000 ounces of gold were being won in a single year from just one small corner of the state.

The gold rushes and development of a thriving rural industry contributed much to the development of Victoria in general and to Melbourne in particular.

The Keynote Is Diversity

Despite Victoria's size, it is not surprising to find a huge diversity of terrain, climate, and vegetation. There are rain forests and deserts, snowfields and tobacco plantations, vineyards and potato fields, vast wheat prairies and frost-protected market gardens. Yet it is all reasonably compact when viewed in the overall Australian context. It is possible to drive from a cold and wet Melbourne winter into the sunshine and desert dryness of Mildura in one day. In two hours' drive, you can be on the snow fields. In summer, escaping the high humidity and soaring temperatures of Melbourne you can soon be amid the mountain freshness of the alpine region.

Once outside Melbourne, there are few built-up areas to negotiate. Thus the driver can proceed easily at the permitted maximum speed of 100km/h (63 mph) for hour upon hour and encounter little traffic or delays. Not only are all main roads paved, but so are the majority of minor roads. Dirt roads are encountered only when diverting into more remote regions—perhaps exploring the Grampians or taking some of the rain forest tracks of Gippsland. For such expeditions, a four-wheel-drive vehicle is the best form of transport in all but the driest time of year.

The climate varies greatly over the state. The weather in Melbourne will often be vastly different from what towns a few miles away on the other side of the Great Dividing Range are experiencing. It has been said that Melbourne can experience all four seasons in one day, so greatly and rapidly does its weather change. However, extremes are rare apart from a few summer days when the temperature rises to about 100°F. Equally rare are temperatures below freezing point.

Travelers are likely to be delayed by fog only on an average of 20 days a year, and this will generally turn out to be a mere morning mist that disappears within a few hours. Rainfall is just under 660mm (27 in.) a year, falling an average of 143 days. The north of the state is far dryer than the south; and the eastern half is much, much wetter than the western half. Officially, the weather is described as "mild in the main but disconcertingly changeable." The most stable, pleasant months seem to be March to June and October and November.

Such mixed weather leads to mixed vegetation growing amid a highly varied terrain; volcanic in part, arid and flat for thousands of acres, seven mountain peaks rising above 6,000 feet and a coastline that varies from gaunt, wreck-strewn cliffs to tranquil lakelands. A third of the state is covered by mountain wilderness and bushland—ideal for bushwalkers but dangerous country for the unwary and inexperienced.

The waters offshore present many opportunities for boating, fishing, surfing and simple swimming. Sharks are a hazard only occasionally and undercurrents can be dangerous on certain beaches. It is essential, therefore, to use only those beaches which are patrolled by life-saving clubs or which are clearly designated as safe in all respects.

Victorians tend to flock to the beaches and lakes throughout the high summer, leaving the inland roads almost deserted. They show a great fondness for power boating, water skiing, and fishing so that piers, jetties, and launching ramps are forever busy throughout the summer weekends. The climate makes outdoor living by tent or camper a pleasant pastime.

Access to Victoria tends to be direct into Melbourne for anyone coming by rail or air. Interstate express coach services terminate in Melbourne too. Motorists will cross the border from the neighbouring states of South Australia and New South Wales at any of a number of points on major highways. But they should be prepared for confiscation of any fruit they are carrying—a measure designed to eradicate the fruit-fly menace.

Exploration of the state has been made easy by the creation of 8 distinctly separate and well-defined tourism regions. Two of these contain Melbourne and its environs; the remainder cover the country areas. Each has its own visitor-information center in addition to the information centers to be found in the larger towns. But before starting any exploration of the inland regions one first needs to be introduced to Melbourne.

MELBOURNE

Sprawling out from the hinge of the great jaw of land around Port Phillip Bay, Melbourne is a city that lets you discover it at your own pace. There is no great need to rush, nor is there a license to "lie back." The pulse of the city is whatever you want it to be.

It is a city of sports and symphonies, art museums and sidewalk sales, acres and acres of parks, and clean, safe streets. Restaurants are abundant and diverse. Joggers and cyclists move along the city's 100-plus kilometers of bike paths, while trams move along the over 137 miles of track. It is a city that spreads peace of mind—a reflection of the sure, safe fifties overlayed with the excitement and technology of the eighties.

And it is a city of people.

Coming first from England and in subsequent decades immigrating from Ireland, China, Greece, Italy, Russia, Germany, France, the Slavic countries, the Middle East, Vietnam, and Japan, Melbourne residents continue to make the city a unique melting pot, where cultures coalesce rather than clash. It is a place where an architecture paying homage to its early Victorian English roots stands in silent approval as modern high-rise buildings mingle with exotic pagodas, temples, and spires.

It's a lovely, lively city, and much of the pleasure it affords lies in its discovery bit by secret bit.

Melbourne's central square-mile business and commercial area is a grid of main streets interlaced with a network of arcades that entail plenty of walking if they are to be explored to the full. Here you will find elegant boutiques, many extremely small and very specialized one-person businesses, and innumerable bistros and restaurants. Redevelopment has been rapid over the past decades and appears certain to continue for some time yet. High office blocks are changing the skyline from its previously fairly low profile, and the city's underground-railway system is now running at five major stations.

One city block of the main shopping area, Bourke Street, has been experimentally turned into a pedestrian mall that may later be extended another block. Grandiose plans for a city square eventually reached fruition when the queen performed the opening ceremony in May 1980.

In past years, residents and visitors could take a lift to the top of one of the many high-rise buildings for a fine overall view of the city. Now, owing to increasingly strict safety regulations, such opportunities are greatly restricted.

Further exploration can be done by tram (streetcar), a transportation system that is the subject of frequent debate but seems destined to remain. Tram routes cover most of the main city streets and spread for many miles out into the surrounding suburbs.

Within the city center are several superb parks and gardens, some of which are considered by authorities to be the best of their type anywhere in the world. The white "Christmas cake" edifice of Government House is set in one of these gardens, and in another is the cottage in which Australia's discoverer, Captain Cook, spent his childhood. The house was brought from England in 1934.

The Royal Park houses the zoological gardens—the place in which to walk among Australian animals in their natural setting amid native flora.

Because Melbourne hosted the 1956 Olympic Games it is well endowed with near-city sports arenas. Most impressive of these, however,

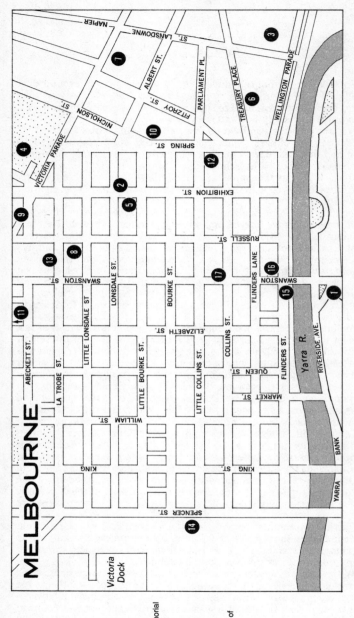

MELBOURNE

Points of Interest

1) Arts Centre
2) Comedy Theatre
3) Conservatory
4) Exhibition Buildings
5) Her Majesty's Theatre
6) John F. Kennedy Memorial
7) St. Patrick's Cathedral
8) State Library/Nat'l Museum
9) Trades Hall
10) State Parliament
11) City Airline Terminals
12) Windsor Hotel
13) Royal Melbourne Inst. of Technology
14) Spencer St. Station
15) Flinders St. Station
16) St. Paul's Cathedral
17) Melbourne Town Hall

VICTORIA

is the Melbourne Cricket Ground, which dates back many decades. To watch a cricket match (in summer) or a football match (in winter) in this gladiatorial setting is to see the Victorians in their true clothing. The big sporting occasions are rumbustious, noisy, emotional events in which the crowd of 120,000 is rarely silent and the wisecracks flow like water.

Beaches are a short tram ride away from the city center, affording Melbournians the luxury of having a swim for lunch, if they are so inclined. The beaches are wide and clean and often crowded. The area around Kerferd Road and Albert Park is "tops optional"; it is said it's easy to recognize the unwarned newcomers—they're the ones with their necks locked at a 90-degree angle. Kerferd Road also has a pier, though somewhat weather worn, and ample parking. There are also plenty of changing areas, a life-saving club, and several refreshment kiosks.

Lie Down and Look Up

Also on the city fringe is the imposing new arts center, gaunt, gray, and windowless from the outside but a sheer delight inside, where garden courtyards display sculpture and admit natural light. Lie down on the carpeted floor of the great hall for the best view of the world's largest stained-glass ceiling, a magnificent achievement by local artist Leonard French.

A further insight into the Victorian (and Australian) character is gained by visiting Tattersalls in Flinders Street. This is the local lottery center. Public drawings are held at regular intervals, although the gambling high spot of the week is at 9:30 every Saturday night when seven out of 40 numbered balls decide who has won more than $1 million in the newest pastime of Tattslotto. Millions of dollars are invested each week on just this one form of gambling. Much more is spent on horse racing (Melbourne has several tracks and almost daily racing), dog racing, and trotting.

Once a year, Melbourne lets its hair down and stages a festival called Moomba—allegedly Aboriginal for "Let's get together and have fun." Slow to develop, it is now a mammoth open air event of music, dancing, art shows and concerts. There are water skiing on the river, parades in the streets, paintings in the parks, and concerts in the gardens. It attracts artistes from other parts of the world and is recommended as a good time to be in Melbourne. It takes place over 10 days at the end of February and the first week of March.

The city is the center of the country's "rag trade" and boasts many elegant dress shops. There is quality (and expensive) shopping to be had at "the Paris end" of Collins Street (that's the bit where there are a few trees and a couple of sidewalk cafes) and in the chic suburb of Toorak. Although Melbourne contains the largest department store in the southern hemisphere (Myer) it also has by contrast a wealth of small shops that provide the goods and services not available from the large concerns. The small family-run retailer is a prominent feature of Melbourne life which ensures that the shopper can find virtually any item or service required. Free enterprise at its best is seen on the Esplanade at the bayside suburb of St. Kilda every Sunday morning when, on payment of a small fee, anyone can set up their pavement stall to sell their wares. Craftwork of all descriptions dominates the scene here.

High spots of the Melbourne year, apart from Moomba, are the Melbourne Show (a funfair and agricultural gathering) in September and the Melbourne spring racing carnival with the running of the Melbourne Cup (the first Tuesday in November), bringing the entire nation, including Parliament, to a halt.

PRACTICAL INFORMATION FOR MELBOURNE

See also information on the Melbourne Leisure Region, for more nearby sights and activities.

HOW TO GET THERE By air: Most international passengers arrive through Tullamarine International Airport; in the same complex are the major Australian domestic airlines, *Ansett, East-West,* and *Australian Airlines.* International airlines serving Melbourne are *Air Nauru, Air New Zealand* (which has direct flights from New Zealand ports), *Alitalia, British Airways, Continental, Garuda, KLM, Cathay Pacific, Malaysian Airlines Systems, Lufthansa, Philippine Air Lines, Qantas, Thai International, Singapore Airlines,* and *United.*

By rail: Main trunk routes are Albury from New South Wales and Sydney and from Western Australia (Perth) through South Australia (Adelaide). The train runs overnight, nightly between Melbourne and Adelaide and nightly and daily between Melbourne and Sydney. There is also a service between Melbourne and the federal capital, Canberra, via Yass, Mondays to Saturdays.

By sea: Sea passengers arrive at Station Pier, Port Melbourne, but services from overseas are now almost nonexistent. Cruise ships, too, make only rare calls and all major companies now operate out of Sydney. *P & O, Sitmar,* and *CTC Lines* are the main providees of cruises and line voyages. (See Facts at Your Fingertips for Australia.)

ACCOMMODATIONS. Melbourne, more than any other Australian city, is one of old-world, Victorian charm and modern metropolis conveniences. And nowhere is this more in evidence than in its many fine hotels. Some rise up to form a part of its magnificent skyline, and others have been restored from 19th-century buildings and are protected by the National Trust. Most major hotels are within the downtown core, with its stores, shops, and restaurants. And it's safe to walk there at night.

Traditionally, reservations are difficult during Melbourne Cup week (early November), Australian-rules football's grand final (late September), and Moomba festival time (February to March).

Hotels are listed below by their year-round or peak-season rates, in the following categories, based on double occupancy: *Super Deluxe,* $A130 and up; *Deluxe,* $A115–$A130; *Expensive,* $A90–$A115; *Moderate,* $A60–$A90. All hotels and motels offer reduced rates on weekends.

Free lists of hotels can be obtained from Victoria Tourism (*Victour*), 230 Collins St., Melbourne.

DOWNTOWN MELBOURNE

Super Deluxe

Hilton International Melbourne. 192 Wellington Pde., East Melbourne; (03) 419–3311. High-rise, restaurants, lounges, bars, disco, nightclub attracting international stars, pool, meeting rooms.

Hyatt on Collins. 129 Collins St., Melbourne; (03) 657–1234. New (October 1986) world-class, high-rise luxury hotel with health and recreation center including tennis court, pool, spa, a business center, Regency Club (four floors of exclusive accommodations), food court with eight international restaurants, full kosher kitchen for private functions, meeting rooms.

Menzies at Rialto. 495 Collins St., Melbourne; (03) 62–0111. Restaurants, bar, indoor pool, meeting rooms, garage. Lots of old-world character within its facade.

The Regent Melbourne. 25 Collins St., Melbourne; (03) 630–321. Rising from the 35th floor of the eastern tower of the Collins Place complex, the Regent offers the best views of the city. No pool but excellent restaurants, lounges, bars, shops, meeting rooms, and valet garage.

VICTORIA

Rockmans Regency. Cnr Lonsdale & Exhibition sts., Melbourne; (03) 662–3900. High-rise, restaurants, bar, heated indoor-outdoor pool and spa, garage. They provide a very personal service with a touch of class.

Windsor. 103 Spring St., Melbourne; (03) 63–0261. Building protected by National Trust. Totally renovated but still in the style and grandeur of bygone days. Restaurants, lounges, bar; no pool. Across street from Parliament House and Fitzroy Gardens.

Deluxe

Chateau Melbourne. 131 Lonsdale St., Melbourne; (03) 663–3161. High-rise, licensed restaurant, heated pool, sauna, meeting rooms.

Gordon Place. 24 Lt. Bourke St., Melbourne; (03) 663–5355. Luxury apartments, licensed restaurant, shops, bar, heated pool, spa. Classified by National Trust. New Orleans–style feeling. Excellent location on edges of scenic Chinatown within the downtown area. No car park.

Park Royal on St. Kilda Road. 562 St. Kilda Rd., Melbourne; (03) 529–8888. New high-rise, restaurants, lounge, bar, small pool, spa and sauna on top floor, butler service, meeting rooms, airport pickup service. Few minutes from downtown on tree-lined St. Kilda Road.

Southern Cross. 131 Exhibition St., Melbourne; (03) 63–0221. Restaurants, lounges, bar, heated pool, tennis court, garage. Something of a landmark in Melbourne; 70 shops in plaza adjacent to hotel.

Expensive

Noahs Melbourne. 186 Exhibition St., Melbourne; (03) 662–0511. Licensed hotel, heated pool, restaurants, lounge, bar, garage.

Royal Parade Travelodge. 441 Royal Pde., Parkville; (03) 380–9221. Licensed restaurant, pool, meeting rooms. Near zoo and Royal Park.

St. Kilda Rd. Travelodge. St. Kilda Rd. and Park St., Melbourne; (03) 699–4833. High rise, licensed motel, pool, restaurant. Close to arts center.

Telford Old Melbourne. 5 Flemington Rd., North Melbourne; (03) 63–0261. Licensed hotel, heated pool, meeting rooms, garage.

MELBOURNE AIRPORT

Expensive

Melbourne Airport TraveLodge. Centre Rd. (opposite international terminal); (03) 338–2322. Licensed restaurant, pool, meeting rooms, baby-sitting.

RESTAURANTS. It is said one could take lunch and dinner at a different restaurant in Melbourne every day of the year and still not sample them all.

There is no doubt that one of the most accessible legacies of Melbourne's much-touted multicultural society is its diversity of ethnic restaurants.

Little Bourke Street could be a busy side lane on Kowloon; Lygon Street, Carlton, a local via Condotti; and Swan Street, Richmond, in places reminds the traveler of Athens. Victoria Street, Collingwood, is home to myriad Vietnamese restaurants, and Acland Street, St. Kilda, has Jewish delis and bagels.

The price classifications of the following restaurants are based on the cost of an average three course dinner for one person for food alone; beverages, tax, and tip would be extra. *Inexpensive* means less than $A10; *Moderate*, $A10–$A25; *Expensive*, $A25–$A40; *Exclusive*, over $A40. Abbreviations for credit cards are A, American Express; DC, Dinners Club; M, MasterCard; and V, Visa. Abbreviations for meal codes are: L, Lunch; D, dinner; BYO, bring your own alcohol. Note: Most all restaurants in Melbourne, small or large, require reservations for lunch and dinner.

CITY AND SUBURBS

Exclusive

Stephanie's. 405 Tooronga Rd., Hawthorne East; 20–8994. French. The owner, Stephanie Alexander, is one of Australia's most brilliant and innovative chefs. Her restaurant is one of Melbourne's grandest. Three dining rooms in an ornate Italianate mansion. Closed Sunday and Monday.

Le Restaurant. 35th Floor of Regent Hotel, 25 Collins St., Melbourne; 63-0321. French. The service, elegant decor, and superlative view combine to make a dinner here most memorable. Lunch is half the price of dinner. Closed Sunday. A, DC, M, V.

Fanny's. 243 Lonsdale St., Melbourne; 663-3017. French. Distinguished restaurant for 25 years. Upstairs is an elegant, luxurious room offering outstanding seasonal menus from fish to stuffed quail legs in pastry. Downstairs Bistro offers a less formal atmosphere and is cheaper. Closed Sunday. L, D. A, DC, M, V.

Glo Glo's. 3 Carters Ave., Toorak; 241-2615. Modern French. Sophisticated and expensive but one of Melbourne's showpieces. D only; Closed Sunday. A, DC, M, V.

Windsor Hotel (Grand Dining Room). 115 Spring St., Melbourne; 63-0261. French. Dinner in this room that has been restored to its original 1883 spendor is a grand experience. L, D. AE, DC.

Expensive

Clichy. 9 Peel St., Collingwood; 417-6404. French. Offers a choice of styles. Restaurant on the left offers distinguished original food in the French manner. Wine bar and bistro offers simple food with a flair at lower prices. L, D. Closed Sunday. A, DC, Mw V.

Cafe Florentino. 80 Bourke St., Melbourne; 662-1811. Italian-French. Jackets and ties are needed in this traditional restaurant, which has a full house most nights. The Bistro Grill is downstairs and offers modestly priced pasta, and the Bistro Cellar is good for late breakfasts. L, D. A, DC, V.

Mietta's Melbourne. 7 Alfred Place, Melbourne; 654-2366. French. Upstairs in this restored 100-year-old building is an elegant French restaurant with varied specialties such as roast pheasant, venison, and fresh snapper. Downstairs is the lounge, which is primarily a meeting place for drinks. L, D. A, DC, M, V.

Kenzan. Lower Ground Fl., Collins Place, 45 Collins St., Melbourne; 662-2933. Japanese at its best in Melbourne. Offers sashimi and sushi. L, D. Closed Sunday. A, DC, M, V.

The Tandoor. 517 Chapel St., South Yarra; 241-8247. Melbourne's most fashionable Indian restaurant. It's lively and noisy and has excellent food. L, D; BYO. A, DC, MC, V.

Vlado's. 61 Bridge Rd., Richmond; 428-5833. Steakhouse, touted by many to have the best steaks in the world. L, D. BYO. Closed Sunday. A, DC, M, V.

The Willows. 462 St. Kilda Rd., South Melbourne; 267-5252; French. Grand old building, classified by National Trust, houses a most distinguished French restaurant. L, D. Closed Sunday. A, DC, M, V.

Gordon Place. 24-32 Little Bourke St., Melbourne; 663-5355. Elegant courtyard restaurant surrounded by four stories of tiered balconies. Pasta, seafood, and meat dishes with daily specials and excellent wine list. L, D. A, DC, M, V.

Moderate

Bamboo House. 47 Little Bourke St., Melbourne; 662-1565. Chinese. In Chinatown, delicacies served occasionally include Nanjing salt duck, drunken chicken, or Peking duck. L, D. A, DC, M, V.

Flower Drum. 103 Little Bourke St., Melbourne; 663-2531. Chinese. Fresh abalone is exceptional and fresh lobster from the tank a specialty. L, D. A, DC, V.

Savini. 619 Nicholson St., North Carlton; 387-6437. Italian. Combination of ingredients and presentation is similar to Franco-Italian. L, D. BYO. Closed Sunday. A, DC.

Avanti. 235 Rathdowne St., Carlton; 663-6706. Italian in a charming Victorian terrace. The menu offers homemade pasta, fresh fish, seafood, and meat dishes. L, D. BYO. Closed Sunday. A, DC, M, V.

Shahnai. 359 Brunswick St., Fitzroy; 417-5709. Indian. Specializes in Kashmiri food. L, D. BYO. DC.

Kuni's. 27 Crossley Lane, Melbourne; 63-9243. Japanese. On a little side street, between Little Bourke and Bourke streets. Small and always busy; sushi bar. L, D. BYO. Closed Sunday. A, DC, M, V.

Tolarno. 42 Fitzroy St., St. Kilda; 534-0521. French bistro. Lively and a favorite of many. L, D. A, DC, M, V.

Ilios. 174–178 Lygon St., Carlton; 347-2555. Greek. Good chicken and fish dishes and excellent moussaka. L, D. BYO. A, DC, V.

Tu Du. 143 La Trobe St., Melbourne; 662-2625. Most popular Vietnamese eating place. Specialties include crab claws in prawn batter, stuffed chicken wings or fish, and vegetarian dishes. L, D. Closed Sunday. BYO. A, DC, M.

Stavros Tavern. 183 Victoria Ave., Albert Park; 699-5618. Greek. Food, dance, and song. Authentic Greek tavern with good food. D only. BYO. A, DC, V.

Que Huong. 176 Bridge Rd., Richmond; 429-1213. Vietnamese. Well-run family concern. Satays and sizzling chili prawns are popular. BYO. L, D. A, DC, V.

Inexpensive

Fungi's. 441 Toorak Rd., Toorak; 241-1822. Excellent Pritiken dishes as well as cappucino with sweets, cafeteria style. Casual. Open daily, 10 A.M.–midnight. L, D. BYO. M only.

The Treble Clef. Concert Hall, Victorian Arts Centre, St. Kilda Rd., Melbourne; 617-8264. Good for breakfast or simple snacks throughout the day, 7 A.M.–8 P.M. A, DC, M, V.

Trotters. 400 Lygon St., Carlton; 347-5657. Casual, food prepared ahead. Popular spot for lunch and early Saturday mornings. Open daily with varied hours; call ahead. L, D. BYO. M.

Athenaeum Cafe. 294 Collins St., Melbourne; 63-9041. Casual basement cafe with solid Aussie tucker (food). Open only till 7:30 P.M.; closed Sunday.

HOW TO GET AROUND. From the airport: Downtown Melbourne is 20km (12 mi.) and 30 minutes from Tullamarine International Airport. Taxi fares are $14 to $18 (see below). *Skybus,* a private concern, operates buses every 30 minutes between the airport and several locations in the city at a cost of $5. Major car-rental companies have counters at Tullamarine Airport (see below).

By taxi. Taxis cost $1.10 and rise $.63 per kilometer, plus a $.30 telephone-booking fee. During the night hours and over the weekend the rates rise about $.10 per kilometer. Among the larger cab companies are *Silver Top* (345-3455); *Regal* (810–0222); *Arrow* (417–1111); and *Embassy* (329–9444). Taxis can be hired off the street, at taxi ranks, at major hotels, or by phoning one of the companies

By Metropolitan Transport System. "The Met," Melbourne's public transport system, enables you to change from tram to train to bus for the price of one ticket. Tickets can be purchased on any one of the three services. Ticket prices are based on how many neighborhoods you are traveling in and for how long, with 2-hour, daily, and weekly travelcards available. A 2-hour ticket in the city is $1.10. Call The Met customer service, 617-0900, for information, or pick up a timetable at the Met store in the Royal Arcade.

By tram. Melbourne's famous electric tram system is the most extensive in the world. It comprises 325km of track in the inner-city areas and suburbs. Trams can be hailed at stops (look for red, black, and white tram stops) and operate until midnight. For information call 617-0900.

By rail. From Flinders Street Station an extensive network of electric trains service inner and outlying suburban areas. The inner city area is serviced by an underground rail loop. For information, 61–001.

By bus. The inner city and suburban areas are serviced by modern buses. For information call 617-0900.

By car. Leading car-rental companies include *Astoria* (347–7766); *Budget* (320–6222); *Hertz Australia* (338–4044); *Thrifty* (663–6366).

Rules for Victorian motorists: Keep to the left. When turning left, drivers must give way to any vehicle on the right or to any vehicle making a right-hand turn in front of them.

Two unusual road rules apply while driving in Melbourne, which has trams operating on its major roads. Always pass a tram on the *left;* but when a tram has stopped you *must* stop also unless there is a railed safety zone for tram passengers. Then you may overtake with care—again on the left.

At various intersections within the city, drivers wishing to turn *right* must keep well in the *left* lane, drive forward, then wait for the traffic signals to change before proceeding with the turn. This is so that you do not impede tram-traffic flow.

The AACV (Royal Automobile Club of Victoria), 123 Queen St., Melbourne (607–2211), is the major source of information on all aspects of road travel and transport in Victoria.

TOURIST INFORMATION. *Victour*, 230 Collins St., Melbourne, VIC 3000; (03) 602–9444. *Melbourne Tourism Authority*, Level 20, Nauru House, 80 Collins St., Melbourne, VIC 3000; (03) 654–2288.

TOURS. Bus Tours. A wide range of day and half-day sightseeing tours in and around Melbourne are available and recommended through three major tour operators: *AAT Kings*, 181 Flinders St., 666–3363; *Australian Pacific Tours*, 181 Flinders St., 63–1511; and *Ansett Pioneer Tours*, corner of Franklin and Swanston Sts., 668–2422. Competition between them is keen, and consequently the service is good.

An especially good value is the City Explorer, sponsored by the *Age*, The Ministry for Planning & Environment, and Australian Pacific Tours, which is a circular tour of Melbourne on a luxury double-decker bus, $5 adults, $3 pensioners, $2 children. For details call 63–1511 or the *Age*, 602–9011.

Victorian Arts Centre. Spectacular $225-million complex of buildings that include National Gallery of Victoria, Theatres Building (under spire), and the Melbourne Concert Hall. Guided tours of the center are conducted every day of the year except Christmas Day and Good Friday. Tours leave regularly from the Theatres Building, Level 6 from the Shop, between 10:30 A.M. and 4 P.M., and last approximately one hour. Tickets can be obtained for a combined tour of the three theaters within the Theatre Building and the Melbourne Concert Hall. $2.75 adults, $1.75 students, 617–8211. A 90-minute Backstage Tour, a nontechnical look at the backstage world of the theaters and concert hall, is conducted on Sundays, 11:45 A.M. and 1:45 P.M., for $6. Book during the week at 617–8211. Evening at the Victorian Arts Centre includes a tour, dinner at one of the restaurants within the complex, and a show of your choice—a play, an opera, or the ballet. Cost varies from $45 to $60, depending on the show. Must be booked in advance and during the week 9 A.M. to 5 P.M., 617–8211.

Yarra River Cruises. *Yarra Princess*, operated by Melbourne Cruisers (63–2054), cruises daily, 12 noon, 2 P.M., 3:30 P.M., from Berth 3, Princes Walk, Melbourne, toward Como Island or downstream toward West Gate Bridge and the Port of Melbourne. These one-hour cruises are in a modern glass-enclosed boat and cost $5 adults, $2.50 children. Both cruises can be combined (with a break in between), $9 adults, $4 children. (Cruises are subject to public demand.) The *Leisuretime* or *Pleasuretime* offer sightseeing cruises up and down the Yarra as well. Moored at berths 1 and 2, Princes Walk, and are operated by Quay Melbourne River Cruises, 654–1233. One-hour cruises run daily (subject to public demand) and cost $5 adults, $4 pensioners, $2.50 children (under 5 free).

Stock Exchange of Melbourne. The gallery of the stock exchange is open to the public from 9 A.M. to 5 P.M. during the week. Tours can be arranged by contacting 351 Collins St., Melbourne; 617–8611,

Walking Tours. A variety of pamphlets that will guide you through historic Melbourne is available from the National Trust's bookshop at Tasma Terrace, Parliament Place, Melbourne, 654–4711, open Mon. through Fri. 9 A.M to 5 P.M. Victour, 230 Collins St., Melbourne, 619–4444, can provide a tour pamphlet that shows what different buildings on the walking tour looked like in the 19th century. *Melbourne Out and About Heritage Walking Tour*, 241–1085, includes a close look at Melbourne's historic buildings with a full commentary by History Fine Arts graduates, 90 minutes (pickup arranged).

SEASONAL EVENTS. February–March: Melbourne's biggest carnival, *Moomba*, street processions, open air theatre, dancing, art displays, water skiing on the Yarra River, fairs, competitions. The whole city swings. Chinese New Year Celebrations on Little Bourke St. around February 9.

VICTORIA

July: *Annual Sheep and Woolcraft Show* at the Showgrounds in the third week of July.

September: *Grand Final, Australian rules football,* at the Melbourne Cricket Ground on the last Sat. in the month.

October: Melbourne's annual *marathon* is held on the second Sun. in Oct.

November: Everything stops on the first Tues. in Nov. for the *Melbourne Cup* race at Flemington. The only horse race in the world that's a public holiday.

PARKS AND GARDENS. The parks and gardens in and around Melbourne are among of the most impressive features of this city within the Garden State of Australia. More than one-quarter of the inner city area has been set aside as open space for passive recreation. Indigenous trees, plants, and flowers, as well as exotica from other parts of the world, weave a living tapestry that leaves you with a feeling of space and country, within this thriving modern city.

Royal Botanic Gardens, in Domain Park, are rated as one of the finest examples of landscaped gardens in the world. The present design and layout of the gardens are the brainchild of W. R. Guilfoyle, curator and director of the gardens from 1873 to 1910. Within the 100 acres are 12,000 species of native and imported plants and trees, sweeping lawns, and ornamental lakes with islands and many ducks and swans who love to be fed. The oldest section is Tennyson Lawn, where there are four English elm trees more than 120 years old. A fern gully built around an old billabong (pond) contains an American swamp cypress, the tallest tree in the gardens. You can discover the gardens on your own along their many curved paths or with free guided walks that leave every Tues. and Thurs. at 10 A.M. from Plant Craft Cottage, near Gate H, Alexandra Ave., 63–3235. Pamphlets are available from the Herbarium (corner of Birdwood Ave. and Dallas Brooks Dr.), the kiosk, or the brochure box at Gate F. Incidentally, the kiosk, near the ornamental lakes, is a great place to stop and have Devonshire Tea (for hours and information call 266–8067). The main gate to the gardens (Gate F) is on Birdwood Ave., near Dallas Brooks Dr. There are other entrances at Gate A, corner of Anderson St. and Alexandra Ave., Gates B and C, along Anderson St., and Gate H, along Alexandra Ave.; 63–9424. Hours: daily 7 A.M. to 7:45 P.M. in the summer and 8:30 A.M. to 5:15 P.M. in the winter. Admission free.

Also of interest within Domain Park is a floral clock, in **Queen Victoria Gardens,** that talks as well as tells time. The clock's recorded message gives a brief history of the gardens in and around Melbourne. It is situated opposite the arts center on St. Kilda Rd. in one of the Domain's many informal gardens. There are no specific hours—you can take it all in free and at your leisure.

Fitzroy and Treasury Gardens. Attractions of interest within these lovely old gardens (90 acres) include Captain Cook's cottage, which was transported from the famous explorer's home in England to its present site in 1934, as part of Victoria's centenary celebration; a conservatory; the Fairy Tree, carved by Ola Cohn between 1931 and 1934 as a gift to the children of Melbourne; and a model Tudor village presented by the residents of Lambeth, London, in gratitude for food and parcels sent there by Victorians after the war. The View Room in the middle of the gardens is open for breakfast from 7 A.M. to 1 P.M. (417–2544). The gardens are bounded by Wellington Parade, Clarendon, Albert, and Lansdowne sts. They are open 24 hours a day, and admission is free.

Carlton Gardens. The tree-lined paths, artificial lakes and garden beds in this 40-acre English-style 19th-century garden-park form a backdrop to the Exhibition Building. The gardens are bounded by Victoria Parade, Nicholson, Carlton, and Rathdowne sts.

Royal Park is the largest park in Melbourne. It is sports-oriented, with ovals for playing Australian rules football—called "footie"—as well as fields for field hockey, cricket, and baseball and courts for netball and tennis. There's also an 18-hole golf course. It is near the zoo (see Zoos), bounded by Flemington Rd. Gatehouse St., the Avenue (off Royal Parade), and Park St. on the north.

Flagstaff Gardens, opposite the Victoria Market, more or less, boast—apart from good views over the docks and city—a monument to some of the earliest pioneers of the colony, who were buried near the spot. Among the undulating hills and flower beds are the Melbourne Bowling Club and tennis and basketball courts. Bound by Latrobe, William Dudley, and King sts.

ZOOS. Recently, the International Union of Directors of Zoological Societies proclaimed the *Royal Melbourne Zoo* as one of the finest in the world. Dating back as far as 1857, this is also one of the oldest zoos in the world. The zoo has recently undergone some major changes. The grounds have been transformed into gardens, and most of the enclosures have been renovated into "open-environment settings." With the enclosure renovation, many of the animals, some of which have not bred before, are beginning to breed. A map is essential and available at entrance gate for $2. Animals of particular interest are those unique to Australia, such as the koala, kangaroo, wombat, emu, and echidna. There are a lion park and a reptile house. The zoo is open every day of the year, 9 A.M. to 5 P.M. Admission $4.40 adults, $2.20 children (over 3 years). The zoo is 4km (2.5 mi.) north of Melbourne, on Elliot Ave., Parkville.

PARTICIPANT SPORTS. With the many parks in and around Melbourne it's only natural that people get out and get involved with sports. Sports seem to be not just for kids or for organized groups but for families, the average bloke, and the elderly. There is something for everyone to participate in and plenty of room to do it.

Bicycling. No one has measured, but it is safe to say that Melbourne and the surrounding area has more than 100km (60 mi.) of special bike paths through parks and along the river and bay. Some of the more scenic routes include the Yarra River bike path, in the heart of the city, and the Bayside bike path, along the beaches at Port Phillip Bay. Bikes can be rented at a number of locations including *Como Leisure Hire,* on the Yarra bank, corner of Williams Rd. and Alexandra Ave., South Yarra (527–6340). Open Sat. 11 A.M. to dusk, Sun. 9 A.M. to dusk, public and school holidays 10 A.M. to 5 P.M. Cost per hour $4 adults, $3 children; $20 deposit required. Helmets available for children.

Hire-a-Bicycle has locations at the Yarra bank, opposite the Royal Botanic Gardens at Alexandra Ave. in South Yarra; Kevin Bartlett Recreational Reserve, the Boulevard, Burnley; and Jess Park, Waverly Rd., Glen Waverley. For information, call 429–3049 or 288–5177. Hours: Sat., Sun., and public holidays, 10 A.M. to dusk. Cost per hour $4 adults, $2.50 children, per 4 hours $9 adults, $7 children; $10 deposit (2 bikes), $20 (more than 2 bikes). Another bicycle-rental agency is *World Wares,* 132 Nepean Hwy., Seaford (786–2488). Hours of business: Mon. through Fri. 9 A.M. to 9 P.M., Sat. 9 A.M. to 3 P.M. Prices start at $8 a day, $20 per week; deposit is half the hiring cost. 10-speed racing bikes and helmets ($5) available.

A comprehensive guide listing the paths and descriptions of each can be obtained for around $5 from the *Bicycle Institute of Victoria,* 285 Lt. Lonsdale St. (1st Floor of the Environment Centre), Melbourne.

Canoeing. Closest and easiest access to the Lower Yarra River is Studley Park. The *Studley Park Boathouse,* Studley Park, Kew (861–8707), rents canoes, kayaks, and rowboats. They are open daily 9:30 A.M. to 6:30 P.M. (hours dependent on the weather). Rates for 2 people $9 per hour, $4.50 per extra hour, 3 people $10 per hour, $5 per extra hour.

Diving. Port Phillip Bay is excellent for experienced divers, and the Portsea Hole, about 60 miles south of the city, is ideal for the less experienced. There are a few places around to rent, buy, or service any diving gear. One you might try, which also offers lessons, is *Western Diving Services.* For information, call 397–6045 or 370–9258.

Golf. Melbourne has the largest number of championship golf courses in Australia and private courses like Metropolitan, Royal Melbourne, and Kingston Heath in the sand belt, are world renowned. With more than 60 public and private golf courses in the metropolitan area, it isn't hard to find a course. A sampling of area courses open to the public: *Albert Park Golf Course,* Queens Road, Melbourne (51–5588); *Brighton Municipal Golf Course,* Dendy St., Brighton (592–8688).

Other courses include *Ivanhoe Golf Course,* the Boulevard, East Ivanhoe (49–2310); *Sandringham Golf Links,* Cheltenham Rd., Cheltenham, 598–3590; *Yarra Bend Golf Course,* Yarra Bend Park Rd., Fairfield, 481–0171.

Horseback Riding. The *Cheltenham Riding School,* 15 Byng Ave., Cheltenham, 551–2552, runs one-hour trail rides Sat., Sun., and public holidays, 9 A.M. to 4 P.M. Cost: $7 per hour. *Barringo Valley Trail Rides* (45 minutes from city),

VICTORIA

Shannons Rd., New Gisborne, (054) 26–1778, has escorted trail rides over Mt. Macedon ranges—in the same area is Barringo Wildlife Reserve.

Jogging. Melbourne's parks and gardens, the Yarra River bank, and Port Phillip Bay offer a variety of grades and surfaces, environments and distances for casual joggers as well as serious runners. Among the more popular courses are the Tan, beginning at Anderson St. and Alexandra Ave. and continuing for 4km (2.5 mi.) around the perimeter of the Royal Botanic Gardens; Albert Park Lake Run in Albert Park, 5km (3.1 mi.), and the Bay Run, along Port Phillip Bay, starting at Kereford Rd. and Beaconsfield Parade in Albert Park and continuing on to Bay St. in Brighton. This run winds its way along a footpath parallel to the bay and is around 18km (11 mi.) round trip.

Melbourne's most prestigious marathon, *Budget Melbourne Marathon*, is on the second Sunday in Oct. The route is from suburban Frankston to the arts center in the city. For further information contact Budget Melbourne Marathon, Olympic Park, Swan St., Melbourne, Victoria 3002 (428–7808).

There is also a running tour of Melbourne guided by former Canadian Olympian Bob Bruner. For more information, call 528–4249.

Sailboarding-Windsurfing. Sheltered locations around Port Phillip Bay such as Middle Park, Elwood, Sandringham, Black Rock, and Frankston are ideal for surfboarding. Rentals are available at those locations.

Swimming. Visitors to Melbourne wanting to swim would be best advised to try the historic *Melbourne City Baths,* corner of Swanston and Victoria sts. (663–5888). Meticulously renovated, the baths provide all the gym, sauna, spa, aerobics, and squash facilities one could want. There are a learners' pool and a 30m public pool with a shallow end.

Tennis. Tourists have an advantage over locals in renting courts during the day. Night rentals, however, are just about booked. Public tennis courts for hire in and around the city include *City of Camberwell Tennis Centre* (16 outdoor Supergrass courts), Corner of Bulleen and Thompson roads, Bulleen (850–4500); *East Melbourne Tennis Courts* (four outdoor courts), Powlett Reserve, Albert St., East Melbourne, 417–6511; *Fawkner Park Tennis Courts* (6 outdoor courts), Fawkner Park, Toorak Rd., South Yarra, 26–1953; *Leggets Tennis and Squash Centre* (9 outdoor courts), 132 Greville St., Prahran, 529–3322, and *Universal Indoor Tennis Centre* (5 indoor synthetic-grass courts), 100 Wellington St., Collingwood, 419–8911. For more locations and details consult the yellow pages under Tennis Courts for Hire.

SPECTATOR SPORTS. Many of the big events happening in Melbourne involve sports. One of these events, *Melbourne Cup Day,* is even a national holiday! In a city of more than 3 million people you'll probably find about 3 million opinions on sports ranging from Aussie-rules football to cricket, soccer, basketball, baseball, horse racing, dog racing, golf, tennis, even lawn bowling.

Australian-Rules Football (Footie). Each of the 12 teams within the V.F.L., the national league, play at *V.F.L. Park*, Wellington Rd., Mulgrave (approximately 17km from city), 654–1244, or at their individual home grounds every Sat. during the Mar.–Sept. season. Tickets are purchased on the day of the game and are $7 for adults and $1 for children. The season culminates with the Grand Final, which is usually the last Sat. in Sept., at the Melbourne Cricket Ground (M.C.G.), Brunton Ave., Yarra Park (just on the outskirts of the city). More than 100,000 people usually turn out to experience this event.

Cricket is played during the summer months, Oct. through Feb., and all big international and interstate cricket matches are played at the Melbourne Cricket Ground, Brunton Ave., Yarra Park (654–5511). The stadium has lights for night games and can accommodate 100,000 people. Tickets are sold at the gate and through Bass, 11–500.

Golf. The *Australian Open* is held the third week in Nov. and in '87 will be at the Royal Melbourne Golf Club, Cheltenham Rd., Black Rock, 598–6755.

Greyhound Racing can be seen every Mon. night at Olympic Park, Oval no. 2, Olympic Park, Swan St., Melbourne (428–2145). Cost: $3 adults, $1 pensioners. Every Thurs. night at Sandown Park (30km from city), Lightwood Rd., Springvale (546–9511). Cost: $3 adults, $1 pensioners.

Horse Racing. Racing is popular throughout the year, and Melbourne has the distinction of being the only city in the world that has a public holiday for a horse race—the *Melbourne Cup,* which has been raced on the first Tues. in

Nov. since 1867. For three minutes (the average duration of the race) virtually the whole population of Australia stops to listen to the race on radio. Melbourne has four top-class race courses: *Flemington Race Course* (3km from city), Epsom Rd., Flemington (376–0441), Australia's premier race course and home for Melbourne Cup; *Moonee Valley* (6km from city), McPherson St., Moonee Ponds, 370–2655. Their feature event is Cox Plate which is held in Oct.; *Caulfield Race Course* (10km from city), Station St., Caulfield (572–1111). Its feature events are Blue Diamond in Mar. and Caulfield Cup in Oct.; *Sandown Race Course* (25km from city), Racecourse Dr., Springvale (572–1111), whose feature event is the Sandown Cup in Nov.

Soccer is played nearly year-round at Olympic Park, Ovals 1 and 2, Swan St., Melbourne (537–2533).

Tennis. The *Australian Open,* one of four Grand Slam events in the world, is held at Kooyong Stadium, Glenferrie Rd., Kooyong. As soon as the new $60-million National Tennis Centre is completed the Australian Open will move to its new home. The 1987 Australian Open will be Jan. 12 through 25 at Kooyong. Call 267–3866 for tickets.

CHILDREN'S ACTIVITIES. For thrills and excitement try *Luna Park,* Lower Esplanade, St. Kilda; 534–0653, an amusement park modeled after New York's Coney Island. Main attractions include the Big Dipper and the Scenic Railway. Hours: Fri. 7:15 to 11:15 P.M., Sat. 1:30 to 5:30 P.M. and 7:15 to 11:15 P.M., Sun. 1:30 to 5:30 P.M. Admission: Entrance (excluding rides) is $2.50, single rides cost $2 for adults and $1 for children. Unlimited-ride passes (includes admission) cost $9 adults and $7 children. A $25 family pass entitles 2 parents and 2 children (or one parent and three children) to unlimited rides.

Diamond Valley Railway Ltd., Lower Eltham Park, Eltham, 439–1493 or 836–6996, is a miniature passenger-carrying railway featuring steam, diesel, and electric trains. Hours: Sun., public holidays, and Wed. (school holidays only) 1 P.M. to 5 P.M. Admission: $1 adults, $.80 children.

Puffing Billy. Owned and operated by the Emerald Tourist Railway Board, Puffing Billy is a genuine relic of past days. It's a quaint steam train still running regularly in the scenic Dandenong mountains. You can get there by train, from Flinders St. Station in Melbourne to the Puffing Billy Station in Belgrave, or by car. For information call 602–9011 or 870–8411 for a recorded announcement.

For older children and something different try canoeing. The *Studley Park Boathouse,* Studley Park, Kew, 861–8707, offers canoes and kayaks for hire (paddles and life jackets included in the hire). Rates for canoes: 2 people $9 per hour, $4.50 per extra hour.

HISTORIC SITES AND HOUSES. The churches, cathedrals, and old stone buildings of Melbourne depict the well-ordered life that has often led to its being considered the best-preserved 19th-century city in the world. The National Trust of Australia (Victoria) is a voluntary group committed to that preservation. There are a number of National Trust properties open for inspection in the Melbourne area.

Como is significant as a substantially intact house circa 1840 to 1875, making it a choice example of Victorian architecture. A considerable proportion of the furnishings remain, as well as a 5-acre 19th-century garden. It is a fine example of gracious living and of Australia's pastoral wealth. Situated on Como Ave. (off Toorak Rd.), South Yarra (3 mi. south of the city). Inquiries: 241–2500. Hours: daily 10 A.M. to 5 P.M., closed Good Friday, Christmas Day. Admission: $3 adults, $1.50 children and pensioners.

Rippon Lea. Begun as a 15-room Romanesque style house in the 1860s, it grew to a 33-room polychrome brick mansion by 1887. The surrounding gardens landscaped like the great gardens of England are the outstanding feature of the estate. Situated at 192 Hotham St., Elsternwick (5 mi. south of the city). Inquiries: 523–9150. Hours: Daily 10 A.M. to 5 P.M.; June 16 through Aug. 18, Wed. through Sun. 11 A.M. to 5 P.M. Admission: $3 adults, $1.50 children and pensioners, children under 5 free.

LaTrobe's Cottage was the settlement's first government house. A prefabricated timber house brought from England in 1839 by Charles La Trobe, who went on to become lieutenant governor. The present site is not the original, but the small cottage has been faithfully re-created, and contains many of La Trobe's

VICTORIA

possessions. Situated on Birdwood Avenue, in Kings Domain, by the Royal Botanic Gardens (1 mi. south of the city), 63–5528. Hours: Mon. through Sun. 10 A.M. to 4:30 P.M.; May to Sept. 11 A.M. to 4:30 P.M. Closed Anzac Day, Christmas Day, Good Friday. Admission: $2 adults, $1 students and pensioners.

Old Melbourne Gaol, constructed from 1841 to 1861, had a total of 104 hangings, including that of Ned Kelly in 1880. It was closed in 1929, and sections were progressively demolished, until the the National Trust saved the one remaining cell block as a penal museum. On Russell St. between LaTrobe and Victoria Parade, opposite the Russell St. Police Station; 654–3628. Hours: Mon. through Sun. 10 A.M. to 5 P.M. Closed Good Friday and Christmas Day. Admission: $3 adults, $1.50 children and pensioners, $7.50 family.

Polly Woodside is a deepwater commercial square-rigged sailing ship. Built of riveted wrought iron, it was launched from Belfast in 1885 for the South American trade. The ship is now restored and moored as the centerpiece of the National Trust's Melbourne Maritime Museum. Situated 2 mi. southwest of Melbourne at the corner of Normanby Rd. and Phayer St., South Melbourne; 699–9760. Hours: Mon. through Fri. 10 A.M. to 4 P.M., Sat. and Sun. noon to 5 P.M. Admission: $4 adults, $1.50 children and pensioners, $10 family.

Shrine of Remembrance is the state of Victoria's war memorial, built to honor Australia's war dead. It is said that St. Kilda Rd. was diverted so that the shrine could be visible from the city. Nearby are the Sidney Myer Music Bowl, the Government House, the Royal Botanic Gardens, and La Trobe Cottage. Situated between Domain and St. Kilda Rds., in Domain Park; 63–8415. Hours: Mon. through Sun. 10 A.M. to 5 P.M. Closed Christmas Day. Admission: free.

St. James' Old Cathedral, one of three cathedrals that dot Melbourne's skyline, was designed by Melbourne's first architect, Robert Russell, and built of sandstone and bluestone in 1842. At the corner of King and Batman sts.; 328–4090. It is open to the public Mon. through Sun. 10 A.M. to 4 P.M.

St. Patrick's Cathedral is Australia's largest cathedral. Construction on this Gothic cathedral began in 1850 and ended with the addition of the spires in 1939. At the corner of Gisborne St. and Cathedral Pl., East Melbourne; 662–2233. It is open daily for mass, and private tours are available upon request.

St. Paul's Cathedral (1877) was designed by an English architect who never came to Australia. This grand Gothic-revival cathedral remains the most important Anglican center in Melbourne. At the corner of Swanston and Flinders sts.; 63–3791.

MUSEUMS. National Gallery of Victoria. Melbourne's cultural life attained an exciting new dimension in Aug. 1968, when the first unit of the National Gallery of Victoria, Victorian Arts Centre, was built. This massive bluestone and concrete edifice designed by noted Australian architect Sir Roy Grounds appears to be standing in a pool of water.

Of particular interest within the gallery is the Great Hall, with its dramatic 10,000-piece stained-glass ceiling by Melbourne artist Leonard French. The best way to view the tribal art displayed in the glass is to lie on the floor. (Don't worry—it's the "in" thing to do!)

Some of the gallery's holdings, including its old master paintings, prints and drawings, and antiquities, are unparalleled in Australia, and its works by Tiepolo, Rembrandt, Poussin, Blake, and Durer, together with a rare collection of Greek vases, are world renowned.

The Australian school is well represented with such works as Tom Roberts' *Shearing the Rams,* circa 1890, and Sidney Nolan's modern-day *Bourke and Wills at the Gulf.* Highlights of the European collection include Tiepolo's *Banquet of Cleopatra* (valued at $10 million) and a series of Durer engravings and Blake watercolors.

Other works by leading Australian artists are also on display throughout the other two buildings that make up the arts center. Tours can be arranged, or you can just browse at your own pace. 180 St. Kilda Rd., Melbourne; 618–0222. Hours: Tues. through Sun., 10 A.M. to 5 P.M. Closed Mon. except on public holidays. Admission: $1 adults, 50 cents children, $2 family, pensioners free.

Banyule Gallery, housed in a historic early-Victorian homestead overlooking the Yarra River, is a branch of the National Gallery of Victoria. It accommodates regular exhibitions drawn from the main branch's permanent collections and touring exhibitions from other states and overseas. 60 Buckingham Dr.,

Heidleberg (8 miles n.e. of Melbourne); 459–7899. Hours: Tues. through Sun. 10 A.M. to 5 P.M. Closed Mon. except public holidays. Admission: $1 adults, 50 cents children, $2 family, pensioners free.

Australian Centre for Contemporary Art presents a program of exhibitions, events, and services that focus exclusively upon 20th-century and contemporary art. Dallas Brooks Dr., The Domain, Melbourne; 63–6422. Hours: Tues. through Fri. 10:30 A.M. to 5 P.M., Sat. and Sun. 2 to 5 P.M. Closed Mon. and public holidays. Admission: free.

Gryphon Gallery exhibits contemporary art and crafts from Australia and Asia. In the Melbourne College of Advanced Education, Carlton Campus, corner of Grattan and Swanston sts., Carlton (enter from Gate 4, on Grattan St.); 341–8587. Hours (during exhibitions): Tues. through Sat. 10 A.M. to 4 P.M., Wed. 10 A.M. to 7:30 P.M. Closed Mon.

Heide Park and Art Gallery, set in a peaceful, welcoming environment on the Yarra River, is a memorial to John and Sunday Reed, former owners of the property. Artists represented include Arthur Boyd, Charles Blackman, Joy Hester, Mirka Mora, Sidney Nolan, and Danila Vassilieff. 7 Templestowe Rd., Bulleen; 850–1849. Hours: Tues. through Fri. 10 A.M. to 5 P.M., Sat. and Sun., and public holidays and Sun., noon to 5 P.M., Closed Good Fri. and the Christmas period. Admission: $1, students with ID 50 cents, pensioners and children under 12 free.

SCIENCE AND HISTORY

Museum of Victoria. Recently renovated, this museum now houses a unique blend of the past, present, and future. On display are curiosities and rare finds from Victoria's past, as well as technological discoveries and exhibitions for today and beyond. One very popular exhibit is the world-famous race horse Phar Lap, who died under mysterious circumstances prior to its first race in the United States. The State Library of Victoria is housed in the complex as well. There is a children's museum within the building, which displays a special permanent exhibition called Experilearn. Location: 322–328 Swanston St. (between LaTrobe and Little Lonsdale sts.), Melbourne; 669–9888. Hours: Open 7 days a week, 10 A.M. to 5 P.M. Closed Christmas day, Anzacs Day, and Good Friday. Admission: free.

Melbourne Fire Brigade Museum features public displays of all forms of fire-fighting equipment of the past, as well as uniforms, photographs, and memorabilia. Location: 48 Gisborne St., East Melbourne; 662–2907. Hours: Sun. only, 10 A.M. to 4 P.M. Admission: $1.50 adults, 80 cents children and pensioners, children under 4 free.

Exhibitions displaying Jewish history, culture, religion, and lifestyle can be found in the **Jewish Museum of Australia,** Corner of Toorak Rd. and Arnold St. (behind the Melbourne Synagogue), South Yarra; 266–1922. Hours: Wed. and Thur., 11 A.M. to 4 P.M., Sun. 2 to 5 P.M. Closed Jewish holidays. Admission: $1 adults, 50 cents children.

The Performing Arts Museum, the only one of its kind in Australia and one of the few in the world, has on display more than a quarter of a million items of performing-arts memorabilia. The museum also operates a video library of rare and unusual tapes. In the Melbourne Concert Hall at the Victorian Arts Centre, 100 St. Kilda Rd., Melbourne; 617–8211. Hours: Mon. through Sat. 11 A.M. to 6 P.M., Sun. noon to 6 P.M. Closed Christmas Day and Good Friday. Admission: $2 adults, $1 children, $4 family.

Melbourne Maritime Museum combines a land-based maritime museum and the *Polly Woodside,* a commercial square-rigged sailing ship, moored near the museum. Corner of Normandy Rd. and Phayer St., South Melbourne; 699–9760. Hours: Mon. through Fri. 10 A.M. to 4 P.M., Sat. and Sun. noon to 5 P.M. Admission: $4 adults, $1.50 children, $10 family.

Moorabbin Air Museum features antique and vintage aircraft from before World War II to the '50s. The collection includes a Wirraway, a Mark I Beaufighter, and a Curtis Kittyhawk. Moorabbin Airport, Cheltenham; 580–6222. Hours: Mon. through Fri. 9 A.M. to 5 P.M., Sat. and Sun. noon to sunset. Admission: $2 adults, $1 children, $5 family.

Museum of Chinese Australian History offers as one of its main displays, DaiLoong, the world's largest dragon. 22 Cohen Pl. (a tiny side street off Little Bourke St.), Melbourne; 662–2888. Hours: Mon., Wed., Thurs., and Fri. 10 A.M.

to 4:30 P.M., Sat. and Sun. noon to 4:30 P.M. Closed Tues. Admission: $3 adults, $1.50 children and students, $7 family.

Other museums worth a visit include **Richmond Post Office Museum,** 90 Swan St., Richmond (428–7207). Open every day except Tues. and Sat. 10 A.M. to 4 P.M., Sun. noon to 5 P.M. **Victorian Racing Museum,** Gate 22, Station St., Caulfield Racecourse; 572–1111. Open race days, Tues., and Thurs., 10 A.M. to 4 P.M. Admission: free. **Railway Museum,** Champion Rd., North Williamstown; 596–3249 or 397–7412. Hours: Sat. and Sun. only, 1 to 5 P.M. Admission: $1.50 adults, 70 cents children and pensioners. **Meyer Museum,** 6th floor, Meyers Department Store, 314 Bourke St., Melbourne; 66–111. Open shopping hours. Admission: free.

ART GALLERIES. A host of smaller, individually owned galleries can be found in the city and surrounding suburbs. Some of these include *United Artists,* 42 Fitzroy St., St. Kilda (in Tolarno French Bistro building); 534–5414, and *Australian Gallery,* 33–37 Derby St., Collingwood; 417–4303. Other respected galleries include *Gerstman Abdallah Fine Arts International,* 29 Gipps St., Richmond (429–9172); *Rhumbarallas* (in the back of Rhumbarallas Cafe), 342 Brunswick St., Fitzroy (417–2327); and *Realities,* 35 Jackson St., Toorak (241–3312).

Affordable three-dimensional galleries (glassware, jewelry, ceramics, and sculpture) with works by leading Australian artists include *Distelfink Craft Gallery,* 423 Burwood Road, Hawthorn (818–2555); *Maker's Mark Gallery,* 85 Collins St., Melbourne, (63–3254); and *Meat Market Craft Center,* 42 Courtney St., North Melbourne (329–9966).

Note: For specific hours and details of current exhibitions consult the Entertainment Guide in the Fri. edition of the *Age*. Also, the Melbourne yellow pages are quite complete and can be invaluable.

SHOPPING. Street upon street of boutiques and leading fashion houses have established Melbourne as the fashion capital of Australia. The haute couture overseas labels are available in upper Collins St. (referred to as the "Paris end"), Little Collins St., the arcades (charming burrows off the major street in downtown), and Toorak Village in the suburb of Toorak. Australian designer labels are also available on High St., Armadale, and on Toorak Road, South Yarra. Chapel St., South Yarra, and Lygon St., Carlton, cater more to the eclectic clientele. And on Greville St., Prahran, you can find quality vintage clothing and accessories. Trading Hours: Mon. to Thurs., 9 A.M. to 5 P.M., Fri. till 9 P.M., Sat. 9 A.M. to noon. only.

Figgins Diorama, at 171 Collins St., Melbourne (654–1744), is an exclusive fashion store of more than 40 individual boutiques presenting the best in fashion and accessories from Europe and America. *Georges,* at 162 Collins St., Melbourne (63–0411), is Melbourne's oldest, most exclusive department store.

David Jones (right beside Myer in the Bourke St. Mall), at 310 Bourke St., Melbourne (669–8200), is another distinguished department store. *Myer Melbourne,* at 341 Bourke St., Melbourne (6–6111), is the largest department store in the southern hemisphere, and *G.J. Coles,* at 299 Bourke St., Melbourne (667–4111), is a general retailer.

You can shop for Australian made goods at the *Australiana General Store,* 1227 High St., Armadale (20–2324)

An institution in the Melbourne lifestyle is the open-air atmosphere and bargain prices of the old-fashioned markets. The *Queen Victoria Market* at the top of Elizabeth Street, Melbourne, is the largest and is open Tues. to Thurs. 6 A.M. to 2 P.M., Fri. 6 A.M. to 6 P.M., Sat. 6 A.M. to noon, and Sun. 9 A.M. to 4 P.M. It sells everything from vegetables to clothing. The *South Melbourne Market,* at the corner of Coventry and Cecil sts. (699–4077), is open Wed. 6 A.M. to 2 P.M., Fri. 6 A.M. to 6 P.M., Sat. 6 A.M. to noon, and Sun. 9 A.M. to 4 P.M.

A shopping tour for the true shopping enthusiast: *Rosalind's Shopping Tours* (267–1335) is a group shopping tour for wholesail prices and includes transport and lunch. *Shopping Spree Tours* (568–3889) offer escorted shopping tours to some of Melbourne's best manufacturers and importers; includes lunch.

AUSTRALIA

MUSIC. *Melbourne Symphony Orchestra.* MSO, under the dynamic baton of Hiroyuki Awaki, performs virtually year-round in the new 2,500-seat Melbourne Concert Hall, in the arts center, 100 St. Kilda Rd. (609–8370).

Victorian State Opera and Australian Opera. Both companies conduct regular seasons, with performances from many world-renowned stars, including Pavarotti and Australian-born Joan Sutherland. Seasons usually vary in time of year and length (best to call when you arrive), but all performances take place in Melbourne Concert Hall, 100 St. Kilda Rd. (617–8211). Further inquiries, phone Bass, 11–566.

The Australian Ballet. Occupying the 2,000 seat State Theatre, the company provides five programs yearly. It has had the honor of having many of the greats, from Pavlova to Nureyev, grace its stage. For information, call 376–1400.

Musica Viva, a national organization that organizes chamber-music concerts, presents 16 concerts a year, 8 at Dallas Brooks Hall, 300 Victoria Pde., East Melbourne, and 8 at the Melbourne Concert Hall, 100 St. Kilda Rd. All inquiries 11–566.

If you are in the contemporary-music scene you may see many favorite international performers at any one of the several major musical venues in the city: *Melbourne Concert Hall,* in the arts center, 100 St. Kilda Rd. (11–566); *Melbourne Sports and Entertainment Centre,* Swan St., Melbourne (429–6288); *Royal Melbourne Showgrounds,* Epsom Rd., Ascot Vale (about 3 mi. from the city; 376–3733).

Open-air concerts, beginning in the summer (Dec. thru Mar.), can be seen at the *Sydney Meyer Music Bowl,* Kings Domain, Melbourne. For information call, 11–566 or 617–8211. There is also a *Free Entertainment in the Parks* program, which begins in early Oct., yearly. Phone 328–2168 for recorded program listings.

Jazz is well-represented in Melbourne in such venues as *Bell's Hotel,* corner of Moray and Coventry sts., South Melbourne (690–4360); *Tankerville Arms,* corner of Johnston and Nicholson sts., Carlton (417–3216); *Bridge Hotel,* 642 Bridge Rd., Richmond (428–3852); *Chez Jazz,* 328 Kings Way, South Melbourne (690–1522). Note: some of the venues include music and meals; some have cover charges. Also, there is a program *Jazz after Dark,* every Fri. and Sat. night at 11 P.M. ($5 cover) in the foyer of the Studio Theatre, at the arts center, 100 St. Kilda Rd. For information, call 617–8211.

If you are really adventurous and want to sample some of the up-and-coming local contemporary groups, there is a network of venues where groups such as Men at Work, Little River Band, Air Supply, Split Enz, and INXS got their start. Among them are *Aberdeen Hotel,* 324 St. Georges Road, North Fitzroy (489–8353); *Armadale Hotel,* 1068 High St., Armadale (509–0277); *Billboard,* 170 Russell St., Melbourne (663–2989); and *The Venue,* 17 Upper Esplanade, St. Kilda (534–5179). Other musical nightspots include *Palace Entertainment Complex,* Lower Esplanade, St. Kilda (534–0655), and *City Limits* (in the Sandown Hotel), corner of Corrigan Rd. and Princess Hwy., Noble Park (546–5755).

For a complete listing to Melbourne's musical night spots, pick up a copy of the Friday edition of the *Age* and consult their Entertainment Guide supplement.

STAGE. *Melbourne Theatre Company.* The MTC, Melbourne's first and most successful theater company, has two seasons per year, during which they perform one-third classical, one-third overseas, and one-third Australian works. They can be seen at their own *Russell Street Theatre,* 19 Russell St., the *Athenaeum Theatre,* 188 Collins St., and the new *Playhouse,* in the Theatres Building at the arts center (the building with the "Eiffel Tower" on the top). For information and bookings, call 654–4000.

Playbox Theatre Company. The city's second largest company, Playbox stages around ten productions a year, which are primarily new and contemporary. Since their own theater burned down in 1984, and until a new one is built, they perform at *St. Martin's Theatre,* 28 St. Martin's Lane, South Yarra (267–2477), and at the *Studio,* in the Theatres Building at the arts center, 100 St. Kilda Rd. (63–4888).

Anthill Theatre. French director Jean-Pierre Mignon created the Australian Nouveau Theatre—ANT—to present radical versions of French classics, as well as neglected modern European works, and they manage to throw in their own reconstruction of an Australian play. The *Anthill Theatre* is a former church hall at 199 Napier St., South Melbourne (699–3253).

Australian Contemporary Theatre Company. Centered in a large former church, still referred to as the Church, A.C.T. is noted for its unusual productions of new Australian plays. At 500 Burwood Rd., Hawthorn. For information, call 819–1818 or 819–2644.

Universal Theatre. This would be called off-off Broadway in the States; the Universal Theatre is the home of the daring, adventurous, avant-garde production. U.T. is in an atmospheric, moody, oddly shaped theater that manages to seat 300 on three sides of its corner stage. Upstairs, there's a recently renovated *Universal 2*, for smaller shows. Address: 13 Victoria St., Fitzroy (419–3777).

Historic old theaters within the city offering stage plays and musical comedies include the *Princess Theatre*, 163 Spring St. (662–2911); *Her Majesty's Theatre*, 219 Exhibition St. (663–3211); and the *Comedy Theatre*, 240 Exhibition St. (662–3233).

Half-Tix. There is a Half-Tix ticket booth in the Bourke St. Mall, city center, which sells tickets at half price on the day of the performance to a wide range of theater attractions. Hours: Mon. to Fri. noon to 6 P.M., Sat., 10 A.M. to 2 P.M. Phone: 63–9420.

NIGHTLIFE–ENTERTAINMENT. Melbourne takes on a different feeling at night. Whether discoing in the Underground or taking in a comic at the Last Laugh, there's always something to dance to, laugh at, and generally have a ball doing.

Theater Restaurants. *Last Laugh Theatre Restaurant,* 64 Smith St., Collingwood; 419–6226. Offers the best in contemporary entertainment, including stand-up comics and avant-garde musical performers. Tues. through Sat. from 7:30 P.M. to 3 A.M. Casual style, licensed. Upstairs is *LeJoke*, a smaller room featuring five or six acts a night, mostly stand-up comics. *Comedy Cafe,* 177 Brunswick St., Fitzroy; 419–2869. Offers zany humor and a lively atmosphere. BYO. Open Tues. through Sat. *Tikki and John's,* 169 Exhibition St., Melbourne; 663–2585. The best of traditional music-hall entertainment. Licensed and open Tues. through Sat. Jan. through Oct., and Mon. through Sat., Nov. and Dec. *Bull 'n' Bush and Naughty Nineties Music Hall,* First fl., Glen Arcade, 675 Glenferrie Rd., Hawthorn; 818–1509. A two-hour music hall variety-vaudeville show followed by dancing. Open Wed. through Sat. BYO.

Discos, Nightclubs. *Melbourne Underground Discotheque,* 22 King St., Melbourne; 62–4701. Decor is unusual, with renovated railway carriages. Offers food, drink, and dancing. Its hours vary and door charge is up to $9 per person.

Inflation Discotheque, 60 King St., Melbourne; 62–3674. This club seems to attract a younger group and includes dance floor, restaurant, lounge, and various bars. Open Mon. and Wed. to Sun. from 8 P.M. to 4 A.M. or later. Door charge is $5 to $9.

VICTORIA BEYOND MELBOURNE

Victoria is a conveniently compact state. You are no more than six hours' drive from sandy beaches, snowy mountains, untouched forests, desert, rivers, lakes, ghost towns, modern cities, farms, and myriad other slices of life, nature, and history that go to make exploring Victoria not only exciting and adventurous, but very accessible. Victoria has a network of roads and highways second to none in Australia. The roads are well stocked with gas stations, diners, rest stops, and scenic overlooks. Just obey the speed limits as posted—maximum throughout the state is 100kp h (60 mph)—and remember to drive on the left side of the road, and you'll do just fine.

Victoria is broken down into eight regions. Aside from Melbourne–inner city and Melbourne–leisure regions, there are: southeast;

northeast; gold central; west coast; Wimmera; and Murray. An in-depth look at each region follows, using Melbourne as a starting point.

Melbourne Leisure Region

Phillip Island

Phillip Island (Isle of the Fairy Penguin) is 85 miles south of Melbourne via Princes, South Gippsland, and Bass Highway.

The fairy penguins, the smallest members of the penguin family, struggle ashore at Summerland Beach under the blaze of powerful spotlights, after a day at sea gathering food. For this alone, Phillip Island is one of the most popular tourist attractions in Australia. Word of warning: No matter what time of the year you decide to watch the penguins, make sure you wear plenty of warm clothing.

Other features on the island include a colony of seals, seen through telescopes from the Nobbies kiosk, and koalas, seen at the many koala reserves on the island.

Mornington Peninsula

Mornington Peninsula stretches 120 miles to the farthest point south of Melbourne, via Nepean Highway. To take advantage of the coastal scenery, detour at Mornington, and pick up Marine Drive through Mt. Martha to Dromana. A playground for Melbourne's summer holiday makers, this boot-shaped promontory with its sandy sheltered bayside beaches is ideal for swimming, boating, and soaking up the sunshine.

At Arthur's Seat near Dromana take a chairlift ride for scenic views. Sorrento is an area full of history, seen in the buildings and first settlers' grave. The beach is ideal for swimming and fishing.

Portsea is a pretty town; the back beach is popular with surf lovers. A ferry runs from Portsea and Sorrento to Queenscliff on the other side of the bay. There are many excellent public golf courses on the Peninsula; it is a golfers' paradise.

Cape Schanck Coastal Park stretches along the coast and includes vast stretches of ocean beach, curious rock formations, and rugged cliffs. Thick coastal tea tree covers much of the park. The National Parks Service has developed a beautiful walk to Bushrangers Bay.

The Dandenongs

Thirty miles east of Melbourne via the Burwood Highway to Ferntree Gully are the rolling hills of the Dandenongs, renowned for their tree-fern gullies, magnificent views, tall forests, and exotic trees and plants. There are ornamental flower farms growing tulips and the hills are the home of the spectacular lyrebird—all less than an hour's drive from Melbourne.

The William Ricketts Sanctuary on the Mt. Dandenong Tourist Road, in Olinda, displays a lifetime of sculpture in a natural setting. William Ricketts has devoted his life to the faces and legends of the Australian Aborigine.

Sherbrooke Forest is the home of the lyrebird. For a delightful afternoon, have lunch or tea at Burnham Beeches and then follow one of the walking tracks into the forest.

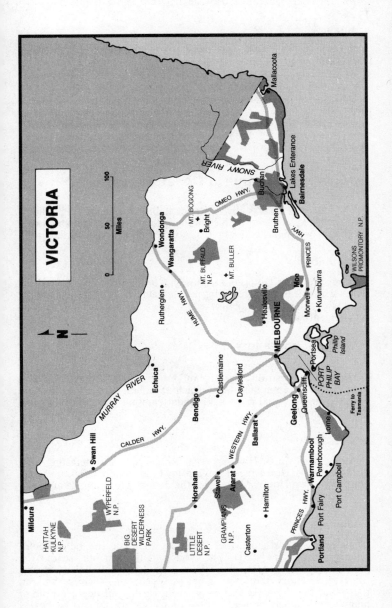

A popular attraction is Puffing Billy at Old Monbulk Road in Belgrave. The small vintage steam train takes travelers on a scenic tour, through tree-ferned gullies between Belgrave and Emerald.

Healesville

Healesville is 35 miles east of Melbourne via Maroondah Highway. Healesville is a destination point for many international visitors because of its important Australian native-fauna sanctuary. The sanctuary accommodates more than 200 species of Australian birds, kangaroos, wombats, koalas, and the duck-billed platypus in a natural bush setting.

Nearby, Marysville offers many beauty spots including Steavenson Falls and some of the world's tallest hardwoods.

Southeast Coast Region

The southeast coast is alive with possibilities for an exciting holiday. With excellent accesses via the South Gippsland and Princes highways the visitor will find no shortage of holiday attractions and facilities.

Korumburra

Along the South Gippsland Highway, Korumburra is the site of Coal Creek Historical Park, featuring a re-created coal mine and mining town of the 1890s. Korumburra is also noted for its dairy industry and for its giant earthworms.

Wilson's Promontory

Via the South Gippsland Highway, Wilson's "Prom" is at the southernmost tip of Australia. The "Prom" has just about everything: bushland, granite formations, magnificent beaches, birds, wildlife, and bushwalking. Its tidal river is a popular camping spot, with flats and cabins available.

Moe

Along the Princes Highway east, Route 1, is an interesting little industrial town, featuring Old Gippstown, an outdoor folk museum, and Loren Iron House. Moe is also the doorway to Walhalla and Baw Baw National Park.

Walhalla

Some 50km north of Moe, Walhalla was once the richest goldmining town in the state. When the gold thinned out, so did the population. Still, there are many points of interest, including the steam-tramway terminal, the long tunnel extended mine—which you can tour—and the Walhalla Cemetery, an intriguing hillside gravesite of many of the area's pioneers, some of whom are said to be buried vertically. The ski slopes and bushwalking trails of Baw Baw National Park are only 5km away.

Of special interest is the alpine walking track, a 400km (250-mi.) track that extends from Walhalla, through Baw Baw National Park, to

VICTORIA

the New South Wales border and takes several weeks to complete. For more information, contact the National Park Information Service.

Gippsland Lakes

Via Route 1, Princes Highway East, this network of lakes paralleling the southeast coast forms one of the largest inland waterways in Australia. A unique splay of scenic, serene, blue waters, these lakes are also the site of the popular resort towns of Bairnsdale, Paynesville, Metung, and Lake's Entrance. Houseboats, yachts, and cruisers are available for rental. It's an ideal environment for water sports and fishing; for nature watchers, the area abounds with exotic flora and fauna. The best view of the lakes is from the cliffs at Nyerimilang Park, about 10km northwest of Lake's Entrance. From there, you can see the deep blue Reeves Channel and the network of Fraser, Flannagan, and Rigby islands. The single biggest activity at the lakes is fishing, with likely catches being bream, flathead, and skipjack.

Snowy River National Park

East along Princes Highway (about 240 mi. from Melbourne), via Bruthen and Buchan, is the entrance for Snowy River National Park. Made popular by Banjo Patterson's poem "Man from Snowy River" and the recent film of the same name, the Snowy winds down from New South Wales, through the park, on its way to the Tasman Sea. It is a river of many faces and moods, at times peacefully sleeping in languid pools, other times whitewater angry and raging. The park offers you a chance to experience its extremes and observe some of its inhabitants, including wallabies, wombats, the rare brush-tailed rock wallaby, and the Gippsland crocodile, which looks like a fierce little dragon but is actually quite harmless. While there, you can also visit the scenic Tulloch Ard Gorge and the popular McKillop's Bridge, which has quiet swimming pools and sandy beaches.

On your way to the Snowy River National Park, you might want to stop at Buchan Caves, in Buchan, for one of their five daily tours.

Northeast Region

The Northeast region is known as the all-seasons resort area. Visitors can ski the Victorian Alps during the winter and go bushwalking along those same slopes during the summer and autumn. The "high country" is a labyrinth of forests with fertile river valleys and plains dotted with gold mines and some great trout fishing. It is also the home of such famous—or infamous—characters as the Man from Snowy River and the bushrangers Dan Morgan, Harry Power, and the most romanticized outlaw in Australian folklore, Ned Kelly.

It is a region that offers sweet-bearing vineyards, and the freedom of soaring along swift air currents in a glider.

Mt. Bogong is the highest elevation in the state, and perfect for the serious back-packer or in a four-wheel-drive vehicle.

Ski resorts at Mt. Buller, Mt. Buffalo, Mt. Hotham, and Falls Creek offer accommodations and great skiing during August to mid-September.

Beechworth

The town of Beechworth holds a Golden Horseshoes Festival every year to commemorate the member of parliament who once rode through the town on a horse shod with golden shoes. Beechworth then had a population of 8,000, with 61 hotels and a theater that attracted performers from all over the world. Today, it has 3,500 inhabitants and is noteworthy for the excellence of its trees, parks, and gardens. Several buildings remain from the gold-rush days. They include a fine powder magazine, Chinese funeral ovens, and the honey-colored government buildings of the 1850s.

Thirty miles from Beechworth is the tobacco-growing center of Bright, which plays an important role as a staging post for visitors to the ski resorts in winter. The town trumpets the oncoming autumn with the Bright Autumn Festival; it's worth the trip to watch the leaves.

Mt. Buller

Mt. Buller Alpine Village, 150 mi. northeast of Melbourne, with an elevation of 5,907 ft., is Australia's largest resort and one of Victoria's most developed ski areas. There are a dozen ski runs of varying difficulty. It's an ideal place for a day ski jaunt from Melbourne. Other ski-resort areas worth a try are Falls Creek, 225 mi. northeast of Melbourne; Mt. Buffalo, 190 mi. northeast of Melbourne; Mt. Hotham, 232 mi. northeast of Melbourne.

Rutherglen, 165 mi. northeast of Melbourne, is the place to go for good wine right from the cellar. Rutherglen is the premier wine town in Victoria and is literally surrounded by vineyards. It celebrates a winery walkabout each Queen's Birthday weekend.

Gold Central Region

Born out of the gold-rush days of the 1850s, this tourist region is in the center of Victoria and, in a way, at the center of its history. Gold fever spread all over the country and the promise of instant wealth brought in prospectors from as far away as China.

The region is one of the most rewarding tourist areas in the state. You can amble into one of the re-created mining towns, pan for gold, take a dip in or a sip from one of area's mineral springs, and, to top it off, have a bit of pluck from one of the wineries along the way. The area is also a marketplace for original crafts and antiques.

Ballarat

Via the Western Highway, 67 mi. west of Melbourne, Ballarat is unique in Australian history in that it was the site of the Eureka Rebellion, a small but significant skirmish between miners and the law. Legislation regarding miners' rights and representation resulted from it. The city was also one of the gold-mining centers of the state and the home of the Welcome Nugget, the second largest single gold nugget in the world. It weighed 63,000 grams (139 lb.). A small monument marks the location in the city where it was found.

Gold was not the only industry in Ballarat. For about 35 years, until 1906, it was also a very successful manufacturer of locomotives for the Victorian government. It was also the home of a large brewery and a

VICTORIA

small lingerie business, both of which still thrive today under new names and corporate ownerships.

In Ballarat, Sovereign Hill is a must-see. It is a re-creation of a goldmining town of the 1850s, built on the site of the Sovereign Hill Quartz Mining Company. It is divided into three sections: the Red Gully Diggings, which show the activity associated with early alluvial mining; Sovereign Hill Township, which exemplifies the support services and social functions that sprang up during the boom times, and the Mining Museum, which incorporates guided tours into mine shafts and tunnels, a ride on a coach, and demonstrations on panning for gold. You can even buy a miner's right and pan for gold yourself.

Near Sovereign Hill is the Gold Museum, which houses a priceless collection of gold from the local diggings and around the world.

The botanic gardens, which encircle Lake Wendouree, are thick with lush plants and exotica, as well as fine sculptured works of marble donated by several men who made their fortunes in the Ballarat gold fields. The Begonia House, in the gardens, is the focus for the Begonia Festival held yearly, February-March.

Incidentally, Lake Wendouree was human made and was the site of the 1956 Olympic rowing events. You can get a beautiful feel for the lake and a great glimpse of the city by taking a ride on the paddle cruiser *Sarah George*.

Daylesford-Hepburn Springs

Sixty miles northwest of Melbourne, along the Western Highway and the Midland Highway, are Daylesford and Hepburn Springs. Nestled snugly into the slopes of the Great Dividing Range, they are well-known for their spa water. In fact, the area has the highest concentration of mineral waters in Australia.

In Daylesford, see the Daylesford Historical Society Museum, containing some remnants of its earlier gold-mining days, as well as some Aboriginal artifacts. Also see Jubilee Lake, where boating and swimming are available.

In Hepburn Springs, don't miss Hepburn Mineral Springs Reserve, where you can get mineral, electrical, herbal, and steam baths with massages. There is also a 5km round-trip walk from the reserve to the Hepburn Reservoir. Also of interest is the Hepburn Blowhole, along the Hepburn Springs to Daylesford walking track.

Castlemaine

Seventy-five miles from Melbourne, northwest along Calder Highway–Rte. 79 to Elphinstone, west, is Castlemaine. The quaint former mining town is now known for Castlemaine Market, on Mostyn Street. Built in 1862, the market's architectural design is Greco-Roman. Though it was actually used as a marketplace until 1967, it is today a museum that blends interesting artifacts with audiovisual displays.

The town also has a major regional-art gallery and museum, with the works of noted Australian artists on display, on Lyttleton St.

Two Castlemaine hotels have been classified by the National Trust: the Cambell Street Motor Lodge and the Midland. Both buildings are of historic value and have been preserved in their original design.

Bendigo

Ninety miles northwest of Melbourne, via the Calder Highway, Bendigo was one of the richest gold centers in the world. The first strike was in 1851, and the rush of activity that followed lasted into the twentieth century. The three Deborah Mines were still working in the 1950s, but by then, because of escalating operating costs and a thinning out of the veins, the fever was long gone. What remained was the architecture and artifacts of a fast-paced, affluent past.

While in Bendigo, take a ride on the Vintage Talking Tram, which operates from the Central Deborah Gold Mine to the Chinese joss house (about 5 mi.). A taped commentary informs the riders of points of interest along the way.

The Chinese joss house (temple of worship) is uniquely authentic, having been built by Chinese miners during the days of the great rush. This finely preserved structure is a National Trust site.

Central Deborah Gold Mine, the last mine to have operated in Bendigo, is open for daily tours. Items to be seen are rock drillers, boilers, a stokehold, and a winding engine. The miners' change rooms are intact.

And about 3½ mi. from Bendigo, in Epsom, is Bendigo Pottery. There, you can buy from one of Australia's oldest potteries. The pottery has become so well-known within the state that it has become a tourist attraction.

West Coast Region

Beginning with Geelong and the Bellarine Peninsula, just across Port Phillip Bay from Melbourne, and continuing west to the South Australia border, the west coast region is a living kaleidoscope of nature and history. Along the Great Ocean Road, arguably the most scenic road in Australia, built by veterans as a war memorial to those who died in World War I, one is awe-struck by the raw, rough beauty of nature juxtaposed with the quaint gentleness of seascape towns. The forbidding Twelve Apostles, a group of monolithic rock formations, rise up out of the sea, creating great gorges, caves, and havens for all sorts of wildlife. The lush, verdant Otway Rain Forest seems untouched by all but its own wildlife. The rugged coastline is home to the fishers of Port Fairy, Peterborough, Portland, and Port Campbell and a graveyard for many seafarers of other times who tried to navigate the hellish currents lurking beneath its beauty. The city of Warrnambool is a wool and dairy center whose ranges and rolling hills overlook the ships that sail into its port. Wherever you walk or drive along the west coast region, it's like being in a living postcard. And it's really something to write home about.

Geelong

Some 45 mi. SW of Melbourne, on the Princes Highway, Route 1, is Geelong. The second largest city in Victoria, Geelong is an industrial center, with a Ford Motor Plant, a busy shipping port, and a fine blend of modern and historic architecture. It sits on the western shores of Port Phillip Bay.

From Geelong you can head south to Torquay and the beginning of the Great Ocean Road or southeast along the Bellarine Highway, to the Bellarine Peninsula. All along the peninsula you can discover sheltered beaches, seaside villages, and historic landmarks and architecture. Queenscliff and Point Lonsdale, on the headland at the entrance to the bay, provide comfortable accommodations in old hotels and guesthouses.

Torquay

Torquay is 55 mi. southwest of Melbourne, via the Princes Highway, Route 1 west, to Geelong; then follow the signs, heading due south, to Torquay and the Great Ocean Road. Torquay is Australia's premier surfing and wind-surfing resort. Its Bell's Beach is world famous for its Easter surfing contests. Each October, there are international wind-surfing contests. It's a Valhalla for the serious fisher or the leisurely sailor. It also offers an 18-hole golf course, squash courts, horseback riding, bush walking, and clifftop walking paths.

Lorne

At the edge of the Otway Range, this lovely little town is the site of a wild celebration every New Year's Eve. Some make their reservations a year in advance. It's a favorite spot of Melbournians for surfing, sailing, and sunbathing.

If you're heading west from Lorne, don't miss the Otway National Park. It is part of the Otway Ranges, a rain forest that has some precipitation about 200 days a year. It is a very natural, primitive environment, with ferns and shrubs that seem to define the color green. Be warned that some of the roads are not paved; it can get a little bumpy and very slow-moving.

Warrnambool

Some 160 mi. west of Melbourne, is Warrnambool, a wool and dairy-farm center. It's a friendly city of robust, hardy people who live off the land and on the sea. Be sure and see Flagstaff Hill Maritime Village, which shows the significance of the seaport in Australia's heritage. In the village, you can visit a lighthouse built in 1853 and still in use today; wander through an old fort built in 1887 for fear of a Russian invasion after the Crimean War; or board the *Reginald M,* a trading ship from the South Australian Gulf.

Port Fairy

Some 180 mi. west of Melbourne on the Princes Highway via Warrnambool, or along the Great Ocean Road to Warrnambool (connects with the Princes Highway), is one of the most charming places in the region. Port Fairy is the second oldest town in Victoria and a sheer delight for its sturdy old bluestone buildings set close to the banks of the River Moyne. Originally a whaling station, it still thrives as the base for a fishing fleet that keeps local hotels well supplied with fresh crays and lobster.

Head inland for Casterton and Hamilton, and the route passes along the Glenelg River and across rolling, studded gum-tree country, to Warrock Homestead, a complete township remaining as it was when first built and settled more than 100 years ago. All the buildings are classified by the National Trust and are still in daily use by the fourth generation of the same family that first settled there. Through Hamilton, noted for its art galleries, the road leads back down the Hamilton Highway to Melbourne.

Wimmera Region

The Wimmera region, settled in the 1860s, is a land of contrasts. The layout is generally level, with the notable exception of the Grampian Mountain Range, rising up out of the landscape like a great, rocky dragon. In the shadow of this imposing range, which is the highlight of the region, there are deserts, rivers, sleepy little towns, and bustling little cities.

The cities of Ararat and Stawell both act as gateways to the Grampians.

Ararat

About 120 mi. northwest of Melbourne, on the Western Highway, is Ararat. Surrounded by wheat fields, grazing land for sheep and beef, and wine vineyards, Ararat is also noted as being a festive, sports-minded town.

About 10 mi. north of Ararat is the Great Western Vineyard, well-known for its champagne, which is matured in underground galleries similar to those in Champagne, France. Guided tours are available.

Stawell

Stawell is 140 mi. northwest of Melbourne, on the Western Highway. A service center to the Grampians National Park, Stawell also has some attractions of its own, including the World in Miniature Park, Wallaroo Wildlife Park and hot-air balloon tours of the Grampians and the wine country.

The Grampians

The Grampians are 155 mi. west of Melbourne, off the Western Highway to Halls Gap (can also be approached from the southwest via Hamilton). Long famous for its rugged mountain ranges, rock formations, and spectacular wildflowers, the Grampians became Victoria's largest and newest national park in 1984.

The Grampians were formed millions of years ago, when sandy sediments were tilted, uplifted, and eroded to form the north-south ranges evident today.

Wildflowers are the most obvious features of the Grampians flora, offering more than 860 native species. Wildlife abounds too. Gray kangaroos, red-neck wallabies, koalas, echidnas, possums, and emus are common, and more than 200 species of birds have been recorded.

The Glenisla Homestead, on the fringes of the park, is a restored authentic homestead, circa 1870, that is available for overnight accommodations. The manager of the Homestead offers tours throughout the Grampians that include a close look at the mysteriously beautiful Aboriginal rock paintings, believed by some experts to be thousands of years old.

At Zumstein, within the park, you can stop and pet tame kangaroos.

Roads and walking tracks near Halls Gap provide access to many attractive sites in the Wonderland and Mt. William ranges as well as providing accommodations, shops, and restaurants.

Horsham

An irrigation program that began in 1953, around the Horsham area, has made that land rich and fertile, one of Victoria's grain-producing centers. Some of the flatlands provide ample grazing acreage for Horsham's well-regarded livestock industry. To reach Horsham, drive 185 miles northwest of Melbourne, on the Western Highway.

Murray Region

The Murray is Australia's biggest river, forming a natural border between Victoria and New South Wales. It is 1,609 mi. long and empties into the Indian Ocean, on the west coast of the continent. It is the main feeder for the many rivers and streams that vein their way down Victoria from the New South Wales border and creates an oasis on the threshold of the great Outback. Its tributaries and lakes provide a nesting place for indigenous and rare bird life. And in the Murray Valley, you will find some of the best vineyards in the country.

As much as the Murray River is the life force of much of the region, it is also a part of the lifestyle. One can dine on delicious cuisine while cruising its winding paths on old-fashioned paddle steamers and cabin cruisers, venture forth on ultramodern water-jet boats, or, for the more leisurely inclined, rent a houseboat and do your own thing.

Echuca

Some 120 mi. north of Melbourne, via the Hume Highway, to the Northern Highway, north, is Echuca. Echuca is at the junction of the Murray, Campaspe, and Goulburn rivers and is the closest Murray River town to Melbourne. Echuca was Australia's major inland port during the 19th-century river-trade era. Still in evidence of this era are restored riverboats, barges, the Bridge and the Star hotels, and the famous Red Gum Wharf. Rich River Festival, mid-October, is yet another reminder of the riverboat days.

Swan Hill

The Swan Hill Pioneer Settlement is one of Australia's top tourist attractions, and with good reason. No detail is overlooked in providing visitors with an in-depth look at what life was like for the inland pioneers of the 19th century. The focal point of the settlement is the landlocked, three-decked paddlewheeler, the *Gem,* at one time the largest cargo-passenger boat on the Murray. It houses a licensed restaurant, an art gallery, and a souvenir kiosk. Swan Hill is 215 miles north of Melbourne on the Murray Valley Highway via Northern Highway and 100 miles north of Echuca.

In the settlement itself, visitors can wander into the pioneers' homes or shop at the general store. You can visit a steam workshop and see how a steam boiler drives a whole range of workshop machines.

Many believe that the most exciting aspect of the settlement is the sound-and-light show, which uses state-of-the-art lighting effects and real-life sounds to re-create the decades of pioneer history at Swan Hill. The show goes on every night.

A full tour of the settlement would cover about 50 buildings and items of interest, and a suggested walk is available at the entry gate.

Anyone interested in taking it all in at a leisurely pace, however, should consider staying over at one of the many lodges and campsites in the area.

Mildura

About 335 mi. northwest of Melbourne, on the Calder Highway, is Mildura, known as the center for its citrus, wine, and dried fruit industry, as well as for its houseboat tours along the Murray. Many of the vineyards are open for touring and tasting. The famous Mildara and Lindeman's wines are produced in this area. Mildura also boasts of more sunshine hours per year than Queensland's Gold Coast.

PRACTICAL INFORMATION FOR VICTORIA BEYOND MELBOURNE

See also Practical Information for Melbourne.

HOW TO GET AROUND. *By air:* Ansett and *Australian Airlines* have regular services between Melbourne and all state capitals plus Canberra and Alice Springs and Darwin, linking with intrastate airlines at each place for onward travel to smaller towns. *East-West* flies between Sydney and Melbourne and from Melbourne to other cities in Australia. Tullamarine, 10 mi. northwest of the city, is the international and domestic airport and is equipped to take any commercial aircraft now flying in the world. The second, and former major airport, Essendon, 6 mi. northwest of Melbourne, can take all aircraft up to Boeing 727 and DC 9s and is mainly used by commuter and charter airlines. Such are *Executive Airlines,* Merimbula/Melbourne and Melbourne/Launceston/Devonport; *Kendell Airlines,* operating between the New South Wales towns of Cooma, Wagga, and Griffith to Melbourne and from the coastal towns of Merimbula (NSW) and Mallacoota (Victoria) to Melbourne.

By rail. All train travel into cities of Victoria operates out of Melbourne. Melbourne's two major railway stations are Spencer St. Station (for interstate and country trains) and Flinders St. Station (for suburban trains). V/Line is the state's largest transport authority and operates daily rail services to Sydney and Adelaide, with connections to other capital cities. All major Victorian cities and many smaller country centers can be reached by regular rail service. For information call 6–1001 or 62–0771.

By car: Road travel is the most popular form of travel for holiday-makers in Australia. Victoria gets more than its share of vacationers because of the top class road system within the state. The rules are the same as those for the interstate: keep to the left; give way to oncoming traffic on your right. This latter rule is superseded in Victoria when the road you are on has a priority road sign—broad upward arrow crossed by a narrow line. Traffic entering your road on your right has to give way.

By bus. Express coach companies *Ansett Pioneer Express* and *Greyhound* operate interstate services from Melbourne and there are several local bus lines. For information regarding bus travel in Victoria, call 654–5311.

TRAILER TIPS. Victorians love to go camping and caravanning (trailer camping). This state has, per square mile, probably the best road system of all and plenty of parks to cater to holidaying families. Thus, beware of Victorian coastal parks at peak seasons—December, January, and Easter holidays.

Many parks are then crowded or untidy, or both, with vacationers living cheek by jowl in crowded conditions they would not tolerate in their own homes. Inland during these times, and everywhere during the rest of the year, parks are of a high standard with laundry, barbecues, and hot showers. A deposit for a key to the facilities is usually requested.

Because there are so many parks, and for very detailed information on attractions, facilities and how and where to book, consult the *RACV Australian Outdoor Guide,* which you can buy from this motoring organization, 123 Queen Street, Melbourne. For information, call 607–2211.

Most parks will garage your camper for you; they have minimum-stay periods over the peak holiday season. Most have also on-site campers but the price quoted is for two to four people for a site without power. LPG means bottled gas available.

The Melbourne Leisure Region

ACCOMMODATIONS. *Expensive* double rooms cost $A90 and up; *moderate* accommodations are $A60–$A90; *inexpensive,* under $A60.

DANDENONGS. Burnham Beeches Country House. *Expensive.* Sherbrooke Rd. (adjacent to Alfred Nicholas Memorial Gardens), Sherbrooke; (03) 755–1903. Licensed restaurant, indoor heated pool, hot spa, tennis court, meeting rooms, lounge. A stately country house–hotel built in the 1930s, finest domestic example of art deco in Australia.

HEALESVILLE. Healesville Motor Inn. *Inexpensive.* 45 Maroondah Hwy., Healesville; (059) 62–5251. Light breakfast.

PHILLIP ISLAND. Cowes Colonial Motor Inn, *Moderate,* 192 Thompson Ave., Cowes; (059) 52–2486. **Homestead Motor Inn.** *Inexpensive.* Pool.

SORRENTO. Koonya. *Moderate.* Nepean Hwy., Sorrento; (059) 84–2281. This hotel offers licensed restaurant and breakfast.

RESTAURANTS. Price classifications are based on the cost of an average meal for one person, not including tax, gratuity, or beverage. *Expensive,* $A30 and up; *moderate,* $A10–$A25; *inexpensive,* under $A10.

BELGRAVE. Fawlty's. *Moderate.* 580a Monbulk Rd., Belgrave; 754–7463. Imaginative menu includes calamari with lemon butter in an abalone shell. BYO. Open Wednesday to Sunday for dinner only. All cards.

DANDENONGS. Burnham Beeches. *Expensive.* Sherbrooke Rd., Sherbrooke; (03) 755–1903. French. Luxurious country-house estate open every day for lunch and dinner. Setting is beautiful. Most major cards.

HEALESVILLE. Mt. Rael. *Moderate.* Yarra Glen Rd., Healesville; (059) 62–4107. Country-style. Beautiful view from verandah. Open Wednesday to Sunday for lunch; Friday to Sunday for dinner. Diners Club and MasterCard. BYO.

MOUNT MARTHA. Flouch's. *Expensive.* Lochiel Ave., Mount Martha; (059) 74–2733. Modern French. Restaurant furnished with simple elegance. Menu changes every six weeks. All major cards. Lunch on Sunday only. Dinner Tuesday through Saturday. BYO.

SORRENTO. Knockers. *Moderate.* 182 Ocean Beach Rd., Sorrento; (059) 84–1246. Grills-fish. Very popular. Blackboard menu changes daily. Mainly char-grilled steaks and fresh fish. Open daily for dinner from 6 P.M. MasterCard. BYO.

AUSTRALIA

TOURIST INFORMATION. *Victour,* 230 Collins St., Melbourne; 619–9444. *Phillip Island Information Centre,* Phillip Island Tourist Rd., Newhaven (1km from the bridge); (059) 56–7447.

TOURS. Bus: A wide variety of daily tours to the Dandenongs and Phillip Island are available through *AAT* (666–3363), *Australian Pacific* (63–1511), and *Ansett Pioneer* (668–2422). Victour, 230 Collins St., Melbourne (619–9444) can provide brochures for each tour company and make bookings.

Air. *Penguin Express,* Essendon Airport; (03) 379–2122. This service, which has won tourism awards, includes pickup from and delivery back to hotel, a scenic 30-minute flight to Phillip Island and return, entrance fees, and bus transport to beach and back for $120 a person (at time of writing).

SPECIAL SIGHTSEEING. *The Penguin Parade* at Phillip Island can be seen every day of the year at dusk. Tickets can be purchased at the penguin-reserve office, which opens 30 minutes before the parade and closes an hour after dusk. To avoid long lines purchase tickets at the Phillip Island Information Centre near San Remo, which is open daily, 9 A.M. to 5 P.M.

Healesville Sanctuary, Badger Creek Rd., Healesville; (059) 62–4022. It is open daily, 9 A.M. to 5 P.M.

For information regarding the *Puffing Billy* train ride in Belgrave, call 754–6876. *The William Ricketts Sanctuary* on Mt. Dandenong Tourist Rd. near Churinga is open daily from 10 A.M. to 5 P.M.

Werribee Park, situated about 30km southwest of Melbourne, is an opulent mansion built in Italianate style in 1873–1878. After exploring the interior, visitors may picnic on the grounds, play golf and tennis, and visit an animal park. The Mansion is open Mon. to Sun. from 10 A.M. to 5 P.M., and the grounds stay open until 8 P.M.

The Southeast Region

HOTELS AND MOTELS through this portion of Victoria are not fancy or large. Area around Gippsland Lakes (3½ hours from Melbourne) has the most accommodations but is best known for holiday flats. Camping is the best way to enjoy Wilson's Promontory and its surrounding beauty. Categories, for double occupancy, are: *Expensive,* $A50 and up; *moderate,* $A35–$A49; *budget,* $A25–$A34.

BAIRNSDALE. Mitchell Motor Inn. *Expensive.* 291 Main St. (Princes Hwy.); (051) 52–5012. This homestead motor inn offers 26 units, refrigerators, licensed restaurant (closed Sunday), room service, laundry, pool, communal hot spa, and playground. Nearby is the tourist center for Gippsland Lakes.

Bairnsdale Motor Inn. *Moderate.* 598 Main St. (Princes Hwy.); (051) 52–3004. This Flag Inn offers 34 units, refrigerator, barbecue, laundry, pool, and playground.

LAKES ENTRANCE. Abel Tasman Motor Lodge. *Expensive.* 643 Esplanade (Princes Hwy.); (051) 55–1655. This motel offers 11 units, refrigerator, laundry, and pool. This accommodation is first-class for the area and has won many tourism awards.

MALLACOOTA. Mallacoota Inlet Hotel-Motel. *Moderate.* Maurice Ave.; (051) 58–0455. This 27-unit motel-hotel offers licensed restaurant, pool, laundry. Tuna, marlin, and barracuda fishing off coast of Mallacoota.

METUNG. McMillan Holiday Village. *Expensive.* 165 Metung Rd.; (051) 56–2283. Luxury self-contained 1-, 2- and 3-bedroom cottages. Features barbecue, recreation and video room, laundry, 2 pools, tennis court, and boat-moor-

VICTORIA

ing facilities. Minimum booking 2 days, but 1 week during Easter and school holidays. This accommodation is the most popular in the area and has won many awards for its excellence.

MOE. Moe. *Moderate.* 45 Lloyd St., (051) 27–1166. This homestead inn offers 28 units, 2 suites, licensed restaurant (closed Sunday), pool, community spa, and 2 hot spas. North of Moe is skiing at Mt. Baw Baw and the ghost town of Wahalla

MORWELL. Farnham Court. *Moderate.* Princes Hwy., (051) 34–6544. This motel offers 33 units, licensed restaurant (closed Sunday), barbecue, and sauna.

WILSONS PROMONTORY. Tidal River Area. *Moderate.* Tidal River, 56km southeast of Fish Creek; (03) 619–9444. 1- and 2-bedroom holiday flats (linen required). Bookings for flats only through *Victour* (see Tourist Information). Bookings open June 1 for Christmas.

CAMPING. *Wilson's Promontory National Park* has camping facilities and cabins available at Tidal River, 56km southeast of Fish Creek; (056) 80–8538. Sites $3 to $6 for three persons, $1.10 for each additional person. Cabins $16 per day, 500 sites, none power, 6 cabins, accommodate up to 4 (everything required). Reticulated river water, septic toilets, hot shower, laundry, barbecue, playground, kiosk, supplies, ice, cafe, gasoline, public telephone. No open fires permitted from April 30 to November 1. Hikers must obtain permit from park office. There is an entrance fee.

TOURIST-INFORMATION CENTERS. *Korumburra Information Centre,* Silkstone Rd. Korumburra, Victoria, 3950, (056) 55–2376, or *Bairnsdale Information Centre,* 240 Main St., Bairnsdale, Victoria, 3875, (051) 52–3234.

TOURS. *Snowy River Outriders,* Box 399, Orbost, 3888; (051) 54–1089, operate weekend and 6- to 8-day tours through spectacular country along the Snowy River including Tullock Ard, where eagles soar high overhead and parrots and smaller bush birds fly through the gums.

Cruise tours of the Gippsland Lakes: *Peels Tourist and Ferry Service,* Esplanade, Lakes Entrance, (051) 55–1246; *Sheltons Sea-Fairies,* Raymond Island, (051) 56–6621.

HISTORIC SITES AND MUSEUMS. *Gippsland Aboriginal Art Museum,* 191 Princes Hwy., Lakes Entrance, (051) 55–1505. Open daily 9 A.M. to 5 P.M., $1 adults, 50 cents children. *Old Gippstown Folk Museum,* Princes Hwy., Moe, (051) 27–3082, open Thurs. through Mon., 10 A.M. to 5 P.M., $5 adults, $2.50 children, $13 family. *St. Mary's Roman Catholic Church,* 242 Main St. (adjacent to Bairnsdale Information Centre), Bairnsdale, best to view the murals and ceilings during the day, free.

The Northeast Region

ACCOMMODATIONS. The mountain areas have a higher standard of accommodation because of their English-style ski chalets. Since the ski area is so popular, Victour Travel Centre, 230 Collins St., Melbourne, 3000 (telephone 03–619–9444), has an Alpine section that handles only accommodations and ski packages for the alpine region.

AUSTRALIA

The rest of the northeast region is dotted with many small towns that have fairly good accommodation. Categories, based on double occupancy, are: *Expensive,* $A50 and up; *moderate,* $A35–$A49; *budget,* $A25–$A34.

BEECHWORTH. The Rose Cottage. *Moderate.* 42 Camp St.; (057) 281–069. Most charming bed-and-breakfast inn.
Tanswells Commercial. *Moderate,* 30 Ford St.; (057) 228–1480. Classified by National Trust. Licensed hotel with restaurant.

BRIGHT. Colonial Motor Inn. *Moderate.* 54 Gavan St., Bright; (057) 55–1911. Heated swimming pool with family suites available.
High Country Inn. *Moderate.* 13 Gavan St., Bright; (057) 55–1244. Licensed restaurant, lounge, sauna, pool, hot spa. Skiing nearby.
John Bright Motor Inn. *Moderate.* 10 Wood St., Bright; (057) 55–1143. Family suites available.

FALLS CREEK. Sundance Inn. *Expensive.* Alpine Rd., Falls Creek; (057) 58–3391. Licensed hotel with restaurant, pool, sauna, hot spa, tennis court. Skiing in season.

MT. BUFFALO. Mt. Buffalo Chalet. *Expensive.* Mount Buffalo National Park; (057) 55–1500. BYO restaurant, lounge, sauna, pool, and tennis court. Off-season rates available.
Tatra Inn. *Expensive.* Cresta, Mt. Buffalo National Park; (057) 55–1322. Licensed restaurant, meeting rooms, lounge. Off-season rates available.

MT. BULLER. Arlberg. *Expensive.* 53 Summit Rd., Mt. Buller; (057) 77–6260. Licensed restaurant, lounge, sauna, hot spa, meeting rooms. Off-season rates available.
Howqua Dale. *Expensive.* (50km before Mt. Buller) Mansfield; (057) 77–3503. Modern homestead, bed and breakfast. Offers gourmet meals, pool, horse riding, tennis, game room, library.
Pension Grimus. *Expensive.* 4 Breathtaker Rd., Mt. Buller; (057) 77–6396. Open snow season only. Licensed restaurant, lounge, sauna, hot spa, ski hire.

RUTHERGLEN. Red Carpet Inn. *Moderate.* Murray Valley Hwy., Rutherglen; (060) 32–9776. BYO restaurant, pool. Wineries nearby.
Walkabout. *Moderate.* Murray Valley Hwy., Rutherglen; (060) 32–9572. Above-ground pool.

WANGARATTA. Merriwa Park. *Moderate.* Ryley St. (Hume Hwy.); (057) 21–5655. BYO Flag Inn with BYO restaurant and pool.
El Portego. *Moderate.* 52 Ryley St. (Hume Hwy.); (057) 21–6388. Pool.

WODONGA. Provincial. *Moderate.* 12 High St. (Hume Hwy.); (060) 24–1200. Flag Inn with licensed restaurant and pool.

TOURIST INFORMATION. *North East Visitor's Centre,* Hume Hwy., Wangaratta, Victoria, 3677; (057) 21–5711; *Tourist Information Centre,* Goulburn Valley Hwy., Nagambie, Victoria, 3608; (057) 942–647.

TOURS. *V/Line Travel* offers rail-coach day tours from Melbourne to the wine country around Rutherglen every Tuesday for $46 per person; historic Beechworth every Tuesday, Wednesday, and Thursday for $47 per person (this is a special group tour) and to Bright for the annual Autumn Festival (late April to early May) for $49 per person. For details regarding these tours contact Victour, 230 Collins St., Melbourne; (03) 619–9444.

Bogong Jack Adventures, Box 209, Wangaratta, 3677; (057) 21–2564, have a variety of adventure tours in northeast Victoria from their base in Wangaratta: cycling in the wine region; bushwalking-trekking on the Bogong High Plains; weekend ramble to see alpine wildflowers; four-wheel-drive tour and walking on

VICTORIA

the high plains; four-wheel-drive fishing tour along alpine rivers; variety of nordic skiing and snowcraft packages in the Mt. Buffalo, Falls Creek area; horse riding in Bogong High Plains. For more information contact Bogong Jack Adventures at the above address or Victour at 230 Collins St., Melbourne, 3000.

Victoria has soaring centers operating seven days a week at Euroa and Benalla. Both are surrounded by cattle- and sheep-grazing country, and both are near mountains, which provide good air currents and breathtaking scenery.

Euroa Soaring Centre offers hourly glider hire as well as 5-day live-in packages for around $380 per person. For more information write to Euroa Airfield, Drysdale Rd., Euroa, Victoria, 3666, or to Victour, 230 Collins Street, Melbourne, 3000.

NATIONAL PARKS. The Victorian Alps are spectacular year-round. During ski season and the holiday period, sites within the parks must be booked in advance. The Victorian Government Travel Centre, 230 Collins St., Melbourne, 3000; (03) 619–9444, provides booking services and information on all aspects of travel in the parks. The following are a few of the many national and state parks within this region.

Mount Buffalo National Park is a long-established national park that provides cross-country and downhill skiing in winter, magnificent views, walking, and camping. The campground is very popular in summer.

Bogong National Park has the highest peaks in Victoria. The park provides outstanding opportunities for cross-country skiing, bush walking, camping, and scenic drives. Falls Creek and Mt. Hotham ski resorts adjoin the park.

Fraser National Park is situated on the western shores of Lake Eildon, 17km from Alexandra. This park is popular for camping, boating, fishing, and walking. Three camping areas with showers, toilets, laundries, fireplaces, and tables cater to tents and campers, and there is a launching ramp for boats. Fees are charged, and for holiday seasons campsites should be booked well in advance.

WINERIES AND VINEYARDS. There are approximately 20 wineries within the Rutherglen-Wangaratta area. Victour, 230 Collins St., Melbourne, (03) 619–9444, has a recommended guide (free) of select wineries in Victoria. It is complete with directions to the wineries and their hours of business. The following list is just a few of the wineries in this area.

Brown Brothers Milawa Vineyard, (16km southeast of Wangaratta), off main Glenrowan–Mytleford Rd., Milawa; (057) 27–3400. Hours: Mon. to Sat. 9 A.M. to 5 P.M., Closed Christmas, Boxing Day, New Year's Day, Good Friday and Anzac Day.

Bailey's of Glenrowan, turn off at Glenrowan, cross railway bridge, and follow notices (057–66–2392). Hours: Mon. to Fri. 9 A.M. to 5 P.M., Sat. and public holidays 10 A.M. to 5 P.M.

All Saints Winery is 9km north west of Rutherglen, continue north off Corowa Rd., 1km east of Wahgunyah. Winery classified by the National Trust.

HISTORIC SITES AND MUSEUMS. *Drage Airworld Wangaratta*, (057) 21–8788, open daily 6:30 A.M. to 9:30 P.M., displays dozens of vintage airplanes. *Burke Memorial Museum*, on Loch St. in Beechworth (28–1420), is open daily 9 A.M. to 4:30 P.M. The museum honors Captain Robert O'Hara Burke, who was a member of the ill-fated Burke and Wills expedition.

The Gold Central Region

HOTELS AND MOTELS. Categories determined by price: *Expensive*, $A60 and up; *moderate*, $A35–$A50; *budget*, less than $A35.

BALLARAT. Bell Tower. *Moderate.* Western Hwy.; (053) 34–1600. This Flag Inn offers 66 units, 7 suites (up to $160), licensed restaurant (closed Sunday except for long weekends), room service, sauna, laundry, heated pool, hot spa, tennis courts.

Colony Motor Inn. *Moderate.* Melbourne Rd.; (053) 34–7788. This Homestead Motor Inn offers 40 units, BYO restaurant, laundry, pool, hot spa, tennis court.

Mid-City. *Moderate.* 19 Doveton St., North, (053) 31–1222. This Flag Inn offers 67 units, 4 suites (up to $60), licensed restaurant (closed Sunday), laundry, heated pool.

DAYLESFORD–HEPBURN SPRINGS. Bellinzona Country House. *Moderate.* Main Rd., Hepburn Springs; (053) 48–2271. This charming bed-and-breakfast old-style guesthouse offers 24 rooms, licensed restaurant, sauna, indoor heated pool, community spa, and squash and tennis courts.

Central Springs Inn. *Moderate.* Corner Camp and Howe sts. (Wills Square), Daylesford; (053) 48–3134. This Homestead Motor Inn, classified by the National Trust, offers 16 units, BYO restaurant, and playground.

BENDIGO. All Season Motor Inn. *Moderate.* 479 McIvor Hwy.; (054) 43–8166. This Flag Inn offers 47 units, 2 suites (up to $65), licensed restaurant (closed Sunday), laundry, pool, and rec room.

Heritage Motor Inn. *Moderate.* 259 High St., (054) 42–2788. This inn offers executive suites with spas (up to $60), laundry, pool, community spa.

RESTAURANTS. Bendigo has two outstanding restaurants. *The Copper Pot.* 8 Howard Pl.; (054) 43–1362. Has a reputation as one of Victoria's finest. Licensed, French-international, about $25 for 2 for lunch, about $60 for dinner. AE, BC, DC. *Jolly Puddler.* 101 Williamson St.; (054) 43–9859. Friendly, relaxed, out-of-town restaurant is basically French. Licensed, about $24 for two for lunch, $50 for dinner. AE, DC, MC.

Ballarat has *La Scala*, known throughout Victoria as a fine restaurant, 120 Lydiard St.; (053) 31–4848. Licensed, this magnificently restored old bluestone warehouse has a downstairs nightclub. Expensive, about $50 for 2, with an international menu. AE, DC, MC.

TOURIST INFORMATION. 202 Lydiard St., North Ballarat, Victoria, 3350, (053) 32–2694; 26 High St., Kangaroo Flat, Victoria, 3550, (054) 47–7161.

TOURS. By bus. *A.A.T.*, (03) 666–3363; *Australian Pacific*, (03) 63–1511; and *Ansett Pioneer*, (03) 668–2422, have regular days tour from Melbourne into Ballarat, Bendigo and Castlemaine–Hepburn Springs area. Cost ranges from $28 to $32 adults. Victour, 230 Collins St., Melbourne, (03) 619–9444, can provide brochures and take bookings.

By rail. *V/Line Travel*, (03) 619–1500, has regular rail/coach tours from Melbourne to Ballarat, $23, and to Bendigo, $30. For true luxury, *The Melbourne Limited*, 595 Melbourne Rd., Spotswood (near Melbourne), 3105, Victoria, (03) 391–9599, has a 2-day tour, once a month, from Melbourne to Bendigo, on board a luxury train for $120.

SEASONAL EVENTS. February–March. The world-renowned *Ballarat Begonia Festival*. **April.** Bendigo's *Easter Fair* dating back to 1871.

WINERIES. *Yellowglen Vineyards*, White's Rd., Smythesdale (south of Ballarat); (053) 42–8617. Open Mon. to Sat. 10 A.M. to 5 P.M., Sun. noon to 5 P.M. Closed Good Friday.

VICTORIA

SPA–MINERAL SPRINGS. Daylesford–Hepburn Springs area is the home of some of the finest mineral waters in the world. Mineral Springs Reserve, at the end of Main St. in Hepburn Springs, features *Hepburn Spa Complex.* The spa complex, situated in the middle of a volcanic basin, was first opened in 1895. Totally renovated, the spa complex offers private baths in the natural health-giving waters for $6.50, herbal, pine, valerian, or jet baths for $7.50. The facilities also offer hydro mineral spa massages, skin care and mud, bubble, and sinusoidal electric baths. For information, call (053) 48–203

ART GALLERIES. The *Ballarat Fine Art Gallery,* 40 Lydiard St.; (053) 31–5622. Open Tues. to Fri. 10:30 A.M. to 4:30 P.M., Sat. 12:30 to 4:30 P.M., Sun. 12:30 to 4:30 P.M. A regional gallery of Victoria; comprehensive collection of Australian art.
Bendigo Art Gallery, View St.; (054) 39–7309. Open Mon. to Thurs. 10 A.M. to 5 P.M., Fri. to Sun. and public holidays 2 to 5 P.M. Outstanding regional gallery with a collection of both Australian and European paintings.

SPECIAL INTEREST SIGHTSEEING. Ballarat. *Sovereign Hill,* Bradshaw St.; (053) 31–1944. Open daily 9:30 A.M. to 5 P.M., closed Christmas Day. In the *Botanical Gardens,* Wendouree Pde., see Begonia House or ride Ballarat's Vintage Trams. *Old Curiosity Shop,* 7 Queen St., (053) 32–1854, has walls decorated with crockery chips and dolls' heads. Open daily 9 A.M. to 5 P.M. *Golda's World of Dolls,* 148 Eureka St., (053) 31–4880, is a private collection of 1,500 dolls from more than 50 countries. Open Sat. 1 to 5 P.M., Sun. and holidays, 10 A.M. to 5 P.M.; closed Fri. *Kryal Castle* (east of Ballarat), Forbes Rd., Warrenheip, (053) 34–7388, sets you back to medieval times. Open daily 9:30 A.M. to 5 P.M.
Bendigo. *Bendigo Pottery,* Epsom (north of Bendigo), (054) 48–4404, is one of Australia's oldest potteries. The pottery has become so well-known within the state that it has become a tourist attraction. Open weekdays and public holidays and offers hourly tours from 10 A.M. to 3 P.M. and half-hour tours on weekends from 1:30 to 4 P.M. *Hartland's Eucalyptus Distillery,* Whipstick Forest (signposted from Huntly, 12km north of Bendigo) is a remarkable survivor of an industry that in other times was second only to wool. For information, call (054) 48–8227.

The West Coast Region

ACCOMMODATIONS. The highlight of the west-coast area is traveling the Great Ocean Rd. You might have to sacrifice a little in luxury accommodations, but the scenery more than makes up for it. Categories, based on double occupancy, are: *Expensive,* $A50 and up; *moderate,* $A35–$A49; *budget,* $A25–$A34.

APOLLO BAY. Apollo, *Moderate,* Moore St., Apollo Bay; (052) 37–6492. Contains 12 units, BYO restaurant, laundry, heated pool, communal hot spa.
Beacon Point Motel Lodges, *Moderate,* Apollo Bay; (052) 37–6218. Set in the Otway Ranges, these self-contained lodges offer log fires, tennis court, restaurant adjacent, baby-sitters, playground, and table tennis.

GEELONG. International Geelong. *Expensive.* Cnr Gheringhap and Myer sts., (052) 21–6844. This Homestead Motor Inn offers 131 units, 6 suites (up to $120), licensed restaurant, room service, heated pool, communal hot spa, laundry.
Buena Vista Motor Inn. *Moderate,* 68 High St. (Princes Hwy.), Belmont; (052) 43–6766. This Flag Motor Inn offers 36 units, licensed restaurant, room service, heated pool, laundry. Near beach, tennis, bowling, and croquet.

HAMILTON. Botanical Motor Inn. *Moderate.* Cnr Thompson and French sts., opposite Botanical Gardens, (055) 72–1855. This Flag Inn offers 33 units, licensed restaurant (closed Sunday and public holidays), heated pool.

LORNE. Erskine House. *Expensive.* Mountjoy Pde., Lorne; (052) 89–1409. This grand old guest house on the beach offers 75 rooms, BYO, restaurant, laundry, tennis court, croquet lawns or lawn bowling, and 18-hole putting green.

OTWAY RANGES. Exclusive Log Cabins. *Moderate.* Glen Aire, (052) 37–9231. Situated off the Great Ocean Road in the Otway Ranges, these self-contained cabins can accommodate up to 6 people. Twelve Apostles and excellent trout fishing in the Ford or Aire rivers nearby.

PORT CAMPBELL. Port Campbell Motor Inn. *Moderate.* 12 Great Ocean Rd.; (055) 98–6222. A Homestead Motor Inn member with 13 units. The Port Campbell National Park across the highway offers an excellent walk along the cliff tops through heath and coastal shrub. Dramatic coastal scenery and unique rock shapes including the Twelve Apostles and London Bridge.

PORT FAIRY. Seacombe House Motor Inn. *Moderate.* 22 Sackville St., (055) 68–1082. Classified by National Trust, this inn has a hotel section, 1- and 2-bedroom, self-contained cottages, and a BYO restaurant

QUEENSCLIFF. Vue Grand. *Expensive.* 46 Hesse St.; (052) 52–1544. This bed-and-breakfast private hotel has 41 rooms and a licensed restaurant, indoor heated pool, hot spa, laundry.

WARRNAMBOOL. Central Court. *Moderate.* 581 Raglan Pde. (Princes Hwy.), (055) 62–8555. This Flag Inn offers 38 units, B.Y.O. restaurant (closed Sunday), laundry, pool.
Warrnambool. *Moderate.* 65 Raglan Pde. (Princes Hwy.), (055) 62–1222. This Homestead Motor Inn offers 12 units, pool, communal hot spa, laundry.

TOURIST INFORMATION. *Old Telegraph Station,* 83 Ryrie St., Geelong, Victoria, 3220, (052) 97–220; *Information Centre,* Lonsdale St., Hamilton, Victoria, 3300, (055) 72–3746

TOURS. *Australian Pacific,* (03) 63–1511, offers round-trip day tours (12 hours) from Melbourne to Port Campbell–Twelve Apostles approximately once a month, $40 adults. They also offer a round-trip day tour (9 hours) from Melbourne to Lorne and the Great Ocean Road once a month, $32 adults. *V/Line Travel* (rail and coach), (03) 619–1500 or (03) 62–3115, has special group day-tours available from Melbourne to the Otway Ranges (12 hours) Tue., Wed., and Thurs. for $40 a person; Port Campbell (12 hours) for $40 per person; Geelong (7 hours), Tue., Wed., and Thurs. for $23 per person and Warrnambool (12 hours), Tue., and Fri., for $37 per person. Contact *Victour,* 230 Collins St., Melbourne, (03) 619–9444, for complete details and bookings.

GARDENS. *Geelong Botanical Gardens,* along Garden St., are set in Eastern Park, which overlooks Corio Bay. These well-planned gardens feature an aviary.

SPECIAL SIGHTSEEING. *Casterton. Warrock Homestead,* sign posted 6km east of Casterton, off the Glenelg Hwy., is open daily 10 A.M. to 5 P.M. A town as it was more than 100 years ago.
Geelong: At *Ceres Lookout* (12km south of Geelong) on Barrabool Rd. in Ceres is a magnificent view of Geelong and bay.
The Heights is a prefabricated timber mansion imported from Germany in 1855 that is open to the public on Wed., weekends, and public holidays from 2 to 5 P.M. It has 14 rooms, stables, and a lookout tower. Location: 140 Aphrasia St., Newton Geelong. For information, call (052) 21–3906. Another home that

VICTORIA 193

registers the impact of Barwon Valley is *Barwon Grange*. It was built by a merchant-ship owner. Fronting the Barwon River, the homestead is noted for its fretted timber and fine verandah. Location: Fernleigh St., Newton, Geelong. It is open weekends, Wednesday, and public holidays from 2 to 5 P.M. For information, call (052) 21–3906.

Fairy Park in Anakie (30km northwest of Geelong) is a hillside complex of fairytale and fantasy scenes in miniature castles, caves, and tunnels. The park opens at 10 A.M. For information, call (052) 84–1262.

Warrnambool. *Flagstaff Hill Maritime Village,* at the Port of Warrnambool, shows the significance of the seaport in Australia's heritage. The village was created around two original lighthouses and a light-keeper's cottage. In the harbor, the visitor may board the *Speculant* (1909), a former ferry, and *Reginald M,* a trader from the South Australian Gulf. Open daily, 9:30 A.M. to 4:30 P.M.

ART GALLERIES. *Hamilton Art Gallery,* Brown St., Hamilton. Works by noted Australian artists such as Sidney Nolan and Charles Blackman, plus a collection of ancient Mediterranean pottery and antique porcelain. Open Tues. to Fri. 10 A.M. to 5 P.M., Sat. 10 A.M. to noon and 2 to 5 P.M., Sun. and public holidays 2 to 5 P.M.

Geelong Memorial Art Gallery is open Mon. to Thurs. 10 A.M. to 5 P.M., Fri. 10 A.M. to 8 P.M., Sat., Sun., and public holidays 1 to 5 P.M. It features Frederick McCubbin's *A Bush Burial* and paintings of Geelong and the district.

The Wimmera Region

ACCOMMODATIONS. Categories determined by price: *Expensive,* $A60 and up; *moderate,* $A35–$A50; *budget,* less than $A35.

ARARAT. Ararat Colonial Lodge. *Moderate.* 6 Ingor St. (Western Hwy.); (053) 52–2411. Offers 19 units, BYO restaurant (closed Sunday), pool. Homestead Motor Inn member.

HALLS GAP. Hall's Gap Colonial Motor Inn. *Moderate.* Dunkeld Rd.; (053) 56–4344. Member of Homestead Motor Inns, offers 33 units, licensed restaurant, laundry, pool. Main entrance to Grampians National Park.

HORSHAM. Glenisla Homestead. (45 mi. south of Horsham), Henty Hwy. A century-old homestead situated within full view of the Grampian Mtns. Host Eric Barber offers authentic pioneer history of the area and guided tours, (053) 80–1532.

Golden Grain Motor Inn. *Moderate.* Dimboola Rd. (Western Hwy.); (053) 82–4741. Recreation room, laundry, indoor heated pool, communal hot spa. Member of Homestead Motor Inns.

May Park Motor Lodge. *Moderate.* Corner Darlot and Baillie sts.; (053) 82–4477. This Homestead Motor Inn offers 23 units, indoor heated pool, playground.

STAWELL. Goldfields Motor Inn. *Moderate.* Western Hwy., (053) 58–2911. This Flag Inn offers 23 units, B.Y.O. restaurant (closed Sun.), pool.

TOURIST INFORMATION. *Grampians Information Centre,* Stawell World In Miniature, London Rd., Stawell, Victoria, 3380; (053) 58–2314. *Horsham Information Centre,* O'Callaghan's Parade, Horsham, Vic., 3400; (053) 82–3778.

BALLOONING. *Outdoor Travel Centre,* 377 Little Bourke St., Melbourne, 3000; (03) 67-7252, offers hot-air balloon adventure packages Mar. through Oct. A one-day ballooning package includes accommodation, breakfast, gourmet picnic lunch, winery tour or bush walk, and hot-air ballooning and costs $160. Transportation to and from Melbourne.

SPECIAL-INTEREST SIGHTSEEING. *Wimmera-Mallee Pioneers Museum,* 1km south of Jeparit and 35km north of Horsham, open daily 9:30 A.M. to 4:30 P.M., is a 10-acre complex with historic buildings, period furnishings, and countless antiques. The *North Western Agricultural Machinery Museum,* Warracknabeal (35 mi. north of Horsham), open Mon. to Sat. 10 A.M. to 5 P.M., Sun. 1 to 5 P.M., depicts the history of the wheat industry with giant steam-powered chaff cutters, combine harvesters, and tractors. In *Stawell's World in Miniature Tourist Park* are seven Asian countries, a Papua New Guinea stilt village, Bunjils Shelter, and several other portrayals. Open daily 9 A.M. to 5 P.M. Location: London Rd., Stawell, (053) 58-1877.
Vineyard Tour. *Seppelt Great Western,* Moyston Rd., 10 mi. northwest of Ararat on Western Hwy.; (053) 56-2202. Tours: one-hour tours Mon. to Sat. 9:30 A.M. to 3 P.M. Closed Christmas Day, Australia Day, Good Friday. Open on Sun., only on long weekends and school holidays, 12:15 P.M. to 2:45 P.M. This winery is known for its extensive underground champagne cellars, which have been classified by the National Trust.

The Murray Region

HOTELS AND MOTELS. Good accommodations are found mainly in the towns along the Murray River. Categories, price determined on double occupancy, are: *Expensive,* $A50 and up; *moderate,* $A35-$A49; *budget,* $A25-$A34.

ECHUCA. Hopwood Motor Inn. *Moderate.* Northern Hwy., (054) 82-2244. This Flag Inn offer 30 units, licensed restaurant, room service, pool, playground.
Rich River Country Club, Moderate, Barham Rd. (across New South Wales Border via Moama bridge), Moama; (054) 82-4411. Offers 40 two-room suites, heated swimming pool, hot spas and gym, licensed restaurant (closed Tuesday and Wednesday), golf.

SWAN HILL. Campbell Motor Inn. *Moderate.* 396 Campbell St. (Murray Valley Hwy.); (050) 32-4427. This Flag Inn offers 27 units, BYO restaurant (closed Sunday), laundry, pool, playground.
Swan Hill Motor Inn. *Moderate.* 405 Campbell St. (Murray Valley Hwy.); (050) 32-2726. This Flag Inn offers 67 units, two suites, licensed restaurant (closed Sunday during off season), room service, sauna, laundry, pool.

MILDURA. Grand Hotel. *Expensive.* 7th St., opposite railway station; (050) 23-0511. This hotel offers 116 rooms, 3 suites, licensed restaurant (closed Sunday), room service, rec room, sauna, laundry, heated pool, communal hot spa.
Four Seasons Mildura Resort. *Moderate.* 373 Deakin Ave.; (050) 23-3823. This Homestead Motor Inn offers 98 units, licensed restaurant, room service, sauna, laundry, heated pool, tennis court.

TOURIST INFORMATION. *Swan Hill Tourism Centre,* McCallum St., Swan Hill, Victoria, 3585; (050) 32-3033. *Mildura Tourist Information Centre,* 60 Deakin Ave., Mildura, Victoria, 3500; (050) 23-4853 or 23-3619. *Echuca Tourist Information Centre,* Customs House, 2 Leslie St., Echuca, Victoria, 3625; (054) 82-5252.

VICTORIA

TOURS. *Australian Pacific Tours,* 181 Flinders St., Melbourne, (03) 63–1511, have full-day tours (8:55 A.M. to 8 P.M.), Melbourne-Echuca-Melbourne, every Wednesday. Included is a cruise on the Murray River for $32 per person.

Victour, 230 Collins St., Melbourne, (03) 619–9444, offers occasional riverboat specials to Echuca at $34 per person.

V/Line Travel (by rail), 589 Collins St., Melbourne, (03) 619–1500, offers round-trip day tours to Echuca for $36 a person. Tour includes a cruise on the Murray River with lunch afloat.

Wine-Vineyard Tours. The Mildura area produces about half the grapes commercially grown in Australia. *Mildara Wines,* on the cliffs at Merbein, 11km from Mildura (can be reached by road or by river at Chaffey Landing), (050) 25–2303; self-guided tours and tastings Mon. to Fri. 8 to 11:15 A.M. and 1 to 4:15 P.M.

Lindemans Cellars, 28km southeast of Mildura via Nangiloc Rd., (050) 24–0303, tastings, sales, tours Mon. to Fri. 9 A.M. to 5 P.M., Sat. 10 A.M. to 1 P.M., closed Sun., Good Friday, Anzac Day, Christmas, Boxing Day, and New Year's Day.

HOUSEBOATING ON THE MURRAY RIVER. Several houseboat fleets are in operation offering various types of vessels for hire that range from 4 to 12 berths and are luxuriously appointed. No special license is required to operate these vessels, since they do not exceed 10 knots. Conditions of hire all require $200 to confirm a booking, with the balance payable 60 days prior to the commencement of holiday. Security bonds vary with operators—$100 to $300 cash—are required on arrival, and are refunded if the boat is returned clean and in good condition. Minimum hire period is 3 nights, except for school holidays, when the minimum is 5 nights.

Driving and handling instructions are always given by the owners to the hirers when they board the vessel. Most vessels are fitted with radio transceivers. The boats are propelled by various types of units, the most common being the jet drive, which allows navigation of shallow waters. Rates, based on 3 nights during the summer (Dec. to May 31) are about $460 to $580.

Contact *Mildura Holiday Houseboats,* Box 249, Mildura, 3500, telephone (050) 23–4771 or 23–5541; *Adventure Houseboats,* Box 213, Buronga, New South Wales, 2648, telephone (050) 23–4787 or 23–1344 (have executive houseboats that sleep 10).

PADDLE STEAMER CRUISES. Echuca is home port of the paddle steamer *Emmylou.* This authentic paddler takes up to 20 passengers on 2-day, 2-night cruises that include all meals and full use of ship's facilities, from $220 per person. Reservations and information through Echuca Travel Centre, 203 Hare St., Echuca, Victoria, 3564, telephone (054) 82–2177, or Victour in Melbourne.

P.S. Pride of the Murray has one-hour day cruises that depart Port of Echuca daily, 11 A.M. and 1 P.M. Cost: $5 adults, $2.50 children. Booking office: 57 Murray Esplanade, Echuca, telephone (054) 82–5244 or (054) 83–5383. *Tisdall Princess,* 28 Heygarth St., Echuca, (054) 82–2141, offers lunch or dinner cruises on the Murray on weekends during off season, and Tue., Wed., Fri., Sat., and Sun. during peak season. Cost: $20 adults, $14 children for lunch cruise; $30 adults, $18 children for dinner cruise.

P.S. Melbourne departs every day except Sat. from Mildura Wharf, 10:50 A.M. to 1 P.M. and 1:50 to 4 P.M. Comprehensive commentary included. For information, call (050) 23–2200. *Showboat Avoca* cruises at midday, noon to 2 P.M. with commentary, Fri. night for a disco, 8 P.M. to midnight, and Sat. evening for dinner cruise, 7:30 to 11:30 P.M. All cruises depart from Mildura Wharf. For information, call (050) 23–7077.

Five-day cruises are available on *P.S. Coonawarra.* For information, write Ron's Tourist Centre, 41 Deakin Ave., Mildura, 3500, or call (050) 23–6160.

SPECIAL SIGHTSEEING. Echuca. *Port of Echuca;* entry is via the Star Hotel, where ticket purchased entitles the bearer to visit the Star Hotel, Echuca Wharf and Bridge Hotel, open daily 9:15 A.M. to 5 P.M.

Swan Hill. *Swan Hill Pioneer Settlement,* Horseshoe Bend, (050) 32–1093. Open daily 8:30 A.M. to 5 P.M., with sound-and-light show nightly. Closed Christmas Day.

Murray Downs Homestead, 1.5km over bridge from Swan Hill, (050) 32–1225, set in more than 4 acres of formal gardens, dates back to the early 1840s. One tour daily at 2 P.M. and during public and school holidays, 9 A.M. to 5 P.M. Another homestead within in the Swan Hill area is *Tyntyndyer Homestead,* built in 1846 and classified by the National Trust. Situated 16km north of Swan Hill, 3.2km north of Beverford on Murray Valley Hwy.; (050) 37–6506. Tours daily 9 A.M. to 4:30 P.M.

Amboc, a mohair farm featuring a range of garments made by local craftspeople, is open daily. On Murray Valley Highway, Mystic Park (28km south of Swan Hill). For information, call (050) 54–3310.

QUEENSLAND

by
DAVID SWINDELL

David Swindell travels frequently throughout Australia. He writes about the country for a variety of publications, including Travel & Leisure *and* Frequent Flyer.

There are vast differences between Queensland and the rest of Australia, differences that not only set the state apart from the rest of the country, but make it Australia's boom state in terms of both tourism and industry. It is said, in fact, that about a thousand newcomers a month settle in Queensland—a lot in a nation of only 15 million people. Certainly more than that come to the state as tourists, for several of Australia's top tourist attractions here—the Great Barrier Reef, the Gold Coast, the Whitsunday Islands, the Coral Sea, and the Sunshine Coast, to mention a few. Indeed, Queensland is Australia's "Sunshine State," as its license plates declare, a little like Florida, a little like California, a little like Hawaii in the 1950s, and a little like the Caribbean.

On the books at least, Queensland is Australia's most conservative state. Gambling has only recently been legalized, and as yet there are only two casinos, but others are in the works. A new law that caused chuckles from Sydney to Perth banned "perverts" from bars and pubs in the state, although just who is a pervert was never spelled out by lawmakers. The state's immensely popular premier (governor), Joh Bjelke-Petersen, is the target of endless jokes outside the state but is admired inside for his controversial right-wing political stands. Under his guidance, tourism has become big business in Queensland and is getting bigger all the time.

Many argue that Queensland's tropical location makes it Australia's most beautiful region. The Tropic of Capricorn slices the state in half, and from its tip at the top of Cape York Peninsula to its southern boundry at the New South Wales state line, eastern Queensland is an endless tropical rain forest, beach, island, and wilderness. In the vast stretches of the Queensland Outback, an area even few Australians have ever seen, lies bush, semidesert, more bush, and more semidesert. It's rough country out there, not unlike the untamed American West of a century ago. Miles of open spaces provide the perfect setting for cattle ranches the size of Rhode Island, and the earth yields some of the world's most abundant supplies of coal, copper, zinc, bauxite, copper, silver, lead, and gold. But it's an isolated corner of the world, one where neighbors often pay Sunday visits to each other in light planes. And it's of little interest to vacationers.

There can be no arguments about Queensland's size. The statistics are staggering: big enough to hold four Japans, with room left over; bigger than Alaska and Washington state combined; large enough to swallow up France, Belgium, and Holland three times over. Numerically translated, Queensland is 1,727,000 square kilometers (667,000 square miles) in area and has a population of 2.5 million, the great majority of whom live along the coast in such cities as Brisbane, the state capital and Australia's third largest city; Cairns, gateway to the northern reaches of the Great Barrier Reef and one of the world's foremost big game fishing and scuba diving centers; and Townsville, jumping-off point to the Whitsunday Islands.

If international airports are any measure of a destination's appeal to tourists, Queensland has more than any other Australian state—Brisbane, Cairns, and Townsville. There is definitely a reason for having three gateways in the state: the Great Barrier Reef. Either God, the Australian government, or both left it up to Queensland to be the guardian of one of the world's most priceless treasures and its largest living thing. And where hundreds used to come for a glimpse of the reef, the opening of new airports, with flights directly overseas, has opened up the Great Barrier Reef to many thousands of visitors a year.

The reef is made up of billions of tiny creatures called polyps and is indeed alive. Sea creatures, each seemingly more brilliant than the next, are the reason it is the undisputed best spot on earth for scuba diving and snorkeling. The reef runs along the Queensland coast for more than a thousand miles, from just north of Cairns to about halfway between Townsville and Brisbane. Naturally, resorts have sprung up on the coast and on the islands that sit atop the reef.

While the Great Barrier Reef is Queensland's best-known tourist destination outside Australia, Aussies might just as well prefer a vacation on the Gold Coast, Australia's Ft. Lauderdale–Waikiki–Miami Beach all rolled into one. The Gold Coast begins about a hour south of Brisbane and is essentially that city's closest beach, since Brisbane does not front the ocean but lies inland a few miles on the banks of the Brisbane River. There is a definite carnival atmosphere along the Gold Coast, thanks in large part to numerous family attractions (Sea World here, Lion Safari Park there). The town of Surfer's Paradise, whose name pretty well sums it up, is center of the action, especially during school breaks in Australia when the place looks like the set from *Where the Boys Are.* That is certainly not to say one can't have a laid-back vacation along the Gold Coast, but many people, when they really want to get away from it all, head north of Brisbane instead to a stretch of perfect beach called the Sunshine Coast.

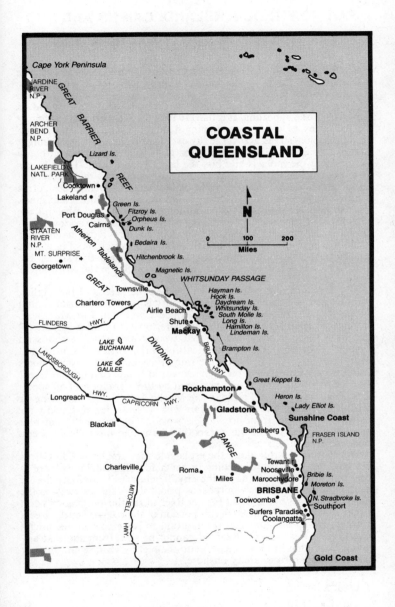

FAR NORTH QUEENSLAND: CAIRNS AND THE FAR NORTHERN GREAT BARRIER REEF

Cairns is capital of the region called far north Queensland, or the "Deep North" as it is also known. Cairns is closer to Papua New Guinea than to most of the rest of Australia, and a feeling of isolation is keen in the city. That, of course, is precisely why the city and its environs are so appealing. It is hard to imagine the world ever catching up to Cairns, or Cairns ever hoping it might. Tropical birds of near-blinding colors streak across the sky over Cairns the way pigeons might somewhere else, and pelicans and sea gulls work the harbor in hopes of grabbing the morsels and bits the fishers don't want. The city sits in a lush tropical setting on Trinity Bay, surrounded by rain forests and macadamia, sugar, and pineapple plantations. The Coral Sea forms Cairns's eastern boundary. Cairns is apt to catch a sudden and quick rain shower at almost any time, although the sun ducks behind the clouds only momentarily; thus, many of the sidewalks in the downtown business district are wisely covered. Quite a few older homes and buildings in Cairns are built on stilts, the only way to cool down the place in pre–air-conditioning days, and overhead fans that stir up the rich Coral Sea breezes are to this day more popular in the city than air conditioners.

If you're a serious fisher, you've reached the Mecca of the angling world when you come to Cairns. The city is the black marlin capital of the world, and everyone from Prince Charles to Lee Marvin to dozens of captains of industry come here to try to land a "grander," the term given a black marlin that weighs more than a thousand pounds. These sea monsters are plentiful in the waters off Cairns, and every morning, except during the rainy days of winter, fishing boats leave from Marlin Jetty on their expeditions out beyond the Great Barrier Reef to the open seas preferred by these grandest of all sports fish. Boats can be hired right at the Marlin Jetty, but if you've never tried heavy tackle fishing, don't start with a black marlin. Luckily for enthusiastic fishers from around the world, there are many different species of sports fish in the waters off Cairns and more than enough boats so no one gets left behind.

Apart from a stroll along the esplanade that ambles beside Cairns Harbor, the best vantage point in town for birdwatching, there is precious little to see or do in the city. There aren't even any decent beaches in town. Cairns's purpose is primarily as the gateway to the northern reaches of the Great Barrier Reef and as the jumping-off point to the resort islands that lie in this portion of the reef—Lizard, Green, Fitzroy, and Dunk. One fact is important to remember in planning a trip to the Great Barrier Reef—it cannot be seen from shore at any point. You'll have to venture out onto the reef by visiting an island or taking a launch from a city onshore.

Lizard Island

The deluxe resort of Lizard Island accommodates no more than 30 guests at a time in its rather exclusive lodge, which, with full board, costs about $A150 per night. Lizard is a base for black-marlin fishers who can afford its prices, but the island is also a haven for scuba diving and snorkeling. So no one misses the Reef—a scant 16km (10 mi.)

away—a glass-bottom boat is provided by the management and a catamaran is available for sailors. The island is so remote that many think it is the most classic of all Great Barrier Reef islands. Captain Cook landed here in 1770 and named the island for its population at the time—monitor lizards. It has some 24 private sandy coves, an average of almost one private cove per guest. Lizard Island is accessible from Cairns by air, and travel agents can book space for visitors at Lizard Island Lodge.

Green Island

Green Island sits right on top of the Reef, 27km (16 mi.) out to sea from Cairns. It isn't really an island, but a coral cay protruding only a few feet above the water's surface. Boats leave daily from the Marlin Jetty in Cairns for the one-and-a-half-hour trip to Green Island. The voyage is a popular day trip from Cairns. Boats dock at the island and give passengers the rest of the day to swim and snorkel. Snorkeling equipment is available for rent as you get off the boat on the island. There are an underwater observatory for reef viewing and accommodations on the island for those who wish to remain overnight.

Dunk Island

"Paradise found" is how a writer in the last century described Dunk Island, and nothing has changed since. Dunk is a tropical jungle with long white sandy beaches and tall palms and wild orchids and hibiscus growing everywhere. Tennis, golf, and horseback riding complement the usual choice of water-related activities on the island. The resort is first class, with suites and cabanas sitting on the beach, and there are entertainment and dancing in the evening. Accommodations start at about $A600 for two people for a week on the island. Dunk is accessible by air from Cairns or Townsville. Travel agents can book a room on the island.

Fitzroy Island

Fitzroy is called the best-kept secret on the Barrier Reef. It is a resort island but seems to get lost in the shadow of the better-known and better-promoted islands. Reef divers and fishers have long known about Fitzroy, and tourists are discovering that the untouched island is a real find for an out-of-the-way vacation. Trails on the island lead to secluded beaches, and the swimming and snorkeling conditions from any of them are perfect. Australia's only clam farm is on the island; it raises clams to restock the reef. Moderately priced, comfortable accommodations are available on the island. Fitzroy is accessible by sea from Cairns; the trip takes about 45 minutes.

Cape York Peninsula

The Cape York Peninsula is one of the world's last great wildernesses, but unless you have a car and don't mind driving on an unpaved road, you won't be able to see most of this region. In fact, four-wheel-drive vehicles are recommended for most of the way on the Peninsula Development Road, which runs from Lakeland, north of Cairns, to the tip of the Peninsula at Somerset. Several Australian tour operators take camping safaris into the Cape York region, and Queensland Government Travel Center offices can book these trips. Besides the flora and fauna, the most interesting thing about the peninsula is its history. It has been home to Aboriginals for eons and prehistoric rock paintings near the town of Laura have been carbon dated to 13,200 B.C. A guided tour of some of the more accessible prehistoric-art galleries can be arranged in Cairns with the Queensland Government Travel Center.

Kuranda

Every morning at 9 A.M. a train leaves Cairns Railway Station bound for the town of Kuranda in the mountains of the rain forest to the northwest. Kuranda is an old sugar plantation town, but what is of most interest is the train trip itself. The railway line was carved through the jungle between 1884 and 1888, passing over deep gorges and thunderous waterfalls and miles of cane fields, and was the only way sugar cane got to the port of Cairns in the early years. Today the train is just for tourists, and the engineer obligingly stops along the way so passengers can take photos. The 18km (10 mi.) trip is a popular excursion from Cairns, and the train sits in Kuranda for about an hour while passengers poke around the town. The Jilli Binna Museum on Coondoo Street, a short walk from the station, displays interesting exhibits about the Aboriginal tribes of far north Queensland. No reservations are accepted for the train. Just show up at Cairns Station, buy the inexpensive ticket, and board the train. On Sundays, a second train leaves Cairns at 9:30.

Atherton Tablelands

The Atherton Tablelands is the name of the region along the plateau of the Great Dividing Range that separates Cairns and the tropics from the vast emptiness of the Queensland Outback. The tablelands are reached by road from Cairns, or you can leave the Kuranda train in Kuranda and board a sightseeing bus for the trip. The tablelands is an agricultural region, full of scenic drives that look like the farming areas in California. The weather here is much cooler than by the coast, and humidity is low. Maps, available at gas stations in the tablelands or from the Queensland Government Travel Centre in Cairns, show the most scenic drives.

Cape Tribulation

North of Cairns is the region known as Cape Tribulation, and it is here that many of Australia's finest beaches are found. Driving north along the Cook Highway, you'll come to the closest beaches to Cairns—Trinity Beach, Clifton Beach, Machan's Beach, Palm Cove, and others. In Palm Cove, the Australian Bird park, open daily, is a natural habitat for many of the tropical birds native to far north Queensland. The entire cape region is a continuous rain forest with a beautiful coastline, and you can pull your car off the road and take a dip anywhere you like. Keep one thing in mind, however—you cannot go swimming in the waters of this part of far north Queensland in summer, because they are infected with "stingers," a particularly deadly jellyfish. At other times of the year, waters are safe.

Port Douglas

Port Douglas is one of the towns on Cape Tribulation that has special appeal for visitors. Time passed the town by long ago when Cairns came into prominence as the main city of far North Queensland, but Port Douglas has all the character of a grand dame of the tropics. There are several restaurants and motels in the town, all of which are inexpensive and usually do not require advance bookings. Port Douglas is 62km (37 mi.) north of Cairns. Its stretch of beach is considered by many as the most inviting on Cape Tribulation. Day cruises operate from Port Douglas to the Outer Great Barrier Reef, about an hour and a half away, and to the several of the low isles along closer stretches of the Reef.

Cooktown

On the Endeavour River about 324km (194.4 mi.) north of Cairns, Cooktown stands on the spot where Captain James Cook repaired his ship *Endeavour,* during his voyage of discovery in 1770. For a short while in the 1870s, it was the scene of a gold rush. Today, it is a sleepy tropical town with a certain charm. *Air Queensland* operates day tours from Cairns, including flights over the Great Barrier Reef.

PRACTICAL INFORMATION FOR FAR NORTH QUEENSLAND

HOW TO GET THERE AND HOW TO GET AROUND. By air. Cairns is a long way from just about everywhere, so air travel is the only choice for most vacationers. *Ansett* and *Australian Airlines* fly to Cairns from Townsville and Brisbane, and both airlines have connections in those cities to the rest of Australia. It's sort of hard to reach Cairns from inside Australia on a nonstop flight because Australia's non-deregulated industry nips competition in the bud. However, *Qantas* flies nonstop between Cairns and Honolulu several times a week and has connections at Honolulu to San Francisco and Los Angeles. *Air Queensland* connects Cairns to Townsville and Brisbane and other cities and towns in the state and also flies to the Lizard Island Gold Coast and the Sunshine Coast, but most likely with a stop or connections along the way. Air Queensland also operates day flights from Cairns that fly over the Great Barrier Reef and the Outer Reef for people in a big hurry. Dunk Island can be reached by air from Cairns or Townsville.

By train. *Railways of Australia* operates the Sunlander to Cairns from Brisbane every day except Sunday. A 9 A.M. train leaves Cairns Railway Station each morning for Kuranda; on Sundays a second train leaves at 9:30.

By bus. *Ansett Pioneer* and *Greyhound Australia* have regular services to Cairns from Townsville, Brisbane, and other cities in Queensland.

By boat. Boats leave daily from the marlin jetty in Cairns for the 1½-hour trip to Green Island. It's a 45-minute trip by boat from Cairns to Fitzroy Island. Boats can also take visitors from Port Douglas to the outer Great Barrier Reef.

By car. Four-wheel-drive vehicles are recommended for the trip into the Cape York Peninsula. The Peninsula Development Rd. runs from Lakeland, north of Cairns, to Somerset, at the tip of the Peninsula. The tablelands, west of Cairns, offer many scenic drives. Get maps from gas stations or the Queensland Government Travel Center, Cairns.

ACCOMMODATIONS. Hotels and motels are classified as: *deluxe,* more than $A85 per night for two people; *expensive,* more than $A60 per night for two people; *moderate,* more than $A50 per night for two; and *inexpensive,* less than $A50 per night for two. Prices on island resorts usually include food, therefore are higher than these categories.

CAIRNS

Pacific International Hotel. *Deluxe.* 43 Esplanade, 4870; (070) 51–7888. All rooms have balconies and ocean views. Restaurants, bars, health club, pool.
Tuna Towers. *Expensive.* 145 Esplanade, 48285; (070) 51–4688. Motor inn with restaurant, bar, pool.
Cairns Holiday Inn. *Moderate.* 259 Sheridan St., 4870; (070) 51–4611. 2km from town. Restaurant, pool.
Tuna Lodge. *Moderate.* 127 Esplanade; 4870; (070) 51–4388. Bar and restaurant; refrigerators in rooms.
Four Seasons Cairns. *Moderate.* Esplanade and Alpin Street; (070) 51–2311.
Cairns Motor Inn. *Inexpensive.* 187 Sheridan St.; (070) 51–5166.

Day (from $A40 for two people per night) and weekly (from $A250 per week for two) rates are offered by self-catering apartment units, which have fully equipped kitchens for cooking meals: *Cairns City Gardens Apartments.* Lake and Minnie streets; (070) 51–8000. **Sunshine Villa Holiday units,** 163 Grafton St., (070) 51–5288; **Tropic Villa,** 285 Lake St.; (070) 51–6022; **Villa Marine Luxury Holiday Units,** 8 Rutherford St.; (070) 55–7158.

DUNK ISLAND

Great Barrier Reef Hotel. *Deluxe.* (070) 68–8199. Tropical resort with bars, restaurants, pools, tennis courts, and a variety of sports.

GREEN ISLAND

Green Island Reef Resort. *Deluxe.* (070) 51–4644. Informal resort. Restaurants, bars, water sports, glass-bottom boats.

LIZARD ISLAND

Lizard Island Lodge. *Deluxe.* (070) 50–4222. Dining room and bar, water sports, sheltered beach.

PORT DOUGLAS

Peter Morton's New Motel. *Moderate.* Port Douglas Rd.; (070) 98–5320; **Archipelago Motel.** *Inexpensive.* Macrossan St.; (070) 98–5387; **Rusty Pelican Inn.** *Inexpensive.* Davidson St.

DINING OUT. Restaurants are classified as *expensive,* $A50 or more for two; *moderate,* $A25–$A49 for two; and *inexpensive,* less than $A25 for two. These are dinner prices, with wine, so expect lunch prices to be lower. BYO means bring your own beer, wine, or spirits, as the restaurant does not have a liquor license. The restaurant will serve the drinks, provide the mixers, and pour the wine.

CAIRNS

Barnacle Bill's. *Expensive.* 65 Esplanade; 51–2241. Known for its grilled barrimundi, a fish native to the waters of far north Queensland.
Pacific International Hotel. *Expensive.* 43 the Esplanade; 51–7888. Seafood and Continental cuisine.
Tawny's. *Expensive.* Marlin Jetty; 51–1683. Known for its Coral Sea trout; on the waterfront.
Kee Kong. *Moderate.* 59 Spence St.; 51–2772. Chinese.
Mr. Blue. *Moderate.* 227 Sheridan St.; 51–3726. BYO. Seafood and Australian cuisine.
The Pancake. *Inexpensive.* 43 Spence St.; 51–6551. Basic food. BYO.

QUEENSLAND

TOURIST INFORMATION AND TOURS. The *Queensland Government Travel Centre,* 12 Shields St., Cairns, (070) 51–4066, is your one-stop place for information and booking tours in and around Cairns and to resorts on Great Barrier Reef islands in far north Queensland.

CRUISES. If you don't plan to spend a few days at a resort on an island along the Great Barrier Reef, you can take a cruise to points along the reef from either Cairns or Port Douglas. There are day trips to Green Island and Fitzroy Island from Cairns. Also from Cairns, Hayles sails launches that depart every day at 9:30 A.M. from the Marlin Jetty bound for the Outer Reef. There's a quick stop at Green Island, and the vessel cruises on to Hastings Reef, where passengers are transferred to a "subsea viewer," a craft with an underwater glass chamber that hovers above the reef. Price is $A55 for the day, half for children. Call Hayles at (070) 51–5644 for bookings. The M.V. *Quicksilver* sails daily at 10:30 A.M. from Port Douglas Wharf to the Outer Reef, where passengers are invited to swim, snorkel, or scuba dive. Price is about $A50 for adults, half for children. Phone (070) 51–5547 in Cairns or (070) 98–5373 in Port Douglas for bookings. Also from Port Douglas, the *M.V. Martin Cash* sails to parts of the reef closer to shore for snorkeling and scuba diving. Price is about $A27 for adults, half for children. You can board the boat in Port Douglas or take a bus operated specifically for the boat that leaves from Cairns. Use the *Quicksilver* numbers (above) for reservations and information.

SPORTS. Equipment for most sports can be rented; instruction available. Cairns is the black-marlin capital of the world. Hire boats from the marlin jetty. Lizard Island is also a base for black-marlin-fishing enthusiasts. And there are plenty of other sport fish available throughout the area.

The Barrier Reef is, of course, heaven for snorkelers and scuba divers and all water-sport enthusiasts. On Dunk Island you'll find fishing, water skiing, diving, windsurfing, snorkeling, and swimming. Tennis and golf and horseback riding are also available. Fitzroy Island offers fishing, water skiing, sailing, diving, snorkeling, swimming, and tennis. Snorkeling equipment can be rented as soon as your boat from Cairns reaches Green Island. Here you'll also find fishing, diving, and swimming. Aside from the excellent game fishing on Lizard Island, you'll find diving, snorkeling, water skiing, windsurfing and tennis.

BEACHES. Many of Australia's finest beaches are found north of Cairns (in the area known as Cape Tribulation) off Cook Hwy. These include *Trinity Beach, Clifton Beach, Machan's Beach,* and *Palm Cove* (site of the Australian Bird Park). However, all along Cape Tribulation there's beautiful coast; swim anywhere you'd like, but remember not to swim in summer when jellyfish are prevalent.

PROTECTING THE REEF. The Great Barrier Reef is protected by law. It has been developing for centuries, but humans have the capability of destroying it in moments. Thus, the Australians have laid down the law to people viewing the reef: (1) Don't remove coral; (2) wear rubber-soled shoes for reef walking (rubber soles do not damage living coral); (3) don't touch or pick up reef creatures, including shellfish (this law is as much for people as for the reef, because many of these creatures are dangerous); (4) return any boulders you may have overturned to their original positions (you may be upsetting a reef creature's home); (5) for your own health, don't neglect stings, cuts or coral scratches (always ask for first-aid treatment immediately). These regulations are enforced throughout the Great Barrier Reef region.

NIGHTLIFE. Don't expect to paint the town in Cairns. There are pubs aplenty all over the place, but most close at about 11 P.M. There is a nightclub, *Scandals,* on Lake Street, which stays open until 3 A.M., but you may be yawning long before that at this place. A night on the town in Cairns consists of a good meal, a walk along the esplanade and around the marlin jetty, and to bed early.

NORTHERN QUEENSLAND: TOWNSVILLE AND THE NORTHERN GREAT BARRIER REEF

Townsville has always been an important gateway to the Great Barrier Reef and the Whitsunday Islands, but not until its international airport opened in 1981 did the area boom in terms of international visitors. Townsville has a population of just over 100,000, making it Australia's largest city of the tropics. (Brisbane is considered semitropical.) By itself, Townsville is not an exciting tourist destination, but that is changing. Sheraton has recently opened the first casino in North Queensland (see Accommodations, below) and is soon to open Great Barrier Reef Wonderland, a theme park attraction that "transports" people to the reef without their ever leaving the mainland. There are several fine beaches in the area—Pallarenda, 6km (3.5 mi.) from downtown; Saunders Beach, 22km (13 mi.) from downtown, and Balgal Beach, 50km (30 mi.) from the city center.

But Townsville definitely owes its fame to the Great Barrier Reef. The city is closer to reef islands than any other in the country, with Magnetic Island only 8km (5 mi.) away. Other Barrier Reef islands within striking distance of Townsville are Orpheus, Hinchinbrook, and Bedarra islands.

Bedarra Island

Hideaway, the resort on Bedarra Island, is so well secluded that it cannot be seen from the water—a wall of palms surrounds the place. Once Hideaway is found, it could be mistaken for a private estate, since it has only eight bungalows and accommodates no more than 20 people at a time. Guests have their choice of swimming, snorkeling, sailing, water skiing, or doing nothing. It's not cheap here. Weekly rates, including meals, start at a bit more than $A1,000 for two. Bedarra is accessible from Townsville via Dunk Island. Accommodations on the island can be booked through a travel agent.

Hinchinbrook Island

Hinchinbrook is part of a large national park and, therefore, is not as built up as the other reef islands. There are moderately priced bungalows on the island for 30 people, but don't expect the deluxe treatment here. Again because it is a national park, there are long stretches of open and unspoiled beaches and many tropical birds buzzing overhead. It's a real paradise, but the only organized activities are the ones you organize yourself. Hinchinbrook is accessible by air from Townsville.

QUEENSLAND

Orpheus Island

Orpheus is another exclusive Barrier Reef resort where only the prices are more startling than the natural beauty. Expect to pay $A1,000 or more for accommodations and meals for two for a week. Only 25 couples at a time can be accommodated on the island.

There's a freshwater swimming pool and all water sports one expects on the Great Barrier Reef. Seven secluded beaches guarantee you won't be in a crowd. Guests are free to use the island's tennis courts, paddleboats, catamarans, and windsurfers. Orpheus is accessible by air from Townsville, and accommodations can be booked on the island by a travel agent.

Magnetic Island

Because it is so close to Townsville, Magnetic may be the most visited of the Great Barrier Reef islands. It has 23 bays and beaches, 10 of which are easily accessible and consequently the most crowded. There are graded paths that criss-cross the island for bushwalkers, a nine-hole golf course, tennis, horseback riding, and all water sports. There are several motels and guesthouses on the island, none of which are pricey. There are a few shops where you can buy reef souvenirs, and minimokes and taxis are available for transportation on the island. A passenger ferry operates regularly between Townsville and Magnetic Island, and a vehicular ferry operates twice daily, so you can bring over your rental car. Inquire on the island about motel and guesthouse vacancies.

PRACTICAL INFORMATION FOR
NORTHERN QUEENSLAND

HOW TO GET THERE AND HOW TO GET AROUND. By air. *Qantas* operates international direct flights to Townsville from North America and Europe that usually have a connection at Cairns or Brisbane or another Australian gateway. *Ansett* and *Australian Airlines* fly to Townsville from Brisbane and Cairns and from all cities in Australia with connections. *Air Queensland* flies to Townsville from several points in Queensland. Seaplanes will take you from Townsville to Hinchinbrook and Orpheus.

By rail. *Railways of Australia*'s Sunlander stops in Townsville on its regular run between Brisbane and Cairns.

By bus. *Ansett Pioneer* and *Greyhound Australia* operate express motor-coach services to Townsville from many cities in Australia.

By car. Townsville is on the Bruce Highway, the main north–south route along the Queensland coast.

By boat. A launch will take you to Bedarra from Dunk Island; passenger and vehicular ferries operate regularly between Townsville and Magnetic Island.

ACCOMMODATIONS. Accommodations are classified *deluxe,* $A75 or more per night; *expensive,* $A60–$A74 per night; *moderate,* $A40–$A59 per night; and *inexpensive,* less than $A40 per night. Prices are for two people sharing a room. (Rates on island resorts usually include meals.)

AUSTRALIA

BEDARRA ISLAND

Hideaway. *Deluxe.* Water sports; meals included. Contact your travel agent.

HINCHINBROOK ISLAND

Hinchinbrook Island Hideaway. *Moderate.* Box 3, Caldwell, Qld. 4816; (070) 66-8585. Dining room, pool.

MAGNETIC ISLAND

Mediterranean Holiday Village. *Moderate.* Mandeley Ave., Nelly Bay 4816; (77) 78-5200. Restaurant, cocktail lounge, pool, tennis; golf nearby.

ORPHEUS ISLAND

Orpheus Island Resort. *Deluxe.* Ingham 4850; (77) 777-377. Elegant resort. Fine dining; rates include most sports. Attracts couples.

TOWNSVILLE

Sheraton Breakwater Island Casino Hotel. *Deluxe.* Breakwater Island. Phone any Sheraton reservation number. The only legalized gambling casino in north Queensland.
Townsville International. *Deluxe.* Flinders Mall; (077) 72-2477. Heart of downtown; rooftop pool; restaurants, bars.
Lowths. *Expensive.* Flinders and Stanley sts. (077) 72-1888. Attractive hotel in center of town. Restaurant, bars, disco.
Townsville TraveLodge. *Expensive.* 75 the Strand; (077) 72-4255.
Palms. *Moderate.* 44 Bowen Rd.; (077) 79-6166.
Town Lodge Motor Inn. *Moderate.* 15 Victoria St.; (077) 71-2164.
Coachman's Inn. *Inexpensive.* 33 Flinders St.; (077) 72-3140.
Coolabah. *Inexpensive.* 75 Bowen Rd.; (077) 79-2084.

RESTAURANTS. An *expensive* meal in Townsville costs about $A50 for two with wine and drinks, *moderate* between $A25–$A49, and *inexpensive* less than $25. These are dinner prices; expect to pay less for lunch and quite a bit less for breakfast. Breakfast is usually served at hotels and motels and is quite reasonable.

The Restaurant. *Expensive.* 458 Flinders St.; 72-5242. More than 100 dishes and 150 wines to choose from.
Affaire De Coeur. *Expensive.* 1 Sturt St.; 72-2742. French gourmet cooking.
Ancient Mariner. *Moderate.* 428 Flinders St.; 72-3324. Seafood.
Hong Kong. *Moderate.* 455 Flinders St.; 71-5818. Chinese.
Nevada's Steakhouse. *Moderate.* 119 Charters Towers Rd.; 71-5345. As the name says.
Captain's Table. *Inexpensive.* 43 Flinders St.; 71-3428. Seafood.
Seaview Hotel. *Inexpensive.* The Strand; 71-5005. Australian home cooking.

TOURIST INFORMATION AND TOURS *Queensland Government Travel Centre,* 303 Flinders Mall, Townsville, (077) 71-3077, can answer all your travel questions about North Queensland and book many tours and cruises to Reef islands.

SPORTS. Rentals and instruction for most sports are readily available on Bedarra Island. You'll find fishing, sailing, snorkeling, swimming. Hinchenbrook Island offers fishing, diving, sailing, windsurfing, snorkeling, and swimming. Magnetic Island has a full array of sports: fishing, water skiing, diving, sailing, windsurfing, snorkeling, swimming—as well as tennis, golf, and

QUEENSLAND

horseback riding. On Orpheus Island you'll find fishing, water skiing, diving and snorkeling, windsurfing and sailing, tennis, and golf.

BEACHES. In addition to the beautiful beaches on the reef islands, there are several fine beaches close to Townsville: Pallendra, 3 mi. from town; Saunders, 13 mi.; and Balgal, 30 mi.

CRUISES. The *Reef Link* sails from Townsville to a pontoon moored over the Great Barrier Reef daily for snorkeling, diving, and fishing. A short stop at Magnetic Island is included. Call *Reef Link* in Townsville at (077) 72–5733 for current rates and schedule.

THE WHITSUNDAY ISLANDS AND COAST

The Whitsunday region of the Great Barrier Reef consists of a string of resort towns that begins south of Townsville and continues along the Bruce Highway to the town of Mackay, 326km (106 mi.) to the south, and the Whitsunday Islands, 74 in all, most uninhabited, that are part of the Whitsunday Island National Park. There are resorts on Hook, Hamilton, South Molle, Daydream, Hayman, Lindeman, Long, and Brampton islands. Airlie Beach and Shute Harbor are the main resort towns on the Whitsunday coast, and from these two towns and Mackay, the Whitsunday Islands resorts are reached.

Airlie Beach

Airlie Beach is a laid-back kind of resort lined with beautiful beaches and several attractions suitable for the family. The Whitsunday Aquarium on Jubilee Pocket Road displays much of the sea life that lives on the reef and screens an informative movie about the Great Barrier Reef daily. The aquarium is open daily 9 A.M. to 5 P.M. Not far away is another fun place for the family, Flame Tree Grove on Shute Harbour Road. Here, there are several acres of tropical rain forest with marked trails for bushwalking. It's a good place to see the rich bird life in this part of Queensland. Flame Tree Grove is open every day but Wednesday, 9 A.M. to 5 P.M. But most people don't come to the Whitsunday region to trek about from attraction to attraction. They come here for sun and sea and water-related activities. Hotels and motels in Airlie Beach can advise you how to participate in any activity you desire—snorkeling, scuba diving, sailing, windsurfing, water skiing, boating, tennis, golf, and on and on.

Shute Harbour

Shute Harbour is a small town with a natural harbor that is a haven for many of the yachts and sailboats that cruise the Whitsunday Passage, the stretch of water between the mainland and the islands that is considered by many yachters as one of the most beautiful sea lanes in the world. Shute Harbour is the main departure point for cruises and yacht charters to the Whitsunday Islands.

Mackay

Although Mackay has become a sort of transit center between the southern Australian capitals and the Great Barrier Reef region, it is a pleasant resort in its own right. The city, facing the Pacific and surrounded by lush green sugar-cane fields, is situated on the banks of the Pioneer River. An excursion to the Eungella Range, 80km (48 mi.) west of Mackay, is well worth it even if it means spending a night in the town. Eungella National Park, 1,200m (3,960 ft.) above sea level, is a tropical rain forest in cool mountain air. The name is Aboriginal and means "land of clouds"—which need not be taken literally. The park abounds in palms, elkhorns, staghorns, parasite figs, ferns, orchids, flowering vines, and shrubs.

Hook Island

Hook Island is one of the largest islands along the Great Barrier Reef. It has an underwater observatory where people can walk and view close up coral and sea life on the reef. There are a large number of moorings on the island where yachters can pull in for the night. Abundant camping facilities and low-cost cabins make Hook Island the favorite of the Whitsundays for vacationers on a budget. There's a restaurant on the island. Hook Island is accessible by boat from Shute Harbour.

Hamilton Island

On this island is the largest and most sophisticated resort in the Whitsundays. A new hotel recently opened, giving the island the capability of accommodating 1,000 people a night in hotel rooms, suites, apartments, or Polynesian-style bungalows. The marina docks 200 boats, and there are pools, spas, tennis and squash courts, five restaurants, and four boutiques for shoppers. Every conceivable water-related activity is at hand on the island (even jet s .s) and boats are ready to take anglers to the rich waters of the Outer Reef for big-game fishing. The island has its own helicopter, which takes snorkelers and divers to a floating pontoon on the reef for some of the best viewing in the Whitsundays. Back on the island, a 200-acre wildlife reserve has koalas, deer, kangaroos, and emus that can be seen close up. The Coral Cat, a floating hotel that sits over the reef, is also at Hamilton Island's guests' disposal. Guests fly out to the Coral Cat by helicopter or take a launch from the island and spend a few days right on top of the Great Barrier Reef. This is a particular favorite of divers and fishers. In the waters where the Coral Cat is moored, it is possible to walk on top of the reef. The ship has 21 double cabins and one suite, a restaurant, a bar, a lounge, and a sundeck. Hamilton Island is also the only Great Barrier Reef island with an airport that can take jet aircraft, and Ansett flies there daily from Brisbane and Sydney. Light aircraft also fly to Hamilton Island from Shute Harbour. Any travel agent can book a room on Hamilton Island.

South Molle Island

Here's one Whitsunday Island that didn't forget the kids and is, therefore, a favorite resort for families traveling with children. Many children's activities are planned each day, and the resort has a playground, a wading pool, trampoline, and a game room. Some lodge units

QUEENSLAND

on the island have been especially outfitted for families with children, and a baby-sitting service is available in the evenings. For adults, South Molle provides a legion of activities by day and operates cruises to the Outer Reef and through the waters of the Whitsunday Passage. At night, everything from disco to bingo is available. There is a choice of accommodations on the island ranging from inexpensive dorm-style rooms to pricey beachfront units with private patios. South Molle is accessed by boat or helicopter from Shute Harbour, and there are boat connections from the jet airport on Hamilton Island. Any travel agent can book a room on South Molle Island.

Daydream Island

One of the smaller islands in the Whitsunday chain, Daydream is the perfect out-of-the-way tropical escape, yet close enough to shore to be easily accessible. Daydream has all the water-related activities available in the islands and is equipped with its own glass-bottom boat for up-close reef viewing for those who don't snorkel or dive. At night, the island is one of the liveliest along the reef, with a disco, a cabaret, movies, and fancy dress balls as a few of the diversions. Accommodations are reasonably priced—around $A500 for two for a week. Daydream Island is a 20-minute cruise from Shute Harbour.

Hayman Island

Hayman is the most northerly island in the Whitsundays to be transformed into a resort. About $100 million was spent to convert the island into a luxury, five-star vacation dream spot, and all the effort paid off. Hayman's Blue Lagoon is the playground for all sorts of watersports. At low tide it is possible to walk on the reef at this point. There are graded tracks across the island for bushwalking, and Hayman is an ornithologist's delight, since some 80 species of tropical birds live on the island. There are rates from about $A500 to $A1,000 for two for a week, depending on accommodation choice. Hayman is reached by boat from Shute Harbour. Any travel agent can book a room on the island.

Lindeman Island

Lindeman is where the golfers go. Its six-hole course is especially tricky, since it hugs the island's rocky coast. There are seven sandy beaches on Lindeman and some 20km (12 mi.) of scenic walking tracks. It's the oldest resort in the Whitsunday group, established in 1929. It is ideal for families traveling with children, because activities are well-planned and supervised for children from 3 to 14 years old. You can spend less than $A500 for two for five nights on the island, and family rates are available. Lindeman is accessible by air from Mackay or by boat from Hamilton Island jetport. Any travel agent can book a room on Lindeman Island.

Long Island

The Whitsunday 100 resort on Long Island is youth oriented, with lots of time set aside for sailing during the day and then dancing until dawn. And although the atmosphere is laid back for the younger set, it may be too fast paced for older travelers. Palm Bay, also on Long Island, is a more typical vacation spot for older folks. Accommodations at Whitsunday 100 are budget priced in deference to the youth market and are only slightly higher at Palm Bay. Long Island is accessible by boat from Shute Harbour or by boat from the Hamilton Island jetport.

Brampton Island

At the southern entrance to the Whitsunday Passage lies Brampton Island. It is an all-around activities islands, with golf, tennis, and the usual assortment of water-related activities. Scuba-diving expeditions and fishing charters and cruises leave from the island. Sing alongs, dancing, and parties fill the nights. Two people can spend five days on the island for about $A350. Brampton is accessible by air or sea from Mackay.

PRACTICAL INFORMATION FOR THE WHITSUNDAY REGION

HOW TO GET THERE AND HOW TO GET AROUND. By air. *Ansett* and *Australian Airlines* fly to Mackay from Brisbane, Townsville, and other cities in Australia, and from there *Air Whitsunday* operates flights to many of the islands. Amphibian and light aircraft fly from Shute Harbour to many of the islands. *Ansett* flies to Hamilton Island from Brisbane and Sydney.

By sea. Cruises operate from Mackay, Airlie Beach, and Shute Harbour to all resort islands in the Whitsunday group.

By rail. *Railways of Australia* operates the Sunlander passenger train to Mackay from Brisbane in the south and Cairns in the north.

By bus. *Ansett Pioneer* and Greyhound Australia serve Mackay and Shute Harbour.

By car. The Bruce Highway is the main north–south route along this portion of the Queensland coast and it passes Mackay. It also passes the town of Prosperine, where the road to Shute Harbour and Airlie Beach begins.

ACCOMMODATIONS. Accommodations are classified as *expensive,* more than $A60 per night; *moderate,* $A40–$A59 per night, and *inexpensive,* less than $A40 per night. Prices are for two people sharing a room. Many of the prices on the island resorts include food and are higher than these categories.

AIRLIE BEACH

Coral Sea Resort. *Expensive.* 25 Ocean View Ave.; (079) 46–6458.
Airlie Beach Hotel-Motel. *Moderate.* Shute Harbour Rd.; (079) 46–6233.
Wanderers Paradise. *Moderate.* Shute Harbour Rd.; (079) 46–6446.
Airlie Beach Motor Lodge. *Inexpensive.* Lamond St.; (079) 46–6418.

BRAMPTON ISLAND

Brampton Island Resort. *Moderate.* (070) 57–2595. Entertainment and recreational facilities, including tennis, golf, waterskiing, and glass-bottom boats.

DAYDREAM ISLAND

Daydream Island Resort. *Moderate.* (079) 46–9200. Restaurant; bar; pool; sauna; tennis; scuba instruction; cruises.

QUEENSLAND

HAMILTON ISLAND

Hamilton Island Resort. *Expensive.* (79) 46-9144. Polynesian-style accommodations with restaurants, bars, and nightly entertainment. Extensive water sports: snorkeling, waterskiing, parasailing, boating, diving, tennis.

HAYMAN ISLAND

Royal Hayman Hotel. *Expensive.* (79) 46-9100. Lively luxury resort. Restaurants; lounges; disco, cabaret; swimming pools; tennis; water sports.

LINDEMAN ISLAND

Lindeman Island Hotel. *Moderate–Expensive.* (79) 46-9333. Restaurant; bar; shops; entertainment. Golf, tennis, and water sports.

LONG ISLAND

Happy Bay Island Resort. *Moderate.* (79) 46-9400. Dining room and cocktail lounge. Tennis; 4-hole golf; pool.

MACKAY

Coral Sands Motel. *Moderate.* 44 McAlister St.; (079) 51-1244.
Marco Polo. *Moderate.* 46 Nebo St.; (079) 51-2700.
Teleford Coach House. *Moderate.* 40 Nebo St.; (079) 57-6526. Restaurant, pool.
Hospitality Inn. *Inexpensive.* 2 McAlister St.; (079) 51-1666. Overlooking river in center of town. Pool. BYO restaurant; refrigerators in rooms.
The Mackay. *Inexpensive.* Imperial Arcade; (079) 57-6985.

SHUTE HARBOUR

Coral Point Lodge. *Expensive.* Harbour Ave.; (079) 46-9232.
Shute Harbour. *Moderate.* Shute Harbour Rd.; (079) 46-9131.
Motel Shute Harbour. *Inexpensive.* Shute Harbour Rd.; (079) 46-9131.

SOUTH MOLLE ISLAND

Telford South Molle Island Resort. *Moderate–Expensive.* (79) 46-9433. Rooms and bungalows. Family units available. Restaurants, bar, entertainment. Tennis, golf, water sports including dive program; children's activities.

RESTAURANTS. Dinner for two is classified *expensive* if the price is $A50 or more, including wine; *moderate,* between $A25 and $A49; and *inexpensive,* less than $A25. Lunch and breakfast are priced less.

AIRLIE BEACH

Coral Sea. *Expensive.* Coral Sea Resort; 46-6548. Seafood.
Spice Island Bistro. *Moderate.* 66 Shute Harbor Rd; 46-6585. Beef, lamb, and curry dishes.
Coconut Palms. *Inexpensive.* 20 Shute Harbour Rd.; 46-6465.
The Wildlife Seafood Restaurant. *Inexpensive.* Jubilee Pocket Rd.; 46-6124.

MACKAY

Kismet's. *Moderate.* Sydney and Victoria; 57-6844. Seafood, pheasant, quail.
Lychee Gardens. *Moderate.* Wellington and Victoria; 51-3939. Chinese.
Valencia. *Moderate.* 44 McAlister St.; 51-1244. Spanish and seafood.
Alpapa's Italian Restaurant. *Inexpensive.* 186 Shakespeare; 51-5107.
Splendor. *Inexpensive.* 208 Victoria; 57-4545. Basic food.

SHUTE HARBOUR

There are restaurants at hotels and motels in Shute Harbour.

TOURIST INFORMATION. The *Queensland Government Travel Centre* has all the information you need for a vacation in the Whitsunday Islands. The office is on River Street in Mackay, phone (079) 57-2292. The *Mackay–Whitsunday Tourism Council*, Nebo Rd., Mackay, phone (079) 52-2038, also has tourist information about the region.

CRUISES/FLIGHTS. Naturally, there are numerous cruises through the Whitsunday Islands that can be joined at Mackay, Airlie Beach, and Shute Harbour, as well as regular boat services between these towns and the Whitsunday Islands. Cruises are also available to some of the uninhabited islands in the chain. Air-charter companies fly light planes and seaplanes from the small airports in Mackay and Shute Harbour to islands on the reef and on sightseeing flights over the reef. Hamilton Island has its own helicopter fleet for sightseeing flights.

DIVING. Though it is quite possible to scuba-dive all along the Great Barrier Reef, the sport is most readily available in the Whitsunday Islands. There are three types of diving vacations offered in the Whitsundays—staying on one of the Whitsundays and using the resort's facilities; joining one of the diving vessels that sail out over the reef from Mackay and Shute Harbour on day or longer diving expeditions; and joining a scuba diving course on the mainland that provides instruction and on-reef experience. The latter is advised for novices. PADI, NAUI, YMCA, or other internationally recognized certificates are required for scuba diving in Australia. A medical certificate of good health is required of people who want to take diving lessons in Australia. Several tour wholesalers in North America and the U.K. operate diving tours to the Great Barrier Reef. Any travel agent can book them. The Queensland Government Travel Centre (see above) has details on all three types of diving vacations.

BAREBOATING. Also particularly popular in the Whitsunday Islands is bareboating, a sail-yourself yacht-charter plan. Experienced yachters can rent a sailboat from any number of companies in Mackay, Shute Harbour, or Airlie Beach. Those who don't know how to sail can hire a skipper to go along. Bareboating is especially popular with groups of friends traveling together, since it becomes quite economical when several people pitch in on the cost. The Queensland National Parks and Wildlife Service has established camps throughout the Whitsunday Islands where yachters can moor and come ashore. Camping permits are required. The Queensland Government Travel Centre (see above) has bareboating-rental details.

For availability of other **sports,** see Accommodations, above.

SOUTHERN QUEENSLAND

The Southern Great Barrier Reef

Toward the end of the 2,041km-(1,258 mi.)-long Great Barrier Reef are three more resort islands—Great Keppel, Heron, and Lady Elliot islands. They are reached from the mainland towns of Rockhampton, Gladstone, and Bundaberg. None of the towns is of overwhelming interest to tourists, except as jumping-off points to the islands, but each

QUEENSLAND

has a curiosity worth a mention. Rockhampton sits astride the Tropic of Capricorn and enjoys a near-perfect climate, much like Hawaii's. Quay Street in the center of town is one of the few surviving Australian townscapes from the colonial period of the last century and is protected by the National Trust. Gladstone is famous for its huge aluminium plant, and Bundaberg is known for rum.

Great Keppel Island

This island is preferred by the younger set because of its round-the-clock atmosphere. There are 17 separate sandy beaches on this island, and they're usually well populated by a fun-loving crowd. All the requisite water activities are found on Great Keppel. In the evening, a resident rock band plays until the wee hours. Two people can stay a week on the island for approximately $A500. Great Keppel is reached by air from Rockhampton. Any travel agent can book a room on the island.

Heron Island

Heron is a true reef island, alive with wildlife and so beautiful that it is often the choice of photographers shooting the Barrier Reef islands for brochures or magazines. Among the natives are such unusual birds as noddy terns, reef herons (hence the name), and silver gulls. Little green reef turtles, harmless creatures, are all about. Heron Island is perhaps the first choice of serious scuba divers. Diving boats leave twice daily for the reef and for Outer Reef. A marine-geology headquarters is also on the island. Nights are quiet, but there is dancing to the music of a resident band two evenings a week. Heron is reached from Gladstone by helicopter. Accommodations on the island begin at about $A500 for two for five nights and continue upward to more than $A1,000 for a suite. Any travel agent can book a room on Heron Island.

Lady Elliot Island

Lady Elliot Island is the most southerly coral cay of the Great Barrier Reef and the closest reef island to Brisbane. The island is small and unassuming. Cabins and tents are used for accommodations, but that helps keep the cost in check—$A250 to $A300 for five nights for two people. The island is reached by air from Bundaberg. Any travel agent can book a cabin or tent on Lady Elliot Island.

Brisbane

How you judge Brisbane, Queenslands's capital, will largely depend on the time of year you're there. In summer, the city broils, but other times of the year the climate is pleasant, although there is never any doubt that you're in a semitropical city. Brisbane is a new city, built largely since 1864, when a fire leveled it. One of the few surviving prefire buildings is the observatory on Wickham Place, built by convict labor in 1829 as a windmill used in grain processing. Few other buildings in Brisbane are of particular interest, but two of the most imposing are City Hall and the Queensland Parliament in the city center.

What is of interest in Brisbane is the outdoors, for it is a beautifully landscaped city with jacarandas, tulip trees, flame trees, coral trees, oleanders, frangipanis, bougainvillea, and many other trees, flowers, and shrubs growing everywhere. You merely have to walk around to get the picture, but for a heavy assault on the senses, visit the 50-acre botanic garden in the center of town on the banks of the Brisbane River. You might also have a quick look at the Queensland Art Gallery and the Queensland Museum, both within the confines of the Queensland Cultural Centre in the heart of town.

The city and the river that meanders through it were named after the Scottish soldier and astronomer Sir Thomas Makdougall Brisbane (1773–1860), governor of New South Wales from 1821 to 1825. The waterway was discovered by two escaped convicts in 1823, and the penal settlement was established the following year on its banks, 32km upstream from its entry into Moreton Bay. Thirty-five years later, Queensland, named after Queen Victoria at her suggestion, became a separate colony. Brisbane, its capital, was still a primitive town.

There are several sanctuaries not far from the city. Lone Pine Koala Sanctuary is a half hour drive west of City Hall. Its animal population includes koalas, kangaroos, wombats, and emus. A platypus can be seen between 3 and 4 P.M. Bunya Park, 24km north of the city, surrounds an artificial lake and features a mystery maze to "The Bunyip." The African Lion Safari at Yatala on the Pacific Highway has lions, tigers, leopards, bears, and other animal species including Australia's only liger (a cross between a lion and a tiger).

There are a few spots near the city center where one can obtain impressive bird's eye views of Brisbane, and beyond. From Bartleys Hill, 5km away, one can see the city, the port, the Taylor Range and, in the distance, the Great Dividing Range. Mt. Coot-tha, 8km (4.8 mi.) from downtown, commands similar views. It has a restaurant that serves reasonable meals and, at dinner, offers an unforgettable view of the city's sea of lights. Mount Gravatt, 10km (6 mi.) from downtown, presents panoramic views as far away as the Glasshouse Mountains (72km) and the border ranges of New South Wales. The Sir Thomas Brisbane Planetarium and a tropical plant dome are housed in the Mt. Coot-tha Botanic Gardens.

Brisbane is, of course, a young city where anything dating back more than a century is "antique" and deemed worth preserving. Most of it—such as Newstead House in Newstead Park, the oldest preserved home in Queensland, where the State's Royal Historical Society has its headquarters—is pleasant enough but will hardly arouse rapturous enthusiasm in the visitor. Although many who knew Brisbane before World War II now lament the disappearance of its quiet provincial life and its early-to-bed, early-to-rise schedule, the visitor may enjoy the city's present tempo—vibrant without being hectic.

Moreton Bay, Stradbroke, Tangalooma

About a 20-minute drive from Brisbane is the vast and sheltered expanse of Moreton Bay, Brisbane's marine playground. It's an area strewn with islands. Three of them—Stradbroke, Moreton, and Bribie—are quite large and inhabited, but several smaller ones are also inhabited and cultivated, yielding considerable crops of vegetables and tropical fruits. The mainland shores are studded with resorts, well equipped for all kinds of water sports including swimming, sailing, and fishing.

South Stradbroke Island resort is reached by launch or seaplane from the Gold Coast. Launches leave from Surfers Paradise and Southport and the seaplane departs from Paradise Waters.

Stradbroke, the southernmost of the three large islands in the bay, is 61km (36.6 mi.) long. In 1896, huge waves driven by a wild cyclone gouged a channel across it so that now the island is cut in two. Named after the Earl of Stradbroke, who discovered it in 1823, it is an important sand-mining center, and large amounts of titanium, zircon, and rutile are extracted from its beaches. Air and launch services operate from Brisbane to North Stradbroke, and ferry boats for motorists ply between the coastal villages of Redland Bay and Cleveland. There are good swimming beaches on the bayside, such as Dunwich and Amity Point, and several surfing beaches facing the ocean. A small national park, with Lake Kaboora in its center, offers pleasant, easy bush-walks amid a riot of wildflowers.

North of Stradbroke is Moreton Island, which is connected to Brisbane by a launch and air to the island's main center, Tangalooma. The unique feature of the island named by Matthew Flinders in 1799 is the huge sand hills—reputedly the biggest in the world—which rise up to 279m (Mount Tempest). The main sports are swimming, fishing, and surfing.

Bribie Island is at the northern end of Moreton Bay and 63km (37.8 mi.) from Brisbane. It is one of the few spots in Australia where the colonizers met with fierce resistance from the Aborigines who practiced cannibalism. Bribie is connected by a concrete bridge with the mainland at Toorbul Point at the southern end of Pumicestone Passage. There is also a daily coach service to and from Brisbane. The island is a wildlife sanctuary with large numbers of native animals and plants; wild boronia which flowers between August and December is a special attraction. There are two small settlements at the southern end of the island, Bongaree and Woorim. A golf course, bowling greens, and water sports are provided for visitors.

It takes only an hour's comfortable drive south from Brisbane to reach Australia's number one playground, the Gold Coast. This 42km (25.2 mi.) stretch of narrow land—in one part it is only half a kilometer wide—serves one purpose: to help the annual influx of 2,000,000 visitors relax and have fun. The Gold Coast is sometimes criticized as garish and flashy, a sort of upstart Miami. It is not a place for people who seek quiet and isolation to recover from the hectic tempo of modern life.

It is a place for people to enjoy their vacations *with* other people, not in solitude—at least not in that part of the Gold Coast where dozens of multistory luxury hotels and motels stand cheek by jowl with modest guest houses. Where camper parks and supermarkets stand near expensive boutiques. Where self-service cafes stand next to elegant restaurants. Where one may dress formally, informally, or with casual abandon. For that part of the Gold Coast tries to provide for all tastes and all pockets. Well, nearly all of them.

But only a short distance from the beaches and the adjacent funlandia there is another Gold Coast along the human-made canals and the foothills of the mountains. This is the area where, in recent years, residential land developers have reaped huge profits. The Gold Coast region has the fastest growing population in the whole of Australia—13 percent a year. The permanent population of a few thousand a decade ago now exceeds 112,900.

Tourists are not alone in flocking there to enjoy an average of 287 sunny days a year and a mean temperature of 75°F (24°C). Thousands retire there; the number of these new settlers increases yearly. Besides climate and its many amenities, the Gold Coast has an added attraction for the not so young—Queensland has abolished death duties, an advantage property salespeople are quick to point out. Prices of houses and home units (apartments) are not inexpensive; though real estate values have dropped somewhat recently, development of the region, which began in the 1950s, continues. Until about 30 years ago, the Gold Coast was mainly farm country with a few hotels, guest houses, and villas of well-to-do Brisbanites along the sea shore.

The main season is the winter months—June, July, and August—when people from the southern states as well as overseas flock to the

Gold Coast. Nevertheless, the climate is quite pleasant throughout the year—December and January are especially popular—but February, March, and April may produce some spectacular downpours.

Where Fun Abounds

Southport, 80km (48 mi.) by road from Brisbane, marks the northern entry to the Gold Coast. The string of beaches along the Gold Coast include Surfers Paradise, Broadbeach, Mermaid Beach, Currumbin, Kirra, and Coolangatta. The Gold Coast is, of course, well supplied with facilities for water sports as well as with bowling greens, tennis courts, and golf courses. A new hotel-casino, Conrad International Hotel and Jupiters Casino, recently brought legalized gambling to the Gold Coast.

One of the region's least expected attractions is the mountainous hinterland—the MacPherson Range, with several national parks and wildlife sanctuaries. All are within easy driving distance of the coast and can be visited in a day. Most have well-marked paths leading to lookouts over sweeping vistas, deep ravines, and waterfalls. Among those you might visit are:

Numinbah Valley National Park. Roads from Southport, Broadbeach, or Burleigh lead through the charming hillside settlement of Nerang to the park 27km (16.2 mi.) away. The valley, situated between the steep face of the Springbrook Plateau and the forests of Lamington National Park, is irrigated by the Nerang River, which flows through it. The river forms natural swimming pools, and there are many picnic areas on its banks.

Springbrook, about 40km (24 mi.) from the coast, contains two national parks. The best way to approach this plateau is from Burleigh Heads through Mudgeeraba. Five kilometers beyond Mudgeeraba is the small Gold Coast Historical War Museum (with displays of tanks and other military equipment) and a boomerang factory where visitors over the age of seven can try their skill with this ancient Aboriginal weapon. Several attractions along this road serve meals.

Lamington National Park, 32km (19.2 mi.) from the coast, can be reached by two roads, one of which terminates at O'Reilly's Green Mountain guesthouse and the second at Binna Burra, where comfortable accommodations are available. Lamington is Queensland's best-known national park and one of Australia's most beautiful reserves, with some unique flora. The peaks of the mountains range up to 1,200m (3,960 ft.) high where the Antarctic beech—remarkable trees, some of them 3,000 years old—have survived the vicissitudes of time and climate. The region is the creation of violent volcanic actions in prehistoric times, and rain forests, flowering trees, and ferns thrive in the rich soil. Well-graded paths lead to the interior of the park from O'Reilly's and Binna Burra, where rather basic accommodation is also available.

Tamborine Mountain, 42km (25.2 mi.) from the coast, has 10 national parks with peaks of up to 650m (1,155 ft.). The parks preserve varieties of vegetation and have many picturesque waterfalls. Its most interesting plant, the macrozamia palm, which grows on the western slopes, has retained its characteristics through millions of years. Some of the palms on Tamborine mountain are more than 1,000 years old.

The Sunshine Coast

About 105km (63 mi.) north of Brisbane, there is another 60km (36-mi.) stretch of beaches, inlets, lakes, and mountains which, a few years ago, acquired the name of Sunshine Coast.

The Sunshine Coast begins opposite Bribie Island in the south (see sections on Brisbane and Moreton Bay), and in the north, it ends somewhere near Double Island Point. But its tourist and holiday sector is between Caloundra and Noosa. Scenically, this region is even more beautiful than the Gold Coast. And its hinterland—while it cannot match the grandeur of Lamington National Park—is also attractive in a more mellow way. Sunshine Coast resorts, however, are much quieter than those on the Gold Coast. They are less commercialized and—if sophistication is measured by the number and quality of hotels, restaurants, and nightclubs—less sophisticated.

The Sunshine Coast is more for people who want to be physically active yet relaxed during their vacation. Sports facilities (water and land) are as good north of Brisbane as they are south of the state capital. The costs of a vacation are about the same in both places. Hence, whether people choose one or the other is very much a question of personal taste.

The Bruce Highway is the main traffic artery that connects Brisbane with the Sunshine Coast. The highway runs inland, but good bitumen roads branch off to the coast, which is an average distance of 20km (12 mi.) away. The turnoff from the Bruce Highway to the Bribie Island Bridge is 45km (27 mi.) north of Brisbane. It is near Caboolture, which is noted for a fine 18-hole golf course. Continuing along the highway, 24km (14.4 mi.) farther north are the 10 steep trachyite cones of the Glasshouse Mountains, named in 1770 by Captain Cook, who was reminded by the cones of the glass furnaces of his native Yorkshire. From Nambour (108km (64.8 mi.) from Brisbane) roads lead to the coast, to the mountains of the Blackall Range, and to the small, attractive Mapleton Falls and Kondalilla National Park. Gympie, another 72km (43.2 mi.) away, is the northernmost inland limit of the Sunshine Coast with good road connections to the chain of lakes north of Noosa where water skiing facilities and large flocks of water birds (including black swans, wild ducks, and cranes) may be found.

Sunshine Coast Resorts

There are a number of seaboard resorts along the Sunshine Coast going from south to north. Caloundra, at the meeting place of Pumicestone Passage and the Pacific Ocean, has a series of excellent beaches extending over a dozen kilometers. Best for water skiing, swimming, and boating are Golden Beach and Bulcock Beach. For surfing, try Kings and Dickey, which are regularly patrolled by surf lifesavers. Mooloolaba, at the mouth of the Mooloolah River, is one of the best fishing spots along the Sunshine Coast (the name means "the snapper's place"). It has facilities for all water sports and an excellent boat harbor. The resort is the finishing line of the Sydney-Brisbane Yacht Race and of the Single Handed Trans-Tasman Race. It is also the site of the annual Winter Series off-shore races and the base for a professional fishing and prawning fleet.

Alexandra Headland has fine sand beaches. A road from there leads to the Bruce Highway and Buderim, a fast developing settlement now favored as a permanent retirement place for well-to-do "southerners." Buderim has a good golf course and Australia's only ginger factory. Adjacent to Alexandra Headland is Maroochydore, situated on the Maroochy River, with first-rate surfing beaches. At the estuary of the Maroochy River is a completely protected inlet that provides still-water swimming. A mass of cotton trees, decked in yellow blooms most of the year, borders the cove. For about 5km (3 mi.) between Cotton Tree and Bli Bli the tree lined road runs along the Maroochy River and provides spots for picnickers. There is good fishing in the river, especially in winter. Coolum beach lies at the foot of Mt. Coolum, where there are fine panoramic views of the coast and hinterland.

Noosa Heads has excellent surf because Laguna Bay faces north, rather than east. The still water of the estuary lagoon of the Noosa River offers pleasant swimming, good surf, and estuary and rock fishing. Noosaville, on the Noosa River, is the gateway for tours to the famous multicoloured sands in the 170m (627-ft.) cliff face at Teewah. At Tewantin, on the Noosa River, a barge crosses the river and carries vehicles for trips to Teewah. Only four-wheel-drive vehicles can make that journey.

Noosa National Park at Noosa offers a fine view from its crest, Tingirina Lookout, and the picturesque spots along the park's oceanside walk, including Boiling Pot, Hell's Gates, Fairy Pool, Paradise Caves, Devil's Kitchen, and Alexandra Bay. North of Tewantin, a chain of lakes stretches for some 80km (48 mi.); the largest of them is Lake Cootharaba, which is reached by a road running from Tewantin to Boreen Point. The lake is crossed by a launch (an 11km (6.6-mi.) trip) and from the other shore, a 2km (1.2-mi.) walk leads to the sands. The lake offers swimming, fishing, and sailing.

There are two national parks worth seeing in the Blackall Range—a short distance from the seashore of the central Sunshine Coast; Nambour is a suitable starting point for visits to both. The Mapleton Falls National Park, about 10km (6 mi.) from Nambour, is a rain forest with fascinating birdlife and well-marked tracks to splendid viewing areas. Kondatilla Park, about 22km (13.2 mi.) from Nambour (via Montville), is heavily timbered with all kinds of trees including bunya pines. The Kondalilla Falls cascades 75m (236 ft.) into a rain forest valley. Easy walks lead to the head of the falls and to forest pools where the "living fossil," the Ceratodus (lung fish), may be found.

PRACTICAL INFORMATION FOR SOUTHERN QUEENSLAND

HOW TO GET THERE AND HOW TO GET AROUND. By air. *Qantas* flies to Brisbane from North America and Europe with connections in Sydney or Cairns. *Ansett* and *Australian Airlines* fly there from all cities in Australia, and *Air Queensland* connects Brisbane with other cities and towns in Queensland. Ansett, Australian Airlines, and *East-West Airlines* fly to Coolangatta, airport for the Gold Coast region, from Brisbane, Sydney, Melbourne, and Adelaide, with connections for all other major cities in the country. *Air New South Wales* and East-West fly from Sydney to Maroochydore, airport for the Sunshine Coast, and Air Queensland flies there from Brisbane. *Noosa Air* flies from Brisbane to Noosa, main resort on the Sunshine Coast. Ansett and Australian Airlines fly from Brisbane to Rockhampton, and Australian Airlines flies Sydney-Rockhampton. Heron Island is reached by helicopter from Gladstone. Lady Elliot Island is reached by air from Bundakery. There are planes from Brisbane to North Stradbroke and Moreton Island.

QUEENSLAND

By rail. *Railways of Australia* operates the Brisbane Limited daily between Sydney and Brisbane, a 16-hour overnight trip, and the Capricornian daily between Brisbane and Rockhampton, a 14-hour overnight trip.

By bus. Ansett Pioneer and *Greyhound Australia* operate to Brisbane, Rockhampton, Coolangatta, Surfers Paradise, Maroochydore, and Noosa, with regular express and local motorcoach services from across Australia. Buses also connect Brisbane with Bribie Island.

By car. The Bruce Hwy. is the main road connecting Brisbane with the Sunshine Coast. The Gold Coast is an hour's drive south of Brisbane.

By boat. Launches connect South Stradbroke Island with Surfers Paradise and Southport; seaplanes connect Paradise Waters and South Stradbroke. Launches connect Brisbane with North Stradbroke; ferries connect the coastal villages of Redland Bay and Cleveland.

ACCOMMODATIONS. Hotels and motels are classified as *deluxe,* more than $A80 per night for a double room; *expensive,* $A60–$A79; *moderate,* $A40–$A59; and *inexpensive,* less than $A40.

BRISBANE

Sheraton Brisbane. *Deluxe.* 249 Turbot St.; (07) 835-3535 and any Sheraton reservations number. Brisbane's top hotel. Overlooks city, park, gardens. Restaurants, bars. Pool, gym.

Brisbane Parkroyal. *Expensive.* Alice and Albert streets, (07) 221-3411. Overlooking river. Restaurant, bar, pool.

Crest International. *Expensive.* King George Square; (07) 229-9111. Modern hotel with restaurants, bars, entertainment. Pools, saunas, gym.

Gateway. *Expensive.* 85 North Quay; (07) 221-0211. Panoramic views; restaurants, bars, pool.

Gazebo Ramada. *Expensive.* 345 Wickham Terrace; (07) 831-6177. Rooftop restaurant; bar; pool and terrace.

Brisbane TraveLodge. *Moderate.* 355 Main St.; (07) 391-5566. ½ mile from city. Restaurant; bar. Pool in garden.

Canberra. *Moderate.* Ann and Edward sts.; (07) 32-0231. In heart of city. Restaurant. Economy units available.

Embassy. *Moderate.* Edward and Elizabeth sts.; (07) 221-7616.

Regal. *Moderate.* 132 Alice St.; (07) 31-1541.

Dorchester. *Inexpensive.* 484 Upper Edward St.; (07) 831-2967.

Marrs Town House. *Inexpensive.* 391 Wickham Terrace; (07) 831-5388.

Tourist. *Inexpensive.* 555 Gregory Terrace; (07) 52-4171.

Self-catering apartments: **Paramount.** *Moderate.* 649 Main St., (07) 391-1109. **Summit Holiday Apts.** *Moderate.* Leichardt and Allenby sts.; (07) 839-7000. **Mariner's Lodge.** *Inexpensive.* 235 Main St., (07) 391-5656. **Spot Holiday Units.** *Inexpensive.* North Quay, (07) 229-4411.

GOLD COAST

Conrad International Hotel and Jupiters Casino. *Deluxe.* Gold Coast Highway, Broadbeach; (075) 50-3722 or any Hilton reservations number. The smartest place to stay on the Gold Coast, and the most expensive. On landscaped gardens, yards from the beach. Variety of restaurants and bars; 3 pools; sauna, gym.

Chevron Paradise. *Expensive.* Ferny Ave., Surfers Paradise, (075) 39-0444. Restaurant, lounge, pool, gym. 1 block from beach.

Chateau Quality Inn. *Expensive.* Esplanade, Surfers Paradise; (075) 38-1022. Overlooking beach. Pool; golf and water sports arranged.

Telford Chateau Royale. *Moderate.* 1 Garrick St., Coolangatta; (075) 36-7111.

Telford Resort. *Expensive.* Ferry Ave., Surfers Paradise; (075) 59-4444.

Greenmount Beach Resort. *Expensive.* Hill St., Coolangatta; (075) 36-1222.

Ambassador Inn. *Moderate.* 2 Elkhorn Ave., Surfers Paradise; (075) 31-6045.

Happy Holiday Inn. *Moderate.* 2 Albert Ave., Broadbeach; (075) 50-1311.

Heron. *Inexpensive.* Gold Coast Highway, Mermaid Beach; (075) 52-6655.

AUSTRALIA

Mayfair. *Inexpensive.* Gold Coast Highway, Surfers Paradise; (075) 39-9699.

Madison. *Inexpensive.* Gold Coast Highway, Surfers Paradise, (075) 31-7324.

Self-catering apartments: **Aloha Apts.** *Expensive.* 8 Trickett St., Surfers Paradise; (075) 38-1922. **Golden Orchid Resort.** *Expensive.* 18 Orchid Ave., Surfers Paradise; (075) 38-6799. **Surfside 6.** *Moderate.* **Esplanade,** Surfers Paradise; (075) 31-7166. **Telford Equinox.** *Moderate.* 3458 Main Beach Parade, Surfers Paradise; (075) 38-3288. **Palmrose Court.** *Inexpensive.* 19 Leonard Ave.; Surfers Paradise, (075) 38-1953.

GREAT KEPPEL ISLAND

Great Keppel Island Resort. *Moderate.* (79) 39-1744. Motel-type units. Dining room and bars. Pools, tennis, water sports.

HERON ISLAND

Heron Island Resort. *Moderate–Expensive.* (79) 78-1488. Dining room, bar, lounge, pool; water sports; glass-bottom boats.

SUNSHINE COAST

Boolarong Motel. *Moderate.* Alexandra Parade, Alexandra Headland; (071) 43-3099.

Caloundra Hotel. *Moderate.* Bullock St., Caloundra; (071) 91-1388. **Surf Air International Hotel.** *Moderate.* David Low Highway, Mooloolaba, (071) 48-7177. Overlooking beach. Restaurants and bars. Pool, gym. Watersports and golf nearby.

Wayamba Motel. *Moderate.* Wirraway St., Maroochydore; (071) 43-3833.

Caloundra Safari Motel. *Inexpensive.* Orsova Terrace, Caloundra; (071) 91-3301.

Dolphine Motel. *Inexpensive.* 6 Cooma St., Caloundra; (071) 91-2511.

Motel Mediterranean. *Inexpensive.* David Low Highway, Mooloolaba; (071) 44-4499.

Newport. *Inexpensive.* Parkyn Parade, Mooloolaba; (071) 44-4445.

Self-catering apartments: **North Wind Holiday Apts.** *Inexpensive.* 125 Esplanade, Mooloolaba; (071) 44-3258. **Los Nidos Apts.** *Inexpensive.* Hastings St., Noosa; (071) 47-3420. **Chantilly Apts.** *Inexpensive.* Hastings St., Noosa; (071) 47-4244. **Mylos Apts.** *Moderate.* Maroubra St., Alexandra Headland; (071) 43-4625.

CAMPING. The Queensland Government Travel Centre staff can tell you where campsites are in southern Queensland.

FARM VACATIONS. The Queensland Government Travel Centre in Brisbane provides up-to-date listings of farms and ranches in the state that accept paying guests.

RESTAURANTS. At finer restaurants in Southern Queensland, you'll pay $A50 or more for dinner with wine for two people *(expensive),* from $A25–$A49 for a *moderate* meal and less than $A25 for an *inexpensive* dinner. Lunch and breakfast are cheaper. Along the Gold Coast, there are zillions of burger stands and fast-food joints, just as you'd expect in a fast-paced resort.

BRISBANE

Ask for the free publication "Dining Out Brisbane" available at most hotels and tourist-information offices. Major credit cards are welcome at most Brisbane restaurants.

QUEENSLAND

Allegro. *Expensive.* Central Station Plaza; 229-5550. Continental cuisine, live music.
Barrier Reef Seafood Restaurant. *Expensive.* 138 Albert St.; 221-9366.
Black Duck. *Expensive.* 80 Jepson St.; 370-2646. Nouvelle Chinese.
Chevaliers. *Expensive.* 55 Railway Terrace; 369-8043. French.
Czars. *Expensive.* 47 Elizabeth St.; 221-3486. Russian.
George and Martha's. *Expensive.* Crest International Hotel; 229-9111. Excellent continental cuisine.
Harrower's. *Expensive.* Park Rd. and Coronation Dr.; 369-0088. French.
Milano. *Expensive.* 78 Queen St.; 229-3917. Italian.
Misho's. 39 Elgin St.; 356-9370. Seafood, lobsters, sand crabs, mud crabs.
Top of the Restaurant. *Expensive.* Gazebo Ramada Hotel, 831-5051.
Alexanders. *Moderate.* Metropolitan Motor Inn; 831-6000. Home-style cooking.
Breakfast Creek. *Moderate.* 1982 Breakfast Creek Rd.; 52-2451. Seafood.
Mrs. Brown's. *Moderate.* Wintergarden Mall; 221-7892. Family restaurant.
Squirrels. *Moderate.* 190 Melbourne St.; 44-4603. Vegetarian.
Cubana. *Inexpensive.* Wallace Bishop Arcade; 31-2906. Coffee shop.
Wild Willy's. *Inexpensive.* Acacia Ridge Hotel; 275-1444, and Loganholme Tavern, 209-8022. Family bistro.

GOLD COAST

The Loft. *Expensive.* 542 Thomas Dr., Chevron Island; 38-1836. French.
Oskar's Garden. *Expensive.* Elkhorn and Orchid, Surfers Paradise; 38-5244. Seafood.
Eliza's. *Expensive.* 19 Cavill Ave., Surfers Paradise; 38-2186. Seafood; live entertainment nightly.
The Carvery. *Moderate.* Trickett St., Surfers Paradise; 59-1299. Steaks.
Golden Dragon. *Moderate.* Boundry and Griffith sts., Coolangatta; 36-3357. Chinese.
Marty's. *Moderate.* Griffith and Warner streets, Coolangatta; 36-4804. Seafood.
Oskar's on the Beach. *Moderate.* Marine Parade, Coolangatta; 36-4621. Seafood.
China Bowl. *Inexpensive.* Gold Coast Hwy., Surfers Paradise; 39-0846. Chinese.
La Marinara. *Inexpensive.* Gold Coast Hwy., Palm Beach; 34-1306. Seafood and spaghetti.

SUNSHINE COAST

Annabelle's. *Expensive.* Hastings St., Noosa, 47-3204. Seafood.
Pierre's. *Expensive.* Noosa International, Noosa, 47-4822. Seafood, continental cuisine.
La Terrasse. *Expensive.* Esplanade, Maroochydore; 43-3924. Steak and seafood.
Barry's on the Beach. *Moderate.* Hastings St., Noosa, 47-3726. Seafood, steaks, burgers.
The Islander. *Moderate.* 18 Bowman Rd., Caloundra; 91-1499. Seafood.
Pelorus Jack's. *Moderate.* Bullock St., Caloundra; 91-4767. Hot and cold dishes; entertainment.
Pioneer Restaurant. *Moderate.* Stewart St., Alexandra Headland; 43-1811. Steaks and seafood.
Rob Reed's. *Moderate.* Parkyn Parade, Mooloolaba; 44-4810. Home cooking; BYO.
The Downtowner. *Inexpensive.* Bullock St., Caloundra, 91-5609. Home cooking.
The Mango Tree. *Inexpensive.* Hastings St., Noosa, 47-3909. Home cooking.
Rogue's. *Inexpensive.* Esplanade, Caloundra; 91-3749. Basic food; BYO.
Roma Pizza. *Inexpensive.* Sunshine Beach, Noosa; 47-3602.

PUBLIC TRANSPORTATION IN BRISBANE. City buses operate all over town. For fares and schedules, visitors may call 225-4444. Ferries operate across the Brisbane River on these routes: West End Terminal–St. Lucia; Edward St.–Kangaroo Point; New Farm Park–Norman Park; Hamilton–Bulimba; Customs House–East Brisbane; Hawthorne–New Farm. Phone 399-4768 for fare and schedule information. Taxis are available at hotels and taxi stands and in a pinch may be hailed off the street.

CAR RENTAL. The following companies have rental offices in Brisbane, on the Gold Coast, and at airports in the region: *Hertz* (07-221-6166), *Budget* (07-52-0151), *Manx Auto Rental* (07-52-7288), *Letz* (07-262-3222), *National* (07-854-1499), and *Avis* (07-52-7111). On the Gold Coast and Sunshine Coast there are many local auto-rental companies that hire cars, minimokes, and campervans; they are all listed in the yellow pages.

TOURIST INFORMATION. *Queensland government travel centers* in Brisbane, Rockhampton, Gold Coast, and Sunshine Coast have pertinent information for tourists to the region and can book most tours throughout Southern Queensland. Brisbane: 196 Adelaide St., phone (07) 31-2211; Rockhampton: 119 East St., phone (079) 27-8611; Gold Coast: Australian Airlines Building, 2nd floor, 30 Cavill Ave., phone (075) 38-5988; Sunshine Coast: Alexandra Parade, Alexandra Headland, phone (071) 43-2411.

TOURS. Queensland government travel centers book the following tours: **From Brisbane.** City shopping and sightseeing tours that last half or a full day; half-day tours to Lone Pine Sanctuary; day tours to the Sunshine Coast, Gold Coast, and Lamington National Park. Cruises on Moreton Bay and on the Brisbane River are also available. Half-day tours cost about $A10; full-day trips cost $A20–$A30.

From the Gold Coast. Half-day tours to Seaworld, Dreamworld, and other attractions along the Gold Coast; evening nightlife tours; full-day tours to Brisbane and the Sunshine Coast; half-day cruises on the canals that run inland from the coast; shopping tours to Brisbane; full-day tours to Lamington National Park.

From the Sunshine Coast. Sightseeing flights and bus tours of the Sunshine Coast that range from a few hours to a full day.

WILDLIFE SANCTUARIES. *African Lion Safari,* Pacific Hwy., Yatala. The big cats—including Australia's only "liger" (a cross between a lion and tiger). *Bunya Park,* 24km north of Brisbane, surrounds an artificial lake. Move freely around a variety of animals, ranging from koalas to kangaroos. Daily 9 A.M.–3 P.M. *Lone Pine Koala Sanctuary,* ½ hr. west of Brisbane. Native Australian animals—including koalas, kangaroos, wombats, emus. See a platypus between 3 and 4 P.M. Open 9:30 A.M.–5 P.M.

SPORTS. All water sports can usually be arranged through your hotel or by inquiring with the local Queensland government travel center. Gold Coast beaches are regularly patrolled by lifeguards. Tennis courts are everywhere in southern Queensland; again inquire at hotels or tourist-information offices. There are gold clubs that welcome guests on the Gold Coast at Southport, Tweed Heads, and Surfers Paradise and on the Sunshine Coast at Caloundra and Maroochydore. In Brisbane, visitors are welcome at the courses in Victoria Park and Long Pocket. The yellow pages of the Brisbane telephone directory list other golf clubs. For tennis information in Brisbane, contact the Queensland Lawn Tennis Association in Sheard Park. The Wednesday edition of the *Brisbane Telegraph* lists fishing clubs that accept visitors, and the Queensland Government Travel Centre can book deep-sea-fishing trips from Brisbane and the Gold and Sunshine coasts.

QUEENSLAND

BUSHWALKING. There are four sources for bushwalking information for the state of Queensland: *Queensland government travel centers* (see above); *Queensland Dept. of Forestry,* 41 George St., Brisbane; *Queensland Federation of Bushwalking,* Box 1537, Brisbane; and the *Brisbane Bushwalking Club,* Box 1949, Brisbane.

MUSEUMS. *Newstead House,* Newstead Park, Breakfast Creek Rd. Oldest preserved home in Queensland. Relics from the early colonial days. Mon.–Thurs., noon–3:30; Sun. 2–5 P.M. Closed Sat.

Queensland Art Gallery, South Bank, South Brisbane. A good collection of Australian art—as well as some international works.

Queensland Museum. Corner Gregory Terrace and Bowen Bridge Rd. Natural history and technological exhibits. Daily to 5 P.M.

Newstead House, Newstead Park, Breakfast Creek Rd. Oldest preserved home in Queensland. Relics from the early colonial days. Mon.–Thurs., noon–3:30; Sun. 2–5 P.M. Closed Sat.

SHOPPING. There are many stores in Brisbane and legions of souvenir stands at the Gold Coast. In Brisbane, *David Jones* and *Myers* are the two main department stores; they are on Queen Street Mall in the center of the business district, along with many other shops. One of the largest selections of Australian opals in Brisbane is found at *Darrell James,* 260 Adelaide St. Most stores and shops in Brisbane accept major credit cards.

NIGHTLIFE. Brisbane is hardly Australia's swingin'est city. Surfers Paradise, on the other hand, may well be. As for the Sunshine Coast, it is quiet in the evenings.

Brisbane. There are piano bars at the *Sheraton Hotel* and the *Crest International Hotel.* Dinner theaters are especially popular in this city. Try *Dirty Dick's,* Judge and Weetman streets (07-369-0555); *Duval's,* George and Margaret streets (07-229-499), or *Maria's,* Hacienda Hotel (07-52-4858). Programs are also listed in Brisbane newspapers, as are movie listings. The *Queensland Ballet* and the *Brisbane Symphony* play at the Queensland Cultural Centre and live theater performances are staged at the Arts Theatre, 210 Petrie Terrace (07-36-2344) and Her Majesty's Theatre, 197 Queen St., (07-221-2777). *This Week in Brisbane* is a publication that lists what's on in the city and it is available free at hotels, tourist-information offices, and stores throughout the city. There's a cabaret at *Leo's Restaurant,* 160 Edward St. (07-221-2307), and on board a boat that cruises the Brisbane River—*Tangalooma Flyer Cabaret Cruise,* phone (07) 48-2666 for reservations. Discos that stay open into the wee hours, usually only Wednesday to Saturday nights, are *General Jackson's,* Crest International Hotel; *Images,* Albert and Turbot sts.; *Sybil's Dome Roon,* 383 Adelaide St.; and *Sybil's Club 25,* same address.

Gold Coast. Surfers Paradise is where the action is at night, and quite a few honkytonks are open late. Floor shows are staged at *Tiki Village,* Cavill Ave.; *Roaring Twenties,* Gold Coast Hwy.; and the *Chevron Paradise Hotel* and the *Broadbeach International Hotel.* Newspapers also list the evening's diversions.

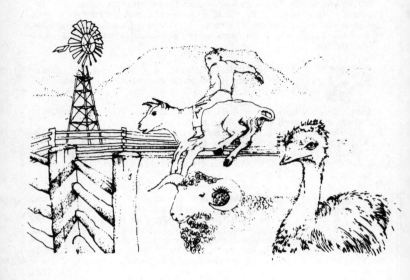

SOUTH AUSTRALIA

by
CHRIS FARRANT

Journalist Chris Farrant writes for a South Australia media magazine and plays lead guitar with the rock band Greenwich.

South Australia is the driest state in the driest continent in the world. Approximately 99 percent of its population lives in the southern half of its 984,200 square kilometers, leaving much of the north of the state as it was 150 years ago, when South Australia was first proclaimed a British colony.

Renowned for its wines, opals, seafoods, festivals, and Formula One Grand Prix, South Australia is a land of contrasting terrain. To the north are the Flinders Ranges, which join the Adelaide Hills and run 800 kilometers to the south coast near Cape Jervis. Although they are the dominant feature of the landscape, the mountain range's highest point barely exceeds 1,000 meters above sea level. Beyond the mountain range is the arid, sparsely settled Outback, ranging to the border of the Northern Territory.

To the south is the Fleurieu Peninsula, running 80 kilometers from Adelaide, and the popular tourist centers of Wirrina, Normanville, and Victor Harbor.

To the southeast, the coastline consists of long, sweeping beaches protecting the tidal Coorong River and merging to ragged cliffs and rocky outcrops. The principal centers of this area are the fishing ports of Robe, Kingston, and Port MacDonnell. Near the Victoria border is Cape Northumberland, the southernmost point of the Australian mainland.

SOUTH AUSTRALIA

Through the east of the state meanders the mighty River Murray. Stemming from tributaries in New South Wales and Victoria, the river travels 2,450 kilometers before entering the sea at Lake Alexandrina, 90 kilometers southeast of Adelaide. Features along the river include the citrus-growing towns of Loxton and Waikerie.

To the west are Yorke and Eyre peninsulas. Much of this area is used for farming, with Port Lincoln at the bottom of Eyre Peninsula home to a tuna-fishing industry. The western beaches of Eyre Peninsula are pounded by spectacular surf up to the breathtaking coastline along the Great Australian Bight. Inland from here is the Nullarbor Plain, a vast, dry expanse stretching over the border into Western Australia.

ADELAIDE: THE CAPITAL

Once known as the City of Churches, Adelaide now has a reputation as the Festival City. Much smaller than its eastern-states counterparts Sydney and Melbourne, Adelaide has a unique layout designed by its first surveyor-general, Colonel William Light.

The city square mile is bordered by four terraces and picturesque parklands. Only five minutes' walk away is the River Torrens, where paddleboats are available for hire to give a closer view of the surrounding gardens and bird life.

The Mount Lofty Ranges provide the backdrop to Adelaide. These hills, only 30 minutes' drive from the city, are ideal for picnics and scenic drives. The legacies of tragic bush fires that swept through this area on Ash Wednesday, 1983, (February 12) can still be seen in the form of blackened trees, although most of the plant life has grown back.

Adelaide is home to one of the most beautiful sports arenas in Australia—Adelaide Oval. Cricket and Australian-rules football are played here. Adelaide also hosts the prestigious Formula One Grand Prix motor race; the circuit here is claimed by some to be the best in the world.

The Adelaide Festival Centre, built overlooking the River Torrens, is the venue for the Adelaide Festival of Arts, a gala event staged every two years (even numbers) in March. Various concerts, plays, and outdoor events are held here all year round.

PRACTICAL INFORMATION FOR ADELAIDE

TELEPHONES. The area code for Adelaide is 08.

HOW TO GET THERE. By air. Domestic Airlines that service Adelaide are: *Ansett Airlines,* 150 North Terrace, Adelaide, 5001; (08) 212–1111; for the airport office, (08) 217–7222. *Australian Airlines;* 144 North Terrace, Adelaide, 5001; (08) 217–3333; airport, (08) 216–1911.

International Airlines: *Air New Zealand.* 144 North Terrace, Adelaide, 5001; (08) 212–3544. *British Airways,* 33 King William Street, Adelaide, 5000; (08) 211–7566. *Qantas,* 14 King William Street, Adelaide, 5000; (08) 218–8541. *Singapore Airlines,* 40 Currie Street, Adelaide, 5000; (08) 212–3656; airport, (08) 352–1555.

By bus. Adelaide is serviced by: *Ansett Briscoes,* 101 Franklin Street, Adelaide, 5001; (08) 212–7344. *Greyhound,* 111 Franklin Street, Adelaide, 5001; (08) 212–1777. *Premier,* 111 Franklin Street, Adelaide, 5001; (08) 212–0777. *STA Roadliner,* 171 Morphett Road, Morphetville; (08) 217–4455.

By car. You can reach Adelaide via good roads from Melbourne, Sydney, Brisbane, Darwin, and Perth.

By train. From Melbourne on the Overland daily; (08) 294–5577.

ACCOMMODATIONS. Price ranges for two people in a double room are: *Deluxe:* $A100 and up; *Expensive:* $A60–$A100; *Moderate:* $A40–$A60; *Inexpensive:* $A40 and under.

Grosvenor. *Deluxe.* 125 North Terrace, Adelaide, 5001; (08) 51–2961. Near city center, opposite casino. Budget rooms also available.

Hilton. *Deluxe.* 233 Victoria Square, Box 1871, Adelaide, 5001; (08) 217–0711. 386 rooms. Florist, jeweler, hairdressing salon, swimming pool, spa, health club, regular cabaret, three restaurants, two bars.

Lakes Resort. *Deluxe* 141 Brebner Drive, West Lakes, 5021; (08) 356–4444. 37 luxury rooms, 5 executive rooms. Swimming pool, spa, restaurant, piano bar, view of lake, close to shopping center.

Adelaide Park Royal. *Expensive.* 226 South Terrace, Adelaide, 5000; (08) 223–4355. 93 rooms, licensed restaurant, cocktail bar, view of parklands.

Gateway Inn. *Expensive.* 147 North Terrace, Adelaide, 5001; (08) 217–7552. 225 rooms, restaurant, piano-cocktail bar.

Arkaba Court. *Moderate.* 232 Glen Osmond Road, Fullarton, 5063; (08) 79–1645. 45 rooms, restaurant, swimming pool, spa, sauna, in-house video.

Earl of Zetland. *Moderate.* 158 Gawler Place, Adelaide, 5001; (08) 223–5500. 30 rooms, downstairs bar, meals available.

Royal Coach. *Moderate.* 24 Dequeteville Terrace, Kent Town, 5067; (08) 42–5676. 42 rooms, dining room, heated swimming pool, sauna, cocktail lounge.

Sands. *Inexpensive.* Swimming pool, restaurant, modern facilities.

RESTAURANTS. Price categories are based on a meal for two with a bottle of wine: *Deluxe:* $A80 and up; *Expensive:* $A60–$A80; *Moderate:* $A40–$A60; *Inexpensive:* $A40 and under.

Ayers House. *Deluxe.* 288 North Terrace, Adelaide; 224–0666. *Henry Ayers,* open: lunch 7 days, dinner Tues.–Sat. French silver service. *Conservatory,* open: Lunch 7 days, Dinner Tues.–Sat. Garden brasserie. All major credit cards.

Drumminor. *Deluxe.* 61 Golden Grove Road, Ridgehaven; 264–1033. Open: Lunch Mon.–Fri., Dinner Mon.–Sat. International menu. Specialties include spaghetti marinara, trout. All major credit cards.

Pavilion on the Park. *Expensive.* Veale Gardens, South Terrace, Adelaide; 212–1991. Open: Lunch Mon.–Fri., Dinner Mon.–Sat. Light French cuisine. All major credit cards.

Swains. *Expensive.* 249 Glen Osmond Road, Frewville; 79–6449. Open: Lunch Mon.–Fri., Dinner Mon.–Sat. Seafood. Specialties: seafood platter. All major credit cards.

Bangkok. *Moderate.* 28 Regent Arcade, Adelaide; 223–5406. Open: Lunch Mon.–Fri., Dinner Mon.–Sat. Authentic Thai cuisine. All major credit cards.

HMS Buffalo. *Moderate.* Adelphi Terrace, Glenelg North; 294–7000. Open: Lunch Sun.–Fri., Dinner 7 days. Seafood. Specialties: buffalo seafood platter. All major credit cards.

Oyster Bed. *Moderate.* 320 North East Road, Klemzig; 261–0911. Open: Lunch Mon.–Fri., Dinner Mon.–Sat. Seafood and steaks. All major credit cards.

St. Paul's. *Moderate.* Pulteney Street, Adelaide; 223–4255. Ground-floor restaurant featuring seafood. A la carte, smorgasbord, and bistro facilities also available. All major credit cards.

Gouger Cafe. *Inexpensive.* 98 Gouger Street, Adelaide; 51–2320. Fish and other seafood.

Paul's Restaurant. *Inexpensive.* 79 Gouger Street, Adelaide; 51–9778. Fish and other seafood.

HOW TO GET AROUND. Adelaide Airport is situated 4 kilometers (2½ mi.) west of the city. Taxis, buses, and public transport are available from domestic and international terminals. Public transport operates along Burbridge Road, which leads east-west along the northern side of the airport. Taxi fare from the airport is approximately $4.

SOUTH AUSTRALIA

By car. There are highways into Adelaide from all four state borders. **Car rentals.** *Avis,* Adelaide Airport, (08) 43–4558; 108 Burbridge Road, Hilton, (08) 354–0444. *Budget,* Adelaide Airport, (08) 352–6199, 274 North Terrace, Adelaide; (08) 223–1400. *Hertz,* Adelaide Airport, (08) 352–6566; 233 Morphett Street, Adelaide, (08) 51–2856. *Ranger,* 274 Anzac Highway, Keswick; (08) 297–5255. *South Australian Hire Cars,* 67 Hewitt Avenue, Toorak Gardens, (08) 31–6794. *Thrifty,* Adelaide Airport, (08) 43–3554; 100 Franklin Street, Adelaide, (08) 211–8788.

By moped. To hire mopeds, contact *Action Moped Hire,* 269 Morphett Street, Adelaide, (08) 211–7060.

Public Transport. Adelaide has a system of buses, trains, and trams. For information on buses and trains, call *South Australian Transport Authority;* they can supply you with timetable and route information; (08) 210–1000.

Adelaide has one tram service, which runs from Victoria Square to popular Glenelg Beach. For timetable information, 210–1000.

By taxi. Contact *Amalgamated,* 223-3333; *Suburban,* 211-8888; *United Yellow,* 223-3111.

TOURIST INFORMATION. *South Australian Government Travel Centre.* 18 King William Street, Adelaide, 5000; (08) 212–1644.

TOURS. Tours are run on full- and half-day bases. The main operators are: *Ansett Pioneer,* 101 Franklin Street, Adelaide, (08) 212–7344. *Australian Sightseeing,* 111 Franklin Street, Adelaide, (08) 211–8522. *Premier,* 111 Franklin Street, Adelaide, (08) 217–0777. *Riviera,* 6–10 Wakeham Street, Adelaide, (08) 223–5022. Also check with South Australian Government Travel Centre for any tours available. (08–212–1644).

ITINERARIES

Torren Gorge and Birdwood. Tours twice per week, full- or half-day. Full-day cost: adult, $23; child, $13. Half-day cost: adult, $14; child, $6.50. Includes the Torrens Gorge in the Adelaide Hills and the toy factory at Gumeracha. Then to Birdwood, where the museum contains a varied collection of Australian inventions and souvenirs. The National Motor Museum has more than 300 vehicles on display (Museum: 68–5006); (Australian Sightseeing).

City by Day. Tours 6 days a week, half day. Cost: adult, $14; child, $6.50. Includes the picturesque streets, reserves, and parks, historic and important buildings, and nearby North Adelaide (Premier).

City by Night. Tours twice per week, 3-hour evening trip. Cost: adult, $13; child, $6. Travels into Adelaide Hills to look down on the city lights at night. (Ansett Pioneer). A similar tour, including dinner at Eagle on the Hill Restaurant, runs once per week. Cost: adult, $26; child, $13 (Riviera).

Parks and Beaches. Tours twice a week for half a day. Cost: adult, $14; child, $5.50. Beginning at Port Adelaide, the tour runs along the metropolitan coast past safe swimming beaches and then to scenic national park (Ansett Pioneer).

GARDENS. Adelaide's parklands, which border the city center, feature well-grassed areas with attractive flower arrangements and native trees and shrubs.

Adelaide Botanic Garden. North Terrace, Adelaide; 228–2311. Open: weekdays from 7 A.M.; weekends and public holidays from 9 A.M. Closing times vary with seasons and weather. The garden features a huge range of native and exotic plants. Visitors can follow paths around the garden and feed the ducks at the lake. Food and drinks are available from the kiosk.

Mount Lofty Botanic Garden. Access via Lampert Road or Mawson Drive. Open: 10 A.M.–4 P.M. daily. As well as the native plants here, the garden features many ornamental species from around the world. Two artificial lakes have been created to assist with the irrigation of the garden. Picnic areas are supplied.

Adelaide Himeji Garden. Corner of South Terrace and Glen Osmond Road, Adelaide. Open: 8 A.M.–4 P.M. daily. Features gardens of Japanese design and style.

ZOOLOGICAL GARDENS. *Adelaide Zoo.* Frome Road, Adelaide; 267-3255. Open: 9:30 A.M.–5 P.M. daily. Cost: adult, $4.50; child, $2.30. Set along the River Torrens, the zoo features walk-through aviaries, a children's zoo, a reptile house, and a vast collection of Australian fauna from all over the world.

SPORTS. Cricket. Australia's premier sport during summer. For spectators, there are the local district competition, the interstate Sheffield Shield matches, and the international test matches. Adelaide Oval, north of the city on King William Street, is the main arena.

Australian-Rules Football. The main winter sport. Matches are played mainly on Sat., the most popular venues being Football Park at West Lakes and Adelaide Oval.

Swimming. Adelaide is fortunate to have 33 kilometers of safe, sandy swimming beaches, stretching from North Haven to Hallet Cove.

Golf. *Belair,* Upper Sturt Road, Belair; 278-7534. Cost: $6, club hire $5. *Patawolonga,* Glenelg North; 356-4811. Cost: $5.50. *North Adelaide,* par 3, War Memorial Drive, North Adelaide; 51-2359. Cost: $3.50, club hire 50 cents per club; 18-hole course, 267-2171. Cost: $6.

MUSEUMS, GALLERIES, AND HISTORIC SITES. South Australian Museum. North Terrace, Adelaide; 223-8911. Open daily. Collection of Australian birds, animals and prehistoric skeltons. Also has an interesting astronomy section and world-famous Aboriginal collection.

Art Gallery of South Australia. North Terrace, Adelaide; 223-7200. Open daily. Features an international collection but concentrates mainly on Australian art.

Aboriginal Arts Shop. 26–30 Currie Street, Adelaide; 212-2171. Open daily. Presents a comprehensive range of traditional and contemporary Aboriginal arts and crafts.

Hahndorf. 35 kilometers from Adelaide by car along the South-Eastern Freeway, which is well sign-posted. This charming town, nestled in the Adelaide Hills, was settled in the 1830s by immigrants of German descent. The traditions and crafts of these people still exist. Copper work, pottery, art, clothes, souvenirs, and food, including fruit and vegetables, cakes, and small goods, are available in the many shops that line the main street. *The German Model Train Display,* at 47 Main Street (388-7953), and the *Beerenberg Strawberry Farm,* just south of Hahndorf along the main road (388-7272) are also highlights here.

SHOPPING. *Rundle Mall.* In the heart of the city, the mall hosts a huge range of department stores, arcades, and specialist shops. Late-night shopping on Fri.

Adelaide Central Market. Victoria Square. The largest produce market in the southern hemisphere. An enormous range of fresh fruit, vegetables, fish, meat, cheese, and small goods available. Open Tues. 7 A.M.–6 P.M., Fri. 7 A.M.–10 P.M., Sat. 7 A.M.–1 P.M.

FOR THE CHILDREN. *Downtown.* 65 Hindley Street, Adelaide; 51-2692. Roller skating, dodgem cars, amusement machines, various games, and sports. Open daily.

Magic Mountain. Colley Reserve, Glenelg; 294-8199. Trading hours vary according to season and weather. Water slide, putt-putt golf, video games and pinball, dodgem cars, various rides.

NIGHTCLUBS AND MUSIC. For the younger crowd, live bands can be seen at many pubs around Adelaide, mainly on Fri. and Sat. nights. Information is available in daily newspapers.

Arkaba. 150 Glen Osmond Road, Fullarton, 79-3614. Disco Fri. and Sat. nights. Age group 18–30.

SOUTH AUSTRALIA

Old Lion. 163 Melbourne Street, North Adelaide; 267-3766. Live bands and discos Thurs., Fri., and Sat. nights. Age group 18-30.

SOUTH AUSTRALIA BEYOND ADELAIDE

The Northern Region

Barossa Valley

The Barossa Valley, 75 kilometers (47 mi.) north of Adelaide, is Australia's wine-producing capital. The area was settled by German immigrants in the early 1800s and maintains much of its 19th-century charm.

The main wineries here are centered around Tanunda, Angaston, and Lyndoch, where the magnificent red and white wines can be sampled and bought. Visitors can also inspect the vineyards and learn about the process of winemaking.

The commercial center of the valley is Nuriootpa. The town was first settled in 1840 by miners traveling north to the Burra copper mines.

Clare

Clare, the other main wine-producing district of the mid-north, is 150 kilometers (93 mi.) from Adelaide. Especially famous for its white wines. Other features include the Martindale Hall and nearby Spring Gully National Park.

Burra

This small town was originally developed around the copper-mining industry. The area abounds in history and artifacts from the 19th century. Fishing enthusiasts can pursue trout in the creeks here.

Flinders Ranges

The ranges are visited every year by thousands of campers and hikers who come to view the native plants and animals and to take up the challenge of conquering the rugged terrain. Crystal-clear streams wind through the mountains along breathtaking gorges and spectacular waterfalls.

The Outback

South Australia's vast Outback consists of wide expanses of desert sands between the small settlements scattered many kilometers apart. The area is hot and dry in the summer, but one good rain can turn arid creek beds and dirt roads into muddy quagmires. Visitors are warned to take care when these conditions prevail and also to carry ample supplies of fuel, food, and water when traveling by car.

Opal Mines

Situated at Coober Pedy and Andamooka, 930 kilometers (578 mi.) from Adelaide. Opals were first discovered here 60 years ago. Coober Pedy is an Aboriginal name meaning "hole in the ground," which is where many of Coober Pedy's townsfolk work and live to escape the searing heat. Visitors can study the mining process or purchase the gems, most of which are sold uncut to overseas buyers.

Lake Eyre

Australia's largest lake is actually a dry salt pan during parts of the year. During the floods of 1973, the lake was 70 kilometers wide and 130 kilometers long, but in 1954 it was so dry that the late Donald Campbell set a land-speed record on it.

The Southern Region

Wine Coast

Only 45 kilometers (28 mi.) from Adelaide is another wine-growing region. Around McLaren Vale and Clarendon are dozens of vineyards and wineries set against the picturesque Adelaide Hills with a view of St. Vincent Gulf. The wineries are close enough together for an afternoon tour to take in most of them. Apart from sales and tasting, lunches are also served by some. Visitors can also pass through the almond-growing district of Willunga.

Fleurieu Peninsula

The lower region of the peninsula is a big drawing card for fishers and bushwalkers. Normanville and Second Valley are popular visiting spots, with fishing at its best at Rapid Bay Jetty and Cape Jervis. Tommy ruffs, garfish, and squid are the main catches.

Victor Harbor

This town is probably South Australia's most popular tourist center. Set in a protected bay surrounded by small islands, Victor Harbor has many attractions. The city center comprises a busy main street with numerous shopping facilities.

Visitors can stroll around Granite Island, which is linked to the mainland by a causeway. Kangaroos roam free on the island, and chairlift rides and food-and-drink facilities are available. Fishers often frequent the Screwpile Jetty and breakwater where garfish, salmon, trout, and the occasional large mulloway can be caught.

To the southern end of the bay is the Bluff, a steep hill that slopes to the pounding surf below. A rigorous climb to the top of the Bluff gives a spectacular view of the surrounding coastline and township.

Ten kilometers farther south are the surf beaches at Waitpinga and Parsons. Hardy fishers work the beach during winter in search of salmon. Swimming here is not advised.

SOUTH AUSTRALIA

Murray Mouth

The mouth of the River Murray, situated in Encounter Bay at the junction of Lake Alexandrina and the Coorong, is another popular fishing and camping spot. The area offers both surf and estuary fishing but is accessible only by four-wheel-drive vehicles. Those less adventurous can try their hand at boating and water skiing on Lakes Alexandrina and Albert.

Kangaroo Island

The island is situated across Backstairs Passage from Cape Jervis. It is the third largest island in Australia and its 451 kilometers of coastline offer both protected beaches and rugged cliffs with a national park at the western end of the island. Popular tourist spots include American River, the stalactite and stalagmite caves at Kelly Hill, Admiral's Arch, Dudley Peninsula, and the seals at Seal Bay.

The Southeast Region

From the Murray mouth runs the Coorong, a saltwater estuary that hugs the coastline for 120 kilometers. The Coorong attracts both professional and amateur fishers and is home to many species of bird and animal life. Between the Coorong and the sea is a long, sweeping beach inaccessible to conventional vehicles.

Kingston and Robe

From Kingston, 300 kilometers (186 mi.) from Adelaide, the coastline becomes rockier and the sea rougher. The cliffs and outcrops are broken up by the occasional beach or sheltered bay. Kingston and Robe are the principal towns of this area and host busy crayfishing industries, supplying the delicacy to much of the state. At Kingston is the giant human-made lobster in front of the restaurant where the local wares can be bought to take home or for a sit-down meal.

Mount Gambier

The last major town before crossing the Victorian border is Mount Gambier, 470 kilometers (292 mi.) from Adelaide. This district hosts Australia's largest commercial pine forests and the Blue Lake, situated in the mount itself. The mount is actually an extinct volcano with a lake inside the cone. The lake mysteriously changes color from gray to brilliant blue each year around the end of November, changing back in June.

Other highlights of the southeast include the wines and cheeses of Coonawarra and the caves at Naracoorte.

The Eastern Region

The main geographical feature of the east of South Australia is the River Murray. The mighty waterway winds its way toward the coast through varying terrain and is home to several towns along the way, many of them depending on the river for their livelihood.

All parts of the river are popular with water skiers, boating enthusiasts, and fishers. Boat-launching facilities are available in most towns. Fish found in the Murray include scallop, redfin, bony bream, catfish, perch, the rare Murray cod, and the noxious European carp, which exists in plague proportions in the river but is extremely poor eating. For shore and boat fishers, the best baits are tiger worms, which can be bought from fishing shops or dug from moist soil, and shrimps, which can be scooped from reeds along the river in a small net. The best spots to fish are deep holes or near the bank where there are reeds and overhanging trees. Yabbies and freshwater crayfish can also be caught from the river.

Renmark

This is the first major town the river passes through as it enters South Australia. Renmark is 260 kilometers (162 mi.) from Adelaide and is the center of the state's largest irrigation area. Oranges and grapes are grown here, and the town has its own winery and distillery. Renmark is the most important source of grapes for the Australian brandy industry. With the addition of fruit canning and juice processing, Renmark is the produce capital of the River Murray.

Orange Towns

Loxton and Berri, 250 kilometers (155 mi.) from Adelaide, and Waikerie, 200 kilometers (124 miles) from Adelaide, are the main producers of oranges in the riverland. Local wares can be bought in all towns, and the huge playground at Monash is worth a visit.

Murray Bridge

A popular spot for water skiers, the town is centered around the two bridges that span the river. Flood levels from the 1950s are marked on the railway bridge showing the incredible heights to which the water rose. Spacious camping grounds and holiday shacks line the river next to the wharf where cruise steamers dock. Only an hour's drive from the city, Murray Bridge and surrounds can be visited and explored comfortably in a day trip.

The Western Region

To the west of Adelaide are St. Vincent and Spencer Gulfs, which wash the shores of Yorke and Eyre peninsulas. Beyond is the spectacular but isolated coastline that leads to the border of Western Australia.

SOUTH AUSTRALIA

Yorke Peninsula

Much of the state's rural farming area is situated on the peninsulas. The flat inland plains are suited to crop growing, with wheat and barley being some of the main produce.

The coastline of Yorke Peninsula is varied. At the top are calm beaches and expansive sand flats. Past Port Vincent and Stansbury, the beaches are segmented by cliffs and continue around the foot of the peninsula to the western side, which is more exposed to the elements. Pondalowie Bay and Corny Point are noted surfing spots, and Port Giles, Edithburgh, Brown's Beach, and Wallaroo are popular with fishers.

Eyre Peninsula

The geography of Eyre Peninsula is very similar to that of Yorke Peninsula, but Eyre is more sparsely settled. The principal towns are Whyalla and Port Lincoln, where the fishing industry thrives.

The western side of the peninsula is pounded by the waters of the Great Australian Bight. The beaches here provide exciting surfing that is often dangerous, not only because of the rough conditions, but also because of sharks.

The Far West Region

Ceduna, 780 kilometers (485 mi.) from Adelaide, is the last major town in South Australia along the Eyre Highway, yet is still 480 kilometers (298 mi.) from the Western Australian border. It has been the scene for captures of huge white pointer sharks, the most memorable weighing in at 1,179 kilograms (2,596 lb.).

Beyond Ceduna is the Nullarbor Plain. As the highway approaches the coast near the border, the magnificent coastline can be seen as the flat plain plunges straight down to the surf below.

PRACTICAL INFORMATION FOR SOUTH AUSTRALIA BEYOND ADELAIDE

HOW TO GET THERE AND HOW TO GET AROUND. See also Practical Information for Adelaide. Most areas of South Australia are accessible by paved roads. For all long trips, especially in the north and far west, supplies, water, and spare parts (such as radiator hoses, spare tires, etc.) should be taken. Speed limits in South Australia are—60km per hour (37 mph) in built-up areas and 110km per hour (68 mph) on the open road in country areas. A limit of 80km per hour (50 mph) applies when entering and leaving most country towns. All speed limits are clearly sign-posted.

By air. *Eyre Charter.* 66 Bruce Terrace, Cummins, 5631; (086) 86–2062. *Kendell.* 43 Thompson Street, Wagga Wagga, New South Wales, 2650; (069) 21–2131. (This airline runs services in South Australia.) *Lloyd Aviation.* Adelaide Airport; (08) 352–6944. *Opal Air.* 150 North Terrace, Adelaide, 5001; (08) 217–7222; Adelaide Airport, (08) 352–3337.

AUSTRALIA

ACCOMMODATIONS. Rates are generally less expensive than in Adelaide. For a double room, *Expensive*, $A60–$A100; *Moderate*, $A40–$A60; *Inexpensive*, $A40 and under.

NORTH

Barossa Motel. *Moderate.* Murray Street, Tanunda, 5352; (085) 63–2988. Air conditioning, swimming pool, laundry, licensed restaurant.

Tanunda Hotel. *Moderate.* 51 Murray Street, Tanunda, 5352; (085) 63–2030. Air conditioning, meals available, bar.

Vineyards Motel. *Moderate.* Stockwell Road, Angaston, 5353; (08) 64–2404. 20 units, modern facilities.

Christison Park Caravan Park. *Inexpensive.* Main North Road, Clare, 5453; (08) 42–2724. 8 on-site vans, kiosk, telephone, barbecue.

FAR NORTH

Mill Motel. *Moderate.* 2 Railway Terrace, Quorn, 5432; Quorn 48–6016. All modern facilities.

Opal Motel. *Moderate.* Coober Pedy; (086) 72–5054. Self-contained units, air conditioning, restaurant.

Outback Motel. *Moderate.* Wilpena Road, Hawker, 5434; Hawker 111. Air conditioning, hire cars, modern facilities.

Melrose Caravan Park. *Inexpensive.* Box 80, Melrose, 5483; (086) 66–2060. 4 on-site vans, barbecue, tennis courts.

SOUTH

Cavalier Inn. *Moderate.* 7 the Strand, Port Elliot, 5212; (085) 54–2067. Licensed restaurant, swimming pool.

Goolwa Holiday Estates. *Moderate.* Collingwood Street, Goolwa, 5214; (085) 55–2824. Modern facilities.

Goolwa Lakeside Tourist Resort. *Moderate.* Noble Avenue, Goolwa, 5214; (085) 55–2737. Units and caravan park. 12 units, 6 on-site vans, swimming pool, boat ramp, barbecue, telephones.

Wintersun Motel. *Moderate.* Hindmarsh Road, Victor Harbor, 5211; (085) 52–3533. All modern facilities.

Crown Hotel. *Inexpensive.* 2 Ocean Street, Victor Harbor, 5211; (085) 52–1022.

Second Valley Caravan Park. *Inexpensive.* 2 Park Street, Second Valley, 5204; (085) 59–4054. 2 on-site vans, kiosk, barbecue, telephone.

KANGAROO ISLAND

Island Tourist Lodge. *Moderate.* Telegraph Road, Kingscote, 5223; (0848) 2–2100. Air conditioning, swimming pool, games room, licensed restaurant.

Ozone Motel Hotel. *Moderate.* Commercial Street, Kingscote, 5223; (0848) 2–2011. Air conditioning, swimming pool, modern facilities.

Penneshaw Caravan Park. *Inexpensive.* 18 Falinga Terrace, Penneshaw, 5222; (0848) 3–1075. 4 on-site vans, boat ramp, barbecue, telephone.

SOUTHEAST

Guichen Bay Motel. *Moderate.* Victoria Street, Robe, 5276; (087) 68–2001. 16 units, playground, licensed restaurant.

Motel East Lynn. *Moderate.* 44 North Terrace, Mount Gambier, 5290; (087) 25–2354. Modern facilities.

Motel Mount Gambier. *Moderate.* 115 Penola Road, Mount Gambier, 5290; (087) 25–5800. 33 units, air conditioning, modern facilities.

Kingston Caravan Park. *Inexpensive.* Marine Parade, Kingston, 5275; (087) 67–2050. 11 on-site vans, kiosk, barbecue, tennis courts, telephone.

Longbeach Tourist Park. *Inexpensive.* The Esplanade, Robe, 5276; (087) 68–2237. 10 on-site vans, kiosk, barbecue.

SOUTH AUSTRALIA

Southern Ocean Caravan Park. *Inexpensive.* Foster Street, Beachport, 5280; (087) 35-8153. 6 on-site vans, kiosk, barbecue.

EAST

Barmera Hotel. *Expensive-Moderate.* Barwell Avenue, Barmera, 5345; (085) 88-2111. Luxury and budget units, swimming pool, licensed restaurant, view of Lake Bonney.
Berri Hotel-Motel. *Moderate.* Riverview Drive, Berri, 5343; (085) 82-1411. Modern facilities.
Fountain Motel. *Moderate.* Renmark Avenue, Renmark, 5341; (085) 86-6899. Air conditioning, swimming pool, restaurant.
Loxton Hotel-Motel. *Moderate.* East Terrace, Loxton, 5333; (085) 84-7266. Close to river. Modern facilities.
Berri War Memorial Riverside Caravan Park. *Inexpensive.* Riverside Avenue, Berri, 5343; (085) 82-1718. 18 on-site vans, boat ramp, barbecue, kiosk, telephone.
Commercial Hotel. *Inexpensive.* Railway Terrace, Morgan, 5320; (085) 40-2107. Modern facilities.
Lake Bonney Caravan Reserve. *Inexpensive.* Barmera, South Australia, 5345; (085) 88-2234. 18 on-site vans, boat ramp, barbecue, bike hire, tennis courts, telephone.
Princess Highway Caravan Park. *Inexpensive.* 313 Princess Highway, Murray Bridge, 5253; (085) 32-2860. 10 on-site vans, swimming pool, kiosk, barbecue.
Riverfront Caravan Park. *Inexpensive.* Habels Bend, Loxton, 5333; (085) 84-7862. 6 on-site vans, boat ramp, kiosk, barbecue, telephone.

WEST

Ardrossan Hotel-Motel. *Moderate.* 36 First Street, Ardrossan, 5571; (088) 37-3008. Modern facilities.
Edithburgh Motel Holiday Flats. *Moderate.* Henry Street, Edithburgh, 5583; (088) 52-6162. Near coast. Kiosk, modern facilities.
Esquire Motor Inn. *Moderate.* 27 Lydia Terrace, Wallaroo, 5556; (088) 23-2303. 37 units, licensed restaurant and bar, view of ocean.
Patio Motel. *Moderate.* 196 Bay Road, Moonta Bay, 5558; (088) 25-2473. Licensed restaurant, air conditioning, modern facilities.
Sea Breeze Hotel. *Moderate.* Tumby Terrace, Tumby Bay, 5605; (086) 88-2362. Modern facilities.
Stansbury Holiday Motel. *Moderate.* Adelaide Road, Stansbury, 5582; (088) 52-4147. Near coast, modern facilities, wagons for hire.
Ardrossan Caravan Park. *Inexpensive.* Park Terrace, Ardrossan, 5571; (088) 37-3262. 5 on-site vans, kiosk, boat ramp, telephone.
Kirton Point Caravan Park. *Inexpensive.* Hindmarsh Street, Port Lincoln, 5606; (086) 82-2537. 8 on-site vans, 10 cabins, boat ramp, kiosk, barbecue, telephone.
Port Vincent Caravan Park. *Inexpensive.* Box 113, Port Vincent, 5581; (088) 53-7073. 4 on-site vans, boat ramp, barbecue, telephone.
Streaky Bay Caravan Park. *Inexpensive.* Streaky Bay, 5680; (086) 76-1126. 9 on-site vans, 6 cabins, kiosk, barbecue, telephone.

TOURS. Major operators for the following tours are: *Ansett Pioneer,* 101 Franklin Street, Adelaide, 5001; (08) 212-7344. *Riviera,* 6-10 Wakeham Street, Adelaide, 5000; (08) 223-5022. Check with South Australian Government Travel Centre for any other tours available and where bookings can be made; (08) 212-1644.

ITINERARIES

Clare Valley. Once per week, full day. Cost: adult, $28; child, $14. Visits the wine region, Martindale Hall, which was featured in the film *Picnic at Hanging Rock,* and the historic town of Mintaro (Riviera).

Barossa Valley. Once per week, full day. Cost: adult, $25; child, $12. Tours the principal towns of the valley, stopping at wineries and returning through Torrens Gorge (Riviera).

Barossa Valley Champagne Flights. Half-day. Cost: $160 per person. Morning and afternoon flights available, weather permitting. Hot-air balloon trips over the wine region, with champagne supplied afterward. (Balloon Adventures, Box 382, Tanunda, 5352; (08-24-4383). Flinders Ranges Camel Treks. One-day tour (April to November). Cost: $40 (includes lunch). Follows Moralana Creek across the plains into the ranges and then to Wilpena Pound. 4-day tour. Cost: $325. Explores the Wilpena Pound Range and the more inaccessable areas. 7-day tour. Cost: $595. Follows Moralana Creek to Lake Torrens, then through sandy plains into the ranges. (Transcontinental Safaris, The Ravine Wildlife Park, PMB 251, Kingscote, Kangaroo Island, 5223; 0848-9-3256.) Bookings can be made through the South Australian Government Travel Centre, tel. 08-212-1644.

Trekabout Safaris. Several tours lasting from 4 to 16 days. Costs from $252 to $1,320. Tours are four-wheel-drive safaris that visit places including Flinders Ranges, Andamooka and Wilpena Pound. (Trekabout Safaris, 30 Berryman Drive, Modbury, 5092; tel. 08-264-3770.

Victor Harbor/South Coast. Once per week, full day. Cost: adult, $19; child, $5. Follows the south coast to Victor Harbor and visits Granite Island, the Bluff, and the Southern Vales (Ansett Pioneer).

Goolwa and Murray Mouth. Once per week, full day. Cost: adult, $36; child, $18. Tours through the Mount Lofty Ranges to Goolwa and Lake Alexandrina. Includes lunch on a cruiser (Ansett Pioneer).

Murray Mouth Bus Tours. Various tours run throughout the week. Prices vary seasonally. Four-wheel-drive bus tours the beach and surroundings. Evening fishing trips are available. Tel. (085) 55-2355.

Murray River. Once per week, full day. Cost: adult, $33; child, $15. Tours through Hahndorf and Adelaide Hills to Mannum, then luncheon cruise on the Murray River (Ansett Pioneer).

CAMPING HIRE. *Adelaide Party and Camping Hire.* 46 Glynburn Road, Hectorville, (08) 336-2466, or 1491 South Road, Darlington, (08) 298-6311. Boats, canoes, roof racks, water skis, life jackets available for hire. *SA Camping Hire.* 64 Maple Avenue, Forestville, (08) 297-8003. Tents, stoves, camping accessories available for hire.

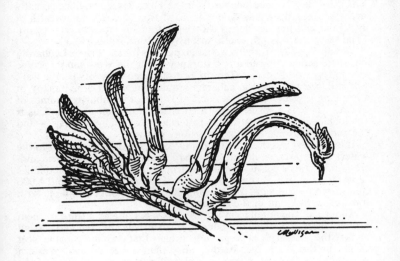

WESTERN AUSTRALIA

Home of "the Most Fortunate People"

When English seafaring buccaneer William Dampier stumbled across the far western edges of the Australian continent he described the inhabitants he found there as "the miserablest people in the world." He informed the British government that the land seemed unsuitable for agriculture; it was barren and useless so far as this seventeenth century navigator was concerned.

Dampier's comments provoke a good-natured smile from today's inhabitants of Western Australia, for they consider themselves the most fortunate people of all who live on this vast continent.

It was with good reason that Western Australia was officially called "the State of Excitement."

A State on the Move

It is here, in a region about the size of western Europe and accounting for a third of the entire country, that many of Australia's greatest developments are taking place. Within its million square miles lies one of the world's richest storehouses of mineral wealth—deposits of iron, bauxite, nickel, natural gas, oil, and gold. It has vast wheatlands, abundant forests, and seas rich with all manner of fish as well as even more oil and gas.

It has a pleasant, equable climate and its capital, Perth, has more sunny hours, even temperatures, and clear days than any other Australian city. It is closer to Asia than to the rest of the nation, and its inhabitants set themselves apart from much that the rest of Australia thinks and does, seeing secession as a real and feasible possibility.

One rich and free-thinking grazier has, in fact, already done just that. The self-titled "Prince Leonard" of the Hutt River Province actually declared his property as having seceded from the Commonwealth of Australia and has developed a thriving tourism industry as a result. (The secession was not taken seriously by authorities.)

Not all West Australians would go quite as far as "Prince Leonard"; but there is definitely an air of vibrancy about the West and its people that is less readily detected in the rest of the country. Its people walk tall and *are* tall. (Exotic cabarets around the world derive many of their long-legged chorus boys and girls from the suburban homes of Perth.) There is a spring in the step of the rush-hour crowds. This is the luckiest state in what has been termed "the lucky country"—and the people who live there know it only too well.

It looks west out over the Indian Ocean toward Africa, south to the waters of Antarctica, northeast toward India and southeast Asia and, from its northern coast, is separated from Indonesia by only 300 miles of water. It measures some 2,000 miles from north to south and 1,000 miles from east to west. Yet its inhabitants total about a million, with most of them living in the southwest.

About half the population is under 24 years of age; a third of them are teenagers. They marry young and have their children early. It all adds to the general air of go-go youthfulness that is an inescapable facet of life in the West. Yet hardly more than a decade ago, Western Australia was a quiet, sleepy and almost neglected backwater of the country. It took a mineral boom, a vast inflow of capital to foster the boom, and an inrush of migrants to transform the state into its present exciting condition.

Iron Ore and Wildflowers

Lying beneath the stark ochre-red rocks of the Hamersley Ranges is enough high-grade iron ore to meet all the world's needs for many years to come. Some of the ore is so rich in mineral content that it is possible to weld two pieces together prior to any refining process.

Mountains are being moved—and new ones created—by mechanical shovels that can shift up to 24,000 tons of ore a day. A visitor to the huge mining projects of the Hamersley region moves in a world of Goliaths, dwarfed by giant machines and the vast landscape. New towns, ports and railways have sprung up to provide the support services for the mining projects. Places once remote and inaccessible have come within reach of all.

In the far north, on the border with the Northern Territory, is the far-sighted Ord River irrigation scheme designed to change grazing lands into fertile crop-growing country. From this has come the creation of a 286-square-mile reservoir containing nine times the amount of water of Sydney's impressive harbor. Old homesteads of early settlers now lie beneath the waters of Lake Argyle, which has become a holiday center for anyone wanting to see the grandeur and fauna of the tropical north.

But not everything is modern, mechanized development, extracting ton after ton from the earth. Pearling luggers still set out from the coast that once drew divers from all over the East to make Broome one of the busiest ports along the entire Western Australia coast. Until 1978, whalers set out from Albany on a strictly controlled search for the great sperm whales of the southern oceans. Now whaling has stopped, but the station remains as a tourist attraction. The sea also provides good living for exporters of tuna and crayfish tails.

Once a year, much of the state bursts into color as the wildflowers bloom. Areas north and south of Perth bring coachloads of sightseers to see the brilliant kaleidoscope that covers the ground from Geraldton to Albany. From August through November is the time to go.

The true traveler who wants to see Western Australia in its entirety will probably enter the state in the northeast on the route out of Darwin, tour right down the coastline (with an occasional detour inland), stop awhile in Perth, and then continue on around the southwest and across the Nullarbor Plain into South Australia. For some of the year, such a journey would be impractical. Western Australia has a wet season and a dry season in its more northerly regions. And when it's wet, it really is just that. Monsoonal rains teem down and roads can become impassable. Total annual rainfall is generally less than received in Perth, but it tends to come all at once with the summer months (November through February), when the humidity is high and travel by road is not recommended.

THE PERTH AREA

When the first manned spacecraft was orbiting the earth, it was the middle of the night as the crew tracked across Australia. As they passed over Perth, the city turned on all its lights. It was then that the spacemen knew that, far below, there were people thinking of them.

Such a gesture is typical of the gregarious, expansive people who live in Perth. Maybe it is the isolation, maybe the feeling of space; but whatever the reason, the Sandgropers—as they are jibingly called by other Australians—tend to be the most open, relaxed and easy going of all Australians. One could also attribute to the equable climate and clear air the tendency of West Australians to be bigger, taller, and bonier than their fellows in other parts of the country.

Geography, terrain, and climate have set Perthians aside from the rest of Australia. The city they live in is unique for its isolation: a million people living on the fringe of a continent, 1,750 miles from their nearest city neighbor (Adelaide) and staring across an ocean where the next landfall (Mauritius) is 3,600 miles away.

The city hugs the banks of the Swan River, climbs a hill to the beautiful King's Park, and closes off some of its city streets so that pedestrians can stroll unhindered by a vehicular population that rivals Los Angeles for the world's highest per capita level of car ownership.

A Mellow, Sun-Blessed City

Although often referred to as a planned city, Perth has none of the sterile orderliness of other places, notably Canberra, that come into this category. Its early designers set about blending the city with the benefits already bestowed by nature. The site was originally selected by Captain James Stirling in 1827 on orders from the same Governor Darling who had also ordered the setting up of a military post farther down the coast at Albany. Early British government reluctance to assist in the creation of another settlement was overcome when Thomas Peel formed a group willing to underwrite the migration of 10,000 people. Stirling named the city after the Scottish birthplace of the then secretary of state for war and the colonies, Sir George Murray. Thomas Peel proved to be a poor organizer and could not even create work for the 300 emigrants he brought out from England in 1829. Growth was slow. It took the gold rush of 1892 to spark progress. Suddenly the pace quickened, a port was established at Fremantle, and the coming of the railway from the other side of the continent in 1915 put the final seal

AUSTRALIA

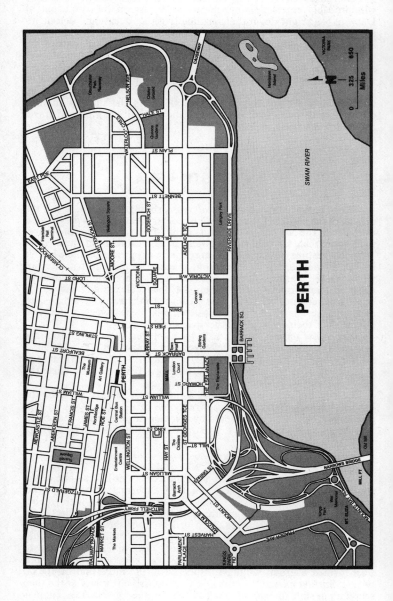

WESTERN AUSTRALIA

on the establishment of modern-day Perth. It is now a mellow, sun-blessed city, spacious, green, and floral. Its crowning glory is the King's Park, a thousand acres of mostly natural bushland spreading out over a hill looking down into the city's business and commercial heart. Few would argue with the claim by Perth citizens that this is the best city parkland in Australia. For this, they thank Governor Sir Frederick Weld, who first proposed preservation of the area as far back as 1871.

The city's oldest surviving building is the old courthouse in Stirling Gardens. The Old Mill in South Perth was built a year earlier (1835) and has undergone restoration work to take it back to its original appearance. Inside are relics from pioneer days. Convict labor was used to build the Town Hall in the style of an English Jacobean marketplace. It stands on the corner of two of the city's main streets, Hay and Barrack. Further reminders of England are to be found on a walk along London Court, a Tudor-style shopping arcade linking Hay Street Mall with St. George's Terrace.

Tour, 82 miles north of Perth to New Norcia. Here, the Benedictine order of monks still runs a mission first set up in 1846 to help aborigines. At one stage in its history the monastery was separated from the Perth diocese and became responsible directly to the Vatican. Later it gained status as a diocese in its own right. Now it is a self-supporting property, farming some 20,000 acres.

South of Perth are coastal resorts that provide good surfing, swimming, and fishing. Rockingham is 28 miles away, and Mandurah involves a 50-mile drive. Twenty-five miles to the northeast and set among hills is Mundaring Weir, and at Yanchep (32 miles north from Perth) there is a pleasant holiday and picnic complex complete with native fauna and limestone caves.

Fremantle

On the world map, with the staging of the America's Cup yachting challenge, Fremantle, 19km from Perth, is the chief port of WA and has made giant strides in building and restoring many of the historic buildings. It won a Pacific Area Travel Association award two years ago as an example of excellence in preservation and style. It can be reached by road via Canning Highway or Stirling Highway, with frequent MTT bus services traveling through suburbs en route. Passenger rail services travel from Perth to Fremantle on a line that was closed by one government and opened by the next. Tour operators often include Fremantle on their itineraries.

Victoria Quay is Australia's most modern passenger-shipping terminal, built when passenger ships came through here. Now Fremantle is lucky to see one overseas liner in six months, and the terminal has found other, varied uses. The port is a small cargo handler but has a good reputation for cleanliness.

Fishing Boat Harbour, seaside of Esplanade, is the anchorage for fishing fleets (numbers range up to 500), which include a Japanese tuna fleet fishing far south. Success Yacht Harbour, a marina off Marine Tce., South Fremantle, is headquarters for the Fremantle Sailing Club; it has a safe, locally quarried limestone breakwater for 500 sail and power boats. There's an impressive clubhouse. It is home to the fleet in the Plymouth-to-Fremantle Parmelia Yacht Race, and start and finish of annual Fremantle-to-Bali (Indonesia) and Fremantle-to-Albany yacht races. A spectacular new yachting complex has been built as home base for the world's best 12-meter yachts readying themselves for the America's Cup challenge.

There are numerous special events. Each October the fishing fleet is blessed and a statue of the madonna paraded from St. Patrick's on

Adelaide St. down to Fishing Boat Harbour, where beflagged boats await the start of fishing season. Fremantle Week celebrates the sporting and cultural life of the area; it ends with monster fireworks display on the Oval (fireworks are banned in WA except for such events). Foundation Day, the first Monday in June, is marked with a ceremony at the spot that Captain Fremantle planted the Union Jack in 1829.

The area is noted for old buildings of three periods: pre-convict (1829–1850): a 12-sided "round house" was designed as a prison and completed 1831. It's at the top of High St., near the beach, and open most days. Colonial Georgian Period (1850–1869): convict-built Fremantle Gaol still operates as a prison. Of interest is the fine stone work and arched main gateway with clock. Warder's Quarters are stone cottages on Henderson St., still used by warders. The Old Customs House, Cliff St., was built of local limestone, about 1852. Late Victorian Period: St. John's Church and Square is considered the "true heart of Fremantle"; the flagstones came to WA as a ship's ballast. Town Hall, corner William and Adelaide sts., was opened as part of Queen Victoria's Jubilee.

Fremantle has a very active art and cultural scene, with numerous galleries and art centers. There are also modern museums in this "living museum" of a port, one up to the minute because of the America's Cup fever. Noted sailor Rolly Tasker, sailmaker, has the America's Cup Museum, with a complete set of models of the yachts that competed for the cup from 1851 to 1983.

If you get tired of walking around you can catch a tram—once the transport system of Perth and Fremantle. The Fremantle Tram operates tours in and around Fremantle from the City Tram Stop, corner Queen and Adelaide sts. If the children want a break (and you do, too) Timothy's Toys, Croke Lane, has hand-made wooden toys manufactured on the premises.

Rottnest Island

Only 20km off the coast from Perth and Fremantle is Rottnest Island, which attracts thousands of locals annually. The island was first found about 300 years ago, and many want it to stay just the way it was then. Commodore Vlamingh noticed it in 1696 as he sailed past what is now Perth and Fremantle. The name is derived from Rat's Nest. The sailor thought the odd marsupial quokkas were rats, but these quaint creatures are protected today on the island, which is a sanctuary. The hotel built in 1864 was the summer home of the governors of WA and is often referred to as the Quokka Arms—or other endearing terms linked with beer drinking and loud fun. No cars (other than those on council business) are permitted, and locomotion is by bicycle or foot power. Special buses tour the island, and you can hire boats, swim in many a secluded cove, or just relax. The Rottnest Island Board, (09) 292–5044, runs the place and rents out more than 250 villas and cottages for four, six, or eight people. They are like gold in school holiday periods but are strictly leased and policed. Good savings can be had in off-season times (May to August). You can fly there very cheaply or take a ferry—the recommended way to get into the holiday mood. Ferries sail daily from Barrack St. jetty, Perth, calling at Fremantle jetty on the way.

PRACTICAL INFORMATION FOR THE PERTH AREA

HOW TO GET THERE AND HOW TO GET AROUND. See Practical Information for Western Australia beyond Perth. Local **buses** and **trains** can take you between Perth and Fremantle. For information contact the MTT office, St. George's Tce., Perth; 325–8511.

The historic **Fremantle tram** will take you around town; call 328–4542 or *Holiday WA* (see Tours).

Ferries will take you from Perth and Fremantle to Rottnest Island. It costs $26 round-trip for adults from Perth; call 325–6033 in Perth or 335–7181 in Fremantle.

ACCOMMODATIONS. Luxury hotels began popping up like mushrooms in Perth from 1985 onward, and the city of just over a million people has more five-star properties than any other in Australia. With the casino hotels due to open in 1986, the city will have a huge supply of deluxe and top quality rooms—something that worries those who feel there has been huge overbuilding in the euphoria of winning the America's Cup yachting classic. But it does give the most remote city in Australia a huge choice, and visitors could not be disappointed with standards and service. As a guide the rates are, for a single room, *deluxe* $A90-plus, *expensive* $A80–$A100, *moderate* $A50-plus, *inexpensive* under $A50. Most top hotels feature tea and coffee-making facilities, refrigerator, and color TVs.

Ansett International Hotel. *Deluxe.* 10 Irwin St., WA 6000; (09) 325–0481. Central location.

Merlin. *Deluxe.* Corner Plain St., Adelaide Tce., WA 6000; (09) 323–0121. Among Australia's top hotels; 20 minutes to city center walking, overlooking Swan River.

The Orchard. *Deluxe.* 707 Wellington St., WA 6000; (09) 327–7000. Central. Wide range of gourmet food.

Parmelia Hilton. *Deluxe.* Mill St., WA 6000; (09) 322–3622. Central.

Sheraton Perth. *Deluxe.* 207 Adelaide Tce., WA 6000; (09) 325–0501. Pleasant 10-minute walk to city center. Overlooking Swan River.

Chateau Commodore. *Expensive.* 417 Hay St., WA 6000; (09) 325–0461. Central.

Kings Ambassador Hotel. *Expensive.* 517 Hay St.; (09) 325–6555. Central.

Perth Ambassador Hotel. *Expensive.* 196 Adelaide Tce., WA 6000; (09) 325–1455. Central.

Perth Park Royal. *Expensive.* 54 Terrace Rd., WA 6000; (09) 325–3811.

Riverside Lodge. *Moderate.* 150 Mounts Bay Rd., WA 6000; (09) 321–4721. Delightful setting, pleasant walk to city center.

Town House. *Moderate.* 778 Hay St., WA 6000; (09) 321–9141. Central.

Adelphi. *Inexpensive.* 130 Mounts Bay Rd., WA 6000; (09) 322–4666. Budget accommodation.

Airways Hotel. *Inexpensive.* 195 Adelaide Tce., WA 6000; (09) 323–7799. Restaurant; parking; near Sheraton.

CAMPING. See Practical Information for Western Australia. Listed here are some of the camper parks close to Perth. *Caravan Village,* 2462 Albany Highway, Gosnells, (09) 398–2746, train and bus to Perth near entrance, 30 minutes out of city, powered sites $6 double, on-site vans $16. *Caversham Park,* Lot 1 Benara Rd., Caversham (09) 279–6700, 12km north, buses from entrance, powered sites $8 double, on-site vans. *Banksia Tourist Village,* Midland Rd., Midland (09) 274–2351, 19km east, swimming pool, games room, powered $7.50 double. *Cherokee Village,* 10 Hocking Rd., Kingsley (09) 409–9039, 20 minutes out on bus route to city, powered $7.50, on-site vans about $20 double. *Orange Grove Caravan Park,* 19 Kelvin Rd. (09) 453-6226, 20 minutes out, pool, children's playground, bus to city, powered $7 double, on-site vans $18 double. *Perth Tourist Caravan Park,* Hale Rd., Forrestfield (09) 453-6677, 20 minutes out, powered $9 double, on-site vans $17. *Springvale Caravan Park,* Lot 10 Maida Vale Rd., High Wycombe, (09) 454-6829, 16km out, pool, dogs on leash, powered $6 double, on-site vans about $16 double.

RESTAURANTS. When it comes to eating the prime meats, fish, fruits, and vegetables grown in the state, there appears to be an infinite number of ways of preparing and serving food. Those who know once said there were, for instance, more Chinese restaurants in Perth than in the rest of Australia. And because of WA's close proximity to southeast Asia—the state's nearest neighbors if you believe the many who want to secede from the rest of Australia—it is no wonder there is such a big Asian influence on WA's eating habits. The eating houses run the gamut from corner cafes serving pies and chips, fast, fast take-aways, hamburgers and hot dogs to the upper-upper establishments that embellish their pure-white crockery with "nouvelle cuisine"— that colorful and sparse decoration posing as food that crept in from Europe several years ago. Generally, prices are reasonable for a capital city unless you lash out in the five-star hotels and challenge the chef. In the larger restaurants credit cards are, for the most part, accepted. Look for the stickers on the door, just like anywhere else. Restaurants are in the city of Perth, unless noted otherwise.

Chinese. *Canton Restaurant,* 532 Hay St.; 325-8865. *Golden Eagle,* 130 James St.; 328-5420. *Golden Swan.* 91 James St., Northbridge; 328-3248. *Imperial Palace,* Milligan-Wellington St.; 321-4573. *Orchard Noodle House,* Milligan-Wellington; 321-4573. *Emperor's Court,* 66 Lake St.; 328-8860. *Princess Court,* 326 Hay St.; 325-1230. Or give yourself a treat and drive 20 minutes along Freeway South to 897 Canning Hwy., Canning Bridge; 364-8470—the *Prince of China.*

French. *La Bonne,* 957 Hay St.; 321-2469. *Burgundy's of Perth,* 623A Wellington St.; 322-1610. *Chez Pele,* 254 Adelaide Tce.; 325-6210. *The French Restaurant,* Orchard Hotel, 707 Wellington St.; 327-7000. *Luis',* 6 the Esplanade; 325-2476; 29 years of popularity.

Indian. *Bengal Curry House,* 48 High St., Fremantle; 335-2400. *India Restaurant,* 10 Lake St.; 328-4171.

Indonesian. *Cinta,* Orchard Hotel complex, floor 1, Wellington-Milligan St.; (09) 322-1487; live entertainment at night. *Opa's,* 85 Francis St., (09) 328-8884; Dutch and Indonesian, blackboard specials, live music, dancing.

Italian. *Ciceros,* 105 Francis St., Northbridge; 328-5361. *Mamma Maria's,* 105 Aberdeen St., Northbridge; 227-9828. *Tinelli's at the Orchard,* Wellington St.; 481-1370. *Uncle Dominic's,* 291A William St.; 328-6654. *Vino Vino,* 27 Lake St.; 328-5403.

Japanese. *Hana of Perth,* Mill St. (opposite Parmelia Hilton); 322-7098; traditional tatami rooms, sushi counter, Kirin beer, sake, Japanese whiskey, Monday–Saturday; top value. *Jun and Tommy's Sushi Bar,* 117 Murray St.; 325-7341 (cafe style). *Shima Restaurant,* Orchard Hotel, 67 Milligan St.; 322-5688.

Mexican. *La Siesta,* 398 Oxford St., Mt. Hawthorn; (09) 444-0653; short taxi ride. *Mexican Cantina,* 26B Chapman Rd., Bentley; (09) 451-3550, taxi ride.

Vietnamese. *Kim Anh,* 178 William St.; (09) 328-9508. *Thanh Tan,* 489 Beaufort St., Highgate; (09) 227-8517; excellent food, unbelievably low prices.

Recommended restaurants for setting, value, reasonably priced wines, popularity. *Hilite 33,* 44 St. George's Tce., St. Martin's Tower; (09) 325-4844; revolving restaurant, country-style buffet or French cuisine. *Janica and Me,* 376 Fitzgerald St.; (09) 328-6220. *King's Park Restaurant,* King's Park Rd.; 321-7655; overlooking city from famous park, very popular, lunch 7 days 12–2:30 P.M. *Lombardo's,* Fishing-boat harbor, Fremantle; (09) 430-4346; middle of yachting action, great views. *Matilda Bay,* 3 Hacket Dr., Crawley; (09) 386-5425; favorite on banks of Swan. 10-minute scenic drive. *The Mediterranean Garden Restaurant,* 414 Rockeby Rd., Subiaco; (09) 381-2188. *Minty's Restaurant and Cocktail Bar,* 309 Hay St., East Perth; (09) 325-5743. *Oyster Beds,* 26 Riverside Rd., East Fremantle; (09) 339-1611. *Pier 21,* 3 John St., Fremantle;

WESTERN AUSTRALIA

(09) 336–2222; overlooking Fremantle harbor. *Ruby's,* 37 Pier St.; (09) 325–7474; class.

Vegetarian. *Magic Apple,* 447 Hay St.; 325–8775. *Niggles,* 104 Wray Ave, Fremantle; 335–8614. *Stripes Gourmet,* 313B Vincent St.; Leederville; 444–0016. *Zorba the Buddha,* 6 Collie St., Fremantle; (09) 335–7035.

TOURIST INFORMATION. See Practical Information for Western Australia.

TOURS. Day tours in and around Perth: *Australian Pacific Tours,* (09) 325–9377: Yanchep Sun City tour through suburbs along West Coast Highway beside Indian Ocean for 16km to Yanchep Sun City Marina, once the launching place of America's Cup challengers, Atlantis marine park for dolphin, sea lion, seal performances, Yanchep National Park, koalas, emus, kangaroos, black swan, park-ranger guided tour of caves, $25, runs Monday, Thursday, Saturday. Wildlife-Heritage Tour: to Cohuna Wildlife Park in Darling Ranges, feed kangaroos, emus, black swan, see wombats, pelicans, peacock, large walk-through aviaries, to scenic Araluen Park, Churchman's Brook Reservoir, Pioneer Village, recreation of past days and ways, Elizabethan Village, replica of Shakespeare's birthplace, artifacts more than 300 years old, village green, stocks, $25, Tuesday, Thursday, Saturday. *Avon Valley Tours,* 5 Ascot Place, Belmont, (09) 277–3667: El Caballo Blanco for dancing stallions, state's longest chairlift, historic Swan Valley and vineyards, Darling Ranges, wine tasting at 1870 Coorinja Vineyard, $20, Monday (via York, WA's oldest inland town, Wednesday and Friday). *Feature Tours,* 2 Cambridge St., Leederville 6007, (09) 381–4822, toll-free 008–999–819, telex 94835: America's Cup Museum, Millionaires' Mile, maritime museum, fish-and-chip lunch, flea market, prison museum, good round-up of Fremantle today and yesterday, morning tea, lunch, free drink included, $30, Friday. Perth by Night Tour: wining, dining, dancing, entertainment, dinner, drinks, selected night spots, $35 Wednesday, Thursday, Friday. *Parlorcars* (09) 325–5488: bird life, black swan, garden suburbs, Indian Ocean beaches, university campus, Kings Park gardens, $23, Monday; Sunday bush and hills: for lunch in log cabin atmosphere Chalet Healy, Araluen National Park, visit Mundaring Weir, $35. *Cygnet Tours,* 91 Berwick St., Victoria Park (09) 362–2494: Mandurah cruise, Murray Valley, 6 hours with 2 hours cruising, hotel lunch, $31, Wednesday. *Freemantle Tram* is a tour of that town, call 328–4542 or *Holiday WA.*

River Cruises. *Captain Cook Cruises,* No 2 Pier, Barrack St., Perth WA 6000, (09) 325–3341: lunch cruise, 10:15 A.M.–1:00 P.M. Tuesday to Friday, to Fremantle inner harbor, morning tea, smorgasbord, $15; scenic harbor cruise, 1:45–4:45 P.M. daily, tea or coffee, Fremantle Harbour, fishing harbor where America's Cup yachts prepared, wine tasting, $10.

Wine Tours. Western Australia is establishing a big reputation as a wine-producing state with some whites rivaling those from the more established and better-known eastern states' vineyards. Although small by comparison, the wine production is big on taste. Several tours take in vineyards in the southwest, but for Perth visitors and dwellers the Swan River cruise up to the nearer vineyards are extremely popular. Among the wines waiting to be tasted are cabernet sauvignon, shiraz, cabernet rose, verdelho, rhine riesling, burgundy, and port. Contact *Wines of the West Promotion Centre,* Grapevine Cellars, 2 Great Eastern Highway, Rivervale WA 6103 (09) 362–3200: WA wines for tasting free, snacks, maps, information books on wine, 8:30 A.M.–8:30 P.M. Monday to Saturday, minutes from city center on MTT buses 297, 300, 302, 304, 306. *Lady Houghton Champagne Cruise,* Barrack St. Jetty, Perth WA 6000, (09) 325–6033 or *Holiday WA* (09) 322–2999. Day cruise: morning tea, commentary on scenic Upper Swan, white wines, champagne, cheese, biscuits, lunch at Mulberry Farm with wine, entertainment, music, dancing, etc., on cruise back, $27, 9:45 A.M.–4:45 P.M. Evening cruise: champagne, wines, hors d'oeuvres, dinner, floor show, music, etc., $30, 6 P.M. Friday and Saturday nights. *Miss Sandalford Vineyard Cruise,* Pier 4, Barrack St., Perth 6000 (09) 325–6033, or *Holiday WA,* (09) 322–2999: river-history commentary on Upper Swan cruise, morning tea, wine, cheese, biscuits, Woodbridge Manor historic site, wine tasting at Sandalford vineyard, lunch, $27. Evening cruise: 6 P.M. departure, hors d'oeuvres, wine, Sandalford, four-course meal, $30 Friday and Saturday to midnight. Both vessels air-conditioned. *Ace Travel Agency,* 34 Cheriton St., East Perth, (09) 328–

4542, telex AA92841, Swan Valley wineries via Caversham wildlife park, mussel pool, steam train ride, lunch, two vineyards for tasting, Halls Museum, diamond-cutting factory, $30 Sunday.

SPORTS. Western Australia is a great sporting state and has shown the world the way in hockey (the Australian side of the championship team was dominated for years by WA champions) and cricket, where the Australian side was heavy with Western Australian bowlers, batsmen, and a record-breaking 'keeper. Whatever the time of the year you'll find activity on ovals, golf courses, water, and horse-racing tracks and in stadiums.

1986–87 is, of course, dominated by the **America's Cup sailing championship.** On September 26, 1983, at Newport, Rhode Island, Australia won the America's Cup, ending 132 years of American domination of the sea classic. Elimination series in October '86 were held between four Australian syndicates vying for the honor to defend the trophy against the world. They included Alan Bond's America's Cup Defence 1987 (he won the trophy); Syd Fischer's Eastern Australian Syndicate; the South Australian Challenge for the Defence of the Cup; and WA millionaire Kevin Parry's Task Force '87. Syndicates from six countries—United States, Great Britain, New Zealand, France, Canada, and Italy—mounted a challenge with eliminations taking place in October '86.

The challenge and defense are sailing on the sparkling waters of the Indian Ocean at Fremantle, 15 minutes by car from Perth. At one point, less than a mile offshore, the rigorous courses consist of eight 3.5-mile legs, a more grueling test than the previous six 4.5-mile legs.

A host of spectator boats, power, sail, even luxury ocean-going cruise ships will go out to the course each day to give the public a close view of proceedings. It will be hard to see which yacht is which from the sandhills along the coastline between Fremantle and the northern beaches, but powerful binoculars and telescopes will be used by thousands who enjoy the sun and sand to keep an eye on the champions.

The final challenge between an Australian boat and the successful challenger will begin January 31, 1987, with the best of seven races deciding the winner. It should be all over by mid-February. Generally, at this time of year there are few clouds and little rain; temperatures average 85°F. Spectators should remember to protect themselves from the Australian summer sun.

During summer first-class **cricket** can be seen at the Western Australian Cricket Association (WACA) oval near the causeway, one outlet across the Swan from the city. The oval is a 20-minute walk from the city center, about the same from the Merlin and Sheraton hotels.

Saturday is **horse race** day, and Perth has two modern courses close to the city with bars, restaurants, and grandstands and a computerized betting system known to all as "the tote." The harness races are held at Gloucester Park; the WACA oval entrance is just across the street—on Friday nights it alternates races with the Fremantle track. Greyhounds run, too, Saturday night on a specially built raised track.

In winter the sports are **Australian rules football, rugby league,** and **rugby union,** with a myriad of other team games.

For information on local sports: *WA Football League* (09) 381–5599; *Lawn Tennis Association* (09) 481–0377; *Trotting Assoc.* (09) 325–8822; *Cricket Assoc.* (09) 325–9800; *Turf* (horse-racing) *Club* (09) (09) 322–1311; *Greyhound Racing* (09) 458–4600; *WA Golf Club* (09) 349–1602; *Hockey Assoc.* (09) 451–3688; *Ladies Bowls* (09) 325–8439; *Ladies Golf Union* (09) 368–2618; *Softball Assoc.* (09) 459–1804; *Gymnastics Assoc.* (09) 328–1408; *Volleyball Assoc.* (09) 362–6339; *Swimming* (09) 328–4978; *Cycling* (09) 387–4648; *Disabled Sports* (09) 361–8006; *Gliding* (09) 349–9859; *Parachuting* (09) 330–7270; *Rugby League* (09) 381–4473; *Trout and Freshwater Angling* (09) 332–7779; *Speedboat Club* (09) 401–6725.

Beaches are easily accessible up and down the coast.

MUSEUMS. See also Galleries, below. "Art for Everybody" is the boast of the new *Western Australian Art Gallery,* an octagon bordered with an expansive concourse with waterway. Different galleries inside can be changed in shape and size to fit any collection. Sculpture includes Henry Moore's *The Reclining Figure,* Rodin's *Adam,* Jean Arp's *Dreaming Star,*

WESTERN AUSTRALIA

Greco's *Head of Man*, Renoir's *Tete de Venus*, Hepworth's *Two Forms in Echelon*. Tribal art from Burma, Thailand, Indonesia; an outstanding Aboriginal art collection—posts, figures, carvings, bark paintings; historic collection including prints taken from engravings of Sir Joseph Banks with Captain Cook on his first voyage around the world; prints and drawings from Rembrandt, Toulouse-Lautrec, Spencer, Callot, Whistler, Warhol. Fully licensed restaurant. City free bus stops outside gallery, 47 James St., Perth, 328–7233. Admission free; open daily 10 A.M.–5 P.M.; easy walking distance from city. $3 taxi ride.

Western Australian Museum. Francis St. A variety of historical and natural history displays, including an Aboriginal gallery. The Old Perth Gaol is part of the museum.

FREMANTLE

America's Cup Museum. Rolly Tasker Building, 43 Swan St., North Fremantle, 430–4323. Contains models of all the yachts competing for the trophy between 1851 and 1983. Open daily 9:30 A.M.–5 P.M. Admission charge.

Fanny Samson's Cottage Museum. 33 Cliff St., 335–7444. Built 1829 as a warehouse for a family business. Contains mementos of the company. Call for appointment.

Fremantle Motor Museum. 4 Josephson St., off High St., 335–5546. Historic cars, jazz, and sculpture make an interesting display. Open Thurs.–Sun., 10 A.M.–6 P.M. Admission charge.

Fremantle Prison Museum. 335–4911, ext. 332. Graphic depiction of the convict era. Open Sat. 1–4 P.M., Sun. 11 A.M.–4 P.M.; by appointment weekdays (call Mon. and Wed. A.M.)

Western Australia Maritime Museum. Cliff St. Marine history: pieces from shipwrecks; former residence of a convict controller, built 1852. Open Fri.–Mon. and holidays 1–5 P.M.

Fremantle Museum. 1 Finnerty St.

 GALLERIES. *Alexander Galleries* features Australian artists, 12 Aberdeen St., 328–8589.

Lister Gallery features Australian artists; open daily 10–5, 248 St. George's Tce.

William Curtis Gallery shows oil paintings, 252 St. George's Tce.

FREMANTLE

Art Gallery, 335–5855, Pioneer Reserve between Phillimore and Short sts., open Wednesday–Sunday 12–5 P.M., features famous Australian painters.

Bannister Street Craftwork, 33–5915; open Tuesday–Friday 10 A.M.–5 P.M., other days 12–5:30 P.M.

Editions Gallery, 23 Pakenham St., 335–8483. Weekdays 10 A.M.–4 P.M., Sunday 2–5 P.M.

Fremantle Arts Centre, 335–8244, Finnerty St., in museum complex, pottery, painting, handicraft of locals. Open daily 10 A.M.–5 P.M., Wednesday 7–9 P.M.

Gallery of Original Arts-Artifacts, Croke La., 336–1281. Aboriginal works, paintings, sculpture; open Tuesday–Friday 10 A.M.–5 P.M., weekends 2–5 P.M.

Joan Campbell's Pottery Workshop, Round House, High St., 335–1999. Open daily 10 A.M.–5 P.M., weekends 12–5 P.M.

Praxis Gallery, 33 Pakenham St., 335–9770; open Tuesday–Saturday 11 A.M.–5 P.M., Sunday 2–5 P.M.

FLEA MARKETS. Several are held each Sunday around Perth and near suburbs. Worth a look for those interested in junk as well as fruit, vegetables, homemade jams, etc. Bentley—held every Sunday, La Plaza Shopping Centre, Albany Highway; Fremantle—Cnr. Henderson and South Tce., Friday 9 A.M.–9 P.M., Sat. 9 A.M.–5 P.M., Sun. 11 A.M.–5 P.M.; Melville—Canning Highway, Melville Shopping Centre, every Sunday 7–11:30 A.M.; Midland Markets, the Crescent, every Sunday 8 A.M.–4:30 P.M.; Subiaco Car Park Market, Sat., Sun. 9 A.M.– 5 P.M., Station St.; Thornlie—Spencer Rd., every Sunday in Thornlie Square Shopping Centre, 9 A.M.– noon; Victoria Park Hotel, Albany Highway, has stalls and live entertainment, Thurs., Fri., 11 A.M.–9 P.M.; Sat. 11 A.M.–7 P.M., Sun. 11 A.M.–5 P.M.

CASINO. The largest one-room casino in the southern hemisphere has been doing great business at Burswood Island, across the Swan from the city, an easy taxi ride ($4–$5) or take the bus and stroll. The gambling floor was opened in record time, and a huge international-style five star hotel is rapidly rising next door. The whole area will become a resort with sports and more. Gambling is available 24 hours a day with roulette, two-up, blackjack, keno most popular. The floor features a restaurant ($14 champagne breakfast) dance floor, entertainment, and drinks at bar prices. It has become the social center of the city, forcing many nightclubs to cut cover charges.

NIGHTCLUBS. These are in Perth unless noted otherwise. *Angels Teenage Disco,* 52 South St., Fremantle, 325–9397. *Aurora Night Club,* 232 William St., 328–1748. *Beethovens,* 418 Murray St., 321–6887; *Civic Theatre Restaurant,* 380 Beaufort St., 328–1455. *Clouds,* Sheraton, 207 Adelaide Tce., 325–0501. *Connections,* 81 James St., 328–1870. *Crazy Cats,* 434 William St., 328–3581. *Disco Tomorrow,* lower lobby, Merlin Hotel, 99 Adelaide Tce., 323–0121. *Eagle One,* 139 James St., 328–7447. *Entertainment Enterprises,* 65 Lake St., Northbridge, 227–9199. *Garfields Cafe,* 135 James St., 328–5636. *Gobbles,* 613 Wellington St., 322–1221. *Hannibals,* 69 Lake St., Northbridge, 328–1065. *Juliana's Supper Club,* Hilton, Mill St., 322–3622. *Knight Klub,* 137 Melville Parade, Como, 367–2680. *La Riviera,* 137 Melville Parade, Como, 367–2680. *Pinocchio's Nite Club,* 393 Murray St., 321–2521. *Red Parrot,* 89 Milligan St., North Perth, 328–9870. *Romano's Night Club and Restaurant,* 187 Stirling St., 328–4776. *Scotts F Night Club,* 237 Hay St., East Perth, 325–6850. *The Underground,* 268 Newcastle St., 328–6770.

WESTERN AUSTRALIA BEYOND PERTH

The fact that much of this state is so sparsely populated means that distances between towns are often great. Improvements to major road links have opened up many areas to the visitor, but some of Western Australia's most rugged and beautiful attractions are best reached by air.

Great Southern Region

Although Perth is the state capital, with far the largest concentration of population, it was 250 miles to the south, in the former whaling port of Albany, that the first settlement of Western Australia took place. The town spreads around Princess Royal Harbour and is protected from the stormy southern oceans on three sides.

Forty-four soldiers and convicts, sent by the governor to thwart French attempts to colonize the area, were the first to settle in Albany in 1826. They landed on Boxing Day, December 26. Development was slow until the whaling fleet moved in during the 1840s. There was a period of growth right through to the present century, but when Fremantle became established as the port for Perth, Albany's development slowed. Today, it is a town of historical interest, the starting point for travel into the wildflower regions of the southwest and for tours to see the south coastal areas.

The state's oldest residence, Old Farm, can be seen on Strawberry Hill. Orchards, wheatlands, and fields of clover are the hallmark of the Albany region. So, too, are its thriving herds of cattle, its tuna fleet, and the acres of potatoes.

The booming waves of the Southern Ocean pound along the coastline down South with spectacular results in many parts. Blow holes send plumes high into the blue sky, and huge granite shapes have been

WESTERN AUSTRALIA 251

gradually sculptured into strange images, caves, and bridges. The fury of waves contrasts with the quieter karri and tinglewood forests, lazy rivers perfect for canoeing, fantastic wildflowers, which draw people from all over the world—book well ahead for tours—national parks among the farm and grazing lands.

Other favorite holiday spots in the Great Southern Region include Denmark, a favorite family holiday area with fishing, beaches, and the Winniston Park antique collection, complete with the Royal Golden Bed used by Mary Queen of Scots in 1554; Mt. Barker, a lazy farming area which has become the wine-growing center producing fine riesling, cabernet, chardonnay, and shiraz; and Walpole/Nornalup with green forests and rivers, inlets and estuaries.

Snow is sometimes an unexpected sight on the bluffs of the Stirling Ranges, and there are some unusual coastal rock formations where the ocean hammers incessantly against the shores.

Butting on to the eastern boundary of the Albany region is the area known as Esperance, running right along the shores of the Great Australian Bight as far as the South Australian border. As recently as 1954 there were only 36 farmers in these 57,000 square miles of mostly open country; today there are more than 600 farming in excess of a million acres. It is a land that is only now beginning to blossom and develop, experiencing its first real prosperity since gold was discovered in the 1890s.

The only town of any size is also called Esperance, after the frigate that brought Huon de Kermadec into the bay in 1792. John Eyre passed by in 1841, but permanent settlement did not take place until Andrew Dempster obtained a lease over 100,000 acres in 1866. It was the gold rush of 1893 that brought the first real increase in population. Prosperity came to Esperance as it became a seaside resort and an outlet for the frustrations and fortunes of the Goldfields miners.

A burgeoning wheat-growing project was killed off by the Depression, and the farmers left the land. Now the farmers are returning, and the land is realizing its potential of becoming one of Australia's biggest producers of beef, fat lambs, wool, wheat, oats, barley, and linseed.

The southern seaboard of seemingly endless rolling plains presents a wild and windswept scenery not to be found anywhere else in Australia. There are three million acres of rolling heath with a rainfall of 16 to 24 inches. Farther inland is the dryer, harsher mallee scrub country—another three million acres of it—where the rainfall is a mere 13 to 16 inches.

Nevertheless, the Esperance area is expanding rapidly as a trading and business center and is one of the best examples of the vitality that is so typical of Western Australia. It remains a popular holiday center, for it boasts some of the best unspoiled coastal scenery anywhere on the Australian seaboard.

On the western side of the Albany region, taking up the southwest corner of the state, is the South West Region. This was another early sighting by French mariners, explored by Captain Freycinet in 1803 but first occupied from the land by an expedition that set up a military post in 1829. Like the English countryside with its rolling green hills, forests, farmlands, flowers, and rivers, this region is the most popular with visitors and locals alike. It is a beautiful corner of the vast state, with vineyards, beautiful beaches, cave formations, big timber, and winding, scenic drives. Here you can watch surfers battle the giant waves at Yallingup, world famous for its rollers, ride a vintage steam train, picnic and fish, or wander and drive through the giant karri trees, the only place in the world where the beautiful iron-hard red jarrah grows, and see the tinglewood soar high. Collie plays a major role in supplying WA with coal for its giant power stations. The oldest stone church in Western Australia is at Busselton. A workman's cottage that became a church in 1848 is at Australind, and the well-lit Yallingup Caves are worth an inspection.

Central Hinterland: A Tidal Wave in Granite

Inland from the Bunbury and Albany regions is the area designated as the Central Hinterland. Here, grain and wool provide the economic backbone. More grain is grown and more wool is clipped here than anywhere else in the state. It covers an area roughly equal to the whole of the North Island of New Zealand. Farms here comprise millions of acres and account for more than a third of all the cleared land in Western Australia. The main center is the Avon Valley township of Northam, 66 miles by road northeast of Perth, although one of the oldest rural settlements in the state is the smaller center of York. York is named after the English city and has now been preserved and restored as a historical attraction.

The railways play a vital role in the Central Hinterlands' daily life. Tracks and sidings fan out from Northam to provide the link by which the grain is sent after harvest from the wheatfields to the ships waiting alongside the wharves in Fremantle. The prairie country comes to life at each harvest and then sleeps for the rest of the year. Huge silos dot the landscape, storehouses for grain awaiting the next train.

This is one of the regions where road travel by private car is quite feasible. Good roads enable you to drive the 218 miles to the eastern wheatlands township of Hyden to see the extraordinary granite overhang quite accurately named Wave Rock. Estimated to have been formed 2,700 million years ago, the rock appears like a huge tidal wave, several hundred yards long, about to break over the dry, flat country that surrounds it. To make the journey worthwhile stop, too, to see other nearby weird and wonderful rocky formations such as the Humps and Hippo's Yawn. In Bates Cave there are Aboriginal rock paintings.

Taking up more than 307,000 square miles inland from these three regions is the ore-rich desert of the Kalgoorlie region. Bigger than Texas, it is home to fewer than 50,000 people. Yet, at the height of the gold rush in 1905, there were 200,000 people on the gold fields. New fortunes are being created today by the discovery of nickel, mined now not by the small-time prospectors of the type who first opened up the area, but by giant corporations who are building completely new treed and landscaped towns in the midst of a previously barren and inhospitable land.

The Lure of Gold

Alluvial gold was first discovered at Coolgardie in 1892 by prospectors William Ford and Arthur Bayley. A year later, Irishman Patrick Hannan made a strike that was reported around the world. With Thomas Flanagan and Dan Shea he made a strike that simply involved collecting nuggets from the surface of the sandy gullies. In a few days they collected 200 ounces of gold, and the boom began. The town of Kalgoorlie grew from this boom and sits on what is considered the richest square mile of rock ever known. To date it has given up close to 40 million ounces of gold, and the locals still maintain there is much more to come.

Life on the goldfields was rugged. Living conditions were primitive and unsanitary. Intense heat with little shade added to the miners' discomfort. Many died. It was only when a water supply was piped through the 350 miles from the Darling Ranges in 1903 that many of the problems of disease and drought were relieved. Just how pitifully

WESTERN AUSTRALIA

men were prepared to live in the expectation of making a fortune is depicted in a highly graphic museum in the main street of the pioneer town Coolgardie. Here are the tents, the utensils, tools, mementos, and records of the pioneers. It is a moving portrayal of an era when, according to one reporter, one half of Coolgardie was busy burying the other half, so high was the mortality rate. Burial was a primitive business. Anything would be used as a coffin. Miners went to their graves encased in coffins that bore the names of tinned foods or liquor. One carried the inscription "Stow away from boilers," obviously in the belief that he had made his peace with his Maker.

Today Coolgardie bustles with tourists and the local inhabitants have turned to less bloodthirsty pastimes. The town has three motels, a hotel, a safari village, a guesthouse, and a caravan park—still a little short of the 23 hotels and three breweries of its heyday. Legend has it that in those times, water was more expensive than whiskey!

The town then had two stock exchanges and two daily and four weekly newspapers and was second in size only to Perth and Fremantle. But today, a genuine atmosphere of ghostliness pervades the shimmering air. The town has been left to die, but the echoes of its tough, rumbustious founders work easily on the imagination.

Kalgoorlie survived the gold rush. Twenty-four miles to the east of Coolgardie, it is still a town of grandiose boom-time buildings, wide streets, and pioneering spirit. It owes its modern prosperity as much to the gold that is still being won as to the more recent discovery of nickel.

The name of Paddy Hannan has been preserved in street names, a statue, and a tree. The tree is said to mark the spot where the fortunate Irishman made his first strike. As a relic from the more permissive gold-rush days, Kalgoorlie boasts one of the few red-light districts tolerated by the authorities, although it's not featured in the tourist brochures.

Kalgoorlie's twin town Boulder is worth seeing on the Boulder Loop Line, which takes travelers on the railway that brought supplies and mine props. Today you can try your luck with the traditional gold pan or the modern metal detector, which has found thousands for many a weekend prospector. All you need is luck and a miner's right from the Mines Department.

Southeast of Kalgoorlie, 35 miles down the highway, is the model town of Kambalda, built by the Western Mining Corporation for workers at Australia's first commercial nickel mining venture. Kambalda is living proof that the desert can bloom and flower. You drive through a well-wooded but harsh plain, not unlike that of the old goldfields of southeastern Australia, to be greeted by tree-lined streets, green lawns, and gardens full of flowering shrubs. There are salt pans to be visited at Lake Lefroy and it is possible to go down a former gold mine specially set up to show visitors old and new methods used in the extraction of the precious metal.

Reminiscent of the pioneering days are the covered wagons and camels to be seen around Coolgardie. They are no longer used but are preserved as a reminder of an era only a couple of generations away.

Geraldton: Shipwrecks and Copperfields

Move coastward and northward from the Kalgoorlie region and you arrive in the area of Geraldton. This sprawls over 113,000 square miles and boasts some of the best year-round Mediterranean-style climate in the whole state.

It is an area rich in reminders of the state's early history. The coastline is littered with wrecks from the first exploration attempts.

Best known is that of the *Batavia,* which sank in 1629 and from which relics are slowly being recovered and restored for public display. The *Zuytdorp* (wrecked in 1712) and the *Zeewyck* (1727) are two other vessels among the many that provide sport and excitement for divers. Offshore are the Abrolhos Islands, charted and named by the 16th-century Portuguese navigators. The islands are renowned for the excellent fishing grounds. Cray-fishing is a thriving export industry that has attracted millions of dollars of investment money into the main town, Geraldton. The size of the commercial fishing fleet is strictly controlled, and there is a closed season from August 15 to November 15.

While the rest of the country was undergoing gold fever, the area around Geraldton was experiencing the first flush of being the center of major copper deposits. The Wanerenooka copper lode was discovered as early as 1842. Lead mining began at Northampton in 1848. Copper has been successfully mined since 1940. Worthwhile excavations of barytes, beryl, ochre, and tantocolumbite ores have also been made. A field of natural gas was discovered at Dongara in 1970, and a pipeline now leads from there to supply consumers in Perth.

The coast is the fishing paradise of Western Australia—snapper, grouper, shark, tuna, marlin, sailfish, and mackerel. Clean white beaches, tame dolphins at Monkey Mia near Shark Bay, prawns at Denham.

The huge overseas telecommunication-satellite station at Carnarvon is 29.6 meters in diameter and known to locals and the tourists it attracts as the big dish. Banana plantations and tropical fruits abound, and rich, irrigated lands produce fruit and vegetables for the local and Perth-Geraldton markets.

Close by is where the Dutch explorer Dirk Hartog made one of the first landings and explorations of the Australian coast. That was in 1606. Ninety-three years later came William Dampier with his findings that he had discovered a country that appeared to be useless, barren, and peopled by the most miserable beings. The streets of Carnarvon were planned with a width of 44 yards so that camel trains, which proved the mainstay of communications until the 1920s, could turn around easily.

The Gascoyne Agricultural Station, 6 miles from town, gives an insight into the research and development taking place in an area that has far from reached its full farming potential. There are blowholes on Quobba Station (42 miles from Carnarvon), and 15 miles farther on, Cape Cuvier presents the unusual sight of multicolored cliffs, 400 feet high, being pounded by the Indian Ocean.

Carnarvon, Exmouth and Onslow, farther north on the coast, are favorite winter retreats for "southerners" escaping the cooler days around Perth and the southwest. Exmouth sits on the North West Cape and is support town for the Harold Holt naval communications station. Learmonth, 35km (21 mi.) south, in Exmouth Gulf, was a U.S. submarine base in World War II. Onslow, an allied refueling base in war, is base now for deep-sea fishing and is sometimes called "cyclone city" because of cyclones that hit the coast during wet season. The dry season from April to September makes up for it. Gascoyne Junction, 164km (100 mi.) east of Carnarvon, is center of mining, and pastoral lands and gateway to Kennedy Range, home of Mt. Augustus, twice the size of Ayers Rock, 1,750 million years old, a spectacular monoclinal formation and largest known.

The Pilbara: Bursting at the Seams

Travel north from Carnarvon and you reach the most exciting pioneering region of all Western Australia: the Pilbara. It is one of the most highly mineralized regions on earth. It is bursting at the seams

WESTERN AUSTRALIA

with ore of all types and grades. It is a vast, scarred and ancient land, sunburned and brooding. The predominant color is rust-red ochre. It is an awe-inspiring, terrifying land of gorges, gullies, rifts and valleys that stretch to a very far horizon. Cavernous holes are being gouged out of the ground, and mountains are being blasted aside and new mountains being created from the resultant rubble. It is a frontier land; pioneering country of the first order. The mining companies have built entire new towns, constructed hundreds of miles of railways, and created ports capable of taking the world's biggest ships.

The region's main outlet for its products, Port Hedland, is one of Australia's fastest-growing towns. First founded by pearl fishers in 1857, it now handles massive bulk ore carriers of 100,000 tons or more. Its an unlovely, untidy rambling town, which still needs to be seen by anyone wanting to grasp the enormity of the mineral boom that has brought rapid civilization to a land where, until very recently, only a few Aboriginal tribes and hardy Outback graziers were prepared to settle and live. Port Hedland is today what Cossack used to be: the most important port on the coast.

Much of Cossack had disappeared beneath the dunes until a determined restoration program was undertaken. Today the courthouse is perhaps the best example of this work. Cossack can be found 5 miles off the highway between Roeburne and Port Sampson, south of Port Hedland. At its height, it boasted a population of about 400, with an additional 1,000 people living there when the pearling fleet was "laid up" between May and September.

Inland from Port Hedland is the town that has the reputation of being the hottest place in Australia. Other settlements in the area might, however, dispute Marble Bar's dubious claim to fame. But many of them were not in existence when it recorded, in 1923-24, the longest known heat wave. For 160 consecutive days the temperature exceeded 100°F. It is quite common for the thermometer to register over 120°F on many days between October and March. Yet in winter, frosts are not unknown. Marble Bar has been described by reputable commentators as "a grim, lonely little settlement," and they say it is typical of much of the Western Australian Outback. So it is a place for visiting by those seeking out the unique aspects of this often weird and wonderful land.

Many of the names that appear on a present-day map of the Pilbara would not have been there even a quarter of a century ago. And most of the landmarks that then were named had little significance to anyone but land surveyors and geographers. In the middle of the Pilbara are the Hamersley Ranges and the Hamersley Range National Park, adjacent to Mt. Meharry—the highest point in WA at 1,245m (4,046 ft.). Most popular of all the gorge areas is Wittenoom, with giant ant hills, waterfalls, and site of an old blue asbestos mine. A town sits at the mouth of a gorge and cliffs run for about 30km (18 mi.). Millstream National Park, a tropical oasis on the Fortescue River, has deep natural pools, water lilies, palms, even fruit bats. Millstream National Park is adjacent to Chichester National Park; popular at Chichester is the Python Pool, a natural freshwater pool sanctuary for wildlife. In the wet season, water pours over the cliff face and growth is lush, tropical.

The Kimberley

Divided into the West and East Kimberley, this is one of the world's oldest areas, estimated to be more than 2,500 million years old. Gorges and cliffs, mountains and river beds have been molded into spectacular scenery. Dinosaurs roamed the area and left footprints 130 million years ago in sandstone along coast. You can see them at low tide at

Cable Beach, Broome, first visited by Dampier in 1699. The unique town with its multiracial society was home to the pearl fleets, which numbered 300 to 400 luggers and employed 3,000 men to supply most of the world's mother-of-pearl shell. Many of the pearlers were Japanese, Malays, and Filipinos, and each year at famous Shinju Matsuri (Festival of the Pearl) the town remembers the good old days. Today it is the center for cultural pearl project at Kuri Bay.

Cut across 222km to Derby, port and center for West Kimberley, famous for giant boab trees—the huge hollow trunk of one was used as a prison—and gateway to Gorge country. Nearly 200km inland is Fitzroy Crossing, with the rock faces of Geike Gorge best seen from April to November. Cut through ancient fossilized coral reef, the Gorge, on the Fitzroy River, is in a national park. Freshwater crocodiles can be seen on a river trip. Tunnel Creek national Park features another strange experience in a strange land—a half-mile natural limestone tunnel which can be negotiated using lanterns that scatter flying foxes overhead in the central cave. Windjana Gorge in Napier Range soars 90 meters from the river bed. Rock paintings by Aboriginals can be found with the help of a guide among rocks of this outstanding geographical attraction.

The East Kimberley is known as the land of big waters, pioneers, and wildlife. The largest human-made sight is Lake Argyle, where the huge area of valley and gorge on Ord River was dammed to make a water catch area larger than Sydney Harbour. The largest natural sight is Wolf Creek Crater, 133km from Halls Creek. Here is the world's second largest meteorite crater, where 50,000 years ago the earth was hit. The crater can be reached by road during the dry season (April to October). Halls Creek is scene of WA's first big gold rush. Kununurra, Aboriginal word for "big water," is the town for Ord River scheme and agricultural research station. Only 97km away is Wyndham, a port established in 1886 to cater to the Halls Creek gold rush, now used to ship out beef to world centers.

Because of the need for a reliable surface-transportation system, fine "beef roads" now run across the Kimberley, making touring by car a much more feasible proposition than it was a few years back. However, the inexperienced would always be well advised to leave the driving to someone else; keep your car in the garage and take a seat on a coach, safari vehicle, or aircraft instead. To do this, head first of all to Perth.

PRACTICAL INFORMATION FOR WESTERN AUSTRALIA BEYOND PERTH

HOW TO GET THERE. By air. Perth is international gateway from southeast Asia and Europe into Australia. It is served by *Qantas* from U.K. and Singapore, Bali, Bangkok, Tokyo; *British Airways* from London via Bombay; *Cathay Pacific Airways* from Hong Kong with connections to Rome, Paris, Tokyo, Vancouver, San Francisco; *Malaysian Airline System* from Kuala Lumpur; *Singapore Airlines* from Singapore; *Thai International* from Bangkok; *South African Airways* from Johannesburg and Mauritius; *Garuda* from Bali and Jakarta; *Air New Zealand* direct from Auckland with connections to Honolulu and Los Angeles. All Asian airlines terminate in Perth. Qantas, *South African Airways,* and British Airways continue to Melbourne and Sydney. Domestic airlines *Ansett, Australian Airlines,* and *East-West* link Perth with capital cities in other states. Ansett WA, *Sky West,* and East-West serve northern towns with some TAA operations.

WESTERN AUSTRALIA

By bus. Daily connections with interstate capital cities across the long Nullarbor via Adelaide, South Australia. *Across Australia* coachlines, 30 Pier St., Perth WA 6000 (09) 325-3288; *Ansett Pioneer,* 26 St. George's Tce., Perth, WA 6000 (09) 325-8855; *Deluxe Coachlines,* AMP Arcade, Hay-William sts., Perth, WA 6000 (09) 322-7877; *Greyhound,* 14 Wynyard St., Belmont, WA 6104 (09) 478-1122; *Parlorcars,* 30 Pier St., Perth, WA 6000 (09) 325-5488. Meal stops made at regular intervals; baggage limited; no alcohol on board; videos on some lines; some nonsmoking, others 50-50; toilet-equipped; reclining seats; tinted windows.

By car. There is one main highway into Western Australia from the eastern states—the Eyre Highway, which crosses from South Australia at Eucla on the Great Australian Bight. It is fully paved and passes through tiny settlements with historic backgrounds until Norseman, the "gateway" to WA and first big settlement. The road branches down to Esperance and along the coast into the southwest becoming the South Western Highway through Albany, Busselton, Bunbury, and Mandurah to Perth. Or from Norseman the road goes to Kalgoorlie and Coolgardie; the Great Eastern Highway continues through wheatbelt towns of Merredin, Kellerberrin, and Northam, to Perth. From Perth going into the northwest, take the Brand Highway up the coast to Geraldton from the Muchea turnoff or continue along the Great Northern Highway farther inland through Mt. Magnet, the flying-doctor base and alternate airport for Perth, Meekatharra, into outback hardlands via Newman, Marble Bar to Port Hedland —the major export port, which is the meeting point with the North West Coastal Highway. From Port Hedland the Great Northern curls up to Broome and Derby, crosses to Fitzroy Crossing and Halls Creek, and continues farther up through Kununurra to Wyndham, which is the end of the line. Drivers heading for the east can take the Duncan Highway from Halls Creek through the Northern Territory into Queensland.

Cars must be in top running condition because of vast distances covered. On long trips carry spares and drinking water. Crossing the Nullarbor from Caiguna you travel over one of the longest straight stretches in the world. Service stations are situated at regular intervals for gasoline—the longest distance between service is 191km (118 mi.) from Balladonia to Norseman. There are motor hotels at Eucla, Mundrabilla, Madura, Cocklebiddy, Caiguna, and Balladonia. Take your time; take it easy. Up north check road conditions before leaving, especially in the *wet* season (November to March). *Note:* Plant and food matter *cannot* be brought into Western Australia because of quarantine to protect plants and crops against pests. Such items will be confiscated at Norseman Agricultural Check Point.

By rail. One of the great rail journeys of the world can be enjoyed between the Pacific Ocean on Australia's east coast and the Indian Ocean in Western Australia. The *Indian Pacific* luxury train runs from Sydney to Perth, Sunday, Thursday, Saturday, leaving 3:15 P.M. and arriving 7 A.M. three days later after crossing the continent. It does the return trip Sunday, Monday, Thursday departing Perth 9 P.M. and arriving Sydney 3:50 P.M. First-class fare, one way, $A595; economy (second class) $A442, with all meals and sleeping compartments. Passengers can sit up for $A211 and buy meals from buffet car. *Trans Australian* leaves Perth for Adelaide, capital of South Australia, Wednesday and Saturday 9 P.M., arriving 44 hours later; departs Adelaide Wednesday and Saturday 6 A.M., $A394 first class, $A291 second, $A105 sit up. Trains go via Kalgoorlie. There are no train services to the northwest.

HOW TO GET AROUND. By air. Western Australia's vast size (about a third of whole continent) makes air the best way to get around. *Ansett WA,* division of Ansett Australia, services most big areas in the northwest and south. Contact Ansett, 26 St. George's Tce., Perth, WA 6000 (09) 325-0201; divisions in Broome, Carnarvon, Derby, Exmouth Gulf, Geraldton, Kalgoorlie, Karratha, Kununurra, Newman, Paraburdoo, Port Hedland, Tom Price, Wickham. *East-West Airlines,* 28 the Esplanade, Perth, WA 6000 (09) 322-3900; divisions Karratha, Port Hedland. *SkyWest Airlines,* Floor 6, 140 St. George's Tce., Perth, WA 6000 (09) 426-4555. *TAA,* 55 St. George's Tce., Perth, WA 6000 (090) 336-2122; branches at Port Hedland and Fremantle. Small charter airlines include *Avior Airlines,* 431 Great Eastern Highway, Redcliffe, WA 6104, (09) 277-7422. *Travair Aerial Services,* 11/13 Mends St., South Perth, WA 6151, (09) 367-7255 runs DC-3 tours and charters.

By train. For train lovers there are some services available. The short Perth to Fremantle service is for commuters and runs regularly during the day. There is also a service to Armadale in the hills to the south. One of Australia's fastest trains, the Prospector, does service Kalgoorlie. Contact *Westrail Travel Centre,* City Rail Station, Wellington St., Perth 6000, (09) 326–2690, for information.

By bus. Bus is the most popular way after private car to get around the state. Luxury, air-conditioned coaches travel to most areas of the northwest, southwest and inland. See Tours section, below.

By car. For those without a vehicle, car rental is the answer with all popular modern makes in all sizes. *Avis Australia,* 46 Hill St., Perth, WA 6000, (09) 325–7677, telex AA92993; *Budget Rent a Car,* 960 Hay St., Perth, WA 6000, (09) 322–1100, telex AA93188; *Barron Rent a Car,* Merlin Hotel, Adelaide Tce., Perth, WA 6000, (09) 325–1833; *Hertz,* 39 Milligan St., Perth, WA 6000, (09) 321–7777, telex AA93562, airport, (09) 277–9614; *Thrifty Rent-a-Car,* 33 Milligan St., Perth WA 6000 (09) 481–1999. Prices range from $A6 a day (*Rent-a-Heap,* 368 Guildford Rd., Bayswater, WA 6053, (09) 271–7216) to $A15 for some four cylinder cars in the city (*Letz Rent-a-Car,* 190 Great Eastern Highway, Belmont, (09) 478–1999.). Weekly rates from $A120 (*Bayswater Hire Cars,* 160 Adelaide Tce., Perth 6000, (09) 325–1000) in city to $A196 in country (*Carousel Rent-a-car,* 1971 Albany Highway, Maddington, WA 6109, (09) 459–9999). Most rates include unlimited kilometers.

By camper. Called caravans, these are the other answer for driving yourself around WA. Lowline "pop-ups" to big six-wheelers are available, and parks are readily available throughout the state. *Budget Campervans,* 529 Scarborough Beach Rd., Innaloo, (09) 445–1200; *All-Ways Caravan Hire,* 1922 Albany Highway, Maddington, (09) 459–3000; *Modern Caravans,* 152 Wanneroo Rd., Tuart Hill, (09) 349–1022; *Fleetwood Holidays,* 317 Great Eastern Highway, Belmont, (09) 478–2600.

ACCOMMODATIONS. There is great variety of accommodation possibilities throughout the regions of Western Australia, and some surprisingly good ones in some coastal and northern areas—although there's nothing very plush outside the metropolitan area. Cost guide: *Expensive,* $A80-plus; *moderate,* around $A50; *inexpensive,* $A20 to $A40, room only per person unless otherwise stated.

ALBANY

Travel Inn. *Moderate.* 191 Albany Highway; (097) 41–4144. **Esplanade Motor Hotel.** *Inexpensive.* Middleton Beach; (097) 41–1633. **Hospitality Inn.** *Inexpensive.* 234 Albany Highway; (097) 41–2200.

BROOME

Continental Hotel. *Moderate.* Weld St.; (091) 92–1002. Pool, restaurant. **Mangrove Hotel-Motel.** *Moderate.* Dampier Tce.; (091) 92–1303. Pool, restaurant. **Tropicana Motel.** *Moderate.* Cnr Saville and Robinson St.; (091) 92–1204. Video, tea-coffee facilities, pool, restaurant. **Roebuck Bay Hotel.** *Inexpensive.* Dampier Tce.; (091) 92–1221. Pool, licensed dining room, restaurant.

BUNBURY

Bussell Motor Hotel. *Moderate.* Bussell Highway; (097) 21–1022. **Lighthouse Inn.** *Moderate.* Carey St., (097) 21–1311. **Admiral Motor Inn.** *Inexpensive.* 56 Spencer St., (097) 21–7322. **Anne Hathaway Motor Inn.** *Inexpensive.* Ocean Drive; (097) 21–2427.

BUSSELTON

Busselton Amaroo Motor Lodge. *Inexpensive.* 31 Bussell Highway; (097) 52–2038, **On the Vasse Motor Resort.** *Inexpensive.* 70 Causeway Rd.; (097) 52–3000, **Vasse Hotel.** *Inexpensive.* 44 Queen St.; (097) 52–1455.

WESTERN AUSTRALIA

CARNARVON

Hospitality Inn. *Moderate.* West St.; (099) 41-1600. **Carnarvon Auto Motel.** *Inexpensive.* North West Highway; (099) 41-1532. **Port Hotel.** *Inexpensive.* Robinson St.; (099) 41-1704.

DERBY

Boab Inn. *Moderate.* Loch St.; (091) 91-1044. Restaurant, pool, tea-coffee facilities. **King Sound Motel.** *Moderate.* Delewarr St.; (091) 91-1166. Video, pool, room service, restaurant-dining room.

ESPERANCE

Hospitality Inn. *Moderate.* The Esplanade; (090) 71-1999. **Pier Hotel.** *Inexpensive.* The Esplanade; (090) 71-1777, **Travellers Inn.** *Inexpensive.* Goldfields Rd.; (090) 71-1677.

EXMOUTH

Norcape Lodge Resort. Truscott Cres.; (099) 49-1334. Family apartments, rooms for one to five $90; $540 a week; room only one person $60, suites $75. **Potshot Inn.** *Moderate.* Murat Rd.; (099) 49-1200.

GERALDTON

Batavia Motor Inn. *Inexpensive.* 54 Fitzgerald St.; (099) 21-3500, **Freemasons Hotel.** *Inexpensive.* Marine Tce.; (099) 21-1688. **Hospitality Inn.** *Inexpensive.* 169 Cathedral Ave.; (099) 21-1422.

KALBARRI

Kalbarri Beach Resort. *Moderate.* Corner Grey and Clotworthy sts.; (099) 37-1061. **Palm Lodge Resort motel.** *Inexpensive.* Porter St.; (099) 37-1008. **Kalbarri Motor Hotel.** *Inexpensive.* Grey St.; (099) 37-1000.

KALGOORLIE

Hospitality Inn. *Inexpensive.* Lower Hannan St.; (090) 21-2888. **Midas Hotel.** *Inexpensive.* 409 Hannan St.; (090) 21-3088. **Palace Hotel.** *Inexpensive.* Cnr Hannan and Maritana St.; (090) 21-2788, **Star and Garter Hotel-Motel.** *Inexpensive.* 497 Hannan St.; (090) 21-3004.

KARRATHA

International Hotel. *Expensive.* Millstream Rd.; (091) 85-3111. Dining room, restaurant, pool, in-house movies. **Walkabout Hotel.** *Moderate.* Lot 1079 Searipple Rd.; (091) 85-1155. Pool, TV, radio, tea- and coffee-making facilities.

KUNUNURRA

Hotel Kununurra. *Moderate.* Messmate Way; (091) 68-1344. Tea-coffee facilities, pool, restaurant, room service. **Lake Argyle Inn.** *Moderate.* Lake Argyle Tourist Village; (091) 68-1064. Pool, restaurant, room service. **Swagman Inn.** *Moderate.* Duncan Highway; (091) 68-1455. Tea-coffee facilities, pool, dining room.

PORT HEDLAND

Hedland Hotel. *Moderate.* Cnr Lukis and McGregor St.; (091) 73-1511. Pool, video movies, restaurant, tea-coffee facilities. **Hospitality Inn.** *Moderate.* Cnr Webster and Sutherland St.; (091) 73-1044. Restaurant, tea-coffee facilities, pool. **Walkabout Motel.** *Moderate.* North West Coastal Highway (opposite airport); (091) 72-1222. Tea-coffee, pool, restaurant.

ROEBOURNE

Victoria Hotel. *Inexpensive.* Roe St.; (091) 82-1001,

 CAMPING. Even in such a vast state as Western Australia with countless thousands of square miles of land, there are rules on caravaning (using a camper) and camping. The WA government says you can camp outside an established caravan park only where the owner has no objection; there is no local regulation against camping; a nuisance will not result because of the sanitary arrangements; you stay there for three nights or less; and there is no caravan park within a radius of 16 kilometers (10 miles). Dogs or other pets are banned from entering or being kept in any "on site" caravan park (i.e., where campers are provided). In cottages, chalets, flats, or on-site caravans blankets and linen must be provided by clients. In some instances you provide all cooking utensils, cutlery, and crockery. Check first.

ALBANY

Emu Beach Caravan Park, 7km from town, Emu Point; (098) 44-1147. $6.50 for two; powered $7.50, on-site vans $18-$26, flats about $30. *Middleton Beach,* 3km out, (098) 41-3593. On-site vans $20, powered sites $7, unpowered $4. Safe beach, walking pleasure. *Mt. Melville Caravan Park,* 1km out, 3km from beach; (098) 41-4616. On-site vans $20, powered sites $9 (weekly $58), pets allowed.

BROOME

Broome Caravan Park, Box 551, Lot 1207 Wattle Dr.; (091) 92-1776. Powered $10 double, on-site vans $38, weekly $230, chalets $45 double. *Bali Hai Caravan Park,* 4km out; (091) 92-1375. Powered $9.50 double, chalets $60 foursome. Laundry, food.

BUNBURY

Bunbury Village Caravan Park, 6km out on Bussell Highway; (097) 25-7100. Disabled facilities, on-site vans, camping areas. Vans $18 a night, sites $6 for two. **Koombana Park,** near town; (097) 21-2516. Powered sites $7 for two, on-site vans $16 for two.

BUSSELTON

Lazy Days Caravan Park, 452 Bussel Highway; (097) 52-1780. On-site vans $14-$20, camping sites $6 for two. *Mandalay Holiday Resort,* Geographe Bay; (097) 52-1328. Cottages $100-$150 week, on-site vans $18 for two, campsites $7 double, plus $1 for powered site; close to beach.

CARNARVON

Carnarvon Caravan Park, PO Box 286, 4km from town; (099) 8101. Powered site $9, on-site vans about $20, chalets about $30 double. *Marloo Caravan Park,* 3km out; (099) 41-1439. Shaded sites, grass. Powered $7 double, on-site vans $50 plus. *Norwesta Caravan Park,* corner Robinson and Angelo sts.; (099) 41-1277. Powered about $8, on-site vans $35 plus.

DENMARK

Denmark Ocean Beach Caravan Park, 7km from town; (098) 48-1105. Tennis courts, barbecues, playgrounds, on-site vans $18 to $30, camp sites $6.50, cottages about $25 a day. *Rivermouth Caravan Park,* Inlet Drive, 1km out; (098) 48-1262. $6 unpowered sites for two, on-site vans $20, cottages $12 plus.

WESTERN AUSTRALIA

DERBY

Derby Caravan Park, town center, Rowan St.; (091) 91-1022. Powered $9 double, on-site vans $30 double.

ESPERANCE

Esperance Shire Caravan Park, 2km from town; (090) 71-1251. Snack food. 50 meters from beach, no on-site vans. $6.80 a day with power, $42 a week. Grassy, shaded area. *Bathers Paradise Caravan Park,* Westmacott St. (off Goldfields Rd.), 3km from town, powered site $7 daily, on-site vans $16. 150 meters to beach. *Bushland Caravan Park,* 6km out; (090) 71-1346 Box 801. Minutes from town, beaches. Powered sites $7 double, on-site vans about $15, chalets about $22 plus.

EXMOUTH

Exmouth Caravan Park, Lefroy St.; (099) 49-1331. Powered $8, on-site vans $20 plus. *Norcape Lodge Holiday Resort,* Truscott Cres.; (099) 49-1334. Powered $10 double, $60 weekly. Pool, shop, restaurant.

GERALDTON

Geraldton-Belair Gardens, West end Marine Terrace; (099) 21-1997. Powered sites $7, camp sites $5, on-site vans from $18, chalets $22. Safe beach, barbecue. *Separation Point Caravan Park,* 1.5km from town. Swimming, fishing, surfing. Powered $7, on-site vans $20.

KALBARRI

Anchorage Caravan Park, near town; (099) 37-1181. Powered sites $8, on-site vans about $20. Pool, barbecue, playground. *Tudor Caravan Park,* Lot 473 Porter St.; (099) 37-1077. Powered sites $8, on-site vans $22-$25, $150 weekly, cabins $22.

KALGOORLIE

Kalgoorlie Caravan Park, Central; (090) 21-4455. Powered sites $8. *Golden Village,* 2km out; (090) 21-4162. Powered sites about $8, on-site vans about $20. *Goldminer Tourist Park,* 4km out; (090) 21-3713. Powered $8, on-site vans $25 double, chalets $25 double.

KARRATHA

Karratha Caravan Park, PO Box 126; (091) 85-1012. Powered sites about $8 double; no dogs. *Pennant Tourist Park,* cnr Mystery and Searipole Rd.; (091) 85-1825. Powered sites $8. Snack food, ice, no pets.

KUNUNURRA

Adventure Park, 1km from town; (091) 68-1280. Powered about $9 double, pool, shop. *Kona Park,* Levee Bank Rd. (091) 68-1031. Powered $10.50, shop. *Lake Argyle Tourist Village,* 75km out; (091) 68-1064. Powered about $9 to $12 double.

PORT HEDLAND

Cook Point Caravan Park, Athol and Taylor sts.; (091) 73-1271. Near ocean. Powered $7 double, on-site vans $12 plus, petrol, supermarket, gas. *Port Hedland Caravan Park,* Lot 945, North West Coastal Highway, near airport; (091) 72-2525. Powered $6.50 double. Barbecue, pool, kiosk.

ROEBOURNE

Roebourne Caravan Park, Box 144; (091) 82–1063. Powered $8 double, on-site vans $20. Barbecue, pool, food. *Harding River Caravan Park*, 4km out, center of tourist attractions; (091) 82–1063. Powered $8, on-site vans $20. Pool, shop, playground, gas barbecues.

WYNDHAM

Caravan Park, 1km out, (091) 61–1064. Powered $8.50 double.

TOURIST INFORMATION. Holiday WA tourist information centers pride themselves in their up-to-date information. Contacts are: Perth: Holiday WA, 772 Hay St., Perth, WA 6000, (09) 322–2999, telex AA93030; Shop 26 Merlin Centre, Adelaide Tce., Perth, WA 6000, (09) 325–3200, telex AA93030. Fremantle: 41 High St., Fremantle, WA 6160, (09) 430–5555. Adelaide: 108 King William St., Adelaide, SA 5000, (08) 212–1344, telex AA82812. Melbourne: 2 Royal Arcade, Vic 3000 (03) 63–3692, telex AA32147. Sydney: 92 Pitt St., Sydney, NSW 2000, (02) 233–4400. Brisbane: Level 2, City Mutual Building, 307 Queen St., Brisbane, Qld 4000, (07) 229–5794, telex AA41286. Auckland: Australian Tourist Commission (ATC), 15th floor, Quay Tower, 29 Customs St. West, (09) 79–9594, telex 21007. Frankfurt: ATC, Neue Mainzerstrasse, D6000, Frankfurt/Main, Federal Republic of Germany, (0611) 23–5071, telex 416634. Los Angeles: ATC, 3550 Wilshire Blvd., CA 90010–2480 USA, (213) 380–6060, telex 674940. London: ATC, floor 4, Heathcoat House, 20 Saville Row, W1X 1AE, (01) 439–2773, telex 266039. New York: ATC, Suite 467, 630 5th Ave., International Bldg., NY 10111–0043 USA, (212) 489–7500, telex, 640747. Singapore: ATC, floor 8, Orchard Towers, 400 Orchard Rd., 235–2295, telex 38420. Tokyo: ATC Sankaido Building, 7F, 9–13 Akasaka, 1-Chome Minato-ku, 107 (03) 585–0705 telex 26785.

GREAT SOUTHERN REGION

Albany: Tourist Bureau, 171 York St., PO Box 764, WA 6330 (098) 41–1088, telex AA91988. Denmark: Tourist Bureau, Strickland St., WA 6333, (098) 48–1265, open daily. Mt. Barker: Tourist Bureau, Lowood Rd., WA 6324, (098) 51–1163.

ESPERANCE REGION

Esperance: Tourist Bureau and Travel Centre, Box 554 Museum Park, WA 6450, (090) 71–2330.

SOUTH WEST REGION

Main towns have information bureaus. Bunbury: Travel Information Centre, Box 176, (097) 21–4737. Busselton: Tourist Bureau, Civic Centre, WA 6280, (097) 52–1091. Collie: Tourist and Travel Bureau, Throssell St., WA 6225, (097) 34–2051, open each day; maps, brochures. Manjimup: 95 Giblett St., WA 6258, (097) 71–1831, also serves Walpole area; open each day. Margaret River: Cnr Tunbridge Rd. and Bussell Highway, WA 6285, (097) 57–2147, open daily, also serves Augusta area. Pemberton: Brockman St., Box 93, WA 6260, (097) 76–1133, open daily, serves Northcliffe.

GOLD FIELDS

Kalgoorlie: Tourist Bureau, 250 Hannan St., WA 6430, (090) 21–1413, closed Sunday. Coolgardie: Tourist Bureau, Box 11, Bayley St. (town center), (090) 26–6090, open daily.

WESTERN AUSTRALIA

GERALDTON REGION

Geraldton: Tourist Bureau, Civic Centre, Cathedral Ave., Box 187, WA 6530, (099) 21-3999. Closed Sunday. Public holidays 10 A.M. to noon. Kalbarri: Travel Service, Grey St., WA 6532, (099) 37-1104, open daily, Sunday, public holidays 10 A.M.-noon.

CARNARVON REGION

Denham: Shire Information Centre, Box 126, Hughes St., WA 6537, (099) 48-1218. Carnarvon: District Tourist Bureau, Carnarvon Civic Centre, 11 Robinson St., WA 6701, (099) 41-1146, closed Sunday. Exmouth: Tourist Bureau, Box 149, Maidstone Crescent, WA 6707, (099) 49-1176.

PILBARA

Port Hedland: Tourist Bureau, 13 Wedge St., Box 664, WA 6721, (091) 73-1650, open daily in tourist season. Roebourne: Tourist Bureau, 173 Roe St., WA 6718, (091) 82-1060, closed Sunday.

KIMBERLEY

Broome: Tourist Bureau, corner Bagot Rd./Great Northern Highway, WA 6725, (091) 92-1176, telex AA99847. Derby: Tourist Bureau, Clarendon St., WA 6728 (091) 91-1426. Kununurra: Visitors Centre, Coolibah Drive, WA 6743, (091) 68-1177, telex 99403, open daily in season.

TOURING. Forget about distances when you are thinking of touring in Western Australia. They are vast, but if you want to see some of the most breathtaking scenery in the world you have to go north—three or four hours by jet, several days by touring coach with overnight stops. It's closer down south to the sweeping, rolling hills, green forests, giant trees, beautiful beaches, and coastline. The best time is around August and September, when the west lives up to its publicity as the Wildflower State. Close to Perth are the hills of the Darling Ranges with valleys, streams, farms, sheep, cattle, sleepy towns, and historic sites. Southwest to Augusta, Bunbury, Busselton for day trips centered on these towns; go fishing or wine tasting in the Margaret River vineyards; picnic among the giant jarrah. Into the Great Southern to rugged mountains, coastal scenery. On through wheat and barley fields for native flora and fauna in national parks of the central south. Find the Goldfields, Kalgoorlie and Coolgardie, and the ghost towns where only the wind is left to swing the barroom doors. Or head north from Perth into the strange, eerie beauty of the Pinnacles, unique limestone formations that were once giant trees buried for thousands of years in drifting sand. And up farther to the port of Geraldton, the holiday resort of Kalbarri, and the magnificent coastline and gorges of the Murchison. The distances stretch farther now—here you can see Mount Augustus, the world's biggest rock (yes, bigger than Ayers Rock!) and the beautiful Ningaloo Marine Park, a 260km stretch of coral reef that rivals in quality and color the Great Barrier Reef. Then the Pilbara, where humans move mountains of iron ore and ships can carry hundreds of thousands of tonnes each trip, and the crew need motor scooters to cover the deck. The Kimberley and the old pearling town of Broome; incredible landscape of the forbidden Bungle Bungle Ranges discovered by tourists a year or so ago; herds of cattle and diamond mines and the largest human-made stretch of water in the land—Kununurra and Lake Argyle, bigger than Sydney Harbour. You'll need time and money because of sheer distance covered, but it's a valuable and exciting experience.

All tours unless otherwise stated from Perth, with prices at 1986. Check with operators for any rate changes.

By air: *Ansett WA,* 26 St. George's Tce., Perth, WA 6000, (09) 323-1113, or Smith St. Mall, Darwin, NT, (089) 80-3229. Tours to Pilbara: Hamersley Range Park, red gorges, ore projects, ghost town of Cossack, all meals, share twin $1,098, jet return to Port Hedland, coach touring. To Kimberley: Broome, Derby, gorges, Ord River, Lake Argyle, Kununurra, all meals, share twin,

$1,498, jet return, coach. To Mt. Augustus: world's largest rock, bird life, flowers, wildlife, five days, all meals, return jet to Carnarvon, coach, $612. To Goldfields: Kalgoorlie, Kambalda, Coolgardie, gold, nickel mining, ghost town, return air, three days, $318.

Skywest Airlines, floor 6, 140 St. George's Tce., Perth, WA 6000, (09) 426–4555. Tours to Albany: whale and shell museums, giant trees, coastal sights, wildlife reserve, Aboriginal fish traps, five days, $449. To Esperance: wildlife park, pink lake, national park, pre-Cambrian granite outcrops, pure white sand beaches, parrot farm, six days, $485. To Geraldton: Outback country, shearing shed, gold fossicking, wheat and sheep farms, three days $321. To Kalgoorlie: gold-detector search for wealth! Ghost towns, gold-treatment plant, visit to "two up" gambling school to see penny coins tossed, three days, from $294.

By coach: *Ansett Pioneer,* 26 St. George's Tce., Perth WA 6000, (09) 325–8855, 63 Smith St., Darwin, NT 5790, (089) 81–6433. To Albany; Geraldton, via Pemberton, Yanchep, Kalbarri: combining coastal scenery, forests, wildflowers, fishing, twelve days, $910. To Darwin via Geraldton, Carnarvon, Exmouth, Karratha, Tom Price, Wittenoom, Port Hedland, Broome, Fitzroy Crossing, Halls Creek, Kununurra with jet back to Perth, seventeen days, $1,960.

Australian Pacific, floor 1, 25 Barrack St., Perth, WA 6000, (09) 325–9377, telex AA95424. Gorge country: by air to Exmouth, coach to Dampier, Hamersley Range, Gorges, Tom Price, Port Hedland, Broome, Fitzroy Crossing, Geikie Gorge, Kununurra, Wyndham, Lake Argyle, Katherine, Darwin, fifteen days, $1,585.

Amesz Camping Safaris and Expeditions, 223 Collier Rd., Bayswater, WA 6053, (09) 271–2696 (toll free 008–99 9204). To Pilbara: Dampier, Karratha, Cossack, national parks, gorges, iron ore, Port Hedland, seven days, tents, $816 includes return jet travel. *Bryan Casey Adventure Tours,* 9 Habgood St., East Fremantle, WA 6000, (09) 339–94291. To Pilbara: Geraldton, Hutt River Province, Kalbarri, Carnarvon, Exmouth, Dampier, Karratha, Roebourne, Wittenoom, Newman, 13 days, $550, tents in bush or caravan parks. *Deluxe Coachlines,* AMP Arcade, corner Hay and William sts., Perth, WA 6000, (09) 322–7877, telex 94457. To South West: Esperance, Albany, coastline whaling station, shell-gemstone museum, five days, departs Sunday, $230. *Pathfinder Tours,* 7 Wild Close, Bullcreek, WA 6155, (09) 332–3332, toll free 008–999–304. To Geraldton, Carnarvon, Wittenoom, Port Hedland, Broome, eight days, return jet, $853. *Parlorcars,* 30 Pier St, Perth 6000, (09) 325–5488, telex 92805. To Albany, Manjimup, Margaret River, ranges, coast, horse farm, tall timber, Blackwood River cruise, five days, $442; To see wildflowers, Albany, Stirling Ranges, Manjimup, Margaret River, six days September and October, $567. To Kalgoorlie, Esperance, Albany, Manjimup, Margaret River, gold mining with coastal scenery, nine days, $863. Wildflower special, August–October, Jurien Bay, Geraldton, northern sandplains, national parks, wide range native flora, five days, $457. *Pinnacles Travel Centre,* Cnr Hay and Irwin sts., Perth 6000, (09) 325–9455, toll free 008–999–069. To Swan Valley Vineyards, wildflowers, Pinnacles limestone formations, Geraldton, Kalbarri gorges and national park, Murchison River, Shark Bay, Monkey Mia (where dolphins sometimes swim to shore to play), rock lobster fishing port of Dongara, six days, $480.

By rail. *Westrail Travel Centre,* Wellington St., Perth, 6000, (09) 326–2690, toll free 008–099–150, telex 95735. To Goldfields, Prospector express to ghost town Coolgardie, "two-up" gambling school, gold detecting, return daylight through beautiful Avon Valley, four days, $253. To southwest via Busselton in Australind train via Busselton for coach touring.

NATIONAL PARKS. Most of the designated reserves are to be found reasonably close to Perth: the rest of the State is just one great big wide open space. The *Penguin Island Reserve National Park,* 30 miles south of Perth and half a mile offshore from Safety Bay, justifies its name by being a sanctuary for penguins. Canoeing is good at the *Walyunga National Park,* where the Swan River pours out through the Darling Ranges. Caves are a feature of the *Yanchep National Park,* 30 miles north of Perth. The Yonderup Cave was an aboriginal burial ground. The park contains boating facilities, a golf course, wildlife reserves, and picnicking amenities. The *John Forrest National Park* is 3,500 acres of natural bushland in the Darling Ranges. It is 20 miles from Perth, off the Great Eastern Highway. Historic buildings and bird life are the main interest

WESTERN AUSTRALIA

in the *Yalgorup National Park,* situated between Bunbury and Mandurah and about 60 miles south of Perth. Giant karri, jarrah, and red gum trees are seen at their best in the *Walpole-Nornalup National Park,* 260 miles southeast of Perth. Go to *Hamelin Bay Park,* close to Augusta (200 miles south of Perth) for fishing and swimming. You need a four-wheel-drive vehicle to gain access to the limestone pinnacles and white-sand drifts of the *Painted Desert, Pinacles, Nambung National Park* 110 miles north of Perth. For extremely rugged coastal scenery there is the *Cape Le Grand National Park,* 20 miles out of Esperance on the state's most southerly shores. *Millstream National Park,* on the Fortescue River, has deep natural pools and wildlife. *Chichester National Park,* also on Fortescue River, features the Python Pool—a natural freshwater wildlife sanctuary. *Hamersley Range National Park,* in the Pilbara, is adjacent to Mt. Meharry. *Geike George National Park* is near Fitzroy Crossing, on the Fitzroy River; there are crocodiles here. *Tunnel Creek National Park* is the place to see flying foxes in a natural limestone tunnel.

SPORTS AND BEACHES. Western Australia is the place for the outdoor life. The wide-open spaces make it perfect for camping and hiking. Tours mentioned above will help you plan adventure holidays.

Beautiful **beaches** abound. *Yallingup* is a favorite with surfers; *Denmark* a favorite with families; *Kalbarri* is a favorite holiday resort for anyone.

If **diving** is your interest, contact *Dive in Australia,* 680 Beach St., San Francisco, CA 94109, (415) 928–4480. The *Geraldton* area is littered with shipwrecks and makes a fascinating divers' area. *Nigaloo Marine Park* is a 260km stretch of coral reef that rivals the Great Barrier.

Off the coast, the saltwater **fishing** is legendary. Snapper, grouper, shark, marlin, sailfish, and mackerel keep fishing enthusiasts happy. The Abrolhos Islands are known for their fishing excellence.

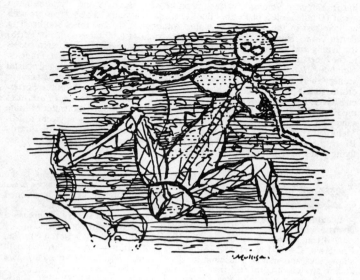

THE NORTHERN TERRITORY

Two bored young men sunning themselves on a rock in Darwin Harbour decided to ask the local radio station to play a request tune for one of their friends. The request, they said, came from the Rocksitters Club, Darwin Harbour.

Inquisitive listeners to the program enquired about the club. Some set out to find it. A number succeeded and were welcomed as members. The joke had become reality. But the membership list soon closed, because the rock could only seat 30 or so bodies plus their supply of refreshments.

Rocksitters and Dry Regattas

And so the Rocksitters Club came into being and one more crazy dimension was added to the already oddball way of life to be found in the Northern Territory. Maybe it is the climate; perhaps the isolation and loneliness. But certainly this vast, tropical, unpeopled 523,000 square miles of Australia seems to have more than the average number of eccentric and unusual happenings.

The Territorians are almost aggressive in their eccentricity, determined to set themselves aside from the rest of Australia by fostering a laconic, rough-and-ready image of themselves that comes as close as anyone is likely to get to the popular idea of the tall, gaunt, leathery tough Australian bushman of the imagination.

The Territorians swagger and boast. Their talk matches the size and vastness of the land to which they cling. They are used to extremes of sun, rain, and distance, and they emphasize this familiarity in their conversations with strangers. But beneath it all they are still by and large suburbanites. They swagger off home to their air-conditioned suburban villas, dig the garden, check the freezer, and settle down to an evening's television. It is an intensely social and sociable life they lead, for they have most of the comforts of their big-city siblings thousands of miles to the south but few of the distractions.

Thus the Rocksitters Club was a welcome newcomer. It fitted in with a pattern formed by such notable occurrences as the Beer Can Regatta (which creates work and entertainment from the territory's most used commodity), the Bangtail Muster and—high spot of them all—the Henley-on-Todd Regatta.

The Todd is the river that flows intermittently through the center of Alice Springs. More often than not it is simply a sandy indentation straggling between the gum trees. It is in this dried-up creek bed that the residents of Alice Springs hold their annual version of the august international rowing regatta that occurs each year on England's River Thames.

There are a few slight differences between the two events. Because of lack of water, the Territorians depend on foot power to propel their craft. The rowing eights and yachts have no bottoms; the crews have to pick up their craft and run. It is a slapstick, raucous, hearty carnival and typifies the Northern Territory. Spectators watch safe in the knowledge that the Alice Springs Surf Life Saving Club (so it is a thousand miles to the nearest beach!) is on hand to rescue any capsized craft.

Darwin and a Town Called Alice

Alice Springs, a desert city, is one of two main centers of population in the Northern Territory; the other, a thousand miles "up the track" to the north, is Darwin, a city rebuilt after being almost completely destroyed by a cyclone that struck on Christmas Day, 1974.

The two are completely dissimilar. "The Alice"—as it will always be known—is now a far cry from the bush shanty town depicted in Nevil Shute's *A Town Like Alice* but remains a cattle town nonetheless. Darwin, however, is a port and administrative center. The majority of its population are public servants living there on detachment rather than with any view toward permanent residency.

Darwin receives heavy monsoonal rain from November to March, and humidity is extremely high. Alice Springs escapes the monsoons but has high summer heat. Darwin is surrounded by lagoons and thickly wooded swamplands with buffalo, crocodile, and an exotic bird population. Around Alice Springs are the rich red hills of the desert ranges and limitless deserts stretching hundreds of miles in all directions.

To the west 465km is a real oasis—the multi-million-dollar tourist complex of Yulara near Ayers Rock. There's nothing much south, but Tennant Creek is 500km north, then 400km farther, Daly Waters, another 151 to Mataranka, an on 105 to Katherine are main points of human congregation. Jabiru, 251km east of Darwin, serves rich uranium mines of Arnhem Land.

Pioneers of the 1800s

The first land exploration of the area now occupied by the territory came when Charles Sturt ventured into the desert regions to the south of Alice Springs in the 1840s. Nothing much more was discovered about the region until John McDougall Stuart made three expeditions between 1860 and 1862. On one of these, in 1860, he became the first white man to cross the Macdonnell Ranges. His route took him some 30 miles to the west of Alice Springs. Settlement began only when work started 11 years later on building an overland telegraph line from

Adelaide to Darwin. John Ross then selected Heavitree Gap (still the main approach to the town) as the best way to bring the telegraph through the ranges. Discovery of the actual springs was made soon afterward. They were named after the wife of the man responsible for construction of the telegraph line, Sir Charles Todd.

Alice Springs thus happened because of its usefulness as a staging post. Darwin, however, received more urgent and earlier attention because of its importance as a strategic link between Great Britain and Australia. The coastline thereabouts was first properly explored in 1802 by Mathew Flinders. Between 1824 and 1849 three attempts were made to establish permanent settlements. All three—at Raffles Bay, Port Essington, and Melville Island—failed. It was probably as true then as it is today that the optimists of the dry season soon become the pessimists of the wet season; the monsoons have killed off many high hopes, and development has always been slow.

Naturalist Charles Darwin, who made several scientific expeditions on board the *Beagle,* is the man after whom the town is named. The *Beagle* was the ship sailed by Captain J. Stokes when he discovered the port in 1839.

This event was followed by a further period of inaction until a shipful of settlers arrived from South Australia in 1869 to populate a town site that had been selected three years earlier. At that stage the town was named Palmerston. Only in 1911 was Darwin given his accolade.

Farms of a Million Acres

The overland telegraph reached the town in 1872, a gold rush seduced thousands into heading north for a short-lived period of hope, and farmers seeking cheap labor opened up million-acre properties for their cattle. All this resulted in Darwin's quickly achieving a population of 10,000. Alice Springs, meanwhile, languished and had only 27 white residents as recently as 1927.

It was the coming of the railway north across the desert from Adelaide in 1929 that set in motion the first real settlement in the Alice. The train is known as the Ghan: a tribute to the many Afghan camel drivers who formed the mainstay of overland trade and communication until quite recent times. Camels still roam the Outback areas and race annually in the Alice Springs Camel Cup. There is also a thriving export trade to Middle East countries. Visitors have several chances close to Alice Springs of taking a short ride on these snarling, bumpy beasts.

In more recent times Alice Springs has leaped ahead, largely owing to its popularity as a staging post for touring into central Australia but also in part owing to the location of an American communications center on the outskirts at Pine Gap.

Darwin: Wet or Dry, It's Hot

Darwin's progress has been less steady. Setbacks have been many. The early enthusiasm for its pastoral potential waned under the hardships of tropical living, largely because of the inability of settlers from temperate zones to adapt either their way of life or their methods of farming to a climate made up of just two distinctly different seasons. It was either wet or dry—and always hot.

Nowhere is this better described than in the classic of Australian folklore, *We of the Never Never,* Mrs. Aneas Gunn's story of settlement of a Northern Territory cattle station at the turn of the century. It is a touching story of hardship and heroics, of dismay and determination, that needs to be read by anyone wishing to come to grips with the character of the Northern Territory.

THE NORTHERN TERRITORY

Darwin boomed briefly, thanks to gold, then died, then boomed again as pastoralists set up huge cattle stations based on the exploitation of cheap native labor. But the optimism petered out, and the city's growth slowed again. World War II turned Darwin into an important military base. The northern outpost of the country, it was closest to any invading forces. It suffered 64 bombing raids, becoming only one of two Australian areas to be hit. The other was the pearling town of Broome, Western Australia. This was a traumatic experience for a country that has always been so far removed from the areas of battle. A postwar slump set in and it took the discovery of uranium at nearby Rum Jungle, plus an ill-fated scheme to develop rice plantations at Humpty Doo, to bring back a sense of purpose to the area. In recent times the city's growth has been due as much to the influx of public servants as to any other factor. The cyclone devastated the city, but reconstruction work brought it back to its previous level of development, and a flourishing new city has risen from the rubble.

Exploring the Northern Territory

Highways lead in from Western Australia (to Katherine), from Queensland (to Tennant Creek), and from South Australia (to Alice Springs). There will always be a certain amount of backtracking no matter which route travelers follow—unless they take the unwise step of venturing out across the desert. The best scheme is to enter from the south, tour up the track to Darwin with occasional diversions, and then backtrack into Western Australia or Queensland. From Alice Springs there are roads (mostly unpaved) out to the gorges of the Macdonnell Ranges, to Ayers Rock, and to the Olgas. It is a 250-mile drive across the desert to reach the great sandstone monolith of Ayers Rock. Its great hump rises 1,143 feet from the desert. Its base measures 5½ miles.

The rock is notable for its significance as an Aboriginal shrine and for the way it continually changes color. Much of its base is covered in vegetation, and just to drive around it is to witness scenes of great variety and rapid change. Be there at sunset and you will see the colors shift through the spectrum until darkness descends and there is nothing left but a huge, brooding, elongated dome that defies explanation or description. Just 20 miles farther on is an equally inexplicable phenomenon: the cone-shaped domes of the Olgas. Less famous than Ayers Rock, they are just as unusual and just as fascinating.

Take the road out of the Alice to the Jay Creek Native Settlement and you pass the boulder that marks the grave of John Flynn, the man who set up the Flying Doctor Service, now headquartered in Alice Springs. Travel on to Standley Chasm but be sure to get there at noon. The overhead sun pours down into this narrow defile and turns the sandstone walls into every shade of gold, ochre, orange, russet, and red.

Going north up the Track (it's never given its proper name of Stuart Highway), the first settlement reached is Tennant Creek—313 miles away. This is one of the oldest gold-and-copper-mining centers in the territory. It has become an important staging post on the journey north, since it is just 16 miles south of the junction with the Barclay Highway coming in from the east through Queensland. On the approach to Tennant Creek, 60 miles out of town, you pass the Devil's Marbles. This group of huge granite boulders were believed by Aboriginals to be eggs laid by the mythical rainbow snake.

Continue up the track through Renner Springs, Elliott, and Newcastle Waters to reach the settlement of Daly Waters. It is a good place to take a break for fishing and boating. Rivers from here on abound with fish of an extremely succulent and meaty variety. Cooked fresh over an open fire in the clear, clean air of this unindustrialized vastness, they take on a flavor known to only a few among modern day man.

Sunny Beaches and Sheer Cliffs

When you reach the next outpost of civilization at Larrimah you are still about 320 miles from Darwin. This township is the end of the railway line that runs south from Darwin, with no link on to the southern states. It was built primarily to serve the needs of the cattle stations so that they could move their beasts more quickly to market. Forty miles further on, and five miles off the highway, is the Mataranka cattle station, which provides limited accommodation for tourists. Set amid palm groves and warm springs, it is notable for the Elsey Memorial Cemetery, which contains the graves of the hardy settlers mentioned in *We of the Never Never*.

Drive on for 64 miles and you reach the busy, prosperous small community of Katherine at the junction of the road north and the route in from Western Australia. It is at the heart of the inland Australia's best network of rivers, gorges, and places of significance in Aboriginal mythology. Kintore Caves, 17 miles to the northwest, are of great anthropological importance. The Katherine Gorge, 22 miles to the northeast, is a magnificent waterway of calm waters, sheer cliffs, secluded sandy beaches, abundant wildlife, and, in its upper reaches, complete solitude. Crocodiles can be seen sunning themselves and gliding into the water. The fishing is excellent. Boat-cruise passengers are entranced by the perfect reflections of trees and cliffs in the blue-green water. Early morning or late afternoon are the ideal times to visit.

Thirty-two miles north of Katherine is the chain of waterfalls cascading into deep rock pools at Edith Falls. The freshwater crocodiles that make their homes in the rock pools are a protected species. To travel through the tropical greenery to the higher falls and pools usually entails use of a four-wheel-drive vehicle plus some walking.

From Katherine the route north goes through the historic mining center of Pine Creek to Adelaide River, 72 miles south of Darwin. Here is the cemetery in which are buried the civilians and members of the armed forces killed during the 1942–43 Japanese air raids on Darwin.

On the final run into Darwin, through Batchelor and Rum Jungle, you will see roads off to left and right. These are the routes to take to the great Aboriginal reserve of Arnhemland, to the falls and hot springs of Knuckey's Lagoons, Tumbling Waters, Berry Springs, and Robin Falls. But first establish your base in Darwin.

Exploring Darwin

Darwin sits on a peninsula with its commercial and business heart overlooking the harbor and much of its residential area concentrated in the suburbs of Parap and Fannie Bay looking out over Fannie Bay.

There is no mistaking its role as a port and administrative center. This is reflected in the number of four-square, imposing public buildings and the number of ships lying at anchor. It is short on sights for visitors to see. Most interest lies in coming into contact with the people and their way of life. The city is an ideal base from which to explore the tropical coastland rather than being of great interest in its own right. It is the base and starting point for operators of tours and safaris, many using four-wheel-drive vehicles, into the plains, forests, and swamplands that enfold the city on all but its seaward side. Its botanical gardens, however, are an unrivaled reserve of tropical luxuriants. At East Point reserve, four miles from downtown, there are an artillery museum and the guns that defended the city during World War II.

Exploring Alice Springs

The Stuart Highway becomes Todd Street for the couple of miles or so that it slices through the Alice. This is the main shopping street, the site of many hotels and restaurants and the place from which to get your bearings to all other points of interest. Todd Street is a rich melange of smart suburban housewives, high-booted cattlemen, Aborigines, rubbernecking tourists, and the weatherbeaten roughnecks who sample the high life in town for a few days, then head off back to the solitude of the desert. For all its spruce new homes and sparkling supermarkets, the Alice is still a frontier town. You can sense it in the air, see it in the people.

Travel not more than a couple of miles in any direction and you are on the border of a seemingly limitless desert, hot and inhospitable. One of the most noticeable buildings on Todd Street is the John Flynn Memorial Church. The service he founded, the Flying Doctor, has its base nearby (between the hospital and the jail!) and can be visited. Stop, too, to attend a lesson at the School of the Air, a unique service by which the children hundreds of miles away on isolated cattle stations gain their education. A mile out of town, close by the actual Alice Springs, are the restored remains of the original telegraph station that led to the founding of the town. It contains a graphic portrayal of the laying of the line from Adelaide to Darwin. Alice Springs boasts a commercial date farm and the Pitchi Richi sanctuary two miles from town has the only wine-producing vineyard in the desert center and a comprehensive collection of Aboriginal artifacts.

Alice Springs has developed a strong reputation as a center for artists. For such a small town it contains quite a number of galleries. Many concentrate on Aboriginal artists while others are outlets for the creations of their owners.

You will see Alice and its surroundings at their best from April to October. But August is the high spot. This is when carnival follows carnival and there are picnic races such as the three-day event at Hartz Ranges. It is these occasions that one sees the Territorian in his or her true colors. And it's a sight not to be missed!

PRACTICAL INFORMATION FOR THE NORTHERN TERRITORY

HOW TO GET THERE. By air. Alice Springs and Darwin are served by the two main domestic carriers *Australian Airlines* (TAA) and *Ansett* from all capital cities. *East-West* flies Perth–Ayers Rock–Sydney. *Air-WA* flies Perth–Ayers Rock–Alice Springs–Cairns (Queensland). National airline *Qantas* flies into Darwin. Airlines have discounted air fare schemes including standby and airpass for a number of different destinations at low fare. Contact TAA, Ansett, any city, or the NT Government Tourist Bureau, 31 Smith St. Mall, Darwin, NT 5794, (089) 81–6611.

By rail. Two direct train services into Alice Springs—Ghan from Adelaide in 24 hours (first-class sleeper; economy sleeper; situp); connections available with Trans Continental from Sydney and Perth. The Alice from Sydney through NSW and South Australia in 48 hours—restaurant; lounge cars; twin rooms with shower; toilet; video movies; electronic organ. The Sunlander from Brisbane to Townsville twice weekly connects with Inlander to Mt. Isa—air conditioned; first and economy; single; twins. From Mt. Isa to Alice by coach or plane.

AUSTRALIA

By bus. *Ansett-Pioneer, Deluxe,* and *Greyhound* have regular services to Northern Territory from capital cities. Special passes allow unlimited travel to and around the territory for 14, 30, and 60 days. Contact NT Tourist Bureau for latest offers. Interstate tour operators: *Ansett Briscoes,* 101 Franklin St., Adelaide, SA 5000, (08) 51–2975; *Australian Pacific Tours,* Box 118, Hampton, Victoria 3188, (03) 598–5355; *Camping Connection,* Box 526F, Hobart, Tasmania 7001, (002) 23–5777; *Centralian Staff Holidays,* 1 James St., Clayton, Vic. 3168, (03) 543–7629; *Deluxe Coachlines,* Cnr. Castlereagh and Hay sts., Sydney, NSW 2000, (02) 212–4888; *Newmans Carah Coaches,* Box 5353, Sydney, NSW 2000, (02) 231–6511.

ACCOMMODATIONS. Millions of dollars have been spent in the territory over the past two years in luxury hotel and casino building. The Sheraton hotel group has invested very heavily in Yulara (Ayers Rock) with a five-star 230-room property and in Alice Springs with a 238-room luxury hotel that opened mid-1986. In Darwin the 235-room luxury Beaufort-Darwin has just opened. Its ultramodern architecture matches that of the Diamond Beach Casino, the other top property. New hotels and motels are going up in both Alice and Darwin, but building costs are high and rooms are expensive in better accommodations. Following rates are for a double room. *Deluxe,* \$A100 and up; *expensive,* \$A80–\$A100; *moderate,* \$A50–\$A70; *inexpensive,* \$A25–\$A45.

ALICE SPRINGS

Diamond Springs Casino and Country Club. *Deluxe.* Barrett Drive; (089) 52–5066, toll-free (008) 08–6112. Pool, gambling, tour desk, theater, amphitheater, tea-coffee facilities, in-house movies, 75 rooms.

Sheraton Alice Springs. *Deluxe.* Barrett Drive; (098) 52–8000. 238 rooms, pool, tea-coffee facilities in room, in-house movies, tour desk, adjacent 18-hole golf course.

Alice Motor Inn. *Moderate.* 27 Undoolya Rd.; (089) 52–2322. Well maintained, good furnishings. Pool, tea-coffee facilities, color TV in rooms; licensed to sell liquor.

Alice Tourist Apartments. *Moderate.* Gap Rd.; (089) 52–2788. Self-contained units with queen-size beds, four bunks in separate bedroom, cooking facilities in room, pool.

Elkira Motel. *Moderate.* 134 Bath St.; (089) 52–1222. Quality furnishings, well appointed, pool, excellent dining room, tea-coffee making in room.

Larapinta Lodge. *Inexpensive.* 3 Larapinta Drive; (089) 52–7255. Tea-coffee facilities, pool, well appointed.

Melanka Lodge. *Inexpensive.* Todd St.; (089) 52–2233. Tea-coffee, pool. Backpacker special: \$12 single.

AYERS ROCK/YULARA

Four Seasons. *Deluxe.* Yulara; (089) 56–2100. Resort with in-house movies, pool, excellent restaurant, tea-coffee facilities. 100 rooms.

Sheraton Ayers Rock. *Deluxe.* Yulara; (089) 56–2200. Resort with movies, pool, restaurants, tour desk. Design won Australian award for architecture. Solar panels a feature. 230 rooms.

Ayers Rock Lodge. *Inexpensive.* Yulara; (089) 5–6217. Double units, 4-bedded, dormitory, cot hire, linen hire. Meals, barbecue facilities available, swimming pool.

DARWIN

Beaufort Darwin Centre. *Deluxe.* The Esplanade; (089) 81–1188. All rooms have view over Darwin Harbour. Pool, tea-coffee facilities, convention, bars, restaurant.

Darwin TraveLodge. *Deluxe.* 122 The Esplanade; (089) 81–5388. All facilities. Special weekend rates \$65.

Diamond Beach Casino. *Deluxe.* Gilruth Ave.; (089) 81–7755. Toll free (008) 89–1118. All resort facilities, gambling. Children under 14 free.

THE NORTHERN TERRITORY

Sheraton Darwin. *Deluxe.* 32 Mitchell St.; (089) 81–1155, telex 85991. All facilities, special weekend rates.
Lameroo Lodge. *Expensive.* 69 Mitchell St.; (089) 81–9733. Bus terminal on premises, meals available. Swimming pool, laundry facilities.
Marrakai Apartments. *Expensive.* 93 Smith St.; (089) 81–2819. Serviced apartments with swimming pool, most facilities, cooking in rooms.
Asti Motel. *Moderate.* Cnr. Smith and Packard sts.; (089) 81–8200. Reasonably priced meals in restaurant. Most facilities.
Darwin Motor Inn. *Moderate.* 97 Mitchell St.; (089) 81–1122. Pool, bar, fridge, licensed restaurant, continental breakfast included, near casino.
Don Hotel. *Moderate.* 12 Cavanagh St.; (089) 81–5311. Swimming pool, entertainment, restaurant.
Aspa City Motel. *Inexpensive.* 38 Gardens Rd.; (089) 81–8200. Well maintained; pool; restaurant.
Capricornia Motel. *Inexpensive.* 44 East Point Rd.; (089) 81–4055. Breakfast only available. Tea-coffee facilities, color TV.
Leprechaun Hotel. *Inexpensive.* Opposite Darwin Airport, Stuart Highway, Winnellie; (089) 84–3400. Sauna-spa, communal kitchen, fridge, coffee-tea facilities.

GULF COUNTRY

Borroloola Inn. *Moderate.* Borroloola; radio telephone 1257. Laundry, restaurant, licensed, parking, swimming pool.

GOVE

Arnhem's Hideaway Hotel. *Moderate.* Nhulunbuy; (089) 87–1813. No private facilities; tea-coffee making; licensed restaurant; pool; parking.
Walkabout Hotel. *Moderate.* Westall St., Nhulunbuy; (089) 87–1777. Pool, private facilities, licensed restaurant, entertainment, parking, laundry facilities.

KATHERINE

Crossways Motel. *Moderate.* Cnr Katherine Tce. and Warburton St.; (089) 72–1022. Includes continental breakfast; pool, entertainment, disco Friday and Saturday nights.
Katherine Hotel-Motel. *Moderate.* Katherine Tce.; (089) 72–1622. Pool, handicapped facilities, restaurant, licensed, sauna-spa.
Gardean Holiday Village. *Inexpensive.* 1475 Cameron St.; (089) 72–2511. Family 2 X 2, $45. Pool, licensed restaurant, room service.
Paraway Motel. *Inexpensive.* O'Shea Terrace; (089) 72–2644. Spacious units, pool, handicapped facilities, licensed restaurant.
Riverview Motel and Caravan Park. *Inexpensive.* 440 Victoria Highway; (089) 72–1011. Tea-coffee making, fridge, color TV, 10% discount stay of three nights.

KAKADU NATIONAL PARK

South Alligator Motor Inn Resort. *Expensive to inexpensive.* Arnhem Highway; (089) 79–0166. Pool, licensed restaurant, handicapped facilities, tea-coffee making. Safari accommodations available.

MATARANKA

Mataranka Homestead Tourist Park. *Inexpensive.* Mataranka; (089) 75–4544. Laundry facilities, licensed restaurant, sauna-spa, no rooms with private facilities.

TENNANT CREEK

Bluestone Motor Inn. *Moderate.* Paterson St.; (089) 62–2617. Private facilities, licensed restaurant, swimming pool.
Eldorado Motor Lodge. *Moderate.* Paterson St.; (089) 62–2402. Private facilities, licensed restaurant, pool.

AUSTRALIA

Goldfields Hotel-Motel. *Moderate.* Paterson St.; (089) 62-2030. Licensed restaurant, color TV, laundry facilities.
Safari Lodge Motel. *Moderate.* Davidson St.; (089) 62-2207. Fridge, color TV, tea-coffee free in room.
Tennant Creek Hotel. *Moderate.* Paterson St.; (089) 62-2006. Licensed restaurant, tea-coffee facilities, rates include breakfast in motel.

CAMPERS AND CARAVANS. More and more travelers are taking caravans (campers) to the territory, where the caravan parks are modern, comfortable, and plentiful. However, many others—mostly the young—like to pitch a tent and "live under canvas." All the main areas in the territory have parks that cater to these people whether they arrive by car or on foot as hitchhikers. Some have permanent tents on site that are rented out at a nominal sum (about $20 per person per week) on an unpowered site. All parks listed here have swimming pools, meals available (or nearby), communal shower and toilet facilities, barbecues, electricity included in the charge, ice available, community laundry with washing machines, unless otherwise stated. Telephone ahead to check on availability, especially for Yulara (Ayers Rock) and Kakadu National Park, which are limited in camping sites, and most popular. The Northern Territory Government Tourist Bureau produces a travelers' guide to caravan parks, which is free. Contact the bureau at offices listed; see Tourist Information, below.

ALICE SPRINGS

Alice Travelers Village. Stuart Highway; (089) 52-8955. Powered sites $7 a night, unpowered $3.50; cabins/units $8 per person per night, 4-share basis. *Carmichael Tourist Park,* Larapinta Drive; (089) 52-1200. Powered $10, unpowered $8; units $25-$35; on-site vans $25. *Greensleaves Tourist Camp,* Burke St.; (089) 52-8645: $35, tents $18 a week per person, on-site vans $70 a week. *Heavitree Gap Caravan Park;* (089) 52-2370, $9, $4, vans on site $22. *MacDonnell Range Tourist Park,* Ross Highway; (089) 52-6111: $11, $4, on-site vans/cabins $34. *Stuart Caravan Park,* Larapinta Drive, (089) 52-2547: $9.50, $8, on-site vans $24.

AYERS ROCK/YULARA

Ayers Rock Campgrounds, Yulara Tourist Resort (089) 56-2055, telex 81085: $14 per person a night, extra person $5, weekly $98 and $35 on powered sites; unpowered $10, extra person $5 a night; on-site vans $38.50, extra person $5, weekly $270, $35.

DARWIN

Coolalinga Tourist Park, 26km Stuart Highway, Howard Springs; (089) 83-1026. Powered $8.50, extra person $3.50, weekly $45, extra person $15 plus power. *Kampgrounds of Australia,* McMillans Rd., Malak (suburban) (089) 27-2651. Powered $11, extra person $2, weekly $40 plus power, extra person $15, no swimming pool. *Malak Caravan Park,* McMillans Rd., Malak (089) 27-3500. Powered $11 (4 people), weekly $40 plus power; no pool. *Overlander,* McMillans Rd., Berrimah (suburb) (089) 84-3025. On-site vans $10-$20, units $12 ($60 a week), powered $7, weekly $43 plus power; unpowered $5 two adults, weekly $30, swimming nearby.

KATHERINE

Gorge Caravan Park, Katherine Gorge National Park; (089) 72-1253, telex 85425: powered sites 2 adults $9, extra $3.25; unpowered $6.50, $3.25. Camping area available (no sites), swimming nearby. *Springvale Homestead,* Shadforth Rd., Katherine; (089) 72-1355, telex 85425: 2 adults $9, extra $3.25; $6.50, $3.25; cabins/units 2 adults $40, $7. *Riverview Motel and Caravan Park,* 440 Victoria Highway, Katherine; (089) 72-1011: powered $7, extra person $1; air conditioning extra $42 weekly; unpowered $4, extra person $3, weekly $24 and $12; on-site vans $20, extra person $5, weekly $100 and $25; swimming nearby.

THE NORTHERN TERRITORY

KAKADU

Cooinda Inn Caravan Park, Kakadu; (089) 79–2545: powered $15 per van per night, unpowered $10; camping. *South Alligator Motor Inn,* Kakadu; (089) 79–0166, telex 85732: powered $10, extra person $3, unpowered $6, $1.50; cabins/units $22 to $50.

MATARANKA

Mataranka Homestead Tourist Park; (089) 75–4544, telex 85425: powered $6.50, extra person $3.25; unpowered $6.50, $3.25; air conditioning extra $3.25; cabins/units twin $46, extra person $3, triple $53. Swimming nearby, electricity extra.

TENNANT CREEK

Tennant Creek Caravan Park, Stuart Highway, Tennant Creek; (089) 62–2325: powered $9, extra person $3, unpowered $7 couple, extra adult $3. On-site vans $24, extra person $3; cabins/units $12, extra person $3. *Outback Caravan Park,* Peko Rd.; (089) 62–2459: powered $9, extra person $2.50, unpowered $3.50, on-site vans $20–$25, extra person $2.50. *Threeways Roadhouse,* 25km north; (089) 62–2744: $7, $1; $4, $1; on-site vans $20; cabins/units $25 single, $30 double.

DRINKING LAWS. It can be a long way between cold drinks in the territory, but drinking laws are liberal. Hotels and motels 10 A.M.–2 A.M. daily, restaurants 11:30 A.M.–2 A.M., bottle shops Sunday to Friday, noon to 10 P.M., bottles only, Saturday 9 A.M.–10 P.M.

RESTAURANTS. Alice Springs. *Alice's Bistro,* coffee shop, international, Sheraton Alice Springs. *Casino Grill Room,* Barrett Drive, 52–5066. *Chopsticks Chinese Restaurant,* Ermond Arcade, (089) 52–3873. *Jules Coffee Pot,* Shop 10, Todd Plaza. *Mandarin Chinese Restaurant,* Coles Complex, (089) 52–5899. *Maxim's,* Todd Tavern, Todd St., (089) 52–5399. *Mia Pizza Bar–Italian Restaurant,* Larapinta Drive, Diarama Village, (089) 52–2964. *The Bradshaw Room,* top dining, Sheraton Hotel, (089) 52–8000. *Turner House,* 13 Hartley St., (089) 51–5775, licensed. *The Other Place,* Todd Tavern, Todd St., (089) 52–5399, counter meals, lunch, dinner. *Terrace Restaurant,* Elkira Motel, 135 Bath St.; (089) 52–1222. Fine dining. *Stuart Room Restaurant,* F. White Gum Park Tearoom, opposite Simpsons Gap off Larapinta Drive, (089) 52–4066. Licensed.

Ayers Rock/Yulara. *Four Seasons* and *Sheraton* coffee shops and dining rooms cater to guests and public. Prices reasonable. Yulara shopping center between these two serves quick meals cafe style with take-aways.

Darwin. *Diamond-Beach Hotel Casino,* Gilruth Avenue, (089) 81–7755. Coffee shop 24 hours, Chinese restaurant, licensed, credit cards, noon–2 P.M. weekdays; check for dinners. *Darwin TraveLodge,* 122 the Esplanade, (089) 81–5388. *The Four Seasons Rooftop Restaurant,* Dashwood Crescent, (089) 81–5333, recommended, day-night views. *Telford Top End,* corner Esplanade, Mitchell and Daly sts., (089) 81–6511. Bistro for casual dining room. *The Sheraton Darwin,* 32 Mitchell St., (089) 81–1155, telex 85991. *Expensive.* International dining. Danish, French, Malaysian, Indonesian, Chinese, steak houses, seafood specialists, fish and chip shops, and quick snack bars available in town.

HOW TO GET AROUND. By air. *Australian Airlines, Ansett, Airlines of Northern Territory* link all main towns and some settlements even in remotest areas. Charter operators *Tillair,* Katherine, have mail and freight flights of up to 7 hours calling at outback stations; passengers can join. See Tours section. *Tiwi Tours* offer flights to Bathurst and Melville Islands from Darwin. Also see Tours.

By bus. *Ansett-Pioneer, Deluxe, Greyhound* have "unlimited mileage" passes for 14, 30, and 60 days between $250 and $700 for NT exploration. They can be bought from offices in any capital city. Government tourist bureaus have latest information. See Tourist Information. Vast range of coach touring available from national companies and local bus operators in most areas. You can camp out at night and coach by day or stay in motels or hotels depending on degree of comfort and adventure desired.

By car. Two main highways into the territory are the Stuart, which connects with Adelaide, South Australia, and the Barkly, connecting with Brisbane, Queensland. Both are paved. *Australian National Rail* offers car transport to Alice Springs from Adelaide. Well-maintained, all-weather roads take you to most major tourist attractions. Important to stay on recognized routes and check facilities available before setting out. MUSTS are reliable vehicle, reliable map. Ask for advice if in doubt. Basic spare parts: tire, spare tube, tire repair kit, coil, fan belt, condenser, radiator hoses, distributer points. If plan is to travel away from main roads take EXTRA spare tire and tube, extra jack with large base plate (to stop sinking in sand or mud), engine oil, tools, ax, shovel. Always carry plenty of water, extra gas. Darwin, Katherine, Tennant Creek, Alice Springs linked with 1,600km bitumen-paved Stuart Highway. Main road Ayers Rock–Alice Springs, 465km paved. On Stuart and Barkly highways gas stations, stores, accommodations at least every 200km. All main roads are regularly patrolled by Northern Territory police. Most drivers see all they want and never leave paved roads. **Car rentals: Darwin:** *Avis* (phone 81–9922), *Budget* (84–4388), *Hertz* (81–6686), *Thrifty* (81–8555). **Alice Springs:** *Avis* (52–4366), *Budget* (52–4133), *Hertz* (52–2644), *Thrifty* (21–1303). **Katherine:** *Avis* (72–1445), *Budget* (72–1280). **Ayers Rock:** *Avis* (52–4366). Prices range $17–$85 daily. *Budget Campervans:* Alice Springs: (527–6444) from $85–$115 fully equipped.

TOURIST INFORMATION. The *Northern Territory Government Tourist Bureau* has offices in Darwin and Alice Springs to provide information on all facets of touring. Write NTGB, 31 Smith Street Mall, Darwin, NT 5794, (089) 81–6611, telex: AA85027. 51 Todd St., Alice Springs, NT 5750, (089) 52–1299, telex: AA81277. In other states: South Australia: 9 Hindley St., Adelaide, SA 5000, (08) 212–1133, telex: AA82506. Victoria: 99 Queen St., Melbourne, Vic. 3000, (03) 67–6948, telex: AA31450; 84 Walker St., Dandenong, Vic 3175, (03) 794–7755, (03) 794–7755, telex: AA34912. Queensland: 260 George St., Brisbane, Qld 4000, (07) 229–5799, telex: AA42848. New South Wales: 89 King St., Sydney, NSW 2000, (02) 235–2822, telex: AA26825; 44 Macquarie St., Parramatta, NSW 2150, (02) 633–9400, telex: AA23376. Western Australia: 62 St. George's Tce., Perth, WA 6000, (09) 322–4255, telex: AA94467. Australian Capital Territory: 35 Ainslie Ave., Canberra City, ACT 2601, (062) 571–177, telex: AA61948. Tasmania: 93 Liverpool St., Hobart, Tas 7000, (002) 34–4199, telex: AA57012. Overseas offices in Japan, London, Frankfurt, Singapore, Auckland, and North America: 3550 Wilshire Blvd., Los Angeles, CA 90010, USA 800–4–Outback. Telex: (230) 3720296.

SEASONAL EVENTS. It must be the weather that gives the Northern Territory its share of characters, odd events, and wry humor. Highlights of any year tend toward the off-beat rather than recognized culture. Where else would you find, for instance, the *World's Barefoot Mud Crab Tying* championship than in Darwin (August) or the *Henley-on-Todd Regatta,* where sand takes the place of water (Alice Springs, August)? Other annual mysteries include *Darwin's Froggolympics* (January), the *Bangtail Muster Parade of Weird Floats* in Alice Springs (May), *Camel Cup,* Alice Springs (May), *Beer Can Regatta,* in which otherwise normal people spend months joining together beer cans to make very imaginative boats to sail off Mindil Beach (June), and the *rodeo round,* when the rough riders and drovers come to town to see how long they can sit in the saddle—Mataranka (August), Alice Springs and Katherine (August), Darwin (August). But when they are not practicing running along a dry riverbed in a bottomless boat for the Todd event, the Alice Springs people indulge in an annual festival (October), art exhibition (November), show (July), Old Timers' Fete (August), and a Melbourne Cup race meeting (November).

THE NORTHERN TERRITORY

Darwin has its show (July) and racing carnival (August). Events subject to change without notice. Check government tourist bureaus.

TOURS. Operators offer vast range of tours ranging from half-day and day coach trips to four-wheel-drive Outback adventures, camping, fly-in safaris, camel treks, wildlife boat cruises, balloon safaris—even holidays where you learn to "live off the land." You can take a camel to lunch, have an evening under the stars with stockman damper and billy tea around a roaring fire, sample bush food including the Aboriginal delicacy of witchetty grubs, climb to the top of Ayer's Rock, see cave paintings, go on hunting safaris to shoot buffalo and pigs with gun or camera, fish for the fighting barramundi in quiet rivers and creeks, swim under cascading waterfalls among palm trees in the middle of a red desert, or fly low in light aircraft around gorges and crags following winding river courses. Some of the tours include:

ALICE SPRINGS

By coach. *AAT Kings,* 74 Todd St., Alice Springs, NT 5750, (089) 52–5607: Half-day, day sightseeing town and gorges $22–$55. *Ansett Trailways,* Todd Mall, (089) 52–2422: Alice Explorer half-day $10, day $15, two days $20. *Arura Safari Tours,* 113 Todd St., (089) 52–3843: Ghost town, goldfields, rock carvings, all inclusive $175. *CATA Tours,* Todd St., (089) 52–1700: four-wheel-drive to Palm Valley oasis, Aboriginal mission, $39. *Frontier Tours,* 13 Mills St., (089) 52–3448: camel ride to winery for barramundi or buffalo-steak dinner, $38. *Rod Steinert's Dreamtime and Namatjira Tours,* Schaber Rd., (089) 52–4610: follow Aboriginal man and woman through bush to find water, animals, shelter, food, $75. AAT Kings, Ansett Trailways, CATA Tours run two- and three-day tours to Ayers Rock $250–$350.

By balloon. *Balloon Safaris,* 41 Gap Rd., (089) 52–1322: fly and tour $100-plus range.

AYERS ROCK/YULARA

By coach. *Ayers Rock Touring,* Yulara, daily from visitor center to rock, ranger tour, $15.

By air. *Ayers Rock Air Services,* Yulara, scenic flights on demand around $90. *Opal Air Tours,* Yulara, on request; Ayers Rock to Coober Pedy opal town, South Australia, two days, $300.

DARWIN

By coach. *Ansett Pioneer,* 63 Smith St., (089) 81–6433; city sights $22, wildlife $28, morning river safari for crocodiles, bird life $35, two days to Kakadu National Park $270, three days $405, Katherine Gorge day trip $88. *Dial a Safari,* Box 381, (089) 81–1155; waterfall, tin mine ruins, rivers, plains, wetlands, four-wheel-drive, $85. *Terra Safari Tours,* 14 Knuckey St., (089) 81–1006: sunset, champagne and chicken, night cruise on Adelaide River, crocodile spotlighting, snake feeding, $55. Extended tours up to three days Kakadu about $300.

Special interest. *Back of Beyond,* Box 12, Pine Creek, (089) 76–1221: hunting buffalo, pigs, one day $400 (spectators $50). *Wimray Safaris,* Box 1634, (089) 27–3917: photographic wildlife-fishing, daily from $130.; one-day barramundi fishing, from $130; five-day buffalo, fly-in, bush camp, isolated $2,500 all inclusive (nonhunter $500), guide.

KATHERINE

By coach. *Brolga Tours,* Box 83, Katherine, NT 5780, (089) 75–4516: Cutta Cutta caves, ranger guide, $13. *Katherine Gorge Tourist Agency,* c/o Ampol Service Station, Katherine, NT 5780, (089) 72–1044: Gorge cruise, daily $10; Gorge tour, daily $16; area special, three nights, Gorge, caves, thermal pool Mataranka, from $174.

By air. *Tillair,* c/o NT Tourist Bureau, 31 Smith Street Mall, Darwin, NT 5794, (089) 81–6611: mail-freight flights, four areas, up to 7 hours, 11 stations, no meals, $120.

KAKADU NATIONAL PARK

Cooinda Inn, Box 170, Jabiru, NT 5796, (089) 79–2545: boat cruise, birds, crocodiles. On request, $15.

MATARANKA

Never Never Land Tours, PMB 110, Mataranka, (089) 75–4516: thermal pool, Rainbow Springs, waterfalls. On request.

TOP END CRUISES

Bark Hut Inn, PMB 51, Winnellie, (089) 76–0185: Mary River wetlands, buffalo station, $15. *Go Tours,* Box 4352, Darwin, NT 5794 (089) 81–4306, 7-hour Adelaide River cruise, bird life, crocodiles, flora, river systems, barbecue lunch, $55.

MELVILLE/BATHURST ISLANDS

Tiwi Tours, 27 Temira Crescent, Darwin, NT 5790, (089) 81–5115: full-day, two islands, Aboriginal community, mission, about $180; half-day Bathurst Island, community, about $120; both include airfares.

NATIONAL PARKS: There are nearly 40 parks and reserves in the vast Northern Territory. Best known are *Uluru* (Ayers Rock–Mt. Olga National Park) in Central Australia and *Kakadu National Park* at the "Top End." Uluru is 465km southwest of Alice Springs, easily accessible by plane, coach, hire car, or private vehicle. Drive south along Stuart Highway for 198km, turn right at Erldunda Roadhouse and west along Lasseter Highway for 265km. Three roadhouses service route—Erldunda, Mt. Ebenezer, and Curtin Springs. All stock super gas and diesel fuel. Coach tours, air tours, express coach services operate daily from Alice Springs. Entrance fee to Park $1.50. Children free. Permit not required. Multimillion-dollar tourist complex Yulara ("place of the howling dingo") built just outside park boundary. Two international standard hotels, bunkhouse and dormitory accommodation, camper park, and camping ground with showers, toilets, laundries, on-site vans, barbecues, swimming pools. No tents provided. Ranger office and visitor-information center open 8 A.M.–10 P.M. daily. Contact Conservation Commission of Northern Territory, Gap Rd., Alice Springs, NT 5750; (089) 50–8211. Main parks near Alice Springs: *Ormiston Gorge and Pound,* 132km west on good road. Spectacular scenery; year-round waterhole; camping allowed; barbecue facilities; toilets. *Finke Gorge Nature Park,* 150km, photographer's delight where wind and water have carved forms in red sandstone. Camping, toilets, barbecue.

"Top End Region" dominated by 12,000-square-kilometer Kakadu National Park owned by Aboriginal people of Alligator Rivers region. About 200km east of Darwin on all-weather road. On World Heritage list. Most arrive by motor vehicle. Some spur roads impassable during wet season (November to April). Contact National Park HQ, Box 71, Jabiru, NT 5796; (089) 79–2101. River system and coastal plain, boating, fishing, Aboriginal art, walking, camping, picnic facilities. Spectacular waterfalls of Jim Jim and Twin Falls. Area contains all wildlife common to NT—buffalo, bird life. Dangerous to swim in creek, rivers, or billabongs because of crocodiles. Watch children near water. Don't leave food refuse around.

Main parks near Darwin: *Holmes Jungle Nature Park,* 15km off Vanderlin Drive; World War II army convalescent camp; beautiful rain-forest area. *Daly River Nature Park,* 225km, scenic river, fishing, boating, camping allowed. *Fogg Dam,* 63km, wildlife refuge, abundant bird life, monsoon forest. *Katherine,* 320km southeast of Darwin, center for Katherine Gorge Park, 30km, boat tours on spectacular gorge through sandstone, camping facilities (Katherine Gorge Tourist Agency, (089) 72–1810). *Cutta Cutta Caves,* 27km, guided tours limestone caves 10:30 A.M. and 1:30 P.M. daily, October to March; check times with conservation commission (089) 22–0211.

HOT SPRINGS. There is a wide area of thermal activity near Darwin. *Howard Springs,* 30km, spring-fed pool, monsoon forest, picnic area, birds, fish, wallabies, swimming, no camping, picnic facilities. *Douglas Hot Springs,* 200km, camping, barbecue, toilets, popular weekend destination, swimming. *Mataranka Pool,* 105km south of Katherine, monsoon forest, swimming, spring water maintains temperature of 34°C, caravan and camping, day tours from Katherine $45 Wednesday, Saturday (KGTA 089-72-1810).

WILDLIFE. The Northern Territory abounds in wildlife—buffalo, crocodile, snake, kangaroo, dingo, wallaby, bird, fish, donkey, camel—which can be seen (except for the wily dingo) on many tours if you keep an alert eye on the bush. In Alice Springs you can see camels at the *Camel Farm,* Larapinta Drive, and even go riding on them for fun or to dinner at a nearby winery. In Darwin crocodiles can be watched at the *Crocodile Farm,* 40km out of town on the Stuart Highway, (089) 88–1450. Snakes are handled and displayed at *Graeme Gow's Reptile World,* 6km along Arnhem Highway, (089) 88–1661. Many varieties of fish collect each day at *Doctor's Gulley* on the esplanade, a popular tourist attraction at high tides. Check times morning and afternoon with *Aquascene* (089) 81–7835. One you *don't* want to see is the deadly box jellyfish, between October and May, so *don't* swim in northern waters except in protected areas.

ABORIGINAL LANDS. The Aboriginals were in Australia for thousands of years before the whites. In the past few years intensive campaigns have been mounted over their land rights, and many areas of the Northern Territory are now owned and governed by Aboriginals with white advisors. The question has caused a wide division throughout Australia, mainly in Western Australia, Queensland, and the territory, where the majority of Aboriginals live. The handing over of Ayers Rock to the Aboriginals is the biggest issue, since the Rock is Australia's top tourist attraction. There were cases of professional photographers' being refused permission to film around and on the rock, and areas have been fenced off from tourists, although normal tour operations continue. If you wish to enter Aboriginal lands you must get permission from the Aboriginal community that owns them. Applications in writing must be submitted at least four weeks before the intended visit so they may be considered. If granted, carry the permit at all times. Further information from: Central Land Council, Box 3321, Alice Springs, NT 5750, (089) 52–7554; Northern Land Council, Box 3046, Darwin, NT 5794, (089) 81–7011; Tiwi Land Council, Nguiu, Bathurst Island, via Darwin, NT 5791, (089) 78–3957. Several places and things have special significance to Aboriginals. They are called sacred sites. The law protects them, and there are penalties for entering, defacing, or damaging.

SPORTS. The tropical lifestyle of Top End and clear heat of central Australia mean the outdoor life and a great variety of sporting activities. Around Darwin fishing, canoeing, swimming, hunting, bowling, athletics, rugby league, and rugby union football, soccer, Australian rules football, cricket, hockey, tennis, basketball, baseball, netball, volleyball, squash, golf, horse racing. There are more than 50 sporting clubs in Alice Springs including the above plus horse and pony clubs, motorbike scrambles, gliding, parachuting, aero and gun organizations. WARNING: No swimming in the sea around coast during the wet season (November to April) because of venomous sea wasp; its sting can kill. No swimming in Top End's creeks and rivers because of crocodiles.

Popular Darwin sporting events include City to Surf fun run; Walkabout of 25km; St. Patrick's race club meeting (March); squash championship (May); Darwin Cup racing (July); Yacht racing (August). Alice Springs: squash championships; race meeting (May); camel cup (May); MacDonnell Range race meet (October). Visitors can join in tennis club matches in Alice Springs, Tennant

Creek, Katherine, Darwin, and Jabiru. Golf at Alice Springs, Tennant Creek, Katherine, Darwin, Jabiru, and Gove. Squash in Alice Springs, Tennant Creek, Katherine, Darwin City, Howard Springs, and Milner. Lawn Bowls in Alice, Katherine, Gove, and Tennant Creek. Hats, sun lotions, sun blockout creams a must; sun will be warmer and stronger than people may expect.

HISTORIC SITES. Australia is a young country—just about 200 years ago the first whites set up a colony in New South Wales. Explorers and cattlemen took some time to move into the territory with its harsh deserts and craggy mountains. They found many signs of the original inhabitants and left their own mark. These historical features are preserved in trust for the future.
Alice Springs: *Ewaninga Carvings,* 39km south, petroglyphs not understood by today's Aboriginals. *Arltunga Goldfields Reserve,* 111km east in MacDonnell Ranges, ruins of gold-mining township. Camping facilities, four-wheel-drive recommended. *John Flynn's Grave,* memorial to founder of Flying Doctor Service, 6km west. *Lasseter's Grave,* Memorial Drive. Old cemetery, burial place of Harold Lasseter, who perished in desert 1931 searching for fabulous lost reef of gold; also grave of Albert Namatjira, first famous Aboriginal painter. *Old Pioneer Cemetery.* Headstones tell of pioneers dying of "foul air."
Katherine: *Old Elsey Cemetery,* Mataranka Springs, 105km, pioneer graves. *Nott's Crossing,* Katherine, site of original township, where Mrs. Aeneas Gunn wrote Australian classic *We of the Never Never.*
Darwin: *Stuart Memorial,* honoring John McDouall Stuart, who crossed Australia from south to north in 1861; route became Overland Telegraph Line and Stuart Highway. *Ross Smith Memorial* obelisk commemorates first landing in Darwin of flight from England 1919 by Ross and Keith Smith.

MUSEUMS. Life was hard in the early days of the Northern Territory. There was no air-conditioning or jets, and distances were vast and unexplored. There are many museums and memorials to the pioneers and their achievements. All tell a story of courage in the face of danger and the unknown.
Alice Springs: *Aviation Museum,* Memorial Drive, in the Connellan Hangar on Alice Springs' original airport. Engines, photographs early aviation, aircraft recovered from desert, video. Monday to Friday 8:30 A.M.–4 P.M.; Saturday, Sunday 9:30 A.M.–4 P.M. *John Flynn Memorial Church,* Todd Mall. Australian Inland Mission's first medical center. *Old Timers Museum,* Stuart Highway. Exhibits date from 1890s; daily 2 P.M.–4 P.M. (phone 52-5742 any other time for appointment). *Pitchi Richi Sanctuary,* near Todd River southern causeway. Open-air museum with Aboriginal artifacts, sculptures by William Ricketts. *Old Telegraph Station,* 3km north, off Stuart Highway. Historical reserve, with early photos, papers, documents, original buildings restored with great taste; equipment salvaged and displayed with imagination. *Historical Museum,* Magic Spark Radio Museum, Camel Farm Complex, Emily Gap Rd. Nostalgic look at communication equipment; 9 A.M.–5 P.M. daily, evenings by appointment. *Stuart Auto Museum.* Old vehicles, telephones, phonographs, motorcycles, etc.; 9 A.M.–5 P.M. daily, admission charge.
Darwin: *Artillery Museum.* Blockhouses, command posts, observation towers—reminder of Darwin bombing in World War II when 243 died in 64 raids. War artifacts, photos, newspaper clippings. *Fannie Bay Gaol Museum.* "Time capsule" of nearly 100 years ago with few alterations. *Northern Territory Museum of Arts and Natural Sciences.*

ART GALLERIES. A great variety of Aboriginal and Outback art can be found in Alice Springs and Darwin. Aboriginal painting is very popular with Australians and overseas visitors, but you must know what you are buying. Hermannsburg Mission School watercolors featured in Alice Springs' *Panorama Guth,* art gallery featuring 360-degree painted landscape of surrounding countryside. Open 9 A.M.–5 P.M., Monday to Friday, Saturday 9 A.M. to noon and 2–5 P.M., Sunday 2–5 P.M. Admission $1. *Diarama Village,* Larapinta Drive, Alice Springs. Myths and legends of Aboriginals plus excellent selection of art works. *Araluen Arts Centre,* Alice Springs. Performing- and visual-arts center features two art galleries, craft center. In Katherine: *MiMi Aboriginal Arts and Craft Centre,* Pearce Street.

TASMANIA

An Island State

by
JENNIFER PRINGLE-JONES

Jennifer Pringle-Jones is an award-winning writer whose credits include three books on Tasmania.

From a physical point of view, the 68,000-square-kilometer island state of Tasmania is more like New Zealand than Australia's other states and territories. Some Australians claim that Tasmanians are a race apart but locals in the island—the second Australian area settled by British explorers—fiercely defend their picturesque state, which in recent times has drawn an increased number of visitors and settlers attracted by its quality of life.

The pace is slower here than in the larger states, nineteenth-century history has been combined with twentieth-century development in a way not found elsewhere in Australia, and Tasmania has a greater percentage of its area in national parks. No place in Tasmania is more than 115 kilometers from the sea—with the associated fishing, boating, and other recreational pursuits.

Falling within the temperate zone, Tasmania has four distinct seasons as well as temperature variations between the milder coastal areas and the highlands.

Generally speaking, summer wear for beach or sightseeing should be light, with provision for something extra to put on in the cool of the evening. There is no winter freeze, although temperatures in both Launceston and Hobart can fall to freezing point overnight. Spring and fall can produce changeable conditions, and hikers are warned that weather can be treacherous in highland areas.

Buildings and vehicles are normally heated. Heavy clothing is required only if you are spending time in the open—at race meetings or walking round Port Arthur. Office buildings, hotels, motels, and bigger shops are air-conditioned for summer.

There is no wet season, but a light raincoat or umbrella should be packed irrespective of time of year.

Nightlife clothing depends where you go, but smart casual clothes will do for both sexes in most places. For men a jacket is necessary for evening admittance to the casinos and to some hotels.

The best way to see the state is by bus, rental car, or camper-van, the newest of which have facilities which include showers, color television, and even video cameras. There are no passenger trains, but other means of sightseeing range from charter flights in light aircraft to bicycles and even donkeys! One of Tasmania's greatest assets is the variety it offers within its boundaries (which, incidentally, extend as far south as Macquarie Island in the Antarctic zone). The mountainous western region gives way to highland plateaus filled with lakes (renowned for trout fishing), long, sandy beaches in the east, total wilderness of World Heritage status in the southwest, and lush coastal plains in the northwest. Forestry, tourism, and mining are the main income earners, but wherever you go it is impossible to avoid history.

Van Diemen's Land

Getting back to the beginnings, the real reason why Tasmania was settled was that the British didn't want the French to have it, even though it had been discovered by a Dutchman.

Abel Tasman discovered the island in 1642 and named it Van Diemen's Land, and that was that for 130 years. Between 1772 and 1803, when it was finally settled, no fewer than 10 exploring expeditions landed many Frenchmen, not to mention Captain James Cook, and George Bass, who proved in 1798 that Tasmania was an island.

The last such explorer was Nicholas Baudin in 1802. He had previously enjoyed great hospitality from the British in Sydney. While extending this hospitality, the British governor in New South Wales wrote to the then secretary of state for the colonies, Lord Hobart, suggesting that a new colony should be formed down south.

Approval was given, and Lieutenant Governor David Collins set out from the other side of the world. Before he could get there, however, New South Wales Governor King, hearing rumors of French intentions to settle in southern Tasmania, decided to beat them to it and sent Lieutenant John Bowen, who landed at Risdon, now a Hobart suburb, in 1803. Next year Collins arrived, landed in the same place, but decided on Sullivans Cove as the settlement headquarters, naming it Hobart Town. The British decided the settlement should also claim the northern half, and this was subsequently done at Port Dalrymple. Thus, the island had two governors for a while. The island grew up in 1865, when responsible government was established and the name of the colony changed to Tasmania.

Historical associations still remain, however, for there is a distinct feeling among Tasmanians of belonging to either the south or the north, mostly because Hobart to the south and Launceston to the north have quite different characters and are the only two really well-populated cities.

If you are traveling in Tasmania you will find that the state divides itself up quite naturally into a variety of areas. Ideally, one should allow about a week to see the island, but compromises are possible if time is short. Although distances are not great, roads are often narrow and twisting because of the hilly terrain.

The main points of entry are at Devonport (for sea travel) and Launceston or Hobart, the capital, for air travel. Launceston, in the north, is the most convenient base because roads from here lead west, east, and south.

Launceston: "Garden City"

Launceston was given its name by the founder, Colonel Paterson, after the U.K. Cornish birthplace of the then Governor King. This city, second largest in Tasmania, is situated at the confluence of the South and North Esk rivers, which here become the Tamar, named after the river flowing by the English town. About 20 miles downstream, you might like to look at the Batman Bridge, one of the world's first cable-stayed truss bridges, which is dominated by the 330-foot-high steel-frame tower.

In Launceston take a day out to the Cataract Gorge and ride the chairlift. The nearby Penny Royal Cornmill and the Gunpowder Mill offer a taste of colonial life with a little piratical high adventure thrown in. Both feature good accommodation and restaurants.

Historical establishments such as the Colonial Motor Inn (built in 1847 as the Launceston Grammar School) and the Batman-Fawkner Inn (whose first landlord, John Fawkner, planned the settlement that grew into Melbourne) contrast with modern complexes such as the Launceston Federal Country Club Casino, 10 kilometers from the city center at Prospect.

To travel to the east coast head up the East Tamar Highway to George Town (past the Comalco Aluminum plant at Bell Bay) or east toward Scottsdale. At Nabowla, near Lilydale, the world-famous Bridestowe Lavender Farm is open for inspection between Boxing Day (December 26) and the third week in February, when flowers are in bloom.

The natural beauty of the northeast is its best asset. Scottsdale, the main town, services a rich agricultural district, timber and food-processing industries, and hops growing. Most of the hops produced at Tonganah, 7 kilometers along the Tasman Highway, are exported to overseas breweries. In the nineteenth century this was a bustling tin mining district with a large Chinese population. At Derby are a recreated tin-mining shanty town and Cribshed Tearooms.

East Coast Beach Beauties

Long, sandy beaches, often with only nature to keep them company, are found all along the east coast. St. Helens, the largest town in the region, is a base for fishing fleets (crayfish, scallops, abalone, and scalefish). Visitors are well catered to with a variety of accommodations and eating places. Charter boats are available for fishing, and the area is noted for its wildflowers (especially orchids) and abundant bird life.

Other towns worth a visit are Bicheno (don't miss the East Coast Bird and Wildlife Park or the Sea Life Centre—see fairy penguins, too, near Diamond Island); Coles Bay, one of Tasmania's prettiest spots; and Swansea, where Australia's only restored bark mill operates daily. Visitors also can play billiards or eight ball between noon and 3:30 P.M. and from 7 to 9 P.M. from Monday to Saturday on Australia's only remaining full-sized billiard table, in the 1860 community center.

Triabunna is a fishing port and departure point for trips to Maria Island, site of Tasmania's second penal settlement and now a national park. The visit to Maria Island can be done in one day and is certainly worthwhile for history lovers. (Take your own provisions.)

Orford is a holiday resort and base for hire boats (canoes, dinghies, and paddleboats). Sandstone from cliffs along the highway was used in many of Melbourne's early buildings.

On the way into Hobart, you'll see Buckland, whose most notable feature is the Church of St. John the Baptist, built in 1846. The beautiful east window is said to have been originally designed for Battle Abbey in England on the site of the Battle of Hastings. (The abbey was badly damaged and never restored, and the window was given to the first rector of Buckland.)

If you don't want to backtrack before you go into Hobart, take the Port Arthur Road crossing Eaglehawk Neck with its tessellated pavement and spuming blowhole. The Neck, a narrow strip of land joined to the Tasman Peninsula and containing the Port Arthur penal settlement, made escape for prisoners almost impossible. Guards with ferocious dogs would patrol the Neck. (One prisoner nearly made it by swimming the narrow stretch underwater. But it was his unlucky day. He swam against the tide; a hawk-eyed guard noticed ripples flowing against the stream, and it was back to the prison again.)

Port Arthur is possibly the most interesting relic of Australia's days as a penal colony. It has a walkway through it as well as an audiovisual performance and a museum. The scenery around is quite beautiful. Guides explain that contrary to what most people think, compared with the poor free working people in England of their time, the prisoners were well off. They had food and clothes and not too exhausting work, whereas their compatriots overseas would be starving, ill treated, and overworked until they literally dropped.

Modern attractions with an old-time theme include the Bush Mill, complete with a working shingle splitter, blacksmith, steam-powered sawmill, and steam railway.

There are also a wildlife-and-nature park and the Port Arthur Marine Park, with indoor and outdoor aquariums and a wide range of sealife including live crayfish, sharks, stingrays, and seals.

Ideally, you should stay at least one night on the Tasman Peninsula, where accommodations include a camper park, motels, and self-contained cottages.

It takes an hour and a half to drive from Port Arthur to Hobart, but it is worth detouring from the highway and traveling to the historic town of Richmond. The turnoff is about 2 kilometers past the Llanherne Airport, which services Hobart. The site of an early penal institution, Richmond has Australia's best-preserved convict jail (open for inspection); the oldest Roman Catholic church, St. John's; the oldest bridge still standing (built by convicts in 1823); and excellent art galleries and craft shops (all in restored nineteenth-century buildings).

Hobart: by Harbor and Mountain

Hobart is the second oldest capital city in Australia, founded 16 years after Sydney, in 1804. Life here always has centered on the magnificent Derwent estuary and harbor, one of the world's finest deepwater harbors. Initially it was a port for landing free settlers, convicts, and their supplies, but later it was exploited as a base for South Sea whalers. Now Hobart is noted as a port for exports such as newsprint and timber, as the finishing point for the annual Sydney to Hobart Yacht Race, for its casino (the first legal one in Australia), as the gateway to the Antarctic (suburban Kingston has headquarters of the Australian Antarctic Division), and as a city that combines the benefits of modern times with a feeling for the past, in the form of its rich heritage of buildings dating from the early years of settlement.

Hobart nestles between the harbor and majestic Mount Wellington (1,271 meters). A drive to the peak affords panoramic views, but beware of the road condition and do not go at night in winter. If there is heavy cloud cover, opt instead for Mount Nelson, which is lower and readily accessible all year round.

Places that shouldn't be missed include the former seafaring village, now suburban Battery Point; Salamanca Place, with its rows of sandstone buildings that once served as warehouses—also the scene of a lively outdoor market every Saturday morning; the Royal Tasmanian Botanical Gardens; the Tasmanian Museum and Art Gallery (noted for its colonial-art collection); the Wrest Point Hotel Casino; and an architectural gem, the Theatre Royal. Hobart is a good starting point for tours to the Huon Valley and Bruny Island in the south and to the Derwent Valley in the west.

Reminders of the Past

Heading south on the Channel Highway you come to Oyster Cove, where the last of the full-blood Tasmanian Aborigines spent their final days in the 1870s.

There is a good eating spot at the fishing port of Kettering, and the highway later joins the Huon Highway, which services this orcharding and farming district.

At Hastings you can swim in a thermal pool, explore caves, and fossick at nearby Lune River for gemstones.

Casey's Living Steam Museum at Dover is the only fully steam-operated museum in Australia; exhibits are powered by the original marine-type boiler. (Closed in July.)

Hops and on to the West

The Derwent Valley, cut by the Derwent River and flanked by poplars and native eucalyptus, is a photographer's paradise. The New Norfolk area is famous for its hops, and the history of the industry is depicted in the Oast House Museum.

A Lake That Drowned

If mountain scenery and humans' use of natural power interest you, divert from New Norfolk into Maydena and travel the private road up through geologically ancient country to the hydroelectric scheme at Strathgordon and the drowned Lake Pedder, whose end caused much controversy among conservationists a few years ago (1974). You can stay overnight at Strathgordon in the Lake Pedder Chalet (but book ahead), see the mighty dam, and visit the underground Gordon power station.

Backtrack again through Bushy Park and continue on the mountainous twisting road through the Derwent River valley (sheer delight in colors in autumn) and into Queenstown. This mining town has been scoured out of the rocks and is not beautiful, but to visit the mines and stand on top of the workings can be impressive. Beware of windy days, for the gales will suck the breath out of you if you stand on the rim of the open cut.

Strahan, 18 miles south, is now merely an echo of its glorious past during the copper boom. Even so, it is used today as the starting point for the breathtaking Gordon River trip by motor launch on which Tasmania's first penal prison, Settlement Island, can be seen.

Zeehan, on the way back to the north coast, and Burnie saw their greatest prosperity between 1903 and 1908 in the mining boom; their prosperity, is now being revived by the reopening of the Renison Bell Tin Mine nearby. Many buildings of that era are now in use, including the once famous Grand Hotel (now apartments), Gaiety Theatre, post office, some banks, and St. Luke's Church. The West Coast Pioneers' Memorial Museum houses one of the world's finest mineral collections.

Burnie, in the northwest, is an industrial town, but the surrounding "cape country" is full of green, rolling hills descending steeply to a wild and rocky coastline. The many small towns rely on the processing of farm products for their livelihood.

Burnie's pioneer museum is worth a visit, and locomotive enthusiasts will enjoy a drink at the Loco Bar in the Burnie Town House Motor Hotel, where they'll be surrounded by photographs of early railwaymen and their steam engines.

In this area, visit cheesemakers, carpet factories, and paper mills. At Devonport see the Tiagarra Aboriginal project, which traces the history of the extinct Tasmanian Aboriginals and preserves some of their art, crafts, and rock carvings.

The Devonport area is the center of cave visits at Gunns Plains—but make sure they will be open—and Mole Creek, open daily and featuring glowworms. King Solomon caves are also open daily.

Temptation, Recreation, Salvation, Damnation

Once back in Launceston take the Midland Highway down the middle of the island—a road through several worthwhile historic small towns. See Campbell Town and Ross—one of the state's finest and most attractive historic villages, whose dominant feature is the convict-built Ross Bridge. Stand in the center of Ross and look at the four corners: Man O Ross Hotel, said to represent temptation; Town Hall, recreation; the church, salvation; and the Gaol, damnation!

Traveling south to Oatlands, look for topiary (tree figures) lining both sides of the roads. Oatlands got its name because it reminded the early Governor Macquarie of his native Scotland and the grain that grew there, but as late as 1827 it was still only a site with a board bearing the name. Much of its development took place in the 1830s and it is said today that almost everyone in the town lives in a historic building.

Many of the towns between Launceston and Hobart have been bypassed by the upgraded Midland Highway, but you will be amply rewarded for the few extra minutes' travel if you take the deviations.

At Melton Mowbray there is a turnoff to the historic town of Bothwell, center of a rich grazing district and a base for trips to the highland lakes, a mecca for trout fishers.

This, then, is the body of Tasmania. If you have extra time and money, try the outlying islands of King and Flinders in the north, reached by air services. These will be attractive just for their peace and scenery.

PRACTICAL INFORMATION FOR TASMANIA

Facts and Figures. Named after Dutchman Abel Tasman, who discovered the island in 1642, Tasmania was settled by the British in 1803. Initially it was a penal colony, but ironically, many of the 74,000 convicts whose destiny led them to Van Diemen's Land (the name was changed to Tasmania later) were key contributors to development and even survival in the outpost.

The state has a population of 450,000, the main centers being Hobart, Launceston, Burnie, Devonport, and Glenorchy (part of Greater Hobart). Being Australia's southernmost state, Tasmania offers cooler weather in summer than many mainland states and very little humidity. The nights are cold in winter, but days usually are clear and crisp. Snow falls on the highlands but rarely in low-lying areas. The rainfall is heaviest in the west, but Hobart averages only 25 inches per annum.

Tasmania was once noted for its apples, but its fame these days rests with its forestry, mining (iron ore, copper, tin, lead, zinc), and tourism.

TELEPHONES. There are three separate telephone directories (004 code for the northwest, 003 for the north, and 002 for the south).

HOW TO GET THERE. By boat. *The Abel Tasman,* a vehicular ferry, has accommodation for 828 passengers and up to 440 cars. Cabins range from $A180–$A186 in the peak period (December and January) to $A143–$A166 in the bargain season (May to August). There are three trips weekly (Monday, Wednesday, and Friday), from Melbourne to Devonport. Advance bookings are essential; the peak period is booked about one year ahead.

By air. From New Zealand, there are *Quantas* flights each Monday between Auckland and Hobart, and on Saturday, *Australian Airlines* and *Air New Zealand* have flights between Christchurch and Hobart. Passport required. Nationally, Tasmania is serviced by *Ansett, Australian Airlines, Air New South Wales,* and *East-West Airlines,* plus intrastate carrier *Airlines of Tasmania.* Flights several times daily from Melbourne into Devonport and Wynyard on the northwest coast, Launceston in the north, and Hobart in the south take up to one hour. Competition between airlines has increased recently as a price war heats up, and as a result, there are now a number of flights each day direct between Sydney and Hobart. It is best to check the latest situation with an agent of Tasbureau, the Tasmanian government tourist agency.

ACCOMMODATIONS. In addition to conventional hotels and motels, an extensive network of self-contained accommodations has been established in colonial buildings and farms and in historic towns. These are ideal for family groups and usually have facilities for up to 6 people. Deluxe suites at the hotel casinos in Launceston and Hobart top the range.

Prices for double rooms: *Expensive,* $A50 upwards; *moderate,* $A35–$A50; *inexpensive,* $A20–$A35. SC stands for self-catering (linen, crockery, cutlery provided).

BERRIEDALE

Highway Village Motel. *Moderate.* 897 Brooker Highway; (002) 72–6732. Liquor room service. Licensed restaurant. Own boat ramp and jetty.

BICHENO

Homestead Holiday Estate. *Moderate.* Tasman Highway; (003) 75–1161. Liquor room service. Licensed restaurant. Near golf course, fishing beach.

TASMANIA

Silver Sands Hotel/Motel. *Moderate.* Burgess St.; (003) 75–1266. Liquor room service. Licensed restaurant. Pool. Overlooking beaches. Near golf course. Member Flag chain.

Holiday Village. *Moderate.* The Esplanade; (003) 75–1171. SC, pool, lake, games room.

BOAT HARBOUR

Seaway Motel. *Moderate.* Boat Harbour Beach; (004) 45–1107. Off-season rates available. Licensed restaurant. Near beach, national park, golf and bowling courses.

BURNIE

Voyager Motor Inn. *Expensive.* Corner of North Terrace and Wilson sts.; (004) 31–4866. Liquor room service. Licensed restaurant. Opposite beach. Near golf, bowls, tennis. Member Flag chain.

Four Seasons Town House. *Moderate.* 139 Wilson St.; (004) 31–4455. Liquor room service. Licensed restaurant. Member Zebra chain.

Motel Emu. *Moderate.* 12–16 Bass Highway; (004) 31–2466. Pool.

Top of the Town Hotel/Motel. *Moderate.* 195 Mount St.; (004) 31–4444. Liquor room service. Licensed restaurant. Sauna. Near beach, golf course.

Bayview Hotel. *Inexpensive.* 10 Marine Tce.; (004) 31–2711. Counter meals available. Cabaret Saturday night. Central, near beach.

DERWENT PARK

Hotel Carlyle. *Inexpensive.* 232 Main Rd.; (002) 72–0299. Rate includes hot breakfast. Licensed restaurant.

DEVONPORT

Gateway Motor Inn. *Expensive.* 16 Fenton St.; (004) 24–4922. Liquor room service. Licensed restaurant. City center. Near beach.

Motel Argosy. *Moderate.* Tarleton St.; (004) 27–8872. Liquor room service. Licensed restaurant. On main highway. Member MFA Homestead chain.

Shearwater Country Club Hotel/Motel. *Moderate.* Port Sorell; (004) 28–6205. Liquor room service. Licensed restaurant. Pool. Own golf course, tennis courts. Near beach.

Sunrise Motel. *Moderate.* 140 Fenton St.; (004) 24–1631. Near beach. A member MFA Homestead chain.

Hotel Formby. *Inexpensive.* 82 Formby Rd.; (004) 24–1601. Some cheaper rooms without facilities. Licensed restaurant. Near beach, golf course.

EAGLEHAWK NECK

Penzance Motel. *Moderate.* Pirates Bay; (002) 50–3272. Liquor room service. Licensed restaurant. 24-hr food service. Near beach, two golf links, historic buildings.

Lufra Hotel Motel. *Inexpensive.* Arthur Highway; (002) 50–3262. Licensed restaurant. Surf beach. Near historic Port Arthur.

GEORGE TOWN

Mt. George Motor Hotel. *Moderate.* 106 Agnes St.; (003) 82–1057. Includes hot breakfast. Licensed restaurant. Near beach, golf course.

GLENORCHY

Balmoral Motor Inn. *Moderate.* 511 Brooker Highway; (002) 72–5833. Off-season rates available. Liquor room service. Licensed restaurant. Near racegrounds, trotting, showgrounds.

HADSPEN

Rutherglen Holiday Village. *Moderate.* Bass Highway; (003) 93–6214. SC. Zoo, horse riding, pool, tennis, restaurants.

HOBART AND ENVIRONS

Four Seasons Downtowner. *Expensive.* 96 Bathurst St.; (002) 34–6333. Liquor room service. Licensed restaurant. 24-hr food service. City center.
Four Seasons Westside. *Expensive.* 156 Bathurst St.; (002) 34–6255. Liquor room service. 24-hr food service. Member Zebra chain.
Hatcher's Hobart Motor Inn. *Expensive.* 40 Brooker Highway; (002) 34–2911. Licensed restaurant. Central. Member Innkeepers chain.
Hobart Pacific Motor Inn. *Expensive.* Kirby Court, Knocklofty; (002) 34–6733. Liquor room service. Licensed restaurant. Pool. Panoramic views.
Lenna Motor Inn. *Expensive.* 20 Runnymede St.; (002) 23–2911. Liquor room service. Licensed restaurant. 24-hr food service. Overlooking harbor, at historic Battery Point.
Wrest Point Hotel-Casino. *Expensive/Deluxe.* 410 Sandy Bay Rd., Sandy Bay.; (002) 25–0112. Prices depend on whether room in wing or in casino tower. Liquor room service. Licensed restaurant in revolving tower. 24-hr food service. Pool. Air-conditioned. Near beach, river.
Argyle Motor Lodge. *Moderate.* Cnr. Lewis and Argyle sts.; (002) 34–2488. Near city and Oval.
Astor Private Hotel. *Moderate.* 157 Macquarie St.; (002) 34–6384. Pleasant, homey atmosphere. Central location, licensed restaurant.
Barton Cottage. *Moderate.* 72 Hamden Rd., Battery Point. SC colonial accommodation. (002) 23–6808.
Black Buffalo Hotel. *Moderate.* 14 Federal Street, North Hobart; (002) 34–7711. Liquor room service. Licensed restaurant. 24-hr food service.
Blue Hills Motel. *Moderate.* 96a Sandy Bay Road.; (002) 23–1777. Not licensed.
Brisbane Hotel. *Inexpensive.* 3 Brisbane St.; (002) 34–4920. Rate includes hot breakfast. Licensed restaurant.
Four Seasons Motor Lodge. *Moderate.* 429 Sandy Bay Rd., Sandy Bay. Licensed restaurant.
Hadley's Hotel. *Moderate.* 34 Murray St.; (002) 23–4355. Some cheaper rooms without private facilities. Liquor room service. Licensed restaurant. 24-hr food service.
Marquis of Hastings Hotel/Motel. *Moderate.* 209 Brisbane St.; (002) 34–3541. Licensed restaurant.
Motel Mayfair. *Moderate.* 17 Cavell St.; (002) 34–1670. No restaurant. Near city center.
Prince of Wales Hotel. *Moderate.* 55 Hampden Rd., Battery Point; (002) 23–6355. Licensed restaurant. Set in historic area.
Southport Town House. *Expensive.* 167 Macquarie St.; (002) 34–4422. Liquor room service. 24-hr food service. Central city.
Taroona Motor Hotel. *Moderate.* 178 Channel Highway; (002) 27–8748. Liquor room service. Licensed restaurant. One minute from beach, five from casino.
Black Prince Hotel. *Inexpensive.* 145 Elizabeth St.; (002) 34–3501. Liquor room service. Licensed restaurant. City center.
Waratah Hotel. *Inexpensive.* 272 Murray St.; (002) 34–3685. Licensed restaurant. Central.

HOWRAH

Shoreline Motor Hotel. *Moderate.* Corner of Howrah and Rokeby roads, Shoreline Drive; (002) 47–9504. Liquor room service. Licensed restaurant.

KING ISLAND

King Island Boomerang Motel. *Moderate.* Currie; (004) 62–1288. Adjacent bowls, tennis courts.

TASMANIA

LAUNCESTON

Launceston Federal Country Club Casino. *Deluxe/Expensive.* Country Club Ave.; (003) 44–8855. Casino, licensed restaurants, cabaret, pool, saunas, golf, tennis, squash.
Colonial Motor Inn. *Expensive.* Cnr. George and Elizabeth sts.; (003) 31–6588. Licensed restaurant.
Four Seasons Great Northern Motor Inn. *Expensive.* 3 Earl St.; (003) 31–9999. Licensed restaurant features old tram.
Penny Royal Watermill. *Expensive.* 145 Paterson St.; (003) 31–6699. Atmospheric, restored and converted old watermill. Liquor room service. Licensed restaurant. Near the Gorge. Has antique and gift shop and corn-mill museum.
Abel Tasman Motor Inn. *Moderate.* 303 Hobart Rd.; (003) 44–5244. Includes light breakfast. Near golf course, airport.
Batman Fawkner Hotel. *Moderate.* 39 Cameron St.; (003) 31–7222. Liquor room service. 24-hr room service. No restaurant. Central.
Coach House Motel. *Moderate.* 10 York St.; (003) 31–5311. Kitchen facilities in rooms. Member Flag chain.
Commodore. *Moderate.* 13 Brisbane St.; (003) 31–4666. Liquor room service. Licensed restaurant. Opposite city park.
Hotel Tasmania. *Moderate.* 191 Charles St.; (003) 31–7355. Liquor room service. Licensed restaurant.
Launceston Hotel. *Moderate.* 107 Brisbane St.; (003) 31–9211. Liquor room service. Licensed restaurant. 24-hr room service.
The Old Bakery Inn. *Moderate.* Cnr. York/Margaret sts.; (003) 31–7388. Colonial.
Hillview House. *Moderate.* 193 George St.; (003) 31–7388. Colonial.
Parklane Motel. *Moderate.* 9 Brisbane St.; (003) 31–4233. Kitchen facilities in room. Opposite parkland. Central. Member, Flag chain.
Riverside Motor Inn. *Moderate.* West Tamar Rd.; (003) 27–2522. Includes light breakfast. Licensed restaurant. Near golf, swimming pool, tennis courts.
St. James Hotel. *Moderate.* 122 York St.; (003) 31–6122. Licensed restaurant.
Village Motor Inn. *Moderate.* Westbury Rd.; (003) 43–1777. Liquor room service. Licensed restaurant. Pool. Member Flag chain.

MONTAGUE BAY

Motel Panorama of Hobart. *Moderate.* Tasman Highway; (002) 43–8555. No restaurant. Near golf course, swimming pool, beach.

MOONAH

Lenton Lodge Motel. *Moderate.* 238 Main Rd.; (002) 72–5044. No restaurant. Near race courses.

MOUNT NELSON

Mount Nelson Motor Inn. *Moderate.* 571 Mt. Nelson Rd.; (002) 23–5399. Off-season rates available. Licensed restaurant. Overlooks city.

NEW NORFOLK

Amaroo Motel. *Moderate.* Lyell Highway; (002) 61–2000. Off-season rates available. Liquor room service. Licensed restaurant. Near golf course.

NEW TOWN

Valley Lodge Motel. *Expensive.* 11 Augusta Rd.; (002) 28–0125. Licensed restaurant. Pool.
Hobart Tower Motel. *Moderate.* 300 Park St., nr football ground; (002) 28–4520. Off-season rates available.
Seven Mile Beach. *Moderate.* The Pines Resort; (002) 48–6222. SC, pool, surfing, tennis.

AUSTRALIA

Graham Court Holiday Apartments. *Inexpensive.* 15 Pirie St.; (002) 28–0283. Kitchen facilities in rooms. No restaurant. Central.

NUBEENA

Cascades Hospital Cottage. *Moderate.* SC colonial; former convict outstation. Koonya, Tasman Peninsula; (002) 50–3121.
Fairway Lodge Country Club. *Moderate.* Main Rd., Nubeena; (002) 50–2171. Pool, tennis, golf, barbecues, sauna, SC.

OATLANDS

Ellesmere Cabin. *Moderate.* (002) 54–4140. Timber cottage on grazing property. SC.
Waverly Lodge. *Moderate.* (002) 54–1264. Restored cottages on rural property. SC.

PORT ARTHUR

New Plymouth Holiday Village. *Moderate.* Stewarts Bay; (002) 50–2262. SC log cabins.
Four Seasons Motor Hotel. *Moderate.* (002) 50–2102. Licensed restaurant. Member of Zebra chain.
Fox and Hound. *Moderate.* Arthur Highway; (002) 50–2217. Licensed restaurant.

QUEENSTOWN

Four Seasons Silver Hills Motel. *Moderate.* Penghana Rd.; (004) 71–1755. Licensed restaurant.
Penny Royal Queenstown. *Moderate.* Batchelor St.; (004) 71–1005. Motel or self-contained units.
Southport Motor Hotel. *Moderate.* 1 Orr St.; (004) 71–1888. Licensed restaurant. Central.
Westcoaster. *Moderate.* Batchelor St.; (004) 71–1033. Licensed restaurant.

SAVAGE RIVER

Savage River Motor Inn. *Inexpensive.* (004) 46–1177. Licensed restaurant. Near Pieman River.

SCAMANDER

Four Seasons Motor Hotel. *Moderate.* Tasman Highway; (003) 72–5255. Licensed restaurant. Pool. Near ocean beach.
Surfside Motel. *Moderate.* Tasman Highway, Beaumaris; (003) 72–5177. Licensed restaurant. Pool. Near beach, golf course. Member MFA Homestead chain.

SMITHTON

Bridge Hotel-Motel. *Moderate.* Montagu St.; (004) 52–1389. Licensed.

ST. HELENS

Bayside Inn. *Moderate.* 2 Cecilia St.; (003) 76–1466. Coffee makers, color TV, electric blankets, refrigerators. Licensed restaurant.
Club St. Helens. *Inexpensive.* 49 Cecilia St.; (003) 76–1131. Dining, games rooms.

SWANSEA

Swan Motor Inn. *Expensive.* Franklin St.; (002) 57–8102. Liquor room service. Licensed restaurant. On beach. Near golf, bowling.
Rose Cottage. *Moderate.* Tasman Highway; (002) 57–7576. SC.

ULVERSTONE

Beachway Motel. *Moderate.* Heathcote St.; (004) 25-2342. Rate includes hot breakfast. Pool.
Stone's Hotel. *Inexpensive.* 33 Victoria St.; (004) 25-1197. Rate includes hot breakfast. Liquor room service. Licensed restaurant.

WALHEIM, CRADLE MOUNTAIN

Pencil Pine Lodge. *Moderate.* In boundary Cradle Mountain National Park; (003) 63-5164. Hotel or cabin facilities. Licensed restaurant. Abundant wildlife.

WYNYARD

Four Seasons Motor Lodge. *Moderate.* Goldie St.; (004) 42-2351. Liquor room service. Licensed restaurant. Near beach, golf.

ZEEHAN

Heemskirk Motor Hotel. *Moderate.* Main St.; (004) 71-6107. Licensed restaurant.

DINING OUT Credit cards or personal checks are accepted at most restaurants (exceptions are indicated). *MasterCard* is the most popular, followed by *American Express* and *Visa*. Price ranges (3-course meal, excluding wine): *Expensive* $A30 and up; *Moderate:* $A20–$A30; *Inexpensive:* $A10–$A20.

BURNIE

Kaddys. *Expensive.* 16 Cattley St.; (004) 31-8333. International a la carte. Monday–Saturday. Licensed.
Raindrops Room. *Expensive.* 9 North Terrace; (004) 31-4866. Extensive menu, children's servings available. Licensed. Serves breakfast, lunch and dinner.

CARRICK

Christies. *Moderate.* Main Rd., Carrick; (003) 93-6311. French. Licensed.

COLES BAY

The Chateau. *Inexpensive.* Freycinet National Park; (003) 57-0101. Family place, fresh vegetables.

CLEVELAND

St. Andrews Inn. *Moderate.* Midland Highway; (003) 91-5525. Country fare and seafood. Licensed.

DEVONPORT

Rubys. *Expensive.* 28 Forbes St.; (004) 24-6431. Licensed. International cuisine, intimate cottage atmosphere.

HADSPEN

Casey's. *Expensive.* Bass Highway; (003) 93-6214. A la carte. Tuesday–Saturday.

AUSTRALIA

HOBART

Dear Friends. *Expensive.* 8 Brooke St.; (002) 23-2646. Silver service. A la carte.

Dirty Dick's Steak House. *Expensive.* 22 Francis St., Battery Point; (002) 23-3103. Old world atmosphere. Steak size to suit appetite. Licensed.

Drunken Admiral. *Expensive.* 17 Old Wharf; (002) 34-1903. Seafood in appropriate "old salt" atmosphere. Licensed.

Mures Fish House. *Expensive.* 5 Knopwood St., Battery Point; (002) 23-6917. Fresh seafoods in intimate cottage. Licensed. Bookings essential. No cards.

Revolving Restaurant. *Expensive.* Wrest Point; (002) 25-0112. International cuisine, panoramic views, lunch and dinner.

Sakura Room. *Expensive.* 85 Salamanca Place; (002) 23-4773. Licensed. Tuesday–Saturday.

Chinese Lantern. *Moderate.* 186 Collins St.; (002) 34-9595. Special lunches and banquets. Licensed.

Cooneys. *Moderate.* 301 Macquarie St.; (002) 23-4770. A la carte, restored colonial house.

Mondo Piccolo. *Moderate.* 196 Macquarie St.; (002) 23-2362. Italian dishes, veal a specialty. Licensed, lunch and dinner.

Stuckis. *Moderate.* 23 Stoke St., New Town; (002) 28-1885. Fondues a specialty. German fare in Willem Tell Restaurant.

Aberfeldy. *Inexpensive.* 124 Davey St.; (002) 23-7599. Family fare.

Dr. Syntax Hotel. *Inexpensive.* 139 Sandy Bay Rd.; (002) 23-6258. Counter meals 6–8 P.M.

Taroona Hotel Fernery. *Inexpensive.* Channel Highway, Taroona; (002) 27-8748. Good for families.

LAUNCESTON

Quigleys. *Expensive.* 96 Balfour St.; (003) 31-6971. Tasmanian wines a feature.

Penny Royal Watermill. *Moderate.* 147 Paterson St.; (003) 31-6699. Traditional English food in Owls Nest Restaurant.

Rosies Tavern. *Moderate.* 158 George St.; (003) 31-6588. A la carte.

Shrimps. *Moderate.* Corner of George St.; (003) 34-0584. Licensed, seafood specialty.

Aristocrat. *Inexpensive.* Cnr Charles and Paterson sts.; (003) 31-2786. Specializes in Greek dishes. BYO.

Woofies. *Inexpensive.* Macquarie House, Civic Square; (003) 34-0695. A la carte, licensed.

PORT ARTHUR

Fox and Hounds. *Moderate.* Arthur Highway; (002) 50-2217. A la carte.

PORT SORELL

Shearwater Country Club Hotel-Motel. *Moderate.* (004) 28-6205. Holiday club atmosphere, barbecues near pool, smorgasbords. Dining and dancing at night.

QUEENSTOWN

Goldrush Restaurant. *Moderate.* Westcoaster Motor Inn; (004) 71-1804. Local fish and Tasmanian cheeses. Licensed.

ROSS

Scotch Thistle Inn. *Expensive.* Church St.; (003) 81-5213. Old world charm. Good food and wines. Tuesday–Saturday.

RICHMOND

Prospect House. *Expensive.* (002) 62-2207. Game a specialty. À la carte Sunday-Wednesday.
Ma Foosies. *Inexpensive.* 46 Bridge St.; (002) 62-2412. Morning, afternoon teas and lunches. Restored dwelling.

SMITHTON

The Bridge Hotel. *Inexpensive.* Montagu St.; (004) 52-1389. Choose your own steak.

SWANSEA

The Swan Motor Inn. *Moderate.* Franklin St.; (002) 57-8102. À la carte.

TOURIST INFORMATION. A number of private companies and carriers operate information services, but the most comprehensive is through *Tasbureau.* In Tasmania offices are in all main centers: *Hobart:* 80 Elizabeth St.; (002) 30-0211. *Launceston:* Corner of St. John and Paterson sts.; (003) 32-2101. *Devonport:* 18 Rooke St.; (004) 24-1526. *Burnie:* 48 Cattley St.; (004) 30-2224. *Queenstown:* 39-41 Orr St.; (004) 71-1099.

All offices open during the day Monday to Friday and in the morning on Saturday and public holidays. Hobart and Launceston offices also open on Sunday morning.

You can also find Tasbureau information outside Tasmania. *Melbourne:* 256 Collins St.; (03) 653-7999. *Sydney:* 129 King St.; (02) 233-2500. *Brisbane:* 217-219 Queen St.; (07) 221-2744. *Adelaide:* 32 King William St.; (08) 211-7411. *Canberra:* 5 Canberra Savings Centre, City Walk; (062) 47-0070. *Perth:* 55 William St.; (09) 321-2633. *Auckland:* 15th floor Quay Tower, Corner of Customs and Albert sts.; (649) 79-5535. *Christchurch:* 71 Armagh St.; (643) 79-1563. *Singapore: Australian Tourist Commission,* 17th floor, Goldhill Square, 101 Thomson Rd.; (65) 255-4555. *Los Angeles: A.T.C.,* Suite 1740, 3550 Wilshire Boulevard; (213) 380-6041. Inquiries also can be made at A.T.C. offices in London, New York, Frankfurt, and Tokyo (see Facts at Your Fingertips for Australia).

The *Tasmanian Visitor Corporation* is the umbrella body of the private sector and is actively involved in promotion and organization of conferences. It has offices in Hobart (7 Franklin Wharf; (002) 31-0055) and Launceston (59 Brisbane St.; (003) 31-3151). The T.V.C. replaces the former Tasmanian Tourist Council and the Tasmanian Convention and Visitors' Bureau.

HOW TO GET AROUND. By coach. *Tasmanian Redline Coaches* is the largest coach line and buses cover the state daily. The company has offices in: Hobart: 96 Harrington St.; (002) 34-4577. Launceston: 112 George St.; (003) 31-9177. Devonport: 9 Edward St.; (004) 24-2685. Burnie: 177 Wilson St.; (004) 31-2660. Smithton: 13 Smith St.; (004) 52-1262 Queenstown: Orr St.; (004) 71-1011.

Services operate from Hobart and Launceston airports to the city and to major accommodation centers for a nominal cost. Taxis from the airports are about $A14. A 14-day open ticket for Tasmania costs $A75.

By air. *Airlines of Tasmania* (book through Tasbureau) fly between Hobart, Queenstown, Wynyard, Devonport, Flinders, and King Islands. Private charter companies with light aircraft operate from Cambridge Airport near Hobart, and Launceston, Devonport, and Wynyard airports.

By car and camper. Cars, campervans, motor caravans, and minibuses are available for hire in Launceston, Devonport, Burnie, Wynyard, and Hobart. The largest companies are *Auto-Rent/Hertz* (in Hobart, (002) 34-5555; Launceston, (003) 31-2099; Devonport, (004) 24-1013; Burnie/Wynyard, (004) 31-4242); *Budget* (Hobart, (002) 34-5222; Launceston, (003) 34-0099; Devonport, (004) 24-7088; Burnie, (004) 31-3577; Wynyard; (004) 42-3033; Queenstown, (004) 71-2222); *Avis* (Hobart, (002) 34-4222; Launceston, (003) 31-1633; Devonport, (004) 27–9797; Wynyard, (004) 42–2512, George Town, (003) 82–1882); *Thrifty* (Hobart, (002) 23–3577; Launceston, (003) 91–8105; Devonport, (004) 27–9119; Wynyard, (004) 42–3407). Most rental companies have unlimited-mileage rates. Gas suppliers work on a roster system weekends and on public holidays, so it is best to fill up in advance.

The speed limit in towns is 37 mph (60km/h); outside is 68 mph (110km/h). Sounding of horns, except in an emergency, is forbidden in built up areas. Main highways are paved (except parts of the Lake Highway), but many tourist routes include unpaved sections. Double white lines indicate it is dangerous to pass.

TOURS. *Tasmanian Government Tourist Bureau (Tasbureau)* operates bus tours round the state, taking 7 to 15 days. These tours, together with those of mainland operators *Australian Pacific, Trans Otway, AAT, Pioneer,* and *Centralian Staff,* are packaged together with flights from Melbourne and the seagoing *Abel Tasman.* Similarly, there are flight-inclusive packages offered by Tasbureau and the airlines *Ansett* and *TAA,* from Melbourne. Under-30s coach tours and camping tours are operated by Australian Pacific, and camping tours by Centralian Staff and AAT.

The *Arcadia 11* travels the Pieman River to the Pieman Heads on the rugged West Coast daily except Tuesday, from Corinna. There's a two-hour picnic stop at the Heads, where the river meets the Indian Ocean. Other interesting river cruises operate out of Strahan up the Gordon River; magnificent river reflections and a visit to a 19th-century convict settlement are highlights. Details of all trips from Tasbureau.

Par Avion provides scenic flights over Cradle Mountain, northwest, west, and southwest coasts and Bass Strait Islands, from Hobart and Devonport. Details from Cambridge Airport, (002) 48–5390.

Tasbureau can tell you about the seven-day, personally escorted excursions through Cradle Mountain National Park from Waldheim Chalet. These operate during summer months only. *Goondooloo* motor launch cruises along the Tamar River near Launceston operate daily from December to April; Paddlesteamer *Lady Stelfox* leaves several times daily from Ritchies Landing near the Penny Royal complex in Launceston.

Tasmanian Chairlifts in Launceston run a chairlift ride of 500 yards along the beautiful Cataract Gorge, about a mile from the city center. The central span of more than 300 yards is believed to be the greatest single span of any chairlift in the world. Impressive at any time, the gorge is best seen in spring for the color of the flowers.

Each main center in Tasmania has half- and full-day tours to surrounding attractions. Devonport has car trips out to the hydroelectric scheme, to Gunns Plains Caves, Mole Creek Caves and scenic coastal tours.

From Burnie, all day tours by car run through magnificent mountain and forest scenery to Queenstown, to Savage River, where mines can be inspected (women wear slacks and low-heeled shoes) and through rich farming communities to Launceston. Table Cape Boat Harbour tour gives an interesting run along the superb seascapes of Burnie's coast to the dramatic headland of the Nut and historic settlement of Stanley. The tour to Fern Glade goes through dense forest and is bordered by manferns and the Emu River.

From Launceston, half-day tours visit historic Entally House, and for mountain and coastal views to Mt. Barrow. City sights tour includes Cataract Gorge, National Trust House, Clarendon, and a tour along the Tamar river with constant river and orchard views. Whole day trips from Launceston take in St. Helens on the east coast, visiting St. Columba Falls; the Great Lake 3,000 ft. above sea level and Poatina power station; the verdant farmland and rugged coastal scenery en route to Table Cape.

Longer one-way tours last two or three days, finishing in Hobart. The shorter of these travels the gentler rolling farmland scenery of the east coast with its old villages. The three-day tour goes along the northwest coast and then south down the west coast to Queenstown. When available, a day-long cruise up the lovely Gordon River is included; at other times, more time is spent on the northwest coast.

At Port Arthur *MV Bundeena* travels several times daily out to the Isle of the Dead, the burial ground when Port Arthur was a penal settlement. A jet boat operates every 90 minutes on the Derwent River from New Norfolk. Phone (002) 61–3460 or Tasbureau for details. Bookings essential for the jet boat.

TASMANIA

In Hobart unusual tours include a guided walk round historic Battery Point. They begin at 9:30 a.m. each Saturday in Franklin Square, near the GPO, and are operated by the National Trust. Details from the Trust gift shop in Galleria Salamanca, 33 Salamanca Place; (002) 23–7371. For a nominal sum the Metropolitan Transport Trust issues daily off-peak zone tickets that can take travelers through Greater Hobart areas. Tickets are available on any M.T.T. bus. Derwent harbor cruises operate throughout the year from the Hobart Wharf. Companies include *Commodore Cruises*, (002) 34–9294; *Derwent Explorer Charter Co.*, (002) 34–4032; *Transderwent*, (002) 23–5893.

Industrial tours. Many factories encourage visitors, and since this is a tourist-orientated state, people with special interests will probably be accommodated if they contact firms directly, irrespective of whether they are open for general inspection. Places worth seeing include Bell Bay *(Comalco Aluminum)*, Launceston *(Waverley Woollen Mills* —tours and sales room), Port Latta (iron-ore pelletizing plant), Savage River (iron ore mining), Queenstown (Mt. Lyell Mining and Railway Company—copper mining), Russell Falls (trout farm near Mt. Field National Park), Claremont (Hobart suburb, base for Cadbury Schweppes Australia—chocolate manufacture). Details of times and conditions of tours from Tasbureau offices.

In the mountainous center of Tasmania, the *Hydro-Electric Commission* provides viewing galleries for visitors at the following stations: Liapootah, Tarraleah, Tungatinah and Trevallyn. Guided tours are available at the Poatina underground power station in the north of the state and at Strathgordon. Contact the Hydro-Electric Commission at 4–16 Elizabeth St., Hobart, for details; (002) 30–5111.

SEASONAL EVENTS. Regattas, and golf and fishing tournaments are held year round all round Tasmania. Main events are: **January:** *Aquatic Carnival*, Stanley. **February:** *Royal Hobart Regatta Association Carnival* on the River Derwent. **October:** The *Launceston Agricultural Show*, about October 5, followed by *Royal Hobart Show*, about October 18–22. **November:** Woolnorth *Rodeo*. **December:** *Sydney to Hobart Yacht Race* starting from the New South Wales capital on Boxing Day (December 26) and usually finishing three days later, in Hobart's fine old Constitution Dock (see Spectator Sports). At about the same time the *Westcoaster*, Melbourne to Hobart yacht race, is run. Latrobe *Wheel Race*—one of biggest cycling carnivals in Australia.

PARTICIPANT SPORTS. Winter skiing, bush walking, climbing, golf, yachting, pheasant shooting, and above all, fishing are the sporting attractions Tasmania has to offer the visitor.

The Tasmanian snowfields have the advantage of being within about one hour's drive from the main cities, so visitors can stay in town and be on the fields early next day.

Main **skiing** grounds are at Ben Lomond, 40 miles from Launceston, and Mount Field, 50 miles from Hobart. At the moment, no top class accommodation is available on the actual skifields but facilities are being developed by ski clubs and tows are in operation. Equipment for hire.

Contact the Tasbureau for information on conditions, accommodation, and equipment hire. Or advance inquiries may be sent to Southern Tasmania Ski Association, GPO Box 702-G, Hobart, or the Northern Tasmanian Alpine Club, Box 641, Launceston 7250.

For **golf,** *Hobart's Rosny Park* is the only public course offering prebooked starting times and equipment for hire. Tasmania has 60 courses, of which half require membership of an affiliated club; about 20 mostly in resorts and country clubs welcome visitors on payment of a green fee.

Fishing: Game fishing has three active clubs: *Game Fishing Club of Northern Tasmania* with headquarters in Launceston; *The Tuna Club* of Tasmania in Hobart; and the *St. Helens Game Fishing Club.*

The most common game fish is the southern bluefin tuna, caught off the east coast from St. Helens southward, from late November to end of June. Other tuna common in these waters are striped tuna and the albacore.

The Yellowtail Kingfish is now being sought after; they are usually caught off the east coast but have been found around Cape Portland and the northeast coast. The Broadbill Swordfish has been sighted and Blue Pointer and one White

Pointer sharks have been captured by game fishers. Charter boats can be hired at St. Helens, Triabunna and Pirates Bay.

Saltwater fishing is available all around Tasmania. The main species caught are Australian salmon, trumpeter, perch, trevally, flounder, whiting, rock lobster, flathead, rock cod, and black bream.

Along the northwest coast, estuary fishing is popular in the Duck, Inglis, Leven, Forth, Mersey, and Rubicon rivers; in the northeast in the Mussel, Roe, and Ansons Bay; at St. Helens, Scamander, the Douglas River, near Bicheno, Coles Bay, Swansea, Little Swanport, and Prosser Bay on the east coast; in the Pittwater and Derwent rivers in the south; in the Huon River, at Dover, and Southport in the Huon-Channel area; and in the Tamar River.

Surf fishing is found from the beaches of the north and east coast and on Flinders and Bruny Islands. The waters of the west coast are generally too rough.

Carp, trumpeter, and members of the parrotfish family can be found by skin-diving and spear-fishing enthusiasts. Rock lobsters and abalone are the only saltwater fish on which there are restrictions on the number bagged. Also, licenses are required for these.

Trout fishing: Tasmania's waters were stocked, first with browns, in 1864, and then with rainbows in 1896. There are about 2,500 miles of streams and rivers within 40 miles of Launceston especially the Patrick River, the Macquarie River, and Brumbys Weirs, which are renowned for dry-fly fishing. In the central lakes, trolling and spinning are productive in lakes such as Sorell and Arthurs. The Lagoon of Islands has excellent rainbow. Catches of up to 10 kilos have been taken from Lake Pedder, now proving to be one of the state's best fishing areas.

Southward, the Derwent system of impoundment gives good fishing, to trolling and spinning. Fly fishers should try Bronte and Dee lagoons.

Bushwalking and climbing: Plenty of opportunities for both in the numerous national parks through Tasmania. Several local organizations welcome visitors and in some cases provide guide facilities. Contact *Hobart Walking Club; Launceston Walking Club; North West Walking Club; Tasmanian Caverneering Club; Federation for Field Naturalists; Tasmanian Air Tours Association;* or the nearest Tasbureau office. See National Parks.

SPECTATOR SPORTS. Horseracing is held year-round. In Launceston and New Norfolk there are pacing events each Saturday; in Hobart pacing is every alternate Saturday from May to September and every Friday night during the summer. Gallops meetings conducted by turf clubs alternate each Saturday between Elwick (Hobart) and Mowbray (Launceston). There is a nominal entry charge.

Australian-rules football is played statewide from April to September, on Saturdays. There are three leagues, with matches in Hobart, Launceston, and Queenstown and on the northwest coast at Burnie, Devonport, or Latrobe. Details of venues and teams are published in daily newspapers each Friday. For further details contact the State-Wide League in Hobart (002-34-9177). Tickets at gates.

Cricket is played in summer at the T.C.A. ground in Hobart, the N.T.C.A. in Launceston, and at Devonport. As well as grade cricket (also at suburban and country grounds), national and international matches are held on a seasonal basis. Details in daily newspapers, the *Mercury*, the *Examiner*, and the *Advocate*.

Boating activities in Hobart on the River Derwent range from sailboating through small-class yachts to the maxis. The finish of the Sydney–Hobart Race (which starts on Boxing Day) draws thousands of spectators along the foreshore and at the docks. A special wharf area is cleared to accommodate up to 180 yachts from around the globe, and they are usually in port from about December 29 to January 4. This is a peak period for visitors, so accommodation should be booked in advance.

TASMANIA

PARKS AND GARDENS. Launceston is known as Tasmania's Garden City. *City Park* dates back to the late 1820s and features a zoological section with specially designed monkey quarters, and John Hart Conservatory. It covers a large block from Brisbane St., a short walk from the main shopping center. *Cataract Gorge,* just 10 minutes' walk from the shopping center, retains its wild beauty, and adjacent reserves are ideal for picnics, swimming, and canoeing (hire facilities).

The *Royal Tasmanian Botanical Gardens* on Queens Domain in Hobart, about five minutes' drive from the city center and next to Government House (not open to the public), are open daily (free admittance). The conservatory is regarded as the best in the commonwealth, and its features include a Huon pine sculpture commemorating French exploration in Tasmanian waters. Allow at least 1½ hours to see it, since areas of interest are spread out. (Meals and light refreshments from a kiosk.)

FAUNA PARKS. Tasmania today has no major zoo, but it has developed a series of small zoos, wildlife sanctuaries, and deer parks to display both native and introduced fauna to its visitors and local public. The modern concept of presenting native and introduced fauna in a mostly open-range situation, has proved to have great appeal.

At the deer parks, animals and birds go free in their native habitat; yet they are never too distant for the public to view or photograph. People can drive or walk through the parks to observe deer, kangaroo, wallaby, and birds and fowl as they exist naturally.

Tasmanian Wildlife Park, 20km from Deloraine at Mole Creek in the northwest, has animals roaming free, a nocturnal house, and a koala village. Open daily, (003) 63–6162.

Tasmanian Devil Park, at Taranna, near Port Arthur on the Tasman Peninsula, has native animals and a rare film of a Tasmanian tiger (the last known tiger died in a Hobart Zoo in the 1930s).

The *Longford Wildlife Park,* just out of Launceston, features fallow deer and Tasmanian marsupials, including the giant Forester kangaroos, in their natural habitat. A road winds through the park, and there are trails for bushwalking. Picnic, barbecue, and kiosk facilities. Closed Monday and Friday, except in school holidays, and open weekends only from mid-June to end of August. It's along Pateena Rd. (signposted directions from Bass Highway just past Prospect); (003) 91–1630.

Hadspen Park, at Rutherglen Holiday Village, west of Launceston on the Bass Highway, includes Tasmanian devils, wombats, and a large range of birds.

Bonorong Park at Brighton, just north of Hobart and a short detour from the Midland Highway, has native Tasmanian animals and barbecue and picnic facilities, (002) 68–1184.

East Coast Birdlife and Animal Park at Bicheno on the east coast features pelicans, emus, rainbow lorikeets, and rare and territorial birds. Walk around the park or travel by minitrain. Open daily; (003) 75–1311.

Talune Wildlife Park has native and farm animals. Travel to Gardners Bay on the Channel Highway in the south and then follow signs to Mike Jagoe's 30 hectare farm. See woodturning and Tasmanian crafts as well; (002) 95–1775.

NATIONAL PARKS. Tasmania's Scenery Preservation Act of 1915, the oldest legislation of its kind in Australia, has resulted in the state's having the highest percentage of its land in Australia set aside as national parks, state reserves, and conservation areas—a total of 6.1 percent.

Part of a geologically ancient country, Tasmania has, in one of its many national parks, a primitive wilderness area explored only by the hardy bushwalker. It is quite possible to walk where no other modern human has trod, even in these travel-conscious times. *South West National Park,* 1,105,000 acres (442,000 hectares) is the largest in Tasmania. This park incorporated the flooded Lake Pedder, now a storage lake created by the hydroelectricity authority. Guided walks are conducted by private operators. It is wild rugged windy country. Don't venture in without a guide.

Cradle Mountain–Lake St. Clair National Park 330,000 acres (132,000 hectares) is accessible by road at the southern end via Derwent Bridge. Superb lake and mountain scenery, with good fishing, forests of eucalypt and pine, extensive plains and mountains bedecked with summer alpine flowers are contained in the park. This park also has Tasmania's highest mountains. Furnished accommodation (no linen) cabins are available at *Lake St. Clair* at the southern end, although everything is supplied in chalets and cabins at *Cradle Mountain* at the northern end, where access is available by road. Prepare for bad weather. Blizzards can occur even in midsummer. Discuss with ranger.

Mt. Field is 50 miles (82 kilometers) from Hobart on a sealed road and has recreation and picnic area at entrance. Russell Falls are reached in 10 minutes' walk; giant eucalypts border this track. By driving 16 miles into the park, visitors can get good skiing in winter at Lake Dobson. A ski tow is operated by Southern Tasmanian Ski Association. Four rustic cabins can be rented. *Ben Lomond National Park*, 61 kilometers from Launceston, accessible by road, is developing as a ski resort by ski clubs, and ski tows are in operation. *Mt. William National Park,* covering 34,700 acres (13,800 hectares), 15 kilometers northeast of Gladstone, is the place to see the Forester kangaroo, but access is limited, and there is no accommodation.

On the east coast adjoining the town of Coles, *Freycinet National Park,* 19,000 acres (7,541 hectares) provides a combination of a seaside resort, bushwalking, and mountain climbing. Red granite outcrops and magnificent coastal scenery are features. Caravan and camping facilities are provided and a ranger is stationed here.

Franklin/Lower Gordon Wild Rivers National Park, subject of international attention since its listing as a world heritage area, features the untamed Franklin River and the enormous white quartz peak of Frenchman's Cap, southeast of Strahan. Experienced rafters can travel the Franklin during summer. Details from National Parks & Wildlife Service, 16 Magnet Court, Sandy Bay, Tasmania 7005. Ideal wilderness for bushwalkers entering from the Lyell Highway, but conditions change without warning. Huts at Lake Vera and Lake Tahune.

Hartz Mountains Park, 21,000 acres (8,620 hectares), 80 kilometers southwest of Hobart via Huonville and Geeveston, is good for a one-day trip from the capital city. High moorland dotted with picturesque lakes and seasonal wildflowers attract visitors.

Rocky Cape is a small park of 7,500 acres (3,000 hectares) on the northwest coast, accessible from the Bass Highway about 30 kilometers west of Wynyard. Geology is the main interest of this park—many formations are more than 700 million years old. The park is also renowned for rare botanical specimens peculiar to the area and caves frequented by Aborigines about 9,000 years ago.

Tasmania has two island national parks: *Mt. Strzelecki* and *Maria.* The latter is off the east coast and was originally a penal settlement. The quaint little settlement of Darlington is in a good state of preservation, and some dwellings are still occupied. Interesting marine fossils, splendid mountains and sheer cliffs on the coast are features. It is accessible by boat from Triabunna or by light aircraft from Hobart and Launceston. Mt. Strzelecki is the only national park on Flinders Island, with its entrance 15 kilometers from Whitemark. A walking track leads to the 750-meter peak.

Rangers are stationed at all national parks, and there is a nominal entry fee. Bushwalkers have to register and later sign out at the end of their walk. It cannot be stressed too much that weather in these parks often changes without warning. It's best to aim for huts overnight (details of location from rangers), but in the southwest you may have to pitch tents. Further information from *National Parks and Wildlife Service,* Magnet Court, Sandy Bay, Hobart; (002) 30–8033, or *Tasmanian Wilderness Society,* which runs a shop at 155 Liverpool St., Hobart; (002) 34–9370.

CAMPING. Camping is not permitted in any roadside picnic areas or rest areas in Tasmania. Most campgrounds charge a fee. Tasmania can be cold and downright rainy and miserable in winter, so keep camping for summer and those golden autumn and tangy spring days only.

TASMANIA

MUSEUMS AND ART GALLERIES. Hobart. *Tasmanian Museum and Art Gallery*, 5 Argyle St. European and Australian glass, silver, china, emphasis on Tasmanian Aborigines and early colonial activities. Open daily except Christmas Day, Good Friday, and Anzac Day. *Allport Collection*, State Library, 91 Murray St. Colonial art, furniture, silver. Open weekdays. *Salamanca Art Gallery*, Salamanca Place. Closed Sundays. *Van Diemens Land Folk Museum*, 103 Hamden Rd., Battery Pt. (also known as Narryna).

Launceston. *Queen Victoria Museum and Art Gallery*, Wellington St. Includes a Chinese joss house used last century by Chinese miners in northeastern Tasmania. Open daily, afternoons only on Sunday, except Christmas Day, Good Friday, and Anzac Day.

Regional museums and galleries open daily include Swansea, *Bark Mill Museum;* Plenty, *Piscatorial Museum at Salmon Ponds* (live fish, too); Zeehan, *Mine Museum;* Burnie, *Pioneer Museum;* Evandale, *Colonial Art Gallery;* Richmond, *Saddlers Court Gallery;* Deloraine, *Bowerbank Mill*.

HISTORIC SITES. When Australians want to see history, they go to Tasmania. On your wander around Tasmania, make a point of looking in at Bothwell, Evandale, New Norfolk, Oatlands, Pontville, Ross, and Stanley; Longford was recently classified.

Consistently Tasmania's number-one historic attraction is *Port Arthur*, once the major penal settlement. The old asylum has been developed and has a visitor-reception center with audiovisual presentations, scale model, and small museum.

Isle of the Dead, originally Opossum Island, became the burial ground for convicts and free people from Port Arthur. Boat trips across to the island from Port Arthur daily except July.

Bowen Park. Risdon Cove. A $1.2-million development honoring the founders of the first European settlement in Tasmania. Open daily. Films, displays, and audiovisuals.

Evandale. Clarendon House, Nile, completed 1838, one of the great Georgian houses of Australia, designed in the grand manner and set in an extensive formal garden. Open daily except Christmas Day, Good Friday, and July.

Deloraine. Bowerbank Mill, Bass Highway. One of several flour mills, built 1853, whose production finally ceased in the 1930s. Now an art gallery exhibiting work by Tasmanian artists and craftsmen. Open Tuesday to Sunday.

Hadspen. Military museum with vehicles, uniforms, photographs. Daily.

Richmond. A pleasant drive from Hobart through grazing country that once served as the state's "wheatbelt" brings the visitor to this historic township featuring Australia's oldest bridge, beautiful churches, galleries and tea shops.

George Town. The Grove, 25 Cimitiere St. Once the home of the port officer, the house has been lovingly restored and is open for inspection daily. Closed July. The owner and staff dress in period costume to guide, and supply refreshments.

Hadspen Village. Entally House, old home of great charm, furnished with prized antiques and set in delightful park. Collection of horse-drawn vehicles in outbuildings. Open daily except Christmas Day and Good Friday.

Bush Mill. Tasmania Peninsula. A replica of a 19th-century steam timber mill. Open daily. Audiovisuals and tea-rooms.

Hobart. Narryna (also known as Van Diemen's Land Memorial Folk Museum), built 1836, with many original features preserved. Open daily, closed for four weeks in winter. *Shot Tower, Taroona*, 11 kilometers south of Hobart. Built to make shot for firearms. Interesting museum, locally made souvenirs. Panoramic views from top of tower.

Launceston. Franklin House, Franklin Village, Georgian house once a home and then a school. Open daily except Good Friday and Christmas Day. *Bonney's Inn* at Deloraine offers good food in a charming atmosphere, well suited to the pace of life in this small rural town.

New Town. Runnymede, 61 Bay Rd. National Trust property, recreated home of 1860s. Open except Mondays, closed July.

New Norfolk. Old Colony Inn, Montague St. One of Tasmania's most famous historic features, built 1835, but doubtful if it ever was actually used as a pub.

Contains fine antiques and collection dating back to penal era. Huge walnut tree in the delightful grounds reputed to be 170 years old. Open daily.

Westbury. *White House, Village Green.* Originally a store, now contains collection of 17th-and 18th-century furniture. Garage houses early motor cars and horse-drawn vehicles. Display of miniature furniture, glass and china, model toys and playthings from 1850. Open daily except July and early August.

Gunpowder Mills, near Cataract Gorge, is simulation of 19th-century gunpowder mill with foundry, arsenal, and ships of war. Open daily.

SHOPPING. Shops in Hobart, Launceston, Devonport, and Burnie are open on Saturday morning, with limited trading in Hobart and Launceston on Friday evenings. Supermarkets and hairdressers in large centers open Thursday and Friday evenings, and small general stores operate 7 days a week. In Hobart, *Corbys Pharmacy* on Macquarie St. operates a 24-hour service (002) 23–3044. The *Salamanca Market* in Salamanca Place, Hobart, is an event each Saturday morning that shouldn't be missed. Tasmania is noted for its art and crafts outlets. Local materials such as Huon pine, sassafras, myrtle, and other timbers are crafted into items as diverse as letter racks and salad bowls. Craft stores worth a visit include: **Hobart:** *Aspect Design,* Salamanca Place. Open weekdays and Saturday morning. *Fragments,* 133 Elizabeth St.; *National Trust Gift Shop,* Galleria, Salamanca Place (weekdays and Saturday morning). *Handmark Gallery,* 44A Hamden Rd., Battery Point (seven days weekly).

Launceston: *National Trust Old Umbrella Shop,* 60 George St. (weekdays and Saturday morning). *Tasmanian Design Centre,* adjacent to City Park (open daily).

Ross: *Wool and Craft Centre,* Bridge St. (good for raw and spun wool and knitted goods).

Scottsdale: *Art and Craft Centre* (specializes in north-eastern gemstones), open Monday–Saturday.

Carrick: *The Gallery,* Bass Highway.

Ulverstone: *Weeda Copperware,* 39 Forth Rd. (hand-beaten copper items).

Richmond: *The Granary and the Bridge Inn* (variety of crafts, including locally grown mohair).

Port Arthur: *The Bush Mill Craft Shop.*

MUSIC. The *ABC* (Australian Broadcasting Commission) features major orchestral concerts at the converted Odeon Cinema in Liverpool Street and also organizes youth concerts at the same place. The ABC and the *Conservatorium of Music* run regular lunchtime concerts at the State Library Auditorium, Murray Street. *This Week in Tasmania,* available at accommodation places, is a good guide to current performances and staging of rock, jazz and Musica Viva concerts. The *Tasmanian University Musical Society* also stages unusual concerts.

THEATER. The three main theaters for local and imported productions are the *Launceston Princess Theatre,* Brisbane St., (003) 31–7156; *The Burnie Civic Centre,* Wilmot St., (004) 31–2075; and Hobart's historic, acclaimed *Theatre Royal,* 29 Campbell St., (002) 34–6266 (this architectural gem, with its magnificent dome featuring hand-painted portraits of famous composers, plush velvet chairs, and an atmosphere steeped in history dating back to 1834, is also open for tours).

There are cabaret shows and nightly performances by international stars as well as comedy and review specials at the *Wrest Point Hotel Casino and Convention Centre* four miles from the Hobart city center at Sandy Bay (002) 25–0112, and at the *Launceston Federal Country Club Casino,* at Prospect, near Launceston, (003) 44–8855. Costs range from $15 up for the show, depending on the guest performer, and dinner can be ordered a la carte in the entertainment area or from one of the other restaurants in the complexes.

BARS. Under Tasmania's licensing laws, the most liberal in Australia, owners of licensed hotels or restaurants may elect their own hours of trading, provided certain minimums are observed. As a result, trading hours vary enormously on all days except Sundays, when trading is restricted to between noon and 8 P.M.

CASINOS. Hobart boasts Australia's first legal casino at *Wrest Point Hotel,* open seven days a week from 1 P.M. until 3 A.M., where blackjack, French and American roulette, mini-baccarat, keno, mini dice, and two-up are played to a maximum $500. A special suite operates on the lower ground floor for gamblers wishing to play for higher stakes. Launceston's new *Federal Country Club Casino* offers gamblers the same choice of games and true "country club" pursuits on its acres of grounds. Both offer a range of accommodation and restaurants, discos, indoor and outdoor sports facilities, such as swimming and tennis (plus horseriding at Launceston). Wrest Point is at 410 Sandy Bay Rd. (002–25–0112) and Launceston Casino is at Prospect, 19km from the city center. (003–44–8855).

NEW ZEALAND

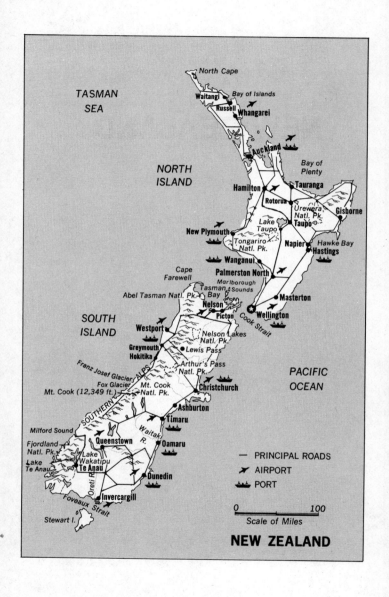

FACTS AT YOUR FINGERTIPS FOR NEW ZEALAND

TOURIST INFORMATION. The *New Zealand Tourist and Publicity Department* was founded in 1901 to develop tourist amenities and stimulate tourism, and today it has Travel Commissioners in various parts of the world, from whom information on accommodations, transport, tours, and all aspects of travel may be obtained. *North America:* Suite 970, Alcoa Building, One Maritime Plaza, San Francisco, CA 94111, (415) 788–7404; Suite 1530, Tishman Building, 10960 Wilshire Boulevard, Los Angeles, CA 90024, (213) 477–8241; Suite 530, 630 Fifth Avenue, New York, NY 10111, (212) 586–0060.

Britain: New Zealand House, Haymarket, London, S.W. 1Y 4TQ, (01) 930–8422.

Australia: United Dominion's House, 115 Pitt Street, Sydney NSW 2000, (02) 233–6633; C.M.L. Building, 330 Collins Street, Melbourne, Victoria 3000, (03) 67–6621; Watkins Place, 288 Edward Street, Brisbane, Queensland 4000, (07) 221–3722; 16 St. George's Terrace, Perth, West Australia 6000, (09) 325–7347.

Japan: Toho Twin Tower Building, 2F, 1–5–2 Yurakucho Chiyoda-ku, Tokyo 100, 508–9981.

Germany: New Zealand Government Tourist Office, 6000 Frankfurt A.M., Kaiserhofstrasse 7, Federal Republic of Germany, 0692 88189.

Canada: New Zealand Consulate-General, 701 West Georgia St., IBM Tower, Vancouver, B.C. V7Y 186, (604) 684–2117.

Singapore: 13 Nassim Rd., Singapore 1025, 235–9966.

Within New Zealand the department operates *New Zealand Travel Offices* (previously known as Government Tourist Bureaus) in: Auckland, 99 Queen St., (09) 798–180; Rotorua, 67 Fenton St., (073) 85–179; Wellington, 27 Mercer St., (04) 739–269; Christchurch, 65 Cathedral Square, (03) 794–900; Dunedin, 131 Princes St., (024) 740–344; Queenstown, 49 Shotover St., 143.

These offices not only provide information but also offer a complete travel service in advising on and reserving sightseeing and in planning itineraries and making reservations if required. Such a service is, of course, also provided by the many travel agents, but the New Zealand Travel Offices are widely used by New Zealanders themselves for domestic travel arrangements.

Maps, touring information, and accommodations guides are also available from Automobile Association offices. See "Hints to the Motorist," below.

PASSPORTS, VISAS, CUSTOMS. A passport valid for 3 months beyond intended stay is required, except for nationals of Australia and the Commonwealth countries who have permission to reside indefinitely in Australia and New Zealand, but passports are necessary for reentry into Australia.

No visas required for tourists from U.S. (except American Samoa), Japan, New Caledonia, and Tahiti for stay of up to 30 days; citizens of West Germany, Iceland, and Malta for stay of not more than three months; citizens of Belgium, Denmark, Finland, France, Liechtenstein, Luxembourg, Monaco, Netherlands, Norway, Sweden, and Switzerland for stay of not more than six months. Commonwealth citizens require only temporary entry authority, which may be granted on arrival; those not wholly of European origin must obtain it before departure. Sufficient funds for length of stay and onward ticket required.

Visa applications at nearest New Zealand embassy or consulate or at British consulates. Allow two weeks by mail.

There is no restriction on the amount of foreign currency that may be brought into or reexported from New Zealand. No customs duty is payable on personal effects, or on a reasonable amount of photographic equipment. No duty on: 1 qt. of liquor; 1 qt. of wine; 200 cigarettes or 50 cigars.

NEW ZEALAND

CLIMATE. Subtropical in the North Island; temperate in the South Island. The north has no extremes of heat or cold, but winter can be somewhat cold in the south. The seasons are reversed from the northern hemisphere: summer from December through February; fall from March through May; winter from June through August; spring from September through November.

Average Temperature (°Fahrenheit) and Humidity

Auckland	Jan	Feb	Mar	Apr	May	June	July	Aug	Sept	Oct	Nov	Dec
Average max. day temperature	74°	75°	73°	68°	63°	59°	58°	59°	62°	64°	68°	71°
Days of rain	6	5	6	8	10	12	12	11	9	9	8	7
Humidity, percent	64	65	65	65	70	71	69	69	66	65	64	66
Christchurch												
Average max. day temperature	71°	71°	67°	63°	57°	52°	51°	54°	59°	63°	67°	69°
Days of rain	5	4	5	4	6	6	6	4	4	5	5	5
Humidity, percent	57	59	63	65	71	70	70	63	61	56	55	58

Although there are good ski fields in both the North and South islands, snowfalls are largely confined to the mountainous area. Christchurch and Dunedin are the only two cities likely to experience an occasional fall of snow, which is usually light and quickly disappears.

PACKING. Take light- or medium-weight clothing during the summer (December-April) and medium weight at other times. Include a sweater for possible use at nights during the spring and fall to offset occasional cool days or when sightseeing in the mountainous regions. Include a raincoat for occasional rainy days.

New Zealanders tend to dress casually and informally, but a jacket and tie are usually worn when dining at top hotels and restaurants.

Shorts for men and women and slacks for women are acceptable. In general, dress as you would at home.

Don't forget sunglasses, sun hat, and sunburn protective creams (or buy them here). New Zealand is renowned for the clarity of its light—meaning that sunburn can occur more quickly and imperceptibly here than in many other places.

WHAT WILL IT COST? By comparison with most other countries, New Zealand is not expensive. The biggest variation is in accommodations. Rates for a room at the very top city hotels can be from NZ$100 up, at a very good motel from NZ$50 to NZ$70. At good, clean, comfortable quality hotels, rates could drop to NZ$70, and at motels to NZ$50. There are also a number of small guest houses with common bathrooms and toilets, often providing breakfast, for around NZ$30 to NZ$40.

Typical expenses per person (one-half of a double room) could be:

Room at moderate hotel or motel	NZ$40.00
Breakfast (cooked) at hotel or motel (no tip)	7.00
Lunch at coffee shop (no tip)	4.00
Dinner at moderate restaurant (no tip)	14.00
Sightseeing bus tour (full day)	24.00
Evening drink	2.00
Admission to museums (mostly free)	2.00
	NZ$93.00

FACTS AT YOUR FINGERTIPS

Late last year the government introduced a goods-and-services tax (GST) of 10 percent on all saleable items and services. It was not possible to obtain prices with the GST added at the time this edition was compiled, but 10 percent should be added to the prices quoted. Other than this there are no national or city taxes on accommodations or meals. A $2 airport tax is payable on departure overseas but not for domestic traveling.

CURRENCY. The monetary unit is the New Zealand dollar. Following recent devaluation, it is worth approximately 52 United States cents. An American virtually buys everything at half price. The rate varies as the New Zealand dollar is "floating." Paper money is in denominations of $1, $2, $5, $10, $50, and $100; coins in 1-cent, 2-cent, 5-cent, 10-cent, 20-cent, and 50-cent pieces.

American Express, Diners Club, Bankcard, MasterCard, and Visa travelers checks and credit cards are universally negotiable.

Prices quoted are in New Zealand dollars, unless otherwise noted.

HOW TO GET THERE. The international airports at Auckland, Wellington, and Christchurch have direct services to Australia, but most international flights arrive at Auckland. *Air New Zealand, United Airlines, Continental Airlines,* and *UTA French Airlines* have regular flights from North America (Air New Zealand and *CP Air* from Vancouver; *Qantas* flies from North America and Europe via Australia; *British Airways* from England; Air New Zealand and *Japan Airlines* from Japan; *Trans Australia Airlines* from Hobart to Christchurch. Check with your travel agent.

STOPOVERS. Air carriers have opened many Pacific doors with their new on-line stopover privileges. You must work with your travel agent, but to give you an idea of how this works investigate "circle" fares. Low season is always the best bargain dollarwise, and circle fares mean multi-destinations for you. Remember these are special fares; you cannot change carriers. Stopover or multi-destination examples: *Air New Zealand's* low-season fare of $1000 from Los Angeles includes stopovers in Honolulu/Fiji/Auckland with return via Cook Islands and Tahiti/Los Angeles. For $100 more you can add Wellington and Christchurch and continue to Sydney or Brisbane with a return to Auckland, Cook Islands, and Tahiti/Los Angeles.

HOW TO GET ABOUT. By air: *Air New Zealand* has frequent services between the major centers. Scheduled flights to some of the outstanding scenic areas are run by *Mount Cook Airlines* and *Newmans Air.*

Kiwi Air Pass: The Kiwi Air Pass, which must be purchased prior to arrival in New Zealand, allows 14 days of travel to: Bay of Islands, Auckland, Rotorua, Christchurch, Mt. Cook, Queenstown, and the Southern Lakes. (Not valid for flightseeing, ski-plane, or charter operations.) Reservations are essential and must be made at the Mount Cook Airlines offices in New Zealand. Tickets must be issued against the pass only by Mount Cook in New Zealand, and only for each separate stage of the itinerary. Rates are for air travel only, all other charges at passenger's expense. Contact Mount Cook Line, Suite 1020, 9841 Airport Blvd., Los Angeles, CA 90045; (213) 684-2117.

By rail: The main towns and cities of both islands are connected by rail, and many of the routes are scenically attractive. Wellington and Auckland have commuter train services. *New Zealand Railways* Travelpass allows unlimited rail travel throughout both islands. You can buy more than one pass if you want to travel, stay somewhere for a time, then travel again. Contact New Zealand Tourist Offices (see Tourist Information, above).

By bus: Scheduled coach service throughout the country. Rates run around NZ$16 to NZ$22 for a half-day trip; NZ$19 to $46 for a full day, depending on length of journey. Reservations required. Contact the Mount Cook Line or *Newmans Coachlines,* Box 3719, Auckland, or 10351 Santa Monica Blvd. #305, Los Angeles, CA 90025; (213) 552-0901. A *Kiwi Coach Pass* is available for reductions on bus fares.

By ferry: Ferries link North and South islands; travel is between Wellington and Picton and takes about 3½ hours. The service (52 miles across the Cook Strait) is operated by New Zealand Railways aboard four ferries for passengers, automobiles, and railway freight cars. Daily sailings from Wellington are at 10 A.M. and 4 P.M. daily, and 6:40 P.M. Monday through Saturday; 8 A.M. Wednesday through Sunday, with somewhat similar departures from Picton. Crossing takes 3 hours 20 minutes. Lounges, cocktail bars on board. Cabin berths available on some ships at extra charge. One-way passenger fare NZ$20. The voyage is scenic: the first 40 minutes are in Wellington Harbour, followed by a two-hour traverse of the lower end of the North Island thru Cook Strait, after which the ship enters the narrow gap of Tory Channel and steams for an hour down the sheltered deep-blue waters of Queen Charlotte Sound to Picton. In Wellington call 725–3990 or contact New Zealand Tourist Offices listed above under "Tourist Information."

HINTS TO THE MOTORIST. Except for the fact that traffic keeps to the left on the road and that automobiles are therefore left-hand drive, visitors should find no difficulty driving in New Zealand. All the main highways and secondary roads are well formed and sealed and well sign-posted, and state highways are numbered—a red shield being used for the main highways and a blue shield for secondary roads. Four-lane motorways are confined to approaches to main centers. Distances are given in kilometers.

The maximum speed limit is 100 kilometers per hour, but this is reduced to 50 kilometers in cities and more populous areas. A sign "L.S.Z." (Limited Speed Zone) means there is no speed limit set, but that the speed should be governed by road conditions and the traffic at the time.

School patrols control traffic at school crossings, and school buses should be passed with great care; you should stop if a bus is discharging children. A stop sign at an intersection means exactly what it says.

Giving way to other traffic is governed by what is known as the right-hand rule, which means that in general you always give way to traffic approaching from your right unless the other automobile is approaching you head-on and wants to turn across you or is approaching a give way sign (usually marked with double white lines on the road) on your right.

Most main highways have a broken white line at the center of the road, which means you can pass if the road is clear ahead. A double solid yellow line means don't pass, and a double yellow line with one solid and the other broken means that you can pass with care if the broken line is on your side.

Being a semi-mountainous country, New Zealand has few long, straight stretches of road. This makes for more interesting driving, but it also means that traveling times are often longer than might be expected from the distance to be covered.

Allowing for refreshment stops, gas replenishment, and occasional stops to admire the scenery, budget on an average of 50 to 60 kilometers per hour for comfortable driving.

Gas stations are scattered along the main routes, but make sure your tank is topped up before driving from Te Anau to Milford Sound and back. The return trip is only about 150 miles, but there is no habitation or gas station.

Watch out for sudden encounters with a herd of cows being driven home for milking or a flock of sheep being moved from one field to another. The farmer's dogs will usually clear a pathway for you.

New Zealand is tough on drinking and driving and has compulsory breathalyzer and blood tests.

The automobile association has branches at all the main centers and offers a comprehensive range of traveling brochures, maps, and accommodations guides. The main offices are at: Auckland, 33 Wyndham St. (774–660); Wellington, 344 Lambton Quay (851–745); Christchurch, 210 Hereford St. (791–280); Dunedin, 450 Moray Pl. (775–945).

SELF-DRIVE RENTAL AUTOMOBILES

Several well-known rental firms operate in New Zealand. *Hertz, Avis, Budget,* and *Letz* have depots in the main cities and provincial centers and at airports. Rates vary very little and depend on the type of size of the automobile. Japanese cars tend to predominate.

A current domestic or international driver's license is required. Driver's licenses from the U.S., Australia, Canada, and the U.K. are valid. All firms must offer comprehensive automobile insurance coverage, which costs about $5 a day, and third party personal insurance is compulsory.

Average rental rates are $41 a day for a Honda Civic and $45 for a Toyota Corolla with an additional 16 cents per kilometer; $65 a day for an automatic Ford Telstar with 20 cents per kilometer. There are reductions for longer hire periods. A four-berth camper van costs from $63 to $125 a day, depending on the season.

TAXIS. Taxis in New Zealand do not cruise for hire and are obtained from a sign-posted taxi stand or by phone. All fares are based on metered charges so that it is not necessary to establish a fare when engaging a taxi. Tipping drivers is not necessary and is not usually done unless they have given special service.

ACCOMMODATIONS. Accommodations in New Zealand are equal to international standards in terms of amenities and creature comforts, but hotels are not as large or elaborate as is often the case in some other countries. The emphasis is on cleanliness and comfort rather than ostentation.

Similarly, rates are not as high and the category of "expensive" (a relative term) means they are top grade and expensive from a New Zealander's point of view but not necessarily to an overseas visitor. The highest rate for a standard room in a moderate hotel would be about NZ$90, although rates in a more elaborate hotel would be from NZ$100 up.

Motor inns are of modern design and have single or family suites with a high standard of appointment, on-site parking, usually a restaurant attached, and liquor service.

Motels have self-contained units. Some include fully equipped kitchens. Hotels and motels usually have tea- and coffee-making facilities. Rates range from NZ$40 to NZ$60 for a double room.

Motor camps offering community washing, cooking, and toilet facilities are available at the principal cities and resorts, but campers are required to provide their own tents and equipment. **Cabin accommodations** are available at some. Tent and caravan sites cost from $3 to $7 and cabins from $5 per person per night according to the standard and season.

For all accommodations early reservations are recommended during the peak demand period of Christmas, January, and Easter, when most New Zealanders go on holiday. With the increase in tourist arrivals advance reservations are advisable from October through April, particularly in some of the remote but outstanding scenic areas.

The *Tourist Hotel Corporation* has a chain of hotels at such areas as Waitangi, Waitomo Caves, Wairakei, Tokaann, Tongariro National Park, Mount Cook, and Milford Sound, and has a reservations telephone number in Wellington (733–689), which can be dialed without long-distance charges from Auckland.

FARM HOLIDAYS. If you're traveling by self-drive car you shouldn't miss the opportunity of spending at least one night on a farm, where you'll be treated as one of the family, sharing meals with the hosts and, if you wish, taking part in daily farm activities. Several organizations can arrange such visits, and most farming families in the schemes are more interested in meeting people than in making money. Visitors can choose the type of farm in which they are interested—dairying, sheep, cattle, cropping, and high-country farming.

Some homes provide private bathroom facilities for guests, though in other homes you are expected to share with the family. In all cases hygiene standards are high, and facilities will be convenient to the guest room.

The daily cost per person usually covers dinner, bed, and breakfast, and the average price will range from NZ$50 to NZ$70.

Reservations are essential and can be made through a travel agent or with: *N.Z. Farm Holidays*, Private Bag, Parnell, Auckland (09–394–780); *Farm Home and Country Home Holidays*, Box 31–250, Auckland (09–492–171);

Town and Country Home Hosting, Box 143, Cambridge (071–27–6511); *Rural Holidays New Zealand,* Box 2155, Christchurch (03–61–919); *Home Stay/Farm Stay,* Box 630, Rotorua (073–24–895); *N.Z. Home Hospitality,* Box 309, Nelson (054–84–727).

FOOD. New Zealand food has earned acclaim for its quality. Lamb, especially spring lamb from October to January, is probably the most popular dish, but other favorites are beef (roasted or as steaks), pork, and, in some restaurants, venison, which comes from deer farms.

The country's extended coastline yields good catches of fish; five delicious varieties are blue cod, snapper, John Dory, grouper, and orange roughly. Seasonal delicacies are oysters (Auckland rock oysters are small and sweet, and Steward Island oysters much larger and plumper and stronger in taste), crayfish, scallops, and whitebait (a type of small smelt).

Vegetables are fresh and good and in variety. Try kumara, a native sweet potato.

Good locally produced fruit is always available, especially during the summer months. Don't miss kiwi fruit, which originated in China but is now widely grown and exported. Another interesting fruit is the tamarillo, a pear-shaped red or orange fruit.

For dessert, New Zealand claims as its own the Pavlova cake, a special type of large meringue cake with lashings of whipped cream. And, of course, the traditional apple pie is everywhere.

Visitors often say that New Zealand milk shakes are especially enjoyable because of the quality and richness of the milk. There are milk bars everywhere.

New Zealand also has a good variety of domestic wines, some of which have won international awards.

DINING OUT. Dining out can be fun, but as with hotels don't expect large, ostentatious restaurants with elaborate service. Most restaurants favored by New Zealanders are small and, particularly in Auckland, often in unprepossessing buildings where the interior has been renovated and redecorated into cozy intimate oases catering to 80 people or less.

Emphasis is on good food rather than surroundings and obsequious service. Not that service is lacking; it's just more casual, which is the New Zealand way of life. Waiters and waitresses are often university students earning extra money, and if they do not have the polish of professional waiters and waitresses, they are friendly and enjoy meeting and talking with patrons. Servility does not rate at all, but civility and friendliness do. You don't *have* to tip, but if you do it is appreciated, not as something routine and expected but as an expression of thanks for good service and attention.

Many of the restaurants are licensed to serve liquor; some are not, but diners can bring their own. Check with the restaurant when reserving a table, which is advisable, especially on weekends.

Prices vary, of course, but the difference between a moderate and expensive restaurant is not that great. An average price for two at a moderate restaurant for soup, appetizer, main course, dessert, and coffee would be around NZ$50 to NZ$60. Restaurant bills are not taxed.

There are plenty of restaurants offering cooked lunches, but try a New Zealand–style lunch: patronize one of the ubiquitous coffee shops or tea shops where you select from cabinets displaying meat pies and pieces of deep-fried fish, cold meat or chicken with a mixed green salad, sandwiches with a bewildering range of fillings, assorted small cakes and fruit salads, and tea, coffee, or soft drinks. An average filling lunch would cost from $4 to $6.

Or, if it's summer and you'd like to be like many office workers, buy a take-away lunch and eat it in one of the nearby parks or beaches.

DRINKING LAWS. New Zealand's drinking laws may be confusing to a visitor. The government has set up a commission to rationalize the morass of rules and regulations, but it will be two or three years before this is completed.

FACTS AT YOUR FINGERTIPS

Liquor at a bar or at tables may be purchased only at licensed hotels, which have public bars, lounge bars, and cocktail bars; some have entertainment. Individual bottles of spirits or beer can be purchased only from the "bottle store" of hotels, but minimum quantities of two gallons can be bought at lower rates from liquor wholesalers.

Hotel hours vary slightly, but are generally from 10 A.M. to 10 P.M. Monday to Saturday inclusive, but no liquor can be sold to the public on Sundays. However, if you are a guest in a hotel you can be served drinks after 10 P.M. for as long as the hotel keeper wants to keep the house bar open, and on Sundays. You can also be served drinks on Sunday if you are having a meal at a hotel.

Liquor, including beer, cannot be sold at supermarkets or other stores. On the other hand, New Zealand and imported wines can be sold as individual bottles from wine shops, which cannot sell spirits or beer.

The term *licensed restaurant* means it can serve you spirits or wine with your meal, and the term *BYO* means the restaurant cannot serve you liquor but you can bring your own bottle of wine. The minimum age for the consumption of liquor is 20.

TIME ZONE AND BUSINESS HOURS. New Zealand standard time is 12 hours ahead of Greenwich Mean Time; 17 hours ahead of New York; 20 hours ahead of San Francisco. In other words, 12 noon in New Zealand is 4 P.M. the previous day in San Francisco, 7 P.M. in New York, and 2 P.M. in Honolulu. New Zealand is also two hours ahead of Sydney, Australia. From the last Saturday in October to the first Sunday in March the clock is put forward one hour.

Shops and banks are open five days a week and closed on Saturday and Sunday, but some shops are open on Saturday until noon. Shops are usually open from 9 A.M. to 5:30 P.M. and until 9 P.M. on Fridays. If you are cooking your own meals it is wise to stock up for the weekend on Friday, although small food shops with a basic range of goods (milk, canned food, butter, soap powder, tobacco, etc.) and known as "dairies" are open seven days a week.

FESTIVALS AND SPECIAL EVENTS. January: *Auckland Cup Galloping* race meeting; *National Lawn Bowling Tournament* (varies); *N.Z. International Grand Prix*, Auckland; *Wellington Cup Galloping* meeting; *National Yearling Sales* (bloodstock sale of about 450 selected yearlings, held concurrently with Wellington Race meeting); *Anniversary Day Yachting Regatta* (Auckland), reputed to be the largest one-day regatta in the world.

February: *Auckland Cup Harness* racing meeting; *Festival of the Pines* (New Plymouth), music, ballet and cultural arts in outdoor amphitheater; *International Vintage Car Rally* (varies).

March: *Golden Shears Sheep Shearing Championships* (Masterton), with leading shearers competing; *Ngaruawahia Annual Regatta* (Hamilton), the only Maori Canoe Regatta held; *Wellington Galloping* race meeting.

March/April: *Easter Show* (Auckland), a mixture of displays of home services, manufactured goods, and farm animals, horse riding events, carnival sideshows and outdoor attractions.

April: *Rugby* football and *winter sports* seasons (other than skiing) open; *Highland Games* (Hastings), an elaborate gathering of participants in traditional Scottish costume for competitions in bagpipe playing, Scottish dancing, and Scottish sport such as tossing the caber and shot putting; *Metropolitan Harness* racing meeting (Christchurch).

May: *Skiing season* opens (depending on snowfalls); *World Ploughing Championships* (Christchurch), a contest in which the winner, pulling a plow behind a tractor, plows the cleanest and straightest series of furrows over a given area of grassland.

June: *Great Northern Hurdles and Steeplechase* meeting (Auckland); *Agricultural Fielddays* (Hamilton), displays of equipment.

July: *Wellington Hurdles and Steeplechase* meeting.

August: *International Ski Championships* (varies); *Grand National Hurdles & Steeplechase* meeting (Christchurch).

September: *Cherry Blossom Festival* (Hastings and Alexandra), a parade of decorated floats to celebrate the full blossoming of cherry blossom trees.

October: *Hawke's Bay Agricultural Show* (Hastings); *Waikato Agricultural and Pastoral Show* (Hamilton). Commonly abbreviated to A & P Shows, these are farmers' shows where stock are paraded and judged for prizes. Produce, including home cooking, is displayed. There are usually horse-riding events and always carnival-type entertainment and sideshows. Much like a U.S. state fair. New Zealanders take their own vacations mid-December through April, and tourist attractions tend to be more crowded at these times.

November: *New Zealand Cup* race meeting and *Trotting Cup* race meeting (Christchurch); *Canterbury Agricultural and Pastoral Show* (Christchurch).

SIGHTSEEING. If you're interested in escorted tours, contact your travel agent. Operators of escorted tours include: *Brendan Tours,* 510 W. Sixth St., #1232, Los Angeles CA 90014; *Club Pacific,* 790 27th Ave., San Francisco, CA 94121; *Fourwinds,* 175 Fifth Ave., New York, NY 10010; *Globus Gateway,* 727 W. 7th St., #1040, Los Angeles, CA 90014; *Hemphill Harris,* 16000 Ventura Blvd., #200, Encino, CA 91436; *Japan Travel Bureau,* 45 Rockefeller Plaza, New York, NY 10111; *Maupintour,* 900 Mass Street, Lawrence, KS 66044; *Dateline Tours,* Box 1755, Newport Beach, CA 92663; *Voyages of Discovery,* 1298 Prospect, La Jolla, CA 92037; *World Adventures,* 2183 Fairview Rd., #106, Costa Mesa, CA 92627.

Independent tours are run by: *Islands in the Sun,* 760 W. 16th St., #L, Costa Mesa, CA 92627; *Expanding Horizons,* 17581 Irvine Blvd., #115, Tustin, CA 92680; *Jetset Tours,* 8383 Wilshire Blvd., #432, Beverly Hills, CA 90211; *Koala Tours,* 2930 Honolulu Ave., #200, La Crescenta, CA 91214; *Network Travel Planners,* 202 Main St., Venice, CA 90291; *Newmans Tours,* 10351 Santa Monica Blvd., #305, Los Angeles, CA 90025; *Rainbow Adventure Holidays,* 23241 Ventura Blvd., #216, Woodland Hills, CA 91364; *Silver Fern Holidays,* 31729-C, 48th La. S.W., Federal Way, WA 98003; *SOPAC,* 1448 15th St., Santa Monica, CA 90404; *Tour Pacific,* 1101 E. Broadway, #201, Glendale, CA 91205.

Because trips to the main cities alone will not do justice to the variety of attractions this country has to offer, listed here are some sample itineraries to help you get the most out of your trip. *North Island* (4 days): Day 1, Arrive Auckland; day 2, Auckland to Waitomo Caves to Rotorua; day 3, at Rotorua; day 4, Rotorua to Auckland. *South Island* (5 days): Day 1, arrive Christchurch; Day 2, Christchurch to Queenstown by air; day 3, at Queenstown; day 4, Queenstown to Mount Cook to Christchurch; day 5, depart Christchurch. *Both Islands* (10 days): Day 1: Arrive Christchurch; day 2, Christchurch to Lake Te Anau by air; day 3, day trip to Milford Sound by road; day 4, Lake Te Anau to Queenstown by air; day 6, at Queenstown; day 7, Queenstown to Mount Cook by air; day 7, Mount Cook to Rotorua by air; day 8, at Rotorua; day 9, Rotorua to Waitomo Caves to Auckland by road; day 10, depart Auckland. *Both Islands* (17 days): Day 1, Arrive Auckland; day 2, at Auckland; day 3, Auckland to Paihia (Bay of Islands); day 4, at Paihia (catamaran or launch cruise or day trip to Cape Reinga); day 5, Paihia to Auckland; day 6, Auckland to Waitomo Caves to Rotorua; days 7 and 8, at Rotorua; day 9, Rotorua to Christchurch by air; day 10, Christchurch to Lake Te Anau by air; day 11, day trip to Milford Sound; day 12, Lake Te Anau to Queenstown; days 13 and 14, at Queenstown; day 15, Queenstown to Mount Cook by air; day 16, Mount Cook to Christchurch by air; day 17, depart Christchurch or fly to Auckland for departure.

SPORTS. Because of its temperate climate and the abundance of its mountains, rivers, lakes, and the surrounding sea, New Zealand has a wide range of outdoor activities within a relatively compact area. The easiest way to enjoy them is to check with the New Zealand Tourist Offices (see Tourist Information, above), both locally and before your trip.

Sports most favored by overseas visitors because of their excellence are *trout fishing, salmon fishing,* and *big game fishing* and *hunting* (see Fishing and Hunting, below).

Backpacking: There are guided hiking trips in several parts of the country, but the most popular are the three- or four-day alpine "walks" over the Milford Track in Fiordland, walks through the Routeburn and Hollyford Valleys from Queenstown, and the Wanganui River Walk. Contact Routeburn Walk, Ltd.,

FACTS AT YOUR FINGERTIPS 315

Box 271, Queenstown (phone 100). For the Hollyford Valley Walk: Fiordland National Park, Box 29, Te Anau.

For the Milford Track hike, contact Tourist Hotel Corp. of New Zealand, Box 2840, Wellington. Departures from Te Anau on Mondays, Wednesdays, Fridays with extra parties scheduled as required. Trek is sold as a five-day/four-night package ending at Milford Sound. Prices: Adults NZ$450. In the U.S., contact Southern Pacific Hotel Corporation, 1901 Avenue of the Stars, Suite 880, Los Angeles, CA 90067; (213) 557-2292.

Dane's Back Country Experiences, Ltd., Box 230, Queenstown, NZ (phone 1144), are backcountry specialists in whitewater rafting, hiking, fishing, airplane tours in the back country. Tours from three hours to five days.

Information about the national park system, walks, and scenic reserves can be obtained from tourist information offices or Dept. of Lands and Survey, Private Bag, Wellington; (04) 735-022.

Boating. Mainly in Auckland and the Bay of Islands, yachts may be chartered fully equipped with or without crews; only food and bedding are required.

Fiordland Cruises Ltd., Manapouri, operate three-day cruises in Doubtful Sound in Fiordland. Charges include transport, accommodations and meals.

Jet boat trips are operated on many rivers, ranging from one hour to a full day. Inquire locally.

Golf: Even small towns have golf courses, at which visitors are always welcome. Green fees range from about $5 to $10 per game. Golf is very popular and played year-round. Equipment can usually be rented.

Mountaineering: Probably no country can offer such a wide scope and variety of mountaineering as the Southern Alps, where Sir Edmund Hillary, the first to climb Mount Everest, did much of his early training. Mount Cook and Westland, from the nature of their country, attract more overseas climbers than other places.

River Rafting: Heavy-duty inflatable rubber rafts similar to those used on the Colorado River are used for journeys down rivers and through countryside not normally seen. Trips vary from three hours to 12 days. See also Backpacking.

Snorkeling and Scuba Diving: While good diving is available out of most cities and towns, the Poor Knights, off the coast of Tutukaka in Northland, offers the most spectacular diving.

Skiing: New Zealand has fine ski fields, close to accommodations centers, and with the complete absence of tree hazards. The main season in the North Island is from about mid-July to the end of October and in the South Island from early July to the end of September. The main ski fields are at *Mount Ruapehu* in the North Island and at *Coronet Peak*, and the *Remarkables*, Queenstown, and *Mount Hutt*, near Christchurch.

Alpine Guides (Mount Cook) Ltd., Box 20, Mount Cook, or New Zealand Government Tourist Bureau, Alcoa Bldg., Maritime Plaza, San Francisco, CA 94111, provides information on heliskiing, glacier skiing, Nordic skiing, and Alpine skitouring. Guided climbing, mountaineering courses and raft trips are available in summer.

Surfing: New Zealand's extremely long coastline offers surfers a wide variety of reef point, river bar and beach breaks. The best surfing is in Northland, the west coast of the North Island, Bay of Plenty, Gisborne, Wellington, and the east coast of the South Island.

SPECTATOR SPORTS

There are virtually no professional sports in New Zealand, and organizations stick zealously to their amateur status. The climate allows almost all outdoor sports to be played throughout the year. Just about any sport you can think of (except baseball, the substitute being softball, and ice hockey) has its followers. Most popular in summer are **cricket, tennis, swimming, yachting,** and **sailing.** Field sports are played in public parks, with no admission charges. In winter the passion is **Rugby football, soccer football,** and **hockey**—again in free public parks except for the main Rugby match, for which there is an admission charge of $3 or so. Another passion is **horse racing** (gallops and harness racing) and there are race meetings somewhere every Saturday. The best way to find out what's happening where you are is to check the local newspapers. Admission charges in race courses vary but are very reasonable.

FISHING AND HUNTING. *Deep-sea fishing* is one of New Zealand's most outstanding sports and fishing facilities are well developed. Boats, complete with all equipment, may be chartered at five major ports, all on North Island within 200 miles of Auckland.

Trout fishing is excellent in New Zealand's numerous rivers and lakes, which are abundant with rainbow and brown trout. Season varies somewhat in different areas, but all areas are open from Oct.-Apr., and Lakes Rotorua and Taupo have open season all year. A special trout-fishing license for overseas visitors valid for one month is available at $12 from any NZTP office. Guides: NZ$18–$NZ24/hr.

Hunting. Experienced, registered guides providing all camping, hunting and transportation equipment can be obtained by writing to the Fishing and Hunting Officer, Tourist and Publicity Dept., Private Bag, Rotorua. Guides (costing around NZ$350 per day, plus food and equipment) will usually arrange for entry permits to National Parks or private land. Duck, Canadian geese, swan, pheasant and quail have a three-week to two-month season beginning the first Saturday in May. See also the essay on Fishing and Hunting.

BEACHES. No place is more than 70 kilometers in a direct line from the sea, which means there are accessible beaches from one end of New Zealand to the other. The list of swimming beaches would be endless. No beach can be privately owned, and all can therefore be used by the public. The main cities and provincial centers have their favorite beaches for swimming and picnics and most are safe for bathing—some have lifeguard patrols.

Apart from the many beaches just north of the city, Auckland is notable for half a dozen popular beaches starting a couple of kilometers from the city center (Mission Bay, Kohimarama, St. Heliers), and similarly in Wellington there is Oriental Bay just three kilometers from the city. All are faced by expensive homes and apartment blocks.

SHOPPING. The best buys for the visitor are greenstone jewelry and sheepskin. Greenstone is a type of jade, deep or pale green in color. For centuries, the Maori made weapons and ornaments from it, and it is now used for attractive rings and brooches. Other, less expensive ornaments are fashioned from the irridescent blue-green shell of the *paua,* a large shellfish similar to the abalone. New Zealand sheepskins make wonderful floor mats, jackets, soft toys, and automobile seat covers, which keep the seat cool in summer and warm in winter.

Many imported products are sold duty-free to visitors throughout the country.

GAMBLING. Gambling is illegal. There are no casinos and no poker machines. The exception is that bets on horse racing may be placed on a totalisator (pari-mutuel system) at a racecourse or at one of the many Totalisator Agency Board's offices (the T.A.B.) in a city or town.

HINTS TO HANDICAPPED TRAVELERS. Within recent years considerable attention has been given to catering to the handicapped traveler in New Zealand, and the main hotels, motels, department stores, and public toilets have special facilities. Parking areas and buildings have spaces marked and reserved.

POSTAGE. To North America, letters and postcards cost 80 cents for the first 10 grams; aerograms 60 cents. Domestic postage is 30 cents for a surface letter and 45 cents for airmail.

FACTS AT YOUR FINGERTIPS

ELECTRICITY. The current in New Zealand is different from that in the United States—220–240 volts, A.C., 50 cycles—and the wall sockets require a three-prong plug (the two top prongs are set at an angle, so the set of adapter plugs you have may not work here). All the larger hotels and many of the motels have electric shaver sockets in the bathroom designed to accept two-prong plugs and adapted to 110 volts. Bring an adapter if you need one; they are hard to find here.

TELEPHONES. To call New Zealand, you'll need to first dial the country code (64) then the area code for the particular city. When calling within New Zealand city to city dial zero before the city's code. Auckland is 9; Wellington, 4; Christchurch, 3. Other codes and costs are listed in the front of directories.

The telephone service is controlled by the New Zealand Post Office, and telephones are rented at a flat fee. There is no charge for local calls except from pay phones (10 cents). A station-to-station call to North America costs $8.40 for three minutes, $2.80 for each added minute.

If you want to know the cost of a call, dial the tolls operator and ask for a price required call—shortly after the call is completed the operator will phone and advise you. Hotels and motels require that long-distance calls be placed through the switchboard operator.

A ringing tone is "Burr-Burr-Pause-Burr-Burr"; a busy tone is "Buzz-Pause-Buzz"; an unobtainable number is "Pip-Pip-Pip-Pause-Pip-Pip-Pip" (call the operator for assistance).

Emergency numbers (police, ambulance, fire, etc.) are listed in the front of directories, as are doctors and hospitals.

NEW ZEALAND

Land of the Long White Cloud

by
JOHN P. CAMPBELL

A New Zealander, the author has traveled to every part of his country through his work with the New Zealand Tourist and Publicity Department. Currently focusing on travel writing, he contributes to a number of publications, including Travel Digest.

To think of the South Pacific is to conjure up visions of tropical isles, warm sandy beaches, waving palms, exotic forests, colorful Polynesians and lilting music. As a South Pacific country New Zealand has all these; yet it also contradicts the popular image. Its scenery rivals the best of other parts of the world, but it also has fine modern cities and is a major exporter of food and manufactured products.

The atlas shows New Zealand as a slender, slanted outline close to the bottom of the world. Astride a line midway between the equator and the south pole, it appears small and isolated in the vast Pacific Ocean. In shape, it resembles California; in size it exceeds Britain and equals the area of Colorado. On the map, New Zealand seems to be dwarfed by the neighboring continent of Australia; but Australia lies 1,200 miles to the west, and it is a source of pained but resigned irritation to New Zealanders that the two are often linked by the misleading term "Australasia". Naturally, there is some affinity between the two peoples, but Australia and New Zealand are quite distinct, each having an individual character and landscape.

NEW ZEALAND

New Zealand comprises three main islands: the North Island (44,197 square miles); the South Island (58,170 square miles); and Stewart Island (676 square miles). From north to south the country is about 1,000 miles long, and no point is more than 70 miles from the sea. Two-thirds is mountainous; a region of swift-flowing rivers, deep alpine lakes and dense subtropical forest—known locally as "bush."

New Zealand has the best of climatic worlds. The climate ranges from subtropical in the north to temperate in the south. There are no extremes of heat or cold, and snow is usually confined to the mountains and high country. Rainfall levels vary, but since rainy days are evenly distributed throughout the year, there is no unduly wet season to be avoided.

Topsy-Turvy Topography

To those living in the northern hemisphere New Zealand is an upside-down country. The north is warmer than the south and the seasons are reversed: summer is from December to March, fall from April to May, winter from June to August, and spring from September to November. Even the visitor's sense of time needs adjustment. New Zealand has a universal time zone, set 12 hours ahead of Greenwich Mean Time; which puts it ahead of most other places too: noon in New Zealand is 7 P.M. the previous day in New York, for instance. In the summer period, the difference is increased by one hour by New Zealand daylight-saving time, which extends from the last Sunday in October to the first Sunday in the following March.

For thousands of years, after its last land bridges sank beneath the Pacific, New Zealand remained isolated. Evolution went its curious way, undisturbed by man or beast except for sea-blown birds from other lands. Safe from predators, some birds became lazy and abandoned flight. Gradually their wings atrophied to small stumps and they walked the earth for their food. Best known is the kiwi (pronounced *kee-wee*, and named for its cry), which has become, although unofficially, New Zealand's national emblem. New Zealanders are sometimes referred to, and refer to themselves, as Kiwis. About the size of a young turkey and rounded in shape, the kiwi has strong legs and an unusually long bill with two nostrils close to the tip, which it pokes about in the undergrowth in search of grubs. Being nocturnal, it is seldom seen in the wild, but there are several places where it can be viewed in specially constructed houses.

An emu-like bird ten feet in height, the *moa*, once grazed in New Zealand. A main source of Maori food, and materials for clothing, it was hunted to extinction. The tuatara lizard, about 18 inches long and with a third vestigial eye, is a living fossil. It evolved before the giant dinosaurs roamed the earth, lives a hundred years or more, and still exists as a protected species on certain offshore islands.

Finding the Forgotten

About 75 percent of New Zealand's native flora is unique, and includes some of the world's oldest plant forms.

This was the virginal land first sighted by the adventurous Polynesian voyagers some 600 years ago. They called New Zealand by a more colorful name—*Aotearoa* ("Land of the Long White Cloud"). To them, near death from thirst and starvation in their sea-battered canoes on a migratory voyage across hundreds of miles of ocean, the land first appeared as a long, low white cloud on the horizon. To Abel Tasman, the first European to sight New Zealand, it appeared as "a great land uplifted high."

Both descriptions are apt. As you approach by air, New Zealand often does appear as a long low cloud joining the sky and the sea, especially when you are flying from Australia to Christchurch and the long line of the Southern Alps rises to meet you.

New Zealand was unknown to Europeans until 1642 when Abel Tasman, the Dutch navigator, sighted it when seeking a southern continent. He had trouble with the Maoris, however, and sailed away after drawing a wavy line as a crude chart. He gave the land the name of *Nieuw Zeeland*. No one was interested until 1769, when Captain Cook and a Frenchman, De Surville, rediscovered it almost simultaneously; though neither was aware of the other's presence on the opposite side of the islands. It was Cook who circumnavigated New Zealand and found that Tasman's wavy line was actually a group of islands. In general, his chart is amazingly accurate.

From 1790 onward adventurous Europeans arrived to take lumber, flax, whales and seals, and lonely settlements grew up in Northland and on the West Coast of the South Island. They were wild, lawless and isolated. The main European settlement and headquarters for the whaling fleets was Russell (then known as *Kororareka*) in the Bay of Islands. It became known as "the hellhole of the Pacific."

The newcomers traded muskets with the Maoris, and the traditional inter-tribal wars became bloodbaths. But the newly-introduced European diseases took a heavier toll. Thousands of Maoris, having no immunity, died from epidemics of normally minor ailments, such as influenza and measles.

Arrival of "Law and Order"

Pressure was growing on Britain to make New Zealand a colony. Finally, the British government acted by sending Captain William Hobson as governor. On February 6, 1840, a week after his arrival, he officiated at the signing of the Treaty of Waitangi, by which the Maoris ceded sovereignty to the British Crown in return for the protection of law and order and the rights of ownership of their traditional lands and fisheries for all time.

This event is regarded as the beginning of modern New Zealand history, and the date is still observed as New Zealand's National Day.

Then features of American history began to repeat themselves. Disputes over land developed between the settlers and the Maoris, culminating in the "Land Wars" of 1860. They flared up spasmodically for years, and the last sparks were not extinguished until 1872. The settlers cleared the land and turned to sheep farming, but the invention in 1882 of refrigeration enabled the export of meat, butter, and cheese.

New Zealand's success in agriculture is due to its ability to grow superb grass and clovers, an equable climate, land management, and regular applications of fertilizer from the air (known as topdressing).

Agricultural exports provide the major source of the country's income. It has become the biggest exporter of sheep meat and dairy products in the world and the second largest exporter of wool. These three agricultural commodities account for 75 percent of the country's total exports, and a wide and expanding range of annual crops is also grown.

New Zealand is ideally suited to sheep farming. High-country farms concentrate on wool, while the more fertile lowlands (carrying up to 5 sheep per acre and sometimes even more) raise lamb and mutton. With over 55 million sheep, it is not surprising that New Zealand is the third largest producer and second largest exporter of wool in the world. It is also the world's largest lamb and mutton exporter, contributing 65 percent of the market, and rears 6.5-million beef cattle.

NEW ZEALAND

Because of the equable climate, dairy stock do not have to be housed in winter, and grass grows the year round. There are some 2,080,000 cows in milk in New Zealand. Butter and cheese are the main dairy exports, followed by casein and skim milk powder.

Most grain crops are grown for local consumption, a wide range of fruit is grown for export, and tobacco is grown and blended with imported leaf for the local market.

New Zealand also exports a wide range of manufactured articles to many parts of the world. About a quarter of the labor force is involved in manufacture, though most of the factories are small by overseas standards.

The biggest growths have been in light engineering, electronics, textile and leather goods, rubber goods, plastics, building materials, pottery and glassware, and furniture. One of the largest developments has been in carpets.

Large exports of pulp, newsprint, wood chips, and lumber come from one of the world's largest manmade forests, the Kaingaroa Forest of more than 364,000 acres of *radiata* pine, which mature in about 25 years (much faster than in their native American habitat).

Influence of the Military

Though far from Europe, New Zealand has not escaped its conflicts. In World War I New Zealand fought beside Britain, and World War II cost another heavy contribution in manpower and resources. Its land forces fought in Greece, Crete, North Africa, Italy, and the Pacific, more than 140,000 served overseas.

New Zealand became vulnerable as the Japanese began moving across the Pacific, but it did not recall its troops from the Middle East. Instead, it became a base for American forces. The Second Marine Division was based in Wellington, and it was from there that they embarked for what was to become the bloodbath of Guadalcanal. Many New Zealanders whose sons were fighting overseas took Americans into their homes and adopted them as their own, and when news of the grim casualties came back an air of grief enveloped the city. Many of the wounded returned to Wellington for recuperation, and some returned after the war, married New Zealand women, and settled.

Although established as a British colony, New Zealand quickly achieved self-government and has long been fully independent nation, and remains a member of the British Commonwealth by choice. The head of state is Queen Elizabeth II, who is represented by a resident governor-general, appointed for a term of five years. The present governor-general, Sir Paul Reeves, appointed in 1985, is a Maori.

The New Zealand Parliament has a single chamber, the House of Representatives, with 92 members, among whom are four Maori members elected directly by Maori voters. The head of government is the prime minister, who is always the leader of the successful political party.

From the 1880s, New Zealand has often led the way in social welfare. In 1984, the New Zealand Labor party came into power, pledging to make the nation a nuclear-free zone. This has led to a certain amount of tension between New Zealand and U.S. governments, since it could mean that American warships will be banned from New Zealand waters.

Seeing the Best of New Zealand

It is easy to be misled by looking at New Zealand on an atlas. It appears smaller than it really is, especially when compared with its much larger neighbor Australia. But don't allow its size to persuade you that it can be seen in three or four days by taking excursions from the main cities. Its varied attractions are scattered throughout the thousand-mile length of the two islands and are often remote from major cities.

Visitors will miss a great deal if they do not allow enough time to see the best of both the North and South islands. It is possible to glimpse some of the highlights in a week, but having invested in the cost of reaching New Zealand the wise traveler will allocate at least ten days or two weeks, or perhaps even longer.

Climatically and scenically, the islands are like two entirely different countries. The only satisfactory way to enjoy these attractions is to travel progressively from place to place.

New Zealand's charms lie in the countryside, mountains and fiords rather than in the cities. In terms of European settlement, New Zealand is less than a century and a half old; so there are no ancient sights.

Certainly, at least one day should be spent in the major cities, each of which has its own individuality and charm, but most of the time should be devoted to the scenic areas.

Driving for Fun

The main cities are linked by road, air and rail, but many of the most beautiful regions are in the mountain fastnesses and can be reached only by road or air. Because of the varied countryside, road travel is exciting. There are no long monotonous distances to be covered. Because of the hilly to mountainous terrain the roads weave through an ever-changing landscape, bordered by lush green pastures dotted with sheep and cattle, or clothed in native forest.

All the main roads and most of the secondary roads are paved, well maintained, and signposted, with route numbers. New Zealand has changed to the metric system, and all road signs are now in kilometers. To convert kilometers to miles, divide by 8 and multiply by 5; e.g., 100 km per hour (the legal speed limit) equals 60 mph.

Getting around Fairly Easy

New Zealand has an efficient network of air, road, rail, and sea transport. The major domestic air carriers are the government-financed Air New Zealand, which uses Boeing 737 jets and F27 Fokker Friendship turbo-jet aircraft and services the main cities and provincial centers. Servicing the prime scenic resorts such as Rotorua, Mount Cook, and Queenstown are Mount Cook Airlines and Newmans Air. Mount Cook Airlines also continues to Te Anau in Fiordland. Modern motor coaches are used on coach tours and scheduled services, and the New Zealand Railways, government owned, link the main and subsidiary centers. Group tours are operated by several companies. Rental cars are available at all the main centers, but the visitor should note that traffic travels on the left of the road. Motor caravans and campervans may be rented at the main centers.

The New Zealanders

A survey of visitors' impressions carried out by the Pacific Area Travel Association showed that memories of "a warm, friendly people" did much to account for New Zealand's popularity with travelers in the South Pacific. Friendliness is undoubtedly one of its greatest charms. New Zealanders are fiercely proud of their country, and they enjoy sharing its delights with others. To them, a visitor is a guest—not just another tourist. The growth of tourism has not affected the New Zealander's spontaneous willingness to go out of her or his way to welcome and assist the visitor. Their good nature has enabled the people to become a distinctive, unique nation.

The early settlers, and those who followed them, left Britain to escape from overcrowded slums, the limitations imposed by class barriers, and the lack of economic opportunity. These motives have formed the New Zealand character and an egalitarian society. Few are very rich and none are really poor. There are no slums or tenements, and by overseas standards, unemployment is relatively low.

The Unimportance of Position

An egalitarian attitude is universal. New Zealanders do not take kindly to servility. New Zealanders cannot abide being addressed by their surnames only; to them, this would imply inferiority. Honorifics (Mr., Mrs., etc.) are always used until first-name terms are reached—which happens quickly, if not immediately. They value and respect people for themselves, not social status or wealth, which leave them unimpressed.

The Maori People

No one really knows where the Maori (pronounced "Mau-ree," not "May-ori") originally came from. Tradition has it that they sailed to New Zealand in a migratory voyage from a land they called Hawaiki, which was not Hawaii but is thought to have been the Society Islands near Tahiti. It is generally believed that the islands of the Pacific were inhabited by people from Asia, although one theory is that the first settlers came from South America. All three propositions are matters of scholarly discussion and debate.

One thing is sure—the Polynesians were among the greatest long-distance sailors in the world. Legend relates that the first Polynesian voyager to sight New Zealand was Kupe about A.D. 950, who returned to Hawaiki and gave sailing instructions which were later followed by the migrating canoes. It is said that the next to come was Toi, in about 1150.

One of the reasons for our lack of positive knowledge is that the Maori had no written language. History was passed down by word of mouth, usually in the form of chants (*waiata*). There was room, therefore, for imaginative embellishment.

Maori tradition has it that the great migration from eastern Polynesia took place about 1350 in seven canoes. No one knows why the migration took place, but it may well have been due to overpopulation and a shortage of food. If the great migration theory is believed, however, it is clear that the Maori knew of the existence of New Zealand and navigated to it in a voyage covering hundreds of miles—a remarkable achievement.

It now seems likely, however, that the canoes arrived over a period of years, even centuries, rather than all at once in a "Great Fleet." It's thought that the original settlers probably arrived by the eighth century. The earliest arrivals are known as *moa* hunters. They had an abundance of food from the *moa* (a huge bird), other flightless birds, and fish from the sea. Their villages were unfortified, they seem to have had no weapons. Later, conflict did develop.

The Maori brought with them the *kumara,* a variety of sweet potato, the dog, and the rat. These were the first mammals to live in New

Zealand. The Maori had an abundance of fish and birds and established agriculture.

From these beginnings emerged a distinctive Maori culture and well-ordered tribal society, led by hereditary chiefs and a powerful priesthood.

The Maori lived in small villages retreating to hilltop fortifications (*pa*) during times of war. They built sleeping and eating houses and a main meeting house, all focused on a main courtyard, the *marae*. The *marae* was an important part of the village. It was here, in front of the meeting house (*whare runanga*), that matters of importance were debated and decided and that visitors were received.

Lore of the Tribes

The *marae* retains that importance and function today. Though they now live in European-style homes, any large settlement of Maoris will have a meeting house and a *marae* on which any important visitors will be received, and an ancient and impressive greeting ritual is still followed.

Intensely proud, the Maroi also practiced *mana* and *utu* (revenge). *Mana* was all-important and any insult or slight, however trivial, demanded retribution.

Intertribal warfare was frequent, either for *utu* or for more desirable land. The Maori man reveled in fighting and excelled in hand-to-hand combat, for which he fashioned weapons. He did not use throwing spears. Instead, he used the *taiaha,* a sort of wooden broadsword about five feet long with a blade for cutting and a hilt sharpened for thrusting. The *taiaha* was wielded with two hands. For even closer combat the Maori warrior used a *patu* and a *mere,* clubs about the length of a man's forearm. They were made either of wood, whalebone, or the very hard greenstone.

Before engaging in battle warriors would perform a *haka.* While it has the appearance of a war dance, the *haka* was really a limbering-up exercise, much like a boxer uses to limber up before the start of a fight. Today the *haka* is a popular item in Maori concerts and is often performed as a symbol of New Zealand by sports teams competing overseas.

For clothing and baskets the Maori used the leaves of native flax. They were stripped and dried and woven into cloaks or rolled into long tubes to make skirts (*piupiu*). The chiefs' cloaks were decorated with the feathers of birds.

The Maori developed a distinctive style of wood carving, which he used lavishly. All Polynesians carved in wood but seldom reached the artistic standard of the Maori. The design was not haphazardly chosen; each had a meaning and each carving told a story. The human figure was distorted and grotesque so as not to offend the gods by making a true image of a human being.

For a time it appeared that the carver's art would be lost, but the government established the Maori Arts and Crafts Institute at Rotorua, which has enabled exponents of carving to continue the tradition.

Tattooing was traditional to the early Maori. As a sign of status the warrior was heavily tattooed on cheeks, nose, and forehead in an intricate design of whorls. Women, too, were tattooed, but mainly on the chin (*moko*). It was a painful process. The skin was cut, not pricked, with a chisel and coloring was rubbed into the wound. Tattooing has long died out, but the designs are now painted on to the face for performances at Maori concerts.

Pride, Dignity, Intelligence

The basis for the integration of the Maori into European society was laid when the Treaty of Waitangi was signed by 45 Maori chiefs in the Bay of Islands on February 6, 1840. In essence, it recognized that the chiefs' lands belonged to the Maori and stated that any land they would be willing to sell would be sold only through the British Crown, which implied that the Crown was concerned with saving the Maoris from being cheated in private land deals.

The principles were laudable, but of course the treaty did not work. Representatives of the Crown wanted to buy the land for next to nothing; four years after the treaty was signed the Crown abandoned its right of preemption, and settlers were doing their own buying on their own terms.

The stage was set for what was to become a period of bitterness and strife. The wars over the sale and confiscation of land dragged on from 1860 to 1872. The conflict was a series of skirmishes rather than a national war over an unbroken period; it did not completely involve both races. Some Maori tribes were, in fact, friendly to the government. Although land matters are still not fully resolved, land classified as Maori property totals about 4 million acres and is administered by Maori interests.

Songs, Dances, Oratory

At the personal level, cultural pride embraces preservation of ancestral land and traditional arts, including wood carving, weaving, and oratory. The Maori loved oratory almost as much as fighting, and to listen to a Maori elder speaking on a *marae* in Maori is to hear poetry, even if the words and meaning are not fully understood.

Double Heritage of Culture

From the early days there was a good deal of intermarriage between Maori and pakeha, which has intensified over the last three decades. One result has been a greater drawing together of the two races in a desire to foster their bicultural heritage. As Witi Ihimaera, well-known Maori author, says in his book *Maori:*

"Today, one in every twelve persons in New Zealand is of half or more Maori origin. In addition, the non-Maori population includes another 50,000 people who are part but less than half Maori. On top of this, it can be safely estimated that most New Zealand families have relatives with Maori blood and more than cursory contact with Maori people.

"In effect, most New Zealanders now have a double heritage of culture. Rather than maintain the division between Maori and pakeha, many New Zealanders now seek a compromise world where Maori culture has an equal place with pakeha culture in New Zealand, where New Zealand is as bi-cultural as they are.

"There has been, therefore, a growing identification of many New Zealanders with Maori culture. This identification has tended to contest the question of what, in fact, constitutes a Maori. Intermarriage has meant that today there are few, if any, full-blooded Maori in New Zealand. For present census purposes he is one who states that he has half or more Maori blood. By the same token, none other than verbal evidence is required to substantiate a claim to being a Maori, which means that a Maori is a Maori if he says he is.

"The usual visual evidence of a brown skin is no longer the sole criterion, and some Maori today have such non-racial characteristics as green eyes and red hair. Such has been the success of integration."

The Arts in New Zealand

In spite of the image of New Zealand as a generally sporty, outdoorsy nation, a majority of New Zealanders demand an increasing number of cultural services.

New Zealanders buy more books per capita than any other country. They buy more recorded music per capita than any other country except Sweden. Surveys show that more than 80 percent of the adult population actively support the range of cultural activities which concern the Queen Elizabeth II Arts Council, the principal government body dealing with the arts.

While New Zealand's population is just over 3 million people, it counts 4,000 craft potters who earn part or all of their living from their craft, another 40,000 who make and sell some pots, and an equal number who study pottery at adult-education or higher education classes.

In towns with a population of more than 5,000, there is generally at least one amateur theater group, a craft center, public library, and a brass band or music group.

Information on the various arts activities occurring in and around different New Zealand cities and towns can be obtained from the visitors' bureau in each center.

The rise of New Zealand writers in all fields of fiction, drama, and poetry, the proliferation of strongly individual visual artists, the production of New Zealand feature films, the emergence of New Zealand composers and choreographers, the establishment of local television drama series featuring New Zealand writers, actors, and directors, and the growth of characteristic New Zealand rock music, has meant a flowering of activities which collectively have created greater interest than ever in the arts.

Major examples of Maori carving can be found in the large collections in the Auckland Museum and National Museum in Wellington, both of which include a larger meeting house (*whare nui*), and in museums in Gisborne, Napier, Nelson, Christchurch, Dunedin, Wanganui, Rotorua, Invercargill, New Plymouth, Te Awamutu, Hamilton, and Whakatane.

At the Maori Arts and Crafts Institute in Rotorua, visitors can watch young carvers learning the art under masters. Carving objects of nephrite jade (greenstone) and bone is also a long-standing tradition that is flourishing.

New Zealand Theater

After the demise of the national professional company The New Zealand Players in 1960, six full-time professional theaters were gradually set up. Wellington's Downstage (1964), Auckland's Mercury Theatre (1968) and Theatre Corporate (1973), Christchurch's Court Theatre (1971), Fortune Theatre in Dunedin, and Centrepoint Theatre in Palmerston North (both 1974), are now backed up by cooperative theaters such as Circa and the Depot in Wellington and New Independent Theatre and Working Title in Auckland.

New Zealand Films

After making only three feature films in the 10 years prior to 1975, the New Zealand film industry began to produce feature films at the average rate of three to four a year.

New Zealand Music

The establishment of the New Zealand Symphony Orchestra in 1946 as a division of the public broadcasting organization gave impetus to local classical music making. The orchestra now gives more than 100 concerts a year with international and local guest conductors and soloists. Regional professional orchestras in Auckland, Wellington, Christchurch, and Dunedin present many local concerts.

After a troubled history in the 1960s, the New Zealand Opera Company ceased to function. Professional opera was revived in 1978 and has now been incorporated into the Mercury Theatre's annual repertoire.

New Zealand Visual Arts

A network of 10 major public art galleries throughout the country from Auckland to Dunedin constantly show major exhibitions and smaller projects of New Zealand historical and contemporary art, while dozens of dealer galleries in the main centers have continuous shows by major and minor painters, usually for a fortnight at a time.

Recent growth in photography and print making has seen the establishment of several specialist galleries dealing in these media.

New Zealand Crafts

As many as 4,000 registered craftspeople create ceramics, weaving, hand-made jewelry, and carved craft objects throughout New Zealand, but particularly in areas such as Coromandel and Nelson.

New Zealand is particularly strong in its creation of handcrafted ceramics, developing a plethora of individual styles from the original strong Japanese classical influence of visiting potters.

In woolcraft, wall hangings and rugs are a characteristic concern of New Zealand craftspeople. Jewelers are experimenting with indigenous materials such as bone, paua shell, and stone, which are also being used by carvers.

New Zealand Writing

Among modern writers, Sylvia Ashton-Warner, with her educational interests, Janet Frame in her powerful explorations of the individual's mental universe, Maurice Shadbolt and Maurice Gee in personal sagas, and Witi Ihimaera and Keri Hulme reaching into Maori spirituality, have all explored parallel themes of the country's development through a largely biographical fiction.

New Zealand Dance

The Royal New Zealand Ballet is one of the oldest professional performing arts organizations in New Zealand, having celebrated its 30th anniversary in 1984. In spite of having had its costume store burned out at one point, and being reduced to a handful of dancers through financial constraints at another, it has survived to present a lively mix of classical and contemporary internationally and locally choreographed repertoire, which it tours regularly throughout New Zealand, in an average of 70 performances annually.

New Zealand's premier modern-dance company, Limbs, which is based in Auckland, equally has a large repertoire of New Zealander–choreographed dances, which it tours and expands each year.

NATIONAL PARKS

A Legacy of Grandeur

As early as the beginning of this century New Zealand began preserving some of its most outstanding natural assets: It now has ten national parks, totaling over 5¼ million acres (one-thirteenth of the total land area) and encompassing forests and valleys, mountains and glaciers, inland lakes and coastal bays. Three are in the North Island and seven in the South Island.

Overall administration is carried out by the National Parks Authority, although each park has its own controlling board. The objective, set out in an act of Parliament in 1952, is to preserve these areas in their natural state for the benefit and enjoyment of the public.

Inevitably, the tourist must visit or pass through some of these parks, as they contain many of New Zealand's most beautiful and unusual attractions.

Without exception, the parks suffer from the depredations of animals. There were no mammals indigenous to New Zealand and, misguidedly, the early settlers introduced deer, opossum, stoat, and weasel and, in the Mount Cook region, chamois and Himalayan thar. Having no natural enemies and finding the environment much to their liking, the immigrant species multiplied rapidly until they became menaces to the native vegetation and bird life. They still destroy the forest cover, resulting in erosion on steep slopes and flooding of rivers, while birds fall prey to stoats, weasels, and domestic cats that have run wild. Some of these have been declared noxious animals, but the nature of the terrain makes it almost impossible to implement an effective control program.

Tongariro National Park

The nucleus of Tongariro, New Zealand's first national park, was set aside in 1887 when a far-seeing Maori chief, Te Heuheu Tukino, gave the summits of three mountains to the government to avoid inevitable sale to Europeans. "They shall be," he said, "a sacred place of the Crown and a gift for ever from me and my people."

Almost in the center of the North Island, the park has extremes of climate and terrain, ranging from forest to desert-like areas and geothermal activity. This central upland plateau has as its most prominent land forms three volcanic peaks rising almost in a straight line from north to south: Mt. Tongariro (6,345 ft.), a series of mildly active craters; symmetrical Mt. Ngauruhoe (7,515 ft.), the most active volcano; and Mt. Ruapehu (9,175 ft.), the highest mountain in the North Island, with an intermittently active crater from which radiate small glaciers. The park has an area of nearly 171,000 acres.

Tongariro National Park is the most accessible and easily seen of all the national parks. It straddles two main highways between Lake Taupo and Wellington on the east and Wanganui and New Plymouth on the west. It can, in fact, be circumnavigated by road with continuous views of the mountains.

Tongariro is also the most used of the national parks. Although only the upper part of Mt. Ruapehu is coated with snow in the summer and fall, the lower slopes are heavily covered in winter and form the North Island's most popular skiing resort. Skiers come from as far as Auckland and Wellington. About 40 mountain clubs have provided buildings in an alpine village from which a system of chair lifts, T-bars, and tows take skiers higher up the slopes.

The Tourist Hotel Corporation (THC) Chateau Tongariro is conveniently placed close to the main highway.

Egmont National Park

The second to be established, Egmont National Park of 82,836 acres surrounds the symmetrical cone of Mt. Egmont (8,260 ft.) and dominates the extensive and fertile farming country of Taranaki. It is easily reached by good roads from the main highways and is popular for skiing and climbing. Three roads run up into the park: from New Plymouth to the North Egmont Chalet; from Stratford to the Stratford Mountain House and plateau; and from Hawera to Dawson Falls and the Dawson Falls Tourist Lodge.

Geologists consider that Egmont may have been active about 220 years ago, but it is now dormant and its dense rain forest helps control the watersheds of 31 rivers that radiate from its slopes. The Maori hold the peak to be sacred. Skiers and mountaineers respect it as an excellent training ground.

Urewera National Park

By tradition the home of the Tuhoe tribe ("the children of the mist"), Urewera National Park lies in a remote region between Rotorua and Wairoa, on the east coast, and at 495,000 acres is the third largest of New Zealand's national parks and the largest in the North Island. A maze of confusing watersheds, it is noted for its Maori history, for the size of its area of virgin forest, and for its lake, Waikaremoana ("sea of rippling waters"), a vast, star-shaped lake of intense blue water and countless bays and coves some 2,000 feet above sea level.

The heavily wooded ranges include forest typical of the original vegetation. So vast and unbroken are the forests that the traveler does not have to go far from roads and tracks before he feels that no one has been there before him.

Access to the park is by a highway linking Rotorua and Wairoa, but it is a slow, winding road which must be taken with care. There is no hotel, but there are camping facilities near the Wairoa end of the lake.

Mt. Cook National Park

The area of Mt. Cook National Park (172,739 acres) is not large by New Zealand standards, but its essence and quality are determined by the height and sheerness of the ranges and by the size and length of the glaciers, the great valleys they have gouged, and the rock debris they have spread. Waving tussocks, blue-green lakes fed by glacier water, tawny rocks and glistening snow add to the grace and breadth of the scene. The park is linked to Westland National Park by the ice-covered chain of the Main Divide of the Southern Alps.

The park is dominated by Mt. Cook, at 12,349 ft. New Zealand's highest mountain, and clustered around it are 17 peaks over 10,000 ft. The area has been a training ground for many mountaineers who have represented New Zealand in the Antarctic, the Andes, and the Himalayas.

The Alps were pushed up late in New Zealand's geological history, and have been sculpted into their present form by glaciers and streams. The degree of glaciation is outstanding high. There are scores of glaciers within the park, but the most impressive are the Tasman (18 miles), the Murchison (11 miles), the Hooker (7 miles), and the Mueller (8 miles).

An exciting sightseeing event is a skiplane flight with a landing at about 7,500 feet on the vast snowfield at the head of one of the glaciers.

Accommodation is available at the THC Hermitage complex almost at the foot of Mt. Cook. Although the Hermitage and Glencoe Lodge are at 2,500 ft., snow does not cover the ground except occasionally in winter, and no special warm clothing is needed.

The Hermitage is roughly halfway between Christchurch and Queenstown, and is reached by road or the regular services of Mount Cook Airlines.

Mt. Aspiring National Park

South of Mt. Cook, Mt. Aspiring National Park is wild and rugged and visited mainly by enthusiastic hikers and hunters. The boundaries of its 680,000 acres extend along a 100-mile front, and its width is seldom more than 20 miles, but it effectively divides the eastern side of the South Island from the West Coast. The Haast Pass road to the West Coast traces the park's northern tip.

Like other South Island parks, Mt. Aspiring consists of glaciers and rocky mountains, thick bush, river flats and gorges, waterfalls and passes. It has some rivers so accessible that families may camp on the flats, and others so rough and inaccessible that only hardy hunters or hikers can reach them.

The park derives its name from its dominant feature, Mt. Aspiring, which rises to 9,931 ft. It is a distinctive peak, sheer and icy and rising to a needle point, not unlike Switzerland's Matterhorn.

The mountains may be comfortably seen across the lake from Wanaka, where the THC runs a well-appointed hotel. There are also motels.

Wanaka is reached by an alternative route from Mt. Cook to Queenstown, where the traveler turns off at a right angle at Tarras, reaching

Queenstown through Wanaka and over the Crown Range. Wanaka is passed in the course of, or can be the starting point for, the journey through the Haast Pass to the west coast.

Fiordland National Park

Fiordland National Park is the grandest and largest of all—over 3 million acres, virtually untouched and in some places unexplored. It is larger than the total area of the other nine parks and one of the largest in the world. Its western boundary is a shoreline intended by countless fiords and bays. So difficult of access is the land that it was here as recently as 1948 that a small colony of *Notornis* (*takahe* in Maori), a swamp bird thought to be extinct, was rediscovered. It is also the only place in New Zealand where wapiti are established in the wild.

Fiordland has a wealth of history covering nearly two centuries and a great variety of people, from navigators, sealers, and whalers to explorers, surveyors, and miners. After rounding the southern point of the South Island on his first voyage, Captain Cook sailed *Endeavour* in March 1770 past the west-coast sounds but could not make harbor. At one place "dusk" intervened and at another the weather was "doubtful"; accordingly he named the sounds Dusky Sound and Doubtful Sound. On this voyage Cook left a few names on the map but never a footprint on the land.

The highlight of Fiordland is Milford Sound, a 10-mile-long, narrow waterway biting into precipitous granite cliffs rising thousands of feet. Milford can be seen on a 1½-hour scenic flight from Queenstown or Te Anau or can be reached by road from Te Anau by a journey of 75 miles through exciting alpine scenery. The vastness of the sound is best appreciated from a launch cruise.

For those who enjoy hiking, the most rewarding way to explore Fiordland is on the three-day, 33-mile walk over Milford Track, with overnight stays at accommodation huts. The trace passes the Sutherland Falls which, at 1,904 ft., are among the highest in the world.

The gateway to Fiordland, either by road or by the Milford Track, is Te Anau on the shores of the lake of that name.

The THC runs a comfortable hotel at the head of Milford Sound, and at Te Anau there is the THC Te Anau Hotel as well as several well-appointed motor hotels and motels.

Westland National Park

Westland National Park is dominated by the mountains and the sea. Its eastern boundary is the main divide of the Southern Alps, and from the sea on the west come rains that feed the forest and glaciers. The park's 219,000 acres are a mixture of high, snow-clad peaks, steep glaciers, lush rain forest, deep gorges, and cattle-farming country.

Westland's glories are the thick, verdant rain forests, attractive even in the rain, the backdrop offered by the long line of high, snow-covered peaks, and lovely, unexpected lakes.

The Franz Josef and Fox glaciers, flowing from vast snow fields shadowed by peaks more than 9,000 ft. high, are among the largest glaciers in the temperate zone. They descend for seven and eight miles, respectively, past flanks of luxuriant bush to less than 1,000 feet above sea level and only ten miles from the sea.

By glacial standards the rate of flow is fast—1,000 feet an hour. The rate of flow varies according to the pressure of ice built up in the snow basins high in the mountains. The specific rate of flow varies in different parts of the glacier, like the current of a river. The ice surges over itself,

NATIONAL PARKS

breaking and grinding and being forced up into pressure ridges by the movement of the flow.

The boundaries of the park are skirted by the traveler driving along the West Coast between the western portal of the Haast Pass and Hokitika.

There are hotels and motels at the Franz Josef and Fox glaciers.

Arthur's Pass National Park

Arthur's Pass National Park comprises 243,000 acres and extends on both sides of the main divide of the Southern Alps between Canterbury and the west coast. Its scenery, climate, vegetation, and development reflect its spread over contrasting areas.

Easily accessible, the park attracts people to its river flats, its forests, and, in winter, its snowy mountains. The main transalpine railroad, with its 5¼-mile Otira tunnel, and the main transalpine highway take a large number of people through the park.

Only 93 miles by road from Christchurch, Arthur's Pass is the shortest overland route to the west coast and Hokitika, only 63 miles farther on. It is a popular skiing area in winter, and there are day excursions by road and rail from Christchurch.

The road over the pass can be closed by snowfall, floods, or landslides in winter, but it is open for most of the year. Farther north, the Lewis Pass has easier gradients and is less vulnerable to storms, but the scenery is less spectacular.

There is a small township, called Arthur's Pass, near the summit.

Nelson Lakes National Park

Nelson Lakes National Park is a very popular recreation area for New Zealanders. Nelson people used it as such long before it became a national park and a tradition of a holiday at Lake Rotoiti was well established. It is much used in this way today as there are excellent facilities for camping, boating, swimming, hiking, trout fishing, and hunting.

Comprising 141,127 acres, Nelson Lakes is predominantly a park of bush-clad mountains, quiet valleys, swift-flowing rivers and streams, the seven-mile long Lake Rotoroa, and five-mile long Lake Rotoiti. Forests here mark a stage in the transition of vegetation from the rain forests of the West Coast to the dry grasslands east of the main divide. The bush is principally beech forest.

Abel Tasman National Park

Just north of Nelson, Abel Tasman National Park, with only 47,373 acres, is the smallest of the parks. Much of it is coastline and outlying islands, and its unspoilt golden beaches make it popular with New Zealanders for camping holidays. Access is either by sea or by land, but there are no hotel or motel accommodations.

FISHING AND HUNTING

Trout, Marlin, Shark, Chamois, and Thar

New Zealand has long been renowned for its outstanding trout and big-game fishing and for its hunting for deer, chamois, and thar. Even though the number of local anglers is increasing, the quality of trout fishing remains consistently high and big-game fishing still yields some excellent fish. Hunting, however, is becoming more difficult because of measures to control herds and reduce damage to the natural forests and as a result of the development of an overseas market for venison.

Fantastic Trout Fishing

By overseas standards New Zealand is underfished. Its innumerable fast-flowing rivers and streams of clear mountain water and cold, clear lakes proved an ideal environment for the brown trout ova introduced and hatched in 1869 and the rainbow trout ova brought from Russian River, California, in 1877. Both species bred swiftly and were subsequently liberated throughout the country.

Fishery management by national and local wildlife authorities has maintained these qualities through sound conservation and hatching methods, and size and quality of trout are, in many cases, even improving.

So fast do trout grow in New Zealand that they rarely reach maturity until 14 inches long. In fact, all trout under this length must be returned to the water.

As an instance of this rapid growth, rainbow fingerlings weighing less than half an ounce each (forty to the pound) were liberated in 1971 in Lake Tarawera. When taken by anglers nine months later they weighed an average of 3½ to 4 pounds. Some grew 7 pounds in sixteen

FISHING AND HUNTING

months. The wildlife authorities estimate that each year about 700 tons of trout are taken by anglers from Lake Taupo alone, the average weight being 4.4 pounds.

A check taken a year or two ago indicated that about 6,000 anglers visited New Zealand and caught about 14,000 trout, or better than two trout per angler—better still when it is realized that most fishers returned unwanted trout to the water alive. These 14,000 trout at a conservative estimate weighed 14 tons, which proves that the claim "tons of trout" is no exaggeration.

For seven years Rotorua conducted a trout fishing competition for one week each year. Over the seven weeks, 5,018 trout were weighed and found to total 17,654 pounds—nearly 8 tons, or over a ton of trout each week. The fish averaged 3.52 pounds.

Lake Tarawera has a reputation for producing more 10-pound trout than any other lake in the world. The summer average, when the fish are feeding deep in this lake, is 5 pounds; but in May and June, when the trout come up from the deep and gather at the stream mouths to spawn, fly fishing comes into its own. In May and June of a recent year fish of 9 to 10 pounds were caught almost daily. The biggest was a female weighing 13.2 pounds.

The average brown trout passing through a fish trap on a Lake Taupo spawning stream weighs 6.71 pounds. In the South Island, browns average 2 to 3 pounds, although in such rivers as the Mataura, Clinton, and Hollyford, 5-pound fish are commonly caught.

The daily limit per angler differs slightly from one district to another but is usually eight to ten trout a day, and trout under 14 inches long must be returned alive to the water. There is no limit on brown trout taken from Lakes Rotorua and Taupo. Rainbow trout taken in Lake Rotorua average from 2 to 4 pounds and in Lake Taupo from 3½ to 6 pounds. In Lake Tarawera the rainbow trout average 5 pounds, but weights of 8 to 10 pounds are not uncommon.

Whopper after Whopper

The main fishing areas of New Zealand are the lake systems of the North Island, including Lakes Rotorua and Taupo. Here the quarry is the rainbow and the usual method of fishing is with wet fly (streamer).

Most streams flowing into lakes are designated for fly fishing only, and sinking lines with lure-type flies are most favored. Trolling is popular and most productive, and during the summer floating lines are used for rising trout. Spinning is also popular.

In the South Island the brown trout is predominant and most plentiful in the southern lakes, rivers and streams of Southland. It is taken mainly by dry fly, or nymph. Rainbows and landlocked salmon as well as sea-run browns are also taken in the southern lakes. Here, spinning, trolling, and wet fly are used with success. Rainbows and browns average 2 to 2¼ pounds but run to 5 pounds in some areas. Rainbows of 10 pounds can be found and 11-pound browns are not unusual.

Although several areas, notably Lakes Taupo and Rotorua, are open all the year round, the main season is from October to the end of April (in some districts as late as the end of June).

Most serious anglers who try to avoid the January vacation period find that dry fly fishing is good in October, December, February, and March. Wet fly fishing in lakes, mainly at stream mouths, is good from October to December and in February–March and is excellent in rivers when trout start their spawning runs, from April through September. Trolling and spinning are both good from October through March.

Fishing licenses are reasonably priced. In most areas day licenses cost $3 and, for a week, average $10. A tourist license is available to visiting anglers at a cost of $50. This allows the holder to fish anywhere in New Zealand for one month (with the exception of one Maori-owned lake where an additional day license is needed).

Accommodations in the popular fishing areas are good, with many hotels and motels of high standard at Rotorua, Taupo, Turangi, Wanaka, Queenstown, Te Anau, Gore, and Invercargill. There are also fishing lodges at Lakes Okataina, Tarawera, Rotoroa, Makarora, and at Tokaanu. Camping and caravan sites are plentiful, and many small country hotels in fishing areas make the angler especially welcome. The roads to most fishing areas are good.

Scattered throughout the most popular areas are 60 or more professional guides. They provide all equipment needed, including first-class rods, lines, and reels. Many supply hipboots. Most have boats, from fiberglass 14-footers to 50-foot overnight launches, and many have passenger-licensed automobiles.

The average price of a top fly fishing guide supplying all equipment and vehicle to reach streams is $250 to $300 per day. Trolling guides operating 15-ft. boats with canopy and two motors run a daily average of $250 to $300. Fifty-ft. launches charter at $350 to $600 a day, or $36 to $60 an hour, plus $100 for overnight trips, plus meals, and can sleep up to six, who share that rate.

BIG Big-Game Fishing

The coastal waters of New Zealand teem with fish of all descriptions. Those that can be regarded as big game are broadbill swordfish; blue, black, and striped marlin; mako, thresher, and hammerhead shark; yellowtail (or kingfish, as it is known locally); and tuna. Excellent light-tackle sport can be enjoyed with smaller varieties such as bonito, skipjack, and the famous *kahawai* (sea trout).

Big game fish are found mostly on the eastern coast of the North Island between North Cape and Cape Runaway in an area warmed by the Pacific tropical current. Here are found the big game fishing bases of Whangaroa, Bay of Islands, Tutukaka, Mercury Bay, Tauranga, Mayor Island, and Whakatane. All are less than 200 miles from Auckland and visitors with limited time can fly to them by amphibian aircraft.

New Zealand's big-game-fishing grounds are world famous for producing big fish; in fact, striped marlin, the most prolific of all marlin in these waters, average around 250 pounds. Black marlin average around 250 pounds. Black marlin average from 400 to 600 pounds: a 976-pound black marlin held the world record from 1926 to 1953. Pacific blue marlin range from 300 to 600 pounds.

New Zealand all-tackle records are: broadbill, 673 pounds; black marlin, 976 pounds; blue marlin, 1,017 pounds; striped marlin, 465 pounds; yellowtail, 111 pounds; thresher shark, 922 pounds; tiger shark, 947 pounds; hammerhead shark, 460 pounds; mako shark, 1,000 pounds; yellowfin tuna, 168 pounds; bluefin tuna, 519 pounds.

The trend in New Zealand fishing circles is to lighter tackle. For many years most charter boats used 130-pound (and heavier) line but most now carry 80-pound line, while enthusiastic sportspeople are taking records on lines of 50, 30, and even 20 pounds.

Top of the light-tackle fish are the yellowfin tuna, which run from 40 to 100 pounds. Second are the yellowtail closely followed by the skipjack, bonito, and *kahawai*. The *kahawai* is in fact eagerly sought by fishers using fly rods and fly lure. Seasoned trout anglers say that *kahawai* fights better, pound for pound, than trout.

Kahawai is also the popular bait fish used by big game fishers when trolling or drifting for marlin and shark. It is found in huge schools,

FISHING AND HUNTING

often up to an acre in extent. At times, *kahawai* can be seen "boiling" on the surface at all points of the compass.

Charter boats are available at all the big-game bases mentioned. Most are fitted with two chairs, outriggers, and ship-to-shore radio. Most boats are operated by owner-skippers who are fully conversant with the fishing and other conditions in their areas. Costs are around $450 a day.

Membership of any of the big-game-fishing clubs runs from $5 to $10 annually. It entitles one to use all facilities and to enjoy the general conviviality of such clubs everywhere. Visitors are made especially welcome. The season is from mid-January through April.

Hunting

Because of vastly reduced wild-animal populations there are now few guides. The daily rate is $350, plus equipment and food, and an hourly rate of $600 for a helicopter (3 seats) to locate game and gain access. World-class trophy animals—chamois, thar, and deer (red, sika, and fallow)—can be hunted from lodges on game-management areas, where all hunting is controlled. Trophies of each species are guaranteed. The average price for each animal starts at $2,000 and increases on a point system, depending on the rating in the world record books.

Interested hunters can obtain lists of all guides from the Fishing and Hunting Officer, New Zealand Government Tourist Bureau, Private Bag, Rotorua.

THE NORTH ISLAND

"The Fish of Maui"

by
JOHN P. CAMPBELL

New Zealand is a land of startling scenic contrasts. The North Island has its weird geysers and bubbling mudpools, where underground steam sizzles through cracks in the ground as if from Nature's pressure cooker. Huge clouds of steam billow from the vast underground reservoir, which is now tapped to provide power for electricity.

The South Island has the dramatically impressive beauty of its Alps and fiords, its forests and rivers, and its enchanting lakeland. But the North Island has its share of rolling pastureland and verdant forest-clad hills, so easy on the eye and restful to the senses.

In ancient Maori mythology the North Island is *Te Ika a Maui* ("the fish of Maui"). While fishing with his brothers, Maui, who was descended from the gods and had magical powers, fished the North Island from the sea. Disobeying his orders not to touch the fish, his brothers gnawed at it to assuage their hunger, causing the fish to writhe and thresh about and giving the island an undulating or mountainous landscape.

Auckland (pronounced "Orkland"), the arrival point for most visitors, divides the bulk of the island from the long peninsula of Northland. Being nearer to the equator than the remainder of New Zealand, Northland has a subtropical climate, with superlative seascapes and uncluttered beaches. It is a dairying region, with some sheep farms, but also has large citrus and tropical fruit orchards. It is the birthplace of

THE NORTH ISLAND

New Zealand as a nation, for it was here that the Maoris signed the Treaty of Waitangi, acknowledging British rule.

Most visitors travel south from Auckland through the center of the island to Rotorua to see the thermal activity, and to meet Maori people in one of their principal homes. A detour of some 46 miles is necessary to visit the Glow-worm Grotto of the Waitomo Caves (definitely not to be missed), but this is always included on organized tours and is easy to visit either in a rented car, or by coach.

Wherever you travel in the North Island you'll pass through dairying and sheep-raising country, and it begins soon after you leave Auckland. On the road you'll notice a number of large stainless-steel tankers, some with trailers. They are not carrying gas or oil, but milk. These tankers collect milk from the farms every day and take it to factories, which make butter, cheese, dried milk powder, and other dairy products. One of the largest of these, a tall, gleaming modern building, is passed at Te Rapa just before reaching Hamilton, which stands on the banks of the Waikato River and is New Zealand's largest inland city.

To the left lies Tauranga, the Bay of Plenty and Poverty Bay on the east coast; to the right New Plymouth and Taranaki on the western bulge.

"An Endless Golf Course"

Beyond Hamilton you pass through some of the most fertile farming land in New Zealand. The rolling pastures and grass-covered hills are incredibly green and dotted with fat, white woolly sheep—they appear like mushrooms in the distance—and sleek dairy cows. The countryside looks like an endless golf course, so immaculately kept are the pastures. They always draw comment, and coach drivers often joke that "as soon as they upgrade the local golf course they are going to turn it into a farm."

The lush fields result from scientific farming. High quality grasses and clovers are sown, but the soil still needs additional fertilizer. Superphosphate, occasionally mixed with other ingredients, is spread annually, and often twice a year. This once laborious task is now done from the air—"aerial topdressing" it is called. This has become a fine art. Aircraft can now land, load a ton of superphosphate, and be airborne again within one minute. Only by aerial topdressing can much of New Zealand's hill country be kept fertile. The chances are that you'll see aerial topdressing being done as you travel.

Abruptly leaving farmland behind, the road enters thick bush and climbs over the Mamaku Range. This magnificent stand of native forest remains just as it was hundreds of years ago. As you peer through the tangled undergrowth, and admire the graceful trees climbing from the deep valleys, you cannot help wondering how the Maoris first found their way through it. You'll also understand why people still get lost in it, and why animals introduced to New Zealand, such as deer, pigs and opossums, which have no natural predators, multiply so prolifically and have been declared noxious animals.

Rotorua is the center of a hot thermal belt which begins in the Bay of Plenty some 40 miles to the east and continues to Tongariro National Park. Rotorua's thermal area, though vigorously active, is concentrated, and rather surprisingly, surrounded by rich green farms.

It was not always so. Until comparatively recent times the land, consisting to a large degree of volcanic ash and pumice, would grow little but scrub, but scientists discovered that the addition of small quantities of cobalt would make the soil productive. Topdressings of this and superphosphate have resulted in the development of highly intensive farming. The landscape has been transformed from a dull brown to a deep green.

World's Largest Human-Made Forest

It was also found that the pumice and volcanic soil supported pine trees, which mature here in 20 to 25 years, much faster than in other countries. The farming of these trees for lumber and pulp is now one of New Zealand's largest industries. Near Rotorua is the Kaingaroa Forest; 364,000 acres of pines, claimed to be the largest human-made forest in the world. There are other large forests at nearby Kinleith.

The trees are husbanded and harvested much like other crops. Replanting programs are followed, and the government maintains a Forest Research Institute at Rotorua. All New Zealand newspapers, and many in Australia, are printed on newsprint made at a large plant at Kawerau, a few miles from Rotorua. Understandably, the plant makes use of natural underground stream for some of its power. You'll see the fringe of the forest as you drive from Rotorua to Wairakei and Taupo, and pass through towering avenues of pines.

Fire is a constant danger, and in the dry summer months fire watchers are stationed in hilltop observation towers, and aerial inspections carried out. In the forests large roadside signs indicate the present degree of fire danger. Thoughtful people do not throw cigarette butts out the automobile or coach windows. One cautionary sign says: "Chaperone your cigarette—don't let it go out alone."

If time presses, you can fly from Rotorua to Wellington or Christchurch, or even to Mount Cook and Queenstown, but the road journey south is full of interest.

Only 56 miles (90km) from Rotorua is Taupo, on the northern shores on the lake of that name. Once little more than a sleepy village catering mainly for anglers (the lake is famous for the quantity and size of its trout) and summer holiday makers, Taupo is today a thriving modern town. It owes its prosperity to the development of farming and the growth of forestry.

Entering the town you descend an incline and cross a narrow bridge over sluice gates. This is the beginning of the long Waikato River, which flows out of the lake. Here, unlike the muddy river seen on the journey from Auckland, the waters are crystal-clear with an icy blue-green tinge, for they flow from the vast snowfields and glaciers at the opposite end of the lake.

In spite of its commercial activity, Taupo is still a mecca for anglers. More than 700 tons of trout, mainly rainbow, are taken from the lake each year!

The road follows the eastern shores of the lake for 32 miles (45.5km) to Turangi at the southern end. At Waitahanui, where a stream flows into the lake, you'll probably see a score or more anglers standing waist-high in the water, and almost shoulder to shoulder. At this particularly productive point, the congestion is known as the picket fence.

The road then winds through a narrow gorge, thought to have been formed by an earthquake, and climbs to a plateau, at the end of which is an especially beautiful vista of the lake and the sacred island of Motutaiko, a Maori burial ground. On a fine day the lake is colored in pastel shades, as if a rainbow had been laid on the waters.

Like Taupo, Turangi was once a sleepy trout-fishing village, but it is now the center of a large hydroelectric development nearing completion.

Hard-to-Pronounce Mountains

Within a few miles you enter the boundaries of the Tongariro National Park, with its three mountains—Ruapehu, Ngauruhoe and Tongariro. To the right, the road follows the western slopes to the Chateau, the North Island's most popular skiing resort, but the more direct route to Wellington is to the left. Some delightful forested valleys with tumbling mountain streams are passed before a long plateau is reached. This is known as the Desert Road, but it is nothing like a conventional desert. Overshadowed by three mountains and swept by winds, the area is arid and grows nothing but scruffy tussock in its pumice soil, although pine plantations are now being established. Anyone familiar with true desert would object to the description, but to New Zealanders, accustomed to grass-covered land, it is a barren wasteland. Near the center of the plateau the road is 3,600 ft. above sea level, and is occasionally blocked by snow in winter. Waiouru, at the southern end, is the North Island's main military base.

Hill-Country Farming

Green pastures soon appear again, but the terrain is steep and rugged —a good example of what New Zealanders describe as "hill country farming." The hills were once covered with thick forest, which was burnt off and replaced with good grasses and clovers. Sheep clamber up the steep slopes like mountain goats.

Slowly, the hills give way to rolling pastures, and finally to an extensive plain which slopes from the mountain ranges to the sea. It is an area of concentrated sheep farming and dairying, and once again the large number of sheep in the fields demonstrates the fertility of the land.

Just past Waikanae, some 40 miles (64.4km) from Wellington, there are fine views to the right of Kapiti Island off the coast. Once a stronghold of the infamous Maori chief Te Rauparaha, it is now a bird sanctuary. The land which appears, rising from the sea as you follow the coast to enter the suburbs of Wellington, is the northern tip of the South Island.

Most visitors tend to follow this central route and omit the delightful areas of the Bay of Plenty and Hawke's Bay on the eastern coast, and Taranaki on the west coast, because of the additional traveling time required. If time is not an important factor, it is a good plan to travel through the center of the island on the way south, and to return to Auckland from Wellington along the eastern or western coast.

In Hawke's Bay, Hastings and Napier are reached in one day by road or in 2 hours by air. The area is one of the largest vegetable and fruit producing regions in the country, and Napier is a delightful seaside city. From Napier one can travel through mountain passes to Taupo and Rotorua, or go up the east coast to Gisborne and through to Tauranga, in the Bay of Plenty, from which it is an easy drive to either Rotorua or Auckland.

The west coast route passes through the river city of Wanganui and on to New Plymouth, nestling beneath the slopes of Mount Egmont in Taranaki. The Glow-worm Grotto at Waitomo Caves lies close beside the main road to Auckland.

AUCKLAND

Rome was built on seven hills, Auckland on seven or more extinct volcanoes. Auckland is New Zealand's largest city, with a population of over 800,000. Situated on a narrow isthmus, it separates two seas, the Pacific Ocean and the Tasman Sea, and two harbors, the Waitemata and the Manukau.

Dominating the Waitemata Harbor ("Sea of Sparkling Waters") is Rangitoto Island, a long, three-humped, former volcanic island, whose shape never changes from whatever angle it is viewed.

Like parts of the United States, Auckland was bought for a song. History records that 3,000 acres of land were purchased from the Maori for $110 in cash, 50 blankets, 20 pairs of trousers, 20 shirts, 100 yards of cloth, 10 waistcoats, 10 caps, 20 hatchets, a bag of sugar, a bag of flour, 10 iron pots, 4 casks of tobacco, and a box of pipes.

A large population and an abundance of flat land gradually drew industry to Auckland, which is today New Zealand's largest industrial and commercial center. Thoughtful planning has, however, prevented most of the newer factories from becoming unsightly blotches and the new homes from being too stereotyped.

The growth of industry called for more labor, and, seeking opportunities for employment and education, thousands of Pacific Islanders, who also hold New Zealand citizenship, have flocked to Auckland. From the Cook Islands, Tonga, Western Samoa, the Tokelau Islands and from Niue Island they came, to make Auckland the largest Polynesian city in the world.

Unlike the Europeans who settled earlier, the Polynesians have tended to retain their own culture and customs and to live in their own communities. On Sundays especially you will see the women in long skirts and flowered straw hats, and the men in neat suits with white shirt and tie going to their own churches. Walk the length of Karangahape Road, to the north of the business center of the city, and you'll rub shoulders with as many Polynesians as Europeans.

They are mostly a happy, carefree people, but some have yet to adjust to the European way of life. They tend to congregate with their own compatriots, and some of the hotel bars have identified with them by painting their exteriors in the brilliant colors the Polynesians love, particularly reds and purples.

Queen Street: Narrow Valley Floor

Some New Zealanders consider that Auckland is humid in summer. There is some truth in this, but the humidity is nothing like as enervating as the humidity of New York, and there is usually the relief of a sea breeze.

Most of the principal hotels are close to Queen Street, the main street, which runs along a narrow valley floor, with side streets climbing off it like herring bones. Queen Street is a series of small shops, interspersed with larger department stores and some interesting arcades. One of the largest is the Downtown Shopping Centre (opposite the chief post office at the bottom of Queen Street), which has 70 shops under one roof, including a duty-free shop.

Almost opposite is the Old Auckland Customhouse at the corner of Customs and Albert Streets, where the architecture of the 1880s has been preserved and craft shops added. Just up Queen Street from the

THE NORTH ISLAND

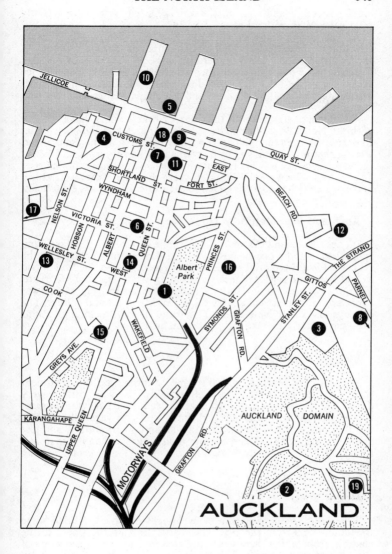

Points of Interest

1) Art Gallery
2) Botanical Gardens
3) Carlaw Park (Rugby League)
4) City Markets
5) Ferry Terminal
6) His Majesty's Theater
7) Old Customhouse
8) Parnell Village Shopping Center
9) Post Office
10) Princes Wharf
11) Queen's Arcade Shopping Center
12) Railroad Station
13) St. Matthews Church
14) Strand Arcade
15) Town Hall
16) University
17) Victoria Park Market
18) Visitors Bureau and Downtown Airlines Terminal and Shopping Center
19) War Memorial Museum

chief post office and also on the left is Queens Arcade, a recently refurbished area with 45 shops.

At 128 Queen Street is the Plaza Shopping Centre, which has a selection of specialty stores but has an emphasis on food services. At the Gourmet Food Gallery numerous stalls offer Mexican, Indonesian, Turkish, and French fare, together with roasts, fish and chips, an ice cream parlor, and a coffee shop. Just across the street is the C.L.M. Mall, catering to clothing, shoes, and fabrics, as well as caneware and costume jewelry.

Aucklanders are proud of their harbor bridge which links the city with the North Shore (a popular residential area and the main outlet to the north), even though they flippantly refer to it as the Coathanger. Previously the only link was by ferry or a long journey by road. Opened in 1959, the bridge is 3,348 ft. long, and its 800 ft. navigation span rises 142 ft. above the water. Within ten years the traffic flow had trebled, and extra lanes had to be to added to each side. It now has eight lanes.

Auckland War Memorial Museum

In the Auckland Domain, a large expanse of parkland and sportsfield, a short taxi or bus ride from downtown Auckland, is the Auckland War Memorial Museum. It is a memorial to the dead of two World Wars and is noted for its outstanding masterpieces of Maori art. The great carved house Hotunui and the only surviving Maori war canoe are centerpieces to a large display of Maori art and culture. The displays also cover New Zealand's natural history, including its bird life—particularly the extinct giant Moa bird.

Victoria Park Market

Victoria Park Market has transformed a former garbage treatment plant site into an attractive marketplace thronged with visitors every day of the week—a sort of high quality flea market. A wide range of specialty shops sell prepared food, fresh fruit and vegetables, books, health foods, arts and crafts, clothing, ceramics and pottery, and just about everything else. There are four food outlets and an international food hall. It is about three kilometers from the city center and an inexpensive taxi ride.

Mount Eden

The 643-ft. symmetrical cone of an extinct volcano is Mt. Eden, some four kilometers from the city. The road spirals up the slopes to the summit, from which there is a complete circle of panoramic views of the city and outlying areas. From here one can look at two oceans with a turn of the head; on one side the Tasman Sea, on the other the Pacific Ocean. A table shows the direction and distances of the main cities of the world. Just below the lip is the deep red lava crater, fringed by grass, where sheep graze placidly.

One Tree Hill

This hill, 6 kilometers from downtown, catches the eye from the city, with its single tree and a 70-ft. obelisk honoring Sir John Logan Campbell, "the father of Auckland." On the crest of the hill is the Auckland Observatory. Like Mt. Eden, it was formerly a Maori fortified village.

THE NORTH ISLAND

Parnell Rose Garden and Village

Famous for its rose gardens and profusion of blooms in season (November), this sight is only 2 kilometers from the city.
Parnell Village, a couple of miles from the city, should not be missed. Here, an imaginative developer has transformed what was formerly a rather run-down part of Auckland into a delightful replica of early colonial days—not merely as a tourist attraction but as an attractive collection of shops.

Kelly Tarlton's Underwater World

Another Auckland highlight is Kelly Tarlton's Underwater World, which is far from a routine aquarium. The impression of actually being an underwater diver is strong as one takes the 8-minute trip on a conveyor through a 40-foot-long tunnel lined with acrylic windows. Over 30 species of fish, including sharks and stingrays, swim beside and above you in a natural environment. There are also fish pools and a 12-minute audiovisual show. The complex is opposite Orakei Wharf, on a bus route and close to the city.

Greenstone Factories

Greenstone, a type of jade, is distinctive to New Zealand and was widely used by the Maori to make weapons and ornaments. It is so hard that it has to be cut with diamond saws. It may be seen being cut and fashioned into modern ornaments at the factory of Greenstone Distributors Limited, 26 Honan Place, Avondale (8 kilometers outside Auckland), and at Finnegan's Paua and Greenstone Factory, corner of Gundry and Ophir Streets, Newton (five minutes by taxi from downtown).

Zoological Gardens

By overseas standards the Auckland zoo is not outstanding, but New Zealand's unique bird, the kiwi, can be seen in a special nocturnal house. The kiwi forages for food only at night, and a special house has been built and lit to resemble its native habitat.

Museum of Transport and Technology

Don't let this forbidding title put you off. This is a fascinating collection of equipment and machines that have now largely disappeared, including a working tramway, a railway, vintage cars and carriages, and wartime guns and aircraft. It also contains the remains of what was probably the second aircraft to fly. A New Zealander, Robert Pearse, designed and built an aircraft, which he twice flew in March 1904, just three months after the Wright brothers made the world's first powered flight. There is still argument whether Pearse did, in fact, fly first. Ancient vehicles have been painstakingly restored, and mounted on rails are old trolley cars and railroad locomotives. The camera and telephone exhibits are outstanding. If you grew up in the 1920s and 1930s you'll feel a pang of nostalgia to see the old type of gas pumps still bearing names like "Voco," and "Super Plume Ethyl" and even five-gallon cans labeled "Texaco" and "Shell." In another part of the museum about a mile away memories of World War II are revived by a Lancaster bomber, one of the type which carried out the daring raid on the Moehne, Eder and Sorpe dams in the Ruhr. Nearby are a Kittyhawk and a Vampire jet.

Vineyards

The Henderson area is renowned for its vineyards. They began in the 1890s when an immigrant from Lebanon, Assid Abraham Corban, brought with him a 300-year-old tradition in wine making and viticulture. Today, there are dozens of vineyards in a compact area, from large corporation enterprises to small individual holdings. A tour of some of the vineyards to taste the local product on the site is full of enjoyment.

NORTHLAND

"The winterless north" is how residents describe the long peninsula pointing north from Auckland. (Remember that seasons are reversed in the southern hemisphere). The claim is not strictly true, but the region is subtropical, and certainly warmer in winter than other parts of New Zealand. It is a productive dairying area and also contains New Zealand's only oil refinery, at Marsden Point.

Northland is often bypassed, as it is time consuming to travel. Even though the route is circular, it takes six or seven days if sufficient time is allowed for sightseeing. Yet it repays a visit. Even just three days will allow a visit to the most interesting area, the Bay of Islands.

In pre-European times much of the land was covered with a unique tree, the kauri. Of huge size, it is branchless for much of its length, and was therefore especially favored by the early whalers for masts and spars. The Maoris made canoes more than 100 ft. long from it. And the Europeans plundered it—a tragedy, as it is a slow-growing tree and takes a thousand years to reach full maturity. Today, the remaining forests are rigidly protected. There are three stands where the kauri may be seen in all its magnificence—the Waipoua State Forest and Trounson Park on the western side, and Puketi State Forest, near Waitangi, in the east. Waipoua State Forest has the greatest kauri of all—Tane Mahuta ("God of the Forest"—167 ft. tall and 14 ft. thick, with the lowest branches 60 ft. from the ground, and an estimated age of 1,200 years.

Through splits in its bark the tree exudes a gum which runs down the trunk and into the ground. It hardens into solid lumps of amber-colored, clear resin, which is today used for carved ornaments. In the latter part of the last century, however, it was much used for making varnishes, and thousands of Yugoslavs came to New Zealand as gum diggers. They dug for the gum in the ground and scaled the straight trunks to extract it from the branch forks. Modern synthetics replaced the gum, and many of the Yugoslavs became absorbed into other occupations or became grapegrowers and wine-makers, a calling they still follow.

A little more than halfway up the narrow peninsula on the east coast is the Bay of Islands—a large semicircular indentation serrated by many bays and beaches, as if some giant sea monster had bitten into the coast with a mouth of jagged teeth. Within the bay are some 150 islands—the exact number is a matter of dispute.

This is the birthplace of modern New Zealand history. It was here that the Treaty of Waitangi, establishing British rule, was signed on February 6, 1840. Waitangi Day is observed as New Zealand's National

THE NORTH ISLAND

Day, and a colorful ceremony is always held on the sweeping lawn outside the Treaty House, now a historical reserve. It was here, too, that Christianity was first introduced to the Maori. On Christmas Day 1814 the Rev. Samuel Marsden conducted the first Christian service to be held in the country.

Farther north on the west coast is the long stretch of Ninety Mile Beach (actually only 64 miles), and further up on the northernmost tip of New Zealand, Cape Reinga.

Between December and April marlin and shark appear off the eastern coast, and two points share popularity with other places farther south for big game fishing.

Exploring Northland

Traveling up the east coast, your objective will probably be the Bay of Islands, but pause to try the thermal springs at Waiwera, which means "hot water," and see the busy city of Whangarei. Here the Clapham Clock Museum in Lower John Street is world-renowned for its collection of clocks, and should not be missed.

In the Bay of Islands, Paihia, close to the Treaty House, and Russell stand on opposite sides of the bay. There are regular launch services connecting them, but vehicles have to be punted across a stretch of water. Because of its wider range of accommodations Paihai has become the holiday center.

Russell, once known as Kororareka, is redolent with evidence of early history. It was once known as the hellhole of the Pacific, when in the early 1800s whaling ships began calling for provisions. They traded with the Maoris with muskets and liquor, and brawling was commonplace. Nevertheless, after the signing of the Treaty of Waitangi it became New Zealand's first capital and was renamed Russell, but in 1841 the seat of government was moved to Auckland.

Russell still maintains an old-world charm. Dominating the waterfront is what is known as Pompallier House, a graceful Colonial-style building which could almost have come from the deep South of the United States. It is commonly thought of as the home of Bishop Pompalier, a Frenchman and the first Roman Catholic bishop of the Southwest Pacific, who arrived in 1838 to establish the first Roman Catholic mission. Actually, he never lived in it but in a building which has long disappeared. The present building bears no resemblance to the original two-storey structure made of rammed earth that was used to house the mission's printing presses. They produced several religious booklets printed in Maori. After the mission moved to Auckland it was used as a tannery for a time, but then sold to a local official, who transformed it into a fine residence. It was subsequently acquired by the government, and the Historic Places Trust has turned it into a museum, which contains a number of interesting exhibits.

Outstanding sidetrips from Russell (or Paihia) are cruises to outlying islands by launch (formerly known as "Fullers Cream Trip") or by the motor-powered large *Tiger Lily* catamaran. The big thrill is a Piercy Island turnaround, with its famous "hole in the rock." Here the sea surges through a funnel-like hole about 30 ft. long, 50 ft. high, and 40 ft. wide, and, with masterly maneuvering, the catamaran is edged slowly through the gap. Both the catamaran and the launch have comfortable cabins, hostess services, and bars. Take your lunch or order one when buying your ticket.

Across the bay is Waitangi, the birthplace of New Zealand history. On a grassy lawn sloping to the sea the Treaty of Waitangi was signed.

The Treaty House is fascinating. It was built as a home by the newly-appointed British resident, James Busby, in 1833, and is typical of the type of home favored by the more prosperous of the early settlers. In addition to a collection of historic items, it contains the first piano brought to New Zealand. In front of the house a kauri flagstaff marks the place where the treaty was signed.

Of greater interest, however, is a Maori meeting house *(whare runanga)* which is unusual in that it contains carvings from many different tribes; a meeting house usually has only the carvings of its own tribe. Beside it is a 117-ft. war canoe built for the 1940 centennial celebrations. It is made in three jointed sections, cut from huge trees.

Relics from the Bottom

Two miles (3.2km) beyond the Treaty House is Mount Bledisloe (376 ft.), from which there are wide views of the Bay of Islands.

It is worth pausing near the Waitangi Bridge to see the Museum of Shipwrecks, housed in an old wooden ship sitting on the river bottom. Here a collection of what diver Kelly Tarlton has brought up from the sea bed is exhibited.

Just a few miles away is the township of Kerikeri, one of the first mission stations. It is a prolific citrus-growing area, but a rich soil and kind climate also favor other subtropical fruits.

Almost on the river bank is the Mission House, the oldest building in New Zealand, which has been carefully restored, and the old Stone Store, still a store and in part a museum.

It's a full-day bus trip to New Zealand's northernmost tip, Cape Reinga. Part of the route is along the hard sand of Ninety Mile Beach and then up a shallow river bed. From the lighthouse at the cape you can watch the Pacific Ocean meet the Tasman Sea in a flurry of angry water. It was from here, the Maoris believed, that the spirits of the dead departed on their journey back to their Pacific homeland, Hawaiki.

Ninety Mile Beach is famous in New Zealand as a source of the toheroa, a type of clam which grows up to 6 inches long and from which is made a delicious green soup. Unfortunately, this is hard to get, as restrictions have been imposed to conserve the toheroa beds, which were being depleted. More plentiful, however, is the tuatua, a similar but smaller type of clam, which is also mouth-watering.

The return to Auckland from the Bay of Islands is usually made down the west coast and through the Waipoua State Kauri Forest.

Waitomo Caves

Resist the temptation to say, "when you've seen one cave you've seen them all." Certainly the Waitomo Caves have stalactites and stalagmites like so many others, but they also have a feature which is unique —the Glowworm Grotto. Neither words nor pictures can capture the beauty and the atmosphere. A visit is a remarkable experience.

With a guide, you descend to a deep cavern through which flows a quiet, sluggish stream. You are warned to keep silent, because the glowworms extinguish their lights at noise. At a landing you take your place in a flat-bottomed boat, the electric light is extinguished, and the guide slowly pulls the boat by wires around a cornice and into a vaulted cavern festooned with thousands and thousands of pinpricks of light— tiny individually, but collectively strong enough for you to see your companions in the darkness. Except for the occasional sound of dripping water the silence is complete. Above and around you myriads of glowworms shine their steady blue-green light, the dark, still waters glistening with their reflections like a star-studded carpet.

The Waitomo glowworm is an unusual species, quite unlike the glowworms and fireflies seen in other countries. While most other glowworms shine their lights as a mating lure, the Waitomo glowworm lights up to attract food. The hungrier it is, the stronger the light. Visitors are able to see the glowworms at close hand in what is called the "demonstration chamber" close to the grotto. Guided tours of the cave run every hour from 9 A.M. to 4 P.M., (0813) 88–228, for $6.

The Waitomo Caves are 126 miles (203km) from Auckland and 46 miles (74km) off the main route to Rotorua. Such is their beauty that they are always included in an itinerary unless lack of time makes it impossible. It is possible to include the caves in a tour of other parts of the region, and they are also a convenient stopover point if one is driving from Auckland to New Plymouth or Rotorua.

Rotorua

Rotorua is an area of contradictions. Gentle scenic beauty and violent thermal activity exist side by side. It has long been regarded as New Zealand's prime attraction, both for overseas visitors and New Zealanders themselves.

It has also remained one of the traditional homes of the Maori people, and it is the best place to meet them and to gain an insight into their philosophy and culture. But don't expect to see them living in native reservations or around the streets in their native costumes. They are completely integrated into modern society and live, dress, and work the same way as Europeans. Far from there being any segregation, they mingle freely and on equal terms. But to entertain the visitor they don their traditional costumes to give Maori concerts at night. Few are fulltime entertainers; most of the men and women you see performing hold regular jobs as secretaries, shop assistants, radiographers, technicians, or clerks. The woman you see performing intricate and graceful dance movements may serve you your breakfast in the morning.

(A reminder: Maori is pronounced "Mau-ree", not "May-ori." Not that offense is taken at a mispronunciation, but you might as well give a good impression by saying it right.)

Rotorua, 149 miles (239.8km) south of Auckland, once relied on tourism, but forestry and farming are now major industries, and the city's population has grown to over 47,000. Don't be concerned at the smell as you approach. Because of the underground thermal activity there is frequently a pungent odor of hydrogen sulphide: the locals sometimes jocularly refer to it as Sulphur City. But the natural gas is harmless, and one quickly becomes accustomed to the smell.

For many years Rotorua was a popular spa resort, and many went there to bathe in the mineral waters. Modern medicine tends to discount the curative power of the waters, but it does not dispute their value in relieving minor aches and pains. There is nothing more relaxing than soaking in a hot thermal pool after a day's sightseeing. You'll sleep soundly. The Polynesian Pools near the center of the city have a variety of baths, and many hotels and motels have their own pools, as do some private homes.

Don't be alarmed by discolorations on the water taps and fittings. They are not dirty. Chemicals in the water tend to tarnish certain metals; in fact, you can often identify "Rotorua money" by the dullness of the silver coins.

The Hot-Water Belt

Rotorua sits on a huge bed of hot water and steam. You'll see it seeping from banks and culverts, from gutters beside the sidewalks, from clumps of bushes, and even from the middle of flower beds. It is not uncommon to see hot and cold pools side by side. In fact, hot earth is one of the natural hazards in the main golf course.

Residents of the "hot water belt" take full advantage of this by sinking a bore and harnessing the steam to heat their homes and pools, and even do some of their cooking. You'll often see thin pipes rising from gardens to let off surplus steam.

Rotorua is at the southern end of the 32-square-mile lake of that name. Unfortunately, the name is not as evocative as it sounds. It simply means "second lake" (*roto* means lake and *rua* means second). When the migrating Maori canoe *Arawa* landed on the east coast an exploring party moved inland. They found a large lake, Rotoiti ("first lake"), and then a larger lake, Rotorua.

The Arawa tribe settled in the Rotorua area, and it is still their homeland.

In the center of Lake Rotorua is Mokoia Island, the scene of the greatest of Maori legends, a love story that ended happily. Against the wishes of her parents, a Maori maid, Hinemoa, who lived on the shores of the lake, fell in love with a young chief, Tutanekai, who lived on the island. Her efforts to sail to her lover in a canoe were foiled, and night after night she listened to the sounds of Tutanekai playing his flute to guide her. Finally she could stand it no longer and under the cover of darkness slipped into the water and swam the long mile to the island, guided by the sounds of the flute. Exhausted and cold, she dragged herself up the beach and sank into a natural thermal bath, which bears the name Hinemoa's Pool.

Tutanekai, who had retired for the night, was unable to sleep and sent a slave to a cold spring near the pool for a calabash of water. Disguising her voice, Hinemoa asked the slave for a drink of water. He passed the calabash, which she promptly smashed. He returned to Tutanekai and reported the insult, and Tutanekai seized his club and rushed to the pool to challenge the stranger, only to find his beloved. He placed his cloak around her and embraced her and led her to his hut, and they were married and lived happily ever after.

The love story is still related in song, and two streets in the city have been named after the lovers.

As Maori names are used so extensively in Rotorua, it is helpful to know how to cope with these seemingly tongue-twisting words. Break the words into syllables, give each vowel its full value, and remember that every word must end in a vowel and that "wh" sounds like an "f". For example, Whakarewarewa breaks down into *Whaka-rewa-rewa*, Tutanekai into *Tu-tan-e-kai*. Hinemoa into *Hine-moa*, Whakaue into *Wha-cow-e*, Ohinemutu into *O-hine-mutu*, and Tamatekapua into *Tama-te-ka-pua*.

Apart from its thermal activity, Rotorua is also a popular area for trout fishing in the nearby lakes and streams.

Exploring Rotorua

No area in New Zealand has such a wide variety of sightseeing. Two or three days, or more if possible, should be spent here to enjoy all the area offers. Excursions are well organized and inexpensive.

Information and brochures on sightseeing and tours may be obtained from the New Zealand Travel Office, 67 Fenton Street, 85–179; the Rotorua Promotions and Development Society, Box 90, 84–126, or individual sightseeing operators.

THE NORTH ISLAND

Whakarewarewa

Commonly shortened to Whaka. It is essential that the tourist visit this weird thermal area, only a couple of miles from the city center. There are two entrances, but it is recommended that you enter through the replica of a fortified Maori village (a *pa*) beside the main highway. An ornately carved gateway straddles the thick palisades to the village. The two figures at the gateway depict the famous lovers, Hinemoa and Tutanekai.

From the entrance a well-kept path bordered by native shrubs twists its way through outcrops of steam and boiling mud and silica terraces. Tiny geysers hiss beside you, and spouts of boiling mud leap from the mud lakes like jumping frogs. In the center of the area is Pohutu Geyser, New Zealand's largest, which plays to about 100 ft., often for long periods. Its activity is heralded by the "Prince of Wales Feathers", three jets which play spasmodically to a height of 40 ft. Below all this feverish activity a small cold stream flows placidly along the floor of the valley. Just before you leave the thermal area you pass a number of Maori graves, concrete-encased above the ground because of the earth's heat, and reach a collection of hot pools in which the Maoris who live nearby still cook their food. Meat and vegetables are placed in a woven flax basket and immersed in the boiling water, or in a wooden or concrete box set into the earth to trap the steam; a sort of natural pressure cooker.

Maori Arts and Crafts Institute

This is situated beside the main entrance to the Whakarewarewa thermal area and should not be missed. It is not a museum, but a living preservation of Maori art and culture. As the Maori acquired the European way of life there was a danger that the Maori arts would disappear; so, with government assistance, the institute was formed some 20 years ago.

For a three-year course of training under a master carver, the school accepts four students of less than 18 years of age, chosen from four Maori tribes. They are paid the same wages as apprentice carpenters. Some of their smaller carvings can be purchased, but the larger pieces are destined to replace deteriorating carvings at meeting houses in various parts of the country.

Women are not permitted to carve by Maori ethics, but at the institute they demonstrate traditional Maori weaving with flax, the making of *piupiu* skirts (flax leaves rolled into tight tubes), and basket and mat making. Instructors now go all over New Zealand to teach. The institute is funded by the fees paid to enter Whakarewarewa. There is a kiwi house near the institute where live kiwis may be seen.

Government Gardens

It was left to the government to beautify Rotorua in the early days (there were not enough local residents to meet the cost), which it did by forming what are still known as the Government Gardens, close to the center of the city, facing Hinemaru Street. Rotorua was then much favored as a spa resort, and, in an effort to emulate the elegance of European resorts, a large and incongruous Elizabethan-style bathhouse was built, and surrounded with lawns and flower gardens.

It is no longer used as such and contains an art gallery, museum, and restaurant. The formal flower gardens are delightful, and, surprisingly, steam often rises from stone cairns in the middle of them. There are also well-kept greens for playing lawn bowls and croquet in summer.

Some 3,000 temperate to tropical orchids, 300 of which will be blooming at any one time, are displayed in the Fleur International Orchid Garden in the Government Gardens. Among them are plants valued at up to $5,000 and new locally-developed hybrids. The orchids are displayed in two large plant houses heated by natural underground steam. Landscaped pathways lead through tropical foliage and native bush with waterfalls and streams. Adjacent is a free-flight parrot aviary. Hours are from 10 A.M. to 10 P.M. daily.

Polynesian Pools

Rotorua's natural thermal waters can be enjoyed at the Polynesian Pools in the Government Gardens. There are two public pools, one for adults and one for children, and 20 well-appointed private pools, all fed by the soft alkaline mineral waters of nearby Rachael Spring. There are also the Priest and Radium Springs, with their eight pools of different temperatures, bubbling out of the pumice. This spring water is acidic, and is well-known for relieving arthritis and similar ailments.

Ohinemutu Maori Village

Ohinemutu is truly a Maori village in that only Maoris live there. But do not expect to find native huts; they live in European-style houses. Nevertheless, it is one of the most fascinating places in Rotorua. Although it is on the edge of the cold waters of the lake, the land is pitted with harmless little geysers, and steam rises from crevices. In the courtyard stands a bust of Queen Victoria, surrounded by four decorated pillars and shielded by a canopy decorated with Maori designs and carving.

Two buildings are of special interest. Almost on the shore of the lake is St. Faith's Anglican Church, built in Tudor style in 1910. You cannot escape a feeling of reverence as you enter. The layout is traditional, but the decorations are distinctly Maori. Rich Maori carving is everywhere —on the pews, the pulpit and the altar. Hymn books are in Maori.

As you approach the sacristy move to the right and sit in the front pew. Before you is a large window fronting the lake. On it is etched the figure of Christ—a Maori Christ wearing a chief's robe—at such an angle that he seems to be walking on the waters. Near the entrance to the church hang several historic military flags.

If you can, attend a service. To listen to the liquid and sonorous Maori language and the harmonious singing is an emotional experience. It is also an opportunity to mingle with the Maori people in their own environment.

Opposite the church is the Tamatekapua meeting house, an ornately carved building containing some venerated work dating from about 1800. The house is named after the captain of the Arawa canoe, and the carved figures in the interior represent passengers in the canoe. The figure on the top of the center post is Ihenga, who claimed the hot lakes district for the Arawa people. Another figure represents Ngatoroirangi, the canoe's navigator and *tohunga* (priest).

Fleur Orchid House

The Fleur Orchid House in Hinemaru Street and backing into the Government Gardens is one of Rotorua's newest attractions. It contains hundreds of orchids. Some are raised locally, some are imported

THE NORTH ISLAND

from overseas, and some are virtually priceless. The orchids are most tastefully displayed amid rockeries and ferns, and there is vivid greenery and color all the year round. The Fleur Orchid House (476–699) is open daily from 10 A.M. to 10 P.M., admission $4.

Kuirau Domain

Just a short stroll from the city is Kuirau Domain, a pleasantly grassed area which has the inevitable boiling mud pools, steam vents and small geysers. More unusually, it has a shallow pool of thermal water which is used as a foot bath. It does indeed invigorate tired feet.

Maori Concerts

A Maori concert is an unforgettable experience. Their original chants *(waiata),* which usually describe the history and ancestry of the tribe, are monotonal, rather like a church litany, but they warmly embraced the European tone scale, giving to the melodies their own harmonic variations. Maori singing is truly sweet and rhythmic.

Maori concerts are given in full costume in most of the larger hotels, at the Maori Cultural Theater, the Tudor Towers in the Government Gardens and Ohinemutu. The THC Rotorua International Hotel adds spice by giving a Maori feast every Sunday evening, followed by a concert. For a reasonable charge nonguests can attend the meal and entertainment, but reservations are essential.

Pork, chicken, ham and vegetables are cooked in a *hangi* (oven) in the hotel grounds. A large hole is dug and partially filled with river stones which have been heated to a high temperature. Water is thrown on them to make steam, the food in flax baskets or other containers is placed on top, and covered with soil. That is the true Maori oven, but in Rotorua the natural superheated underground steam dispenses with the need for heating stones. The principle and effect are, however, the same. The food is taken into the concert area and eaten informally.

The concert always begins with the traditional Maori ceremony of welcome. Grimacing fearfully and brandishing a *taiaha* (a long club), a warrior from the host tribe advances to the visitors with a sprig of greenery. He places this at the feet of the leader of the visitors and cautiously retires. If the visiting leader picks up the greenery he comes in peace; if not, it is war. Needless to say, the sprig is always picked up at a concert. The host tribe then greets the visitors with a song of welcome—*Haere mai, Haere mai, Haere mai,* thrice welcome. The ceremony is held in respect, and guests are asked not to applaud.

So musical are the Maoris that they do nothing without singing. Lilting melodies accompany the graceful *poi* dances by the women as they deftly twist and twirl balls of plaited flax.

It is impossible not to feel the blood stirred by the war dance *(haka)* performed by the men. The chant is in a simple rhythm and the tempo is kept by stamping feet—the Maori did not use drums. Every part of the body is brought into action in a set routine, even to protruding and wagging the tongue. The *haka* was intended to strike fear into the hearts of the enemy, but was also a "limbering up" exercise for hand-to-hand battle.

The concert always ends with the traditional Maori song of farewell, "Now is the hour" *(Po ata rau).* It is not strictly a Maori melody, but Maori and *pakeha* alike have adopted it as a traditional New Zealand song. They sing it first in Maori and then in English, and as its plaintive notes die it is impossible to escape a feeling of sadness at parting.

Waimangu Round Trip

The Waimangu thermal valley gives a good idea of how the earth was formed. It contains both furious thermal activity and quiet bush with grass-covered slopes rising from placid pools. The main valley can be seen from a mini-coach on a half-day trip. An extension, which includes some walking, adds launch cruises on Lake Rotomahana, with its steaming cliffs, and Lake Tarawera, where you meet a bus for the return to Rotorua.

The Waimangu Valley was created by the violent eruption of Mount Tarawera in 1886. In the early hours of June 10 the northern peak blew up, splitting the range into a series of massive craters. The noise was heard hundreds of miles away. Ash and debris were strewn over 6,000 square miles, and the Maori villages of Te Wairoa, Te Ariki, and Moura were destroyed. Maori legend tells that a phantom canoe was seen in Lake Tarawera just before the eruption.

Among other things, the eruption destroyed the famous Pink and White Terraces, glittering staircases of silica, and the Waimangu Geyser, once the world's largest, which played to a height of 1,600 ft.

But other remarkable sights remain or were created. The Waimangu Cauldron occupies a crater formed by a later and milder eruption and is a boiling lake of about 10 acres. The flow at the outlet is more than a thousand gallons a minute. Above the lake rise the jagged Cathedral Rocks, red-tinted and gently breathing steam. Ruaumoko's Throat (he was the god of the underworld) has an atmosphere of suppressed unearthly violence. Roughly circular, the crater is the bed of a pale blue steaming lake of unknown depth which overflows periodically at a rate varying from 200 to 3,000 gallons a minute. At times the water recedes 50 ft. to uncover the beautiful white walls of the crater. Bird's Nest Terrace is aptly named, but has miniature geysers and a silica terrace formation. Surrounded by vegetation, the Warbrick Terraces are layers of orange, brown, black, white and green caused by algae and mineral deposits falling from the top platform.

Te Wairoa Buried Village

In contrast to geysers and hot mud pools, the Te Wairoa Buried Village is tranquil but interesting.

Once the starting point for the trip to the Pink and White Terraces, the village of Te Wairoa was buried under eight feet of ash in the eruption. It has now been partly excavated—a sort of miniature Pompeii. There are many interesting relics, but as one walks through the heavily grassed pastures fenced by tall poplar trees and English cherries it is hard to visualize the devastation which occurred.

Of special interest are the remains of a *tohunga's whare* (priest's house). The tohunga, who was reputed to be 110 years old, did not predict the coming disaster and was therefore blamed for it by the tribe, who refused to allow him to be rescued from his buried house. After four days they relented. Incredibly, he was still alive, but died a few days later. Relics of the eruption are still being excavated and are on display in a museum, which also includes displays of kauri gum and polished New Zealand rocks.

THE NORTH ISLAND

Tikitere

Appropriately named Hell's Gate, Tikitere is an area of furiously bubbling pools and seething mud, including a mud waterfall. It is an eerie place, but intriguing.

Mount Tarawera Tours

When Mount Tarawera erupted it blew a 9¾-mile rift along almost its entire length, leaving a jagged chasm with walls up to 800 ft. high. From the air, it is an awesome sight, and there are helicopter and fixed-wing aircraft tours that include a circuit of the mountain and a flight across the crater as part of a scenic tour, which takes in the surrounding native forests and lakes, the vast pine forests, the Blue and Green Lakes and aerial views of the city. Some aircraft land on a strip at the summit of the mountain. Another way of viewing the crater is by a four-wheel-drive cruiser that travels from Rotorua up the side of the mountain to the summit.

Lake Okataina

Lake Okataina, 19 miles from Rotorua, must be one of the loveliest lakes in New Zealand. Steep hills, thickly clad in subtropical forest, enclose the blue-to-turquoise waters and delightful sandy beaches. The place is alive with native birds, and deer roam the forest. Of human habitation there is only a tourist lodge, a launch and runabouts for enjoying a cruise and for fishing, for the lake is renowned for the abundance and size of its rainbow trout.

The name means "place of laughing", but you are more likely to relax and absorb its serenity and beauty. The approach is impressively beautiful, through thick native forest and a tunnel of native fuschia, whose flowers form a red carpet on the roadway in the spring.

Trout Pools

Even if you don't catch trout you can see them at close quarters at Rainbow Springs and Paradise Valley Springs. Here they live a protected life in crystal-clear pools in native bush, gradually evolving from tiny fingerlings to 8- and 10-lb. monsters. In some springs the path is below the pool, one side of which has a thick plate-glass window, through which you can see the fish cavorting beneath the water. It is enthralling to watch the trout, like performing dolphins, leaping from the water to seize small pellets of meat held above the pool on the end of a stick. Rainbow Springs also has a kiwi house where a live kiwi may be seen.

Taniwha Springs

Taniwha Springs, 7 miles from Rotorua, has dozens of busy waterfalls, gushing springs, glittering sandsprings, and several trout pools set in native bush. A short climb takes you to an old Maori fortified village site. It takes its name from a legendary water monster, the "taniwha."

Skyline Skyrides

An outstanding attraction is Skyline Skyrides, just a few miles from Rotorua center. A 900-meter gondola lift, with a vertical rise of 200 meters, takes you up the slopes of Mt. Ngongotaha to a panoramic view and a restaurant and cafe. Descent can be by the gondola or a 1-km-long luge, or slide ride.

Agrodome

Even if you think you've seen enough sheep as you've traveled through New Zealand, a visit to the Agrodome, five miles from Rotorua, is well worthwhile. Here you can meet them at first hand and watch performing sheep take the center stage and show off their rich fleeces. Top-class shearers describe the characteristics of 19 different breeds and demonstrate shearing techniques. But the sheep dogs steal the show as they muster sheep into a holding pen, often without a bark being heard.

Heli-Jet Tours

A Heli-Jet tour is an adventure, but safe. It is an unusual combination of helicopter sightseeing and a ride in a jet boat. A helicopter takes you to the unspoiled Lake Rotokawau, nestling amid towering native forest and tree ferns. You step from the helicopter into a waiting jet boat and then speed at up to 50 mph over the lake before returning to the airport by the helicopter. The tour takes about 1½ hours.

Waiotapu

While much of the thermal activity at Rotorua is vigorous, the phenomena at Waiotapu are quieter, but beautifully colored. The area is 19 miles from Rotorua and is conveniently visited when driving from Rotorua to Wairakei and Taupo.

Wairakei

There is no settlement of Wairakei—just a comfortable Tourist Hotel Corporation hotel, a superb golf course, and a dramatic example of how man has harnessed Nature's vast underground heat for his own benefit. This is the site of the Wairakei Geothermal Steam Power Project, where scores of bores have been driven several thousand feet into the earth to tap huge underground reservoirs of super-heated steam, which is then piped to a powerhouse to make electricity. The steam drives turbines, which feed 192,600 kilowatts into the national supply.

You'll know when you approach Wairakei, 50 miles south of Rotorua. Huge clouds of steam pipes arch over the road, and a sign warns of a visibility hazard from drifting steam.

The complex is unusual, to say the least, and its like can be seen in few parts of the world. A roadside information center graphically demonstrates the project, and an impressive view of the steam field can be obtained from the crest of a hill behind the area.

Lake Taupo

Six miles beyond Wairakei lie Taupo and the lake. On the way, a detour should be made to view Huka Falls on the Waikato River. The falls are not particularly high, but they are spectacular. Compressed into a narrow rock channel, the river boils and surges before it gushes over a 35-ft. ledge into a maelstrom of white and green water.

Lake Taupo, New Zealand's largest lake, is 25 miles long and 17 miles wide and about 1,100 ft. above sea level. It is almost the geographical center of the North Island. The Maoris called it *Taupo Moana* (the Sea of Taupo).

To anglers throughout the world the name Taupo is synonymous with trout, for it is famous for the abundance and excellence of its fishing both in the lake and in the numerous rivers and streams flowing into it. It is said that over 700 tons of trout are taken from the lake each year! The average weight is 4½ lb., and 7- and 8-lb. fish are not uncommon. Charter boats are available for hire from the small natural harbor.

Until recent years the township of Taupo, at the northern end of the lake, was a sleepy village catering mainly for anglers and holidaymakers, but the development of farming and forestry have transformed it into a clean modern business town of some 13,000 people. It has also become a popular retirement place, with many fine homes.

From the lake's edge there are good views of the mountains in Tongariro National Park. Off the southeastern shore of the lake is the island of Motutaiko, an ancient Maori burial place and therefore sacred.

Tongariro National Park

The most popular national park in the North Island, Tongariro National Park, some 60 miles south of Taupo, encloses 175,000 acres of brown tussock plains and native forest. Dominating the park are three mildly active volcanoes—Mount Ruapehu (9,175 ft.); permanently snowcapped; Mount Ngauruhoe (7,515 ft.); and Mount Tongariro (6,458 ft.). Curiously, it is the lesser mountain which gives its name to the park. They huddle close together, as if for protection.

Ruapehu still has a steaming lake in its snow fringed crater. Ngauruhoe, an almost perfect cone, still sends up occasional puffs of steam; and Tongariro, which blew its top countless years ago, still has warm slopes in places.

The park is a tribute to Maori generosity and wisdom. In 1886, to avoid other tribal claims and the inevitable sale of the land to Europeans, Te Heuheu Tukino, hereditary chief of the Ngati Tuwharetoa tribe, gave the land to the government ("It shall be a sacred place of the Crown and a gift for ever from me and my people"). There is a succinct tribal proverb: *"Ko Tongariro te Maunga; ko Taupo te Moana; ko Te Heheu te Tangata"*—"Tongariro is the mountain; Taupo is the sea; Te Heuheu is the man".

There are many Maori legends about the mountains, but the most popular is that there were once more of them in the park, and all were in love with the womanly Mount Pihanga, to the north. They fought, and the vanquished were banished, but they could move only during the hours of darkness, and now remain in parts of the North Island where daylight touched them. One, Mount Taranaki, hurried westward, scouring the course of the Wanganui River as he went, and by daylight reached the position by the sea where he still stands.

From late spring through fall the mountains are bare of snow except for the upper slopes of Ruapehu, but in winter all are deeply snowcovered. Ruapehu is the North Island's most popular ski resort and has chairlifts and ski tows to the upper ski fields. Many ski and mountain clubs have huts here.

There are pleasant walks through the native bush, and at the National Park Headquarters there is a fine exhibit of the park's geology, flora and fauna. There is also a good golf course, and tennis courts.

Tauranga

Finding the Maoris of the east coast of the North Island hospitable, Captain Cook named the area the Bay of Plenty. In the production of dairy products, meat, and fruit, it is still a region of plenty. Its principal city and port is Tauranga, with a population of 48,000. Not far away is Maketu, the landing place of the *Arawa* canoe in the great migration from Hawaiki.

Tauranga's genial climate made it chiefly a retirement area, and center for holidays and big game fishing. Now its character is changing, but it has lost nothing of its charm. It is now a modern, thriving city, supported by the export of lumber from the man-made pine forests near Rotorua, 55 miles away, and farming.

Two narrow entrances open to a sheltered harbor. The city is on the western side, and opposite, at the tip of a peninsula, is Mount Maunganui, standing like a sentinel at the entrance. Sweeping beaches and good swimming make this a popular holiday resort. Off the coast is Mayor Island, the main big game fishing center.

Tauranga was the site of the most chivalrous battle in the wars with the Maoris. In 1864, to prevent supplies and reinforcements reaching Maoris who were fighting inland, the government sent troops to build two redoubts. Hearing this, the Ngaiterangi tribe hurried back and built a *pa* some miles inland. But no soldiers came. Mystified, the chief, Rawairi Puhirake, sent a letter to the commanding officer at Tauranga advising him of the presence of the *pa* and the fact that his followers had built 10 miles of road "so that the soldiers would not be too weary to fight." Still no soldiers came, so a second *pa* was built closer to Tauranga. It become known as Gate Pa as it stood near the entrance to the Christian mission.

The first two British assaults failed, and as night fell a remarkable incident of chivalry occurred. Hearing a wounded British officer begging for water as he lay near the outer ramparts of the *pa*, a Maori woman crept through the British lines with a rusty can, filled it at a small creek, and made the dangerous journey back to give it to the officer and four others. The British finally managed to storm the *pa*, but the Maoris had slipped quietly away to fight again elsewhere.

Tauranga Mission House

Better known as the Elms, it was built between 1838 and 1847 by Archdeacon A. N. Brown, and contains the original furnishings.

Tauranga District Museum

A blacksmith's shop, a colonial section, and an exhibition depicting the development of Maori culture and the growth of Tauranga are featured at the Tauranga District Museum.

Gisborne

Because of its closeness to the International Date Line, Gisborne claims to be the most easterly city in the world, and the first on which the sun shines.

It was at Gisborne that Europeans first landed on New Zealand soil. Knowing that he must be near land, Captain Cook offered a gallon of rum to the first man to sight land, and promised that the part seen would be named after him. On October 7, 1769, Nicholas Young, a

THE NORTH ISLAND

twelve-year-old cabin boy, sighted a headland, which was promptly named Young Nick's Head.

Two days later Cook led a party ashore at Kaiti Beach—the spot is marked with a memorial. A series of misunderstandings led to bloodshed, and Cook sailed away. He named the area Poverty Bay "because it afforded us no one thing we wanted."

Contrary to Cook's description, Poverty Bay is anything but poor, but a highly productive area for lambs, corn, vegetables, citrus fruit, grapes and wine.

Kaiti Hill Lookout

From the summit of Kaiti Hill there are splendid views of the city and the long sweep of the bay, including Young Nick's Head. At the foot of the hill is one of the largest Maori Meeting houses in New Zealand.

"Star of Canada" House

The bridge of a 7,280 ton ship in a city street! In 1912 the *Star of Canada* was wrecked on Kaiti Beach. The superstructure was salvaged and reconstructed as a house, which is now used as a private residence.

Napier

Napier is a phoenix city, risen from the ashes. Without warning on February 3, 1931, a severe earthquake shook the province of Hawke's Bay, and was felt further afield. Much of the city and many houses in the suburbs were flattened and fire ravaged a good deal of what remained. Hills crumbled and crevices opened in the roads. The Ahuriri lagoon was raised and over 8,000 acres of new land arose from the sea bed. Today, factories and the airport are on this new land.

Out of the chaos order was restored in a surprisingly short time. Napier was rebuilt as a modern city, and now has a population of 50,000.

Standing at the center of the wide sweep of Hawke's Bay, Napier's pride is the Marine Parade fronting the city. Lined for two miles with graceful Norfolk pines, it has beautiful sunken gardens, a dolphin pool, a concert auditorium, a roller skating rink and an aquarium.

On the parade stands the graceful bronze statue of Pania of the Reef. Maori legend has it that Pania, one of the Sea People, left them to live with her human lover, Karitoki. But she yielded to the constant calls of her people to return, and swam out to meet them. From the caverns of the sea they came to draw her down, keeping her forever from her lover. And so Pania sits, gazing forlornly out to the sea.

Exploring Napier

Regular sightseeing tours are run by Cox World Travel and also by taxi companies. Features at Napier are the formal botanic gardens and the lookout from Bluff Hills, affording panoramic views of the bay.

Cape Kidnappers Gannet Sanctuary

Cape Kidnappers, a cliff-faced promontory jutting into the sea at the southern end of Hawke's Bay, was named by Captain Cook because here the Maoris tried to kidnap his interpreter, a Tahitian boy.

Only recently has an overland route been opened to the gannet sanctuary. 22 miles (35.5km) from Napier, it is the world's only mainland gannet colony. At the cape visitors can obtain excellent views of the gannets, and walk quite close to the nesting birds. There are between 12,000 and 13,000 birds at the sanctuary in the height of the season, which is between November and February.

A fully-grown gannet weighs about 5 lb. and has a wing span of 5 ft. Eggs are laid in October, and take about six weeks to hatch. The chicks are fully fledged at 12 weeks and fly after 16 weeks. Migration of the chicks and dispersal of the adult birds occurs in February and March, and by April most birds have gone. Because of the rugged nature of the terrain, visits can be made only in special vehicles on tours run by Gannet Safaris.

Hastings

13 miles (21km) south of Napier is Hastings, with a population of 51,000. There is friendly rivalry between the two cities; each has, for instance, its own daily newspaper.

It is a well-kept city, proud of its parks, gardens, and streets. Closer to the fertile sheep farming country of Hawke's Bay and to large vegetable and fruit farms, Hastings is more of a commercial center. There are a number of food processing plants, including Wattie's Canneries, which cans and quick-freezes huge quantities of vegetables and fruit. It is the largest and most complex plant of its kind in the southern hemisphere. Nearby meat-packing plants process about three million head of sheep and cattle annually.

Although most New Zealand wine is produced in the Auckland area, there are large vineyards near Hastings and Napier. The larger wineries, which welcome visitors, include Greenmeadows, a Catholic mission which is possibly New Zealand's oldest vineyard. It produces a variety of excellent table wines. Vidals Wines were founded in 1902 in converted racing stables; their wines are now well known and also sold in Australia. At nearby Havelock North, T.M.V. Wines runs the oldest commercial vineyard in the country. North of Napier, Glenvale Wines are one of the largest producers.

Hastings is the host city for two popular annual events: the Cherry Blossom Festival in October and the Highland Games at Easter, when the city resounds to the skirl of bagpipes and competitions are held in Highland dancing and sports.

New Plymouth

The perfect cone of Mount Egmont (8,260 ft.) dominates the province of Taranaki, which was also the Maori name for the mountain. It is a dormant, but not extinct, volcano. The ash from its ancient eruptions has made the land fertile, particularly for dairying, and Taranaki exports large quantities of cheese.

Below the northeastern slope of the mountain is the city of New Plymouth (population 43,000). Though a commercial center, it is a well-planned and attractive city.

It is also New Zealand's main hope for new sources of energy. Oil was found in the suburb of Moturoa as early as 1856, only seven years after the first discoveries in the United States, but the yields were small. Drilling in what is known as the Maui field, some distance off the coast, is raising hopes of a more bountiful supply. In 1962 natural gas was discovered at Kapuni and is now piped to various points of the North Island and provides considerable quantities of oil condensate for shipment to the oil refinery at Whangarei, north of Auckland.

THE NORTH ISLAND

Pukekura Park

Once a wasteland, this area was transformed by voluntary labor into a delightful park. One of the outstanding features is a small lake, surrounded by tree ferns, with the cone of Mount Egmont forming a perfect backdrop. At night an elaborate illuminated fountain plays in the lower of the park's two lakes and makes a colorful spectacle.

Adjoining Pukekura Park is Brooklands Park, where a natural amphitheater can seat over 16,000 people. A lake in front of the soundshell mirrors performances of drama, ballet, opera and music for the Festival of the Pines held in January and February.

Taranaki Museum

An excellent collection of early Maori sculpture and Maori carvings done with original stone tools may be seen in this museum, which also contains the stone anchor of the Tokomaru canoe, part of an early canoe fleet.

Pukeiti Rhododendron Trust

Any lover of flowers will be enthralled by this world-famous 900-acre park of rhododendrons and azaleas 18 miles (29km) from New Plymouth. It is at its best between September and November. There are about 900 species, all of which grow better in this climate than in their native habitat. Japanese nurserymen have been sending seedlings to the extensive nursery of Duncan & Davies; from which, after two years, they are shipped back, having grown as much as they would in five years in Japan.

Wanganui

One of New Zealand's oldest cities, Wanganui (population 38,000), stands near the mouth of the Wanganui River, which rises in the Tongariro National Park in the center of the North Island. The river was used as a canoe highway by the Maoris, and until recent years was navigated for more than 100 miles by launch, but this mode of transport gradually declined as roads were built.

The real beauty of the river is a 20-mile section upstream from Pipiriki, 49 miles (79km) from Wanganui, known as the Drop Scene. Here the river is confined to narrow, fern-clad gorges, where small waterfalls cascade down through the bush, and the water is churned into foam by rapids. The full-day trip is now done by jet boats.

Durie Hill

Panoramic views of the city and surrounding countryside can be obtained from the tower on Durie Hill (300 ft.). A road leads to the summit, which can also be reached by an elevator inside the hill.

Wanganui Museum

The Wanganui Museum has a good Maori collection, and New Zealand's first church organ, which has no keyboard and is operated like a pianola by a rotating cylinder.

Sarjeant Gallery

The Sarjeant Gallery displays a good selection of British and New Zealand painters of the nineteenth and twentieth centuries.

WELLINGTON

"Like San Francisco" say Californians when they survey the city from the surrounding hills. And it *is* rather like San Francisco. Its wide, circular harbor lies in a basin of steep hills, the shops and offices cluster near the waterfront, and it even has a cable car! As the lights glow at night it resembles Hong Kong.

Wellington stands at the southwest tip of the North Island, and only a 20-mile stretch of water, Cook Strait, separates it from the northern tip of the South Island. The gap is bridged by 4,000 ton passenger-vehicle ferries which cross the strait frequently every day.

It is known as Windy Wellington. Cook Strait seems to funnel every breeze that blows and expand it into a wind. Most are gentle to moderate, but in the spring and fall they become strong. They are not unbearable, and at least they prevent air pollution. Other cities have a joke: "You can always identify a Wellingtonian because he grabs his hat when he rounds a corner."

Wellington is the capital city, and a large proportion of Wellingtonians work in government departments, whose head offices are here—rather like Washington D.C. Many national business concerns also have their head offices in Wellington, though there is a gradual migration to Auckland, where the factories are tending to concentrate.

The combined urban areas have a population of about 354,000, making it the second largest city. The number in the city boundaries is, however, much less, as there are large residential and light industrial areas in the adjoining Hutt Valley and Porirua basin. Lower Hutt and Upper Hutt are cities in their own right.

Wellington is justly proud of its magnificent harbor, a huge circular basin reached through a channel from Cook Strait and hemmed by steep hills. As the settlement grew from its small beginnings problems arose. There just wasn't enough flat land. The extension of the business areas was achieved by reclaiming land from the harbor. One of the main streets, Lambton Quay, is no longer a waterfront and is now about a quarter of a mile from the docks. From the waterside the hills rise so steeply that in some of the modern buildings you can enter a shop or office block at street level, ascend in an elevator to the second or third floors and exit at a door, still at street level.

Finding sites for homes also posed problems, and many houses climb dizzily up the hills, clinging to apparently sheer slopes. Many are built on stilts, and some even have their own small private cable cars.

There was only one way for the city to go—up. Wellington's two and three-story office and shop buildings are giving way to small skyscrapers. The height of the buildings was originally kept low, not because tall buildings were not originally needed, but as a precaution against possible earthquakes. Modern design and construction have, however, overcome the latter danger.

Named after the Duke of Wellington, who won the Battle of Waterloo between the British and the French, Wellington was settled by a company formed in England by Edward Gibbon Wakefield. The first

THE NORTH ISLAND

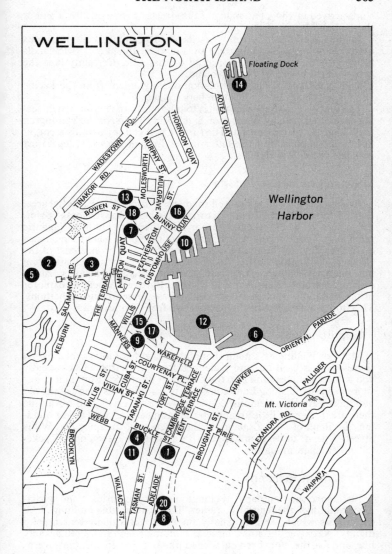

Points of Interest

1) Basin Reserve (Cricket and Soccer)
2) Botanical Gardens
3) Cable Car
4) Carillon & Hall of Memories
5) Carter Observatory
6) Freyberg Pool
7) Government Buildings
8) Government House
9) N.Z. Travel Office
10) Main Docks
11) National Art Gallery and Museum
12) Overseas Shipping Terminal
13) Parliament House
14) Picton Ferry Terminal
15) Post Office
16) Railway Station
17) Town Hall
18) War Memorial
19) Wellington Airport
20) Zoo

ships arrived in 1840, and many of the streets are named after them or the British leaders of the day.

In 1865 Wellington became New Zealand's capital. It adopted as its motto *Suprema a Situ,* supreme by situation. In spite of Auckland's faster growth, it still holds proudly to that title. Certainly it is the geographical center of New Zealand.

Like Auckland, it has a population of Polynesians from the Pacific Islands, although in smaller numbers.

The best way to see Wellington is to take one of the half-day sightseeing coach tours run by Wellington Sightseeing Tours, or the Wellington City Transport Corporation. The former will call, by arrangement, at hotels and motels, and the latter leaves from Rotary Garden Court opposite the Town Hall.

Summit of Mount Victoria

Reached by a winding but well-made road through a residential area, the 558-ft. summit of Mount Victoria is the best known vantage point. From here the whole city and harbor seem to spread out like a gigantic relief map. To the west, the northern tip of the South Island can be seen on a clear day. In the roofed observation deck is a bronze bust of the Duke of Wellington staring austerely, not at the city named after him but, strangely enough, away from it. A short distance away is a stone cairn memorial to Rear Admiral Richard Byrd, an American explorer of the Antarctic who used New Zealand as a base for his expeditions. The stones embedded in the cement are from Antarctica.

Lambton Quay

Much of Wellington's main shopping area either follows the original shoreline or is built on land reclaimed from the harbor. Occasionally you will see plaques sunk into the pavement inscribed "Shoreline." For shopping, a stroll along Lambton Quay is absorbing, as many of the old buildings have been demolished and new ones erected, and for a mile there are intriguing little arcades, terminating at the city's tallest building, the Bank of New Zealand, at the junction of the quay and Willis Street. With its underground plaza, it's a little like New York's Rockefeller Center in miniature.

Parliament Buildings

Just above the Cenotaph, Wellington's war memorial, stand parliament buildings, the legislative center. The main marble buildings lack the towers which were originally intended but still present a solid dignity. At one end is a new circular building which looks remarkably like, and has therefore been christened, the Beehive. Inside, the government messengers will conduct you on a tour of the legislative offices.

Government Buildings

Below Parliament Buildings is one of the largest wooden buildings in the world. Of 100,300 square feet, the government buildings, which house several departments, are a source of pride to Wellingtonians.

Alexander Turnbull Library

Just a short block up Bowen Street (behind the Cenotaph), a walk of 100 yards or so brings you to the Terrace (a long street parallel with

THE NORTH ISLAND

Lambton Quay and the site of many of Wellington's tall commercial buildings). At Number 44 is the Alexander Turnbull Library. This is as much a museum as a library in that it contains a priceless collection of historic documents and many rare first editions. Included in the displays are the original signed sheets of the Treaty of Waitangi.

Old St. Paul's Cathedral

The Church of England's new cathedral faces Parliament Buildings on the corner of Hill and Molesworth Streets, but on Mulgrave Street, just a couple of blocks north, is Old St. Paul's Cathedral. This is one of the finest examples of a wooden church built in the early days. It was so much part of Wellington's history, and so beloved, that it is now preserved as a national shrine. The interior is exquisite.

Kelburn Lookout

A ride on the cable car should not be missed for the magnificent views of the city and harbor from the 480-ft. summit at Kelburn. The entrance to the city terminal is along a lane off Lambton Quay. Unlike the San Francisco cable cars, the car simply climbs a hill and then returns. It travels at a constant angle of about 15 degrees. Try to get seats on the left-hand side as the car ascends, and in front for the best views as the car descends. The car passes through three short tunnels and makes three intermediate stops before reaching the summit. The cars run frequently, and the return trip can be made after you have enjoyed the view.

Memorial Gates to the Second American Marine Division

As the Japanese began moving down the South Pacific, the Second American Marine Division made Wellington its headquarters. They were based at McKay's Crossing (a railroad crossing) near Paekakariki, some 30 miles north of Wellington on the main highway. From here they embarked for the bloodbath of Guadalcanal. The Memorial Gates, recalling the 17 months spent there by the division, stand at the entrance to the former camp.

Tramway Museum

Close by is a Tramway Museum, founded to preserve Wellington's trolley cars, now replaced by buses. The old trolley cars still run on a ¾-mile track in Queen Elizabeth Park.

Botanic Gardens and Lady Norwood Rose Garden

From a bus stop at the start of Lambton Quay (look for a bus with a "Karori" destination sign), a three-minute ride will take you to the entrance of the Botanic Gardens, 62 acres of native bush and exotic plants. Tulip Day especially (early October) demands a visit. Just a short distance down from the entrance to the gardens is the Lady Norwood Rose Garden, which is a profusion of blooms from summer thru fall. There is also a begonia house (open 10 A.M. to 4 P.M.).

National Museum and Art Gallery

On a mount overlooking the city and harbor stands the National Museum and National Art Gallery, fronted by the War Memorial

Carillon Tower, with its Shrine of Remembrance. It is a landmark which can be seen from most parts of the city. The Maori section contains many authentic carvings and artifacts, including a meeting house which is considered to be the finest surviving example of its kind. There are some relics of Captain Cook, including the original figurehead from his ship *Resolution,* which he used on his second and third voyages to New Zealand. The colonial section shows early European life in New Zealand and features an "Early Wellington House" complete with furnishings. The museum is not directly serviced by public transport but is an inexpensive taxi ride from the city.

Directly opposite the city center is the dormitory seaside suburb of Eastbourne and to the northeast a four-lane motorway leads to the Hutt Valley, which is a mixture of light industry and pleasant suburban homes. Through the valley meanders the Hutt River.

First suburb to be reached, six miles out, is Petone, on the shores of the harbor, and it was here that the early settlers first landed. Just four miles farther on is the garden city of Lower Hutt, and some ten miles farther is Trentham, site of Wellington's main racecourse, leading to the city of Upper Hutt just beyond.

The route continues through farming areas, over the winding Rimutaka Hill and down to the Wairarapa Plains, one of the country's finest sheep-farming areas. The main town of Masterton (population about 20,000) is about 1½ hours' drive from Wellington.

Wellington's main highway north, however, branches to the left at Ngauranga, some five miles out of the city, climbs the steep Ngauranga Gorge and continues on a motorway until it descends to the sea on the west coast of the island at Paekakariki.

This is the start of "the Golden Coast" (or the Kapiti Coast) with its uncluttered and pleasant bathing beaches. Particularly popular with Wellingtonians is Paraparaumu Beach, some 35 miles out of the city and a developing retirement area on this coast.

Just off the beach is Kapiti Island, once a stronghold of the marauding Maori warrior Te Rauparaha and now a bird sanctuary.

In clear weather the northern tip of the South Island may be seen across Cook Strait to the south.

PRACTICAL INFORMATION FOR THE NORTH ISLAND

ACCOMMODATIONS. New Zealand does not have "super luxury" hotels, but the better hotels are somewhat similar to the Hilton type, although styles vary. The average room rate ranges from NZ$85 to NZ$145, and motels from NZ$45 to NZ$60. The cities and scenic resorts are well served with good quality hotels and motels, but advance reservations, especially from Christmas through February, are advisable.

Many motels have fully equipped kitchens where you can cook your own meals; others have only tea and coffee-making facilities; some serve breakfast.

Some remote scenic areas are served by Tourist Hotel Corporation hotels (prefixed by the letters THC), which have high-quality accommodations, in the middle of mountains, lakes or fiords.

AUCKLAND

Airport Inn. Ascot and Kirkbride rds., Mangere (close to airport); (09) 275–7029. 100 rooms, restaurant, bar, pool.

Airport TraveLodge. Ascot and Kirkbride Rds.; (09) 275–1059. 253 rooms, high quality. Restaurants, bars, parking, pool.

Barrycourt Motel. 10–20 Gladstone Rd., Parnell; (09) 33–789. 126 rooms. Restaurant, bar.

Earls Court Motor Inn. 104 Gladstone Rd., Parnell; (09) 774–477. 25 serviced units, 2km (1¼ mi.) from city. Restaurant, bar.

Hyatt Kingsgate. Prince St. and Waterloo Quadrant; (09) 797–220. 327 rooms, restaurants, bars, Jacuzzis, jogging track. One of the most expensive Auckland hotels.

Mon Desir Hotel. 144 Hurstmere Rd., Takapuna (on the North Shore); (09) 495–139. 37 rooms, restaurant, bar pool, sauna.

Quality Inn. 150 Anzac Ave.; (09) 798–509. 110 service units. Central location.

Regent of Auckland. Albert St., central; (09) 398–882. 332 rooms, restaurants, bars, parking, top quality.

Rose Park Motor Inn. 100 Gladstone Rd., Parnell; (09) 773–619. 110 units. Restaurant, bar.

Royal International Hotel. Victoria St. W.; (09) 31–359. 98 rooms, restaurant, bars, refrigerators in rooms.

Sheraton-Auckland Hotel. 85 Symonds St.; (09) 795–132. 410 rooms, 28 executive rooms. Top quality, central location, pool, bars, parking, sauna, spa, gym.

South Pacific Hotel. Customs St.; (09) 778–920. 184 rooms, restaurants, bars, refrigerators in rooms.

Takapuna Beach Motel. The Promenade, Takapuna; (09) 493–356. 28 units and studios with kitchens, bars; restaurant close by.

TraveLodge. 96 Quay St.; (09) 770–349. 198 rooms, restaurant, bars, parking.

Vacation Hotel. 187 Campbell Rd.; (09) 664–179. 222 rooms, restaurant, bar, parking, 5 mi. from city.

White Heron Regency. 138 St. Stephen's Ave.; (09) 796–860. 75 rooms, restaurant, bar.

BAY OF ISLANDS (PAIHIA)

Autolodge Motor Inn. Marsden Rd.; (0885) 27–416. 50 rooms, restaurant, bar, pool, parking.

Bushby Manor Motor Inn. Marsden Rd.; (0885) 27–527. 17 suites, nearby restaurant, pool, parking.

Casa Bella Motel. McMurray Rd.; (0885) 27–387. 16 units, parking.

Paihia Sands Motor Lodge. Marsden Rd.; (0885) 27–707. 8 units, restaurant, parking.

THC Waitangi. (0885) 27–411. 111 rooms, restaurants, bar, parking.

GISBORNE

Quality Inn. Huxley and Tyndall rds., Box 113; (079) 84–109. 26 rooms, restaurant, bars.

Sandown Park Motor Hotel. Childers Rd.; (079) 84–134. 35 rooms, restaurant, bars.

HAMILTON

Quality Inn Glenview. Ohaupo Rd.; (071) 436–049. 18 rooms, all facilities, restaurant, cocktail bar.

Quality Inn, Riverina Hotel. Grey St. across the river; (071) 69–049. 12 doubles, 31 singles, restaurant, cocktail bar.

Waikato Motor Hotel. Main highway at Te Rapa; (071) 494–959. 18 rooms, all facilities, restaurant, cocktail bar.

HASTINGS

Angus Inn Motor Hotel. Railway Rd.; 88–177. 58 rooms, restaurant, bar, parking, 5 minutes' walk to the city's center, adjacent to the racecourse.

Fantasyland Motels. Sylvan Rd.; 68–159. 19 rooms, private facilities but no restaurant or bars.

NAPIER

Masonic Hotel. Marine Parade; (070) 58–689. 18 rooms with facilities, 49 without, restaurant, bars.

Tennyson Motor Inn. Emerson St.; (070) 53–373. 42 rooms, restaurant, bars, parking.

TraveLodge. Marine Parade; (070) 53–237. 60 rooms, restaurant, bars, parking.

NEW PLYMOUTH

Devon Motor Lodge. 382 Devon St.; 86–149. 135 rooms, cabaret, pool, sauna, gym.

The Plymouth. Leach, Hobson, and Courtenay sts.; 80–589. 75 rooms, suites. Restaurants, bars, parking.

Quality Inn. 15 Bell Block; 70–558. Restaurant, bars, pool.

Westown Motor Hotel. Maratau St.; 87–697. Restaurant, bars, pool.

ROTORUA

Geyserland Motor Hotel. Fenton St.; (073) 82–039. 76 rooms, restaurant, bars, thermal pool, massage facilities golf course, pool.

Kingsgate. Eruera St. (073) 477–677. Deluxe resort with 233 rooms, Health center, some Jacuzzis, restaurants, bars, parking.

Muriaroha Lodge. 411 Old Taupo Rd., 2 miles from city center; (073) 88–136. Small, intimate, family-operated, exclusive hideaway on secluded grounds, beautifully landscaped. 7 suites and 2 bungalows furnished with antiques. Restaurant, bar, parking. Relatively expensive.

Okawa Bay Lake Resort. Lake Rotoiti, 12 miles from Rotorua on shores of Lake Rotoiti; phone Okere Falls 599 through long-distance operator. 44 rooms. Restaurant, bar, sauna, marina. Ideal for trout anglers. Relatively expensive.

Quality Inn. Fenton Park.; (073) 80–199. 74 rooms, restaurant, bars, heated pool.

Sheraton-Rotorua Hotel. Fenton St.; (073) 81–189. 144 rooms, restaurants, bars, roof-top pool, entertainment, spa, parking; top quality.

THC Rotorua Hotel. Froude St.; (073) 81–189. 150 units, restaurant, bars, refrigerators in rooms, thermal baths and pool.

THE NORTH ISLAND

TraveLodge Motor Inn. Eruera St.; (073) 81–174. 210 rooms, restaurant, bar, thermal pool.
Voyager Resort. Ranolf St.; (073) 88–149. 42 hotel rooms, 44 motel rooms. Restaurant, bar, parking.
There are also a large number of good quality motels, all rooms with private bath and toilet, some with thermal pools.

TAUPO

Berkenhoff Tourist Hotel. Corner Duncan and Scannell sts.; (074) 84–909. 1½ miles from town, restaurant, bar, parking.
De Brett Thermal Hotel/Motel. Napier Hwy.; (074) 87–080. 2 miles from town, restaurant, bar, parking.
Huka Lodge. 2 miles from town on banks of Waikato River; (074) 85–791. Mainly for anglers, restaurant, bar, parking.
Manuels Motor Inn. Lake Terrace; (074) 85–110. Restaurant, bar, parking, pool, fishing, sauna.
Suncourt Motor Hotel. Northcroft St.; (074) 88–265. 52 units, restaurant, bar, parking.
Tui Oaks Motor Inn. Lake Terrace; (074) 88–305. 23 units, serviced rooms and units. Restaurants, bars, parking.

TAURANGA

18th Avenue Motels. 50 18th Ave.; (075) 83–179. 21 rooms, no bars or restaurant, but breakfast available.
Tauranga Motor Inn. 15th Ave. and Turret. Rd.; (075) 85–041. 22 new units with thermal pools, cooking facilities.
Willow Park Motor Hotel. Willow St.; (075) 89–119. 44 rooms, restaurant, bar, parking.

TONGARIRO NATIONAL PARK

THC Chateau Tongariro. A Tourist Hotel Corporation hotel on the slopes of Mount Ruapehu; phone 899 Ruapehu. 84 rooms, all facilities, heated, restaurant, bars.

WAIRAKEI

THC Wairakei Hotel. 48–021 Taupo. 75 rooms, restaurant, bar, thermal swimming pool, golf.

WAITOMO CAVES

Waitomo Country Lodge. 17 rooms, restaurant, cocktail bar.
THC Waitomo Hotel. Phone 948 Te Kuiti. Run by the Tourist Hotel Corporation, an oldish but redecorated hotel featuring solid comfort and good meals, 26 rooms with facilities, 17 without, restaurant, cocktail bar.

WANGANUI

Bryvern Motor Inn. 321 Victoria Ave.; (064) 58–408. Restaurant, bars, parking.
Hurley's Grand International Hotel. 99 Guyton St.; (064) 50–955. Restaurant, bars.
Wangunui Motel. 14 Alma Rd.; (064) 54–742. Restaurant, bar, pool.

WELLINGTON

Burma Motor Lodge. Burma Rd., Johnsonville, 8 miles from city; (04) 784–909. 63 rooms, restaurant, bar, parking.
Hotel St. George. Willis St.; (04) 739–139. 88 rooms, restaurant, bars, central.
Hotel Waterloo. Waterloo Quay and Bunny St.; (04) 728–255. 85 rooms, restaurant, bar, opposite railroad station.

James Cook Hotel. The Terrace; (04) 725–865. 270 rooms, restaurant, bars, parking.
Melksham Towers. Brougham and Ellis Sts.; (04) 851–569. Motel flats, 39 units. No liquor facilities or restaurant.
Parkroyal Hotel. 360 Oriental Bay; (04) 859–949. 70 rooms, high quality, restaurants, bars, parking.
Quality Inn. 100 Oriental Parade; (04) 850–279. 122 rooms, restaurant, bar.
Sharella Motor Inn. 20 Glenmore St.; (04) 723–823. 66 rooms, restaurant, bar, parking, ½ mile from city.
Shaw Savill Lodge. Kemp St., Kilbirnie; (04) 872–189. 122 rooms, restaurant, bar, parking, 4 miles from city, 1 mile from airport.
Terrace Regency. 345 The Terrace; (04) 859–829. High quality, 122 rooms suites, pool, bars, restaurant, parking.
Wellington Travelodge. 40 Oriental Parade; (04) 857–799. 78 rooms, restaurant, bar.
West Plaza Hotel. 110–116 Wakefield St.; (04) 731–440. 102 rooms, restaurant, bar, central.

Home hospitality can be arranged by **Cottage Meals & Tours.** Don and Margaret Hoare, (04) 889–124, organize meetings and dining with New Zealanders in their homes and also home-stay stopovers. Sample charges: Bed and breakfast $56; dinner, bed, and breakfast $70; home-cooked dinner $38 (all based on 2 persons). Tour with car and driver, $22 per hr.

RESTAURANTS. New Zealand has few first-class restaurants of the quality one would expect to find in the larger cities of Europe and America. However, over the past few years, restaurants serving more interesting and sophisticated cuisine have flourished. Good food is not hard to find, for New Zealand has an abundance of excellent and relatively inexpensive raw materials. Steak, lamb, and seafood are world-renown. New Zealand wine, like American, is variable in quality, but some reds and a great many white wines are well worth trying.

All the major hotels contain restaurants, and the larger cities, especially Auckland and Wellington, contain smaller establishments that serve attractive meals. You may pay anything from NZ$20 to NZ$40 per person for a three-course meal, but the cost is usually determined by the quality of the food rather than the reputation of the chef, or current fashion in dining. The most elegant restaurants can be more expensive.

By New Zealand law, restaurant staff are paid a living wage and do not depend upon tips for their livelihood. It is not necessary, then, to leave a tip, but your kindness will be appreciated if you do.

There are a number of smaller restaurants of the diner variety where a meal of steak and French fries can be had for as little as NZ$8. In these, however, you cannot obtain alcoholic beverages. Many more expensive restaurants also lack a liquor license, but some will allow you to bring in your own wine.

AUCKLAND

Antoine's. 333 Parnell Rd.; 798–756. Traditional French colonial atmosphere, French cuisine.
Bonaparte Restaurant. Victoria and High sts.; 797–896. Empire period decor, French cuisine and traditional New Zealand dishes.
Carthews. 151 Ponsonby Rd.; 766–056. American cuisine, creole cooking.
Clichy Restaurant. 3 Britomart Pl.; 31–744. French provincial atmosphere, all French cuisine.
Da Gino. 66–68 Pitt St.; 770–973. Appropriate Italian decor and exclusively Italian food.
Fisherman's Wharf. Northcote Point; 483–955. Harborside nautical atmosphere, predominantly seafood menu.
Gamekeeper's. 29 Ponsonby Rd.; 789–052. Hunting lodge decor, game and local foods.
Le Gourmet. 1 Williamson Ave., Ponsonby; 769–499. Late-Victorian decor, limited specialized menu.
Harleys. 25 Anzav Ave.; 735–801. New Zealand food, with embellishments. B.Y.O.A.

THE NORTH ISLAND

Hoffman's. 70 Jervois Rd., Herne Bay; 762–049. Award-winning restaurant with cocktail lounge and open fireplaces. Closed weekends.
Number Five. 5 City Rd.; 770–909. Top quality, superlative French nouvelle cuisine.
Oblio's. 110 Ponsonby Rd., Ponsonby; 763–041. An "indoor garden" restaurant, tasteful decor, and good food.
Orient. Strand Arcade, Queen St.; 797–793. Elegant Chinese decor with Chinese cuisine.
Orsini's. 50 Ponsonby Rd.; 764–563. Fine food in elegant surroundings.
Papillon. 170 Jervois Rd., Herne Bay; 765–367. Well-prepared and beautifully presented food; courtyard for pleasant summer dining. B.Y.O.
Sardi's Restaurant & Piano Bar. Queens Arcades; 790–876. Good food in ultra smart surroundings.
Union Fish Company. 16 Quay St.; 796–745. Old renovated warehouse, unpreposing exterior but seafood is tops.
Yamato. 183 Karangahape Rd.; 771–424. Traditional Japanese food.

NAPIER

The Beachcomber. 90 Marine Parade; 58–303. Nothing pretentious but good Indonesian food. BYO.
Italian Restaurant. Emerson St.; 54–181. Strictly Italian food and inexpensive.
Pickwick's Restaurant. Marine Parade; 56–120. Top quality with imaginative menu featuring New Zealand food.
La Ronde. Marine Parade; 58–180. French-style cuisine, limited but good menu.

NEW PLYMOUTH

L'Escargot. 51 Devon St.; 84–812. French provincial, small and compact.
Juliana's. 393 Devon St. E.; 88–044. Flambé a specialty.
Rafters. 282a Devon St. E.; 88–731. Intimate dining and good food.
Ratanui Colonial Restaurant. 498 Carrington Rd.; 34–415. Old homestead out of town; graceful dining with fine silverware.

ROTORUA

Aorangi Peak. Mountain Rd.; 86–957. 7 miles from the city, magnificent views, good food.
Becky Brown's. Travel-center end of Tutanekai St., 87–071. New Zealand game and seafood, licensed.
Bushman's Hut. 167 Tutanekai St.; 83–285. Decorated as such, seafood and wild game.
Caesars. Arawa St.; 70–984. Modern decor, international menu, licensed.
Colonel's Retreat. Little Village, Tryon St., Whakarewarewa; 81–519. International menu, jazz some nights.
Friar Tuck. Arawa and Tutanekai sts.; 81–492. Quiet atmosphere and good steaks.
The Gourmet. 41 Arawa St.; 87–237. French cuisine, BYO.
Hoo Wah. 85–025. Chinese food, dine and dance Saturday.
Keets Licensed Cafe. Hinemoa St.; 83–721. Opposite post office, live music.
Landmark. 1 Meade St.; 89–376. Early colonial decor, elegant; top New Zealand food.
Lewishams. 115 Tutanekai St.; 81–786. Tastefully quiet, good service, good food.
Rendezvous. Hinemoa St.; 89–273. Seafood a specialty, colonial atmosphere.
Rumours. Pukuatua St.; 477–277. Continental–nouvelle cuisine, modern decor, BYO.
Sinbad's Licensed Seafood Restaurant. Geyser Court, Eruera St.; 85–107. Seafood and live entertainment Thursday and Saturday.
Suaves Restaurant & Cocktail Bar. Memorial Dr.; 82–001. Lakefront, cocktail and piano bar.
Tudor Towers. Government Gardens; 81–285. Cabaret and dancing.

TAURANGA

Checkers Restaurant. 265 Otumoetai Rd.; 69–955. A la carte, BYO.
Olivers Restaurant. 111 Devonport Rd.; 86–704. Seafood and international cuisine.
Sierra Bianca. Marine Parade, Mount Maunganui. Continental dishes, steaks, lobster.
Top Hat International Restaurant. Main Road, Mount Maunganui. Steak and seafood.

WANGANUI

Bonne Maison. 321 Victoria Ave.; 58–408. French classical and nouvelle in turn-of-the-century surroundings.
Golden Oaks. 112 Liverpool St.; 58–309. European and New Zealand food.
Joseph's Restaurant. 13 Victoria Ave.; 55–825. Traditional New Zealand food.

WELLINGTON

Acropolis. 37 Dixon St.; 859–057. Specializes in Greek food.
Bacchus Restaurant. 8 Courtenay Pl.; 846–592. Quiet, intimate, wide range of dishes.
Beefeater's Arms. 105 The Terrace; 738–195. Tudor decor, popular for business lunches. Specialty is rib of beef on the bone.
The Coachman. 46 Courtenay Pl.; 848–200. Small and exclusive, concentrates on good food, quiet atmosphere. Specialties are duckling, scallops, and crayfish.
Il Casino and Il Salone. 108 Tory St.; 857–496. Good traditional Italian cuisine.
Genghis Khan Mongolian Restaurant. 25–27 Majoribanks St.; 843–592. Mongolian style barbecue fare set in a pleasant decor.
Grain of Salt. 232 Oriental Parade; 848–642. Contemporary decor, French cuisine with excellent harbor views.
Marcel's. 104 Courtenay Ple.; 842–519. Swiss-Austrian cuisine, featuring game and continental meals. Pleasant atmosphere.
Nicholson's. Rotunda Pavilion, 245 Oriental Parade; 843–835. European cuisine, set on the harbor waterfront with excellent views, contemporary decor.
La Normandie. 116 Cuba St.; 845–000. Elegant old-fashioned decor, New Zealand game a specialty.
Orsini's. 201 Cuba St.; 845–476. Elegant, open fires in winter, quiet dining; seafood and steak.
Otto's Hafen Restaurant. Overseas Passenger Terminal; 845–436. Harbor views, specializes in fresh seafood.
Pierre's Restaurant. 342 Tinakori Rd.; 726–238. Early settler decor, small, intimate, French cuisine, no liquor license so bring your own wine.
Plimmer House. 99 Boulcott St.; 721–872. Gracious dining, Victorian decor, specialties are beef and seafood. Reservations.
The Roxburgh. 18 Majoribanks St.; 857–577. Small, intimate, international fare, German emphasis; open fire in winter.
Shorebird. 301 Evans Bay Parade; 862–017. Fresh fish caught from restaurant's own boat.
Skyline. At top of cable car; 758–727. Good food, views of city.
The Out and About Company (729–726) arranges luncheons in homes, as does **Cottage Meals and Tours** (889–124).

GETTING AROUND. Most towns are small and can be seen on foot. To get to attractions outside the cities, visitors should rent cars, join tours, or use local taxi companies.

THE NORTH ISLAND

AUCKLAND

At the airport. Auckland's international airport (15 miles from the city) is adjacent to the domestic terminal so that transfers are common to both. An *Airporter* bus operates half-hourly services from the city and airport seven days a week, and taxis are available outside the terminals. The current fares are $4 by Airporter bus and $25 by taxi. The Airporter will also pick up passengers from certain hotels; call 275–0789.

By taxi. The two main taxi companies are: *Alert Taxis* (32–899) and *Auckland Co-Op Taxi Society* (792–792).

By rental car. The main Auckland firms are *Hertz*—in the U.S., 800–654–3131; in Auckland, 154 Victoria St. W., 34–924; *Avis*—in the U.S., 800–331–2112; in Auckland, 22 Wakefield St., 792–545; *Budget*—in the U.S., 800–527–0700; in Auckland, 26 Nelson St., 734–949.

BAY OF ISLANDS
(Paihia)

Paihia Taxis (27–506).

NEW PLYMOUTH

New Plymouth Taxis (75–665).

ROTORUA

Rotorua Taxi Federation (85–069).

WANGANUI

Wanganui Taxis (54–444).

TOURS. Auckland. Tours of the area are operated by *Trans Tours (The Gray Line),* 792–420. *Scenic Tours Ltd.,* 64–0189, offers half-day tours that include city sights, Mount Eden, Domain Park and gardens, Auckland Museum, Parnell Village, waterfront drive, harbor bridge. Depart from Downtown Airline Terminal (by TraveLodge Hotel), 9:30 A.M. and 2:30 P.M.; $20. *Auckland Morning Tour,* is run by *Mutual Fourways,* 22 Wakefield St., 792–096. Tours include Tamaki Drive, Kelly Tarlton's Underwater World, Ellerslie Racecourse, Mount Eden, Parnell Village, Albert Park; pickup can be arranged; $19. *Shuttle Service,* 640–189, visits Kelly Tarlton's Underwater World, Heritage Park, Victoria Park Market. Depart from Downtown Airline Terminal on the hour from 10 A.M. to 4 P.M., $8. *City Of Sails Tour,* H&H Group, 796–056, covers Harbor Bridge, Takapuna Beach, Mission Bay, Mount Eden, Auckland Museum, Parnell Village, Departs Downtown Airline Terminal, 9:15 A.M. and 1 P.M.; $19.

A full-day tour of Auckland/Waitomo Caves, is available from *New Zealand Railways Road Services,* 792–500. Coaches depart from the depot at the railway station at 9:15 A.M. and return at 6:30 P.M. Cost, including a visit to the Glowworm Grotto, $30.

Napier. *Cox World Travel* runs a morning tour of Napier, Hastings, and Havelock North from 9:30 A.M. to 12:30 P.M. on Mon., Wed., and Fri., and an afternoon tour from 2 P.M. to 5:45 P.M. for sightseeing and visiting 8 major wineries. Call 58–574.

New Plymouth. Half- and full-day tours are run by *Newman's Sightseeing,* 23A Devon Mall (84–622).

Rotorua. *New Zealand Travel Office,* Fenton St. (85–179), and *Rotorua Promotions,* Haupapa St. (84–066), will provide information. Almost all Rotorua's attractions can be reached by private automobile, but several companies operate regular sightseeing tours. Reservations may be made with the New Zealand Travel Office and often at hotels and motels or with individual operators. Most are half-day trips. N.Z. *Road Services,* Travel Center, Amohau St., next to the railway station, 81–039, extension 374. Tour 1: (Rotorua Grand

Tour), 4 hours, visits Rotorua city sights, Agrodome, Rainbow Springs, Whakarewarewa, Maori Arts & Crafts Institute; $20. Tour 2: Herb Gardens and Whakarewarewa, 4 hours; $15. Tour 3: Skyline Rides and Whakarewarewa, 4 hours; $17. Tour 4: Waimangu Thermal Valley, Waiotapu and Lady Knox Geyser, 5 hours; $21. Tour 5 (full-day tour): Waiotapu, Lady Knox Geyser, Waimangu Thermal Valley, and Te Wairoa Buried Village; $29. Tour 6: Te Wairoa Buried Village, three hours; $12. Tour 7: Agrodome and city highlights, 3 hours; $16. Tour 8: Agrodome and Fleur Orchid House, 3 hours; $16. Tour 9: City highlights and herb gardens, 2½ hours; $13.50. Tour 10: Skyline Rides and city highlights, 2½ hours; $15.50. Tours 1 to 4 are morning tours departing at 9.30 or 10 A.M., and Tours 6 to 10 are afternoon tours, departing from the travel center at 1:45 P.M. and the New Zealand Travel Office at 2 P.M.

Panorama Tours, Amohau St., 80–594, have morning and afternoon tours visiting Whakarewarewa, Rainbow Springs, Ohinemutum Kuirau Gardens, and Government Gardens, 3½ hours; departs New Zealand Travel Office 8:45 A.M. and 1:45 P.M.; $21. Waimangu Thermal Valley and Lake Rotomahana, are visited on morning and afternoon tours, departing 8:45 A.M. and 1:45 P.M.; $22. Agrodome, Rainbow Springs, and Government Gardens morning tour, 3½ hours, departs 8:45 A.M., $21. Te Wairoa Buried Village and Hell's Gate afternoon tour, 3½ hours, departs 1:45 P.M.; $20. Jet Boat Panorama is a half-day tour visiting Hell's Gate and takes a 1½-hour jet-boat ride on the Rangitaiki River; departs 9 A.M.; $67.50. There's a Rainbow Springs, Agrodome, and Whakarewarewa morning tour, 4½ hours, departs 8:45 A.M.; $28.

Tarawera Mountain Sightseeing Tour: 89–333. Half-day tour by four-wheel-drive cruiser to the summit of Mount Tarawera for a close-up view of the massive crater, four hours, 9:15 A.M. and 2 P.M. from N.Z. Travel Office; $28.

Waimangu Thermal Valley: The valley, about 16 miles from Rotorua, may be visited as a half-day trip with a return by the same route or may be extended to a full-day trip with launch cruises on Lake Rotomahana and Lake Tarawera and then by coach to the Te Wairoa buried village and the Blue and Green Lakes and back to Rotorua (a circular route). Visitors walk through the valley, but a minibus is available for the return trip. For both trips coaches depart from the New Zealand Travel Office at 8:45 A.M. The half-day trip costs $22, and the full-day trip $30. Take a packed lunch on the full-day trip or arrange with the coach driver to have a packed lunch, $5, available on the launch.

Wellington. The best way to see Wellington is to take a half-or full-day tour. The Wellington City Council has half-day tours leaving the Public Relations Office on Mercer Street (opposite the Town Hall) at 2 P.M. daily. *Hammonds Sightseeing Tours* (847–539) has morning (10 A.M.–12:30 P.M.) and afternoon (2–4:45 P.M.) tours; an afternoon tour to the Gold Coast (2–4:45 P.M.) on Saturdays; and a full-day tour to the Wairarapa (departing 9:30 A.M.) on Sundays. Buses depart from the New Zealand Travel Office on Mercer Street.

Capital Elite Tours (727–281) have a Harbor City Coastline Tour (9:45–11:45 A.M.), a *City Sights Tour* (12:15–2:15 P.M.) and a *Hutt Valley Excursion* (2:30–4:30 P.M.) on Mon., Tues., Thurs., and Fri.; full-day drive through the Akatarawa hills and forest on Saturdays (9:45 A.M.–5:30 P.M.); and a full-day Wairarapa tour (9:45 A.M.–5:30 P.M.) on Sundays. Buses leave from the Public Relations Office.

SPECIAL-INTEREST SIGHTSEEING. Auckland. There are a number of **harbor cruises,** which give excellent views of the city's skyline, ranging from the regular 45-minute ferry trips across to Devonport to more extensive cruises by launch, catamarans, and yachts. *Pride of Auckland Cruises,* 734–557, operates large sailing catamaran accommodating 60 people, for two-hour cruises. Depart Quayside Launch Landing, Quay St., 10 A.M. to noon, coffee cruise, $21; lunch cruise 12:30 to 2:30 P.M., $21 plus $9 for lunch; afternoon coffee cruise, 3 to 5 P.M., $21; dinner cruise, 6 to 9 P.M., $40 including meal. *Captain Cook Cruises,* Quay St., 774–074, offer large launch harbor cruises. Morning tea cruise 9:45 to 11:30 A.M., $18; volcanic island cruise, 9:45 A.M. to 2:30 P.M., $38; lunch cruise, noon to 2:15 P.M., $28; afternoon tea cruise, 2:30 to 4 P.M., $18; evening cruise, Mon. to Thurs., 6:45 to 9:15 P.M., $24; sunset cocktail cruise, Fri., Sat., and Sun., 6 to 8 P.M., $22.

Scenic Flights are offered by *Capt. Al's Fantasy Flights,* Ardmore Airfield, 299–6456. Half-hour flights over city and outlying areas. Courtesy coach will pick up groups from hotels or motels, $89.

THE NORTH ISLAND

Takina Tours, 279-8020, have a Maori-culture tour, taking in Mount Eden, visit to Maori *marae* (Maori village meeting place), migration landing spot, Maori concert, and meal on *marae* by special arrangement. Check on starting times and places; $25 for tour only.

The **Glenbrook Vintage Railway** (the term railroad is not used in New Zealand) is for railroad buffs and features a locomotive and railroad cars lovingly restored by enthusiasts. It is 58 kilometers south of Auckland city, and there is no organized transport. The train runs on several miles of track and the 40-minute ride operates from late October to June. Phone contact is 669-361.

Wine Tours. New Zealand wines are beginning to build a reputation, and a number of vineyards are within 30 kilometers of Auckland. Wine tours which visit the vineyards for free wine tasting, lunch, and cheeseboards are operated by A.G.M. Promotions (398-670) from 10 A.M. to 3 P.M. Mon. through Sat., with pick-ups from hotels/motels. Reservations are essential. Six vineyards are visited on each tour, but vary from day to day.

Napier. An interesting sidelight is a visit to a **sheepskin factory** *(Classic Decor Limited,* Thames Street, Pandora; phone 59-570) where you can see sheepskins going through the entire process of washing, cleaning, and shaping and finally made into floor rugs, car seat covers, soft toys and moccasins. Tours are at 11 A.M. and 2 P.M. Mon. through Fri. Your own transport is needed, though a taxi transport would not be expensive. Further information from the *Napier Public Relations Office,* Marine Parade (57-182).

Northland. No visit to Paihia or Russell would be complete without a **cruise,** either a half-day or a full-day, in the huge area enclosed by dozens of appealing and unspoiled islands and jutting headlands with inviting bays and beaches. A fast and exciting cruise is in one of the large diesel-powered catamarans operated by the Mount Cook Line, *Tiger Lily I, Tiger Lily II,* or *Tiger Lily III,* which have cruising speeds of 20 knots and cover about 40 nautical miles. Air-conditioned suspension ensures a smooth ride in most conditions. The main cruise is to Cape Brett and Piercy Island and if weather permits a passage through the famous Hole in the Rock, a narrow tunnel where the promentary meets the sea, and a gentle entry into the Cathedral sea cave.

The catamaran has a bar serving spirits, beer, soft drinks and tea or coffee, but lunch must be ordered or take a picnic lunch with you. The half-day cruise departs Paihia at 9:30 A.M. and 12:30 P.M. daily (3-hour cruise), $19; and the 4-hour super cruise departs at 10 A.M. and 2 P.M., $21. Contact the Mount Cook Line office in the shopping mall (27-811).

A similar but more leisurely cruise is by Fullers "Cream Trip" on a large launch seating 170 people with wide windows and comfortable seating. The launch delivers mail and supplies to outlying islands. Lunch is taken at a licensed restaurant in Otehei Bay. The launch has a bar and hostess service. The cruise leaves Paihia at 9:45 A.M. and returns at 3:30 P.M. Contact *Fullers P&O Cruises* beside the wharf (27-421).

Rotorua. *Skyline Rides,* just 5 kilometers from the city center, can easily be seen from the road. A 900-meter gondola lift with a vertical rise of 200 meters takes you up the slopes of Mount Ngongotaha for panoramic views and a restaurant and cafe. Descent can be by gondola or by a 1-kilometer-long luge ride on a type of cart which has steering and braking and follows a curving track. Call 70-027.

Lake Cruise departs from lakefront wharf, 479-852. Cruises to Mokoia Island in the center of the lake in the launch *Ngaroto.* Coffee cruise 10 A.M. to noon and 2 to 4 P.M., $18; lunch cruise 12:30 to 4 P.M., $25 including lunch; barbecue cruise 7 to 10 P.M., $25 including barbecue.

Ahuwhenua Farm Tour, 32-632, Bryce Rd., 12 miles southwest of Rotorua. Developed by two proud Maori farmers, the Ahuwhenua property is a 180-acre dairy farm milking 150 cows. Tour of farm and milking. Lunch provided. Visits by bus organized. $20.

Aerial Sightseeing: Because of the varied nature of its scenery, the Rotorua region lends itself well to aerial sightseeing. From the airport, 12 min. from the city, *Rotorua's Volcanic Wunderflites* (56-079) operates several aerial tours taking in Taupo and its lake, the thermal area, White Island (a still-active volcanic island off the east coast), the lake areas, forests, and Mount Tarawera. Costs range from $30 for a 15-minute flight to $370 for the Grand Volcanic Presentation. Similar flights are operated by *The Helicopter Line* (59-477), the prices rising from $90 for the Volcanic Experience Flight to $130 for the Grand Tour and $275 for the White Island Experience. From the downtown lakefront,

Float-Plane Air Services operate sightseeing flights from $30 for 30 minutes to $145 for a landing on Matahina Hydro Lake and a jet-boat ride.

Wanganui. An offbeat side trip is a 2½-hour cruise up the river on the restored paddlewheel steamer *Otunui* (originally built in 1907) to Holly Lodge Estate Winery. The steamer leaves the City Marina at the end of Victoria Ave. (the main street) at 10 A.M. and returns at 12:30 P.M. Further information from Hospitality Wanganui (53–286).

Wellington. The *Kelburn Cable Car* (call 722–199) gives magnificent views of the city and harbor from the 480-foot summit at Kelburn. The entrance is on Cable Car Lane, almost opposite the T & G Building, off Lambton Quay. Cars run about every 10 minutes.

SPORTS. See also Facts at Your Fingertips for New Zealand and the introductory essay on fishing and hunting in New Zealand.

Boating. Contact *Charter Cruise Company,* Box 3730, Auckland, 734–557; *New Zealand Adventure Center,* Box 72–068, 399–192; or *South Seas Yacht Charter,* Box 38–366, Howick, Auckland; 534–2001.

Diving. Diving is a year-round sport in New Zealand, although it is most popular in summer. There are a variety of charters, but visitors may wish to contact *Sportsways Aqua Lung Center,* 234 Orakei Rd. Remuera, Auckland; 542–117 or 546–268.

Golf. Visitors are welcome at the *Chamberlain Park Public Golf Course,* Linwood Ave., Mt. Albert, Auckland; 866–758.

Skiing and **river-rafting** packages are available through *Live-Life New Zealand Action Tours,* Box 4517, Auckland; 768–936. See Skiing, below.

BAY OF ISLANDS

Diving. Clear water in the Bay of Islands makes diving an exciting experience. Complete equipment and advice are available from *Paihia Dive & Charter,* Box 210, Paihia; 27–551.

Fishing. The Bay of Islands was made famous some years ago as a base for big game fishing by the author Zane Grey, who had his base at Otehei Bay on Urupukapuka Island. The most plentiful are striped marlin (which may weigh up to 150 kilograms), black marlin (often attaining more than 230 kilograms), and mako shark (over 100 kilograms). Best months are from Jan. to May. Charter boats are available from $350 to $450 a day from *Game Fishing Charters,* Maritime Building, Paihia; 27–311.

ROTORUA

Rotorua is one of New Zealand's most famous **trout fishing** areas, where fish average 4 lb. and often go up to 10 lb. Fly fishing requires skill, but you don't need any experience to catch a trout on Lake Rotorua, Lake Tarawera, or Lake Okataina. All you have to do is to drag a line with a lure behind a launch until a trout abandons caution and takes it. After that it's up to you to play it in carefully. If you are lucky, your hotel will probably cook and serve the fish for you. It's your only way of tasting trout as, being classified as a sporting fish, it cannot be sold commercially and therefore does not appear on hotel or restaurant menus.

There are a dozen or so fishing guides (members of the New Zealand Professional Fishing Guides Association) who offer trout-fishing excursions for rates averaging $45 an hour. Advertisements appear in the local tourist newspaper, or contact the government tourist bureau.

SKIING. Most fields have a ski season that extends from mid-June to early October. In addition to the commercial ski areas listed here, there are also ski clubs that welcome visitors. Contact the New Zealand Tourist and Publicity Dept. (see Facts at Your Fingertips) for further information.

Mt. Ruahepu in the center of the North Island boasts the most developed ski field in New Zealand, the *Chateau Ski Field,* with 2 double-chair lifts, three T-bars, and 3 pomas. Special areas for beginners. The ski field is 4½ hours from Auckland or Wellington. Accommodations available at Chateau Tongariro. For

THE NORTH ISLAND

more information contact Chateau Tongariro, Tongariro National Park. Use a long-distance operator to call: MRP 809.

On the southwestern slopes of Mt. Ruahepu, 11 miles from the Ohakune township, lie the *Turoa Skifields*. The skifields offer 2 triple-chair lifts, 1 T-bar, 1 beginner's lift. For information phone 225 from Ohakune; 775–406 from Auckland. The information center is at 12 Clyde St., Ohakune.

HOT SPRINGS. In **Rotorua,** visitors to the *Polynesian Pools* in the Government Gardens can enjoy the mineral waters for as long they like. Some pools are open air, some enclosed, some private. Call 81–328.

THEME PARKS/HISTORIC SITES. *Heritage Park* is some 12 kilometers from Auckland at 3 Harrison Rd. (off the Ellerslie/Panmure Highway at Mount Wellington). A comparatively new development with a strong Maori influence, it is a theme park displaying agriculture, flora, fauna, and culture. Live entertainment includes a Maori concert party, a myths and legends show, a farm animal show, and art and craft displays. Open daily from 9:30 A.M. to 5:30 P.M., $7; *hangi* Sat. 7 P.M. to midnight, reservations essential, $20. Phone 590–424.

The *Tauranga Historic Village,* corner of Cameron Rd. and 17th Ave., Tauranga, is typical of early New Zealand townships and has period shops, cobblestone streets, and wares of a bygone age. Vintage transport is on display and there are rides on a train, a double-decker bus, or a horse and cart. Included is a gold-mining village, a Maori village, a military barracks and pioneering machinery. Hours are from 9 A.M. to 4 P.M. Phone 81–302.

ZOOS AND AQUARIUMS. *Auckland Zoological Park,* Motiono Rd., Western Springs, Auckland, is 5 minutes from downtown. The park contains a collection of exotic and native species and has a kiwi house. Open 9:30 A.M.–5:30 P.M. Small admission charge. Phone 761–415.

Kelly Tarlton's Underwater World is a bus ride from Auckland on Tamaki Drive, near Orakei Wharf. A 40-foot-long tunnel lined with large windows gives visitors a close-up view of sharks and stingrays—over 30 species of fish in all. Phone 580–603. Open 9 A.M. to 9 P.M., small admission charge.

MAORI HERITAGE. The *Maori Arts and Crafts Institute,* on Rotorua's southern edge near the entrance to the Whaka Reserve, preserves ancient Maori skills among young people. Visitors are welcome and there is a shop attached. Open 8 A.M.–5 P.M.; the carving school is closed on weekends and school holidays. Phone 89–047.

Ohaki Maori Village, near Waitomo Caves in Te Kuiti, is a model village where visitors can learn about pre-European Maori life. For information call 86–610.

One of the most enjoyable experiences in Rotorua is to attend a *Maori concert* and if possible to sample food cooked in the Maori way in an earth oven (a *hangi*). The traditional Maori way is to heat stones in a pit, into which the food—meat, fish, and vegetables—is placed in woven flax baskets. The pit is then covered and the food left to steam. In Rotorua, however, natural super-heated underground steam is used in many cases, which saves a great deal of time, though the principle is the same. You can enjoy a Maori concert and/or *hangi* at the following: *Rotorua Maori Cultural Theater,* 85–912 or 86–591, 7 P.M. daily, $6, bookings not required. *Tamatekapua Meeting House,* Ohinemutu Village, 8 P.M. daily, $6, no bookings required.

Maori Arts & Crafts Institute, (see above), concerts 12:15 P.M. daily from mid-Oct. to the end of Mar.; thereafter May and Aug. school holidays only; $5. *Maori Hangi and Concerts* (reservations essential). *THC International Hotel,* corner Froude and Tyron sts., Whakarewarewa, 81–189, 6:30 P.M. daily, $23. *TraveLodge,* Eruera St., 81–174, 7 P.M. daily, $25. *Tudor Towers,* Government Gardens, 81–285, 7 P.M. daily, $19. *Geyserland Resort,* Fenton St., Whakarewarewa, 82–039, 6 P.M. daily, $20. *Sheraton Hotel,* Sala St., 87–139, 7 P.M. daily, $25.

See also Museums and Galleries, below and Special-Interest Sightseeing and Tours, above.

 MUSEUMS AND GALLERIES. There is more to New Zealand than spectacular scenery, and rainy days can become a perfect time to learn more about the country's art and artifacts.

AUCKLAND

Auckland City Art Gallery. Wellesley and Kitchener sts.; 792–020 or 069. One of the finest public art collections in New Zealand, the holdings at the gallery include European art, contemporary international prints, and New Zealand art past and present. Mon.–Thurs., 10 A.M.–4:30 P.M.; Fri. to 8:30 P.M.; Sat. and Sun. 1–5:30 P.M. Free.

Museum of Transport and Technology. A few miles from city center, in great North Rd., Western Springs; 860–198. A fascinating collection of methods of transportation, among other items. Accessible by city bus. Open daily, except Christmas, 9 A.M.–5 P.M. Admission charge.

War Memorial Museum. In the Auckland Domain; 30–443. Noted for its outstanding collection of Maori art, the museum is also a memorial to the dead of the two world wars. Displays also feature New Zealand's natural history. Open daily 10 A.M.–5 P.M., from 11 A.M. Sun. Accessible by Auckland bus.

GISBORNE

Gisborne Museum and Arts Centre, 18–22 Stout St. (83–832), features Maori works as well as natural exhibits. Local artists and craftspeople also display their works here. 10 A.M.–4:30 P.M., Tues.–Fri.; from 2 P.M. on Sat., Sun., holidays. Small admission charge.

HAMILTON

Hamilton Arts Center, corner of Victoria and Marlborough sts. (390–685), features changing exhibits of contemporary art.

Waikato Museum of Art and History, 150 London St. (392–118), displays art as well as Maori and European history exhibits. Tues.–Sat., 10 A.M.–4:30 P.M.; from noon, Sun. and holidays. Admission is free.

NEW PLYMOUTH

Govett-Brewster Art Gallery (85–149) is considered by many to be one of the most exciting art galleries in the country.

Taranaki Museum (89–583) displays a fine collection of Maori artifacts.

ROTORUA

Rotorua Art Gallery and **City of Rotorua Museum** (86–382) are inside Tudor Towers within the Government Gardens. The art gallery displays works of native New Zealand and international artists. Small admission to each.

WANGANUI

Wanganui Regional Museum is in the Civic Center, at the end of Maria Place. The largest regional museum in New Zealand; here is displayed a large Maori collection and historical exhibits. Open weekdays 9:30 A.M.–4:30 P.M.; weekends 1–5 P.M. Small admission charge. Call 57–443.

WELLINGTON

Alexander Turnbull Library, 44 the Terrace, houses records from early New Zealand: books, pamphlets, newspapers, manuscripts, prints, paintings, photographs. 9 A.M.–5 P.M.; to noon Sat. Call 722–107.

THE NORTH ISLAND

Artours, 727–018, run by the New Zealand Crafts Council, are guided tours to arts and crafts galleries and studios; from 9 A.M. to 5 P.M. Mon. to Sat., groups 4 to 6, $85 and $60 per person.

The National Art Gallery (phone 859–703) and **National Museum** (859–609) are on Buckle St. The art gallery features paintings by New Zealanders, but also has a large collection of European works. The museum displays exhibits of South Pacific, New Zealand, and Maori history. 10 A.M.–4:45 P.M. daily. Accessible by bus from Wellington if you're willing to walk a little. Admission is free at both.

Southward Vintage Car Museum. Vintage car buffs should certainly not miss this. Situated two miles north of Paraparamumu (37 miles from Wellington) on Otaihanga Road, the museum has one of the largest and most comprehensive collections of vintage automobiles in the southern hemisphere. The collection comprises some 250 vehicles, more than half of which are on show at any one time. There is, for instance, a 1915 Indianapolis Stutz, a 1907 Holsman, a 1904 Wolseley, a 1913 Maudslay, and a 57C Bugatti, and even one of gangster Al Capone's cars with bullet holes in the glass.

ARTS AND ENTERTAINMENT. In Auckland, visitors can enjoy the range of theatrical productions offered by the *Mercury Theater,* 9 France St., 33–869, and *Theater Corporate,* 14 Galatos St., 774–307. Watch the local papers for other cultural events, such as performances by *The Symphonia.*

A variety of theater experiences are offered by the *Downstage Theater* in **Wellington.** In the Hannah Playhouse on Cambridge Terr. (849–639), the group is very popular and tickets should be reserved well in advance.

THE SOUTH ISLAND

"The Mainland"

The starting point of a journey through the extraordinary scenery of the South Island is usually Christchurch, which is reached by air from just about everywhere in New Zealand. It is a good point of arrival, as it typifies the different characteristics of the two islands. While Christchurch is a busy commercial city, it is more gracious than those in the North Island and the pace of life seems more relaxed. Its intensive civic pride is exemplified by numerous city gardens and parks and by the lovely gardens of private homes.

The South Island is larger than the North, and the South Island people like to refer to it as the Mainland.

To the south, the main highlights are Mount Cook, Queenstown, Lake Te Anau, Lake Manapouri, and Milford Sound. All can be reached by good roads, but almost a full day is required between each point, and most visitors use the regular services of Mount Cook Airlines or Newmans Air with their turbo-jet planes. The pilots add enjoyment by giving detailed commentaries as points of special interest are passed.

On a time-restricted itinerary it is possible to fly to Mount Cook, take a ski-plane flight with a landing on the glacier, and be back in Christchurch that night, having included a glimpse of Queenstown. Changing planes at Queenstown one can even fly into Milford Sound. All, of course, depends on favorable weather, as this is alpine country, and weather can be changeable. But having come this far in the South Pacific, one should make the most of it and allow a week or more, to enjoy some outstanding scenic spectacles and sightseeing experiences.

As the plane leaves Christchurch the vast checkerboard of green and brown cultivated fields of the Canterbury Plains unfolds, and soon the

THE SOUTH ISLAND

plane is flying along the long chain of the permanently snow-clad summits of the Southern Alps. As far as the eye can see there is a jumbled mass of rugged peaks.

In a little over half an hour the plane crosses the divide at about 7,500 ft., and as it does so, the majesty of Mount Cook and the sister mountains clustering around her are suddenly revealed. Below is the 18-mile-long Tasman Glacier, down which the plane flies. Sheer icy cliffs rise beside and above you as the plane gradually loses height to land at the airport, whose altitude is 2,500 ft. The clarity of the air makes the mountains seem almost at the wing tip; in fact they are a mile or more away.

From the Mount Cook airport the plane flies down the length of the Tasman River and over the green-blue glacial Lake Pukaki and swings to the right. On the left is the alpine plateau of the Mackenzie Country, named after a Scottish sheep stealer who found a pass to it through the mountains; to the right is lovely Lake Ohau. Soon the blue waters of Lake Wakatipu and tree-studded Queenstown come into view, and the plane sweeps over the deep valleys, silver rivers and fertile farms to land.

From here, smaller planes fly the exciting scenic round-trip flight to Milford Sound, where one can stop overnight, and return next day by road. Alternatively, continue to Te Anau, and make that a base for a trip to the sound by road.

That is the aerial tour for the visitor in a hurry, but he will miss some of New Zealand's most enchanting travel experiences. Mount Cook demands a day to absorb the grandeur of the surrounding mountains, and savor the ski-plane flight to the full. As one visitor put it, "Queenstown is good for the soul." An unhurried sampling of the wealth of beautiful and unusual sidetrips amply repays a visit of three days.

Milford Sound cannot be appreciated in all its majestic glory and grandeur on a flying visit, for unless a half-day is allowed for a launch cruise down the sound a truly moving experience is missed.

Lakes Te Anau and Manapouri offer their own unique attractions. Each has its individual charm: Manapouri for its somber beauty and Te Anau for its glowworm cave. The road from Te Anau to Milford Sound must rank as one of the most spectacular scenic drives in New Zealand.

The Fertile Southland

Farther to the south are Southland, so fertile that farmers can run up to eight sheep to the acre, and Invercargill, the southernmost city, famous for its succulent oysters. To the east is Dunedin, founded by the Scottish immigrants, and proud of its title of the Edinburgh of the South.

If you look at a relief map of the South Island you will see quite clearly how the Southern Alps form a backbone for much of the length of the island. Only three passes give access to the west coast. Consequently, this delightful region is too seldom visited, for it is a place of magnificent seascapes, tranquil alpine lakes, verdant subtropical forest, and the Franz Josef and Fox glaciers.

From Christchurch the West Coast can be reached through the Lewis Pass and Arthur's Pass, both distinguished for natural beauty, and from Queenstown through the Haast Pass, spectacular in an entirely different way. A popular route, especially for organized tours, is from Christchurch to the glaciers, through the Haast Pass to Lake Wanaka and Queenstown, Lake Te Anau and Milford Sound, back to Queenstown, and then on to Mount Cook and back to Christchurch.

The northern part of the South Island above Christchurch, which is highly popular with New Zealanders, is often omitted by overseas visitors as it is apart from the main route. The Marlborough Sounds, a maze of sunken valleys, has hundreds of miles of inland waterways which afford excellent fishing. Nelson, a placid city, is the heart of a large fruit- and tobacco-growing area, with some of the most delightful beaches to be found anywhere and a climate that lures people into retirement there.

Although they have a common bond, the North and South islands are entirely different. The South Island undoubtedly has the greater number of scenic attractions.

CHRISTCHURCH

"Gracious" is a fitting term for Christchurch, the South Island's largest city. With a population of over 300,000, it is the hub of the extensive Canterbury district and the main point of arrival for travelers from the North Island and many from Australia.

Christchurch is often described as the garden city of New Zealand and richly deserves its title. Within its confines are about a thousand acres of parkland and gardens, and through the city itself meanders the small and restful Avon River, fringed with willows and bordered by sloping grassy banks. Householders take pride in their gardens, and competitions are held every year for the finest garden and best-kept street.

It has also been said of Christchurch that it is "more English than the English and the most English city outside England. Certainly many aspects of it and many of its buildings are reminiscent of England, for it was planned that way.

It was settled under the auspices of the Church of England and was planned for English people belonging to the Anglican Church. In 1850 the "First Four Ships" brought a group of English settlers to the port of Lyttelton, and the Canterbury pilgrims made their historic trek over the steep Port Hills to the fertile plains beyond. The older Canterbury families proudly trace their lineage to these ships, just as Americans are proud to claim that their forbears came over on the *Mayflower*.

The settlers found their city already surveyed and laid out in broad regular streets, some named after Church of England bishoprics, such as Worcester, Hereford, and Gloucester. Canterbury's planners saw the colony as part of England transplanted to New Zealand.

Colonization went ahead rapidly. By 1865 all the available land on the Canterbury Plains had been cultivated and sheep farms carried more than a million sheep. In the 1880s the success of refrigerated shipping revolutionized farming in Canterbury. Small towns and villages, the centers of farming areas, grew up, an irrigation system solved the problem of watering stock, new areas were opened up by railroads, and the large holdings were divided to make land available for small farms. Today, Canterbury is New Zealand's chief wheat-growing district, as well as the home of world-famed Canterbury lamb.

Christchurch was planned and built around the beautiful Christchurch Cathedral. Like many of the city's early buildings, the cathedral is Gothic in design and built of rough gray local stone. The bells duplicate the upper ten of St. Paul's Cathedral, London. Gothic architecture, undergoing a revival when the first buildings of Christchurch were erected, was used for many of the early structures: schools, the museum, the old provincial-council chambers and Canterbury University College. There is a charm and stability about these early stone buildings, sheltered by English trees planted by the city's forefathers.

To the south of the city rise the Port Hills. From the 24-mile scenic Summit Road extending along their crests there are fine views of the Canterbury Plains and the Southern Alps and, to the east, the peaceful bays of Lyttelton Harbor and the hills of Banks Peninsula. The French established a colony on the peninsula in 1840, and had they done so a little earlier they could well have claimed New Zealand for France before the Treaty of Waitangi was signed, establishing British sovereignty over all New Zealand. The French attempt was abandoned nine years later.

Christchurch has long been a New Zealand base for exploration of the Antarctic. The British explorer Robert Falcon Scott, whose party of five reached the South Pole in 1912, left from here (his statue stands by the Avon River), and it is now the headquarters of Operation Deep Freeze. From the international airport nonstop 2,200-mile flights are made in summer to McMurdo, the main United States base in Antarctica. New Zealand exercises control over the Ross Dependency and maintains Scott Base, near McMurdo.

Scenic Tours

Afternoon bus tours are run by the Christchurch Transport Board. Easy two-hour morning and afternoon escorted walking tours of the city's main attractions or escorted tours in your own vehicle are available from Personal Guiding Services at $US10.50 for a half-day. Contact the New Zealand Travel Office or Canterbury Information Center.

Christchurch Cathedral

The graceful Christchurch Cathedral dominates the heart of the city. The foundation stone was laid in 1864, just 14 years after the arrival of the first organized settlers sponsored by the Church of England. From the balconies to the bell chamber (133 steps up) there are magnificent views of the city and a glimpse of the Southern Alps on a clear day. Choral evensong is sung by the Cathedral Choir on Tuesdays and Wednesdays at 5:15 P.M.; and by the Boy Choristers on Fridays at 4:30 P.M. The tower is open from 9 A.M. to 4 P.M. weekdays and Saturdays and 1 P.M. to 4:30 P.M. on Sundays; admission 50 cents. The cathedral is open for prayer or a visit from 8 A.M. to 5 P.M.

Cathedral Square

Cathedral Square stands at the very heart of the city, and all the main streets radiate from it. Once a busy bus terminal, it has now been cleared of traffic and made into a delightfully decorated pedestrian area. A "speaker's corner," where those who have a cause to advocate can give their message, is popular at lunchtime.

The Christchurch Wizard has become a nationally known institution as an orator, entertainer, and fun maker. Dressed in a sorcerer's robe with a wide-brimmed coned hat he performs at 1 P.M. on weekdays in the square and orates on subjects that interest him at the time. He is witty and provocative but never offensive. If he feels strongly enough he will impose a "curse." It is all good fun, and the Wizard obviously enjoys the performances as much as the crowd does.

Christchurch Town Hall

This is less an administrative building than a cultural complex containing a concert auditorium, a theater, a banquet room, and a restaurant. It was opened in 1972 and is one of the finest in the Southern Hemisphere. It incorporates the latest in theater and auditorium design, and its pleasing exterior is set off by a small lake and fountain.

Canterbury Museum

An entire Christchurch street after the style of the 1850s can be explored. Shop windows display their goods, cottages are fully furnished, and there is even an old fashioned horse cab. The ornithological section is particularly well designed, with birds displayed in realistic dioramas.

The Hall of Antarctic Discovery contains a well-displayed history of Antarctic exploration and a superb collection of equipment used by successive parties which have visited Antarctica. A graphic idea of the scientific knowledge that has resulted can be gained from static and moving diagrams, dioramas of penguins, seals, and whales, and sound recordings of them.

Botanical Gardens

In keeping with the garden-city reputation, the Botanical Gardens are a delight. A section is devoted entirely to New Zealand plants, and the rose, water, azalea, and rock gardens are outstanding. Tropical plants may be seen in the begonia house, and there is a splendid display of cacti in the succulent house.

McDougall Art Gallery

Just behind the museum is the McDougall Art Gallery, which contains classic paintings of the Maori by the noted artists Lindauer and Goldie.

Sign of the Takahe

Henry George Ell, who died in 1934, was a visionary. He planned a series of rest houses along the Summit Road of the Port Hills and began three. Only one, the Sign of the Takahe (a New Zealand bird), was completed. It takes the shape of an English baronial hall of the Tudor period. Made of stone quarried from the Port Hills and from native timbers, the building was fashioned by hand. Its fine carvings, coats of arms, heraldic shields and stained glass windows bring a touch of old-time England to these southern hills.

Ferrymead Historic Park & Transport Museum

Still in the process of development, this technological museum is a journey into the past. There are displays of old trolley cars and railroad locos and horse-drawn vehicles. The Hall of Wheels houses vintage autos and machinery and early century appliances.

Orana Wildlife Park

Animals from various parts of the world have been assembled in this 10-acre drive-through wildlife park, not far from the center of the city. Lions, tigers, camels, and others roam freely in a natural environment.

Willowbank Wildlife Reserve

This reserve contains probably the largest collection of birds and animals in the South Island and includes mountain lions, camels, donkeys, and deer. A farmyard section has Scottish highland cattle, primitive sheep and other ancient livestock breeds, as well as old farm implements and vehicles.

Mount Cook

This towering pinnacle of 12,349 ft. is New Zealand's highest mountain. The Maoris called it *Aorangi* (the Cloud Piercer). But it is now, of course, named after Captain Cook, who never actually saw it.

Mount Cook is in the very heart of New Zealand's most spectacular mountain region, almost in the center of the long chain of permanently snow-capped Southern Alps stretching down much of the South Island. Yet it does not stand alone—surrounding it are 17 peaks, all exceeding 10,000 ft.—and Mount Sefton, Mount Tasman, and Mount La Perouse are only a little lower.

Rising to what appears to be a sharp point (though there are three peaks on the summit ridge), Mount Cook is indeed a monarch among mountains, its steep slopes glistening with ice and snow. Those who first saw it thought that it would never be climbed. It was—but not until Christmas Day 1894. It has since been climbed many times, and by the first woman, Freda du Faur, in 1913. It was here that Sir Edmund Hillary, the first to conquer Mount Everest, did much of his early mountaineering.

Glaciers abound on the mountain slopes, including the 18-mile Tasman Glacier, longest in the southern hemisphere. From the hotel, 2,500 ft. above sea level and well below the snow line, it is not uncommon to hear the dull roar of an avalanche high in the mountains, particularly on Mount Sefton.

Two natural inhabitants are of interest. The area is one of the homes of the kea, a New Zealand bird rather like a large parrot with deep green plumage and a vivid crimson breast. They are amusing birds, inquisitive and fearless, but beware of leaving anything bright or shiny about; it will quickly disappear or be pecked to pieces by their strong beaks. The name comes from the sound of their cry. Although they are not large, they have the reputation of being sheep killers. It is said that a flock will chase a sheep until it is exhausted and then alight on its back and dig with their cruel beaks for the kidneys.

Seldom seen except by hunters, thar and chamois also inhabit the mountains. Liberated in 1904, they found the environment similar to their native Himalayas, and thrived to such an extent that they have been declared noxious animals because of the damage they do to vegetation.

Growing profusely on the alpine slopes are the delicate white flowers of what are known as Mount Cook lilies. This is not, however, a true lily but a variety of *ranunculus lyallii*. It is used as the insignia of Mount Cook Airlines.

Arriving by road (or flying from Mount Cook to Queenstown) you pass through or over a large plateau of brown tussock and grass bounded by long ranges of hills. This is the Mackenzie Country, named after a Scottish sheep stealer. Mackenzie, who spoke only Gaelic, found a pass through the mountain barrier in the mid 1800s and would sneak with his dog down to farms in the lower levels, round up sheep, and drive them back to the plateau. Caught eventually, he was given a five-year jail sentence. He begged to be allowed to take his dog with him to prison but was refused. The dog was taken south, and her offspring were eagerly sought by shepherds. Mackenzie escaped three times in the first year and was finally released on condition that he leave the country and never return.

Good sheep dogs were indispensable to the early settlers in this remote and spartan area. At Lake Tekapo, at the edge of the Mackenzie Country and just off the main road from Christchurch on the way to Mount Cook, stands a bronze statue of a sheep dog, erected as a tribute.

Here too is the charming rural Church of the Good Shepherd, built of stone as a memorial to the pioneer sheep farmers of the region. The backdrop to the altar is a large window, filled with a magnificent panorama of the blue-green waters of the glacial lake and the mountains behind.

Ski-Plane Flights

A wonderful way to see the New Zealand scenery. Where else in the world can you take off at 2,500 ft. and within 20 minutes land at about 7,000 ft. on the vast snowfields at the head of a glacier? Many tourists go to Mount Cook as much for this flight as to see the mountain.

The aircraft has wheels for use at the Mount Cook airport, but it is also fitted with retractable skis. You take off from the airfield in front of the hotel, and within minutes you are flying amid peaks sheathed in perpetual ice, over snow valleys, and beside glittering icefalls. The slopes seem close enough to touch, but distances are deceptive in the clear mountain air, and they are actually at least a quarter of a mile away. Below you the rock-strewn surface of the Tasman Glacier gives way to pure ice, hundreds of feet deep, and then you are above the huge snowfields at the head of the glacier.

The skis are lowered, and the plane glides on to the snow and hisses to a stop. You get out into the soft snow—and find yourself in complete silence, in a place that once only mountaineers could reach. Armchair mountaineering if you like, or, as one visitor put it, instant Hillary. Only the most insensitive could fail to be emotionally stirred.

After a time to take photographs the plane takes off again and you fly around Mount Cook, with a view of the two glaciers flowing down the opposite side into native forest and the Tasman Sea. Then down the Meuller Glacier and back to the airport. Known as the Grand Circle, the flight takes an hour, and no special clothing is needed.

The ingenuity of a New Zealander made this flight possible. The late Harry Wigley (later Sir Henry), head of Mount Cook Airlines and its coach-touring company, had flown light planes in this region before and after the war, during which he was a well-known pilot. He designed his retractable skis had his company workshops make a prototype, and on September 22, 1955, Wigley and one of his men made the first ski-plane landing. As he writes in his book *Ski Plane Adventure:*

"For several seconds not a word was said. We just sat and looked at each other. Then we slowly opened the doors and stepped out into the deep, soft, powder snow almost up to our knees. We felt like two blowflies sitting on the South Pole."

THE SOUTH ISLAND

Now landing on the glacier is commonplace. Ski-plane flights are very popular and dependent on the weather, so it is wise to reserve as soon as possible after you arrive at the Hermitage or Glencoe Lodge or with the Mount Cook Line at the airport; 849. The cost is $76.

Skiing and Mountain Climbing

Skiing and mountain climbing in the area are superb. Alpine Guides, at Mt. Cook Village, offer heli-skiing, glacier skiing, ski touring, cross-country skiing, and a school of mountaineering.

National Park Headquarters

Here you can see collections of mountaineering equipment and exhibits of local flora and fauna and specimen rocks peculiar to the region.

Christchurch to Mount Cook by Road

Mount Cook is 211 miles (339.5km) from Christchurch by road—a good day's drive. For about 60 miles (96.5km) the road heads straight through the rich Canterbury Plains, which were formed by the wearing down of the high country by snow or glacier-fed rivers rising in the Southern Alps. Some of these are quite large, and all are swift-flowing and change their courses continuously—hindering the efforts of soil conservation authorities, who have tried to confine the waters to regular channels with protection works of willow and embankments, but a delight to anglers, as the rivers are the haunt of brown trout and quinnat salmon. The Selwyn River is unusual in that it flows underground for much of the year.

The road then swings inland into the rolling lamb country of Canterbury and Fairlie, nearly a thousand feet above sea level, and in coaching days a staging place on the journey to Mount Cook. It then follows the pleasant Opihi Valley and climbs through Burke's Pass to 2,000 ft. The long chain of the Southern Alps is now clearly in view.

A gentle downhill grade brings you to Lake Tekapo, 15 miles long and 620 ft. deep, the site of a glacier that flowed in prehistoric times. 30 miles (42km) on is Lake Pukaki, 1,588 ft. above sea level. Both Lake Tekapo and Lake Pukaki are sites of extensive hydroelectric developments.

On the 36-mile (52km) run to Mount Cook the road follows the shore of Lake Pukaki for 15 miles and then heads up the mountain-flanked Tasman Valley to the Hermitage complex. In clear weather the views of the high alps are breathtakingly beautiful.

Mount Cook to Queenstown by Road

After following the Tasman River for 36 miles (52km) to Lake Pukaki, turn right and head south. For 26 miles the road crosses comparatively flat country, through which the Ohau River flows. The river drains Lake Ohau, another glacial lake and also a source of the Waitaki River.

After leaving the township of Omarama there is a fairly steep ascent to the 3,300-ft. summit of the Lindis Pass through hills covered with brown tussock and grass, then a descent through the Lindis Gorge. From ancient times a well-worn track used by the Maoris ran from Wanaka over the Lindis Pass and down the banks of the Waitaki River to the coast.

From the township of Tarras, after 112 miles (180km), there are two routes to Queenstown. To the right the road leads to Lake Wanaka and then climbs over the 3,676-ft. Crown Range, dropping down to Arrowtown and continuing to Queenstown. The more popular route, however, is straight on to Cromwell at the junction of the Clutha and Kawarau rivers. This was the scene of intense gold mining activities in the 1860s, and dredging is still carried on in the Clutha River.

The next 22 miles is through the winding Kawarau Gorge, with its many relics of the gold-mining days. Of special interest are the Roaring Meg Stream, which operates a tiny powerhouse, and, about a mile farther on, a natural bridge across the river, used for years by the Maoris. The remainder of the journey is through pleasant farm country. At the crest of a hill, pause to admire tree-ringed Lake Hayes, famed for its lovely reflections.

As the route is sparsely populated, it is a good plan to have the hotel give you a box lunch, as there are many lovely picnic spots.

Queenstown

Picturesque is a word too frequently used in tourist brochures; yet it is difficult to find a more appropriate adjective for Queenstown. It is a small, well-kept township of 3,000 permanent residents but thronged with visitors throughout the year. Most leave with regret that they have not allowed enough time to enjoy it more. Though reliant on tourism for its prosperity, it has avoided gross commercialism. The outstanding quality of the scenery and the variety of sightseeing make exploitation unnecessary.

Queenstown delights the mind as well as the eye. It stands on the middle shores of Lake Wakatipu, facing two imposing peaks and flanked by the saw-toothed 7,500-ft. range of the Remarkables. It is often difficult to believe one is not at an alpine lake in Switzerland.

Queenstown can be enjoyed in all four seasons. In winter it resounds to the laughter of young skiers, in spring the trees begin to show their greenery, in summer it is a place for swimming, sunbathing, and boating, and in the fall it is a blaze of color. The early settlers planted deciduous trees in this originally treeless area, and as fall arrived the willows and poplars, elms and larches, sycamores and maples splash the brown landscape with a riot of color.

Lake Wakatipu, shaped like a giant letter S, is 52 miles long and varies from one to three miles in width. It is 1,016 ft. above sea level, and its greatest depth is 1,310 ft., which means that its floor is 294 ft. below sea level. It has been called the Lake That Breathes, as its waters rise and fall 3 inches every 15 minutes. The Maoris noticed this and created a legend. In revenge for carrying off his bride-to-be an angered lover set fire to a giant as he lay sleeping in the fern. The pain of the fire caused the giant to draw up his knees, and so intense was the heat that he sank deep into the earth and burned until nothing remained but his ashes and his heart, which kept beating. The rains and rivers filled the chasm, but the outline of the lake retained his figure. The waters of the lake, says the legend, still pulsate to the beating of the giant's heart.

Hard-headed scientists, however, give a more prosaic explanation. The pulsations, they say, are caused by wind or variations in atmospheric pressure. A pity. The Maori legend is more colorful.

High in the affection of Queenstown residents and much admired by visitors is the T.S.S. *Earnslaw,* a steamer built in 1912 and still in service. Her gleaming white hull and red funnel capped with a black band blend harmoniously with the mountain and lake backdrops. The Lady of the Lake, they call her. Of 335 tons, she was prefabricated in

THE SOUTH ISLAND

Dunedin in 1912 and assembled at Kingston, at the southern end of the lake. Until a road was cut around the lake comparatively recently, she was the only means of servicing the lakeside farms, and she worked hard transporting not only stores but also sheep and cattle. If you have time, don't miss a half-day or full-day cruise up the lake. If you're mechanically minded, you'll enjoy peering down at the engine room, with its gleaming, lovingly maintained machinery, watching the boilers being stoked with coal to drive the twin screws and smelling the pungent clean smell of hot oil.

In spite of the then difficult access the first settlers established sheep farms, but in 1862 an event occurred which changed the history of the area. Gold, in plentiful supply, was found, and New Zealand's biggest gold rush began. The Shotover River was termed the richest river in the world. Thousands of miners converged from many parts of the world.

Gradually, the bounteous supplies dwindled, and the miners either settled or left. A little gold is still found, but the finest gold in Queenstown today is the burnished leaves on the trees in fall. Everywhere, however, are interesting relics of those days of gold fever—abandoned workings, crude stone cottages, culverts to carry water for washings, and the huge mounds of stone tailings from the dredges.

Exploring Queenstown

Queenstown has such a wide range of beautiful and unusual side trips that a week could be spent doing something new every day.

Lake Cruises

Several cruises are operated by the historic T.S.S. *Earnslaw*. A one-hour lunch cruise departs at 12:30 P.M. daily August to June; a longer cruise, giving views of the lake shores and the head of the lake and a visit to Mount Nicholas Sheep Station, departs at 2 P.M. August to June; and you can dine on board on an evening cruise departing at 7 P.M. December thru March. There are also faster, enclosed hydrofoil cruises. Book cruises through Fiordland Travel Services on the wharf on Beach St. (phone 570).

Also on the wharf is an underwater observatory where you climb down 15 feet below the water into a viewing lounge to see wild trout, quinnat salmon, longfin eels, and ducks living free in their own environment.

Skyline Chalet

From almost anywhere around Queenstown you'll see a chalet perched on Bob's Peak 1,530 ft. above the town. It is reached by an aerial cableway with small gondolas, and from the restaurant at the top there are spectacular panoramic views. Open 10 A.M. to 9 P.M.; small admission charge.

Queenstown Domain

Sometimes called the Government Gardens (they were developed by the government), the Queenstown Domain extends along a peninsula occupying one side of the bay and presents a colorful display of bright flower beds, lily ponds, exotic shrubs and trees, and a sports area. Near the tip is a large glacial boulder commemorating five Antarctic explorers.

Queenstown Motor Museum

Close to the base terminal of the cableway, this museum displays a very good collection of vintage cars—a 1903 De Dion, a 1909 Renaults and a 1922 Rolls Royce Silver Ghost, to name a few. 9 A.M. to 5:30 P.M.

Queenstown Sound and Light Museum

An audiovisual lasting about 20 minutes in three rooms, each presenting a different aspect of early immigration and early colonial life in Queenstown during the gold-rush days. Room 1 is in a ship's cabin, Room 2 in a gold mine, and Room 3 in a canvas hotel with a display wall incorporating silent movies, slides and artifacts. 10 A.M. to 5:30 P.M.; $3.

Deer Park Heights

Deer, chamois, thar, wapiti, and mountain goats may be seen close at hand in a natural setting about 10 miles from Queenstown. In the April mating season you can hear the stags roaring their challenge to each other.

Farm Visits

Dominating the opposite side of the lake are two lofty peaks—Walter Peak (5,936 ft.) to the right and Cecil Peak (6,477 ft.) to the left. Both are sheep and cattle ranches. A half-day trip to Walter Peak Station by launch, the only means of access, is worthwhile. Hosts explain how the steep hills are farmed and how trained sheep dogs are able to muster the animals from "the tops." Sheep dog demonstrations are given. Launches leave from the jetties. Departures 9:30 A.M. and 2:15 P.M.; $20.

Beyond Queenstown

Obtain a free copy of *Queenstown Sightseeing and Activities Guide* from the New Zealand Tourist Office, 49 Shotover Street, phone 143. (Note: At the time of writing Queenstown, which has a resident population of under 3,000 people, still has a manual telephone exchange in which the number required has to be given verbally to the operator; hence the low numbers.)

The *Guide* describes full- and half-day trips, lake excursions, river trips, scenic flights and other activities and gives prices and optional times. The New Zealand Tourist Office can also make sightseeing reservations and can arrange onward travel and accommodations.

Another useful and convenient center for obtaining information as well as a departure point for many sightseeing coaches is the Mount Cook Travel Office at the bottom of the mall on the corner of Rees St. (phone 366).

(It is more convenient to reserve at any of the above offices than to try to contact individual operators.)

Coronet Peak

One of New Zealand's most popular ski fields, Coronet Peak, is 11 miles from Queenstown. There are no regular tours, but you can drive in your own automobile. From the road terminus at 3,800 ft. a chair lift rises 1,600 ft. to the summit, from which there are spectacular views. Coronet Peak is snow covered only from June through September, and summer visits are worthwhile. The Coronet Cresta Run is a thrilling toboggan ride on brake-controlled sleighs down 1,800 feet of a stainless steel track.

Skippers Canyon

While highly interesting, this trip should be taken only by those with strong nerves. A warning road sign "Extreme Care Necessary" does not exaggerate. But if you go by one of the regular tour coaches it is safe, though scary. The narrow road twists around a steep gorge past abandoned gold-prospecting sites and relics to a turning point. It was from this part of the Shotover River that a great amount of gold was taken. Tours available.

Cattledrome

Just past the Edith Cavell Bridge is the Cattledrome, where cattle have been trained to walk into the large exhibition hall and mount steps to their allotted pens. Seven breeds of beef cattle and three cows of leading dairy breeds are displayed. A focal point is the milking of the cows by machine at eye level. The show includes a film, *The Grass Growers,* showing how New Zealand has led the world in developing pastures. Shows are held at 9:30 A.M. and 4:15 P.M., and tours are available.

An extension of the Cattledrome tour takes in Arrowtown, with time to explore the gold-mining/pioneer museum and preserved village. Departs 2 P.M.; $24.

Trail Rides

For those who like horseback riding, the half-day trail rides operated by Moonlight Stables from Arthurs Point into the old gold-mining district of Moonlight are something unusual. Transport is by courtesy coach to and from the stables. Departures 9:30 A.M. and 2 P.M.; $24 (half-day).

Trout Fishing Safaris

The lakes and rivers around Queenstown abound in rainbow and brown trout and quinnat salmon. If you're an expert you can arrange to be taken on a guided fly-fishing tour, and if you're just an amateur but would like to try your luck you can go trolling or spinning from a jet boat. Fishing gear is supplied on all charters.

Hang-Gliding Simulator

The hang-gliding simulator enables you to fly a hang glider without the fear of falling to earth. The glider allows full freedom of flight but is safety-harnessed to a 750-ft.-long cable which descends from a 90-ft.-high hill, and the pilot is also safely strapped in. After a brief period of instruction on how to control the flight you can speed down the cable at about 20 mph until gently brought to rest at the base. The simulator is about 12 miles from Queenstown on Malagan's Rd. (the main road to Arrowtown). And transport departs at 9 A.M., 10:30 A.M., noon, 1:30 P.M., 3 P.M., and 4:30 P.M. The cost is $40 an hour with a guaranteed minimum of four flights. Phone Arrowtown 343.

The Ultimate Game

The thrill of stalking an enemy (and being stalked) is realistically created in the Ultimate Game, which is played (usually by teams) in a dense pine forest interspersed with small clearings. Dressed in overalls of different colors and protective goggles, each team tries to ambush, force to surrender, or shoot its opponents with plastic-coated colored water pellets fired from a gas-powered pistol. "Casualties" report to the game controller to register points. Teams can be organized. The site is almost opposite the Arrowtown intersection on the main road to Queenstown. Courtesy transport can be provided. The cost is $25 for an average playing time of 1½ hours. Phone 557.

Whitewater Rafting

The swift Shotover and Kawarau rivers with their turbulent boulder-strewn stretches are ideal for whitewater rafting. The upper canyon of the Shotover River is between rock walls, the lower canyon has twists, turns, and rapids, and the Kawarau is punctuated with rapids. Trips range from 3 to 4½ hours and prices from $64 to $80. All equipment is provided. Rafting operators are Challenge Rafts, Danes Back Country Rafts, Kawarau Raft Expeditions, Queenstown Rafts, Value Tours Rafting and Wild Water Expeditions.

Arrowtown

Just 12 miles from Queenstown, Arrowtown, now little more than a village, was once a booming gold-rush town. Its main street is lined with sycamores, which lay a golden carpet of leaves in the fall. Many of the old stone cottages and wooden buildings have been preserved and are still lived in, giving this sleepy village an air of realism while it still retains its history.

Guided Hiking

Two outstanding guided scenic hikes (known here as walks) operate from Queenstown. The Routeburn Walk covers 25 miles of track or trail over four days through Fiordland and Mount Aspiring National Parks, with accommodations and meals provided in mountain lodges. The four-day Hollyford Valley Walk is also through alpine scenery, although in a different direction. The walks are from November through April.

Queenstown to Te Anau By Road

The road follows the Frankton Arm of Lake Wakatipu to the airport and then drops gently down to the Kawarau Dam Bridge over the outlet of the lake. The dam was constructed in 1926 to lower the waters of the Kawarau River so that the alluvial gold-bearing deposits could be worked. The scheme was not successful and has long been abandoned.

For a time you follow the flanks of the Remarkables and the eastern shore of the lake before arriving at Kingston, about 30 miles from Queenstown at the southern tip of the lake.

The way then lies through the barley-growing and seed-producing region of Garston, and after passing several little settlements descends to Five Rivers, which is little more than a gas station. Watch for the

THE SOUTH ISLAND

signposted right-hand turnoff to Te Anau, as the main highway continues to Lumsden and farther south, and if you are not alert you could fly past it and add miles to your journey by having to turn inland at Lumsden. If you set your speedometer at zero at Queenstown it should be reading about 97 kilometers at Five Rivers.

The main road from Lumsden is joined at Mossburn, 20 miles on, and a right-hand turn is made for Te Anau. Much of the journey is through rolling farm country and some tussock. On the left are the Takitimu Ranges, said in Maori legend to be the petrified hull of the canoe "Takitimu."

Te Anau is 118 miles (190km) from Queenstown, and it is a pleasant 2½- to 3-hour drive.

Fiordland

Some of New Zealand's most spectacular mountain and lake scenery is found in Fiordland National Park on the southwest corner of the South Island. Over three million acres in area, it is one of the largest national parks in the world, and the terrain is so precipitous and heavily forested that parts have never been explored. The land still holds secrets. In 1948 a bird long believed to be extinct, the Takahe *(notornis)*, was discovered in a remote valley. It is now being nurtured to preserve the species. In 1947 a glowworm cave was discovered.

A flight over Fiordland will show why much of it is virginal. Towering peaks and sheer rock walls are jumbled together as if to keep humans at bay. The steep rock walls slide into narrow valleys, and the luxuriant rain forest is almost impenetrable.

In Dusky Sound Captain Cook rested his crew after a two-month voyage, made tea from the manuka shrub, brewed a sort of beer, and boiled a native celery plant as antidotes to scurvy. It was here, too, that the first house was built by a European, bagpipes were first played (by one of the sailors), and the first musket was fired by a Maori.

Queenstown and Te Anau are the starting points for a journey into Fiordland. The highlight is Milford Sound, which can be seen in a 1½-hour scenic flight, but to really appreciate the dramatic and outstanding scenery you should travel by road down the eastern shore of Lake Wakatipu to Lake Te Anau and thence through the mountains to the sound.

From October through April there are full-day return trips by coach, although a one- or two-day stopover at Te Anau is well worthwhile. Alternatively, you can travel by road to Milford Sound, stay overnight, and return to Queenstown by air.

The road journey to Milford Sound is more exciting than the return, as the scenery opens before you more impressively. A two- or three-hour launch cruise down the sound should certainly be undertaken.

Milford Sound

Milford is magnificent—there is no other way of describing the primeval grandeur of this region sculptured by Nature. The majesty of the scenery makes the visitor feel insignificant.

Thousands of years ago great glaciers gouged out the land from granite rock, forming a deep basin. As the glaciers receded, the sea flowed in, filling a great depression. From the water's edge almost vertical cliffs rise several thousands of feet. They are mostly bare rock, yet here and there vegetation clings somehow to the sheer slopes. In many places valleys high above the sound end abruptly in a U shape. These are known as hanging valleys and were formed when the glaciers feeding the main glacier receded and disappeared.

Milford Sound is 10 miles long and about 1½ miles wide at its broadest point. At its deepest the floor is 1,280 ft. below sea level. So deep are the waters that the largest cruise ships can enter the sound, but there is only one place, Harrison Cove, where they can anchor.

Like a forbidding guardian, Mitre Peak rises 5,560 ft. to dominate the sound. Opposite, the Bowen Falls explodes in a great spout of water which soars high into the air before tumbling 520 feet into the sound in a flurry of spray. Farther down are the Stirling Falls (480 ft.), which flow from hanging valleys in a series of leaps before they too plunge into the sea.

To appreciate the beauty of Milford Sound to the full a regular launch cruise should be taken. Only in this way can a sense of the vastness of the encircling cliff faces and the towering heights of the mountains be gained. Scenic flights are also a wonderful way to view the sound and can be arranged from Queenstown.

Milford Sound has one irritating defect—it is heavily populated with voracious sandflies, so go armed with insect repellent.

The Road to Milford Sound

The road to Milford Sound from Te Anau is probably the most scenically exciting in New Zealand, and should be traveled if possible. The distance is only 75 miles, but it will take you three hours or so—not that the road is difficult or dangerous, but there are many points where you will want to stop to admire the view or take photographs.

Shortly after leaving Te Anau, the road crosses the Upukerora River, a noted trout stream, and for the 17 miles to the Te Anau Downs sheep ranch there are views of the South Fiord, Center Island and the Middle Fiord. The road then enters the Eglinton Valley and follows the Eglinton River for some miles. A magnificent forest of beech trees, some from 70 to 90 ft. high, flanks the road between the serrated peaks of the Earl Range on the left and the Livingstone Range on the right.

Suddenly, you enter the Avenue of the Disappearing Mountain. At the end of a long avenue of beech trees a mountain slowly disappears from view instead of growing larger as one would expect. This effect is caused by an almost imperceptible rise in the road, and is startling to say the least.

From Cascade Creek Camp, 47 miles (69.5km) from Te Anau, the outstanding beauty of Fiordland begins. Two small forest-ringed lakes, Gunn and Fergus, are passed, and then the divide is reached. As you round a big bend the Crosscut Range comes into view and a little farther on Mt. Christina, over 7,000 ft., suddenly appears, its sparkling peak rising above the skyline framed by forest.

High, stark granite cliffs, snow-capped and laced with waterfalls, close in as the road follows the floor of the Hollyford Valley and gradually climbs to a large basin of stark granite cliffs.

Like a pinpoint in the massive barrier, the portal of the Homer Tunnel appears. The construction of the tunnel was a daunting undertaking. In winter the area is subject to mountain avalanches, and twisted hunks of reinforced concrete testify to their destructive force where a protective canopy was caught in an avalanche and crumped out of recognition. There is, however, no danger, as the road is closed when there is a danger of avalanches.

Although it is perfectly safe, the tunnel appears a little fearsome at first sight. There is no graceful facade—it is simply a hole in the rock. Its walls are of rough-hewn rock and there is no lighting. Headlights have to be used, and the traffic is one-way for 25 minutes of each hour. When almost at the center you can hear the roar of a hidden waterfall.

THE SOUTH ISLAND

The Homer Tunnel is 3,000 ft. above sea level at its eastern portal and descends for three-quarters of a mile at a grade of 1 in 10. It is only 12 ft. high and 22 ft. wide. As you emerge from the tunnel it is as if the backdrop of a stage were being raised to reveal the beautiful Cleddau Valley.

The road snakes down the moraine in a series of zig-zags and, still dropping, follows the floor of the valley, flanked by lovely forest and occasional waterfalls. The towering mountains of the Sheerdown Range, Mt. Underwood, the Barrier Range and Barren Peak almost enclose the valley. From Tutoko Bridge there are fine views of Mt. Tutoko (9,042 ft.). Then, as you round a corner, Milford Sound springs suddenly into view, like a slide being thrown on to a screen.

The Milford Track

"The finest walk in the world" is the description often given to this three-day, 33-mile hike from Te Anau to Milford Sound. It was not until 1888 that a Scottish immigrant, Quintin Mackinnon, discovered a mountain pass that made land access possible to Milford Sound. This route is now one of the most popular hikes in New Zealand, if only because of the spectacular scenery through which it passes.

The walk is made in three stages, with comfortable overnight accommodation in well-equipped huts. With a guide, it is taken in easy stages and is within the capabilities of anyone who is reasonably fit and used to walking. The season is from mid-December through March. As parties are restricted to 40 persons, reservations are necessary.

The lake steamer leaves Te Anau in the early afternoon and takes you to the head of the lake, from which a half-mile bush track leads to Glade House, where the first night is spent.

The first section of the Milford Track has been likened to a Sunday-afternoon stroll, for the path is broad and rises only 500 ft. in 10 miles. After crossing the swing-bridge over the Clinton River you follow the river through the Clinton Canyon. On the left are the Pariroa Heights, which reach 5,000 ft. For the last mile of the journey the saddle of the Mackinnon Pass can be seen framed in the converging walls of the canyon ahead. The night is spent at Pompolona Huts.

The track becomes steeper after leaving Pompolona and the beech forests give way to ribbonwood. The bushline is left behind as you approach Mackinnon Pass, and at 3,400 ft., the saddle, the highest point in the journey is reached.

The view from the Mackinnon Pass is ample reward for the climb. Three thousand feet down on one side is the bush-clad canyon of the Arthur River, and on the other, just as sheer, is the great cleft of the Clinton Canyon, the bed of an ancient glacier, pointing the way back to Lake Te Anau. Lake Mintaro glitters far below, and the Clinton River threads its way along the valley floor, with the rock walls of the canyon towering thousands of feet on either side. More intimate beauty is provided by the sub-alpine flowers which grow in the pass—mountain lily and daisy and the thin wiry snowgrass make a wonderful show among the rugged hills. Descending from the pass, the track leads under several mountains and ends at Quintin Huts, where the night is spent after the 9¼ mile hike.

A sidetrip to the Sutherland Falls is normally included. The track enters the bush from beside the huts and rises gradually through beautiful ferns and beech trees. The roar of the falls steadily increases, and after a walk of a little over a mile they come into view.

The third day consists of an 11-mile walk and a launch journey of two miles to the jetty in Milford Sound.

Most hikers travel back to Te Anau by motor coach.

Lake Te Anau

Built on the edge of the lake, the township of Te Anau is the land gateway to Fiordland and Milford Sound. At the foot of high, rugged, forest-clad mountains, the lake has three long narrow arms. It is the South Island's largest lake, being 33 miles long and six miles wide at the widest point. Its greatest depth is 906 ft., making the floor 212 ft. below sea level.

Lake Te Anau shares with Waitomo the distinction of having a glowworm cave, but the two differ in many respects. While the Waitomo glowworms extinguish their lights when disturbed by noise, the Te Anau glowworms continue shining above a noisy torrent of water.

Te Anau is a contraction of the Maori name *Te Ana-au,* which means "cave of swirling water." No one knew of this cave until in 1947 a curious resident, Lawson Burrows, went exploring and entered a cavity where water was flowing out of a hill.

A visit to the cave is now an essential part of Te Anau stopovers. The trip takes about 2½ hours and can be undertaken after dinner.

The caves are reached after a half-hour launch cruise. The entrance is low, and one has to crouch for about 20 yards to reach a higher chamber where the river plunges over a human-made dam, necessary to float a steel punt. A series of concrete ramps are climbed and a second boat boarded to enter the glowworm grotto itself. As at Waitomo, the ceiling and walls are covered with thousands and thousands of brightly shining glowworms.

Lake Te Anau is a popular weekend resort for residents of the city of Invercargill, about 100 miles away, many of whom have cottages on the lake shores and boats on the waters. It is popular, too, with anglers, as its waters are full of rainbow and brown trout and Atlantic salmon.

From Te Anau, day trips can be taken by coach or hired automobile to Milford Sound, and scenic flights are also operated.

Te Anau is not far away from New Zealand's "Kentucky country," the Hokonui Hills. There were no feuds, but illicit whisky was distilled there some years ago. Objecting to paying tax on liquor, a Scottish family decided to make their own. The terrain of the hills is such that a successful surprise raid was difficult, but occasionally the "revenooers" paid a visit. They sometimes found the still, but seldom the distillers, who had quietly melted away. The story is told that on several occasions the stills were dismantled and sold to recover costs. And who bought them? The distillers, of course, who took the parts back to the hills for reassembly and went happily back to distilling. Older residents still talk about the potent Hokonui whisky.

The crude but distinctive label featured a skull and crossbones with the words:

> Ergo Bibamus
> Free from all Poisons
> OLD HOKONUI
> Passed All Tests except the Police
> Bottled by ME for YOU
> Produce of SOUTHLAND
> Supplied to all Snake Charmers

You might be able to pick up a label—but not the whisky. Full-day coach trips to Milford Sound, 10 A.M. to 6 P.M., with a launch cruise on the sound, are operated by Fiordland Travel Services (on the lakefront by the jetty), 7416, for $50. Fiordland Travel also operates the 2½-hour afternoon and evening trips to the Te Anau-au glowworm caves at $17.

THE SOUTH ISLAND

Lake Manapouri

"The lake of the sorrowing heart" is the meaning of the Maori name. The legend tells of two sisters who, near death in the high forests, held each other and wept. Their tears divided the hills and formed the lake.

Flanked by the Cathedral Mountains, it is studded with small islands clad in native bush. It has many moods. On a clear morning or in the late afternoon it can be peaceful and serene, with the tranquil beauty of its surroundings mirrored in the waters and the stillness broken only by the call of the tui or bellbird. Or it can have an air of mystery when lying beneath a curtain of mist.

Lake Manapouri is long and narrow. With a coastline of over 100 miles, it is 20 miles long and six miles wide at its widest point, and the deepest part is 872 ft. below sea level. Rainbow and brown trout and Atlantic salmon are plentiful in the lake.

Lake Manapouri became the focal point in one of New Zealand's most heated controversies over the environment. Some 10 years ago the government decided to divert some of the lake waters to a power house, mainly to produce the large amount of electricity required by a new aluminum smelter 100 miles away. This meant raising the level of the lake by several feet to provide water storage, thus burying vegetation at the water's edge and submerging some of the small beaches. A vociferous and effective body, the Guardians of the Lake, was formed, and a petition with some 265,000 signatures was presented to Parliament. The battle was not completely won, but significant modifications were made to the plan.

The hydroelectric plant is unusual in that the powerhouse is 700 ft. underground. The lake waters are channeled down into the powerhouse and discharged into Doubtful Sound on the west coast of the island. Fiordland Travel Ltd. runs a four-hour trip which is full of beauty and interest. Leaving the natural boat anchorage at Pearl Harbor, near the Manapouri township, the launch *Fiordland* threads its way through the islands to West Arm. From here passengers are taken by coach down a 1¼-mile road, which spirals down to the powerhouse 700 ft. below. The powerhouse is a cavern hewn out of solid rock, 364 ft. long by 59 ft. wide. The water drawn from the lake falls nearly 600 ft. to turn the turbines and then passes through a 6¼-mile tailrace to discharge in Deep Cove in Doubtful Sound.

An extension of this trip goes by coach over the 2,200-ft. Wilmot Pass and down into Deep Cove. This trip, 10 A.M. to 6 P.M., is also operated by Fiordland Travel Services and costs $72.

Invercargill

Invercargill (population 50,000) is New Zealand's southernmost city. The Maoris called it Murihiku ("the end of the tail"). The name is formed from the combination of "Inver," from the Gaelic "mouth of the river," and "Cargill," after Captain William Cargill, the first superintendent of the province of Otago. Most of the settlers were of Scottish descent and have left their mark on those streets named after Scottish rivers or places.

For 30 years Invercargill was a "dry" area, a prohibition city where no liquor could be sold, but some 25 years ago it went "wet" in an experiment that has now been followed in several parts of New Zealand. Instead of allowing private enterprise to establish liquor stores, a licensing trust was formed, and all profits are devoted to improving the city's amenities.

For many years the southland area was the largest oat-producing region in New Zealand, but now that the horse has been replaced by machinery it concentrates on sheep raising and dairying. Four large meat-packing plants process nearly six million lambs annually, most of which are exported from the port of Bluff, 17 miles to the south, where an 84-acre island was built in the harbor to provide docks and loading facilities. Across the harbor a large smelter produces 110,000 tons of aluminum annually, powered by electricity from Lake Manapouri.

Fifteen miles across the restless waters of Foveaux Strait lies Stewart Island, New Zealand's third and most southerly island. Stewart Island is so small and sparsely populated that even New Zealanders are inclined to overlook it and forget that New Zealand comprises three and not two islands. It has a population of less than 400, concentrated in one area, and only about 16 miles of road. Rugged and heavily forested, it is indented with many lovely bays and beaches and is a bird sanctuary. The Maoris called the island *Rakiura* ("sky glow") from the superb sunsets for which it is famed.

Off the coast, mutton birds (sooty shearwaters) are harvested in April and May. The birds are very fatty and have a very strong fishy taste.

Not so, however, the large, plump Stewart Island oysters dredged from the waters of Foveaux Strait. They are much larger than rock oysters and perhaps not as sweet, but if oysters are your dish you'll find a dozen almost a full meal. They are marketed throughout New Zealand, but there is a special gastronomical joy in eating oysters freshly dredged from the strait.

DUNEDIN

Dunedin shows a Scottish influence. The original plan of the new Edinburgh to be founded in Otago was made by the lay association of the Free Church of Scotland. It was to be a truly Scots settlement where the Kirk would be the basis of community life.

Like Christchurch, the city was surveyed and laid out before the colonists arrived. The surveyor was instructed to reproduce features of the Scottish capital, and Dunedin has as many associations for the Scots as Christchurch has for the English. Many of the streets bear familiar names—Princes, George, King, Hanover, Frederick, Castle, and Queen streets—and the little boulder-strewn stream flowing through the north-east corner of the city is called the Water of Leith.

In the early 1880s gold was discovered in the province. Thousands of prospectors poured in from all over New Zealand and from Britain, Australia, and even California. Dunedin's population jumped from 2,000 to 5,000 and the population of the Otago Province from 12,000 to 75,000.

Dunedin was the center where prospectors met and prepared to leave for the gold fields. The township became blocked with shanties and tents packed on to all vacant sections. Miners swarmed down every track leading to the gold fields, traveling by bullock wagon, on horseback, and on foot. As much as $200 a week (a substantial sum in those days) could be made, and in the first four wild years Otago exported $14,000,000 worth of gold.

Dunedin boomed. But even in the middle of this dizzy prosperity the canny Scots citizens gave thought to the future, and when inevitably the boom ended the settlement had something permanent to show for the years of precarious good fortune.

THE SOUTH ISLAND

The citizens needed all their determination and resourcefulness in the years that followed, for they had to find new and more permanent means of making their living. They established flourishing industries and developed fruit growing and farming in the province. New prosperity was found after the first shipment of frozen meat left Port Chalmers in 1882.

Today Dunedin has a population of about 120,000 and is New Zealand's fifth largest city. Its progress has been steady, if less spectacular, over the last three-quarters of a century. Stone buildings replaced the wooden shanties of gold-boom times, and Dunedin's beautiful churches and schools are among the finest in the country.

First Church, Gothic in design, stands in Moray Place right in the center of the city, and when the spire is floodlit the building is an impressive sight. St. Paul's Cathedral dominates the Octagon. The main block of the Otago University, the oldest university in New Zealand, is also Gothic; a stately gray stone building with a tall clock tower.

Railroad Station

Railroad enthusiasts will find the railroad station fun ("railway" is the New Zealand term). Its architect was dubbed Gingerbread George, and the station is a fitting monument to him. He seems to have wanted to leave nothing undecorated. Heraldic lions corner the massive copper-capped tower, the NZR (New Zealand Railways) cypher is engraved on window panes everywhere, ornate scrolls surround the ticket-office windows, and stained-glass windows depict locomotives approaching at full steam.

Lanarch Castle

Built in 1871 and copied from an old Scottish castle, Lanarch Castle is a living memento of the Victorian way of life. William Lanarch had married the daughter of a French duke, and, being wealthy, he set out to provide her with the sort of lavish home he thought she should have. It is said to have cost about $300,000, which was a very considerable sum in those days. The interior is a mass of ornate carving and mosaics, elaborately decorated ceilings, and marble fireplaces. The most notable feature is a Georgian hanging staircase. There is even a dungeon, where Lanarch is said to have locked up poachers caught on the property. It is situated on the Otago Peninsula nine miles from the city and is included in sightseeing tours or can be visited by taxi or private automobile.

Olveston

This stately mansion, built between 1904 and 1906, stands in a beautiful setting of trees and formal gardens. In the Dutch influenced Jacobean style, Olveston has some 35 rooms, and contains an unusual collection of domestic art: paintings, ceramics, ivory, bronze, silverware, and furniture. It is only one mile from the city.

Royal Albatross Colony

Taiaroa Head, at the tip of the Otago Peninsula about an hour's journey from the city, is the only place in the world where this magnificent bird breeds close to human habitation and can be seen at close quarters. One of the largest of birds, it has a wing span of about 11 ft., weighs up to 15 pounds, stands about 30 inches high, has a bill about 7 inches long, and may live 70 years. It does not breed until it is about seven years old and then only on alternate years.

The birds arrive from their migration in September and settle down to lay a single egg, which is white, is about 5 inches long, and weighs about a pound. The parents share sitting duty for about 11 weeks, and the chick may take three days to struggle free from the shell. It is not fully fledged for about a year, when it flies as far as Tahiti in search of squid. Eight years pass before it returns to start a new breeding cycle.

The colony is rigidly protected, and bookings must be made in advance through the New Zealand Tourist Office, 131 Princes Street; parties are restricted to 10 persons. The season is usually late November through mid-March but may be canceled without notice to protect the birds. There is no public transport, so you may need a taxi or rental car. From January, when the chicks have hatched, there is an afternoon coach tour, usually on Mondays, Wednesdays, and Saturdays only.

Weather conditions at the colony are often boisterous, and 40 to 50 knot winds are not unusual. Warm clothing and walking shoes are recommended. Binoculars are available for observing the birds.

The Roads to the West Coast

Like a long spine, the Southern Alps divide the west from the east coast. There are only three ways across them—the Lewis Pass and Arthur's Pass from Christchurch and the Haast Pass from Queenstown and Wanaka.

By the Lewis Pass, the northern route, it is 208 miles (335km) to Greymouth. The ascent to and descent from the 2,840-ft. summit lie through glorious beech forests.

By Arthur's Pass it is 159 miles (258km) to Greymouth. The first pass to be negotiated is Porter's Pass which, at 3,102 ft., is 77 ft. higher than Arthur's Pass on the main divide. It is the boundary between Canterbury and Westland and the center of Arthur's Pass National Park. The mountains are pierced by a 5¼-mile railroad tunnel, an outstanding engineering feat. One portal appears at Otira as you leave the pass.

Neither pass poses difficulties to the driver, although the descent from the summit of Arthur's Pass to the west coast is winding and steep.

The Haast Pass, at 1,849 ft., is the lowest of the alpine passes and many find it more restful to the eye. The road passes through beautiful forest and mountain scenery, with good views of Mount Brewster (8,264 ft.) and the Brewster Glacier. As there is no settlement of any size between Wanaka and the Fox Glacier 180 miles away, take a picnic lunch.

The opening of the Haast Pass road in 1965 has opened a circular route from Christchurch through to the West Coast, to the glaciers and through the Haast Pass to Queenstown. Before then it was necessary to return from the glaciers to Greymouth in order to reach Queenstown.

Franz Josef and Fox Glaciers

The main attractions of the west coast are the Franz Josef Glacier and the Fox Glacier, which flow down from the Southern Alps. Only 24 miles apart, they are the lowest in the southern hemisphere and are unusual in that they descend to the edge of native forest. Both have receded in recent years, but the recession does not make them less beautiful. Scenic roads lead almost to the terminal faces, from which

THE SOUTH ISLAND

you can take a guided walk on the ice if conditions are suitable. Boots are provided by the hotel. The walk at the Franz Josef is now quite a rugged one.

The Franz Josef Glacier was named after the Emperor Franz Josef of Austria by the geologist Sir Julius von Haast in 1862.

The glacier's broken surface ends abruptly in a terminal ridge. Here the ice beneath the covering shingle is gray, but only a short distance above it is clear white. From an ice cave at the foot of the glacier the turbulent Waiho River ("smoky water") gushes out and flows for 12 miles to the coast. The water appears milky from the particles of rock ground to dust by the glacier, and a layer of mist sits above the surface, formed by the sudden chilling of the warm air as it meets the ice-cold river. A short distance from the source of the river is a small hot mineral spring, which emerges beside cold water.

The glaciers start at the crests of the Southern Alps and are fed by heavy snowfalls brought by westerly winds. The steep mountain slopes account for the glacier's precipitous fall—about 1,000 ft. a mile.

Unlike other New Zealand glaciers, the Franz Josef's surface is almost clear of debris. The surface is marked by deep crevasses and jagged pinnacles, owing to tension caused by the more rapid motion of the middle of the glacier or by its movement over steep slopes in the rock floor of the valley. The crevasses are usually confined to the upper layers of the ice where the pressure is not great enough to force the ice to flow.

Ice is solid, but the movement of a glacier resembles that of a viscous fluid. The movement of the Franz Josef Glacier varies from 1½ to 15 ft. a day.

Be sure to visit the small church in the bush, St. James Chapel. A large window behind the altar gives a magnificent view of the bush and mountains.

Aerial sightseeing trips are run from the air strip, and ski planes are used for landings on the glacier snowfields.

The Fox Glacier was named as a compliment to Sir William Fox, who visited it during his term as premier of the colony. The Fox River emerges from the terminal face and flows westward to join the Cook River on its journey to the sea. The Cook River Flat is good sheep and cattle country.

Nearby Lake Matheson is famous for its reflections of Mt. Cook and Mt. Tasman. The best time to see these is in the early morning. The return walk through the native bush surrounding the lake takes about 40 minutes.

Hokitika

Hokitika now has a population of only a little more than 3,000, but in 1864 and 1865 it was a booming gold-rush town of thousands. In those years over 1.3 million ounces of gold were exported. But the rush declined as quickly as it had begun when rich deposits were exhausted. Although small quantities of gold may still be found, Hokitika now mainly relies on farming and lumber.

But it was left with one natural asset—greenstone, a type of jade. New Zealand Greenstone, as it is called, is found in rivers near Hokitika, and helicopters are used to bring out boulders from inaccessible sites in the mountains. A 12-ton boulder was recently dragged from the sea.

Greenstone is extremely hard and can be cut only by diamond saws. The Maoris called it *pounamu* and used to raid the area to obtain it for their war clubs and ornaments. A visit to the Westland Greenstone Factory to watch the stone being cut, fashioned, and polished is well worthwhile. Greenstone jewelry and ornaments may be purchased at the factory (as in most souvenir shops throughout New Zealand), but, like other kinds of jade, it is not inexpensive.

Hokitika is also a prime source for a popular New Zealand delicacy —whitebait. A type of smelt, it is netted in spring at the mouths of and on the banks of rivers as it swims upstream. The fish is usually cooked in batter as fritters or patties.

Greymouth

Greymouth, with a population of just under 8,000, is primarily a coal-mining town and the main business center of the west coast. Seven miles south is Shantytown, a convincing replica of a gold-field town at the height of the boom. Authenticity has been observed as far as possible, in both the buildings and the replicas on display. Some of the buildings were restored from those actually used, and an 1897 locomotive hauls a couple of passenger cars a short distance through the bush.

Traces of gold are still found in the area, and you can try your luck in panning for gold at Shantytown. Even if you don't find a nugget, which occasionally happens, you can be reasonably sure of leaving with a few glittering specks in a tiny phial of water. Transport can be arranged through the West Coast Public Relations Office, Mawhera Quay.

Marlborough Sounds

North of Christchurch and at the northern tip of the South Island are the Marlborough Sounds, an enormous jigsaw puzzle of sunken valleys forming over 600 miles of waterways. Three of the largest are Queen Charlotte, Pelorus, and Kenepuru sounds, Pelorus being the most extensive (34 miles long). The hills, headlands, and peninsulas rising from the sheltered waters are in many cases densely wooded, and everywhere there are secluded bays and beaches. Some of the hills have been turned into sheep farms which can only be reached by water.

Understandably, the sounds are a popular holiday center for both Wellington and Christchurch residents, for although they are 217 miles (339.5km) by road from Christchurch they are only 52 miles from Wellington by sea. The opportunities for swimming, sailing, boating, and exciting sea fishing are limitless. Those who like the amenities of a township will base themselves at Picton (population normally about 3,000, but rising to 10,000 at the height of the holiday season between Christmas and the end of January); those who prefer relaxing in quiet scenic beauty by the sea "away from it all" or enjoy boat fishing or surf-casting will choose a place like the Portage in Kenepuru Sound.

The ubiquitous Captain Cook entered Queen Charlotte Sound in 1770 and anchored his ship *Endeavour* near the northern entrance in "a very safe and convenient cove" (Ship Cove). On an island he hoisted the flag and announced he was taking possession of New Zealand in the name of King George III, after whose queen the sound is named. Cook returned to the sound four times.

Passenger-vehicle steamers of over 4,000 tons sail regularly each day from Wellington to Picton. The voyage takes 3½ hours, but only two hours are spent in Cook Strait itself. The last hour is entrancing, after the steamer has swung through a narrow entrance and cruises down the narrow sound, whose banks are dotted with sheep farms.

From Picton there are launch cruises to various parts of the sound and organized fishing trips.

THE SOUTH ISLAND

Nelson

Only 40 minutes by air from Wellington and 73 miles by road from Picton, Nelson is one of the sunniest places in New Zealand, with 2,407 sunshine hours a year. Its climate and lovely beaches make it highly popular for holidays and retirement.

In 1858, although it had a population of less than 3,000, Nelson was declared a city by Queen Victoria when she ordained that it should be a bishop's see. A cathedral was duly built. Today Nelson has a population of over 42,000.

Nelson is the hub of one of New Zealand's largest fruit-growing areas. Orchards are to be seen everywhere, and it exports over a million cases of apples each year, mainly to Britain. It is here, too, that New Zealand's tobacco is grown, as well as hops for brewing.

Nelson is proud of being the birthplace of Lord Rutherford, the first man to split the atom. He received his early education at Nelson College and went on to do research into radioactivity at McGill University, Montreal, and later at Cambridge University, England. He was born at Brightwater, 12 miles south of Nelson.

Near outlying Takaka is one of the largest fresh water springs in the world, Pupu Springs. Water bubbles out of the sand at a reputed 200 million gallons a day and a constant temperature of 52°F.

PRACTICAL INFORMATION FOR THE SOUTH ISLAND

**ACCOMMODATIONS.** Average room rates for hotels on the South Island run NZ$85–NZ$145. A motel is less expensive, averaging NZ$45–NZ$60 for a double. THC means Tourist Hotel Corporation—high-quality rooms in the more remote areas.

CHRISTCHURCH

Admiral Lodge Motor Hotel. 51 Pages Rd.; (03) 899–014. 20 rooms and motel flats. Restaurant, bar, parking.

Avon Motor Lodge. 356 Oxford St.; (03) 791–180. 108 rooms. Restaurant, bars, parking.

Blenheim Road Motor Inn. 280 Blenheim Rd.; (03) 487–063. 20 rooms and efficiency units. Licensed restaurant; bar; pool; parking.

Canterbury Inn. 110 Mandeville St.; (03) 485–049. 45 rooms. Restaurant, bar, parking.

Chateau Regency. 187 Deans Ave.; (03) 488–999. 98 rooms; suites available. Restaurant, bars, parking.

Christchurch TraveLodge. Memorial Ave.; (03) 583–139. 110 rooms. Restaurants, bar, parking, pool.

Clarendon Hotel. 78 Worcester St.; (03) 798–440. 76 rooms. Restaurant, bars.

Coker's Hotel. 52 Manchester St.; (03) 798–580. 37 rooms. Restaurant, bars.

Commodore Motor Inn. 447 Memorial Ave.; (03) 588–129. 105 rooms. Restaurant, bars; close to airport and putting green.

Cotswold Inn. 88–90 Papanui Rd.; (03) 553–535. New unusual hotel; six wings built to resemble a 16th-century inn. 50 luxury suites; restaurants; bars; parking.

DB Redwood Court Hotel. 340 Main North Rd.; (03) 529–165. 22 rooms. Restaurant, bars, parking.

Gainsborough Motor Lodge. 263 Bealey Ave.; (03) 798–660. 52 rooms. Restaurant, bar, parking.

Hotel Russley. Roydvale Ave.; (03) 588–289. 69 rooms. Restaurant, bar, pool. Adjacent golf course.

Kingsgate Vacation. Colombo St.; (03) 795–880. 90 rooms. Restaurants, bars.

Latimer Motor Lodge. 195 Worcester St.; (03) 796–760. 29 rooms. Restaurant, bars, parking.

Noah's Hotel. Corner Worcester St. and Oxford Terr.; (03) 794–700. 214 rooms; some suites. Restaurants, bars.

Shirley Lodge Motor Hotel. 112 Marshlands Rd.; (03) 853–034. 63 rooms. Bar, restaurant, parking.

White Star Motor Inn. 252 Barbados St.; (03) 790–540. 30 rooms. Restaurant, bars, parking.

DUNEDIN

Abbey Lodge Motor Inn and Motels. 680 Castle St.; (024) 775–380. 38 rooms, 12 motel apartments. Restaurant, bar, parking.

Adrian Motel. 101 Queens Dr., St. Kilda (close to beach); (024) 52–009. 10 units, swimming pool, spa.

Alcala Motel. Corner George and St. David sts.; (024) 779–073. 21 motel flats; parking.

Commodore Hotel. 932 Cumberland St.; (024) 777–766. 12 motel units. Attractive decor, parking, close to restaurants.

Leisure Lodge Motor Inn. Corner Great King and Duke sts.; (024) 775–360. 50 rooms. Restaurant, bar.

THE SOUTH ISLAND

Pacific Park Motor Inn. 23 Wallace St.; (024) 773-374. 60 rooms, restaurant, bar.
Regal Court. 755 George St.; (024) 777-729. 11 motel flats in different ethnic styles; parking.
Southern Cross Hotel. Princes St.; (024) 770-752. 94 rooms. Restaurant, bars.
Quality Inn. Upper Moray Pl.; (024) 776-784. 55 rooms, restaurant, bar.

FRANZ JOSEF GLACIER

THC Franz Joseph Hotel. Phone 719 Franz Josef. 45 rooms. Restaurant, bars, parking.
Westland Motor Inn. Hwy. 6, Box 33; phone 729 Franz Josef. 47 rooms. Restaurant, bar, parking.

FOX GLACIER

Fox Glacier Hotel. Phone 839 Weheka. 53 rooms. Restaurant, bars, parking.
Kingsgate Hotel. Phone 839 Weheka. 55 rooms. Restaurant, bar, game room, shop.

GREYMOUTH

Ashley Motel & Motor Inn. 70-74 Paroa Rd.; phone (027) 5135. 54 serviced units. Restaurant, bar, parking.
King's Motor Hotel. 88 Mawhera Quay.; (027) 5085. 177 rooms. Restaurant, bar, pool, parking.
Quality Inn. Greymouth Hotel. 68 High St.; (027) 5154. 26 rooms. Restaurant, bar, disco.
Revington's Hotel. Tainui St.; (027) 7055. 25 rooms, restaurant, bar.

HOKITIKA

Quality Inn. Westland Hotel. 2 Weld St. phone 411. 28 rooms. Restaurant, bar, parking; close to railway terminal.
Hokitika Hotel. 22 Fitzherbert St.; 292. 3 rooms; 13 units with kitchens. Breakfast available.

INVERCARGILL

Ascot Park Hotel/Motel. Corner Tay St. and Racecourse Rd.; (021) 76-195. 77 rooms, 23 motel units. Spa, heated indoor pool, restaurant, bar, parking.
Don Lodge Motor Hotel. 77 Don St.; (021) 86-125. 24 rooms. Restaurant, bar, parking.
Grand Hotel. 76 Dee St.; (021) 88-059. 62 rooms. Restaurant, bar.
Kelvin Hotel. 16 Kelvin St.; (021) 82-829. 82 rooms. Restaurant, bars.
Swan Lake Motor Inn. 217 North Rd.; (021) 59-135. 15 motel-type rooms, restaurant.

MARLBOROUGH SOUNDS

Quality Inn Hotel. High St., Picton; phone (057) 452. 20 rooms, restaurant, bar, parking.
The New Portage Hotel. Kenepuru Sound; (057) 161. 11 rooms with facilities, 22 rooms share baths. Restaurant, bar, parking; informal atmosphere.
Picton Motor Inn. Waikawa Rd., Picton; (057) 444. 70 units. Boating available. Pool, restaurant, bar, parking.
Whaler's Inn. Picton 1002. 34 rooms, Restaurant, bar, parking.

MILFORD SOUND

The Tourist Hotel Corporation has a well-appointed and comfortable hotel (the **THC Milford**) with restaurant and bar at the head of the sound, but as that is the only accommodation available, advance reservations are essential. Telex 4300, or cable WELCOME.

MOUNT COOK

As Mount Cook is within a national park, only the Tourist Hotel Corporation is permitted to operate hotels. **The Hermitage,** regarded as the best resort hotel, is so built that each room has excellent views of Mount Cook and other mountains and is furnished to a very high standard. It has restaurants, bars and parking. Phone (05621) 809 or cable WELCOME.

Nearby **Glencoe Lodge** (phone 809, telex 4308, or cable WELCOME), **Mount Cook Motels** and **Mount Cook Chalets** (same phone) are less luxurious, with lower rates. The popularity of the area, and its remoteness from a town of any size, makes it essential to reserve accommodations in advance.

NELSON

Quality Inn Hotel. Trafalgar Square; 82–299. 95 rooms. Restaurant, bar, pool, parking.

QUEENSTOWN

A-Line Motor Inn. 27 Stanley St.; phone 316. 56 rooms. Restaurant, bar, lake view.
Hotel Esplanade. 32 Peninsula St.; 585. 21 rooms, restaurant, bar, on lake shore.
Kingsgate. Frankton Rd.; 940. 83 rooms, top quality.
Lakeland Regency. Lake Esplanade; 207. 116 rooms. Restaurant, bar.
Mountain View Lodge Motel. Frankton Rd.; 153. 1 mile from town, 32 motel apartments, restaurant, bar, parking.
Country Lodge. Fernhill Rd, ½ mile from town; 930. 25 rooms. Restaurant, bar, parking.
TraveLodge. Beach St.; 1000. 140 rooms. Restaurant, bar, parking, sauna; on lake shore.
Vacation Hotel (Frankton). Vewlett Crescent; 565. 87 rooms, restaurant, bars. 5 miles from Queenstown; adjacent to airport.
Vacation Hotel (O'Connell's). Beach St.; 286. 65 rooms. Restaurant, bar.

TE ANAU AND MANAPOURI

Campbell Autolodge. 42 Te Anau Terr.; phone (0229) 7546. 23 rooms, motel flats. Restaurant, parking.
Fiordland Motor Lodge. Hwy. 94; (0229) 7511. 106 rooms, motel flats. Restaurant, bar, parking.
Luxmore Lodge. Milford Rd.; (0229) 7526. 69 rooms, restaurant, bar, parking.
Quality Inn. Manapouri. 56 rooms. Restaurant, bar, parking, lake swimming.
THC Te Anau Hotel. Lakefront; (0229) 7411. 102 rooms. Restaurant, bars, parking.
Vacation Hotel Te Anau. Te Anau Terr.; (0229) 7421, Box 133; 96 rooms. Restaurant, bar, parking, jacuzzi. Summer resort.
Village Inn. Mokoroa St.; (0229) 7911. 42 rooms, restaurant, bar, parking.

RESTAURANTS. Dinners on the South Island range from NZ$15 to NZ$30 per person for a three-course meal, not including drinks, tax, tip, though the most elegant restaurants can run higher. Many restaurants do not have liquor licenses but will allow you to bring your own wine; call ahead if this is a concern.

CHRISTCHURCH

Allegro. 108 Hereford St.; 793–250. Elegant decor, Italian food.
Cascade Restaurant. Main foyer of Town Hall; 790–738. Modern atmosphere, Chateaubriand a specialty, smorgasbord.

THE SOUTH ISLAND

The Civic Regency. 198 Manchester St.; 67–779. Elegant, refurbished civic chambers specializing in Continental and Chinese cuisine.
Dux-de-Lux. Corner Montreal and Hereford sts.; 66–919. Vegetarian.
Guardsman Restaurant. 103 Armagh St.; 68–701. Contemporary dining, barbecued lamb cutlets a specialty.
Kurasaki. Colombo St.; 67–092. Japanese food and atmosphere.
Leinster. 158 Leinster Rd.; 558–866. Game food, varied. B.Y.O.
Michaels. 178 High St.; 60–822. French Mediterranean food.
Paul Revere's. 813 Armagh St.; 799–099. Traditional cooking.
Sign of the Takahe. Dyers Pass Rd., Cashmere Hills; 324–052. Elegant atmosphere and European cuisine. A taxi ride from town.
Waitangi Room. Noah's Hotel, Oxford Tce.; 794–700. Excellent food, efficient formal service. One of the city's top restaurants.

DUNEDIN

Blades. 450 George St.; 776–548. Simple, intimate; excellent French food.
Carnarvon Station. Prince of Wales Hotel, 474 Princes St.; 770–389. Impressive, authentic railroad setting.
The Huntsman. 309 George St.; 778–009. Old English setting, booth seating, specializes in steaks.
Rogano. 388 Princes St.; 775–748. Specializes in seafood.
La Scala. Alton Ave., Musselburgh; 54–555. Attractively furnished, specializes in Italian food.
Savoy. Corner of Princes St. and Moray Pl.; 778–977. Victorian-style furnishings, specializes in New Zealand foods.
Terrace Cafe. 118 Moray Pl.; 740–686. Small and quaint; specializes in vegetarian dishes.

INVERCARGILL

Crawford House. 40 Don St.; 84–776. Central European cuisine.
Donovan Licensed Restaurant. 220 Bainfield St.; 58–156. Game food a specialty; courtesy car available.
Gerrard's Restaurant. Corner Leven and Esk sts.; 83–406. Try the blackboard specials.
Strathern Inn Restaurant. 200 Elles Rd.; 89–100. Edwardian-style decor, a la carte specialties.

QUEENSTOWN

Caesar's Restaurant. Plaza Arcade, Beach St.; 1385. Italian and New Zealand cuisine.
Country Lodge. Fernhill, 3 miles from township; phone 930. Views down south arm of the lake, whitebait a specialty.
Gourmet Express. 62 Shotover St.; 1407. American-style coffee shop, open 7 A.M. to 9 P.M. for breakfast, lunch, dinner. Good food, very moderate.
La Rochelle. Beach St.; 1345. French cuisine.
Packers Arms. About 4 miles out of Queenstown; 929. Genuine old stone cottage tastefully decorated; venison ragout a specialty.
Roaring Meg's Restaurant. 57 Shotover St.; 968. Informal atmosphere; specializes in scallops, salmon, whitebait, venison, and lamb.
Sablis Restaurant. Beach St.; 145. French cuisine.
Skyline Restaurant. Top of cableway; 123. Panoramic views and good cuisine, specialty is crayfish mornay.
Upstairs/Downstairs. Arcade in center of town; 203. Modern restaurant with semi-Victorian decor, specialty is fillet steak with tomato, cheese, and onion.
Westy's. Center of town in the mall; 609. Gourmet food, yet casual atmosphere.

TE ANAU

Kepler's Restaurant. Corner Milford Rd. and Mokonui St.; 7909. Game and seafood.

Southern Touch Restaurant. Corner Milford and Bligh rds.; 7248. New Zealand food a la carte.

GETTING AROUND. Christchurch. The Christchurch international and domestic airport is seven miles from the city center. Taxis are available from outside the terminal, and the average cost to a city hotel or motel is NZ$12. *Pacific Tourways* operates a shuttle service, costing NZ$1.50, to the main hotels and motels, with a pickup service on request for airline departures.

The principal taxi firms are *Blue Star Taxis* (799–799) and *Gold Band Taxis* (795–795).

Dunedin. The Momana Airport is 18.5 miles (30km) from the city. An airport bus costs NZ$6 per person each way, and buses depart and arrive opposite the Southern Cross Hotel, High St.

For taxis, phone *City Taxis* (771–771) or *Dunedin Taxis* (777–777).

Invercargill. *Blue Star Taxis* (86–079).

Queenstown. *Taxis* (112).

TOURS. Christchurch. *Red Bus Scenic Tours* (Christchurch Transport Board; 794–600) offers a two-hour tour of city highlights, 10 A.M. daily, $7.50. 3-hour hills and harbor tour, including Summit Rd. and short cruise, 1:30 P.M. daily, $9.50. All tours depart from kiosk, Cathedral Square.

Canterbury Scenic Tours (69–660): half-day city-sights tour, 9 A.M. and 1:30 P.M. daily, $18. Evening city tour, 6:30 P.M. to 9 P.M. October to March, $18. Full-day tours: Akaroa and cheese factory, 9 A.M. to 5 P.M., $54; Hanmer Springs thermal resort 80 miles north), $65. Pickup from hotels in metropolitan area.

H&H Travel Lines (The Gray Line), 40 Lichfield Street (799–120). Garden City Tour, 10:30 A.M. to 12:15 P.M., $14. Historic Summit Tour, 1:15 to 3:45 P.M. $17. Tours depart Canterbury Information Center.

Pacific Tourways, 502A Wairakei Road (599–133). Garden City Tour, 9 A.M. to 11:30 A.M., 2 to 4:30 P.M., $18. Full-day tour to Akaroa, 9 A.M. to 5:30 P.M., $60. Four-day tour with 45-minute scenic flight and lunch on a high-country sheep station, 8 A.M. to 8 P.M., $190. Full-day tour to Mount Cook and Queenstown, Tues. and Sat., departs 8 A.M.; $395 including accommodations and breakfast.

Town & Country Tours (63–289). Banks Peninsula and Akaroa Tour, 9:30 A.M. to 5 P.M., $55. Arthur's Pass and visit to a sheep station, 9 A.M. to 6 P.M., $70. Country-style tour, including visits to a pottery and honey factory, 9:30 A.M. to 5:30 P.M., $65. Tours depart from Clarendon Hotel, Worcester St., or pickup by arrangement.

Dunedin. The two daily sightseeing tours by coach include: *Newton's Coachways'* city and suburbs tour (52–199), which leaves the Dunedin visitors center at 1 P.M. and covers either Larnach Castle, Olveston, and Glenfalloch or the Royal Albatross Colony and seals and penguins (in season).

H & H Panoramic Tours (740–674) leaves the visitors center at 9:30 A.M. and takes in a half-day of city sightseeing and a guided visit to Olveston.

Franz Josef and Fox Glaciers. If you're not absolutely terrified of small aircraft and the weather is favorable you will miss an unforgettable experience if you don't take a scenic flight. The *Mount Cook Line* has 10 different flights by ski plane over the Franz Josef, Fox, Tasman, Meuller, and Hooker glaciers and over the main divide to Mount Cook. Some flights include a landing on the huge upper mountain snowfields by ski plane. At Franz Joseph call 714; at Fox 5 812.

Glacier Helicopters, which holds a snow-landing-by-helicopter concession, operates flights over the Franz Josef, Fritz, Victoria, and Fox glaciers. Flights are from 10 to 30 minutes. At Franz Josef call 879.

Invercargill. City tours are run by *Panorama Tours* (82–419), starting at their terminal at the corner of Don and Kelvin sts. at 1:15 P.M.

Marlborough Sounds. Half- and full-day cruises are operated by *Friendship Cruises,* London Quay, Picton (phone 175). Fishing trips can be arranged, and small boats with outboards may be hired. For sailing in the sheltered waters of the Sound, 24-ft. motor sailers may be hired from *Southern Maritime Charters,* London Quay. Further information is available from the *Marlborough Public Relations Association,* Blenheim; phone (057)84–480.

Milford Sound. See Queenstown, below.

THE SOUTH ISLAND

Mount Cook. Tours of this mountain region can be arranged from Christchurch through *Guthrey's* (79–3560) and *Pacific Tourways* (599–133). For a ski plane flight, contact the *Mount Cook Line*.

Nelson. Personalized half- and full-day tours are conducted by *Nelson Day Tours* (76–674).

Queenstown. Sightseeing tours of Queenstown sites, such as the Cattledrome Arrowtown, and Skippers Canyon can be arranged by contacting New Zealand Tourist Office, 49 Shotover St., phone 143, or Mt. Cook Travel Office, at the bottom of the Mall on Rees St., phone 366.

Coach tours are operated by *Fiordland Travel* ($68), *H&H Travel Lines* ($66), and New Zealand Road Services ($62). The first two will pick up from hotels if prebooked.

Fiordland Travel also operates a daily coach trip to lake Manapouri, the underground power station, and over the Wilmot Pass to Doubtful Sound (with a launch cruise on the sound). The tour departs at 7:15 A.M. and returns at 8 P.M. and costs $92. A lunch may be purchased at the Lake Manapouri cafeteria for $4.

H&H Travel Lines runs a coach tour to the Routeburn and Greenstone valleys at the head of the lake. The tour departs at 9 A.M. and returns at 3 P.M. Dec. to Apr. Take your own lunch. Fares are $30 to Routeburn and $35 to Greenstone.

Milford Sound

Mount Cook Airlines will fly you over the spectacular scenery at Milford Sound, land you there for a brief exploration, or land you there for a 2-hour cruise down the Sound. Book at the Mount Cook office Rees and Ballarat sts. (366) or *Milford Sound Scenic Flights* at any travel office or the airport.

Three coach lines operate daily return trips to Milford Sound. It is a long day, as the coaches leave Queenstown at 7:30 A.M. and return at 8 P.M., but the spectacular scenery makes it worthwhile. There's time for a launch cruise down Milford Sound. Book at the *Railways Road Services Office, H. & H. Tours,* or the *Government Tourist Bureau,* 43 Shotover St. (143).

The Remarkables

The newly developed ski field high in the Remarkables is in a previously inaccessible area. The road snakes up the edge of the mountain range to the base facilities at 4,500 ft., from which 6-seat gondolas take you up 15,000 ft. more. A short climb then takes you to Lookout Point, from which there are magnificent 180-degree panoramic views. The skiing area is clear of snow until about May, but its absence does not detract from the rugged beauty of the landscape. Mount Cook Line coaches have daily tours at 2:30 P.M., and the cost is $18.50.

SPECIAL-INTEREST SIGHTSEEING. Dunedin. *Speight's Brewery* is one of the smallest breweries in New Zealand and is strictly regional, servicing, Otago and Southland. But not long before the war its beer was shipped around the country, had won numerous international awards, and had an enviable reputation for quality. In northern ports its coastal ship became known as the Mercy Ship.

A rather unusual trip is a tour of the brewery at 200 Rattray St., just three blocks from the Octagon, at 10:30 A.M. Mon.–Fri. for $2. Bookings are essential (779–480). The visitors center contains a collection of historic photographs and displays, and on the tour visitors can see how barrels were made, see beer brewing in gleaming copper vessels, fermenting in open kauri vats, lagering in cold storage, being filtered and bottled in the packaging hall, and being loaded into the draught beer tankers—a feature of beer distribution in New Zealand. The tour is up to 1½ hours long and, appropriately, concludes with a visit to the Board Room for a glass of Speight's Beer.

Queenstown. Visits to the *Walter Peak* sheep and cattle farms and the *Cecil Peak* sheep, cattle, deer, and horse farm make fascinating excursions. A half-day trip to either ranch by launch (the only means of access) is well worthwhile. Hosts explain how the steep hills are farmed and how sheep dogs are able to muster the animals from "the tops." Sheep-dog demonstrations are given. Walter Peak operates its own launch, which leaves the Queenstown launch jetty at

9:30 A.M., returning at 12:30 P.M. (reservations from any travel office), and the Cecil Peak launch leaves at 9:30 A.M. and 2:15 P.M., returning at noon and 4:45 P.M. Tickets are available from any travel office or the launch captains.

Aerial gondolas will take visitors 1,530 ft. above town to *Bob's Peak*, where a restaurant affords spectacular views. The terminal is at the corner of Isle and Brecon sts. The gondola operates 10 A.M.–5 P.M. and from 6:30 P.M. until the restaurant closes at midnight.

Earnslaw Cruises. It is hard to resist making a trip on this stately vintage steamer, which has plied the lake since 1912 and dominates the bay with its thin red funnel, its white hull, and its column of black smoke (just about the only pollution around Queenstown but excused because of the steamer's historic value). A midday one-hour lunch cruise from 12:30 P.M. (Aug. to June) is a restful break from other sightseeing and costs $12. There is also a one-hour evening cruise (Dec. 26 to Mar. 31) departing at 6 P.M. with the option of dining aboard for $12. Book at ferry wharf; Fiordland Travel Services; phone 570.

Jet Boats. Several jet boats operate either from Queenstown Bay or the outlet of the Kawarau River and down the river *(Alpine Jet, Goldstream Jet, Kawarau Jet, Pro Jet, Queenstown River Jet,* and *Twin Rivers Jet).* Durations range from 1 to 1½ hours and cost from $23 to $30. All depart hourly and courtesy transport from the Mount Cook Travel Office is provided if necessary (see Tours).

For added thrills there are combinations of jet boats and helicopters such as *Helijet* (1½ hours, $55), *Pro Jet/Heliflight* (1½ hours, $53), *Pro Jet/Helishuttle* (1½ to 2 hours, $62, *Pro Jet/Raft* (3 hours, $64), *River Jet/Helisights* (two hours, $69), *River Jet/Raft* (3½ hours, $64), *Triple Thriller* (3½ hours, $80), and *Ultimate Three* (3½ hours, $80). Regular departures, but times should be checked with New Zealand Travel Office or Mount Cook Travel (again, see Tours).

Shotover Jet. Of all the jet-boat rides the *Shotover Jet* is the most spectacular and the most thrilling. It speeds along a stretch of the Shotover River which at first glance would appear to be unnavigable. Invented by a New Zealander, the boat has no propeller but is driven by a concentrated jet of water under high pressure, rather like a jet aircraft. They can travel in only 4 inches of water and maneuver quickly and easily through shallows and rapids, even turning in their own length.

Carrying up to nine passengers, the boat speeds through a narrow gorge, dodging boulders, over rapids and along shallow stretches only 1 foot in depth. Passengers wear life jackets, but this is purely a precautionary measure and there is no real danger. If the boat did happen to strike a boulder it would dent but not puncture. The trip starts below the Edith Cavell Bridge at Arthur's Point, about 3 miles from Queenstown, to which transport is provided at the Mount Cook Tourist Offices. Cost $35.

Hydrofoil Cruise. A fully enclosed hydrofoil runs 20-minute cruises ($12) at 11:30 A.M. and 1:15 P.M. and 50-minute scenic cruises ($22) at 10:30 A.M., 2 P.M., and 3 P.M. from the jetty at the bottom of the mall.

Hovercraft Cruise. An unusual way to see the Kawarau River is by the Queenstown Hovercraft, which floats on a cushion of air from dry land on to the lake and down the river and over shingle banks. Runs every hour, $30. Book at Mount Cook Travel office.

Helicopter Flights. Helicopter flights vary from the Queenstown-sights trip to the more spectacular Grand Circle flights, which include a landing at almost the summit of the Remarkables. Fares are from $30.

WILDLIFE. Dunedin. To see the world's only mainland breeding spot for albatross, visit the *Royal Albatross Colony,* Taiaroa Heads, Otago Peninsula, 740–344 or 775–020. Accessible by tour, private car, or public transportation.

Christchurch. The *Willowbank Wildlife Reserve,* 60 Hussey Rd. (596–336), has the South Island's largest collection of birds and animals—including mountain lions, camels, Scottish highland cattle, primitive sheep, and other breeds of ancient livestock. Open daily, it's a 15-minute drive from city center.

THE SOUTH ISLAND

SPORTS. See also Facts at Your Fingertips, the introductory essay on fishing and hunting, and Mountain Climbing and Skiing below.

QUEENSTOWN

Hiking. *Danes Back Country* (Box 230; phone 1144) sponsors hiking trips. The *Routeburn Walk* is a guided hike covering 25 miles and lasting 4 days. The trail is through Fiordland and Mt. Aspiring National Parks. Accommodations and meals provided. Contact Routeburn Walk, Ltd., Box 271, Queenstown (phone 100). The 4-day *Hollyford Valley Walk* also takes hikers through alpine scenery. Contact Fiordland National Park, Box 29, Te Anau.

Horseback riding. *Moonlight Stables* operates trail rides from Arthurs Point into an old gold-mining district. A coach carries visitors to and from the stables, beginning at the top of the mall on Camp St. Details from the New Zealand Travel Office (phone 143).

Rafting. Whitewater rafting has become highly popular in both the North and South islands and especially at Queenstown. Contact the New Zealand Travel Office.

TE ANAU

Milford Track. Often called "the finest walk in the world," this three-day, 33-mile hike takes walkers from Te Anau to Milford Sound. Well-equipped huts provide overnight accommodations. Season is mid-Dec. through Mar. Contact Tourist Hotel Corp., Box 2840, Wellington, or THC, Box 2207, Auckland, (09) 773–689.

MOUNTAIN CLIMBING. Contact *Mountain Guides, New Zealand,* Box 93, Twizel, (05) 620–737, or, for climbing in Mt. Cook National Park, *Alpine Guides,* Box 20, Mt. Cook National Park, (05) 621–834.

SKIING. *Mount Hutt,* two hours from Christchurch, offers varied terrain and 8 lifts, appropriate for all grades of skiers. Accommodations are also available less than an hour from the mountain in Ashburton. For more information contact Mt. Hutt International, Methven, Alpine Tourist Co., Box 446, Christchurch, (03) 792–720.

Mount Cook Ski Region. The highest peak in New Zealand offers a wide range of skiing adventures, including heliskiing, ski touring, and glacier skiing. Accommodations available. Write to the Ski Desk, THC Mt. Cook, Mt. Cook, New Zealand.

Highly popular are *Coronet Peak* and the *Remarkables* ski field at Queenstown. Contact the Mt. Cook Company.

Ideal for beginners is *Tekapo Ski Field.* A first-class ski school, rentals, and accommodations are available. Heli-skiing nearby. Contact Tekapo Ski Field, Box 7, Lake Tekapo, (05) 056–852.

For skiing, including helisking and glacier skiing trips, contact *Alpine Guides,* Box 20, Mt. Cook, (05) 621–834; *Live-Life New Zealand, Ltd.,* Box 4517, Auckland, (09) 768–936; *Mountain Guides New Zealand,* Box 93, Twizel, (05) 630–737.

MUSEUMS AND HISTORIC SITES. Christchurch. *The Arts Center of Christchurch,* in old neo-Gothic building on Worcester St. (60–989), Monday–Friday 8:30 A.M.–5 P.M. A living center including theater, ballet, cinema, craft workshop, potters, cane and stained-glass workers and printmakers.

Brooke Gifford Gallery, 112 Manchester St. (65–288), Mon.–Fri. 10:30 A.M.–5 P.M. Exhibitions of contemporary New Zealand painting and sculpture.

Canterbury Museum, on Rolleston Ave. (68–379), houses a good, permanent Antarctica exhibit, along with displays of New Zealand's history, natural life, and Maori culture. Open Mon.–Sat., 10 A.M.–4:30 P.M.; opens 2 P.M. Sun. Admission is free; donations encouraged. Just behind the museum is the *McDougall*

Art Gallery housing exhibits of Australasian and European Art. 10 A.M.–4:30 P.M. Mon.–Fri.; 1–5:30 P.M. weekends.

Canterbury Society of Arts, 66 Gloucester St., 67-261, Mon.–Fri. 10 A.M.–4:30 P.M. Displays of New Zealand and overseas art.

Ferrymead Historic Park is a working museum of transport and technology situated on 100 acres at 269 Bridle Path Rd., Heathcote, near the Cashmere Hills. Exhibits include vintage machinery, automobiles, horse carts, trolley cars, railroad locomotives, aircraft, home appliances, musical instruments, and models. A ride in a vintage train or trolley car is the way to reach a vintage township with an operating bakery and printing works. It is open daily from 10 A.M. to 4:30 P.M. and can be reached by bus from Cathedral Square. For more information call 841–708.

Robert McDougall Art Gallery, adjacent to the Canterbury Museum, Rolleston Ave. (50–915), 10 A.M.–4:30 P.M. daily. Painting, drawings, prints, sculptures, and ceramics by British, oriental, Australian, and New Zealand artists.

Dunedin. The *Otago Early Settlers' Museum,* at 220 Cumberland St. (close to the Railway Station; call 775–052), shows early colonial household items in authentic settings, including 19th-century toys and costumes and early pianos and printing equipment. Open 9 A.M.–4:30 P.M. weekdays; 10:30 A.M.–4:30 P.M. Sat; Oct.–March; from 1:30 P.M. Sun. Small admission charge.

The *Otago Museum* on Great King St. (three blocks from the Octagon; call 772–372), contains a good collection of Polynesian and Melanesian exhibits and also ceramics and New Zealand birds. 10 A.M.–5 P.M. Mon.–Fri.

The *Dunedin Public Art Gallery* in Logan Park (a short taxi ride) is the oldest art gallery in New Zealand and has a good coverage of New Zealand and foreign paintings. Open 10 A.M.–4:40 P.M., Mon.–Fri., 2–5 P.M. weekends and holidays.

Out on the Otago Peninsula, 9 miles beyond Dunedin on Highcliff Rd., stands *Lanarch Castle,* where the declaration was signed giving women the right to vote (1893: a precedent in the western world). The castle was built by William Lanarch for his first wife. The restored interior is elaborately decorated with architectural touches from all periods. The carved dining room ceiling took some 14 years to complete. (Lanarch shot himself when his third wife ran away with his son.) Newton's Sightseeing Bus includes the castle on a tour—or you can take your own car. Accommodations and dining available. Open 9 A.M.–5 P.M. in winter; until dusk at other seasons. Phone 761–302.

Olveston was another unique home, built around 1905. One mile from Dunedin, on Cobden St., off Queens Dr. (773–320), it reflects the elegant lifestyle of the businessman who built it. The building, a Jacobean work of art in itself, houses art treasures from around the world. Reservations recommended for guided tours. Newton's Sightseeing Tours also include this.

Queenstown. *Arrowtown* is 14 miles northeast of Queenstown—and a trip into the past. Once filled with gold miners from all over the world, the town remains one of the prettiest in New Zealand. There are the Lake District Centennial Museum, a pub that once served the miners, an old stone jail, and a variety of shops. H & H coaches depart from the Camp St. depot at 2 P.M.

The *Queenstown Motor Museum,* 25 Brecon St. (phone 752), is a 5-minute walk from the center of town. The display here is of vintage, veteran, and classic vehicles. Open daily; small admission charge.

The *Sound and Light Museum* on Beach St., is an audiovisual show, recreating Queenstown's past. Walk-through displays, simultaneous slides and movies, as well as sound effects, make for an interesting 20 minutes. Small admission charge.

ARTS. See Museums and Historic Sites, above.

THE
SOUTH PACIFIC

THE PACIFIC WAY

An Introduction to the South Pacific

by
JAN PRINCE

A resident of Tahiti since 1971, Jan Prince works as a free-lance journalist and tour guide. Her voyages to the remote islands of French Polynesia provide first-hand information for her articles.

An expatriate German lady, who lives on the French Polynesian island of Moorea, sailed away from her native Berlin a few years ago with her husband aboard their 28-foot yacht. Their intention was to circumnavigate the world.

When fate stepped into their lives in the form of an interesting job offer in Moorea, the couple talked it over, decided to give up their nomadic life, and combined the best of both worlds—an apartment ashore with their yacht safely anchored practically at their front door.

"I write to my friends back home and tell them about my life here," she said. "I tell them in the mornings I have a swim in the crystal-clear lagoon, I shower under the most refreshing water in the world, I wrap a piece of brightly colored material around my body, put fragrant flowers in my hair, and go to work. And in the evening I try to wear shoes."

This fortunate lady then pointed to the panoramic view that surrounds her while she performs her job as assistant hotel manager. There was the thatch-roofed hotel situated in well-manicured gardens adjacent to an ultramarine bay, overlooked by fern-covered mountains and a picture-postcard sky.

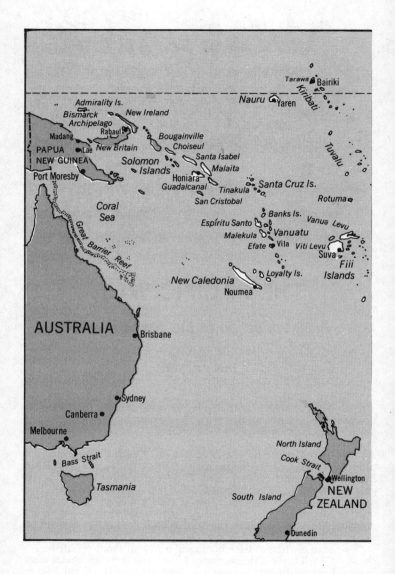

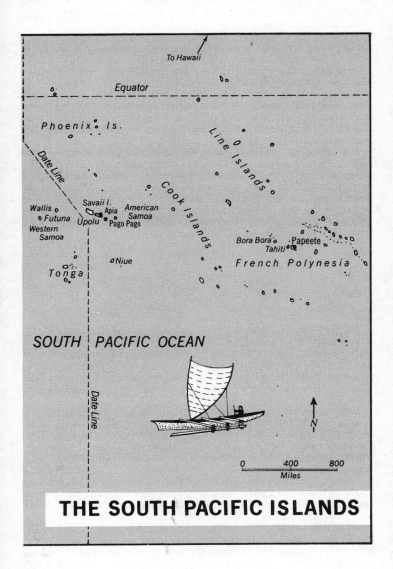

THE SOUTH PACIFIC ISLANDS

If this sounds like paradise to you, be assured that the South Pacific Islands have inspired even the most taciturn of visitors to express themselves in phrases of "purple prose" when they succumb to the spell of the islands.

For two hundred years Europeans and North Americans have dreamed of the South Seas—adventure and romance in a setting of palm-shaded green islands, white-sand beaches, and blue lagoons, plus a life of ease among friendly natives. For the men and boys, the picture also included lovely island girls.

Writers such as Herman Melville, James Michener, Robert Louis Stevenson, Jack London, W. Somerset Maugham, and Joseph Conrad have planted many a seed of desire and wanderlust. Paul Gauguin, Zane Grey, Captain William Bligh, and Father Laval have become well-known heroes or villains.

The impact of movies showing the South Sea Islands has been so motivating that several people moved down here to live forever after seeing films such as *Taboo, Sadie Thompson* (also known as *Rain*), *Return to Paradise*, one or more of the versions of *Mutiny on the Bounty*, and the very popular *South Pacific*.

And in this age of easy travel by jets and luxury ocean liners the possibility of escaping to the romantic South Seas Isles has become a reality for voyagers from many countries.

Defining the South Pacific

The South Pacific Islands number into uncounted thousands of tiny emeralds sprinkled about in the southern region of the earth's greatest body of water. The Pacific Ocean covers 64,000,000 square miles, or one-third, of the earth's surface. Some theorists believe that most of this area was at one time a large Pacific Continent and the numerous little islands simply the highest peaks of the mountains covering that vanished land.

Two imaginary lines divide the Pacific Ocean into quarters: the equator and the International Date Line. Voyagers who cross the equator by ship or yacht enjoy the ritual of paying tribute to Neptunis Rex, undisputed king of the ocean. Any "Pollywogs" on board the vessel, who are crossing this line for the first time, are duly initiated into King Neptune's Court by the "Shellbacks," who have already experienced these rites. The occasion calls for celebrations, practical jokes played on the initiates and blamed on Davy Jones, plus the posting of a letter enclosed in a bottle and dropped into the ocean at the "equatorial mail buoy."

All of the island groups presented in this book are located in the Pacific basin, south of the equator, with the exception of some of the Kiribati archipelago, which straddle the Line (as the equator is sometimes called).

The Date Line is a zig-zag line that approximately coincides with the 180th meridian, and it is where each calendar day begins. The date advances one day when you're crossing in a westerly direction and falls back one day when you're crossing in an easterly direction. One of the deviations from the 180th meridian leads the International Date Line back to the tiny Kingdom of Tonga. The dignified islanders living in these friendly and benign islands are the first people in the world to greet a new day. Consequently, many of their tourist handouts and stamps proudly carry the slogan "Tonga—Where Time Begins."

The Island People

Whether home is a half-drowned atoll or a mountain several thousand feet above sea level, the South Pacific Islander normally belongs to one of three racial groups: Micronesian, Melanesian, or Polynesian.

Nesia means island. Micronesia indicates tiny or small islands; Melanesia translates as the islands where black- or dark-skinned people live; and Polynesia means many islands.

The Polynesians have become well known for their physical beauty and the friendly welcome they extend to visitors. They live in the most romanticized islands. The Polynesian island groups presented in this guide include the Samoas, Tonga, Niue, the Cook Islands, French Polynesia, Tuvalu, Wallis, and Futuna.

The Melanesians, who outnumber the Polynesian population by eight to one, are Oceanic Negroids. Their color varies from light brown to ebony, their hair rather coarse. Features can be gentle or somewhat fierce, with thick lips and wide or hooked noses. The Melanesians occupy islands farther west than Polynesia and have retained their creative and artistic skills, with their cultural practices still an integral part of life today. These islands of Melanesia include Fiji, New Caledonia, Vanuatu, the Solomons, and Papua New Guinea.

Most of the Micronesian atolls and miniscule islands are found in the Northwest Pacific, with only the poor but now independent Republic of Kiribati or Tungaru, as the I-Kiribati people call it, represented in this guide. The Micronesian people, often sturdy and heavy-set, have similarities to the Polynesians and to the Filipinos. As a group they are not as closely related to each other as are the Polynesians or the Melanesians, and their customs, religion, and culture differ widely from one group to another.

Origin of Species

One of the questions that is still a much discussed subject among archaeologists, ethnologists, anthropologists, and other scholars is when, why, and how the first inhabitants of the Pacific Islands got there. These islands are small and often isolated by hundreds, even thousands of miles of open ocean.

The general consensus among those who study this subject is that the early pioneers of the South Pacific came from the Southeast Asian mainland, walking across a landmass that existed in the final Ice Age, to reach the Indonesian islands of Sumatra, Java, and Borneo. From here the first boats filled with wanderers seeking new homes are thought to have traveled the short distance to New Guinea, as far back as 27,000 years ago.

New migrations began, many years later, bringing voyagers all across the South Pacific to eventually settle on every speck of land that could support life. They brought with them their women and children, pigs and dogs, coconuts and taro, breadfruit tree cuttings and roots, shrubs and trees, as well as flowering plants, which were to be used for food, clothing, medicines, and other household needs.

The islands first settled are known today as the Bismarck Archipelago, the Solomon Islands, Santa Cruz Islands, New Caledonia, Vanuatu, the Loyalty Islands, and Fiji. Although a few Polynesian villages exist today in the western South Pacific, this area is predominantly Melanesian.

The group of people called Micronesian are credited with having invented the outrigger canoe and are believed by many people to have been the greatest sailors the world has ever known. They sailed eastward in their huge double ocean going canoes, using the wind, ocean currents, and the heavenly bodies as their guides, referring to their crude stick charts to navigate to new islands. Carrying 100–500 people on board these canoes made of lashed planks with sails of pandanus matting, they settled on the least hospitable atolls. After departing Southeast Asia they are thought to have traveled through the Philippines to the Caroline and Marshall Islands, and some of them eventually migrated south to mingle with the people who lived in Samoa, Tonga, and perhaps Fiji. The slow progress eastward was usually made by no more than a few canoes at a time, historians believe, and occurred over a period of 5,000 years. Departure from a settled island was probably necessitated due to food and water shortage or because of internal fighting.

The Polynesian culture is said to have evolved in the central Pacific, either in Fiji, Tonga, or the Samoas. From this "cradle" of Polynesia more explorations were made even farther eastward, and the Marquesas Islands became the home of a tall and stately race of proud and cultured Polynesians. Carbon-14 dating places man in the Marquesas at least 120 years before the birth of Christ.

From the Marquesas Islands voyaging canoes were sent south and west to the Tuamotu Archipelago and Mangareva, north to the Hawaiian Islands, and even farther eastward to discover and populate Easter Island. The great Polynesian migrations then proceeded southwest, with canoes departing from the religious and cultural center of Raiatea in the Society Islands. With canoes from other Polynesian villages, the explorations eventually ended in New Zealand, where the Maori culture still flourishes.

European Conquerors: Ships without Outriggers

Centuries before man left the environs of the Mediterranean to discover that the earth was indeed round, the cultures of the South Pacific were well established, complete with an entire retinue of gods, demigods, myths, legends, a hierarchy of social and religious chiefs, and well-defined customs.

In 1513 A.D. Vasco Nuñez de Balboa crossed the Isthmus of Panama and sighted the mighty Pacific Ocean. This Spanish explorer was followed just a few years later by one of his countrymen when Ferdinand Magellan led the ships *Victoria* and *Trinidad* across the Pacific in 1520–21.

During the succeeding centuries the Pacific was visited many times by the Spanish, Portuguese, English, Dutch, Russians, French, Americans, and Germans, who sometimes claimed proprietorship of islands already possessed by other countries.

Some of the islands and atolls where the Europeans attempted to land proved to be inhabited by hostile natives who refused to allow the foreigners to come even close to shore. Other natives showed a definite willingness to be friendly, offering gifts of coconuts, fresh water, fish, and other food items, as well as their wives and daughters, in exchange for trinkets and nails from the sailors.

Following the famous voyages of Captain Samuel Wallis, Captain James Cook, and Admiral Louis Antoine de Bougainville in the late 1760s, word of the South Sea Islands began to circulate around England and France, exciting the imagination of Europe.

When a real live "noble savage" was brought back to France by Bougainville from the island he called "La Nouvelle Cythere," this Tahitian visitor who first "discovered" Paris became the pet of the court ladies, as well as the subject of much curiosity and many examinations executed by the French doctors and scientists.

Interest in the South Pacific Islands also spread among those who agreed to give up the familiar comforts of a life in civilization to sail away to cannibal islands to bring the word of salvation to heathen souls. The early missionaries, who came out from the London Missionary Society in 1797, were followed by French Catholics. In the process of rescuing the souls of the heathen savages, they did eliminate most of the cannibalism, but the missionaries also managed to help destroy not only the native culture, but also eliminated thousands of the islanders themselves, who did not adapt to the confines of clothes nor to the restriction of their happiness. This joy had always been expressed through the rituals of song and dance, by playing musical instruments and decorating bodies with tattoos and cosmetics. The sexual mores of the islanders were not at all to the taste of the missionaries, and these practices, which included public intercourse, were also forbidden.

Battles were fought as the native societies resisted the European invasion. Some of these resistance wars were aided by another type of "discoverer." These were the misfits and social outcasts of Western culture, who came ashore as deserters from whaling ships. Many of these were rough and ready men who had left their lonely lives on the Line to find adventure, danger, power, and island maidens. Other men who arrived as castaways on the beautiful islands and tiny, sun-drenched atolls of the South Sea were pirates and buccaneers, treasure hunters, convicts, mutineers, and victims of shipwrecks.

Some of them supplied the natives with guns and alcohol, further complicating the lives of the missionaries and colonialists. A few of these violent yet colorful escapists also realized their dreams of living as supreme rulers of a private kingdom on a Pacific island, where they fathered innumerable offspring with several of their native "wives."

As more ships began to arrive in the South Pacific scores of natives were killed by the white man's guns simply for the sport of it, while others were carried away from their islands by "blackbirding" ships who sought laborers for the plantations of Australia, Peru, New Caledonia, Fiji, Hawaii, and Samoa. Some islanders went willingly, seeking work, while others were shanghaied onto the ships and sold into slavery. Most of them never returned to their island homes.

Perhaps the cruelest and certainly the most effective method of annihilating the South Pacific islanders was the introduction, often intentional, of communicable diseases. A terrible epidemic of smallpox eliminated two-thirds of the population of Nuku Hiva in the Marquesas Islands when a ship stopped there in 1867 and dropped off some sailors dying with this disease. By the early 1920s only 1,500 survivors remained in this island group, which had been inhabited by some 120,000 beautiful and proud Polynesians in 1767.

Influenza, measles, tuberculosis, pneumonia, venereal disease, typhoid fever, cholera, malaria, guns, and alcohol also proved to be efficient destroyers of society in these tropical islands.

Imported South Sea Islanders

Even while such "labor recruiters" as Bully Hayes were busily depleting the manpower on some islands by blackbirding the young men and women to other shores, new faces appeared in the South Pacific by the importation of workers from settlements farther west.

Chinese were brought to Tahiti, Fiji, and Papua New Guinea. Indian laborers went to live in Fiji; New Caledonia received workers from Japan, Vietnam, and Indonesia; American Samoa's fishing industry received workers from Japan and Taiwan; North Vietnamese were imported to Vanuatu and Papua New Guinea also received some Malays and Ambonese.

Most of these imports have remained to become leading merchants and solid citizens of the island communities. The Asian and Indian cuisines have been integrated with the local foods to offer tempting culinary choices for residents and visitors alike.

The Pacific War

For many people in the world some of the islands of the South Pacific became meaningful during World War II. Guadalcanal, Rabaul, Tarawa, Santo, and Bougainville were names transformed from obscurity to the front pages of the hometown newspaper, to become familiar household words as the war continued.

This era between 1941–45 marks a significant part of the history of the South Seas, still remaining today in many islands in the form of rusting pieces of war machinery that were abandoned on the white-sand beaches, in the coral lagoons, and in the verdant mountains of the islands that were used as military bases during the war.

International airports exist today on land that was originally cleared by the Allied Forces to build their airstrips. Roads, wharves, bridges, and Quonset huts are still being used by the islanders, while the old cannon and anti-aircraft guns are routinely pointed out as items of interest during guided tours on some islands.

The war touched almost every island group in some way, either by direct battle in places like Papua New Guinea, the Solomon Islands, and some atolls of Kiribati, or by use as forward bases that remained outside the hostile areas.

Most of the islands' principal villages have war memorials for the foreign forces who fought for their freedom and for their own island men, who joined the Allied troops at home and abroad to fight for the common cause.

During the years following the Pacific war, as the South Pacific Islands are developing and tourism is becoming an important factor in the local economies, war memorabilia has been included in the sightseeing possibilities of Papua New Guinea and the Solomon Islands.

Tourists: Modern Discoverers

During the early 1960s, many of the passengers who stepped down from international flights into the warmth of a tropical morning were the same men who had years before watched the magic of dawn appearing over the horizon on some lovely island while they stood guard at their military bases.

These war veterans returned to the South Seas with their families, to renew old friendships with their Polynesian and Melanesian buddies, sometimes speaking Pidgin or Polynesian, and always being treated to the typical feasts of the South Pacific. They eagerly ate the roast suckling pig, breadfruit, taro, yams, bananas, and other foods that had been baked in an underground oven, using their fingers to eat in the island fashion, drinking the cool liquid of the green coconut. The wives and children of these American, New Zealand, and Australian visitors, perhaps with less sentimental enthusiasm for the occasion, quietly longed for the taste of more familiar foods.

As tourism has developed in some of these South Pacific Islands, so has the variety of food available to these visitors expanded. Although a hamburger can now be found in most capital cities and resort hotels, there are no fast food establishments so popular in the United States.

Neither is there a Hilton Hotel nor a Holiday Inn, although the former group is looking for property and the latter chain once had a hotel in Tahiti. In Fiji and New Caledonia, where the majority of vacationers are from Australia and New Zealand, the accommodations vary from international class resort hotel complexes to the comfortable but simple oval bungalows with thatched roofs called "bure" in Fiji and "gites" in New Caledonia.

The most expensive hotel in the South Pacific is the Hotel Bora Bora, which caters to "up-market" guests. Their clientele includes many honeymooners and repeat visitors, who happily pay $300 a day to stay in an overwater bungalow, or "fare," built of bamboo and pandanus.

The best way to visit the South Pacific is, of course, the most leisurely way. Hundreds of cruising yachts from all over the world pass through the islands each year, with some boats stopping only long enough to get provisions for the next leg of the journey, while others linger until the authorities ask them to move on.

Their contact with the villagers in remote islands is often rewarding for all concerned, with the yachtsmen often getting involved in the daily lives of these friendly people.

Outgoing visitors are frequently invited to join in the volleyball and soccer games that are played every afternoon during the week by the teenagers and young adults of the South Pacific. They may be invited along on fishing expeditions, hunt for tiny shells that are strung into pretty necklaces, learn to weave hats, mats, and baskets from palm fronds, eat delicious seafoods direct from the shell while standing on a technicolored reef, and in the evenings, sit beside their friends under a starlit sky, watching the Southern Cross as they listen to melodic island tunes being played on guitars and ukuleles.

These technically knowledgeable yachtsmen often assist their Polynesian and Melanesian friends by repairing pieces of machinery and equipment that were simply discarded because of some minor default.

An increasing number of overseas visitors choose to fly to one island group and spend their time in the homes of the islanders. Lifelong friendships have been formed from these associations, with the tourists later becoming hosts in their own homes and introducing the South Seas Islanders to life on the big continents.

A fly and cruise program is also a great way to explore the islands, although the people contact is more limited. Several programs are now available to the tourist, with opportunities to see the capitals and some more distant islands.

This can be experienced aboard a bare-boat charter, copra/passenger schooners, or aboard deluxe-class ships of many sizes that offer a variety of package programs tailored to those with limited time.

Visitors go deep-sea fishing, scuba diving, sailing, windsurfing, parasailing, snorkeling, and waterskiing. They take glass-bottom boat rides to visit the lagoons and speed-boat rides to walk on the coral reef. They sign up for shark-feeding excursions that require them to actually descend into a clear lagoon, and watch through masks as a fantastic array of sea creatures, including lagoon sharks, come around for a free meal of fish. And they enjoy different taste treats themselves by dining out in the local restaurants.

Tourists can go on private or group picnics to discover secluded coves and mountain retreats, explore caves and grottos, photograph panoramic views of the lagoons, and watch the sunset from a deserted beach, with perhaps a friendly dog for company.

Others toast the setting sun from the comfort of their hotel terrace, with cocktails and hors d'oeuvres to accompany the music played by the hotel musicians, who are clad in clean white trousers with brightly patterned shirts, or dressed with the simple cloth wrap that is the normal attire of the South Seas. This piece of material is known as *lava lava, sulu sulu,* or *pareu.*

The visitors themselves are usually dressed in some version of island fashions, by this time, and happily sip their cool rum punches or maitais while breathing in the fragrance of their floral crowns or leis.

During their stay in the islands the enthusiastic and curious tourists find time to poke around in the often quaint shops for souvenirs of hand-blocked fabrics, T-shirts, wood carvings, ceremonial masks, tapa wall hangings, shell jewelry, perfumes, postcards, and in some islands such as Tahiti, fresh vanilla or liqueurs made from the local fruits. In Tahiti there is also a marvelous selection of the very expensive black pearl that is farmed in the Tuamotu Archipelago.

Duty-free shopping has also arrived in the South Pacific, with some bargains available in cameras, radio equipment, calculators, and luxury accessories in Port Vila, Vanuatu, Tonga, American Samoa, and Fiji, and French perfumes and other items sold at reasonable prices in Tahiti and New Caledonia.

The visitors who spend at least a few days in the South Pacific usually find time to visit the public markets, which provide excellent opportunities to learn about the lifestyles of the local people. For those who are curious to taste *kava* or *yaqona*, an informal opportunity can sometimes be presented at the market by paying a minute sum for a cup of the muddy liquid. Kava has recently been banned as an import item to the United States, so for those who find a liking for the "piper methysticum" root, remember it's best to satisfy the desire while traveling in the islands.

Attending Sunday church services in the islands is highly recommended for all visitors who enjoy people watching and beautiful music. The religions that were originally rejected by the cannibalistic ancestors of today's South Sea Islanders have been wholly accepted over the years and are today used as a social gathering and opportunity to blend their voices in song.

A variety of religions abound in these islands and the list is still increasing annually. In Western Samoa there are more than 200 churches, with the congregations swapping religions according to who gives the best parties, so the islanders say, jokingly.

The observant visitor will note that although the churchgoers are very attractively dressed, often in white, and the women wear fancy hats made from the leaves of pandanus, coconut, bananas, and even from gift-packaging ribbons, they do not ever wear flowers to church.

Flowers, ferns, and other leaves are worn when a person is celebrating. These occasions are often expressed by giant feasts, followed by ceremonies, including speeches, the exchange of gifts, and exciting dance shows.

Although the casual visitor to the islands seldom has the occasion to participate in the private celebrations, such as births, weddings, or the arrivals and departures of officials and friends, they usually do experience the feasts, flowers, music, and dancing at some time during their stay. In New Caledonia these feasts are called *bougna;* in Samoa they have the *fia fia;* Fiji presents a *magiti;* and in French Polynesia it's a *tamaara'a.* On the other islands this feast is called simply "island night." They are all far more authentic than the highly touristic luaus of Waikiki.

The most pleasant months in the South Pacific are from June through October, with a month or two added on for more temperate climates such as Tonga and New Caledonia. However, most tourists simply come when the opportunity arises, which is the most logical answer. Even during the summer season there are perfectly clear days, with intermittent sunshine and cooling breezes to help make the term "paradise" a more realistic one.

The Pacific Way

Since 1962, when Western Samoa became an independent sovereign state, the islands of Nauru, Fiji, Tonga, Papua New Guinea, Solomons, Tuvalu, Kiribati, and Vanuatu have also proudly raised their independent flags and decided their own national anthems, creeds, and even their names, congratulating one another that victory had been won in relatively peaceful conditions, for most of them. The other South Pacific Island groups have also become self-governing or have made giant steps forward in deciding their own internal affairs.

"The Pacific Way" is a phrase often used by politicians and speakers, an expression playing on the ambivalence of the word "pacific," which shows the will of the Pacific Islanders to reach a consensus in a polite, dignified manner.

The Pacific Way also means that one maintains a sensitivity to local feelings and customs. For the tourist this includes complying with the dress codes and rules of etiquette. Most of the "don'ts" are listed in the chapters on the Samoas, Tonga, and the Cook Islands, which comprise the conservative "Bible Belt" of the South Seas.

Politicians and prognosticators say that the Pacific will be the center of the new world, and it is here that the crucial problems of the approaching 21st century will be worked out. They add that even though the newly emerging micro-nations of the South Pacific are making positive steps toward independence from colonial powers, their value to the great nations is based more on their strategic location rather than any economic possibilities.

On a per-capita basis the small islands of the Pacific receive more aid than anyone else on earth. To change the financial balance, as their populations increase rapidly, these economically vulnerable governments are looking for ways to support themselves. Diplomatic relations have been established with foreign governments and fishing rights with major powers have been signed to help develop the natural riches of the vast ocean surrounding these tiny island nations.

Some of these accords have caused concern and alarm among the neighbor governments in the Pacific, such as the August 1985 agreement that Kiribati signed with Russia, allowing 16 Russian trawlers fishing rights among the Phoenix Islands.

Equally as important as becoming and remaining independent, the island governments want a nuclear-free Pacific. This desire has been expressed in many anti-nuclear demonstrations against France's nuclear tests, conducted since 1966 on the atoll of Moruroa in the Tuamotu Archipelago. Protests by the Greenpeace movement have been joined by Australians, New Zealanders, and many South Pacific Islanders. These demonstrations are often outright protests of France's continuing presence in the Pacific, which they feel does not fit in with "The Pacific Way."

The islands of Vanuatu realized more economic independence in mid-1985 when gold fever became the exciting news. Significant gold discoveries brought dozens of prospecting companies from Australia and the United States. The Solomons, Fiji, and Papua New Guinea have also yielded up gold and copper deposits, with copper comprising a sizeable percentage of Papua New Guinea's exports.

Most of the other countries of the South Pacific are now coming to the realization that their best products are themselves. The gentle, shy, yet friendly, people of the South Pacific, along with the natural beauty of the sea, lagoons, topography, and flora, have become the assets that are now being promoted to the tourist market as a place to get away from it all.

Some government leaders have not readily accepted the idea and still have no interest in promoting themselves. Some admit freely that they would just rather have the money and let the tourists stay home. Others have stepped forward, very hesitatingly making an appeal for tourism on a limited basis.

Western Samoa asks that travel agencies send only their best tourists —"travelers of taste and character." Tonga wants visitors who will be interested in Tonga—"the gentle visitor, not the boisterous tourist . . . people who love it the way it is." The Cook Islands hope for people who are "friendly and understanding," who will, in return, find the islanders most kind, pleasant, and easy to get along with. These happy, friendly people are typical of the South Seas Islanders of today. Although they maintain their easy-going, family-oriented lifestyle, in every respect these Polynesians are very much a part of today's world. Behind their relaxed composure they feel the same concerns for their families, homes, communities, country, and fellow man that citizens of the most developed countries feel. And the myth of the lazy, carefree native, which has been confused with a laid-back, casual approach to unnecessary worries, will be put to rest when the observant visitor sees how hard the average native does work, usually beginning in the early hours of the morning, while most of us are still enjoying the comfort of our beds.

Island Attractions

Tonga has its own "Stonehenge," or seasonal calendar, called the Ha'amonga Trilithon. Vanuatu boasts of active volcanoes on Tanna and land divers at Pentecost Island. Fiji has 3,000 species of plants, including the fuchsialike "tagimaucia" that blooms beside a crater lake in the high Taveuni jungle, and is found nowhere else in the world. Likewise, on top of Temehani Mountain in Raiatea grows the unique "Tiare Apetahi" flower that "pops" open with the first light of dawn.

In the Solomon Islands lives the Megapode bird, which burrows a hole two feet deep into the sand where it deposits its eggs. American Samoa has a 5,400 foot cable that supports an aerial tramway, thrilling visitors as they climb higher and higher over Pago Pago Harbor, providing an exciting panorama of mountains, lagoon, reef and ocean.

Papua New Guinea offers the most varied selection of people, languages, cultures, adventures, and magnificent scenery, rich jungle life, high plains and mountains, plus off-shore islands with their own diversity of beauty and culture. The "sing-sing's" of the Highlands are world renowned, as well as the frequent tribal wars.

A word of caution to the visitor—do not get in the way of the warring tribes during the midst of their battles. These gaily painted and feathered figures will happily stop to pose for a picture, then rush off to attack the enemy. So far no tourists have been reported injured in these skirmishes, and certainly the traffic in Tahiti is far more dangerous to the visitor, as well as to the residents of this speed-happy island, than the chance of any mishaps in Papua New Guinea, or in any other island.

So, to set the pace for your trip to the fabled Isles of the South Seas, just keep in mind the normal precautions of travel in tropical zones. Have the necessary inoculations and medicines to prevent illnesses of the region, such as malaria, yellow fever, and cholera—normally confined to Papua New Guinea, the Solomon Islands, and Vanuatu, with cholera appearing in some parts of Fiji.

Take care when walking or swimming in the lagoons, by wearing protective footgear and following local advice on safe places to swim and which fish to eat. Be careful of the local drinking water and even more cautious of the tropical sunshine, which can be deceptively bright, causing sunburns even on hazy, overcast days.

Carry along a good mosquito repellant, and, for more remote places, take a good flashlight and batteries, as electric power isn't always available or reliable.

Finally, remember that the South Pacific area as a whole is still largely undiscovered. There remain scores of white-sand beaches, emerald lagoons, and stately coconut palms waiting to provide the perfect backdrop for your island paradise.

Also there exist many wonderful people who are happy to be painted or photographed, exotic dances to be filmed, native handicrafts to be purchased, and feasts to be tasted. The proud and free, smiling and friendly people of the South Pacific are waiting to discover you, to welcome you to their dream islands, where life is lived for the simple joy of living.

FRENCH POLYNESIA

The Bustling Paradise

by
JAN PRINCE

Flowers! The heady, sweet scent of tropical blossoms permeates the air you breathe as you enter Tahiti. Whether you come by airplane or ship, you are greeted by leis of Tiare Tahiti gardenias or the fragrant frangi pani. Smiling Tahitian beauties welcome you to their island in their high musical voices as they place the flowers around your neck and you are happy to have arrived in Paradise. After clearing immigration and customs and learning that there is "No Tipping!" in Tahiti, you cheerfully proceed to your hotel by taxi or escorted tour bus. If it should be in the daylight hours when you arrive, you will be sitting back in the car when you suddenly become aware of something—what is that noise?

Welcome to modern day Tahiti! That's just what it is—noise. Hundreds of motorcycles, motorbikes, Vespas, trail bikes, automobiles and trucks all zoom along, zigzagging in and out of the traffic, trying to get there first. There is even a small section of freeway cut through the mountains now, giving two lanes that are usually made into five lanes by the speed happy motorists.

Look out into the lagoon and there is more noise. Even the traditional outrigger canoes have engines on them, as well as the power boats and, the most annoying of all, the racing boats that whine round and round the once calm (oh, how long ago!) lagoon.

The other noise that tourists once complained about is still here also—that of the roosters crowing at all hours of the night and the

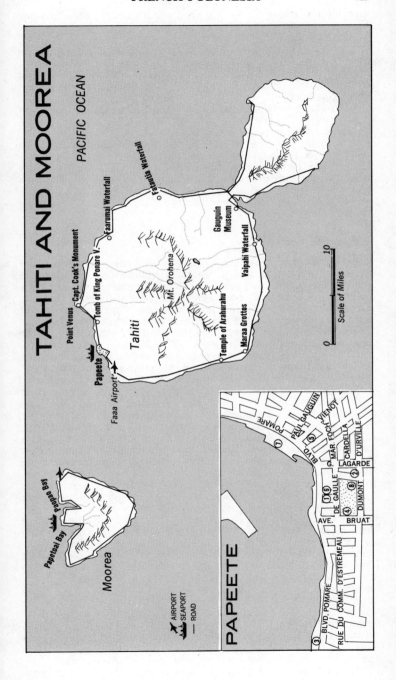

mynah birds fussing outside the hotel windows in the early morning hours. Compared to the machines, though, these natural noises are like music to the ears.

Take a stroll downtown. What has happened to dear old "Papeete town"? It has almost vanished forever. Gone are the old landmarks, many of the centuries old trees, and whole blocks of once familiar Chinese stores, replaced by modern shopping centers or buildings under construction.

When the most famous bar in the South Pacific, Quinn's, was torn down in 1973, "Papeete town," as it was known to hundreds of seamen, voyagers, adventurers and South Seas characters, ceased to exist. The urge to build shopping centers and apartment buildings seemed to affect everyone with money to invest, and a rash of fires on the waterfront speeded up the process of changing the face of Papeete. And that's what it is now; Papeete, a true city, bustling and noisily busy. The town that was once the land of *"aita pea pea"* (who cares?) and *"haere maru"* (take it easy) has become the city of *"depêchez-vous"* and *"ha'a viti viti"* (hurry up).

Paradise Found

But don't despair. Take heart, for the good old days do still exist and can easily be found outside of Papeete. There are some 130 islands in the vast area known as French Polynesia. To some people all this is collectively known as Tahiti, meaning more a state of mind than any geographic location. However, it is not necessary to leave the island of Tahiti to seek your ideal of a tropical setting. Just get away from the downtown area, take a tour around the island and you will find all the beauty, tranquility and color you could wish for.

Go to Point Venus and see where the first known Europeans set foot on the island that later came to be known to the world as "paradise." This famous spot is today a lovely park with a lighthouse, monuments, permanent artisan exhibits and a *fare pote'e,* a traditional Polynesian style meeting house. The wonderful swimming here and the large black-sand beach with mountain views make it a favored location for many, including topless female sunbathers. It was here, on June 23, 1767, that Captain Samuel Wallis of the British Royal Navy, and his crew of 150 men aboard H.M.S. *Dolphin,* anchored in Matavai Bay, five days after first sighting the tall mountains of Tahiti and following the coastline to seek a safe anchorage. The exhausted and scurvy-ridden men aboard the 32-gun frigate had left England eight months before in search of Terra Australis Incognita, the great land mass that King George III and his geographers were convinced lay somewhere between Cape Horn and New Zealand, in balance with the northern hemisphere. Imagine their surprise and joy the following morning when they found their ship surrounded by "upwards of five hundred canoes" containing four thousand athletic paddlers and loaded with fruit, coconuts, fowl and young pigs. But the most astonishing sight to their sea-weary eyes was that of the fair young girls, standing in the middle of each canoe, nude to the waist, "who played a great many droll, wanton tricks." While the hungry sailors were enjoying the free strip-tease, the Tahitians began to hurl fist-sized stones at the men on board the "Dolphin." The sailors retaliated by firing the ship's cannons at the canoes, killing forty or fifty of the Tahitians and sinking a great number of the canoes. After a second attack that the men of the ship easily won, the Tahitians decided to be friendly and peaceful.

As Wallis was too weak from scurvy to claim the new land in the name of the King, the second lieutenant, Tobias Furneaux, hoisted a pennant on a long pole and took possession of the island, calling it

"King George's Island." The remainder of the five-week visit was spent trading earrings, nails and beads for foodstuffs. However, the men of the *Dolphin* began to wholeheartedly engage in "a new sort of trade . . . it might properly be called the old trade," according to George Robertson, master, whose journal is the best account given. When the men had emptied their sea chests to exchange their possessions for the ladies, they began to pull out the iron nails and cleats from the ship. The initial cost of such carnal exchange was a 20 or 30 penny nail. This rose to a 40 penny as demand outgrew the supply, and some women demanded as much as a seven- or nine-inch spike. Very soon two-thirds of the men had no nails to hang their hammocks on. The *Dolphin* sailed back to England soon afterward, without looking further for the southern continent.

Here at Point Venus is a marker for Captain Wallis and another one for the French explorer Louis Antoine de Bougainville, who was the second visitor from Europe to claim Tahiti for his country. Bougainville, captain of the French ships *Boudeuse* and the *Etoile,* had been searching also for the mythical Terra Australis Incognita and sought refuge on the windward side of the island off the district called Hitiaa, arriving nine months after Wallis' departure. His short visit, lasting only from April 6–14, 1768, was very much a repetition of the reception Wallis had received. One unusual incident marked this landing, when the Tahitians spotted among the 314 officers and men of the two ships a woman who had made the voyage disguised as a man. When one big Tahitian man grabbed her up to run off to the hills, her secret became known. Her name was Jeanne Baret and she had sailed as the personal valet of Bougainville's botanist, amongst all those French sailors, without any of them knowing there was a woman on board. She became the first white woman to visit Tahiti and to circumnavigate the world.

Bougainville, not knowing that his new island had already been "discovered" by Wallis and claimed for England, proclaimed French sovereignty over the island he called New Cythere or the New Island of Love. He found many similarities between the ancient worship of Aphrodite-Venus, whose birthplace was the Greek island of Cythere, and the Tahitian love rites.

Before Bougainville sailed away, his botanist named the scarlet and violet paper-like flowers they saw growing in such profusion Bougainvillea, after his captain. And when the *Bodeuse* left, there was a young Tahitian man from Hitiaa named Ahutoru, who sailed with her. He became the first Tahitian to discover Europe.

The following year Tahiti had her third visitor. Lieutenant James Cook, who later came to be known as England's most famous explorer, anchored in Matavai Bay in H.M.S. *Endeavour* on April 13, 1769. After 25 years at sea, half in the merchant marine, Cook had so impressed his superiors in the Royal Navy (he is credited with originating the art of making charts) that they took the almost unprecedented step of transferring him to the command of a very important mission, promoting him from the ranks to lieutenant.

This expedition assigned to Cook was to take an astronomer either to the Marquesas Islands or to New Zealand for the purpose of observing the transit of the planet Venus across the disc of the sun. This event was to take place on June 3, 1769, and there would be no further opportunity to witness such a phenomenon again until 1874. Astronomers were anxious to take advantage of this rare occurrence as it would enable them to ascertain the distance of the earth from the sun, the fundamental base line in all astronomical measurements, and which was imperfectly known. Expeditions organized by the Royal Society had been sent to various parts of the world, but Cook's was the only one to the southern hemisphere and was therefore of special importance.

Two months before Cook left for the South Seas, Wallis returned to England with the disappointing news that he had not found the great southern continent. When he learned of the imminent voyage Cook was to command, Wallis suggested King George III's Island as the ideal spot to establish an observatory. There Cook and his men would find hospitable natives and an abundance of food and water.

Cook's expedition consisted of eighty-four officers and seamen and eight civilians. The civilians included Joseph Banks, a young botanist who later became president of the Royal Society; Dr. Daniel Solander, an eminent Swedish botanist and zoologist who had studied with the great Linnaeus; and astronomer Charles Green, who, in addition to supervising the observation of Venus, provided Cook with precise estimates of longitude, indispensable on such a discovery voyage.

When Cook and his noteworthy assistants anchored in Matavai Bay, seven weeks before the transit of Venus was expected, the "Endeavour" was given an enthusiastic welcome by the Tahitians. Crowds of natives greeted the ship with the now customary friendliness and immediately recognized four of the officers who had visited the island with Wallis.

The first thing Cook did upon arrival in what was then known to the English as King George III's Island was to erect a fort to protect the astronomer and his instruments. He chose the same site that Wallis had selected, the strip of land between the beach and the river. In less than three weeks' time the 150 foot long and 80 foot wide fort was finished, complete with five foot high walls and two four-pounder cannons.

These precautions proved superfluous, however, for the Tahitians, especially the women, were so friendly and hospitable that the British sailors forgot their duties. Cook had posted regulations concerning trade with the natives to prevent a repetition of Wallis's nail-removing fiasco. It was ordered that no iron be exchanged except for provisions. He also asked his men to treat the natives with "all imaginable humanity" and to use every fair means of cultivating their friendship. The natives appreciated this treatment and came to know the Englishmen affectionately by their "Tahitianized" surnames—Tute (Cook), Opane (Banks), Tolano (Solander), and so forth.

The major problem Cook encountered was constant pilfering. From time to time he was obliged to take one or more of the chiefs hostage against the return of pilfered objects. The most important item taken was the quadrant, an essential instrument for astronomical observation. Although the instrument was eventually returned, the culprit had removed it from its box and taken it apart to see what made it tick and it proved of no use in the operation.

On the day of the observation, there was not a cloud in the sky and the scientists were able to witness every phase of the transit from the fort at the place named Point Venus in honor of the occasion. However, it was subsequently found that the readings taken in Tahiti and other places were of little value because of unforeseen optical distortion caused by the irradiation of the sun.

Cook's expedition stayed in Tahiti for three months, during which time he learned much about the Tahitian way of life. He made precise observations of native customs, manners, religion and law. He described the people's appearance (explaining their tattoos), cooking methods, foodstuffs and apparent social and political order. He also made a trip around the island and drew a complete and accurate map of the whole coastal region of Tahiti.

By this time Cook had learned what the natives called their island and began using the name he understood it to be—Otaheite. When he asked them the name, they replied, "This is Tahiti," and in their language it sounded like Otaheite. Actually, the full name is *Tahiti-nui-i-te-vai-uri-rau,* "Great Tahiti of the many-colored waters."

Several of the things Cook learned about the Tahitian way of life shocked the 41-year-old seaman. "It is this," he said in his Journal, "that more than half of the better sort . . . have enter'd into a resolution of injoying free liberty in Love, without being Troubled . . . by its consequences. These mix and Cohabit together with the utmost freedom, and the Children who are so unfortunate as to be thus begot are smothered at the Moment of their Birth." He noted that couples lived together for years, destroying all children. His reference was to the Arioi Society that was in existence at that time, and their meetings during which "the Women in dancing . . . give full Liberty to their desires." He was also aghast that "both sexes express the most indecent ideas in conversation without the least emotion" and that "chastity . . . is but little valued. The Men will very readily offer the Young Women to Strangers, even their own daughters, and think it very strange if you refuse them; but this is merely done for the sake of gain."

However, the Tahitian people were suffering consequences of having enjoyed free liberty in love. Cook found, to his distress, that many of them, as well as his own men, were suffering from venereal disease. How they had caught it is a toss-up between the men on Cook's ships or the former discoverers. The English blame the French and vice-versa.

In years to come, the ravages of venereal disease, as well as other illnesses the Europeans introduced to the islands such as tuberculosis, small pox, measles and alcoholism, as well as the guns they brought to the natives, helped to reduce the population at an alarming rate. Cook gave the estimate of the population at over 200,000. Just 36 years later it was determined to be 8,000.

Cook and his men sailed away from Tahiti on July 13, 1769. Heading westward, he discovered the islands of Huahine, Raiatea, Tahaa and Bora Bora. He named them the Society Islands "because they lay contiguous to one another." He then sailed on to New Zealand and Australia, discovering many islands in the process. He was to return to Matavai Bay again, as Captain Cook, on three separate occasions in 1773, 1774 and 1777, during his second and third voyages of exploration. Today there is a monument to this great discoverer at Point Venus.

"Breadfruit Bligh" and the Bounty

In the following years many ships called at Tahiti, some anchoring in Matavai Bay and others stopping at Tahiti-iti, the peninsula which means "little Tahiti." One of the most famous ever to drop anchor in these waters was the H.M.S. *Bounty,* commanded by Lieutenant William Bligh. The *Mutiny on the Bounty* saga is well known as it was imaginatively told by co-authors James Norman Hall and Charles Nordhoff, two Americans who moved to Tahiti after fighting in World War I. The *Bounty* story, starring Marlon Brando, Trevor Howard, and the Tahitian beauty, Tarita, was filmed at Point Venus in 1961, and a 1980's version, with English and Australian actors, was filmed on Moorea.

Bligh, who had been to Tahiti previously with Cook on his third voyage, aboard the *Resolution,* was married to a lady whose uncle had a number of large plantations in Jamaica, was well connected in government circles and was the owner of several ships. A petition was made to King George III by English merchants in the West Indies, asking that the breadfruit tree be transplanted from Tahiti to their islands. Cook and others had spoken highly of the breadfruit as a substitute for bread and had told of how healthy and strong the Tahitians were, who ate it as their staple diet. The merchants believed it would be a cheap and nourishing means of feeding their slaves. The petition was approved and Bligh was appointed to command the voyage. There was no problem in signing on a crew as the reputation of the friendly and voluptuous Tahitian ladies was well known in Europe by that time.

By the time the *Bounty* arrived in Matavai Bay, October 26, 1788, there had already been problems aboard between captain and crew. For five months they stayed in Tahiti, waiting for the breadfruit to reach the right stage for transplanting. During this lengthy stay the discipline slackened while the sailors lived among the happy Tahitians, who were not accustomed to let work interfere seriously with their many pleasures and amusements.

As the time drew nearer for their departure, Bligh became excessively severe with his men. And on April 4, 1789, when the *Bounty* weighed anchor and steered towards the leeward islands of the Society group, he carried a reluctant crew.

The magic of Tahiti proved too strong a magnet and Bligh's insults to his officers, especially to acting Lieutenant Fletcher Christian, too harsh to endure. Thus, on the early morning of April 28, Bligh was awakened by four of his men, hauled out of bed, tied up and dragged on deck. There he learned that a mutiny was being staged, under the leadership of Christian, and he was put into a launch, along with eighteen of his officers and men, a 28-gallon cask of water, 150 pounds of bread, some wine and rum, a compass, a quadrant, some canvas, lines and sails. Then the mutineers cast the boat adrift in the open ocean, a few miles from Tofua in the Tongan Islands. Bligh made one of the most notable open boat voyages in history, sailing 3,600 miles to Timor and Batavia in the Dutch Indies, losing only one man during this grueling voyage. Six others died after reaching safety.

The mutineers first tried to settle at Tubuai, in the Austral Islands, but the natives were so hostile that the *Bounty* turned back to Tahiti three days later to resupply and reconsider what to do next. The twenty-five men who remained in the *Bounty* consisted of two parties: those who had taken an active part in the mutiny and those who had not. On June 6 the ship once again anchored in Matavai Bay, where she remained for ten days, loading pigs, goats, a cow and a bull, dogs, cats and fowl. When she sailed for Tubuai again, the mutineers were accompanied by nine Tahitian men, eight women and nine children, many of whom were stowaways.

Life with the aggressive Tubuaians proved impossible (about 100 natives were killed in skirmishes), so the mutineers finally decided to retreat to Tahiti. Some of the men remained there and Fletcher Christian led eight of his fellow mutineers, with six Tahitian men, one little girl and twelve Tahitian women, aboard the *Bounty* and they sailed away to eventually settle on the uninhabited island of Pitcairn. There they burned the ship and were not heard of again for 18 years.

Meantime 16 of the original *Bounty* crew lived in Tahiti, some taking wives and having families. Here they were discovered in March, 1791, when H.M.S. *Pandora* sailed into Matavai Bay, in search of the mutineers. Two of the *Bounty* men had died by the time the *Pandora* reached Tahiti, but Captain Edward Edwards arrested the remaining 14. On their way to England for their trial, the *Pandora* was shipwrecked and four were drowned. A court martial inquiry was held in England and three men were condemned to death and hanged, while the remaining seven were allowed to live as free men. During his confinement, one of the men, Peter Heywood, wrote the first Tahitian dictionary while awaiting trial.

Even after all the troubles he had been through on the *Bounty,* old "Breadfruit" Bligh didn't give up on his mission. He appeared again in Matavai Bay on April 10, 1792, as Captain Bligh and commander of H.M.S. *Providence* and her armed tender, the *Assistance.*

When he arrived there was a native war going on and he was afraid it would make it hard for him to collect the breadfruit. Finally he went ashore to supervise the building of storage sheds for his plants.

During the three months he was in Tahiti on this visit, Bligh had ample time to note the changes that had occurred. He was disappointed to learn that "little of the ancient customs of the Otaheitans remains . . . It is difficult to get them to speak their own language without mixing a jargon of English with it, and they are so altered that I believe in future no Europeans will ever know what their ancient customs of receiving strangers were." He also felt that their method of dress had degenerated and they were "no longer clean Otaheitans, but in appearance a set of ragamuffins with whom it is necessary to observe great caution."

By July 18, Bligh had collected 2,126 breadfruit plants and about 500 others and set sail for the West Indies with no major problems. There, in St. Vincent and in Port Royal, Jamaica, the breadfruit seedlings were planted. But when the trees grew and bore fruit, the Negro slaves, for whom the breadfruit was intended, disliked the taste and refused to eat it.

Heathen and Missionary

Thirty years after Captain Wallis discovered Tahiti, a shipload of an entirely different type of conquerors arrived in Matavai Bay. These were the missionaries. Composed of Presbyterians, Methodists, Episcopalians and Independents, the newly formed London Missionary Society left England in 1797, bound for Tahiti. This island was chosen as their first foreign country because they felt the society should begin its work in some place where "the difficulties were least."

By the time their ship, the *Duff,* anchored in Matavai Bay, on March 5, 1797, a Sunday morning, more than a hundred natives were dancing and capering on the decks, crying "*tayo, tayo*" (friend). Even though they were unarmed, the captain ordered the ship's guns to be hoisted. The Tahitians cheerfully assisted in placing them in their carriages.

As the 18 missionaries settled into their new quarters on Point Venus, formerly the house of Lieutenant Bligh, they began to realize the immensity of their task in imposing bleak, puritanical ideas on the uninhibited, idolatrous islanders. They soon became aware that there was "more to apprehend from being caressed and exalted, than from being insulted and oppressed."

There were only four ordained ministers in the group, while the rest were carpenters, weavers, tailors, shoemakers, bricklayers, and a harness maker. Most of them were in their early twenties and only five of them were married and had their families with them. Therefore, it is not surprising that the first problem to face the new settlers was how to deal with the beautiful and alluring Tahitian women. Even though they agreed that it would be sinful to marry a heathen woman, some of the men succumbed to the weakness of the flesh and committed the unforgivable sin of fornication.

The missionaries' life was not an easy one, in that they never learned the Tahitian language well enough to preach the gospel in an intelligible manner. The natives would scoff and ridicule them and laugh when they tried to convince the Tahitians that Jehovah was the only true God and their pagan rites and human sacrifices should be abolished. It took the missionaries more than 15 years to make their first convert, even though they had some 2,300 natives attending their meetings and instructions. Some of the Tahitians felt that the missionaries should pay them to attend the mission schools. The missionaries also quarreled among themselves and many of their number left for other islands or back to England. They made the mistake of taking sides in the local power struggles and usually supported the wrong chief for the wrong reasons.

After baptizing the powerful chief, Pomare II, whom the missionaries thought of as king of Tahiti, the other people followed suit and their idols and temples were destroyed in favor of the Christian religion.

For almost forty years the Protestant missionaries enjoyed tremendous success in Tahiti before any competition arrived. They had gained strong political control and some had lined their pockets well.

Therefore, when a small band of Catholic missionaries arrived in Tahiti with the intent of opening a new mission, the Protestants used all their influence to prevent this from happening. The first Catholic group landed on the island of Mangareva, 900 miles away, in 1835. One of them was sent to Tahiti disguised as a carpenter. The Protestants protested when they learned his true mission and they were even more incensed when two French Catholic priests arrived on the scene the following year.

The priests were asked to leave the island but refused. Queen Pomare IV, the illegitimate daughter of Tahiti's first Christian convert, who was now in power, wrote a letter to the French priests, ordering them to leave on a ship that was in port. When they again refused, the two men were forcibly removed from the island and placed aboard the ship.

The Brink of War

This action began a series of events that almost brought England and France to the brink of war. When the French government learned of this affair, it was decided that the "scandalous treatment" of the two priests could not go unpunished. Thus the frigate *Venus,* under the command of Captain Abel Du Petit-Thouars, was ordered to proceed to Tahiti to demand "a full reparation" from the Queen for "the insult done to France in the person of our compatriots." The punishment called for the Queen to write a letter to the King of France, apologizing; an indemnity of 2,000 Spanish dollars was to be paid for losses suffered by the two priests and the French flag was to be hoisted and saluted with twenty-one guns. The Queen wrote the letter but had neither the money nor the flag nor the powder. Du Petit-Thouars provided the flag and the gunpowder for the salute and George Pritchard, the most prominent missionary, and two other English residents gave the money.

The French Commander also proposed that a treaty of perpetual peace be drawn up between Tahiti and France and that Frenchmen of every profession would be allowed the right to come and go and to trade in all the islands composing the government of Tahiti. He also proposed that Frenchmen should be "received and protected as the most favoured foreigners."

As soon as the *Venus* had sailed, Queen Pomare and four of her principal chiefs wrote to Queen Victoria asking for British protection. This was not the first time the Queen of Tahiti, persuaded by George Pritchard, had asked the Queen of England to make Tahiti a British protectorate. But England was having her own troubles with France and Queen Victoria "expressed deep concern at the difficulties under which Queen Pomare appeared to labour," but decided it would be impossible for her to "fulfill, with proper punctuality, any defensive obligations towards the government and inhabitants of Tahiti." For that reason, she was unable to make Tahiti a protectorate of Great Britain, but she would always be glad to "give the protection of her good offices to Queen Pomare in any differences which might arise" with any foreign power.

Queen Pomare began having serious problems with a foreign power very soon after this letter was received from the Queen of England. A Frenchman who was also a Catholic, M. Moerenhout, had been appointed as the French Consul. While the queen was visiting in Raiatea and while the former missionary, George Pritchard—who was now the British Consul—was away in England, Moerenhout took advantage of the opportunity to trick four of the chiefs into signing a document he had composed, asking that Tahiti be made a French protectorate.

When the French government received this request, they found it suited their needs at the time, since they were looking for a base in the Pacific for the warships, whalers and merchant vessels sent out from France. They had already decided to take possession of the Marquesas Islands. So Rear Admiral Du Petit-Thouars, aboard the flagship "La Reine Blanche," was chosen to establish the French protectorate in Tahiti as well.

Despite the protests of Queen Pomare and her chiefs, who admitted they didn't understand what the document was about that they had signed, the French began to install themselves very firmly on the island. With threats and troops, Du Petit-Thouars obtained the signature of the Queen on a letter accepting "the proposal to place the government of Queen Pomare under the protection of His Majesty Louis Philippe, King of the French." He then set up a provisional government of three—the Commissioner Royal, a military governor and a captain of the port of Papeete.

When news of the French protectorate reached England six months later, the matter was brought up in Parliament, and the decision was made to accept the French protectorate as long as the Protestant missionaries would be allowed to carry on with their work.

However, when it was learned in England and in France that Du Petit-Thouars had not merely established a protectorate in Tahiti but had actually taken full possession in the name of the French king, this far-away island became the main topic of conversation on both sides of the Channel. The issue was debated even more heatedly when it was learned that the Tahitian flag had been replaced by the French flag after 500 French troops surrounded the palace, and Queen Pomare had been dispossessed and forced to flee to the safety of an English ship in the Papeete harbor. But all of England was outraged when Pritchard arrived on July 26, 1844, in H.M.S. *Vindictive* with the news that he had been arrested and deported.

The matter was heatedly discussed in all circles and given much publicity in the newspapers of both countries. Both the French and English governments found it difficult to avoid war as both sides felt they had been humiliated. Finally King Louis Philippe offered to pay Pritchard 25,000 francs out of his own pocket, hoping that he could maintain the "entente cordiale" with Great Britain. This offer was rejected and accord was maintained between the two governments when France apologized to England for the treatment given Pritchard and an "equitable indemnity" was paid for his loss and sufferings.

This affair was kept alive in the French parliament for three more years and contributed to the eventual overthrow of the government and monarchy in the famous revolution of February 24, 1848.

While England and France were carefully avoiding war back in Europe, the Tahitians were staging a lot of skirmishes with the French troops in Tahiti, and sometimes getting the upper hand. Their queen sought refuge in Raiatea, where she wrote to Queen Victoria, pleading for help in regaining her sovereignty. The letters were never answered and she realized that she would have to fight alone. The natives, however, never gave up hope that Britain would come to their aid. They could not believe that England had deserted them and they refused to submit to the French protectorate.

The protectorate had been re-established and the Queen's sovereignty restored in early 1845, after France and England had come to terms over the George Pritchard affair. But Queen Pomare refused to return to Tahiti under French rule. Finally, in February, 1847, she gave up the useless struggle when she heeded the advice of a Tahitian chieftainess and agreed to accept the French protectorate. Thus she was brought back to Tahiti, where she was little more than a figurehead until her death on September 17, 1877.

King Pomare V, the last of the dynasty to carry this title, was totally unfit for even the most nominal duties of kingship. He preferred drinking and gambling and had none of his mother's pride in the Tahitian heritage. Therefore, it was easy to get him to abdicate, with the promise of an annual pension for himself, his wife and two brothers.

The century-old rule of the Pomares formally came to an end on December 30, 1880, and Tahiti became a full-fledged French colony, when the French government accepted Tahiti and her dependencies as forming one and the same country with France.

In 1903 the whole of the French establishment in the Eastern Pacific was declared one colony and was called French Oceania. In 1957 the status was changed from a colony to a Territory and the name was changed to the present, French Polynesia.

Modern Polynesia

Before you leave Point Venus and the site where white man first stepped ashore to change the lives of these 'noble savages,' take a moment to look up at the green peaks of Mt. Orohena, Tahiti's tallest mountain of 7,353 feet. Follow the line of the mountains around to where the hotel Tahara'a is situated on top of the famous "One Tree Hill," so named by Captain Cook. Here you have the continuity of the magic of Tahiti, bridging the unknown past with the uncertainty of the future. Eight million years have passed since these mountains first rose from the blue waters. Radio-carbon dates indicate that human history began in what we now know as the Society Islands around A.D. 850. As there was no written language until the missionaries devised an alphabet for the natives, very little is known about their origins. Scientists have learned some interesting things about their ancient culture by studying their language and by excavations that have revealed their temples, called "maraes," and their stone adze heads, fishhooks and artifacts.

In modern times, after more than 200 years of white man's influence, the Tahitian and Polynesian culture is very much alive. A leisurely drive around the island of Tahiti reveals many of the same attractions that brought romanticists to these shores—writers and artists such as Robert Louis Stevenson, Jack London, Somerset Maugham, Rupert Brooke, Paul Gauguin, Henry Adams—who were, each in his own way, trying to capture the "same charm of light and air." There are the several rivers and waterfalls; the fern-covered mountains; coconut plantations and taro fields; the simple Tahitian *fares* painted in rainbow colors; the soft featured and golden skinned women, clad in their bright *pareos* and with flowers behind their ears, holding a baby on their hips and gossiping alongside the road; and there are the friendly and athletic men who still fish on the reefs at night and play their guitars and drums. The *tamure* and other traditional dances are still performed with skill and enthusiasm even though the modern French Polynesian eagerly adopts the latest dances from Europe or America and performs them with vigor and an abandon seen nowhere else.

It is true that the faces of Tahiti have changed from the days when Wallis and de Bougainville and Cook first came ashore. With the arrival of the Europeans in 1767 and the Chinese—who were first introduced to these islands during the American Civil War to work in the cotton plantation where the golf course is today—there has been more racial intermingling than in any other part of the Pacific except Hawaii. With the exception of the Chinese community, who are the merchants of these islands and who still try to maintain their tradition of marrying within their own race (although it is increasingly difficult to control), there are no financial, racial or social barriers.

Even though many of the couples who live together are not legally married, the population continues to grow, so that more than half the population of 175,000 in French Polynesia is under the age of 20. There is no stigma for an unmarried girl to have a baby and there are few unwanted babies. Tahitians love any tiny infant, cat, or dog, as long as they are very young. Life is not so easy for the growing youngster or animal, however, in many cases. And the growing rate of juvenile delinquency in downtown Papeete is equivalent to the population explosion.

As you end your tour of Tahiti you find that you have stepped back into modern day Papeete, just in time for the evening rush hour to begin as the workers go home from their offices. The euphoria that surrounded you around the island as you walked through the botanical gardens, picked a flower, watched the surf breaking on the reef, listened to the wind whistling through the casuarina trees at the edge of a black sand beach, drank the cool liquid of a coconut, or viewed the mountains of Tahiti from the plateau at Taravao on the isthmus, begins to dissipate as you enter the downtown area with its high rise shopping centers and parking meters.

But if you can keep that magic around you and get to the waterfront area undisturbed by the noise and the incredibly undisciplined traffic, then you will be amply rewarded as the sun begins to set behind the peaks and spires of Moorea, that land of "Bali H'ai," just 12 miles across the bay. As you sip a tall cool one at one of the sidewalk cafés and watch the sky turn all shades of red, pink and orange, the last of the traffic disappears and you can see the outrigger canoes in the harbor, where their vigorous paddlers are practicing for their next race. When you finish your drink and before you return to your air conditioned hotel room, walk down the waterfront to the corner across the street from the Tahiti Tourist Board. Here, in a thatched-roof *fare,* you will find a tradition that has existed ever since there have been Tahitians. The old women are sitting on the floor, making crowns of flowers for the merrymakers to wear when they go out that evening, dining and dancing. This scene is one of the last remnants of "Papeete town."

For the curious traveler who doesn't adhere to the belief that "if you've seen one island, you've seen them all," French Polynesia is a veritable treasurehouse. Because it covers such a large area of the eastern Pacific and the five archipelagoes are at different latitudes, choices can be made from the high volcanic islands of the Society group, the low coral atolls of the Tuamotus, the remote and mysterious islands of the Marquesas, or the temperate climate of the distant Australs.

Many a visitor has made the mistake of allowing too little time for visiting the outer islands of French Polynesia and quite often the complaint is heard, "Oh, how I wish I had come here first."

At the Tahiti-Faaa airport in Tahiti there are lockers where it is possible to store luggage while visits are made to the other islands. Also the hotels are very good about keeping your bags while you are away from Tahiti.

The islands most frequently visited are those with first class hotels. They are: *Tahiti, Moorea, Bora Bora, Huahine,* and *Raiatea* in the Society Islands; and *Rangiroa* and *Manihi* in the Tuamotus. The following information will enable you to determine which ones suit your desires most, and includes some of the lesser known islands.

Moorea

This sister island just 12 miles from Tahiti is the most frequently visited one after Tahiti. Many tourists say it is worth the airfare to Tahiti just to see Moorea's spectacular bays. There are several launches that leave daily from the Papeete harbor for the 45-minute crossing, returning to Tahiti in the afternoon. Also there is an air taxi service that will land you on Moorea in just seven minutes flying time. Once there, you can choose from several hotels, most of which are located on white sand beaches.

In Moorea, as on the other islands, most of the activities are centered around the clear waters of the lagoon. A coral reef several yards offshore protects the lagoons from the pounding surf and, as a result, the lagoons are usually as calm as a giant swimming pool.

If you're not a swimmer, snorkeler or diver, then you can ride a bike around the island or take a tour arranged by the hotels. It is also well worth the money to rent a car and drive the 37 miles around the island and up into the valley of Opunohu, passing coffee plantations and pineapple fields. Be sure to drive up to Le Belvedere, a lookout spot where you will be well rewarded with a magnificent view of Moorea's jagged mountains and Cook's Bay, also called PaoPao and of Opunohu Bay, also known as Papetoai Bay. On all the tours the mountain called "Bali H'ai" by the tourists will be pointed out. This is a needle shaped mountain named Mou'aroa that appeared in the movie *South Pacific* as the mythical Bali H'ai.

Most of the nighttime activities take place in the hotels, where there are regular Tahitian feasts, called *tamaaraas,* dance shows or singing to the accompaniment of guitars and ukuleles. For those with rental cars it is fun to dine out at one of Moorea's excellent restaurants, and then to hotel hop, checking out the evening's action at each hotel bar.

Bora Bora

More "purple prose" has been written about this little island than any other in the South Pacific and justly so. Situated 143 miles northwest of Tahiti, it can be reached in 55 minutes by Air Polynesie, plus another 45 minutes by launch from the airport to the main village of Vaitape. Or you can go by an air-conditioned ferry that leaves Tahiti twice weekly, stopping at Huahine, Raiatea, and Tahaa enroute, and arriving in Bora Bora the following day.

The island is fringed by small islets, called "motus," and boasts one of the clearest and most colorful lagoons anywhere, with a variety of coral gardens that can be viewed through glass-bottom boats or while snorkeling and diving. The two highest mountains, Mt. Otemanu at 2,379 feet and Mt. Pahia at 2,165 feet, can be seen from many vantage points as one travels the 17 miles around the island on a partially paved road.

There are three rental car locations that have bicycles and motorbikes, as well as jeeps and cars. Bicycles are a popular method of transportation in Bora Bora and can facilitate the many stops you will need to make to visit the villages, the old barracks and seaplane base built by the Seabees, the ancient temples, called "maraes," or to inspect the curios at the many souvenir stands around the island. You will want to stop for a drink at the Bloody Mary Restaurant and make reservations to return for a seafood dinner, cooked and served in a setting right out of a South Seas movie.

The largest hotel, the Hotel Bora Bora, offers all types of water sports, and frequent Tahitian dance shows or slide shows. The Club Mediterranée, with over-water bungalows, also has a full range of activities, including picnics and swimming on a nearby *motu*. The Hotel Marara was built to house a movie crew while filming a Dino DiLaurentiis movie, *The Hurricane*. Upon completion of the film the Marara (Tahitian for flying fish) was opened to the public, and is now operated by Sofitel, owned by the group ACCOR. It faces toward Tahaa and Raiatea. Next door is the Hotel Ibis, built as Climat de France, but taken over in July 1986 by the ACCOR group. The Hotel Oa Oa has eight bungalows near the principal village and the Revatua Club is on the opposite side of the island from all the other hotels. You can rent a luxurious bungalow at the Bora Bora Condos; the Hotel Matira has housekeeping bungalows, complete with individual outrigger canoes, built beside the island's prettiest beach.

If you just want to lie back and take life easy, this island is an ideal place to do just that. There is no hustle and bustle unless you want to create it yourself. Serenity is the password on Bora Bora, which means "firstborn-of-silent-paddle."

Huahine

Quickly becoming one of French Polynesia's most popular tourist islands, Huahine is only 40 minutes by air from Tahiti, or just an overnight trip by inter-island schooner.

This quiet and peaceful island, which is actually two islands, called Huahine-Nui (big Huahine) and Huahine-Iti (little Huahine) is only 20 miles in circumference. There are mountains over 2,000 feet high and two lakes, where it is easy to dig for clams and crabs. Most of the island's population of 4,000 fish and farm for a living and produce watermelons and cantaloupes for the market in Tahiti.

The principal village, called Fare, is reminiscent of an old western town from some cowboy country. There are a handful of Chinese stores lining the tree-shaded waterfront, plus a billiards parlor, two banks, the Air Polynesia office, and a couple of small boutiques, one with lovely pottery made by an American man and his Tahitian wife. The 2-story Hotel Huahine overlooks the harbor and beach and Lovina's small hotel sits next door to a photo shop. Pension Enite serves great meals behind the Snack Te Marara, which also is popular for its hamburgers and Hinano beer and is a good place to hang out and talk with yachting people.

When the Raromatai Ferry and copra/cargo/passenger boats *Temehani II* and *Taporo IV* arrive from Tahiti or return from Bora Bora and Raiatea, there is much excitement in the village, with truckloads of Tahitians coming to town for market day. The rest of the week the village takes on a somnolent air with only a few people strolling under the big almond trees.

The first class Hotel Bali H'ai Huahine can be reached in just five minutes from the village by walking on a path alongside the strip of white sand beach that stretches from the village past the hotel.

Rental cars or mopeds can be ordered at the Hotel Bali H'ai, Hotel Huahine, or with Lovina. Budget Rentals has Mehari jeeps. Also there are guided tours from each place around the island, or visits to the village of Maeva, a Polynesian village that is a sort of "open-air" museum. Many interesting Tahitian temples or "maraes" are located in or near this village.

Five miles from Fare is the Hotel BelleVue, with 15 colonial-style bungalows and eight double rooms, a swimming pool, and a restaurant that features locally caught seafood prepared Chinese-Tahitian style.

At the south end of Huahine-Iti two hotels were opened in mid-1985 near the pretty village of Parea. The Huahine Beach Hotel and the Relais Mahana are built beside long white sand beaches and offer attractive bungalows each, plus restaurant, boutique, all water sports, and other activities. Parea has a few "pensions" where guests share the Polynesian lifestyle, including children and dogs.

Raiatea

This second largest island in the Society group is only a 45-minute flight from Tahiti or an overnight passage aboard the "Raromatai Ferry," an air-conditioned passenger and car ferryboat that departs Tahiti twice weekly. The inter-island schooners *Temehani II* and *Taporo IV* also service the Leeward Society Islands, with a true Polynesian atmosphere.

Although there are not many white sand beaches to be found on this island, many visitors favor Raiatea because of the friendly people and the historic landmarks. It was from the river called *"Faaroa"* located here that the original Maoris set off for New Zealand. This was also the former educational and religious center for the ancient Tahitians, and the most famous temple or *marae* called *Taputapuatea,* is located on the southeast point of the island.

The Hotel Bali H'ai chain offers first class accommodations with many over-water bungalows, all water sports, bicycles, a swimming pool and games area, as well as being the center for the nightly social events and dancing.

The Raiatea Village, with 12 bungalows complete with kitchenettes, opened in late 1983 by the Faaroa River. In the center of Uturoa is the Hotel Motu, with clean rooms for the budget traveler, plus a very good French restaurant upstairs. Although this small hotel is not close to the village it does offer a peaceful beauty.

There are various tours available with the hotels, including speedboat trips to the nearby island of Tahaa, where time seems to have stopped a hundred years ago.

A lot of fun can be had just by walking or biking into the principal town of Uturoa. There are Chinese shops to explore and the public market, in the center of town, is interesting to visit during the early morning hours of market days. Even though Raiatea has a population of 7,400 and Uturoa is the second-largest town in French Polynesia, there is little nighttime activity except on weekends, when the young Raiateans head for the disco or local nightclub to dance the night away.

Another kind of dancing is performed on special occasions at the Hotel Bali H'ai, when the firewalking ceremonies recreate the ancient rites of walking barefoot across white-hot stones.

Tahaa

Tahaa is the sister island of Raiatea, sharing the same lagoon. It is nearly circular in shape and is only 15 miles in circumference, half the size of the main island of Raiatea. From Tahaa you can easily see Huahine, Raiatea and Bora Bora. It is necessary to go to Raiatea first if flying and take the *Ramanui* or one of the other small ferry boats that arrive in Raiatea early each morning and return to Tahaa before noon.

Most tourists visit Tahaa for the day only, but it is now easier to find a room for the night. The Tahaa Iti Village is an old hotel recently taken over by a French couple, offering excellent cuisine, marvelous views of Bora Bora and the sunset. Tahaa Lagon, across the mountains or around the bay, is a small and new French bungalow/restaurant complex. Marina-iti is a good stopover place for those chartering yachts. And a few rooms are still available with local families in some villages. The *Raromatai Ferry* and the copra ships *Temehani II* and *Taporo IV* call at Tahaa.

Maupiti

This small and beautiful island lies 37 kilometers (22 miles) west of Bora Bora and is surrounded by a protective barrier reef with off-shore *motus* lying between the main island and the coral reef. Air Polynesie has an airstrip on one of these islets, with flights from Tahiti and Raiatea to Maupiti each Monday and Thursday morning and from Bora Bora to Maupiti and return to Raiatea and Papeete on Monday and Thursday afternoons. The cargo/passenger boat *Taporo I* leaves Raiatea for Maupiti each Tuesday at midnight, arriving through the dangerous pass into the tranquil harbor the following morning at 6 A.M. and departing for Raiatea by way of Bora Bora three hours later. Maupiti's 800 residents are mostly watermelon farmers and fishermen, or they produce copra, pandanus, taro, yams, tapioca, and bananas. This tranquil island has mostly been kept a secret; there are no big hotels. White-sand beaches and excellent snorkeling are found around the motus, where a few tourist bungalows have been built. Accommodations are also available in the main village, in small pensions. Activities, besides water sports, include walking or biking around the island, which is only 5.7 miles in circumference, and visiting the archeological ruins and *marae* temples that are remnants of a former powerful civilization. There are nursery and primary schools, a city hall, infirmary, post office, and a few general stores.

Tetiaroa

Tetiaroa is the atoll that belongs to Marlon Brando, just a 17-minute flight from Tahiti. Due to extensive damage during several hurricanes in 1983, the hotel was closed and is presently open for day tours and one-night weekend stays only. Accommodations include 13 bungalows and 4 A-frame rooms built of coconut trees. Beautiful beaches and an interior lagoon are the natural attractions here. The hotel is managed by Marlon Brando's son Teihotu.

Tuamotus

The Tuamotu archipelago, also called the Low or Dangerous archipelago and comprising 78 low islands called coral atolls, is scattered over several hundreds of miles of the eastern Pacific that is part of French Polynesia.

Thirty of these atolls are uninhabited, while the rest are very sparsely populated. The islands rise only some six to twenty feet above the water and are surrounded by coral reefs with rarely a pass or break in the reef; when there is a pass it is usually navigable only at certain tide levels. The reefs are graveyards for the many boats that didn't make it through the passes. Life on these remote atolls is simple and often lonely, because of the lack of people or visiting boats. The diet of the people consists mostly of fish, coconuts and canned food.

There is airplane service to several of the atolls—Rangiroa, Manihi, Arutua, Hao, Tatakoto, Pukarua, Reao, Nukutavake, Fangatau, Fakahina, Vairaatea, Tureia, Puka Puka, Kaukura, Mataiva, Apataki, Napuka, Fakarava, Takapoto, Anaa, Makemo and Tikehau—but there are no first class hotels on any except at Rangiroa and Manihi. There are facilities available with Tahitian families on the other atolls, for those travelers who don't require too many comforts and services.

Rangiroa is a perfect example of a coral atoll. The reef encloses a lagoon 42 miles long and 14 miles wide at its extreme width. Air Polynesie has flights six days a week from Tahiti to Rangiroa and in only one hour you are there, in a completely different world, surrounded by blindingly white sand beaches, with the multi-colored lagoon on one side and the pounding surf of the Pacific on the other side of this narrow strip of land.

The atoll life can be observed in the villages of Tiputa and Avatoru on Rangiroa, where there are the churches, schools, the usual Chinese stores and ancient bakery still producing long loaves of French bread daily. Tiputa can be reached by speedboat from the Kia Ora Hotel in a few minutes. Avatoru is located on the same atoll as the airport and the hotel can be reached by car. There is a pass into the lagoon at both Avatoru and Tiputa. Many visitors and locals enjoy swimming through the passes as the extremely powerful tide rushes through. You can see hundreds of tropical fishes, as well as sharks, who are swept along with the current.

The hotels Kia Ora Village, Rangiroa Village, and La Bouteille a la Mer are located on the main atoll, and the small hotel Sans Souci is across the lagoon on a private islet.

These atolls of the Tuamotus are often ravaged by hurricanes or cyclones. Their limpid lagoons have been found to be the perfect place to farm the famous South Seas black pearl, which is sold in Tahiti.

For the diver, a trip to these waters is a dream come true, for it offers some of the finest diving in the world.

Marquesas

The twelve islands that comprise *Les Îles Marquises* are little known to the world and are considered to be strange and mysterious by the outsider. The first white man to discover any of these high volcanic islands was Alvaro Mendana de Neira of Spain, who arrived in 1595 and discovered four of the southernmost islands. He named the group in honor of the Viceroy of Peru's wife, the Marquesa de Mendoza.

Before the missionaries converted the people to Christianity, the Marquesans fought many wars among themselves and were noted cannibals, but the diseases and vices introduced by white man had a more devastating effect on the population than earlier practices had. The population was once more than 100,000 but numbers 6,500 today.

For 40 years prior to the French government taking over, the Marquesas group was ravaged by whalers, traders, blackbirders (slave traders) and others. Finally the Marquesan chiefs asked France to help, and a treaty was signed between the chiefs and Admiral du Petit-Thouars in May 1842.

Today, the Marquesans are noted for their native handicrafts, especially for their wood carvings. They also earn money from copra and the sale of shells.

The island of Nuku Hiva can be reached by airplane from Tahiti. This 5-hour flight normally runs each Saturday with a stopover in Rangiroa. There are additional flights often added during high season, operating on Thursdays. It is advisable to make reservations well in advance. There are internal flights within the Marquesas islands, connecting Nuku Hiva with the islands of Hiva Oa, Ua Pou and Ua Huka. The Aranui, a 264-foot long cargo/copra/passenger ship departs Tahiti each month for 16-day round trips to the Marquesas, with two brief stops in the Tuamotus enroute. This is the best way to visit the Marquesas; the ship is comfortable, clean, and air-conditioned, with a French chef, and the Aranui calls at each principal Marquesan island and at isolated valleys.

There are a few small hotels on some of the islands, as well as a room or two in village homes. For those adventurous enough to visit these still-peaceful islands where wild horses, cattle, goats, sheep, and pigs roam through the mountains, the trip will be an experience.

Australs

For those who want to see French Polynesia but prefer their climate a bit cooler than is usually found in the Society Islands, then perhaps the Austral group will be just what you're seeking.

The five inhabited and two uninhabited islands form a chain that extends from the southwest to northwest over a distance of about 800 miles. The nearest island to Tahiti is Rurutu, which is 300 miles south, placing it in a temperate zone where potatoes and strawberries grow in addition to mangoes and papayas.

Rurutu, as well as Tubuai, can be reached by plane from Tahiti in less than 2 hours. The flights leave on Mondays and Thursdays, returning the same day. A passenger-cargo schooner, the *Tuhaa Pae II*, makes regular trips between Tahiti, Rurutu, Tubuai, Raivavae and Rimatara. The round trip takes 10–12 days. A 15–17 day round trip is made between Tahiti, the above islands and Rapa every three months.

On the island of Tubuai there are numerous accommodations in Tahitian-style bungalows close to the beach. There are bicycles, horses and outrigger canoes to rent for exploring this oval-shaped small island that is only six miles long by three miles wide. This is the island where the *Bounty* mutineers attempted to make a settlement but were forced to leave when the natives became violent. Today, the people of the Australs are very friendly and love to include the visitor in their daily events.

On Rurutu there is a hotel that opened in February, 1982. Each of the 16 bungalows includes a sunken bathtub, lush carpets, bedding and towels. A freshwater swimming pool and excellent food are part of the hotel's offerings for the visitor who wishes to explore Rurutu in comfort and style. There are also lodgings available with the local people in the three villages of Moerai, Avera and Hauti. Here the islanders build their own schooners and carry their produce of taro, arrowroot, copra and vanilla to the other islands to sell. The woven hats from Rurutu are very well made and bring a high price in the stores of Papeete.

Anyone planning to visit these islands of the Austral group that Captain Cook discovered should bring a heavy cardigan and warm clothes, especially during the months of May through October.

PRACTICAL INFORMATION FOR FRENCH POLYNESIA

FACTS AND FIGURES. French Polynesia covers an area as big as Europe without Russia (1,545,000 sq. miles) and consists of some 130 islands with a land area of only 1,544 sq. miles. These islands, many of which are uninhabited, are divided into five archipelagoes: the Society Islands (Windward and Leeward Islands), the Austral Islands, the Tuamotu-Gambier Islands and the Marquesas Islands. Total population is 175,000.

Tahiti, the largest island, is the seat of government and the capital, with Papeete (pronounced Pah-pay-ay-tay, meaning 'water (from a) basket') the major city and harbor. Population for Tahiti is 123,000, consisting of Polynesians of Maori origin representing 69%, Polynesians mixed 14%, Asians 4% and Europeans (including Americans) 13%.

French Polynesia is administered as an overseas Territory of the French Republic. The High Commissioner is appointed by France to serve for three years. A 1984 revision to the constitution allows more internal autonomy, with a local president and council of 10 ministers elected by the 41 Territorial Assembly members for 5 years. The Territory is represented in France by a senator and two deputies to the National Assembly.

WHEN TO COME. There are only two real seasons in French Polynesia—the warm and rainy season from November to April and the cooler and drier season from May through October. The daytime temperature in the hotter time of the year averages 82°F. and during the cooler months the average is 76°F. The flowers and fruits are at their best during the warmer months but the tropical winds are usually blowing during the months of April through August.

Average Temperature (°Fahrenheit) and Humidity

Papeete	Jan	Feb	Mar	Apr	May	June	July	Aug	Sept	Oct	Nov	Dec
Average max. day temperature	86°	86°	86°	85°	83°	82°	82°	82°	82°	83°	84°	85°
Days of rain	14	11	9	8	7	7	6	5	6	8	9	13
Humidity, percent	79	79	79	79	80	79	78	76	77	77	79	79

WHAT WILL IT COST? Due to the fluctuation of the American dollar the exchange rates vary daily. At time of publication the average rate of US $1–125 CFP (French Pacific Francs).

LANGUAGE. The official language is French, although Tahitian is usually spoken by the Polynesian population, especially away from Papeete. English is spoken in many of the shops and in all the hotels. Keep in mind, however, that this is French Polynesia, and the English you hear will not always be perfect. Try to learn a few words of French and Tahitian and you'll have more fun as well as a warm response to your efforts.

TIPPING. Signs are posted at the airport in Tahiti in three languages, "No Tipping." In other places, such as hotels and travel brochures, you will read that tipping is contrary to Tahitian hospitality. This is true and it is

FRENCH POLYNESIA

not the custom to tip; however, the employees of the larger hotels in Tahiti, as well as tour escorts and drivers, do graciously accept occasional tips.

PASSPORTS AND CUSTOMS. All passengers entering French Polynesia must be in possession of a valid passport and outbound ticket. Visas, issued by the French Consulates and Embassies, are required by all visitors except citizens of the European Economic Community, Switzerland, Liechtenstein, Andorra, and Monaco. This is not an immigration country and foreigners looking for work are discouraged from applying for long-term visas. A few retired or independently wealthy Americans have moved to these islands and bought property, with the approval of the local government. A work visa is necessary before non-French citizens can be employed in French Polynesia. Professionals such as teachers, nurses, architects, etc. need French diplomas and licenses before working here.

No shots required.

Cruising Yachts

Special formalities apply to those visitors arriving in yachts. Official ports of entry into French Polynesia are: Tahiti and Moorea in the Windward Islands; Raiatea, Huahine, and Bora Bora in the Leeward Islands; Nuku-Hiva, Ua-Pou, and Hiva-Oa in the Marquesas Islands; Tubuai, Rurutu, and Raivaevae in the Austral Islands; and Rangiroa in the Tuamotu-Gambier Islands. A special passport is necessary from the Customs Officer or Gendarmerie in the arriving seaport or bay, normally valid for three months, with extensions usually available following application in Tahiti. Return airplane tickets are required for everyone or an equivalent sum of money can be deposited into an account.

WHAT TO TAKE. Pack lightweight summer clothes, which are used all year round in the tropical weather of Polynesia. A light sweater or jacket feels good in the evenings during the cooler months of June through October. Rarely is a man seen wearing a jacket and tie in Tahiti. The standard attire for men even at dinner parties is simply slacks and shirt. The women usually wear pretty, long dresses in the evenings and normal resort wear around the hotels. *Pareos* or *pareus* (brightly colored and versatile) are worn in most of the outer islands around the hotels, but Tahiti is more cosmopolitan. Tennis shoes or plastic beach sandals for walking on the coral reefs and in the lagoons. If you're going to some of the more remote islands, such as the Marquesas or Tuamotus or Australs, take your own supply of tobacco, cigarettes, and booze. Suntan lotion, dark glasses, and mosquito repellant come in handy, also. Bring lots of money because this place is *très cher!*

TIME ZONE. Tahiti is Greenwich Mean Time minus 10 hours; 2 hours behind U.S. Pacific Standard Time.

ELECTRICITY. Most of the hotels use 220 volts, 50 cycle, with 110 volt outlets for razors only. Some of the older hotels still use 110 volts. Converters can sometimes be borrowed from reception desks in the hotels. A small, portable voltage converter with input holes for American appliances and round output plugs for standard French outlets can be purchased at hardware stores in the States and in Tahiti. Most outlets in Tahiti have two round holes.

WATER. Some tourists seem to have problems with the water, so drink bottled mineral water wherever you are.

THE SOUTH PACIFIC

HOW TO GET THERE. By air. By the end of 1986 the airport at Tahiti-Faaa is expected to be served by at least seven international airlines plus three charter flight operations. *UTA French Airlines* leaves Los Angeles four times weekly direct to Tahiti with an extra flight added during peak seasons. UTA also flies to Tahiti from Sydney, Noumea, and Auckland three times weekly and operates a DC-10 weekly flight between Tahiti and Honolulu, departing Honolulu each Monday and returning the following Sunday. *Air New Zealand* flies from Los Angeles to Tahiti twice a week, using B747 aircraft, and has three weekly flights from Auckland, one of which stops in Fiji and the Cook Islands. *Qantas Airways* flies B747M's from Los Angeles to Tahiti three times weekly, and three weekly flights arrive from Melbourne and Sydney, Australia. *Lan Chile* arrives on Wednesdays from Santiago, Chile, and Easter Island. *South Pacific Island Airways* flies from Honolulu and returns each Monday. *Continental Airlines* has announced twice weekly flights from Los Angeles to Tahiti, Auckland, Sydney and return. *Air France* (Paris–L.A.–Tahiti) and *People Express* (L.A.–Tahiti) have also begun flights.

By sea: Several international ships call at Tahiti but on an infrequent basis, offering connections from Europe, South Africa, Panama or Australia. These ships are from the lines of Sitmar, Cunard, Holland America, Norwegian America and Bank Line. A few cruise ships leave from San Francisco or other California ports, as well as New York and Florida, and stop in Tahiti. Royal Viking Lines, the *Pacific Princess, Queen Elizabeth II,* and *Sagafjord,* among other passenger ships, cruise to Tahiti and beyond. A few Windjammer Barefoot Cruise boats, such as *Yankee Trader,* pass through infrequently.

Charters and excursions. *Airline Marketing Tours* (AmiTours), 1211 Coast Village Rd., Santa Barbara, CA 93108 (805–565–1448), working in conjunction with *American Hawaii Cruises,* sells budget-priced one-week Tahiti packages, using available seats aboard AHC's charter flights on Transamerica Airlines. Roundtrip airfare between Los Angeles and Tahiti and 7-night Tahiti-Moorea hotel bargains cost $699 per person at publication. This program does not include any shipboard accommodations.

Morris Travel, 433 W. Lawndale Dr., Salt Lake City, Utah 84115 (801–487–9731), beginning Oct., 1986, offers weekly flights from Salt Lake City to Tahiti via San Francisco. Programs starting at $699 for a one-week, seven-night stay will be available for passengers flying from San Francisco, and the starting price from Salt Lake City is $749.

The French charter company *Minerve,* Compagnie Francaise de Transports Aeriens, 4, Rue Cambon, 75001 Paris (42–96–16–86), offers roundtrip air fare from Paris to Tahiti via San Francisco for 7,500 French francs, or approximately US$1,090.

Ted Cook's Islands in the Sun, 760 W. 16th St., Suite L, Costa Mesa, CA 92627 (Nationwide 800–854–3413, California 432–7080, Orange County 714–645–8300) is a wholesale tour operator with a variety of package plans, tours, and excursions to the South Pacific. Their brochure includes one complimentary night at Tahiti's new Hotel Ibis, plus six free nights at the Captain Cook Beach Hotel on Moorea to anyone booking the 7-day S.S. *Liberté* cruise through their company. Other savings are offered for cruises aboard the *Majestic Tahiti Explorer.*

Ron Armstrong, *World Adventure Tours,* 2183 Fairview, Suite 106, PO Box 3009, Costa Mesa, CA 92627 (Nationwide 800–222–8687; California 800–221–8687; from area codes 213 and 818, 800–492–2828; and Orange County 714–645–8873) is a wholesale tour operator specializing in the South Pacific, with many programs featuring French Polynesia.

ACCOMMODATIONS. Accommodations in French Polynesia range from the air-conditioned, carpeted deluxe rooms with telephones and room service, similar to what you can find throughout most of the world, down through your thatched roofed bungalow "fares" and your Tahitian pensions, where you share a room and the bathroom may be outdoors with cold water showers or a barrel of water that you splash on with half a coconut shell. The Hotel Sofitel Maeva Beach and the Ibis Hotels in Tahiti and Moorea have television sets in the rooms, as well as in-house video programs. Some of the hotels in Tahiti and the outer islands now have a big-screen video for evenings and rainy-day entertainment.

In Tahiti, most of the hotel rooms are conventional in that they are in buildings easily identified as hotels. In the outer islands, the resort hotels normally have individual gardens and overwater bungalows and rooms, many of which are built of bamboo with pandanus roofs and a porch or veranda. These all have large bathrooms with showers. Bathtubs are found only in the deluxe hotels in Papeete and one or two others of the expensive category. Swimming pools are becoming more popular, even in some of the outer islands, although they are still not standard amenities. However, there is usually a lagoon nearby where one can swim in clear water.

The listings below are ranged according to price categories. The rates for the island of Tahiti are based on double occupancy, without meals and the ranges are *Deluxe,* $210 and up; *Expensive,* $90–$115; *Moderate,* $60–$89; *Inexpensive* $32–$55. The rates for all accommodations in the outer islands vary widely and are often more expensive than deluxe-rated hotels in Tahiti. The classification given is based on double occupancy, without meals, although in some remote islands meals are included. *Deluxe Overwater Bungalow,* $200–$355; *Expensive,* $96–$250; *Moderate,* $60–$95; *Inexpensive,* $20–$55. Hotel Tax is 7%.

Listings begin with Tahiti; other islands and (island groups) follow alphabetically.

TAHITI

Hotel Sofitel Maeva Beach. *Deluxe.* P.O. Box 6008, Faaa Airport, Tahiti; 42.80.42, Telex 214FP. On the west coast of Tahiti, on a man-made white sand beach, 4.5 miles from Papeete. One 7-storied building, 230 rooms and suites, totally air conditioned with elevators, 2 restaurants (one of them gourmet class), 2 bars, meeting room, beauty parlor, boutiques, 5 acres of gardens, swimming pool, tennis, all water sports, TV sets in all rooms with in-house video and direct distance dialing telephone system. Tahitian dance shows several times weekly. Very French hotel.

Tahara'a. *Deluxe.* P.O. Box 1015, Papeete, Tahiti; 48.11.22, Telex 225FP. Five miles northeast of Papeete, 8 miles from airport, this hotel is built on the famous "One Tree Hill," commanding one of the finest views in Tahiti. 200 air-conditioned rooms and suites, all with terraces overlooking Matavai Bay and the island of Moorea. Elevators, coffee shop, gourmet restaurant, bar, banquet-and-bar facility, meeting room, beauty parlor, boutiques, 10 acres of gardens, swimming pool, tennis, skeet shooting, jogging trail, beach club and lovely cove with black-sand beach at bottom of cliff reached by stairs built into the cliff or by beach buggy from hotel entrance. Varied water sports including sunset cruises. Tahitian dance shows several times weekly. Hotel is American owned and operated.

Tahiti Beachcomber. *Deluxe.* P.O. Box 6014, Faaa, Tahiti; 42.51.10, Telex 276FP. On the west coast of Tahiti, 4.3 miles from Papeete with good view of Moorea. 200 rooms, including overwater bungalows and suites, air conditioned, elevator in 3-story building, pool, tennis, 9-hole golf course, all water sports, conference room, boutique, beauty parlor, 2 bars, coffee shop, gourmet restaurant, refrigerators and coffee maker in rooms, free slide shows and video movies, Tahitian dance shows, Friday night gastronomic seafood buffet and show on white sand beach beside lagoon. Very pretty location.

Ibis Punaauia. (Formerly Climat de France.) *Expensive.* P. O. Box 576, Papeete, Tahiti; 42.60.40, Telex 428FP. Located at PK. 7,800 on hill between Hotels Te Puna Bel Air and Sofitel Maeva Beach, overlooking lagoon and Moorea. 40 rooms with TV and video, swimming pool, two tennis courts, restaurant and bar.

Royal Tahitian. *Expensive.* P.O. Box 5001, Pirae, Tahiti; 42.81.13. 2.5 miles east of Papeete, with 45 motel-style rooms and beach bungalows, situated in large tropical garden, air conditioned, beach restaurant and bar. A normally very quiet hotel, except on weekends when locals come to enjoy the good swimming in the gentle swells of open ocean that sweep onto the long, curving black-sand beach.

Ibis Papeete. *Moderate.* P.O. Box 4545, Papeete, Tahiti, Telephone 42.32.77, Telex 319FP. Tahiti's newest hotel (opened Jan. 1986) is located at intersection of Blvd. Pomare and Ave. Prince Hinoi in the middle of downtown Papeete, across street from Moorea boat dock. 72 sound-proofed air-conditioned rooms have color TV, in-house video, and include 4 rooms for handicapped. 90-seat

Le Restaurant serves continental cuisine and "Ibisburgers" on second floor, and bar is on street level.

Matavai. (Formerly Holiday Inn.) *Moderate.* B.P. 32, Papeete, Tahiti; 42.61.29 or 42.67.67, Telex 222 FP. Located 1.2 miles from center of Papeete at Tipaerui, 3 blocks inland from lagoon. 146 rooms, some with kitchenettes, air conditioning, elevators, pool, squash courts, meeting room, game room and boutique, restaurants, bars, night club with special Friday night Polynesian dinner and dance show, and on Saturday nights one of Tahiti's most popular Tahitian bands plays music for dancing.

Pacific. (Formerly Kon-Tiki.) *Moderate.* P.O. Box 111, Papeete, Tahiti; 43.72.82. Medium-sized highrise across street from pier for Moorea boats, located on Blvd. Pomare in downtown Papeete. 44 air-conditioned rooms with private balconies facing harbor or mountains, with La Bellevue Restaurant on top floor and Laserium disco at street level.

Princesse Heiata. *Moderate.* P.O. Box 5003, Pirae, Tahiti; 42.81.05. Located off Ave. Prince Hinoi, 2.5 miles east of Papeete in district of Pirae. Two blocks from large black-sand beach with good swimming area, swimming pool and pool bar in gardens, restaurant, and bars inside that are turned into all night after-hours disco on weekend nights. This hotel, with 25 rooms and 11 bungalows, is very popular with French Foreign legionnaires and other military personnel.

Puunui. *Moderate.* P.O. Box 7016, Taravao, Tahiti; 57.19.20, Telex 410FP. This 54-room hotel, located on the peninsula of Tahiti-iti (little Tahiti) in the district of Vairao, is built on a mountain 1,353 feet high, overlooking Tahiti's southwest coast. Operated by Best Western Hotels, it is run as a family-style hotel with junior suites, which include kitchenettes. A swimming pool, restaurant, bar, boutique, and meeting room are included in the mountain portion of the hotel, with a beach bar, restaurant, marina, and sports area bordered by a white-sand beach and lovely lagoon on the sea level. Water activities includes motor boat trips to Tahiti-iti's beautifully unspoiled rugged coast where there are no roads and nature reigns supreme. Picnics on the "motu" can be combined with snorkeling and fishing expeditions.

Royal Papeete. *Moderate.* P.O. Box 919, Papeete, Tahiti; 42.01.29. On Blvd. Pomare in downtown Papeete, across from Moorea boat dock. An old hotel with a new wing and soundproof walls, has 85 rooms and is popular with business people and those who want to be in the midst of the city without the noise. Owned and operated by local Chinese family. Totally air conditioned, with popular restaurant, bar, disco and night club "La Cave," where Tahitian dance band performs on weekends. Favorite night spot for most of Tahiti's young social set.

Tahiti. *Moderate.* P.O. Box 416, Papeete, Tahiti; 42.95.50 or 42.61.55. On the lagoonside, at Auae, 1.2 miles from Papeete. This was once the most popular hotel in Tahiti, before the 3 deluxe hotels were built. Renovations have upgraded the quality and rates during the past few years. Very Polynesian style, with immense thatch roof covering reception, boutique, restaurant, bar, and huge dance floor, where balls are held every weekend. Overwater restaurant, swimming pool, swimming dock (no beach), lovely gardens, and lacy woodwork-trimmed buildings in South Seas colonial style. The 92 rooms and 18 bungalows are spacious with verandahs or terraces, air conditioners, and refrigerators. Live Paumotu music several nights a week.

Te Puna Bel Air. *Moderate.* P.O. Box 354, Papeete, Tahiti; 42.82.24 or 42.09.00. On west coast of Tahiti, between Hotels Tahiti Beachcomber and Sofitel Maeva Beach, sharing same white-sand beach and reef-protected lagoon. 48 rooms are in motel-style buildings with 28 Tahitian style thatched-roof bungalows, many air conditioned or kitchen equipped. Natural spring-fed swimming pool, restaurant, bar, tennis court, beach snack bar, and swimming pool.

Le Petit Mousse. *Inexpensive.* P.O. Box 12085, Papara, Tahiti; 57.42.07. A very popular restaurant with 12 bungalows alongside the lagoon in the district of Papara on Tahiti's west coast, almost 20 miles from downtown Papeete. Food is French, Italian, and "Pied Noir", or North African. Nautical activities include outrigger canoes, sailboards, pedal boats. Tennis courts and golf course nearby. At 5,000 CFP a night for two persons, bungalows are said to be the cheapest in French Polynesia; the smiles are free of charge.

Mahina Tea. *Inexpensive.* P.O. Box 17, Papeete, Tahiti; 42.00.97. A 10-minute walk from center of Papeete, behind Gendarmerie on Rue St. Amelie. A simple and clean pension with 16 rooms and 6 studios, private baths or shared, with hot water, TV downstairs, and reduced rates for longer visits.

FRENCH POLYNESIA

Shogun. *Inexpensive.* 10 Rue du Commandant Destremeau, Papeete, Tahiti; 43.13.93, night phone 48.08.75. Located above the Boutique Keiko one block from the waterfront in Papeete, between Ave. Bruat and Rue de la Canonniere Zelée. 7 rooms and 2 suites can be rented by day, week, or month. Complete with air conditioning and bathrooms, these conveniently located rooms are only a couple of blocks from the principal shopping district of Papeete.

Chez Guinette Fineau-Tautau. *Inexpensive.* Located at Angle Rue de General Castelneau and Rue de Pont Neuf, no. 4 (second house on the right on Pont Neuf), Papeete, Tahiti; 43.74.99. No reservations required for this in-transit way-station type lodging. There are 11 cot-sized beds in 2 rooms, with people often sleeping on the front and back terraces, swelling the numbers of lodgers sometimes to 2 dozen backpackers and world travelers from all nations. Guests share bathroom and cooking facilities and usually eat together at the big table on the front terrace.

Chez Nicole Guest House. *Inexpensive.* P.O. Box 4810, Papeete, Tahiti; 42.48.00. This family-style pension is located on Rue St. Amelie, just behind the Gendarmerie at the end of Ave. Bruat, a 10-minute walk from the center of Papeete. The 3 single or double rooms share a common bathroom and open onto a clean and attractive terrace.

Chez Siki. *Inexpensive.* Write to Tehia Teahui, PK. 19,20 (cote mer-chemin Avia), Paea, Tahiti; 53.35.32. A good place for those who want to experience a visit in a Tahitian home. Siki is Tahitian, and speaks fluent English and French, and his wife speaks French and German. Two rooms with a double bed each and bathroom in common, hot water and electricity, located in family house on beautiful lagoon with white sand beach in district of Paea, 12 miles west of Papeete. All meals included if desired and big "tamaara'a" Tahitian feast on Sundays provided there are enough people. Siki is a great musician, dancer, entertainer, fisherman, and cook.

Chez Tea Hirshon. *Inexpensive.* PK. 17,5, Punaauia; 58.23.30. Beach house and garden house for rent on Tahiti's "gold coast," located on one of the island's prettiest private properties. White-sand beach, protected clear lagoon, and sunset view of Moorea just 10 miles west of Papeete.

AUSTRAL ISLANDS

Rurutu

Hotel Rurutu Village. *Moderate.* P.O. Box 16, Rurutu, Austral Islands, French Polynesia; telephone 42.93.85 (Tahiti) or 392 Rurutu, Telex 311 FP. 16 bungalows outside village of Moerai, with carpets, sunken bathtubs, luxurious bedding and draperies, freshwater swimming pool, tennis court, bar and excellent restaurant, small library, shallow lagoon, and white-sand beach in front of hotel, island excursions, horse rentals.

Chez Atai Aapae. *Inexpensive.* Village of Moerai, Rurutu, Austral Islands, French Polynesia; telephone Rurutu 455. 4 double rooms with a kitchen and bathroom.

Chez Catherine. *Inexpensive.* C/o Mme. Catherine Ariiotima, Moerai Village, Rurutu, Austral Islands, French Polynesia; telephone 377 Rurutu. This pension, with 10 double rooms and private baths, is located in the center of the village, with all meals served in restaurant on premises. Catherine also operates a pension in Vitaria village, next to the mountain, across from beach and lagoon. This is a 2-bedroom house with a kitchen and bathroom, with sleeping accommodations for 10 maximum. With or without meals.

Chez Maurice. *Inexpensive.* C/o Maurice Lenoir, Avera, Rurutu, Austral Islands, French Polynesia; telephone 426 Rurutu or 43.60.19 (Tahiti). In Avera village, behind the Protestant temple, a few steps from a white-sand beach and lagoon. One huge house that can sleep a group of 13 people maximum, with equipped kitchen, electricity, a communal bathroom, and furnished linens. No meals included.

Chez Patrice. *Inexpensive.* C/o Patrice Teinauri, Moerai Village, Rurutu, Austral Islands; telephone Rurutu 443, or 58.23.30 (Tahiti). A 2-bedroom house with bathroom and equipped kitchen, with or without meals, rented to couples or families only. Located in Moerai Village with lagoon swimming from white-sand beach.

Tubuai

Ermitage Sainte Helene. *Inexpensive.* C/o Mme. Tehinarii Ilari, Village de Mahu, P.O. Box 79, Tubuai, French Polynesia; no Telephone. 3 houses for 4 persons maximum each, with bathrooms, hot water and equipped kitchens, in Mahu Village. White-sand beaches and lagoon swimming, boats, bicycles, picnics, excursions arranged.

Chez Caroline. *Inexpensive.* C/o Caroline Chung Thien, P.O. Box 94, Mataura Village, Tubuai, French Polynesia; telephone 346 Tubuai. 2 houses with 3 double rooms each, plus bathrooms, hot water, and equipped kitchens. In principal village of Tubuai, close to all activity and white-sand beaches and lagoon. Bicycles and excursions by boat or car.

Chez Taro Tanepau. *Inexpensive.* C/o Tahimata Tanepau, Mataura Village, Tubuai, French Polynesia; telephone 382 Tubuai or 43.87.32 (Tahiti). 2 houses with 2 double rooms each, equipped with bathrooms and communal kitchen. Available by day, week, or month, and located in Tubuai's principal village, with excursions and lagoon swimming principal activities.

BORA BORA

Bora Bora. *Expensive.* Nunue, Bora Bora; 67.70.28 or 67.71.28. For reservations, P.O. Box 1015, Papeete, Tahiti; 48.12.06, Telex 225FP. This upmarket hotel is perhaps the most expensive in all the South Pacific, and certainly the most beautiful in French Polynesia. 15 acres of tropical gardens are bordered by a very long, sugar-white beach with some of the best snorkeling anywhere among colorful fish and coral formations. 80 large, attractively decorated thatched-roofed Polynesian-style bungalows are nestled among tropical flowers and palm trees or built over the water on stilts. Overhead fans, hair dryers, coffee makers, and refrigerators in rooms. 2 bars, 2 restaurants (one serving gourmet cuisine), beach snack bar for light lunches, boutique, conference and lounge room, village-type store for supplies. Hotel supplies lots of complimentary equipment for activities: bicycles, outrigger canoes, snorkel equipment, games, tennis, basketball, volleyball, rides on outrigger sailing canoe, video movies, slide shows, billiards, table tennis, garden tours, *pareu* demonstrations, lessons in dancing the *tamuré*, or making *poisson cru*. Also available are glass-bottom boat tours, sunset catamaran cruises, reef trips, island picnics, speedboat excursions, scuba diving and sailing or fishing expeditions.

Ibis Bora Bora. *Expensive.* P.O. Box 252, Vaitape, Bora Bora; 67.71.16, Telex 302FP. Located next to Hotel Sofitel Marara on beautiful white-sand beach in Amanahune community, this hotel, formerly Climat de France, has 9 blocks of 4 rooms each on the beach side and across the road in several acres of gardens. Restaurant, bar, boutique, nightly giant screen video programs, boat dock and all water activities in marvelous lagoon.

Oasis du Lagon. *Expensive.* C/o Archipel, P.O. Box 2007, Papeete, Tahiti; 43.13.43 or 43.32.07. A developing condominium timeshare project located on Motu Roa, a long atoll-shaped islet between the Pacific Ocean and the lagoon facing Bora Bora's Anau village. Miles of white-sand beaches, swaying palms, and exquisite swimming waters surround this recently opened resort. When completed, the project will contain 14 luxurious hurricane-proof villas, each villa comprised of 3 independent Polynesian-style facilities, housing 2–3 persons in one deluxe suite and 4–5 persons in two duplex bungalows, with one swimming pool per villa group. Color TV, video equipment, hi-fi, radiotelephones, desalination unit and solar equipment are part of the project, with a large club house and mosaic tiled swimming pool. Amenities and services include boating, tennis, bicycles, automobile rentals, floating solarium, central library, all water sports activities, taxi-boat, 24-hour security, maids, delivery, laundry, Polynesian and international catering, baby sitting, answering service, and telex. Bungalows can be rented by day, week or month.

Hotel Sofitel Marara. *Expensive.* P.O. Box 6, Vaitape, Bora Bora; 67.70.46, Telex 326FP. This 64-bungalow hotel was built in 1978 to house crew for film *Hurricane.* Thatched-roof bungalows, with overhead fans and refrigerators, are located in gardens, along white-sand beach and on stilts over water near village of Anau. Tennis courts, swimming pool, nightly shows and disco, European food and ambiance. Emphasis is on water activities—there's a special speedboat

FRENCH POLYNESIA

excursion around island, with visits to reef and very popular shark-feeding show, where you can actually go into water with sharks.

Bora Bora Bungalows. *Moderate.* P.O. Box 98, Vaitape, Bora Bora; 67.71.33. Luxury condos, built as Polynesian-style bungalows on stilts over lagoon and on hillside, facing airport and offering fantastic sunset views. Two bedrooms with sleeping capacity for 4–5 persons, completely equipped for cooking, with laundry facilities, maid service, and taxi available on premises.

Bora Bora Yacht Club. *Moderate.* P.O. Box 17, Vaitape, Bora Bora; 67.71.50 or 67.70.69. Less than 2 miles from Vaitape village, at Pointe Fare Piti is the Fare Iati, as the yacht club is known in Tahitian. Three overwater bungalows provide a double bed in each, with bathroom. attractive furnishing and terraces overlooking the deep lagoon, where yachts anchor 6 floating bungalows are available for those who want complete privacy; these are built in the thatched-roof Polynesian style, and are equipped with a kitchen, shower and toilet, bar, loggia, and sleeping accommodations for 4, plus a small boat to travel back and forth to shore.

Club Méditerranée. *Moderate.* P.O. Box 575, Papeete, Tahiti; 42.96.99, Telex 256FP. On lagoon less than a mile from Vaitape village, 45 minutes by boat from Bora Bora airport. The 41 twin units are built as Polynesian style thatched-roof bungalows on stilts over the lagoon. Large restaurant, bar, nightclub, and boutique. Disco dancing nightly, sailing, picnics, glass-bottom boat, excursions on lagoon and to mountains, private swimming dock. No beach, but there are several shuttle boat trips made daily to the beautiful Motu Tapu, where there are blinding white-sand beaches and good swimming.

Fare Toopua. *Moderate.* C/o Madame Annie Muraz, P.O. Box 87, Vaitape, Bora Bora; 48.26.12 (Tahiti). Situated on Motu Toopua, a small island 5 minutes by speedboat from Vaitape village. 2 bungalows with mezzanine and a bedroom, bathroom, equipped kitchen in each bungalow. White-sand beach and lovely lagoon at your doorstep, with aluminum dinghy available upon deposit. Minimum stay 3 days, with monthly rentals available.

Hotel Matira. *Moderate.* P.O. Box 31, Vaitape, Bora Bora; 67.70.51. Some of the 28 bungalows are kitchen equipped and are located on Matira Plage, Bora Bora's most beautiful white-sand beach. Others are built across the street from the beach in the gardens or on the hillside, 5 miles from Vaitape village and 45 minutes by boat from airport. Restaurant Matira, Bora Bora's only Chinese restaurant, serves 3 daily meals to the hotel guests, if desired, and the offices for the hotel are also located here.

Hotel Oa Oa. *Moderate.* P.O. Box 10, Vaitape, Bora Bora; 67.70.84. Next door to Club Med, less than a mile from Vaitape and 45 minutes by boat from Bora Bora airport. 8 bungalows situated on lagoon with restaurant, bar, meeting room. Popular with visiting yachts. Glass-bottom boat, windsurfing, and many other water sports.

Revatua Club. *Moderate.* P.O. Box 159, Vaitape, Bora Bora; 67.71.67, Telex 417FP. Located between Anau and Faanui districts, about 35 minutes by car from Vaitape and 8 minutes by speedboat. A new hotel, opened Dec. 1985, with 16 double or triple rooms on the mountain side, and an overwater restaurant, bar, and boutique, all built in the 1930s colonial style. The rooms all face the lagoon and are complete with fans, bathrooms, and a small terrace. *Chez Christian* restaurant, the hotel's dining room, offers the best French cuisine in Bora Bora—with seafood specialties—at rather expensive prices. Activities include canoe trips on the lagoon, picnics on a private *motu,* windsurfing, snorkeling, small boating, waterskiing, fishing from the hotel's pontoon or on the reef; daily shuttle service to Vaitape village.

Hotel Royal Bora Bora. *Moderate.* P.O. Box 202, Vaitape, Bora Bora; 67.71.54. Located in the village of Vaitape, this old hotel next to the lagoon (no beach) has 8 bungalows in the Polynesian style, plus 3 tiny rooms with 2 single beds each. The bungalows have bathrooms but the rooms have toilet and shower facilities in common. Accommodations are sold MAP only. Rental bicycles and scooters available, with tours of the island and picnics on a *motu* arranged upon request.

Bungalows Are. *Inexpensive.* C/o Madame Are Siou Moun, Matira, Nunue, Bora Bora; 67.70.73. 5 bungalows with 2 double rooms each, living room, equipped kitchen and bathroom with hot water and electricity, located across road from a beautiful white-sand beach between Hotels Bora Bora and Matira. Excursions and picnics can be arranged as well as transport to Vaitape village. 3 of the bungalows are available only July–August.

Chez Aime. *Inexpensive.* C/o M. Aime Mare, Vaitape, Bora Bora, (no telephone). No reservations taken. In Vaitape village about 55 yards from the boat dock, on the mountain side, Aime's house of 6 sleeping rooms, 1 bathroom (no hot water), and a kitchen can sleep 18. Good for budget travelers, who often join Tahitian family in daily activities, such as fishing, expeditions into valley, shelling, etc. Swimming across street in lagoon.

Chez Fredo. *Inexpensive.* C/o Alfredo Doom, Vaitape, Bora Bora; 67.70.31. In Vaitape village, a 5-minute walk from boat dock, on mountain side. 4 housekeeping bungalows on lagoon, plus a house with 3 rooms where you can rent a single bed with kitchen privileges. Low rate for bed and breakfast. Popular with international budget travelers and French military from Tahiti.

Chez Nono. *Inexpensive.* C/o Noel Leverd, P.O. Box 12, Vaitape, Bora Bora; 67.71.38. 1 double bungalow and 2 small bungalows, including equipped kitchens and bathrooms at a private home at Pointe Matira Beach. Activities arranged upon request, including trips on the lagoon by motor boat, sailboards and transfers to Vaitape village.

Chez Robert Tinorua. *Inexpensive.* Nunue, Bora Bora; 67.72.92. The last house at Pointe Matira, with Bora Bora's most beautiful white-sand beach and lagoon at the doorstep. A modern house with two bedrooms, kitchen, bathroom, living/sleeping room, and big terrace overlooking beach and lagoon. Can sleep 9 maximum, but water shortage poses problems in dry season of July–October. Outrigger canoe visits around lagoon, to reef, picnics on *motu* or around the island.

HUAHINE

Bali Hai Huahine. *Expensive.* P.O. Box 2, Fare, Huahine; 68.82.77. For reservations: P.O. Box 26, PaoPao, Moorea; 56.13.59, Telex 331FP. Near village of Fare (0.6 mile) on long white-sand beach and adjacent turquoise lagoon. 1.8 miles from airport. First-class Tahitian-style bungalows on stilts, very nicely constructed and decorated with indoor gardens in all bathrooms, which are sunken to ground level. Hotel is in midst of several acres of gardens and lakes, crisscrossed with bridges over fish-filled lakes and pools decorated with lily pads and water hyacinths. Excavations on premises have revealed important archeological finds from prehistoric Polynesian society, with artifacts displayed in hotel's mini-museum. Restaurant, boutique, bar, excellent swimming in lagoon, with *Liki Tiki* excursions for snorkelling and shelling, plus sunset cruises. Large swimming pool, tennis courts, games room, Tahitian music nightly. Long pants required for men after 6 P.M.

Huahine Beach Hotel. *Expensive.* P.O. Box 39, Fare, Huahine; 68.81.46, Telex 418FP. American-owned hotel in Parea village on Huahine-iti, approximately one hour's drive from airport and Fare. Opened June 1985 with 8 bungalows along white-sand beach and in gardens by lagoon, with 8 more bungalows and a swimming pool under construction across road at publication 1986. Thatched-roof Polynesian style bungalows, with hardwood floors, carpeted bedrooms, sunken bathrooms, large sitting area, and large terrace. Accommodations include king, queen, twin, and one handicapped room. Separate bar with stools, wide screen TV with video movies, stereo system and video game. Diningroom overlooks lagoon and beach, with salt water pond containing lagoon fish just outside. Activities include night fishing from hotel pier, deep sea fishing, outrigger canoes, inner tubes, Hobie cat, windsurfing, snorkelling, excursions to nearby motu, bicycling, 6-mile jogging path into valley, special barbeques, and Tahitian *Himaa* cooking.

Relais Mahana. *Moderate.* P.O. Box 30, Fare, Huahine; 68.81.54, Telex 300FP. This 12-bungalow hotel is situated on Huahine's most beautiful white-sand beach, which stretches for miles alongside a magnificent coral-flowered lagoon. This is at Avea Bay, one mile from Parea village on Huahine-iti, 1-hour by car from the Huahine airport or Fare village. Efficiently operated by a French family from New Caledonia, the food, ambiance, and language are definitely French. The clean, modern rooms can sleep 3 persons, with one bungalow designed for the handicapped. Restaurant, bar, boutique, tennis court, long pier, excellent snorkelling, windsurfing, pedal boats, outrigger canoes, Hobie cat, water-skiing, ping-pong, and games. Bicycles, rental scooters, and cars available on premises. Disco dancing in lounge each evening.

Hotel Bellevue. *Inexpensive.* P.O. Box 21, Maroe, Huahine; 68.82.76 or 68.81.70. In district of Maroe, 3.6 miles from Fare and 6 miles from Huahine

FRENCH POLYNESIA

airport, on hillside overlooking Maroe Bay. 1-story building with 8 rooms and 15 bungalows built around a swimming pool. Solar electricity, restaurant featuring local seafood caught by Chinese-Tahitian owner, who will take guests along on his fishing expeditions, or take them by boat to a *motu* where there are white sand beaches and great swimming and snorkelling. Hotel also has small bar, ping-pong, *petanque,* and tours of the island.

Pension Enite. *Inexpensive.* C/o Martial Lafourcade, Fare, Huahine; 68.82.37. This pension is very popular because of its great cuisine, served next to lagoon and white-sand beach at Fare, right at the entrance to the main village. There are 6 rooms in a big building with beds for 17 people, with bath facilities in common. Besides the restaurant and bar there are excursions around the island and windsurfing. 2-day stay required and meals are AP.

Hotel Huahine. *Inexpensive.* C/o Pierre Colombani, Fare, Huahine; 68.82.69. 2-story building with 10 rooms in the center of Fare, overlooking harbor. Some rooms contain private bathrooms with cold water, which is scarce during dry months of July–October. Beds are very uncomfortable, sagging in middle, and maid service is nonexistent while rooms are occupied. Hotel is very popular with international surfers and budget travelers who find a certain charm about the place.

Chez Lovina. *Inexpensive.* C/o Lovina Bohl, Fare, Huahine; 68.81.90. In the middle of "downtown" Fare, right on the harbor front, Lovina has 7 clean and attractively decorated rooms for rent with electricity, private bathrooms, and double beds. She also has 3 housekeeping bungalows for rent, by the ocean and in a garden. Lovina speaks English, serves meals and gives tours if desired. Great lagoon swimming and white-sand beach across street to right of hotel.

Chez Rine. *Inexpensive.* C/o Ah Foussan, Fare, Huahine; 68.82.79. 5 rooms upstairs over the post office in Fare, one block from the waterfront. Electricity, bathrooms. Swimming and white-sand beach 5-minute walk from here.

Tarapapa Motel. *Inexpensive.* C/o Adolphe Bohl, Maeva, Huahine; 68.81.23 (Huahine) or 48.12.52 (Tahiti). 10 housekeeping rooms in Maeva district, at Lake Fauna Nui, 7 km. (4.2 miles) from Fare village. 1 building of 4 rooms is located on lake side and another building of 6 rooms is across street, next to a food store. All rooms are equipped with electricity, kitchens, bathrooms, fans, TV, double beds, and terraces. Excursions can be arranged with owners. Beautiful white-sand beach and lagoon swimming found on ocean side of long *motu* opposite the lake.

Chez Temeharo. *Inexpensive.* C/o Madame Amelie Temeharo, Parea, Huahine; 68.81.87. In village of Parea, 28 km. (17 miles) from airport and Fare. 5 rooms in big two-story house in center of village. All toilet and shower facilities in common and meals are served family style in large dining room. Long and beautiful white-sand beach 5-minute walk from pension and trips to nearby *motu,* picnics, and other excursions can be arranged.

MANIHI

Kaina Village. *Expensive.* P.O. Box 2560, Papeete, Tahiti; 42.75.53 (Tahiti), Telex 339FP. Located on the same *motu* where the airport strip is located, this hotel is across the lagoon from the main village. 14 overwater self-contained *fares* have balconies from which you can watch the colorful fish feeding on coral formations in the aquamarine lagoon. A superb restaurant, separate bar and billiards room, boutique, lagoon excursions, line fishing; visits to village, pearl farm, fish park; and picnics on lovely *motu*. All the white-sand beaches and excellent lagoon swimming anyone could wish for.

Chez Rei Estall. *Inexpensive.* Turipaoa, Manihi, Tuamotu Archipelago, French Polynesia; no telephone. 2 rooms in private house in Turipaoa village. Electricity, toilets and shower in common with family, as well as meals.

Chez Marguerite Fareea. *Inexpensive.* Turipaoa, Manihi, Tuamotu Archipelago, French Polynesia; no telephone. 15 minutes by boat from airport to village, with complimentary transfers. 2 double rooms, electricity, bath facilities, and meals shared with Paumotu family.

MARQUESAS ISLANDS

Fau Hiva

Chez Tehau Gilmore. *Inexpensive.* Omoa Village, Fatu Hiva, Marquesas Islands, French Polynesia; no telephone. House with 2 bedrooms he rents very low priced, no meals included. In village with river running behind that is often used for bathing purposes as well as swimming and catching fresh river shrimps. Prepare food yourself or arrange with nearby families. Black volcanic-sand beach often has very rough undertow and heavy breakers.

Chez Francois Peter, Chez Kehu Kamia, and **Chez Joseph Tetuanui.** C/o Omoa Village, Fatu Hiva, Marquesas Islands, French Polynesia. 3 private homes in Omoa Village who rent 2 bedrooms each to visitors. Meals included if desired. Join in family activities, rent horses or go on a wild pig hunt.

Chez Veronique Kamia and **Chez Yvonne Tevenino.** C/o Hanavave Bay, Marquesas Islands, French Polynesia. 2 houses in Hanavave Bay with rooms to rent in their homes, meals included. Swim from black-sand beach at beautiful Bay of Virgins beneath shadow of sculptured mountain peaks.

Hiva Oa

Atuona Mairie Bungalows. *Inexpensive.* C/o Guy Rauzy, Atuona Village, Hiva Oa, Marquesas Islands, French Polynesian; telephone AT332. 5 bungalows operated by the town hall of Atuona in center of village, equipped with kitchens, refrigerators, bathrooms, and electricity.

Chez Bernard Heitaa. *Inexpensive.* C/o Puamau Village, Hiva Oa, Marquesas Islands, French Polynesia; no telephone. Private house with 2 bedrooms, kitchen, bathroom in common, and electricity. Located in the valley of Puamau, with the possibility of visiting stone *tiki's* by land rover. Swimming in surf bordered by black volcanic-sand beach just below village homes. Full board pension available.

Nuku Hiva

Keikahanui Inn. *Moderate.* C/o Frank and Rose Corser, P.O. Box 121, Taiohae, Marquesas Islands, French Polynesia; telephone TA383. Almost a mile from the boat pier, situated on a bluff overlooking Taiohae Bay and a long black volcanic-sand beach. 3 Polynesian-style bungalows with private bathrooms, hot water, and refrigerators; one 3-bedroom house with equipped kitchen, bathroom, and hot water; and 2 bedrooms for 2–3 people each, with bathrooms. No credit cards accepted. Horses for rent and 4-wheel-drive vehicle for excursions

Hotel Moana Nui. *Inexpensive.* P.O. Box 9, Taiohae, Nuku Hiva, Marquesas Islands; telephone TA 330. Located 1 km. from dock in main village, facing ocean, across road from long black-sand beach with pretty bay for swimming. 7 simple rooms, some with bathrooms, bar and restaurant downstairs. Reservations required for meals, which are usually steak and French fries.

Chez Fetu. *Inexpensive.* C/o Fetu Peterano, Taiohae Village, Nuku Hiva, Marquesas Islands, French Polynesia; telephone TA 366. 300 meters from boat dock in the Vallee Française, two houses, with accommodations for 3 people each, including equipped kitchens and private bathrooms. Swimming from black-sand beach at Taiohae Bay, or nearby white-sand beach close to village.

Chez Katupa Matu. *Inexpensive.* Hatiheu Village, Nuku Hiva, Marquesas Islands, French Polynesia; no telephone. This pretty little village is one hour by boat from Taiohae Bay or a good day's ride across the rutted mountain roads. 4 bungalows with bathrooms and petrol lamps in village facing ocean, black-sand beach noted for *nonos* (stinging sand flies). Meals are served in pension's well-known restaurant and include fresh river shrimp and lobsters. Rental horses to visit *tiki's* or excursions into valley.

Tahuata

Chez Naani Barsinas. *Inexpensive.* Vaitahu Village, Tahuata, Marquesas Islands, French Polynesia; no telephone. 3-bedroom house in village with salt-and-pepper sand beach and bay swimming in front of village. Meals served, with

FRENCH POLYNESIA

emphasis on fresh fruits and fish, lobster, and river shrimp. Boat excursions arranged.

Ua Huka

Chez Vii Fournier. *Inexpensive.* Hane Village, Ua Huka, Marquesas Islands, French Polynesia; no telephone. A house with 2 double rooms, toilet, kitchen with refrigerator, plus a "passage hut" with 2 beds and a toilet for those in transit. Monthly rentals available. Meals taken with family. Excursions to *tiki's* in valley. Black-sand beach at foot of village offers swimming in open surf.

Chez Miriama Fournier. *Inexpensive.* Vaipaee Village, Ua Huka, Marquesas Islands, French Polynesia. 3-bedroom house with bathroom, electricity, and kitchen. Meals can be served by family and excursions arranged. Swimming from black-sand beach and often strong current of open bay.

Chez Joseph Lichtle. *Inexpensive.* Vaipaee Village, Ua Huka, Marquesas Islands, French Polynesia; no telephone. 3-bedroom house, kitchen, electricity, toilet, in village of Vaipaee. Meals and monthly rentals if desired. Horses available for hire.

Chez Joseph Lichtle. *Inexpensive.* At 5 km. from Vaipaee, in Haavei, Mr. Lichtle has a lovely setting with a long white-sand beach, gentle swells, and 2 bungalows along beach and a house on the hill overlooking beautiful bay and bird island. Meals are provided from his plentiful garden, fruit trees, and livestock supply, plus an abundant ocean. No other houses around.

Chez Laura Raioha. *Inexpensive.* Vaipaee Village, Ua Huka, Marquesas Islands, French Polynesia; no telephone. A big 4-bedroom house with double accommodations in each room, plus kitchen, electricity, and communal bathroom. Meals served if desired, and horseback riding provided. In village, with swimming from black sand beach in open swells.

Chez Yvonne et Jules Hituputoka. *Inexpensive.* Hakahau, Ua Pou, Marquesas Islands, French Polynesia; telephone HA 332. 2 houses for rent by day, week, or month, with 2 or 3 rooms, electricity, bathrooms and equipped kitchens. Meals served if desired. Houses in Hakahau Village, with black-sand beach and often rough swells a few blocks from village. Possibility of rental horses and land rover with driver for excursions into valleys and to visit lovely white sand beaches.

Chez Rosalie. *Inexpensive.* C/o Mrs. Rosalie, Village of Hakahau, Ua Pou, Marquesas Islands, French Polynesia; no telephone. Lively pension in center of Hakahau village with accommodations for 4 persons in big family house. Meals taken with family and excursions arranged.

Chez Francois Teikitutoua. *Inexpensive.* Village of Hakahau, Ua Pou, Marquesas Islands, French Polynesia; telephone HA 342. House with 4 rooms, 2 bathrooms, kitchen, electricity, and meals in village, a few blocks from black-sand beach. Excursions arranged.

Chez Louis Teikitutoua. *Inexpensive.* Hakahau Village, Ua Pou, Marquesas Islands, French Polynesia; telephone HA 312. 2 houses in village with 1 bedroom each, plus kitchen, refrigerator and bathrooms. Meals taken with family.

MAUPITI

Hotel Auira. *Inexpensive.* C/o Mme. Edna Terai, Maupiti, French Polynesia; No telephone. 8 bungalows built in Polynesian style with double bed. 3 of these are located on very white sand beach, with private bathrooms and the 5 garden bungalows share facilities. Hotel has restaurant and is located on Motu Hu'apiti, across the lagoon from main island.

Chez Papa Roro. *Inexpensive.* C/o Teroro Raioho, Maupiti, French Polynesia; no telephone. Located in the main village of Vai'ea, 500 meters from schoolhouse, with 1 house with 4 rooms and private baths, 1 house with 6 rooms and communal baths and 1 big house with 3 rooms and a common bathroom. Restaurant and bar on premises and swimming in lagoon across street.

Pension Tavaearii. *Inexpensive.* C/o Mme. Vilna Tavaearii, Motu Tiapaa, Maupiti, French Polynesia; no telephone. Accommodations for 16 people in 2 bungalows with 4 double rooms each, plus 3 showers and 2 toilets in common, a communal dining room, solar lighting and petrol lamps. Located on Motu Tiapaa, an islet across the lagoon from main island, with beautiful white sand beaches and excellent swimming in lagoon. Outrigger canoes and windsurfing.

Chez Teha Teupoohuitua. *Inexpensive.* Maupiti, French Polynesia; no telephone. A big house by the lagoon in the village of Farauru, with a capacity for 14 people in 5 rooms and toilet and shower facilities in common. Full pension meals.

Chez Anua Tinorua. *Inexpensive.* Maupiti, French Polynesia; no telephone. 2 double rooms in family home close to the schoolhouse in principal village of Vai'ea. Complete pension with Tahitian family.

MOOREA

Bali Hai Moorea. *Expensive.* B.P. Box 26, Moorea, French Polynesia; 56.13.59, Telex 331FP. At entrance to Cook's Bay on small white-sand beach, 6 miles from Moorea's airport. 63 Tahitian-style bungalows in 4 acres of gardens, along beach, and over the fish-filled lagoon. Busy and popular bar, restaurant, boutique, outrigger canoes, bicycles, volley ball, tennis, diving, excursions on raft *Liki Tiki,* frequent picnics, friendly management and personnel. Sunday noon Tahitian feast with folk-dance show. Swimming pool with barstools in the pool. Tahitian music nightly.

Captain Cook Hotel. *Expensive.* P.O. Box 1006, Papetoai, Moorea; 42.48.33 or 56.10.60, Telex 211FP. 18 miles from Moorea airport in district of Haapiti on very long white-sand beach. 24 air-conditioned rooms are in 2-story motel-type buildings, with 19 bungalows alongside the beach. Restaurant, large bar, boutique, picnics to the *motu,* glass-bottom boat excursions, all water sports and rainy day games. American owned hotel.

Climat de France. *Expensive.* P.O. Box 1052, Papetoai, Moorea; 43.08.81 or 56.15.48, Telex 339FP. Next door to Hotel Residence Tipaniers, along white-sand beach in Haapiti district. 40 rooms in motel-style buildings, with air conditioning or fans, plus 37 bungalows with kitchenettes. Rooms are homey and cheerful, with fridges and some bathtubs. Restaurant, bar, swimming pool, tennis, water-skiing, windsurfing, and all other water sports. Nightly movies on large video screen, often in French.

Sofitel Kia Ora Moorea. *Expensive.* P.O. Box 6008, Faaa Airport, Tahiti; 56.11.73 or 56.12.90, Telex 390FP. 82 thatched-roofed, attractive and spacious bungalows are spread throughout almost 25 acres of coconut palm trees, lush tropical gardens and a white-sand beach almost a mile long. Moorea's most deluxe resort hotel includes executive suites, 2 restaurants, gourmet cuisine, 2 bars, well-stocked boutique, all water sports in clear turquoise lagoon, glass-bottom boat, outrigger canoes, picnics, tennis, frequent Tahitian shows and *pareu*-tying demonstrations. Watch the sun rise behind Tahiti each morning from this beautiful site 5 minutes from Temae Airport in Moorea.

Club Bali Hai. *Moderate.* B.P. 26, Moorea, French Polynesia; 56.13.68 or 56.13.59, Telex 331FP. Located on a small white-sand beach near village of Pao Pao at famous Cook's Bay with fabulous panorama of mountains and bay. Formerly Hotel Aimeo, this 19-unit hotel is now managed by the Bali Hai group as a vacation interval ownership program. Swimming pool, tennis court, restaurant, two bars, outrigger canoes and *Liki Tiki* cruises.

Club Mediterranee. *Moderate.* B.P. 575, Papeete, Tahiti; 42.96.99, Telex 256FP. 45 mins. by bus from Moorea airport on large white-sand beach at Haapiti. The completely rebuilt village has 700 beds, a huge restaurant, bars, boutique, disco, theater, and sports complex, plus almost constant organized activities.

Hibiscus. *Moderate.* P.O. Box 1009, Papetoai, Moorea; 56.12.20 or 56.14.09. 29 *fare*-type thatched-roof bungalows scattered spaciously throughout palm-dotted gardens, with huge banyan tree shading part of the immense white sand beach beside a clear lagoon. Next door to Club Mediterranee in Haapiti district, this hotel is noted for its *l'Escargot Restaurant* and *Sunset Beach Bar.* Swimming pool and all water sports avaialble.

Ibis Moorea. *Moderate.* B.P. 30, Moorea; 56.10.50, Telex 361FP. 76 rooms built in "neo-colonial" style with restaurant, bar, color TV in rooms, swimming pool, Hobie cats, sailboards, sunset cruises, "gym-tonic" classes and game room, with picnics to the *motu.* Located in Cook's Bay next door to *Keke III* dock. Part of French hotel chain ACCOR.

Moorea Lagoon. *Moderate.* B.P. 11, Moorea; 56.14.68 or 56.11.55, Telex 327FP. Hotel reopened July 1986 under new ownership and management. All of the 45 thatched-roof bungalows, built along a pretty, white-sand beach and scattered amidst 12 acres of gardens, are being rebuilt, with new furnishings and

FRENCH POLYNESIA

bathrooms. Located between Cook's Bay and Opunohu Bay, 9.5 miles from village of Pao Pao, with restaurant, bar, boutique, bicycles, outrigger canoes and *Aqua 6* surface submarine for underwater viewing.

Moorea Village. *Moderate.* P.O. Box 1008, Papetoai, Moorea; 56.10.02. 19 miles from Moorea airport on large white-sand beach at Haapiti. This hotel is Tahitian owned and operated, with 50 thatched-roof bungalows, including 15 with kitchenettes. Swimming pool, tennis courts, restaurant, bar, boutique, picnics on the *motu* and all water sports. *Maa Tahiti* (Tahitian food) served each Sunday at noon, followed by Tahitian dance show. This hotel is popular with local families from Tahiti and French military personnel.

Hotel Residence Les Tipaniers. *Moderate.* P.O. Box 1002, Haapiti, Moorea; 56.12.67. In district of Haapiti next door to Climat de France and close to Club Mediterranee, on long white-sand beach with beautiful lagoon. 20 bungalows, 9 equipped with kitchenettes, plus excellent restaurant featuring Italian, French, and Polynesian specialties. Beach snack bar and water skiing center.

Residence Linareva. *Moderate.* P.O. Box 205, Temae, Moorea; 56.15.35. Telex 537FP. 4 housekeeping bungalows in Polynesian style on long white-sand beach in Haapiti district. Each *fare* is equipped with electricity, color TV, barbeque grill, bathroom, kitchenette, and linens. Accommodations for 3–8 people, with outrigger canoes, sailboards, bicycles, Hobie cats, sunfish boat, motor boat, and scuba diving facilities. Minimum of 2 nights required.

Coconut House. *Inexpensive.* P.O. Box 2329, Papeete, Tahiti or Maharepa, Moorea; 56.15.44. 12 bungalows in the district of Maharepa, a 5-minute walk from Hotel Bali Hai. On mountain-side of road, with white-sand beach and lagoon across street. Hotel has very popular restaurant, bar with piano, boutique, swimming pool, hot water, video, outrigger canoes, and snorkeling equipment.

Le Kaveka. *Inexpensive.* P.O. Box 13, PaoPao, Moorea; 56.18.30, Telex 361FP. Located next to *Keke III* boat dock in Cook's Bay, this 26-bungalow hotel has an overwater bar and restaurant, plus a marina with aquatic sports activities. Small white-sand beach. Very good salad bar with barbequed steaks.

Hotel Residence Tiahura. *Inexpensive.* P.O. Box 1068, Papetoai, Moorea; 56.15.45, Telex 537FP. Located 300 meters before Club Med, across street from long white-sand beach. 24 Polynesian-style bungalows, 18 with equipped kitchenettes including small refrigerators. Windows are not screened. Swimming pool, boutique, small restaurant-grill, and snorkeling equipment.

Chez Albert. *Inexpensive.* PaoPao, Moorea; 56.12.76. Situated in the village of PaoPao, across street from Club Bali Hai, on mountain side. Family operated motel-type rooms with communal or private bathrooms. Total of 19 rooms including 2 houses, some equipped for cooking. Two night minimum is required and no credit cards accepted.

Chez Billy Ruta. *Inexpensive.* Haapiti, Moorea; 56.12.54 or 56.16.98. These 11 bungalows, beside the lagoon and white-sand beach near Club Med, are complete with 2 single beds each, bathrooms, and linens. Three of the bungalows have kitchenettes. Billy is noted for his *tamaara'a's*, Tahitian feasts complete with his family dancers performing the traditional folk shows.

Fare Mato Tea. *Inexpensive.* P.O. Box 1111, Papetoai, Moorea, (no telephone listed). Located at PK. 28,7, Haapiti, past Hotel Moorea Village, on white-sand beach and lovely, quiet lagoon. 7 bungalows, built of concrete, contain equipped kitchens, bathrooms, hot water, and linens. Accommodations for 4–6 people and monthly rentals are possible.

Hotel Pauline. *Inexpensive.* Afareaitu, Moorea; 56.11.26. About 5 miles from Moorea airport, on mountain side, near the Mairie or city hall of Moorea's capital village, Pauline's is noted for its local-style cuisine. 7 rooms are located in an old South Seas gingerbread-style home complete with verandah. Bathrooms and showers are in common. Beds are rather lumpy and tend to dip into a V in the middle. Pauline's house is also a sort of Polynesian museum, with stone *tiki's* from Moorea's valleys.

RAIATEA

Bali Ha'i Raiatea. *Expensive.* P.O. Box 43, Uturoa, Raiatea; 66.31.49. For reservations, P.O. Box 26, Moorea, French Polynesia, Telephone 56.13.59, Telex 331FP. Built on the lagoon 0.6 miles from village of Uturoa, 2 miles from airport. 36 units, built Tahitian style as rooms in a 1-story building or bungalows over the water and beside the lagoon. No beach. A sitting pool, bar, restaurant, boutique, game room, bicycles, volley-ball, table tennis, outrigger canoe shuttle to nearby white-sand beach *motu*, boat excursions to Fa'aroa River and nearby island of Tahaa, frequent fire walking ceremonies and children's folkloric dance show.

Le Motu. *Inexpensive.* P.O. Box 549, Uturoa, Raiatea; 66.34.06. 7 basic but clean rooms, plus a very good French restaurant located on second floor of old building in middle of downtown Uturoa. Billiards parlor and disco night club downstairs. Frenchman Roger Bardou came from New Caledonia with his family and took over the abandoned Hotel Hinano building, cleaned it up and refurbished the rooms, which can sleep 3 maximum, and have private showers and lavabos, with common toilets next to the hallway. The restaurant faces the public wharf and public gardens, with flamboyant trees outside. Water-skiing, windsurfing, deep-sea fishing, guided tours, picnic trips to the *motu*, boating excursions available, plus rental scooters and cars. Cuisine is seafood, French and Tahitian specialties.

Raiatea Village. *Inexpensive.* P.O. Box 282, 12 bungalows with kitchenettes located at Fa'aroa River in district of Avera, 11 km. (6.6 miles) from downtown Uturoa. Owned and operated by Tahitian family, who provide transport to the airport, plus excursions around the island, lagoon trips, visits to archeological sites and serve meals if requested. Clean and attractive bungalows are built along a man-made white-sand beach beside the lagoon or just behind in the gardens. Snorkeling equipment, outrigger paddle canoe, bicycles and rental cars available on premises.

Pension Ariane Brotherson. *Inexpensive.* P.O. Box 236, Uturoa, Raiatea; 66.33.70. 2 rooms for 3 persons each located in a private home, complete with meals, at P.K. 8, Avera, 4.8 miles from Uturoa center. Share the bathing facilities and meals with Tahitian family, and swimming across the street in clear lagoon. Bicycles, island tours, and all nautical activities available.

Chez Sylvere Commings. *Inexpensive.* P.O. Box 190, Uturoa, Raiatea; 66.32.96 or 66.30.92. 3 double rooms with communal bath located in private home 3.6 miles from Uturoa center, in Quartier Tcheco at Uturaerae. Half or full pension available and windsurf boards and bicycles for rent.

Pension Marie-France. *Inexpensive.* C/o Marie-France Philip, P.O. Box 272, Uturoa, Raiatea; 66.37.10. 2 rooms in a Tahitian home on the lagoon 3 minutes from the center of Uturoa. Electricity, with bath facilities in common, all meals if desired, plus picnics and lagoon diving excursions with professional instructor.

Pension Yolande. *Inexpensive.* C/o Madame Yolande Roopinia, Avera, P.K. 10, Uturoa, Raiatea; 66.35.28. Popular accommodations with Tahitian family 6 miles from airport on pretty lagoon. One large Polynesian-style bungalow with 4 rooms and 3 single beds each, plus a bathroom and equipped kitchen and electricity. Also a smaller bungalow on the beach with beds for 3 people, plus a bathroom. MAP available, plus picnics on the nearby *motu*, excursions to the *marae* (Tahitian temple), windsurfing and sailing, outrigger paddle canoes, and bicycles available.

RANGIROA

Hotel Kia Ora Village. *Expensive.* P.O. Box 706, Papeete, Tahiti; 42.86.72 or 42.86.75, Telex 306FP, telephone on premises 384 Rangiroa. 30 first-class attractively designed and decorated bungalows, situated along a very white sand beach and dotted throughout several acres of gardens and coconut palm forests. 15 minutes by boat from Tiputa village and 15 minutes by bus from Avatoru village, 10 minutes by bus from airport. Very good restaurant, overwater bar, boutique, barbeque, all water activities, including glass-bottom boat, diving facilities and lessons, snorkeling through the passes with sharks and fishes swimming below in the very swift current. Tahitian music several nights a week. Friendly management who take good care of their clients.

La Bouteille a La Mer. *Moderate.* P.O. Box 17, Avatoru, Rangiroa; 43.99.30 or 334 Rangiroa, Telex 537FP. 11 beach bungalows in typical thatched-roof and bamboo-wall design, on very long white-sand beach beside turquoise lagoon, very close to airport. Family-style meals, French atmosphere, with emphasis on do-it-yourself entertainment, with water sports the main theme.

Hotel Rangiroa Village. *Moderate.* P.O. Box 8, Avatoru, Rangiroa; telephone 383 Rangiroa. 9 traditional bungalows on white-sand beach. 0.5 miles

FRENCH POLYNESIA

from Avatoru village. Restaurant, bar, water sports, and lagoon excursions. Tahitian owned.

Village Sans Souci. *Moderate.* C/o Greg & Louise Laschelle, Avatoru, Rangiroa; 42.48.33 (Tahiti). Life on a *motu* can be experienced in this 15-bungalow complex located one hour by speedboat from Avatoru village, across immense lagoon. These simple *fares* are made of coconut thatch and have petrol lamps, communal toilets with cold water showers, do-it-yourself housekeeping. Linens provided. Complete pension plan with emphasis on fresh seafood from plentiful lagoon surrounding motu islet. Activities include fishing, snorkelling and scuba diving.

Chez Jean & Temarama Ami. *Inexpensive.* Avatoru, Rangiroa; no Telephone. Located on lagoon 3 miles from airport, close to Avatoru village. 3 houses with 2 double rooms each, toilets and showers in common, part-time electricity. Full pension, with fresh fish the principal food, and meals taken with local Paumotu family.

Chez Jimmy Estall. *Inexpensive.* Tiputa, Rangiroa; telephone 316 Rangiroa. Several traditional individual bungalows, complete with electricity and bathrooms, located between the ocean and the lagoon, 2 km. from the city hall of Tiputa. Family-style meals served at long picnic tables under thatched shelter. Lagoon excursions and fishing expeditions arranged. Very pleasant pension hotel.

TAHAA

Marina Iti. *Moderate.* P.O. Box 158, Uturoa, Raiatea; 66.31.01, Telex 537FP Atin-Marina-Iti. At the entrance of Apu Bay in Vaitoare, this attractive pension on a point facing the sunset is easily accessible when arriving by boat from Raiatea. Open, spacious sitting lounge, with bamboo and rattan South Pacific-style furnishings. Three rooms with bathroom in common, *table d'hôte* French cooking, all sorts of excursions on the lagoon and water sports. Operated by three French yachtsmen.

Chez Mata Marae. *Inexpensive.* Patio, Tahaa (no telephone). 2 rooms in a private home in the village of Patio, next to the Protestant temple. Showers and toilets in common. Meals taken with Tahitian family.

Tahaa Iti Village. *Inexpensive.* Tiva, Tahaa; 65.61.00 Located between villages of Tiva and Tapuamu, facing Bora Bora and providing clear view of magnificent sunsets. 7 small thatched-roof bungalows are built on stilts over the beautiful, clear lagoon where tropical fishes can be seen feeding among the colorful coral gardens. These old bungalows, now being reconstructed, are very simple, with tiny balconies and bathrooms and showers in common in the gardens. A new thatched-roof building is the dining room and kitchen, where one of French Polynesia's best chefs serves up sumptuous meals, *table d'hôte.* Tours of the island, excursions on the lagoon, picnics on the *motu,* outrigger canoes, bicycles, and mountain hiking can all be arranged.

Tahaa Lagoon. *Inexpensive.* P.O. Box 151, Haamene, Tahaa; 65.61.06. Family pension and *Restaurant Hibiscus* operated by Gilbert and Marie-France Marchand, a young French couple who have owned restaurants in many parts of the world. 4 newly built individual bungalows, restaurant, bar, and boutique on the mountain side between the bays of Haamene and Faaaha. A fun atmosphere, with picnic trips to the *motu,* fishing on the reef, windsurfing, bicycling, tours of the island, and rental cars. Full pension possible, with escargots, lobster and fondue Bourgignonne on menu. No beach, and bay here is rather choppy due to wind gusts sweeping through.

TETIAROA

Tetiaroa Village. *Moderate.* P.O. Box 2418, Papeete, Tahiti; 42.63.02. This is Marlon Brando's private atoll, 17 minutes by airplane from Tahiti. The hotel consists of a private airstrip, plus 13 thatched-roof bungalows complete with electricity, private bathrooms and hot water, plus 4 A-frame bungalows with none of the above, sharing facilities in common. There is a dining room, reception area, boutique, and kitchen with a beach bar on the blindingly white sand beach, close to a magnificent lagoon. Weekend accommodations, plus day tours for minimum of 6 people. Activities include trips to bird island by boat across turquoise lagoon, sailboards, snorkeling equipment, Hobie cat, and boat rental with driver.

THE SOUTH PACIFIC

CAMPING. There are no organized campgrounds in French Polynesia, as Americans and Europeans are accustomed to think of them. Occasionally someone with a cleared piece of land will allow a few tents to set up a campsite, and a few more are soon added. At present there is no "official" campground on Tahiti, but on Moorea there is a location next to the Club Med, with fresh water and spartan facilities, but a lovely beach and lagoon, and bus service is available to the boat dock. A dozen or so tents are always set up in Huahine, in a clearing beside the beach and lagoon between the Hotel Bali Hai and the village of Fare. No fresh water or bathrooms available on the premises. On Bora Bora there is a campground run by Philippe Selio Vaino, two km. south of Anau Village. Hot and cold running water available for a nominal fee and daily bus service to the village of Vaitape, plus the bonus of fresh fruit and coconuts often provided by the owner. On a white-sand beach beside the lagoon. Campers are backpackers and no prior reservations are made for tent sites.

RESTAURANTS. Dining out in Tahiti is one of the most popular pastimes for visitors and residents alike. Since there are so many cultures, it naturally follows that the choices of foods available are varied and interesting ones. The most popular restaurants for visitors are usually those serving French food—Papeete is noted for its French restaurants. Chinese food is a favorite anywhere and Tahiti is no exception, as shown by the many Chinese restaurants scattered over town. Tahitian food is a little harder to find, because it is usually prepared at home by the families. Many of the hotels do feature Tahitian feasts or "tamaaraas" frequently to give the visitor a taste of smoked breadfruit, taro, "fei" or mountain bananas, "fafa," their version of spinach which is very good when cooked with chicken and served with their young suckling pig, and "poisson cru," or marinated fish served with coconut milk, or "poe," a starchy pudding made of papaya, mango or banana.

Good old fashioned steak and French fries can be purchased almost anywhere that serves food and the quick-service hamburger shops have discovered Tahiti, with the opening of Big Burger and several stand-up sidewalk shops. A very popular place to eat, especially at night with the locals, yachties or those on low budgets, is on the "trucks" called "Les Roulottes." These are lunch wagons that are parked on the waterfront where the boats load for Moorea. Some have stools and they all serve basically the same foods—steak and fries, chicken and "poisson cru," brochettes or shish-kabobs, which are heart of veal barbequed on the spot. For breakfast or a snack, try the French pastries found in the "salons de thé."

Price categories are as follows: *Deluxe*, over $20. *Expensive*, $14–20. *Moderate*, $6–$14. *Inexpensive*, $4–$6.

Bloody Mary's. *Expensive.* Located on Bora Bora between Vaitape Village and Hotel Bora Bora; 67.72.86. This highly popular seafood restaurant and bar has a huge thatched roof, white-sand floor, rough-hewn tables and coconut log stumps. Fresh fish, lobsters and other seafoods are barbequed on grill while clients watch. Chicken and steaks also available. Many world-famous people have dined here. Free transportation from hotels. Reservations requested. Closed Sundays. Accepts major credit cards.

Chez Christian. *Expensive.* Located on Bora Bora between villages of Anau and Faanui at Hotel Revatua Club; 67.71.67. An overwater 1930s colonial-style restaurant that serves excellent seafood, French cuisine, and extravagant desserts. Open daily. Reservations preferred. Accepts *American Express, Carte Bleue, Visa.*

Coco's. *Expensive.* On the lagoon at P.K. 13, Punaauia, 7.8 miles from Papeete; 58.21.08. A colonial-style restaurant and separate bar/lounge owned by two Frenchmen. French nouvelle cuisine is served, featuring such dishes as *aiguillettes de canard* and *choux farcis aux noisettes d'agneau au miel et citrons verts.* Closed Sunday evening and Monday. Reservations a must. Accepts *American Express* and *Visa.*

La Cremaillére. *Expensive.* On Blvd. Pomare in Quartier Patutoa, 2 blocks from lagoon heading inland, 42.09.15. Excellent nouvelle cuisine Française served in this small, air-conditioned restaurant off the tourist track, in a neighborhood close to Papeete. Serves lunch and dinner. Closed Sundays. Reservations recommended. Accepts *American Express* and *Visa.*

FRENCH POLYNESIA

Le Gauguin. *Expensive.* Located in Hotel Sofitel Maeva Beach at P.K. 7,5 Punaauia; 42.80.42, ext. 87. Elegant atmosphere, good service and gourmet French cuisine make this one of Tahiti's nicest places to dine. Open every night. Reservations required. Accepts *American Express, Diner's, Master Card,* and *Visa.*

Jade Palace. *Expensive.* Located on ground floor of Vaima Center on Rue Jeanne d'Arc, immediately across street from Tahiti Tours, ½ block inland from Papeete waterfront; 42.02.19. This is the Chinese restaurant most tourists are directed to by hotel travel desks, so reservations are required. Open for lunch and dinner, closed Sundays. Accepts *American Express, Diner's, Visa.*

Lagoonarium. *Expensive.* Seafood restaurant built over lagoon at P.K. 11,5 in Punaauia, 7 miles from Papeete; 43.62.90. Tahitian dance shows Friday nights and Sundays at 2:00. Visits to underwater observatory included. Closed Mondays. Reservations recommended. Accepts *American Express, Diner's,* and *Visa.*

La Maribaude. *Expensive.* On the heights of Pamatai, overlooking Papeete, Moorea, and Point Venus. Take Pamatai Road from circle island road and follow up mountain about 15 minutes until you see the entrance to restaurant; 42.82.52. French gastronomic cuisine featuring salmon with butter and leeks, chicken legs stuffed with foie gras, and duck breasts. Swimming pool, cool mountain air, and jazz music with dinner every Friday night. Free roundtrip transportation. Closed Sundays. Reservations required. Accepts all major credit cards.

Moana Iti. *Expensive.* On Blvd. Pomare on Papeete waterfront, between Ave. Bruat and Rue de la Canonniere Zelée; 42.65.24. Excellent French cuisine, with specialties including *paté de la maison,* rabbit simmered in red wine sauce, and steak au poivre. Closed Sundays. Reservations recommended. Accepts *American Express, Carte Bleue, Diner's,* and *Master Card.*

Nuutere. *Expensive.* Located in Papara district at P.K. 32.5, 20 miles west of Papeete on mountain side; 57.41.15. A wonderful gastronomic destination for those with transportation. A pleasant restaurant featuring French cuisine with a Bretonne touch. Many mouth-watering chef's specialties, plus fresh seafood dishes and T-bone steaks. Closed Tuesdays. Reservations requested. Accepts *Visa.*

La Petite Auberge. *Expensive.* At the Pont de l'Est, on Rue des Remparts, just around corner to right from Rue de Marechal Foch, going east from Papeete toward Mamao; 42.86.13. A small, intimate French country-style inn with air conditioning and service not usually found in Tahiti. The most "French" restaurant on the island, featuring cuisine from the provinces of Normandy and Brittany, with a fine selection of wines. Duck conserve a specialty. Serves lunch and dinner. Closed Saturdays. Reservations required. Accepts *American Express, Diner's,* and *Visa.*

Acajou. *Moderate.* Downtown Papeete, on corner of Blvd. Pomare and Rue Georges Lagarde; 42.87.58. This indoor/outdoor restaurant is usually filled with a lively group of American tourists or the European-Chinese-Tahitian-American residents of Tahiti. Owner-chef Acajou, formerly with Pitate, is famous for his French onion soup, seafood cassoulet, steak roquefort, shrimp in champagne sauce, and delicious pepper steaks. Serves breakfast all day, plus lunch and dinner. Closed Sundays. Reservations recommended. Accepts *American Express, Diner's Club,* and *Visa.*

Amandine. *Moderate.* Centre Aline, Blvd. Pomare on Papeete waterfront, in interior courtyard behind Tahiti Art; 43.85.53. A favorite lunch or refreshment stop for shoppers and office workers, this small *salon de thé* is also a patisserie and confiserie, serving deliciously baked French pastries and chocolate candies, ice cream, and sorbets, plus 30 kinds of perfumed teas. Closed Sunday. No reservations. No credit cards.

Le Belvedere. *Moderate.* Located 600 meters (1,800 feet) high in the mountains, up the Fare Rau Ape valley in Pirae district east of Papeete; 42.73.44. This restaurant offers the best bargain for tourists as the price includes transportation to and from hotels, a delicious meal with wine, coffee and dessert, a swimming pool, and happy atmosphere. The beef fondue is a specialty. Second and third helpings of beef, French fries, salad, and wine are cheerfully brought on request. Other selections include French onion soup, mahi mahi, cous-cous, and pepper steak. The ride up the mountain is an unforgettable experience as the bright yellow Le Truck winds around the numerous curves, overlooking all of Papeete and the harbor. Closed Tuesdays. Reservations required for transport. Accepts *American Express, Diner's, Visa,* and travelers checks.

Dahlia. *Moderate.* In Arue district, east of Papeete, at P.K. 4,200, lagoon side, just after Camp d'Arue French military base; 42.59.87. This very popular restaurant is always busy because it serves the best Chinese food in Tahiti. Try roast suckling pig in coconut milk, or crystal shrimps. Open for lunch and dinner, but get there before 1:00 or 8:30 P.M. Closed Sundays. Reservations recommended. *American Express, Carte Bleue, Diner's, Visa.*

Dragon d'Or. *Moderate.* On Rue du Colette, across from Papeete City Hall between Rue Paul Gauguin and Rue de Ecole des Freres de Ploermel, two blocks inland from harbor; 42.96.12. A very popular, well-established Chinese restaurant that serves excellent cuisine for lunch and dinner. French dishes also available. Closed Mondays. Reservations requested. Accepts *American Express, Carte Bleue,* and *Visa.*

Le Gallieni. *Moderate.* Located in Hotel Royal Papeete on Papeete waterfront street, Blvd. Pomare; 42.01.29. Noted for excellent breakfasts. California prime-rib featured for lunch or dinner each Thursday, Friday and Saturday, with other specialties including cous-cous, pineapple duck, and hot apple pie. Reservations needed for specialty days. Open every day. Accepts *American Express, Carte Bleue, Diner's, Master Card, Visa.*

Lou Pescadou. *Moderate.* On Rue Anne-Marie Javouhey, 2 blocks inland from Papeete waterfront; 43.74.26. Mediterranean, Provençale, and Italian cuisine and very noisy, lively, popular pizzeria, where free drinks are served while waiting for a table. Open for lunch and dinner, first come, first served. Closed Sundays. Accepts *American Express, Visa.*

Mandarin. *Moderate.* On Rue des Ecoles, 2 blocks inland from Blvd. Pomare and Papeete waterfront; 42.99.03. A nicely decorated, air-conditioned restaurant serving excellent Cantonese specialties. Ask to be seated in the dining room upstairs, which is even more elegant and offers excellent service. Closed Sundays. Reservations recommended. Accepts *American Express, Diner's, MasterCard,* and *Visa.*

Restaurant du Musée Gauguin. *Moderate.* Built over the lagoon at K.M. 50,500 in the district of Papeari, 30 miles from Papeete, overlooking the Tahitiiti peninsula; 57.13.80. A favorite luncheon stop for people touring the island, this beautifully located restaurant is close to the Paul Gauguin Museum. Roger and Juliette Gowan serve fresh and deliciously prepared hot and cold dishes, shrimp curry, and other seafood specialties, varied buffets, plus fruits and homemade pies. Most tourist groups eat here. Open every day for lunch, closed for dinner. Group reservations required. Accepts *American Express, MasterCard* and *Visa.*

Les Tipaniers. *Moderate.* Located at Hotel Residence Les Tipaniers on Moorea, in Haapiti district near Club Med; 56.12.67. Unpretentious surroundings with excellent Italian cuisine. Fresh pasta, lasagne, pizza and other Italian favorites, plus Continental cuisine. Closed Tuesdays. Reservations preferred. All major credit cards accepted.

Les Roulottes. *Moderate.* Located on Papeete's boat docks, all along the quay and parking area next to Papeete harbor. These lunch-wagon type vehicles usually have stools for sit-down eating. Many of them serve barbequed shish kabobs, steaks, and chicken legs, while others serve Chinese food, pizzas, hamburgers, crêpes, waffles and ice cream, Tahitian food, and veal on a rotisserie. A fun way to watch the people pass by while dining under the stars, before, during or after a night on the town. Most of the roulottes begin serving dinner as soon as the sun goes down and continue to the wee hours of the morning, or all night on weekends. No reservations. No credit cards.

TOURIST INFORMATION SERVICES. There are two dozen travel agencies in French Polynesia that can provide information and assistance for anyone wishing more specific information on Tahiti and Her Islands. Some of the larger ones are: *Tahiti Nui Travel,* B.P. 718, Papeete, Tahiti, 42.68.03; *Tahiti Tours* (the American Express Agency), B.P. 627, Papeete, Tahiti, 42.78.70; *Tahiti Voyages,* B.P. 485, Papeete, Tahiti, 52.57.63; *Voyagence* (also known as *AmiTahiti*), B.P. 274, Papeete, Tahiti, 42.72.13; *Marama Tours,* B.P. 6266, Faaa Airport, Tahiti, 43.96.50; and *Paradise Tours,* B.P. 2430, Papeete, Tahiti, 42.49.36. The best source for general information and

FRENCH POLYNESIA

brochures about French Polynesia is the *Tahiti Tourist Promotion Bureau*, B.P. 65, Papeete, Tahiti, 42.96.26. Inquiries regarding lodging with local families in the islands, how to immigrate to Tahiti and/or get a job, how to visit the islands as cheaply as possible, or whether you can bring your pet with you should be addressed to either the Tahiti Tourist Promotion Bureau in Papeete or their office at Tele Flora Bldg., 12233 West Olympic Blvd., Suite 110, Los Angeles, CA 90064, (213) 207-1919, or telex 497 1603. (There is no ZIP code used in the addresses in French Polynesia.)

Embassies and Consulates. No embassies exist in French Polynesia and the consulates, which are primarily honorary titles, represent European and Scandinavian countries, with the addition of Chile and the Republic of Korea. There are no consulates for the United States, Great Britain, Canada, New Zealand or Australia. The nearest American Embassy is located at P.O Box 218, Suva, Fiji.

HOW TO GET AROUND. By air. *Air Polynesie*, 42.24.44, the domestic airline, connects Tahiti with neighboring islands (Moorea, Huahine, Raiatea, Bora Bora, Maupiti), distant islands of the Gambiers, and remote archipelagoes (Tuamotu atolls of Rangiroa, Manihi, Takapoto, Anaa, Makemo, Tikehau, Hao, Kaukura, Apataki, Mataiva, Fakarava, Tatakoto, Pukarua, Reao, Nukutavake, Fangatau, Napuka, Arutua, Fakahina, Vahitahi, Tureia, and Pukapuka; Austral Islands of Rurutu and Tubuai; and the Marquesas Islands of Nuku Hiva, with connections to Ua Pou, Ua Huka and Hiva Oa), using F-27 turbo-prop and Twin Otter planes. There is also an air taxi service between Tahiti and Moorea, operated by *Air Tahiti*, 42.44.29, with planes leaving frequently throughout the daylight hours.

By sea. (See also "Cruises," below.) Between Tahiti and Moorea—the *Keke III* (tel. 42.80.60), an air conditioned, sleek motor launch with bar and hostesses, makes three round trips daily. Departures from the Papeete boat dock to the nearest Moorea harbor of Vaiare Bay leave Tahiti at 7 A.M. and 5:15 P.M. for a 45-minute crossing, and the "tourist special" departs each morning at 9:15 for the 60-minute trip to marvelous Cook's Bay, leaving for Papeete at 4 P.M. The *Moorea Ferry II* (tel. 43.73.64), which takes passengers and motor vehicles, departs from its private pier at Motu Uta every day except Tuesdays for Vaiare Bay, leaving Tahiti at 8 and 11 A.M., with a supplementary departure every Friday at 5 P.M. The *Tamarii Moorea II* (tel. 56.13.92) car and passenger ferry leaves from its anchorage near the *Keke III* on Papeete's boat dock, departing Monday through Saturday at 9:15 A.M., 1:30 and 5:30 P.M. for Vaiare Bay in Moorea. The schedule changes on Sundays, when the boat leaves Tahiti at 9 A.M., 4:45 and 8 P.M.

The Leeward Society Islands of Huahine, Raiatea, Tahaa, and Bora Bora are served from Tahiti by a car ferry and two passenger/cargo ships. The *Raromatai Ferry* (Compagnie Maritime des Iles Sous Le Vent, B. P. 9012, Papeete, Tahiti, 43.90.42), which offers a restaurant plus a choice of airplane-type seats, semi-private or private cabins with beds, leaves Motu Uta dock in Papeete each Tuesday and Friday at 8:30 P.M., arriving in Huahine the following morning at 6 A.M. and continuing the stops in Raiatea and Tahaa, finally completing the 17-hour trip to Bora Bora at 1:30 P.M. One-way fare for a seat is 4.000 CFP and 10.000 CFP for private cabin. The *Temehani II* (Societe de Navigation Temehani, Motu Uta, Tahiti, 42.98.83) and the *Taporo IV* (Compagnie Francaise Maritime de Tahiti, B.P. 368, Papeete, Tahiti, 42.63.93) offer a less expensive way to visit the Leeward Islands, while providing an insight into the normal lifestyle of Polynesians voyaging from island to island, plus the color and excitement of a cargo freighter. The *Temehani II* leaves Motu Uta in Tahiti each Monday and Thursday at 5 P.M., arriving the following morning in Huahine. Accommodations include berths or a place on the bridge. Bring your own food and drinks. The *Taporo IV* leaves Tahiti each Monday and Wednesday at 5 P.M. and each Friday at 6 P.M. for the Leeward Islands, with stops made in Tahaa on the last two voyages of the week. This ship, which is usually crowded with islanders, has a snack bar, TV, and couchette berths in an open room, or a place on the bridge to put down a bedroll or sleeping mat. Rates vary from 1.100 CFP to 2.100 CFP, according to destination and sleeping arrangement. The *Taporo I* (Societe Taporo Teaotea, B.P. 129, Uturoa, Raiatea, 66.35.52), based in Raiatea, operates between Raiatea and Tahaa, Bora Bora and Maupiti, with one voyage every three months to Schilly, Bellinghausen, and Mopelia, returning to Raiatea in three days.

The far-off Marquesas Islands can be reached from Tahiti by the 264-ft. air-conditioned 17-cabin passenger/cargo/copra ship *Aranui* (Compagnie Polynesienne de Transports Maritimes, B.P. 220, Papeete, Tahiti, 42.62.40), which departs Tahiti every 25 days for a 17-day voyage through the Taumotu atolls of Rangiroa and Takapoto to the Marquesas Islands of Ua Pou, Ua Huka, Nuku Hiva, Hiva Oa, Tahuata, and Fatu Hiva. Not recommended for those who need all the comforts of a passenger liner, but highly recommended for adventurers of all ages, as this offers the best way to visit islands that still merit the cliche "paradise." Rates begin at 118.800 CFP for a mattress on the bridge deck and range up to 326.700 CFP for the ship's best cabin for two persons, all meals and land excursions included. The less tourist-oriented and less expensive ship, *Taporo V* (B.P. 368, Papeete, Tahiti, 42.63.93), departs Tahiti every 15 days for a direct voyage to the Marquesas, arriving back in Tahiti 8 days later. A one-way fare on the bridge costs 5.500 CFP and in a cabin 9.625 CFP, with meals at 1.700–2.200 CFP per day. The Austral Islands of Tubuai, Rurutu, Rimatara, and Raivaevae are served by the *Tuhaa Pae II* (Societe Anonyme d'Economie Mixte de Navigation des Australes, B.P. 1890, Motu Uta, Papeete, Tahiti, 42.93.67), with two voyages per month and a stop in distant Rapa once every two months. The average round-trip without Rapa lasts for 6–7 days and costs 9.800 CFP on the bridge and 16.000 CFP for a berth in a cabin. Meals are 2.400 CFP per day.

The Tuamotu Archipelago is served by several small ships called *goelettes* that take merchandise to these atolls and bring back copra and fish to Tahiti. It is sometimes possible to secure deck space and occasionally a berth on these cargo vessels, but do not expect anything fancy or comfortable. The *AuuraNui* (Sane Richmond, B.P. 9196, Papeete (Motu Uta), Tahiti, 43.92.40), plies its trade in the northeast and central Tuamotus, with voyages lasting three weeks. The *Manava II* (Societe des Transports Maritime des Iles, B.P. 1816, Papeete, Tahiti, tel. 43.83.84), also covers some of this area with 15–17 day voyages. And the *Tameni* (C/o Jean Charles Tekuataoa, B.P. 2516, Papeete, Tahiti, 43.86.82) makes 3–4-week passages to the southern Tuamotus and the Gambier archipelago. Fares for these voyages are determined by the super cargo.

By car. On the islands of Tahiti and Moorea it is relatively easy to rent cars and four-wheel drive vehicles of recent vintage. *Avis* (tel. 42.96.49) and *Hertz* (42.04.71) have offices at the Tahiti-Faaa International Airport and at the larger hotels of Tahiti. Other rental agencies in Tahiti are: *Andre* (42.94.04); *Budget* (42.66.45); *Europcar National Car Rental* (42.48.97); *Pacificar* (42.43.64); *Robert* (42.97.20); *Tahiti Rent A Car* (42.74.49); *Toyota* (43.70.22); and *TTT* (42.87.66), with chauffeur if desired. Automobiles, jeeps, vespas, and bicycles can be rented at all the Moorea hotels, as well as at the Temae Airport and at the boat docks in Vaiare and Cook's Bay. Agencies in Moorea include: *Arii Rent A Car* (56.11.01, 56.10.01, or 56.16.02); *Pierre* (56.12.48); and *Billy Ruta* (56.16.98). On Bora Bora, cars, jeeps or mini-mokes, vespas or mobylettes, and bicycles can be rented through the hotels or at the 3 agencies on the island: *Bora Bora Rent A Car* (67.70.03); *Chez Alfredo Doom* (67.70.31); and *Otemanu Locations* (67.70.94). Bicycles or cars are definitely recommended as opposed to vespas or other motorized two-wheeled vehicles, as many tourists have ruined their vacations by suffering severe accidents or at the least "road rash." On Huahine, *Kake Rent-A-Car* (68.82.59) has mini-mokes, cars, scooters, and small Hondas; *Budget Rent A Car* (68.81.47) rents cars only; and *Dede,* in Fare, rents Honda motorcycles and small scooters. On Raiatea contact Suzanne Guirouard at *Garage Motu Tapu* (66.33.09) for car rentals or *Charles Brotherson* (66.32.15) for motorcycle, scooter, and bicycle rentals. On the island of Tahaa car rentals or excursions can be arranged through the *Tahaa Iti Village* (65.61.00) or the *Tahaa Lagon* (65.61.06). Henri Tupaia in Poutoru rents cars and Petit Tetuanui in Tiva arranges excursions. On other islands ask at your hotel or with the mayor of the village concerning transportation needs. Major credit cards are accepted in Tahiti and Moorea and at the Budget agency in Huahine, but most of the other rental agencies accept only cash and require a deposit.

By taxi. There is taxi service available in Tahiti, Moorea, Huahine, Raiatea, and Bora, the most visited islands. The fares are high and in Tahiti the prices double between the hours of 11:00 P.M. and 5:00 A.M. Taxis can usually be found outside the airport in Tahiti, outside the larger hotels, in front of the Centre

FRENCH POLYNESIA

Vaima at the corner of Blvd. Pomare and Rue Jeanne d'Arc in downtown Papeete, behind the public market downtown, and in front of the Jasmine Bar on Blvd. Pomare. To call for a taxi telephone 43.19.61. In Moorea, *Frederic Pahi* (56.17.15) offers taxi service, or you can ask the hotels to call a taxi; in Raiatea, *Rene Guilloux* (66.31.40) has taxis; *Ioata* (68.80.94) and *Enite* (68.32.37) provide taxi service in Fare, Huahine, and in the other islands just ask at your hotel desk.

By Le Truck. Local buses, called Le Truck, offer an inexpensive and often entertaining way to get around Papeete, and to and from your hotels in Tahiti. They leave from the central market downtown and go in all directions, making stops all along the way, up back roads and alleys, taking people home. There is no set schedule for these trucks except for those going to the other side of the island, and you don't want to be on these Le Trucks unless you have a definite way to return when you want to. Service operates from very early in the morning throughout the day and for the hotels on the west coast, up until midnight or sometimes later. You pay the driver when you get off. Public transportation by Le Truck is offered also on Huahine and Raiatea, but not on Moorea or Bora Bora, although Le Trucks are used to transport passengers between the boat docks and the hotels.

INTER-ISLAND CRUISES. (See also "How to Get Around by Sea," above.) *American-Hawaii Cruises,* 550 Kearny St., San Francisco, CA 94108, (415–392–9400) or AmiTahiti, B.P. 21397, Papeete, Tahiti, (42.72.13). Operates the 715-passenger ship SS *Liberte* on 7-day cruises plus pre- and/or post-cruise land programs. Departures from Papeete at 11 P.M. each Saturday for Bora Bora, Huahine, Raiatea, and excursions to Tahiti, returning by Moorea to Papeete. Ship includes casino, pool, nightclub, conference center, and closed circuit TV sets, on-board entertainment, and American films, excursions ashore plus rental bicycles for do it yourself exploring in the islands.

Association des Professionels du Tourisme Nautique des Iles Sous le Vent is comprised of several charter yachts and sports fishing boats in the Leeward Society Islands. Members include 56-ft. Columbia ketch *Aita Peapea,* 55-ft. catamaran *Katiana,* 65-ft. cruiser *Danae III,* 72-ft. motor yacht *Maliga,* 37-ft. sloop *Vanessa,* fishing boats *Toerau, Mokalei, Aquaholics,* and *Te Aratai II,* plus the Moorings fleet of charters. P.O. Box 590, Uturoa, Raiatea; 66.35.93, Telex 422FP.

Aranui, B. P. 220, Papeete, Tahiti, Tel. 42.62.40, offers 17-day cruises to the Marquesas Islands, departing Papeete every 25 days in 264-ft. A/C 17-cabin passenger/cargo/copra ship. See How to Get Around for details.

Exploration Cruise Lines, 1500 Metropolitan Park Bldg., Olive Way at Boren Ave., Seattle, Wa. 98101; 800–426–0600; in Seattle, 624–8551, Telex 32–9636, offers island hopping aboard the *Majestic Tahiti Explorer.* First-class 4-, and 5- and 7-day cruises from Tahiti to Moorea, Huahine, Bora Bora, Tahaa and Raiatea, aboard 152-foot, 44-stateroom, 4-deck ship. Fly and cruise programs available in cooperation with UTA from Los Angeles.

Moana Adventure Tours, Nunue, Bora Bora. Glass-bottom boat trips, water skiing, speedboat rides, visits to coral reef, fishing, scuba diving inside lagoon and outside reef. Write to Erwin Christian, C/o Hotel Bora Bora, Nunue, Bora Bora, 67.70.28.

Sea and Leisure, B. P. 3488, Papeete, Tahiti; 43.97.99. This floating office along the Papeete waterfront, across from the Post Office, has information on every aspect of water sports in Tahiti and her Islands. Boats, fully equipped for deep-sea fishing for marlin, sailfish, tuna, and other game fish can be chartered here. Sailboats, Hobie Cats, surfboards, and windsurfing equipment, glass-bottom boats, waterskiing and diving expeditions can all be arranged.

The Moorings, 1305 U.S. 19 South, Suite 402, Clearwater, FL 33546; 800–535 –7289 or 813–535–1446. World's largest yacht charter company operates a bareboat sailing fleet of 20 yachts based in Raiatea. Formerly South Pacific Yacht Charters, the sailing fleet consists of specially designed Moorings yachts, plus a few Endeavor 37-ft. boats, Nautical 39-ft. boats and Peterson CSY 44-ft. yachts. Provisions, captain, cook, and crew available if desired, for chartering in the Leeward Islands of the Society group. Telephone in Raiatea is 66.35.93.

Tahiti Aquatique, BP6008, Faaa, Tahiti; 42.80.42. Double Polynesian canoe used as glass-bottom boat for lagoon cruises, snorkeling, sunset or "funset booze cruise," dinner cruises. Complete line of nautical sports including scuba diving and underwater photography lessons. Located at Maeva Beach Hotel.

Tahiti Cruising Club, B.P. 1604, Papeete, Tahiti; 42.68.89. Skippered- or bare-boat sailing in new or recent yachts ranging 32–83 ft. long. Hotel accommodations, airline connections, and all other conveniences arranged for you.

TOURS. Circle Island Tour. Any travel agency or hotel desk in Tahiti can arrange a tour of the island, with or without meals and/or admissions to the museums, for a half day or full day. The average tour leaves the hotel at 9:30 A.M., stopping at One Tree Hill, historic Point Venus, pointing out the Blowhole of Arahoho, cascading waterfalls deep within the lush green valleys, the marker of Bougainville's landing in Hitiaa and rainbow-colored Tahitian homes surrounded by gardens of dancing color. A visit to the Paul Gauguin Museum in Papeari can be included before or after lunch, followed by a walk through the Harrison Smith Botanical Gardens or a smaller garden with verdant tropical foliage and a roaring waterfall. The latter half of the tour passes by the Atimaono Golf Course with a refreshing stop at the cool fern grotto of Maraa Point, then a roadside view of Tahiti's lovely and wealthy west coast districts of Paea and Punaauia, with old Polynesian style homes of pandanus and woven bamboo beside the lagoon and multimillion dollar modern homes in the mountains. The tour ends at the hotel, usually around 3:30 or 4 P.M.

Interior Mountain Tours. Sea and Leisure or Mer et Loisirs, in the floating office across from the Papeete Post Office (43.97.99), can arrange exciting, challenging, and unusual tours for those who wish to explore Tahiti's interior valleys, climb mountains, walk across the island, or investigate old lavatubes, burial caves, and hidden grottos. These excursions are classified according to the difficulty of accomplishment and can take from 1–4 days. Four-wheel drive vehicles are used for the most popular tours.

Helicopter Tours. *Pacific Helicopter Service* (43.16.80 and 43.84.25) and *Tahiti Helicopters* (43.34.26 or 42.61.22) provide aerial sightseeing of Tahiti's ancient volcanoes, spectacular mountain peaks, lush valleys, and tropical waterfalls. Pilots are trained for still and motion photography flights.

SEASONAL EVENTS. Two of the major events on Tahiti's annual schedule are listed here. In **July,** *Tahiti's Festival* is in full swing when the month begins and the pace accelerates with competitive sports, singing, and dancing events. All over French Polynesia there are parades, games, contests and colorful shows, with special food, dancing and gambling *baraques* constructed for the occasion. The highlight of the festival is the International Pirogue Race, with competing teams from many countries.

In **December** is *Tiare Tahiti Day.* Tahiti's national flower, the white gardenia, is featured, with a gardenia being presented to everyone on the streets of Papeete, in the hotels and at the airport, culminating in an all-night ball with Tiare Tahiti flowers decorating the ballroom, the tables and even the performers.

SPORTS. Many sports are available in conjunction with your hotel. See Accommodations. The climate is very favorable all year for outdoor sports, and the lagoons are the centers of sporting activities. In Tahiti there are sailboats for rent by the hour, day or week at *Tahiti Cruising Club,* B. P. 1604, Papeete, Tahiti; Tel. 42.68.89 and Sea and Leisure's floating office on the waterfront across from the Papeete Post Office, 43.97.99. There are water sports facilities located at the Hotel Tahiti Beachcomber (43.86.23) and at Tahiti Aquatique, located at the Hotel Sofitel Maeva Beach, (42.80.42). Both locations have small sailboats, water-skiing, sightseeing lagoon tours, glass-bottom boat rides, line fishing in the pass or on the coral reef, and deep sea-fishing expeditions. Tahiti Aquatique also offers diving instruction and expeditions.

On the waterfront in downtown Papeete there are numerous deep-sea fishing boats for hire, and the Haura Club, Tahiti's official organization for sports fishing, holds annual International Billfish Tournaments, associated with the International Game Fish Association. Contact Dave Cave, P. O. Box 582, Papeete, Tahiti, 42.49.29 or 42.89.10.

FRENCH POLYNESIA

American snorkeling and shelling expert Ron Hall, B. P. 98, PaoPao, Moorea, Tel. 56.11.06, guides Moorea visitors to the best snorkeling and shelling spots, giving extensive lessons for beginners. Snorkeling and diving expeditions can also be arranged at Hotel Linareva in Moorea, 56.15.35; with Erwin Christian of Moana Adventure Tours in Nunue, Bora Bora, 67.70.28; and with the Hotel Kia Ora Village on the Tuamotu atoll of Rangiroa, RA 384, where guests enjoy diving in the passes along with hundreds of sharks and fishes.

Airplane rentals are possible through the Aeroclub de Tahiti, B.P. 1500, Papeete, Tahiti, Tel. 42.58.02.

The Vol-Libre Polynesian Club, B.P. 5374, Pirae, Tahiti, 43.72.01, a **hang-gliders** association, offers another form of flying.

A **bowling alley** is located between Papeete and the Tahara'a Hotel (42.93.26).

For the **golf** enthusiast, the course at Atimaono (57.40.32), 45 minutes by car from the center of Papeete, is open year round and is located between the lagoon and the mountains in a very colorful setting. There are 18 holes (6,950 yards) and par is 72 for men and 73 for women. A club house with bar and snack bar, pro-shop, lockers, driving range, clubs, hand cart rentals and lessons are all provided.

Mountain climbing expeditions can be arranged through Sea and Leisure, the floating office across from the Papeete Post Office, B. P. 3488, Papeete, Tahiti, 43.97.99.

Riding. Horseback riding and lessons are available in Tahiti at the *Club Equestre* (42.70.41) and *L'Eperon de Pirae*, (42.79.87), both located next to the Hippodrome in the district of Pirae. Wendy Pratt, a young American woman, operates Te Anavai Ranch in the district of Papeari, (Tel. 57.20.20), giving riding lessons and leading trail rides through Tahiti's most beautiful tropical forests. La Petite Ferme on Huahine is located between the airport and the Hotel Bali Hai, B. P. 12, Huahine, Tel. 68.82.98). Riding lessons, hourly rides, and 2-4 day camping trail rides can be arranged. Horses are a common mode of transportation in the Marquesas and horses, with or without saddles, can easily be rented on all the Marquesan islands.

Tennis. There are tennis courts and clubs at Hotel Tahara'a (48.11.22); Hotel Tahiti Beachcomber, (43.86.23); Hotel Sofitel Maeva Beach, (42.80.42); Hotel Te Puna Bel Air, (42.09.00); and at the Tennis Club in Fautaua, (42.00.59). On Moorea there are tennis courts at the Hotel Bali Hai, (56.13.59); Club Bali Hai (56.13.68); Hotel Sofitel Kia Ora Village, (56.12.90); Club Mediterranee, (56.15.00); Climat de France, (56.15.48); and Moorea Village, (56.10.02). The Hotel Bora Bora has a tennis club (67.70.28); and the Hotel Bali Hai (68.82.77) and Relais Mahana (68.81.54) in Huahine have tennis courts.

SPECTATOR SPORTS

Soccer, the favorite sport of Tahitians, can be seen on almost all the islands. In Tahiti, enthusiastic crowds gather at the Fautaua Stadium or the Stade Pater, both located in Pirae, near Papeete, on week nights and during weekends to cheer their team to victory. As there are many athletic clubs in Tahiti, it is best to call the local newspapers (*La Depêche de Tahiti*, 42.43.43) to find out what sporting events are taking place and where. Reservations and advance purchase of tickets are not needed. *Horseracing.* Tahitian-style horseracing is held on special occasions at the Pirae Hippodrome, where jockeys sometimes ride bareback, wearing only a brightly colored Pareo and a crown of flowers. Parimutuel betting exists, but the payoffs are very small. *Cockfighting* is another Sunday afternoon event. Although officially illegal, the fighting rings are out in the open and all the hotels can help you to find out where the action is taking place. Recent spectator sport to thrill the trail bike enthusiasts is the opening of an international motorcross course at Taravao. Other regularly scheduled spectator sports include *archery, bicycling, boxing, outrigger canoe racing, volleyball, sailboat racing* and *track* events.

 MUSEUMS AND GALLERIES. *Musée de Tahiti et Des Îles,* 58.34.76, at Pointe des Pêcheurs in Punaruu P.K. 15.7, about 10 miles from town, is located on the site of a former *marae* and has displays of the ocean floor and the Polynesian islands. The bountiful nature that exists in these islands is featured—life on the coral reefs and in the lagoons, in the highlands and on the atolls, as well as the flowers and trees. The history of Polynesia after the arrival of the Europeans is also a main theme here. Open 9:30 A.M.–5:30 P.M. daily except Mondays. Admission charge. The *Paul Gauguin Museum,* B.P. 7029, Taravao, Tahiti, 57.10.42 or 57.10.58, is located 30 miles southeast of Papeete at P.K. 51.2 in the district of Papeari. This is Tahiti's most famous museum. The story of this famous artist's life and artistic activities is told with the help of photographs, reproductions of his most famous works, documents and furniture. Open every day 9 A.M.–5 P.M. Admission charge. *Tahiti Perles Center,* 43.85.58, on Blvd. Pomare, next to Protestant Temple of Paofai, is a jewelry store and a new museum for the black pearl. Open Mon.–Fri. 7:30 A.M.–noon and 1:30–5 P.M., Sat. 9 A.M.–noon. Closed Sun.

Art galleries in Tahiti are: *Galerie Winkler,* 42.81.77, located on Rue Jeanne d'Arc between the waterfront street of Blvd. Pomare and the Catholic Cathedrale; *Galerie Atea-45,* 42.72.33, on Rue du Commandant Destremeau, across street from La Pizzeria's back entrance; *Galerie Vaim'antic,* 43.68.96, located on the lower plaza of the Vaima Center in Papeete; *Galerie Noa Noa,* 42.73.47, on Blvd. Pomare in front of the Tahiti Tourist Office; *Galerie Jean-Jacques Laurent,* 42.04.32, adjacent to Vaim'antic in the Vaima Center and occupying part of the Galerie Winkler; and *Galerie Oviri,* 42.63.82, located at P.K. 12,700 in Punaauia, on the mountain side, fourth house on the left.

In Moorea the *Galerie Aad Van Der Heyde* is located at P.K. 7 in PaoPao (56.14.22); *Galerie Api* in the district of Haapiti (56.13.57) combines artwork with hand-painted clothing. On Bora Bora, at the entrance to Point Matira, is the *Jean Masson Museum,* featuring the works of this famous French artist, whose widow, Rosine Temauri, also exhibits her own paintings and hand-painted clothing.

GARDENS. The *Harrison W. Smith Botanical Gardens* are located adjacent to the Gauguin Museum in Papeari, 30 miles from Papeete. In these 340 acres you will find hundreds of varieties of trees, shrubs, plants and flowers from tropical regions throughout the world.

SHOPPING. With the introduction of shopping centers in Papeete, the merchandise displayed in the stores is very much what you find in Parisian boutiques, including the price tag. There are no real bargains to be found here. French perfumes are less expensive than in the United States. There are some local products such as the exquisite Marquesan wood carvings, the dancing costumes, shell jewelry and Tahitian perfumes that will make nice gifts or souvenirs of your visit to Polynesia. An especially nice inexpensive purchase is the Monoi Tiare Tahiti, which is the coconut oil scented with Tahiti's national flower. This can be used as a moisturizing lotion, a perfume, suntan lotion, mosquito repellant, hair dressing, massage lotion—some people have even considered drinking it! The brightly patterned *pareu* fabrics that make the traditional Tahitian *pareo* are available in dozens of shops.

Tahiti's biggest export is the South Seas black pearl, which is also the most sought-after souvenir item. Exquisite jewelry fashioned of black pearls, 18-karat gold and frequently with diamonds, or unset pearls of all sizes, shapes, quality and prices can be purchased in French Polynesia. Shops selling these pearls are found on practically every block in downtown Papeete, in addition to all the hotel boutiques on all the tourist islands.

The *Centre Vaima,* located in the middle of downtown Papeete, occupies a city block between the Blvd. Pomare on the waterfront, Rue Jeanne d'Arc, Rue du General De Gaulle and Rue Georges Lagarde. This 3-level shopping complex is the largest in Papeete. Here you will find *Popsy,* a *tres chic* boutique for ladies; *Armandissimo,* with Italian and French ready-to-wear for men and women; *Choisir* for elegant gifts, handbags, crystal, and china; *Polynesian Curios* for local wood carvings and mother-of-pearl jewelry; *Islands Treasures* for authentic Polynesian artifacts and dance costumes; *Optique Surdite* for instant repair of eyeglasses or purchases of French-style sunglasses; *Vaima Junior* for children's clothes; *Anemone and Vaima Shirts* for hand-painted Tahitian style clothing; *Cordo Express* for repair of luggage, handbags, and shoes; *Elegancia* for French shoes; *Polynesie Perles* for black pearls; *Vaima QSS Photo* for one-hour photo development; *La Cave à Cigars* for cigars from Havana, Brazil, and Sumatra; *Tahiti Duty Free Shop* for French perfumes; *Le*

FRENCH POLYNESIA

Kiosque for international newspapers and magazines; and *Aux Ducs de Gascogne* for foie gras, patés, French Armagnac, and other gourmet items.

Aline's, Tahiti's only department store, has a small shopping mall. It is located one block from the Vaima center, on Blvd. Pomare. Also on this waterfront street, between the Vaima center and Aline's, is *Tahiti Art,* with exclusive and lovely fabrics, dresses, and shirts. *Marie Ah You,* on Blvd. Pomare one block toward the public market from the Vaima center, sells elegant original gowns, using their own designs of fabric and fashion. For beautiful Tahitian fabrics to sew yourself, try *Tapa Tissus,* on Rue du General de Gaulle, across from the Vaima center.

The boutiques on Moorea carry a good selection of the hand-painted muumuu type dresses, as well as bikinis, T-shirts, beach cover-ups, and other elegantly casual wear, created by the artisans who live on this neighboring island. Try *Shark's Tooth Boutique,* the boutique at the Sofitel Kia Ora Village, and *Laurie's Boutique,* all on Moorea. On Bora Bora, Alain and Linda sell their own clothing designs and wall hangings, hand painted by brush; and *Martine's Boutique* has a good selection of hand-painted T-shirt dresses. *Moana Art* near the Hotel Bora Bora also carries a line of elegant island fashions. Shops, boutiques, jewelry stores, and art galleries all maintain the normal working hours of the South Seas. This means they are open early in the morning, around 7–7:30; they close for a couple of hours at noon or just before; then are open in the afternoon until 5:30–6:00. Usually they are open on Saturday mornings and closed on Sundays.

NIGHTLIFE. Papeete is a swinging town after dark and the crowds in the restaurants and nightclubs seem to really enjoy themselves. Most of the hotels feature Tahitian dance shows several times a week and a band that plays dance music nightly. For discotheque dancing, go to the *Club 106* above the Moana Iti Restaurant on Blvd. Pomare, between Ave. Bruat and Rue de la Canonniere Zelée; the rather snobby *Rolls Club* in the Centre Vaima, entrance on Rue du General de Gaulle; the select *Le Retro Disco* behind Le Retro Restaurant on the corner of Blvd. Pomare and Rue Georges Lagarde; or the young "jet-set" *Mayana Club* upstairs at the Centre Bruat on the corner of Ave. Bruat and Blvd. Pomare.

La Cave, located at the other end of Blvd. Pomare, on the ground floor of the Hotel Royal Papeete, has both a disco and a large dance hall with a live Tahitian band that plays on weekends and special events. Tourists of all ages will feel comfortable here and will enjoy the ambiance while dancing to a Tahitian beat of fox trots, waltzes and the hip-shaking *tamure.*

The *Hotel Matavai* in Tipaerui also has a live Tahitian band on weekends, with a dance show and a big floor for dancing in the traditional Tahitian style, plus disco dancing later in the evening. *Le Pub,* on Avenue Bruat, is another disco, where office and government workers gather for happy hour cocktails and dance to the latest disco tunes. Next door is *Le Pitate,* at the corner of Ave. Bruat and Blvd. Pomare. This noisy dance hall, with a very lively band, gets going late, as do most of the nightclubs, but is always filled with a mostly Tahitian crowd. Lots of class-conscious people in Tahiti refuse to go there, but it is this editor's favorite night spot and appreciated by most visitors who want to really experience a flavor of the old South Seas.

For another view of Papeete-by-night, try the other end of town, where young French military men often dance with Tahiti's transvestites and watch Papeete's entertaining *mahu's* or third sex, reign in all their flamboyance. *The Piano Bar,* on Rue des Ecoles, welcomes tourists to their transvestite strip show. Also on this street are several other bars and discos, including the *Bounty Club* and *Le Lido,* mostly military hangouts. Several other waterfront type discos and dives are located along Blvd. Pomare, between Ave. Prince Hinoi and Ave. du Chef Vairaatoa. The *Princesse Heiata* is a hotel in Pirae, about 3 miles from downtown, where an after-hours disco operates each weekend until 5 A.M. Very crowded and noisy. The *Hotel Tahiti* often has very nice dinners and dances on Saturday nights, in conjunction with a contest to elect a beauty queen or to celebrate a sports event.

THE COOK ISLANDS

The Goose Gets Fatter

by
GRAEME KENNEDY

Graeme Kennedy is a feature writer for the Auckland Star *specializing in aviation and travel—especially the South Pacific Islands.*

Tiny Rarotonga, in the Cook Islands midway between Hawaii and Auckland, Fiji, and Tahiti, was 15 or 20 years ago the Pacific's most enviable destination. If you'd been there, you could really impress travellers hooked into the Fiji-Tahiti-Hawaii sun circuit, for the Cooks were then an undiscovered place of tropical beauty and peace right off the track and thus able to impart the prestige exclusivity brings.

How things have changed. These days, if you want to meet your neighbor or workmate, go to Raro. Chances are he or she will be there or just got back or is packing to go.

The change started in 1973, when New Zealand built the Cooks an international airport just outside the main town of Avarua on Rarotonga. A trickle of regular visitors began to stay in the handful of motel-guesthouses scattered around the 32-kilometers-circumference, reef-ringed island where you could have whole white sandy beaches to yourself. The trickle became a torrent when the Rarotongan Resort Hotel opened in 1977, funded by the New Zealand government as a means of generating revenue to aid an ailing economy. Within five years, tourist numbers had rocketed to almost 18,000—ironically the Cooks' 1986 population.

THE COOK ISLANDS

Tourism has since peaked in the last two years at around 26,000, with 10,500 visitors coming from New Zealand, attracted by the closeness and the fact that their own currency, weak throughout the world, is used there. Australians came next, with almost 3,500, followed by just over 3,000 Canadians and, curiously, only 937 Americans in 1984–85.

Tourism Minister Dr. Teariki Matenga insists there is "room for more visitors for some time," and his Tourist Authority says that Cook Islanders are aware of "the negative effects of tourism on other Pacific islands and have no intention of becoming like them," but there are already predictions that the Cooks—and that means Rarotonga—could eventually expect up to 2,000 visitors a day and a little more than 100,000 a year.

It is doubtful the Cooks' culture and natural attractions could cope, and already there are calls in Rarotonga for restrictions on building accommodations after the current programs, which include a new resort hotel of up to 300 rooms at Muri Beach, another of 80 rooms in Avarua, and at least two new motels. Meanwhile, the Rarotongan is adding 100 rooms, and the Tamure and existing motels are expanding to catch the boom.

Just getting there on Air New Zealand's virtual monopoly service—one 747 and one 737 a week—has not been easy, although more airline seats are now available with the New Zealand carrier putting on four 767s a week and Cook Islands Premier Sir Tom Davis, long angered by what he saw as Air New Zealand's paltry service, taking matters into his own hands. Under Sir Tom, a Cook Island–born doctor who worked in the United States for NASA on the early space programs, the island nation took control of the New Zealand–donated airport on April 1, 1986, began negotiating its own bilateral air rights, and announced plans for its own international airline, Cook Islands International, to be operated and administered by Australia's Ansett. These increased accommodation and airline plans will bring thousands more tourists to the islands, and many fear it will be a retelling of the old goose-and-golden-egg story.

Now, though—while there's still space on the beach—the Cooks are an attractive proposition. With the New Zealand dollar very low, the exchange rate is extremely favorable, especially for North American and Australian visitors; the lagoons are clean and warm; beaches are uncluttered; and the living is pretty easy.

The Cooks' 15 islands occupy just 93 square miles in 750,000 square miles of ocean from Pukapuka, Rakahanga, and Penrhyn in the north to Rarotonga, Mauke, and Mangaia in the south. In the north, the islands are storybook coral atolls; in the south, all are of volcanic origin, with jungled basalt spires and fine lagoons.

Folklore puts the Cook Islanders' origins back to the early 1300s, when two chiefs, from Tahiti and Samoa, arrived almost at the same time to claim the new land. Without a battle, they divided Rarotonga equally and lived harmoniously, while the territorial boundaries were eventually broken down and the new race emerged. Legend has it that seven canoes of Cook Islanders left Muri Lagoon about 1350 and navigated to New Zealand to begin the Maori race after a growing population on the small island created food shortages and tribal wars.

Captain Cook visited the islands that were to bear his name in the 1770s and was followed by the missionaries and traders in the 1800s. The Cooks became a British colony and remained so until 1901, when they were turned over to New Zealand, whose administration was notable only for its neglect. The small Pacific nation became independent under Premier Albert Henry in 1965. An individualistic and volatile character often accused of nepotism, he was known as Papa at home until his death in 1978, when Sir Tom Davis succeeded him. Rarotongans are proud of their Albert Henry Museum in Avarua, where mementos of the old man's iron reign are displayed.

Avarua is a busy waterfront town with public buildings and shops, old homes in spacious tropic gardens, the inevitable guesthouses, and the almost-anything-goes Banana Court bar, tavern, cabaret, and meeting place still run by former Pacific heavyweight boxing champion Apiro Brown. Outwardly a friendly chap, Apiro has little trouble in his well-run establishment.

Under the towering basalt peak known as the Needle, and its jungle-draped lesser brothers, Rarotonga lies warm and happy, encircled by its reef, lagoon, and villages like Titihaveka, Ngatangiia, Matavera, Arorangi, and Muri. Peaceful and unhurried they can still be, Pacific-enchanting and languid they remain, but one might question their future after watching a new favorite tourist attraction, the round-island pub-crawl, where mostly New Zealanders and Australians are chaperoned on a half-day visit to every drinking establishment on the lagoon road.

There's none of that, of course, on the only other of the Cook Islands accessible to visitors—southerly volcanic Aitu and Mauke and the northern atoll Aitutaki, often claimed to be the most beautiful lagoon in the world, where the flying boats once overnighted on their luxurious four-day haul from Auckland to Tahiti. But more of the Cooks might soon be made available to visitors seeking real seclusion, real peace, and unspoiled beauty as the tourism goose becomes too big, too tough and unpalatable.

PRACTICAL INFORMATION FOR THE COOK ISLANDS

WHEN TO GO. Apart from December through March, when rainfall regularly exceeds 10 inches a month, the Cook Islands have a pleasantly warm and sunny climate, temperatures and humidity peaking with February's average 84°F maximum and easing to a 77°F minimum in August. Stormy weather hits the Cooks infrequently, but the rain can be spectacular. Take a light raincoat even in the dry season.

Average Temperature (°Fahrenheit) and Humidity

Rarotonga	Jan	Feb	Mar	Apr	May	June	July	Aug	Sept	Oct	Nov	Dec
Average max. day temperature	84°	84°	83°	81°	79°	77°	77°	77°	77°	79°	80°	82
Days of rain	15	15	16	14	13	11	10	11	11	12	13	14
Humidity, percent	79	81	80	79	77	77	75	74	73	74	75	76

General hints: The best tourist season is May through October. Temperature is warm and humid, tempered by trade winds.

WHAT TO WEAR. Other Polynesian islands are a good guideline. Light, breezy, and casual day and night, but please, no swimwear or bare chests in public places. Minimum winter temperatures in the 60s in August may require a light wrap or cardigan at night.

THE COOK ISLANDS

HOW TO GET THERE: The most direct route to Rarotonga is with *Air New Zealand,* which operates regular services from Los Angeles through Tahiti and Fiji or from Auckland—four weekly flights with the airline's new Boeing 767s. *Polynesian Airlines* flies in from Western Samoa and *Air Nauru* from Pago Pago and Niue.

ENTRY REQUIREMENTS. All visitors except New Zealanders need passports for stays up to 31 days. Entry permits are not needed provided visitors have onward tickets showing they do not intend to stay longer. Application can be made in Rarotonga for longer visits. Vaccination certificates are not needed.

Duty-free allowance in the Cook Islands is 200 cigarettes, ½ lb. of tobacco or 50 cigars, and two liters of spirits or wine or 4½ liters of beer. The Cooks are free of serious plant and animal diseases and pests, and all plants, fruit and animals brought into the country will be inspected.

CURRENCY: The Cook Islands use the New Zealand dollar, worth about US50¢. Coins are minted for local use, including the dollar coin bearing the image of the god Tangaroa, which has become popular with coin collectors. All credit cards are accepted.

ELECTRICITY. Available voltage is 230 volts, 50 cycles, the same as in New Zealand and Australia. However, a two-pin plug may be required at some accommodations. Provision for 110-volt AC electric shavers is made at several hotels and motels.

TIPPING. This will offend in the Cook Islands.

LANGUAGES. Cook Islands Maori is the local language, but almost everyone is fluent in English.

TIME ZONE. Greenwich Mean Time, plus 10½, or 2 hours behind U.S. Pacific Standard.

ACCOMMODATIONS. *Deluxe* means $NZ100 and up for a double room; *Expensive* $NZ50–$NZ70; *Moderate* $NZ30–$NZ50; *Inexpensive,* below $NZ30.

RAROTONGA

Rarotongan Resort Hotel. *Deluxe.* Box 103 Rarotonga. Phone 25.800. The island's top hotel, with 150 rooms and four beachfront suites 12km from Avarua town. Rooms have one double and one single bed and are fully self-contained with refrigerator and tea-coffee-making facilities. Hotel has restaurants, bars, games room, swimming pool, shop, tennis, wind surfers, and outrigger canoes. Conference facilities are also available. Tour and travel desk and hourly bus service to Avarua.

Ariana Bungalows. *Expensive.* Box 434. Phone 20.521. In Upper Tupapa, eight minutes' drive from town, six self-contained pole-construction cottages and two family units in spacious tropical gardens. Swimming pool, barbecue, store with basic groceries.

Edgewater Resort Motel. *Expensive.* Box 121. Phone 25.437. 84 self-contained units with fully equipped kitchens minutes from Avarua on four-acre private site with sandy safe swimming beach. Squash court, swimming pool, games room adjacent to bar, nightclub, and restaurant.

Lagoon Lodges. *Expensive.* Box 45. Phone 22.020. Just 400m from Rarotongan Resort Hotel, set in two acres of garden with 10 self-contained bungalows, four with two separate bedrooms. Pool, barbecue, opposite lagoon.

Little Polynesian. *Expensive.* Box 366. Phone 24.280. On the white-sand beach at Titikaveka 12km from town, nine self-contained units beside pool; liquor license.

Moana Sunrise Motel. *Expensive.* Depot 8, Ngatangiia, Rarotonga. Phone 26.560. Eight self-contained units 7.3km from Avarua with shore frontage but no beach.

Muri Beachcomber. *Expensive.* Box 379. Phone 21.022. On sparkling Muri lagoon, 10km from Avarua, with six double and four twin self-contained and serviced units. Pool, barbecue on 1.25 acres of garden.

New Beach Hotel. *Expensive.* Box 700. Phone 27.652. Redecorated and modernized, on sandy beach at Arorangi Village 8km from Avarua. Restaurant, airport transfers, bar with 20 self-contained villas.

Palm Grove Lodge. *Expensive.* Box 23. Phone 20.002. In garden setting with swimming pool opposite private beach, two self-contained bungalows, and two island-style units 15.3km from Avarua. Handy to restaurant and shop, regular bus service.

Puaikura Reef Lodge. *Expensive.* Box 397. Phone 23.537. Twelve self-contained units sleeping four each opposite white sand beach 10.8km from town. With freshwater pool and barbecue.

Raina Village Motel. *Expensive.* Box 1047. Phone 20.197. Opposite safe white beach, spa pools, wind surfers, barbecue. 14km from town, four luxury units with own balcony and sun deck.

Tamure Resort Hotel. *Expensive.* Box 17. Phone 22.415. Has 35 newly decorated twin and double rooms on the beach 2.5km from town. All are at ground level and contain tea-coffee-making facilities, refrigerator, fans, and all amenities. The Tamure offers bicycle, motorbike, and car rentals, secretarial service, tour desk, and entertainment four nights a week, usually local dancing.

Arorangi Lodge. *Moderate.* Box 51. Phone 27.379. Eight self-contained units in Arorangi Village, just past airport.

Kii Kii Motel. *Moderate.* Box 68. Phone 21.937. On the beach only 2.6km from Avarua, nine roomy self-contained units that sleep up to four. Swimming pool and barbecue area in gardens.

Mana Motel. *Moderate.* Box 72. Two self-contained units, 3km from Avarua.

Matareka Heights. *Moderate.* Box 587. Phone 23.670. Away from beach, in foothills 3km from town. One communal unit and two self-contained with bathroom facilities.

Onemaru Motel. *Moderate.* Box 523. Across road from swimming beach in quiet gardens 11.7km from Avarua. Two self-contained units with twin beds.

Orange Grove Lodge. *Moderate.* Box 553. Phone 20.050. Close to licensed restaurant 15.4km from town and three minutes' stroll to beach. Set in banana and citrus plantation with free in-season fruit to guests. Two self-contained units with twin beds. Bus service to Avarua.

Punamaia Motel. *Moderate.* Box 326. Phone 24.338. Two-story block of six self-contained units with twin beds 2.4km from Avarua.

Tiare Village Motel. *Moderate.* Box 489. Phone 23.466. Opposite airport on inland road 3km from town, 2km from beach; three fully equipped chalets.

Are-Renga and Airport Lodge. *Inexpensive.* Box 223. Phone 20.050. At the airport 8.5km from Avarua with six self-contained units.

Atupa Orchid. *Inexpensive.* Just two self-contained units 2km from Avarua.

Dive Rarotonga Hostel. *Inexpensive.* Box 38. Phone 21.873. Barry and Shirley Hill run this budget facility with special washing, drying, and storage for dive equipment. Six twin rooms, one double, and two singles. Communal kitchen; lounge, washing and toilet facilities.

Rutaki Lodge. *Inexpensive.* Box 170. Phone 22.115. Just two self-contained units 12.2 km from Avarua.

Whitesands Motel. *Moderate.* Box 115. Phone 25.789. Six self-contained units with cooking facilities 10km from Avarua and 7km from Rarotongan Resort Hotel on sandy beach.

AITUTAKI ISLAND

Aitutaki Resort Hotel. *Deluxe.* Box 342, Rarotonga. Phone 22.713. 25 fully self-contained cottages in tropic garden on own private island, linked to Aitutaki by causeway. Full bar and restaurant with games room, native-craft center, gift

THE COOK ISLANDS

shop, marina, swimming pool, and glass-bottomed boat. All water-sport and diving facilities and adjacent to a nine-hole golf course.

Rapae Cottage Hotel. *Expensive.* Box 65 Rarotonga. Phone 22.888. Close to main Aitutaki village in tropic garden. 12 units with one double and one single bed, two catering for families of up to six. All self-contained and include insect screens, ceiling fans, and sundecks. Hotel has restaurant and bar and features weekly island feast and dancing. Cruises, fishing, and diving available.

Tiare Maori Guesthouse. *Moderate.* Box 65, Rarotonga. Phone 26.300. Six rooms at Ureia, three-minute walk from post office and shop.

ATIU ISLAND

Atiu Motel. *Moderate.* Box 79, Rarotonga. Two self-contained units with tennis courts; motorcycles for hire.

MAUKE ISLAND

Tiare Holiday Cottage. *Inexpensive.* Write Tiare Cottage, Mauke, Cook Islands. Three cottages with share cooking and bathroom block.

HOW TO GET AROUND. There is no transport problem for the tourist on Rarotonga, with public and private vehicles readily available.

A local **bus** company operates an hourly service around the island (21 mi. clockwise, 20 mi. on the inside lane in the opposite direction) from 7 A.M. to 4 P.M. weekdays and 7 A.M. to noon on Saturdays. Most hotels have their own bus services to Avarua.

Cook Islandair's Britten-Norman Islander **aircraft** fly scheduled services from Rarotonga to Aitutaki, Atiu, Mitiaro, and Mauke, and *Air Rarotonga* flies a Beechcraft twin to Aitutaki, Atiu, Mauke, and Mangaia. Charter aircraft are available for island hopping and scenic flights.

A local **shipping** company operates overnight voyages to the outer Cook Islands; however, because of varying cargo demands and weather, services are not definite until a few days before departure.

Rarotonga has several reliable **taxi** services available 24 hours a day. Fares are government controlled and are displayed in each cab.

Most stores and hotels rent **bicycles,** which are convenient, since the round-Rarotonga road follows the lagoon and is quite flat.

Several **rental-car** companies are well established in Rarotonga and are always in high demand. Car bookings should be made before arrival. The major companies: *Budget,* Box 607, phone 20.888; *Cook Islands Rental Cars,* Box 326, Phone 24.442; *Avis,* Box 79; *TOA Rental Cars,* Box 327, phone 20611; *Tipani Rentals,* Box 72, phone 22.327; *Vaima Rentals,* Box 1043, phone 22.2222.

Driving is on the left, and tourists must have a current Cook Islands' driving license, available from the police station in Avarua on presentation of their own license.

TOURIST INFORMATION. *Cook Islands Tourist Authority,* Box 14, Rarotonga; Phone 29.435.

TOURS. Rarotonga, small though it is, offers a variety of organized and special-interest tours including a cross-island walk through the mountainous interior, a round-island sightseer, reef walks, beach barbecues, and a day trip to Aitutaki. Book through *Stars Travel,* Box 75, phone 23.669; *South Seas Travel,* Box 49, phone 22.327; *Tipani Tours,* Box 4, phone 22.792; *Union CITCO,* Box 54, phone 21.780; *Trans Pacific Travel,* Box 511, phone 20.660.

Cruises. Deep-sea fishing is immensely popular out of Rarotonga, and a number of companies offer specialized service. *Samaki Tu.* Dan Webb hires out the 20-ft. *Samaki* to four people for a five-hour trip at $NZ50 a person. Packed lunch provided. Box 468; phone 23.334.

Blue Water Adventures. The 32-ft. *Don Quixote* takes an unspecified number of fishing enthusiasts for a three-hour voyage under the command of Trevor

Nicholson. Lunch and drinks provided at $NZ50 a person. Box 94; phone 21.225.

Aquaholics IV. Chris Mussell hires his boat out at $NZ250 and prefers groups of four. Food and drink are provided—and fish are guaranteed. Phone 22.161.

Don Beer Charters. Don charges $NZ40 a person for a five-hour fishing trip on his 24-ft. *Tangaroa II,* preferring groups of four. Lunch provided but bring your own drinks. Box 384; phone 21.525.

Seafari Charters. Elgin Tetachuk hires the 34-ft. *Seafari* to a maximum of six anglers for $NZ55 each and trips up to five hours. Snack lunch but bring your own drinks. The *Seafari* is also available, at $NZ350, for photographic cruises catering to up to 15 people. Box 148; phone 20.328.

Rarotonga Marine Zoo. The zoo charges $NZ20 a person for three- to five-hour trips on its 20-ft. *Bonny II.* Light lunch and nonalcoholic drinks included. Box 659; phone 22.450.

All deep-sea-fishing cruises share catches with tourist-fishers.

SPORTS. A beachside nine-hole golf course and grass tennis courts are available in Avarua, but most sporting activities in the Cooks are ocean oriented—swimming, diving, sailing, fishing, wind surfing, with equipment available for hire at most hotels and from tour operators.

The intervillage athletic competition, "kumete," is on June 2; the annual international lawn bowls tournament on June 26; the Rarotongan Open Golf Championship in July; the Nike 15km road race on Easter Monday; and the round-Rarotonga road race on November 8. All events attract international competitors.

NIGHTLIFE AND RESTAURANTS. Cook Islanders excel at dancing, singing, and drumming and all major hotels feature regular island nights with feasts of native food. Don't miss an evening or two at the quaint old *Banana Court* tavern-lounge in central Avarua, right alongside the betting shop. Open 11 A.M. to 11 P.M. Mondays and Tuesdays and until midnight other days; closed Sundays. Dancing Wednesday through Saturday nights with live local bands.

Quality restaurants have proliferated on Rarotonga to cater to visitors staying at the high proportion of motels on the island where it is estimated they eat out four or five nights a week. Almost a dozen restaurants have grown up on the round-island road, so that none is more than 20 minutes' drive from anywhere.

Brandis, one of the Rarotongan Hotel's three restaurants, is regarded as the island's best and is popular with tourists and locals alike, offering traditional and European meals. For a change, try the Mexican fare at the *Hacienda,* Chinese at the *Tangaroa* and *Hibiscus House,* Italian at the *Portogino,* and grills and seafood at the *Vaima.*

The *Tamure Hotel* offers good Polynesian and western dishes, and the *Outrigger* specializes in seafood and steaks. Other popular dining spots are *Romiads,* the *Kaena,* and *Metura's Cafe.* A top-class restaurant specializing in seafood is due to open midway through 1986 on the waterfront at Avarua.

DEPARTURE TAX. $NZ20.

AMERICAN SAMOA

Polynesia Imperfect

by
GRAEME KENNEDY

Step out of a cab in Fagatogo after the 30-minute drive along the stunning seascape from Tafuna Airport and you know you're still in Samoa—but a very different Samoa from the one to the west you might have just left. For unlike Apia, with its leisurely, Old World charm and pace, Pago Pago bears the unmistakable stamp of the Stars and Stripes and all that goes with them. This doesn't make American Samoa better or worse—just different.

This U.S. territory (a domestic flight from Honolulu), has a total land area of just 76 square miles spread over six islands ranging from the tiny atoll Swains Island (population 34 at last count) in the north, through the 54-square-mile Tutuila, to the eastern Manua group of Tau, Olosega, and Ofu.

Pago Pago Bay, on Tutuila, recognised as the Pacific's most spectacular deepwater port—and therefore possessing a major U.S. navy base—is dominated by 2,142-foot Mount Matafao to the west and 1,609-feet Mount Alava atop the eastern coast of the bay, reached from Pago's downtown area, Fagatogo, by a cable car on the world's longest unsupported aerial tramway. The town, a mixture of modern and old, clings to the harbor shores under steep jungle curtains, their tops often hidden by the clouds that bring the 120 inches of annual rainfall which prompted Somerset Maugham's classic short story "Rain." The tale was dramatized and filmed as *Sadie Thompson,* after a Pago Pago prostitute and town character whose name now adorns the lounge-bar at the Rainmaker Hotel, built at the port entrance under 1,178-foot Mount Pioa—Rainmaker Mountain.

Pago is a happy town across the bay from three fish canneries where Korean, Japanese, and American deep-sea-fishing fleets come and go with their catches of tuna. With the U.S. sailors, the Asian fishers lend the Polynesian territory an exotic and colorful atmosphere.

The U.S. government pumps millions of dollars into its Samoan territory annually, and it shows. American television is beamed live by satellite into the most remote villages; the first major building you'll pass on the drive in from the airport is the Lyndon B. Johnson Tropical Medicine Center; Fagatogo supermarkets are crammed with American goods; and the U.S. flag flies high over the town.

Less influenced is the Manua group to the east, relatively undeveloped and with only one tourist motel, on Olosega. The territory's highest peak, 3,050-foot Lata Mountain, towers over the main island, Tau, where the twin villages of Si'ufaga and Luma were the object of anthropologist Margaret Mead's studies that led to her book *Coming of Age in Samoa.* Published in 1928, it depicted the Samoan people as sexually guilt-free, relaxed, highly intelligent and adhering to their thousand-year-old lifestyle. Mead died at 77 in 1978, five years before New Zealander Derek Freeman published his *Margaret Mead: The Making and Unmaking of an Anthropological Myth.* He argued that Samoans were, in fact, jealously violent and often turned to rape, murder, assault, and suicide.

It is still debated whether Manua or Savaii was the true ancient Samoa, the cradle of Polynesia from which these handsome people grew. Many legends and stories that are the basis of Samoan tradition and ceremony can be traced to incidents that occurred on Tau island.

Archaeologists believe that Polynesians had established themselves on the eastern shores of Tutuila about 600 B.C. and lived peacefully

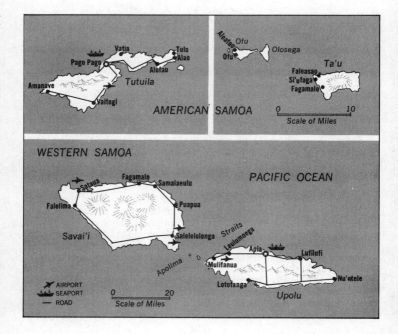

AMERICAN SAMOA

isolated from the western world until Dutch navigator Jacob Roggeveen became the first European to see the islands, in 1722.

Roggeveen sailed on without landing after inaccurately fixing their position, and Samoa remained undisturbed for another 40 years before whites "rediscovered" the islands. They avoided them for decades after learning of the massacre of eleven members of a French scientific expedition led by Captain Jean François La Pérouse at Aasu, near Fagasa, across Tutuila from Pago Pago, in 1787. The site is now known as Massacre Bay, and a monument and cross erected by the French government in 1883 still stands.

The first real outside influence arrived with missionary John Williams and his ship *Messenger of Peace* in 1831. The islanders grasped Christianity with enthusiasm and were prepared when they were caught up in the wave of colonial expansion in the late 1830s. The United States, seeking suitable coaling ports in the Pacific, took over Tutuila in 1900 and the Manua group four years later while Germany gained possession of Upolu and Savaii to the west. With no official colonial administration, President McKinley declared the islands the responsibility of the U.S. Navy, with Commander B. F. Tilley formally accepting the deed of cession from all but one of the major chiefs, Tuimanua, from Tau. He did not sign for five years; then his people were granted the privileges of their new association with the United States.

With World War looming, Tutuila took on a new importance, and Pago became a vital training and staging area for the Marine Corps. Roads, air strips, docks, and hospitals were built, shattering the Samoans' quiet lives for all time. Many Samoans joined the Marines and began the flood of islanders who would migrate to the United States and build new lives there.

The military left in 1945 as suddenly as it had come, and Tutuila reverted to its prewar peace and quiet.

Administration was moved from the navy to the Department of the Interior under President Truman, and for more than 10 years the distant territory stagnated until, in 1961, President Kennedy sent a new governor, H. Rex Lee, to Pago Pago with instructions to get the islands moving. That he did, bringing the islands into the twentieth century and building the foundations for the Polynesian-American society that thrives today.

Tutuila is a surprising piece of the United States. Set in the South Pacific with soaring green-jungled mountains, crashing waterfalls, and superb beaches backed up by an efficient tourism infrastructure—it's not pure Polynesia, but it is fun.

PRACTICAL INFORMATION FOR
AMERICAN SAMOA

WHEN TO GO. American Samoa's rainfall is notorious, with more than 14 inches falling in an average December and more than 12 inches a month until April, when trade winds strengthen, humidity drops, and the dry season begins. Wet-season temperatures average around 80.5°F, falling to the high 70s midyear. Even in the rainy season, long periods of sunshine can be expected.

Average Temperature (°Fahrenheit) and Humidity

Pago Pago	Jan	Feb	Mar	Apr	May	June	July	Aug	Sept	Oct	Nov	Dec
Average max. day temperature	87°	86°	86°	87°	85°	84°	83°	83°	84°	85°	86°	86°
Days of rain	25	22	22	24	20	18	19	18	18	22	21	23
Humidity, percent	76	76	76	76	76	77	75	74	73	76	76	75

General hints: The tourist season starts April-May; June to October are considered the most pleasant. Remember, Samoa is close to the equator, and the weather is tropical, warm and humid. It rains most of the year, but the bursts last only an hour or so.

WHAT TO WEAR. Anything comfortable and informal is the standard, with cotton or light washable clothes ideal all year. A light plastic raincoat is essential. Samoans have their own clothing standards, and bikinis or short shorts should not be worn outside your hotel.

HOW TO GET THERE. *Hawaiian Air* from Honolulu; *Polynesian Airlines* and *South Pacific Island Airways* from Western Samoa; *Air Pacific* from Fiji; and *Air Nauru* from Rarotonga. **Ferry** sails several times a week from Western Samoa. Pago Pago's Tafuna Airport is 6 miles from town.

ENTRY REQUIREMENTS. U.S. nationals need no travel documents; others need passports and visas. You can bring in one gallon of liquor and 200 cigarettes, 50 cigars, or one pound of tobacco.

CURRENCY. The U.S. dollar is used in American Samoa.

LANGUAGE. Both English and Samoan are spoken fluently.

TIPPING. This is not encouraged.

TIME ZONE. GMT less 11 hours; 3 hours behind U.S. Pacific Standard.

ACCOMMODATIONS. Rainmaker Hotel. Doubles run $52–$90; *fales* $62–$100. Box 996, Pago Pago. Phone 633.4241. Set on a point jutting into Pago Pago Bay, under Rainmaker Mountain, with 184 air-conditioned rooms and several beach *fales,* all with music and telephones. Convention facilities, pool, private beach, *Fia-Fia* coffee shop, *The Terrace* dining room, and the famous *Sadie Thompson* lounge bar. Tours arranged, boats and diving gear for hire.

Apiolefaga Inn. $38 double. Box 336, Pago Pago. Phone 699.9124. On coast 10 minutes from airport, 20 minutes to town; restaurant, pool, live band and dancing three nights a week, Polynesian floor show Friday nights. Eight self-contained air-conditioned rooms.

Herb and Sia's Motel. Box 430, Pago Pago. Phone 633.5413. In the center of Pago's shopping area, 15 air-conditioned island-style rooms. Rates on request.

Don and Ilaisa's Motel. Doubles $21–25. Box 932, Pago Pago. At Olosega Beach in the Manua group, with one air-conditioned and four standard rooms. Canoes, vehicles, and diving gear for hire.

AMERICAN SAMOA

HOW TO GET AROUND. Local **airline** services by *South Pacific Island Airways* at Tafuna Airport.

The public "aiga" **bus** operates unscheduled services from Fagatoga to Tutuila's outlying villages but stop running about 5 P.M.

Cabs are plentiful, and fares are government controlled.

Cars can be rented by the day, week, or month from *Scanlan's Rentals, Royal Samoan, Holiday Rental, Budget,* or *Avis,* Box 3457, Pago Pago; phone 699.1630; after hours, 699.1632.

The spectacular cross-harbor **cable car** from Solo Hill, above Government House in Fagatogo, to the summit of 1609-ft. Mt. Alava is not to be missed. The 12-passenger cab soars for one mile on the world's longest unsupported cable span. Open every day except Sunday from 8 A.M. to 4 P.M., the ride costs only a few dollars and offers superb views, especially early morning and late afternoon. Western Samoa and the Manua Islands can be seen from Mt. Alava.

TOURIST INFORMATION. Contact the *Office of Tourism,* Box 1147, Pago Pago, American Samoa.

TOURS. Two major tour companies offer a variety of special-interest and general sightseeing tours of Tutuila and the Manua group.

Both have offices in the Rainmaker Hotel and can arrange harbor sailings for around $25, all-day tours to the coastal villages for about $35, and a traditional village fia-fia for $25.

Spending a night with a Samoan family in a village can be arranged, but visitors should be aware of protocol to be observed as guests. The tourism office in Pago Pago can arrange for a guide to be with you to avoid embarrassment.

Sightseeing by light aircraft to Manua is around $50, with an overnight costing $80.

Contact *Samoa Tours and Travel Agency,* Box 727, Pago Pago. Phone main office 633.5884, Rainmaker office 633.4545. *Samoan Holiday and Travel Centre,* Box 986, Pago Pago. Phone main office 633.5336, Rainmaker office 633.4323,

SPORTS. Most recreation is water oriented, with swimming, surfing, and sailing the most popular pursuits. Snorkeling and scuba diving are excellent, with water visibility often exceeding 100 feet, giving superb views of coral reefs and fish.

Sport-fishing boats, catamarans, and yachts are available for hire—check at the hotel desk.

Ashore, tennis and volleyball courts are available, and visitors are welcomed at Pago Pago's spectacular golf club. Hiking trails through the steep jungle are popular. Two are close to Pago Pago: the trek to the top of Mt. Matafao and the climb to Mt. Rainmaker's peak, although this is for serious climbers only.

For spectator sports, villages and districts compete regularly in rugby and boxing, and competition between the five American Samoa high schools includes American football, basketball, and volleyball. The national sport, though, is kirikiti—a remarkable adaptation of the stately English game of cricket but now including American baseball influences. The number of players in a team will probably never be decided. Robert Louis Stevenson observed a game almost 100 years ago between sides of 100 men, women, and children. It is played with a hand-made rubber ball and a three-sided bat and is accompanied by much singing and dancing on the sidelines. Hotels and the downtown tourist office can advise times and venues.

SHOPPING. The Samoan Village at Pago Pago Park is a collection of fales built by American Samoa's old people and is devoted to traditional handicrafts such as shellwork, weaving, and carving. Aged citizens work at the center and sell their wares there. Good buys include puke and paper-shell necklaces, tapa prints, and woven pandanus ware such as place mats, bags, and baskets. Carved wooden kava bowls and tortoise shell are also of high standard.

American Samoa is a duty-free port, and several stores in Fagatogo and neighboring Utulei, as well as at Tafuna Airport, specialize in perfumes, cameras, and stereo and radio equipment.

NIGHTLIFE AND RESTAURANTS. Like Apia, Pago Pago has a wide variety of entertainment, ranging from the sophisticated *Rainmaker Hotel* to the rollicking atmosphere in the *Sadie Thompson* lounge bar or the *Pago Bar* or the local-favorite, the *Bamboo Room,* a block back from the water in the central bay area. *Samu's Diner* and the *Seaside Garden Club,* both right on the water, are good noisy fun. Other worthwhile nightspots include the *Tumua Palace,* the *Tiki Club,* and the *11th Frame.*

Elegant dining at the head of Pago Pago Bay is offered at *Soli's Restaurant,* built over the water and giving fine up-harbor views. The Rainmaker's *Terrace* dining room and *Fia Fia* coffee shop can provide just about anything from a hamburger to typical American and traditional Samoan meals, and you can eat Chinese at the downtown *Golden Dragon* or *Soli and Mark's* restaurant and disco. Other bay area restaurants offer Italian and Japanese menus.

WESTERN SAMOA

Where It's Really At

by
GRAEME KENNEDY

"You lie on a mat in a cool Samoan hut and look out on the white sand under the high palms and a gentle sea, and the black line of the reef a mile out and moonlight over everything. . . .

"And then among it all are the loveliest people in the world, moving and dancing like gods and goddesses.

"It is sheer beauty, so pure it is difficult to breathe in it."

Rupert Brooke, one of the many men of literature to become besotted by Samoa, wrote those lines almost 100 years ago; yet they remain just as relevant today.

For Western Samoa, the magic islands of Savaii and Upolu is Polynesia at its most pure. Savaii, they say, is the legendary Hawaiki from which the original Polynesian people set out to conquer the Pacific and settle north in Hawaii, south in the Cook Islands and New Zealand, and east in Easter Island.

Now the old migration is reversed, with tourists coming from America and Europe, Australia and Japan, New Zealand and Asia, all lured by the glistening beaches and lagoons that might be models for all others in the South Pacific, the clear freshwater inland lakes, high waterfalls, tumbling rivers, and lush-green highlands—and for Samoa itself. It is often said that the best thing about Samoa is simply being there, feeling the warmth of the people and the land, surrounded by the beauty Brooke and others wrote of and caressed by the heady scents of frangipani, poinciana, ginger flowers, bougainvilleas, and countless other tropical flowers filling the air.

They come to the new Faleolo international airport, opened late 1985 to 747 standards, a 40-minute drive from the island nation's capital, Apia. Since then, motels and cheaper accommodations have sprouted like mushrooms, a new 200-room hotel, the Royal Samoan, is scheduled to open early 1987 and the government has legislated to create a Western Samoan visitors' bureau to regulate and develop a tourism industry compatible with age-old customs and tradition.

Apia, a busy waterfront town of more than 30,000 people on the north coast of Upolu, is flanked to the east by its deepwater port and the impressive Fono (parliament buildings) on Mulinuu Point to the west. Once a center of intrigue where foreign consuls plotted the annexation of the South Pacific by colonial powers, and a gathering place for trading schooners, sealers, and whalers, Apia is still a romantic South Seas port town. Modern office buildings now stand alongside colonial wooden structures, with their wide verandas and palm-treed charm. The old post office and the Burns Philp store are wonderfully preserved examples of early-1900s architecture.

Apia stretches itself, warm and lazy, around the bay to embrace the colorful, noisy New Market, where villagers bring their produce, fish, live turtles, and handicrafts for sale from predawn until late, late night. There are restaurants, bars, memorials, parks, shops, and government offices within Apia's arms, shared with tourist hotels such as the Tusitala and Aggie Grey's, both bearing the names of Samoan legends.

Aggie, 89 years old in 1986 and only recently wheelchair bound, is the Pacific's last living legend, whose name became synonymous with Bloody Mary from Michener's *Tales of the South Pacific*.

Michener and Aggie are good friends, and although his Mary of book, stage, and screen was actually an old tobacco-chewing harridan from the New Hebrides (now Vanuatu), she could easily have been modeled on the incredible Aggie. Aggie first met Michener when he was serving with the U.S. Navy during World War II and, like thousands of others, found a home away from home at Aggie's then-modest guesthouse on the waterfront. A luxury guest fale at her now-magnificent hotel is named for the author, as are others for actress Roberta Hayes and actor Gary Cooper, who shared her hospitality when they starred in the sixties movie adaptation of Michener's *Return to Paradise,* filmed across Upolu at the dramatically beautiful Lefaga Beach. Twice widowed and left with six children at the height of German colonization, Aggie pestered the authorities until she was granted a license to run a club where Samoans could meet, talk, and drink together.

The Americans and their military machine marched up the Pacific toward Japan in the early 1940s, and they all ended up at Aggie's, transforming it into a U.S.-style hamburger bar and beer hall. That was the beginning, and now the soldiers, sailors, and airmen of the war years return as elderly tourists to have another beer with the legend.

The Scottish novelist Robert Louis Stevenson is also a legend in Samoa. They called him Tusitala—the teller of tales—and his tomb atop Mount Vaea, overlooking Apia and the bay, is almost a national shrine. It bears his immortal requiem: "Under the wide and starry sky/dig the grave and let me lie. . . . Home is the sailor, home from the sea, / and the hunter home from the hill."

Stevenson, suffering from tuberculosis, came to Samoa from Honolulu in 1888 in search of a place to recover his health and continue writing.

He wrote to a friend, "I go there only to grow old and die; but when you come, you will see it is a fair place for the purpose." Already famous, with *Treasure Island* published, Stevenson built a fine house at Vailima, at the foot of Mt. Vaea, and wrote prolifically in his last five years, producing novels such as the controversial *The Beach at Falesa, The Ebb Tide,* and *The Wrecker.* He died on December 3, 1894, while preparing a salad for dinner. A steep track has been cut up the mountain to his tomb; tourists are advised to make the journey in the early morning, before the heat of the day. Vailima, beautifully restored, is the official residence of the head of state, the Malietoa Tanumafili. Permission to visit Vailima and its flowered, parklike grounds can be obtained from the Prime Minister's Department in Apia.

But Western Samoa is much more than Apia and Vailima—Michener wrote that even the journey from Faleolo, past the 72 village churches, into town was "the most beautiful drive in the South Pacific." The road hugs the coast past neat villages, rugged seascapes, lagoons, and quiet pools until it bursts into the bustling Apia suburbs. Continuing east, the road weaves through some of the island's most colorful villages and scenery, climbs to Mafa Pass and its stunning views and on to the magnificent 160-foot Falefa Falls before plunging to the white sands and clear lagoon at Aleipata on the eastern tip of the island.

There, soak in the warm Pacific and gaze at the tiny off-shore islands Nuulua, Nuutele, Fanuatapu, and Namua. Return to Apia through dreamlike Mulivai Beach and savor its wide lagoon over a drink at Western Samoa's premier beach resort, the Samoan Hideaway. Also accessible by cross-island road over the highlands from Apia, the Hideaway is run by New Zealander Rob Poole and Australian Frank Byron in very laid-back style, from one of the best beach-bars in the Pacific.

Don't miss the sliding rocks at Papaseea, just five miles from Apia, where natural-rock water chutes give thrilling rides into a cool, shaded freshwater pool similar to that at Piula Cave, where cold, crystal waters flow from beneath the village Methodist church just a 30-minute drive inland from Apia. The same distance is Lake Lanoto'o, where you can swim in clear, fresh water teeming with goldfish. Difficult to reach, but it is worth the effort—engage a guide through your hotel.

The "big island" of Savaii is 1½ hours, or 13½ miles, to the west by ferry from Mulifanua, near Faleolo Airport. It's just seven minutes, by Polynesian Airlines, from Apia's air strip by the golf course at Fagalii, to the main town of Salelologa. Here are beaches and lagoons you've dreamed about—white sand that rarely bears a footprint, bird-filled forests unchanged since time began, lagoons so clear they can't be real. But to shake yourself back into the twentieth century (well, almost), be on the Salelologa wharf when the ferry docks from Upolu. Guitar-playing Samoans, with pigs, chickens, crates of beer, and much singing and laughter make every arrival a festival.

Wonderful islands, these, first sighted by Dutch navigator Jacob Roggeveen in 1722 and named the Navigator Islands by the Frenchman Bougainville 64 years later. Samoa's modern history began, as did many island's, with the pioneer missionary John Williams' arrival in 1830, and a stone cairn in Savaii's Sapapalii village marks the spot where he first set foot on the Samoas. Ten years later, the German trading firm Godeffroy and Sons established itself in the islands to trade in copra and encourage the Samoan people to grow produce for export as well as their own use.

Meanwhile, warring tribal factions under rival kings sought aid from the British, German, and U.S. powers in Apia in the late 1800s, prompting a show of naval force, wiped out by the great 1889 hurricane, which sank all but one ship (British) and ended what could have become a major confrontation. As a result, Germany administered

Western Samoa, the United States the east, and Britain quietly withdrew. Good colonists, the Germans established vast coconut plantations now operated by a Western Samoan quasi-government organization. World War I broke out in 1914, with New Zealand taking charge as the Germans retreated homeward. An unlikely colonial power, New Zealand's administration caused much friction, creating the Samoan chiefs' Mau movement, which culminated in a waterside confrontation in which more than a dozen Samoans were shot dead by New Zealand militia. A change of government in Wellington and the overpowering U.S. influence during World War II were the catalysts to Western Samoa's becoming the first independent Polynesian nation in January 1962. Thus began a gradual, graceful emergence into the twentieth century.

The population of 160,000 now includes the world's largest number of full-blooded Polynesians. Samoan is the purest surviving Polynesian type. A dignified people who love to sing and dance in the traditional way, they have adapted their lifestyle, based on Fa'a Samoa—the way of the ancestors—to western influences. The very basis of Samoan life is the aiga (*eye-ing-a*), or family, which extends far beyond parents and children to embrace a vast group of blood, marriage, and adopted members. At the head of each aiga is the matai, the acknowledged head of the family selected by consensus and responsible for directing the family's future, lands, and other assets.

Within the aiga is an unwritten law binding its members to house, feed, clothe, lend money to, or fight for others in the group if necessary, creating a philosophy toward property incompatible with western ideas. But it works well in Samoa, where most live on the land in the traditional style, growing their own food outside their thatched fales, catching fish in the lagoons, and selling a little produce at the markets for cash. Drive through any Samoan village and you will see women weaving and men carving and tilling their soil in the old way—and you realize that they are not doing this for the tourist.

It is the way of things.

It has been said that if a Samoan man has healthy children, a neat and comely wife, a house of his own, a canoe, a coconut palm, banana trees, and a few pigs, he has the intelligence to know he's well off.

And that isn't bad.

PRACTICAL INFORMATION FOR
WESTERN SAMOA

WHEN TO GO. Since it is close to the equator, Western Samoa's climate is hot and humid, although the fresh trade winds in the May-to-October dry season make life pleasantly comfortable despite an 84°F average. Temperatures average 86° and humidity soars in the November-to-April wet season, when rain will fall more than 75% of the time. Sea temperatures are ideal all year—mostly in the low 80s and rarely falling below 75°F.

Average Temperature (Farenheit) and Humidity

Apia	Jan	Feb	Mar	Apr	May	June	July	Aug	Sept	Oct	Nov	Dec
Average max. day temperature	86°	86°	86°	86°	86°	85°	84°	84°	85°	85°	86°	86°
Days of rain	24	24	19	24	13	13	11	11	21	18	15	22

WESTERN SAMOA

| Humidity, percent | 84 | 85 | 84 | 84 | 83 | 82 | 80 | 80 | 80 | 82 | 83 | 84 |

General hints: There is little climate variation between the two Samoas, although American Samoa has a heavier rainfall. Best time for visit in Western Samoa is June through November.

WHAT TO WEAR. Lightweight summer clothes with a light cardigan or sweater for cooler midyear nights are ideal. Apia is generally informal, and men seldom wear ties. Shirts and shorts are acceptable almost everywhere. In keeping with Samoan custom, women should wear dresses outside their hotel and should not be seen in the main streets wearing bikinis or other bathing suits.

HOW TO GET THERE. National flag carrier *Polynesian Airlines* links Western Samoa with Boeing 737 services to Tahiti, Rarotonga, Pago Pago, Auckland, Fiji, Tonga, and Sydney. Other international airlines operating into Faleolo include *Air New Zealand, Air Pacific,* and *Air Nauru. South Pacific Island Airways* flies daily between Pago Pago and Faleolo.

ENTRY REQUIREMENTS. A passport and onward travel bookings are required for stays of up to 30 days. Longer visits will require an entry permit obtainable from the immigration officer in Apia, Western Samoa, the high commissioner in Wellington, New Zealand, the consulate in Auckland, or from the Samoa mission to the United Nations in New York.

Visitors must make written declarations and are allowed one bottle of spirits and 200 cigarettes. Firearms, drugs, and indecent publications of any kind are prohibited.

Yellow fever vaccinations are necessary at press time.

LANGUAGE. Samoans generally use their own soft, musical Polynesian language, although English is the accepted language for government and commerce. English is widely spoken and understood in the most remote villages.

ELECTRICITY. About 50 square kilometers around Apia is served by hydroelectric and diesel-generated power. Supply is scarce in outlying districts, although some villages and hotels, like the Samoan Hideaway, have their own generators. Current is 240 volts AC, 50 Hz. Electric shaver adaptors are available in most hotels.

CURRENCY. Western Samoa's decimal currency is the *Tala*, broken into 100 sene. At press time, one American dollar buys 2.2 Tala. Foreign currency is accepted at major hotels and larger stores or can be exchanged at the Apia banks during business hours, 9:30 A.M. to 3 P.M. All credit cards are accepted at larger establishments, but check first with smaller restaurants.

TIPPING. This is not done in Western Samoa.

ACCOMMODATIONS. For double rooms, *Expensive* means $US35–50; *Moderate,* $US20–$US30; *Inexpensive,* below $US20.

Aggie Grey's Hotel. *Expensive.* Box 67, Apia. Phone 22.880. The best hotel in the Samoas—and probably in Polynesia outside Tahiti. 130 air-conditioned rooms, suites, and fales on the Beach Rd. waterfront in flower-garden setting with large swimming pool, two bars, and airy, elevated dining room. Now managed by Aggie's son Alan, the hotel will undergo a WST1.5 million renovation during 1986. Old Polynesian charm will be retained.

Tusitala Hotel. *Expensive.* Box 101, Apia. Phone 21.122. Has 96 air-conditioned double rooms on the waterfront, a short walk to the west of downtown. Swimming pool, conference room, bars, dining room.

Vaiala Beach Cottages: *Expensive.* Box 1157. Phone 22.202. This popular swimming beach is 1 mile from downtown Apia, just past the wharf and near the Jade Garden Chinese restaurant with seven cottages in garden grounds. All are self-contained and have cooking facilities. Good diving at Palolo Deep, 300 yds. away.

The Apian Way. *Moderate.* Box 617. Phone 21.482. Next door to the Tiafau with five double and one single. Air-conditioned rooms, restaurant, bar.

Samoan Hideaway. *Moderate.* Box 1191, Apia. Phone 23.800. Samoa's only beach resort. 30 units built on magnificent lagoon at Mulivai, 14 miles across Upolu from Apia. Licensed restaurant, bar, entertainment with traditional feasting, tennis courts, golf course, yachting, wind surfing, and outrigger canoes. Mulivai is famous for its reef diving, and a professional scuba center has been established there.

Tiafau Hotel. *Moderate.* Private Bag, Apia. Phone 21.141. Farther along Mulinuu Point, toward Parliament House, with 30 self-contained, air-conditioned rooms, licensed restaurant, three bars, and swimming pool.

Harbour Light Hotel. *Inexpensive–Moderate.* Box 8. Phone 21.103 or 21.933. 30 air-conditioned rooms, licensed restaurant and bar at wharf end of Apia waterfront.

Betty Moor's Guesthouse. *Inexpensive.* Box 18. Phone 21.085. Inland near wharf and 100 meters from Vaiala Beach with five single rooms, four twins, and two doubles. Share cooking facilities and showers.

Olivia Yandall's Casual Accommodation. *Inexpensive.* Box 4089. Phone 22.110. Two self-contained units, each with one single and two double bedrooms.

Seaside Inn. *Inexpensive.* Phone 22.578. Budget accommodation in Apia.

SAVAII ISLAND

Safua Hotel. *Expensive* (but rates include meals). Box 5002, Salelologa. Phone 24.262. Just north of Salelologa, on the beach in parklike grounds with restaurant, bar, and nine self-contained fales. Visitors are welcome in the nearby picturesque villages of Safua and Lalomalava.

Salafai Inn. *Expensive.* At Salelologa with guest-house-style accommodation, double rooms on spectacular beach. Meals available. Book through travel agents in Apia.

Salimu Hotel. *Expensive.* On beach with canoeing and snorkeling gear for hire. Bookings through travel agents in Apia.

Savaiian Guest Fale. *Expensive* (but rates include breakfast and dinner). At Salelologa, comfortable island-style accommodation. Book through travel agents in Apia.

Vaisala Hotel. Box 5002, Salelologa. Phone 24.262. Built on one of Savaii's prettiest beaches on the northwest corner of the island, featuring 18 self-contained units, restaurant, two bars, facilities for all water sports.

HOW TO GET AROUND. Internal **air services** to Savaii are operated by *Polynesian Airlines* using twin-engined light aircraft.

The *Western Samoa Shipping Corporation* has daily **ferry services** between Upolu and Savaii and a twice-weekly schedule to American Samoa. The service and departure times are irregular, and passengers should contact the corporation by phoning in Apia 20.935.

Public-transport buses are colorful wooden-seated and open-sided old vehicles ideal for tourists looking for a bit of adventure. They leave irregularly from the bus stand at the new market in central Apia. A 30-sene fare will take you through the town area or up into the hills through neighboring villages and plantations. Fares to the most distant villages are a maximum of about WST1.60. Buses also serve the coastal villages on Savaii Island.

Rental cars are plentiful. The license of your own country is acceptable, driving is on the right, and all signs are in English. Car-rental companies include *Pavitt's U-Drive* (phone 21.766), *Gold Star* (phone 21.711), *Avis Rentway* (phone 22.468).

WESTERN SAMOA

A host of richly decorated stereo-blasting **cabs** are available in Apia and include two radio-controlled services. Cabs can be telephoned or picked up at ranks outside the major hotels, downtown, and at the airport.

TOURIST INFORMATION. Contact the *Western Samoa Visitors Bureau*, Box 862, Apia. Phone 20.471.

TOURS. Guided bus and car tours are available to all places of major interest on Upolu. A limited tour service operates on Savaii, and travel agents in Apia should be contacted for information.

Tour companies on Upolu include: *Retzlaff's Tours*. English- and German-speaking guides in this long-established Western Samoan company. All entrance fees included in costs. Box 145; phone 21.724 or 21.725.

Gold Star Travel and Tours. Half-day tours available through Apia, to Stevenson's tomb, sliding rocks, Felafe Falls, and Piula Cave, full day to Mulivai, Aleipata Sands, Paradise Beach, and the Togitogiga Falls. Meals not included. Box 185; phone 20.466.

Samoa Scenic Tours. Specializing in two to four-hour tours, one taking in Apia township, royal tombs, Stevenson's home, Vailima, coffee plantations, the sliding rocks, and other attractions along the north coast to the east to Falefa Falls, plantations, the Mafa Pass, and return via Piula Cave Pool. Private car available. Box 669; phone 22.880.

Janes Tours. Jane Leungwai operates tours throughout Upolu from 2½ to 6 hours, taking in all places of interest and popular spots. Minimum numbers are eight in a coach and four by car. Box 70; phone 20.954 or 20.218.

Union Travel and Tours. Operating station wagons and specializing in groups, Union offers half- and full-day tours of Upolu. Box 50; phone 21.787.

SPORTS. Western Samoa has surprisingly excellent sporting facilities, dominated by the huge Apia Park stadium and tennis-court complex built to accommodate the South Pacific Games in 1983. Almost every village has a sports club, and rugby, soccer, basketball, netball, volleyball, hockey, and American football are played vigorously. Squash is becoming popular, and courts in Apia are a short stroll from Aggie Grey's toward the wharf. Phone 23.780 for reservations.

The *Apia Park tennis courts* are open every day, including Sundays, and cost 50 sene per player per half-hour. Reservations can be made on 22.571.

The *Royal Samoan Golf Club* at Fagalii in suburban Apia is the site of the Royal Samoan Open Golf Championship every August. Visitors are welcome, and arrangements to pay greens fees can be made at your hotel.

Lawn bowls are popular in Samoa and hotels or tour companies can direct you to the *Apia Bowling Club,* which has greens next to the Tusitala Hotel and at Apia Park.

Laser and Hobie cat yachts and wind surfers can be hired from *Samship Charters,* near the Tusitala Hotel. Phone 21.700.

SHOPPING. Samoan families have always made a wide range of articles for their personal use, and these are becoming increasingly popular to tourists for their quality and beauty of woods and fibers. The Samoan siapo (tapa) cloth, made from mulberry bark and painted with natural dyes, is a particular example. Woven mats and baskets, hand-carved bowls, shell jewelry, and bright native prints are all attractively priced in the handcraft store on Beach Rd. and at the family stalls in the New Market in downtown Apia.

The Philatelic Bureau above the main post office sells examples of Samoa's prize-winning postage stamps, and commemorative issues of Samoan coins are available in mint sets from the Treasury Department.

All duty-free items are available from two stores at Faleolo Airport.

THE SOUTH PACIFIC

NIGHTLIFE AND RESTAURANTS. Apia is a swinging nighttime town, with more liquor licenses, rock bands, bars, and clubs per square mile than any other Polynesian island outside Hawaii. Add to those the thundering fia-fias held almost nightly at one hotel or another, and you've got a lot of nightlife.

FIA-FIAS

Fia-fia literally means "fun" and an opportunity to take in a huge slice of Western Samoan culture and excitement in one gulp. Friday night at *Aggie Grey's Hotel* is the scene for the islands' most spectacular fia-fia, with centuries-old drumming underlining warlike dancing led by heavily-tattooed Dominic, who doubles as a headwaiter in the hotel dining room. He is followed by the women's performance, often led by Aggie's granddaughter Alana, who demonstrates the traditional siva—a dreamy and sensuous dance not unlike Hawaii's hula. The climax of the show is a drumming, whirling fire dance, an electrifying performance. Next comes the feasting—mountains of whole spit-roasted pig, chicken, fish, hams, salads, and that Polynesian delight palusami, young taro-leaf tops steamed with coconut cream to be savored with any dish.

Other worthwhile fia-fias are at the *Samoan Hideaway*, the *Tiafau*, and the *Tusitala*.

COCKTAILS

Predinner drinks are almost compulsory in Samoa, and Apia abounds in pleasant bars, most on the waterfront and facing the sunset. Try *Otto's Reef* (phone 22.691), but don't expect the Ritz, just good drinks and plenty of fun, especially if Otto is there. The *Tusitala's* bar is cavernous and, open both sides, attracts the cooling evening breezes. Almost next door is the *Beachcomber*, relatively new and happily run American-style by Tessa and Horst. The bar at *Aggie's* is comfortably airy.

RESTAURANTS

Eateries are many and varied, from the seemingly endless range of western and Samoan dishes offered at *Aggie's* to the authentic Chinese menu at the *Jade Garden*, a stately old colonial home near the beach at Vaiala, just outside Apia (phone 22.489), and the fine steaks at *Amigo's*, on Vaea St. at Saleufi (23.140). The *Apia Inn*, on Beach Rd. overlooking the harbor, is air-conditioned, with cool decor and splendid service specializing in European dishes (21.010), and the *Poly-Eurasian Restaurant* (21.996) has a menu to match its name.

LATE NIGHT

Late-nighters in Apia have no excuse to simply sit in their hotel rooms—you can rock way past midnight here.

Start at *Jerome's Cove*, just a short stroll toward the wharf from Aggie's, where Jerome Grey (no relation) hosts a cabaret-bar at the top of a flight of steep wooden steps. Grey is a superb musician. He returned home in the early eighties after playing jazz piano for several years in San Francisco and wrote the island's unofficial anthem, "We Are Samoa." Dancing; good drinks and prices (22.769).

A five-minute walk in the cool night breezes toward town brings you back to *Otto's*, where, on Friday and Saturday nights and for a WST1 door charge, you can hear top Apia rock bands playing their own compositions. Very loud but much fun. Just two doors down is the *Love Boat* (24.065), an upstairs restaurant-bar with dancing and live music that opened only four years ago. If you miss it, don't worry too much.

Get a WST1 cab from the Love Boat into Apia and *Donovan's Reef* (23.187), a wonderfully wild and wacky bar with live band and dancing. Donovan's is a must—but be wary of the exterior flight of wooden steps when you're leaving.

There are several other so-called nightclubs in Apia, featuring deafening disco and live music in dark, gloomy interiors. Don't go.

For something totally different in late-night entertainment, head for the *New Market* and follow your nose. Food stalls abound, it seems, open 24 hours a day and offering such Samoan fare as barbecued mutton flaps and chicken backs with fried vegetables and island chop suey—vermicelli with meat, soya sauce, and spices—all starting at around WST3. Don't expect china and silver cutlery, but it's fun.

DEPARTURE TAX. WST 20.

TONGA

Ancient Polynesia Still

by
GRAEME KENNEDY

The Pacific's only surviving monarchy and the only island group never colonized, Tonga sprawls poor but proud just east of the international date line between 15 degrees and 23.5 degrees south, a scattering of 169 islands in 140,000 square miles of ocean.

With a total land area of just 258 square miles and only 36 islands inhabited, the 92,000 native Tongans subsist as Polynesia's poorest people. The biggest problem is a lack of land. Under Tongan law, every male over 16 is entitled to an 8¼-acre allotment on which to plant crops and eventually raise a family. There is simply not enough land to go around, but large-scale emigration is prevented by strict entry laws and quota systems in favored countries, notably New Zealand.

So Tongans are trapped at home—with a 3.6 percent annual population growth and a fragile agricultural economy based on erratic export prices for copra, bananas, and coconut products. Tonga is actively encouraging tourism as a reliable source of foreign exchange, although the economy is still propped up by cash aid grants and development projects from wealthier nations, especially New Zealand, Australia, and West Germany. Tonga, though, offers the tourist no more—and in many areas a lot less—than other Polynesian destinations, and this is probably why the kingdom welcomed fewer than 4,000 guests last year.

Tonga's outer island groups, especially Vava'u and Ha'apai, have wonderful beaches and superb lagoons—but so do other Pacific islands that have much more rewarding exchange rates with the U.S., Australian, or New Zealand dollars.

But Tonga is quaint and historic. Its ruler, King Taufa'ahau Tupou IV, is able to trace his origins back to the Tu'i Tonga chiefs who reigned more than 1,000 years ago, and archaeologists believe the islands were inhabited as early as the fifth century. The first Europeans there were the Dutch navigators Schouten and Lemaire in 1616. They were followed by Tasman, Wallis, and Cook, who named the group The Friendly Islands. Captain Bligh had cause to remember Tonga—the *Bounty* mutiny occurred in Tongan waters.

The missionaries arrived in the 1820s, and their influence helped in 1845 to end the savage tribal wars that had raged for 50 years. King George Tupou I was proclaimed ruler, beginning the dynasty that survives today under Tupou IV—a big 22-stone (308-pound) man who needs two aircraft seats whenever he flies overseas, which is often. Tongans accept and revere their royal family, despite the vast and obvious differences in living standards and wealth: Three-quarters of the working population are employed on plantations, and others seek a livelihood from the sea. Able navigators and fishers, Tongans until recently still hunted whales with hand harpoons.

The women are skilled at mat weaving, basket work, and producing tapa cloth, although the younger population, eyes opened to the twentieth century by tourism and stories from their contemporaries who have experienced the great mecca that is Auckland, New Zealand, often show little interest in continuing with traditional pursuits.

Men and women in Tonga wear the skirtlike *tupanu,* or *vala*—men to the knee and women to the ankle. Women wear a decorative waistband, the *kiekie,* and men a woven mat, the *ta'ovala,* tied with belts of coconut fiber. Both are signs of respect for elders and the royal family.

Since the first missionaries came to Tonga around 180 years ago, Christianity has dominated local life and stamped it with attitudes approaching priggishness. Until recently, swimming and dancing were banned on Sundays and even now any loud activity is discouraged on Sundays, when no public transport operates, international airline flights are banned, inter-island shipping is canceled—and you won't find a drink anywhere outside the bigger hotels. Almost every Tongan will attend church on Sunday, and harmonized hymn singing is almost the only sound heard throughout the islands. The official church is Wesleyan, with Tupou IV its head, but almost all denominations are represented here. The Mormons, especially, have a huge following.

Tongatapu, the most populous island (with 61,000 people), is quite flat and covered by coconut plantations. It has cliffs to the south but a wide lagoon embracing 12 small islands along its northern coast. Here is Tonga's capital, Nukualofa, a ramshackle town with a handful of modern buildings housing the Bank of Tonga and some administrative departments. The king's 120-year-old Victorian-style royal palace and chapel, surrounded by tall Norfolk pines, dominates the waterfront just along from Queen Salote Wharf, where cruise ships occasionally tie up. Almost in the center of town are the much-photographed royal tombs, where Tongan royalty has been buried since 1893.

Other monuments left by ancient kings remain on Tongatapu. At the ancient capital of Mu'a is the Langi—the vast terraced tombs where the Tu'i Tonga were laid to rest in huge slabs of hewn rock to create the closest thing to a pyramid in Polynesia.

Farther around the coast, at Tongatapu's northeast corner, is the 1,000-year-old Ha'amonga trilithon—a 5-meter-high gateway of carved coral rock topped by a 6-meter rock lintel. The stones are estimated to weigh about 40 tons each, and legend says they were brought by canoe to Tonga from Wallis Island. Deep-etched lines in the crosspiece point directly to the rising sun on the longest and shortest days, indicating that the ancient kings might have used the trilithon as an early seasonal calendar.

Across the island and nine miles from Nukualofa are the blowholes, known as *Mapu-'a-Vaea,* or Chief's Whistle, for the whistling noise made by the surf as 18-meter geysers blast into the air as far as you can see along the coastal cliffs. Near Mu'a, on the inland lagoon and 12 miles from town, is the old 'ovava tree under which Captain Cook rested when he visited Tonga in the *Endeavour* more than 200 years ago. A monument was placed at the spot in 1970.

Along the north coast on roads made reasonable by overseas aid programs, one of the strangest tourist "attractions" on any island is a collection of tall trees at the beachside village of Kolovai, where thousands of bats, or flying foxes, spend the day hanging upside-down, chattering and smelling. They are sacred and can be hunted only by members of the royal family. Visitors will miss little by avoiding the bats' pungent, stringy, tough flesh.

Eua Island, 40 kilometers southeast of Tongatapu, is a complete contrast to the main island, with rolling hills, high cliffs, and streams tumbling through a natural forest that is the home for a variety of tropical birds, particularly the Eua parrot, kingfishers, and blue-crowned lorikeets. Population is around 4,000.

The Haapai group, 160 kilometers north of Tongatapu, is a flat, thin archipelago featuring the live volcano Tofua and the extinct Kao. It has many fine beaches, lagoons, and reefs and is home to about 10,000 Tongans.

Another 112 kilometers north is the Vavau group, the finest among the Tongan islands and with a population around 13,000. The seas around the main island are sprinkled with 17 others, smaller and separated by deep, narrow channels leading into the fiord-like approach to the main town, Neiafu. This natural harbor has been known for centuries as Port of Refuge and is one of the Pacific's most beautiful. The Paradise International Hotel lies at its head, and jungle-clad Mount Talau rears above, giving spectacular views across freshwater Lake Tuanuku and the group's larger islands, Pangai Motu, Kapa, Nuapapa, and Hunga.

A Tongan friend once explained that "Nukualofa is the worst of our country—but Vavau is the best."

He was not wrong.

PRACTICAL INFORMATION FOR TONGA

WHEN TO GO. Tonga's climate is slightly cooler than that of most other tropical islands, but it shares their seasonal division into "summer" wet and "winter" dry seasons. The dry months are May, June, and July, when the average temperature falls to 21, 22, and 23°C—about four degrees below the wet-season averages. Rainfall drops from around 2,450mm in Feb. to only .860mm in June. In the capital, Nukualofa, the mean annual temperature is 24.7°C, humidity 76.9%, and rainfall 1,775.5mm. Temperature, rainfall, and humidity increase in the northern island groups.

Average Temperature (°Fahrenheit) and Humidity

Nukualofa	Jan	Feb	Mar	Apr	May	June	July	Aug	Sept	Oct	Nov	Dec
Average max. day												

TONGA

temperature	83°	84°	83°	82°	79°	78°	76°	76°	76°	78°	80°	82°
	Jan	Feb	Mar	Apr	May	June	July	Aug	Sept	Oct	Nov	Dec
Days of rain	17	17	20	15	14	12	12	12	12	12	12	14
Humidity, percent	76	78	79	77	74	74	72	72	71	70	71	73

General hints: Best tourist months are May through November. Heavy rains begin in December and last through March; humidity is high in this period. It's a good idea to have a sweater along for the cool July and August evenings.

WHAT TO WEAR. Tongans, like other Polynesians, adhere to the teachings of the early missionaries in their attitudes to modesty. The law here forbids any person from appearing in a public place without a shirt or blouse, and this is strictly enforced. Brief shorts, bikinis, and other swimwear are fine at the beach or poolside but are frowned upon in public. Although Tonga is cooler than other tropical islands, casual dress is recommended; however, a light pullover or stole should be packed for evenings in the June-to-September dry season. Bring an umbrella or a light raincoat at any time of the year.

HOW TO GET THERE. *Polynesian Airlines* and *Air New Zealand* fly into Tonga's Fuaamotu Airport from Pago Pago, Apia, and Auckland, New Zealand. *Air Pacific* flies in from Auckland, Nadi, and Suva. Negotiations were begun late 1985 for Australia's Ansett Airlines to back an airline venture linking Tonga to Sydney direct, but no progress had been made by mid-1986.

ENTRY FORMALITIES. Visitors must have passports, ongoing tickets, and adequate funds to qualify for a 30-day permit, extensions to which can be granted up to a maximum of six months. Visas are required by all but citizens of Commonwealth or European Economic Community countries. Health certificates are no longer required in Tonga.

CURRENCY. Tonga's unit of currency is the *pa'anga*, which is tied to no fixed rate of exchange with any other country. It is totally worthless outside Tonga. The *pa'anga* is divided into 100 units called *seniti*, so that the terms dollars and cents ($T) are frequently used. Foreign currency and traveler's checks can be changed at the Bank of Tonga in Nukualofa or Vavau. $US1 gets you about $T1.45.

ELECTRICITY. Electricity is diesel generated and available in Nukualofa and at larger hotels. Current is 230 volts AC, 50 Hz.

TIPPING. This is not encouraged in Tonga.

LANGUAGE. Most Tongans understand and speak some English, but that does not necessarily end the language problem. A Tongan "yes" can mean a "no," since Tongans will often say what they think will please you rather than what they mean. This can be frustrating.

TIME ZONE. GMT plus 13 hours; 21 hours ahead of U.S. Pacific Standard.

ACCOMMODATIONS. The Tongan Visitors Bureau regularly inspects accommodations offered to ensure they maintain standards justified by the prices charged. Most have flush toilets, but don't expect hot water in the smaller, cheaper guesthouses. Boil water before drinking in areas outside Nukualofa. Tonga offers a variety of hotels, motels, and guesthouses, but Tonga veterans will advise you to pay a little extra rather than try to subsist in "budget" accommodations.

EUA ISLAND

Leipua Lodge. Mr. Lilo Vaka'uta, Box 1, Ohonua, Eua. 3km from the wharf and 15 minutes' drive from Kaufana Airport; four rooms with two single beds and three rooms, each with a double bed. Rate $T4—with all meals, an extra $T4.

HAAPAI ISLAND

Evaloni Guest House. Miss Sitali, Huakau, Pangai, Haapai. Five minutes' walk from wharf, with two single rooms and one double at $T10 single and $T18 double.

Fonongava'inga Guest House. Mr. Pita Vimahi, Pangai, Haapai. In town, with four single, two double rooms. $T8 single, $T16 double includes all meals.

Niuatoputapu Island Fita Motel. Fita Motel, Hihifo, Nivatoputapa, Haapai. Four fale units sharing bathroom, dining room, and lounge on the Hihifo waterfront for $T4.50 single and $T8 double. Good swimming, barbecue, picnics.

Seletute Guest House. Mrs. Seletute Falevai, Pangai, Haapai. ½ km from Taufa'ahau Wharf, with two single rooms at $T24 and two doubles at $T20 per person. All meals included. Horse and bicycle rentals; airport transport $T3.

TONGATAPU ISLAND

Angie's Guest House. Neiafu, Vavau. Next door to the Tufuolou, Angie's has two double bedrooms and two single beds. Rates are $T3.50 single, $T7 double.

Beach House. Box 18, Nukualofa; 21–060. Less than 1km from Nukualofa overlooking harbor, with 10 double rooms sharing two bathrooms, dining room, lounge, veranda, and gardens. Rates from $T15 with all meals. Bed and breakfast only $T7.50.

Captain Cook's Vacation Apartments. Six self-contained two-bedroom units 1.5km from the town center with rates from $T25 single to $T31 double.

Fafa Island Resort. Box 42, Nukualofa; 22–800. A 30-minute launch trip after a 6.4km drive north of Nukualofa gets you to this comfortable island with good swimming, snorkeling, and diving beach. Fafa has eight fales, with bar and restaurant listing French and local meals. Wind surfing, boating, and fishing trips available on request. Rates from $T12 single and $T16 double; extra bed $T6. Transport to the island is $T6.

Falemaama Motel. Box 387, Nukualofa; 22–560. A quiet spot down on the lagoon 4km from the center of Nukualofa with nine two-bedroom fales, all with full kitchen facilities and three with hot showers. Rates $T8 single, $T12, double or $T50 a week with hot shower, $T40 with cold.

Fasi-Moe-Afi Guest House. Box 316, Nukualofa; 22–289. Alongside the tourist bureau and charging $T5 and $T7 single and $T8 and $T12 double. Coffee shop open daily.

Friendly Islander Motel. Box 142, Nukualofa; 21–900. One of the better ones, 3km from Nukualofa, with swimming pool and 12 modern suites with fully equipped kitchens, private balconies, fans, radios, and telephones. Prices range from $T22 single to two-bedroom suites at $T35.50, plus $T5 for an extra child.

Good Samaritan Inn. Box 306, Nukualofa, 41–022. Twenty-four fale units spread along Kolovai Beach, 20km from Nukualofa. Share bathroom; dining room, lounge, and barbecue. Rates from $T5. Family fale for five to seven people $T30 a day. Full French-style restaurant available.

Haatafu Beach Motel. Box 490, Nukualofa; 41–088. Overlooking impressive Haatafu Beach and Marine Park 21km west of Nukualofa, offering seven two-bedroom fales and restaurant. Share bathrooms; dining room, barbecue. Rate $T6.50. Tongan floor show in restaurant.

International Dateline Hotel. Box 39, Nukualofa; 21–411. Famous old Pacific hotel on the waterfront in Nukualofa with 76 rooms ranging from $T35–$T39 single to $T41–$T45 double and triple; a couple with one child may stay from $T47–$T51 per night. Swimming pool in fine garden setting, tennis court. Meals average $T10 for dinner.

TONGA

Joe's Tropicana Hotel. Just round the corner from the Dateline, with 14 private-facility rooms from $T20 single and $T30 double, including meals. Joe's has two bars and a restaurant.

K's Guest House. Near Nukualofa shopping center, with five double and four single rooms ranging from $T12 to $T24, meals included.

Moana Hotel. Box 169, Nukualofa; 21-440. Overlooking Faua Harbour 2km from town, the Moana has four double fales, each with private bathroom. Rates from $T5 single and $T9 twin.

Nukuma'Anu Hotel. Box 390, Nukualofa; 21-750. On the waterfront 2km from downtown and featuring one-, two-, and three-bedroom individual fales ranging from $T21 to $T44 daily.

Pangaimotu Island Resort. Box 740, Nukualofa; 21-155. Tonga fales set on 32-acre island 15 minutes by boat after a 2km drive from Nukualofa. Good swimming and snorkeling with rates $T5 single and $T9 double. Lunch $T6.

Ramanlal Hotel. Box 74, Nukualofa; 21-344. Center of commercial district with 25 self-contained and air-conditioned rooms with fully equipped kitchens, including bar, phone, refrigerator. Hotel has nightclub and restaurant. Rates $T34 single, $T39 double.

Sela's Guest House. Box 24, Nukualofa; 21-430. Twelve double and two single rooms sharing bathrooms, dining room, and lounge 2km from town. Rates $T12 a day, meals included. Also four self-contained units at $T20 a day.

Sunrise Guest House. Box 132, Nukualofa; 22-141. On the waterfront at Kolomotua, 1.5km from town, the Sunrise has three single rooms at $T16 and three single at $T30, meals included.

Tufumolou Guest House. Mrs 'Ofa Lafaele, Neiafu. Situated at the foot of Mount Olopeka at Neiafutahi on the beach known as Old Harbour; three double rooms with four single beds available. Rates $T3.50 single, $T7 double. Dinner $T7.

VAVA'U ISLAND

Paradise International Hotel. Box 11, Neiafu; 111. Until the late seventies known as the Port of Refuge Hotel, the Paradise is Tonga's lush hideaway—no other accommodation comes anywhere near it for ambience and beauty. It overlooks Port of Refuge Harbour—named by the early navigators for its sheltered and picturesque inlet dotted with islands and dominated by the group's capital, Neiafu. The Paradise Hotel has 32 units, all with private bathrooms and access to freshwater swimming and paddling pools, garden patio, dining room, and a small sandy beach. First-class rooms are $T39 single, $T46 double, with economy rooms $T28 single and $T34 double. Extra bed $T6; children under three free. Cable address is, appropriately, PARADISE.

Potauaine Tu'iniua Guest House. Mr. Pota Uaine, Neiafu. In the town center with 7 rooms with 4 single beds each. Rates $T4 to $T8.

Stowaway Village. Box 5, Neiafu. In Neiafu, with single rate from $T5 to $T8 and double from $T9.50 to $T15.50.

Vava'u Guest House. Box 148, Neiafu. Opposite the Paradise, with rates from $T4.50 single and $T6 after $T2 transport from airport. Bus tours of main island arranged from $T4.

TOURIST INFORMATION. Tonga Visitors Bureau, Box 37, Nukualofa, tel. 21-733.

HOW TO GET AROUND. Depending on the island you are visiting, transportation can range from comfortable sedan to bicycles and horses. On the main island of Tongatapu, buses, taxis, rentals, and the colorful—if uncomfortable—open-air three-wheel taxis known as *ve'etolu* are available. Public transport is very limited on the other islands and, along with shipping and air services, does not operate on Sundays. The other six days of the week, buses are cheap and run regularly through Nukualofa and Tongatapu. Inter-island ferries operated by the Shipping Corporation of Polynesia, Warner Pacific Lines, and several private companies link Nukualofa with the other island groups, but advance bookings cannot be made because schedules often change due to weather or other commitments.

THE SOUTH PACIFIC

Rental cars, mostly Japanese, are available from *Gateway Rental Cars* (Box 956, tel. 21–215), *Friendly Island Rental Car* (Box 142, tel. 21–900), and *Nukualofa Motors,* Taufaahau Road, Fanga.

Cabs are readily available, but be warned—fix a price for the trip before departure.

Domestic air services are provided by Tonga Air to Eua, Haapai, and Vavau. The airline has recently ordered a Spanish-built twin-turboprop 22-seater for its longer routes and was negotiating with the New Zealand government to provide air strips suitable for its operation.

Because Tongatapu is quite flat, bicycles are an ideal form of transport and can be hired cheaply in Nukualofa. Horses can be hired from Queen Salote Wharf when cruise ships are in. On other occasions, the Tonga Visitors Bureau can assist.

TOURS. *Tongatapu Island.* Tour operators provide a wide range of sightseeing and excursion tours and will be happy to bend regular itineraries to suit personal preferences. The Tonga Visitors Bureau, however, warns that some "operators" are not always reliable and visitors should arrange movements well in advance and have them confirmed in writing, especially outside Tongatapu.

All ground-tour operators on Tongatapu take groups on the most popular excursions. These include:

The Nukualofa Capital tour to the royal palace, the royal tombs, the Langa Fonua handicraft center, the Talamahu fruit and vegetable market, and the Havelu desiccated-coconut factory. Time is 2 hours and distance 16km.

The historical tour through the ancient capital of Mua and the burial grounds of the old kings to the trilithon and Captain Cook's landing place. Time is 3 to 4 hours and covers about 50km;

A cultural tour that enables visitors to meet Tongans in their villages and watch them preparing meals, making tapa cloth, and weaving baskets or mats. Time is 2½ hours, and distance depends on which villages are chosen;

The Hufangalupe tour to one of Tonga's most attractive sea vistas with a huge natural-coral bridge, towering cliffs, sandy beach and profuse bird life, which takes about 90 minutes and covers 30km;

Local identity Oscar Kami's Oholei Beach Feast, which is the one Tonga attraction not to be missed (visitors dine on traditionally cooked suckling pig, crayfish, and fruit in Hina's Cave, a natural theater formed from an ancient ocean blowhole) 5 hours for the 40km tour and feast;

The spectacular blowholes, the hideously impressive trees with flying foxes hanging like bunches of grapes at Kolovai, and lunch, a swim, and snorkeling at either Haatafu Beach or the Good Samaritan Inn; can be either a half- or full-day tour.

Tongatapu's ground tour operators include *Oholei Beach Tours* (Box 330, Nukualofa, tel. 21–707), *Jones Travel* (Box 34, Nukualofa, tel. 21–422), *Vital Travel and Tours,* (Box 838, Nukualofa, tel. 21–616), *Maamafo'ou Tours* (Box 229, Nukualofa, tel. 21–425), *Teta Tours* (Box 215, Nuku'alofa, tel. 21–688).

Pangaimotu Cruises operates the 2½-hour cruise and visit to Pangaimotu Island, which features swimming on fine white beaches, snorkeling, water skiing, and picnic lunches under the coconut palms. Check with Earl Emberson, Box 740, Nukualofa.

Nuku or Leo's Island is about an hour's launch trip from Nukualofa for a day trip of fishing, swimming, snorkeling, and picnicking on the perfect island to do just about anything. Contact *South Seas Travel and Cruises,* Box 581, Nukualofa.

Vava'u Island. Most Nukualofa-based tour operators will organize special trips on Vava'u. Give yourself either 3 hours or all day for the visits to Keitahi and Eneio beaches—both superb white sandy tracts and crystal-clear coral water. Visitors are driven across the island from Neiafu through native villages and plantations for picnics.

Give yourself 3 hours for the scenic coastal drive through the villages of Feletoa, Tefisi, and Longomapu and enjoy the stunning views of Port of Refuge Harbour and its many islands.

Just 14.5km from Neiafu, visitors can savour *lapila,* or kingfish, caught by hand and pan fried on the shores of the freshwater lake Teanuku. Set about 3 hours aside for this excursion.

Vava'u's highest peak is Mount Talau, towering behind Neiafau. A steep path leads climbers to the table-top summit for a wonderful view of the town and many of the group's other islands. Three hours should suffice for this side trip.

Thousands of swallows find the multicolored cave on the island of Kapa their sanctuary during autumn. Take 2 hours by boat, down the spectacular Port of Refuge Harbour, to drift inside their amazing grotto.

Experienced divers are enthusiastic about the drowned caves on the island of Nuapapu, where guides take them down through a heart-shaped entrance into an ethereal, blue-lit cavern. Veterans of this dive say the allotted 3 or 4 hours is not long enough.

Haapai Islands. There are very few organized tours here, but worth visits are Felemea village, on Uiha Island, where visitors can take part in octopus hunts, *kava* ceremonies, feasting, dancing, and other post-partying pursuits.

Pangai town, once the seat of the Tongan royal family, is a delightful old village, skirted by white, sandy beaches, and will always merit an hour's stroll.

SPORTS. Tongans have been represented at international competition level by boxers, rugby players, and handballers, but visitors should confine their sporting activities to the water—there are few facilities available for other pursuits. A low-standard nine-hole golf course is on the inland lagoon a few miles south of Nukualofa, and tennis courts are found mostly in the residences of foreign high commissioners.

NIGHTLIFE AND RESTAURANTS. Don't look for a lot of nightlife in Tonga, where until recently even swimming was banned on Sundays and you could have been thrown in jail for dancing and singing on Sunday. With tourism, times have changed, however, and visitors now have ample opportunity to kick up their heels—even if it is all a bit basic.

Loud, pop-style bands are featured at the *Dateline* and *Joe's Tropicana* on Fridays and Saturdays. Dine-dance nights are also held occasionally at the *Yacht Club* in Nukualofa, the *Tong Hua* Chinese restaurant, and the *Good Samaritan Inn.*

Restaurants and snack bars have increased in Nukualofa with the growing numbers of tourists. They include the *Basilica Restaurant,* for snacks or full meals under the basilica in the cultural center at St. Anthony of Padua, Taufaahau Rd.; The *Beach House,* for home cooking in the old Vuna Rd. boardinghouse; *Cafe Fakalato,* which offers snacks and meals on Wellington Rd.; *Dateline Hotel,* with a full restaurant, poolside snack bar, and Thursday-night barbecue; *Fasi-Moe-Afi Cafe,* offering a sea-front garden setting for substantial snacks on Vuna Rd.; *Good Samaritan Inn,* serving seafood and French dishes at Kolovai Beach; *Joe's Tropicana,* with its seafood specialties in the Latai Room; *John's Place,* serving snacks and take-away food in Taufahau Rd.; *Ha'atafu Beach Motel,* with its restaurant offering superior meals and service; *Onetale Snack Bar,* serving simple fare opposite Talamahu Market on Salote Rd.; and *Sela's Guest House,* with traditional Tongan food.

Off Tongatapu, some hotels offer meals, including the *Kaukinima Motel* and *Leipue Lodge* on Eua, the *Seletute Guest House* on Haapai, and, on Vavau, the *Paradise International Hotel* and the *Stowaway Village.*

DEPARTURE TAX. $T2.50.

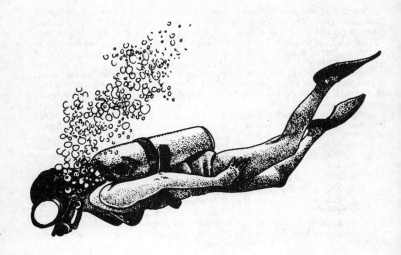

NIUE ISLAND

Hidden Coral Wonderland

by
GRAEME KENNEDY

Fly into Niue, and your first sighting will be of a badly made concrete sponge cake sitting quite alone in an awesome vastness. It appears dry and harsh (which it is) and inhospitable and totally uninteresting (which it certainly is not.) Initial impressions of Niue are misleading—you must look within this fascinating island to find its magic.

Niue is the world's largest single block of coral—259 square kilometers (about 100 square miles) of it sitting atop a giant of an undersea volcano in the middle of a triangle formed by Samoa, Rarotonga, and Tonga. With a population of around 3,000, Niue is bigger than either Rarotonga or Tongatapu. Most of the inhabitants live on the western side of the island near its busy little main center, Alofi.

Unlike its neighbors, Niue has no jungle-draped mountains sweeping down to glistening white lagoons, no rivers, lakes, or waterfalls. But treasures are hidden here.

Over the centuries, rainwater has leaked through the coral, leaving stunningly beautiful sea caves in the high cliffs with their feet on a coral shelf, creating magnificent subterranean grottoes, caverns, and freshwater lakes 100 feet below the arid surface.

Niue was once a coral atoll embracing the tip of its volcano pedestal. In some prehistoric movement of the earth's crust, Niue was thrust upward, and the lagoon is now a central plateau, the old reefs and islets forming a rugged escarpment rising more than 200 feet above the sea.

The cliffs, pierced by cathedral-like sea caves open to the coral shelf and the Pacific, are the treasures. The underground lakes in their vaulted caverns, accessible from the old interior lagoon, are wonders of the South Pacific.

Niue was first sighted by Captain Cook in 1774. He named it Savage Island when his attempted landing was fiercely opposed by the natives, who, having enough trouble eking out an existence from their sparse land, did not want to deal with strangers.

The name was changed when the world got to know the natives better—but even that took some time since missionaries, traders, and administrators passed the island by until the early nineteenth century. The Niueans remained aloof from the rest of the world until Samoan missionaries brought Christianity to the island in 1846, followed 17 years later by the London Missionary Society, who defended their tiny land from invaders.

In 1900, Niue was granted protection by the British crown, and the following year it was annexed to New Zealand, to be administered as part of that country's overseas territories. The island has run its own affairs since 1974 through a legislative assembly that meets regularly in Alofi under the leadership of longtime premier Sir Robert Rex. Visitors are sometimes surprised to find that Rex is an affable, stately man who enjoys a whiskey with friends and visitors alike in the modern Niue Hotel.

Since the early sixties, Niue has been moving into the twentieth century, with computer technology, satellite communications, and modern health and education services. The opening of Hanan International Airport was a big event for Niue, but tourism was then unknown.

Tourism Minister Frank Lui realizes that the island's fragile social fabric could be torn apart by a torrent of relatively wealthy foreign visitors, and he has always opted for controlled development. The small number of beds available on the island is a built-in control in Lui's efforts.

Meanwhile, New Zealand businessman Colin Payne has taken a long lease of the 20-room Niue Hotel and is encouraging scuba divers to experience some of the clearest and most colorful water in the Pacific. With virtually no beaches, underwater visibility is uncluttered by sand, and the lack of rivers means no soils or other pollution in seas teeming with tropical fish and Technicolor-bright corals.

Niue is no place for the elderly and infirm, although the Tourist Department is undertaking to build negotiable paths and steps down the cliffs to the more spectacular caves and seascapes.

I think of Avaiki as a Walt Disney sea cave; the colors and natural architecture suggestive of scenes from *Fantasia*. Here, vast limestone caverns open like a theater stage onto the Pacific breakers exploding on the reef edge 50 meters away. The theater balcony opens onto a crystal pool, alive with tiny fish darting like liquid sapphire. You can swim here under stalactites that hang like rock icicles, droplets of water continuously falling and sounding like tiny bells. It has relatively easy access from the round-island road, 4.5 kilometers from Alofi.

Just 150 meters north is Palaha, the soaring sea cave, for all the world like a gigantic opera house, with a huge arch supported by giant pillars of long-dead coral.

On to Hio, a pocket-sized coral-sand beach, a craggy clamber from the road near the village of Vaipapahi, and one of the very few beaches on Niue. It is quite beautiful and worth the effort of getting there.

The road swings up into the escarpment, through air heady with the perfume of lime and passionfruit plantations to Hikutavake, village of old people and children who do not smile until you do—then you can't stop them. Here is the majestic Matapa Chasm, a towering cleft in the cliff and the legendary bathing place for the ancient kings. Here you can float in gentle swells, which are calmed by bus-sized boulders blocking the chasm entrance from the big Pacific seas that explode against the cliffs outside.

The arches at Talava are another of the dozen or so wonders of Niue on the northeast of the island, where huge coral bridges leap over acres of deep clear pools on the coral shelf; again, a place for the sprightly. Access is through a narrow, slippery cavern, which emerges high up the towering cliff-face with the Pacific thundering at its base and exposing a coral amphitheater. At the landward side of the coral arena, a rock hole scarcely large enough to admit a person plummets straight down for almost 15 feet, then angles away in a limestone tunnel barely high enough to crawl through. This is not for claustrophobics, but those who undergo the ordeal are rewarded with a sight few Europeans have seen—a subterranean cave lit from above with an ethereal beauty, a pool so clear that tiny pebbles on the bottom 12 feet down are magnified among brilliant white sand, those electric-blue mini-fish, and greenery creeping in with the sunlight.

Catch your breath and go on to Togo, about 2½ miles north of the east-coast village of Hakupu, where you cross a cliff-top moonscape of jagged gray dead coral until there, in its midst, you find a white coral sand oasis 50 feet below sheer rock cliffs. Coconut palms rise beside a freshwater pool and stream rising from somewhere under the coral.

Pass through the Huvalu Forest and through neat villages like Avaseli, Liku, Lakepa, and Mutalau, and wonder at the magnificent old churches that dominate the clifftop landscape. But the jewel of Niue is a magic cave named Vaikona. The rough track into Vaikona starts 2½ miles south of Liku. Walking it, with the stink of old coral in your nose and thorns and spikes barring your way, you wonder why you have bothered to come. But Vaikona is the one natural challenge you must conquer if you go to Niue. Drop through a rock hole on the high jungle floor barely wide enough to squeeze through and carefully make your way across an underground cliff face, wet and slippery from the incessant water dripping from the limestone just above your head. How far down if you slip? It's mercifully too dark to see. Edge forward until, at last, you turn a corner and stand atop yet another cliff at least 15 meters below the surface, and you are faced with one of the most breathtaking sights you will ever see—above or below the earth.

A vast cavern opens before you, and a jagged crack in the "ceiling" high above sends shafts of sunlight lancing to the bottom of a deep, clear lake at the bottom of this massive vault. The jungle has found its way in, and vines and deep green leaves cling halfway down the limestone walls. You swim in the cold, clear water and wonder at what forces centuries ago created this beautiful place. Then the climb back out doesn't seem so hard.

It is sad that today almost 9,000 Niueans have deserted their homeland and settled among the bustle and bright lights of New Zealand's biggest city, Auckland. But there are jobs there, and New Zealand aid money can provide only so much employment out of Alofi. Yet those who remain are a pleasant people, busying themselves with their government jobs, their sports, and their bush gardens, blocks of land up in the interior where they grow taro, bananas, coconuts, limes, and passionfruit for their own needs and a little for export to Auckland's Karangahape Rd. shops. Everyone—even cabinet ministers and Sir Robert Rex himself—adheres to the old custom of spending time each week weeding, digging, planting, or harvesting in their high, hot bush gardens.

Niueans also go to sea in outrigger canoes—stored in high cliff caves, away from the pounding seas—and catch tuna and Spanish mackerel, big game fish that fight and test every inch of the Niueans' courage and skill. And they have one of the world's rare delicacies simply walking around, ready to be picked up (carefully), cooked, and eaten. It's the coconut crab, or *uga*—pronounced *"oonga"*—a creature as delectable as it is ugly. It eats only coconut meat, tearing the nut apart with its huge claws, and its white flesh is delicately flavored by the tropical fruit.

Bees thrive on Niue and, feeding mainly on passionfruit and lime flowers, produce a unique, thin, dark honey of tantalizing taste.

It is unfortunate that Niue is really for the fitter tourist, seeking off-the-beaten-track sights and experiences. It's not easy to get to, but it all seems worthwhile when, after a day of magic, you sit in the bar of the Niue Hotel sharing a tall, cool drink with the premier.

PRACTICAL INFORMATION FOR NIUE

WHEN TO GO. Like all tropic islands, Niue has two seasons—the wet season from December to March and the dry season in the remaining eight months, when temperatures average 24°C. after wet-season highs of 27°C. Niue has the southeast trades, which create warm temperatures by day and a comfortable coolness by night. Average rainfall is 2,780mm a year. Humidity is highest during the wet season.

WHAT TO WEAR. The early missionaries left their mark on Niue, and swimwear is still unacceptable in public, such as in the shops. The coral and rugged terrain make thongs unsuitable, and sneakers or tennis shoes are recommended. Casual, comfortable clothing is standard for day and night—walking shorts, socks, and short-sleeved shirts for men and light cotton frocks for women. A light pullover will be useful in the cooler evenings.

HOW TO GET THERE. Weekly flights by *Air Nauru* operate from American Samoa, Auckland, and the Cook Islands. Check travel agents for latest fares and schedules.

ENTRY REQUIREMENTS. Passports are required for 30-day visitors' permits. Onward travel booking is essential; permit extensions can be obtained from the police department in Alofi. Visas and health inoculation certificates are not required. Baggage searches are mandatory to protect Niue's fragile agriculture-based economy from imported pests.

CURRENCY. The New Zealand dollar is Niue's official currency, and all banking needs are conducted through Niue's Treasury Department in Alofi. A bank authorization is required for the export of foreign currencies, and they must be declared on departure.

LANGUAGE. Niueans speak their own Polynesian dialect and are fluent in English.

ACCOMMODATIONS. Built in 1957 for the South Pacific Forum meeting, the Niue Hotel is 3km south of Alofi and has 20 modern and self-contained rooms on the cliff top overlooking the Pacific. It has a full-sized swimming pool and a dining and entertainment center offering excellent meals including local dishes and a weekly smorgasbord, usually on Tuesdays. Lunch boxes are provided for day tours. Island nights, with traditional dancing, are features at weekends. Rates are $NZ55 single, $NZ58 double or twin, $NZ96 executive suite (sleeps 5). Box 80, Alofi; tel. 91 or 92. The **Hinemata Motel** consists of three rooms serviced daily, with shared kitchen and bathroom. On the coast near Alofi. Budget rates. Box 81, Alofi; tel. 167. The **Vesta Guest House** consists of three double rooms with washing facilities. Meals available; hotel is also adjacent to store with take-away food. Ideal for budget traveler. Box 85, Alofi. A three-room house with shared facilities between Alofi and the Niue Hotel, the **Pelenis Guest House** serves European and island-style meals with complimentary fresh fruit in season. Guests are encouraged to accompany the owner, Mr. Talagi, in his daily routine—to church and his plantation—to experience authentic island life. Box 11, Alofi; tel. 135.

TOURIST INFORMATION. The *Niue Tourist Board,* Box 67, Alofi, and the *Niue Consular Office,* Box 68–541, Newton, Auckland, New Zealand, are both good sources of information.

GETTING AROUND. There is no regular transport service on Niue, but cabs and rental cars and motorcycles are readily available. A local guide may be necessary to take you to some of the more out-of-the-way places of interest. Cabs charge around $NZ1 a kilometer and can be called on either Alofi 58 or 70W. Rental cars cost between $NZ35 and $NZ45 a day and motorcycles between $NZ15 and $NZ25 a day. Bicycles are about $NZ7 a day.

Rental-car companies are *Niue Rentals,* tel. 58; *Maile Rentals,* tel. 271 or 85, and *Russell and Ama,* tel. 167 or 608.

TOURS. *Niue Adventure Tours* offers almost every Niuean sport, leisure, and cultural activity in its range of tours. Uga-hunting and bat- and pigeon-shooting expeditions cost $NZ25 a person. Tropical-fish collecting is $NZ30, and fishing at night for flying fish is $NZ50. Scenic tours by van are $NZ20 a person, and scuba diving is $NZ60. Niue Adventures offers a wide range of fishing and diving tours with all equipment, including air tanks, masks, fins, underwater cameras, and fishing tackle available for hire. An air tank fill is $NZ5. Contact *Niue Adventures;* Box 141; tel. 102.

SPORTS. Niueans are versatile and enthusiastic sportspeople, engaging in organized competition in softball, soccer, rugby, netball, and a local version of cricket played with a club-shaped bat and a hard rubber ball by teams of 30. Watch a game at any village in the evenings. All visitors are welcome at the *Niue Sports Club,* opposite the airport-entrance road, where they can try their skill on the nine-hole golf course or grass tennis courts. Clubs, tees, balls, and bag can be hired from $NZ5 to $NZ10 a day. Two tennis racquets, and two balls cost $NZ8 a day. The sports club has a friendly, well-stocked bar where visitors are honored guests.

SHOPPING. Niue is known throughout Polynesia for the high quality of its woven wares. Basic materials are young coconut palm fronds and the leaves of the pandanus palm. Woven with great style and finish, mats, baskets, and hats are colored with natural dyes and can be bought at moderate prices. In the Alofi stores, visitors can buy a wide range of products, generally more cheaply than in Australia or New Zealand. Duty-free shopping has not been introduced to Niue, but the low duties levied do allow bargain buying.

DEPARTURE TAX. $NZ10.

WALLIS AND FUTUNA

French Fantastic

by
GRAEME KENNEDY

The road to Aka-Aka from the coastal flatlands and the long coral runway of Hihifo Airport sweeps upward past green leafy hillsides. Old horses and young pigs scamper in and out of the banana and taro and onto the manicured lawns that seem to float around villages, and fine old white colonial buildings hang in a blue-green haze at the coastal main town of Mata-Utu, on the mideast shore of this handsome island.

Your jeep climbs, juddering on the potholed white coral road and groaning upward through jungle so lush it is impossible to see more than a few yards ahead; yet above you're told there are deep, cold freshwater lakes held in extinct volcano craters and drenched in tropical flowers inhabited by parrots, lorikeets, and other vivid native birds.

With every turn of this road, the lagoon expands in both view and beauty far below until there is an explosion of color that strikes the senses like a physical blow. Blues, greens, reds, yellows, and startling whites of the coral shimmer under a transparent sea in which tiny islets with palm trees float inside the reef, where the Pacific thunders in white detonations almost a mile out.

You stop, breathless, at Lomipeau—a modest yet unique restaurant, open sided so that the jungle, lagoon, and ocean present a living mural. Warm scented zephyrs flirt with the red-and-white-checked tablecloths while you wait with a cold drink at the matey little bar.

It is the home of Christian Ruotolo, the darkly handsome fiftyish French-Algerian who made this his home after years of pouring wine for other tourists from Italy to Noumea. He knew what he was doing when he moved 21,000 kilometers from Paris, 2,200 kilometers from New Caledonia to this beautiful, tiny tropic island to the north of Fiji and the Samoas. Christian and his Wallisian wife, Paola, have been here since the mid-seventies and have gradually expanded their little restaurant; it now has 15 air-conditioned double rooms and is a large part of the entire Wallis tourist plant. In a typical menu, the Ruotolos offer baby lagoon scallops pampered in oil, garlic, and parsley; New Zealand lamb with taro and island herbs; and French vanilla ice cream drenched in Kahlua or Cointreau, all washed down with good Bordeaux for around 2,200 French Pacific francs (about 15 U.S. dollars).

Wallis is a treasure island of fewer than 10,000 people, a far outpost of France which pours millions of francs every year into this little-known territory for one purpose—to keep control of the strategically important runway at Hihifo. The islanders don't seem to mind the French motives, for they are secure and happy. With the territory comes Futuna, just over an hour's flight to the southwest, more mountainous and jungled than Wallis but with the same perfect white beaches and lagoons. The bones of the Pacific's first saint, St. Peter Chanel, now rest at the Futuna village of Poi, where he was hacked to death in 1841.

Discovered by English navigator Captain Samuel Wallis during his 1766 to 1770 voyage of exploration to find the mythical great southern continent in the Pacific (he also discovered Tahiti), the archipelago that bears his name was made a French protectorate in 1886 as the major powers scrambled for new colonies. The United States built the air strip at Hihifo during World War II and more than 5,000 American servicement were once based there. Wallis and Futuna became a French overseas territory in 1961.

A popular port of call for wandering South Seas yachtspeople, Wallis has never been on the convenient tourist trails. One jet flight comes to Wallis each week, in an aging Caravelle from Noumea through Fiji's Nadi. But a trickle of visitors do come, enough to maintain Lomipeau and the splendid Tanoa on the beach at Alele, on the island's northeast coast. The spectacular lagoon laps its rear doorstep, where Lyon natives Jean-Pierre and Josette Defer manage broken French-English with their guests over sunset drinks before dinner. They gather the island shellfish *mulitiki* from the lagoon each morning and, after gently sautéeing and garnishing them with spices and garlic, serve them as an admirable substitute for the traditional Gallic escargot. It's a dish not to be missed.

In the late seventies, there were plans to build a Club Med–style resort at the Tanoa, but they seem to have been forgotten. I'm pleased about that.

PRACTICAL INFORMATION FOR
WALLIS AND FUTUNA

WHEN TO GO. Expect hot, humid, rainy weather in the traditional Pacific wet season from November through March, with temperatures up to 31° C; it will be more comfortable from June/July through September, with an average high of 24°C. Farther north past both Fiji and the Samoas, the oppressive wet-season heat is countered by refreshing midyear trade winds.

WALLIS AND FUTUNA

WHAT TO WEAR. Light, comfortable, informal clothes are adequate all year-round. Bring a sweater for cooler evenings and a plastic coat or umbrella for unexpected showers. Shorts and swimwear are not acceptable as evening wear at restaurants.

HOW TO GET THERE. Noumea-based *Air Caledonie International* operates a weekly Tuesday service to Wallis's Hihifo Airport via Nadi in Fiji; return service is on Thursday. A shipping service leaves Noumea about every 35 days.

ENTRY FORMALITIES. No visa is required, but passport and onward or return tickets are necessary, for stays of up to 30 days. Yachtspeople should contact the high commissioner, 1, ave. Marechal Foch, Noumea, New Caledonia, before their voyage.

ELECTRICITY. As in all French Polynesia, electric current is 220 volts AC, 50 Hz. A two-prong plug is necessary.

TIPPING is not encouraged.

LANGUAGE. Most Wallisians speak French and their own Tongan-based Polynesian dialect. Fluent English speakers are difficult to find.

CURRENCY. Wallis and Futuna's monetary unit is the French Pacific franc (CFP). Notes are CFP5,000, CFP1,000 and CFP500. Coins are CFP100, 50, 20, 5, 2, and 1. One U.S. dollar is about CFP150.

TIME ZONE. GMT plus 11 hours; 20 hours ahead of U.S. Pacific Standard.

ACCOMMODATIONS. About 6km from Hihifo Airport and 800m from the center of the main town, Mata-Utu, at Aka-Aka, the **Hotel Lomipeau** has 15 air-conditioned rooms with private facilities, television, and radio. Marvelous restaurant, with bar and tour desk. Rates: Single CFP6,500, double CFP7,500. Box 84, Aka-Aka, Wallis Island; tel. 22–221. On the lagoon at Alele with 18 air-conditioned rooms, the **Tanoa Hotel** has several self-contained beachside bungalows, a dining room, and dancing, only minutes from anywhere. Run by Jean-Pierre and Josette Defer—both originally from Lyon, although they settled on Wallis after visiting French Polynesia as tourists. Rates: air-conditioned room, single CFP3,000, double CFP3,500. Bungalow, single CFP2,000, double CFP2,500.

GETTING AROUND. Unscheduled village buses run around Wallis from Mata-Utu, where limited rental cars are available at moderate cost. Check at hotel desk. *Air Caledonie International* operates a 1-hour-15-minute Britten-Norman Islander service to Futuna on Mondays, Wednesdays, and Fridays. Internal transport on Futuna is haphazard.

TOURIST INFORMATION. New Caledonia Tourist Office, 25, ave. Marechal Foch, Noumea, New Caledonia (tel. Noumea 27–2632).

TOURS. Individual tours around the lagoon, to the crater lakes, to villages, and for general sightseeing can be arranged through your hotel desk to suit personal preferences and timetables.

SPORTS. You've come to the wrong island if you're looking for championship-standard golf courses and Wimbledon-style tennis courts. You have it right, though, if you're after superb snorkeling and diving, sailing, or any other water sport you can think of. All equipment can be hired through your hotel.

NIGHTLIFE AND RESTAURANTS. Nightlife is extremely limited on Wallis and unknown on Futuna. Hotels, especially the Tanoa, have live bands and dancing once or twice a week, and a native disco with no known name on the hill outside Mata-Utu is a happy, noisy place. Elaborate Wallisian dancing and *kava* ceremonies are not to be missed.

The Tanoa dining room specializes in seafood, and Hotel Lomipeau specializes in an imaginative French-style menu with tantalizing Polynesian overtones. Several smaller eateries of unknown origin flourish in Mata-Utu.

FIJI ISLANDS

Crossroads of the South Pacific

by
JAMES TULLY

James Tully was Pacific Affairs writer for the Auckland Star *before becoming assistant editor in 1985. He has traveled widely in the Pacific and visited Fiji several times. He studied the region in depth when obtaining his postgraduate degree in history at Auckland University.*

A cluster of tropical islands straddling the 180th meridian, 1,100 miles south of the equator, Fiji is usually portrayed as a Pacific paradise—an ideal destination for the traveler seeking an escape from urban civilization.

Fiji, the tourist cliché continues, is a sun-drenched land of unpolluted, uncrowded islands with friendly people and the bonus of duty-free shopping.

Seasoned travelers usually dismiss the rhapsodic descriptions of travel agents, but the proof of the publicity is in the visiting.

With Fiji the cliché is remarkably accurate. But of course, there is far more to this fast-developing mini-state at the crossroads of the South Pacific.

Fiji is an archipelago of more than 300 islands, ranging from tiny coral atolls and rugged limestone islets, to the two islands of Viti Levu and Vanua Levu, which together comprise 85 percent of the group's total area of 7,022 sq miles. About 105 of the islands are inhabited.

The group lies on the main North American air route to Australia and New Zealand, 3,183 miles from Honolulu and 5,611 from San

Francisco. Suva, the capital, is 1,960 miles by air from Sydney to the southwest and 1,317 miles from Auckland to the south.

Most of Fiji's approximately 700,000 people live on the coasts, especially in and around the capital Suva and the other sugar-producing towns. Sugar is the main commercial crop and export.

Suva is the only place in Fiji which gives the visitor an impression of urban bustle, with its busy docks, light industrial zone, and thriving shopping center.

It is mainly in the towns that the visitor can see the ethnic variety of Fiji society. There are powerfully built Fijians dressed in wrap-around sulus, numerous Indians, men in western clothes, women in colorful saris, and a scattering of Europeans, Chinese, and other Pacific Islanders.

Fijian legend tells of the great chief Lutunasobasoba leading his people across the seas to the new land of Fiji. Archaeological evidence suggests that Fiji was first settled about 3,500 years ago. Linguistic evidence suggests that the original inhabitants—the Lapita people—came from Vanuatu or possibly the eastern Solomons.

The islands were discovered gradually by European seafarers over a period of about 300 years. The Dutch explorer Abel Tasman sighted islands and reefs in the Fiji group in 1643, and English navigators, including Captain James Cook in 1774, discovered others. Most of the credit for the European discovery of the islands goes to Captain William Bligh, who sailed through the group after the *Bounty* Mutiny in 1789.

European contact increased steadily through the nineteenth century: traders in search of sandalwood, settlers in search of land, missionaries in search of souls. The rapid conversion of the Cannibal Isles to a gentle and generous Christianity was a miracle of missionary endeavor.

Because of the unstable conditions of life, a British consul was appointed in 1857 to aid the traders and missionaries in Fiji. Seventeen years later the islands were voluntarily ceded to Great Britain, which continued to administer them until independence in October 1970.

The Alien Majority

Annexation in 1874 not only cemented the British presence, but heralded an era of migration that was to change the nature of Fiji society profoundly.

When the first Australian and British planters sought labor for their cotton and sugar plantations they found that Fijians had no wish for money and no relish for labor other than tribal enterprises.

By the 1860s the growth of the plantation economy had created a demand for human labor that outstripped supply. The solution was to import labor, mainly from the New Hebrides and the Gilbert Islands, until the British government forcibly disapproved of "blackbirding." Fiji's first governor, Sir Arthur Gordon, took the initiative after 1874 by introducing contracted labor from India.

Under contract, Indians were imported to Fiji as "coolies," with a right to repatriation to India. Only a third of the 62,837 Indians imported between 1879 and 1916 elected to return home.

In 1923 there were only 39,000 Indians in Fiji, but with free migration until the 1930s and a high birth rate, they outnumbered Fijians by 1946. Today they make up just over half the population.

Indians form the majority in the towns and dominate commercial and professional life. The nation's shopkeepers, taxi drivers, importers, lawyers, and doctors are mostly of Indian descent. In the country they produce most of the sugar cane and rice, on land leased from Fijians. Indians own only about 2 percent of the freehold land available in Fiji.

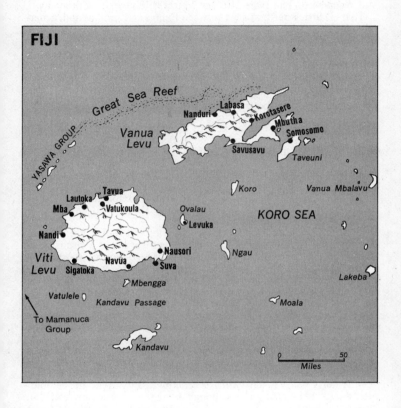

Though some of the age-old customs remain, particularly in rural areas—marriages may still be arranged by the parents—the migration to Fiji brought changes in the Indian community. The Hindu caste system was shed, and women were freed from many restrictions hallowed by custom and religion.

To speak of Indian culture in Fiji implies the existence of a subcontinent of India. All the provinces are represented. Ten Indian dialects are still recognised. There are Hindus, Muslims, Sikhs and Christians.

There is little inter-marriage between Fijians and Indians and, generally speaking the two races do not mix socially, yet race relations have been harmonious since independence.

Fire Walking: A Double Act

It is an odd coincidence that two races—one indigenous, the other "imported"—should both practice the rare rite of fire walking.

Fijian fire walking arises from a belief in a legendary spirit god who passed on the gift of resisting heat to the Sawau tribespeople, who live in four villages on the southern side of Beqa Island, just off the main island of Viti Levu. It is said that only the Sawau people can walk on the white-hot stones with impunity—but the tribe has been known to adopt outsiders who have been able to perform the ceremony successfully.

Visitors can see the men of Sawau walk barefooted over stones heated by an enormous log fire at special occasions on Beqa Island or at several hotels on the Coral Coast.

Fijian fire walking has its origin in legend, and Indian fire walking is done for religious reasons. Trial by fire is regarded as a cleansing of the spirit, and the ceremony is the climax of a 10-day ritual practiced by the Madrasis sect of the Hindu religion.

During the ceremonies held by the followers of *Maha Devi* (the Divine Mother) all are clad in yellow. Devotees selected to walk on the hot coals daub their faces with vermilion dye and yellow turmuric powder, which they consider a symbol of prosperity and power to destroy disease. Their bodies are pierced with needles and skewers. The fire walking is preceded by 10 days of abstinence.

Young children are sometimes carried through the fire in the arms of devotees to satisfy vows taken by their parents when the children fall seriously ill.

Only fairly recently have tourists been invited to attend the ceremonies, usually held in August. Although admission charges are made "in keeping with the spirit of the times" the ritual remains, for the devotees of Maha Devi, a religious penance and not merely a tourist attraction.

Kava Drinking

Throughout Fiji—and also in most parts of Polynesia—the drinking of *yaqona* (pronounced Yanggona), or *kava,* is a common ceremonial and social custom.

Yaqona is made from the root of the pepper plant. In the past the drink was prepared by the young maidens of a village, who chewed the pieces of root into a soft, pulpy mass before water was added. Today the root is pounded in a pestle and mortar or ground to powder by a machine. After the addition of the water, the gritty pieces of root are strained by passing the liquid through a bundle of vegetable fiber.

The *yaqona* ceremony is still important in the Fijian way of life, but *yaqona* has also become a social drink. *Yaqona* drinking is very common in Fijian villages, and it is usual for the men to gather round the kava bowl *(tanoa)* and swap yarns as the astringent liquid is passed around in the *bilo,* a half coconut shell.

In old Fiji, birth, marriage, and death all called for correct ceremonies; as did installation of chiefs, welcoming important visitors, and launching canoes.

The ceremony is performed by the hosts, and the *yaqona* mixed in the presence of the guest of honor is presented in a complicated ritual. This ceremony is not performed indiscriminately by Fijians and cannot be regarded as a spectacle. Not all visitors to Fiji are fortunate enough to see it. However, social drinking of *yaqona* is very informal.

The Road Ahead

Fiji is the most populous and economically advanced of the South Pacific island groups and the most important communication center.

Though a new figure on the world stage, Fiji has participated enthusiastically in the various international organizations to which it belongs—the Commonwealth, the United Nations, the South Pacific Forum, the South Pacific Conference, and the Lome Convention, which links it with the European Economic Community (Common Market). For six years a battalion from the Royal Fiji Military Forces served in Lebanon as part of the United Nations peace-keeping force.

Fiji is a parliamentary democracy with an elected House of Representatives (Lower House) and an appointed Senate (Upper House). The Senate's general purpose is to review legislation from the Lower House, and it has one particularly important power as far as the Fijian people are concerned—to adjudicate matters involving their land.

The complicated electoral system is designed to ensure a racial balance and guarantee the status of Fijians as the original inhabitants of a country where they are outnumbered.

Fiji's first and only prime minister is Ratu Sir Kamisese Mara, a hereditary chief, educated at Oxford University in England. He is a scholarly statesman of world stature who has personally guided Fiji into nationhood.

Ratu Mara's Alliance government was actually defeated in the April 1977 elections. But the governor-general reappointed him prime minister because he felt Ratu Mara was the man best able to command a majority in the House after an election which saw the mainly Indian National Federation party win 26 seats to the Alliance's 24. At a new election in September 1977 the Alliance swept back to power with 36 seats. They were reelected in July 1982.

Fiji's economic growth has centered on agriculture, chiefly sugar, and tourism. The Government-owned Fiji Sugar Corporation crushes the cane and partly refines it for export. Sugar accounts for 75 percent of domestic exports, and the industry employs about 22 percent of the labor force.

Tourism is the second largest industry, though in 1984 gross earnings from tourism exceeded sugar exports by $51 million.

Other major export earners are gold (from the Emperor Mine at Vatakoula), copra, fish, and coconut oil. Beef production is increasing. The timber industry, focused on pine, is expected to become the third major export earner.

The country's ninth development plan lays heavy emphasis on the growth of tourism, timber exports, and export-oriented manufacturing industries. An 11.5 percent annual growth in tourism is predicted.

A continuing theme in Fiji's development has been the need to reduce the drift to the towns, where there has been insufficient work for the unskilled.

The government hopes to slash the rate of population growth between 1986 and 1990.

Exploring Fiji

Nadi International Airport on the west coast of Viti Levu is the gateway to Fiji. This is an area of dry hills, sweeping plateaus, and mountains. The feeling of being in the tropics is strongest on the shoreline where palm trees sway. The rainfall on this the "dry" side of the island is about 60 inches annually, half that of the eastern side.

Not far from the airport are a dozen or so first-class hotels. Duty-free shops lining Nadi's main street are the only real attraction for the tourist. But Lautoka, 20 miles to the north, is of more interest. Fiji's second largest city and port is the setting-off point for several small island resorts and cruises to the almost untouched Yasawa Group.

Life is casual on the island resorts off Nadi and Lautoka. Visitors stay in Fijian-style thatched or tile-roofed *bures*. There are white sand beaches for sunning and swimming. The calm waters behind the coral reefs offshore are safe for diving and snorkeling.

Beachcomber Island, just five sandy acres, is the most informal of the resorts and is popular with the younger set. Other resorts include Plantation Island, Treasure Island, Castaway Island, Club Naitasi, Mana Island, and Musket Cove.

Viti Levu is circled by a 317-mile road. The part running westward from Suva to Lautoka is called Queen's Road, and the other section King's Road.

Heading from Nadi to Suva 132 miles away, you will immediately notice that you are in the sugar belt. The tall green cane stretches for miles. Narrow railway lines take trucks laden with cut cane to the huge sugar mill at Lautoka.

A little way out of Nadi there is a rough winding road that climbs into the Nausori highlands, from which there are arresting views of the southwest coast of Viti Levu.

Forty miles from Nadi is Sigatoka, market center for the fertile Sigatoka Valley. A 33-mile gravel road follows the meandering river upstream past scallop-shaped river flats checkered with crops. There are large terrace forts on the valley sides.

Beyond Sigatoka the road hugs the so-called Coral Coast. This 60-mile stretch of white sand beaches has been developed into a major resort area, with almost a third of Fiji's hotel beds.

Of special interest is the Pacific Harbour Development, a "leisure-oriented satellite town" 30 miles from Suva. In this Mediterranean-type resort, the first of its kind in the South Pacific, you may own or rent a villa. There is an 18-hole, par-72 championship golf course, the only one in the South Pacific to be fully irrigated and offer electric golf carts.

Nearby is Navua, a sleepy riverside town from which you can cruise upriver, through rapids, to a Fijian village.

By now you are in the wet belt around Suva and the open grasslands have become thick forest and evergreen grass. Heavy black rain-bellied clouds seem always to be overhead.

A mixture of old colonial and brash eighties, Suva sits on a point jutting into Laucala Bay: a busy port, thriving commercial center, and focus of government.

The downtown shopping area has dozens of duty-free shops with electrical gear, cameras, hi-fi sets, perfumes, jewelry, sports equipment.

For a more peaceful atmosphere there are the museum and botanic gardens in the domain next to Government House, home of the governor-general. The museum has an excellent collection of Fijian artifacts including pottery fragments from sand dunes at the mouth of the Sigatoka River dated as being about 2,000 years old.

The University of the South Pacific, sited on what was once an air-force base at Laucala Bay, is a regional educational center for the South Pacific. Students from many island groups study there.

Five miles from Suva is Orchid Island, an island in a river with extensive collections of tropical plants as well as plots of coffee, tea, and vanilla. Fauna includes mongoose, rare iguanas, monkeys, and local snakes.

Seven miles from Suva is Colo-I-Suva forest park with its nature walks, picnic areas, and swimming holes in Waisila Creek.

A short hop by air takes you from Suva to Ovalau Island, where you can visit the historic town of Levuka, the original capital of Fiji.

The King's Road passes through Nausori, site of Suva's airport, and heads northeast up the coast to Korovou, where the road branches through Lodoni to Natovi, where a ferry service to Ovalau operates. Or you can cut inland from Korovou to Vunidawa on the Rewa River.

King's Road continues around the island to Rakiraki, Tavua, and Ba before joining Queen's Road at Lautoka. Two roads branch off at Tavua Bay—one to the timber-milling highlands of Nadarivatu, the other to the gold-mining town of Vatakoula.

Vanua Levu and Taveuni

The great appeal of the accessible outer islands, Vanua Levu and Taveuni, is their peace and beautiful scenery.

The main villages on Vanua Levu are Savusau, in the south, and Labasa, in the north. In between are coconut plantations, tropical vegetation, and a mountain tableland.

Labasa (population 5,200) is the busier of the two, with its market and sugar mill. Vanua Levu's major road goes south from Labasa to Nabouwala at the island's southernmost point.

Savusavu is a sleepy little town of 2,600 people and a handful of shops. A good road called the Hibiscus Highway travels east to Karoko via Buca Bay, where there are swimming and snorkeling.

Fiji's third largest island, Taveuni, is not on the main tourist trail. Visitors stay at the only hotel at Waiyevo. The 35-mile road that connects copra plantations takes the visitor through rural villages that have changed little in the last 100 years. Behind Waiyevo is a mountain with a small crater lake. The unique tagimaucia flower is found only on the shores of this lake. Resembling the fuchsia, the plant has bunches of red flowers with white centers.

On the north end of Taveuni there are mysterious earth works of a large scale. The island is one of several areas in Fiji where there are rock carvings.

The limestone caves on Sawa-i-Lau Island have ancient writing on their walls.

PRACTICAL INFORMATION FOR FIJI

HOW TO GET THERE. The international airport at Nadi in western Viti Levu is the gateway to Fiji. A shuttle service links it with the capital, Suva, where Nausori Airport can handle narrow-bodied twin-engined jets and light aircraft.

Fiji's national carrier, *Air Pacific,* runs scheduled flights to New Zealand, Australia, Vanuatu, the Solomons, and Tonga. It has regular services between Nadi and Suva.

Other international carriers that fly to Fiji are *Air New Zealand, Qantas, Continental Airlines, Canadian Pacific Air, Japan Air Lines, Air Nauru, Air Vanuatu, Air Caledonie,* and *Polynesian Airlines.*

CLIMATE. Warm and pleasant without great extremes of heat or cold. The temperature averages 25°C (79.5°F) November to April and 24.4°C (75.7°F) May to October.

Rainfall varies markedly. It is usually abundant in the wet season (November to April), especially over Viti Levu and Vanua Levu, but deficient the rest of the year, especially in the dry zone on the western and northern sides of Viti Levu and Vanua Levu. Tropical cyclones, which have caused considerable damage in recent years, are most likely to hit Fiji between January and March.

Average Temperature (°Fahrenheit) and Humidity

	Jan	Feb	Mar	Apr	May	June	July	Aug	Sept	Oct	Nov	Dec
Nadi												
Average max. day temperature	88°	88°	87°	87°	85°	84°	83°	83°	84°	85°	86°	88°
Days of rain	21	19	24	20	17	14	10	12	14	14	16	17
Humidity, percent	75	78	80	80	77	79	76	71	69	66	67	69
Laucala Bay (Suva)												
Average max. day temperature	86°	86°	86°	84°	82°	81°	79°	80°	80°	81°	83°	85°
Days of rain	12	13	15	14	9	7	6	5	8	8	10	10
Humidity, percent	81	81	83	82	80	81	79	78	79	78	78	79

CURRENCY. Fiji's unit of currency is the Fiji dollar. Denominations of Fiji notes are $20, $10, $5, $2, $1. In April 1986 the United States and Fiji dollars were close to parity: $US1 = $F1.08.

ENTRY FORMALITIES. All visitors to Fiji must have a passport valid for at least six months from date of entry. They must produce an onward ticket out of the country, and proof may be required of sufficient funds for maintenance while in Fiji.

Visas are required from nationals of only a few countries. A temporary visa may be obtained to stay for one month, and it may be extended up to six months. Business travelers are required to obtain a work permit after seven days from date of arrival.

Inoculations are not required unless visitors are entering from a designated infected area. Children under a year are exempt.

LANGUAGE. English is the commonly spoken language.

ELECTRICITY. The current is 240 volts AC. Plugs are three pronged, set at an angle. Most electrical supply shops sell adaptors. Hotels generally have 110-volt converters for appliances.

COMMUNICATIONS. Fiji is particularly well served with a modern communications network handling telephone, telegraph, and telex services worldwide.

FIJI ISLANDS

TIPPING. Tipping is optional.

DRINKING LAWS. A wide range of beers, wines, and spirits are available at licensed outlets—hotels, restaurants, and clubs. Local liquor laws should not inconvenience adult (over 20) visitors.

TIME ZONE. GMT plus 11 hours; 20 hours ahead of U.S. Pacific Standard Time.

USEFUL ADDRESSES. *Fiji Visitors Bureau,* head office: Thomson Street, Suva. GPO Box 92. Telephone 22–867 Suva and 72–433 Nadi Airport. Other bureau offices are in Auckland, Box 1179, telephone 732–134; Sydney, 38 Martin Place, telephone 231–4251; Los Angeles, 6151 West Century Boulevard, suite 524, telephone (213) 417–2234, telex 759972; London, 34 Hyde Park Gate SW7 5BN, telephone 584–3661; Tokyo, NOA Building (10th floor) 3–5.2 Chome, Azabudai, Minato-ku, telephone (03) 587–2038.

Fiji Hotel Association, Box 2001, Government Buildings, Suva. Telephone 38–1093.

American Embassy, 31 Loftus St., Suva. Telephone 31–4466.

FESTIVALS. *Bula Festival:* an annual event in Nadi Town each July (Bula means welcome). *Hibiscus Festival:* Held in Suva each August to coincide with the first week of the school holidays; this is a carnival week of traditional entertainment, sports, and shows. The week ends with the Hibiscus Ball and the crowning of Miss Hibiscus. *Sugar Festival:* Lautoka, the sugar city, celebrates the harvest in September. *Diwali:* the Hindu festival of lights (October–November) is preceded by an annual spring cleaning of houses. Oil lamps and colored lights decorate the houses. Hindus celebrate the holy festival with devotion—fasting is observed, and prayers and offerings of sweets and fruits are given to Lakshmi, the goddess of wealth.

ACCOMMODATIONS. Fiji offers a wide range of accommodations from luxury resorts to dormitories at cheap rates. The traveler with a limited budget has plenty of choice. Based on prices for double accommodations, hotels are graded: *Deluxe* $100 plus; *Expensive,* $F60–$F100; *Moderate,* $F30–$F59; *Inexpensive,* up to $F30. (All room rates subject to 5% government tax.)

VITI LEVU ISLAND

Ba

Ba Hotel. *Inexpensive.* Box 29, Ba; 7–4000. Modest 13-room hotel with bar, restaurant, and swimming pool. Recommended stopover only.

Coral Coast

The Fijian Resort Hotel. *Deluxe.* Private Bag, Nadi Airport; 5–0155. 364 rooms. Luxury resort on 100-acre island 35 miles from Nadi. A one-stop holiday spa. Outstanding hotel staff. Good food. Dining rooms, bars, shops, tennis courts, 2 swimming pools, 9-hole golf course, lawn bowling, water sports, horse riding, dancing nightly, fire walking.

Hyatt Regency. *Deluxe.* Box 100, Korolevu; 5–0555. 249 rooms. Delightful beach setting with human-made off-shore island. Dining rooms, bars, shops, tennis courts, 9-hole pitch and putt, water sports, entertainment, fire walking.

Hide-a-Way Resort. *Expensive.* Box 233, Sigatoka; 5–0177. 15 bures. Beachside hotel on more modest scale. Informality stressed. Dining room, bar, shop, swimming pool. Dormitory accommodation available: $F8. Complete renovation underway.

520 THE SOUTH PACIFIC

Man Friday Resort. *Expensive.* Box 20, Korolevu; 5–0185. 28 bures. Traditional-style thatched bures by beach. Restaurant, bar, mini-golf, water sports, entertainment.

Naviti Beach Resort. *Expensive.* Box 29, Korolevu; 5–0444. 144 rooms. Attractive hotel at water's edge. Dining room, bar, tennis courts, water sports, swimming pool, 9-hole golf course, shops, fire walking.

Reef Hotel Resort. *Expensive.* Box 173, Sigatoka; 5–0044. 72 rooms. Close to coral reef. Restaurant, bar, stables, swimming pool, golf course, coral viewing.

Tambua Sands Beach Resort. *Moderate.* Box 177, Sigatoka; 5–0399. 19 bures beachside. Dining room, bar, swimming pool. Dormitory available: $F8.

The Crow's Nest. *Moderate.* Box 270, Sigatoka; 5–0230. 18 apartments beachside. Dining room, bar, swimming pool, snorkeling, children's playground.

Budget accommodation ($F5–$F22): **Sigatoka Hotel.** Box 35, Sigatoka; 5–0011. 3 rooms. **Waratah Lodge.** Box 86, Korotoga; 5–0278. 5 bures. Swimming pool, restaurant. **Vakaviti Units and Cabins.** Box 5, Sigatoka; 5–0526. 5 units and dormitory. Swimming pool, cooking facilities.

Deuba

Pacific Harbour International Resort. *Expensive–Deluxe.* Postal Agency, Pacific Harbour; 4–5022. 84 rooms and 20 villas. Magnificent resort on coast with championship golf course; air strip, shopping complex, cultural center, and resident doctor. Villas fully self-contained. Swimming pool, tennis courts, water sports, entertainment, fire walking.

Fiji Palms Beach Club Resort. *Expensive.* Postal Agency, Pacific Harbour; 4–5050. 14 self-contained apartments. Swimming pool. Access to Pacific Harbour. Time shares available.

Tropic Sands Beach Resort. *Moderate.* Postal Agency, Pacific Harbour; 4–5155. 32 rooms. Self-contained beachside units and bures. Full kitchen facilities.

Coral Coast Christian Camps. *Inexpensive.* Postal Agency, Pacific Harbour; 4–5178. 6 rooms and 8 budget cabins close to beach. No alcohol permitted.

Lautoka

Anchorage Beach Resort. *Moderate.* Box 9472, Nadi Airport; 6–2099. Beachside near "Sugar City." Dining room, bar, swimming pool, water sports. Dormitory accommodations available at $F12 (cooking facilities).

Cathay Hotel. *Moderate.* Box 239, Lautoka; 6–0566. 42 rooms. Dining room, bar, swimming pool. Golf and tennis can be arranged. In Lautoka town.

Lautoka Hotel. *Moderate.* Box 51, Lautoka; 6–0388. 36 rooms. No-frills hotel also in Lautoka town. Swimming pool, dining room, cocktail bar.

Saweni Beach Hotel. *Moderate.* Box 239, Lautoka; 6–1777. 12 self-contained units on beach, 12 minutes from Nadi. Dormitory $F6. Dining room, bar.

Lautoka-Offshore

Matamanoa Island Resort. *Deluxe.* Box 9729, Nadi Airport; 6–0511. 20 bures on lovely beach. Dining room, bar, swimming pool, water sports, coral viewing.

Castaway Island Resort. *Expensive.* Box 9246, Nadi Airport; 6–1233. 15 miles offshore. 66 bures. Dining room, bar, swimming pool, tennis, water sports, gymnasium, sauna, spa, day trips to neighboring islands, deep-sea fishing.

Club Naitasi. *Expensive.* Box 9147, Nadi Airport; 7–2266. Relatively new resort on Malolo Island. 28 bures and 9 luxury villas. Dining room, bar, swimming pool, cooking facilities, water sports, half tennis court. Beach beautification program underway.

Mana Island Resort. *Expensive.* Box 610, Lautoka; 6–1455. 22 miles offshore. 132 bures beachside on delightful bay. Dining room, bar, swimming pool, water sports, water scooters, tennis.

Musket Cove Resort. *Expensive.* Private Bag, Nadi Airport; 6–2215. 24 attractive self-contained bures. Dining room, water sports, weekly three-island cruise, swimming pool. 16 luxury villas will be ready for 1987.

FIJI ISLANDS

Plantation Island. *Expensive.* Box 9176, Nadi Airport; 7–2333. 20 miles offshore on Malolo Lailai Island. 90 rooms. Dining room, bar, swimming pool, horse riding, water sports, water scooters. Dormitory $F12.

Treasure Island. *Expensive.* Box 364, Lautoka; 6–1599. Idyllic little island. 69 bure units and bungalows. Dining room, bar, mini-golf, water sports, deep-sea fishing.

Beachcomber Island Resort. *Moderate* (meals included in rates). Box 364 Lautoka; 6–2600. 11 miles offshore, five sandy acres. Popular with young people. 14 bures, 12 lodge rooms, and dormitory ($F35 including meals). Dining room, bar, water sports.

Nadi

The Regent of Fiji. *Deluxe.* Box 441, Nadi; 7–0700. 294 rooms. Luxury beach resort (Denarau Island) for those who like to holiday in style. Dining rooms, bars, shops, swimming pool, water sports, archery range, golf course, tennis courts, resident nurse, entertainment, fire walking.

Fiji Mocambo. *Expensive.* Box 9195, Nadi Airport; 7–2000. 124 rooms. Imposing hotel handy to airport. Dining rooms with varied and interesting menu, bars, tennis, golf range, swimming pool, entertainment, fire walking.

Nadi Airport TraveLodge. *Expensive.* Box 9203, Nadi Airport; 7–2277. 114 rooms. Dining room, bar, swimming pool, tennis. Handy to airport. Ideal transit hotel.

Tanoa Hotel. *Expensive.* Box 9211, Nadi Airport; 7–2300. 102 rooms. Good standard accommodation close to airport. Dining room, bar, tennis, swimming pool, spa, sauna, entertainment. Cooking facilities in villas.

Castaway Gateway Hotel. *Expensive.* Box 9246, Nadi Airport; 7–2444. 93 rooms. Recently renovated comfortable hotel ideal for in-transit stopover. Dining room, bar, TV rental, swimming pool, tennis, spa pool.

Dominion International Hotel. *Moderate.* Box 9178, Nadi Airport; 7–2255. 85 rooms. Attractive hotel set around big swimming pool. Dining room, bar, pitch-and-putt golf, horseback riding available. Tennis court, archery range, and jogging track planned.

Seashell Cove Resort. *Moderate.* Box 9530, Nadi Airport; 5–0309. 14 rooms. 17km from Nadi on white-sand beach. Simple facilities. Swimming pool, tennis, water sports. Dormitory $F8. Camping available.

Skylodge Hotel. *Moderate.* Box 9222, Nadi Airport; 7–2200. 48 rooms. Garden setting. No frills. Dining room. Swimming pool, spa, minitennis, golf pitch. Good budget accommodation.

Fong Hing Private Hotel. *Inexpensive.* Box 143, Nadi; 7–1011. 22 rooms. In Nadi town. Tidy budget accommodation. Restaurant with Chinese and European food.

Johals Motel. *Inexpensive.* Box 213, Nadi; 7–2192. 12 rooms. Modest facilities include swimming pool, dining room, and bar. Dormitory $F5.

Sandalwood Inn. *Inexpensive.* Box 445, Nadi; 7–2553. 25 rooms. Also for the low-budget traveler. Swimming pool. Some rooms share facilities.

Rakiraki

Rakiraki Hotel. *Moderate.* Box 31, Rakiraki; 9–4101. 36 rooms. Good-quality budget accommodation. Attractive garden. Dining room, bar, swimming pool, 9-hole golf course nearby, tennis, bowling green.

Betham's Beach Cottages. *Inexpensive.* Box 1244, Suva; 31–5448. Simple self-contained cottages on Nananu-i-ra Island offshore from Rakiraki. Very much for the budget-conscious. Boat to island daily.

Macdonalds Beach Cottages. *Inexpensive.* Box 340, Suva; 2–7274. Three tidy and attractive bungalows with cooking facilities on Nananu-i-ra Island.

Suva

Suva Courtesy Inn. *Expensive.* Box 112, Suva; 31–2300. 56 rooms. Good-quality hotel in downtown Suva. Dining room, swimming pool, video. Rooms renovated in 1986.

Suva TraveLodge. *Expensive.* Box 1357, Suva; 31–4600. 134 rooms. Best hotel in Suva. On water's edge near town center. Full facilities.

Grand Pacific Hotel. *Moderate.* Box 2086, Government Buildings, Suva; 2–3011. 72 rooms. Somerset Maugham atmosphere, but past its best. Thrift accommodation also available.

Southern Cross Hotel. *Moderate.* Box 1076, Suva; 31–4233. 31 rooms. Apartment-like hotel overlooking downtown Suva. Dining room, swimming pool.

Capricorn Apartment Hotel. *Moderate.* Box 1261, Suva; 31–4799. 25 rooms. Two small apartment-like blocks in downtown Suva, overlooking swimming pool. Facilities include a dial-a-meal service. 10 additional rooms planned for 1988.

The President Hotel. *Moderate.* Box 1351, Suva; 36–1033. 42 rooms. Ocean views from attractive hillside setting. Dining room, bar, swimming pool.

Suva Peninsula Hotel. *Moderate.* Box 888, Suva; 31–3711. 39 rooms. Good-quality accommodation with swimming pool, dining room, room service, and baby-sitters.

Tradewinds Resort Hotel. *Moderate.* Box 1354, Suva; 36–1166. 111 rooms. Ocean front with water sports. Deep-sea fishing and scuba diving. Good restaurant. Fire walking twice a month.

South Seas Private Hotel. *Inexpensive.* Box 157, Suva; 2-2195. 30 rooms. Spartan facilities at budget prices—$F11 twin. Dormitory-style.

Suva Apartments. *Inexpensive.* Box 12488, Suva; 2–4281. 12 rooms. Simple self-contained apartments aimed at the budget conscious.

VANUA LEVU ISLAND

Labasa

Takia Hotel. *Moderate.* Box 7, Labasa; 8–1655. 36 self-contained rooms. Dining room and swimming pool.

Savusavu

Namale Plantation. *Expensive.* Box 244, Savusau; 8–6117. 10 rooms. A working copra plantation with private individual bures to accommodate only 20 people. Serves three full communal meals. Tropical gardens.

Kontiki Lodge. *Inexpensive.* Box 244, Savusavu; 8–6262. 7 bures set amid palms by beach. Emphasis on water sports including deep-sea fishing and sailing.

Nukubati Island

Coral Island Resort. *Expensive.* Box 7, Labasa; 8–6288. 14 self-contained units on shores of picturesque bay. Full range of water sports. Rates include meals.

OVAIAU ISLAND

Levuka

Old Capital Inn. *Inexpensive.* Box 50, Levuka; 4–4057. 5 rooms. Very humble hotel with hot and cold water and restaurant serving English and Chinese dishes. Rates include breakfast.

Rukuruku

Rukuruku Holiday Resort. *Inexpensive.* Box 112, Levuka; 31–1491. 4 bures, 4 cottages. No-frills budget accommodation. Campsite with bathroom facilities alongside.

LAKEBA ISLAND

Lau Provincial Rest House. *Inexpensive.* C/o Provincial Office, Tubou, Lakeba, Lau; Lakeba, ext. 35. 4 rooms. Spartan accommodations with communal kitchen.

FIJI ISLANDS

TAVEUNI ISLAND

Qamea Beach Club. Taveuni Post Office; 8–7220. 8 bures facing the beach in idyllic setting. Top-quality accommodation. Activities include wind surfing and other water sports, village tours, crab hunts.

Castaway Taveuni. *Expensive.* Box 1, Taveuni; 8–7286. 35 rooms. Delightful setting at Waiyevo on Taveuni's west coast. Excellent facilities include swimming pool, sauna, bowling, tennis, water sports, and use of 9-hole golf course.

Maravu Plantation Resort. *Moderate.* Postal Agency, Matei; 401A. 3 self-contained bures by beach. Simple but tidy. Swimming pool, wind surfing, dining room and bar. Five new bures available in 1987.

Matei Lodge. *Moderate.* Matei Post Office; 401G. One luxurious guesthouse with full facilities and one bure on headland with great view. Specializes in game fishing.

Dive Taveuni. *Moderate.* Matei Post Office; 406M. Accommodation for 10 divers who take their pleasures—like their sport—seriously but simply. Tanks and back packs supplied.

Kaba Guesthouse. *Inexpensive.* Box 4, Taveuni; 87–58. 3 rooms. Budget accommodation 10 miles from airport. Cooking facilities.

TOBERUA ISLAND

Toberua Island Resort. *Deluxe.* Box 567, Suva; 4–9177 or 2–6356. 14 bures. Idyllic beach-side accommodation. Dining room specializes in local seafood and native foods. Fishing and excursion boats.

NAIGANI ISLAND

Islanders Village. *Expensive.* Private Bag, Suva; 4–4364. 22 rooms. Good-quality accommodation off northeast coast of Viti Levu an hour by air from Suva. Excursions to Ovalau Island. Dormitory $F10.

YASAWAS

Turtle Island Lodge. *Deluxe.* Box 9317, Nadi Airport; 7–2921. 12 bures. Exquisite island setting ideal for a sun-and-sand holiday. For adults only. Transfer by seaplane. Rates include meals.

RESTAURANTS. Fiji offers a wide variety of food—American-English, Indian, Chinese, Japanese, and Indonesian. Generally the quality is good and prices are very reasonable. Tourists tend to dine at the better-quality hotels, particularly outside Suva and Nadi, where most restaurants can be found. But in the two main cities it's possible to dine out in style or within a tight budget or to buy good quality take-out food.

Hotels and resorts usually hold specialty nights featuring ethnic dishes. Some offer the *lovo*—a traditional feast in which the food is wrapped in banana leaves and cooked slowly in an earth oven with hot stones. A whole pig may be the piece de resistance. One of the most popular local dishes with tourists is *kakoda* —raw Spanish mackerel marinated in lemon juice, coconut oil, peppers, tomatoes, and spices.

You can spend as much or as little as you like. At the top end, dinner for two with wine can cost $F120. The average would be $F20–$F30.

Following is a selection of restaurants not attached to hotels or resorts. As a general rule American-English restaurants will cost upwards of $F30 a couple and Chinese or Indian restaurants will be cheaper.

SUVA

Bambo Terrace. Gokai Building, Thomson St.; 2–6316. Chinese.
Curry Place. 16 Pratt St.; 31–3885. Indian.
The Java Room. 46 Gordon St.; 2–4932. Indonesian.
Le Normandie. 36 Cumming St.; 31–5172. French.
The Pizza Hut. 207 Victoria Parade; 2–2418. Italian.

Red Lion. 215 Victoria Parade; 31–2968. American-English. Excellent.
Samraat Restaurant. Ellery St.; 31–4070. Indian.
Scotts Restaurant. 26 Bau St.; 31–2708. American-English (expensive). A must if you want to dine in style in Suva.
Tiko's Floating Restaurant. Civic Centre; 31–3626. Seafood.
Wan-Q Restaurant. 25 Cumming St.; 2–3155. Chinese food at its best.

NADI

Curry Restaurant. Clay St.; 7–0960. Indian.
India Curry House. Main St.; 7–1717. Indian.
Mama's Pizza Inn. 498 Main St.; 7–0221. Italian.
Poon's Restaurant. Main St.; 7–0896. Chinese.

HOW TO GET AROUND. Nadi International Airport is the gateway to Fiji, and almost all visitors arrive there. *Air Pacific* (tel. Nadi 72–422) maintains a 30-minute shuttle service between Nadi and Suva's airport at Nausori. Typical fare is $F40.

Fiji has more than 15 airports and the main outer islands can be reached by air. Air Pacific has daily services to and from Nadi, Suva, and Labasa. *Fiji Air* (tel. 22–666) is the main island service. *Sunflower Airlines* (tel. 73–016) serves several islands from Nadi. *Turtle Airways* (tel. 72–988) operates island resort transfers and seaplane sightseeing. *Pacific Crown Aviation* (tel. 36–1422) has a helicopter-charter service based in Suva.

The offshore resort islands can also be reached by ship or launch, and transfers are usually part of the accommodation package. Yachts and cabin cruisers are available for charter (see Tours). Government and private shipping companies operate freight and passenger services linking the outer islands, but don't expect luxury. For information on government vessels call the Marine Department (tel. 22–818).

Taxi services are geared to take visitors from Nadi and Suva airports to hotels and resorts on Viti Levu. Taxis are metered in towns and are required to carry a fare table for long distances. It's best to agree on a price before taking a long taxi trip. You can expect to pay about $F11 from Nausori to Suva, $F30–$F50 from Nadi to the Coral Coast resorts, and F$65 to Deuba.

Buses operate right around Viti Levu and on the other main islands as well as town and suburban routes. Bus between Nadi and Suva is $F20. Air-conditioned coaches on this route are operated by *United Touring Fiji* (tel. 72–811), *Queen's Own Deluxe Coach* (tel. 72–056), *Pacific Transport* (tel. Nadi 7–0044, Suva 2–5425). Rental cars are readily available to explore Fiji's 1,950 miles of roads. Visitors with a current domestic license are eligible to drive. There are 11 rental-car agencies, most of which have offices at Nadi Airport, Suva, and Lautoka. You can expect to pay a minimum deposit of the estimated rental charge. Rates vary from about $F30 a day, with unlimited mileage. Agencies include *Hertz* (tel. Nadi 7–2771 or Suva 2–3026), *Thrifty* (tel. 7–2935), *UTC* (tel. Nadi 7–2463 or Suva 2–5616), *Budget* (tel. Nadi 7–2735 or Suva 31–5899), and *Avis* (tel. Nadi 7–2233, Suva 31–3833).

TOURS. Cruises. *Blue Lagoon Cruises* (Box 54, Lautoka; 6–3938/6–1622) offers four- and seven-day cruises to the beautiful Yasawa Islands from Lautoka. Opportunities for swimming, snorkeling, and fishing, plus visits to Fijian village and limestone caves. Four-day cruise from around $F300 plus tax; seven-day from around $F600 plus tax. Rates include meals.

Islands in the Sun (Fiji) Ltd. (Box 364, Lautoka; 6–1500) offers a variety of ways to explore the Fiji islands. You can take a two-day cruise from Lautoka to Mamanuca and Yasawa islands on the 120-foot three-masted schooner *Tui Tai*. Beach excursions provided. Cost: $F220 plus tax, including meals. A cruise and resort package (around $F350 plus tax) offers three nights at Beachcomber Island. You can take a day cruise to Beachcomber Island (around $F135), and there's a day trip from the Naviti Beach Resort on the Coral Coast to Vatulele Island, renowned for its red prawns.

South Sea Island Cruises (Box 718, Nadi; 7–0144) has day cruises to Mana, Plantation, and Castaway islands on the fine catamaran *Island Express*. Bar,

FIJI ISLANDS

boutique, and island-style entertainment. Barbecue or smorgasbord lunch included. The *Jungle Princess* will take you upriver to a wilderness area (around $F1). Game fishing can also be arranged.

Daydream Cruises Ltd. (Box 9777, Nadi Airport; 7–3441) offers shopping tours to Nadi from the Coral Coast and a visit to Malamala Island. Swimming, snorkeling, lunch, and entertainment, around $F31.

Coral Sea Cruise (tel. 36–1250). The glass-bottomed vessels *Coral Sea* and *Tropic Sea* offer coral garden viewing, swimming, and snorkeling, with luncheon. Depart daily from Tradewinds Hotel, Suva, 9 A.M. Costs: around $F26 for a full day; under $F20 for a half day.

Sightseeing Tours. *Orchid Island Fijian Cultural Centre* (Box 1018, Suva; tel. 31–1800). Offers half-day coach tour to picturesque Orchid Island. Opportunity to see Fijian history and culture and enjoy *yaqona* (kava drinking) ceremony.

Rainbow Tours (tel. Suva 31–1233) offers half-day tour of the Rewa Delta including Nasilai village, where Fijian pottery making is demonstrated. Tour includes visit to Hindu temple on return to Suva.

Wilderness Adventures (Fiji) Ltd. (Box 1389, Suva; 31–3500). Offers whitewater rafting on the Ba River daily except Sunday and full-day canoe trip on Navua River. Also four-day treks into interior Uih Levu. Age limit 15 years to 50.

Coral Coast Railway Co. (tel 5–0757). The restored train Fijian Princess provides a 12-mile scenic trip from Yanuca (near the Fijian resort hotel) to Natadola Beach along an old sugar-cane route. $F38 fare includes barbecue lunch. Full-day return excursion.

United Touring Fiji Ltd. (tel. 7–2811) offers a variety of coach tours including a five-day trip around Viti Levu with shopping and sightseeing excursions. A full-day guided tour from Nadi to Suva and return takes in the main scenic attractions of the capital. Pick up at all major Coral Coast resorts. A half-day tour from Nadi explores the Cannon Route—the historic Momi gun battery with its tremendous view of the Mamanuca Islands.

Road Tours of (Fiji) Ltd. (Box 9268, Nadi Airport; 7–2935). Full-day trips to Suva, Pacific Harbour, the Emperor gold mine; and the Sigatoka Valley, the heartland of Fiji's agriculture. Half-day trips include the Lautoka sugar mill, the Sigatoka highlands, and the Vuda lookout north of Nadi. Also offers three-day tours around Viti Levu.

Turtle Airways (tel. 7–2988) operates a daily seaplane sightseeing service from Newtown Beach or Regent of Fiji Hotel to the Nadi offshore resorts. Also charter flights.

Sun Tours Ltd. (Box 9403, Nadi Airport; 7–1266, Suva 31–2300) offers seven-day adventure holidays off the beaten track to Vanua Levu, Taveuni, Ovalau, and Naigani islands. For tourists who don't like to laze around.

SPORTS. With a tropical climate and endless shorelines there are limitless opportunities for boating, fishing, diving, and other water sports. Resorts are geared to meet visitors' needs, and numerous companies offer a wide range of facilities and equipment. Club Naitasi, offshore from Nadi, includes paraflying in its daily activities.

Boat Charters/Fishing. *Marau Gamefishing* (Post Office, Pacific Harbour; tel. 1–5347). The M.V. *Marau* is available for deep-sea fishing from Pacific Harbour at $F350 a day and $F175 a half day. Tackle provided free.

South Sea Island Cruises (Box 718, Nadi; tel. 7–1445). Operates out of Castaway Island and the Regent of Fiji.

Mollie Dean Cruises (Box 3256, Lami, Suva; tel. 36–1652). The 75-foot *Mollie Dean* is available from $F800 a day.

Islands in the Sun (Fiji) Ltd. (Box 364, Lautoka; tel. 6–1500). Several vessels available for charter from the Nadi and Lautoka areas.

Oceanic Schooner Co. (Box 9625, Nadi Airport; tel. 7–2455). Has the 100-foot schooner *Whale's Tale* available for charter, $F600 day or $F800 overnight.

Bowls. The main rinks at the *Suva Bowling Club* on the waterfront has two top-class greens with floodlights. Bowls can be hired. Visitors are also welcome at Lautoka, Levuka, and Vatukoula. The Fijian Resort Hotel and the Regent of Fiji both have eight-rink greens where bowls can be hired.

Diving. *Beqa Divers* (Box 777, Suva, tel. 36–1088) offers diving in Beqa lagoon named by *United States Skin Diver* magazine as one of the world's five top dive spots. Departs Pacific Harbour. $F50 per person; snorkelers $F20.

Dive Taveuni (c/o Matei Post Office, Taveuni, tel. 406M). Small resort that emphasizes diving. Back packs, tanks, and guides provided, $F50 a day.

Diver Services of Fiji Ltd. (Box 502, Lautoka, tel. 6-0496) offers dive and snorkeling trips daily and three-day trip to Waya Island ($F185 all inclusive). Instruction given. Four-day open-water dive course $F150.

Scubahire Ltd (Box 777, Suva, tel 36-1241) operates out Tradewinds Hotel, Suva. PADI training facility offers introductory dives and certification course instruction. Daily dives around Suva's main reef.

Sea Sports Ltd. (Box 65, Korolevu, tel. 5-0598/5-0555) offers Coral Coast diving from the Fijian or Hyatt Regency hotels.

Golf. The country's two 18-hole courses are the *Fiji Golf Club* at Suva and the outstanding international championship course at Pacific Harbour. There are 9-hole courses at Nadi, Lautoka, the Fijian Resort, Naviti Beach Resort, Reef Resort Hotel, and Tavenui Estates. Visitors usually need only pay green fees of a few dollars. Club rental is also reasonable.

Squash. Suva has six squash clubs: *Fiji Club* (tel. 2-5504), *United Club* (tel. 2-2678), *Defence Club* (tel. 2-2131), *Merchants Club* (tel. 2-4257), and *Tamavua Club* (tel. 39-1190). Courts are also at Nadi, Lautoka, and Levuka.

Tennis. Courts can be found at most hotels and resorts with the best facilities at *John Newcombe's Tennis Ranch* by the Regent of Fiji. It has six grass and four all-weather courts. Other good facilities are at The Fijian Resort, the Hyatt Regency and Naviti Beach Resort. In Suva, Victoria Park has courts that can be booked by the public (tel. 31-3428).

SPECTATOR SPORTS

For information about sports and sports organizations the Fiji Sports Council (Box 2348, Government Buildings, Suva) is the best source. The local press gives good coverage of sports.

From May to October, rugby football, soccer, hockey, and netball are the main sports, with local interest strongest in rugby. The national stadium in Suva is the main venue for rugby. After October the focus is on cricket, tennis, athletics, and volleyball.

Horse racing. Two meetings a year usually in June and September at Vatualevu near Nadi. Don't expect anything too sophisticated; some races are even bareback.

GARDENS, MUSEUMS, HISTORIC SITES. Suva. *Fiji Museum*, through the Thurston Gardens near the Grand Pacific Hotel, has many relics of Fiji's history from pre-European days. Open daily 8:30 A.M. to 4:30 P.M. Small entrance fee. *Thurston Gardens* has an outstanding collection of flora.

Colo-I-Suva, a forest park 7 miles from Suva, has nature walks, picnic areas, and swimming holes in Waisila Creek. Special permission is required to stay at this licensed campsite; contact the Forestry Department, tel. 2-2777.

Orchid Island, in a river 7 miles from Suva, has an extensive collection of tropical plants, timber, coral, and seashells. Fauna includes mongoose, iguanas, monkeys, and local snakes. The island also features a traditional Fijian village.

Deuba. *Cultural Centre and Marketplace of Fiji* (Postal Agency, Pacific Harbour; tel. 4-5083) re-creates traditional Fiji with dance theater, fire walking, and a village. Market specialty shops include quality handicrafts.

Nadi. *Waqadra Gardens* is a 70-year-old tropical botanical garden around an old family homestead. Tours at 10 A.M. and 11 A.M. Monday to Saturday.

Viseisei Village, where Fijians are thought to have first landed is near the Vuda lookout. Sights include a native house, a church, and a chief's home.

Momi Battery is the site of World War II guns used to guard Nadi. Great view.

Nadarivatural in the mountainous heart of Viti Levu, is a must for nature lovers. Camping is allowed with permission of Forestry Department.

SHOPPING. Duty-free shopping is a tourist occupation in Suva, Nadi and Lautoka. The duty-free shops pay 10% fiscal tax on all imported goods. Fiji's national association of duty-free dealers advises tourists to shop around on their own initiative and not be guided by touts, guides, taxi drivers,

FIJI ISLANDS

or tour operators. It is also wise to procure cash sale receipts to assist you in obtaining a warranty service back home as well as in going through customs procedures. The Suva Duty Free Merchants' Association has introduced a certificate of membership to be displayed in members' shops. Members promise to protect and safeguard the interests of duty-free customers.

Fijian handicrafts are attractive, relatively cheap, and popular with tourists. Mats, baskets and fans, are woven from pandanus leaves. The boldly decorated tapa cloth is made by beating the inner bark of the paper-mulberry tree until it is of tissue-paper thinness and then joining together several layers of these fine sheets by further beating. Indian artisans produce shell jewelry and ornaments.

There are two types of artifacts made from carved wood. One, carved from hard wood by village craftspeople mostly on outlying islands, includes *yaqona (kava)* bowls, clubs, and other traditional weapons. The other has developed recently and has attracted overseas interest. Carvers use the rain tree (known in America as the monkey-pod tree), a wood with an attractive grain and silken texture, to produce figures, heads, and various inlaid objects. The Ministry of Commerce and Industry's handicrafts section has an office in Ratu Sukuna House, Suva, to display authentic handicrafts. Tel. 211–306.

ENTERTAINMENT AND NIGHTLIFE. Generally entertainment, wining, and dining centers on the resorts and main hotels. The Fijian *make*—a program of song and dance—is a regular feature of most hotels. Fire walking is offered at several resorts.

Suva has a handful of nightclubs to appeal to a variety of ages and tastes. *Lucky Eddies* (Victoria Parade) appeals to the younger set with a disco Monday to Wednesday. *Rockefeller's* (Victoria Parade next door to Lucky Eddies) is more sophisticated and offers dancing 8 P.M. to 1 A.M. *The Engine Room* (Stinson Parade) is a relatively new spot aboard the floating restaurant. *Screwz* (Victoria Parade) is also for the younger set, with live band and disco. *Golden Dragon* (Victoria Parade) has an informal atmosphere for a relaxing evening.

DEPARTURE TAX. $F5.

KIRIBATI AND TUVALU

Recently Independent Nations

by
LOIS K. BRETT

Lois Brett is a California-based writer specializing in the South Pacific.

Until 1976, the Gilbert and Ellice Islands were a British colony, and transportation companies treated them as one territory. But they are now independent and separate, and they have new names: The Gilberts are Kiribati (pronounced "kiribas"), and the Ellice Islands are Tuvalu. Most Kirabati people call their republic Tungaru.

Kiribati and Tuvalu, which includes Ocean Island and the Phoenix and Northern Line islands, are situated in the southwest Pacific around the point where the date line cuts the equator. Although the total land area of these two countries is only about 283 square miles, they are scattered over more than two million square miles of ocean, and distances between them are enormous. Christmas Island (part of Kiribati), due south of Hawaii, is 2,000 miles from Ocean Island. The islands are remote from large centers of civilization and are off the major air routes. Tarawa (the capital of Kiribati) is about 2,500 miles from Sydney, Australia, and 1,400 miles from Suva, Fiji.

All these islands except Ocean Island rise no more than 12 feet above sea level; all are coral atoll lagoons, arcs of coral sand, devoid of hills or streams. Were it not for the masses of towering coconut palms, they would appear as little more than sand banks. If you steamed three miles out to sea, the islands would disappear from your horizon. In most of the atolls the reef encloses a lagoon; on the eastern side are long, narrow

KIRIBATI AND TUVALU

stretches of land varying in length from a few hundred yards to some ten miles and in width from one or two hundred yards to nearly a mile. The sea around the islands and in the lagoon swarms with fish, which form an important part of the islanders' diet. Not much grows here; the vegetation is poor. However, the coconut palm thrives on these islands and supplies a good deal of food and drink. The main diet consists of taro, bananas, uncultivated coconut, breadfruit, and seafood —everything else is shipped in. There is no native fauna, apart from birds.

There are 56,000 inhabitants of Kiribati; most of them are Micronesians. The 8,000 Tuvaluans are Polynesians who occupy nine islands with a land area of only 10 square miles.

The islands were first sighted by Europeans in 1765, but it was not until 1856, with the coming of the missionaries, was there any real European contact. The waters of the Gilbert Islands were a favorite with the whalers. Some of the crews deserted and settled, but there was no great interest in colonizing the islands at the time. In the 1860s "blackbirders" carried off about 400 islanders from the Ellice group for work in Peru. Other islanders were recruited to go to work on plantations in Fiji, Tahiti, Hawaii, and Australia. These incidents almost depleted the islands of their male population. This era also brought European diseases, particularly measles, against which the islanders had little resistance. With the people's consent, the islands became a British protectorate in 1892, in hope of eliminating blackbirding and the islanders' incessant tribal battles. A simple code of laws was drawn up based on earlier mission legislation, and a council of old men became the native courts to administer them.

When phosphate was discovered on Line Island in 1900, Ocean was annexed by Great Britain and placed within the jurisdiction of the the protectorate. With this rapidly growing phosphate industry, headquarters were transferred from Tarawa to Ocean Island. Over the years, other islands were annexed, including Christmas Island in 1919. In 1925 the colony was placed under the jurisdiction of the governor-general of New Zealand. The British drained the riches of the phosphate island of Ocean; today the island is the producer of 99 percent of Kiribati's income, but the phosphate will soon be depleted and leave the islands with no cash income. It is hoped that low-scale tourism will help.

The islands remained a British protectorate until 1941, when the Japanese invaded and took control of the Gilbert Islands. The Ellice Islands escaped because they were off the beaten track the Japanese had established for themselves.

The islands became very familiar to Americans when, two years after the Japanese armed forces landed on Tarawa in 1941, the Americans set up an advanced base on Funafuti in the Ellice Islands. On November 21, 1943, Americans launched their first penetration of Japan's ring of island defenses. At dawn, the United States Second Marine Division landed on the Tarawa islet of Betio. After four days of fierce fighting, the marines overwhelmed a strongly entrenched Japanese garrison. The Japanese lost 5,000 men killed in action or dead by suicide, and the Americans suffered 990 fatalities and 2,296 wounded. This was one of the bloodiest battles in the Pacific, and it was a major turning point in the war for the Americans.

There are three major islands of interest to tourists: Christmas Island, the largest coral atoll in the world, is three hours' air time or 1,300 miles due south of Honolulu. Tarawa and Abemama are near the point where the date line and the equator meet—about a five-hour flight from Christmas Island.

Tarawa

Tarawa is the capital island of Kiribati. You reach the islet of Betio by a half-hour drive from the Otintai Hotel (one of the two hotels on the island). A memorial on Betio honors the American war heroes on a point overlooking the harbor—a short walk from the ferry dock. A small park leads the way to the memorial. Along the shore line at Betio, huge bunkers, overgrown with shrubs and plants, are grim reminders of 40 years ago.

A returning veteran would hardly recognize the island. In World War II, the island was totally destroyed. Not a house or a palm tree was left standing. All the Europeans and most of the local people had either left before the Japanese invaded or were killed. Only a few people were left to do service at Japanese insistence. Today, most of the people of the republic live on Betio. The rest of the people on the island of Tarawa are spread along both the lagoon and the ocean side of the island. There is a fairly good road from Bairiki to Bonriki. Beyond Bonriki, you travel by foot or by boat to the few settlements along the way to the tip of the island at Naa.

Returning veterans will find that Tarawa is a lovely island, studded with thousands of palm trees along the white-sand beaches. They will also find to their pleasant surprise very friendly, shy people who, through some amazing gardening technique, are able to grow taro and bananas and who live mainly on uncultivated coconut, breadfruit, and seafood. Most islanders are outrigger sailors and fishers and spend much of the time on their boats. Fish are caught with traps, nets, and lines or speared in the lagoons, along the reef, and in the open sea. With the lack of large crops and the occasional drought, the people live a difficult but proud life.

American veterans wishing to view World War II battlefields will find that a mass of American and Japanese hardware is still conspicuous along the beaches. Hardware abounds at Nukufetau, Nanumea, Abemama, Tarawa, and Butaritari (which the American military labeled Makin). But a concentration of war relics may be found in Betio, at Tarawa, where 6,000 people occupy one square mile. You can circumnavigate Betio on foot along its beaches in about an hour. The best time to find portable war memorabilia is at low tide—but be sure to wear old tennis shoes to minimize the risk of gashing your feet on anything from shards of barnacle-encrusted Coke bottles of the mid-1940s to torn metal and empty cartridges.

Because the entire nation has only some 70 hotel rooms, there is a limit to the number of visitors Kiribati can handle. Kiribati is not for everyone. There is no place here for the demanding tourist or for those in a hurry. Kiribati is a fragile destination, intent on retaining its culture, and it's best suited to travelers who care about wonderful, underdeveloped places off the beaten track.

What tourists will find, wherever they travel in this country, are people who genuinely enjoy tourists, mostly because they see hardly any. They are unjaded, and their smiles and laughter are irrepressible.

Abemama

Robert Louis Stevenson and his wife loved the island of Abemama and lived here for a while in 1889. It probably hasn't changed much since those days, though now you arrive by plane rather than by boat.

Abemama is a coral atoll with a lagoon of clear, warm water, lots of palm trees, and plenty of white-sand beaches. It's only 100 air miles from Tarawa, and the Trislander flies there every day but Sunday.

The Robert Louis Stevenson Hotel is 9 miles from the airport, near the site where the Stevensons lived. Guests are met and transported from the airport in whatever transportation is available that day. If it is a truck, you toss your luggage in the back and plop yourself on top of it for the trip to the hotel. Along the way, you'll most probably pick up anyone who flags down the truck. Since there are no buses, this is the way people get around. Otherwise, most people stroll barefoot along the roads.

As you turn in to the hotel grounds, you are greeted by a huge overhanging sign that welcomes you to the Robert Louis Stevenson Hotel. It's just the type of hotel where Stevenson might have stayed. The cottages are built in a unique style with walls about four feet high, made of the spines of the coconut tree. Above is a latticed criss-cross open-air window pattern; the roof is thatched. The open-air cottages are on the lagoon surrounded by white sand overlooking the brilliant aqua water.

Abemama is a relaxing spot for couples or families. The atmosphere of the island is catchy. With no modern technology to get in the way, people seem to enjoy the simple things in life. There's time to snorkel, to swim, or to study the stars at night. Food is simple, most probably the fish caught that day or some combination of what comes from the hotel's simple larder, but you will not go hungry. With reminders of Stevenson's pictures in the hotel's lounge–dining room–bar and the whole atmosphere of the place, somehow food doesn't seem to matter.

Each cottage is simple but attractively furnished. There are a lanai, a bedroom where you sleep under mosquito nets, and a bath with only tepid but very refreshing water. (Be sure to bring plenty of bug repellent and soap.) If you imagine living a very simple Robinson Crusoe life but in a comfortable and very relaxing setting, you're at the RLS Hotel. The shy staff tries to entertain you at night but they prefer that you join them in song or contribute what talents you have. There's a piano-organ, and it's a perfect place to have singalongs as you relax under the stars, or in the common room.

The staff can arrange for fishing or snorkeling, but you must bring your own equipment. Pack plenty of books and expect to amuse yourself. Except for exploring and getting to know the local people, there is nothing to do but relax. If you are adventurous, this is one of the most idyllic get-away-from-it-all islands on earth.

Christmas Island

Captain Cook spotted Christmas Island on Christmas Day and so named it in 1777. Around 1837, whalers began to settle, setting up shops. By the 1860s there was a flourishing trade in coconut oil and copra.

Only three hours south of Hawaii, Christmas is a "sleeper" in American terms. Protective legislation makes it and the surrounding areas "tropical oceanic sanctuaries." The seas and the lagoons abound with fish. The island and small islets are also sea-bird sanctuaries, with hundreds of thousands of birds, unmatched by any other island in the Pacific.

Visitors stay at the Captain Cook Hotel, a rather plain, small place. The fishing and the bird watching make up for anything the hotel lacks. The rooms are clean, have small refrigerators and bottled water.

A hotel barbecue is held once a week under the trees near the ocean—charcoal-broiled lobsters, other seafood, chicken, and steak. All seafood is fresh, and the hotel will cook your own catch every night—you can even have your fish for breakfast and lunch if you wish. On barbecue night, the hotel puts on an outstanding Kiribati cultural show. The music and choreography are usually taught by a senior villager, whose pride in retaining the culture is strong. Bring lots of film for this colorful show.

Fishing and bird watching are the big things on Christmas, and Hawaiian Islanders sneak down here for a week at a time for a change of pace. The Captain Cook Hotel has facilities to fast-freeze your catches, including the huge lobsters, all of which can be taken back with you on the plane. (*Air Tungaru* offers a special seven-day fishing package.)

Bird watchers will find Christmas Island a haven. You can walk right up to the nesting birds, who have no fear of humans. A few beautiful white fairy terns will follow you around, then go back for companions, and all will investigate your every move.

There is only one weekly flight, so you must come prepared, but your week's stay will be one of the most rewarding experiences of your life. Bring lots of film; you can't buy it there. Also, this is where a tape recorder comes in handy—to capture the bird-life sounds.

Tuvalu

Nine islands make up Tuvalu, which has been an independent nation since 1978. The group is about 1,200 kilometers north of Suva in Fiji. Funafuti is the capital and main island. All but Niulakita are inhabited—about 1,000 people on each of the islands—for a total population of around 10,000.

The islands were originally named after a nineteenth-century politician, Edward Ellice, member of Parliament and owner of the ship *Rebecca*, in which Captain Arent De Peyster discovered Funafuti Atoll in 1819. A few of the other islands were spotted as early as 1528, but not until the nineteenth century did whalers, beachcombers, and missionaries begin to settle in.

Christianity arrived in the 1860s, and the islanders became British subjects in 1877. For most of the colonial period, the Ellice Islands consisted of a single administrative district with its headquarters on Funafuti. The islands were not captured by the Japanese because they were not included in Japanese plans. However, Americans used the islands as a base in 1942, and it was from there the colony was administered until the Japanese were driven from the Gilbert Islands by the American marines in November 1943. The Americans built the first air strip on Funafuti, and it has since been restored. After the war, many of the Ellice Islanders migrated to the Gilbert group because they needed work, but many stayed behind and started proceedings toward independence. They succeeded in separating themselves legally from the Gilbert and Ellice Islands group and became known as Tuvalu in 1975.

The people are Polynesians, most with a Samoan a heritage. Many Samoan customs and traditions still prevail.

Funafuti, the capital, is a pear-shaped atoll enclosing a lagoon. It is only 13½ miles by 10 miles, with 30 islets. Everyone lives near Fongafale, the main center of the island. It was here that Professor Sir Edgeworth David put down a 1,100-foot bore in 1897–1898 to prove Darwin's theory of the origin of coral islands. The island still has some of the remnants of the British colonial days—administration offices, the jail, and a hospital (the old hospital was destroyed by a hurricane in 1972, but a new one was opened in 1975). Prince Charles, following attendance at Fiji's independence celebration, made a four-day visit to Funafuti in 1970.

There's only one hotel on Funafuti—the Vaiaku Lagi Hotel; it's small and inexpensive. Facilities include dining room, bar, tennis courts, and a few small shops. Swimming is in the lagoon. The hotel is near the beach and only a five-minute walk from the airport. Another hotel may be added in late 1986. Bring your own entertainment to this very pleasant but isolated island.

PRACTICAL INFORMATION FOR KIRIBATI AND TUVALU

WHEN TO COME. The weather stays much the same year round—mid 80sF. Best time to visit is between March and October, the season of the northeasterly trade winds. Westerly gales bring rain and sticky discomfort from November through February.

TRAVEL DOCUMENTS. Kiribati: Passport required. Visa required at Kiribati at no charge. You must have ticket to leave with confirmed onward reservations and necessary document to depart to a third country. *Health requirements:* Cholera and yellow-fever inoculation required. No airport tax.
Tuvalu: Passport required. Visa: $A8.00. You must have ticket to leave and enough funds to stay. Airport tax: $A2.50.

HOW TO GET THERE. Christmas Island: via *Air Tungaru* from Honolulu. **Tarawa:** Air Tungaru from Majuro, Marshall Islands, and Tuvalu to Tarawa; *Air Nauru* from Nauru to Tarawa. **Tuvalu:** *Air Pacific* from Suva and from Tarawa via Air Tungaru. For up-to-date information on air fares and schedules contact: Air Tungaru, Box 274, Bikenibeu, Tarawa, Kiribati; or 4767 Farmers Rd., Honolulu, HI 96816; (808) 735-3994.

DRINKING WATER AND ELECTRICITY. Drink only bottled or boiled water or the palatable and wholly sterile juice from a freshly opened coconut. Electricity is geared for Australian and British-type outlets—three prong, 240 volts, 50 Hz. On Abemama, electricity is by generator. Don't count on it for electric razor or hair dryer.

WHAT TO PACK. Modesty in dress is essential. Lightweight casual clothing, preferably cotton. Bikinis are not recommended except for swimming. Women's shorts are never seen in town. Men usually wear walking shorts and open-necked cotton shirts; long trousers are worn in the evening or for formal occasions. Bring sunglasses, lots of film and tapes (you can't buy them here), Lomotil, insect repellent, batteries, flashlight, and candles. Shoes for beach and coral walking. Perhaps some balloons to share with children or small tablets and pencils to give away.

TIPPING. No tipping unless for extraordinary service.

CURRENCY. At present, the Australian dollar is used. $A1 = $US0.74

LANGUAGES. Local languages and English. Because of a local courtesy, English is not spoken in the company of anyone who does not speak it; thus the tourist should be prepared for one-to-one conversations.

TIME ZONE. Tarawa is GMT plus 11 hours; 20 hours ahead of U.S. Pacific Standard Time. Christmas Island is GMT minus 10, 2 hours behind PST.

ACCOMMODATIONS: Kiribati: The *Otintai Hotel* on Tarawa has 20 a/c rooms. Be sure to book well in advance. Box 270, Bairiki, Tarawa, Republic of Kiribati, Central Pacific. For reservations cable: OTINTAAI; tlx: 1041. $18–$35. There are a good restaurant, and a bar; airport shuttle. Car and motorbike rentals and excursions can be arranged. Rooms in the new wing all have balconies overlooking the lagoon. *Hotel Kiribati* at Betio, 16 rooms. For reservations cable: JKKBS BETIO. Box 504, Bairiki, Tarawa, Republic of Kiribati, Central Pacific. $39–$60. Bar; dining room serves Chinese and English-style meals. Rent cars or motorbikes; airport transportation can be arranged. *Captain Cook Hotel* on Christmas Island has 36 rooms. For reservations cable: COOKHOTEL. $59–$60. Clean, plain rooms with refrigerators. *Robert Louis Stevenson Hotel* on Abemama; for reservations write: Kiribati Visitors Bureau, TX KI 039 a/b Resources, Box 64, Bairiki, Tarawa, Republic of Kiribati, Central Pacific. $22/person, including breakfast. Charming open-air cottages.

Tuvalu: *Vaiaku Langi Hotel*, Funafuti, Republic of Tuvalu, Central Pacific. Be sure to book in advance. Rates start at $A20. A new hotel was to have been built in 1986.

TOURIST INFORMATION. Kiribati: Government of the Republic of Kiribati, Ministry of Natural Resources Development, Box 64, Tarawa, Kiribati. Bairiki, Tarawa, Kiribati, Central Pacific. Tlx KI77039 RESOURCES; cable RESOURCES. **Christmas Island:** Write *Air Tungaru*, 4767 Farmers Rd., Honolulu, HI 96816. Tel. (808) 735-3994. Tlx 296808 AIRTG HR; cable TUNGAIR HNL. **Tuvalu:** Tuvalu High Commission, Box 1495, Suva, Fiji. Tel. 2-2697/8.

TOURS. Christmas Island: *C.H.R. Ltd.*, 4767 Farmers Rd., Honolulu, HI 96816. Contact: Carol Farrow, above address, or tel. (808) 735-3994. Tlx: 296808 AIRTG. According to Bob and Carol Farrow, operators of the tours to Christmas Island, fishing at Christmas is "ranked the number-one spot in the world with fly and spin fishermen." Popular catches include bonefish, trevalle (ulua), and wahoo. Fish can be flash-frozen and taken home. Their 7-day tours cost $1,395, including meals, transportation (air and ground), boats, etc. Flights leave Honolulu every Wednesday at 6 A.M. and return the following Wednesday at 1 P.M. Tour also includes trip to the bird sanctuaries. Also packages available through Air Tungaru; see above.

HOW TO GET AROUND. Kiribati: *Air Tungaru* operates a special service for arriving and departing passengers to and from airport. Fare: $A2.50. Regular buses run between Bonriki and Bairiki. Fare is $A0.65. Bus on Betio circles the atoll frequently. Fare: $A0.30. There is very limited taxi service. Car rentals can be arranged at your hotel. Best to order before you arrive. **Christmas Island:** There is no public transport. Rental trucks or minibus available for hire through Air Tungaru. **Tuvalu:** Write *Tuvalu High Commission*, Box 1495, Suva, Fiji. Tel. 2-2697/8 for information regarding transport and other services, or write to the *Vaiaku Langi Hotel* (see above). Note: It is possible to hire local people for their transport—land or sea. Settle *fairly* on price beforehand. On **Tarawa**, it's possible to take a voyage from Tarawa to a distant island in a *baurua*— a large, twin-sailed ocean-going outrigger canoe, centuries old in design.

SHOPPING. There are few handicrafts: baskets, table mats, fans, or items made from coconut shells. There are also a few weapons and artifacts worth looking for. Among tools of war, the Kiribati shark-tooth sword is claimed to be unique in concept and craft. The swords, in great demand by collectors of both artifacts and militaria, are of polished coconut wood, with drilled shark teeth, filed to razor sharpness, lashed to the two edges. The hilt and sometimes the entire length of the sword is covered with finely woven dye-patterned pandanus into which, for good luck, a plaited strand of a woman's hair is sometimes woven. Sword length varies from 12 to 36 inches.

A prized Tuvalu artifact is the carved wooden *tuluma,* also spelled *turama,* an oval miniature sea chest, 18 to 24 inches in diameter, with hermetically fitting lid, in which treasured possessions were carried on transoceanic canoe journeys. Miniature models (4 to 10 inches in diameter) have been used for decades in the South Pacific as humidors and, in recent times, as containers for cameras. A comparable sea chest in the Gilberts is named *bookai.*

Business Hours: Mon.–Fri. 8 A.M.–noon and 1–5 P.M.; Saturday 7 A.M.–noon.

VANUATU

by
KATHLEEN HANCOCK

New Zealander Kathleen Hancock is a freelance journalist and photographer covering travel, trade, and current affairs in the territories of the South Pacific.

In 1606 Pedro Fernandez de Quiros, the finest navigator of his time, came upon Espiritu Santo, northernmost island of the New Hebrides group. He believed he had discovered the great southern continent hinted at by Ptolemy and Marco Polo, outlined on ancient maps as stretching right across the South Pacific. The Portuguese Quiros was looking for land and gold for his sponsor, King Philip III of Spain, and souls for the Church of Rome.

Not a man to be intimidated by immensities of ocean, he had christened the Pacific the Gulf of Our Lady of Loreto on leaving the coast of Peru. And four months later he made landfall in the northern New Hebrides at Gaua in the Banks Group. Gifts were exchanged with the friendly local people, but in the Spanish manner Quiros took hostages against the chance of sudden attack, putting them in the stocks for the night and, worst indignity of all for a Melanesian, shaving their heads and beards.

Sailing south, Quiros found more land and a great bay with a good port. The terrain was mountainous, and he was sure this was the continent he sought. He named it Terra Australis del Espiritu Santo. A great gathering of Melanesians lined the beach to see the strange creatures in their huge ships of 150 tons. The local people refused to let the Spaniards approach them on the beach but laid down their bows

VANUATU

and arrows and indicated that the visitors could get water, giving them presents of fruit and vegetables.

But soon there was trouble. Muskets were fired in the air to frighten the increasing numbers of excited people who gathered in the surrounding bush. A Spaniard fired too low and killed a Melanesian. There was some parleying. A line was drawn in the sand, and a chief indicated that his people would lay down their arms if the Spaniards would do the same. But Quiros' admiral, one Torres, mishandled the situation, arquebuses were fired, and a chief dropped dead. He was hung from a tree "that he might be seen by all."

From this point there was never a chance of reconciliation between Quiros' men and the people he called "courageous and sociable." He broke the most sacred taboos of the people, beginning with the shaving of heads on Gaua. At Espiritu Santo his men stole carefully husbanded supplies of food from hill villages where they might have bartered for them successfully. Small boys were kidnapped to take home to Spain. And "he even broke the rules of war so far as to kill a chief." (Tom Harrisson: *Savage Civilisation*).

Quiros took possession of the "continent," named the great anchorage the Bay of St. Philip and St. James, set up an altar, and christened the city-to-be Nuova Jerusalema. But there were more killings, kidnappings, and ambushes. Local resistance persisted. Many of Quiros' men fell ill with fish poisoning. Discontent, unrest, and nostalgia for home unsettled the crews. Fifty days after their arrival in Espiritu Santo the *Almiranta* sailed out of what is now called Big Bay, bound for South America and ultimately Madrid. After seven years spent petitioning the King of Spain for recognition of his great discovery and compensation for its cost, Quiros died penniless and without honor.

For some reason Quiros' findings were suppressed, and it was 162 years before these islands were visited again by European explorers. Bougainville sighted Maewo, Pentecost, Espiritu Santo, and Malekula in 1768 and established clearly that this was no continent. Four years later Captain James Cook discovered the southern islands of the group and charted the whole archipelago, giving the islands their inappropriately dour Scottish name.

A mixed bag of missionaries, whalers, and sandalwooders followed Cook; then the "blackbirders" moved in with their ugly trade. By 1885 missionaries and planters, mostly British and French, were settling in increasing numbers on most islands in the group and problems arose over their personal safety. Murders were commonplace, with missionaries and traders the usual victims.

In 1877 John Higginson, an Irish-born trader but a naturalized French citizen, was urging the French Government in New Caledonia to take over the New Hebrides, but this idea met with cries of outrage from the well-established British missions and especially from neighboring Australia. Finally the British and French governments got together in 1888 and set up a joint naval commission to keep law and order in the group. Then German interests appeared on the scene with a vigorous campaign to extend their influence in this part of the Pacific. To counter this threat the French and British governments set up the Franco-British Condominium in 1906.

Joint "Pandemonium"

This jointly controlled administration known in the Pacific as the "Pandemonium" with its two sets of laws, two education systems, and two official languages and pidgin as well, was clumsy and expensive to run and functioned at a pace that any self-respecting snail could have bettered. But it did keep the peace and introduce limited education and a system of hospitals and clinics to a wild and remote part of the Pacific.

News of World War I took three months to reach the remote New Hebrides and had little effect on these islands. But the outbreak of World War II was a different matter. The French administration of the New Hebrides was among the first of France's overseas territories to rally to de Gaulle. And when Japan entered the war in 1941, these islands became a forward base for U.S. troops, with attention concentrated on Espiritu Santo.

The Segond Channel, a strait between Espiritu Santo and Aore, was found capable of harboring hundreds of ships. Roads, airfields, and docks were built. Workshops, floating cranes, hospitals, and sawmills were set up. The rain forest was cleared to establish hundreds of acres of market gardens to feed the troops in the New Hebrides and the Solomons. On Espiritu Santo the village of Luganville (or Santo, as it's commonly known) was the staging point for U.S. army, navy, and Marine forces advancing on the Solomons. In 1943 there were around 40,000 U.S. troops in Santo, later joined by about 1,400 New Zealanders, mostly airmen. Men, ships, and supplies poured into the once sleepy backwater. French planters sent their nubile daughters to a safer island.

Independence was granted by Britain and France to the duly elected government of the New Hebrides on July 30, 1980, and the new state was christened Vanuatu, meaning "our land." In the first flush of independence there was some political unrest on Espiritu Santo and Tanna, but both are now back to normal. Efate was never affected.

The ni-Vanuatu (the new name for the Melanesian inhabitants) are now emerging from a confused and confusing period of sporadic contact with a motley array of European explorers, traders, sandalwooders, missionaries, colonists, civil servants, soldiers, sailors, and airmen. Within the passing of less than a century they have left the stone age behind to confront European living, languages, and legal systems. Whatever the rate of emergence into the hard light of social, economic and political reality, one thing is for sure. The great Melanesian gifts of common sense, goodwill, honesty, and humor will prevail.

These are a sturdy, proud, and independent people, with a strongly developed sense of fair play. Even a fleeting encounter with them is a rewarding experience for the traveler looking for a different scene. In these islands it's worth considering the answer given to an early missionary by a man of Tanna. "Why do you put that paint on your faces?" asked the missionary. "Why do you put those clothes on?" asked the Tannese. "This is our way of clothing; that is yours."

The Economy

Vanuatu is a potentially rich area. These islands are incredibly fertile, and the climate, though tropical, is a pleasant one with a predictable rainfall. Copra heads the list of exports, with fish not far behind and cocoa coming on strong. A good way behind come beef and coffee, but production here is increasing and capable of much greater development. The recent growth of tourism has brought another source of income to the group, and the popularity of the area as a tax haven has also had a considerable effect on the economy.

Most of the meat eaten in Vanuatu is produced locally, and there are great strides being made to improve local herds. Cattle were first introduced as a cheap form of weed control in the coconut plantations, but both European planters and Melanesian villagers have discovered that a little care in sowing good grasses and the purchase of good quality breeding stock makes for an extra source of income at not much additional expense. With the introduction of pedigree Charolais and Hereford bulls, as well as Brahmin cross-bred cattle, herds have improved greatly.

Plantation labor is pretty scarce in these islands. It's one of the few Pacific territories that is underpopulated, and to aggravate this, local workers have long been accustomed to spending fairly long periods in New Caledonia, where nickel is king.

Life in Vanuatu and especially in remote Espiritu Santo still ambles on in the same lazy way that it has for nearly a century. In Vila you can buy luscious brandied cherries at the trade stores and ivory and jade and gold jewelry at the Chinese shops. But in the bush villages elsewhere in the group, pigs are both capital and power. While a jazz combo belts out its rhythms on a hotel dance floor, not far away in the hill villages the thump of a hundred feet shakes the ground in a "custom dance."

Exploring Vanuatu (formerly the New Hebrides)

Captain Cook was never much of an original thinker when it came to christening all those islands he discovered in the Pacific 200 years ago. But he seems to have struck rock bottom when he gave such an unimaginative name to the 80 islands of that enchanting archipelago known as the New Hebrides. Now, of course, his error has been corrected by the new independent government.

This offbeat, slightly raffish, totally fascinating collection of islands lies east of the Coral Sea, scattered north to south in the southwest Pacific like confetti. This is a territory where tourists are not yet processed, where you can still wander along a white beach on the edge of an impossibly blue lagoon with only the lap of the tide to break the silence. The two resort hotels in Vila modestly face the lagoon; a little investigation will disclose a few gourmet restaurants and the ambience is as near to the traditional picture of a South Pacific island as you're likely to find.

On the short flight to Vanuatu from Australia, New Caledonia, Fiji, or New Zealand, it's hard to imagine that in about two or three hours you will be descending over Efate Island's endless acres of coconut palms. Your first hint of the important part these islands played in the Pacific war comes as you disembark at Bauer Field, named in honor of a gallant American airman. Melanesian officials, brown and sturdy, in their new green uniforms, whisk you through the few formalities with a minimum of fuss.

Old Vila hands stay at Le Lagon, that lovely cluster of thatched roofs on Erakor Lagoon. This is a notable hotel in anyone's language. At the height of the winter season, or ticking over quietly between times, Le Lagon never gives any sign of hustle or crowding. You can hobnob with your fellows around the pool, or splash together in that translucent lagoon, meet in the bar or on the golf course. But for lovers of peace and solitude, the rooms and bungalows dotted among huge trees and slender palms provide a blissful escape from the worries of day-to-day life.

The new Iririki Island Resort on the island of that name looks over the harbor to Vila Town. Bungalows nestle among big trees and flowering shrubs, climbing the hill to restaurant and bar. There are a big pool and a small beach, the ambience is upscale and elegant, and the cuisine gourmet, with dancing nightly to the hotel duo.

The Intercontinental Island Inn at Tassiriki is set at the far end of the lagoon. The need for more rooms for visitors to Vila has been obvious for some time, since the word about the fascinations of Vanuatu began to filter through the Pacific, and this new hostelry will certainly help to meet the growing demand. There is an excellent hairdresser here and a lively disco operates nightly in the Ravenga Room. Yachtsmen and diving groups tend to stay in town at *Rossi's* on the waterfront. A snack menu is available on the terrace. Another modestly charming hostelry near Vila township is Solaise—also a favorite gathering place for locals. If economy is uppermost in your mind, one of the small rooms in this single-story complex set around a shady swimming pool could well suit you. Overlooking beautiful Vila harbor, the Vate Marina, a few minutes from the post office, is a good place for budget-conscious travelers. And the old Vate Hotel (renamed The Olympic) right in town has been almost gutted and totally refurbished with excellent cooking facilities. The restaurant on the ground floor is popular with discriminating diners.

If you want a change from your hotel, take off aboard trimaran or ketch for a three-day cruise around Efate and the small offshore islands, visiting tribes, buying mats, diving, fishing, and picnicking. Ask at your hotel's tour desk about this. If one day on the ocean is enough, try a relaxing sail on a cruiser with a picnic lunch and all the sun you can soak up to loosen those knots you came here with.

Excursions by road outside Vila are not as smooth as excursions by sea. But if you are looking for a day out, drive around the island either by rental car or with one of the many tours, stopping at Eton Beach for a swim and lunch.

Closer to Vila, Susan Barnes' Whitesands Country Club at Rentabao offers riding through the rain forest, swimming 200 yards from the Clubhouse. Succulent lunches are available on order. An idyllic scene, the mounts are first rate, and both experts and beginners are welcome. Or you can eat at Nagar Hall right on the beach at Paunagisu, where fresh seafoods, grills, and chicken are featured on a moderately priced menu.

Among resorts near Vila is Hideaway, a minuscule island retreat on a five-acre atoll about half an hour by water taxi from the township, or less if you drive the 15 minutes by road to the jetty that looks over toward the island. But don't settle for a day trip—stay a few nights. Lush vegetation and your own private piece of lagoon make this an informal resort to dream about. Snorkel; go coral viewing on Mele Bay. The surrounding waters are densely populated with marine life—they're also a marine reserve. Diving is becoming a feature of this small resort island. The emphasis is on local foods, admirably cooked.

Erakor Island, set on an atoll opposite Le Lagon, is a delightful little bungalow resort run by Australian Val Ireland in conjunction with Erakor village. Great food, comfortable accommodations, and an extra bonus in the form of a ruined chapel and missionary graves.

Manuro Paradise is different—30 miles from Vila, with the most unusual beach scene in the area. The Pacific has carved a rectangular lagoon through the coral rock, sloping up to a sugar-white beach. Bungalows dot the grassy sward, and the food is great. Check to be sure it's open, though.

Back at Vila, shopping in the little township is an adventure. Travelers browse in the Chinese and Vietnamese shops, dark aromatic treasurehouses. Serious collectors of artifacts and shells investigate Island Crafts and Handikraf Blong Vanuatu. A colorful market opposite the Government Building sells shells, artifacts, clothing, and produce on Wednesday, Friday, and Saturday. The Cultural Center has an interesting display of artifacts and shells.

French influence ensures you'll eat well in this far-flung series of dots on the wide Pacific. There's a handful of excellent restaurants in Vila. Good French cooking is the norm, varied by Italian, Vietnamese, and European. You can also buy delicious cheeses and fresh bread in town

VANUATU

from the two big trade stores—Burus and Philp and Ballande—both on Kumul Highway, the main street, or collect takeaways at the *Solaise Motel*.

It's a relaxed scene in Port Vila. The atmosphere is informal, there's no tipping, and tariffs are very moderate by today's standards. This is a duty-free area too, and bargains abound.

Leave yourself plenty of time in these islands. This is a destination where things tend to crop up, adventures materialize, opportunities arise. You'll meet a new kind of people—warm-hearted, eccentric, generous, and hospitable. It's Jack London country, large as life and twice as crazy.

The Outer Islands—Tanna

The next stop on your exploration program could be Tanna, where Captain James Cook saw the glow from the sacred volcano Yasur miles out to sea. The copper-skinned Tannese call their lush island "the navel of the world." You can fly down to Tanna from Vila with Air Melanésie in about an hour, with a possible way stop at Erromanga, "the martyr isle," dubiously distinguished for wholesale murders of missionaries last century.

The plane approaches Tanna over a coastline jumble of red and black boulders washed by the aqua and emerald colors of the reef. You skim over the treetops of the rain forest. From the air the grassy airstrip looks like a cricket pitch, but it's twice the size of the one I landed on the first time I visited Tanna a few years ago.

At the reed and thatch bungalows at Epul Bay, *Tanna Beach Resort* offers good accommodations, a Vila-class restaurant, and cold beer from the bar. It's a lovely spot—rustic, but civilized. The bungalows are scattered among the coconut palms on grassy slopes rolling to a spectacular black sand beach.

At Whitegrass, Chief Tom Numake's bungalows overlook a rocky cove. A small restaurant serves wine and food, and your host will arrange excursions.

In the hill villages behind Epul Bay a cautious approach will pay dividends. These are proud and dignified people, not to be intruded upon with impunity. But as everywhere, good manners are a key to friendly acceptance. A pocketful of candy helps, too.

Villages are the ultimate in primitive living. Bamboo and nipa huts stand a mere five feet at the ridgepole. A rough barrier of logs keeps the pig population out of the dark and smoky interiors. Once Tannese reserve is breached you may be given oranges, and you can occasionally buy a mat or a Tannese grass skirt. If your village neighbors approve of you, there's a chance you might be invited to a "custom" dance—a nightlong feast of primeval music, color, and excitement.

The island is incredibly fertile. Tanna's ten-foot topsoil grows yams six feet long. In the rain forest the margin of a deep pool makes a perfect picnic spot. The indigo ocean crashes in white foam on glistening beaches, black and white. Herds of magnificent wild horses roam at White Grass, and the mighty stallions snort defiance at you, as you are driven by the tourist bus over the high plateau.

There's even a pocket volcano thrown in, with performance almost to order. The area around the volcano is also the headquarters of the Jon Frum movement, a cargo cult that originated on Tanna during the war. A belief arose that Jon Frum would ultimately appear, probably by plane, in the form of refrigerators, trucks, canned food, cigarettes, and all the enormous variety of material goods that had suddenly begun to pour into these islands as part of the American war effort. Jon Frum symbols, which include crosses painted red, may be photographed but should not be touched. Permission to climb the volcano must be obtained from the neighboring village. Tour Vanuatu and Air Tropicana run day tours.

The Outer Islands—Ambrym

Ambrym has always been a mysterious island with its two live volcanoes, black soil, stone carvings, and monumental slitgongs. Ritual and custom are alive here, and for the first time travelers can find, not only accommodation, but an exciting experience. Superb food, guided trips to bush villages, splendid mounts for riding, hikes up the lava river bed to the base of the volcano (only the intrepid make the final climb), bathing in nearly hot springs—it's a scenario second to none in the South Pacific. Air Melanésie offers a weekend package.

The Outer Islands—Espiritu Santo

You can find a lot of adventure in a couple of weeks in Vanuatu; Espiritu Santo, largest island in the group, presents a picture totally different from either Efate or Tanna.

You fly into Santo from Vila with Air Melanésie or from Honiara with Solair, over a canopy of rain forest, interrupted here and there along the coast by the orderly ranks of coconut plantations. Relics of the Pacific war are everywhere on this island. The remains of fighter planes rust in the dense bush. And the jungle has overtaken the miles of market gardens that once supplied New Zealand and U.S. troops. Now, however, the dogs of war are silent in the Coral Sea, and today Santo sleeps in the sun.

Bokissa Island is a real hideaway, separated from the Santo mainland by the big island of Aore. Fifteen minutes by runabout and you find a Crusoe situation, but with all the amenities. Great swimming and diving, easy walks, a pool, and excursions. Good cooking, a varied library, and all the board games you've ever heard of.

The Hotel Santo will be your base on the mainland. It's small, modern, but full of atmosphere. The locals gather at the bar before lunch and dinner. You'll hear tall tales of the Pacific from Scottish supercargoes, Fijian first mates, Melanesian administration officers, Chinese storekeepers. Look around at the paintings, the montages, the ancient artifacts on the walls. Decoration is by Marcel Moutoun, who completed his paintings for the 22 bedrooms in an incredible two-month burst of effort.

Your choice of restaurants in this little township is limited, but the food is as intriguing as Santo itself. Down at the end of the empty main street, is Pinocchio, a typical French bistro. Little Saigon is new, too, with a Vietnamese menu. The formidable Mme. Harbulot dispenses fresh local food in the French manner at a new venue at Chez Lulu.

This island is a storehouse of local custom and wartime history. It's for travelers who like to find their own adventure. Shorter trips include Fanafo village, and the heavily forested South Santo coast where you may still see a "man bush" in traditional dress walking along the coral road. Santo isn't the thriving copra and cattle center it was before independence—only 200 Europeans remain there now—but for the adventurous traveler it still offers much of interest.

Divers will find plenty to do in Santo. There are myriads of fishy wonders, an infinite variety of shells to be gathered, and also the immense wreck of the 32,000-ton troopship *President Coolidge* to be explored. She lies on her side in the Segond Canal, the bow in 80 feet, the stern in about 240 feet of water. This area is an underwater paradise for both reef and wreck divers. Their contact will be Allan Power, who

VANUATU

can be reached at the hotel. Resident in Santo ten years now, and keeper of the local underwater monuments, Power is a world-famous diver who knows the wrecks and the fish who inhabit them. His underwater photography has been featured in *International Photography*.

In Santo there's lots of lovely gossip, as in all Pacific outposts. The coconut wireless may give a garbled version of the truth, but what it lacks in accuracy, it makes up for in color. Given access to local rumor, you'll never need to open those paperbacks you brought with you. Regional half-truths are much stranger than fiction.

PRACTICAL INFORMATION FOR VANUATU

HOW TO GET THERE. Flights from: New Caledonia—*Air Caledonie International*, four times weekly; New Zealand—*U.T.A./Air Caledonie* or *Air New Zealand/Air Caledonie*, each once weekly; Sydney—*Air Vanuatu*, four times weekly; Honiara—*Solair*, twice weekly; Brisbane—*Air Pacific*, twice weekly; Nadi—*Air Pacific*, twice weekly; Apia—*Polynesian Airlines*; Melborne—*Air Vanuatu*, once weekly.

CLIMATE. Semi-tropical with average of 70° May-October, 80° November-May. Humid and often rainy January-February.

Average Temperature (°Fahrenheit) and Humidity

Vila	Jan	Feb	Mar	Apr	May	June	July	Aug	Sept	Oct	Nov	Dec
Average max. day temperature	85°	87°	85°	83°	81°	80°	78°	79°	79°	82°	83°	85°
Days of rain	22	20	23	20	19	18	17	14	16	15	17	19
Humidity, percent	75	76	78	76	74	73	72	70	70	68	69	69

General hints: Note that the seasons are reversed from the northern hemisphere. May to October are good months for tourists. Humidity is high year-round.

CLOTHING. Informal the year round. Daytime, cotton dresses or slacks for women, slacks or shorts for men. No ties. Evening, light long or short dresses for women; for men, slacks.

CURRENCY. Monetary unit the vatu; current rate: 100 vatu = $US1.04.

ENTRY FORMALITIES. A passport is required of all visitors. No visas required for stays of 30 days or less. Onward tickets required.

HEALTH. Medical services available in most areas likely to be visited. It is advisable to take anti-malarial tablets once weekly, starting one week before arrival and continuing for four weeks after leaving the area. As in all tropical regions, it is advisable to equip yourself with remedies against upset stomachs. There are no dangerous animals or insects in Vanuatu.

WATER. The Government Water Board assures visitors it is safe to drink from the tap, but if you are prone to digestive disorders, it may be best for you to boil tap water or stick to the bottled variety.

LANGUAGES. English and French are spoken. Pidgin English and many other dialects are also used in Vanuatu.

ELECTRICITY. 220–240 volts, 50 cycles, 2 prong plugs.

TIPPING. Not in Vanuatu, please. It is contrary to Melanesian customs.

POSTAGE. The post office is located on Kumul Highway, the main street. Hours: 7:30 A.M.–11:15 A.M.; 1:15 P.M.–4:30 P.M. Saturday 7:30 A.M.–11 A.M. Postage rates: Australia and New Zealand, letters 35 vatu, postcards 30 vatu; U.S., letters 45 vatu, postcards 40 vatu; Europe, letters 55 vatu, postcards 50 vatu.

TIME ZONE. GMT plus 11 hours, or 19 hours ahead of U.S. Pacific Standard Time.

ACCOMMODATIONS. By world tourism standards, only one Vila hotel comes within the *expensive* category, but high standards of comfort and cuisine are found at the moderate level, plus 9-hole golf courses, pools, and an outlook over Erakor Lagoon that is the essence of the South Pacific. The motel-apartment scene is also attractive, especially for families, ranging from apartments right in town to tiny islands where you can swim, snorkel, or just lie in the sun, waiting for the next delicious meal. The price categories are as follows: *Expensive,* $US96–$US123; *moderate,* $US32–$US50; *Inexpensive,* $US16–$US30. Most hotels accept American Express, Diners Club, Visa, or MasterCard, but it's wise to take cash to outer-island resorts.

Vila

Erakor Island. *Moderate.* Box 24; 2983. In the lagoon of the same name. Simple bungalows, great food. 24 hr. boat service to mainland. American Express.

Intercontinental Island Inn. *Moderate.* Erakor Lagoon. Box 215; 2040. 166 rooms, air conditioning, all facilities, room service, 2 restaurants, 2 bars, pool. Shops, hairdresser, tour desk. Golf (9 holes), tennis. Conference facilities. Bank, boutique, disco. All cards.

Le Lagon. *Moderate.* Erakor Lagoon. Box 86; 2313. 115 rooms, 25 bungalows on Erakor Lagoon. Air conditioning, all facilities, refrigerator. Some suites, to accommodate 5. The Michoutouchkine restaurant for fine cuisine and a verandah cafe. 2 bars, pool. All water sports, golf course (9 holes), cruises, films, dancing daily in the *Pilioko* piano bar. Conference facilities. Shops, tour desk. Both restaurants offer excellent cuisine. American Express, Diners Club.

Olympic Hotel, *Moderate.* Box 709; 2464. Right in town, popular with business people. Well-equipped apartments overlooking town and harbor. Secretarial services, telex, American Express, Diners Club.

Coral Apartments. *Inexpensive.* Box 810; 3569. Self-contained studio apartments. 5 minutes' drive along airport road. American Express, Diners Club.

Marina Motel. *Inexpensive.* In town on Erakor Road, Box 56; 2566. 12 air conditioned apartments, pool, harbor view.

Rossi's. *Inexpensive.* Rue Higginson. Box 11; 2528. Oldest established hotel in Vanuatu. 32 rooms, air conditioning, and all facilities. Restaurant, bar. Undergoing extensive modernization. All cards.

Solaise. *Inexpensive.* Rue Picardie. Box 810; 2150. 16 units 5 min. from town, each with shower-room, refrigerator. Light breakfast included. Fans. Restaurant, bar, pool, garden. Weekly rates after two weeks. Varied menu, excellent cooking. American Express, Diners Club.

Out of Town

Hideaway. *Moderate.* Mele Island. Box 875; 2963. 6 miles from Vila, 3-minute ferry service to island. 10 bungalows, restaurants, bar, tariff incl. Swimming, snorkeling, diving, good food. American Express.

Vila Chaumieres. *Moderate.* Box 400; 2866. Bungalows, good facilities, popular bar.

Teouma Village Holiday Resort. *Inexpensive.* Box 651; 3248. Charming garden complex of 2 bedroom apartments on Erakor Lagoon. Safe swimming, baby-sitters. American Express, Diners Club.

Santo

Hotel Santo. *Moderate.* Box 178, Luganville; 250. Ten minutes from airport. 22 rooms. French restaurant, bar, swimming pool, curio shop, game room. Air conditioned. Tours arranged. American Express.

Tanna

Tanna. *Economical.* Box 27, c/o Chief Tom Numake, White Grass; 3510. 9 bungalows at Epul Bay. New management. Licensed bar and restaurant, fresh local food,—lobster, fish, steak. Volcano excursions, wild horses. American Express.

Chief Tom Numake's Bungalows. Address above. Small restaurant and bar. Tours to volcano, wild horses; Tom's a good host.

RESTAURANTS. Vila. Even though Vila is a small town of around 15,000 inhabitants, these include about 10,000 Melanesians, 2,000 Europeans, and a smattering of Vietnamese, Chinese, Gilbertese, Fijians, Tahitians, and Tongans, and eating out is therefore an adventure. It must be stressed that in these remote islands changes are frequent. But you are pretty certain to find good and often superb cuisine in the unpretentious eating houses of your choice. Service will not be swift in this languorous ambience, but it will be pleasant, and after all this is not a place to come if you must rush madly around. We note the best of a surprisingly wide choice of restaurants and snack bars. Most restaurants in the *Expensive* or *Moderate* categories accept major credit cards, but check before you book. Price categories for dinner (wine not included): *Expensive,* $US20–$US27; *Moderate,* $US16–$US18; *Inexpensive,* $US10–$US15.

Expensive

Café de Paris. Rue de Paris; 2913. Small French restaurant right in town. Lots of atmosphere, good food, lively bar.

Kwang Tung. Rue Carnot (Chinese Alley); 2284. Good Chinese cooking. Evenings daily.

L'Houstalet. Erakor Road; 2303. French cuisine.

Michoutouchkine. Le Lagon Hotel; 2313. Extensive menu, wonderful outlook over Erakor Lagoon. Evenings only.

Pandanus. Teouma Road; 2552. Beautiful setting at the head of the lagoon.

Pisces. Opposite Kai Viti Hotel and Palm Court Shopping Centre, Erakor Road; 2453. Excellent cooking, fish a specialty, exceptional service, plus a great view.

Reflections. In Olympic Hotel; 3639. Good cooking.

Reriki Restaurant. At Iririki Island resort; 3388. Elegant, great food, music with dinner. 24-hr. ferry operates here.

Tassiriki Room; Intercontinental Hotel; 2040. Charming restaurant *intime.* Reservations.

Moderate

La Cabane. Wharf Road; 2763. Rustic restaurant, good food, Tahitian ambience, a warm welcome from Felix Tehei. Spontaneous music after dinner most nights.

La Hotte. Airport road; 2135. Lots of atmosphere. Excellent and imaginative food. This well-established restaurant has kept up its standards without too much escalation in costs.

Ma Barkers. Right in town opposite taxi rank; 2399. Familiar menu, excellent fish and grills, well presented. Reasonable.

Rossi's. Next to ANZ Bank on main road; 2528. Blackboard menu at reasonable prices. On The Terrace overlooking Vila harbour.

Teppanyaki. Airport Road; 3373. Piano bar.

Trader Vic's. Beautiful setting on harbor. Fine food.

Waterfront Restaurant. Next door to Yachting World; 3490. A roundhouse set on the shore of Vila Harbour, a step from town centre. Select your own steak, fish, or chicken to be barbecued; big salad bar.

Inexpensive

Binh Dan. Freshwater Road en route to Intercontinental Inn; 2287. Vietnamese specialties; new and popular. Dinner only.
Bloody Mary's. Main Road (Kumul Highway). At the market. Excellent quick food, reasonable.
Chalet. Main Road (Kumul Highway). Excellent snacks. Also main dishes like goulash and wiener schnitzel cooked under the eye of M. Brenner, late of Czechoslovakia via Papua-New Guinea.
Ichise. Wharf Road; 2470/2699. Delicious traditional Japanese food and service. Parties can book small dining room.
Solaise. Rue Picardie; 2150. A blackboard menu in a relaxed ambience, a short walk from the center of town. Pizza, crêpes, fresh-caught fish. Also take-aways.
La Tentation. Salon du Thé in Raffea Building. Sinfully delicious patisseries.
La Terrasse. Main road (Kumul Highway). Snacks, French-café ambience, excellent menu, reasonable.

SANTO

In a township that is little more than a hamlet,—you can still eat well. Check for new restaurants when you arrive—like Vila, but on a much smaller scale, the eating out situation in Santo changes frequently. If the cook hasn't just left, the food will be excellent, and prices will be moderate.

Chez Lulu. Close to Hotel Santo on back road; 4215. Mme. Harbulot's famed cuisine features local foods. Access by boat. Good eating here.
Hotel Santo Restaurant. main street; 250. Not the gourmet restaurant it once was, but reasonably good plain food.
Little Saigon. main street. A shoebox of a restaurant serving tasty Vietnamese food.
Pinocchio. main street. A new addition to the Santo scene. Small French café-bar-restaurant, attractive menu changes daily. Seafood is a specialty.
Oceania. main street. Good Chinese food, next to Hotel Santo.

HOW TO GET AROUND. By air: *Air Melanésie* (tel. 2643) flies regular schedules to many parts of the group; charter services available. *Air Tropicana* (tel. 2836) also covers groups on regular basis or charter.
By car: Taxis, depot in town, available from all hotels. Rental: Avis, tel. 2533; Hertz, tel. 2244, Box 128. National Car Rental at Socametra, tel. 2977; Budget Rent-a-Car, minimokes, tel. 3170. **By bike:** *I.S. Rentals*, for mopeds or motorbikes, is on the corner of Wharf Road, next to Ichise Restaurant.

In Santo, **by bus and car:** Regular bus service from wharf to town on cruiseship days and mini-buses operated by hotels, transfers to Pekoa airstrip. **Taxis:** large number of taxis fitted with meters, reasonable charges. Check fare for longer trips before hire. *Melanesia Rent-a-Car*—contact Mary Miu, tel. 325. And remember to drive on the right.

SEASONAL EVENTS *February 14th.* Jon Frum, Tanna Island. Jon Frum cargo-cult rituals on Tanna Island, mainly at Sulphur village, include dances, parades, feast for the expected return of Jon Frum.
May (generally). Land-Divers of Pentecost Island, several times yearly. Diving from 70-ft. tower built around a tree. Vines are attached to ankles to break the fall. Usually performed by the pagan village of Bunlap (South Pentecost). Arranged by Tour Vanuatu, Vila, at a high cost. The 23-meter *Concoola* conducts 6-day Pentecost Jump cruises, generally in April and May. For information, contact Box 611; tel. 3271.
July 30th. Independence Day, Military parade, speeches, ball at night.
End of August. Toka Dance, Tanna Island. Impressive native feast according to custom. Includes dances, killing of pigs by clubs, etc. Circumcision ceremonies are usually held during this period at Tanna.
September. Tanna Agricultural Show.
October. Vila Agricultural Show.

VANUATU

December 23–25. Christmas festivities. Arrival of Père Noel at Vila. Church services, choir singing and ball in main centers.

Holidays. All government offices, banks, and most private offices are closed on the following days—sometimes on the day before and after, too.

January 1—New Year's Day. Easter. May 4th—Ascension Day. July 30th—Independence Day. December 23rd–25th—Christmas holidays.

TOURS. *Vanuatu Visitors Bureau,* Box 209, Port Vila.

Pentecost Land Divers: This event, usually held in May, can be scheduled for special occasions at different times of the year. A trip worthwhile to see these fabulous Pentecost divers. Men dive from 70-foot tower (head first) with vines attached to their ankles to break the fall.

Vila Township: (1½ hours) Drive covers downtown Vila, residential area, courthouse, college, police barracks and a native village. Before returning to hotel, tour continues to top of Klems Hill for a harbor view of Vila with a short stop at another small village. *Mele Village* (full day): Travel to Mele Village. Meet local people. Trip also includes ride on outrigger canoe. Time for swimming, shelling, snorkeling, or loafing. Picnic lunch (included in price) before returning to Vila. *Efate Safari* (Full day): Travel 76-mile route through some of the most rugged terrain of Vanuatu. Tour east coast past beaches to Forari for a view of the islands of Mao, Pele, and Kukula. Visit Church of All Denominations, drive through several villages and plantations. Picnic lunch before returning to Vila. *Volcano Skyrama* (2½ hours): An extensive view of Vanuatu's volcanoes. *Air Melanesia* aircraft leaves at 5:30 A.M. and flying between the peaks of Mataso Island, heads toward the island of Tongoa to view underwater volcano. Tour continues toward Lopevi, one of the most active volcanoes in the islands, to see red-hot lava flowing down sides into steaming sea. View the island of Ambrym to see smoking volcano Benboy and other nearby volcanoes, back to Vila, passing coast of Malekula, home of primitive Big Nambas tribe. *Glass-Bottom Boats* (2 hours): Tour sea world of Erakor Lagoon aboard *Coral Sea* glass-bottom boat. Underwater life specialist describes tropical coral and sea life. *Primitive Tanna Island* (Full day): Fly *Air Melanesia* or *Air Tropicana* to Tanna Island. Transfer to four-wheel Land Rover for plantation tour, then continue through dense jungle bush through the mountains to Kings Cross (the island center). Cross the ash plain of Siwi Lake to Yasur volcano. Drive almost to crater edge for view of lava. Also visit subterranean volcanic tubes, until recently considered taboo. *Hideaway Island Cruise* (full day): Cruise aboard 41-foot catamaran to Mele Bay to Hideaway Island. Snorkel, swim before lunch at resort before return to Vila harbor via Pango Coast and Fila Island. Departs Sunday, Tuesday, Thursday. *South Pacific Cruises:* 3-day cruise round Efate, outlying islands; or 6–12 days to Ambrym, Pentecost, Santo in sailing ship *Coongoola. Vaterama:* (45 min.) *Air Melanesia* flight with panoramic views of Efate, the capital island of Vanuatu. Follow coast road by air with views of the outlying islands of Mele, Nguna, Mataso, Moso, and Hat Island. Also views of wartime airstrip of Coin Hill and Havannah, with pass over the international hotel Le Lagon. *Air Tropicana* for variety of Air Adventure Tours—Tanna, Santo, Ambrym and local sightseeing round Efate. All these tours may be booked by Tour Vanuatu at their office on Kumul Highway (main street), tel. 2745, 3096, or 3035, or at their offices at the Hotel le Lagon and the Intercontinental Island Inn.

Valor Tours, Schooner Point Bldg., 2nd floor, Spring St., Sausalito, CA 94965. Specializes in veterans' tours with organized programs throughout the South Pacific (and the world). Future plans include sending a number of units who served in the Pacific Theater to that area. They work with national and civic leaders of the host country. Write for complete details on individual or group tours to World War II sites.

Other tour operators include *Tour Vanuatu,* tel. 2745; *Frank King Tours,* tel. 2808; *Pan Tours,* tel. 3160.

TOURS AROUND VILA. Reef, fishing, and sailing expeditions: *Frank King Tours,* opposite the market, next to the government buildings. This tour agency has a great variety of interesting tours including glass-bottom-boat tours, sunset cruise, wine and cheese, coral viewing by underwater floodlight. Also enjoy Frank's *L'Espadon II* luxury cruise, which includes snorkeling, swimming, and lunch on Hideaway Island. *Escapade:* a 43-ft. game fishing cabin-cruiser, twin Diesel fitted for diving, top class fishing equipment, day-trips, and charter. *Nautilus Dive Shop,* N.Z. U.A. instructors, scuba diving, snorkeling for both experts and beginners; tel. 2398. Other tours: *Vila Roundabout Bus Tour; Nature Walks; Frank King's Visitors Club,* free services and restrooms for tourists; opposite the market.

SPORTS. *Vila Tennis Club,* on Freshwater Road; *Le Lagon Golf Club* (free to guests); *Port Vila Golf Club,* Mele Beach (green fees 500 vatu; *Squash Courts* (BESA Club), behind the post office; Horse riding, *Whitesands Country Club,* on the Rentabao Road, past the second lagoon; skin-diving, *Dive Action,* on the waterfront, Box 816, tel. 2837; *Nautilus,* on the Kumul Highway (main road), Box 78, tel. 2398; *Yachting World,* harborside next to Waterfront Restaurant; cruising and big-game fishing on Charlie Laub's *Rendezvous II,* Box 828, tel. 2124, or Gordon Neal's *Pacific Dream,* tel. 2745; *Scuba Holidays,* Hideaway Island, Box 875, tel. 2963.

SHOPPING. Vila may be small, but the real traveler with an inquiring mind, a degree of patience, and a nose for a bargain can have loads of fun in the shops, boutiques, and trade stores in-between swimming in that fabulous lagoon and indulging the flesh in the town's restaurants and nightclubs. Vila is a tax-free area for most luxuries. When budgeting be prepared for local 10% tax on tourist services and a 1,000 vatu (approx. $US10) departure tax.

If artifacts are your thing, and you yearn for a puppet from Malekula, an ancestor figure from Ambrym, or an intricately carved comb from Tongoa, then your first stop in Vila town will be at *Island Carvings,* Judith Wood's crowded shop, now in former U.T.A. premises on the Olympic Hotel Corner. You know you'll get the real thing here—this lively Australian does her own buying on trips that range from Tonga to the Trobriands, with emphasis, of course, on local Melanesian crafts. Prices are realistic and a chat with Judith Wood is an added bonus—she is one of the most knowledgeable dealers in the Pacific.

There are dozens of Chinese merchants up the narrow nameless streets of Vila. Jade, gold, ivory, transistors, tape recorders, portable hair dryers, cameras —all at duty-free prices. At the two big trade stores, British and French, look at kitchen gear, fabrics, and perfume; buy French cheese and pâtés to eat for lunch with a loaf of French bread; investigate the range of French and Spanish wines and bottles of tiny mandarines or plums in cognac. For stereo and electronic gear, *Sound Centre* is helpful.

In the Pilioko building *Sun Fashions* sell informal wear for women. *Rococco* across the main street is good for all kinds of trendy gear. All these are small establishments, the range won't be wide and you'll probably have to hunt for your size. Big news on the fashion scene is Australian Trudy Pohl for top-class leisure and swimwear from Europe and Israel.

Prouds, duty-free shop on the main street, sells jewelry, silver, and trinkets of every kind.

ART GALLERIES. Big news on the thriving Vanuatu art scene is the opening of *L'Atelier* by Suzanne Bastien, longtime resident of Vanuatu, friend of Crocq, Frank Fay, and Tatin, whose last show she organized and set up in Tahiti just before his death in 1982. This charming woman is greatly respected for her knowledge of art in all its forms and her understanding of what is best in an area well-known for its painters. She has the absolute eye of the real art lover. Look in at her gallery opposite the entrance of the Olympic Hotel for as exciting a collection of paintings as you will find anywhere in the South Seas.

A mile or so from Le Lagon Hotel along the road skirting the lagoon lies a trap for art lovers. The thatched "atelier-musée" of Nicolai Michoutouchkine sits among a collection of immense slit-gongs in the midst of a tangle of tropical trees and herbiage. French born, of Russian parentage, Michoutouchkine is a painter of originality and power. You can almost feel the miasmic vapors of the rain forest in his wildly colorful oils. His companion, Pilioko, comes from the island of Wallis, and was once the painter's protégé. These days this muralist, weaver of tapestries, and designer of fabrics stands on his own feet. In their shop in the Pilioko Building you can buy shirts, dresses, and pareos designed by Eliza Keil and hand printed by Vanuatu's most famous couple.

NIGHTLIFE. *L'Houstalet Disco*, Erakor Road; *Le Lagon* (Saturday-night disco and dancing in the Pilioko Piano Bar nightly); *Intercontinental* (disco nightly in the Ravenga Room); dinner dancing at *Iririki Island*, ferry takes 10 min. from Vila.

NEW CALEDONIA

The Island of Light

by
KATHLEEN HANCOCK

Note: On the eve of enlarged Melanesian participation in government, there have been confrontations between French settlers and Melanesian tribes over land disputes and the extent of the franchise in the proposed referendum on independence. Ongoing negotiations among the Chirac-Mitterand government, the settlers, and the Melanesian community will continue until a referendum scheduled to take place not later than December 1987. Consult your travel agent on the current state of affairs.

When Captain James Cook discovered New Caledonia in the course of his second voyage to the Pacific in 1774, he found a stone-age Melanesian culture. The population of this 250-mile-long, cigar-shaped island was estimated to be about 50,000 and consisted of a number of warring tribes speaking more than twenty mutually unintelligible dialects. Papuan/Australoid in racial type, the New Caledonian was a rugged warrior, and in times of war a headhunter and a cannibal.

However, the tribe that met Cook when he landed at Balade on the east coast were unarmed and shy.

D'Entrecasteaux followed in Cook's wake some years later. He heard the night cries of seabirds on reefs north of the Loyalty Group off the big island's east coast and hastily made off in the other direction to anchor at Balade in 1793. However, unlike Cook, he found the people surly, dishonest, and warlike and could hardly believe Cook's report of them. But it seems that this extraordinary alteration in the tribes of Balade was caused not by any basic change in the nature of the New Caledonians, but by the famine, drought, and intertribal wars that had intervened.

No one worried much about New Caledonia for the next 50 years. Then French Catholic missionaries established themselves at Balade in 1843, but pillage, arson, and murder were the order of the day, and cannibalism was commonplace. Many a sandalwooder was killed, baked, and eaten with a side dish of yams. However, a little research into early accounts of the goings on of sandalwood crews and traders reveals that their behavior wasn't calculated to create a friendly climate in these islands, and it was generally their own fault that they ended up in the earth oven.

Hot on the heels of the missionaries, John Paddon, English ex-seaman, set up as a trader in New Caledonia, and in 1845 he bought Ile Nou and established his trading station there. Dealing in sandalwood, whale oil, and tortoise shell, he brought groups of settlers from Australia to the as yet unclaimed island in his own ships. It looked as though the scene was set for a new British colony.

But the British delayed; neither the Colonial Office nor Queen Victoria was interested in acquisition. And the French had their own ideas about this remote island. The massacre of 17 naval personnel in the northwest in 1850 had enraged public opinion in France. Further, the establishment of a naval base in the southwest Pacific seemed a good thing. Finally, most pressing of all, the setting up of a prison colony with a climate less hostile than the pestilential vapors of infamous Guiana was felt in Paris to be an urgent matter.

So in 1853 the tricolor was raised at Balade by Admiral Febvrier Despointes. Ten years later the first shipload of convicts were building their own prison on Ile Nou, sold by Paddon to the French for a tidy sum. About this time the French realized that three British missionaries were firmly established in the Loyalty Islands only 50 miles off the New Caledonian mainland. A small "force de frappe" set off for Lifou, where they were confronted by 500 islanders led by the Rev. Macfarlane, a fiery Scots parson. After a bit of skirmishing, the better-armed French subdued the islanders and their leader, declaring the group French territory.

Until penal transportation was abolished in 1898 there were, in any year, between 7,000 and 10,000 able-bodied criminals in the colony, engaged for the most part in mining the nickel that had been discovered by Jules Garnier in 1865. They were also employed on public works—many of New Caledonia's older public buildings date back to this time.

The deportees' lot was regarded in those days as not too uncomfortable. It wasn't unusual to see 50 prisoners controlled only by a man in uniform carrying a white umbrella. And 20 years later, George Griffiths, an English traveler, found Nouméa's nonchalant acceptance of the concerts provided by the prison band in the Place des Cocotiers "quite bizarre." He remarked that the "chef d'orchestre" had cut the heart out of a man he considered his rival in his wife's affections, got her to cook it, and dined off it with her before revealing its origin.

Legend has it that a Comte des Baue, at Les Beaux, in Provence established this gastronomic precedent, serving the head of his wife's lover to his adulterous spouse.

But not all the deportees were common criminals. The Communards, who were sent out in the thousands after the collapse of the Paris Commune, were birds of a very different feather, honest workers and intellectuals for the most part. The Arabs who were exiled after the Kabyle revolt in Algeria were also political prisoners. But few of these were imprisoned at Ile Nou. Some were confined on the Ducos peninsula, but most finished up on the Isle of Pines, where they enjoyed comparative freedom on one of the loveliest and healthiest islands in the Pacific. The great majority of Communards were pardoned and returned to France after the amnesty of 1879.

For a good while after annexation, the Melanesians resisted the French, but there was only one uprising of any importance—the great "canaque revolt" of 1878, which cost the French 200 lives during a guerrilla campaign lasting more than a year. There is no record of Melanesian losses, but many villages were burned and crops destroyed during a long-drawn-out campaign that finally drew to a close when the Canala chiefs threw in their lot with the French.

From this time on the great mineral wealth of New Caledonia was developed in earnest. To fill the gap in the labor pool, Indonesian, Japanese, and Indo-Chinese indentured laborers were brought into the country on contract. Many of the Japanese remained when their time was up, intermarrying with European and Asian women. Most of the Vietnamese, however, chose to return after the end of World War II, when the French held a referendum enabling them to make a choice between returning to southeast Asia or remaining in the Pacific.

The Modern Scene

The outbreak of war in the Pacific led to great changes in this French colony. The island was stunned by the fall of France and shocked by the presence of the Vichy government in Nouméa. Feeling ran high, and finally Henri Sautot, French Resident Commissioner in the nearby New Hebrides, now Vanuatu, took steps. Supported by most of the populace of Nouméa and a great force of "broussards," or bush farmers, from the interior, he deposed the pro-Vichy regime and firmly placed New Caledonia on the side of Free France. In March 1942 he cordially received General Patch, who arrived in the sleepy harbor with 40,000 men in 15 large battleships, 10 cruisers, and several escort vessels.

Nouméa became an important American base, rated second for tonnage in the Pacific after San Francisco. Admiral Nimitz called the country the bastion from which the American offensives in the Solomons and the Philippines were launched. In New Caledonia they described it differently. "You couldn't pee behind a tree without peeing on an American," they complained. And no wonder, with something upward of 250,000 American troops in and around Nouméa at one time. But let it be said that there is still a great reservoir of good feeling and gratitude toward the thousands of Americans and New Zealanders who passed through New Caledonia during the war years.

As in all French territories, there's much excited political talk in Nouméa. At the time of writing France is offering the territory a referendum in 1987 that will enable its citizens to choose between self-government and complete independence.

Education is free and compulsory for all up to the age of 16. The little blue minibuses that scurry round Nouméa day and night are used by citizens of every color and income level. Round the tables at the city's restaurants and nightclubs you'll see blue-black Somalis and pale Europeans; sloe-eyed Vietnamese and sturdy Melanesians; dusky Martiniquai and Chinese-Tahitians. It's an atmosphere you can breathe in.

The Economy

Upcountry New Caledonia is pretty well a solid lump of minerals for the whole of its 200-mile length. It's a case of scratch a mountain and you find a mine in this big cigar-shaped island. Nickel, iron, cobalt, chrome, coal, manganese, antimony, copper, lead, and gold—you name it, they have it. Heading the list however, in vast quantity, is nickel, closely followed by chrome. The drop in world demand for chrome in the sixties caused the bottom to fall out of chrome mining, in spite of large deposits that are 50% pure ore. Today nickel has hit another low, and tourism is playing the major part in the country's economy. However, the big chrome mine at Tiébaghi has now reopened, mainly supplying the Chinese market.

Following their occupation of New Caledonia in 1853, the French wasted little time in investigating the mineral resources of the island. Jules Garnier, a government mining engineer, was sent out in 1863 and covered on foot and on horseback practically the whole of the wild and mountainous terrain of the new colony. He reported huge deposits of iron ore, copper, and chrome, but he is famous principally for his discovery of the nickel ore that now bears his name—Garnierite. His report on his findings, published in 1867, is a historical document, and he also developed methods of smelting nickel ore that were used by the first smelters built near Nouméa.

Garnier's discoveries were followed by the establishment of the Société le Nickel by John Higginson, an Irish-born entrepreneur who later became a French citizen. "Le Nickel" was well-established by the late 1870s, and until a few years ago the company enjoyed a virtual monopoly in New Caledonia. There are a good many independent mine operators, known locally as "petit mineurs," in spite of fortunes running into millions. The "petit mineurs" sell a lower grade ore direct to Japan, where it is processed in Japanese smelters, but this market is threatened today by recent nickel finds in the Philippines and Malaysia that are worked by cheap labor.

Most of the big mines are on the island's east coast, where the nature of the terrain makes the delivery of ore to ship a comparatively simple matter. Mining is open cast, usually high in the mountains or on plateaus well above the narrow shoreline. The ore is recovered by excavators, bulldozers, and power shovels and carried by immense 45-ton trucks to conveyors that send it directly down to the nickel ships on the coast. This economical and efficient method of working the rich deposits was born of necessity. New Caledonia could not produce a labor force large enough to cope with the demand, and almost total mechanization was the only answer.

The "Société le Nickel" draws on many countries for the raw materials required to operate this huge concern. Tankers bring fuel from the Persian Gulf; coal for the coking plant comes from Australia; gypsum is bought from Mexico; New Zealand provides timber for the company's housing schemes.

New Caledonia can view with satisfaction her reserves of ore which have been estimated to be the world's greatest. And "le Nickel" proposes to reopen one of the shut-down furnaces shortly. This promise, together with the reopening of the chrome mine at Tiébaghi, has given New Caledonia's faltering economy a welcome boost.

There are said to be many millionaires among Nouméa's 60,000 citizens. But in spite of all the money lying around, most New Caledonian housewives do their own work. They have to, because the labor shortage that has existed here for nearly a century, together with the highest wage scale of any other Pacific island territory, combine to reduce the domestic labor pool to less than a puddle.

Basic foods are pegged against inflation, and of course, in this French community, wine heads the list of basics. Bread is about the same price as in the U.S. The big difference here is that it comes warm, crusty, and fresh from the ovens twice daily, including Christmas Day, saints' days (of which there seem to be one a week), and all other holidays.

Compared to their Australian and New Zealand neighbors, New Caledonians pay a modest income tax. There's a solid payroll tax for all employers, worked out at from 25% to 30% of the pay packet. This tax, from which all wage earners are exempt except for a 5.5% contribution toward old-age pensions, covers the child benefit, pensions, maternity allowances, a workers' housing scheme, and sundry other social-security measures. If you're self-employed—a doctor or lawyer, for instance—you don't incur this tax, but you don't benefit from social security either.

Two notable developments in New Caledonia have been the increase in the population, which rose from 87,000 in 1963 to around 140,000 in 1979, and the development of tourism during the last ten years. The Melanesian population has risen during this period from about 41,000 to around 60,500, while an influx of immigrants, mostly from France and also from former north-African colonies, has boosted the European sector from 33,000 to around 50,000. Today Polynesians from Wallis and Tahiti number 17,000, and Vietnamese, Indonesians, ni-Vanuatu, and others amount to nearly 12,000.

In the last 15 years or so tourism has seen its position in this territory change from that of a Cinderella neglected in favor of its rich, ugly sister, mining, to a position where it's regarded as a welcome partner in the economy. Nearby Australia and New Zealand provide most of the holiday visitors to New Caledonia, but the slightly scruffy charm of the city of Nouméa, combined with the beauty of the beaches, the reef, and the outer islands, is rapidly making this a destination for travelers from further afield, mainly Japan. Considering the world economic scene, the cost of a holiday in these parts hasn't escalated nearly as much as might have been expected.

It does seem that things are pretty good for most people in this mineral-rich island. As far as tourists are concerned, exchange rates are extremely favorable at the time of writing for visitors from Australia and the U.S., owing to the fall of the French franc.

Government

Today New Caledonia is a French Overseas Territory and an integral part of France. This status was gained in 1958 following the crisis in French politics that brought General de Gaulle to power. In response to de Gaulle's call for a yes/no vote, 96% of the registered voters turned out, and 74% of these opted for the new status.

All New Caledonian citizens of whatever race have French nationality, electing a president of France and sending to Paris two deputies, a senator, and a representative to the Economic and Social Council. The Mitterand government has made a start in buying back large tracts of land to hand over to the Melanesian people, the cost being shared by the territory and metropolitan France. Participation in government has also been increased for New Caledonians.

South Pacific Commission

Nouméa is also headquarters of the South Pacific Commission, housed in the old U.S. Army buildings at Anse Vata Beach. The commission is a kind of small United Nations of the South Pacific, and it is a heartening example of cooperation between the nations who administer territories in the South Pacific, the island territories themselves, and the increasing number of independent Pacific nations. Its staff of experts advise and assist the territories in their area with problems of health, social, and economic development. It is a nonpolitical

NEW CALEDONIA

body and gives its services only on demand. A visit to its operational headquarters at Anse Vata is well worthwhile for those interested.

Food and Drink

Eating is a passion in New Caledonia, and you'll probably be given plenty of advice on where to find the best *crabe farcie,* the best *quenelles,* the best *couscous.* But since there are around 126 bistros, restaurants, and shrines to haute cuisine on the island, there's not the slightest possibility of your being able to sample the lot. Moreover, the scene changes frequently—they do say in these parts that a new restaurant opens every week and an old one closes. Space forbids a full catalog of eating in Nouméa in our Practical Information section, later. But one thing's for sure—you'll eat well. Costs can vary from moderate to as high as you care to go, but whichever way you play it, you'll revel in the cuisine. And when your liver or your wallet protests, Nouméa's excellent delicatessens and groceries will provide you with a delicious picnic lunch for a very small outlay. With a *baguette* of crunchy bread, a *tranche* of Valmeuse, and a bottle of *vin ordinaire,* it's no hardship to economize at lunchtime.

See the *Dining Out* section for editor's choice. Check closing days—they vary.

Exploring New Caledonia

There are lots of good reasons for a holiday in New Caledonia. Obvious ones like sun and sea and fishing, gourmet cooking, the beat of the *tamoure* in dark Tahitian nightclubs, and the scruffy charm of the city of Nouméa all spring instantly to mind. But what you don't expect to find is courtesy, kindness, and that easygoing amiability that's a peculiarly Pacific thing. In this intriguing French Pacific territory, believe it or not, even the taxi drivers are polite!

Early explorers had a name for this island that lies above the Tropic of Capricorn on the fringe of the Coral Sea. They called it the Island of Light. And whether you fly in from Australia, New Zealand, or Fiji, your first sight of land is breathtaking. The strange colors of mineral deposits streak fairytale peaks. A hundred promontories curve their way out to sea. Ten miles offshore the second biggest reef in the world glows jade and turquoise in the translucent ocean. As the aircraft loses height, you glimpse occasional sugar-white beaches between the green belt of coconut palms and the aquamarine waters of the great lagoon.

You're in a different world the moment you step out of the plane at Tontouta. Gendarmes in *képis* and very short shorts give the place a foreign-legion air. But there's nothing military about their duties here —they simply hurry you through entry formalities.

Even at the airport you get a taste of the fascinating complex of peoples that makes up the population of this Pacific outpost. Chic Frenchwomen mingle with brown Melanesians. There's a sprinkling of Indonesian sarongs, and a few tiny women wear the floppy black pants and white jacket of Tonkin. A group of Tahitians straight out of Gauguin stand next to a blue-black Somali off to Paris in a neat business suit.

A new shorter road to Nouméa cuts through rolling country covered with niaouli, cousin of the Australian eucalyptus. The bony, mineral-rich mountains make a dramatic backdrop to the scene. Breadfruit and banana grow by the wayside, and the gardens around the occasional bungalows vibrate with op-art colors—hot-pink hibiscus, magenta bougainvillea, scarlet poinsettia, and citron-yellow allamanda riot everywhere.

Nouméa

For most tourists their first sight of Nouméa is a big surprise. You expect to find a drowsy, humid, tropical town meandering round the shores of the harbor. But the reality is quite startling. Nouméa is a busy little city where the thermometer hovers pleasantly in the mid-seventies. The town clusters round a central square shaded by flame trees. A few tall palms give the Place des Cocotiers (Coconut Square) its name. Colonial buildings of faded pink stone nudge sparkling new structures of glass and concrete. There are chic boutiques with ready-to-wear from the great fashion houses of France. Dark little Indonesian or Tahitian shops are hung with shell necklaces, pandanus hats, and batik or pareu cloth. Chinese stores sell everything from incense burners to men's socks. In the back streets bougainvillea and Burmese honeysuckle spill over garden walls. Here and there among the shuttered houses you catch a glimpse of a cool courtyard.

The citizens of this tropical island are a multiracial mixture—French, Melanesian, Indonesian, Tahitian, Arab, Martiniquais, Somali. In this atmosphere integration is no problem. The population is divided up almost half and half European and Melanesian, with a sizable section of Polynesians from Tahiti and the Wallis Group. Vietnamese, Indonesians, and "others" make up the rest.

One of the foremost attractions of Nouméa is the transport system. From the bus depot on the Baie de la Moselle little blue minibuses scuttle round town and out to the beaches and suburbs. There is no timetable—the bus leaves when it's full and the standard fare will take you anywhere in town or the suburbs. The drivers—of every race and racial mixture—are an obliging lot, and a round-trip on a bus is an entertainment in itself.

Within the precincts of the town you realize that there's nothing sleepy about this little Paris of the Pacific. It moves! At 6 A.M. all Nouméa starts thinking of work, for shops and offices open at 7:30 A.M. and for a good half hour before that cars, scooters, and mopeds whizz along the narrow streets in a continuous stream. Most of the population seems to be on wheels, but the standard of living is high in these parts and no one rides the lowly bicycle. At this hour of the morning the balmy air is filled with a truly Gallic blaring of horns and screeching of brakes.

Mind you, all this bustle is largely on the surface—indulged in, one suspects, because of the lovely noise it makes. There's always plenty of time in this part of the Pacific, and the Caledonians have their own ideas about the important things in life—there'd be a riot if those long loaves of bread didn't issue from the bakers' ovens all day long.

The hubbub comes to an abrupt end at 11 A.M. Nouméa goes home, with a loaf of the mid-day baking under arm, and settles down for a lengthy French lunch and siesta. This is where the visitor has to look sharp. Eleven-thirty is the hour for lunch—and alas for the hapless tourist who wanders into a restaurant around 1:30 P.M. hoping to be fed!

New Caledonians live on and in the water. The yacht harbor is a forest of masts. Swimming in the limpid waters that surround this big island, skin diving off the reef, toasting on the white beaches—this is the New Caledonian way of life.

From the bays just out of town you can board a cruiser or catamaran for a day trip to Amedée atoll—a good way of enjoying all the charms of this informal sport-loving island. This isn't a trip for worshipers of muscular activity, it's for lotus eaters—though you can swim around the tiny atoll if you feel inclined. No, it's a place to lie on the sugar-white sand under a hau tree, dunking yourself in the translucent sea at intervals. Either the *Samara* or *Mary D* makes a good trip. *Samara,* captained by Jack Owen, provides the best lunch, cooked by his delightful Tahitian-Chinese wife, Christine, and accompanied by songs from the Tahitian crew. A new addition to Nouméa's nautical scene is the ingenious Aquascope. Crouched off the Club Med jetty like a huge aluminum seabird, this unique machine has a windowed underwater viewing area in its belly—it will take you into the lagoon to get a real close-up of the fishy and coral inhabitants.

Patrick and Minerva Helmy are charming bilingual hosts aboard the *Mary D,* for day trips to Amedeé Island. And there's atoll living for naturists on M'Ba Island not far offshore in the great lagoon, offering swimming, snorkeling, volleyball, and other games (through *Hoki Mai* Cruises). You can eat superbly in Nouméa and dance on any night of the week. You'll try Tahitian fish, Indonesian curries, Italian pasta, Spanish paella, and Chinese specialties. You can sample every style of French cooking. The traditional French preoccupation with food and wine leads, of course, to a traditional French health problem. To hear one of the locals bemoaning the state of his liver while consuming an epicurean meal washed down by copious draughts of good red wine—this is an experience. "Too much exercise," mutters the sufferer, spearing another delectable morsel.

Between Anse Vata beach and the Baie des Citrons, Dr. Catala's world-famous aquarium attracts scientists from all over. A new wing dramatically displays the vivid colors of the unique collection of living deep-sea corals, creating the effect of actually being submerged on the night-dark floor of the ocean home of these extraordinary creatures. You will probably have to be dragged away from the fishy and coral wonders that are displayed here with such taste.

On weekends sturdy Melanesian women provide a free show with their cricket matches at the square near the gendarmerie. French citizens of every race and color play *Pétanque,* a kind of bowls, under the spreading palms in the Place des Cocotiers. Eating can be expensive at night, but it often costs no more than cuisine of an equivalent standard at home. And a picnic lunch will more than even things up. In addition, you can dance all night in the city's *boîtes* for the price of a drink or two. Tipping is absolutely forbidden in this civilized island.

Down at the docks you can still find the traditional bead-curtained bistros, where a beer or an aperitif can lead to an amiable encounter with the locals. And there's entertainment at the wharves where inter-island ferrys are crowded with outer islanders in a dazzle of gay *muumuus.*

Outside Nouméa

But however intriguing Nouméa may be, it's not the whole story. If you're one for open spaces, Melanesian villages, trade stores, and deserted beaches fringed with rustling palms, then you've got to make another choice. You can fly to Poindimié on the east coast with Air Calédonie and from there potter up north, either by country bus, if you're rugged, or by rental car.

Up country, inns are small and informal; the plumbing works, in spite of a tendency for the towel rail to fall to the floor. The food is generally first rate, with the accent on local fish, crab, and oysters. It will be good French bourgeois cooking, and what more could you want? In these parts you come across old churches that look like illustrations to a book of fairytales, and the Melanesian villages have a picture-book quality too.

Finally a geological surprise awaits the visitor to Hienghène, farther up the coast. The road winds through light forest hung with exotic parasites, along shores bordered with casuarina and coconut palms. Bronze hedges of beefsteak plant mark the sites of villages gay with hibiscus, cassia, poinsettia, and tiare. Blue begonia and magenta bougainvillea clamber over the tiny huts roofed with layers of white bark.

Suddenly Hienghène's stark seascape explodes in the lagoon. Oddly unrelated to the mainland, sheer black rocks rise abruptly from the sea to a height of more than 400 feet. From one side you can see them as the towers of Notre Dame. From another you get a picture of a gigantic sitting hen.

A new road has recently been built from Hienghène to loop around the top of the island, connecting up with the west coast road at Koumac. The northern scenery above Poum is spectacular—white beaches, offshore atolls, a denser rain forest—the road up the west coast is paved as far as Koumac, and work is proceeding on the mountain pass between Bourail and Poindimié. Unpaved roads are reasonable, and the surface is good.

Tribal life in upcountry New Caledonia goes on much as it always has—gardens are tended, a new house built from time to time. Coffee plantations shelter under the bigger trees of the forest all the way up the island, and at the right time of the year, villagers busy themselves drying the beans for market. In the valleys and on the east coast the old life of the bush still survives—it's a warm and friendly place. A fisher on the reef may offer you part of the catch without the least thought of reward. The *gite,* or country lodging, usually a Melanesian project, is a new development upcountry with basic accommodation in well-built thatched *farés. Alfresco* meals are available, and the cooking will be simple but good, with an emphasis on fresh fish and game. All in all, an experience for the adventurous.

The east coast is a favorite area for campers, especially for French families from Nouméa. Apart from mosquitos, there are no stinging or biting things in this favored island.

From Hienghène you can fly straight back to Nouméa if you wish, over the great mountain chain that marches down the center of the island's two hundred and forty-odd miles. Huge deposits of the island's great mineral wealth lie just beneath the surface of the gaunt mountain tops. From the small Air Calédonie plane you can see the winding russet trails traced by prospecting bulldozers. At Thio the towers and turrets of the immense opencast nickel mine look from the air like the red ruins of some ancient city, but as you fly southeast you soon see the familiar ribbon of white coral sand edging the blue-green bays and inlets.

Beyond Nouméa

You can't really leave this area without staying a night or two at an outer island. Ilot Maître, 30 minutes from Nouméa, within the great reef, is easiest to get to. White-roofed bungalows are dotted among the light bush of this little atoll, whose waters are a marine reserve. On the lee side a sandy beach, on the windward side rock pools for fossicking. The cuisine is first rate, served in a beamed, high-ceilinged restaurant overlooking the lagoon. Birds are returning to this island—it's a charming place to unwind.

Isle of Pines

The day trip to the Isle of Pines with Air Calédonie shows you some of the loveliest beaches in the Pacific. Its sugar-white sand skirts blue-green lagoons, and its beauty is world famous. Lunch is included on this excursion, and divers will also find plenty of scope at the Nauticlub, where Swiss-born Albert Thomas and Hilary Root from New Zealand offer picnics (local fish barbecue, diving, swimming and shelling, on off-shore islets). Diving instruction is available, and the rustic ambiance is warm and friendly.

Since the closure of the *Relais de Kanumera,* a number of gites, or rural lodgings, have been built on this lovely island. They are small complexes of 3 to 5 bungalows, which are well constructed by members of the local tribes. Meals can be provided—by arrangement—or you can do for yourself. At the Bay of Ouameo, M. Lepers, a former plumber from Paris, dispenses simple but hearty hospitality at the Gite de Kodjeue—nine sturdy bungalows, excellent meals at a long table under a thatched shelter, a safe beach, plus fishing, pirogues and a grocer's shop, cooking facilities, and a refrigerator cater to cook-your-own types. M. Lepers has extended his domain to a charming rustic restaurant just a step from the fabulous white beaches of Kuto and Kanumera. He will drive guests over for the day—great food and a changing room for swimmers. Also available are trips to Grottoes (Captain Cook's vessel is said to have been spied at sea by islanders peeping through a gap in the wall of one of these caverns) or a visit to the century-old mission at Vao. Nataiwatch is in a leafy grove a few yards from a white beach, and each bungalow is allotted its own private shower and toilet in a nearby block. Here your host is Guillaume Kouathe, teacher of carpentry at the local school, whose craft is well displayed in this delightful cluster of five bungalows.

No visitor to the Isle of Pines should leave without exploring the prison ruins, cemeteries, waterworks, and other relics of the "deportation." Most of the ruins are to be found in the light bush near the isthmus of Kuto.

PRACTICAL INFORMATION FOR
NEW CALEDONIA

HOW TO GET THERE. *Flights from:* Paris (via Singapore), *U.T.A.* three times weekly; *U.T.A.* flies two times weekly and *Qantas* once weekly from Sydney; *U.T.A.* has one flight from Auckland (New Zealand) and two flights weekly from Los Angeles via Papeete. *Air N.Z.* has one flight weekly from Auckland. *Air Calédonie International,* once weekly from Melbourne and Brisbane, once weekly from Nadi, five flights weekly from Vanuatu. It is best to check with your air carrier as to which of the smaller lines can meet your needs.

WHEN TO GO. New Caledonian weather is pleasant all year round. December to March are the warmest months, fairly humid but only moderately rainy. Temperatures around 28°C. April to November is generally dryer, with an average temperature of 22°C. June, July, August can be quite cool at times and you may need to pack a sweater or a wrap of some kind for going out at night. Visitors swim all year round. The locals prefer the summer months of November to March.

CLIMATE. Dry season from April to December. Rainy season early February to late March.

THE SOUTH PACIFIC

AVERAGE TEMPERATURE

	Jan	Feb	Mar	Apr	May	Jun	Jul	Aug	Sep	Oct	Nov	Dec
°F	83.5	84.2	82.9	79.7	77.0	74.5	72.3	72.9	74.1	77.9	80.6	82.6
°C	28.6	29.0	28.3	26.5	25.0	23.6	22.4	22.7	23.6	25.4	27.0	28.1

AVERAGE RAINFALL: (inches)

4¾	4	4¾	5	4¼	3¾	3¼	3	2	1½	1½	2¾

WHAT TO WEAR. Light, informal clothes—women will find sophisticated dressing along these lines in the better restaurants. Long trousers for men at night in restaurants and clubs. Only the casino requires jacket and tie.

CURRENCY. The French Pacific Franc (C.F.P.) is used. At press time, the exchange rate is as follows: U.S. $1.00 = 125 C.F.P.; A$1.00 = 89 C.F.P; N.Z.$1.00 = 66 C.F.P; £1 = 188 C.F.P; Fr. fr. 5.59 = 100 C.F.P. *American Express, Visa, Diners Club*, and *MasterCard* are generally accepted, except upcountry and on outer islands, where cash is required. You can contact the American Express agent—Max Shekelton—at Center Voyages, 27 Avenue du Maréchal Foch (tel. 28.40.40).

WHAT WILL IT COST? Room costs in this territory are moderate in Nouméa and reasonable in the outer islands and upcountry. Food can be an expensive item, according to your tastes, but in most restaurants in the cheaper price range, the set menu is pretty reasonable at about 1,200 C.F.P. The top-class gourmet places will charge you about what you'd pay in similar restaurants at home for three courses and coffee. A bottle of beaujolais or riesling will cost around 1,600 C.F.P. a bottle. You will eat fine food, and the wine list will be extensive.

Drinks aren't cheap either, but it's necessary to remember that by most standards they are doubles—then the price doesn't seem too high. Soft drinks and beer are comparatively expensive and cost nearly as much as a carafe of wine. The remedy is obvious. If you're looking for your money's worth alcoholically speaking, a liqueur is the best buy. They are more like triples and you won't forget in a hurry your first sight of a New Caledonia-size cognac or Benedictine. Nightclub drinks are around $US6.00, but there is no cover charge as a rule and you can sit or dance over a drink or two all night without being hassled to buy more.

Local transport is fairly reasonable. The bus ride from Tontouta airport to your city hotel costs 1,500 C.F.P. The remarkable bus service charges a flat rate of 80 C.F.P. from town to Anse Vata beach and runs from 5:30 A.M. to 7:30 P.M. Taxis charge 420 C.F.P. daytime, after 6 P.M. 450 C.F.P., for the 2-mile trip from Anse Vata to the city. Air Calédonie's rates are reasonable. Rental cars are a bit more expensive than Fiji, but cheaper than Tahiti.

The all-day trip to Amedeé Lighthouse will cost around 5,200, C.F.P. which includes lunch, wine, entertainment, great swimming, and snorkeling. A three-hour fishing tour will run to 3,000 C.F.P., while a whole day's scuba diving will set you back about 9,900 C.F.P. It costs 300 C.F.P. to enter the aquarium and the same for entry to the big Olympic swimming pool.

ENTRY FORMALITIES. Valid passport required. Visa not required for stay of up to 30 days provided visitor has return or onward ticket. Visa may be obtained for stay of up to three months, good for multiple entries and extendable upon arrival. Visas may be obtained from French consulate or embassy.

LANGUAGE. French is the official language, but English is widely understood.

ELECTRICITY. A.C. 220 v., 50 Hz. (2 prongs).

TIPPING. No tipping, please.

NEW CALEDONIA

WATER. Modern pipeline supply. Safe in all areas.

TOURIST INFORMATION. *Office du Tourisme,* 25 avenue du Maréchal Foch, phone 27.26.32. Telex: N.C. Turism 063 N M. Tourist information and literature: *Nouméa Visitors Bureau,* Place des Cocotiers, phone 27.27.03. Also: 39 rue Jean Jaurés, Nouméa.

SERVICE NUMBERS. Police: 17. Radio Taxis: 28.35.12 and 28.53.70. Surcharge 50 C.F.P. for telephone taxi.

POSTAGE. For letters, stamps, parcels, cables, and telephone: Baie de la Moselle. Airmail rates: U.K. letters, 89 cents, postcards, 56 cents; U.S. letters, 79 cents, postcards, 51 cents.

TIME ZONE. GMT plus 11 hours; 19 hours ahead of U.S. PST.

HOTELS. Most are smallish and intimate, with tariffs ranging from moderate to very reasonable. The newer hotels at Anse Vata and the Baie des Citrons are right up-to-date, and so are a few of the newer bungalow hotels upcountry and in the outer islands. Outside Nouméa at certain times of the year it's wise to carry your own mosquito repellent and a packet of mosquito coils, though the management can usually supply the latter. Hotel categories: *First Class,* $US60–$US70; *Moderate,* $US45–$US55; *Inexpensive,* under $US40. Room tax (approximately $US1.20) is not included in the categories.

NOUMÉA

Escapade. *First class.* Box 819; 28.53.20. Atoll resort within the lagoon, 25 min. from town by launch. 44 bungalows, swimming, snorkeling, windsurfing, hobie cats, pool, floor shows twice weekly. Excellent restaurant.

Isle de France–TraveLodge. *First Class.* Anse Vata. Box 1604; 26.24.22. 63 rooms, air conditioned, refrigerator, coffee-making facilities. Bath as well as shower. 7 suites with kitchenette. Restaurant, bar, pool with snack service. Conference facilities. Down a quiet cul-de-sac, 3 minutes from Anse Vata beach.

Nouméa Beach. *First Class.* Baie des Citrons. Box 819; 26.20.55. Charming hotel, excellent restaurant and snack bar, sidewalk café overlooking sheltered beach. Also Japanese restaurant. Rates include American breakfast, water sports, cycles.

Le Surf. *First Class.* Anse Vata Beach. Rocher à la Voile. Box 4320; 28.66.88. Delightful ambiance, coffee shop, restaurant. Pool, casino.

Lantana Beach. *Moderate.* Box 4075; 26.18.39. The old Lantana completely rebuilt with two more floors, color T.V., video, bar. No restaurant but many nearby. On Anse Vata Beach.

Nouvata. *Moderate.* Anse Vata Beach. Box 137; 26.22.00. Recently modernized beachfront hotel, 85 rooms, air conditioned, refrigerators. 2 restaurants, one French, one Chinese. Pool, with snack service. Pleasant garden setting. Charlie's American Bar and the excellent French restaurant, both popular rendezvous.

Mocambo. *Moderate.* Baie des Citrons. P.O. Box 678; 26.27.01. Your host will be M. Lombard of La Rotonde restaurant. Completely refurbished. Air conditioning, color TV, tea- and coffee-making facilities. Free transfer to La Rotonde, one of Nouméa's top restaurants. Telex. Conference rooms.

Nouméa Village Hotel. *Moderate.* 1 rue de Sebastopol; 28.30.06. Apartments, parking, restaurant, right in town. Daily poolside buffet lunch good value, free bus to Kuendu Beach.

Le Lagon. *Moderate.* Route de l'Anse Vata. Box 440; 26.12.55. Air conditioning. Private facilities. Attractive rooftop restaurant with terrace overlooking Anse Vata beach. Tea- and coffee-making facilities. Telex, convention facilities for 150. Recently refurbished.

Paradise Park Motel. *Moderate.* Box 9. A charming complex in the Valeé des Colons; set in 3 acres of garden. Big pool, bar, restaurant, coffee shop. Air-conditioning, kitchenette. Shuttle bus to town and beaches 4 times a day.

Le Paris. *Moderate.* Rue Sebastopol in town. Box 2226; 28.17.00. Convenient hotel, a few deluxe rooms, desk, telex, etc. Caters to business clientele, but families welcome, two nightclubs in complex, restaurant, hairdresser.

Hotel La Pérouse. *Inexpensive.* In town, top end of Place des Cocotiers. Box 189; 27.22.51. Small, basic, 30 rooms, 18 with shower, air conditioning extra. Snack restaurant and bar.

Motel Anse Vata. *Inexpensive.* Val Plaisance. 19 Rue Laroque, Box 4453; 26.26.12. 22 fully equipped one-room motel flats with bath and kitchen. Air conditioning, balcony. Residential area, few minutes' walk from Anse Vata Beach. Good food shops and restaurants adjacent.

Club Mediterrannée. Anse Vata Beach. Box 515; 26.12.00. 550 beds, 3 miles from town. The Club Med recipe as before, great for investigating Club Med but investigation of Nouméa and the hinterland frowned on. Plenty of well-organized spontaneity, lots of *yé yé,* as the French have it, good food at set hours. A bargain package.

YOUTH HOSTEL. Situated on a hill behind the cathedral. Box 767; 27.58.79. 60 bunk beds in dormitories. Communal facilities. Lounge, dining room, and recreational center. Members 700 C.F.P. per night, nonmembers 800 C.F.P.

WEST COAST HOTELS

Les Paillottes de Ouenghi. *Moderate.* Boulouparis; 35.17.35. Quiet country retreat on Ouenghi River. 15 bungalows; pool, tennis, riding, canoeing, excellent food. Only 60 kms. from Bourail—a fascinating area for students of history and World War II.

Tontoutel. Airport motel. 35.11.11. Modern, pool, good food.

UPCOUNTRY TRIBAL LODGINGS (GÎTES)

Not to be missed for a night or two or even longer are the gîtes, or rural lodgings scattered in the countryside beyond Nouméa and along the palm-fringed beaches of the outer island, including the lovely Isle of Pines. These rustic bungalows, usually in a group of four or five, are mostly of traditional construction roofed with thatch, soundly made. Most are owned by Melanesians and built on family land. Some have all facilities, including some means of cooking. Others will provide a communal bathroom. One of the most charming, *Nataiwatch* on the Isle of Pines, offers a solution in the shape of six spanking clean showers, washbasins, and toilets. Nataiwatch is set in a leafy glade bordering the fabulous white sand beaches of the Baie de Kuto. Each bungalow is alloted its own three facilities—in effect a relatively private bathroom. Meals are available every day except Sunday if you don't want to cook. M. Georges Lepers has built nine bungalows along the shore of the *Baie de Ouameo* on the same island. He offers riding and a tennis court, and a pool is under construction. The beach is safe, and you'll eat some memorable meals *chez Lepers*—freshly caught lobster and fish are always here, and sometimes turtle figures on the menu. You'll get first-class French bourgeois cooking, and what more could you ask?

There is much to explore in the offshore islands and upcountry, and your host whoever he or she may be, will be an amiable guide. Melanesians are friendly and helpful to tourists. A little French is useful, but some English will be understood; otherwise sign language does very well. The *Office of Tourism* in Nouméa publishes an excellent brochure on the many gîtes in the territory, both upcountry and offshore. Contact the Nouméa Visitors' Bureau in the rue Jean Jaurés for detailed information on any of the fifteen gîtes in the territory or contact Air Caledonie Gîtes, Magenta, Nouméa, tel 25.20.00 or 25.22.42. If you want to get close to the land and the people, this is your chance.

DINING OUT. Limitations of space prevent a comprehensive listing. So we will present our own choices ranged in rough order of price—which leads to another problem.

NEW CALEDONIA

It's not easy to categorize New Caledonian restaurants in terms of cost. First-class and even the second rank of eating houses are not cheap, for the raw material of any meal you eat will cost your host a pretty penny. Most meat and vegetables are imported by air from nearby New Zealand and Australia and sometimes even from the West Coast of the U.S.

The "elegant decor" required for deluxe rating will often be lacking. But instead, your surroundings will be individual and attractive, and the cooking itself in the better restaurants rates a super-deluxe listing. Fine food is a passion in this country and even the humblest shack on a dusty country road may conceal a cordon bleu cook.

We have therefore not attempted to rate restaurants according to the decor but according to food and service—though in this offbeat French territory you will find that service will mostly be slow. Haste is a bad word here, as it is in most Pacific islands. But one thing is certain—you'll be able to indulge in an orgy of gourmet eating and sample Italian, French, Spanish, Indonesian, African, Chinese cooking. And when your liver or your wallet protests, the excellent delicatessens and groceries in town and at Anse Vata beach will provide you with mouthwatering goodies for a picnic lunch for very little cost.

Price categories: Expensive: $US30 and up; *Moderate:* $US18–$US25; *Inexpensive:* $US10–$US16.

(Check closing days—they differ.)

Expensive

Le Berthelot. 13 rue du Port Despointes; 28.32.70. In charming house in the Vallee des Colons. Fine cooking, interesting menu.

Centre Club. 26 avenue de Maréchal Foch; 27.21.13. Good French cooking just off the Place des Cocotiers. Another shrine for gourmets—best cordon blue cuisine in town.

El Cordobes. 1 rue Bichat; 27.47.68. Spanish dishes a specialty. Try their fish clothed in flaky pastry.

Dodin Bouffant. 29 rue Dusquesne; 28.32.26. Named for the Paris restaurant of gourmet fame. Popular with lovers of fine food.

L'Eau Vive. Route du Port Despointes; 28.61.23. Something different—an unpretentious restaurant run by a missionary order of nuns. Superb food. Moderate prices on the ground floor, fairly expensive upstairs. The sisters import their own wine, Faubourg Blanchot.

Le Petit Train. Baie des Citrons; 26.28.11. Baie des Citrons-gourmet cooking, superb outlook.

La Truffière. Rue Gabriel Laroque, Val Plaisance, near Anse Vata Beach; 26.19.82. First-class cuisine, specializing in the dishes of Périgord.

Moderate

Aux Trois Bonheurs. Avenue de la Victoire; 27.25.32. First-class Chinese cuisine.

Brasserie St. Hubert. Place de Cocotiers; 27.21.42. Toulouse-Lautrec setting for this bar-restaurant in an old colonial building at the top of the Square. A reasonable set menu.

Esquinade. Rue de Sebastopol, Baie de l'Orpelinat; 27.25.05. This fish restaurant is a favourite eating place for old Nouméa hands. Attractive decor, good cooking.

La Grande Muraille. 71 route de l'Anse Vata; tel. 26.12.28. Good Chinese food in small colorful restaurant.

Les Helices. Magenta, near local airport; 27.57.41. Specializes in seafood, popular with locals.

Isle de France Restaurant. Rue Boulari; 26.24.22. In the hotel of the same name. Small, attractive, popular bar.

Le Lagon Hotel Restaurant. Route de l'Anse Vata; 26.12.55. In the hotel of the same name. The proprietor and his Vietnamese wife were in the hotel business in Vietnam for many years.

Maeva Beach. Baie des Citrons; 26.28.11. Excellent cooking and a reasonable set menu.

Mayflowers, Nouvata Hotel. Anse Vata Beach; 26.18.70. High-quality Chinese food, friendly.

Nouvata Hotel Restaurant. Anse Vata Beach; 26.22.20. First-class cuisine. Popular with tourists and locals too. Lively bar, the Monins great hosts.

Ocean Palace. Baie de l'Orphelinat; 26.11.16. Excellent Chinese food, Szechuan style.

Santa Monica. Route de l'Anse Vata; 26.10.35. Near Anse Vata Beach. Abuts the nightclub of the same name. Set menu the best value in Nouméa, as is the carafe wine.

La Vacherie. Rue Broche, Magenta; 27.70.44. Phone and they'll send a free car or deduct taxi fare from your bill. Excellent cooking in a rustic ambiance.

La Voile Snack. Anse Vata Beach; 26.68.88. Coffee shop at Le Surf; open 6:30 A.M. to 10:30 P.M.

Eating Out of Town. Almost every wayside café in New Caledonia can offer an attractive meal, but there are a few good restaurants you may like to investigate if you drive to the east coast or even just out of town for the day.

La Siesta. Plum; 43.35.77. A pleasant rustic retreat about ten miles along the Mont Dore road, good food, and a pool.

Vallon Dore. A traditional meeting place for Nouméa's teenagers, chaperoned by watchful parents. Excellent lunches and dinners, and the Sunday tea dance is lots of fun. 14 miles from Nouméa on the Mont Dore road.

Inexpensive Snacks

Béarno. In town, quick service, reasonable. You can get the usual minute steak, but also such dishes as sausages and lentils. De l'Alma.

Biarritz. Right on the beach, especially good for a quick lunch after swimming.

Jamico. Route de l'Anse Vata, Unassuming little snack bar, friendly service, superb omelettes, as well as hamburgers, steak Tartare, etc. Super Vata Shopping Complex.

La Pergola. 12 rue du Général Mangin. Just off the square, attractive decor, steaks, omelettes, and so on. Reasonable prices, cheerful service.

Anse Vata Beach has blossomed lately with snack bars, pizzerias, boutiques, and a couple of excellent cafés. The problem of a light lunch no longer exists in this area.

HOW TO GET AROUND. *By air: Air Calédonie* maintains regular service from Nouméa to various points on New Caledonia and the surrounding small islands. Points served: Isle of Pines; Mare Lifou, Ouvea, and Tiga in the Loyalty Group, the East and West Coasts. Rates from 6,000–11,000 C.F.P.

By sea: Mary D, 60-passenger tourist boat operated all day; scheduled lighthouse cruises every Sunday or on request; also lagoon cruises, diving and fishing trips. 35-passenger boat *Samara* for charter, with Jack and Christine Owen, 33 rue de Paris, Val Plaisance. Day trip on well-run boat, with great food.

Bus system: From the bus depot buses leave every five minutes for the following destinations: Baie des Citrons, Anse Vata, Port Despointes. Trianon, Motor Pool, Magenta Airport. Fare: 75 C.F.P. for any distance, any direction. Pay the driver on leaving the bus. There is a handy bus stop on the square outside new Town Hall.

Car rental: Avis, Europcar, Mencar, Hertz, and *Vata Location* offer reasonable self-drive rates throughout the island. Inquire at your hotel. A current valid driver's license is required. Drive on the right.

Radio-taxis: Phone 28.35.12 and 28.53.70. Fare Anse Vata to town around 420 C.F.P., 450 C.F.P. after 6 P.M. Drive on the right, give way to the right.

FESTIVALS AND SPECIAL EVENTS. *January 1*—New Year's Day is a public holiday and celebrated throughout the country. *Easter* usually starts the sport season with events throughout the New Caledonian winter season. *May 1*—Labor Day: public holiday. *May 20*—Ascension Day: public Holiday. *July 14*—Bastille Day, celebrated throughout the country. Military parade and public ball. *August 28–30,* Agricultural Fair at Bourail. *September 24*—New Caledonia Day. Sports events. *November 1*—All Saints Day. Families place flowers at grave sites. Public holiday. *November 11*—Armistice Day. *Mid-November*—Round New Caledonia Auto Safari. Teams from Australia, New Zealand, and Japan compete in this highly contested car rally. *December 25*—Father Christmas parades through Nouméa streets in the evening.

NEW CALEDONIA

TOURS. Tours of Nouméa can be booked by telephone from local agents. Most Nouméa companies have their own cars for touring; some operate buses. The most popular tours are listed here. Tours around the city and environs range from around $US25 to $US55 or so, the latter price including lunch. The *Isle of Pines* day trip, including air fare, will be around $US92. Reliable tour agencies in Noumea are as follows: *Amac Tours,* 2 rue de l'Alma, Nouméa; tel. 27.41.53, telex 021 NM. *Center Voyages,* 27 bis avenue du Marechal Foch, Nouméa; tel. 28.40.40, telex 146 NM. *South Pacific Tours,* Shopping Center Vata, Nouméa; tel. 26.23.80, telex 150 NM. *Hibiscus Tours,* Nouméa; tel. 28.27.74, telex 184 NM. *Pacific Holidays,* 27 bis avenue du Maréchal Foch, Nouméa; tel. 27.32.58, telex 045 NM.

City-Day Tours of Nouméa and environs: The following tours are available by limousine from local agents. *Nouméa city tour with Aquarium* (3 hours): Includes drive through downtown shopping area and suburbs; the world-famous saltwater Aquarium de Nouméa, with tanks duplicating biological conditions of the reef; St. Joseph's Cathedral, built by convict labor; Place des Concotiers, the central square with its flaming poinciana trees; first settlement of Vallée des Colons; Magenta Bay; Mt. Coffyn Heights for spectacular city-harbor view.

Tuesdays and Thursdays. Mt. Koghi Tour (4 hours): Travel through tropical jungle to Mt. Koghi for view of Nouméa peninsula, lagoon, and barrier reef. Short jungle walk through rainforest to area waterfalls. Visits via Mont Dore to orchid houses and tropical gardens, lunch at *La Siesta,* continuing to the Parc Forestier and a varied display of tropical bird life.*Thursdays Daily 11 A.M.*

Mt. Dore Tour (3 hours): Travel through country, viewing coastal scenery around the Mountain of Gold. Stops at Mission of St. Louis with its native village of thatch-roofed bungalows and dairy farm and La Conception, the oldest church in Nouméa. Daily. *Bougna Feast:* This tour takes you through Nouville peninsula, site of the infamous penal-colony prisons, to Kuenda Beach for a feast of succulent chicken, yams, sweet potatoes, bananas, and papaw baked over hot stones in an earth oven. The meal is prepared by the local Melanesians and served with wine. Kuenau is one of Nouméa's best swimming beaches, and a Polynesian show is included. *Sundays. East Coast Tour* (Full day). Visits cattle-raising area on the west coast, turning at Boulouparis, crossing mid central mountain chain to the east, with a stop at a nickel-producing area. *(Note:* New Caledonia is the third largest nickel-producing country, after Canada and Russia.) Visit old mission villages and ghost towns, then on to coffee- and fruit-growing country and tribal villages. The return journey passes through coffee plantations and cattle stations. Seafood lunch at the justly famed restaurant *Paillottes de Onenghi,* one of Nouméa's favorite weekend spots.

Wednesdays. Amedée Lighthouse Tour. Full-day tour. Travel by launch to Amedée Lighthouse, built during reign of Napoleon and shipped in pieces to New Caledonia. View coral formations and fluorescent fish. Tour lighthouse before lunch is served under banyan trees. Time for swim, snorkeling, siesta. Daily at 7:45 A.M., weather permitting. Approx. $US42 with lunch and wine.

Hoki Mai Cruises offer naturist cruises to M'Ba island in the lagoon, day trips or longer. Day trip approx. $US35.

Air Calédonie, Magenta Airport, Nouméa, B.P. 212, New Caledonia. Offers regular service to various points within the country: Isle of Pines, the Loyalty Group, the East and West Coasts. The Isle of Pines daytrip is well worthwhile $US112, airfare, lunch, and wine. *Nouméa Yacht Charters* offer a full-day sailing cruise in the huge lagoon, visiting atolls. Lunch with wine, fishing, snorkeling. Departures from Baie des Pecheurs every day, weather permitting.

For general help and information, the Nouméa Visitors Bureau is now in the old "Mairie," or Town Hall, rue Jean Jaurés, on the Place des Cocotiers.

SPORTS. Access to the *Tennis Club du Mont, Coffyn,* the *Cercle Nautique,* and the *Cercle d'Etrier* (riding) must be provided by a member. Inquire at your hotel. The new *Squash Club* at the Baie des Pêcheurs welcomes visitors—bring your own whites—all other gear is available on the premises, 21 rue Jules Garnier, Baie des Pêcheurs, tel. 26.22.18. Water-skiing and wind-surfing can be arranged from your hotel. *Nouméa Yacht Charters* provide bareboat and skippered charters, day sail picnics and diving expeditions in superb Beneteau First 30 and First 38 yachts. Provisioning optional, but reasonable. An enchanting sailing area. Box 848, Noumea, telex 055 NM, tel. 26.17.03.

The *Olympic Pool,* just behind Club Med, Anse Vata, is open daily 1–5 P.M., Sun. 10:15 A.M.–4 P.M. Admission charge. Telephone Town Hall, 26.18.43. Bowling can be found at *Le Commodore,* Anse Vata Beach, tel. 26.26.02. 200 C.F.P. per game. Open every day except Mon., 5–11 P.M. *Municipal tennis courts* are open daily 6 A.M.–9 P.M. Tel. 27.52.32. Admission 300 C.F.P. daytime, 500 C.F.P. nighttime. *Nouméa Fishing Center* offers 40-ft. cruising yacht with crew. 8 fishing rods, 2 fighting chairs. For reservations contact Box 1524, tel. (bus.) 28.25.61, or (priv.) 27.16.00, telex 045 NM. *Mekoua Diving,* Box 4–701 Les Marinas, can be contacted through Amac Tours, Box A3, Nouméa, tel. 27.25.81, telex 021 NM, or 3 rue de la Republique. *Nauticlub,* Box 18, Vao, Isle des Pins, tel. 22 Kuto, telex C/– 112 NM Air Cal. Organizes trips for groups of 4 to 8 persons and 10 to 16 persons. Prices include all gear, board including meals and wine. 2 to 4 persons per bungalow. Reservations essential.

AQUARIUMS. Unique in the world for its magnificent fluorescent corals, colorful fishes, and tropical fauna from the nearby lagoon (Anse Vata), from 1:30 to 4.30 P.M. Adults about 300 C.F.P., students 150 C.F.P., children 50 C.F.P.

MUSEUMS. The *Museum of Nouméa* is well worth a visit. Featured is a well-displayed collection of Melanesian artifacts. Open every day, except Monday, 10 A.M.–5 P.M. Admission charge. The museum is at Baie de la Moselle, two blocks from the bus terminal.

ART GALLERIES. There is a great deal of good painting going on in New Caledonia and Mr. Cazalo's *Galerie Galeria* (cr. rues Gallieni and Republique L'Encardrerie, 2 bis rue de Verdun) has the best range by local artists in oil, watercolor, pastel, charcoal, pen, and wash. Look for Nielly, Crocq, Vernande, Michon, Khim, and Bertillon. This gallery is also a treasure house of rugs, tables, carvings, and bibelots from Tibet, Vietnam, Pakistan, and other eastern sources. *Ondine* (5 rue Salonique) is well worth a visit—an intriguing selection of local carvings, pottery, prints, wall hangings, small antiques, and other odds and ends. But telephone first (28.15.21) about opening hours—they vary.

The rue Salonique mounts the hill at the top of the place des Cocotiers, as does the rue Anatole France, where you will find *Crea* and many attractive small souvenirs created from local stone, as well as carvings from the area. At *l'Atelier* (51 rue Jean Jaurés) a selection of water colors portrays the local scene.

SHOPPING. Shopping in Nouméa is fun, and for many, first thoughts in this French territory are of clothes. And clothes, whether dresses or tops or skirts or underwear are an eye-popping temptation as you explore town. On this sport-loving island the emphasis is on casual gear—cotton knits, slacks, swimwear.

Look for the sign "Soldes"—a sale. In Nouméa a sale is a sale. You may pick up a $120 dress for $60 at one of the boutiques displaying the sign.

Océanie, the big supermarket on the rue Clemenceau, is fun to rummage in for everything from Dijon mustard to Italian cotton knits. *Barrau* on the place des Cocotiers, and *Ballande* on rue de l'Alma, both one-time trade stores, are now transformed into department stores—the former is now Prisunic-Barrau. Ballande's kitchenware department will probably fill some gaps in your "batterie de cuisine." This whole store has been refurbished. It carries good sports clothes for men and genuine Lacoste for both sexes.

Perfume is sold almost everywhere in town, but *Rozanne* in the rue Georges Clemenceau just off the square has a tremendous range and is duty free as well. Delightful accessories here too. *Marlene* on the rue de l'Alma and *Bricoles* at the top end of the square are both well-established duty-free shops, and this is one area of shopping where a 30% discount really matters. For wearable ethnic clothing, beautifully made, see *Anna Couture* at 33 bis avenue du Maréchal Foch, just off the place des Cocotiers; this is the New Caledonian answer to

Marie Ah You of Tahiti, but at half the price. Expect to pay 4,000 to 6,000 C.F.P. for delectable muumuus, New Caledonian style.

There are plenty of elegant specialty shops for the well-heeled locals where you can pay the earth—the jewelry at *Veyret* on the rue de l'Alma will make your mouth water. But further up the street *Cendrillon* is a treasure house filled with all kinds of precious trinkets within the reach of most travelers. Opposite, *Anémone* displays a most intriguing selection of costume and semiprecious jewelry. *Hippocampe* in avenue Maréchal Foch for unusual bibelots modestly priced.

French and Italian leather handbags are a great buy in Nouméa and many of the duty-free shops carry them. Real leather is the rule, not the exception, and *Le Bagage Calédonien* in the Place de la Victoire on the Rue de l'Alma, opposite their main store, has a large range at good prices. Ballande's duty-free shop has a wide range of bags, clothing, perfume, cosmetics, and even shoes.

French children's clothes from birth to adolescence are just as enticing. From doll-size dresses for doll-size French babies to chic toddlers' clothing and fashionable gear for teenagers, French designers have something the others haven't got. But watch out for differences in sizing by years. Multiply by two if you're buying for hefty Anglo-Saxon children. Then shoes! Perhaps, with perfume and handbags, these are the best buy in Nouméa. They run from amusing casual footwear to silver and gold slippers that would grace *Maxim's*. You can buy most of the top French shoe designers—Pierre Cardin, J. B. Martin, and Jourdan—starting at US$60. The *Boty* shops and the Bettina Arcade have the biggest range. On the rue de l'Alma, try *First* for Italian and French shoes, and *Les Champs Elysées* for ready-to-wear and sportswear from the Paris couturiéres. Also try *Les Nanas* at 14 rue de Sebastopol for a small but exclusive selection of footwear, on the rue de l'Alma.

In this town the male shopper isn't catered to as extensively as the female, but casual gear is a good buy, if a trifle expensive. St. Trop on the Rue Vauban isn't cheap, but quality menswear here is good value.

The duty-free shopping is geared to make the traveler's life easier. There is an excellent duty-free store at the airport, but you can also obtain a 20% to 30% discount in a number of licensed shops in Nouméa on purchases totalling 2,000 C.F.P. or over. The Duty-Free Shopping Guide, published by the Tourist Office, supplies a list of these shops, a map of Nouméa with them clearly marked, and a set of rules applying to the purchase of duty-free goods before departure. The range includes jewelery, perfume, clothing, handbags, shoes, cosmetics, cameras, and electronic gear. Tourists must not forget to hand in their duty-free receipts to customs at Toutouta on departure.

NIGHTLIFE. *Commodore Star Truck.* This disco is popular with the young. Tea dancing Sundays 3 to 7 P.M. Entry week nights about $US3.00, Friday and Saturday $US4.00, which includes your first drink. Promenade Anse Vata; 26.17.54.

Casino Royal. The only casino in the South Seas. Everything from poker machines to blackjack or roulette. Tie and jacket required for the gaming room. In Le Surf Hotel grounds, Anse Vata Beach; 28.66.88. Open 9 P.M. to 2 A.M.

Charlie's American Bar. On grounds of the Nouvata Beach Hotel. Nostalgic decor harking back to World War II in the Pacific.

Etoile. In Le Paris building right in town, drinks cheaper here than in the Papa Club, favored by tourists looking for chacha, tango, and so on. Ask at your hotel for a card to enter these clubs. 45 rue de Sebastopol; 28.28.29.

Le Black Jack. Private club in the Commodore complex. (But your hotel can get you a card to most of the private clubs in Nouméa, if you can afford the prices.) Popular with Nouméa's gilded youth. Promenade Anse Vata; 28.42.86.

Le Métro Club. Attractive decor, really swings from about 11 P.M. Handy to all beach hotels. Drinks around $US 5. Anse Vata; 26.22.20.

Papa Club. In the Hotel Le Paris Building. All black glass and subdued glitter. Drinks around $US 5. Offbeat shows Thurs., Fri., Sat. around 10 P.M., dancing after 10:30. 45 rue de Sebastopol; 28.20.00.

Santa Monica. An institution in Nouméa and with visitors too. A really Tahitian atmosphere, small, dark, fabulous music from a group, most of whom sit in each night. No entry charge, drinks around $3.50 or so. Pay when you get your drink—there is sometimes confusion if you leave it till later. Anse Vata; 26.19.06.

Le Soleil. Perhaps the most sophisticated discotheque in Nouméa; worth a visit. Drinks around $US6.00. The most danceable music in town. 6 rue de Verdun.

Le Joker. Swinging disco, popular with young Nouméa. Le Surcouf building off rue Sebastopol. In rue Frédéric Surleau.

Nightlife in Nouméa is fun and everyone on this island loves to dance. The standard of the bands is high and in the discotheques the records are French and fascinating. You can dance for an hour or two over a couple of drinks and no one will breathe down your neck or hassle you to order more. As with restaurants, closing days vary, so check with your hotel.

SOLOMON ISLANDS

Battlefields in the South Pacific

by
JEFF GREENWALD and DON HOOK

Jeff Greenwald writes about the South Pacific for a number of publications, including Islands magazine. His book about Nepal, Raja's Neighborhood *has been recently published.*

The Solomon Islands are located in the Southwest Pacific, stretching between Vanuatu and Papua New Guinea in a double chain about 2,000 km. northeast of Australia. There are 922 islands in all, some barely breaking the surface of the sea. The six main islands—Choiseul, Guadalcanal (which contains the capital city of Honiara), Malaita, Makira, New Georgia, and Santa Ysabel span some 800 km. of ocean. The Solomons sit squarely on the edge of the Indo-Australian and Pacific plates, and are thus the scene of much volcanic and seismic activity. So quickly are the islands being uplifted that, even on the highest hills, one can usually find chunks of coral and semi-fossilized shells.

Unlike many of their South Pacific neighbors—Vanuatu and Fiji, for example—the Solomon Islands are not set up to cater to the tourist trade. Only 12,000 tourists visited the Solomons in 1985 (compared to over 200,000 for Vanuatu). As a result, traveling through the islands is not exactly a carefree venture. There is much to see and do, the country is largely unspoiled and the diving is excellent, but unless you stay at one of the few self-contained resorts, it does take a bit of effort and ingenuity to get around. The Solomons are not for everybody; but those who take the trouble will enjoy a real adventure among the archipelago's spectacular lagoons, reefs, and mountains.

The Solomons were first visited by Europeans in 1568 but it took a bloody battle almost 400 years later to introduce the islands to the Western world.

Alvaro de Mendana, on a voyage from Peru, gave the islands their name, hoping to stimulate interest in his discovery by inferring that the legendary King Solomon had gained his wealth in these faraway outposts. Mendana returned in 1595—27 years later—to find a settlement at Graciosa Bay in the Santa Cruz Islands. The village, however, beleaguered by internal strife, was soon abandoned following a fever epidemic. Mendana, himself, was a victim.

Other Europeans, including Abel Tasman, visited the Solomons but it was not until the end of the 19th century that traders and missionaries began to arrive. At the same time, large numbers of the islanders were recruited to work on sugar plantations in Fiji and Australia. Here they were treated like slaves and appalling stories of cruelty drifted back to the Solomon Islands. In retaliation, many Europeans were murdered.

To stop the bloodshed, the British Government established a protectorate in 1893 embracing the islands of Guadalcanal, Savo, Malaita, San Cristobal (or Makira), and New Georgia. The islands of the Santa Cruz group were added later while the Shortland Group, Santa Isabel (or Ysabel), Choiseul, and Ontong Java were transferred by treaty from Germany to Britain in the early 1900's.

The first British resident commissioner, appointed in 1896, set up office on the island of Tulagi, north of Guadalcanal. The headquarters of the British Solomon Islands Protectorate (BSIP) remained at Tulagi until World War Two when, like many other settlements in the Pacific, it was blasted off the face of the earth by American and Japanese shelling.

World War II

The Japanese advance across the Pacific reached the far western islands of the Solomons in early April, 1942. For the first time, places like Guadalcanal, Henderson Field, "Bloody Ridge," and the Coral Sea became household words around the world.

The Japanese began building an airstrip on Guadalcanal in July, 1942. In August, 1942, American marines landed on Red Beach, took the airstrip within 24 hours and, within a fortnight, the strip was operational. It was named after Major Lofton Henderson, an American hero of the Battle of Midway.

Late in August, the Japanese counterattack led to the famous battle of Edson's Ridge (or "Bloody Ridge" as it was known to the troops). The war on Guadalcanal ended early in February, 1943, when the Japanese evacuated the island and gradually, were forced out of the Solomons island by island. Thereafter, Guadalcanal became a huge American supply base and training centre for the remainder of hostilities. Stark reminders of the war are still to be seen—ships, tanks, vehicles, guns, and aeroplanes—rusting away on the beaches and in the jungle. Iron Bottom Sound, between Guadalcanal, Savo and Florida islands, is probably the world's largest graveyard of men, ships, and planes. Memorials have been built at various battle sites and American and Japanese war veterans often return to the Solomons to pay homage to their fallen comrades.

The war brought great change to Solomon Islands. Honiara (on Guadalcanal) replaced Tulagi as the capital; new roads, bridges, and airstrips were built; the land was opened up to tourists and other visitors; and the beginnings of a national unity began to be felt.

People of the Solomons

The country's population is 220,000. About 200,000 are Melanesian. There are also Polynesians, Gilbertese, Europeans and Chinese. Most Melanesians live on the main islands with the Polynesians living in the outlying islands to the south and east.

Although there have been many developments and incursions in the past 100 years, most Solomon Islanders still live in a traditional way, with each family growing its fruits and vegetables, catching its own fish, and building its own house. Some, however, have adopted the urban life of Honiara, attracted by job opportunities and the "bright lights." In addition, many Solomon Islanders are playing an increasingly active role in the development of their country. The Solomon Islands became independent July 7, 1978. The first Prime Minister was New Zealand-educated Peter Kenilorea. The present Prime Minister is Solomon Mamaloni.

Honiara

The first stopping point for any visitor to the Solomon Islands will be Honiara, the capital. Although it is not much of an attraction in itself, Honiara offers a museum, two botanical gardens (one next to the museum, the other behind the prison!) and an interesting Chinatown that has the flavor of the old American Wild West. The local market would be a fun event for the early riser; it's best on Saturday mornings. There are no street addresses per se in Honiara; simply tell your taxi driver where you wish to go.

The city is in close proximity to a number of WWII battle sites such as Mount Austin and Bloody Ridge, and the nearby coastline is strewn with sunken transports and abandoned amphibious vehicles. A starkly modern Peace Memorial sits on a hill about ten kilometers from the city center, affording a fine view of the surrounding hills and unique Guadalcanal grasslands.

Tours around the old battle-sites may be arranged through travel agencies at your hotel or in town, and rental cars are also available, although the roads are often quite rough.

For the vacationer seeking a South Seas idyll, the Tambea Village Resort (45 km. from Honiara) is an unspoilt cove run as a cooperative by locals. There are no telephones, and the 24 Melanesian-style bungalows (lovely and comfortable) are lit by kerosene lamps. Horse riding, bush walking, diving, snorkeling, fishing, and canoeing are a few of the available activities. The more exclusive Anuha Island resort, a half-hour ride over Ironbottom Sound by twin-engine plane, is a tropical paradise with all the trimmings, including superb cuisine. See details in the Accommodations section.

For the intrepid traveler, the hills, rivers and jungles around Guadalcanal—quite close to Honiara, really—offer some excellent hiking. Katambona Gorge and the spectacular waterfall up the Mataniko River are wonderful day trips, although it may be necessary to find a local person who can act as a guide. Both hikes require wading through lively rivers; don't carry anything you don't want to get wet.

A Diver's Dream

For scuba divers and snorkelers, the warm ocean lapping against the northern coast of Guadalcanal contains a superb variety of reefs, walls, marine life, and wrecks. But good diving isn't confined to the area around Honiara; far from it. Many other spots, around Tulagi, Nggela, Anuha, Gizo, and the New Georgia islands, offer terrific underwater adventures. The submerged wreck of the *Toa Maru*—a torpedoed Japanese transport not far from Gizo that still contains overturned tanks, piles of *sake* bottles and stacks of unused ammo—should be made into a National Park.

To Experience the Culture

One of the most fascinating aspects of the Solomons is also one of the most difficult things to get a handle on. This is the cultural heritage (or "custom," as it is locally called) of the islands. The large hotels in Honiara have very good shows of customary and Gilbertese dance once or twice a week, and these are well worth attending.

Most Solomon Island dances and songs depict the early traditions and customs, or are based on history and mythology. For example, there are Melanesian dances about head-hunting raids and sharks. On some islands, the people once worshipped sharks. Bonito fishing in the Eastern Solomons is linked with the traditional rituals of the people, as are the dolphin drives off Malaita.

There is a carving center at Betikama, where various traditional items are hewn from ebony and "kerosene" wood; and a two-day excursion to Malaita may include a visit to Langa Langa Lagoon, where traditional shell-money is made.

To really experience the Solomons, though, it is necessary to get off the beaten path and visit the small villages that punctuate the shorelines and hide in the bush. In addition to their local languages—and there are scores of them—most Solomon Islanders speak *pijin,* which can be picked up by an English-speaking person without too much difficulty. Talk to the old men chewing *betel-nut* on their verandas; greet the village women tending to their children or carrying laundry back from the local water tap. The Melanese are friendly and inquisitive, and they love to "story" with visitors. Ask to see their gardens and "custom-houses," the focal points for village activities. Be sure to ask permission before taking photos; some locals resent the fact that westerners have made small fortunes selling pictures to magazines and books, and consider this a form of exploitation.

If by some lucky chance you are invited to spend the night in a village, don't pass up the opportunity. Chances are you will be put with the village's most well-to-do family, and given a comfortable mattress to sleep on. Food is simple, usually confined to rice, taro, sweet potato, Chinese cabbage, and sometimes fish or chicken. Do not offer your hosts money; a 10-kg. bag of rice (about SBD $8, or $5 USD) from a local shop is a welcome and appropriate gift.

PRACTICAL INFORMATION FOR THE SOLOMON ISLANDS

HOW TO GET THERE. Twice weekly international services are operated by *Air Pacific* from Brisbane, Australia, and Nandi, Fiji. *Air Niugini* and *Air Nauru* also serve the Solomons. The Solomon Islands Regional Airline, *Solair,* flies to Vanuatu and Papua New Guinea as well as operating all domestic inter-island services. As this edition goes to press, Henderson Airport is being extended to accommodate larger jets; check with your travel agent to see if services have broadened as well.

ENTRY REQUIREMENTS. No animal or vegetable products are permitted into the country. Jets are sprayed with a W.H.O.-approved insecticide before passengers may deplane.

A valid passport is required for entry into the Solomon Islands. Entry visas are generally not required for members of the British Commonwealth. As of mid-July, 1986, American citizens and some others do require a visa. Get one through a British Consulate, or upon arrival at Honiara. A 48-hour visa will be given free of charge, but there is a SBD $10 charge to extend this for a period up to two months. Extensions are available at the Immigration Department, a block from the main post office.

Vaccinations are not normally required for entry unless you are coming from an infected area. Visitors are advised that there is a real danger from malaria. An anti-malarial treatment, such as chloroquine or Maloprim, must be commenced two weeks prior to arrival and continued for several weeks after departure, as per your doctor's instructions. These drugs are available over-the-counter in Honiara. In addition, an injection of gammaglobulin is protection against hepatitis.

CURRENCY. As of August, 1986, the exchange rate was 1.7 Solomon Islands Dollars (SBD) for U.S.$1. There are many banks in Honiara, and in all of the provincial centers as well. All prices quoted in this chapter, unless otherwise specified, are in Solomon Island Dollars.

WATER. Safe to drink in most parts of the Solomon Islands.

COMMUNICATIONS. The Post Office provides telecommunications within the Solomons while international telecommunications are provided through SOLTEL, a joint venture between the S.I. government and the United Kingdom. Service and clarity via the satellite link are excellent, inexpensive, and available 24 hours a day, 7 days a week.

ELECTRICITY. Set for 220 volts.

TIPPING. Tipping in the Solomon Islands is not customary. In fact, most local people find the practice patronizing and insulting. Visitors are strictly advised to refrain from it.

574 THE SOUTH PACIFIC

WHEN TO GO. The Solomon Islands lie between 6 and 12 degrees south of the equator, and thus experience a tropical climate all year round. This is moderated by the expanse of ocean around them. Southeast trade winds blow from April to November. During the rest of the year the winds are from the northwest and occasionally develop into cyclones. There are exceptions to these patterns; devastating cyclone Namu struck parts of the Solomons in mid-May of 1986.

On Guadalcanal and the larger islands, evening breezes sometimes lower the temperatures to 66°F (19°C). Day temperatures are usually in the 80s. Rainfall in Honiara averages 85 inches a year, the heaviest rains occurring Jan. to March. Some of the other islands average up to 140 inches per year.

Average Temperature (°Fahrenheit) and Humidity

Honiara	Jan	Feb	Mar	Apr	May	June	July	Aug	Sept	Oct	Nov	Dec
Average max. day temperature	87°	86°	86°	87°	87°	86°	86°	86°	87°	87°	87°	86°
Days of Rain	N/A	N/A	N/A	N/A	N/A	N/A	N	N/A	N/A	N/A	N/A	N/A
Humidity, percent	73	73	80	N/A	N/A	N/A	73	73	73	73	73	73

LANGUAGE. The official language is English, taught in schools throughout the country; but the "official" official language is *pijin*, a unique dialect combining elements of western vocabulary with Melanesian grammar. This is the true language uniting the Solomons, where over 80 separate tribal languages testify to centuries of enmity and polarization. There is a very good primer called *Pijin Blong Umi* (Pijin Belongs to You and Me), for sale at the bookstores. Learning pijin is a fun way to pass the hot afternoons.

ACCOMMODATIONS. There are three main hotels in Honiara, several more around Guadalcanal, and at least one in each of the provincial centers. Most hotels have their own restaurants and bars. Rates given here are several months old, and may be a bit lower than what you experience. (All rates are quoted in Solomon Island dollars. To convert to US dollars, multiply by .58.)

HONIARA

Honiara Hotel. P.O. Box 113, Honiara; telephone 21737. The Honiara is a very friendly hotel with a warm and helpful staff. It is 1.5 km from the center of town on the road leading to the airport. There are a variety of accommodations, from fan-cooled rooms with shared bath to fully air-conditioned rooms with telephone, refrigerator, shower, and toilet. There is a swimming pool, restaurant, bar, and nightly video movie. One-day laundry service is available at reasonable rates. Customary and Gilbertese dancing two nights a week. The hotel is within walking distance to Chinatown, and a 15-minute walk from town. Doubles run $36–$60.

Hibiscus Hotel. P.O. Box 39, Honiara; telephone: 21205. The Hibiscus is in the center of town, close to the post office. During the summer of 1986 major renovations were undertaken to add a pool, lounge and improve other facilities as well. Rates range from $32 to $50 for a double. Family units are also available.

Mendana Hotel. P.O. Box 384, Honiara; telephone 20071, Telex: HQ66315. The Mendana is Honiara's first-class hotel, situated near the center of town on the beach. There is a swimming pool, and all rooms are fully air conditioned with showers, toilets, and telephones. Refrigerators in deluxe rooms. The Mendana has a good restaurant with a special barbeque on Friday nights, and customary dancing. Car rental and travel agencies, as well as a gift shop, beauty parlor and Island Dive Services, are located in the hotel foyer. A very pleasant place.

Doubles from $75–$90. Lunches are $4–$11; dinners run $7–$15.

SOLOMON ISLANDS

GUADALCANAL PROVINCE

Anuha Island Resort. c/o Pacific Resorts Limited. P.O. Box 133, Honiara; A tropic island "paradise" with all amenities and creature comforts. Anuha is a small island just north of Nggela, and the bungalows occupy one corner of it. The entire island is part of the resort, and features some truly breathtaking scenery. All manner of water sports are available and, with the exception of scuba diving and all-day boat cruises, all are included in the price.

There are four classes of bungalows at Anuha. All are comfortable; some, like the honeymooners' suite, are downright lavish. Actually, Anuha would be a great place for a honeymoon; the staff will bring couples to a private island, maroon them there for a day, then pick them up with champagne that evening.

Rates vary widely, depending on the type of bungalow and number of people. A couple in the least expensive accommodation would pay about $110. On the other end of the scale, the honeymoon suite would cost a couple about $200 per night. Write for a rates list.

Meals, prepared by an international chef, are $30/day adults, $20/day children, and the menu is absolutely superb. Drinks are extra.

Transportation to Anuha via Solair costs about $30 round trip.

Tambea Village Resort. P.O. Box 506, Honiara; telephone 22231, Telex: HQ 66338, Cable: TAMVILLE Honiara. Forty-five km. west of Honiara by the scenic coastal road. Tambea features 24 Melanesian-style bungalows, with private toilet facilities. A large dining hall and pleasant bar serve meals and drinks. All kinds of water sports are available, as are hiking, horseback riding, and beachcombing. Scuba and snorkel gear can be hired. Special feast and dancing on Saturday nights. $40 double.

Tavanipupu Island Resort. P.O. Box 205, Honiara; telephone 22907 (office), 22410 (home). Two fully furnished South Seas style cottages 104 km. east of Honiara in Marau Sound. Accessible by air or island trading boats. Each cottage contains four beds with toilets and cooking facilities. Recreations include swimming, fishing and shelling. Cottages are about $200/week with a $20 deposit.

GIZO

Gizo Hotel. P.O. Box 30, Gizo, Western Province, S.I., telephone 60199 or 60119. A western-style hotel with amenities, although water is sometimes a problem. Bar and restaurant, with a special crawfish dinner on Friday nights. Adventure Sports, Gizo's multi-facility dive service, is very close by. Double: $45. A 5% tax is added to these prices.

Phoebe's Guesthouse. Gizo. A clean, small lodge run by a charming local woman. Three bedrooms available; shared toilet, rainwater shower, and kitchen. No meals served, but supplies may be bought in town. The view from the verandah is spectacular. Ask a local person to walk you to Phoebe's; it's about ten minutes from the wharf, up a slight hill. Rates, $15 double.

Q-Island Holiday Resort. c/o Kelton Marketing, P.O. Box 320, Honiara; telephone 22902. A tropical island resort situated at the entrance of Wona Wona Lagoon some 22 km. from Gizo. Fly to Gizo or Munda and take a powered canoe. There is fine swimming, diving, and impressive views of Mt. Kolombangara, a huge volcanic crater-cum-island. The resort features three traditionally styled and self-contained bungalow units located a few yards from the sea. Rates $10–$16 pp. double Meals range from $2 (breakfast) to $5 (dinner).

MALAITA

Auki Lodge. P. O. Box 9, Auki, Malaita Province. Located on the island of Malaita in the Langa Langa Lagoon area. Accesible by boat (6 hrs.) or daily Solair flights (½ hr.) from Honiara. White-sand beach nearby and cool, clear rivers for swimming. Transportation available for tours around Malaita, which is a center for custom crafts and, to the south, music. Six twin rooms and dining facilities. Double: $25.

Malu'u Rest House. C/o Mr. Isamel Ilabinia, North Malaita, Malaita Province. An 80-km. drive from Auki, situated on a ridge overlooking the port area. Booking by advance only. Rate is $8. per person per night.

In addition to the hotels and resorts listed here, there are Provincial Resthouses in many of the provincial centers, including Kira Kira (Makira Prov-

MUNDA

Munda Rest House. C/o Mrs. Agnes Kera, P.O. Box 9, Munda, Western Province. A comfortable hotel in secluded Munda. A restaurant serves meals and drinks; some interesting handicrafts are for sale. Motor-powered canoes may be hired for excursions to Gizo, Seghe and nearby lagoons and coral reefs. Double: $25.

Uepi Island Resort. Via Seghe, Marovo Lagoon, Western Province (book through Tambea Tours, P. O. Box 506, Honiara). The Seghe area is gaining a reputation as the finest dive spot in the Solomon Islands. This may not be the only hotel there by the time you read this book. There is a local dive shop in Seghe where gear may be hired and tours arranged. The resort itself is in the Marovo Lagoon, a short motorboat ride from Seghe itself. It has several modern houses with bathrooms and refrigerators. Each can accommodate one family or a number of guests. There are also two guestrooms with three beds each in the manager's residence. Each house is $23 per adult per night, with a $46 minimum. Guest rooms are $17 per night per person, $25 minimum. Inquire about family rates. Meals are $14 per day. Transport to and from Seghe is available for about $15/adult, $8/child.

RESTAURANTS. Aside from the restaurants serving the hotels, Honiara contains a number of good quality and reasonably priced eating establishments. Check for availability of ingredients before ordering, or you may end up with pot-luck.

Kingsley's Fast Food. Burgers, meat pies, chicken, fish and chips. In the heart of Honiara. Very inexpensive.

The Lantern. Chinese, European, and Asian dinners. Near the public market. Phone 22549.

The Mandarin. Good Chinese food; in Chinatown. Phone 22832.

Nippon. Downtown Honiara. Japanese and Asian food. Phone 23178.

Sea King. Chinese and Asian dishes. Near the Solair office.

All of the local restaurants are moderately priced; a satisfying dinner with a couple of beers will run about $15 per person, slightly less for lunch (the Lantern has good lunch specials). There are also a number of smaller restaurants and other fast-food shops around the downtown area.

HOW TO GET AROUND. Transportation from Honiara's Henderson Airstrip to the hotels in town is available by the *Solair* hotel bus (SBD $3) or by taxi (SBD $10–$15). Once in town, taxis are plentiful and cheap. There are no meters, so you must decide on the fare in advance. Solomon Island taxi drivers are generally very fair-minded people, and will not try to overcharge you. Don't haggle; if a price seems unfair, try another cab.

For day-trips to WWII sites and other points of interest, there are several options. Once again, a taxi may be hired. The prices seem to vary; expect to pay anywhere between SBD $50 and $80 for a full day's hire, gas included. Some drivers may ask for SBD $1 per kilometer, which is ridiculous. Find another cab.

Car rental is available through *Budget* and *Avis*. Check at the hotels and/or travel agencies. $3.00/gallon.

The Solair office in downtown Honiara will arrange bookings for visits to almost all of the outlying islands, with daily service to many of them. Most of their aircraft are small twin-props seating 6–12 passengers, so book as far in advance as possible. (IMPORTANT: If you plan to drive and fly, remember to check your tables. The general rule is: bottom time of less than 1 hour, wait 4 hours; bottom time of less than 4 hours, wait 12 hours.)

SOLOMON ISLANDS

TOURS. *Guadalcanal Travel Service,* P.O. Box 114, Mendana Avenue, Honiara, Guadalcanal, S. I. Can arrange for groups and individuals. Accommodations, diving tours, and snorkeling tours and all other sightseeing arranged. Make reservations well in advance. Booking agent for all international airlines and shipping lines operating in the Solomons.

Hunts of the Pacific Ltd., P.O. Box 104, Honiara, S.I. Visit the battle grounds of WWII, and many primitive islands. Special bird watching, photographic, or skin diving tours arranged for groups. Most all other travel services also available.

Solair. P.O. Box 23, Honiara, S.I. Will arrange for scheduled and charter service throughout the Solomons. Agents for services are Air Nauru and Air Niugini, Air Pacific.

Melan-Chine Shipping Co. Ltd., P.O. Box 71, Honiara, Solomons. Operates freighter/passenger services throughout the Solomons. Room for 40 passengers but cabin facilities for only four; others have deck space. Not recommended for the comfort seeking. There are ships on the line that carry up to 70 passengers with different facilities and schedules.

Valor Tours, Schooner Point Bldg., 2nd floor, Spring St., Sausalito, CA 94965. World War II battle zone specialists with organized programs for units that served in both the Pacific and European Theaters. With the help and cooperation of national and civic leaders of the host countries, plans are underway for a series of reunions for a number of units who served in the Pacific. Visits: Australia, New Zealand, Papua New Guinea, Solomon Islands, Marianas (Saipan), Micronesia (Truk), New Caledonia, Vanuatu, Japan, Korea, Hong Kong, Singapore and Malaysia. Valor Tours will also arrange any individual tour—just tell them where you want to go, for how long, the approximate number of persons traveling together and when you would like to travel. They will plan your itinerary and provide a cost estimate.

Shipping. Local companies operate scheduled services to a number of islands and several other companies provide non-scheduled services. The Government Marine Department runs scheduled and non-scheduled services and like the commercial operators mentioned can carry a limited number of passengers. The most regular services run from Honiara to the Western Solomons and Malaita. (Refer to Inter-Island Ships in Planning Your Trip section.)

Special tours of sunken WWII wrecks are available for divers through *Island Dive Services.* See Sports.

The following are tours most popular with visitors to the Solomons and most can be arranged after arrival; however, it is usually wise to make reservations well in advance if possible. Prices below are approximate.

Town Tour: (1½ hours) Visit Honiara Market, Chinatown, Vavaya Ridge, Botanical Gardens and Kakabona Village. Approx. US$12. *Honiara and Environs:* (4 hours) Visit Solomon Islands National Museum, Botanical Gardens, Point Cruz, Holy Cross Cathedral, Skyline Ridge. Approx. US$30. *Tambea Village Resort:* (full day) Coastal drive along the West Guadalcanal shore, through villages and coconut plantations, visiting Vilu Village enroute. Bungalow facilities available at Cape Esperance. Swimming, shell-collecting, and lunch. Approx. US$35. *Battlefields of WWII and Betikama Carving Centre:* (4 hours) Visit underground hospital, Bloody Ridge, Red Beach, battlefields and Swiss Memorial. Lunch included. Approx. US$35. *East Guadalcanal:* (6 hours) Tours of oil palm, rice and cattle projects, Henderson Field, Bloody Ridge, Red Beach and Henderson Field. Approx. US$35. *West Guadalcanal:* (6 hours) Tour west coastline and plantations, tropical gardens, WWII relics. Picnic lunch included. Approx. US$35. *Alite Village, Manmade Island, Langalanga Lagoon, Malaita:* (Full day) Solair flight over Iron Bottom Sound, Indispensible Strait, old capital Tulagi, Taiyo factory, transfer by war canoe, stone age factory, Malaita shell money. Approx. US$100. *Western Solomons:* (3 days) Departs Honiara Sunday for Gizo, calling at 10 intermediate ports en route. Twin berth-cabin, passengers provide own meals. Arrive Gizo at 6 P.M. Monday; overnight in a/c Kasolo Hotel. Return flight Tuesday.

SPORTS. Honiara has a number of facilities for land sports such as tennis and squash; the locals love to play soccer, and if that's your interest you can probably find a casual match going and join in. The number for the Golf Club is 30181, and the Squash Court is 22230. For the most part, though, the Solomon Islands are famous for their water sports, such as fishing, sailing, canoeing and especially snorkeling and scuba diving.

There are a number of diveshops in Honiara, but the best is *Island Dive Services*, with three separate locations. The central office is in the Mendana Hotel (telephone 22103; Telex HQ66315), and dives to a variety of interesting wrecks are made several times weekly. They also operate out of Anuha Island Resort and Tambea Village Resort. All equipment, including camera gear, is available on a rental basis, and IDS also offers one-day E-6 slide processing for SBD $12. Single dives cost $25 per person (one tank) and $37 (two tanks). The cost includes tank, backpack, weight belt, and choice of a wreck or reef dive. Other gear rental is extra. Full scuba diving courses leading to international certification are available from professional instructors for SBD $250 per person; an introductory dive can be made for $55, all equipment included. Snorkeling trips are $15 per person.

In the Western Province, *Adventure Sports* in Gizo (radiophone 60199 or c/o Gizo Hotel) is a smaller operation which offers dive trips to some truly spectacular reefs, walls, and wrecks. All equipment is available for rental; dive trips cost $30, and include tank, weights, backpack, guide and/or instructor. If you love to dive and want to do a lot of it, good-natured manager/instructor Dan Kennedy might encourage your enthusiasm with a discount. Full open-water certification course is $250; an introductory dive is $50, all equipment included. Highly recommended are the dives to the Toa Maru (a torpedoed Japanese transport lying in 40–135 feet of water) and Wrasse Reef, where you'll see many sharks.

A new diveshop has recently opened up in Seghe, and will be in full swing by the time this guidebook is released. Ask about it at the Tourist Information Office near the Mendana Hotel in Honiara (tel. 22442).

Swimming is possible off most of the islands' beaches, but be careful of sharp reefs and strong currents before going out. Reports of sharks around the Solomons are true, but the danger has been greatly exaggerated.

Other water sports are available at nearly all the island resorts mentioned in the Accommodations section.

SHOPPING. Duty-free shopping is extremely limited, with a few items available at The Trading Company and Quan Hong. All duty-free items must be purchased at least 24 hours before leaving the country.

Shop hours are generally 8 A.M.–12 noon and 1:30 to 5 P.M., although banks and government offices have more limited schedules. It is nearly impossible to do business during the lunch hour unless you have made arrangements in advance.

Woodcarvings, local handicrafts, and traditional jewelry, including shell money necklaces, may be found at the following shops: *B.J.S. Agencies*, phone 22393. *The National Museum*, 22309. *Solomon Islands Handicraft Centre* (in the new Plaza shopping arcade). *Betikama Carvings*, 30223. *Mendana Hotel Gift Shop*, 20071.

Books about the Solomon Islands and South Pacific, as well as cards, maps, magazines, and general fiction, are available at the following downtown bookshops: *Aruligo Book Centre*, Kingsley Arcade, 23174. *The Bookshop*, next to Solair, 21239.

In addition, the Honiara Branch of the University of the South Pacific (USP) carries a number of fascinating books by local authors such as Julian Maka'a, Jully Sipolo, Sam Alasia and Celo Kulugoe. These books provide unique insights into the mind and spirit of the Solomon Islands.

There is a public library just outside of Honiara, and a National Archive with interesting records of the Islands' history. The Solomon Islands Broadcasting Company ("Radio Happy Isles") records and sells cassettes of local music, from panpipes to rock n' roll; ask the taxi driver to take you to SIBC.

There are several good supermarkets in Honiara, including the Honiara Consumers Co-op and Joy Supermarket. You will find a vast variety of shops selling souvenir T-shirts and "lavalavas," the traditional wrap-around garment.

HONIARA NIGHTLIFE. Aside from the two local cinemas—one downtown and one in Chinatown—there is very little to do at night in Honiara, unless you feel like sitting along the avenue and "storying," which is what you'll find the locals doing. Most of the private and hotel restaurants have adequate bars. The *Honiara Yacht Club* is a good place to go for a few beers, as is the *Guadalcanal ("G") Club.* Non-members may be asked to pay a small initiation fee. The hotels often provide entertainment for guests in the form of video movies or dance programs.

DEPARTURE TAX. SBD$10.

PAPUA NEW GUINEA

Adventurous, Exciting, and Exotic

by
LOIS K. BRETT

Papua New Guinea is one of the most exciting destinations in the world. It takes the visitor back to a people and a way of life still closely related to the Stone Age. No matter where you travel here, you will encounter bits and pieces of that long-ago period.

The natives who live along the coasts still travel by boats similar to those used by their ancestors. The people no longer practice cannibalism or headhunting, but they retain many of the ceremonies of their heritage and culture. Papua New Guinea is very much alive with adventure and mystery and is an anthropologist's dream. Scientists are still trying to capture the flavor of these people and still trying to explain how and why they missed the industrial revolution.

The country is a series of exciting destinations from border to border —each uniquely different from the others. Almost all the tribal communities have only just recently stepped into the twentieth century. In a few places, some people have had little or no exposure to the western world or white people.

The more advanced communities are those along the coasts because of their meetings with traders or missionaries in the end of the nineteenth century. Those inland had no opportunity of exchange until just before or during World War II.

The People

In the past, and in some instances even today, each tribe in Papua New Guinea was a unit unto itself—that is, it had almost no contact with other tribes. Each developed a distinct character due to the very diverseness of the land. Distances between tribes were great and still are. In the past, one tribe might have been able to trade with the tribe immediately next to it, but that was it—nothing beyond. With some 700 tribes and so little communication, each tribe developed its own language. Today English is the official language of Papua New Guinea along with Motu and Pidgin English, but many still converse only in their own tribal language.

The unusual mixture of cultures in Papua New Guinea has puzzled anthropologists for years. A widely accepted theory is that the original inhabitants were Negritoes, a small people with Negroid features and hair who migrated down from southeast Asia at the end of the last ice age, 20,000 to 25,000 years ago. Most also agree that later migrations from Micronesia and Polynesia probably forced the Negritoes into pockets in the mountains. The newcomers populated the islands of Melanesia, as far as Fiji, and the coasts of Papua New Guinea.

The last migrations brought many of the Polynesian people who settled in the Trobriand Islands. They came in their great canoes, probably through the Philippines, between 1000 and 2000 B.C. The Micronesian people landed in the Northwest Islands, which lie west and north of Manus Island.

Geography

Papua New Guinea is only half of an island that lies in the middle of a long chain of islands stretching from the Asian mainland into the South Pacific. It forms the eastern half of the second largest noncontinental island in the world (only Greenland is larger).

The country varies remarkably, from vast swampy plains to high, majestic mountains, broad upland valleys, volcanoes, and the rugged central mountain range. The mountains are the source of fast-flowing rivers that descend to the coastal plains to form some of the largest river systems in the world. The Sepik and the Fly are the largest and are navigable for about 500 miles. A line of active volcanoes stretches along the north coast of the mainland in an irregular line through the island of New Britain. Volcanoes and thermal pools are found in the southeastern part of the country and other islands.

Much of the country, except for the intensively farmed highland valleys, is covered by tropical rain forest, alive with orchids and brilliant butterflies and ancient mangrove swamps, where crocodiles are seen. The savannah grasslands teem with cassowaries, wild duck, wallabies, and deer. Most of the mainland and many of the large and small islands are protected by coral reefs and stretches of fine sand beaches. Many people think that the highly developed tourist packages to the highlands are all Papua New Guinea has to offer. Actually, the entire country is worth exploring though not all areas are geared to tourism. Each area is so distinct from the others that many people going from one to another wonder if they are in the same country.

Papua New Guinea is 100 miles north of Australia and lies wholly within the tropics. In the west, it shares a land border with Irian Jaya, a province of Indonesia, and in the east it takes in the islands of Bougainville in the Solomon Islands group.

Because of the mountainous regions, there are no continuous overland routes. All long-distance travel is by air. There are some very good roads around the major cities of Port Moresby and Lae. Otherwise, the roads are from good to very bad, depending on the industry and settlement in the surrounding areas. In the outlying areas, travel is mostly by four-wheel drive.

Because you must travel by air inland, and since there is only one international airport, most flights are by small plane into small airports —some with very short runways. You must book your seats well ahead of time, since space is at a premium, and you should book your travel through a reliable tour operator who can take care of all the details for you. (Because of the expense, it's best to book your PNG air travel in conjunction with your international ticket. To book once you arrive can be very expensive and time consuming because of the limited seating.) This is one country where booking your air travel or exploring far afield on your own is not generally recommended—unless you are the very adventurous type and have lots of time to spare. A list of competent operators offering a variety of tours is listed in the Tours section in Practical Information.

Port Moresby and the Central District

Because it has the only international airport, most everyone enters the country through the capital city of Port Moresby. Port Moresby was first sighted in 1873 by English Captain John Moresby, who named the city after himself, Fairfax Harbour after his father, Sir Fairfax Moresby, and the entrance to the harbor, Basilisk Passage, after his ship, H.M.S. *Basilisk*.

The major settlement in the area at that time was at Hanuabada—a large and busy coastal village, where the people had built their homes high on stilts over the water. Today, Hanuabada is a short and leisurely coastal drive from Port Moresby; you can still see some of the same style stilt houses—most now with tin roofs instead of thatch.

Missionaries were the first Europeans to settle in the country, and the London Missionary Society was first established at Hanuabada. British, Spanish, Portuguese, and German traders soon followed.

Port Moresby was proclaimed a British protectorate in 1884, became the responsibility of Australia, and grew into a small but typically colonial city.

Japanese forces landed on the mainland of New Guinea in 1942, and Port Moresby was heavily bombed. The city was a major objective and the stepping-stone from which the Japanese expected to take Australia. However, they were defeated on the Kokada Trail, only 20 miles from their goal, after fierce battles with Australian troops. When the Allies landed, General MacArthur, American allied commander in the southwest Pacific, made the city his headquarters. Reconstruction after the war was slow, but much of the old town, canoe village, and Koki market are still there. Today you can visit the trail and the war memorial here by taking Serpentine Sogeri Road, once the supply route. Vairata National Park is nearby.

Port Moresby sits on a hilly promontory, Paga Point. From there you can see the coastline and nearby islands and the National Capital District, with its modern, new National Parliament, National Museum and Art Gallery, National Library, and Supreme Court.

It is a sprawling city with the old town near the harbor and the new government center in another section of the city, making it not quite as easy to get around as tourists may like. The best way to see the city is to take one of the many available tours.

Port Moresby has a number of good international and standard-class hotels. The city is proud of its sports—from skin diving to parachute jumping—and its facilities—an international stadium and Olympic

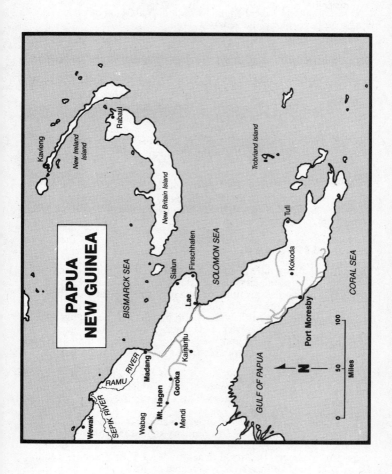

pool. Football, softball, boxing, cricket, and canoe racing are among the spectator sports that draw weekly crowds in season. Other attractions: two golf courses, tennis, bowls, horse riding and racing, rifle shooting, bush walking, swimming, yachting, and motor sports.

Out of Port Moresby

It is possible to take a flight to Tapini, Yule Island, or any of the jungle airstrips along the Kokoda Trail.

A short plane trip from Moresby, Tapini is tucked high in the Owen Stanley Ranges. Several trails welcome bush walkers. Tapini is also accessible to four-wheel-drive vehicles. A small resort hotel and a group of holiday cabins provide accommodation.

To see the city come to life visit Koki Market, especially on Saturdays. Fresh vegetables, fruit, fish, wildlife, and more are sold.

Rigo Road, near the airport, takes you through rolling savannah country. It will take you to the government-owned artifacts retailer Village Arts, the cliffs of Varirata Plateau on one side of the road, Bootless Bay on the other. A ferry can take you across the bay to Loloata Island Resort, for swimming, diving, and boating.

Brown River Road, heading north and west from Moresby, takes travelers through a teak forest, mangrove swamps, cattle ranches, and copra plantations. At Kairuku, you can look across the bay to Yule Island, site of the first Catholic mission in Papua, a hundred years ago. You can reach Yule Island by road, about 80 miles, following the coast through picturesque coconut plantations.

Lae and Morobe Province

An hour's flying time from Port Moresby on the north coast, Lae is the country's second city and an important commercial center and seaport. It is also the terminal for two major road systems—the Highlands Highway to the west, which passes through the Markham Valley and the Kassam Pass to the valleys and plateaus of the Highlands, and the Wau-Bulolo Road, which runs south through timberlands to the site of gold fields at Bulol and Wau. There is a great deal of civic pride in this beautiful little garden town, as well as in the whole of the Morobe Province.

From Nadzab Airport you travel along the Highlands Highway to the busy port city of Lae, gateway to the Highlands, through beautiful coffee, cocoa, and tea plantations. This is an exciting area worth spending several weeks exploring.

Fifty years ago Lae was a little mission station with an air strip developed by the Guinea Gold Company so that freight could be taken into the gold fields. The gold strike of the 1920s and '30s brought gold diggers from around the world to nearby Wau, Edie Creek, and Bulolo. During this time Guinea Airways created air history by flying in dredging equipment in what has been called the greatest airlift the world has ever known.

German missionaries first settled in Finschhafen, a pretty little coast town east of Lae. Germany made the region a colonial territory, and Germans established themselves throughout the Morobe Province. The Tami Islands are easily accessible by boat from town. You can rent boats for game fishing or sightseeing.

The Japanese occupied Finschhafen during World War II, but the Americans drove them out. The area is now occupied by many Australians who moved into the Bulolo Valley after the war. Because the city was never bombed, many of the old German-style buildings remain. Allied soldiers are buried in the beautiful Botanical Gardens complex, 130 acres of parkland within walking distance of the town center. The gardens contain an extensive collection of orchids and are one of the most beautiful spots in the country.

At Mount Lunaman is another war memorial—once a lookout point for the Germans, who named it Fortress Hill. The Japanese army used it for the same purpose, constructing a network of subterranean tunnels within it.

Sialum, not far from Finschhafen, is on a picturesque section of the coast known for its coral terraces. The Paradise Springs Holiday Inn is the focal point of development. Here charter boats are for hire for game fishing.

Wagan or Malhang Beach is five miles from Lae, near the Ampo Mission on Busu Road. The black-sand beach was used as an entry point for the 51st Japanese division in 1943. The remains of the landing barge *Myoko Mari* are still visible. Permission to enter the beach should be obtained from the Wagan villagers.

Ampo Lutheran Mission was the site of the Japanese camp during the war; it is two miles north of the town on Busu Road. Japanese shrines have been erected near the mission by returning servicemen. The church, built in 1933, was used as a field hospital during the war and is one of the few prewar buildings left in Lae.

The Highlands

This area, one of the major reasons people come to Papua New Guinea, is the largest tourist destination. It is a fascinating step back into history. The majority of the country's population live in the highlands; yet this was the last section colonized by Europeans. In fact, the people of the highlands saw their first white man, their first steel tool, and the first wheel in 1937. Civilization here is just one step from the ancients.

The five highland provinces are extremely diverse, both in scenery and in the people—from low plateau country, sparsely populated, in the south, to high mountain country in the north.

Until a short time ago, there were some 700 tribal regions and 700 languages. Only recently have the people of one region known about the people of another, except for their nearest neighbors—whom they were usually battling. Today these same people dress in their fabulous and decorative finery, portray their battle dress, and perform in the famous "singsings". Instead of war, they compete for the best costume and best performance each year. Each province is different from the next in almost every respect.

The Simbu and Eastern Highlands

Some believe that people living in this region some 30,000 years ago had a culture totally different from those who live there today. No one in the outside world knew of the people until 1930, when two Australians, M. J. Leahy and M. I. Dwyer, who were prospecting for gold, explored the eastern fringe of the Goroka Valley.

Shortly after, the Australian government stepped in and established a station at Ramu (now Kundiawa); the station at Goroka was set up a few years later. The Goroka air strip was built by the RAAF during World War II.

As was usually the case in Papua New Guinea, once a region had been discovered, missionaries would move in. The people of the area then called Chimbu were warlike and engaged in many tribal battles and other clan demonstrations. In the 1930s some missionaries were killed and the area was closed to Europeans. Today the tribes are successful farmers and businesspeople with a strong commercial sense for development. However, not until the 1950s did development really begin. Today this area, with the adjoining western highlands, produces most of the high-grade coffee that is Papua New Guinea's second agricultural export.

The last to be developed, this region today is one of the country's major tourist spots. The Eastern Highlands Province, surrounded by Simbu, Madang, Morobe, and the Gulf provinces, is steep, rugged country with fertile river valleys, including the Asaro Valley, home of the world-famous mudmen. The land ranges from lush and dense rain forest on the mountains to light scrub and grass of the rolling foothills. The province is noted for its pleasant climate and its wildflowers. More than 200 acres around Mt. Wilhelm has been set aside as a national parkland, with walking tracks and rest-house facilities for the adventure seeker. The people of this area are a colorful and picturesque group who hold many fascinating singsings.

You can travel by car from Lae on the coast road through the Markham Valley and the Kassam Pass to the eastern highlands, through the center of the extensive coffee plantations and processing factories of the upland plateau. Coconuts, papaw peanuts, sugar cane, and pineapple all flourish in the area. Travel time is five hours to the town of Kainantu, through these plantations and villages. Kainantu has one hotel. Goroka has a number of international- and standard-class hotels.

Asaro is the home of the world-famous mudmen, who perform traditional chants while daubed in gray mud and wearing great helmet masks of mud and fiber. Their costume came about years ago when a tribe they were battling forced them to retreat to the river. When the Asaro tribe climbed out of the river and returned to battle, they were covered with the gray mud, which made them look so fearsome that their frightened enemies fled for their lives.

The J. K. McCarthy Museum features highland masks, weapons, and instruments.

Also in the area are a wool-weaving center, the Lufa Cave paintings, a trout farm, and the Ramu hydroelectric plant. Yonki Township was built to house employees of the Ramu Hydro Electric Scheme, which supplies power to most of the mainland.

All the tribes and clans of the eastern highlands have colorful tribal traditions, and each year groups alternate between Goroka and Mt. Hagen for the Highlands Singsing. The shows are held in August and September of each year and alternate between regions. Up to 10,000 members of clans gather, many walking for days from throughout the highlands for the chance to parade and dance in their magnificent costumes. Many more clan members come from near and far just to watch and enjoy the festivities. The best way for a tourist to guarantee seeing this spectacular event is to take a prepackaged tour.

In the Simbu Province each November, the people hold a festival in celebration of the pig with a series of singsings in several villages. You can drive to see the pig-kill festival by following the highway from Goroka through the eastern highlands, or you can take a scheduled tour from Goroka.

Sporting activities available to the tourist in the eastern highlands include: golf, bowling, swimming, and a sports club in Goroka. Visitors are welcome at the local clubs and can use the facilities. Arrangements can be made on arrival.

Western Highlands Province

From Simbu, the highway enters the western highlands. Mt. Hagen is the provincial capital, in the Wahgi Valley amid coffee and tea plantations. The people of this valley are less westernized than those of Goroka.

The region was discovered in 1896 by a German botanist, Dr. Carl Lautebach, who found it while exploring the Sepik River. The valley he saw is now called Wahgi and the highest peak, Mt. Hagen, he named after the acting administrator of German New Guinea at the time. The botanist did not, however, explore by foot. Consequently, it was to the amazement of the world that in 1933, three Australian patrol leaders wrote that they had "discovered evidence of a fertile soil and teeming populations. A continuous patchwork of gardens—laid off in neat squares like checker boards, with oblong grass houses in groups of four or five, dotted thickly over the landscape. Except for the grass houses, the view below us resembled the patchwork fields of Belgium as seen from the air. Certainly the 50 to 60 thousand new people we had found on the upper Purari were as nothing compared to the population that must live in the valley."

They had discovered a civilization dating back at least 8,000 years, and their findings made news around the world. These clans had a language, culture, and agricultural system unknown to the outside world, including a unique tribal battle system. Missionaries and other Europeans arrived shortly thereafter. The first coffee plantation was established in 1935 and a government patrol post in 1938. During World War II, Mount Hagen served as a staging point and a recreational center for American troops. All through the war a skeletal staff composed of an Australian government officer and a native police officer ran the government from there. After the war the European population began to grow with the coming of regular air service.

The people of the highlands were quite different from those in the coastal plains. Instead of carving, painting masks, or making pottery, they decorated themselves. Decorated shells were money; the other item of value was the ceremonial ax carried by the men during their cult festivals. One type of exchange for a bride then, and even today, is with pigs. Money or other goods are also used in acquiring a mate.

In the early 1960s the Australian administration decided to stage a great annual singsing so ancient traditional enemies could come together on neutral ground. These spectacular shows were a hit from the start and have grown in size ever since. Thousands of warriors perform, glistening with pig grease and charcoal, heads decked with feathers from birds of paradise. Their show has become a major tourist attraction. Besides the major shows at Goroka and Mt. Hagen, smaller singsings are held by many local villages.

One of the best ways to see the highlands, if you are not on a prepackaged tour, is to base yourself in one of the many excellent hotels in the region and travel from town to town by air or road. Activities available to tourists include horseback riding, climbing, trout fishing, golf, bushwalking, and village visiting.

The Baiyer River and Nondugl wildlife sanctuaries offer opportunities to see birds of paradise. Many drives provide the chance to see people in their traditional dress, especially on Sunday.

If you don't have time to stay overnight in the area, it is possible to take a regular daily flight into the region from Port Moresby or Lae to either Goroka or Mt. Hagen.

The Southern Highlands

The first Europeans penetrated the southern highlands in 1935, and a patrol post was set up in 1937 at Lake Kutubu. During the prewar years patrols explored the Tari basin, but it not until 1949 did the government patrols decide to put in an air strip at Mendi. Until the air strip was built all supplies were sent in by airdrop. Between 1954 and 1957 roads were built and the first cars were hauled in from Mt. Hagen. The country of the southern highlands area varies from high mountain ranges to great grasslands. This area has had little contact with westerners, making this an exciting destination for the tourist.

Wewak and the Sepik River

For the adventurous and those interested in primitive art and culture, the Sepik probably has more to offer than any other part of the country. Some of the finest primitive woodcarvings and pottery are here. The towering *haus tambarans* (spirit houses) are the center of the villages, and their huge decorated gables and richly carved pillars are fine examples of the very unique talents of the people. Living in river villages, the people travel from place to place in canoes carved from single tree trunks, rowed masterfully using spade-shaped oars. One of the delightful sights is to watch the children, dressed in spanking-clean European clothes, standing in these narrow canoes, paddling their way to school in the early morning.

The great Sepik River, a mile wide at its mouth and navigable for about 500 miles of its 700-mile length, is a reservoir of animal, reptile, insect, and bird life. The center of the east Sepik region is Wewak, set on white-sand beaches and connected by road to Maprik and Pagwi, on the Sepik River.

In Wewak you'll see the markets, the prime minister's house, and the cultural center. A drive along the north coast will take you to Cape Wom. Wewak was a center of Japanese activity during the war, and in 1960 the Japanese placed a large granite memorial on Mission Hill in commemoration of their war dead.

The road following the coast from Wewak and ending at Aat Dagua brings you through scenic plantation country and villages set on beaches.

The Sepik River, largest in the country, is the main highway of the people; most of them live in villages on the banks of the river. The main direction of the river is west to east, but its course is serpentine. Within the river you'll find lagoons, dead ends, small lakes, and floating islands —land torn from the banks during heavy rains.

The Sepik has been the natural trade route since the Stone Age. The primitive art work of these people is now known throughout the art world. Some of the people and their lives have been lovingly described in the work of anthropologist Margaret Mead.

The West Sepik region, which borders on Irian Jaya, is undeveloped and largely inaccessible to tourists. The provincial capital is Vanimo, near Aitape, known for its abundance of World War II relics and its fine beaches.

Many tourists fly in from Mt. Hagen, join a river craft, and travel downstream to the famous Karawari Lodge, which is outside Wewak on the Karawari River, a tributary of the Sepik. The lodge overlooks the jungle-fringed water.

PAPUA NEW GUINEA

Madang Province

Madang is a picturesque town in the heart of a group of tiny islands with sand beaches and lots of palm trees. Its resorts are known for their international standards and their quiet and unspoiled atmosphere. The site of one of the early German settlements, Madang has flowered streets lined with great shade trees, some of which survived the bombing during the Japanese occupation.

Madang sits on a coral hill in Astrolabe Bay overlooking a magnificent harbor and protected by more than a hundred nearby tropical islands. It is a town of waterways, lagoons, rivers, and bays—all easy to explore on your own. You can picnic on your own private beach or go bush walking or trekking. From here it's even possible to climb Mt. Wilhelm, the highest peak in the country, as well as three other ranges all with established tracks used for centuries by the local people.

Madang Market is colorful and busy. The best time to visit is Saturday. Handicrafts, artifacts, and shell jewelry can be purchased.

There is a small museum with items from the German colonial days to the present time, including small canoes and boats—the only means of transportation before the Germans built roads. The museum is near Smugglers Inn. Open: Mon. to Fri. 8 A.M. to noon and 1 to 4 P.M. A donation is expected.

A harbor cruise or ferry ride will give you your chance to see one of the most beautiful harbors in the country, loaded with colorful coral and many sunken Japanese landing craft. Swimming and snorkeling are available; masks and equipment provided.

The most popular beaches in the area are Lion's Reserve Beach, north of Smugglers Inn, Siar Island; Kranket Lagoon; Pig Island; and Wongat Island. Gear for snorkeling and diving at nearby islands is available at the Madang Resort Hotel and the Dive Centre.

You can take a short flight over Papua New Guinea's highest mountain, Mt. Wilhelm, now a national park teeming with exotic birds. Another air tour takes you over the four active offshore volcanoes, one submerged and three on densely populated islands. You can also get there by boat.

The town is renowned the world over for spectacular diving opportunities—from untouched coral reefs to the relics and wrecks of ships and planes of World War II.

Since Madang is almost on the equator, the climate is ideal, and there is always a pleasant sea breeze to temper the sun's heat.

Four types of people live in the regions: island dwellers, coastal people, riverbottom settlers, and mountaineers, including the Simbai pygmies who inhabit the foothills of the central highlands. All the people of these regions look similar, except for some Simbai tribes, who number only a few hundred and are tucked away in the southwest corner, off the beaten track; many Madang people hardly know that these people exist. Some live in cool thatched houses on short stilts; others live in high stilt houses at the river's edge. Mountaineers live in dwellings that are almost completely enclosed by their roofs.

Interesting to see are the many women who still wear their sago-leaf skirts or narrow stringy skirts; the men wear a meshy net apron in front and a cluster of leaves on their backsides.

The crocodiles that roam the rivers are protected by law. Specified sizes of the animal may be shot and skins exported only with government permit. Visit the crocodile farm in Madang for a close-up look.

Large marine turtles can be seen on the volcanic island of Long at breeding time. Wildlife is abundant.

Boating facilities are available for sailing, wind surfing, water skiing, and game fishing—for mackerel, marlin, barracuda, or shark. Madang is noted for deep-sea fishing. The Madang Hotel has boats for rent, as does the Madang Marine Center. The Madang Golf Course, which runs along the coast, has two tennis courts, a grass-bowling green, and a modern clubhouse with restaurant. Tourists are welcome to use all facilities of the club. You can also rent a car, boat, or bicycle in Madang. Tours can be arranged on land and sea, from a half-day tour on the harbor to a full week's cruise on the Sepik River. Tours take you along the oceanfront to Coastwatchers Memorial Lighthouse, erected by Australia in memory of the coastwatchers who lost their lives during World War II. You travel along pleasant roads by the lagoons, to the old German cemetery to Chinatown to Rotary Lookout, which commands a glorious view of Astrolable Bay. You can see the Rai Coast, pass the Japanese War Memorial, and visit Bilbil Village, where the women of Bilbil specialize in making distinctive pottery prized by tourists as souvenirs.

Other tours travel along the north-coast road past copra and cocoa plantations to Sia Village, which is situated on a peninsula surrounded by scenic waterways. Tour returns by way of Tusbab High School, known for its collection of birds. A singsing group from the school frequently performs at the hotels.

You can visit the vulcanology observatory on North Daughter slopes, along Tunnel Hill Road to Matupit Crater rim.

Milne Bay and The Trobriand Islands

Named after Denis Trobriand, an officer of the D'Entrecasteau Expedition, the islands became world-famous as a result of anthropologist Stanislav Malinowski's work on the people's courtship patterns.

The Milne Bay Province includes some 650 islands and atolls and extend well into the Solomons Sea. The most accessible to the tourist is the Trobriand group and its largest island of Kiriwina. The Trobriands are best known for the Kula Ringa—a ceremonial, traditional trade system operating throughout the islands involving the exchange of white armshells, shell necklaces, pottery, and yams. The Kula ritual is part magic, mythology, and tradition.

The people are also well known for their highly decorative Massim art style with its intricate designs on ebony, gables, yam houses, and war shields. Their canoes and carvings are decorated with cowrie shells.

Nearby Samarai Island, another picturesque island in the region, just off the tip of the mainland, is one of the most attractive islands in the Pacific. In the nineteenth century it was a boom town. In 1878 it became the chief missionary station for the London Missionary Society. Flattened in World War II by Japanese bombs, it has since been rebuilt.

The best way to see the islands is on an organized 3-day, 2-night or 6-day, 5-night tour from Port Moresby. Tours are for those who just want to be lazy and enjoy a South Pacific island experience. Accommodations are included, as are village trips, entertainment by a local band, and traditional dancing by young girls in short grass skirts.

Because of their early contact with Europeans, many people speak and understand English. But the people are special in that they have changed little from their ancestors in lifestyle, customs, and dress. They are subsistence farmers relying on yams and fish. Their wood carvings, known throughout the international art world, are used for local trade. (There, however, be wary—you may have to fight off the touts hawking the local tourist ware.)

Also of interest to visitors are the natural caves in the area and, in particular, the cave at Kalopa, where anthropologists found human remains in a mass burial ground.

Rabaul: New Britain

New Britain is the largest of Papua New Guinea's offshore islands and Rabaul is the beautiful prime attraction.

Archaeological finds of pottery in East New Britain date back to 600–500 B.C. Looking for spice, William Dampier on his 1700 voyage in the *Roebuck* sailed along the east coast of New Ireland and the south coast of New Britain, naming them both, but missed the strait separating them, which was discovered by Philip Carteret in 1767.

In the 1870s a thriving business existed in pearls, rare wood, copra, and *beche-de-mer,* and trading stations were established by British and Germans, mainly on the Duke of York Islands and on the east coast of the Gazelle Peninsula. In 1879, the Samoan "Queen Emma" Forsyth arrived, established a flourishing business in copra, made millions of dollars, and built one of the most beautiful mansions in the South Pacific. Queen Emma's family cemetery can still be seen off the main road in Kokopo.

During the 1870s missionaries made their first contact with the people of East New Britain, but many were killed by natives or died of disease. The northeastern part of the mainland and the islands of the Bismarck Archipelago were proclaimed a German protectorate in 1884. One year later a charter was given to the New Guinea Kompagnie to administer a German colony in the area and in 1899 the German headquarters were moved to what is now called Kokopa. Rabaul became the administrative center in 1910 and remained so until the outbreak of World War I in 1914. The Germans left a heritage in the form of broad tree-lined avenues and the historical remains of the governor's house on Namanula Hill. There's not much left, but the view is outstanding; there are also orchid gardens here.

Thirty years of German control ended abruptly when an Australian naval force landed in Blanche Bay in September 1914, putting Rabaul under military occupation. In 1921 the League of Nations gave Australia a mandate for the civil administration of New Guinea, and Rabaul became the capital.

On January 23, 1942, a large Japanese naval force invaded Rabaul, and during the next three years, heavy bombing by Allied forces destroyed Rabaul completely. The Japanese were forced to build an elaborate system of tunnels and bunkers and virtually lived underground. You can still see the tunnels all along the Gazelle Peninsula. Other relics of the war lie scattered in the bush and on plantations. The town has been rebuilt and is considered one of the most beautiful in the country.

There is a large Chinese community in Rabaul. Exotic bargains are available at fairly low prices.

Rabaul is situated on the Gazelle Peninsula and is known for lush coconut, cocoa plantations, and beautiful scenery. The local Tolai people have had the longest contact with Europeans and are among the more sophisticated people of Papua New Guinea.

New Britain is the largest island in the Bismarck Archipelago, with a mountain range that runs down the center of the island from one end to the other. Because of this mountain range, the southern side receives much less rain than the north coast and gives Rabaul its pleasant tropical climate.

Tours go to the Baining Mountains where you can watch the Fire Walk, a fertility dance, where the performers dress in grotesque masks and dance on hot coals and flames.

Along the north-coast road to Keravat is an experimental farm, a copra drier, a cocoa fermentary, and the Bita Paka War Cemetery, Catholic Mission, and Kokopo—site of Queen Emma's residence; only the stone steps remain but the view is magnificent.

Gaulim is an easy drive from Rabaul; it's home of the Bainings people, whose huge and elaborate masks make excellent souvenirs. Nearby are many World War II relics, including Japanese tanks. The naval command bunker, where Admiral Yamamoto visited before his fatal flight to Bougainville, is now a war museum. At nearby Coastwatcher's Memorial Lookout, there are a Japanese zero fighter and antiaircraft guns. And on the shores of Blanche Bay, a floating crane is beached—captured by Japanese forces in Singapore and towed to Rabaul for their use.

Bougainville (North Solomons Province)

The Spanish explorer Torres in 1606 and later Louis Antoine de Bougainville in 1768 were the first Europeans to spot the area of the North Solomons. When the Catholic missionaries arrived shortly after, a European settlement was attempted but was not very successful. Both Buka and Bougainville were a part of the Solomon Islands group—a British possession. However, the British were not too interested in the islands and traded them to the Germans for the New Hebrides and Tonga.

In 1914 the Australians took back the islands from Germany and the German copra plantation owners, and the islands became British-mandated territory again, along with New Guinea.

Both Buka and Bougainville played important roles in World War II when two coastwatchers, Jack Read and Paul Mason, were able to supply the Allied forces with information about the Japanese and their plans to strike Guadalcanal. American troops landed in the area in 1943, followed by the Australians in 1944. The battles were costly to all sides, but it was a turning point for the Allies in the war in the Pacific.

After the war the islands returned to their sleepy-town status. In 1964 copper, silver, and gold were discovered at Panguna, and Bougainville became an international name again when it hit the world newspapers.

Buka is a small island just to the north of Bougainville; its basketware is noted throughout the art world for the fine quality of artisanship. Most of the work comes from Buin, near the southern coast of Bougainville.

Kieta is the main town and major port, with a small-town atmosphere. There are a few hotels, which cater to people doing business with the mines.

Gulf and Western Province

This area covers the whole of the western part of what was formerly the country of Papua. Most of the region is inaccessible. The Bensbach River runs westward through lowland forest and lush grassland to the Irian Jaya border of Indonesia. The wildlife in the region is fantastic in one of the most remote and unspoiled places in Papua New Guinea. Anyone wanting a rare and exciting opportunity to explore the outreaches of this lush and beautiful country should consider a stay here.

New Ireland

New Ireland is a long, skinny island north of New Britain. Europeans have known of the land as long as they have New Britain. Germans located here and built extensive copra plantations and an excellent road system. The island was captured by the Japanese in World War II, and Kavieng became a major Japanese base. A few Australian coastwatchers, in grave danger, stayed behind and did invaluable service for the Allies. The Allies did great damage to New Ireland, but the Japanese held the island until the final surrender. It has since been restored with productive copra, coffee, rubber, and timber plantations.

Kavieng is the type of town most people dream about when they think of the South Seas. It is a quiet, sleepy village where people wear comfortable south-sea-island dress. Most of the local people are very dark, have very blond, short, curly hair, and are quite friendly. They see few tourists, so they will be most interested in you. Be prepared for an audience wherever you go. As you drive along the road from Kavieng to Namatanai, people will wave. If you have a Polaroid camera, you might share some of your photos. Your hotel can arrange car rental, tours, and fishing trips.

Northern District

The Northern District is where the Kokoda Trail plays a very important role. For Australians, it is more famous than any other battle area in the South Pacific. On this trail the Japanese and the Australians battled it out. The Japanese intended to take Port Moresby, then move on to Australia. The Australians held them 20 miles from Port Moresdy on the Kokoda Trail.

The trail goes through heavy jungles, and neither the Japanese nor the Australians were prepared for the heat, the mosquitoes, or the rugged supply lanes that they had to keep open. Here the New Guinea natives (lovingly called fuzzy-wuzzy angels because of their bravery and strength) worked as carriers. Not only did they carry the ammunition, food, and medicine, but they also carried the wounded over treacherous trails and saved hundreds of Australians.

With 16,000 troops, the Japanese fought viciously to the bitter end. Only 700 survived the battle. The Americans joined the Australians at Oro Bay, which became a headquarters for shipping during the rest of the war. Day trips can be taken to the battlefields.

The Kokoda Trail, about 40 kilometers north of Port Moresby, is not a casual stroll, but a tough five-day hike. Fitness and preparedness are of vital importance. You can also fly to Kokoda from Port Moresby or Popondetta.

Coastal scenery in the Northern Province is spectacular, with deep fjord-type inlets. There is a small but delightful village guesthouse built of local materials at Tufi run by members of the Yariyari clan, who take visitors fishing and sightseeing in their outrigger canoes. You get to Tufi from the airport by canoe. There are lots of white-sand beaches. At Wanigela on Collingwood Bay, there is a plantation resort with a guesthouse.

Wuvulu Island

Wuvulu Island, with its Alaba Lodge, is a destination in itself. The lodge can entertain only 12 to 16 guests at a time. The island, owned by the residents, is idyllic. Jean-Michel Cousteau, James Michener, and William Holden have claimed Wuvulu to be one of the most remarkable areas and one of the finest diving spots, not only in the country, but in the world. The area offers deep, tropical reefs with an amazing variety of marine life. A colorful coral reef surrounds the island. One side is a placid lagoon, and the other side is like a cliff overlooking a chasm a half mile deep. There is also an underwater cave, complete with stalagmites and stalactites.

PRACTICAL INFORMATION FOR PAPUA NEW GUINEA

HOW TO GET THERE. By air: Service from Honolulu on *Qantas* via Sydney and Cairns, Australia. Cheapest fare is through Cairns and then via *Air Niugini* to Port Moresby. Connecting flights from Los Angeles and San Francisco, Brisbane, Cairns, Melbourne, Sydney. Other international destination connections: Christchurch, New Zealand; Honiara, Guadalcanal, Solomon Islands; and Singapore.

CLIMATE. On the coast, the temperature rarely rises above 86°F by day or falls below 73°F at night. The sun is strong between 9 A.M. and 4 P.M.; consequently, it is wise to wear sun screen to match your type of skin during these hours. A wide-brimmed hat will protect your face, especially around noon. Coastal rainfall varies widely; the rainy season in most districts is between November and March. Most of the rain falls at night.

In the highlands areas, the days are warm but nights can be cool–77°F, falling to 57°F. Light woolen slacks and sweaters may be necessary. Because of the higher altitude, ultraviolet rays of the sun are accentuated, and fair skins should be protected.

Average Temperature (°Fahrenheit) and Humidity

Port Moresby	Jan	Feb	Mar	Apr	May	June	July	Aug	Sept	Oct	Nov	Dec
Average max. day temperature	97°	97°	95°	93°	92°	93°	92°	92°	94°	95°	97°	97°
Days of rain	16	18	18	15	8	7	6	7	7	7	8	14
Humidity, percent	77	81	80	82	79	78	77	74	73	69	68	73

HOW TO DRESS. Leave your tie and jacket at home. Summer dresses, slacks, skirts, and blouses for ladies. Women wear loose-fitting cool fabrics and rarely wear stockings. For men, T-shirts, shorts, and sandals are all that's required to wear; slacks and short-sleeved shirts in the evening. Most people prefer drip-dry cottons.

Women should not wear shorts around town or when visiting villages, and *revealing* bikinis on a village beach may attract unwanted attention or, occasionally, even protest. Do not offend—dress modestly. Bring a light plastic raincoat or umbrella and comfortable shoes for walking.

CURRENCY. The Papua New Guinea currency is the *kina* and *toea* —pronounced "keener" and "toya." The currency circulated in K20, K10, K5, and K2 notes and the coin K1 with a hole in the center. The kina is divided into 100 toea, with coins of 1t, 2t, 5t, 10t, and 20t. At press time: 1 Kina = $US1.18.

PAPUA NEW GUINEA 595

Banking hours: Mon. to Thurs. 9 A.M. to 2 P.M.; Fri. 9 A.M. to 5 P.M. No Saturday banking. Airport currency exchange service every day.

Traveler's checks are accepted by most shops and hotels in the major tourist centers. *American Express* and *Diners Club* are accepted by most hotels. *Visa* and *MasterCard* are new and just now being accepted.

ENTRY REQUIREMENTS. Passport and visa required. Stay limited to request. One photo; letter of guarantee from company for business applicants. Single-entry visas available to tourists only on arrival at Port Moresby airport for stays of 30 days or less. If you arrive by sea, you must have a visa beforehand. Ticket to leave and sufficient funds required.

HEALTH. High malaria and dengue-fever risk. Visitors should take anti-malaria tablets for 14 days before arrival, while in PNG, and for at least a month after leaving the country. See your doctor for actual types and dosages required. Since some people have had a reaction to Fansidar, have your physician check you out before taking it. Smallpox vaccination and cholera shot are required to be up-to-date.

LANGUAGE. There are three national languages: English, Pidgin (pronounced pisin), and Motu. English is spoken in all shops, hotels, and restaurants. A Pidgin phrase book is handy in the highlands and coastal areas and can be bought in Port Moresby.

TIME. Papua New Guinea is 18 hours ahead of U.S. Pacific Standard Time, or GMT plus 10.

ELECTRICITY AND WATER. 240 volts mostly 50 Hz AC but DC in some areas. A three-pin plug is used. Water in most areas is safe; however, it is suggested that tourists use the water provided in hotel flasks.

TIPPING. Not customary and not encouraged. Please respect this custom.

COMMUNICATIONS. There is no home-delivery mail service in Papua New Guinea. Everyone has a post-office box and collects her or his mail daily. **Telegrams** are normally phoned through and then left for collection at the post office. **Telephones** are limited to the main centers, but service is good and there is direct dialing to Australia. There are some pay phones in the country, but it is best to make calls from your hotel or at the post office. Local calls are 10 toea. If you want to guarantee hotel reservations, it may be wise to telephone, telex, or cable, since mail tends to be very slow.

When dialing direct to Papua New Guinea from the U.S., dial 011 (international access code) + 675 (country code). When transmitting telex messages from the U.S., the code 794 or 795 for Papua New Guinea must precede the telex number.

Postage rates. Letters within PNG 10t; aerograms 20t; airmail letters per 20gm to: Australia 20t; New Zealand 25t; Europe and North America 45t.

GENERAL HINTS. This is a fragile country—only a few years into tourism. Please remember that how you act toward local people in villages is sometimes their only introduction to western civilization. Treat people as kindly as you react to people at home.

Although most people do not mind being photographed, a polite request is always welcome. **Do not** assume that everyone speaks English or that instant service is a natural happening. In this exotic country, the tropical climate tends to put people and service at a leisurely pace.

Do not be afraid to bargain, especially when purchasing artifacts in villages.

596 THE SOUTH PACIFIC

Do not wander alone at night—*anywhere,* and in particular Port Moresby or nearby suburbs. Individuals are advised not to travel alone into rural areas.

Do drive carefully, especially on the country roads. If you are involved in an accident and someone is hurt, do not stay on the scene but drive directly to the nearest police station.

Do dress appropriately—especially women. Bathing suits and short shorts should not be worn when visiting towns or villages.

TOURIST INFORMATION. There are no tourist bureaus for PNG in the United States. The best place to get information is from the *Air Niuguni* office or from the tour operators mentioned below. In Papua New Guinea: *Air Niugini House,* Jacksons Airport, Port Moresby (tel. 259–000) or Box 7144, Boroko, Papua New Guinea (tel. 272–065; tlx 794/795. Lae also has a tourist bureau.

You can obtain your visa from the following offices, or on arrival at Port Moresby.

United States: *PNG Embassy,* 1330 Connecticut Ave., N.W., Suite 350, Washington, DC 20036. Tel. (202) 659–0858. *PNG Permanent Mission to the UN,* 100 E. 42nd St., Room 1005, New York, NY 10017. Tel (212) 682–6447.

United Kingdom: *PNG High Commission,* 14 Waterloo Pl., London SW1R 4AR.

ACCOMMODATIONS. Some of the hotels in the major tourist towns are deluxe and geared for the international tourist. However, the majority of the hotels are just the comfortable, standard motel-type accommodation. Many have refrigerators in rooms and coffee- and tea-making facilities. Not all have laundry service. Guests should not expect rapid service or the services of a deluxe hotel. Rather, realize that you are in an exotic destination where many of the hotel staff are just being trained in the tourism field and are a generation or less away from the Stone Age. Please take this into consideration when making demands on service. Also, since *everything* must be flown in, food and other amenities are usually expensive.

A few hotels, such as the Karawari, Ambua, Bensbach, or Wululu Lodges are destinations in themselves and are deluxe and unique—not only in furnishings and surroundings but in the structures themselves. Although the rates may be considered high, they include all meals, tours, and entertainment.

Several of the hotels in Port Moresby are in the deluxe international cetegory with fine restaurants, entertainment, and other facilities. Some of the hotels near Port Moresby are popularly used by local people on weekends, as getaways; they are standard but very comfortable hotels with unique beaches and/or retreat facilities.

Hotels in the island communities of New Britain, New Ireland, and Trobriands are geared to international travelers seeking a pleasant South Seas Island adventure but not deluxe accommodations or services. These hotels are comfortable, usually in an ideal setting with a very relaxed atmosphere and service to match, but cannot be compared to those in Tahiti nor Hawaii. Some are steps into the world of Somerset Maugham, James Michener, or Robert Louis Stevenson and are popular with the expatriate community and knowing Australian and New Zealand tourists.

Hotel guide: *Expensive,* K70–K15 and up; *moderate* K50–K70; *inexpensive* K50 and below. See listings below.

PORT MORESBY

Islander Hotel. *Expensive.* Box 1981; tel. 25–5955; tlx 22288; cable ISLANDER. 90 a/c rooms. Near Waigani Government Center and near University. Handsome structure surrounded by pleasant gardens. Banquet facilities, restaurant, water sports, TV, swimming pool, tennis courts. Credit Cards: *American Express, Diners Club.Visa.*

Port Moresby TraveLodge. *Expensive.* Hunter and Douglas streets. Box 3661; tel. 21–2266; tlx 22248; cable: TRAVELODGE. 177 a/c rooms. Restaurant, coffee shop, cocktail lounge, bar, swimming pool, souvenir shop, meeting

PAPUA NEW GUINEA

facilities, nightly entertainment. Accepts most credit cards. On prime hill site overlooking harbor, beaches, and town center.

Davara Hotel. *Moderate–Expensive.* Box 799, city center; tel. 21–2100; tlx 23236; cable DAVPOM. 65 a/c rooms. Restaurant, shops, swimming pool, room service, wind surfing, laundry service. Credit cards: *American Express, Diners Club, Visa.* Close to town center on Ela Beach Road High rise beach resort—one of best in city.

Gateway Hotel. *Moderate to Expensive.* Box 1215; tel. 25–3855; tlx 230821. Near airport. 35 a/c rooms, dining room, 5 bars, room service, disco, in-room refrigerators, laundry service, money exchange. Credit cards: *American Express, Diners Club.*

Huon Gulf Motel. *Moderate–Expensive.* Box 612; tel. 42–8844. 30 a/c rooms. On Markham Rd. near air strip and on high ground near botanical gardens. Motel style. Dining room, 2 bars, swimming pool, function room. Credit cards: *American Express, Diners Club.*

Lae Lodge. *Moderate–Expensive.* Box 2774; tel. 42–2000; tlx 427473. 89 rooms. Banquet facilities, 3 restaurants, swimming pool, tennis courts, TV. A new and an old wing are in a pleasant garden setting. Poolside barbecue, lunch on Sundays. Credit cards: *American Express, Diners Club.*

Melanesian Hotel. *Moderate–Expensive.* Box 756; tel. 42–3744; tlx. 44187. In the city center on 1st St., on high ground in commercial center near airport; nicely situated in pleasant garden surroundings. 89 a/c rooms. Meeting facilities, swimming pool, restaurant, cocktail lounge. Noted for its restaurant. Credit cards: *American Express, Diners Club.*

Pine Lodge Hotel. *Moderate–Expensive.* Box 90, Morobe; tel. 445–220; tlx 44402. In residential area. 11 rooms. Restaurant, swimming pool, golf. Credit cards: *American Express, Diners Club.*

Owen Stanley Lodge. *Moderate.* Box 6036. 8 rooms. Restaurant, meeting facilities, laundry, travel service. Credit cards: *American Express, Diners Club.*

Papua Hotel. *Moderate.* Box 92; tel. 21–2622; tlx 22353. 56 a/c rooms. Restaurant, cocktail lounge, coffee shop, dining room, laundry service. In town center on Musgrave St., excellent restaurant popular with local people. Credit cards: *American Express, Diners Club.*

Tapini Hotel. *Moderate.* (Central District), Box 19; tel. 259–280; cable TAPINI HOTEL. 7 rooms; 3,000 feet up in the Owen Stanley Ranges. Small resort. Dining room, swimming pool, tennis courts, room service, kitchen facilities, video, coffee shop, cocktail lounge. A landing at the Tapini air strip is probably the most dramatic introduction possible to the gigantic mountain backbone of Papua New Guinea.

Boroko Hotel. *Inexpensive–Moderate.* Okari St., Box 1033; tel. 25–6677. 38 a/c rooms. In main suburban shopping center. 5 bars, room service, disco, in-room refrigerators, laundry service, money exchange. With 5 bars, the hotel can get a bit noisy. Credit cards: *American Express, Diners Club.*

Civic Guest House. *Inexpensive.* Box 1139, Boroko; tel. 25–5091. On Mairi Pl. near Angau Dr. in suburban Boroko. 20 rooms, share bath. This clean little guesthouse is popular with tourists.

Kokoda Trail Motel. *Inexpensive.* Box 5014; tel. 21–2266. 16 rooms; at Sogeri, 30 miles from Moresby in the Owen Stanley Range and less than a mile from the beginning of the trail. Built in 1965. Bush-style bungalows in riverside garden setting at cool, airy 1,700-foot elevation. Base for exploring wartime Kokoda Trail country and Variarata National Park. Good value for quiet stay. Fans, pool, licensed dining room.

Loloata Island Resort. *Inexpensive.* Box 5290; tel. 25–8590; tlx 23016. On the beach. 9 rooms, meeting facilities, laundry service, travel services, fishing. Credit cards: *American Express, Diners Club.*

WESTERN HIGHLANDS

Plumes & Arrows Inn. *Expensive.* Box 86, Mt. Hagen; tel. 551–555; tlx 52088. Near the airport. 16 rooms. Dining room, bar, swimming pool, travel services, conference rooms, library, golf, shops. Credit cards: *American Express, Diners Club.*

Highlander Hotel. *Moderate–Expensive.* Box 34; Mt. Hagen; tel. 521–355; tlx 55108; cable HOTELS. 38 rooms. Barber and beauty shops, restaurant.

Baiyer River Sanctuary Lodge. *Inexpensive.* Box 490, Mt. Hagen; tel. 521–482. In national park. Hostel-type accommodations. 8 rooms, kitchen facilities, table tennis, hiking.

Hagen Park Motel. *Moderate.* Box 81, Mt. Hagen; tel. 521–388; tlx 52056; cable HAPARK. 30 rooms. Meeting facilities, restaurant, color TV, doctor on call, disco.

Kimininga Lodge. *Inexpensive.* Box 408, Mt. Hagen; tel. 521–865; tlx 52008; cable KIMININGA LODGE. 37 rooms. Dining room, laundry, parking, video, swimming pool, shop, restaurant.

Kaiap Orchid Lodge. Box 193, Wabag; tel. 522–087; cable KAIAP LODGE. In highlands. 12 rooms. Bar, gardens, parking. Lovely garden setting with lots of orchids. Credit cards: *American Express.*

Tribal Tops Inn. Box 86, Minj; tel. 565–538; tlx 52070. 12 rooms. Dining room, bar, swimming pool, golf course, gardens, travel services. Credit cards: *American Express, Diners Club.*

Wabag Lodge. Box 2, Wabag; tel. 571–069. 12 rooms. Dining room, 2 bars, conference rooms, parking. Polynesian round house bures (cottages). In remote Enga Province. Good touring center by wheel-drive vehicles. Central *Haus Wind* restaurant features open fire for cool nights.

EASTERN HIGHLANDS

Bird of Paradise Hotel. *Moderate.* Box 12, Goroka. 39 a/c rooms. Banquet facilities, barbershop, 2 restaurants, shops, swimming pool, squash courts, video. On main street of town not far from airport. Saturday buffet luncheon. Hotel restaurants are popular with locals. Rooftop bar and lunch snack bar. Credit cards: *American Express, Visa, Diners Club, MasterCard.*

Chimbu Lodge-Kundiawa. Box 191, Kundiawa; tel. 751–144; tlx 75651. Near business area. 22 rooms. Meeting facilities., restaurant, bank, tennis courts, laundry service, room service, color TV. Small country hotel with pretty garden, mountain scenery. Good base for exploring Simbu region. Small but good restaurant. Credit cards: *American Express, Diners Club.*

Kainantu Lodge. Box 31, Kainantu; tel. 771–021; tlx 77632. 17 rooms. Restaurant, tennis court, laundry service, bars, video, color TV, in-room refrigerator. On hill above quiet town on Highlands Highway near Kassam Pass. Motel style. Credit cards: *American Express.*

Lantern Hotel. *Moderate.* Box 769, tel. 72–1776; cable LANTERN. 8 rooms. Dining room bar, restaurant, travel services. Buffet lunch on Sundays. Restaurant offers European, Chinese, and Indian cuisine. In residential area. Well-run, pleasant hotel.

Minogere Lodge. *Moderate.* Box 450, Goroka; tel. 72–1009; cable, GOROKAUNSIL. 57 rooms. Rate includes breakfast. Video. Town swimming pool, steps away, open 9 A.M. to 6 P.M. daily. Hostel-type accommodations run by city council. Short walk from town—central location with good views. Fair prices and good value.

WESTERN HIGHLANDS

Ambua Lodge. Tari. Trans Niugini Tours, Box 371, Mt. Hagen; tel. 521–438; telex. NE 52012. Or: c/o Greg Stathakis, 408 Islay, Santa Barbara, CA 90131. Credit cards: *American Express.* 12 bungalows. Large lounge, bar, and dining area with central fireplace. Built in the Karawari Lodge-style with a highland flavor. You stay in luxury circular accommodation units with private facilities. This new lodge is a destination in itself in the southern highlands. The lodge is at 7,000 feet and overlooks the Tari Basin, home of the "wig men" and birds of paradise. Stay includes visits to villages and cultural events where you are allowed a rare opportunity to study the Huli people, whose lives are still governed by their belief in the ancestral spirits and sorcery. Only since 1951 has a government station been established in the region.

You travel to Ambua Lodge by road from Mt. Hagen. Bird watching (10 species of birds of paradise are found in this region), high-altitude orchids, and bush walks are part of the daily activities. Lodge management is another quality performance by the operator of Karawari and Bensbach and Wuvlulu lodges. An outstanding opportunity to live among the birds of paradise and to see them up close daily. A real adventure and one of the newest offerings in the country.

PAPUA NEW GUINEA

SOUTHERN HIGHLANDS

Mendi Hotel. Box 108, Mendi; tel. 591–188. 14 rooms. Meeting facilities, squash court, TV, Restaurant. In garden setting of valley overlooking small, quiet outpost town. Close to airport. Comfortable motel style. Good restaurant.

WEWAK AND THE SEPIK RIVER

Karawari Lodge. *Expensive.* Write: Trans Niugini Tours, Box 371, Mt. Hagen; tel. 52–1438; tlx NE 52012. Or in the United States: Trans Niugini Tours, c/o Greg Stathakis, 408 Islay, Santa Barbara, CA 90131. Hotel overlooks river and has fantastic view of the mountain regions beyond. 20 rooms, cooled by overhead fans. Sleep under mosquito nets in grand setting. Dining room, bar, swimming pool, shops. Credit cards: *American Express.* Includes meals, entertainment, tours.
The lodge is attractively situated. Each cottage is a self-contained duplex and features extensive use of native building materials. They are clustered alongside the main lodge and built on the style of a traditional *haus tamboran*, or spirit house. Atmosphere is more on the grand-lodge style. As part of the package guests travel from the lodge on river trucks—aluminum river boats, powered by outboard motors. They see reenactments of traditional native ceremonies and observe the day-to-day activities in the villages along the river banks. There are opportunities to explore the extraordinary variety of plant, bird, and animal life. The region is safe. It is difficult to get to—but worth the effort! This is a quality operation. The owners have captured the spirit of the country and have been able to pass this feeling on to their guests.
Wewak Hotel. *Moderate–Expensive.* Box 20, Wewak; tel. 86–2155. 35 a/c and ceiling-fan rooms. On a hill overlooking the sea. Banquet and meeting facilities, restaurant and cocktail lounge, video. Credit cards: *American Express, Diners Club.* Good base for road trip to middle Sepik area.
Angoram Hotel. Box 35, Angoram; tel. 88–3011; tlx 86134; cable ARSHAK. 14 a/c rooms. Garden hotel with bars, dining room, restaurant, TV room. Excellent touring base for the middle Sepik area; canoe trips, visits to local artifact-rich villages.
Sepik International Beach Resort. Box 152, Wewak; tel. 86–2548; tlx 86119; cable WINDJ. On the beach. 20 rooms. Popular restaurant and bar. Fishing arranged. Good traditional open-style restaurant; nice bar.
Sepik Motel. Box 51, Wewak; tel. 86–2422. 14 a/c rooms. Dining room, cocktail lounge, swimming pool, room service, conference room, banquet facilities. Travel services. Credit cards: *American Express, Diners Club.*

MADANG

Madang Resort. *Inexpensive–Expensive.* Coastwatchers Ave. Box 111, Madang; tel. 82–2744; tlx 82707. Situated along the harbor and Yamilon Bay opposite Kranket Island at the entrance to the harbor. Set in 5 acres of landscaped gardens among thousands of native orchids. 60 a/c rooms. Banquet facilities, barbershop, beauty shop, restaurant, swimming pool. More expensive rooms have sea view. Credit cards: *American Express, Diners Club.* The Melanesian Explorer Marina is here for its Sepik Cruise.
Jais Aben Resort. *Moderate–Expensive.* Box 105; tel. 82–3311; tlx NE 82716. 16 rooms. New resort with self-contained units, half with kitchens. Swimming pool and restaurant. Boats for hire and all water sports. Near the beach within a coconut plantation overlooking lovely Nagada Harbor, 12kms from town off the main road on the waterfront. Deluxe rooms along oceanfront—all with screened patio area adjacent to small coral beaches. Dive shop.
Coastwatchers Motel. *Moderate.* Coralita St., Box 324; tel. 82–2684; cable COWAMO. Rates include breakfast. 14 a/c rooms. Dining room, bar, swimming pool, golf course, travel services, boating, video. In beautiful gardens opposite the Coastwatchers Memorial with view over the golf course and Astrolobe Bay. Credit cards: *American Express, Diners Club.*
Smugglers Inn. Box 303; tel. 82–2744; tlx 82722; cable SMUGLER. 45 a/c rooms. Banquet facilities, barbershop, beauty shop, restaurant, swimming pool. Excellent location. Open-air restaurant has view and sea breezes. Lions Reserve Beach is nearby. Credit cards: *American Express, Diners Club.*

Masurina Lodge. *Expensive.* Box 5, Alotau; tel. 611–2212; tlx 61107; cable MASURINA. In residential area. 29 a/c and fan rooms. Dining room, bar. Diving trips and local tours arranged. Credit cards: *American Express.*

Kirwina Lodge. *Inexpensive to Moderate.* Box 2, Losuia. Near the lagoon. 16 rooms. Air conditioned by sea breezes. The lodge is very popular with weekenders from Port Moresby. Can arrange tours and transportation.

NEW BRITAIN

Kaivuna Resort Hotel. *Moderate–Expensive.* Mango Ave., Box 395, Rabaul; tel. 92-1766. In city center. 56 a/c rooms. Restaurants, swimming pool, scuba diving. Open-air bar. Credit cards: *American Express, Diners Club.*

Palm Lodge. *Moderate.* Box 32., Kimbe; tel. 935–001; tlx 93114; cable PALO. Near beach. 20 a/c rooms. Restaurant, swimming pool, TV, travel services. Credit cards: *American Express, Diners Club.*

TraveLodge Rabaul. *Moderate.* On the corner of Mango Ave. and Namaula St., Box 449, Rabaul; 92-2111; tlx 92975. Overlooks harbor. 40 a/c rooms. Queen Emma Dining Room, bar, swimming pool, shops, laundry, beauty shop, minibar. Room service. Most credit cards accepted.

Kulau Lodge. *Inexpensive–Moderate.* Box 359, Rabaul; tel. 92-2115; cable KULAU LODGE. Six units built like local Kunai huts with all conveniences, including refrigerator and room service. Banquet and meeting facilities, restaurant, shops, fishing, snorkeling, boating, laundry service. In pleasant garden setting overlooking ocean, a few kilometers out of town on the North Coast Rd. Credit cards: *American Express.*

Hamamas Hotel. Box 139, PN139, Rabaul; tel. 92–1999; tlx 92959; cable HAMAAMAS. In city center. 56 a/c rooms. TV, conference room, restaurant, two bars, Western and Chinese food.

KIETA

Arvo Holiday Island Resort. *Moderate–Expensive.* (Out of town) Box 44, Arvo Island; tel. 95–1855; tlx 95867; cable ARVO ISLAND. The resort is a short ferry ride from the Kieta Yacht Club. 16 rooms. Kept cool by sea breezes. Pleasant little resort with banquet and meeting facilities, restaurant, tennis courts, scuba diving, fishing, snorkeling, wind surfing. Perhaps the best accommodations in the area.

Davara Hotel. *Moderate–Expensive.* Box 241, Kieta. Near the sea on Toniva Beach. 46 a/c rooms. Bar, restaurant, radio, TV, laundry service, meeting facilities. Swimming pool. Credit cards: *American Express* and *Diners Club.*

Kieta Hotel. *Moderate–Expensive.* Box 228, Kieta; tel. 95–6277; tlx 95843; cable KIETOL. Located near the shopping area. 24 a/c rooms. Restaurant, cocktail lounge, TV lounge, laundry service, in-room refrigerator, room service, tea-coffee-making facilities in rooms.

Buka Luman Sopho. *Moderate.* Buka Passage, Bougainville, Sohano; tel. 966–057; tlx 50014; cable BUKALUMA. 4 rooms. Rates include meals. Bar, video, meeting facilities.

Bensbach Lodge. *Expensive.* Book through Trans Niugini Tours. Like Kawawari Lodge, Bensbach is built entirely from local materials and blends right in with the landscape. Here you become a part of the landscape with its spectacular wildlife. The lodge is comfortable and rooms are spacious and cool, with ceiling fans and refrigerators. Covered verandas link the accommodation wings to the main building, which has dining room, bar, and lounge. Food is excellent, and much care is put into the meals—venison, duck, freshly caught barramundi, and other fresh seafood. Rates include all meals, tours, and sports equipment. Deer, wallaby, and bird life are abundant. Bensbach is a fisher's paradise, and arrangements can be made with local fishers to accompany you to some very special fishing spots. Bensbach Lodge is a destination in itself and is another quality operation by the owners of Kawawari Lodge.

NEW IRELAND

Kavieng Hotel. *Moderate.* Box 4, Kavieng; tel. 942–199; tlx 94904; cable HOTEL. In the center of this capital town. 24 a/c rooms, some with private bath. There are also a few fan-cooled rooms without private bath. Dining room, restaurant, laundry service, bar, parking, color TV, tennis. Relaxing atmosphere

PAPUA NEW GUINEA

and what you'd expect if you've read many stories of the old days in the South Pacific. Credit cards: *American Express, Diners Club.*

Kavieng Club. *Inexpensive.* Box 62, Kavieng; tel. 94–2027. 8 rooms, some with fans, some a/c. Club atmosphere and delightful place to meet local people.

Namatanai Hotel. *Inexpensive–Moderate.* Box 48, Namatanai; tel. 25; cable HOTEL NAMATANAI. 6 rooms. On the waterfront. Fans and private bath, radio. Meals available.

NORTHERN DISTRICT

Lamington Hotel. *Moderate to Expensive.* Box 27, Popondetta; tel. 297–152; cable LAMHOTEL. 18 a/c rooms. Dining room, laundry service, parking, bar, in-room movies, cocktail lounge. Popular with returning Australian veterans.

Waijuga Park Guest House. *Inexpensive.* c/o Post Office Wanigela. 14 rooms. Rates include meals. Canoe trips and glass-bottom-boat trips arranged. Other tours arranged.

Kofure Village Guest House. *Very Inexpensive.* c/o post office or district officer, Tufi. About 1km from airport via outrigger canoe. 18 double rooms. Rates include all meals and entertainment—and fishing.

Mirigina Lodge. *Inexpensive.* c/o post office or district officer, Tufi. 7 double rooms. Rates include meals. Fishing, diving, and sightseeing trips can be arranged. This small lodge is on scenic Cape Nelson. Cabins are of native materials. Situated above the fjord waters at Tufi Station.

WUVULU ISLAND

Alaba Lodge. *Expensive.* Wuvulu Island. For rates and information contact Air Niugini or Trans Niugini Tours. Box 371, Mt. Hagen; tel. 52–1438; tlx 52012. In the U.S.: Trans Niugini Tours, c/o Greg Stathakis, 408 Islay, Santa Barbara, CA 90131. Rates include food, lodging, laundry, land transport, all diving and snorkeling equipment (not regulators), and scuba and fishing boats with guides. This charge also includes air for two dives per day with bottles provided. Booking must be made well in advance.

RESTAURANTS. Hotel food is international; Chinese food is very popular. Most tourist hotels have dining rooms; some have coffee shops or snack bars. A few hotels serve barbecue meals at noon on Saturday and/or Sunday.

The prices of meals are not expensive anywhere, except at the best restaurants in the deluxe hotels in Port Moresby. Most meals are included in the prepackaged tours. Meals average breakfast, K3; lunch, K5; dinner, K10 but will vary depending on whether you are eating in a regular restaurant, a cafe, or an international hotel.

HOW TO GET AROUND. Papua New Guinea's rugged terrain has prevented the establishment of a cross-country road network, but all main centers are connected by frequent air service. In addition, the *Highlands Highway* connects Lae with the major highlands centers of Goroka, Kundiawa, Mt. Hagen, and Mendi. There is also a seasonal road between Lae and Madang.

By air: Offices of the airlines dealing with air travel within Papua New Guinea: *Air Niugini,* Box 7186, Boroka, Papua New Guinea; tel. 25900. In the U.S., write: 5000 Birch St., Suite 3000 West Tower, Newport Beach, CA 92660. Tel. (714) 752–5440.

Aviation Developments PNG Pty. Ltd., Box 1975, Boroko. Tel. 259–655; tlx 22241. Scheduled air tours.

Douglas Airways, Box 1179. Tel. 253–499; tlx 22145; cable AIRTOURS. Five- to 18-passenger charters. Also offers aerial safaris.

Talair, Box 5350, Port Moresby. Tel. 255–799. Scheduled and air charters throughout the country.

Bougair–Bougainville Air offers extensive service from Kieta around the North Solomons to the neighboring islands of Buin, Torokina, Nakunai, and Buka.

THE SOUTH PACIFIC

Because the small planes used in travel throughout the country have limited seating space, it is imperative that all bookings from November through February be booked well in advance; it is wise to book in advance in any period.

Internal air fares within the country are quite high. Major airports with daily flights are: Lae, Rabaul, Kieta, Goroka, Madang, Wewak. Because of the distances involved, there are both large and small airports throughout the country.

By car. Renting is not a problem in major centers. *Avis-Nationwide, Budget Hire Car,* and *Hertz* are represented in Port Moresby, Lae, Rabaul, Mt. Hagen, Madang, Wewak, and Kieta.

By bus. Bus services operate in major towns, including Madang (cost 25 toea); pay when you get off; depot at market; you can also travel out of town), and Port Moresby (for the adventurous only) and the Highlands. Buslines provide a service between Lae and Mt. Hagen.

By sea. For inter-island shipping see also *Planning Your Trip.* The Lutheran Shipping Co. (tel. 82–2577) has weekly service from Lae or Wewak to the islands on Milne Bay. Takes 24 hours; costs K14–K214. Not the most comfortable, but a great way to see the islands.

Sepik-Explorer Houseboats. Contact *Melanesian Tourist Service,* Box 707, Madang. Two houseboats ply Sepik River on 3-day cruises, stopping off at various villages between Angoram, Ambunti, and Pagwi. Good accommodation and food. Excellent opportunity to experience river culture, purchase artifacts. Much used by tour groups.

TOURS. A number of major tour operators deal with all-inclusive package tours to specific areas in the country. Bookings should be made with your travel agent. A number of local tour operators can arrange local sightseeing after you arrive. However, the safe bet is to book through a major operator before arrival in order to guarantee hotel and air reservations. The number of hotel rooms is limited in certain areas, and plane capacity is also limited. You should confirm your reservations well in advance.

Listed below are tour operators who handle packaged tours to the most popular destinations within Papua New Guinea. You can also usually arrange tours through your hotel.

The three largest operators, whose trips are highly recommended:

Trans Niugini Tours, c/o Greg Stathakis, 408 Islay, Santa Barbara, CA 90131; (805) 569–0558. Offers 2- to 15-day package tours throughout the country. Exciting four-wheel-drive trips into remote areas. Special-interest tours; also excursions to Baiyer River Bird of Paradise Wildlife Sanctuary and village cultural tours.

Trans Niugini also arranges trips to the famous Kawari and Bensbach lodges. Or call toll free *Australia Travel Service Tour Pacific* in California (800) 232–2121; U.S. (800) 423–2880; Los Angeles or Canada, call collect: (805) 569–2448.

Travel Plans International, Box 3875, 1200 Harger Rd., Oak Brook, Illinois (800) 323–7600; Illinois (312) 655–5678. Fascinating natural-history and anthropology special-interest tours of the country, as well as special helicopter expeditions—a new way of seeing remote areas that cannot be reached otherwise. Travel Plans International is a creative group operator that handles group and individual tours and provides escorted national and local tours working with Trans Niugini Tours, Melanesian Tours, and Pacific Expeditions (the helicopter operator). They will work with any individual or group wanting to go anywhere in Papua New Guinea.

Melanesian Tourists Services Pty. Ltd., Box 707, Madang. Tel 822; tlx 82707. Unirep, Melanesian Tourist Services, 850 Colorado Blvd, #105, Los Angeles, CA 90041; (213) 256–1991; (800) 521–7242. Interesting *Melanesian Explorer* cruises of Sepik River, the Trobriand Islands, and highlands expeditions. Full- and half-day tours. For individuals or groups.

Air Carriers. *Bougair Air Services Pty. Ltd.,* Box 986, Arawa, Kieta, Bougainville. Arranges flights to government and mission stations throughout Bougainville. Scenic flights of the copper mine at Panguna and Mt. Bagana. Scheduled service between: Kieta and Buin and between Kieta, Torokina, and Kieta, with Tonu–Boku–Wakunai as options, and from Kieta to Torokina. Scheduled flights to Buka via Wakunai, Unus, and Sabah. Write for rates.

Talair Tourist Airlines of Niugini, Box 108, Goroka. Operates 60 aircraft serving major centers and outstations with scheduled service to all provinces.

PAPUA NEW GUINEA

Douglas Airways, Box 1179, Boroko, Port Moresby. Operates 19 aircraft in Gulf, Central, Western and Sepik provinces. Aerial safaris are available. Rates are by size of aircraft and by the hour.

The following tour operators also arrange trips to and within Papua New Guinea. Your may write or call for details, then ask your travel agent to do the rest.

Atlantic and Pacific Tours, 230 N. Maryland Ave., #308, Glendale, CA (818) 240-0538; (800) 421-9020. Individual travel throughout Papua New Guinea.

Wilderness Travel, 1760 Solano Ave., Berkeley, CA 94707; (415) 524-5111; tlx 677 022. Individual and group tours off the beaten track. Trekking and island exploration.

Brendan Tours, 510 W. 6th St., Los Angeles, CA 90014; (213) 488-9191; (800) 421-8446; tlx 215 393.

Burns Philp Travel, Box 87, Rabaul; 92-2645 or 2798; for tours in Rabaul area.

Globus Gateway, 69-15 Austin Street, Forest Hills, N.Y. 11375; (718) 268-4711; (800) 221-0090. Individual extensions to their South Pacific group tours.

Hemphill Harris Travel Corp., 16000 Ventura Blvd, #200, Encino, CA 91436; (213) 906-9086; (800) 421-0454. Escorted deluxe tours as part of their South Pacific tours.

Jet Set Tours, 8383 Wilshire Blvd, #760, Beverly Hills, CA 90211; (213) 651-4050; (800) 421-4603.

Mountain Travel, 1398 Solano Ave., Albany, CA 94706; (415) 527-8100; (800) 227-2384. Emphasis on adventure among peoples, throughout the country. 20 days escorted.

Nature Expeditions, Box 11496, Eugene, OR 97440; (503) 484-6529. Escorted adventure tours throughout the country. Emphasis on culture, with lectures by professionals.

Olson-Travelworld, 5855 Green Valley Circle, #300, Culver City, CA 90230; (213) 670-7100; (800) 421-2255. Deluxe escorted tours as part of South Pacific tour.

Pacific Dateline Tours, Box 1755, Newport Beach, CA 92663; (714) 675-7620; (800) 854-0543. Individual tours covering entire country.

Pacific Expeditions, Box 132, Port Moresby; 25-7803; tlx NE 22292; for tours within PNG.

RTC World Travel, Box 221, Rabaul; 92-2826 or 2849, for tours around Rabaul.

Sobeck Expeditions, Box 7007, Angels Camp, CA 95222; (209) 736-2661. Adventure tours with emphasis on white-water rafting and trekking.

See and Sea Travel, 680 Beach St., #340, San Francisco, CA 94109; Tel (415) 771-0077. Scuba-diving tours.

Society Expeditions, 723 Broadway East, Seattle, WA 98102; (206) 324-9400; (800) 426-7794. Land and sea tours of Papua New Guinea using the World Discoverer and Society Explorer.

Travcoa, 4000 MacArthur Blvd., Newport Beach, CA 92660; (714) 975-1152. Escorted deluxe tours as part of South Pacific tours with in-depth emphasis on Papua New Guinea.

Valor Tours, Schoonmaker Bldg., Sausalito, CA 94965; (415) 332-7850. Emphasis on war-veteran tours to Papua New Guinea and throughout the Pacific.

SEASONAL EVENTS. Papua New Guinea's annual singsings in the highland towns of Mt. Hagen and Goroka have become world famous. They are held alternating years in each province during August and September. But if you can't make these, you may be able to attend other singsings and cultural activities that mark national and local holidays. The following is a guide to scheduled special events held throughout the country. Dates may vary year to year.

End January/early February: *Chinese New Year.* Chinese community in major centers stages festivities with fireworks and traditional dragon dances.

April through June: *Yam Festival.* Held in Kiriwina, a subprovince of Papua. This annual event of the Trobriand Islands is to celebrate the harvest of yams, a staple crop of the area. Singsings, of course, and ceremonial gift exchanges are held.

THE SOUTH PACIFIC

May. *Frangipani Festival,* Rabaul. Three days of celebration including a parade, Mardi Gras, Frangipani Ball, and beauty contest.

June 7: *Marborasa Festival in Madang.*

June: *Queen's Birthday Weekend.* Port Moresby: National Capital Show, cultural, agricultural, and industrial displays. Madang: Maborasa Festival, weekend of cultural events, including music festival, dance and drama performances, and art show.

September 16–18. *National Day.* Celebrated throughout the country, marked by yacht races, singsings, cultural performances, art and craft displays. Hiri Moale (Port Moresby): Festival to mark the early voyages of the Motu people, who traveled along the Papuan coast. Weekend event has canoe races, beauty contast, and singsings. *Papua New Guinea Festival* (Port Moresby): Month-long event with guest performers from other third-world countries participating in traditional- and contemporary-arts program.

September–October: *Tolaii–Warwagira, Kavieng–Malag Festival.* Traditional performances for two weeks. Exciting festival held at East New Britain province's major center. Weekend firework displays, singsings, fire dancers, string-band competition, and performances by choral groups. *Morobe Show* (Lae): Weekend of cultural and agricultural displays. Major singsing is staged on Sunday. Many highland groups travel great distances to participate in the event.

October: *Morobe Festival* in Lae.

November: *Pig Kill Season.* From the beginning of November until Christmas, the Simbu people, near Kundiawa, stage traditional feasts within their village communities. Hundreds of pigs may be killed for one such event. A movable feast marked by singsings moves from village to village. *Pearl Festival* (Samarai Milne Bay Province): Weekend-long festival celebrated by beauty contests, art and craft displays, canoe races, and junior sports events.

December: *Tolai Warwagira, Rabaul,* East New Britain. An annual festival including string-band competitions, yacht races, and performances by drama and choir groups. A major singsing is held near Rabaul during which a *duk duk* dance is performed to represent all *Tubuan* (secret) societies.

SPORTS AND BEACHES. All water sports are extremely popular, snorkeling and diving included. See also Accommodations for resorts that offer sporting activities. *Ela Beach,* 5 minutes from Port Moresby's center, is a popular sunbathing beach. The **Kokoda Trail,** about 40km from Port Moresby, where Australians fought Japanese during World War II, makes an interesting hike. The trail to Owers Corner, where the war memorial is situated, is an easy hike; after this it gets tougher.

Follow the **Sogeri Road,** with its magnificent views, including Rouna Falls, through many rubber plantations. Visitors make it a day outing with a picnic or lunch at the Kokoda Trail Motel (38km from city) where the most popular dish is barbecued crocodile. *Royal Papua Yacht Club* membership includes water skiers, power-boat devotees, big-game fishers, dinghy sailors, and keel boaters, both racing and cruising. Situated on Port Moresby Harbour. Provides extensive amenities and has a dining room serving light meals. Visiting tourists welcome. Phone: 21-4454. You can also contact *Tropical Diving Adventures,* Box 1644, Port Moresby; 25-7429.

In the **eastern highlands,** you'll find golf, bowling, swimming, and a sports club in Goroke that welcomes visitors.

In **Madang Province** scuba diving among coral reefs and wartime wrecks in Hansa Bay can be fascinating. Boating is available; Madang is known for deep-sea fishing. Tourists are welcome at the Madang Golf Course.

In **Milne Bay,** you can rent boats from the Madang Hotel and the Madang Marine Center. The Madang Hotel and the Dive Center (82-2766) can arrange for snorkeling and diving trips. The Dive Center also offers lessons.

The most popular beaches in the area are Lion's Reserve, north off Smuggler's Inn; Siar Island; Kranket Lagoon; Pig Island; and Wangat Island.

In New Britain, the Rabaul Yacht Club. Box 106, Rabaul, welcomes visitors, even non-yachtsman. Good place to have a cool drink and a smorgasbord luncheon while enjoying the sights of Rabaul's Harbor. The three golf clubs on the island, each with its unique setting, welcome visitors to use the courses as the clubs. There are a number of other social and sporting clubs in Rabaul that welcome overseas visitors (golf, aquatic, squash, tennis, snorkeling and sports

PAPUA NEW GUINEA

club). Check with the local tourist office on Park St., 92-1823, or at your hotel for information on local events, festivals, singsings. Tour operators in town can arrange for fishing, sailing and underwater exploration.

Wuvulu Island offers some of the finest diving in the world.

OTHER THINGS TO SEE. Just seeing the country is a fascinating experience in itself. Here we list some particular sites of historic and cultural interest.

PORT MORESBY

National Parliament. The new Parliament House at Waigaini was opened in August 1984 by Prince Charles, heir to the British throne, before a gathering of commonwealth leaders. It is built in *haus tambaran* (spirit house) style. More than 100 members in the national parliament conduct their proceedings in three languages: English, Motu, and Pidgin. If parliament is in session, a visit to the public gallery is recommended. Visitor's gallery open Mon. to Fri. 8 A.M. to noon and 1 to 4 P.M.

National Museum. Opened in 1977 as a gift from the Australian government on independence. The museum, an interesting example of modern architecture, is in the suburb of Waigani, close to the government-office complex. It features excellent displays of pottery and birds of paradise from all the provinces and has a fine collection of Melanesian artifacts. Art is attractively presented; the museum is well worth a visit. Open Tues. and Thurs. from 8:30 A.M. to 3:30 P.M.; Sun. 1 to 5 P.M. No admission charge. Bookshop open Mon. to Fri. 8 A.M. to noon; 1 to 3:30 P.M.; Sundays from 1 to 5 P.M.

National Arts School and Design Center. Good place to watch a painting or sculpture being created by a student or village carvers, or preview the *National Theatre Company* in rehearsal of a play or a dance. Students play ancient Sepik flutes and other native instruments and combine their music into modern folk-rock. The artists live and work together and the work done by the students is on sale to the public. Close to the National Library and the Supreme Court. Open Mon. to Fri. during school hours.

University of Papua New Guinea and the National Botanic Gardens. This modern university has some 3,000 students. Follow the signs to the gardens of one of the world's great orchid collections. More than two-thirds of the world's known species can be seen here. Hybrid double and treble bougainvilleas were developed here. *Botanical Gardens:* Open 8 A.M. to 4 P.M. except Saturdays.

Bomana War Cemetery. Resting place of some 4,000 men from Papua New Guinea and Australia who died fighting for their countries during World War II. Beautifully maintained. About 16km from Port Moresby.

Vairata National Park. On the Sogeri Road about 40km from Port Moresby. This visit can be combined with a trip to the Kokoda Trail (see Sports). During the early-morning hours you can occasionally see the famous and beautiful birds of paradise. In this lush rain forest and nature sanctuary there are a number of hiking trails. From Lookout Point on a clear day you can see all the way to Port Moresby. Picnic facilities are available, and it's possible to camp on Sogeri Plateau.

Moitake Crocodile Farm. Only a few miles from town, behind Jackson's Airport. Crocodiles are bred in captivity, and you can watch their feeding on Friday afternoons.

LAE

Botanical Gardens. The gardens were established in 1949 and occupy 130 acres of parkland within walking distance of the town center. Adjacent to the gardens is the War Memorial and resting place for some 3,000 Allied soldiers. Gardens are also a sanctuary for small animals and birds. Extensive collection of orchids and one of the most beautiful spots in the country.

University of Technology. 11km from Lae on Butibum Road. Note the sharp contrast of the university's modern buildings with the Sepik-style coffee shop and restaurant.

SHOPPING. Papua New Guinea art is known throughout the world. Masks and other creative objects carved in the Sepik region are only a sampling of what to look for. There is also a wide range of crafts made by the people in wood, copper, pottery, shell, and basketwork. Look for the work from the Trobriands or Buka. Artifact shops can be found in every center, or they can be bought from the missions or directly from village craftspeople. *Village Arts,* outside Port Moresby, has a few artifact bargains.

There is stringent control on the export of artifacts of national, historic, or cultural significance, so care should be taken when purchasing articles directly from villagers. A visit to the town market in each center is an experience that should not be overlooked. *Koki Market* in Port Moresby is perhaps the best known. There are two markets at Lae: the *Main Market,* south of the air strip, where Morobe and Highlands people sell their produce and handicrafts, and the *Butibum Market,* on Butibum Road, decorated with traditional murals.

Do not expect local people or small shops to cash traveler's checks; plan on having enough currency to get you through each day. If you plan on bargaining with the local people, make certain you have plenty of smaller-denomination currency.

AIRPORT TAX. There is a 10K international departure tax.

INDEX

Page references to maps appear in **boldface**.

Abel Tasman National Park (N.Z.), 333
Abemama, 530–531
Aboriginal peoples. *See also* Peoples
 of Australia, 49–50, 57–59, 279
 Maori, of New Zealand, 323–326,
  349, 351–353, 377
 of South Pacific islands, 419–420
Abrym, 542
Accommodations, 1, 19–20
 camping and hostels, 21–23
 in homes, farms and ranches, 20–21
 in New Zealand, 311
 in South Pacific islands, 422–423
Adelaide, 227–231
Airlie Beach, 209, 212, 213
Air travel, 1–2, 8–9. *See also*
  Transportation
 to and in Australia, 39
 to Cook Islands, 472, 473, 475
 to Fiji Islands, 517–518
 to French Polynesia, 448, 465
 to Kiribati and Tuvalu, 533, 534
 to and in New South Wales, 115–117
 to and in New Zealand, 309, 380–381
 to Niue Island, 505
 to Papua New Guinea, 582, 594,
  602–603
 to Solomon Islands, 576
 to South Pacific islands, 423
 to Tonga, 497
 to Western Samoa, 489, 490
Aitutaki Island, 476–477
Alice Springs, 267, 271
 accommodations in, 272
 camping in, 274
 restaurants in, 275
 tours of, 277
American Samoa, 479–484, **480**
 automobiles in, 15
 information sources for, 2
 inter-island ships to, 13
 restaurants in, 23
 shopping in, 29
 tours and sightseeing in, 12
 transportation in, 18
America's Cup race, 243, 244, 248
Animals. *See also* Zoos
 in Australia, 47–49
 in Christchurch, 385
 in Dunedin, 399–400, 410
 in New Zealand, 319, 329, 385
 in Northern Territory (Aus.), 279
 in Tasmania, 299
Apia, 486
Aquariums, 377, 566
Arthur's Pass National Park (N.Z.), 333
Arts
 in Australia, 63–65
 Maori, 351, 353
 in Melbourne, 159, 171–173
 in New Zealand, 326–328, 379
 in Sydney, 95–96

 in Tasmania, 302
Auckland, 342–346, **343**
 accommodations in, 367
 museums and galleries in, 378
 restaurants in, 370–371
 tours and sightseeing of, 373–375
 transportation in, 373
Australia, **33**, 35–39, 42, 43–45. *See
  also individual provinces*
 accommodations in, 19–21
 animals and plants of, 47–49
 arts, literature, music and media in,
  63–66
 automobiles in, 15, 41
 camping in, 22
 Canberra, **145**
 climate in, 45–47
 education and science in, 66–67
 government of, 53–57
 history of, 49–54
 information sources for, 2–3
 inter-island ships to, 13–14
 language in, 61–62
 Melbourne, **158**
 New South Wales, **100–101**
 peoples of, 57–61
 Perth, **242**
 Queensland, **199**
 restaurants in, 23
 Sydney, **71**, **82**
 tours and sightseeing in, 12–13,
  40–41
 transportation to and in, 18, 39–40
 Victoria, **175**
 women in, 62–63
Australian Capital Territory, 142–144
 accommodations in, 147–148
 Canberra, 144–147, **145**
 entertainment in, 152–153
 museums, historic sites and galleries
  in, 151–152
 parks, gardens, beaches and zoos in,
  150
 restaurants in, 148–149
 sports in, 150–151
Austral Islands, 445, 451–452
Automobiles, 15–17
 in Australia, 41
 in French Polynesia, 466
 in Melbourne, 163–164
 in New South Wales, 118
 in New Zealand, 310–311, 322
 in the Outback (NSW), 109
 in Queensland, 224
 in Tasmania, 295–296
 in Victoria, 156
 in Western Australia, 257, 258
Ayers Rock, 269, 272, 277

Backpacking. *See also* Camping
 in New Zealand, 314–315
Baggage, 4–5

INDEX

Ballarat, 178–179
Ballooning, 194
Barossa Valley, 231
Bay of Islands (N.Z.), 346–347, 367–368, 376
Beaches
  in Canberra, 150
  in Melbourne, 159
  in New South Wales, 105–106, 134–135
  in New Zealand, 316
  in Papua New Guinea, 604–605
  in Queensland, 205, 209, 219
  in Sydney, **82**, 91–93
  in Tahiti, 430
  in Tasmania, 284–285
  in Western Australia, 265
Bed-and-breakfasts, 20–21
Bedarra Island, 206, 208
Bendigo, 179–180
Bicycling, 19, 166
Blue Mountains (NSW), 99
  accommodations in, 119
  bushwalking in, 135
  information sources for, 116
  museums in, 138
  parks in, 132
  restaurants in, 127–128
  tours in, 129
Bora Bora, 440–441, 452–454
Botany Bay (Aus.), 83
Bougainville, 592
Brampton Island, 212
Brisbane, 215–216, 221–223, 225
Buses, 17–18
  in Australia, 40
  in New South Wales, 116, 118
  in New Zealand, 309
  in Northern Territory (Aus.), 272, 276
  in Tahiti, 467
  in Tasmania, 295
  in Western Samoa, 490
Bushwalking, 225
Bus tours
  of Melbourne, 164
  of Sydney, 74, 90
  of Victoria, 186, 190
  of Western Australia, 264

Cairns, 200, 204
Camping, 21–23
  in French Polynesia, 462
  in New South Wales, 127
  in Northern Territory (Aus.), 274–275
  in Perth, 245–246
  in Queensland, 222
  in South Australia, 238
  in Tasmania, 300
  in Victoria, 184–185, 187
  in Western Australia, 260–262
Canberra (Aus.), 142–146, **145**
  accommodations in, 147–148
  entertainment in, 152–153
  memorials in, 146–147
  museums, historic sites and galleries in, 151–152
  parks, gardens, beaches and zoos in, 150
  restaurants in, 148–149
  sports in, 150–151
Casinos
  in New Caledonia, 567
  in Perth, 250
  in Tasmania, 303
Central Coast (NSW), 103–104
  accommodations in, 120
  information sources for, 116
  parks, gardens, beaches and zoos in, 132, 134, 135
  tours of, 129
Children's activities
  in Adelaide, 230
  in Melbourne, 168
Christchurch, 380, 382–384
  accommodations in, 404
  museums and historic sites in, 411–412
  restaurants in, 406–407
  tours of, 408
Christmas Island, 531–532, 534
Climate
  of American Samoa, 482
  of Australia, 37–38, 45–47
  of Cook Islands, 474
  of Fiji Islands, 518
  of French Polynesia, 446
  of New Caledonia, 559–560
  of New Zealand, 308
  of Northern Territory (Aus.), 267
  of Papua New Guinea, 594
  of Solomon Islands, 574
  of Tasmania, 282–283
  of Tonga, 496–497
  of Vanuatu, 543
  of Victoria, 155–156
  of Western Samoa, 488–489
Clothing, 5, 38–39
Conversions, metric, 28
Cook Islands, 472–474
  accommodations in, 475–477
  automobiles in, 15
  information sources for, 3
  inter-island ships to, 14
  restaurants in, 23
  shopping in, 29
  tours and sightseeing in, 13, 477–478
  transportation in, 18, 477
Cruises, 2, 9–10
  to Australia, 39
  to Fiji Islands, 524–525
  to French Polynesia, 465–468
  paddle steamer, 195
  in Queensland, 205, 209, 214
  in South Pacific islands, 423
Currencies, 7–8
  in Australia, 36
  in Cook Islands, 475
  in Fiji Islands, 518
  in New Caledonia, 560
  in New Zealand, 309
  in Niue Island, 505
  in Papua New Guinea, 594–595
  in Solomon Islands, 573

INDEX

in Tonga, 497
in Wallis and Futuna, 509
in Western Samoa, 489

Dandenongs, 174–176
Darwin (Aus.), 267–270, 272–274, 277
Daydream Island, 211, 212
Drinking water, 25
Driving. *See* Automobiles
Dunedin (N.Z.), 398–403
   accommodations in, 404–405
   museums and historic sites in, 412
   restaurants in, 407
   tours and sightseeing in, 408, 409
   wildlife in, 410
Dunk Island, 201, 204

Egmont National Park (N.Z.), 330
Electricity, 25
   in Australia, 41, 113
   in Fiji Islands, 518
   in French Polynesia, 447
   in Kiribati and Tuvalu, 533
   in New Zealand, 317
   in Papua New Guinea, 595
   in Tonga, 497
   in Wallis and Futuna, 509
   in Western Samoa, 489
Ellice Island. *See* Kiribati and Tuvalu
Entertainment
   in Adelaide, 230–231
   in American Samoa, 484
   in Canberra, 152–153
   in Cook Islands, 478
   in Fiji Islands, 527
   in Melbourne, 172–173
   in New Caledonia, 567–568
   in New South Wales, 141
   in New Zealand, 379
   in Perth, 250
   in Queensland, 225
   in Solomon Islands, 579
   in Sydney, 97–99
   in Tahiti, 471
   in Tonga, 501
   in Vanuatu, 549
   in Wallis and Futuna, 510
   in Western Samoa, 492–493
Entry requirements, 4. *See also* Passports and visas
Espiritu Santo, 542–543, 545, 546
Eua Island, 496, 498

Farm vacations
   in Australia, 127, 222
   in New Zealand, 21, 311–312
Ferries
   in French Polynesia, 441, 442
   in New Zealand, 310
Fiji Islands, 511–518, **513**
   accommodations in, 519–523
   automobiles in, 15
   information sources for, 3
   inter-island ships to, 14
   restaurants in, 23–24, 523–524
   shopping in, 29, 526–527
   sports in, 525–526
   tours and sightseeing in, 13, 524–525
   transportation to and in, 18, 517–518, 524
Fiordland National Park (N.Z.), 332, 393
Fishing
   in Cairns, 200
   in New South Wales, 112, 113
   in New Zealand, 316, 334–337, 376, 391
Foreign independent travel (FIT) tours, 6
Fox Glacier, 400–401, 405, 408
Franz Josef Glacier, 400–401, 405, 408
Freelance tours, 6
Fremantle, 243–244, 249
French Polynesia, 428–430, **429**
   accommodations in, 448–461
   Australs, 445
   Bora Bora, 440–441
   climate of, 446
   entertainment in, 471
   history of, 430–438
   Huahine, 441–442
   information sources for, 464–465
   inter-island cruises in, 467–468
   Marquesas, 444–445
   Maupiti and Tetiaroa, 443
   Moorea, 440
   museums and galleries in, 469–470
   passports and customs in, 447
   Raiatea, 442
   restaurants in, 462–464
   shopping in, 470–471
   sports in, 468–469
   Tahaa, 442–443
   Tahiti, 438–440
   transportation to and in, 448, 465–467
   Tuamotus, 443–444
Futuna, 25, 507–510

Galleries. *See also* Museums
   in Adelaide, 230
   in Canberra, 151–152
   in Melbourne, 171
   in New Caledonia, 566
   in New South Wales, 141
   in New Zealand, 365, 378–379
   in Northern Territory (Aus.), 280–281
   in Perth and Fremantle, 249
   in Sydney, 95–96
   in Tahiti, 469–470
   in Tasmania, 301
   in Vanuatu, 548–549
   in Victoria, 191, 193
Gardens. *See* Parks and gardens
Geraldton, 253–254
Gilbert Islands. *See* Kiribati and Tuvalu
Gisborne, 358–359, 368, 378
Gizo, 575
Glaciers, in New Zealand, 400–401
Gold central region (Aus.), 178–180, 189–191
Gold Coast (Queensland), 198, 217, 218, 221–223
Golden West region (NSW), 113–114

INDEX

Golden West region (*continued*)
  accommodations in, 126
  information sources for, 117
  museums and historic sites in, 140–141
  parks, gardens and zoos in, 134, 135
  sports in, 138
  tours of, 131–132
Grampians, 182
Great Barrier Reef (Aus.), 44, 198
  far north, 200–205
  northern, 206–209
  southern, 214–215
  Whitsunday Islands, 209–214
Great Keppel Island, 215, 222
Great Southern Region (Western Australia), 250–252
Green Island, 201, 204
Greymouth, 402, 405
Guadalcanal, 570, 575, 577

Haapai Island, 496, 498–499
Hamilton (N.Z.), 368, 378
Hamilton Island (Aus.), 210, 213
Handicapped travelers, 30, 316
Hastings, 360, 368
Hayman Island, 211, 213
Healseville, 176
Health certificates, 4
Health facilities, 26–27
Heron Island, 215, 222
Highlands (Papua New Guinea), 585–588, 597–599
Hiking, in New Zealand, 392, 395
Hinchinbrook Island, 206, 208
Historic sites
  in Adelaide, 230
  in Canberra, 144, 151–152
  in Christchurch, 383–384
  in Dunedin, 399
  in Fiji Islands, 526
  in Fremantle, 244
  in Melbourne, 168–169
  in New South Wales, 138–141
  in New Zealand, 347–348, 377, 411–412
  in Northern Territory (Aus.), 280
  in Perth, 243
  Swan Hill, 183–184
  in Sydney, 74–79, 81, 94–95
  in Tasmania, 301–302
  in Victoria, 187, 189
Hobart, 285–286, 290, 294
Hokitika, 401–402, 405
Honiara, 571, 574, 579
Hospitals, 26–27
Hostels, 21–23
Hotels. *See* Accommodations
Housboating, 195
Huahine, 441–442, 454–455
Hunter (NSW), 104–105
  accommodations in, 120–121
  beaches in, 134–135
  information sources for, 116
  museums and historic sites in, 139
  parks in, 132
  restaurants in, 128
  sports in, 136
  tours of, 129
Hunting, in New Zealand, 316, 337

Illawarra (NSW), 102–103
  accommodations in, 119–120
  beaches in, 134
  gallery in, 139
  information sources for, 116
  parks and gardens in, 132
  restaurants in, 128
  shopping in, 141
  sports in, 136
  tours of, 129
Information sources, 2–4
  for Adelaide, 229
  for Australia, 36
  for Canberra, 147
  for French Polynesia, 464–465
  for Kiribati and Tuvalu, 534
  for Melbourne, 164
  for New Caledonia, 561
  for New South Wales, 116–117
  for New Zealand, 307
  for Niue Island, 506
  for Northern Territory (Aus.), 276
  for Papua New Guinea, 596
  for Queensland, 205, 208, 214
  for Tasmania, 295
  for Victoria, 186–188, 190, 192–194
  for Western Australia, 262–263
Inter-island ships, 13–15
  in French Polynesia, 465–468
International Date Line, 418
Invercargill (N.Z.), 397–398
  accommodations at, 405
  restaurants at, 407
  tours of, 408
Isle of Pines (New Caledonia), 558–559

Jenolan Caves (NSW), 114

Kalgoorlie, 253
Kangaroo Island, 233, 236
Kieta, 600
Kimberley, 255–256
Kiribati and Tuvalu, 528–535
  automobiles in, 15–16
  information sources for, 3
  inter-island ships to, 14
  restaurants in, 24
  shopping in, 29
  tours and sightseeing in, 13

Lae, 584–585, 605
Languages, 27
  in Australia, 61–62
  in French Polynesia, 446
  in Kiribati and Tuvalu, 533
  in Papua New Guinea, 581, 595
  in Solomon Islands, 574
  in Tonga, 497
  in Wallis and Futuna, 509
  in Western Samoa, 489
Launceton, 284, 291, 294
Laveuni, 517
Lizard Island, 200–201, 204
Long Island (Aus.), 211–213
Lord Howe Island (NSW), 114–115

INDEX

accommodations in, 126
beaches on, 135
information sources for, 117
sports on, 138
tours of, 132

Mackay, 210, 213
Madang, 589–590, 599–600
Magnetic Island, 207, 208
Mail, 26, 316
Malaita, 575–576
Manapouri, Lake, 397, 406
Manihi, 455
Maori people, 323–326, 349, 351–353, 377, 442
Marlborough Sounds, 402, 405, 408
Marquesas Islands, 444–445, 456–457
Maupiti, 443, 457–458
Medical treatment, 26–27
Melanesians, 419
Melbourne, 157–160, **158**
  accommodations in, 160–161
  children's activities in, 168
  entertainment and theater in, 172–173
  historic sites in, 168–169
  leisure region, 174–176, 185–186
  museums in, 169–170
  parks and gardens in, 165
  restaurants, 161–163
  shopping in, 171
  sports in, 166–168
  tours of, 164
  transportation in, 163–164
Memorials
  in Auckland, 344
  in Canberra, 146–147
  in Papua New Guinea, 585
  in Solomon Islands, 571
  in South Pacific islands, 422
  in Wellington, 365
Metric conversions, 28
Micronesians, 419–420
Milford Sound, 393–395, 405, 409
Milne Bay, 590–591
Money, 7–8. *See also* Currencies
Moorea, **429**, 440, 458–459
Moreton Bay, 216–218
Mornington peninsula, 174
Morobe, 584–585
Motoring. *See* Automobiles
Motorscooters, 19
Mountain climbing, in New Zealand, 387, 411
Mt. Aspiring National Park (N.Z.), 331–332, 385–387
Mt. Cook National Park (N.Z.), 331, 385–387
  accommodations in, 406
  skiing on, 411
  tours of, 409
Munda, 576
Murray Region (Victoria), 183–184, 194–196
Murray Riverina (NSW), 110–111
  accommodations in, 123–124
  information sources for, 116–117
  museums in, 140
  parks, gardens and zoos in, 134, 135

sports in, 136–137
tours of, 131
Museums. *See also* Galleries
  in Adelaide, 230
  in Auckland, 344–346
  in Canberra, 151
  in Christchurch, 384
  in Fiji Islands, 526
  in Melbourne, 169–171
  in New Caledonia, 566
  in New South Wales, 138–141
  in New Zealand, 378–379, 411–412
  in Northern Territory (Aus.), 280
  in Northland (N.Z.), 361
  in Perth, 248–249
  in Queensland, 225
  in Queenstown, 390
  in Sydney, 94–95
  in Tahiti, 469–470
  in Tasmania, 301
  in Wellington, 365–366
Music
  in Australia, 64–65
  Maori, 353
  in Melbourne, 172
  in New Zealand, 327
  in Sydney, 97
  in Tasmania, 302

Napier, 359, 368, 371, 373, 375
National parks. *See* Parks and gardens
Nelson (N.Z.), 403, 406
Nelson Lakes National Park (N.Z.), 333
New Britain (Papua New Guinea), 591–592, 600
New Caledonia, 550–555, 559–561
  accommodations in, 561–562
  automobiles in, 16
  entertainment in, 567–568
  information sources for, 3
  inter-island ships to, 14
  Isle of Pines, 558–559
  Nouméa, 556–557
  outside Nouméa, 557–558
  restaurants in, 24, 562–564
  shopping in, 29, 566–567
  sports in, 565–566
  tours and sightseeing in, 13, 565
  transportation in, 19
Newcastle (NSW), 104
New England (NSW), 107–108
  accommodations in, 122
  information sources for, 116
  museums and historic sites in, 139–140
  parks and zoos in, 133, 135
  tours in, 130
New Guinea. *See* Papua New Guinea
New Hebrides. *See* Vanuatu
New Ireland (Papua New Guinea), 593, 600–601
New Plymouth (N.Z.), 360
  accommodations in, 368
  museums and galleries in, 378
  restaurants in, 371
  tours of, 373

INDEX

New South Wales, 68–69, **100–101**. *See also* Sydney
  accommodations in, 119–127
  beaches in, **82**, 134–135
  beyond Sydney, 99–115
  entertainment and shopping in, 141
  information sources for, 116–117
  museums and historic sites in, 138–141
  parks, gardens, forests and zoos in, 132–135
  restaurants in, 127–128
  sports in, 135–138
  Sydney, 69–99, **71**
  tours of, 129–132
  transportation to and in, 115–118
New Zealand, 318–320. *See also* North Island; South Island
  accommodations in, 19, 21, 311, 367–370, 404–406
  arts in, 326–328
  Auckland, 342–346, **343**
  automobiles in, 16
  camping in, 21–22
  climate of, 308
  Dunedin, 398–403
  electricity and telephones in, 317
  farm holidays in, 311–312
  history of, 320–321
  hunting and fishing in, 316, 334–337
  information sources for, 3, 307
  inter-island ships to, 14
  Maori heritage in, 377
  museums, galleries and historic sites in, 378–379, 411–412
  national parks of, 329–333
  North Island, 338–341
  Northland, 346–362
  peoples and cultures of, 322–326
  restaurants in, 24, 312, 370–372, 406–408
  seasonal events in, 313–314
  shopping in, 29
  South Island, 380–382
  sports in, 314–315, 376–377, 411
  tours and sightseeing in, 13, 314, 373–376, 408–410
  transportation in, 18, 309–311, 372–373
  Wellington, 362–366, **363**
Nightlife. *See* Entertainment
Niue Island, 502–506
Norfolk Island (NSW), 115
  accommodations on, 127
  information sources for, 117
  shopping on, 141
  sports on, 138
  tours of, 132
North Coast (NSW), 105–107
  accommodations in, 121–122
  beaches in, 135
  information sources for, 116
  museums, galleries and historic sites in, 139, 141
  parks in, 132–133
  restaurants in, 128
  sports in, 136
  tours of, 130

Northeast region (Victoria), 177–178, 187–189
Northern Territory (Aus.), 266–267
  accommodations in, 272–274
  Alice Springs, 271
  camping in, 274–275
  Darwin, 267–270
  museums, galleries and historic sites in, 280–281
  national parks in, 278–279
  tours of, 277–278
  transportation to and in, 271–272, 275–276
North Island (N.Z.), 338–341
  accommodations in, 367–370
  Auckland, 342–346, **343**
  Northland, 346–362
  parks, zoos, museums and galleries on, 377–379
  restaurants in, 370–372
  sports on, 376–377
  tours and sightseeing in, 373–376
  transportation on, 372–373
  Wellington, 362–366, **363**
Northland (N.Z.), 338–339, 346–349, 353–357, 359–362
  Rotorua, 349–353
  Tauranga, 358
  Tongariro National Park, 357
  tours and sightseeing in, 375
Northwest region (NSW), 108–109
  accommodations in, 122–123
  information sources for, 116
  parks and zoos in, 133, 135
  tours of, 130
Nouméa, 552, 556–557, 561–562, 565–567

Orpheus Island, 207, 208
Outback (Aus.)
  accommodations in, 123
  information sources for, 116
  museums, galleries and historic sites in, 140, 141
  New South Wales, 109–110
  parks in, 133–134
  South Australia, 231–232
  sports in, 136
  tours of, 130–131

Pacific, **416–417**. *See also* South Pacific islands
"Pacific Way," 425–426
Paddle steamer cruises, 195
Pago Pago, 479–480
Papeete. *See* Tahiti
Papua New Guinea, 580–582, **583**, 594–596
  accommodations in, 596–601
  automobiles in, 16
  Bougainville, 592
  camping in, 23
  Highlands, 585–588
  information sources for, 3
  inter-island ships to, 14
  Lae and Morobe Province, 584–585
  Madang Province, 589–590

INDEX

Milne Bay and Trobriand Island, 590–591
New Britain, 591–592
New Ireland, Northern District and Wuvulu Island, 593–594
Port Moresby, 582–584
restaurants in, 24
seasonal events in, 603–604
shopping in, 29, 606
sports and beaches in, 604–605
tours and sightseeing in, 13, 602–603
transportation in, 19, 601–602
Wewak and Sepik River, 588
Parks and gardens
in Adelaide, 229
in Auckland, 345
in Brisbane, 215–216
in Canberra, 150
in Christchurch, 384
in Fiji Islands, 526
in Melbourne, 157, 165
in New South Wales, 132–134
in New Zealand, 329–333, 351–352, 357, 377
in Northern Territory (Aus.), 278–279
in Perth, 243
in Queensland, 218
in Sydney, 75, 76, 91
in Tahiti, 470
in Tasmania, 299–300
in Victoria, 189, 192
in Wellington, 365
in Western Australia, 264–265
Passports and visas
for Australia, 35–36
for Fiji Islands, 518
for French Polynesia, 447
for Kiribati and Tuvalu, 533
for New Caledonia, 560
for New Zealand, 307
for Niue Island, 505
for Papua New Guinea, 595
for Solomon Islands, 573
for Tonga, 497
for Wallis and Futuna, 509
for Western Samoa, 489
Peoples
of Australia, 49–50, 57–59, 266–267, 279
of Fiji Islands, 512–514
of Kiribati and Tuvalu, 529
of New Caledonia, 550
of New Zealand, 322–326, 349, 351–353, 377
of Papua New Guinea, 580, 581
of Samoa, 480–481
of Solomon Islands, 571, 572
of South Pacific islands, 419–420
of Tahiti, 433, 435, 439
of Tonga, 495
of Vanuatu, 538
Perth, 241–244, **242**
accommodations in, 245
entertainment in, 250
museums in, 248–249
restaurants in, 246–247
tours of, 247–248
Phillip Island, 174

Pilbara, 254–255
Plants, 47, 319, 385. *See also* Parks and gardens
Polynesia. *See* French Polynesia
Polynesians, 419, 420
Port Douglas, 202–204
Port Macquarie (NSW), 106
Port Moresby, 582–584, 596–597, 605
Precautions, for South Pacific islands, 426–427

Queensland (Aus.), 197–198, **199**
far north: Cairns and far northern Great Barrier Reef, 200–206
northern: Townsville and northern Great Barrier Reef, 206–209
southern, 214–225
Whitsunday Islands and coast, 209–214
Queenstown (N.Z.), 387–390
accommodations in, 406
museums and historic sites in, 412
restaurants in, 407
sports in, 411
tours and sightseeing in, 409–410

Rabaul, 591–592
Rafting, 392
Raiatea, 442, 459–460
Rangiroa, 460–461
Rarotonga, 472, 473, 475–476
Remarkables (N.Z.), 409
Restaurants, 23–25, 312
Rotorua, 349–353
accommodations in, 368–369
fishing in, 376
museums and galleries in, 378
restaurants in, 371
tours and sightseeing of, 373–376
Rottnest Island, 244

Samoa. *See* American Samoa; Western Samoa
Santo, 542–543, 545, 546
Savaii Island, 485, 487, 490
Scuba diving and snorkeling
in Great Barrier Reef, 205, 214
in New Zealand, 315
in Papua New Guinea, 604
in Solomon Islands, 572, 578
Seasonal events
in Fiji Islands, 519
in Fremantle, 243–244
in Melbourne, 159, 164–165
in New Caledonia, 564
in New South Wales, 129
in New Zealand, 313–314
in Northern Territory (Aus.), 276–277
in Papua New Guinea, 603–604
in Sydney, 89
in Tahiti, 468
in Tasmania, 297
in Vanuatu, 546–547
in Victoria, 190
Sepik River, 588, 599
Ships. *See also* Cruises
inter-island, 13–15, 465–468
Shopping, 29–30

INDEX

Shopping (*continued*)
  in Adelaide, 230
  in American Samoa, 483–484
  in Auckland, 342, 344
  in Australia, 38–39
  in Canberra, 152
  in Fiji Islands, 526–527
  in Kiribati and Tuvalu, 534–535
  in Melbourne, 159, 171
  in New Caledonia, 566–567
  in New South Wales, 141
  in New Zealand, 316
  in Niue Island, 506
  in Papua New Guinea, 606
  in Perth, flea markets, 249
  in Queensland, 225
  in Solomon Islands, 578
  in South Pacific islands, 424
  in Sydney, 96–97
  in Tahiti, 470–471
  in Tasmania, 302
  in Vanuatu, 548
  in Western Samoa, 491
Shute Harbour, 209, 213, 214
Sightseeing. *See* Tours and sightseeing
Simbu, 585–586
Skiing
  in Australia, 112–113, 177, 178
  in New Zealand, 315, 376–377, 387, 388, 390–391, 411
Snowy Mountains (NSW), 111–113
  accommodations in, 124–125
  historic houses in, 140
  information souces for, 117
  parks in, 134
  sports in, 137–138
  tours of, 131
Snowy River National Park, 177
Society Islands, 433, 438. *See also* French Polynesia; Tahiti
Solomon Islands, 569–571, 573–574
  accommodations in, 574–576
  automobiles in, 16
  culture of, 572
  entertainment in, 579
  Honiara, 571
  information sources for, 3
  inter-island ships to, 14
  restaurants in, 24
  shopping in, 29, 578
  sports in, 577–578
  tours and sightseeing in, 13, 577
  transportation in, 19
South Australia, 226–227
  Adelaide, 227–231
  beyond Adelaide, 231–238
South Coast (NSW), 111–112
  accommodations in, 125–126
  beaches in, 135
  information sources for, 117
  museums and historic houses in, 140
  parks in, 134
  sports in, 138
  tours of, 131
Southeast coast region (Victoria), 176–177, 186–187
Southern Highlands (NSW), 102–103
South Island (N.Z.), 380–382, 391–393

  accommodations in, 404–406
  Christchurch, 382–384
  Dunedin, 398–403
  Invercargill, 397–398
  Lake Ta Anau, 396
  Milford Sound, 393–395
  Mount Cook, 385–387
  museums and historic sites in, 411–412
  Queenstown, 388–390
  restaurants in, 406–408
  sports in, 411
  tours and sightseeing in, 408–410
South Molle Island, 210–211, 213
South Pacific Commission, 554–555
South Pacific islands, 415–418, **416–417**, 426–427. *See also specific islands*
  accommodations in, 19–20
  camping in, 22–23
  Fiji Islands, **513**
  history of, 420–422
  "Pacific Way," 425–426
  Papua New Guinea, **583**,
  peoples of, 419–420
  Samoas, **480**
  Tahiti and Moorea, **429**
  tourism in, 422–424
Special-interest tours, 12–13. *See also* Tours and sightseeing
Sports, 27
  in Adelaide, 230
  in American Samoa, 483
  America's Cup race, 243, 244
  in Canberra, 150–151
  in Cook Islands, 478
  in Fiji Islands, 525–526
  in Melbourne, 157–159, 166–168
  in New Caledonia, 565–566
  in New South Wales, 135–138
  in New Zealand, 41, 314–315, 334–337, 376
  in Niue Island, 506
  in Northtern Territory (Aus.), 279–280
  in Papua New Guinea, 604–605
  in Perth, 248
  in Queensland, 205, 208–209, 224
  in Solomon Islands, 577–578
  in Sydney, 93–94
  in Tahiti, 468–469
  in Tasmania, 297–298
  in Tonga, 501
  in Vanuatu, 548
  in Wallis and Futuna, 510
  in Western Australia, 265
  in Western Samoa, 491
Station tours, 40–41
Stopovers, 9, 309
Sunshine Coast (Queensland), 219–220, 222, 223
Suva, 512, 521–524
Swan Hill, 183–184
Sydney (Aus.), 69–70, **71**, 74–79, 81–83
  accommodations in, 83–84
  entertainment and nightlife in, 97–99
  Harbour, 79–81
  history of, 70–73

INDEX

museums, historic sites and galleries in, 94–96
parks, gardens and beaches of, 91–93
restaurants in, 85–88
shopping in, 96–97
sports in, 93–94
tours of, 90–91
transportation in, 88–89
Sydney Opera House, 70, 75

Tahaa, 442–443, 461
Tahiti, 428–430, *429*, 438–440
accommodations in, 449–451
automobiles in, 16–17
history of, 430–438
information sources for, 3
inter-island ships to, 14
restaurants in, 24, 462–464
shopping in, 29
tours and sightseeing in, 13
transportation in, 19
Tanna, 541–542, 545
Tarawa, 530
Tasmania, 282–287
Aboriginal population of, 58
accommodations in, 288–293
bars and casinos in, 303
museums, galleries and historic sites in, 301–302
parks and gardens in, 299–300
restaurants in, 293–295
shopping, music and theater in, 302
sports in, 297–298
tours of, 296–297
transportation to and in, 288, 295–296
Tauranga, 358, 369, 372
Tavenui Island, 517, 523
Taxis, 18–19
Te Anau, Lake, 396, 406–408, 411
Telephones, 25–26, 317
Tetiaroa, 443, 461
Theater
in Melbourne, 172–173
in New Zealand, 326
in Sydney, 97
in Tasmania, 302
Tipping
in Australia, 42
for cruises, 10
in French Polynesia, 446–447
in Solomon Islands, 573
Tonga, 494–501
automobiles in, 17
inter-island ships to, 14
International Date Line in, 418
restaurants in, 24–25
shopping in, 29
tours and sightseeing in, 13
transportation in, 19
Tongariro National Park (N.Z.), 330, 341, 357, 369
Tongatapu Island, 498–499
Tours and sightseeing, 1, 6, 10–12
of Adelaide, 229
of American Samoa, 483
of Australia, 40–41
of Canberra, 150
of Christchurch, 383

of Christmas Island, 534
of Cook Islands, 477–478
of Fiji Islands, 524–525
of Melbourne, 164
of New Caledonia, 565
of New South Wales, 129–132
of New Zealand, 314, 373–376, 408–410
of Niue Island, 506
of Northern Territory (Aus.), 277–278
of Papua New Guinea, 602–603
of Perth, 247–248
of Queensland, 205, 208, 224
of Solomon Islands, 577
of South Australia, 237–238
special-interest, 12–13
of Sydney, 74, 90–91
of Tahiti, 468
of Tasmania, 296–297
of Tonga, 500–501
of Vanuatu, 547–548
of Victoria, 186–196
of Western Australia, 263–264
of Western Samoa, 491
Townsville, 206, 208
Trains, 18
of Australia, 39–40
in New South Wales, 115, 118
in New Zealand, 309
in Northern Territory (Aus.), 271
in Western Australia, 257, 258
Trams, in Melbourne, 157, 163
Transportation, 6–7
to and in Adelaide, 227–229
by air, 8–9
to and in American Samoa, 482–483
to and in Australia, 39–41
in Brisbane, 224
buses for, 17–18
to and in Canberra, 147, 149–150
to and in Cook Islands, 472, 473, 475, 477
to and in Fiji Islands, 517–518, 524
to and in French Polynesia, 440–445, 448, 465–467
to and in Kiribati and Tuvalu, 533, 534
to and in Melbourne, 157, 160, 163–164
motorscooters and bicycles for, 19
to and in New Caledonia, 556, 559, 564
to and in New South Wales, 115–118
to and in New Zealand, 309–311, 372–373, 408
to and in Niue Island, 505, 506
to and in Northern Territory (Aus.), 271–272, 275–276
to and in Papua New Guinea, 582, 594, 601–602
to and in Perth, 245
to and in Queensland, 203, 207, 212, 220–221
by sea, 9–10
to and in Solomon Islands, 573, 576
to and in South Australia, 235
in Sydney, 88–89
to and in Tasmania, 288, 295–296
taxis for, 18–19

INDEX

Transportation (*continued*)
  to and in Tonga, 497, 499–500
  trains for, 18
  to and in Vanuatu, 543, 546
  in Victoria, 184
  to and in Wallis and Futuna, 509
  to and in Western Australia, 256–258
  to and in Western Samoa, 489–491
Travel agents, 6–7
Trobriand Islands, 590–591
Tuamotus, 443–444
Tubuai, 452
Tuvalu (Tungaru). *See* Kiribati and Tuvalu

Unewera National Park (N.Z.), 330–331
Upper Hawkesbury (NSW), 99–102
  accommodations in, 119
  information sources for, 116
  museums and historic sites in, 138–139
  sports in, 135–136
  tours of, 129

Vanua Levu, 517, 522
Vanuatu (New Hebrides), 536–541, 543
  accommodations in, 544–545
  automobiles in, 17
  information sources for, 3
  outer islands, 541
  restaurants in, 25, 545–546
  seasonal events in, 546–547
  shopping in, 29
  sports, shopping and galleries in, 548–549
  tours and sightseeing in, 13, 547–548
  transportation in, 19
Vava'u Island, 496, 499
Victor Harbor, 232
Victoria (Aus.), 154–157, **175**
  accommodations in, 150–151
  beyond Melbourne, 173–174, 184–185
  children's activities in, 168
  entertainment and theater in, 172–173
  Gold Central region, 178–180, 189–191
  historic sites and houses in, 168–169
  Melbourne, 157–159, **158**
  Melbourne leisure region, 174–176, 185–186
  Murray region, 183–184, 194–196
  museums, 169–171
  Northeast region, 177–178, 187–189
  parks and gardens in, 165
  restaurants in, 161–163
  shopping in, 171
  southeast coast region, 176–177, 186–187
  sports in, 166–168
  tours of, 164
  transportation in, 163–164
  West Coast region, 180–181, 191–193
  Wimmera region, 182–183, 193–194
Vila, 539–541, 544–548
Viti Levu, 516–517, 519–522

Waitomo Caves, 348–349, 369
Walking tours
  of Melbourne, 164
  of Sydney, 90
Wallis and Futuna, 25, 507–510
Wanganui, 361, 369, 372, 376, 378
Water, 25, 533
Water sports, 27, 224
Weather. *See* Climate
Wellington, 362–366, **363**
  accommodations in, 369–370
  museums, galleries and library in, 378–379
  restaurants in, 372
  tours and sightseeing in, 374, 376
West coast region (Victoria), 180–181, 191–193
Western Australia, 239–241
  beyond Perth, 250–265
  Perth, 241–250, **242**
Western Samoa, **480**, 485–493
  automobiles in, 17
  information sources for, 3–4
  inter-island ships to, 15
  restaurants in, 25
  shopping in, 29–30
  tours and sightseeing in, 13
  transportation in, 19
Westland National Park (N.Z.), 332–333
Wewak, 588, 599
Whitsunday Islands, 209–214
Wildlife sanctuaries. *See* Animals; Zoos
Wimmera region (Victoria), 182–183, 193–194
Women, in Australia, 62–63
Wuvulu Island, 593–594, 601

Yachting, 214
  America's Cup race, 243, 244, 248
  in South Pacific islands, 423

Zoos. *See also* Animals
  in Adelaide, 230
  in Brisbane, 216
  in Canberra, 150
  in Melbourne, 157, 166
  in New South Wales, 135
  in New Zealand, 345, 377
  in Queensland, 224
  in Sydney, 80, 93
  in Tasmania, 299